GENERAL MOTORS

DEVILLE/FLEETWOOD/ELDORADO/SEVILLE
1990-93 REPAIR MANUAL

CHILTON'S ™

President	Dean F. Morgantini, S.A.E.
Vice President–Finance	Barry L. Beck
Vice President–Sales	Glenn D. Potere
Executive Editor	Kevin M. G. Maher, A.S.E.
Production Manager	Ben Greisler, S.A.E.
Production Assistant	Melinda Possinger
Project Managers	George B. Heinrich III, A.S.E., S.A.E., Will Kessler, A.S.E., S.A.E., James R. Marotta, A.S.E., S.T.S., Richard Schwartz, A.S.E., Todd W. Stidham, A.S.E.
Schematics Editor	Christopher G. Ritchie
Editor	Michael L. Grady, Martin J. Gunther

CHILTON™ Automotive Books

PUBLISHED BY **W. G. NICHOLS, INC.**

Manufactured in USA
© 1994 Chilton Book Company
1020 Andrew Drive
West Chester, PA 19380
ISBN 0-8019-8420-3
Library of Congress Catalog Card No. 92-054895
6789012345 8765432109

Contents

Contents

SAFETY NOTICE

Proper service and repair procedures are vital to the safe, reliable operation of all motor vehicles, as well as the personal safety of those performing repairs. This manual outlines procedures for servicing and repairing vehicles using safe, effective methods. The procedures contain many NOTES, CAUTIONS and WARNINGS which should be followed along with standard procedures to eliminate the possibility of personal injury or improper service which could damage the vehicle or compromise its safety.

It is important to note that the repair procedures and techniques, tools and parts for servicing motor vehicles, as well as the skill and experience of the individual performing the work vary widely. It is not possible to anticipate all of the conceivable ways or conditions under which vehicles may be serviced, or to provide cautions as to all of the possible hazards that may result. Standard and accepted safety precautions and equipment should be used when handling toxic or flammable fluids, and safety goggles or other protection should be used during cutting, grinding, chiseling, prying, or any other process that can cause material removal or projectiles.

Some procedures require the use of tools specially designed for a specific purpose. Before substituting another tool or procedure, you must be completely satisfied that neither your personal safety, nor the performance of the vehicle will be endangered.

Although information in this manual is based on industry sources and is complete as possible at the time of publication, the possibility exists that some vehicle manufacturers made later changes which could not be included here. While striving for total accuracy, W. G. Nichols, Inc. cannot assume responsibility for any errors, changes or omissions that may occur in the compilation of this data.

PART NUMBERS

Part numbers listed in this reference are not recommendations by Chilton for any product by brand name. They are references that can be used with interchange manuals and aftermarket supplier catalogs to locate each brand supplier's discrete part number.

SPECIAL TOOLS

Special tools are recommended by the vehicle manufacturer to perform their specific job. Use has been kept to a minimum, but where absolutely necessary, they are referred to in the text by the part number of the tool manufacturer. These tools can be purchased, under the appropriate part number, from your local dealer or regional distributor, or an equivalent tool can be purchased locally from a tool supplier or parts outlet. Before substituting any tool for the one recommended, read the SAFETY NOTICE at the top of this page.

ACKNOWLEDGMENTS

Portions of the materials contained herein have been reprinted with the permission of General Motors Corporation, Service Technology Group.

1

GENERAL INFORMATION AND MAINTENANCE

HOW TO USE THIS BOOK

Chilton's Total Car Care Manual for 1990-93 Cadillac Deville, Seville, Fleetwood, Sixty Special and Eldorado is intended to help you learn more about the inner workings of your vehicle and save you money on its upkeep and operation.

The first two sections will be the most used, since they contain maintenance and tune-up information and procedures. Studies have shown that a properly tuned and maintained car can get at least 10% better gas mileage than an out-of-tune car. The other sections deal with the more complex systems of your vehicle. Operating systems from engine through brakes are covered to the extent that the average do-it-yourselfer becomes mechanically involved. It will give you detailed instructions to help you change your own brake pads and shoes, replace spark plugs, and do many more jobs that will save you money, give you personal satisfaction, and help you avoid expensive problems.

A secondary purpose of this book is a reference for owners who want to understand their car and/or their mechanics better. In this case, no tools at all are required.

Before removing any bolts, read through the entire procedure. This will give you the overall view of what tools and supplies will be required. There is nothing more frustrating than having to walk to the bus stop on Monday morning because you were short one bolt on Sunday afternoon. So read ahead and plan ahead. Each operation should be approached logically and all procedures thoroughly understood before attempting any work.

All sections contain adjustments, maintenance, removal and installation procedures, and repair or overhaul procedures. When repair is not considered practical, we tell you how to remove the part and then how to install the new or rebuilt replacement. In this way, you at least save the labor costs. Backyard repair of such components as the alternator is just not practical.

Two basic mechanic's rules should be mentioned here. One, whenever the left side of the car or engine is referred to, it is meant to specify the driver's side of the car. Conversely, the right side of the car means the passenger's side. Secondly, most screws and bolts are removed by turning counterclockwise, and tightened by turning clockwise.

Safety is always the most important rule. Constantly be aware of the dangers involved in working on an automobile and take the proper precautions. (See the portion of this section on Servicing Your Vehicle Safely and the SAFETY NOTICE on the acknowledgment page.)

Pay attention to the instructions provided. There are 3 common mistakes in mechanical work:

1. Incorrect order of assembly, disassembly or adjustment. When taking something apart or putting it together, doing things in the wrong order usually just costs you extra time; however, it CAN break something. Read the entire procedure before beginning disassembly. Do everything in the order in which the instructions say you should do it, even if you can't immediately see a reason for it. When you're taking apart something that is very intricate, you might want to draw a picture of how it looks when assembled at one or more points in order to assure you get everything back in its proper position. (We will supply exploded views whenever possible). When making adjustments, especially tune-up adjustments, do them in order; often, one adjustment affects another, and you cannot expect even satisfactory results unless each adjustment is made only when it cannot be changed by any other.

2. Overtorquing (or undertorquing): While it is more common for overtorquing to cause damage, undertorquing can cause a fastener to vibrate loose causing serious damage. Especially when dealing with aluminum parts, pay attention to torque specifications and utilize a torque wrench in assembly. If a torque figure is not available, remember that if you are using the right tool to do the job, you will probably not have to strain yourself to get a fastener tight enough. The pitch of most threads is so slight that the tension you put on the wrench will be multiplied many, many times in actual force on what you are tightening. A good example of how critical torque is can be seen in the case of spark plug installation, especially where you are putting the plug into an aluminum cylinder head. Too little torque can fail to crush the gasket, causing leakage of combustion gases and consequent overheating of the plug and engine parts. Too much torque can damage the threads or distort the plug, which changes the spark gap.

There are many commercial products available for ensuring the fasteners won't come loose, even if they are not torqued just right (a very common brand is Loctite®). If you're worried about getting something together tight enough to hold, but loose enough to avoid mechanical damage during assembly, one of these products might offer substantial insurance. Read the label on the package and make sure the product is compatible with the materials, fluids, etc. involved.

3. Crossthreading. This occurs when a part such as a bolt is screwed into a nut or casting at the wrong angle and forced. Cross threading is more likely to occur if access is difficult. It helps to clean and lubricate fasteners, and to start threading with the part to be installed going straight in. Then, start the bolt, spark plug, etc. with your fingers. If you encounter resistance, unscrew the part and start over again at a different angle until it can be inserted and turned several turns without much effort. Keep in mind that many parts, especially spark plugs, use tapered threads so that gentle turning will automatically bring the part you're threading to the proper angle if you don't force it or resist a change in angle. Don't put a wrench on the part until it's been turned a couple of turns by hand. If you suddenly encounter resistance, and the part has not seated fully, don't force it. Screw it back out and make sure it's clean and threading properly.

Always take your time and be patient; once you have some experience, working on your car will become an enjoyable hobby.

TOOLS AND EQUIPMENT

Naturally, without the proper tools and equipment it is impossible to properly service your vehicle. It would be impossible to catalog each tool that you would need to perform each or any operation in this book. It would also be unwise for the amateur to rush out and buy an expensive set of tools on the theory that he may need one or more of them at sometime.

The best approach is to proceed slowly, gathering together a good quality set of those tools that are used most frequently. Don't be misled by the low cost of bargain tools. It is far better to spend a little more for better quality. Forged wrenches, 6 or 12-point sockets and fine tooth ratchets are by far preferable than their less expensive counterparts. As any good mechanic can tell you, there are few worse experiences than trying to work on a car with bad tools. Your monetary savings will be far outweighed by frustration and mangled knuckles.

Begin accumulating those tools that are used most frequently; those associated with routine maintenance and tune-up.

In addition to the normal assortment of pliers and screwdrivers, you should have the following tools for routine maintenance jobs:

1. Metric and SAE wrenches, sockets and combination open end/box end wrenches in sizes from 3mm to 19mm, $\frac{1}{8}$ inch to $\frac{3}{4}$ inch and a spark plug socket $\frac{13}{16}$ inch or $\frac{5}{8}$ inch depending on plug type). With Cadillac vehicles, you will most likely find that Metric tools are usually sufficient or required for your purposes. If possible, buy various length socket drive extensions. Most metric sockets available in the U.S. will fit the ratchet handles and extensions you may already have ($\frac{1}{4}$ inch, $\frac{3}{8}$ inch, and $\frac{1}{2}$ inch drive).

2. Jackstands for support.
3. Oil filter wrench.
4. Oil filler spout or funnel.
5. Grease gun for lubrication.
6. Hydrometer for checking the battery.
7. A container for draining oil.
8. Many rags for wiping up the inevitable mess.

In addition to the above items there are several others that are not absolutely necessary, but handy to have around. These include oil dry, a transmission funnel and the usual supply of lubricants, antifreeze and fluids, although these can be purchased as needed. This is a basic list for routine maintenance, but only your personal needs and desire can accurately determine your list of tools.

The second list of tools is for tune-ups. While the tools involved here are slightly more sophisticated, they need not be outrageously expensive. There are several inexpensive tachometers on the market that are every bit as good for the average mechanic as a professional model. Just be sure that the meter goes to at least 1500 rpm on the scale and that it can be used on 4, 6, or 8 cylinder engines. A basic list of tune-up equipment could include:

9. Tachometer.
10. Spark plug wrench.
11. Wire spark plug gauge/adjusting tools.

In addition to these basic tools there are several other tools and gauges you may find useful. These include:

12. A compression gauge. The screw in type is slower to use but it eliminates the possibility of a faulty reading due to escaping pressure.
13. A manifold vacuum gauge.
14. A 12V test light.
15. An induction meter. This is used for determining whether or not there is current in a wire. These are handy for use if a wire is broken somewhere in a wiring harness.

As a final note, you will probably find a torque wrench necessary for all but the most basic work. The beam type models are perfectly adequate although the newer click types are more precise.

Special Tools

Normally, the use of special factory tools is avoided for repair procedures, since these are not readily available for the do-it-yourself mechanic. When it is possible to perform the job with more commonly available tools, it will be pointed out, but occasionally, a special tool was designed to perform a specific function and should be used. Before substituting another tool, you should be convinced that neither your safety nor the performance of the vehicle will be compromised. When a special tool is indicated, it will be referred to by a manufacturer's part number. The following is the principle tool manufacturer for GM and their address:Kent Moore Service Tool Division29784 Little Mack Roseville, MI 48066-2298

SERVICING YOUR VEHICLE SAFELY

It is virtually impossible to anticipate all of the hazards involved with automotive maintenance and service but care and common sense will prevent most accidents.

The rules of safety for mechanics range from "don't smoke around gasoline' to "use the proper tool for the job.' The trick to avoiding injuries is to develop safe work habits and take every possible precaution.

Do's

• Do keep a fire extinguisher and first aid kit within easy reach.

• Do wear safety glasses or goggles when cutting, drilling, grinding or prying, even if you have 20/20 vision. If you wear glasses for the sake of vision, then they should be made of hardened glass that can serve also as safety glasses, or wear safety goggles over your regular glasses.

• Do shield your eyes whenever you work around the battery. Batteries contain sulfuric acid; in case of contact with the eyes or skin, flush the area with water or a mixture of water and baking soda and get medical attention immediately.

• Do use safety stands for any under-car service. Jacks are for raising vehicles; safety stands are for making sure the vehicle stays raised until you want it to come down. Whenever the vehicle is raised, block the wheels remaining on the ground and set the parking brake.

• Do use adequate ventilation when working with any chemicals. Like carbon monoxide, the asbestos dust resulting from brake lining wear can be poisonous in sufficient quantities.

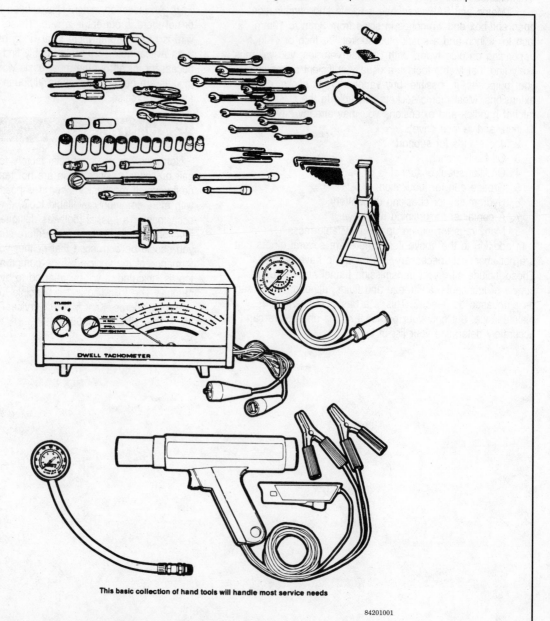

This basic collection of hand tools will handle most service needs

84201001

Fig. 1 This basic collection of hand tools will handle most service needs

• Do disconnect the negative battery cable when working on the electrical system. The primary ignition system can contain up to 40,000 volts.

• Do follow manufacturer's directions whenever working with potentially hazardous materials. Both brake fluid and antifreeze are poisonous if taken internally.

• Do properly maintain your tools. Loose hammerheads, mushroomed punches and chisels, frayed or poorly grounded electrical cords, excessively worn screwdrivers, spread wrenches (open end), cracked sockets, slipping ratchets, or faulty droplight sockets can cause accidents.

• Do use the proper size and type of tool for the job being done.

• Do when possible, pull on a wrench handle rather than push on it, and adjust your stance to prevent a fall.

• Do be sure that adjustable wrenches are tightly adjusted on the nut or bolt and pulled so that the face is on the side of the fixed jaw.

• Do select a wrench or socket that fits the nut or bolt. The wrench or socket should sit straight, not cocked.

• Do strike squarely with a hammer. Avoid glancing blows.

• Do set the parking brake and block the drive wheels if the work requires that the engine be running.

Don'ts

• Don't run an engine in a garage or anywhere else without proper ventilation — EVER! Carbon monoxide is poisonous; it takes a long time to leave the human body and you can build up a deadly supply of it in your system by simply breathing in a little every day. You may not realize you are slowly poisoning yourself. Always use power vents, windows, fans or open the garage door.

• Don't work around moving parts while wearing a necktie or other loose clothing. Short sleeves are much safer than long, loose sleeves. Hard-toed shoes with neoprene soles protect your toes and give a better grip on slippery surfaces. Jewelry such as watches, fancy belt buckles, beads or body adornment of any kind is not safe working around a car. Long hair should be hidden under a hat or cap.

• Don't use pockets for toolboxes. A fall or bump can drive a screwdriver deep into your body. Even a wiping cloth hanging from the back pocket can wrap around a spinning shaft or fan.

• Don't smoke when working around gasoline, cleaning solvent or other flammable material.

• Don't smoke when working around the battery. When the battery is being charged, it gives off explosive hydrogen gas.

• Don't use gasoline to wash your hands; there are excellent soaps available. Gasoline may contain lead, and lead can enter the body through a cut, accumulating in the body until you are very ill. Gasoline also removes all the natural oils from the skin so that bone dry hands will suck up oil and grease.

• Don't service the air conditioning system unless you are equipped with the necessary tools and training. The refrigerant, R-12 is extremely cold and when exposed to the air, will instantly freeze any surface it comes in contact with, including your eyes. Although the refrigerant is normally non-toxic, R-12 becomes a deadly poisonous gas in the presence of an open flame. One good whiff of the vapors from burning refrigerant can be fatal.

HISTORY

The name Cadillac is appropriately that of Antoine de La Mothe Cadillac, the French military commander who founded the city of Detroit in 1701. Cadillac is the oldest manufacturer in Detroit. Henry M. Leland founded the car company in 1902.

The introduction of the first four cylinder engine in 1905 led the industry and enabled Cadillacs to travel at speeds up to 50 mph. From 1908 to 1912 Cadillac won many prestigious awards for the introduction of the electric self starter, electric lighting and ignition system. In 1909 Cadillac was purchased by the then New General Motors Corporation which was greatly enhanced with all weather comfort and became the first manufacturer to offer closed bodies as standard equipment. Between the years 1915 through the late 1930's Cadillac produced some of the finest cars and engines including the first V8 engine and the ever so smooth V12 and 45 degree V16. During World War II, shortly after 1941, Cadillac discontinued car production in order to construct light tanks, combat vehicles and internal parts.

The 1948 model introduced the legendary tail fin which set the trend in automotive styling for nearly two decades. Engineering innovations, conveniences and styling dominated the 50's and 60's. The first front wheel drive personal luxury car was introduced in 1967. The 1970's brought such innovations as an Air Cushion Restraint System (currently known as the air bag), Analog Electronic Fuel Injection, and an on-board microprocessor.

Cadillac has continued its tradition of producing quality luxury vehicles for the 90's and has been awarded many awards such as the Malcolm Baldridge National Quality Award. The 1992 Seville STS is the first car ever to win all three major automotive awards: Car of the Year, Motor Trend; Ten Best List, Car & Driver; Car of the Year, Automobile Magazine. 1993 will also prove Cadillac's creditability with its 32 valve dual overhead camshaft, Northstar 4.6 liter V8 engine. For more than nine decades Cadillac has been a leader in quality and technical innovation.

SERIAL NUMBER IDENTIFICATION

Vehicle

▶ **See Figure 1**

The VIN plate which contains the Vehicle Identification Number (VIN) is located at the top and back of the dash board on the left side and is visible from outside the vehicle on the lower left (drivers) side of the windshield. The VIN consists of 17 characters which represent codes supplying important information about your vehicle. The first character represents the nation of origin. The second character identifies the manufacturer. The third character represents a code used by the man-

Fig. 2 VIN plate location

ufacturer to identify the division. The fourth and fifth characters represent a code used to establish the car line or series. They are a combined code consisting of two letters. The sixth and seventh characters combined represent a code which identifies the body type. On vehicles from model years 1990-93, the sixth character is a code which identifies the body type and the seventh character identifies the type of restraint system used on the vehicle. The eighth character identifies the engine code. The ninth character is a check digit. The tenth character is a code which represents the model year of the vehicle. The eleventh character is a code which represents the assembly plant in which the vehicle was manufactured. Characters twelve through seventeen are the plant sequence number or the number of the vehicle of that model produced at the plant for the model year.

Engine

▶ See Figures 3 and 4

The engine code is represented by the eighth character in the VIN for model years 1990-1993 and identifies the engine type, vehicle plant, model year and manufacturing division. The engine identification code for engines, 4.5L, 4.9L, is either stamped onto the engine block, lefthand side, just behind the flywheel or found on a label affixed to the inboard surface of the left valve rocker cover. The 4.6L Northstar V8 engine label is located on the outboard surface of the upper intake manifold.

Transaxle

▶ See Figures 5, 6 and 7

The transaxle identification plate is stamped into the horizontal cast rib on right rear of the transaxle housing, for all

1990-93 front wheel drive models. The identification plate supplies model year, type of transaxle, Julian date (day of the year), serial number and shift code.

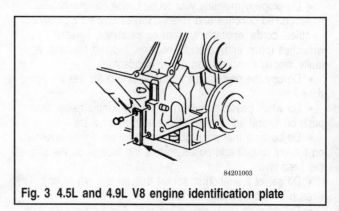

Fig. 3 4.5L and 4.9L V8 engine identification plate

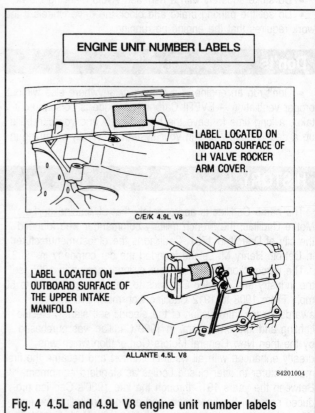

ENGINE UNIT NUMBER LABELS

LABEL LOCATED ON INBOARD SURFACE OF LH VALVE ROCKER ARM COVER.

C/E/K 4.9L V8

LABEL LOCATED ON OUTBOARD SURFACE OF THE UPPER INTAKE MANIFOLD.

ALLANTE 4.5L V8

Fig. 4 4.5L and 4.9L V8 engine unit number labels

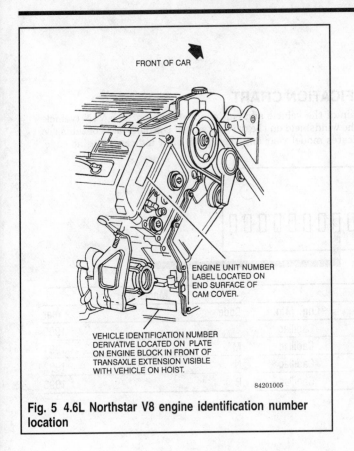

Fig. 5 4.6L Northstar V8 engine identification number location

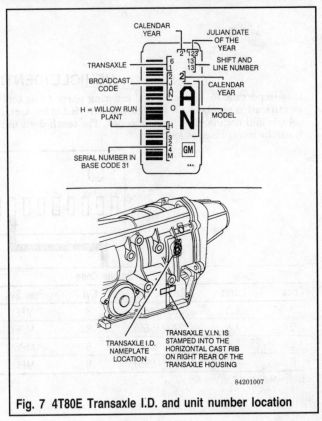

Fig. 7 4T80E Transaxle I.D. and unit number location

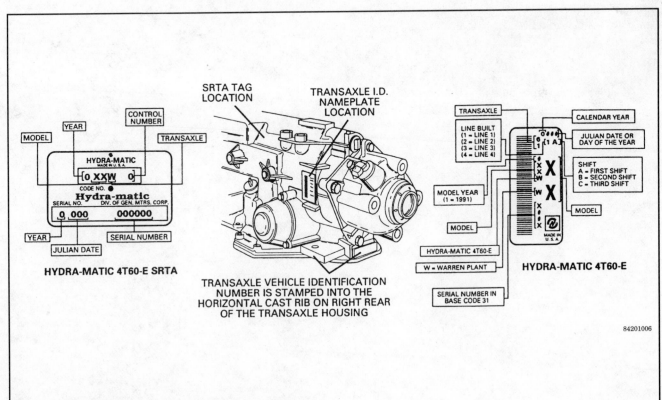

Fig. 6 4T60E Transaxle I.D. and unit number location

VEHICLE IDENTIFICATION CHART

It is important for servicing and ordering parts to be certain of the vehicle and engine identification. The VIN (vehicle identification number) is a 17 digit number visible through the windshield on the driver's side of the dash and contains the vehicle and engine identification codes. The tenth digit indicates model year and the eighth digit indicates engine code. It can be interpreted as follows:

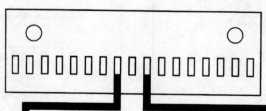

Engine Code							Model Year	
Code	Liters	Cu. In. (cc)	Cyl.	Fuel Sys.	Eng. Mfg.		Code	Year
3	4.5	273 (4467)	8	MPFI	Cadillac		L	1990
9	4.6	279 (4566)	8	MPFI	Cadillac		M	1991
Y	4.6	279 (4566)	8	MPFI	Cadillac		N	1992
B	4.9	300 (4885)	8	MPFI	Cadillac		P	1993

MPFI—Multi-Port Fuel Injection

84201043

ENGINE IDENTIFICATION

Year	Model	Engine Displacement Liters (cc)	Engine Series (ID/VIN)	Fuel System	No. of Cylinders	Engine Type
1990	Deville	4.5 (4467)	3	MPFI	8	OHV
	Eldorado	4.5 (4467)	3	MPFI	8	OHV
	Fleetwood	4.5 (4467)	3	MPFI	8	OHV
	Seville	4.5 (4467)	3	MPFI	8	OHV
1991	Deville	4.9 (4885)	B	MPFI	8	OHV
	Eldorado	4.9 (4885)	B	MPFI	8	OHV
	Fleetwood	4.9 (4885)	B	MPFI	8	OHV
	Seville	4.9 (4885)	B	MPFI	8	OHV
1992	Deville	4.9 (4885)	B	MPFI	8	OHV
	Eldorado	4.9 (4885)	B	MPFI	8	OHV
	Fleetwood	4.9 (4885)	B	MPFI	8	OHV
	Seville	4.9 (4885)	B	MPFI	8	OHV
1993	Deville	4.9 (4885)	B	MPFI	8	OHV
	Eldorado	4.9 (4885)	B	MPFI	8	OHV
	Eldorado ①	4.6 (4566)	9	MPFI	8	DOHC
	Eldorado ②	4.6 (4566)	Y	MPFI	8	DOHC
	Seville	4.9 (4885)	B	MPFI	8	OHV
	Seville ③	4.6 (4566)	9	MPFI	8	DOHC
	Sixty Special	4.9 (4885)	B	MPFI	8	OHV

MPFI—Multi-Port Fuel Injection
OHV—Overhead Valve
DOHC—Double Overhead Cam
① Eldorado Touring Coupe
② Eldorado Sport Coupe optional engine
③ Seville Touring Sedan

84201044

ROUTINE MAINTENANCE

Air Cleaner

The air cleaner keeps the air born dust and dirt from flowing into the engine. If allowed to enter the engine, dust and dirt combined with engine oil may create an abrasive compound which can drastically shorten engine life. Accordingly, the engine should never be run for a prolonged period without the air cleaner in place. A dirty air cleaner blocks the flow of air into the engine and can artificially richen the air/fuel mixture adversely affecting fuel economy and can even lead to damage to the catalytic converter. Insure that the air cleaner to throttle body gasket is in place and that the air cleaner upper housing is properly seated and secured.

The air cleaner should be checked periodically and replaced at least every 20,000 miles, more frequently in dusty driving conditions. Be sure the replacement air cleaner provides a proper fit and is not loose so that air is able to flow around the air cleaner instead of through it.

REMOVAL & INSTALLATION

▶ See Figures 8, 9 and 10

1. Remove the five air cleaner housing wingnuts/bolts from the lower air filter housing.
2. Lift off the upper air filter housing and remove the old air filter.

Fig. 8 Removing the upper air cleaner housing

Fig. 9 Removing the center nut of the upper air cleaner housing

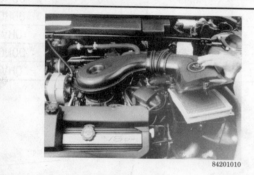

Fig. 10 Removing air cleaner

3. Wipe clean the remaining dirt from both upper and lower housings.

To install:

4. Install the new air filter element, with the flat grid side up.

5. Place the rectangular housing gasket in the ridge of the lower housing.

➡Ensure that the air cleaner to throttle body gasket is in place and that the air cleaner upper housing is properly seated and secured. A missing or mispositioned gasket may cause engine noise or may allow unfiltered air to enter the engine.

Fuel Filter

The fuel filter is located under the front of the vehicle alongside the right body rail. On some earlier models, a tubing flare nut wrench along with a back-up wrench must be used to disconnect the fuel line from the filter. Most later models use quick disconnect fuel pipe connectors.

REMOVAL & INSTALLATION

▶ **See Figures 11 and 12**

Before replacing a fuel filter it is necessary to relieve the fuel system pressure.

1. Disconnect negative battery terminal to avoid possible fuel discharge if an accidental attempt is made to start the engine.

2. Loosen fuel filler cap to relieve tank pressure.

3. Raise and safely support the vehicle.

4. Connect a fuel pressure gauge such as J 34730-1 or equivalent, to the fuel pressure connection. Wrap a towel around fitting while connecting gage to avoid spillage.

5. Install bleed hose into an approved container and open valve to bleed system pressure. Fuel connections are now safe for servicing.

6. Drain any fuel remaining in gage into an approved container.

7. On models equipped with pipe flare nut connections:

   a. Using a backup wrench, remove the fuel line fittings from the fuel filter.

   b. Remove the fuel filter mounting screws and remove the filter from the vehicle.

   c. Discard the fuel line O-rings.

8. On models equipped quick disconnect pipe connections:

   a. Twist the quick connector ¼ turn each direction to loosen any dirt within the connector. If compressed air is available, blow out the dirt from the connector.

   b. Squeeze the plastic tabs of the male end connector and pull apart. Repeat for the other fitting.

9. Remove the fuel filter mounting screws and remove the filter from the vehicle.

To install:

10. On models equipped with pipe flare nut connections:

    a. Install new O-rings to the fuel line fittings.

    b. Using a backup wrench, tighten the fuel line fittings to the fuel filter.

    c. Tighten the fuel filter mounting screws.

11. On models equipped quick disconnect pipe connections:

➡Before installing the new filter, it is important to apply a few drops of clean engine oil to both tube ends of the filter to ensure a proper connection and prevent a possible fuel leak.

    a. Place new filter loosely in position.

    b. Press outlet connector firmly onto the filter male pipe ends until springs snap into place.

    c. Check that connector is locked on by trying to pull the connector away from the male tube end of filter.

    d. Use the same procedure for the inlet connector and check that the connector is locked on.

    e. Install the fuel filter mounting screws to the vehicle.

12. Start engine and inspect for leaks.

84201011

Fig. 11 Quick disconnect fuel line at the fuel filter

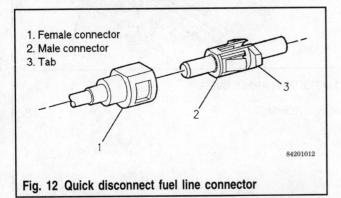

1. Female connector
2. Male connector
3. Tab

84201012

Fig. 12 Quick disconnect fuel line connector

PCV Valve

▶ See Figure 13

A positive crankcase Ventilation (PCV) system is used to provide a more complete collection of crankcase vapors. Fresh air from the air cleaner is pulled into the crankcase, mixed with blow-by gases and then purged through the positive crankcase ventilation (PCV) valve into the intake manifold. The primary control is through the PCV valve which meters the flow at a rate dependent upon manifold vacuum. To maintain idle quality, the PCV valve restricts the flow when intake manifold vacuum is high. If abnormal operating conditions arise, the system is designed to allow excessive amounts of blow-by gasses to back flow through the crankcase vent tube into the air cleaner to be consumed by normal combustion.

On all engines, the PCV valve is located on the rocker arm cover.

REMOVAL & INSTALLATION

1. Remove the PCV valve from rocker arm cover with PCV hose still attached.
2. Run engine at idle speed.
3. Place your thumb over the end of valve to check for vacuum. If there is no vacuum at valve, check for plugged hoses, intake manifold port, or PCV valve.
4. Turn off the engine and remove PCV valve.
5. Shake valve and listen for the rattle of check needle inside the valve. If valve does not rattle, replace valve.

To install:
6. Place new PCV valve in rocker valve cover.
7. Install PCV valve outlet hose on PCV valve and clamp with proper hose clamp.

Evaporative Canister

The Evaporative Emission Control (EEC) System and the charcoal canisters main purpose is to store vapor generated by the vehicle and regulates its consumption during normal driving operation. The charcoal canister prevents fuel vapor from dispelling into the atmosphere.

SERVICING

▶ See Figure 14

1. Disconnect and mark hoses for installation on new canister.
2. Remove purge solenoid electrical connector.
3. Remove the two mounting bolts.
4. Remove canister.

To install:
5. Install canister in bracket. Make sure the canister is positioned with the purge solenoid on top of the canister.
6. fasten the two mounting bolts.
7. Connect the tagged hoses to the proper inlets.
8. Install the purge solenoid electrical connector on the the top of canister.

Battery

▶ See Figure 15

GENERAL MAINTENANCE

Original equipment batteries are maintenance free and do not require checking the electrolyte level. In fact, the cells are sealed on most batteries. As a result, there should be little or no build-up of corrosion on the battery posts, terminals or cables.

If the vehicle is equipped with a replacement battery that is not maintenance-free or has become corroded, inspect and adjust the fluid level as described below.

FLUID LEVEL

1. Remove the cell caps from the top of the battery.
2. Check the electrolyte level and add distilled water as necessary to bring the level up to the bottom of the cell filler opening. Some batteries have a fill mark or a split ring inside the opening.
3. Replace the cell caps, making sure they are properly seated.
4. Wipe up any spilled electrolyte with a shop towel and dispose of the towel in case some of the electrolyte became mixed with water and was absorbed by the towel.

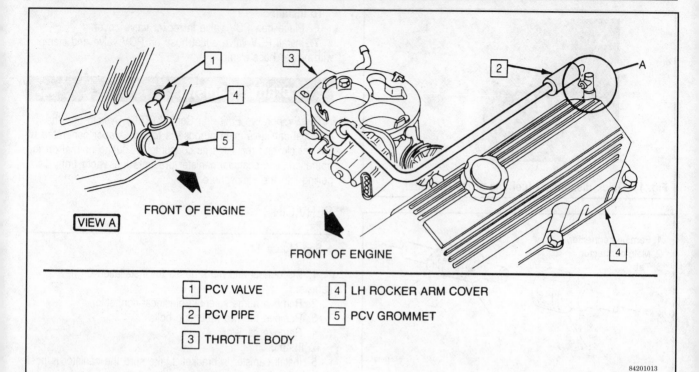

1	PCV VALVE	4	LH ROCKER ARM COVER
2	PCV PIPE	5	PCV GROMMET
3	THROTTLE BODY		

84201013

Fig. 13 PCV valve location

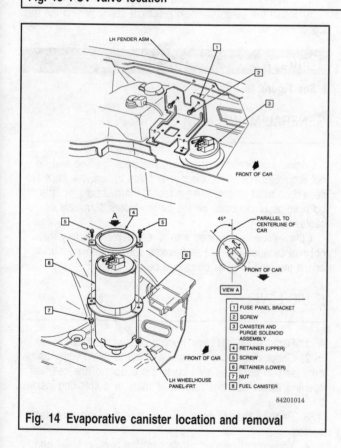

1	FUSE PANEL BRACKET
2	SCREW
3	CANISTER AND PURGE SOLENOID ASSEMBLY
4	RETAINER (UPPER)
5	SCREW
6	RETAINER (LOWER)
7	NUT
8	FUEL CANISTER

84201014

Fig. 14 Evaporative canister location and removal

CABLES

Always use a terminal clamp puller to disconnect the cables from the battery. Attempting to remove the clamp from the battery terminal by prying could crack the battery case.

Clean the cables thoroughly using a terminal brush until the metal is shiny and completely free of corrosion. Special brushes are available to properly clean side-post batteries. If the cables are heavily corroded, they may be cleaned using a solution of baking soda and water. Disconnect both battery cables from the battery before using this method. Immerse the cable in the solution until it stops bubbling.

If the cell caps are removed, make sure none of the baking soda solution is allowed to enter the battery. This could neutralize the electrolyte and destroy the battery.

Rinse well with water and allow to dry thoroughly before reconnecting. Before reconnecting the cables, It is a good idea to remove the battery and inspect the condition of the battery tray. Remove any debris that may have collected under the battery. If the battery tray shows signs of corrosion, remove using a wire brush and apply a coat of acid-resistant paint to protect the tray. After the cables have been reconnected, apply a thin coat of non-conductive grease to the terminal connection to retard corrosion.

TESTING

Some maintenance-free batteries are equipped with a built-in hydrometer. To check the condition of the battery, observe the

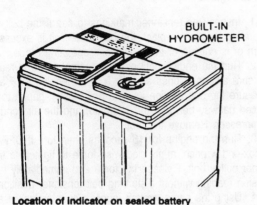

Location of Indicator on sealed battery

Original equipment maintenance-free battery with built-in hydrometer

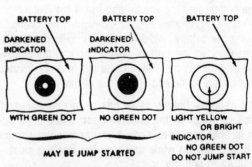

Check the appearance of the charge indicator on top of the battery before attempting a jump start; if it's not green or dark, do not jump start the car

84201015

Fig. 15 Original equipment maintenance-free battery with built-in hydrometer

"eye' on the top of the battery case for the following conditions:

1. If the indicator is dark, the battery has enough fluid. If the eye is light, the electrolyte level is low and the battery must be replaced.

2. If the indicator is green, the battery is sufficiently charged. If the green dot is not visible, charge the battery.

3. If the green dot appears or if the electrolyte squirts out of the vent hole, stop the charge and proceed to Step 4. It may be necessary to tip the battery from side to side in order to get the green dot to appear after charging.

➡**When charging the battery, the electrical system and control unit can be quickly damaged by improper connections, high output battery chargers or incorrect service procedures. Do not charge the battery for more than 50 amp-hours.**

4. Connect a battery load tester and a voltmeter across the battery terminals (the battery cable should be disconnected from the battery for 15 seconds to remove the surface charge. Remove the load.

5. Wait 15 seconds to allow the battery to recover. Apply the appropriate test load for 15 seconds while reading the voltage. Disconnect the load.

6. Check the results against specifications. If the voltage is at or above the specified voltage for the temperature listed, the battery is good. If the voltage falls below specification, the battery should be replaced.

CHARGING

✱✱CAUTION

Batteries give off hydrogen gas, which is explosive. DO NOT SMOKE around the battery while it is being charged. The battery electrolyte contains sulfuric acid. If any of the electrolyte should come in contact with the eyes or skin, flush with plenty of clear water and seek medical attention immediately.

The best method for charging a battery is slow charging, often called "trickle charging', using a low amperage charger. Quick charging a battery can actually cook the battery, damage the plates inside and decreasing the life of the battery. Any charging should be done in a well ventilated area away from the possibility of sparks or open flame. The cell caps (not found on maintenance-free batteries) should be loosened but not removed. If the battery must be quick-charged, check the cell voltages and the color of the electrolyte a few minutes after the charge has begun. If the cell voltages are not uniform or if the electrolyte is discolored with brown sediment, stop the quick charging in favor of a trickle charge. A common indicator of an overcharged battery is the frequent need to add water to the battery.

REPLACEMENT

If the battery is to be removed or replaced always disconnect the negative cable from the battery first using a battery clamp puller. Disconnect the positive cable next. Remove the battery hold-down clamp. Using a battery puller, remove the battery from the vehicle.

Charge the replacement battery, as required, using the slow charge method discussed above. Inspect the battery terminals and cables, and service as required.

Install the battery into the vehicle and install the battery hold-down clamp, making sure not to overtighten the clamp. Overtightening the battery hold-down clamp could crack the battery case. Connect the positive battery cable to the positive battery post and tighten the clamp. Once this is done, connect the negative battery cable and tighten the clamp.

➡**Once the negative battery cable has been connected, do not go back to retighten the positive post. Since the electrical path is now complete, should you accidentally touch the body of the vehicle while touching the positive post an electrical short will occur.**

Serpentine Belt

INSPECTION

A single serpentine belt is used to drive engine-mounted accessories. Drive belt tension is maintained by a spring loaded tensioner. The drive belt tensioner can control belt tension over a broad range of belt lengths, however, there are limits to the tensioner's ability to compensate.

Belt tension and condition should be checked at least every 30,000 miles or 24 months. Check the serpentine belt for cracking, fraying and splitting on the inside of the belt. To properly check serpentine belt tension use a belt tension gauge.

A belt squeak when the engine is started or stopped is normal and does not necessarily indicate a worn belt. If the squeak persists or worsens, inspect the belt for wear and replace as necessary.

REMOVAL & INSTALLATION

1. Insert a ½ inch drive breaker bar into the adjuster arm on the tensioner pulley. Later models require an 18mm box end wrench.

➡**Make sure the drive end of the breaker bar is long enough to fully seat in the tensioner pulley and that both the breaker bar and box wrench are long enough to provide the proper leverage.**

2. Rotate the tensioner counterclockwise and remove the belt.

3. Slowly rotate the tensioner clockwise to release the tension.

To install:

4. Route the belt over the pulleys following the diagram found in the engine compartment.

5. Rotate the tensioner counterclockwise and install the belt over the remaining pulley.

6. Inspect the belt positioning over each pulley to ensure the belt is seated properly in all the grooves.

TENSIONER INSPECTION

▶ **See Figures 16, 17 and 18**

1. Inspect the tensioner markings to see if the belt is within operating lengths. Replace the belt if the belt is excessively worn or is outside of the tensioner's operating range.

2. Run the engine until operating temperature is reached. Be sure all accessories are off. Turn the engine **OFF** and measure the belt tension using a belt tension gauge tool placed halfway between the alternator and the air conditioning compressor. Remove the tool.

3. Run the engine for 15 seconds, then turn it **OFF**. Using a box-end wrench, apply clockwise force to tighten to the tensioner pulley bolt. Release the force and immediately take a tension reading without disturbing belt tensioner position.

4. Using the same wrench, apply a counterclockwise force to the tensioner pulley bolt and raise the pulley to its fully

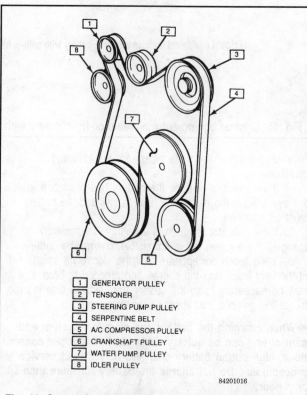

1	GENERATOR PULLEY
2	TENSIONER
3	STEERING PUMP PULLEY
4	SERPENTINE BELT
5	A/C COMPRESSOR PULLEY
6	CRANKSHAFT PULLEY
7	WATER PUMP PULLEY
8	IDLER PULLEY

84201016

Fig. 16 Serpentine belt routing and pulley identification

84201017

Fig. 17 Loosening tensioner and removing serpentine belt

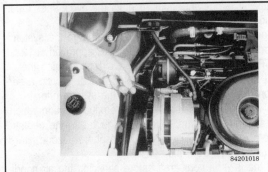

Fig. 18 Adjusting alternator for belt installation

raised position. Slowly lower the pulley to engage the belt. Take a tension reading without disturbing the belt tensioner position.

5. Average the 3 readings. If their average is lower than specifications, replace the tensioner:

Hoses

The hoses should be checked for deterioration, leaks and loose hose clamps every 12,000 miles or 12 months.

REMOVAL & INSTALLATION

▶ See Figures 19, 20 and 21

1. Drain the cooling system into a clean container to a level that is below the hose being removed.
2. Loosen the hose clamps.

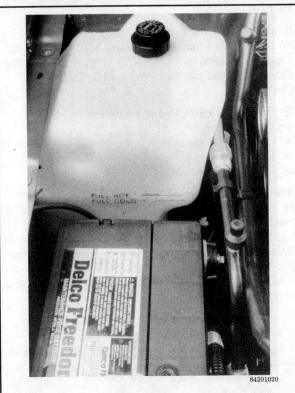

Fig. 20 Coolant overflow bottle

3. Disconnect the inlet hose from the radiator and thermostat housing.
4. Disconnect the outlet hose from the radiator and coolant pump or cylinder block.

Fig. 19 Upper radiator hose location

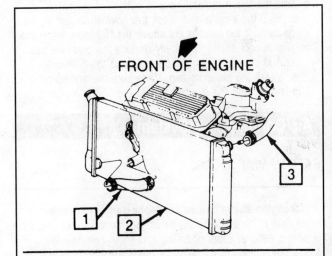

FRONT OF ENGINE

1	LOWER RADIATOR HOSE
2	RADIATOR ASSEMBLY
3	UPPER RADIATOR HOSE

Fig. 21 Upper and lower radiator hose location

To install:

➡**If installing original equipment hoses, make sure to align the reference marks on the hose with the marks on the radiator. A twist in the hose will place a strain on the radiator fitting and could cause the fitting to crack or break.**

5. Connect the outlet hose to the radiator and coolant pump or cylinder block.

6. Connect the radiator hose to the radiator and thermostat.

7. Refill the cooling system to a level just below the filler neck. Install the radiator cap.

➡**The cooling systems on later models may use a surge tank instead of an overflow bottle. The overflow bottle has 1 small hose coming from the radiator filler neck. The surge tank can be recognized by the presence of 2 hoses, 1 from the radiator cap and 1 outlet to the lower radiator hose. The surge tank is also mounted above the level of the radiator cap, making it the highest point in the cooling system.**

8. If equipped with an overflow bottle, perform the following:

a. Fill the overflow bottle to the "Full Hot' mark.

b. Start the engine and allow to come to normal operating temperature.

c. Stop the engine and refill the overflow bottle to the "Full Hot' mark.

d. Check the coolant level frequently over the next couple of days.

9. If equipped with a surge tank, perform the following:

a. Fill the surge tank to the base of the filler neck.

b. Install the pressure cap on the surge tank. Start the engine and allow to come to normal operating temperature or until the upper radiator hose is hot.

c. Stop the engine and check the level of coolant in the surge tank. If the level is not above the "full' line, allow the engine to cool enough to slowly remove the pressure cap.

d. Add coolant to bring the level up to the "full' line.

e. Install the pressure cap. Make sure the arrows on the cap line up with the overflow hose.

Air Conditioning System

SAFETY WARNINGS

Working on automotive air conditioning systems requires a great deal of care due to the nature of the refrigerant and the system pressures (both operating and static). Review the safety precautions listed below before attempting work on the air conditioning system.

• Always wear safety goggles that completely cover the eyes when working on the air conditioning system. Do not trust safety glasses or prescription glasses with safety lens to adequately protect the eyes. Refrigerant released under pressure, contacting the eyes could freeze the eyes causing permanent eye damage. If refrigerant should contact the eyes, seek medical attention immediately.

• If is determined to be necessary to discharge the system, every effort should be made to use an SAE approved R-12 Recovery/Recycling machine so as to avoid discharging the refrigerant to the atmosphere. That could include having a service station remove the refrigerant from the system prior to beginning work. R-12 refrigerant is a chlorofluorocarbon which, when released into the atmosphere, contributes to the depletion of the ozone layer in the upper atmosphere. Ozone filters out harmful radiation from the sun.

Consult the laws in your area before servicing the air conditioning system. In some states it is illegal to preform repairs involving refrigerant unless the work is done by a certified technician.

• Avoid contact with a charged refrigeration system, even when working on another part of the air conditioning system or vehicle. If a heavy tool or sharp object should come in contact with a section of the tubing or heat exchanger, a rupture could occur.

• When it is necessary to apply force to a fitting which contains refrigerant, as when checking that all system couplings are tightened securely, use a backup wrench whenever possible. This will avoid undue torque on the refrigerant tubing. It is advisable, whenever possible, to use tube or line wrenches when tightening these fittings. In the absence of a line wrench, make sure the open end wrench has a firm "bite' on the fitting before tightening.

• DO NOT attempt to discharge the system by merely loosening a fitting or removing the service valve caps and cracking these valves. Precise control is possible only when using the service gauges. If unable to use an approved R-12 Recovery/Recycling machine to remove the refrigerant, place a rag under the open end of the center charging hose to capture any liquid drops that may escape. **Always** wear protective goggles when connecting or disconnecting the service gauge hoses.

• Discharge the system only in a well ventilated area, as high concentrations of the refrigerant can exclude oxygen, which could lead to a loss of consciousness. When leak testing or soldering this precaution is particularly important as toxic gas is formed when R-12 refrigerant comes into contact with a flame.

• Never start a system without first verifying that both service valves are back-seated (if equipped) and that all fittings throughout the system are snugly connected.

• Avoid applying heat to any refrigerant line or storage vessel. Charging may be aided by using water heated to less than 125°F (52°C) to warm the refrigerant container. Never allow a refrigerant storage container to sit in the sun or near any other heat source, such as a radiator.

• Frostbite from liquid refrigerant should be treated by first warming the area gradually with cool water and then gently applying petroleum jelly. Seek medical attention as soon as possible.

• Always keep the refrigerant container fittings capped when not in use. Avoid any sudden shock to the container, which might occur from dropping it or from banging a heavy tool against it. Never carry a refrigerant container in the passenger compartment of a vehicle.

- Always discharge the system completely if the vehicle is to be painted using a baked-on finish or before welding anywhere near the refrigerant lines.

✳✳WARNING

R-12 refrigerant is a chlorofluorocarbon which, when released into   the atmosphere, can contribute to the depletion of the ozone layer in the upper atmosphere. Ozone filters out harmful radiation from the sun.   Consult the laws in your area before servicing the air conditioning system. In some states it is illegal to perform repairs involving refrigerant unless the work is done by a certified technician.

SYSTEM INSPECTION

Checking For System Leaks

Refrigerant leaks can show up as oily areas on the various components, because compressor oil is transported through the entire system along with the refrigerant. Look for oily spots on all the hoses and lines, especially on the hose and tubing connections. If there are oily deposits, the system may have a leak. The diagnosis should be confirmed by an experienced repair person.

Keep The Condenser Clear

Periodically, inspect the front of the condenser for bent fins or foreign matter, such as dirt, leaves, cigarette butts, etc. Straighten bent fins carefully using the edge of a small slotted screwdriver or purchase a coil comb. Remove any debris by first directing water from a hose through the back of the condenser fins. Avoid using a hose with excessive water pressure. Remove the remaining debris with a stiff bristle brush (not a wire brush).

Operate the System Periodically

This step is accomplished automatically in later model vehicles due to the fact that the compressor is automatically engaged when the defrost mode is selected. In the colder weather, be sure to run the defroster for at least 5 minutes, once a week to make sure the refrigerant and, especially, the lubricant are circulated completely.

REFRIGERANT LEVEL CHECKS

Neither the CCOT (Cycling Clutch Orifice Tube) nor VDOT (Variable Displacement Orifice Tube) air conditioning system uses a sight glass to indicate the refrigerant level. The level must be determined indirectly, using a set of manifold gauges.

1. Connect the manifold gauges to the system. Start the engine and run the air conditioning system. Observe the gauge pressures. if the air conditioner is working properly, the pressures will fall within the specifications shown in the performance chart.

2. Cycle the air conditioner **ON** and **OFF** to make sure you are seeing actual pressures in the system. Turn the system **OFF** and watch the manifold gauges. If there is refrigerant in the system, you should see the low side pressure rise and the high side pressure fall during the **OFF** cycle. If the system pressures are fluctuating when the compressor cycles and the operating pressure is within specification and the system is delivering cool air, everything is functioning normally.

3. If you observe low pressures on the high and low sides while the system is operating the system may be low on refrigerant.

GAUGE SETS

▶ See Figure 22

Most of the service work performed on the air conditioning system requires the use of a set of manifold gauges. The manifold gauge set consists of 2 gauges, one to read high (head) pressure and one to read low (suction) pressures in the system.

The low side gauge registers both pressure and vacuum readings. The low side scale registers from 0-60 psi (414kpa) and vacuum readings from 0-30 in. Hg. The high side gauge measures pressure from 0-300 psi (2100kpa).

The manifold valves are designed so they have no direct effect on the gauge readings but serve only to provide a cut off for the flow of refrigerant through the manifold. During all testing and hook-up operations, the valves should be kept in a closed position to avoid disturbing the refrigerant system. System pressures may be observed without opening the valves. Check for limited reference of purging a/c through gauges.

When purging the system, the center hose is uncapped at the lower end and both valves are cracked (opened) slightly with the engine not running. This allows the refrigerant pressure to force the entire contents of the system out through the center hose. During evacuation, both valves are opened to allow the vacuum pump to remove all air and moisture from the system before charging. During recharging, the valve on the high system is closed and the low side valve is cracked open. Under these conditions, the low pressure in the evaporator will draw refrigerant from the relatively warm refrigerant storage container into the system.

Service Valves
▶ See Figures 23 and 24

✳✳CAUTION

Wear protective goggles whenever working on the air conditioning system. Do NOT remove the gauge hoses while the engine is running. Always turn the engine OFF and allow the system pressure to stabilize before removing the gauge set test hose.

To diagnose an air conditioning system problem, the system must be entered in order to read the system pressures. The air conditioning systems on Cadillac vehicles use Schrader type valves, similar to the valves used on automobile tires. The process of connecting the gauge lines set to the system is the same as threading a tire pump outlet hose onto a bicycle tire valve. As the test hose is threaded onto the service port

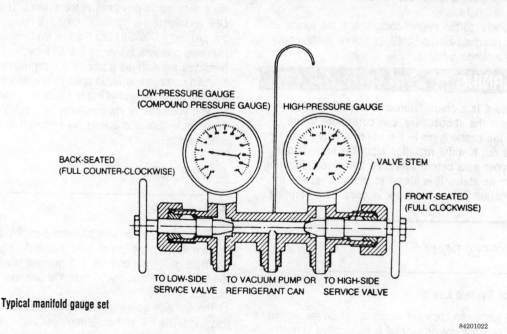

Fig. 22 Typical manifold gauge set

the valve core is depressed, allowing the refrigerant to enter the test hose outlet. When the test hose is removed, the pressure in the system pushes the valve closed.

✳✳CAUTION

Extreme caution must be observed when removing test hoses from the Schrader valves as some refrigerant will normally escape, usually under high pressure. Observe safety precautions.

Using the Manifold Gauges

The following step-by-step procedure should be used to correctly connect the gauge set to the system.
1. Engine NOT running.
2. Remove the caps from the high and low side service ports. Make sure both gauge valves are closed.
3. Connect the blue low side test hose to the service valve on or near the accumulator (large aluminum can).

Fig. 23 Removing dust cap for air conditioning recharge

Fig. 24 Removing dust cap for low side fitting

4. Connect the red high side test hose to the service valve on the refrigerant line that leads from the compressor to the condenser (looks similar to the radiator, mounted in front of the radiator).
5. Start the engine and allow to come to normal operating temperature. All testing and charging of the system should be done at normal operating temperature.
6. Adjust the air conditioner controls to **Max Cold**.
7. Observe the gauge readings.

Storage Of The Gauge Set

When the gauges are not in use, thread the test end of the gauge hoses onto the threaded blank fittings on the manifold assembly. This will keep dirt and especially moisture out of the hoses and manifold. If the gauge set has extra fittings, cap or plug them.

If air and moisture have gotten into the gauges, purge the hoses by supplying refrigerant under pressure to the center hose with both gauge valves open and all openings unplugged. Crack each hose slightly, one at a time, until refrigerant comes out. This will purge the air and moisture from the hoses. Immediately cap the lines as described above.

DISCHARGING THE SYSTEM

❋❋WARNING

R-12 refrigerant is a chlorofluorocarbon which, when released into the atmosphere, can contribute to the depletion of the ozone layer in the upper atmosphere. Ozone filters out harmful radiation from the sun. If possible, an approved R-12 Recovery/Recycling machine that meets SAE standards should be employed when discharging the system. Follow the operating instructions provided with the approved equipment exactly to properly discharge the system.

❋❋CAUTION

Be sure to perform the operation in a well ventilated area.

1. If the system has a charge and the compressor can be operated, run for at least 10 minutes. Turn the engine **OFF**.
2. Attach the gauges.
3. Place a container or rag at the outlet of the center charging hose. The refrigerant will be discharged there and this precaution will avoid its uncontrolled release.
4. Open the low side hand valve on the manifold slightly.

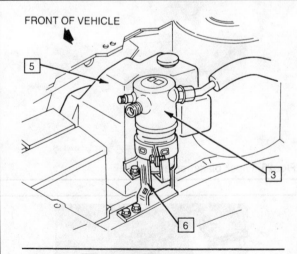

1	A/C HOSE ASSEMBLY
2	BOLT
3	ACCUMULATOR
4	MUFFLER
5	COOLANT RESERVOIR
6	ACCUMULATOR BRACKET

84201025

Fig. 25 Accumulator location and related parts

5. Open the high side hand valve on the manifold slightly.

➡ **If the system is discharged too rapidly, an oily foam will appear in the receiving rag or container. Should this occur, close the valves slowly until the foaming stops.**

6. Close both hand valves on the manifold when the pressure on both gauges read **0**, indicating that the system is discharged.

EVACUATING

If the air conditioning system has been opened to the atmosphere, it should be air and moisture free before being recharged with refrigerant. Moisture and air mixed with refrigerant will raise the compressor head pressure, possibly damage the system's components and will reduce the performance of the system. In addition, air and moisture in the system can lead to internal corrosion of the system components. Moisture will boil at normal room temperature when exposed to a vacuum. To evacuate, or rid the system of air and moisture:

1. Leak test the system and repair any leaks found.
2. Connect an approved charging station, Recovery/Recycling machine or manifold gauge set and vacuum pump to the discharge and suction ports.
3. Open the discharge and suction ports and start the vacuum pump. If the pump is not able to pull at least 26 in. Hg of vacuum there is a leak that must be repaired before evacuation can occur.
4. Once the system has reached at least 26 in. Hg of vacuum, allow the system to evacuate for at least 10 minutes. The longer the system is evacuated, the more moisture will be removed.
5. Close all valves and turn the pump off. If the system loses more than 2 in. Hg of vacuum after 15 minutes, there is a leak that should be repaired.

SYSTEM CHARGING

1. Connect an approved charging station, Recovery/Recycling machine or manifold gauge set to the discharge and suction ports. The red hose is normally connected to the discharge (high pressure) line, and the blue hose is connected to the suction (low pressure) line. If using a manifold gauge set, the center (usually yellow) hose is connected to the charging station or Recovery/Recycling machine.
2. Follow the instructions provided with the equipment and charge the system with the specified amount of refrigerant.
3. Perform a leak test.

LEAK TESTING

▶ **See Figure 26**

There 2 methods of detecting leaks in an air conditioning system: halide leak detection or the open flame method and use of an electronic leak detector. Since burning R-12 creates phosgene gas, which is poisonous, the use of the open flame method is no longer in common use, although it was at one time the only method of leak detection available. Electronic leak detectors are much safer and more accurate, although an electronically created spark is used to detect the presence of refrigerant.

The halide leak detector is a torch-like device which produces a yellow-green color when refrigerant is introduced into the flame at the burner. A purple or violet color indicates the presence of large amounts of refrigerant at the burner.

A electronic leak detector is a small portable device with an extended probe. With the unit activated, the probe is passed along the components of the system which contain refrigerant. Since R-12 refrigerant is heavier than air, passing the probe along the bottom or under the component being tested is a more accurate means of leak detection. If a leak is detected, the unit will sound and alarm signal or activate a display signal depending on the manufacturer's design. Follow the manufacturers's instructions as the design and function of the detector may vary significantly.

✳✳CAUTION

Caution should be taken to operate either type of detector in a well ventilated area, so as to reduce the chance of personal injury, which may result from coming into contact with poisonous gases produced when R-12 is exposed to flame or electric spark.

Windshield Wipers

Intense heat from the sun, snow and ice, road oils and the chemicals used in windshield washer solvents combine to deteriorate the rubber wiper refills. The refills should be replaced about twice a year or whenever the blades begin to streak or chatter.

For maximum effectiveness and longest element life, the windshield and wiper blades should be kept clean. Dirt, tree sap, road tar and so on will cause streaking, smearing and blade deterioration if left on the glass. It is advisable to wash the windshield carefully with a commercial glass cleaner at least once a month. Wipe off the rubber blades with the wet rag afterwards. Do not attempt to move the wipers by hand as damage to the motor and drive mechanism will result.

If the blades are found to be cracked, broken or torn, they should be replaced immediately. Replacement intervals will vary with usage, although ozone deterioration usually limits blade life to about 1 year at the maximum. If the wiper pattern is smeared or streaked, or if the blade chatters across the glass, the elements should be replaced. It is easiest and most sensible to replace the elements in pairs.

There are 3 different types of refills, which differ in their method of replacement. One type has 2 release buttons, approximately ⅓ of the way up from each end of the blade frame. Pushing the buttons down releases a lock and allows the rubber filler to be removed from the frame. The new blade slides back into the frame and locks into place.

The second type of refill has 2 metal tabs which are unlocked by squeezing them together. The rubber blade can then be withdrawn from the frame jaws. A new refill is installed by inserting the refill into the front frame jaws and sliding it rearward to engage the remaining frame jaws. There are usually 4 jaws. Be certain when installing that the refill is engaged in all

of them. At the end of its travel, the tabs will lock into place on the front jaws of the wiper blade frame.

The third type is a refill made from polycarbonate. The refill has a simple locking device at 2 end which flexes downward out of the groove into which the jaws of the holder fit, allowing easy release. By sliding the new refill through all the jaws and pushing through the slight resistance when it reaches the end of its travel, the refill will lock into position.

Regardless of the type of refill used, make sure that all of the frame jaws are engaged as the refill is pushed into place and locked. The metal blade holder and frame will scratch the glass if allowed to touch it.

WIPER REFILL REPLACEMENT

▶ **See Figures 30, 31, 27, 28 and 29**

Normally, if the wipers are not cleaning the windshield properly, only the refill has to be replaced. The blade and arm usually require replacement only in the event of damage. It is only necessary to remove the arm or blade to replace the refill (except on Tridon® refills). The job may be made easier by turning the ignition switch to the **ON** position, then turn the wiper switch **ON**. When the wiper arms reach the center of the windshield, turn the ignition switch to the **OFF** position.

There are several types of refills and your vehicle could have any kind, since aftermarket blades and arms may not use exactly the same type of refill as the original equipment.

The original equipment wiper elements can be replaced as follows:

1. Lift the wiper arm off the glass.

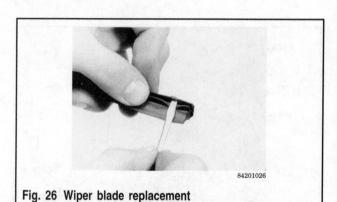

Fig. 26 Wiper blade replacement

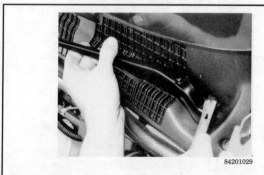

Fig. 27 Removing wiper arm assembly

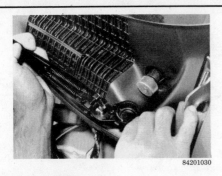

Fig. 28 Wiper arm assembly

2. Depress the release lever on the center bridge and remove the blade from the arm.

3. Lift the tab and pinch the end bridge to release it from the center bridge.

4. Slide the end bridge from the wiper blade and the wiper blade from the opposite end bridge.

5. Install a new element and be sure the tab on the end bridge is down to lock the element into place. Check each release point for positive engagement.

Tires and Wheels

TIRE ROTATION

▶ **See Figures 32 and 33**

Tire wear can be equalized by switching the position of the tires at 6000 miles for new tires and then every 15,000 miles. Including a conventional spare in the rotation pattern can give up to 20% more life to a set of tires.

❋❋CAUTION

DO NOT include the temporary use spare in the rotation pattern.

There are certain exceptions to tire rotation, however. Studded snow tires should not be rotated. Radials should be kept on the same side of the vehicle (maintain the same direction or rotation). The belts on radial tires develop a set pattern. If the direction of rotation is reversed, it can cause a rough ride and vibration.

➡**When radials or studded snows are removed for the season, mark them so they can be reinstalled on the same side of the vehicle.**

TIRE DESIGN

For maximum service life tires should be used in sets of five, except on vehicles equipped with a space-saver spare tire. Do not mix tires of different designs, such as steel belted radial, fiberglass belted or bias/belted, or tires of different sizes, such as P165SR-14 and P185SR-14.

Conventional bias ply tires are constructed so that the cords run bead-to-bead at an angle (bias). Alternate plies run at an opposite angle. This type of construction gives rigidity to both tread and sidewall. Bias/belted tires are similar in construction to conventional bias ply tires. Belts run at an angel and also at a 90° angle to the bead, as in the radial tire. Tread life in improved considerably over the conventional bias tire. The radial tire differs in construction, but instead of the carcass plies running at an angle of 90° to each other, they run at an angle of 90° to the bead. This gives the tread a great deal of rigidity and the sidewall a great deal of flexibility and accounts for the characteristic bulge associated with radial tires.

All Cadillac models are capable of using radial tires and they are the recommended type for all years. If radial tires are used, tires sizes and wheel diameters should be selected to maintain ground clearance and tire load capacity equivalent to the minimum specified tire. Radial tires should always be used in sets of 5 if the spare is a conventional tire. In an emergency, radial tires can be used with caution on the rear axle only. If this is done, both tires on the rear should be of radial design.

➡**Radial tires should never be used on only the front axle as they can adversely effect steering if tires of different designs are mixed.**

TIRE STORAGE

Store the tires at the proper inflation pressures, if they are mounted. All tires should be stored in a cool, dry place. If the tires are stored in a garage or basement, DO NOT, let them stand on a concrete floor. Instead, set them on blocks of wood.

TIRE INFLATION

Factory installed wheels and tires are designed to handle loads up to and including their rated load capacity when inflated to the recommended inflation pressures. Correct tire pressure and driving techniques have an important influence on tire life. Heavy cornering, excessively rapid acceleration and unnecessary braking increase tire wear. Underinflated tires can cause handling problems, poor fuel economy, shortened tire life and tire overloading.

Maximum axle load must never exceed the value shown on the side of the tire. The inflation pressure should never exceed the value shown on the side of the tire, usually 35 psi (241kpa) for conventional tires or 60 psi (414kpa) for a compact spare tire. The pressure shown on the tire is NOT the recommended operating pressure for the tire or vehicle. In most cases, that pressure is far too high and will result in a rough ride and accelerated tire wear. It is the maximum pressure the tire manufacturer has determined that tire can handle under extreme load circumstances. The correct operating tire inflation pressures are listed on the tire placard located on the side of the driver's door.

Check tire inflation at least once a month.

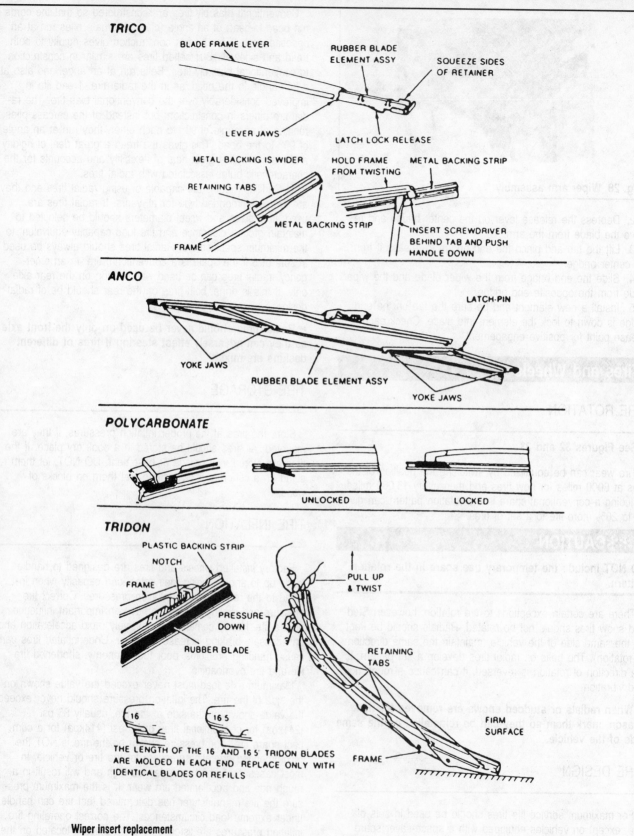

TRICO

BLADE FRAME LEVER

RUBBER BLADE ELEMENT ASSY

SQUEEZE SIDES OF RETAINER

LEVER JAWS

LATCH LOCK RELEASE

METAL BACKING IS WIDER

RETAINING TABS

HOLD FRAME FROM TWISTING

METAL BACKING STRIP

FRAME

METAL BACKING STRIP

INSERT SCREWDRIVER BEHIND TAB AND PUSH HANDLE DOWN

ANCO

LATCH-PIN

YOKE JAWS

RUBBER BLADE ELEMENT ASSY

YOKE JAWS

POLYCARBONATE

UNLOCKED

LOCKED

TRIDON

PLASTIC BACKING STRIP

NOTCH

FRAME

PRESSURE DOWN

RUBBER BLADE

PULL UP & TWIST

RETAINING TABS

FIRM SURFACE

FRAME

16   16 5

THE LENGTH OF THE 16 AND 16 5 TRIDON BLADES ARE MOLDED IN EACH END REPLACE ONLY WITH IDENTICAL BLADES OR REFILLS

Wiper insert replacement

Fig. 29 Wiper insert replacement

84201031

Fig. 30 Wiper arm removal

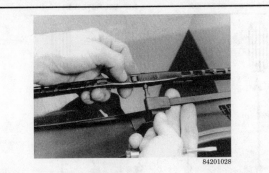

Fig. 31 Wiper arm installation

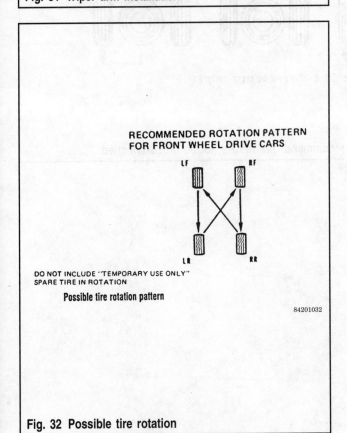

Fig. 32 Possible tire rotation

CARE OF SPECIAL WHEELS

If the vehicle is equipped with aluminum alloy wheels, be very careful when using any type of cleaner on either the wheels or tires. Read the label on the package of the cleaner to make sure that it will not damage aluminum.

FLUIDS AND LUBRICANTS

Fluid Disposal

Used fluids such as engine oil, transmission fluid, antifreeze and brake fluid are hazardous wastes and must be disposed of properly. Before draining any fluids, consult with the local authorities; in many areas waste oil etc, is being accepted as a part of recycling programs. A number of service stations and auto parts stores are also accepting waste fluids for recycling.

Be sure of the recycling center's policies before draining any fluids, as many will not accept different fluids that have been mixed together, such as oil and antifreeze.

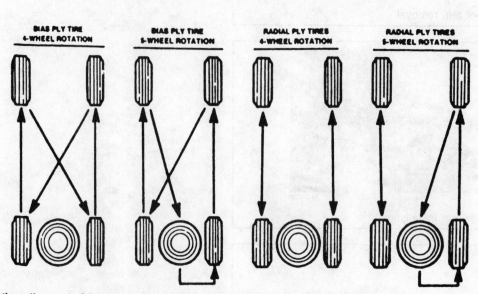

Tire rotation patterns; note that some manufacturers recommend that radials not be cross-switched

84201033

Fig. 33 Tire rotation patterns; note that some manufacturers recommend that radials not be cross-switched

CAPACITIES

Year	Model	Engine ID/VIN	Engine Displacement Liters (cc)	Engine Crankcase with Filter	Transmission (pts.)			Transfer Case (pts.)	Drive Axle		Fuel Tank (gal.)	Cooling System (qts.)
					4-Spd	5-Spd	Auto.		Front (pts.)	Rear (pts.)		
1990	Deville	3	4.5 (4467)	5.5	—	—	22	—	①	—	18	13.2
	Eldorado	3	4.5 (4467)	5.5	—	—	22	—	①	—	18.8	12.1
	Fleetwood	3	4.5 (4467)	5.5	—	—	22	—	①	—	18	13.2
	Seville	3	4.5 (4467)	5.5	—	—	22	—	①	—	18.8	12.1
1991	Deville	B	4.9 (4885)	5.5	—	—	22	—	①	—	18	13.2
	Eldorado	B	4.9 (4885)	5.5	—	—	22	—	①	—	18.8	12.1
	Fleetwood	B	4.9 (4885)	5.5	—	—	22	—	①	—	18	13.2
	Seville	B	4.9 (4885)	5.5	—	—	22	—	①	—	18.8	12.1
1992	Deville	B	4.9 (4885)	5.5	—	—	22	—	①	—	18	12.1
	Eldorado	B	4.9 (4885)	5.5	—	—	22	—	①	—	18	12.1
	Fleetwood	B	4.9 (4885)	5.5	—	—	22	—	①	—	18	12.1
	Seville	B	4.9 (4885)	5.5	—	—	22	—	①	—	18	12.1
1993	Deville	B	4.9 (4885)	5.5	—	—	22	—	①	—	18	12.1
	Eldorado	B	4.9 (4885)	5.5	—	—	22	—	①	—	20	12.3
	Eldorado	9	4.6 (4566)	7.5	—	—	22	—	①	—	20	12.3
	Eldorado	Y	4.6 (4566)	7.5	—	—	22	—	①	—	20	12.3
	Seville	B	4.9 (4885)	5.5	—	—	22	—	①	—	20	12.3
	Seville	9	4.6 (4566)	7.5	—	—	22	—	①	—	20	12.3
	Sixty Special	B	4.9 (4885)	5.5	—	—	22	—	①	—	18	12.1

① Included in transaxle capacity

84201050

Fuel and Engine Oil Recommendations

FUEL

➡Some fuel additives contain chemicals that can damage the catalytic converter and/or oxygen sensor. Read all of the labels carefully before using any additive in the engine or fuel system.

All engines require the use of unleaded fuel only. The octane rating required will vary according to the compression ratio of the engine. For the most part, if the compression ration is 9.0:1 or lower, the vehicle will perform satisfactorily on regular unleaded gasoline. If the compression ratio is greater than 9.0:1, premium unleaded is required. Check the owner's manual for specific guidelines for the engine in your vehicle.

Fuel should be selected for the brand and octane which performs best in your engine. Judge a gasoline by its ability to prevent ping, its engine starting capabilities (both cold and hot) and general all weather performance.

In general, choose the octane the manufacturer recommends. Regardless of the claims made by advertisers as to the improved performance delivered by the use of premium fuel, in most cases the vehicle runs best on the octane fuel recommended by the manufacturer.

➡For all Cadillac engines covered in this manual a premium unleaded gasoline rated at 91 octane or higher is required. An octane rating as low as 87 may be used in a emergency (if heavy knocking does not occur). If your using an unleaded gasoline with a 91 or higher octane rating and you still get heavy knocking, your engine needs service.

OIL

▶ See Figure 34

➡Always use 'SG/CC', or 'SG/CD' Energy Conserving II oils of the proper viscosity.

Two items are important to look for when selecting an engine oil. The quality designation and the viscosity (thickness) rating. Both are printed on the container and usually in the American Petroleum Institute (API) approved logo.

The oil quality must be "SG' and will usually be listed as "API service SG'. It may also be combined with other quality designations such as"SG/CC', or "SG/CD'etc. Energy Conserving II is formulated to help improve fuel economy.

Engine oil viscosity (thickness) has an effect on fuel economy and cold-weather operation (starting and oil flow). Lower viscosity engine oils can provide better economy and cold-weather performance; however, higher temperature weather conditions require higher viscosity engine oils for satisfactory lubrication.

The recommended oil viscosity for all Cadillacs when the temperature is above 0°F (-18°C) is SAE 10-30. Refer to the engine oil viscosity chart for the recommended viscosity grade.

✳✳WARNING

SAE 10W-40 or oils of other quality designations are NOT recommended for use in any Cadillac at any time.

Engine

OIL LEVEL CHECK

▶ **See Figures 35, 36 and 37**

The engine oil level is checked using the dipstick.

➡**The oil should be checked before the engine is started or 5 minutes after the engine has been shut OFF. This gives the oil time to drain back into the oil pan and prevents an inaccurate oil level reading.**

Remove the dipstick from its tube, wipe it clean and insert it back into the tube all the way. Remove it again and observe the oil level. It should be maintained between the upper FULL mark and the ADD mark. Do not allow the oil level to drop below the add line on the dipstick.

✳✳WARNING

Do not overfill the crankcase. It may result in oil-fouled spark plugs, oil leaks cause by oil seal failure or engine damage due to oil foaming.

OIL AND FILTER CHANGE

The manufacturer's recommended oil change interval is 7500 miles under normal operating conditions. We recommend an oil change interval of 3000-3500 miles under normal conditions; more frequently under severe conditions such as when the average trip is less than 4 miles, the engine is operated for

Fig. 35 Engine oil level dipstick markings-keep oil between lines

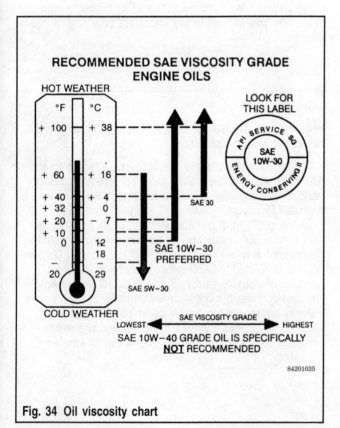

RECOMMENDED SAE VISCOSITY GRADE ENGINE OILS

Fig. 34 Oil viscosity chart

Fig. 36 Engine oil dipstick location

Fig. 37 Engine oil fill location

extended periods at idle or low-speed, when towing a trailer or operating is dusty areas.

In addition, we recommend that the filter be replaced EVERY time the oil is changed.

➡**Please be considerate of the environment. Dispose of waste oil properly by taking it to a service station, municipal facility or recycling center.**

1. Run the engine until it reaches normal operating temperature.

2. Raise and safely support the front of the vehicle using jackstands.

3. Slide a drain pan of at least 5 quarts capacity under the oil pan.

4. Loosen the drain plug. Turn it out by hand by keeping an inward pressure on the plug as you unscrew it. This will prevent hot oil from escaping past the threads until the plug is completely out of the threads.

5. Allow the oil to drain completely and then reinstall the drain plug. Do not overtighten the plug.

6. Using an oil filter wrench, remove the oil filter. Be aware, that the filter contains about 1 quart of hot, dirty oil.

7. Empty the old oil filter into the drain pan and dispose of the filter properly.

8. Using a clean shop towel, wipe off the filter adapter on the engine block. Be sure the towel does not leave any lint which could clog an oil passage.

9. Coat the rubber gasket on the new filter with fresh oil. Spin the filter onto the adapter by hand until it contacts the mounting surface. Tighten the filter ¾ to 1 full turn.

10. Refill the crankcase with the specified amount of engine oil.

11. Crank the engine over several times, then start it. After approximately 3-5 seconds, if the pressure gauge shows zero or the oil pressure warning indicator fails to go out, shut the engine OFF and investigate the problem.

12. If the oil pressure is OK and there are no leaks, shut the engine OFF and lower the vehicle.

13. Wait for a few minutes and check the oil level. Add oil, as necessary, to bring the level up to the **FULL** mark.

14. On those models so equipped, the Oil Life Index must be reset as follows:

   a. Display the 'OIL LIFE INDEX' by pressing the 'INFORMATION' button.

   b. Press and hold the 'STORE/RECALL' buttons until the display shows '100'.

Automatic Transaxle

FLUID RECOMMENDATIONS

When adding fluid or refilling the transaxle, use Dexron®IIE automatic transmission fluid.

LEVEL CHECK

▶ See Figure 38

✱✱WARNING

A false reading of the dipstick is possible if the following instructions are not followed.

You should wait at least 30 minutes before checking the transaxle fluid level if you have been driving as follows:
- When the outside temperatures are above 90°F (32°C).
- At high speed for a long time.
- In heavy traffic (especially in hot weather).
- When pulling a trailer.

To get the right reading the fluid should be at normal operating temperature.

1. Start the engine and drive the vehicle for a minimum of 15 miles.

➡**The automatic transmission fluid level must be checked with the vehicle at normal operating temperature; 180-200°F (82-93°C). Temperature will greatly affect transaxle fluid level.**

2. Park the vehicle on a level surface.

3. Place the transaxle gear selector in **P**.

4. Apply the parking brake and block the drive wheels.

5. Let the vehicle idle for 3 minutes with the accessories OFF.

6. With the engine running, pull the dipstick out and check the fluid level, color and condition.

➡**On the 4.6L Northstar engine, turn the cap at the top of the dipstick counterclockwise to unlock the cap, then pull out the dipstick.**

7. Check both sides of the dipstick and read the lower level. The fluid must be in the cross-hatched area. Push the dipstick back all the way after checking.

8. If the fluid level is low, add only enough of the proper fluid to bring the level into the cross-hatched area on the dipstick, usually less than a pint.

➡**Use only fluid labeled DEXRON® IIE.**

DRAIN & REFILL

➡**Refer to Section 7 for additional automatic transaxle information.**

4T60 and 4T60-E Transaxle

1. Raise and safely support the vehicle.

84201039

Fig. 38 Transaxle fluid level dipstick

2. Place a suitable drain pan under the transaxle fluid pan.

3. Remove the retaining bolts at the front and sides of the fluid pan.

4. Loosen the rear fluid pan bolts approximately 4 turns.

5. Pry the fluid pan loose with a small prybar and allow the fluid to drain.

✳✳WARNING

Be careful not to damage the fluid pan and transaxle case mating surfaces, as damage may result in fluid leaks.

6. Remove the remaining bolts and the fluid pan and gasket.

7. Remove the transaxle screen/filter. The lip ring seal pressed into the case should be removed only if replacement is necessary.

8. Inspect the fluid pan and screen for foreign material, such as metal particles, clutch facing material, rubber particles or engine coolant. If necessary, determine and correct the source of the contamination.

To install:

9. Clean all gasket mating surfaces. Clean the fluid pan and screen in solvent and allow to dry. Inspect the fluid pan flange for distortion and straighten, if necessary.

➡The transaxle case and fluid pan flanges must be clean, dry and free of any oil film prior to fluid pan and gasket installation, or leakage may result. Inspect the washers on the fluid pan bolts before reuse, as shown in Section 7.

10. Install the screen, using a new filter. The filter uses a lip ring seal pressed into the case. The seal should be removed only if replacement is necessary.

11. Install the fluid pan, using a new gasket. Tighten the bolts to 10 ft. lbs. (13 Nm) on 1990 vehicles or 12-13 ft. lbs. (16-17 Nm) on 1991-93 vehicles.

12. Lower the vehicle.

13. Fill the transaxle with 6 qts. of Dexron®II-E transmission fluid.

14. Place the gearshift lever in **P**. Start the engine and let it idle; do not race the engine.

15. Check the fluid level and correct as required. Check the fluid pan for leaks.

4T80-E Transaxle

➡The 4T80-E transaxle has a filter under the side cover that requires service only during a complete transaxle overhaul. However, the scavenging screens under the bottom pan must be cleaned whenever the transaxle fluid is changed.

1. Raise and safely support the vehicle.

2. Place a suitable drain pan under the transaxle fluid pan.

3. Loosen the bottom fluid pan bolts in the reverse order of the torque sequence and drain the fluid from the pan.

4. Remove the drain plug in the case.

➡Removing the bottom fluid pan will only partially drain the transaxle fluid. The remaining fluid is held in the side cover and torque converter. Removing the drain plug in the case after bottom fluid pan removal will drain the fluid from the side cover.

5. Remove the retaining bolts, fluid pan and seal. Discard the seal.

6. Remove the left and right scavenger screens.

7. Inspect the scavenger screen lip seals in the transaxle case for nicks or cuts and replace, if damaged. Inspect the scavenger screens for cuts in the screen or a cracked housing; replace if necessary.

8. Check the fluid pan and transaxle case for dents or nicks in the sealing surface that could cause leaks. Inspect the fluid pan bolts for damaged threads and replace, if necessary.

To install:

9. Clean the scavenger screens and fluid pan in solvent and allow to dry. Clean the fluid pan retaining bolts and the tapped holes in the transaxle case.

➡The fluid pan and case sealing surfaces must be clean and dry for proper sealing. The retaining bolts and tapped holes must be clean and dry to maintain proper bolt torque.

10. Install the drain plug in the case and tighten to 6-10 ft. lbs. (8-14 Nm).

11. Install the left and right scavenger screens.

12. Install the bottom fluid pan using a new seal. Install the fluid pan retaining bolts finger-tight.

13. Tighten the fluid pan bolts in 3 steps. First tighten the bolts, in sequence, to 27 inch lbs. (3 Nm). Then tighten the bolts, in sequence, to 53 inch lbs. (6 Nm). Finally, tighten the bolts, in sequence, to 106 inch lbs. (12 Nm).

14. Lower the vehicle. Add the proper quantity of Dexron®II-E transmission fluid to the transaxle.

15. Make sure the transaxle is in **P**, then start the engine. With a cold powertrain, engine coolant temperature below 90°F (32°C), the fluid level should be in the "Cold' range on the dipstick.

16. When the powertrain is at normal operating temperature, engine coolant temperature 180-200°F (82-93°C), the fluid level should be in the "Hot' crosshatched range on the dipstick.

17. Shut off the engine. To reset the transaxle fluid change indicator, press and hold the "off' and "rear defog' buttons for 5-20 seconds on the climate control simultaneously until the 'TRANS FLUID RESET' message appears in the information center.

Cooling System

FLUID RECOMMENDATIONS

The cooling system should be inspected, flushed and refilled with fresh coolant at least every 30,000 miles or 24 months. If the coolant is left in the system too long, it loses its ability to prevent rust and corrosion.

When the coolant is being replaced, use a good quality ethylene glycol antifreeze that is safe to be used with aluminum cooling system components. The ratio of ethylene glycol to water should always be a 50/50 mixture. This ratio will ensure the proper balance of cooling ability, corrosion protection and antifreeze protection. At this ratio, the antifreeze protection should be good to -34°F (-37°C). If greater antifreeze protection is needed, the ratio should not exceed 70% antifreeze.

LEVEL CHECK

➡**When checking the coolant level, the radiator cap need not be removed. Simply check the coolant level in the recovery bottle or surge tank.**

Check the coolant level in the recovery bottle or surge tank, usually mounted on the inner fender. With the engine cold, the coolant level should be at the ADD or COLD level. With the engine at normal operating temperature, the coolant level should be at the FULL mark. Add coolant, as necessary.

DRAIN AND REFILL

When draining the coolant, keep in mind that cats and dogs are attracted by the ethylene glycol antifreeze and are quite likely to drink any that is left in an uncovered container or in puddles on the ground. This will prove fatal in sufficient quantity.

Always drain the coolant into a sealable container. Coolant should be reused unless it is contaminated or several years old.

✳✳CAUTION

To avoid injuries from scalding fluid and steam, DO NOT remove the radiator cap while the engine and radiator are still HOT.

1. With the engine cool, remove the radiator cap by performing the following:
   a. Slowly rotate the cap counterclockwise to the detent.
   b. If any residual pressure is present, WAIT until the hissing stops.
   c. After the hissing noise has ceased, press down on the cap and continue rotating it counterclockwise to remove it.
2. Place a fluid catch pan under the radiator, open the radiator drain valve and drain the coolant from the system.

3. Close the drain valve.
4. Empty the coolant reservoir or surge tank and flush it.
5. Using the correct mixture of antifreeze, fill the radiator to the bottom of the filler neck and the coolant tank to the FULL mark.
6. Install the radiator cap, making sure the arrows line up over the overflow tube leading the reservoir or surge tank.
7. Start the engine. Select heat on the climate control panel and turn the temperature valve to full warm. Run the engine until it reaches normal operating temperature. Check to make sure there is hot air flowing from the floor ducts.
8. Check the fluid level in the reservoir or surge tank and add as necessary.

FLUSHING AND CLEANING THE SYSTEM

1. Refer to the Drain and Refill procedure in this section and drain the cooling system.
2. Close the drain valve.

➡**A flushing solution may be used. Ensure it is safe for use with aluminum cooling system components. Follow the directions on the container.**

3. If using a flushing solution, remove the thermostat. Reinstall the thermostat housing.
4. Add sufficient water to fill the system.
5. Start the engine and run for a few minutes. Drain the system.

➡**This next step can get messy, so perform the work in a place where the water can drain away easily.**

6. If using a flushing solution, disconnect the heater hose that connects the cylinder head to the heater core (that end of the hose will clamp to a fitting on the firewall. Connect a water hose to the end of the heater hose that runs to the cylinder head and run water into the system until it begins to flow out of the top of the radiator.
7. Allow the water to flow out of the radiator until it is clear.
8. Reconnect the heater hose.
9. Drain the cooling system.
10. Reinstall the thermostat.
11. Empty the coolant reservoir or surge tank and flush it.
12. Fill the cooling system, using the correct ratio of antifreeze and water, to the bottom of the filler neck. Fill the reservoir or surge tank to the FULL mark.
13. Install the radiator cap, making sure that the arrows align with the overflow tube.

Brake Master Cylinder

FLUID RECOMMENDATION

Use only Heavy Duty Brake Fluid meeting DOT 3 specifications. Do NOT use any other fluid because severe brake system damage will result.

LEVEL CHECK

The brake fluid in the master cylinder should be checked every 6 months/6,000 miles (9656km).

Check the fluid level on the side of the reservoir. If fluid is required, remove the screw on filler cap and gasket from the master cylinder. Fill the reservoir to the full line in the reservoir with Heavy Duty Brake Fluid meeting DOT 3 specifications ONLY. Install the filler cap, making sure the gasket is properly seated in the cap. Make sure no dirt enters the system when adding fluid.

If fluid has to be added frequently, the system should be checked for a leak. Check for leaks at the master cylinder, calipers, proportioning valve and brake lines. If a leak is found, replace the component and bleed the system as outlined in Section 9.

Power Steering

FLUID RECOMMENDATIONS

When adding fluid or making a complete fluid change, always use GM P/N 1050017 power steering fluid or equivalent. Do NOT use automatic transmission fluid. Failure to use the proper fluid may cause hose and seal damage and fluid leaks.

LEVEL CHECK

▶ See Figure 39

The power steering fluid reservoir is directly above the steering pump. The pump is located on top of the engine on the right (passenger's) side.

Power steering fluid level is indicated either by marks on a see through reservoir or by marks on a fluid level indicator in the reservoir cap.

If the fluid is warmed up (about 150°F), the level should be between the HOT and COLD marks.

84201040

Fig. 39 Power steering reservoir fill location

If the fluid is cooler than above, the level should be between the ADD and COLD marks.

Chassis Greasing

▶ **See Figures 40 and 41**

Lubricate the chassis lubrication points every 7,500 miles or 12 months. If your vehicle is equipped with grease fittings, lubricate the suspension and steering linkage with heavy duty chassis grease. Lubricate the transaxle shift linkage, parking cable guides, under body contact points and linkage with white lithium grease.

Body Lubrication and Maintenance

Lock Cylinders

Apply graphite lubricant sparingly through the key slot. Insert the key and operate the lock several times to be sure that the lubricant is worked into the lock cylinder.

Door Hinges and Hinge Checks

Spray a silicone lubricant on the hinge pivot points to eliminate any binding conditions. Open and close the door several times to be sure that the lubricant is evenly and thoroughly distributed.

Trunk Lid or Tailgate

Spray a silicone lubricant on all of the pivot and friction surfaces to eliminate any squeaks or binds. Work the tailgate to distribute the lubricant

Body Drain Holes

Be sure that the drain holes in the doors and rocker panels are cleared of obstruction. A small screwdriver can be used to clear them of any debris.

Rear Wheel Bearings

The front wheel drive Cadillac models are equipped with sealed hub and bearing assemblies for the rear wheels. The hub and bearing assemblies are non-serviceable. If the assembly is damaged, the complete unit must be replaced. Refer to Section 7 for the hub and bearing removal and installation procedure.

TRAILER TOWING

Fig. 41 Lower ball joint and tie rod grease fitting location for lubrication

General Recommendations

Your vehicle was designed with the intent of carrying people. Towing a trailer will affect handling, durability and economy. Your safety and satisfaction depend upon proper use of correct equipment. Also, you should avoid overloads and other abusive use.

Information on trailer towing, special equipment and optional equipment is available at your local dealership. You can write to Cadillac Customer Service Department.

Trailer Weight

Trailer weight is the first, and most important, factor in determining whether or not your vehicle is suitable for towing the trailer you have in mind. The horsepower-to-weight ratio should be calculated. The basic standard is a ratio of 35:1. That is, 35 pounds of GVW (gross vehicle weight) for every horsepower.

To calculate this ratio, multiply you engine's rated horsepower by 35, then subtract the weight of the vehicle, including passengers and luggage. The resulting figure is the ideal maximum trailer weight that you can tow.

Hitch Weight

There are three kinds of hitches: bumper mounted, frame mounted, and load equalizing.

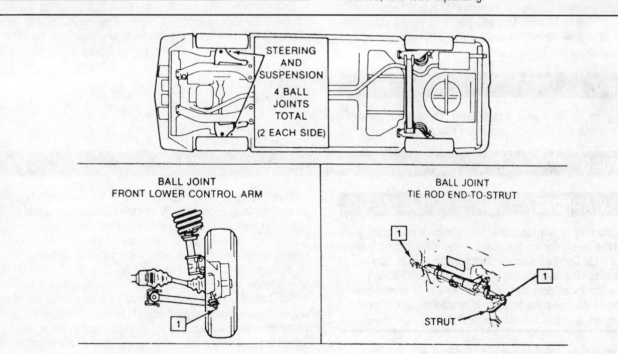

Lubrication points

Fig. 40 Lubrication points

Bumper mounted hitches are those which attach solely to the vehicle's bumper. Many states prohibit towing with this type of hitch, when it attaches to the vehicle's stock bumper, since it subjects the bumper to stresses for which it was not designed. Aftermarket rear step bumpers, designed for trailer towing, are acceptable for use with bumper mounted hitches.

➡**Do NOT attach any hitch to the bumper bar on the vehicle. A hitch attachment may be made through the bumper mounting locations, but only if an additional attachment is also made. Frame mounted hitches can be of the type which bolts to two or more points on the frame, plus the bumper, or just to several points on the frame. Frame mounted hitches can also be of the tongue type, for Class I towing, or, of the receiver type, for classes II and III.**

Load equalizing hitches are usually used for large trailers. Most equalizing hitches are welded in place and use equalizing bars and chains to level the vehicle after the trailer is hooked up.

The bolt-on hitches are the most common, since they are relatively easy to install.

Check the gross weight rating of your trailer. Tongue weight is usually figured as 10% of gross trailer weight. Therefore, a trailer with a maximum gross weight of 2,000 lbs. (907 kg) will have a maximum tongue weight of 200 lbs. (91 kg) Class I trailers fall into this category. Class II trailers are those with a gross weight rating of 2,000-3,500 lbs. (907-1588 kg), while Class III trailers fall into the 3,500-6,000 lbs. (1588-2722 kg) category. Class IV trailers are those over 6,000 lbs. (2722 kg) and are for use with fifth wheel trucks, only.

When you have determined the hitch that you'll need, follow the manufacturer's installation instructions, exactly, especially when it comes to fastener torques. The hitch will be subjected to a lot of stress and good hitches come with hardened bolts. Never substitute an inferior bolt for a hardened bolt.

Wiring

Wiring the car for towing is fairly easy. There are a number of good wiring kits available and these should be used, rather than trying to design your own. All trailers will need brake lights and turn signals as well as tail lights and side marker lights. Most states require extra marker lights for overly wide trailers. Also, most states have recently required back-up lights for trailers, and most trailer manufacturers have been building trailers with back-up lights for several years.

Additionally, some Class I, most Class II and just about all Class III trailers will have electric brakes.

Add to this number an accessories wire, to operate trailer internal equipment or to charge the trailer's battery, and you can have as many as seven wires in the harness.

Determine the equipment on your trailer and buy the wiring kit necessary. The kit will contain all the wires needed, plus a plug adapter set which included the female plug, mounted on the bumper or hitch, and the male plug, wired into, or plugged into the trailer harness.

When installing the kit, follow the manufacturer's instructions. The color coding of the wires is standard throughout the industry.

One point to note is that some domestic vehicles, and most imported vehicles, have separate turn signals. On most domestic vehicles, the brake lights and rear turn signals operate with the same bulb. For those vehicles with separate turn signals, you can purchase an isolation unit so that the brake lights won't blink whenever the turn signals are operated, or, you can go to your local electronics supply house and buy four diodes to wire in series with the brake and turn signal bulbs. Diodes will isolate the brake and turn signals. The choice is yours. The isolation units are simple and quick to install, but far more expensive than the diodes. The diodes, however, require more work to install properly, since they require the cutting of each bulb's wire and soldering the diode in place.

One final point, the best kits are those with a spring loaded cover on the vehicle mounted socket. This cover prevents dirt and moisture from corroding the terminals. Never let the vehicle socket hang loosely. Always mount it securely to the bumper or hitch.

TOWING

✳✳WARNING

Push starting is not recommended for cars equipped with a catalytic converter or automatic transmission which represents ALL Cadillac models. The vehicle can be towed, however, towing the vehicle on a flat bed ("roll back") truck is the most desirable option. The car is safest and the wheels do not have to turn. It is also the most expensive way to tow and not always available.

The second best way to tow the vehicle is with the drive wheels OFF the ground.

Sometimes it is impossible to tow with the opposite wheels on ground. In that case, if the transaxle is in proper working order, the car can be towed with the front wheels on the ground (front wheel drive) for distances under 15 miles at speeds no greater then 30 mph. If the transaxle is known to be damaged or if the car has to be towed over 15 miles or over 30 mph the car must be dollied or towed with the rear wheels raised and the steering wheel secured so that the front wheels remain in the straight-ahead position. The steering wheel must be clamped with a special clamping device designed for towing service. If the key-controlled lock is in the locked position, damage to the lock and steering column may result.

JACKING

The vehicle is supplied with a scissors jack for emergency road repairs. The scissors jack may be used to raise the car via the notches on either side at the front and rear of the doors. Do not attempt to use the jack in any other places. Always block the diagonally opposite wheel when using a jack.

When using floor jacks or stands, use the side members at the front or rear, the center of the rear crossmember assembly or the trailing engine cradle. The engine cradle has been coated with a special finish to protect it. Always position and block of wood on top of the jack or stand to protect the finish when lifting or supporting the vehicle via the cradle.

Whenever you plan to work under the car, you must support it on jackstands or ramps. Never use cinder blocks or stacks of wood to support the car, even if you're only going to be under it for a few minutes. Never crawl under the car when it is supported only by the tire-changing jack or other floor jack.

Small hydraulic, screw, or scissors jacks are satisfactory for raising the car. Drive-on trestles or ramps are also a handy and safe way to both raise and support the car. Be careful though, some ramps may be to steep to drive your Cadillac onto without scraping the front bottom plastic panels. Never support the car on any suspension member or underbody panel.

CAPACITIES

Year	Model	Engine ID/VIN	Engine Displacement Liters (cc)	Engine Crankcase with Filter	Transmission (pts.) 4-Spd	5-Spd	Auto.	Transfer Case (pts.)	Drive Axle Front (pts.)	Rear (pts.)	Fuel Tank (gal.)	Cooling System (qts.)
1990	Deville	3	4.5 (4467)	5.5	—	—	22	—	①	—	18	13.2
	Eldorado	3	4.5 (4467)	5.5	—	—	22	—	①	—	18.8	12.1
	Fleetwood	3	4.5 (4467)	5.5	—	—	22	—	①	—	18	13.2
	Seville	3	4.5 (4467)	5.5	—	—	22	—	①	—	18.8	12.1
1991	Deville	B	4.9 (4885)	5.5	—	—	22	—	①	—	18	13.2
	Eldorado	B	4.9 (4885)	5.5	—	—	22	—	①	—	18.8	12.1
	Fleetwood	B	4.9 (4885)	5.5	—	—	22	—	①	—	18	13.2
	Seville	B	4.9 (4885)	5.5	—	—	22	—	①	—	18.8	12.1
1992	Deville	B	4.9 (4885)	5.5	—	—	22	—	①	—	18	12.1
	Eldorado	B	4.9 (4885)	5.5	—	—	22	—	①	—	18	12.1
	Fleetwood	B	4.9 (4885)	5.5	—	—	22	—	①	—	18	12.1
	Seville	B	4.9 (4885)	5.5	—	—	22	—	①	—	18	12.1
1993	Deville	B	4.9 (4885)	5.5	—	—	22	—	①	—	18	12.1
	Eldorado	B	4.9 (4885)	5.5	—	—	22	—	①	—	20	12.3
	Eldorado	9	4.6 (4566)	7.5	—	—	22	—	①	—	20	12.3
	Eldorado	Y	4.6 (4566)	7.5	—	—	22	—	①	—	20	12.3
	Seville	B	4.9 (4885)	5.5	—	—	22	—	①	—	20	12.3
	Seville	9	4.6 (4566)	7.5	—	—	22	—	①	—	20	12.3
	Sixty Special	B	4.9 (4885)	5.5	—	—	22	—	①	—	18	12.1

① Included in transaxle capacity

84201050

Follow Schedule I if your car is MAINLY operated under one or more of the following conditions:

- When most trips are less than 4 miles (6 kilometers).
- When most trips are less than 10 miles (16 kilometers) and outside temperatures remain below freezing.
- Idling and/or low speed operation in stop-and-go traffic.
- Towing a trailer. ③
- Operating in dusty areas.

Schedule I should also be followed if the vehicle is used for delivery service or other commercial applications.

ITEM NO.	TO BE SERVICED	When To Perform Miles (Kilometers) Or Month Whichever Occurs First	The Services Shown in This Schedule Up To 48,000 Miles (80,000 km) Are To Be Performed After 48,000 Miles At The Same Intervals															
		MILES (000)	3	6	9	12	15	18	21	24	27	30	33	36	39	42	45	48
		KILOMETERS (000)	5	10	15	20	25	30	35	40	45	50	55	60	65	70	75	80
1	Engine Oil & Oil Filter Change ①	Every 3,000 Mi. (5,000 km) Or 3 Mos.	•	•	•	•	•	•	•	•	•	•	•	•	•	•	•	•
2	Chassis Lubrication	Every Other Oil Change		•		•		•		•		•		•		•		•
3	Throttle Boot Mounting Bolt Torque ①	At 6,000 Mi. (10,000 km) Only		•														
4	Tire & Wheel Inspection & Rotation	At 6,000 Mi. (10,000 km) And Then Every 15,000 (25,000 km)		•					•					•				
5	Engine Accessory Drive Belt Inspection ①	Every 30,000 Mi. (50,000 km) Or 24 Mos.										•②						
6	Cooling System Service ①											•						
7	Wheel Bearing Repack (Brougham Only)	SEE EXPLANATION FOR SERVICE ON PAGE 7																
8	Transmission/Transaxle Service																	
9	Spark Plug Replacement ① (See Note)	Every 30,000 Mi. (50,000 km)										•②						
10	Spark Plug Wire Inspection ①											•②						
11	PCV Valve Inspection ①											•						
12	EGR System Service ①											•						
13	Air Cleaner, PCV Filter & A.I.R. Filter Replacement ①											•②						
14	Engine Timing Check ①											•						
15	Fuel Tank, Cap & Lines Inspection ①											•						
16	Throttle Body Inspection ①											•						

① An Emission Control Service

② The U.S. Environmental Protection Agency has determined that failure to perform this maintenance item will not nullify the emission warranty or limit recall liability prior to the completion of vehicle useful life. General Motors, however, urges that all Emission Control Maintenance Services shown be performed at the indicated intervals and the maintenance be recorded.

③ Trailer pulling is not recommended for some models. See Owner's Manual for details.

NOTE: Spark plug replacement on Allante is every 100,000 miles. All services shown in these schedules up to 48,000 miles (80,000 km) should be performed after 48,000 miles at the same intervals.

84201045

Fig. 42 Maintenance Intervals-Schedule 1-1990-91

Follow Schedule II ONLY IF NONE of the driving conditions specified in Schedule 1 apply:

ITEM NO.	TO BE SERVICED	When To Perform Miles (Kilometers) Or Months Whichever Occurs First	The Services Shown in This Schedule Up To 45,000 Miles (80,000 km) Are To Be Performed After 45,000 Miles At The Same Intervals					
		MILES (000)	7.5	15	22.5	30	37.5①	45
		KILOMETERS (000)	12.5	25	37.5	50	62.5	75
1	Engine Oil Change ①	Every 7,500 Mi. (12,500 km) Or 12 Mos.	•	•	•	•	•	•
	Oil Filter Change ①	At first and then every other oil change or 12 mos.	•		•		•	
2	Chassis Lubrication	Every 7,500 Mi. (12,500 km) Or 12 mos.	•	•	•	•	•	•
3	Throttle Body Mounting Bolt Torque ①	At 7,500 Mi. (12,500 km) Only	•②					
4	Tire & Wheel Inspection & Rotation	At 7,500 Mi. (12,500 km) And Then Every 15,000 (25,000 km)	•		•		•	
5	Engine Accessory Drive Belt Inspection ①	Every 30,000 Mi. (50,000 km) Or 24 mos.				•②		
6	Cooling System Service ①	Every 30,000 Mi. (50,000 km) Or 24 mos.				•		
7	Wheel Bearing Repack (Brougham Only)	Every 30,000 Mi. (50,000 km)				•		
8	Transmission/Transaxle Service		SEE EXPLANATION FOR SERVICE ON PAGE 7					
9	Spark Plug Replacement ① (See Note)	Every 30,000 Mi. (50,000 km) Or 36 Mos.				•②		
10	Spark Plug Wire Inspection ①	Every 30,000 Mi. (50,000 km) Or 36 Mos.				•②		
11	PCV Valve Inspection ①	Every 30,000 Mi. (50,000 km) Or 36 Mos.				•		
12	EGR System Service ①	Every 30,000 Mi. (50,000 km) Or 36 Mos.				•		
13	Air Cleaner, PCV Filter & A.I.R. Filter Replacement ①	Every 30,000 Mi. (50,000 km) Or 36 Mos.				•②		
14	Engine Timing Check ①	Every 30,000 Mi. (50,000 km) Or 36 Mos.				•		
15	Fuel Tank, Cap & Lines Inspection ①	Every 30,000 Mi. (50,000 km) Or 36 Mos.				•		
16	Throttle Body Inspection ①	Every 30,000 Mi. (50,000 km) Or 36 Mos.				•		

① An Emission Control Service
② The U.S. Environmental Protection Agency has determined that failure to perform this maintenance item will not nullify the emission warranty or limit recall liability prior to the completion of vehicle useful life. General Motors, however, urges that all Emission Control Maintenance Services shown be performed at the indicated intervals and the maintenance be recorded.
③ Trailer pulling is not recommended for some models. See Owner's Manual for details.
NOTE: Spark plug replacement on Allante is every 100,000 miles. All services shown in these schedules up to 48,000 miles (80,000 km) should be performed after 45,000 miles at the same intervals.

84201046

Fig. 43 Maintenance Intervals-Schedule 2-1990-91

Follow Schedule II ONLY IF NONE of the driving conditions specified in Schedule 1 apply:

ITEM NO.	TO BE SERVICED	When To Perform Miles (Kilometers) Or Months Whichever Occurs First	The Services Shown in This Schedule Up To 45,000 Miles (80,000 km) Are To Be Performed After 45,000 Miles At The Same Intervals					
		MILES (000)	7.5	15	22.5	30	37.5①	45
		KILOMETERS (000)	12.5	25	37.5	50	62.5	75
1	Engine Oil & Filter Change ①	Every 7,500 Mi. (12,500 km) Or 12 Mos.	•	•	•	•	•	•
	Oil Filter Change ①	At first and then every other oil change or 12 mos.	•		•		•	
2	Chassis Lubrication	Every 7,500 Mi. (12,500 km) Or 12 mos.	•	•	•	•	•	•
3	Throttle Body Mounting Bolt Torque ①	At 7,500 Mi. (12,500 km) Only	•②					
4	Tire & Wheel Inspection & Rotation	At 7,500 Mi. (12,500 km) And Then Every 15,000 (25,000 km)	•		•		•	
5	Engine Accessory Drive Belt Inspection ①	Every 30,000 Mi. (50,000 km) Or 24 mos.				•②		
6	Cooling System Service ①					•		
7	Wheel Bearing Repack (Brougham Only)	Every 30,000 Mi. (50,000 km)				•		
8	Transmission/Transaxle Service	SEE EXPLANATION FOR SERVICE ON PAGE 7						
9	Spark Plug Replacement ④	Every 30,000 Mi. (50,000 km) Or 36 Mos.				•②		
10	Spark Plug Wire Inspection ②					•②		
11	EGR System Service ①					•		
12	Air Cleaner, PCV Filter & A.I.R. Filter Replacement ①					•		
13	Engine Timing Check ①					•		
14	Fuel Tank, Cap & Lines Inspection ①					•		
15	Throttle Body Inspection ①					•		

① An Emission Control Service
② The U.S. Environmental Protection Agency has determined that failure to perform this maintenance item will not nullify the emission warranty or limit recall liability prior to the completion of vehicle useful life. General Motors, however, urges that all Emission Control Maintenance Services shown be performed at the indicated intervals and the maintenance be recorded.
③ Trailer pulling is not recommended for some models. See Owner's Manual for details.
④ BROUGHAM ONLY. Replace all other carlines every 100,000 miles (160,000 km).
The services shown in these schedules up to 48,000 miles (80,000 km) are to be performed after 48,000 miles at the same intervals.

84201048

Fig. 44 Maintenance Intervals-Schedule -1992-93

RECOMMENDED LUBRICANTS

USAGE	FLUID/LUBRICANT
Engine Oil	API Service SG, SG/CC or SG/CD of the recommended viscosity
Engine Coolant	Mixture of water and good quality Ethylene glycol base anti-freeze conforming to GM Spec. 1825M
Brake Systems	Delco Supreme 11 Fluid or DOT—3 fluid
Parking Brake Cables	Chassis grease meeting requirements of GM—6031M
Power Steering System	GM Power Steering Fluid or equivalent
Automatic Transmission/Transaxle	DEXRON IIE® Automatic Transmission Fluid
Automatic Transaxle Shift Linkage	Engine Oil
Floor Shift Linkage	Engine Oil
Chassis Lubrication	Chassis grease meeting requirements of NLGI GRADE 2 category LB or GC—LB
Hood Latch Assembly a. pivots and spring anchor b. release pawl	a. Engine Oil b. Chassis lubricant meeting requirements of NLGI GRADE 2 category LB or GC—LB
Hood and Door Hinges, Fuel Door Hinge, Rear Compartment Hinges	Engine Oil
Key Lock Cylinders	Multi-purpose lubricant or synthetic 5W30 engine oil
Weatherstrip	Silicone grease

84201049

Fig. 45 Recommended Lubricants

2

ENGINE PERFORMANCE AND TUNE-UP

TUNE-UP PROCEDURES

A tune-up is performed periodically to make a complete check of the operation of the engine and several associated systems and to replace worn ignition parts. The tune-up is a good time to perform a general preventive maintenance check-out on everything in the engine compartment. Look for things like loose or damaged wiring, fuel leaks, frayed drive belts, etc.

On the vehicles covered in this manual, ignition timing, idle speed and fuel/air mixture are all controlled electronically by the Powertrain Control Module (PCM) and are not adjustable. The choke function has been incorporated into the fuel injection system and is no longer a separate component requiring periodic service and adjustment. With the advent of unleaded fuel and improved manufacturing techniques, spark plugs last longer. A basic tune-up normally consists of replacing the spark plugs, changing the air, fuel and PCV breather filters and performing a detailed visual inspection of the spark plug wires, vacuum hoses, fuel lines and coolant hoses.

Under normal driving conditions, the tune-up should be performed every 30,000 miles (48,300km). This mileage interval should be decreased if the vehicle is operated under severe conditions such as trailer towing, prolonged idling, continual stop and start driving, or if starting or running problems are noticed.

If the specifications on the Vehicle Emission Control Information label in the engine compartment disagree with the Tune-Up Specification chart in this Section, use the figures on the label. The label often includes changes made during the model year.

Spark Plugs

▶ See Figure 1

✳✳CAUTION

The spark plugs used in these vehicles have a lubricated boot release coating baked onto the outer spark plug ceramic. This coating is clear with a slightly waxy feeling. The coating helps prevent the silicone spark plug boot from sticking to the spark plug ceramic. It is important that you wash your hands after handling coated spark plugs and before smoking. The combination of the polymer vapors- the result of contamination of cigarette products and the subsequent burning of the polymer may result in flu-like symptoms and should be avoided.

A typical spark plug consists of a metal shell surrounding a ceramic insulator. A metal electrode extends downward through the center of the insulator and protrudes a small distance. Located at the end of the plug and attached to the side of the outer metal shell is the side electrode. The side electrode bends in at a 90 degree angle so that its tip is even with, and

parallel to, the tip of the center electrode. The distance between these two electrodes (measured in thousandths of an inch) is called the spark plug gap.

In addition to their basic task of igniting the air/fuel mixture, spark plugs can also serve as a very useful tool in telling you about the condition of the engine in your vehicle.

Remove the spark plugs one at a time and examine them. In general, dark deposits on the electrodes indicate too rich a fuel mixture or low intake volume. White electrode deposits indicate either too lean a fuel mixture, advanced ignition timing or insufficient plug tightening. Plugs which exhibit only normal wear and deposits can be cleaned, gapped and reinstalled. However, it is a good idea to replace them at every major tune-up or as recommended on the maintenance chart (see Section 1).

SPARK PLUG HEAT RANGE

Spark plug heat range is the ability of the plug to dissipate heat. The longer the insulator (or the farther it extends into the engine), the hotter the plug will operate; the shorter the insulator, the cooler it will operate. A plug that absorbs little heat and remains too cool will quickly accumulate deposits of oil and carbon since it is not hot enough to burn them off. This leads to plug fouling and consequently to misfiring. A plug that absorbs too much heat will have no deposits, but due to the excessive heat, the electrodes will burn away quickly and in some instances, preignition may result. Preignition takes place when plug tips get so hot that they glow sufficiently to ignite the fuel/air mixture before the actual spark occurs. This early ignition will usually cause a pinging during low speeds and heavy loads.

The general rule of thumb for choosing the correct heat range when picking a spark plug is: if most of your driving is long distance or high speed travel, use a colder plug; if most of your driving is stop and go, use a hotter plug. Original equipment plugs are compromise plugs, but most people never have occasion to change their plugs from the factory-recommended heat range.

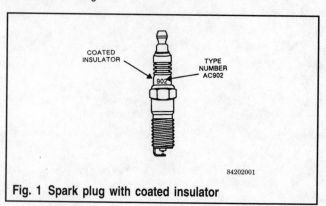

Fig. 1 Spark plug with coated insulator

84202001

REMOVAL & INSTALLATION

▶ **See Figures 2 and 3**

➡️To avoid engine damage, do NOT remove spark plugs when the engine is warm. When you're removing spark plugs, you should work on one at a time. Don't start by removing the plug wires all at once, because unless you number them, they may become mixed up and be installed incorrectly. Take a minute before you begin and number the wires with tape. The best location for numbering is as near as possible to the spark plug boot.

1. Disconnect the negative battery cable.
2. Remove air cleaner components in order to gain access to the spark plugs, if required.
3. Remove the spark plug cable from the plug by twisting the boot slightly while pulling straight outward off of the plug. In order to prevent damage to the spark plug cable, do not pull on the cable itself.

❊❊CAUTION

Never pull on the plug wire alone as you may damage the conductor inside. Remove the cable from the plug by grasping and pulling on the cable boot.

4. Using a spark plug socket, loosen the plugs slightly and wipe or blow all dirt away from the spark plug base. A shop vac is ideal for this job.

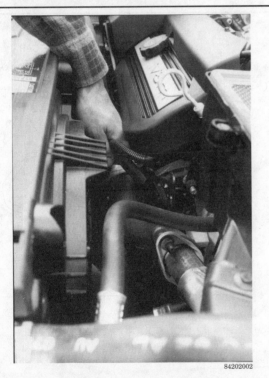

84202002

Fig. 2 To remove spark plug cable from plug, grasp boot on cable and twist slightly while pulling

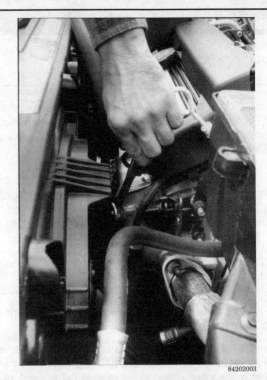

84202003

Fig. 3 Removing spark plug from engine using spark plug socket

5. Unscrew and remove the spark plugs from the engine.
To install:
6. Adjust the spark plug gap to the specifications listed in this Section or on the tune-up label, located in the engine compartment.
7. Lubricate the plug threads lightly with an anti-seize compound and install the spark plug. Tighten the spark plugs to specifications.

❊❊CAUTION

The spark plugs used in these vehicles have a lubricated boot release coating baked onto the outer spark plug ceramic. This coating is clear with a slightly waxy feeling. The coating helps prevent the silicone spark plug boot from sticking to the spark plug ceramic. It is important that you wash your hands after handling coated spark plugs and before smoking. The combination of the polymer vapors- the result of contamination of cigarette products and the subsequent burning of the polymer may result in flu-like symptoms and should be avoided.

8. Install the cable onto the plug. Make sure it snaps in place.
9. Repeat the procedure for the remaining spark plugs.
10. Install the air cleaner components, if removed.
11. Connect the negative battery cable.

Spark Plug Cables

INSPECTION

Your vehicle is equipped with an electronic ignition system which utilizes 8mm wires to conduct the hotter spark produced. The boots on these wires are designed to cover the spark plug cavities on the cylinder head.

Visually inspect the spark plug cables for burns, cuts, or breaks in the insulation. Check the spark plug boots and the nipples on the distributor cap or coil. Replace any damaged wiring. If no physical damage is obvious, the wires can be checked with an ohmmeter for excessive resistance or an open. The resistance specification is 30,000 ohms or less.

REMOVAL & INSTALLATION

➡**To avoid confusion label, remove, and replace spark plug cables one at a time.**

The material used to construct the spark plug cables is very soft. This cable will withstand more heat and carry higher voltage, but scuffing and cutting becomes easier. The spark plug cables must be routed correctly to prevent chaffing or cutting.

4.5L and 4.9L Engines
▶ **See Figure 4**

1. Disconnect the spark plug cables at the distributor assembly.
2. Disconnect the spark plug wires at the spark plugs.

➡**Use care when removing the spark plug boots from the spark plugs. Twist the boot ½ turn before removing and then pull on the boot only. Do not pull on the wire, as it may damage the spark plug cable.**

3. Remove the spark plug channel from the engine.
4. Remove the spark plug wire from the engine.
To install:
5. Position the spark plug wire assembly on top of the engine. Install the plug wire channel.
6. Install the spark plug wire at the spark plug. Make sure the wires are fully seated on the plugs.
7. Install the spark plug wires at the distributor assembly. Secure wires in position.

4.6L Engine
▶ **See Figure 5**

1. Disconnect the spark plug cables at the Ignition Control Module (ICM) assembly.
2. Disconnect the spark plug wires at the spark plugs.

➡**Use care when removing the spark plug boots from the spark plugs. Twist the boot ½ turn before removing and then pull on the boot only. Do not pull on the wire, as it may damage the spark plug cable.**

84202004

Fig. 4 Disconnecting the spark plug cable at the distributor assembly

3. Remove the spark plug channel from the camshaft cover and the intake manifold.
4. Remove the spark plug wire from the engine.
To install:
5. Position the spark plug wire assembly on top of the engine. Install the plug wire channel onto the front camshaft cover and intake manifold.
6. Install the spark plug wire at the spark plug. Make sure the wires are fully seated on the plugs.
7. Install the spark plug wires at the ICM assembly.

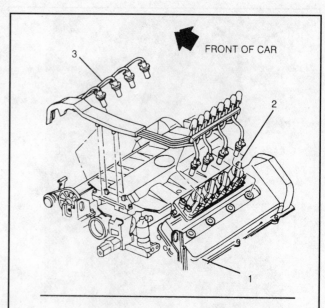

FRONT OF CAR

1	ENGINE
2	IGNITION CONTROL MODULE ASSEMBLY
3	SPARK PLUG WIRES

84202005

Fig. 5 Ignition Control Module (ICM) assembly and spark plug cables — 4.6L engine

GASOLINE ENGINE TUNE-UP SPECIFICATIONS

Year	Engine ID/VIN	Engine Displacement Liters (cc)	Spark Plugs Gap (in.)	Ignition Timing (deg.) MT	Ignition Timing (deg.) AT	Fuel Pump (psi)	Idle Speed (rpm) MT	Idle Speed (rpm) AT	Valve Clearance In.	Valve Clearance Ex.
1990	3	4.5 (4467)	0.060	—	10B	40–50	—	500–550	Hyd.	Hyd.
1991	B	4.9 (4885)	0.060	—	10B	40–50	—	500–550	Hyd.	Hyd.
1992	B	4.9 (4885)	0.060	—	10B	40–50	—	500–550	Hyd.	Hyd.
1993	B	4.9 (4885)	0.060	—	10B	40–50	—	500–550	Hyd.	Hyd.
	9	4.6 (4566)	0.050	—	①	40–50	—	①	Hyd.	Hyd.
	Y	4.6 (4566)	0.050	—	①	40–50	—	①	Hyd.	Hyd.

NOTE: If these specifications differ from those on the Vehicle Emission Control Information label, follow the specifications on the label.
B—Before Top Dead Center
Hyd.—Hydraulic
① Refer to the Vehicle Emission Control
   Information label

84202033

FIRING ORDERS

▶ See Figures 6 and 7

➡ To avoid confusion label, remove, and replace spark plug cables one at a time.

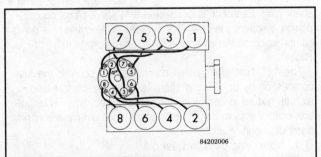

84202006

Fig. 6 4.5L and 4.9L Engines
Engine Firing Order: 1-8-4-3-6-5-7-2
Distributor Rotation: Counterclockwise

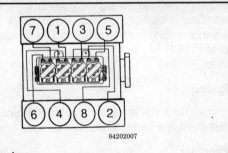

84202007

Fig. 7 4.6L Engine
Engine Firing Order: 1-2-7-3-4-5-6-8
Distributorless Ignition System

ELECTRONIC IGNITION

General Information

4.5L AND 4.9L ENGINES

The ignition system used on these engines is a High Energy Ignition (HEI) system with Electronic Spark Timing (EST). The High Energy Ignition (HEI) system controls fuel combustion by providing a spark to ignite the air/fuel mixture at the appropriate time.

The ignition circuit consists of the battery, the distributor, the ignition switch, the spark plugs and the primary and secondary wiring.

HEI Distributor

The High Energy Ignition (HEI) distributor with Electronic Spark Control (ESC) combines all necessary ignition components in one contained unit. The system includes:
- An integral ignition coil assembly
- A magnetic pick-up coil and pole piece assembly
- A Hall Effect switch
- A solid state ignition module
- An RFI- suppression capacitor and primary winding harness
- A distributor cap and rotor

All spark timing changes in the HEI (EST) distributor are performed electronically by the Powertrain Control Module (PMC). The PMC monitors information from various engine sensors, computes the desired spark timing and signals the distributor to change the timing accordingly. A back up spark advance system is programmed into the ignition module in case of PCM failure. No vacuum or mechanical advance are used.

Ignition Coil

The ignition coil is contained in the distributor cap and connect through a center contact to the rotor.

Capacitor

The capacitor, if equipped, is part of the coil wire harness assembly. The capacitor is used only for radio noise suppression.

Magnetic Pick-up

The magnetic pick-up assembly, located inside the distributor, contains a permanent magnet, a pole piece with internal teeth, and a pick-up coil. A toothed timer core, attached to the distributor main shaft, rotates inside the pole piece. As the teeth of the timer core align with the teeth on the pole piece, a varying current is induced in the pick-up coil. The induced current flow is converted by the HEI module, into a distributor reference pulse.

HEI Module

The HEI module, acting as an electronic ON/OFF switch controls the current flow in the primary winding of the ignition coil. This switching action induces a high voltage in the ignition coil secondary winding which is directed through the rotor and secondary leads to fire the spark plugs.

Hall Effect Switch

A Hall Effect Switch, positioned in the distributor housing, serves as a cam position sensor for the sequential port fuel injection system. The Hall Effect senses the opening point of the intake valve on the number one cylinder and provides that information to the Powertrain Control Module (PCM). Fuel injection is sequenced relative to the engine firing order once No. 1 intake stroke is determined.

Secondary Wiring

The spark plug wires used with the HEI system are composed of four major components:
-An 8mm silicone jacket for high temperature protection. This outer jacket also provides excellent insulation for the high voltage produced in the HEI system.
-A reinforced fiberglass braid for strength.
-An inner core insulation composed of Ethylene Propylene Diene Monomer (EPDM) for strength and voltage insulation.
-A composite High Temperature (CHT) core composed of aramid fibers impregnated with conductive latex and wrapped with conductive silicone.

4.6L ENGINE

▶ See Figure 8

The 4.6L Northstar ignition control system does not use a conventional distributor or a single ignition coil. In this ignition system, both ends of the four ignition coils are connected to a spark plug. Each coil is connected with spark plugs on companion cylinders , ie. 1-4, 2-5, 6-7, 3-8. One cylinder is on its compression stroke when the other one is on its exhaust stroke.

The 4.6L Northstar ignition control system controls the fuel combustion by providing a spark to ignite the compressed air/fuel mixture in each cylinder at the correct time. This ignition control system has several advantages over a mechanical distributor ignition system:
1. No moving parts to wear out
2. No mechanical load on the engine
3. Eliminate of mechanical timing adjustment
4. Improved high engine speed performance

The Northstar ignition control system is composed of the following components:
- Two crankshaft position sensors
- Crankshaft reluctor ring
- Camshaft position sensor
- Ignition control module
- 4 separate ignition coils
- 8 spark plug wires and conduit
- 8 spark plugs
- Knock sensor
- Powertrain Control Module (PCM)

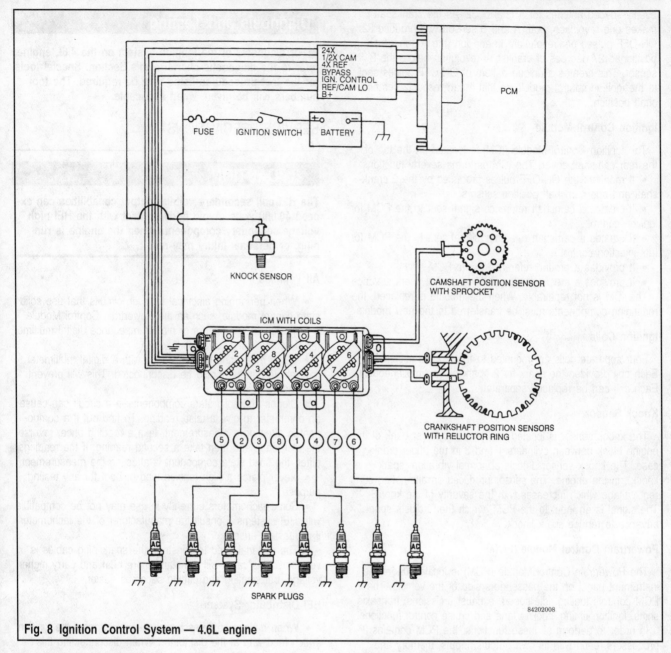

Fig. 8 Ignition Control System — 4.6L engine

Camshaft Position Sensor

The camshaft position sensor is located on the rear cylinder bank in front of the exhaust camshaft. The camshaft position sensor extends into the rear cylinder head and is sealed with an O-ring. The camshaft position sensor is not adjustable.

As the rear cylinder bank exhaust camshaft turns, a steel pin on its drive sprocket passes over the magnetic camshaft position sensor. This creates an ON-OFF-ON-OFF signal sent to the ignition control module similar to the crankshaft position sensor. The camshaft position sensor produces one ON-OFF pulse for every one revolution of the camshaft or every 2 revolutions of the crankshaft. This allows the ignition control module to recognize the position of the camshaft.

Crankshaft Position Sensor and Reluctor Ring

The 2 crankshaft sensors are located on the front of the engine block, between cylinder Numbers 4 and 6. Crankshaft

position A sensor is located on the upper crankcase and crankshaft position B sensor is located in the lower crankcase. Both sensors extend into the crankcase and are sealed into the engine block with O-rings. The crankshaft position sensors are not adjustable.

The magnetic crankshaft position sensors operate similar to the pick-up coil in a distributor. When a piece of steel, called the reluctor, is repeatedly moved over the sensor, a voltage will be created that appears to go ON-OFF-ON-OFF-ON-OFF. This ON-OFF signal is also the signal that a set of breaker points in a distributor would generate as the distributor shaft turned and the points open and closed.

Reluctor Ring

The reluctor ring is cast onto the crankshaft between the No. 3 and No. 4 main bearing journals. The reluctor ring has 24 evenly spaced notches or air gaps and an additional 8 unevenly spaced notches for a total of 32. As the crankshaft makes one revolution, both A and B sensors will produce 32 ON-OFF pulses per revolution. In addition, the A sensor is positioned 27 degrees of crankshaft revolution before the B sensor. This creates a unique pattern of ON-OFF pulses sent to the ignition control module so that it can recognize crankshaft position.

Ignition Control Module

The Ignition Control Module (ICM) is located on the top of the rear camshaft cover. The ICM performs several functions:

- It monitors the ON-OFF pulses produced by the 2 crankshaft and one camshaft position sensors
- It creates a camshaft reference signal sent to the PCM for ignition control
- It creates a camshaft reference signal sent to the PCM for fuel injection control
- It provides a ground reference to the PCM
- It provides a means for the PCM to control spark advance

The ICM is not repairable. When the module is replaced, the remaining components must be transferred to the new module

Ignition Coils

Four separate coils are mounted to the module assembly. Each coil provides the spark for 2 spark plugs simultaneously. Each coil can be replaced separately.

Knock Sensor

The knock sensor is located on the rear cylinder bank of the engine block between cylinders 1 and 3 in the upper crankcase. The knock sensor detects abnormal vibration (spark knock), in the engine. The sensor produces an alternating current voltage which increases with the severity of the knock. The signal is an input to the PCM, which then adjusts spark advance to reduce spark knock.

Powertrain Control Module (PCM)

The Powertrain Control Module (PCM) is located under the instrument panel on the passengers side of the vehicle. The PCM controls fueling, idle speed, exhaust emissions, transaxle shifts, ignition timing, cooling fans and cruise control functions.

In order to perform all these functions, the PCM contains 2 processors, each with its own outputs, inputs, memory and program. The 2 processors function together by sharing input data, but they also function independently by controlling only certain outputs. The functions of each processor can be loosely categorized as engine controls or transaxle controls. The only function performed by both processors is the diagnosis of the serial data line, battery power circuits and the PCM PROM.

As mentioned earlier, the PCM controls spark advance and fuel injection for all driving conditions. The PCM monitors input signals from the following components as part of its ignition control function, to determine the required ignition timing:

- Ignition Control Module (ICM)
- Engine Coolant Temperature (ECT) sensor
- Transaxle Range (TR) switch
- Throttle Position (TP) sensor
- Vehicle Speed Sensor (VSS)
- Knock sensor

Diagnosis and Testing

➡For diagnosis of the ignition system on the 4.6L engine, refer to the diagnostic charts in this Section. Special tools for the test procedures listed may be required. The tool numbers will be given, when applicable.

SERVICE PRECAUTIONS

✳✳CAUTION

The HEI coil secondary voltage output capabilities can exceed 40,000 volts. Avoid body contact with the HEI high voltage secondary components when the engine is running, or personal injury may result.

All Vehicles

- When performing electrical tests on circuits that use solid state control module, such as the Powertrain Control Module (PCM), use a 10 megohm or higher impedance digital multimeter, J-34029-A or equivalent.
- When measuring the resistance with a digital multimeter, the vehicle battery should be disconnected. This will prevent incorrect readings.
- Diodes and solid state components in a circuit can cause an ohmmeter to give a false reading. To find out if a component is affecting a measurement, take a reading once, reverse the test leads and then take a second reading. If the readings differ, the solid state component is affecting the measurement.
- Never pierce a high tension lead or boot for any testing purpose.
- Some tachometers currently in use may not be compatible with HEI systems. Consult the manufacturer of the tachometer if a question arises.
- The material used to construct the spark plug cables is very soft. This cable will withstand more heat and carry higher voltage, but scuffing and cutting becomes easier.

HEI Distributor System

- When making compression checks, disconnect the ignition switch feed wire at the distributor. When disconnecting this connector, do NOT use a screwdriver or tool to release the locking tabs, as it may break.
- No periodic lubrication is required. Engine oil lubricates the lower bushing and an oil filled reservoir provides lubrication for the upper bushing.
- The tachometer (TACH) terminal is next to the ignition switch (BAT) connector on the distributor cap.

➡The tachometer terminal must never be allowed to touch ground, as damage to the module and/or ignition coil can result. Some tachometers currently in use may not be compatible with the HEI system used. Consult the manufacturer of the tachometer if a question arises.

- Dwell adjustment is controlled by the PCM can not be adjusted.
- The material used to construct the spark plug cables is very soft. This cable will withstand more heat and carry higher

voltage, but scuffing and cutting becomes easier. The spark plug cables must be routed correctly to prevent chaffing or cutting. When removing a spark plug wire from a plug, twist the boot on the spark plug and pull on the boot.

VISUAL INSPECTION

On of the most important steps in the diagnosis of a problem is a visual underhood inspection. This can often fix a problem. Inspect all vacuum hoses for pinches, cuts or disconnects. Inspect all wiring in the engine compartment for good, tight connections. Inspect all wiring for burned of chaffed spots, pinches or contact with sharp edges or hot exhaust manifolds. These quick tests take only a few minutes but can save you valuable time, and help you repair the problem.

1. Inspect all vacuum hoses for being pinched, cut or disconnected. Be sure to inspect hoses that are difficult to see such as beneath the upper intake, generator, etc.

2. Check for proper ground connections, ground eyelets connected to ground points and star washer installation, if applicable.

3. Check both battery positive junction blocks for loose retainer nuts.

4. Inspect other wiring in the engine compartment good connections, burned or chaffed spots, pinched wires or harness contact with sharp edges or hot exhaust manifolds.

5. Check for blown or missing fuses or relays missing or installed in the wrong locations.

6. Inspect plug wires for proper routing, connection, cuts or visible signs of arching to ground.

COMPONENT TESTING

Ignition Coil

4.5L AND 4.9L ENGINES

▶ See Figures 9 and 10

1. Detach the wiring connectors at the distributor cap. If necessary, label the position of each wire prior to disconnecting it.

2. Turn the 4 screws and remove the cap and coil assembly from the distributor lower housing.

3. Inspect the interior and exterior of the cap for signs of tracking. If tracking is present, replace the cap.

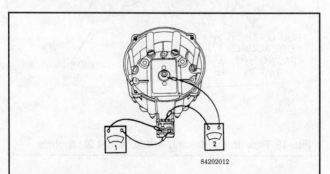

Fig. 9 Testing ignition coil in distributor cap — 4.5L and 4.9L engines

Fig. 10 Removing the distributor cap and coil assembly from the housing

4. Connect an ohmmeter across the coil terminals, which are the outermost terminals located in the recessed boss of the cap.

5. If the reading is not at 0, or nearly 0, replace the coil.

6. Connect the test leads of an ohmmeter to the coil center contact, located in the center of the cap. Connect the other test lead to the center terminal of the 3 wire connector, located on the cap. Make sure to set the ohmmeter to the highest setting.

7. If the reading is infinite, replace the ignition coil.

➡️If no problems are found, then the coil may still be faulty

Hall Effect Switch

4.5L ENGINE

▶ See Figure 11

1. Detach the wiring connectors at the distributor cap.

2. Turn the 4 screws and remove the cap and coil assembly from the distributor lower housing.

3. Inspect the interior and exterior of the cap for signs of tracking. If tracking is present, replace the cap.

4. Connect a 12 volt source and ground, and a voltmeter to the switch as shown. Be careful to observe the polarity shown in the illustration or damage to the Hall Effect switch may occur.

5. Without the blade in the switch, the voltmeter should read less than 0.5 volts. If not, the Hall Effect switch is defective.

6. With the blade in the switch, the voltmeter should read within 0.5 volts of battery voltage. If not, the switch is defective.

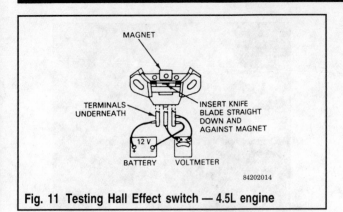

Fig. 11 Testing Hall Effect switch — 4.5L engine

4.9L ENGINE

▶ See Figure 12

The distributor must be removed from the engine in order to perform this procedure. Refer to the procedure listed in this Section for details.

1. Detach the wiring connectors at the distributor cap.

2. Turn the 4 screws and remove the cap and coil assembly from the distributor lower housing.

3. Inspect the interior and exterior of the cap for signs of tracking. If tracking is present, replace the cap. Connect a 12 volt source and ground to the distributor base 3 wire connector, as illustrated.

4. Connect the voltmeter positive test lead to terminal E of the 5 wire distributor harness connector. Connect the negative test lead to terminal D of the 5 wire distributor harness connector.

5. Rotate the distributor shaft and observe the blade passing through the Hall switch. Note readings on voltmeter during the shaft rotation.

6. Without the blade in the switch, the voltmeter should read less than 0.5 volts. If not, the Hall switch or harness is bad.

7. With the blade in the switch, the voltmeter should read within 0.5 volts of battery voltage. If not, the switch or harness is bad.

8. Check the harness and retest. If the problem still exists, replace the switch.

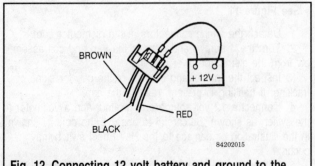

Fig. 12 Connecting 12 volt battery and ground to the distributor base 3-wire connector

Pick-Up Coil

4.5L AND 4.9L ENGINES

▶ See Figure 13

1. Disconnect the negative battery cable.

2. Detach the wiring connectors at the distributor cap.

3. Turn the 4 screws and remove the cap and coil assembly from the distributor lower housing.

4. Remove the retainers and the rotor assembly from the shaft.

5. Remove the pick-up coil leads from the module.

6. Connect an ohmmeter as shown in Test 1 and Test 2 of the illustration.

7. Observe the ohmmeter while flexing leads by hand. This will check for intermittent shorts (test 1) or intermittent opens (test 2). Compare the obtained reading with the desired results:

- Test 1 — Should read infinite at all times
- Test 2 — Should read steady at one value within 500-1500 ohm range.

8. If test results are not as specified, replace the pick-up coil.

Ignition System Diagnostics- 4.6L Engine

1. For diagnosis of the ignition system components on the 4.6L engine, refer to the following diagnostic charts. Use of special tools for the test procedures listed may be required. The tool numbers will be given, when applicable.

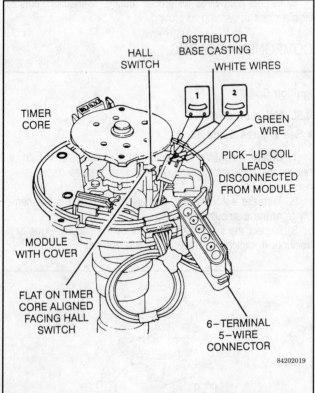

Fig. 13 Pick-up coil testing — 4.5L and 4.9L engines

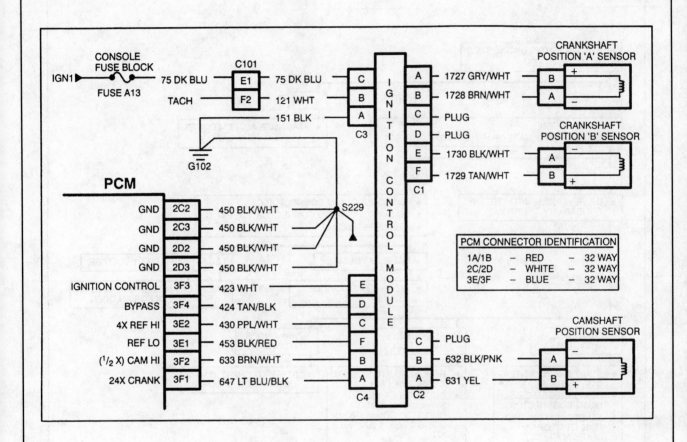

CHART 6D4−1

IGNITION SYSTEM CHECK

CIRCUIT DESCRIPTION:

The Ignition System Check provides a means of testing ignition system performance and references other charts in this section for specific ignition system conditions. This chart requires J 35616 jumper kit.

NOTES ON FAULT TREE:

1. This procedure reduces spark advance. Engine rpm should drop as spark is retarded.

2. This procedure grounds the BYPASS circuit and causes the ignition to operate in MODULE MODE. This will also cause Code 23 to set.

84202034

Fig. 14 Ignition System Diagnostics- 4.6L Engine

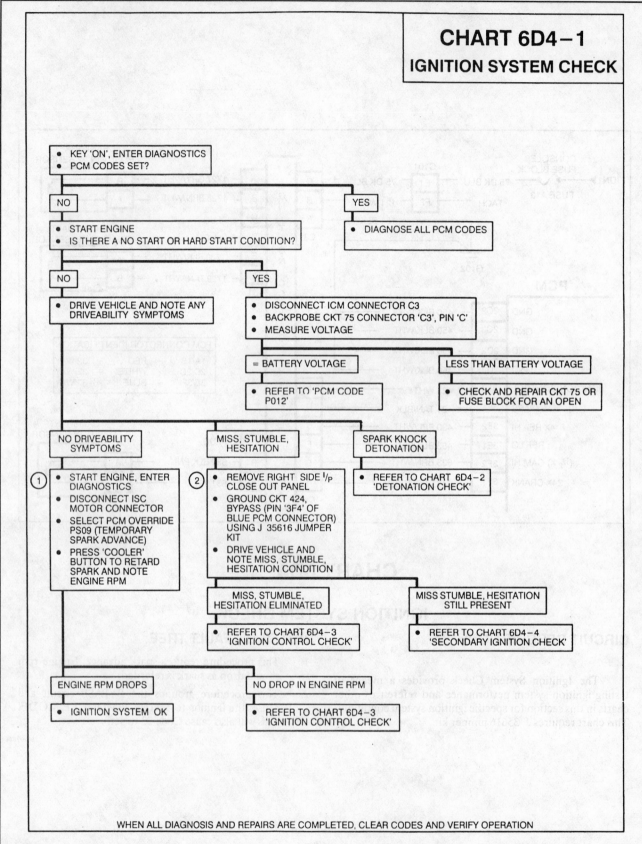

CHART 6D4−1
IGNITION SYSTEM CHECK

- KEY 'ON', ENTER DIAGNOSTICS
- PCM CODES SET?

NO

- START ENGINE
- IS THERE A NO START OR HARD START CONDITION?

YES

- DIAGNOSE ALL PCM CODES

NO

- DRIVE VEHICLE AND NOTE ANY DRIVEABILITY SYMPTOMS

YES

- DISCONNECT ICM CONNECTOR C3
- BACKPROBE CKT 75 CONNECTOR 'C3', PIN 'C'
- MEASURE VOLTAGE

= BATTERY VOLTAGE

- REFER TO 'PCM CODE P012'

LESS THAN BATTERY VOLTAGE

- CHECK AND REPAIR CKT 75 OR FUSE BLOCK FOR AN OPEN

NO DRIVEABILITY SYMPTOMS

MISS, STUMBLE, HESITATION

SPARK KNOCK DETONATION

①
- START ENGINE, ENTER DIAGNOSTICS
- DISCONNECT ISC MOTOR CONNECTOR
- SELECT PCM OVERRIDE PS09 (TEMPORARY SPARK ADVANCE)
- PRESS 'COOLER' BUTTON TO RETARD SPARK AND NOTE ENGINE RPM

②
- REMOVE RIGHT SIDE I/P CLOSE OUT PANEL
- GROUND CKT 424, BYPASS (PIN '3F4' OF BLUE PCM CONNECTOR) USING J 35616 JUMPER KIT
- DRIVE VEHICLE AND NOTE MISS, STUMBLE, HESITATION CONDITION

- REFER TO CHART 6D4−2 'DETONATION CHECK'

MISS, STUMBLE, HESITATION ELIMINATED

- REFER TO CHART 6D4−3 'IGNITION CONTROL CHECK'

MISS STUMBLE, HESITATION STILL PRESENT

- REFER TO CHART 6D4−4 'SECONDARY IGNITION CHECK'

ENGINE RPM DROPS

- IGNITION SYSTEM OK

NO DROP IN ENGINE RPM

- REFER TO CHART 6D4−3 'IGNITION CONTROL CHECK'

WHEN ALL DIAGNOSIS AND REPAIRS ARE COMPLETED, CLEAR CODES AND VERIFY OPERATION

84202035

Fig. 15 Ignition System Diagnostics- 4.6L Engine

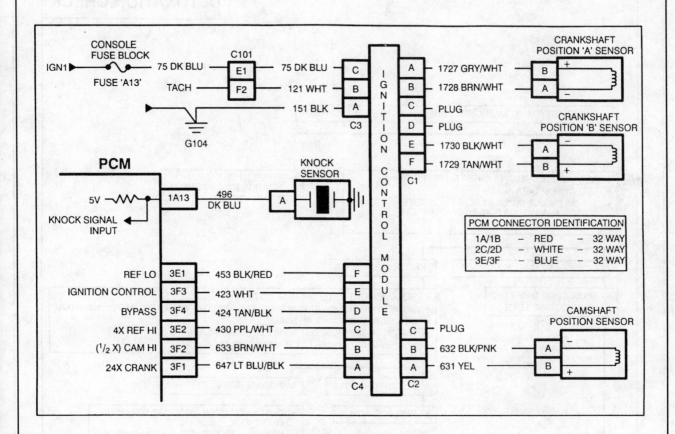

CHART 6D4-2

DETONATION CHECK

CIRCUIT DESCRIPTION:

The Detonation Check test for proper knock sensor operation. Possible causes of detonation include knock sensor, wiring, or PCM faults, poor fuel quality or engine mechanical conditions. This chart requires J 39200 voltmeter and J 35616 jumper kit.

NOTES ON FAULT TREE:

1. Tapping on engine block simulates the noise created by detonation.

2. The knock sensor produces on AC voltage proportional in amplitude to the 'loudness' of the knock condition.

3. The PCM uses the knock sensor information to estimate the octane level of the fuel being used. The PCM selects a spark calibration for either 87, 90 or 93 octane. Early production vehicles have this octane value set to 0.

4. Fuel with an octane level below 87 may cause detonation even with a properly operating engine. Engine mechanical problems such as low oil pressure, worn rod or main bearings or valve train problems may cause a knock condition.

84202036

Fig. 16 Ignition System Diagnostics- 4.6L Engine

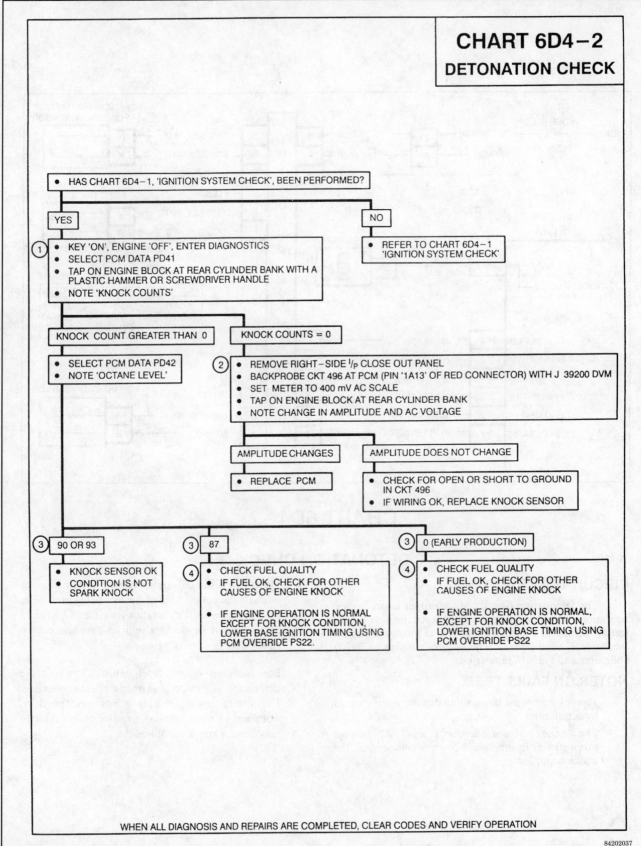

CHART 6D4−2
DETONATION CHECK

- HAS CHART 6D4−1, 'IGNITION SYSTEM CHECK', BEEN PERFORMED?

YES

NO

1
- KEY 'ON', ENGINE 'OFF', ENTER DIAGNOSTICS
- SELECT PCM DATA PD41
- TAP ON ENGINE BLOCK AT REAR CYLINDER BANK WITH A PLASTIC HAMMER OR SCREWDRIVER HANDLE
- NOTE 'KNOCK COUNTS'

- REFER TO CHART 6D4−1 'IGNITION SYSTEM CHECK'

KNOCK COUNT GREATER THAN 0

KNOCK COUNTS = 0

- SELECT PCM DATA PD42
- NOTE 'OCTANE LEVEL'

2
- REMOVE RIGHT−SIDE I/p CLOSE OUT PANEL
- BACKPROBE CKT 496 AT PCM (PIN '1A13' OF RED CONNECTOR) WITH J 39200 DVM
- SET METER TO 400 mV AC SCALE
- TAP ON ENGINE BLOCK AT REAR CYLINDER BANK
- NOTE CHANGE IN AMPLITUDE AND AC VOLTAGE

AMPLITUDE CHANGES

AMPLITUDE DOES NOT CHANGE

- REPLACE PCM

- CHECK FOR OPEN OR SHORT TO GROUND IN CKT 496
- IF WIRING OK, REPLACE KNOCK SENSOR

3 90 OR 93

3 87

3 0 (EARLY PRODUCTION)

- KNOCK SENSOR OK
- CONDITION IS NOT SPARK KNOCK

4
- CHECK FUEL QUALITY
- IF FUEL OK, CHECK FOR OTHER CAUSES OF ENGINE KNOCK

- IF ENGINE OPERATION IS NORMAL EXCEPT FOR KNOCK CONDITION, LOWER BASE IGNITION TIMING USING PCM OVERRIDE PS22.

4
- CHECK FUEL QUALITY
- IF FUEL OK, CHECK FOR OTHER CAUSES OF ENGINE KNOCK

- IF ENGINE OPERATION IS NORMAL, EXCEPT FOR KNOCK CONDITION, LOWER IGNITION BASE TIMING USING PCM OVERRIDE PS22

WHEN ALL DIAGNOSIS AND REPAIRS ARE COMPLETED, CLEAR CODES AND VERIFY OPERATION

84202037

Fig. 17 Ignition System Diagnostics- 4.6L Engine

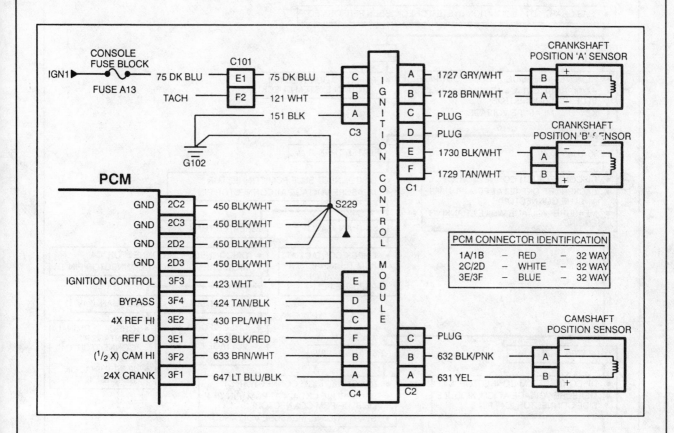

CHART 6D4-3

IGNITION CONTROL CHECK

CIRCUIT DESCRIPTION:

The Ignition Control Check verifies that the IGNITION CONTROL and BYPASS circuits between the PCM and ICM are functioning properly. This chart requires J 39200 voltmeter and J 35616 jumper kit.

NOTES ON FAULT TREE:

1. CKT 424 is the BYPASS circuit and should be low at key 'ON'.

2. CKT 423 is the IGNITION CONTROL, EST, circuit and should be low with the ICM not receiving crankshaft position sensor pulses.

3. CKT 424, BYPASS circuit, should be high with engine running.

84202038

Fig. 18 Ignition System Diagnostics- 4.6L Engine

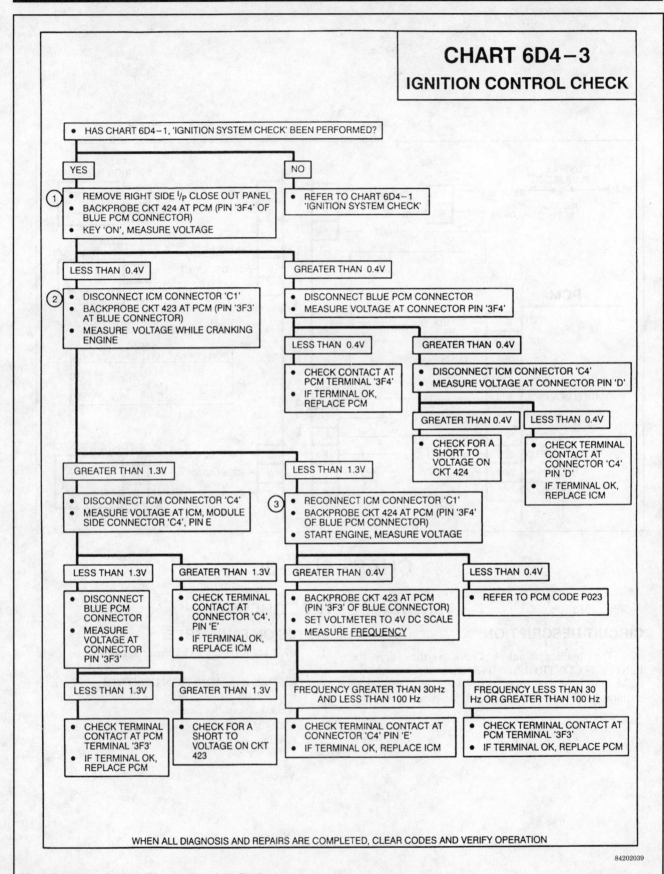

CHART 6D4-3

IGNITION CONTROL CHECK

- HAS CHART 6D4-1, 'IGNITION SYSTEM CHECK' BEEN PERFORMED?

YES

NO

① • REMOVE RIGHT SIDE $^I/_P$ CLOSE OUT PANEL
- BACKPROBE CKT 424 AT PCM (PIN '3F4' OF BLUE PCM CONNECTOR)
- KEY 'ON', MEASURE VOLTAGE

- REFER TO CHART 6D4-1 'IGNITION SYSTEM CHECK'

LESS THAN 0.4V

GREATER THAN 0.4V

② • DISCONNECT ICM CONNECTOR 'C1'
- BACKPROBE CKT 423 AT PCM (PIN '3F3' AT BLUE CONNECTOR)
- MEASURE VOLTAGE WHILE CRANKING ENGINE

- DISCONNECT BLUE PCM CONNECTOR
- MEASURE VOLTAGE AT CONNECTOR PIN '3F4'

LESS THAN 0.4V

GREATER THAN 0.4V

- CHECK CONTACT AT PCM TERMINAL '3F4'
- IF TERMINAL OK, REPLACE PCM

- DISCONNECT ICM CONNECTOR 'C4'
- MEASURE VOLTAGE AT CONNECTOR PIN 'D'

GREATER THAN 0.4V

LESS THAN 0.4V

- CHECK FOR A SHORT TO VOLTAGE ON CKT 424

- CHECK TERMINAL CONTACT AT CONNECTOR 'C4' PIN 'D'
- IF TERMINAL OK, REPLACE ICM

GREATER THAN 1.3V

LESS THAN 1.3V

- DISCONNECT ICM CONNECTOR 'C4'
- MEASURE VOLTAGE AT ICM, MODULE SIDE CONNECTOR 'C4', PIN E

③ • RECONNECT ICM CONNECTOR 'C1'
- BACKPROBE CKT 424 AT PCM (PIN '3F4' OF BLUE PCM CONNECTOR)
- START ENGINE, MEASURE VOLTAGE

LESS THAN 1.3V

GREATER THAN 1.3V

GREATER THAN 0.4V

LESS THAN 0.4V

- DISCONNECT BLUE PCM CONNECTOR
- MEASURE VOLTAGE AT CONNECTOR PIN '3F3'

- CHECK TERMINAL CONTACT AT CONNECTOR 'C4', PIN 'E'
- IF TERMINAL OK, REPLACE ICM

- BACKPROBE CKT 423 AT PCM (PIN '3F3' OF BLUE CONNECTOR)
- SET VOLTMETER TO 4V DC SCALE
- MEASURE <u>FREQUENCY</u>

- REFER TO PCM CODE P023

LESS THAN 1.3V

GREATER THAN 1.3V

FREQUENCY GREATER THAN 30Hz AND LESS THAN 100 Hz

FREQUENCY LESS THAN 30 Hz OR GREATER THAN 100 Hz

- CHECK TERMINAL CONTACT AT PCM TERMINAL '3F3'
- IF TERMINAL OK, REPLACE PCM

- CHECK FOR A SHORT TO VOLTAGE ON CKT 423

- CHECK TERMINAL CONTACT AT CONNECTOR 'C4' PIN 'E'
- IF TERMINAL OK, REPLACE ICM

- CHECK TERMINAL CONTACT AT PCM TERMINAL '3F3'
- IF TERMINAL OK, REPLACE PCM

WHEN ALL DIAGNOSIS AND REPAIRS ARE COMPLETED, CLEAR CODES AND VERIFY OPERATION

84202039

Fig. 19 Ignition System Diagnostics- 4.6L Engine

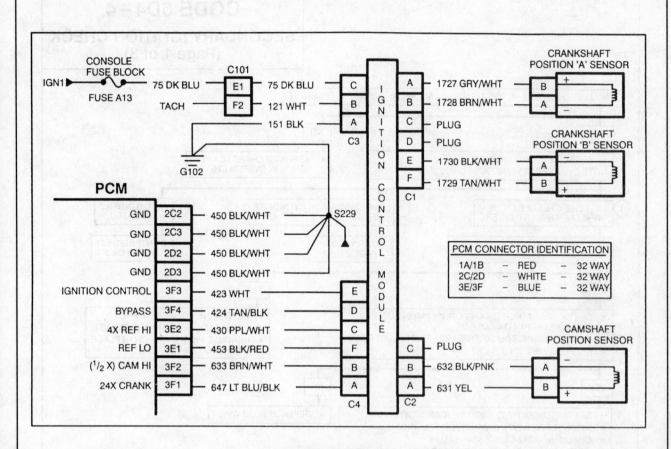

CHART 6D4-4

SECONDARY IGNITION CHECK

CIRCUIT DESCRIPTION:

The Secondary Ignition Check tests for faulty spark plugs, plug wires or ICM/coils. This chart requires J 26792 spark tester (ST-125).

NOTES ON FAULT TREE:

1. After performing the power balance test, if 1 cylinder or non-companion cylinders had no RPM change use Page 1 of 3. If 2 companion cylinders had no RPM change, use Page 2 of 3. Otherwise use Page 3 of 3.

2. J 26792 spark tester (ST-125) presents a more difficult load on the secondary ignition than a normal spark plug. If a miss, stumble or hesitation is being caused by a spark plug not firing, the spark tester should also not fire.

3. The companion spark plug shares the same ignition coil with the spark plug being tested (1-4, 2-5, 6-7, 3-8).

4. A suspected ignition system 'miss' may actually be a fuel system problem.

5. If the no spark condition follows the suspected coil, that coil is faulty. Otherwise, the ignition module is the cause of no spark. This test cold also be performed by substituting a known good coil for the one causing the no spark condition.

6. If the no spark condition follows the suspected coil, that coil is faulty. This test could also be performed by substituting a known good coil for the one causing the no spark condition.

84202040

Fig. 20 Ignition System Diagnostics- 4.6L Engine

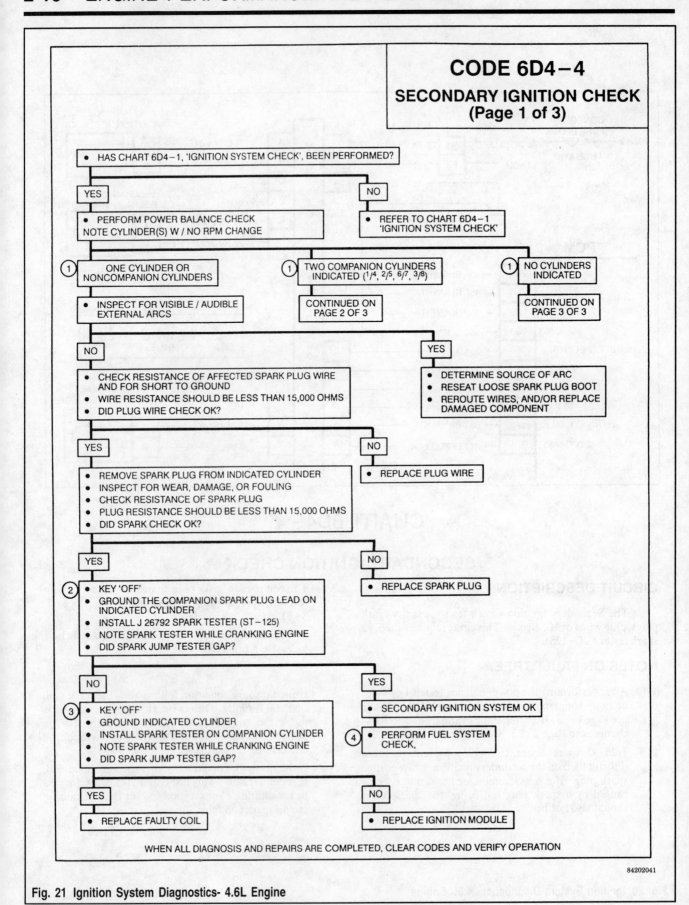

CODE 6D4−4

SECONDARY IGNITION CHECK
(Page 1 of 3)

- HAS CHART 6D4−1, 'IGNITION SYSTEM CHECK', BEEN PERFORMED?

YES
- PERFORM POWER BALANCE CHECK
NOTE CYLINDER(S) W / NO RPM CHANGE

NO
- REFER TO CHART 6D4−1 'IGNITION SYSTEM CHECK'

1 ONE CYLINDER OR NONCOMPANION CYLINDERS

1 TWO COMPANION CYLINDERS INDICATED (1/4, 2/5, 6/7, 3/8)

1 NO CYLINDERS INDICATED

- INSPECT FOR VISIBLE / AUDIBLE EXTERNAL ARCS

CONTINUED ON PAGE 2 OF 3

CONTINUED ON PAGE 3 OF 3

NO
- CHECK RESISTANCE OF AFFECTED SPARK PLUG WIRE AND FOR SHORT TO GROUND
- WIRE RESISTANCE SHOULD BE LESS THAN 15,000 OHMS
- DID PLUG WIRE CHECK OK?

YES
- DETERMINE SOURCE OF ARC
- RESEAT LOOSE SPARK PLUG BOOT
- REROUTE WIRES, AND/OR REPLACE DAMAGED COMPONENT

YES
- REMOVE SPARK PLUG FROM INDICATED CYLINDER
- INSPECT FOR WEAR, DAMAGE, OR FOULING
- CHECK RESISTANCE OF SPARK PLUG
- PLUG RESISTANCE SHOULD BE LESS THAN 15,000 OHMS
- DID SPARK CHECK OK?

NO
- REPLACE PLUG WIRE

NO
- REPLACE SPARK PLUG

2
- KEY 'OFF'
- GROUND THE COMPANION SPARK PLUG LEAD ON INDICATED CYLINDER
- INSTALL J 26792 SPARK TESTER (ST−125)
- NOTE SPARK TESTER WHILE CRANKING ENGINE
- DID SPARK JUMP TESTER GAP?

NO
3
- KEY 'OFF'
- GROUND INDICATED CYLINDER
- INSTALL SPARK TESTER ON COMPANION CYLINDER
- NOTE SPARK TESTER WHILE CRANKING ENGINE
- DID SPARK JUMP TESTER GAP?

YES
- SECONDARY IGNITION SYSTEM OK

4
- PERFORM FUEL SYSTEM CHECK,

YES
- REPLACE FAULTY COIL

NO
- REPLACE IGNITION MODULE

WHEN ALL DIAGNOSIS AND REPAIRS ARE COMPLETED, CLEAR CODES AND VERIFY OPERATION

84202041

Fig. 21 Ignition System Diagnostics- 4.6L Engine

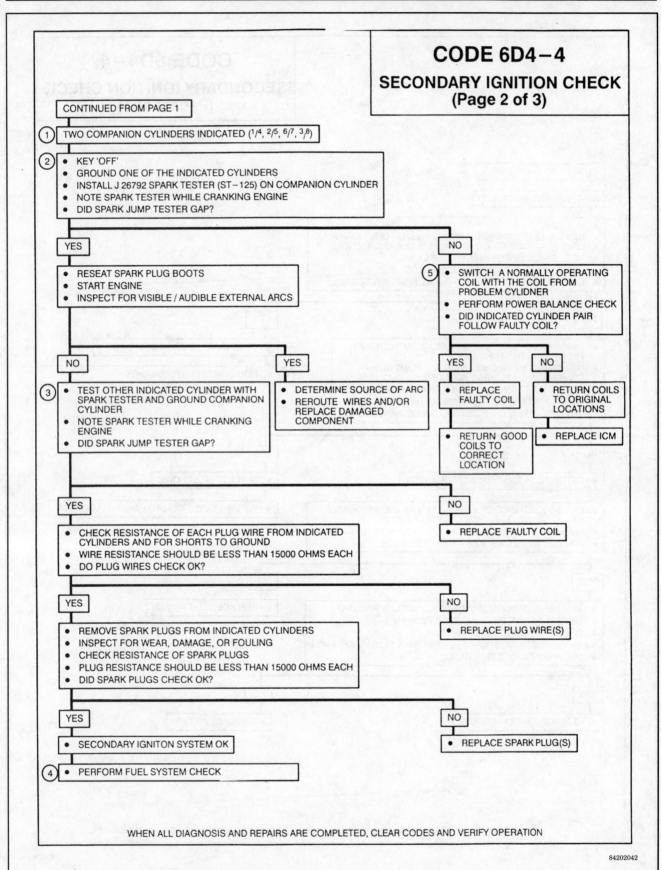

CODE 6D4–4

SECONDARY IGNITION CHECK
(Page 2 of 3)

CONTINUED FROM PAGE 1

① TWO COMPANION CYLINDERS INDICATED (1/4, 2/5, 6/7, 3/8)

②
- KEY 'OFF'
- GROUND ONE OF THE INDICATED CYLINDERS
- INSTALL J 26792 SPARK TESTER (ST–125) ON COMPANION CYLINDER
- NOTE SPARK TESTER WHILE CRANKING ENGINE
- DID SPARK JUMP TESTER GAP?

YES

- RESEAT SPARK PLUG BOOTS
- START ENGINE
- INSPECT FOR VISIBLE / AUDIBLE EXTERNAL ARCS

NO

⑤
- SWITCH A NORMALLY OPERATING COIL WITH THE COIL FROM PROBLEM CYLINDER
- PERFORM POWER BALANCE CHECK
- DID INDICATED CYLINDER PAIR FOLLOW FAULTY COIL?

NO

③
- TEST OTHER INDICATED CYLINDER WITH SPARK TESTER AND GROUND COMPANION CYLINDER
- NOTE SPARK TESTER WHILE CRANKING ENGINE
- DID SPARK JUMP TESTER GAP?

YES

- DETERMINE SOURCE OF ARC
- REROUTE WIRES AND/OR REPLACE DAMAGED COMPONENT

YES

- REPLACE FAULTY COIL

- RETURN GOOD COILS TO CORRECT LOCATION

NO

- RETURN COILS TO ORIGINAL LOCATIONS

- REPLACE ICM

YES

- CHECK RESISTANCE OF EACH PLUG WIRE FROM INDICATED CYLINDERS AND FOR SHORTS TO GROUND
- WIRE RESISTANCE SHOULD BE LESS THAN 15000 OHMS EACH
- DO PLUG WIRES CHECK OK?

NO

- REPLACE FAULTY COIL

YES

- REMOVE SPARK PLUGS FROM INDICATED CYLINDERS
- INSPECT FOR WEAR, DAMAGE, OR FOULING
- CHECK RESISTANCE OF SPARK PLUGS
- PLUG RESISTANCE SHOULD BE LESS THAN 15000 OHMS EACH
- DID SPARK PLUGS CHECK OK?

NO

- REPLACE PLUG WIRE(S)

YES

- SECONDARY IGNITON SYSTEM OK

④ • PERFORM FUEL SYSTEM CHECK

NO

- REPLACE SPARK PLUG(S)

WHEN ALL DIAGNOSIS AND REPAIRS ARE COMPLETED, CLEAR CODES AND VERIFY OPERATION

84202042

Fig. 22 Ignition System Diagnostics- 4.6L Engine

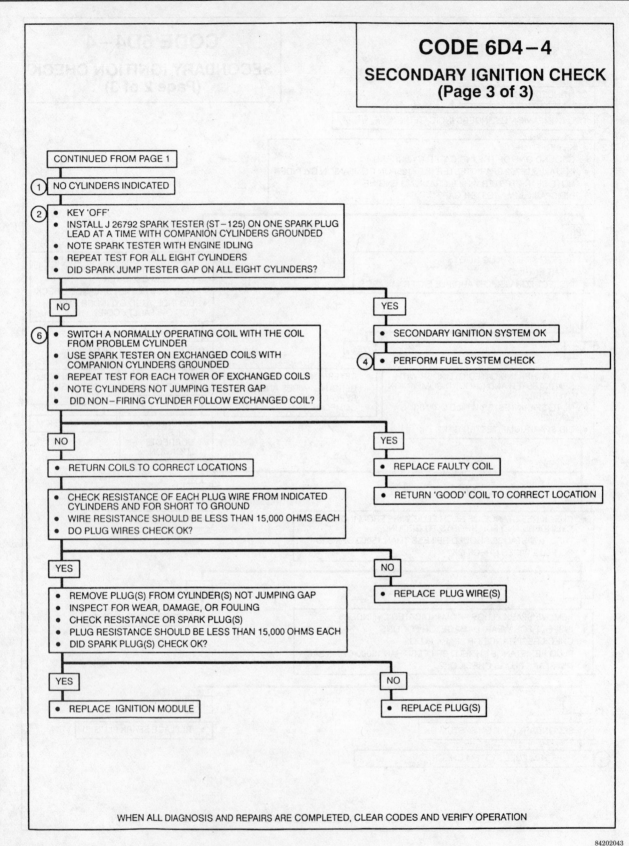

CODE 6D4–4
SECONDARY IGNITION CHECK
(Page 3 of 3)

CONTINUED FROM PAGE 1

① NO CYLINDERS INDICATED

②
- KEY 'OFF'
- INSTALL J 26792 SPARK TESTER (ST–125) ON ONE SPARK PLUG LEAD AT A TIME WITH COMPANION CYLINDERS GROUNDED
- NOTE SPARK TESTER WITH ENGINE IDLING
- REPEAT TEST FOR ALL EIGHT CYLINDERS
- DID SPARK JUMP TESTER GAP ON ALL EIGHT CYLINDERS?

NO

⑥
- SWITCH A NORMALLY OPERATING COIL WITH THE COIL FROM PROBLEM CYLINDER
- USE SPARK TESTER ON EXCHANGED COILS WITH COMPANION CYLINDERS GROUNDED
- REPEAT TEST FOR EACH TOWER OF EXCHANGED COILS
- NOTE CYLINDERS NOT JUMPING TESTER GAP
- DID NON–FIRING CYLINDER FOLLOW EXCHANGED COIL?

YES

- SECONDARY IGNITION SYSTEM OK

④
- PERFORM FUEL SYSTEM CHECK

NO

- RETURN COILS TO CORRECT LOCATIONS

- CHECK RESISTANCE OF EACH PLUG WIRE FROM INDICATED CYLINDERS AND FOR SHORT TO GROUND
- WIRE RESISTANCE SHOULD BE LESS THAN 15,000 OHMS EACH
- DO PLUG WIRES CHECK OK?

YES

- REPLACE FAULTY COIL

- RETURN 'GOOD' COIL TO CORRECT LOCATION

YES

- REMOVE PLUG(S) FROM CYLINDER(S) NOT JUMPING GAP
- INSPECT FOR WEAR, DAMAGE, OR FOULING
- CHECK RESISTANCE OR SPARK PLUG(S)
- PLUG RESISTANCE SHOULD BE LESS THAN 15,000 OHMS EACH
- DID SPARK PLUG(S) CHECK OK?

NO

- REPLACE PLUG WIRE(S)

YES

- REPLACE IGNITION MODULE

NO

- REPLACE PLUG(S)

WHEN ALL DIAGNOSIS AND REPAIRS ARE COMPLETED, CLEAR CODES AND VERIFY OPERATION

84202043

Fig. 23 Ignition System Diagnostics- 4.6L Engine

Distributor

REMOVAL

4.5L and 4.9L Engine
▶ See Figures 24, 25 and 26

During the distributor removal and installation, it is very important that the engine crankshaft not be rotated. If rotated, the reference marks made during removal will have to be disregarded. If the engine is accidentally rotated, the timing will be disturbed. If this is the case, make sure to follow the appropriate distributor installation procedure.

1. Disconnect the negative battery cable.
2. Label and disconnect all wires leading from the distributor cap.

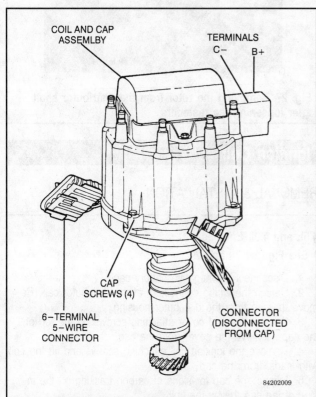

Fig. 24 Distributor assembly — 4.5L and 4.9L engines

Fig. 25 Detach wire connectors at the distributor cap

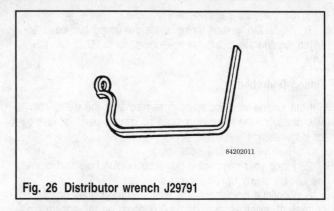

Fig. 26 Distributor wrench J29791

3. Remove the 4 bolts from the distributor cap and move the cap out of the way. Note the position of the distributor cap prior to removal.

➡**Location of the cap doghouse must be in the same area on reinstallation for sufficient clearance for adjustment.**

4. Disconnect the 6 terminal PCM connector from the distributor, if not already done.
5. Using a distributor wrench, remove the distributor hold-down nut and clamp.
6. Using a piece of chalk, mark the rotor-to-distributor body and the distributor body-to-engine positions. Pull the distributor upward until the rotor just stops turning counterclockwise and again note the position of the rotor. Remove the distributor from the engine.

➡**A thrust washer is used between the distributor drive gear and the crankcase. This washer may stick to the bottom of the distributor as it is removed from the engine. Before replacing the distributor, verify that the thrust washer is located in the crankcase at the bottom of the distributor bore.**

INSTALLATION

Timing Not Disturbed

➡**Before installing, visually inspect the distributor. The drive gear should be free of nicks, cracks and excessive wear. The distributor drive shaft should move freely, without binding. If equipped with an O-ring, it should fit tightly and be free of cuts.**

1. To install the distributor, rotate the distributor shaft until the rotor aligns with the second mark, when the shaft stopped moving. Lubricate the drive gear with clean engine oil and install the distributor into the engine. As the distributor is installed, the rotor should rotate to the first alignment mark; this will ensure proper timing. If the marks do not align properly, remove the distributor and reinstall. Be sure to install the thrust washer on the distributor shaft prior to installation.
2. Install the hold-down clamp and distributor clamp nut. Tighten the nut until the distributor can just be moved with a little effort.
3. Connect the 6 terminal PCM harness. Install the distributor cap and secure with the 4 retainer bolts.
4. Connect the coil harness and the ignition switch battery feed wire at the distributor cap.

5. Connect the negative battery cable.

6. Adjust the ignition timing. Once the timing has been adjusted, tighten the distributor hold-down nut to 20 ft. lbs. (25 Nm).

Timing Disturbed

If the engine was accidentally cranked after the distributor was removed, the following procedure can be used for distributor installation.

1. Remove the No. 1 spark plug.

2. Place your finger over No. 1 spark plug hole and crank the engine slowly until compression is felt.

3. Continue cranking slowly until the timing mark on the crankshaft pulley aligns with the 0 degrees on the engine timing indicator. At this point, No. 1 piston is at the TDC of its compression stroke.

4. Position the distributor in the block but do not allow it to engage with the drive gear.

5. Rotate the distributor shaft until the rotor points between No. 1 and No. 8 spark plug towers on the distributor cap. Install the distributor into the engine. If correctly installed, the rotor will point toward the No. 1 tower in the distributor cap when it is fully installed in the engine.

➥**If installed correctly, the rotor should point toward the No. 1 spark plug tower in the distributor cap. If this is not the case, remove the distributor and reinstall until correct rotor positioning is achieved.**

6. Install the hold-down clamp and tighten the nut until it is snug, do not tighten at this time.

7. Connect the ignition feed wire.

8. Install the distributor cap and spark plug wires.

9. Check the engine timing and adjust as required. Once the timing is set to specifications, tighten the distributor hold-down nut to 20 ft. lbs. (25 Nm).

➥**Malfunction trouble codes must be cleared after removal or adjustment of the distributor. Refer to Section 4 of this manual for the proper procedure.**

Distributor Rotor

REMOVAL & INSTALLATION

4.5L and 4.9L Engines

▶ See Figure 27

1. Disconnect the negative battery cable.

2. Turn the 4 screws and remove the cap and coil assembly from the distributor lower housing.

3. Remove the retainers and the rotor assembly from the shaft.

4. Installation is the reverse of the removal procedure.

Fig. 27 Removing the rotor from the distributor shaft after loosening the fasteners

Ignition Coil

REMOVAL & INSTALLATION

4.5L and 4.9L Engines

▶ See Figures 28 and 29

1. Disconnect the negative battery cable.

2. Detach the wiring connectors at the distributor cap. Remove the cap from the distributor housing.

3. Remove the coil cover attaching screws on the top of the cap. Remove the cover from the cap.

4. Remove the ignition coil attaching screws and lift the coil with leads, from the cap.

5. Inspect the cap for signs of carbon tracking on the inside of the cap, below the coil.

6. Remove the ignition coil arc seal. Clean with soft cloth and inspect cap for defects, replace cap as required.

7. Installation is the reverse of the removal procedure.

4.6L Engine

1. Disconnect the spark plug wires for corresponding ignition coils to be removed, at the Ignition Coil Module (ICM) assembly.

2. Remove the ignition coil retaining bolts, 2 per coil.

3. Remove the ignition coils from the ICM assembly.

To install:

4. Install the ignition coils to the ICM. Tighten the 2 retainers to 30 inch lbs. (3.5 Nm).

5. Connect the spark plug wires at the ICM assembly.

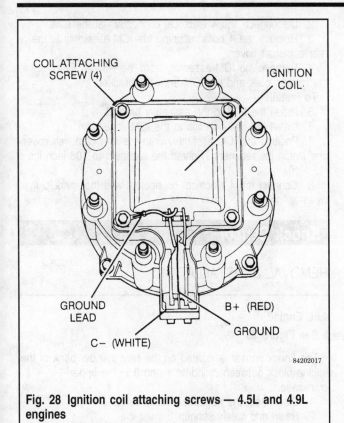

Fig. 28 Ignition coil attaching screws — 4.5L and 4.9L engines

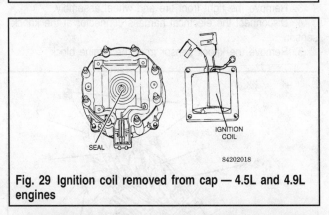

Fig. 29 Ignition coil removed from cap — 4.5L and 4.9L engines

Pick-Up Coil and Module

REMOVAL & INSTALLATION

4.5L and 4.9L Engines

▶ See Figures 30, 31, 32 and 33

1. Disconnect the negative battery cable.
2. Remove the distributor assembly from the engine.
3. Remove the cap and rotor, if still attached to distributor.
4. Mark the distributor shaft and gear so they can be installed in the same position. Support the distributor assembly and, using the correct size punch, drive out the roll pin.
5. Remove the gear from the distributor shaft.
6. Align the flat on the timer core with the Hall switch to facilitate removal. Pull the shaft from the distributor.

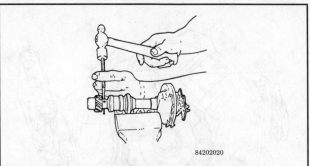

Fig. 30 Support the distributor housing assembly and drive out roll pin using proper size punch

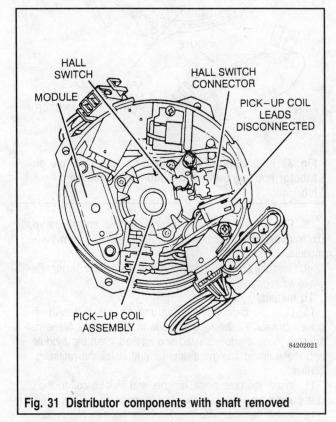

Fig. 31 Distributor components with shaft removed

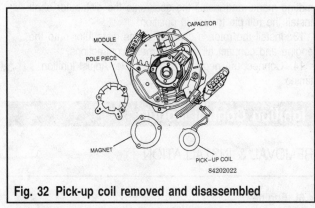

Fig. 32 Pick-up coil removed and disassembled

7. Remove the retainer ring and pick-up coil, magnet and pole piece from the distributor housing.

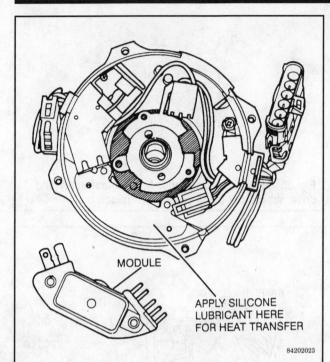

Fig. 33 Installation of the ignition module. Coat the distributor housing under the module with silicone lubricant.

8. Remove the 2 module attaching screws and lift the module from the base. Disconnect the wiring harness from the module.

9. Test the module using an approved module tester. Replace as required.

To install:

10. Coat the distributor housing under the module with silicone lubricant. Fit the module leads to the module. Make certain the leads are fully seated and latched. Seat the module and metal shield into the distributor and install the retaining screws.

11. Install the pole piece, magnet and pick-up coil to the distributor housing. Install the retainer ring.

12. Install the shaft into the distributor housing. Align the mating marks and install the gear onto the distributor shaft. Install the roll pin to lock in position.

13. Install the rotor in cap. Install the distributor onto the engine and connect all wiring harness connections.

14. Connect the negative battery cable. Adjust ignition timing.

Ignition Control Module

REMOVAL & INSTALLATION

4.6L Engine
▶ See Figure 34

1. Disconnect the spark plug wires at the Ignition Control Module (ICM).

2. Disconnect the 4 electrical connectors at the ICM.

3. Remove the 4 bolts retaining the ICM assembly to the rear camshaft cover.

4. Remove the ICM assembly from the vehicle. Remove the ignition coils and the ICM from the bracket.

To install:

5. Install the ICM to the assembly bracket.

6. Install the ignition coils to the ICM assembly.

7. Position the ICM assembly onto the rear camshaft cover and install the retainers. Tighten the retainers to 106 inch lbs. (12 Nm).

8. Connect the 4 electrical connectors and the spark plug wires at the ICM.

Knock Sensor

REMOVAL & INSTALLATION

4.6L Engine
▶ See Figure 35

The knock sensor is located on the rear cylinder bank of the engine block between cylinders 1 and 3 in the upper crankcase.

1. Disconnect the negative battery cable.

2. Raise and safely support the vehicle.

3. Remove the right front tire and wheel assembly.

4. Disconnect the electrical harness connector at the knock sensor.

5. Remove the knock sensor from the engine block.

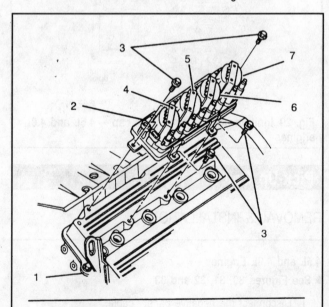

1	ENGINE	4	5–2 IGNITION COIL
2	IGNITION CONTROL MODULE	5	3–8 IGNITION COIL
3	BOLT (12 N•m/106 LB. IN.)	6	1–4 IGNITION COIL
		7	7–6 IGNITION COIL

Fig. 34 Ignition control module with coils — 4.6L engine

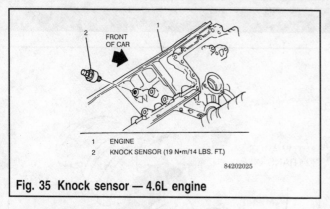

Fig. 35 Knock sensor — 4.6L engine

1	ENGINE
2	KNOCK SENSOR (19 N•m/14 LBS. FT.)

84202025

To install:

6. Install the knock sensor into the engine block and tighten to 14 ft. lbs. (19 Nm).

7. Connect the electrical connector to the sensor.

8. Install the right front tire and wheel assembly.

9. Lower the vehicle.

Camshaft Position Sensor

REMOVAL & INSTALLATION

4.6L Engine

▶ See Figure 36

1. Disconnect the electrical harness connector at the sensor.

2. Remove the retaining bolts and the sensor from the engine.

3. Installation is the reverse of the removal procedure. Tighten the sensor retainer bolts to 89 inch lbs. (10 Nm).

Crankshaft Position Sensor

REMOVAL & INSTALLATION

4.6L Engine

▶ See Figures 37 and 38

The 2 crankshaft sensors are located on the front of the engine block, between cylinder Numbers 4 and 6. Crankshaft

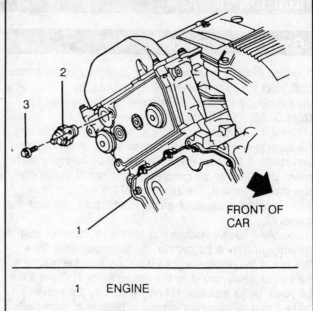

1	ENGINE
2	CAMSHAFT POSITION SENSOR
3	BOLT (10 N•m/89 LB. IN.)

84202026

Fig. 36 Camshaft position sensor — 4.6L engine

position A sensor is located on the upper crankcase and crankshaft position B sensor is located in the lower crankcase.

1. Disconnect the negative battery cable.

2. Raise and safely support the vehicle.

3. Disconnect the electrical connector from the sensor to be removed.

4. Remove the retaining bolt and the sensor.

To install:

5. Install the sensor and the retaining bolt. Tighten the bolt to 89 inch lbs. (10 Nm).

6. Install the electrical connector onto the sensor.

7. Lower the vehicle.

IGNITION TIMING

General Information

Ignition timing is the measurement, in degrees of crankshaft rotation, of the point at which the spark plugs fire in each of the cylinders. It is measured in degrees before or after Top Dead Center (TDC) of the compression stroke.

Ideally, the air/fuel mixture in the cylinder will be ignited by the spark plug just as the piston passes TDC of the compression stroke. If this happens, the piston will be beginning the power stroke just as the compressed and ignited air/fuel mixture starts to expand. The expansion of the air/fuel mixture then forces the piston down on the power stroke and turns the crankshaft.

Because it takes a fraction of a second for the spark plug to ignite the mixture in the cylinder, the spark plug must fire a little before the piston reaches TDC. Otherwise, the mixture will not be completely ignited as the piston passes TDC and the full power of the explosion will not be used by the engine.

The timing measurement is given in degrees of crankshaft rotation before the piston reaches TDC (BTDC, or Before Top Dead Center). If the setting for the ignition timing is 10 BTDC, each spark plug must fire 10 degrees before each piston reaches TDC. This only holds true, however, when the engine is at idle speed.

As the engine speed increases, the pistons go faster. The spark plugs have to ignite the fuel even sooner if it is to be completely ignited when the piston reaches TDC.

The basic ignition timing on the 4.6L Northstar is determined by the relationship of the crankshaft position sensors to the

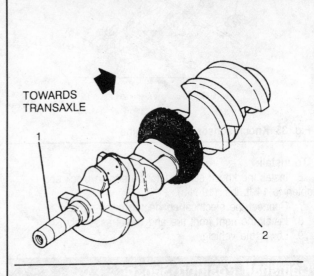

| 1 | ENGINE CRANKSHAFT |
| 2 | RELUCTOR RING |

84202028

Fig. 38 Crankshaft reluctor ring — 4.6L engine

reluctor ring. This relationship is not adjustable and results in a base ignition timing of 10 degrees BTDC.

Timing

ADJUSTMENT

▶ See Figure 39

4.5L Engine

Refer to the tune-up label located in the engine compartment. If the procedure or specifications differ from what is listed below, follow the instructions on the label.

The 4.5L engine incorporates a magnetic timing probe hole for use with special electronic timing equipment. Consult manufacturer's instructions for use of this equipment.

1. With the ignition OFF, connect the pick-up lead of a timing light to the number one spark plug wire. Use as inductive type pick-up. Do not pierce the wire or attempt to insert a probe between the boot and the wire. Connect the timing light power leads according to manufacturers instruction.

➡**Do not time the engine on 7 cylinders as the unburned fuel could cause damage to the catalytic converter.**

2. Jumper pins A and B together at the ALDL connector, while not in diagnostic display.

3. Start the engine and aim the timing light at the timing mark. The line on the pulley will line up at the timing mark. If

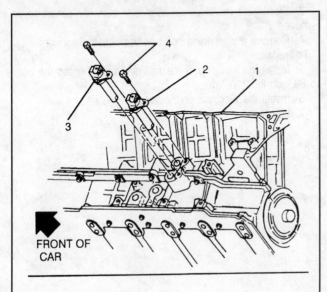

1	ENGINE
2	CRANKSHAFT POSITION "A" SENSOR
3	CRANKSHAFT POSITION "B" SENSOR
4	BOLT (10 N•m/89 LB.IN.)

84202027

Fig. 37 Crankshaft position sensor — 4.6L engine

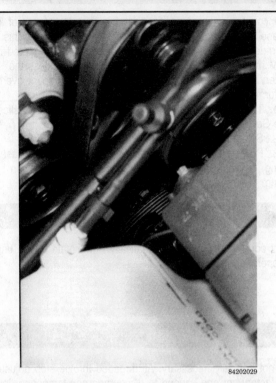

Fig. 39 Ignition timing tab is located above the crank-shaft pulley

a change is necessary, loosen the distributor hold-down nut using distributor wrench J 29791. While observing the timing mark, rotate the distributor until the line indicates the correct timing. Tighten the hold-down nut and re-check the timing.

4. Turn the engine OFF and remove the timing light.

4.9L Engine

▶ **See Figures 40 and 41**

Timing specifications and adjustment procedure for each engine are listed on the underhood Vehicle Emissions Control Information (VECI) label in the engine compartment. Use specifications or procedures from the VECI, if they differ from the specifications or procedure listed in this manual.

The 4.9L engine incorporates a magnetic timing probe hole for use with special electronic timing equipment. Consult manufacturer's instructions for use of this equipment.

Malfunction codes may be set during ignition timing adjustment procedure. Enter diagnostics and clear trouble codes if this occurs. Refer to Section 4 of this manual for more information.

1. Place the transmission in Park.

2. With the ignition in the OFF position, attach a timing light to No. 1 spark plug cable.

➡**Do not pierce the wire or attempt to insert a probe between the boot and the wire. Connect the timing light power leads according to manufacturers instruction. Do not time the engine on 7 cylinders as the unburned fuel could cause damage to the catalytic converter.**

3. With the engine at normal operating temperature and the air conditioning OFF, take off the air cleaner upper housing. The engine should be OFF at this time.

4. Jumper pins A and B at the ALDL connector, while not in the diagnostic display. 'SET TIMING MODE' message will be displayed on the climate control Driver Information Center (CCDIC).

5. Start the engine and aim the timing light at the timing mark. If an adjustment is necessary, loosen the distributor hold-down nut using distributor wrench J29791, or equivalent. While observing the timing mark, rotate the distributor until the line indicates the correct timing. Set base timing at 10 degrees BTDC, at any speed less than 800 rpm.

6. Turn OFF the engine and remove the timing light. Reconnect the number one spark plug wire, if disconnected.

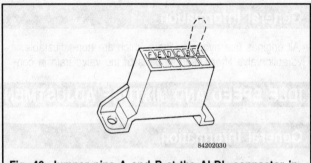

Fig. 40 Jumper pins A and B at the ALDL connector in order to set timing

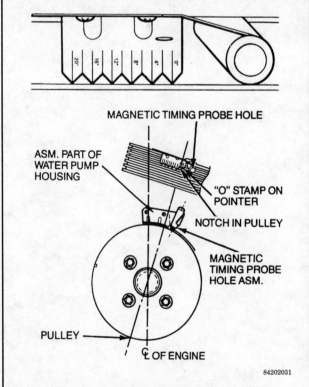

Fig. 41 Magnetic timing probe hole — 4.9L engine

7. Remove the jumper from the ALDL connector and install the air cleaner upper housing.

➡ **Remove the jumper from the ALDL connector when the procedure is complete. If the jumper remains in the ALDL connector, the engine will run at base timing and cause driveability problems.**

4.6L Engine

On the 4.6L engine, the Powertrain Control Module (PCM) incorporates a permanent spark control override, which allows base ignition timing to be lowered electronically if spark knock is encountered during normal operation, due to the use of low octane fuel. Basic ignition timing can be lowered using this override down to 6 degrees BTDC. This override is stored in PCM memory and will remain at the set timing unless the battery is disconnected. To reset the permanent spark override, perform the following:

1. Turn the key to the ON position and enter diagnostics. See Section 4 of this manual for more information.
2. Select the PCM override PS22 (SERVICE SPK.)
3. Press the 'COOLER' button to lower the ignition base timing, or press the 'WARMER' button to increase ignition base timing.

VALVE LASH

General Information

All engines use hydraulic lifters which are non-adjustable. Hydraulic valve lifters keep all parts of the valve train in constant contact and adjust automatically to maintain **0** lash under all operating conditions.

IDLE SPEED AND MIXTURE ADJUSTMENTS

General Information

Idle speed and mixture for all engines is electronically controlled by the Powertrain Control Module (PCM). Adjustments are not normally necessary. All threaded throttle stop adjusters are factory set and capped to discourage any tampering. In most cases, proper diagnosis and/or parts replacement will cure problems concerning idle speed.

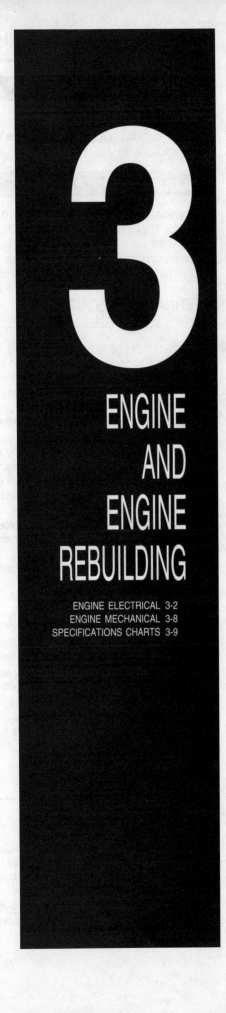

3

ENGINE AND ENGINE REBUILDING

ENGINE ELECTRICAL

For distributor, ignition coil, and ignition module testing and removal and installation procedures, please refer to Section 2, Engine Performance And Tune-Up.

Alternator

All vehicles use a Delco CS-144 for 1990 and Delco CS-144 GEN II for 1991-93. The 'CS' stands for charging system, the '144' denotes the outside diameter of the stator laminations in millimeters and the 'GEN II' denotes design improvements effective with the 1991 model year.

ALTERNATOR PRECAUTIONS

To prevent damage to the alternator, regulator and on-board computer, the following precautions should be taken when working with the electrical system.

1. Never reverse the battery connections or attempt to disconnect or reconnect them with the ignition key ON. Take care not to let metal tools touch ground when disconnecting the positive battery cable.

2. Booster batteries for starting must be connected properly — positive-to-positive and negative-to-negative with the ignition turned OFF. Do not attempt to connect jumper cables from another vehicle while its engine is running.

3. Disconnect the battery cables before using a fast charger; the charger has a tendency to force current through the diodes in the opposite direction for which they were designed. This burns out the diodes.

4. Never use a fast charger as a booster for starting the vehicle.

5. Never disconnect the alternator connectors while the engine is running.

6. Do not short across or ground any of the terminals on the AC generator.

7. Never operate the alternator on an open circuit. Make sure that all connections within the circuit are clean and tight.

8. Disconnect the battery terminals when performing any service on the electrical system. This will eliminate the possibility of accidental reversal of polarity.

9. Disconnect the battery ground cable if arc welding is to be done on any part of the car.

REMOVAL & INSTALLATION

4.5L and 4.9L Engine
▶ See Figures 1 and 2

1. Disconnect the negative battery cable.
2. Label and disconnect the electrical connectors from the back of the alternator.
3. Release the tension from the drive belt and remove the belt from the alternator pulley. Do not remove the belt from any other pulleys.

4. Remove the alternator-to-bracket bolts and the alternator from the vehicle. If necessary, disconnect the ABS ground strap.

To install:
5. Install alternator on vehicle.
6. Reposition drive belt on alternator pulley.
7. Install electrical connectors.
8. Connect negative battery cable.

4.6L Northstar Engine
▶ See Figure 3

1. Disconnect the negative battery cable.
2. Remove the cover from the headlamps and radiator shroud.
3. Remove the air cleaner assembly.
4. Disconnect the left engine torque strut.
5. Disconnect the upper transaxle oil cooler line.
6. Remove the right and left cooling fan.
7. Remove the serpentine belt from the alternator pulley.
8. Remove the bolt from the front top of the alternator.
9. Remove the bolt from the lower front of the alternator.
10. Disconnect the harness connector and output cable from the alternator.
11. Remove the 2 bolts from the alternator rear bracket to the alternator.

➡ **The bolt nearest the exhaust manifold cannot be removed from the bracket but can be backed out to allow for removal of the alternator.**

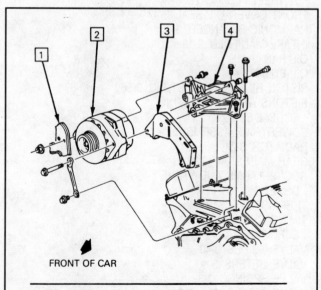

FRONT OF CAR

1	CRUISE SERVO BRACKET
2	GENERATOR
3	DRIVE BELT TENSIONER SUPPORT
4	MOUNTING BRACKET

84203015

Fig. 1 Alternator mounting — 1990-93 Eldorado and Seville with 4.5L and 4.9L engines

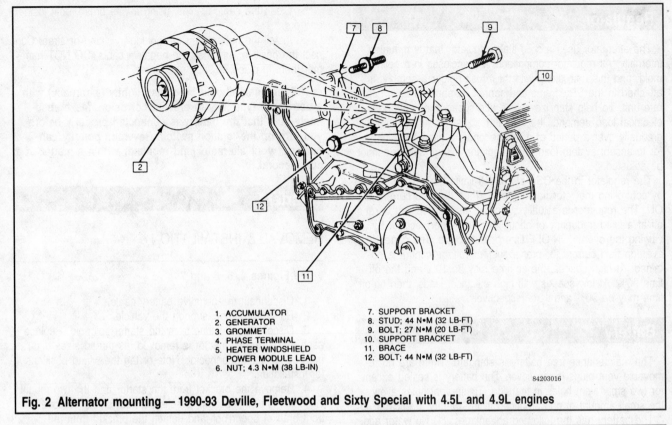

1. ACCUMULATOR
2. GENERATOR
3. GROMMET
4. PHASE TERMINAL
5. HEATER WINDSHIELD
   POWER MODULE LEAD
6. NUT; 4.3 N•M (38 LB-IN)

7. SUPPORT BRACKET
8. STUD; 44 N•M (32 LB-FT)
9. BOLT; 27 N•M (20 LB-FT)
10. SUPPORT BRACKET
11. BRACE
12. BOLT; 44 N•M (32 LB-FT)

84203016

Fig. 2 Alternator mounting — 1990-93 Deville, Fleetwood and Sixty Special with 4.5L and 4.9L engines

12. Remove the A/C splash shield by removing the 3 bolts retaining it to the cradle.

13. Remove the access panel from the bottom side of the radiator support.

14. Disconnect the harness clip from the cradle.

15. Move the alternator out away from the engine and remove from the bottom side of the engine compartment.

To install:

16. Install the alternator to the mounting bracket with the 2 bolts to the rear of the alternator. Hand tighten at this time.

17. Connect the harness clip to the cradle.

18. Install the access panel to the bottom side of the radiator support with the 4 retaining bolts.

19. Install the A/C splash shield and 3 bolts retaining to the cradle.

20. Connect the harness connector and output cable to the alternator.

21. Tighten the rear mounting bolts to 36 ft. lbs. (47 Nm) and the ouput cable to 15 ft. lbs. (20 Nm).

22. Install the bolt to the lower front of the alternator and tighten to 36 ft. lbs. (47 nm).

23. Install the bolt to the front top of the alternator and tighten to 36 ft. lbs. (47 nm).

24. Rotate the drive belt tensioner and install the serpentine belt to the alternator pulley.

25. Install the left and right cooling fan.

26. Connect the upper transaxle oil cooler line.

27. Connect the left engine torque strut.

28. Install the air cleaner assembly.

29. Install the cover to the headlamps and radiator shroud.

30. Connect the negative battery cable.

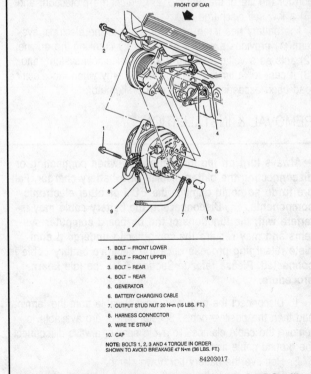

FRONT OF CAR

1. BOLT – FRONT LOWER
2. BOLT – FRONT UPPER
3. BOLT – REAR
4. BOLT – REAR
5. GENERATOR
6. BATTERY CHARGING CABLE
7. OUTPUT STUD NUT 20 N•m (15 LBS. FT.)
8. HARNESS CONNECTOR
9. WIRE TIE STRAP
10. CAP

NOTE: BOLTS 1, 2, 3 AND 4 TORQUE IN ORDER
SHOWN TO AVOID BREAKAGE 47 N•m (36 LBS. FT.)

84203017

Fig. 3 Alternator mounting — 1993 Eldorado and Seville with 4.6L Northstar engine

Regulator

The alternator uses a solid state regulator that is mounted internally. All regulator components are enclosed in a solid mold, and this unit, along with the brush holder assembly, is attached to the SRE frame and cannot be serviced as a separate unit. To help stabilize engine idle speed during changes in electrical load demand, the regulator adjusts system voltage gradually over a period of a few seconds to allow the alternator to accept system load. The regulator voltage setting cannot be adjusted.

The regulator in the CS-144 GEN II limits the system voltage by controlling the rotor field current. When the field current is ON, The regulator is actually switching the field current on and off at a fixed frequency of about 400 cycles per second. By varying the overall ON-OFF time or duty cycle, The correct average field current for proper system voltage control is obtained. At high speeds, the on-time may be 10% and the off time 90%. At low speeds with high electrical loads, then on-off time may be 90% and 10% respectively.

Battery

The maintenance free battery is standard. There are no removable vent plugs in the cover. The battery is sealed except for two small vent holes in the side. These vent holes allow the small amount of gas produced in the battery to escape.

The battery has the following advantages: (1) No water addition for the life of the battery, (2) Overcharge protection, and (3) a low self-discharge rate.

The battery has three major functions in the electrical system: (1) provides a source of energy for cranking the engine, (2) acts as a voltage stabilizer for the electrical system, and (3) it can, for a limited time, provide energy when the electrical load used exceeds the output of the alternator.

REMOVAL & INSTALLATION

➡**Always turn off the ignition switch when connecting or disconnecting the battery cables or a battery charger. Failure to do so could damage the ECM or other electronic components.   Disconnecting the battery cable may interfere with the functions of the on board computer systems and may require the computer to undergo a complete relearning process once the negative battery cable is connected. Please refer to Section 5 for the Idle Learn procedure.**

1. Disconnect the negative (ground) cable from the terminal and then the positive cable. Special pullers are available to remove the cable clamps. To avoid sparks, always disconnect the ground cable first and connect it last.
2. Remove the battery holddown clamp.
3. Remove the battery, being careful not to spill the acid.

➡**Spilled acid can be neutralized with a baking soda/water solution. If you somehow get acid into your eyes, flush it out with lots of water and get to a doctor.**

4. Clean the battery posts thoroughly before reinstalling or when installing a new battery.

5. Clean the cable clamps, using a wire brush, both inside and out.
6. Install the battery and the holddown clamp or strap. Connect the positive, and then the negative cable. DO NOT hammer them in place.

➡**The terminals should be coated lightly (externally) with a petroleum type jelly to prevent corrosion. Make absolutely sure that the battery is connected properly before you turn on the ignition switch. Reversed polarity can burn out your alternator and regulator within a matter of a split second.**

Starter

REMOVAL & INSTALLATION

▶ **See Figures 4, 5, 6 and 7**

1. Disconnect the negative battery cable.
2. Raise and safely support the vehicle.
3. Disconnect all wiring from the starter solenoid. Replace each nut as the connector is removed, as thread sizes differ from connector to connector. Note or tag the wiring positions for installation.
4. Remove the bracket from the starter and the two mounting bolts. On engines with a solenoid heat shield, remove the front bracket upper bolt and detach the bracket from the starter.
5. Remove the front bracket bolt or nut. Lower the starter front end first, and then remove the unit from the car.
6. To install, position the starter into place and secure it with the front bracket, bolts and nuts. Torque the two mounting bolts to 25-35 ft. lbs.

✷✷CAUTION

If shims were removed, they must be replaced to ensure proper pinion-to-flywheel engagement.

7. On engines with a solenoid heat shield, attach the bracket to the starter. Install the bracket to the starter and the two mounting bolts. Install the front bracket upper bolt.
8. Connect all wiring to the starter solenoid and tighten wire lug nuts.
9. Lower the vehicle.
10. Connect the negative battery cable.

SOLENOID REPLACEMENT

1. Remove the screw and washer from the motor connector strap terminal.
2. Remove the two solenoid retaining screws.
3. Twist the solenoid housing clockwise to remove the flange key from the keyway in the housing. Then remove the housing.
4. To re-install the unit, place the return spring on the plunger and place the solenoid body on the drive housing. Turn counterclockwise to engage the flange key. Place the two

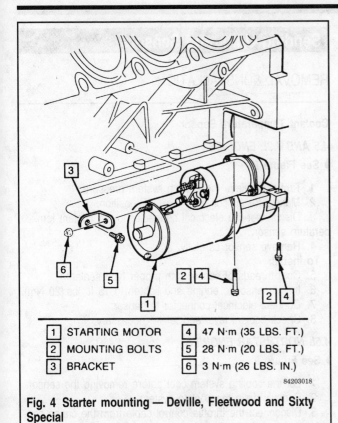

Fig. 4 Starter mounting — Deville, Fleetwood and Sixty Special

1	STARTING MOTOR	4	47 N·m (35 LBS. FT.)
2	MOUNTING BOLTS	5	28 N·m (20 LBS. FT.)
3	BRACKET	6	3 N·m (26 LBS. IN.)

84203018

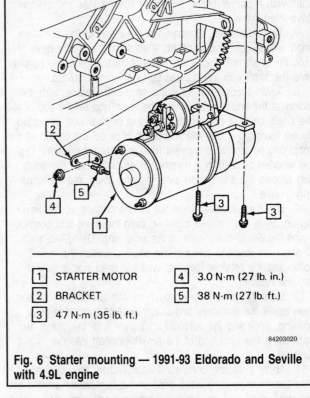

Fig. 6 Starter mounting — 1991-93 Eldorado and Seville with 4.9L engine

1	STARTER MOTOR	4	3.0 N·m (27 lb. in.)
2	BRACKET	5	38 N·m (27 lb. ft.)
3	47 N·m (35 lb. ft.)		

84203020

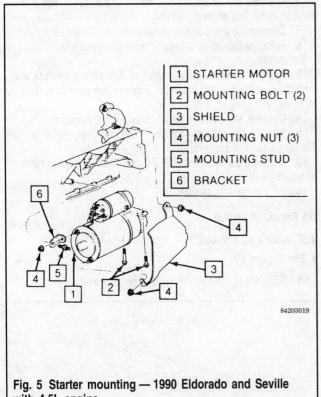

1	STARTER MOTOR
2	MOUNTING BOLT (2)
3	SHIELD
4	MOUNTING NUT (3)
5	MOUNTING STUD
6	BRACKET

84203019

Fig. 5 Starter mounting — 1990 Eldorado and Seville with 4.5L engine

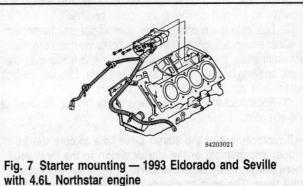

84203021

Fig. 7 Starter mounting — 1993 Eldorado and Seville with 4.6L Northstar engine

DRIVE REPLACEMENT

1. Disconnect the field coil straps from the solenoid.
2. Remove the thru-bolts and separate the commutator end frame, field frame assembly, drive housing and armature assembly from each other.
3. Slide the two piece thrust collar off the end of the armature shaft.
4. Slide a suitably sized metal cylinder (such as a standard 1/2 inch pipe coupling or an old pinion) on the shaft so that the end of the coupling or pinion butts up against the edge of the pinion retainer.
5. Support the lower end of the armature securely on a soft surface, such as a wooden block, and tap the end of the coupling or pinion, driving the retainer towards the armature end of the snap ring.

retaining screws in position and install the screw and washer which secures the strap terminal. Install the unit on the starter.

6. Remove the snap ring from the groove in the armature shaft with a pair of pliers, then slide the retainer and starter drive from the shaft.

7. To reassemble, lubricate the drive end of the armature shaft with silicone lubricant and then slide the starter drive onto the shaft with the pinion facing outward. Slide the retainer onto the shaft with the cupped surface facing outward.

8. Again support the armature on a soft surface, with the pinion at the upper end. Center the snap ring on the top of the shaft, using a new snap ring if the original was damaged during removal. Gently place a block of wood flat on top of the snap ring so as not to move it from a centered position. Tap the wooden block with a hammer in order to force the snap ring around the shaft, then slide the ring down into the snap ring groove.

9. Lay the armature down flat on the surface you're working on. Slide the retainer close up onto the shaft and position it and the thrust collar next to the snap ring. Using two pairs of pliers on opposite sides of the shaft, squeeze the thrust collar and the retainer together until the snap ring is forced into the retainer.

10. Lube the drive housing bushing with a silicone lubricant, then install the armature and clutch assembly into the drive housing, engaging the solenoid shift lever with the clutch and positioning the front end of the armature shaft into the bushing.

11. Apply a sealing compound approved for this application onto the drive housing, then position the field frame around the armature shaft and against the drive housing. Work slowly and carefully to prevent damaging the starter brushes.

12. Lubricate the bushing in the commutator end frame with a silicone lubricant, place the leather brake washer onto the armature shaft, then slide the commutator end frame over the shaft and into position against the field frame. Line up the bolt holes, then install and tighten the thru-bolts.

13. Reconnect the field coil straps to the "motor" terminal of the solenoid.

➡**If replacement of the starter drive fails to cure the improper engagement of the starter pinion to the flywheel, there are probably defective parts in the solenoid and/or shift lever. The best procedure would probably be to take the assembly to a shop where a pinion clearance check can be made by energizing the solenoid on a test bench. If the pinion clearance is incorrect, disassemble the solenoid and the shift lever and replace any worn parts.**

BRUSH REPLACEMENT

1. After removing the starter from the engine, disconnect the field coil from the motor solenoid terminal.

2. Remove the starter thru-bolts and remove the commutator end frame and washer.

3. Remove the field frame and the armature assembly from the drive housing.

4. Remove the brush holder pivot pin which positions one insulated and one grounded brush.

5. Remove the brush springs.

6. Remove the brushes.

7. Installation is the reverse of removal.

Sending Units and Sensors

REMOVAL & INSTALLATION

Coolant Temperature Sensor

4.5 AND 4.9L ENGINES

▶ See Figure 8

1. Properly relieve the cooling system pressure.
2. Make sure ignition is in the OFF position.
3. Disconnect the electrical connector to the coolant temperature sensor.
4. Remove sensor carefully.

To install:

5. Coat threads of sensor with proper type sealant.
6. Install sensor to engine and tighten to 15 ft. lbs.(20 Nm).
7. Connect electrical connector to sensor.
8. Check coolant level and refill if necessary.

4.6L NORTHSTAR ENGINES

▶ See Figure 9

1. Let the cooling system cool before removing the sensor.
2. Partially drain the cooling system
3. Disconnect the throttle control cable from the cruise control servo bracket.
4. Remove the cruise control servo and bracket. Refer to Section 6 for this procedure.
5. Disconnect the coolant sensor electrical connector.
6. Remove the coolant sensor from the manifold.

To install:

7. Apply a non-hardening sealer to the sensor threads and install the sensor in the manifold. Tighten the sensor to 106 inch lbs. (12 Nm).
8. Connect the coolant sensor electrical connector.
9. Install the cruise control servo and bracket. Refer to Section 6 for this procedure.
10. Connect the throttle control cable to the cruise control servo bracket.
11. Fill the cooling system

Oil Pressure Switch

4.5L AND 4.9L ENGINES

▶ See Figure 10

1. Disconnect the locking collar from the switch.

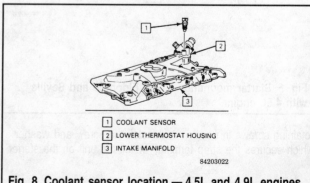

1	COOLANT SENSOR
2	LOWER THERMOSTAT HOUSING
3	INTAKE MANIFOLD

84203022

Fig. 8 Coolant sensor location — 4.5L and 4.9L engines

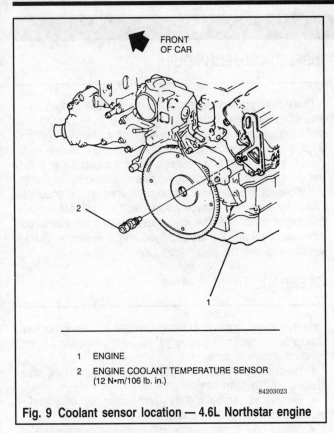

FRONT OF CAR

1 ENGINE
2 ENGINE COOLANT TEMPERATURE SENSOR
  (12 N•m/106 lb. in.)

84203023

Fig. 9 Coolant sensor location — 4.6L Northstar engine

2. Remove the electrical connector.
3. Remove oil pressure switch.

To install:

4. Make sure fittings are properly aligned to allow sensor installation.
5. Wrap Teflon tape or apply Thread lock to threads on sensor.
6. Install new oil pressure switch.
7. Reconnect electrical connector and locking collar onto switch.
8. Start engine check for leaks.

4.6L NORTHSTAR ENGINE

▶ See Figure 11

1. Raise and safely support the vehicle.
2. Remove the electrical connector from the switch.
3. Remove oil pressure switch at the oil filter adapter.

To install:

4. Install oil pressure switch at the oil filter adapter and tighten to 106 inch lbs. (12 (Nm).
5. Install the electrical connector to the switch.
6. Lower the vehicle and check for leaks.

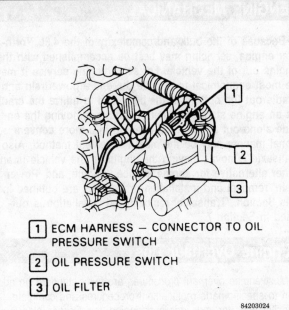

1 ECM HARNESS — CONNECTOR TO OIL PRESSURE SWITCH
2 OIL PRESSURE SWITCH
3 OIL FILTER

84203024

Fig. 10 Oil pressure switch location — 4.5L and 4.9L engines

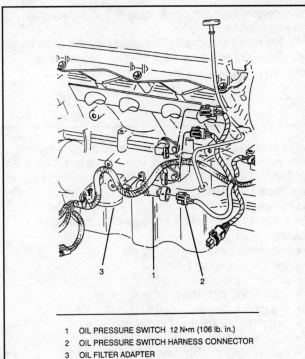

1 OIL PRESSURE SWITCH 12 N•m (106 lb. in.)
2 OIL PRESSURE SWITCH HARNESS CONNECTOR
3 OIL FILTER ADAPTER

84203025

Fig. 11 Oil pressure switch location — 4.6L Northstar engine

ENGINE MECHANICAL

→Because of the bulk and complexity of the 4.6L North-star engine, servicing may best be accomplished with the engine out of the vehicle. For some engine service it may be most economical to remove the entire powertrain and cradle out the bottom of the body and to utilize the cradle as an engine stand. In other situations removing the engine alone out of the hood opening in a more conventional manner may be the most convenient method. Also transaxle removal, leaving the engine in the vehicle is another alternative for engine service. 'Engine' and 'Powertrain' removal and installation procedures are outlined in this Section. 'Transaxle' removal and installation is outlined in Section 7.

Engine Overhaul Tips

Most engine overhaul procedures are fairly standard. In addition to specific parts replacement procedures and complete specifications for your individual engine, this Section also is a guide to accept rebuilding procedures. Examples of standard rebuilding practice are shown and should be used along with specific details concerning your particular engine.

Competent and accurate machine shop services will ensure maximum performance, reliability and engine life.

In most instances it is more profitable for the do-it-yourself mechanic to remove, clean and inspect the component, buy the necessary parts and deliver these to a shop for actual machine work.

On the other hand, much of the rebuilding work (crankshaft, block, bearings, piston rods, and other components) is well within the scope of the do-it-yourself mechanic.

TOOLS

The tools required for an engine overhaul or parts replacement will depend on the depth of your involvement. With a few exceptions, they will be the tools found in a mechanic's tool kit (see Section 1). More in-depth work will require any or all of the following:

• a dial indicator (reading in thousandths) mounted on a universal base
• micrometers and telescope gauges
• jaw and screw-type pullers
• scraper
• valve spring compressor
• ring groove cleaner
• piston ring expander and compressor
• ridge reamer
• cylinder hone or glaze breaker
• Plastigage®
• engine stand

The use of most of these tools is illustrated in this Section. Many can be rented for a one-time use from a local parts jobber or tool supply house specializing in automotive work.

Occasionally, the use of special tools is called for. See the information on Special Tools and Safety Notice in the front of this book before substituting another tool.

INSPECTION TECHNIQUES

Procedures and specifications are given in this Section for inspecting, cleaning and assessing the wear limits of most major components. Other procedures such as Magnaflux® and Zyglo® can be used to locate material flaws and stress cracks. Magnaflux® is a magnetic process applicable only to ferrous materials. The Zyglo® process coats the material with a fluorescent dye penetrant and can be used on any material Check for suspected surface cracks can be more readily made using spot check dye. The dye is sprayed onto the suspected area, wiped off and the area sprayed with a developer. Cracks will show up brightly.

OVERHAUL TIPS

Aluminum has become extremely popular for use in engines, due to its low weight. Observe the following precautions when handling aluminum parts:

• Never hot tank aluminum parts (the caustic hot tank solution will eat the aluminum.
• Remove all aluminum parts (identification tag, etc.) from engine parts prior to the tanking.
• Always coat threads lightly with engine oil or anti-seize compounds before installation, to prevent seizure.
• Never overtorque bolts or spark plugs especially in aluminum threads.

Stripped threads in any component can be repaired using any of several commercial repair kits (Heli-Coil®, Microdot®, Keenserts®, etc.).

When assembling the engine, any parts that will be frictional contact must be prelubed to provide lubrication at initial start-up. Any product specifically formulated for this purpose can be used, but engine oil is not recommended as a prelube.

When semi-permanent (locked, but removable) installation of bolts or nuts is desired, threads should be cleaned and coated with Loctite® or other similar, commercial non-hardening sealant.

REPAIRING DAMAGED THREADS

Several methods of repairing damaged threads are available. Heli-Coil® (shown here), Keenserts® and Microdot® are among the most widely used. All involve basically the same principle — drilling out stripped threads, tapping the hole and installing a prewound insert — making welding, plugging and oversize fasteners unnecessary.

Two types of thread repair inserts are usually supplied: a standard type for most Inch Coarse, Inch Fine, Metric Course and Metric Fine thread sizes and a spark lug type to fit most spark plug port sizes. Consult the individual manufacturer's catalog to determine exact applications. Typical thread repair kits will contain a selection of prewound threaded inserts, a tap (corresponding to the outside diameter threads of the insert) and an installation tool. Spark plug inserts usually differ because they require a tap equipped with pilot threads and a combined reamer/tap section. Most manufacturers also supply blister-packed thread repair inserts separately in addition to a master kit containing a variety of taps and inserts plus installation tools.

Before effecting a repair to a threaded hole, remove any snapped, broken or damaged bolts or studs. Penetrating oil can be used to free frozen threads. The offending item can be removed with locking pliers or with a screw or stud extractor. After the hole is clear, the thread can be repaired.

Checking Engine Compression

A noticeable lack of engine power, excessive oil consumption and/or poor fuel mileage measured over an extended period are all indicators of internal engine war. Worn piston rings, scored or worn cylinder bores, blown head gaskets, sticking or burnt valves and worn valve seats are all possible culprits here. A check of each cylinder's compression will help you locate the problems.

As mentioned in the Tools and Equipment section of Section 1, a screw-in type compression gauge is more accurate that the type you simply hold against the spark plug hole, although it takes slightly longer to use. It's worth it to obtain a more accurate reading. Follow the procedures below.

✳✳CAUTION

When draining the coolant, keep in mind that cats and dogs are attracted by the ethylene glycol antifreeze, and are quite likely to drink any that is left in an uncovered container or in puddles on the ground. This will prove fatal in sufficient quantity. Always drain the coolant into a sealable container. Coolant should be reused unless it is contaminated or several years old.

GENERAL ENGINE SPECIFICATIONS

Year	Engine ID/VIN	Engine Displacement Liters (cc)	Fuel System Type	Net Horsepower @ rpm	Net Torque @ rpm (ft. lbs.)	Bore × Stroke (in.)	Compression Ratio	Oil Pressure @ rpm
1990	3	4.5 (4467)	MPFI	180 @ 4000	245 @ 3000	3.62 × 3.31	9.5:1	①
1991	B	4.9 (4885)	MPFI	200 @ 4100	275 @ 3000	3.62 × 3.62	9.5:1	53 @ 2000
1992	B	4.9 (4885)	MPFI	200 @ 4100	275 @ 3000	3.62 × 3.62	9.5:1	53 @ 2000
1993	B	4.9 (4885)	MPFI	200 @ 4100	275 @ 3000	3.62 × 3.62	9.5:1	53 @ 2000
	9	4.6 (4566)	MPFI	295 @ 6000	290 @ 4400	3.66 × 3.31	10.3:1	35 @ 2000
	Y	4.6 (4566)	MPFI	270 @ 5600	300 @ 4000	3.66 × 3.31	10.3:1	35 @ 2000

MPFI—Multi-Port Fuel Injection
① 26 psi at 30 mph at normal operating temperature

84203124

CAMSHAFT SPECIFICATIONS

All measurements given in inches.

Year	Engine ID/VIN	Engine Displacement Liters (cc)	Journal Diameter 1	2	3	4	5	Elevation ① In.	Ex.	Bearing Clearance	Camshaft End Play
1990	3	4.5 (4467)	2.0358–2.0366	2.0157–2.0165	1.9957–1.9965	1.9756–1.9765	1.9559–1.9567	0.384	0.396	0.0018–0.004	NA
1991	B	4.9 (4885)	2.0358–2.0366	2.0157–2.0165	1.9957–1.9965	1.9756–1.9765	1.9559–1.9567	0.384	0.396	0.0018–0.004	NA
1992	B	4.9 (4885)	NA	NA	NA	NA	NA	0.384	0.396	0.0018–0.004	NA
1993	B	4.9 (4885)	NA	NA	NA	NA	NA	0.384	0.396	0.0018–0.004	NA
	9	4.6 (4566)	1.061–1.062	1.061–1.062	1.061–1.062	1.061–1.062	1.061–1.062	0.370	0.339	0.002–0.003	NA
	Y	4.6 (4566)	1.061–1.062	1.061–1.062	1.061–1.062	1.061–1.062	1.061–1.062	0.339	0.339	0.002–0.003	NA

NA—Not available
① Valve lift

84203125

CRANKSHAFT AND CONNECTING ROD SPECIFICATIONS

All measurements are given in inches.

Year	Engine ID/VIN	Engine Displacement Liters (cc)	Crankshaft				Connecting Rod		
			Main Brg. Journal Dia.	Main Brg. Oil Clearance	Shaft End-play	Thrust on No.	Journal Diameter	Oil Clearance	Side Clearance
1990	3	4.5 (4467)	2.635–2.636	①	0.001–0.015	3	1.927	0.0005–0.0035	0.008–0.020
1991	B	4.9 (4885)	2.635–2.636	①	0.001–0.015	3	1.927 1.928	0.0005–0.0035	0.008–0.020
1992	B	4.9 (4885)	2.635–2.636	①	0.001–0.015	3	1.927 1.928	0.0005–0.0035	0.008–0.020
1993	B	4.9 (4885)	2.635–2.636	①	0.001–0.015	3	1.927 1.928	0.0005–0.0035	0.008–0.020
	9	4.6 (4566)	2.533	0.0005–0.003	0.002–0.019	3	2.124	0.001–0.003	0.007–0.020
	Y	4.6 (4566)	2.533	0.0005–0.003	0.002–0.019	3	2.124	0.001–0.003	0.007–0.020

① No. 1: 0.0008–0.0031
No. 2, 3, 4 & 5: 0.0016–0.0045

84203126

PISTON AND RING SPECIFICATIONS

All measurements are given in inches.

Year	Engine ID/VIN	Engine Displacement Liters (cc)	Piston Clearance	Ring Gap			Ring Side Clearance		
				Top Compression	Bottom Compression	Oil Control	Top Compression	Bottom Compression	Oil Control
1990	3	4.5 (4467)	0.0010–0.0018	0.015–0.024	0.015–0.024	0.010–0.050	0.0016–0.0037	0.0016–0.0037	①
1991	B	4.9 (4885)	0.0004–0.0020	0.012–0.022	0.012–0.022	0.0004–0.020	0.0016–0.0037	0.0016–0.0037	①
1992	B	4.9 (4885)	0.0004–0.0020	0.012–0.022	0.012–0.022	0.0004–0.020	0.0016–0.0037	0.0016–0.0037	①
1993	B	4.9 (4885)	0.0004–0.0020	0.012–0.022	0.012–0.022	0.0004–0.020	0.0016–0.0037	0.0016–0.0037	①
	9	4.6 (4566)	0.0004–0.0020	0.010–0.016	0.014–0.020	0.010–0.030	0.002–0.004	0.002–0.004	①
	Y	4.6 (4566)	0.0004–0.0020	0.010–0.016	0.014–0.020	0.010–0.030	0.002–0.004	0.002–0.004	①

① None, side sealing

84203128

TORQUE SPECIFICATIONS

All readings in ft. lbs.

Year	Engine ID/VIN	Engine Displacement Liters (cc)	Cylinder Head Bolts	Main Bearing Bolts	Rod Bearing Bolts	Crankshaft Damper Bolts	Flywheel Bolts	Manifold		Spark Plugs	Lug Nut
								Intake	Exhaust		
1990	3	4.5 (4467)	①②	85	24①	65	70	③	18	11	100
1991	B	4.9 (4885)	①②	85	25	70	70	③	16	23	100
1992	B	4.9 (4885)	①②	85	25	70	70	③	16	23	100
1993	B	4.9 (4885)	①②	85	25	70	70	③	16	23	100
	9	4.6 (4566)	①④	⑤	①⑥	①⑦	⑧	⑨	20	11	100
	Y	4.6 (4566)	①④	⑤	①⑥	①⑦	⑧	⑨	20	11	100

① Lubricate bolts with clean engine oil
② Tighten in 3 steps:
  1. Tighten, in sequence, to 38 ft. lbs.
  2. Tighten, in sequence, to 68 ft. lbs.
  3. Tighten bolts 1, 3 & 4 to 90 ft. lbs.
③ Tighten in 4 steps:
  1. Tighten bolts 1, 2, 3 & 4, in sequence, to 8 ft. lbs.
  2. Tighten bolts 5–16, in sequence, to 8 ft. lbs.
  3. Retighten all bolts, in sequence, to 12 ft. lbs.
  4. Repeat step 3 until torque level is maintained.
④ Tighten in 3 steps:
  1. Tighten the ten 11 mm bolts, in sequence, to 22 ft. lbs. + 90° turn.
  2. Turn each 11 mm bolt, in sequence, an additional 90° turn.
  3. Tighten the three 6 mm bolts to 10 ft. lbs.

⑤ Tighten in 3 steps:
  1. Tighten the main bearing bolts, in sequence, to 15 ft. lbs. + 65° turn.
  2. Tighten the oil manifold bolts to 7 ft. lbs.
  3. Tighten the upper-to-lower crankcase bolts to 25 ft. lbs.
⑥ 20 ft. lbs. + 90° turn.
⑦ 105 ft. lbs. + 120° turn.
⑧ 11 ft. lbs. + 50° turn.
⑨ Tighten in 2 steps:
  1. Tighten the 4 intake mainfold bolts, in sequence, to 71 inch lbs. + 120° turn.
  2. Tighten the 12 intake mainfold cover bolts, in sequence, to 106 inch lbs.

84203129

Engine

REMOVAL & INSTALLATION

4.5L and 4.9L Engines

1. Disconnect the negative battery cable. Drain the coolant into a clean container for reuse.

2. Remove the air cleaner. Using a scribing tool, match-mark the hood to the support brackets and remove the hood.

3. If equipped with air conditioning, perform the following procedures:

  a. Remove the hose strap from the right-strut tower.

  b. Remove the accumulator from its bracket and position it aside.

  c. Remove the canister hoses from the accumulator bracket.

  d. Remove the accumulator bracket from the wheel house.

4. Remove the cooling fans, the accessory drive belt, the radiator and heater hoses.

5. Label and disconnect the electrical connectors from the following items:

  a. Oil pressure switch

  b. Coolant temperature sensor

  c. Distributor

  d. EGR solenoid

  e. Engine temperature switch

6. Label and disconnect the cables from the following items:

  a. Accelerator

  b. Cruise control linkage

  c. Transaxle Throttle Valve (TV) cable

7. If equipped with cruise control, remove the diaphragm with the bracket attached and move it aside.

8. Remove the vacuum supply hose and the exhaust cross-over pipe.

9. Disconnect the oil cooler lines from the oil filter adapter, the oil line cooler bracket from the transaxle and position them aside.

10. Remove the air cleaner mounting bracket.

11. Properly relieve the fuel system pressure. Disconnect the fuel lines from the throttle body. Remove the fuel line bracket from the transaxle and secure the fuel lines aside.

12. Remove the small vacuum line from the brake booster.

13. Label and disconnect the AIR solenoid electrical and hose connections. Remove the AIR valves with the bracket.

14. Label and disconnect the electrical connectors from the following:

  a. Idle Speed Control (ISC) motor

  b. Throttle Position Switch (TPS)

  c. Fuel injectors

  d. Manifold Air Temperature (MAT) sensor

  e. Oxygen sensor

  f. Electric Fuel Evaporation (EFE) grid

  g. Alternator bracket

15. Remove the power steering pump hose strap from the stud-headed bolt in front of the right cylinder head and the stud-headed bolt.

16. Remove the AIR pipe clip located near the No. 2 spark plug, if equipped.

17. Remove the power steering pump and belt tensioner with bracket attached; wire them aside.

18. Raise and safely support the vehicle.

19. Label and disconnect the electrical connectors from the starter and the ground wire from the cylinder block.

20. Remove the 2 flywheel covers. Remove the starter-to-engine bolts and the starter. Matchmark the flywheel-to-torque converter location. Remove the 3 flywheel-to-torque converter bolts and slide the converter back into the bell housing.

21. If equipped with air conditioning, perform the following procedures:

    a. Remove the compressor lower dust shield.

    b. Remove the right front wheel/tire assembly and outer wheelhouse plastic shield.

    c. Remove the compressor-to-bracket bolts and lower the compressor from the engine. Do not disconnect the refrigerant lines.

22. Remove the lower radiator hose.

23. From the lower right front of the Engine and cradle, remove the driveline vibration damper with the brackets, if equipped, and the engine-to-transaxle bracket bolts. Pull the alternator wire with the plastic cover down and aside.

24. Remove the exhaust pipe-to-manifold bolts with the springs attached and the AIR pipe-to-converter bracket from the exhaust manifold stud.

➡**Be careful not to lose the springs when detaching the exhaust pipe.**

25. Remove the lower right side bell housing-to-engine bolt. Lower the vehicle.

26. Using a vertical Engine hoist, attach it to the Engine and support it.

27. Remove the upper bell housing-to-engine bolts and left front Engine mount bracket-to-engine bolts. Remove the Engine from the vehicle.

To install:

28. Raise the transaxle with a separate jack to engage the engine.

29. Install the Engine into the vehicle, using a suitable Engine hoist. Engage the dowels on the block with the transaxle case.

30. Install the transaxle bell housing-to-engine mounting bolts.

31. Lower and remove the floor jack assembly from the transaxle.

32. Lower the engine, making sure it is seated on the mount properly.

33. Remove the Engine hoist. Raise and safely support the vehicle.

34. Lower the right hand transaxle bell housing-to-engine bolt. Support the engine.

35. Install the left front Engine mount bracket-to-engine bolts and the flexplate-to-converter bolts.

36. Replace the flexplate covers.

37. Install the starter motor and connect the electrical wires to the starter.

38. Connect the AIR pipe-to-converter bracket to the exhaust manifold stud.

39. Install the exhaust pipe to manifold bolts and springs.

40. Connect the alternator and install the plastic cover. Install the right front engine-to-transaxle bracket and tighten the bolts to 30 ft. lbs. (41 Nm).

41. Install the lower radiator hose and replace the air conditioning compressor mounting bolts.

42. Install the air conditioning compressor lower dust shield and the outer wheel house plastic shield.

43. Install the right front tire and wheel assembly. Lower the vehicle.

44. Install the power steering pump and the belt tensioner. Replace the stud headed bolt.

45. Install the power steering hose strap to the stud headed bolt in front of the cylinder head.

46. Connect the electrical connectors to the following:

    a. Idle Speed Control (ISC) motor

    b. Throttle Position Switch (TPS)

    c. Fuel injectors

    d. Manifold Air Temperature (MAT) sensor

    e. Oxygen sensor

    f. Electric Fuel Evaporator (EFE) grid

    g. Alternator bracket

47. Replace the air valve and bracket. Connect the air solenoid electrical and hose connections.

48. Connect the vacuum line to the brake booster.

49. Connect the fuel lines at the throttle body and replace the fuel line bracket at the transaxle.

50. Replace the air cleaner mounting bracket and connect the oil cooler lines to the oil filter adapter.

51. Connect the oil cooler line bracket at the transaxle. Replace the exhaust crossover pipe.

52. Replace the cruise control diaphragm and connect the vacuum line.

53. Connect the accelerator, cruise control and the transaxle throttle valve cables to the throttle lever.

54. Connect the wire connectors to the following:

    a. Oil pressure switch

    b. Coolant temperature sensor

    c. Distributor

    d. EGR solenoid

    e. Engine temperature switch

55. Replace the accessory drive belt, heater hoses and upper radiator hose.

56. Install the cooling fans and connect the air conditioning accumulator bracket.

57. Install the air conditioning accumulator and connect the wires and hoses.

58. Install the hood assembly and replace the air cleaner.

59. Refill the Engine coolant. Connect the negative battery cable.

60. Start the engine, allow it to reach normal operating temperatures and check for leaks.

4.6L Northstar Engine

1. Disconnect the negative battery cable. Remove the air cleaner inlet duct.

2. Matchmark the hood hinge-to-hood and remove the hood.

3. Drain the coolant from the radiator.

4. Remove the left and right torque struts. Install the left front strut bolt back into the bracket.

5. Disconnect the radiator hoses at the water crossover. Remove both cooling fans from the engine.

6. Remove the serpentine accessory drive belt.

7. Disconnect the cruise control servo connections and the ISC motor electrical connector.

8. Disconnect the throttle cable from the throttle body cam. Disconnect the shift cable from the park/neutral switch. Remove the cable bracket at the transaxle.

9. Remove the park/neutral switch and disconnect the power brake vacuum hose.

10. At the rear of the right head, disconnect the cylinder head temperature switch.

11. Remove the bellhousing bolts.

12. Remove the ignition coils and remove the spark plug wires.

13. Raise and safely support the vehicle.

14. Remove the oil pan-to-transmission brace. Remove the torque converter splash shield and the 4 converter-to-flywheel bolts.

15. Disconnect the oil cooler lines from the oil filter adapter.

16. Remove the A/C compressor mounting bolts and disconnect the electrical connectors. Move compressor out of way.

17. Disconnect the electrical connectors from the left side of the engine and move the harness from behind the exhaust manifold.

18. Remove the 2 nuts that secure the motor mount to the engine cradle front crossmember.

19. Remove the exhaust Y-pipe and remove the right front wheel.

20. Remove the crankcase to transmission bracket at the transmission tail shaft. Disconnect the knock sensor.

21. Remove the bolt from the transmission to the cylinder head brace at the cylinder head.

22. Lower the vehicle. Disconnect the fuel inlet and fuel return lines using special tool J37088 or equivalent.

23. Disconnect the injector harness connector and the hoses from the coolant reservoir. Remove the reservoir.

24. Disconnect the cam position sensor. Disconnect the heater hoses from the water pipes at the front of the right cylinder head.

25. Disconnect the battery cable from the junction block and remove the retainer at the cylinder head.

26. Disconnect the starter cable from the junction block.

27. Disconnect the power steering pump pressure and return lines at the pump. Return power steering line retainer from the right front of the crankcase.

28. Disconnect the rear oxygen sensor.

29. Remove the 3 screws securing the wiring harness retainer to right cam cover and position harness out of the way.

30. Connect an engine lifting device to the engine using the support hooks at left and right rear of engine. The torque strut bracket at the left front of the engine should be used as a third lifting hook.

31. Carefully remove the engine from the vehicle.

To install:

32. Lower the engine into the vehicle. Remove the lifting device.

33. Install the 4 bell housing bolts and tighten to 75 ft. lbs. (100 Nm).

34. Raise and safely support the vehicle.

35. Install 2 nuts to the motor mount at the front cradle crossmember. Do not fully tighten.

36. Install bolt to the cylinder head for transmission brace. Do not fully tighten.

37. Install the transmission to crankcase bracket with the 4 bolts. Do not fully tighten the bolts.

38. Tighten the motor mount to cradle crossmember bolts to 30 ft. lbs. (40 Nm). Tighten the transmission brace bolt and transmission to crankcase bolts to 45 ft. lbs. (60 Nm).

39. Install the right front wheel and connect the knock sensor.

40. Install the exhaust Y-pipe.

41. Install the 4 torque converter to flywheel bolts and tighten to 45 ft. lbs. (60 Nm).

42. Install the converter splash shield and install the transmission to oil pan brace. Tighten the bolt to 35 ft. lbs. (50 Nm).

43. Position the A/C compressor in place and install the mounting bolts.

44. Route the electrical harness along the left side of the engine and connect the connectors.

45. Connect the oil cooler lines to the oil filter adapter.

46. Lower the vehicle.

47. Secure the wiring harness to the right cam cover with the 3 screws.

48. Connect the rear oxygen sensor and connect the cam position sensor.

49. Connect the power steering hoses to the pump and secure the return line to the crankcase.

50. Connect the heater hoses to the water pipes.

51. Connect the starter and battery cables at the junction box. Secure battery cable with retainer.

52. Connect and install the coolant reservoir.

53. Install coils and secure with 4 screws.

54. Install the serpentine drive belt and connect the injector harness to the FIS harness.

55. Connect the fuel line connectors. Connect the cylinder head temperature switch to the rear of the right head.

56. Connect the power brake vacuum line.

57. Install the park/neutral switch and shift cable. Adjust switch if necessary.

58. Install the cruise servo and connect the ISC motor.

59. Connect the throttle cable and install both cooling fans.

60. Connect the radiator hoses to the water crossover.

61. Install the torque struts and adjust the preload to zero.

62. Connect the negative battery cable.

63. Refill the engine with coolant. Install the hood and install the air cleaner.

64. Start engine and check for oil, coolant and transaxle leaks.

Powertrain Assembly

REMOVAL & INSTALLATION

4.6L Northstar Engine

➡For some engine service, it may be most economical to remove the entire powertrain and cradle out the bottom of the body and to utilize the cradle as an engine stand.

1. Disconnect the negative battery cable.
2. Remove the air cleaner inlet duct.

3. Remove the left and right torque struts. Install the left front strut bolt back into the bracket.

4. Disconnect the radiator hoses at the water crossover.

5. Remove both cooling fans from the engine.

6. Discharge the A/C system as outlined in Section 1.

7. Disconnect the cruise control servo connections.

8. Disconnect the throttle cable from the throttle body cam. Disconnect the shift cable from the park/neutral switch. Remove the cable bracket at the transaxle.

9. Remove the park/neutral switch and disconnect the power brake vacuum hose.

10. Disconnect the fuel inlet and fuel return lines using special tool J37088 or equivalent.

11. Remove the fuel line retainer at the transaxle case.

12. Disconnect the hoses from the coolant reservoir. Remove the reservoir.

13. Disconnect the heater hoses from the front of the right cylinder head.

14. Disconnect the battery cable from the junction block and remove the retainer at the cylinder head.

15. Disconnect the starter cable from the junction block.

16. Disconnect the power steering pump pressure and return lines at the pump. Return power steering line retainer from the right front of the crankcase.

17. Disconnect the engine harness connectors at the PCM.

18. From under the hood, remove the wiring harness retainer screws at the cowl and pull the engine harness through.

19. Disconnect the high freon temperature switch.

20. Open the relay cover and remove the fan control relays from the relay center.

21. To remove the engine harness connector on the left wheelhouse, remove 1 screw holding the connector halves together and separate. The engine portion of the harness will be removed with the engine.

22. Remove the serpentine accessory drive belt.

23. Raise and safely support the vehicle.

24. Remove both front wheels.

25. Remove both front drive axles as described in Section 7.

26. Disconnect the oil cooler lines at the oil filter adapter.

27. Remove the exhaust Y-pipe.

28. Disconnect the coupling between the steering rack and the column.

29. Disconnect the speed sensitive steering solenoid.

30. Disconnect the power steering switch.

31. Remove the A/C manifold from the rear of the A/C compressor.

32. Separate the traction control controller from the engine cradle and wire controller into position to stay with the body.

33. Move the powertrain dolly such as J 36295 into position and lower the vehicle onto the table.

34. Remove the six engine cradle mounting bolts and remove the powertrain assembly by lifting the vehicle or lowering the table.

To install:

35. With the powertrain on the dolly such as J 36295, move into approximate position under the vehicle which is raised on a hoist.

36. Lower the vehicle onto the powertrain.

37. Align the engine cradle to the body and install the six engine cradle mounting bolts. torque the bolts to 75 ft. lbs. (100 Nm).

38. Raise the vehicle and remove the dolly.

39. Install both front drive axles as described in Section 7.

40. Connect the oil cooler lines at the oil filter adapter.

41. Install the exhaust Y-pipe.

42. Connect the coupling between the steering rack and the column.

43. Connect the speed sensitive steering solenoid.

44. Connect the power steering switch.

45. Install the A/C manifold to the rear of the A/C compressor.

46. Position the traction control controller to the engine cradle.

47. Lower the vehicle.

48. Pull the engine wiring harness through the cowl and install the 2 retaining screws.

49. Connect the engine harness connectors at the PCM.

50. Connect the high freon temperature switch.

51. Open the relay cover and install the fan control relays to the relay center.

52. Position the engine harness connector on the left wheelhouse, install the 1 screw holding the connector halves together.

53. Connect the power steering pump pressure and return lines at the pump. Install the power steering line retainer to the right front of the crankcase.

54. Connect the battery and starter cables to the junction block and install the retainer at the cylinder head.

55. Connect the heater hoses to the front of the right cylinder head.

56. Connect the hoses and install the coolant reservoir.

57. Connect the fuel inlet and fuel return lines.

58. Connect the power brake vacuum hose.

59. Install the park/neutral switch.

60. Connect the throttle cable to the throttle body cam.

61. Connect the cruise control servo.

62. Install both cooling fans.

63. Connect the radiator hoses at the water crossover.

64. Add engine coolant.

65. Install the right and left torque struts and torque the retaining bolts as follows:

➡**It is important during installation that the engine torque struts are not preloaded in their installed position. Adjustment is provided at the point the strut fastens to the core support bracket. Make sure this bolt is loose during assembly. Tighten to 45 ft. lbs. (60 Nm) as the final step of assembly.**

a. Torque strut bracket to cylinder head (M10) bolt: 35 ft. lbs. (50 Nm).

b. Torque strut bracket to cylinder head (M10) stud: 35 ft. lbs. (50 Nm).

c. Torque strut bracket to water manifold (M8) bolts: 20 ft. lbs. (25 Nm).

d. Torque strut bracket to cylinder head (M10) bolt: 35 ft. lbs. (50 Nm).

e. Torque strut to core support bracket bolt 45 ft. lbs: (60 Nm) (see note above).

66. Connect the negative battery cable.

67. Charge the A/C system.

68. Install the air cleaner.

Rocker Arms and Valve Covers

REMOVAL & INSTALLATION

4.5L and 4.9L Engines
▶ See Figures 12 and 13

RIGHT

1. Disconnect the negative battery cable. Remove the air cleaner and the AIR management valve with bracket, move the assembly aside.
2. From the throttle body, remove the Manifold Absolute Pressure (MAP) hose.
3. Remove the right side spark plug wires and conduit.
4. Remove the fuel vapor canister pipe bracket from the valve cover stud.
5. Drain the cooling system to a level below the thermostat housing. Remove the heater hose from the thermostat housing and move it aside.
6. Remove the brake booster vacuum hose from the intake manifold.
7. Remove the rocker arm cover-to-cylinder screws, the cover and the gasket/seals. Discard them.
8. Remove the rocker arm pivot-to-rocker arm support bolts, the pivots and the rocker arms.
9. If necessary, remove the rocker arm support-to-cylinder head nuts/bolts and the support.
10. Clean the gasket mounting surfaces. Inspect the parts for wear and/or damage and replace the parts, if necessary.

To install:

11. Lubricate the parts with clean Engine oil, use a new gasket and coat both sides with RTV sealant, install RTV sealant between the intake manifold-to-cylinder head mating surfaces.
12. Install the rocker arms and pivots to the rocker arm support. Tighten the pivot bolts to 22 ft. lbs. (30 Nm).
13. Install the rocker arm support and place each pushrod into the rocker arm seat.
14. Install the rocker arm support retaining nuts, tighten to 37 ft. lbs. (50 Nm).
15. Install the rocker arm support retaining bolts, tighten to 7 ft. lbs. (9 Nm).
16. Install the rocker arm cover seals and place the molded seal into the groove in the rocker arm cover.
17. Install the rocker arm cover and tighten the mounting screws to 8 ft. lbs. (11 Nm).
18. Connect the brake booster vacuum hose and the EECS pipe bracket.
19. Install the spark plug wires and conduit. Connect the MAP hose to the throttle body.
20. Install the air management and bracket assembly.
21. Replace the heater hose and air cleaner assembly.
22. Connect the negative battery cable. Start the Engine and check for leaks.

LEFT

1. Disconnect the negative battery cable. Remove the air cleaner, the PCV valve, the throttle return spring and the serpentine drive belt.
2. Loosen the lower power steering pump bracket nuts.
3. Remove the power steering pump, the belt tensioner, the bracket-to-engine bolts and the bracket. Move the power steer-

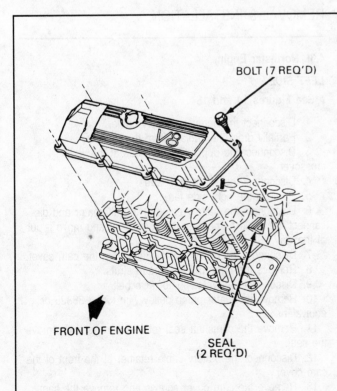

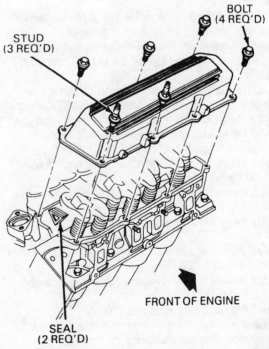

Fig. 12 Left an right valve covers — 4.5L and 4.9L engines

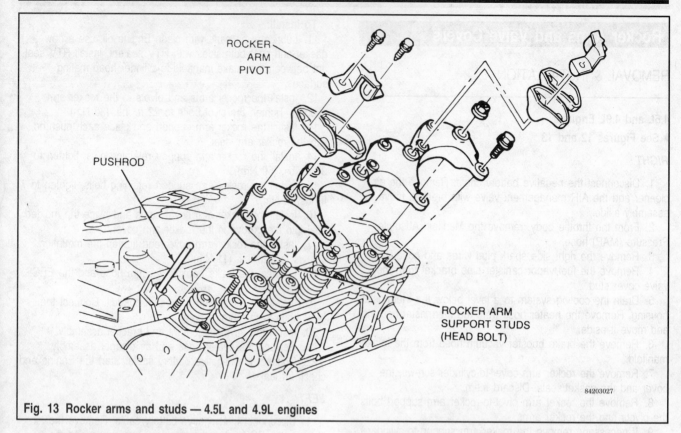

Fig. 13 Rocker arms and studs — 4.5L and 4.9L engines

ing pump assembly toward the front of the vehicle; do not disconnect the pressure hoses.

4. Remove the left side spark plug wires and conduit.

5. Remove the rocker arm cover-to-cylinder screws, the cover and the gasket/seals. Discard them.

6. Remove the rocker arm pivot-to-rocker arm support bolts, the pivots and the rocker arms.

7. If necessary, remove the rocker arm support-to-cylinder head nuts/bolts and the support.

8. Clean the gasket mounting surfaces. Inspect the parts for wear and/or damage and replace the parts, if necessary.

To install:

9. Lubricate the parts with clean Engine oil, use a new gasket, coat both sides with RTV sealant, install RTV sealant between the intake manifold-to-cylinder head mating surfaces.

10. Install the rocker arms and pivots to the rocker arm support. Tighten the pivot bolts to 22 ft. lbs. (30 Nm).

11. Install the rocker arm support and place each pushrod into the rocker arm seat.

12. Install the rocker arm support retaining nuts, tighten to 37 ft. lbs. (50 Nm).

13. Install the rocker arm support retaining bolts, tighten to 7 ft. lbs. (9 Nm).

14. Install the rocker arm cover seals and place the molded seal into the groove in the rocker arm cover.

15. Install the rocker arm cover and tighten the mounting screws to 8 ft. lbs. (11 Nm).

16. Install the spark plug wires and conduit.

17. Install the power steering pump, belt tensioner and bracket assembly. Replace the accessory drive belt.

18. Install the throttle return spring and the PCV valve.

19. Install the air cleaner and connect the negative battery cable.

20. Start the Engine and check for leaks.

Camshaft Cover

REMOVAL & INSTALLATION

4.6L Northstar Engine

LEFT SIDE

▶ **See Figures 14 and 15**

1. Disconnect the negative battery cable.

2. Partially drain the coolant from the radiator.

3. Disconnect the upper radiator hose at the water crossover.

4. Disconnect the spark plug wires.

5. Remove the right side fan.

6. Disconnect the battery cable at the alternator and disconnect the cable harness at the cam cover and move it out of the way.

7. Disconnect the PCV fresh air tube from the cam cover.

8. Remove the right and left torque struts.

9. Disconnect the water pump drive belt.

10. Remove the water pump pulley with tool J 38825 or equivalent.

11. Remove the camshaft seal retainer screws and remove the seal.

12. Disconnect the battery cable retainer at the front of the cam cover.

13. Remove the cam cover screws and remove the cam cover by moving the cam drive end of the cover up and then pivot the entire cover around the water pump drive shaft. Con-

tinue moving the cover upward and pivoting so that the edge of the cover closely follows the left edge of the intake manifold cover.

To install:

14. Install spark plug and cam cover seals.

15. Insert the intake cam through the hole in the cam cover and using your fingers guide the cam cover up over the edge of the cylinder head.

✳✳WARNING

Use care to prevent the exposed section of the cam cover seal from being damaged by the edge of the cylinder head casting.

16. Work the cover into position by allowing the top edge of the cover to follow the left side edge of the intake manifold.

17. Install the cam cover screws and tighten to 7 ft. lbs. (10 Nm).

18. Connect the battery cable retainer to the front of the cam cover.

19. Connect the battery cable at the alternator.

20. Lubricate the seal lips and install the camshaft seal to the end of the intake cam. Seal the screw threads with sealer.

21. Install the water pump pulley with tool J 38825 or equivalent.

22. Install the water pump drive belt.

23. Install the right and left torque struts and torque the retaining bolts as follows:

➡It is important during installation that the engine torque struts are not preloaded in their installed position. Adjustment is provided at the point the strut fastens to the core support bracket. Make sure this bolt is loose during assembly. Tighten to 45 ft. lbs. (60 Nm) as the final step of assembly.

    a. Torque strut bracket to cylinder head (M10) bolt: 35 ft. lbs. (50 Nm).

    b. Torque strut bracket to cylinder head (M10) stud: 35 ft. lbs. (50 Nm).

    c. Torque strut bracket to water manifold (M8) bolts: 20 ft. lbs. (25 Nm).

    d. Torque strut bracket to cylinder head (M10) bolt: 35 ft. lbs. (50 Nm).

    e. Torque strut to core support bracket bolt 45 ft. lbs: (60 Nm) (see note above).

24. Connect the PCV fresh air tube to the cam cover.

25. Install the right side fan.

26. Connect the spark plug wires.

27. Connect the upper radiator hose to the water crossover.

28. Fill the radiator with coolant.

29. Connect the negative battery cable.

RIGHT SIDE

▶ **See Figure 14**

1. Disconnect the negative battery cable.

2. Raise and support the vehicle safely and disconnect the exhaust 'Y' pipe at the converter. Position the converter out of the way.

3. Lower the vehicle.

4. Remove the tower-to-tower brace.

5. Disconnect the 4 DIS wiring connectors and mounting bolts.

6. Remove the DIS and the spark plug wires on the right bank. Tag wires for installation.

7. Disconnect the PCV valve.

8. Remove the purge canister solenoid from the rear of the cover.

9. Remove the 3 screws retaining wiring harness to the cover.

10. Remove the cam cover screws.

11. Safely support the front of the engine cradle and remove the 2 mounting screws at the front of the cradle.

12. Remove the right and left torque struts.

13. Lower the engine cradle (or raise the vehicle) to provide clearance at the rear of the engine compartment.

14. Remove the cam cover and discard the seal if damaged.

To install:

15. Install spark plug and cam cover seals.

16. Install the cam cover and tighten the screws to 7 ft. lbs. (10 Nm).

17. Raise the engine cradle into position and install and tight the 2 mounting bolts to 75 ft. lbs. (100 Nm).

18. Install the right and left torque struts and torque the retaining bolts as follows:

➡It is important during installation that the engine torque struts are not preloaded in their installed position. Adjustment is provided at the point the strut fastens to the core support bracket. Make sure this bolt is loose during assembly. Tighten to 45 ft. lbs. (60 Nm) as the final step of assembly.

    a. Torque strut bracket to cylinder head (M10) bolt: 35 ft. lbs. (50 Nm).

    b. Torque strut bracket to cylinder head (M10) stud: 35 ft. lbs. (50 Nm).

    c. Torque strut bracket to water manifold (M8) bolts: 20 ft. lbs. (25 Nm).

    d. Torque strut bracket to cylinder head (M10) bolt: 35 ft. lbs. (50 Nm).

    e. Torque strut to core support bracket bolt 45 ft. lbs: (60 Nm) (see note above).

19. Install the 3 screws retaining wiring harness to the cover.

20. Install the purge canister solenoid to the rear of the cover.

21. Connect the PCV valve.

22. Install the DIS (4 bolts) and the spark plug wires on the right bank.

23. Connect the 4 DIS wiring connectors.

24. Install the tower-to-tower brace.

25. Raise and support the vehicle safely and connect the exhaust 'Y' pipe to the converter. Tighten the bolts to 20 ft. lbs. (25 nm).

26. Connect the negative battery cable.

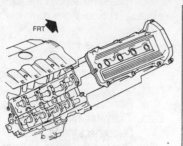 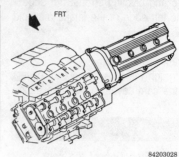

84203028

Fig. 14 Camshaft covers — 4.6L Northstar engine

Thermostat

REMOVAL & INSTALLATION

4.5L and 4.9L Engines
▶ See Figure 16

1. Drain coolant to a level below the thermostat housing.
2. It may be necessary to remove the upper air filter assembly on some models.
3. Remove 2 bolts securing upper thermostat housing to lower housing.
4. Remove upper thermostat housing.
5. Remove thermostat and O-ring from lower housing.
To install:
6. Install thermostat and a new O-ring to lower housing.
7. Install upper thermostat housing to lower housing. Tighten thermostat housing bolts to 20 ft. lbs. (27 Nm).
8. Refill cooling system using a 50/50 mixture of water and ethylene glycol antifreeze.
9. Start engine and check for coolant leaks. Allow engine to come to normal operating temperature. Recheck for coolant leaks.

4.6L Northstar Engine
▶ See Figure 17

1. Drain coolant to a level below the thermostat housing.
2. On 1993 vehicles, remove the front end beauty panel and the air cleaner.
3. Remove 2 bolts securing thermostat housing to intake manifold.
4. Remove thermostat housing.
5. Remove thermostat and O-ring from housing.
To install:
6. Install thermostat and new O-ring to housing.
7. Install thermostat housing to intake manifold. Tighten thermostat housing bolts to 18 ft. lbs. (25 Nm).
8. Refill cooling system using a 50/50 mixture of water and ethylene glycol antifreeze.
9. Install air cleaner and beauty panel, if removed.
10. Start engine and check for coolant leaks. Allow engine to come to normal operating temperature. Recheck for coolant leaks.

Intake Manifold

REMOVAL & INSTALLATION

4.5L and 4.9L Engines
▶ See Figures 18 and 19

1. Disconnect the negative battery cable. Relieve fuel system pressure. Drain the cooling system to a level below the intake manifold. Remove the coolant reservoir. Disconnect the upper radiator hose from the thermostat housing.
2. Remove the air cleaner and the serpentine drive belt. Label and disconnect the spark plug wires from the spark plugs.
3. Remove the cross brace.
4. Remove power steering pump and tensioner bracket assembly and reposition toward the front of engine.
5. Remove alternator and bracket.
6. Remove cruise control servo with bracket and throttle valve cables and position aside.
7. Disconnect wire connections and reposition:
    a. Distributor
    b. Oil pressure switch
    c. Coolant temperature sensor
    d. EGR solenoid
    e. ISC motor
    f. Throttle position switch
    g. If equipped, electric EFE grid
    h. Injectors
    i. MAT sensor
8. If equipped, disconnect the MAP hoses. Remove upper radiator hose and heater hose. Remove air conditioning hose bracket.
9. Disconnect spark plug wire protectors and reposition cap.
10. Mark the distributor rotor position and remove distributor.

➡**Do not crank or in any other way rotate crankshaft with the distributor removed.**

11. Disconnect fuel and vacuum lines from the throttle body. Disconnect the vacuum supply solenoid and lines.
12. Remove valve covers. Remove rocker arms and pushrods.

➡**Pushrods should be marked or retained in sequence so they may be reinstalled in their original positions.**

REMOVAL

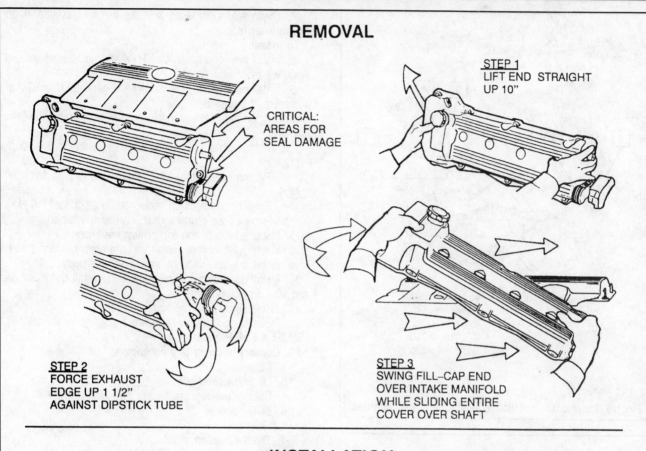

**CRITICAL:
AREAS FOR
SEAL DAMAGE**

STEP 1
LIFT END STRAIGHT
UP 10"

STEP 2
FORCE EXHAUST
EDGE UP 1 1/2"
AGAINST DIPSTICK TUBE

STEP 3
SWING FILL–CAP END
OVER INTAKE MANIFOLD
WHILE SLIDING ENTIRE
COVER OVER SHAFT

INSTALLATION

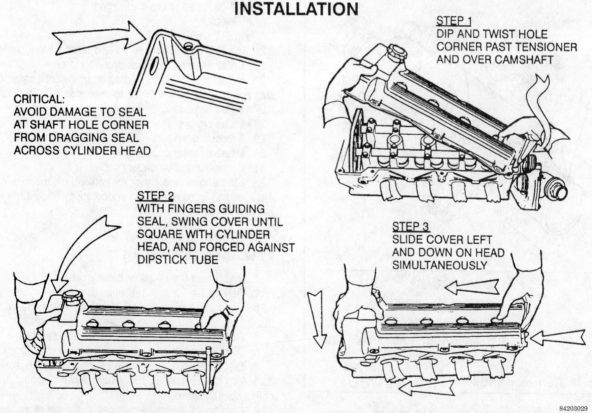

STEP 1
DIP AND TWIST HOLE
CORNER PAST TENSIONER
AND OVER CAMSHAFT

**CRITICAL:
AVOID DAMAGE TO SEAL
AT SHAFT HOLE CORNER
FROM DRAGGING SEAL
ACROSS CYLINDER HEAD**

STEP 2
WITH FINGERS GUIDING
SEAL, SWING COVER UNTIL
SQUARE WITH CYLINDER
HEAD, AND FORCED AGAINST
DIPSTICK TUBE

STEP 3
SLIDE COVER LEFT
AND DOWN ON HEAD
SIMULTANEOUSLY

84203029

Fig. 15 Removing the left side camshaft cover — 4.6L Northstar engine

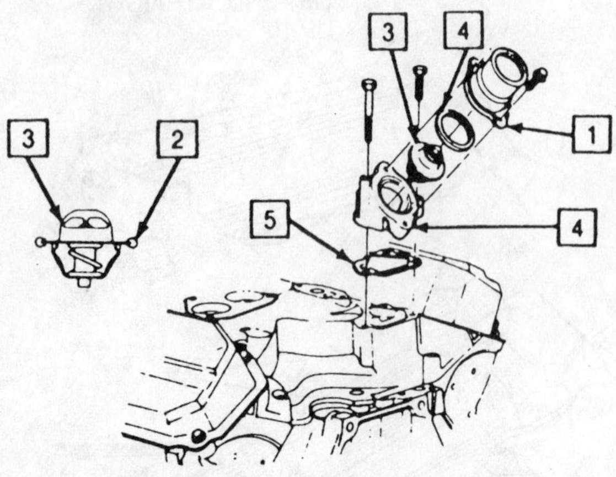

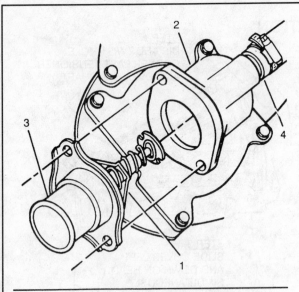

1. Upper housing
2. Gasket
3. Thermostat housing
4. Lower housing
5. Gasket

84203030

Fig. 16 Thermostat installation — 4.5L and 4.9L engines

1 THERMOSTAT
2 THERMOSTAT HOUSING
3 COOLANT PUMP INLET
4 THERMOSTAT BY–PASS HOSE

84203031

Fig. 17 Thermostat installation — 4.6L engines

13. Remove the right front and rear lift brackets. Remove intake manifold bolts and remove intake manifold, gaskets and seals. Discard gaskets and seals.

14. Clean sealing surfaces of intake manifold, cylinder head and cylinder block.

To install:

15. Install new end seals. Use RTV at 4 corners where end seals will meet side gaskets.

16. Install new intake to cylinder head gaskets. Use RTV at 4 corners of end seals.

17. Tighten the intake manifold bolts by performing the following:

   a. Tighten bolts 1, 2, 3 and 4, in sequence, to 8 ft. lbs. (12 Nm).

   b. Tighten bolts 5 thru 16, in sequence, to 8 ft. lbs. (12 Nm).

   c. Retighten all bolts, in sequence, to 12 ft. lbs. (16 Nm).

   d. Repeat Step c until torque level is maintained.

18. Install pushrods and rocker arm assembly.

19. Install valve covers. Install vacuum supply solenoid and lines. Install fuel and vacuum lines to throttle body.

20. Install distributor in original position. Install distributor cap and wire protectors.

21. Install air conditioning hose bracket.

22. Install upper radiator hose and heater hose. If equipped, connect the MAP hoses.

23. Connect following wire connectors:

   a. Distributor
   b. Oil pressure switch
   c. Coolant temperature sensor
   d. EGR solenoid
   e. ISC motor
   f. Throttle position switch
   g. If equipped, electric EFE grid
   h. Injectors
   i. MAT sensor

24. Install cruise control servo and throttle valve cables.

25. Install alternator bracket and alternator.

26. Install power steering pump and tensioner assembly. Install power steering line brace to right side cylinder head.

27. Install serpentine drive belt. Install coolant reservoir.

28. Install cross brace.

29. Fill cooling system.

30. Install air cleaner assembly.

31. Connect negative battery cable.

32. Start engine and check for coolant, oil and fuel leaks. Allow engine to come to normal operating temperature and recheck for leaks.

4.6L Northstar Engine

▶ See Figures 20, 21, 22 and 23

1. Disconnect the negative battery cable.

2. Relieve fuel system pressure as outlined in Section 5.

3. Drain the cooling system to a level below the intake manifold.

4. Remove the intake duct from the throttle body.

5. Disconnect the coolant hoses at the throttle body.

6. Disconnect the 2 electrical connectors at the intake manifold. Also the TP sensor, ISC motor, EVAP solenoid and cruise control servo.

7. Disconnect the vacuum hoses at the brake vacuum booster, fuel pipe bundle and to body.

8. Disconnect the PCV valve at the intake manifold.

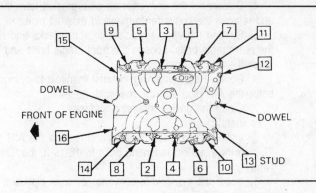

1. TIGHTEN BOLTS 1, 2, 3, & 4 IN SEQUENCE TO 12.0 N·m (8 FT-LBS).

2. TIGHTEN BOLTS 5 THRU 16 IN SEQUENCE TO 12.0 N·m (8 FT-LBS).

3. RETIGHTEN ALL BOLTS IN SEQUENCE TO 16.0 N·m (12 FT-LBS).

4. REPEAT STEP 3 UNTIL TORQUE LEVEL IS MAINTAINED.

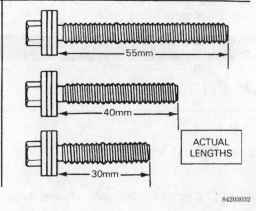

BOLT POSITION	BOLT LENGTH (MM)	BOLT POSITION	BOLT LENGTH (MM)
1	55	9	40
2	55	10	40
3	55	11	40
4	55	12	55
5	30	13	40 W/Studhead
6	30	14	40
7	30	15	55
8	30	16	40

84203032

Fig. 18 Intake manifold and gaskets — 4.5L and 4.9L engines

RTV SEALANT USED AT LOCATIONS MARKED "X"

FRONT OF ENGINE

FWD

RH GASKET

REAR SEAL

LH GASKET

"X"

"X"

"X"

"X"

FRONT SEAL

84203033

Fig. 19 Intake manifold bolt tightening sequence — 4.5L and 4.9L engines

9. Disconnect the accelerator cable at the throttle body and position out of the way.

10. Disconnect the fuel pipe quick connects at the fuel pipe bundle in the engine compartment.

11. Remove the EVAP solenoid bracket at the rear cam cover.

12. Reposition the transaxle range control cable away from the cruise control servo.

13. Remove the 4 intake manifold bolts and lift the intake manifold with the throttle body out of the engine compartment.

14. Remove the intake manifold seals and spacers at the cylinder heads.

15. Remove the fuel pipe retainer at the ISC bracket.

16. Remove the 4 throttle body bolts and remove the throttle body from the intake manifold.

To install:

17. It is important to use a NEW throttle body seal on the throttle body coated with petroleum jelly.

❊❊WARNING

Do not reuse the old throttle body seal because it may not seat properly. Do not use any type of silicone lubricant on the seal or damage could result.

18. Install the throttle body with the 4 bolts to the intake manifold and tighten to 106 inch lbs. (12 Nm).

19. Install the fuel pipe retainer at the ISC bracket.

20. Install the intake manifold seals and spacers at the cylinder heads.

21. Install the intake manifold and throttle body with the 4 intake manifold bolts and tighten to the torque and sequence in the illustration.

22. Connect the coolant hoses at the throttle body and coolant reservoir and add coolant as necessary.

23. Position the transaxle range control cable away at the cruise control servo bracket.

24. Install the EVAP solenoid bracket at the rear cam cover.

25. Connect the fuel pipe quick connects at the fuel pipe bundle in the engine compartment.

26. Connect the accelerator cable at the throttle body.

27. Connect the vacuum hoses at the brake vacuum booster, fuel pipe bundle and to body.

28. Connect the PCV valve at the intake manifold.

29. Connect the 2 electrical connectors at the intake manifold. Also the TP sensor, ISC motor, EVAP solenoid and cruise control servo.

30. Install the intake duct to the throttle body.

31. Connect the negative battery cable.

Exhaust Manifold

REMOVAL & INSTALLATION

4.5L and 4.9L Engines

▶ **See Figures 24, 25, 26 and 27**

RIGHT

1. Disconnect the negative battery cable. Remove the air cleaner.

2. Remove the exhaust crossover pipe. Disconnect the oxygen and coolant temperature sensors.

3. Remove the catalytic converter-to-AIR pipe clip bolt. Remove the upper manifold-to-cylinder head bolts. Raise and safely support the vehicle.

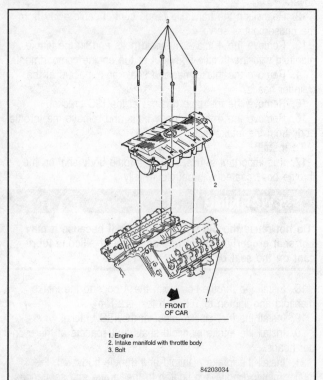

1. Engine
2. Intake manifold with throttle body
3. Bolt

FRONT OF CAR

84203034

Fig. 20 Intake manifold installation — 4.6L Northstar engine

4. Disconnect the converter air pipe bracket from the stud and remove the converter-to-manifold exhaust pipe.

5. Support the engine cradle with screw jacks and remove the rear cradle bolts. Loosen the front cradle bolts and slightly lower the Engine cradle.

6. Remove the remaining exhaust manifold-to-cylinder head bolts, the AIR pipe and the manifold.

7. Clean the gasket mounting surfaces.

To install:

8. Install the exhaust manifold and replace the AIR pipe. Tighten the manifold mounting bolts to 16-18 ft. lbs. (21-24 Nm).

9. Install the manifold-to-converter exhaust pipe and replace the converter air pipe bracket to the stud.

10. Raise the Engine cradle and install the rear cradle bolts. Tighten to 75 ft. lbs (102 Nm).

11. Lower the vehicle. Replace the upper manifold-to-cylinder head bolts.

12. Replace the converter air pipe to AIR pipe clip bolt.

13. Connect the coolant temperature and oxygen sensor connectors. Replace the exhaust crossover pipe.

14. Replace the air cleaner and connect the negative battery cable.

15. Start the Engine and check for leaks.

LEFT

1. Disconnect the negative battery cable. Remove the cooling fan(s) and the exhaust crossover pipe.

2. Remove the serpentine drive belt and the AIR pump pivot bolt.

3. Remove the belt tensioner and the power steering pump brace.

4. Remove the exhaust manifold-to-cylinder head bolts, the AIR pipe and the manifold.

To install:

5. Clean the gasket mounting surfaces.

6. Install the manifold, AIR pipe and exhaust manifold-to-cylinder head bolts. Tighten to 16-18 ft. lbs. (22-24 Nm).

7. Install the belt tensioner and the power steering pump brace.

8. Install the AIR pump pivot bolt and the serpentine drive belt.

9. Install both cooling fans and the exhaust crossover pipe.

10. Connect the negative battery cable.

4.6L Engine

▶ **See Figure 28**

LEFT SIDE

1. Disconnect the negative battery cable.

2. Remove the radiator cover panel. Remove the air cleaner assembly.

3. Disconnect the left and right engine torque struts and position out of the way.

4. Remove the engine cooling fans.

5. Install engine support fixture J 28467-A.

6. Raise and safely support the vehicle.

7. Remove the 2 nuts securing the motor mount to the engine cradle.

8. Remove the 2 bolts securing the motor mount bracket to the crankcase.

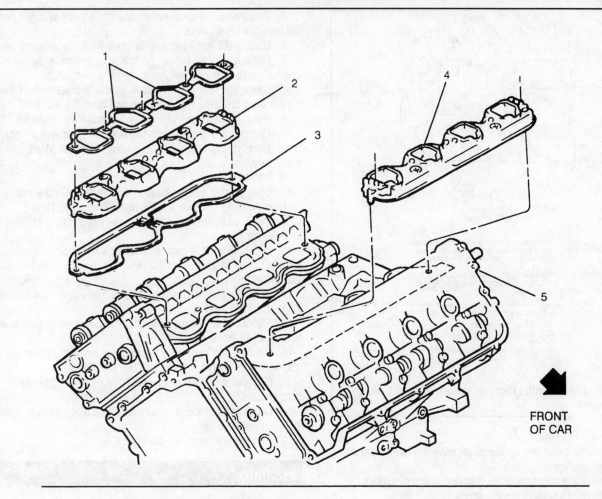

1	UPPER INTAKE MANIFOLD SEAL	4	SPACER WITH SEALS ATTACHED
2	SPACER	5	ENGINE
3	LOWER INTAKE MANIFOLD SEAL		

84203035

Fig. 21 Intake manifold seals — 4.6L Northstar engine

9. Remove the 2 bolts securing the motor mount bracket to the cylinder head.

10. Remove the 2 nuts securing the motor mount to the mount bracket.

11. Disconnect the Y-pipe from the front of the catalytic converter and position the converter out of the way.

12. Lower the vehicle.

13. Raise the engine by adjusting the engine support fixture.

14. Remove the motor mount and bracket.

15. Raise and safely support the vehicle.

16. Remove the rear alternator bracket.

17. Remove the 2 bolts at the manifold outlet flannel.

18. Disconnect the oxygen sensor.

19. Remove the exhaust manifold from the cylinder head and remove the manifold.

20. Remove the gasket. Remove the oxygen sensor from the manifold.

To install:

21. Position the exhaust manifold by inserting the outlet pipe partially into the exhaust crossover pipe and moving the manifold into position.

22. Install gasket to the manifold. Insert 2 screws to hold gasket in place.

23. Tighten the manifold bolts to 20 ft. lbs. (25 Nm).

24. Coat the oxygen sensor threads with Hi temperature anti-seize compound and install the sensor. Tighten sensor nut to 30 ft. lbs. (40 Nm).

25. Connect the oxygen sensor connector. Install the rear alternator bracket. Tighten the crankcase bolts to 40 ft. lbs. (60 Nm) and the alternator bolts to 25 ft. lbs. (30 Nm).

26. Install 2 new bolts at the manifold outlet flange and tighten to 25 ft. lbs. (30 Nm).

27. Position the motor mount and bracket.

28. Loosely install the 2 nuts securing the mount to the bracket.

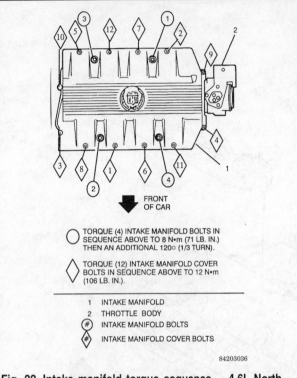

TORQUE (4) INTAKE MANIFOLD BOLTS IN SEQUENCE ABOVE TO 8 N•m (71 LB. IN.) THEN AN ADDITIONAL 120° (1/3 TURN).

TORQUE (12) INTAKE MANIFOLD COVER BOLTS IN SEQUENCE ABOVE TO 12 N•m (106 LB. IN.).

1	INTAKE MANIFOLD
2	THROTTLE BODY
#	INTAKE MANIFOLD BOLTS
#	INTAKE MANIFOLD COVER BOLTS

84203036

Fig. 22 Intake manifold torque sequence — 4.6L North-star engine

29. Lower the vehicle.

30. Loosely install the 2 screws securing the mount bracket at the cylinder head.

31. Lower the engine into the installed position guiding the motor mount studs in the cradle holes.

32. Raise the vehicle.

33. Loosely install the 2 nuts to the bottom of the motor mount.

34. Loosely install the 2 bolts securing the mount bracket to the crankcase.

35. Tighten the fasteners in Step 28, 33 and 34 to 25 ft. lbs. (30 Nm).

36. Install the 2 bolts at the converter to exhaust Y-pipe and tighten to 20 ft. lbs. (25 Nm).

37. Lower the vehicle.

38. Remove the engine support fixture J 28467-A.

39. Tighten the fasteners in Step 30 to 25 ft. lbs. (30 Nm).

40. Install the engine cooling fans.

41. Install the air cleaner assembly.

42. Connect the left and right engine torque struts and adjust and tighten as outlined in the Left Camshaft Cover installation procedure earlier in this Section.

43. Install the radiator trim panel.

44. Connect the negative battery cable.

RIGHT SIDE

1. Disconnect the negative battery cable.

2. Disconnect the rear oxygen sensor at the rear of the right cam cover. Disconnect the harness clip.

3. Raise and safely support the vehicle.

4. Disconnect the Y-pipe from the front of the catalytic converter.

5. Disconnect the suspension position sensor at lower control arm from both sides.

6. Disconnect the intermediate shaft from the steering gear.

7. Place a support below the rear cross member of the engine cradle and remove the 4 cradle to body bolts.

8. Lower the rear of the engine cradle and disconnect the Y-pipe from the exhaust crossover and from the manifold.

9. Remove the manifold nuts and remove the manifold.

10. Remove the gasket from the manifold. Replace if damaged. Remove the oxygen sensor from the manifold as necessary.

To install:

11. Coat oxygen sensor threads with hi-temperature anti-seize compound. Tighten sensor to 30 ft. lbs. (40 Nm).

12. Install gasket, manifold and nuts. Tighten nuts to 25 ft. lbs. (30 Nm).

13. Install exhaust Y-pipe and install 4 new bolts. Tighten the M10 bolts to 35 ft. lbs. (50 Nm) and the M8 bolts to 25 ft. lbs. (30 Nm).

14. Raise engine cradle into position and tighten the bolts to 75 ft. lbs. (100 Nm).

15. Connect the intermediate shaft to the steering gear and tighten to 35 ft. lbs. (50 Nm).

16. Connect the exhaust Y-pipe to the catalytic converter and tighten 2 new bolts to 35 ft. lbs. (50 Nm).

17. Connect the suspension position sensors to the lower control arms.

18. Lower the vehicle and connect the oxygen sensor. Install the harness retainer.

19. Connect the negative battery cable.

Radiator

REMOVAL & INSTALLATION

4.5L and 4.9L Engines

1. Disconnect the negative battery cable.

2. Drain cooling system.

3. Remove the plastic radiator support cover.

4. Remove right and left cooling fans. On Eldorado and Seville remove rear cooling fan.

5. Disconnect coolant reservoir hose at filler neck.

6. Remove upper and lower radiator hoses from radiator.

7. Remove engine oil cooler lines and transaxle oil cooler lines from the radiator.

8. Remove the radiator top support.

9. Remove radiator from car, lifting radiator straight up and out.

To install:

10. Install radiator in vehicle.

11. Install radiator top support. Tighten radiator support retaining bolts to 18 ft. lbs. (25 Nm).

12. Connect transaxle oil cooler lines at radiator. Tighten to 20 ft. lbs. (27 Nm).

13. Connect oil cooler lines at radiator. Tighten to 13 ft. lbs. (18 Nm).

14. Install upper and lower radiator hoses to radiator securing hose clamps.

15. Connect coolant reservoir hose at filler neck.

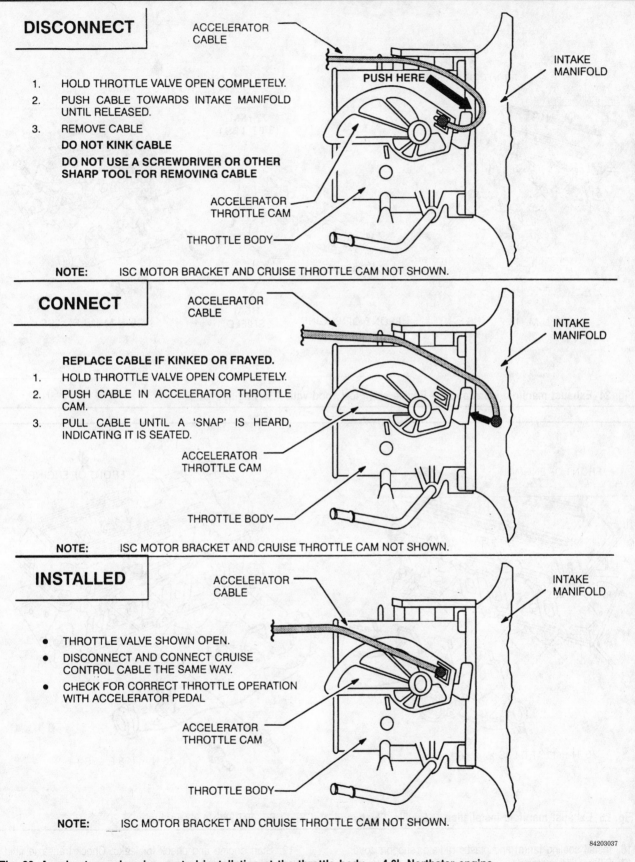

DISCONNECT

ACCELERATOR CABLE

PUSH HERE

INTAKE MANIFOLD

1. HOLD THROTTLE VALVE OPEN COMPLETELY.
2. PUSH CABLE TOWARDS INTAKE MANIFOLD UNTIL RELEASED.
3. REMOVE CABLE
   DO NOT KINK CABLE
   DO NOT USE A SCREWDRIVER OR OTHER SHARP TOOL FOR REMOVING CABLE

ACCELERATOR THROTTLE CAM

THROTTLE BODY

NOTE: ISC MOTOR BRACKET AND CRUISE THROTTLE CAM NOT SHOWN.

CONNECT

ACCELERATOR CABLE

INTAKE MANIFOLD

REPLACE CABLE IF KINKED OR FRAYED.
1. HOLD THROTTLE VALVE OPEN COMPLETELY.
2. PUSH CABLE IN ACCELERATOR THROTTLE CAM.
3. PULL CABLE UNTIL A 'SNAP' IS HEARD, INDICATING IT IS SEATED.

ACCELERATOR THROTTLE CAM

THROTTLE BODY

NOTE: ISC MOTOR BRACKET AND CRUISE THROTTLE CAM NOT SHOWN.

INSTALLED

ACCELERATOR CABLE

INTAKE MANIFOLD

• THROTTLE VALVE SHOWN OPEN.
• DISCONNECT AND CONNECT CRUISE CONTROL CABLE THE SAME WAY.
• CHECK FOR CORRECT THROTTLE OPERATION WITH ACCELERATOR PEDAL

ACCELERATOR THROTTLE CAM

THROTTLE BODY

NOTE: ISC MOTOR BRACKET AND CRUISE THROTTLE CAM NOT SHOWN.

84203037

Fig. 23 Accelerator and cruise control installation at the throttle body — 4.6L Northstar engine

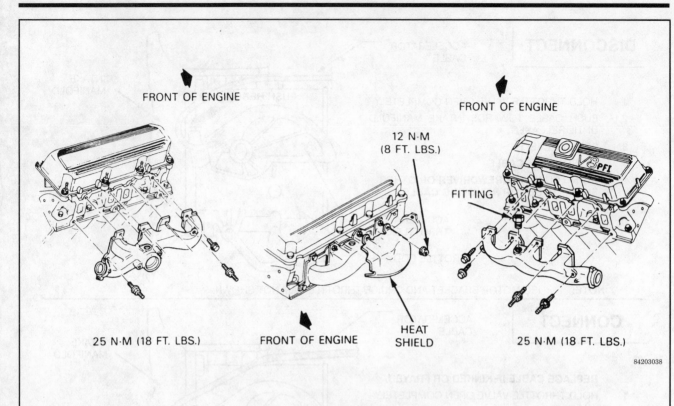

Fig. 24 Exhaust manifold installation — Deville and Fleetwood with 4.5L engine

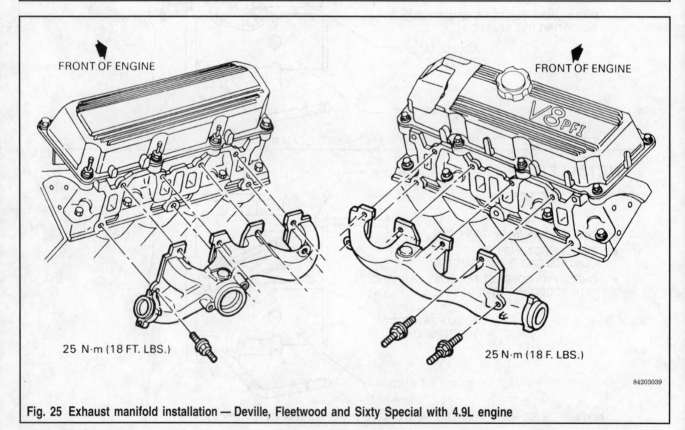

Fig. 25 Exhaust manifold installation — Deville, Fleetwood and Sixty Special with 4.9L engine

16. Install cooling fan(s) and plastic radiator support cover.
17. Fill cooling system.
18. Connect negative battery cable.

19. Start engine and check for leaks. Check transaxle fluid level and add, as necessary. Allow engine to come to normal operating temperature and check again for leaks.

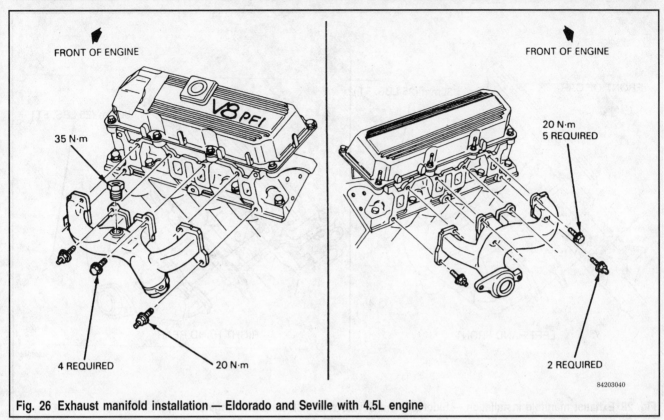

Fig. 26 Exhaust manifold installation — Eldorado and Seville with 4.5L engine

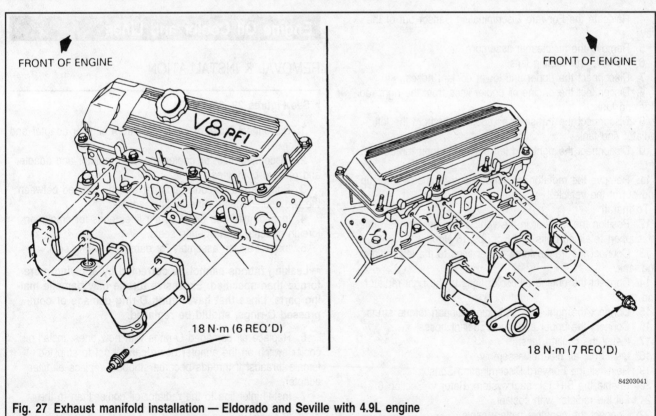

Fig. 27 Exhaust manifold installation — Eldorado and Seville with 4.9L engine

4.6L NORTHSTAR ENGINE

1. Disconnect the negative battery cable.

2. Drain the radiator coolant.
3. Disable the SIR (air bag) system. Refer to Section 6.

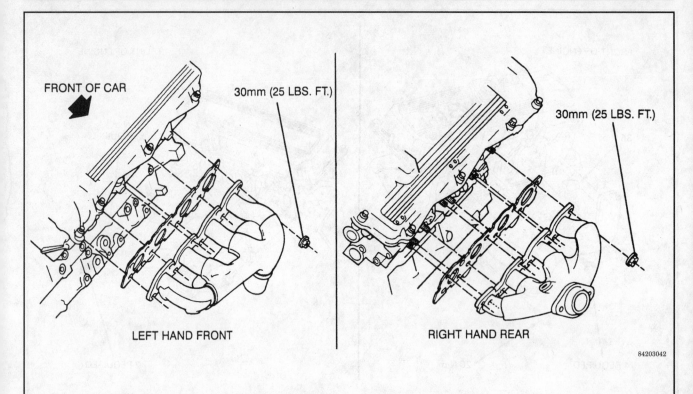

FRONT OF CAR

30mm (25 LBS. FT.)

30mm (25 LBS. FT.)

LEFT HAND FRONT

RIGHT HAND REAR

84203042

Fig. 28 Exhaust manifold installation — Eldorado and Seville with 4.6L Northstar engine

4. Relocate the Forward Discriminating Sensor out of the way.

5. Remove the air cleaner assembly.

6. Remove the cooling fans.

7. Disconnect the upper and lower coolant hoses.

8. Disconnect the engine oil cooler lines from the right radiator end tank.

9. Disconnect the transaxle oil cooler lines from the left radiator end tank.

10. Disconnect the right and left engine support torque struts.

11. Remove the radiator top support and lift the radiator up and out of the vehicle.

To install:

12. Position the radiator in the vehicle and tighten the radiator support retaining bolts to 4.5 ft. lbs. (6 Nm).

13. Connect the transaxle oil cooler lines to the left radiator end tank.

14. Connect the engine oil cooler lines to the right radiator end tank.

15. Connect the right and left engine support torque struts.

16. Connect the upper and lower coolant hoses.

17. Install the cooling fans.

18. Install the air cleaner assembly.

19. Reinstall the Forward Discriminating Sensor.

20. Enable the SIR (air bag) system. Refer to Section 6.

21. Fill the radiator with coolant.

22. Connect the negative battery cable.

Engine Oil Cooler and Lines

REMOVAL & INSTALLATION

▶ **See Figures 29, 30 and 31**

1. Disconnect outlet oil cooler line from oil filter adapter and radiator.

2. Disconnect inlet oil cooler line from radiator and adapter and remove both lines.

3. Remove the oil cooler adapter switch , located between the two cooler lines on the oil filter adapter.

4. Inspect inlet and outlet cooler lines ends for cracks or foreign material in the O-ring seals.

5. Inspect switch assembly for damaged O-ring seal.

➡**Leaking fittings cannot be corrected by applying more torque than specified. Excessive torque may damage mating parts. Lines that have fitting O-ring damage or compressed O-rings, should be replaced.**

6. Replace all damaged O-rings with new ones. Install oil cooler switch on the adapter being careful not to strip the female threads. If threads become stripped, replace oil filter adapter.

7. Install inlet line to the radiator oil cooler then to the adapter.

8. Install outlet line to the radiator oil cooler then to the adapter. Tighten both outlet and inlet cooler line nuts to 12 ft. lbs. (18 Nm.).

9. Start engine and check for leaks.

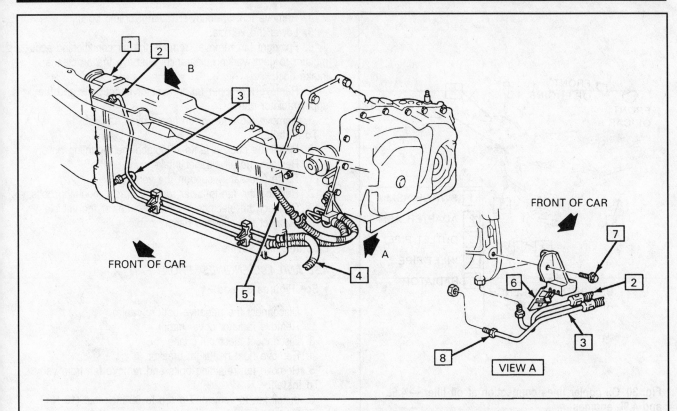

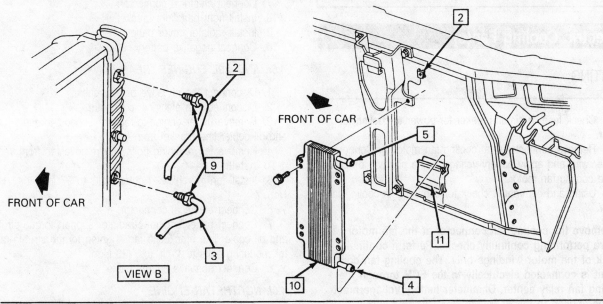

1	RADIATOR AND TRANSAXLE COOLER	7	BOLT
2	OIL SENDING LINE	8	TRANSAXLE INLET AND OUTLET FITTINGS
3	OIL RETURN LINE	9	RADIATOR INLET AND OUTLET FITTINGS
4	TO AUXILIARY COOLER LOWER INLET	10	AUXILIARY TRANSAXLE OIL COOLER
5	TO AUXILIARY COOLER UPPER OUTLET	11	SUPPORT BRACKET
6	CLIP		

84203043

Fig. 29 Oil cooler lines — 4.5L and 4.9L engines

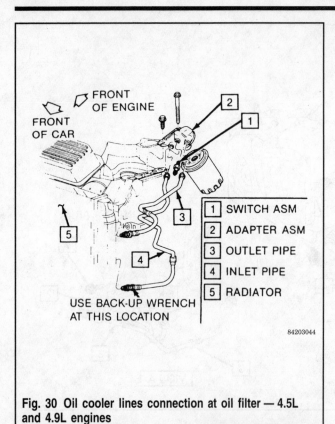

FRONT OF ENGINE

FRONT OF CAR

1	SWITCH ASM
2	ADAPTER ASM
3	OUTLET PIPE
4	INLET PIPE
5	RADIATOR

USE BACK-UP WRENCH AT THIS LOCATION

84203044

Fig. 30 Oil cooler lines connection at oil filter — 4.5L and 4.9L engines

Electric Cooling Fan(s)

TESTING

1. Check fuse or circuit breaker for power to cooling fan motor.
2. Remove connector(s) at cooling fan motor(s). Connect jumper wire and apply battery voltage to the positive terminal of the cooling fan motor.
3. Using and ohmmeter, check for continuity in cooling fan motor.

➡**Remove the cooling fan connector at the fan motor before performing continuity checks. Perform continuity check of the motor windings only. The cooling fan control circuit is connected electrically to the ECM through the cooling fan relay center. Ohmmeter battery voltage must not be applied to the ECM.**

4. Ensure proper continuity of cooling fan motor ground circuit at chassis ground connector.

REMOVAL & INSTALLATION

Deville, Fleetwood and Sixty Special
▶ See Figure 32

1. Disconnect the negative battery cable.
2. Raise and safely support the vehicle.
3. Disconnect the electrical connectors from the rear of the fan assemblies.

4. Remove the fan-to-lower radiator cradle bolts.
5. Lower the vehicle.
6. For right fan removal, remove the air conditioning accumulator to gain working clearance. Remove the air cleaner intake duct.
7. Remove the upper fan-to-radiator panel bolts and the upper radiator panel.
8. Remove the cooling fan assemblies.
To install:
9. Install the cooling fan(s). Replace the mounting bolts.
10. Replace the air cleaner intake duct.
11. Raise and safely support the vehicle.
12. Replace the fan-to-lower radiator cradle mounting bolts.
13. Connect the electrical connectors. Lower the vehicle.
14. Connect the negative battery cable.

Eldorado and Seville

4.5L AND 4.9L ENGINES FRONT FAN
▶ See Figures 33 and 34

1. Disconnect the negative battery cable.
2. Remove radiator cover panel.
3. Disconnect electrical connector.
4. Remove right headlight bracket.
5. Remove fan retaining bolts and remove fan from vehicle.
To install:
6. Install fan to vehicle. Tighten to 88 inch lbs. (10 Nm).
7. Connect electrical connector.
8. Install right headlight bracket.
9. Install radiator cover panel.
10. Connect negative battery cable.

4.5L AND 4.9L ENGINES REAR FAN

1. Disconnect the negative battery cable.
2. Disconnect fan electrical connector.
3. Remove upper engine-to-radiator support torque strut and oil cooler line bracket from fan.
4. Remove fan retaining bolts and remove fan from vehicle.
To install:
5. Install fan in vehicle. Tighten bolts to 97 inch lbs. (11 Nm).
6. Connect electrical connector.
7. Connect upper engine-to-radiator support torque strut and oil cooler line bracket to fan. Tighten torque strut-to-radiator mounting bolts to 17 ft. lbs. (23 Nm).
8. Connect negative battery cable.

4.6L NORTHSTAR ENGINE
▶ See Figure 35

1. Disconnect the negative battery cable.
2. Remove the beauty panel assembly.
3. Remove the left side engine torque support strut.
4. Position upper radiator hose out of the way.
5. Disconnect the fan electrical connector.
6. Remove retaining bolts and remove fan(s).
To install:
7. Install fan(s) to vehicle. Tighten retaining bolts to 88 inch lbs. (10 Nm).
8. Connect fan electrical connector.
9. Reposition upper radiator hose and install left side engine torque strut.

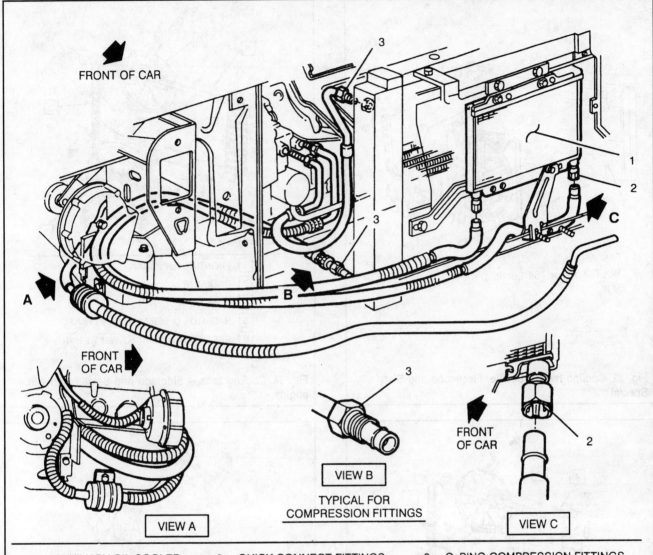

VIEW B

TYPICAL FOR COMPRESSION FITTINGS

VIEW A

VIEW C

| 1 | AUXILIARY OIL COOLER | 2 | QUICK CONNECT FITTINGS | 3 | O-RING COMPRESSION FITTINGS |

84203045

Fig. 31 Oil cooler lines — 4.6L engines

10. Install beauty panel assembly and connect the negative battery cable.

Water Pump

REMOVAL & INSTALLATION

4.5L and 4.9L Engines

▶ **See Figures 36, 37 and 38**

1. Disconnect the negative battery cable.
2. Drain the engine coolant into a clean container for reuse.
3. Remove the air filter assembly. Disconnect and remove the coolant recovery tank.
4. Disconnect and remove the cross brace.

5. Remove the water pulley bolts.
6. Remove the serpentine drive belt and the water pump pulley.
7. Remove the water pump-to-engine bolts and the pump.
To install:
8. Clean the gasket mounting surfaces.
9. Place a new gasket over the water pump studs.
10. Install the water pump. Tighten the water pump bolts as follows:

Water pump-to-engine Torx® bolts to 30 ft. lbs. (40 Nm)

Water pump-to-engine stud nuts to 5 ft. lbs. (7 Nm)
Hex head bolts to 30 ft. lbs. (40 Nm)
Remaining hex head bolts to 5 ft. lbs. (7 Nm).
11. Install the water pump pulley. Install the water pump pulley bolts finger-tight.
12. Install the serpentine drive belt.

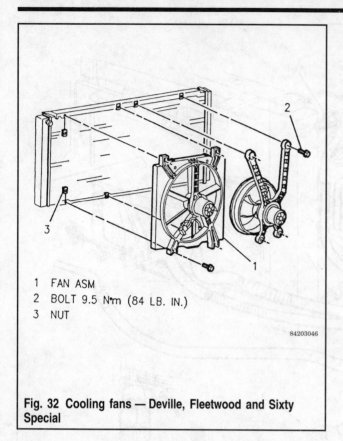

1 FAN ASM
2 BOLT 9.5 N·m (84 LB. IN.)
3 NUT

84203046

Fig. 32 Cooling fans — Deville, Fleetwood and Sixty Special

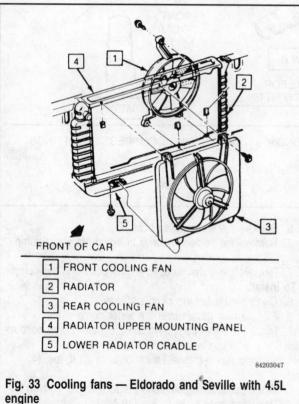

1 FRONT COOLING FAN
2 RADIATOR
3 REAR COOLING FAN
4 RADIATOR UPPER MOUNTING PANEL
5 LOWER RADIATOR CRADLE

84203047

Fig. 33 Cooling fans — Eldorado and Seville with 4.5L engine

13. Tighten the water pump pulley bolts to 22 ft. lbs. (30 Nm).

14. Install the cross brace.

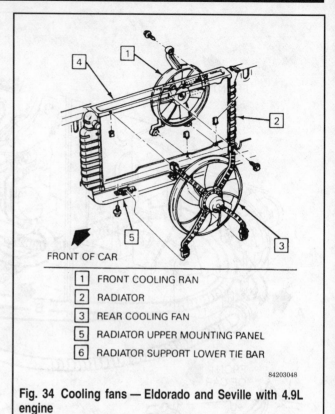

FRONT OF CAR

1 FRONT COOLING RAN
2 RADIATOR
3 REAR COOLING FAN
5 RADIATOR UPPER MOUNTING PANEL
6 RADIATOR SUPPORT LOWER TIE BAR

84203048

Fig. 34 Cooling fans — Eldorado and Seville with 4.9L engine

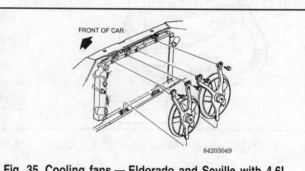

FRONT OF CAR

84203049

Fig. 35 Cooling fans — Eldorado and Seville with 4.6L Northstar engine

15. Install the connect the coolant recovery tank. Install the air filter assembly.

16. Connect the negative battery cable.

17. Fill cooling system and check for leaks. Start the engine and allow to come to normal operating temperature. Recheck for leaks. Top-up coolant.

➡Because the engine block and radiator are aluminum, make sure the antifreeze solution is approved for use in cooling systems with a high aluminum content. GM recommends the use of a supplement/sealant 3634621 or equivalent, specifically designed for use in aluminum engines to protect the engine from damage.

4.6L Northstar Engine

▸ See Figure 39

1. Disconnect the negative battery cable.

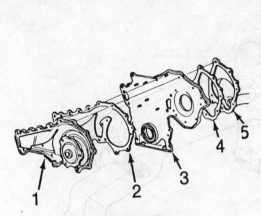

1. WATER PUMP
   ASSEMBLY
2. WATER PUMP GASKET
3. FRONT COVER
4. WATER PUMP INLET
   GASKET
5. WATER PUMP INLET

84203050

Fig. 36 Water pump assembly — 4.5L and 4.9L engines

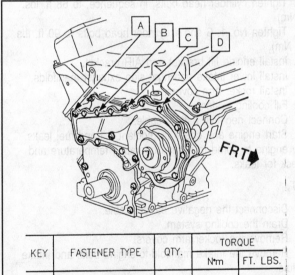

KEY	FASTENER TYPE	QTY.	TORQUE	
			N•m	FT. LBS.
A	TORX SCREW	4	40	30
B	NUT	7	7	5
C	STUD	1	40	30
D	HEX SCREW	7	7	5

84203051

Fig. 37 Water pump fasteners and torques — Deville, Fleetwood and Sixty Special

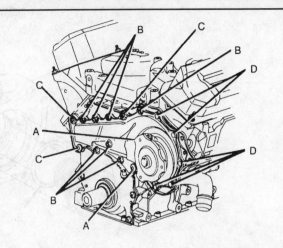

KEY	FASTENER TYPE	QTY.	TORQUE	
			N•m	FT. LBS.
A	TORX SCREW	2	40	30
B	NUT	7	7	5
C	HEX SCREW	3	40	30
D	HEX SCREW	5	7	5

84203052

Fig. 38 Water pump fasteners and torques — Eldorado and Seville with 4.5L and 4.9L engines

2. Drain the engine coolant into a clean container for reuse.
3. Remove the air cleaner assembly.
4. Remove the water pump pulley bolts.
5. Remove the water pump drive belt and the water pump pulley.
6. Remove the water pump-to-engine bolts and the pump.
To install:
7. Clean the gasket mounting surfaces.
8. Place a new gasket over the water pump studs.
9. Install the water pump and tighten the housing bolts to 5 ft. lbs. (7 Nm).
10. Install the water pump pulley. Install the water pump pulley bolts finger tight.
11. Install the drive belt.
12. Tighten the water pump pulley bolts to 22 ft. lbs. (30 Nm).
13. Install the air cleaner assembly.
14. Connect the negative battery cable.
15. Fill cooling system and check for leaks. Start the engine and allow to come to normal operating temperature. Recheck for leaks. Top-up coolant.

➡Because the engine block and radiator are aluminum, make sure the antifreeze solution is approved for use in cooling systems with a high aluminum content. GM recommends the use of a supplement/sealant 3634621 or equivalent, specifically designed for use in aluminum engines to protect the engine from damage.

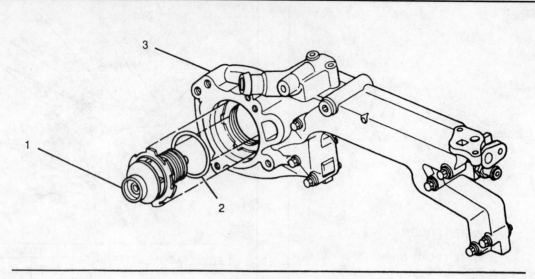

1   WATER PUMP ASM.

2   O–RING SEAL

3   WATER PUMP HOUSING ASM.

84203053

Fig. 39 Water pump assembly — Eldorado and Seville with 4.6L Northstar engine

Cylinder Head

REMOVAL & INSTALLATION

4.5L and 4.9L Engines

▶ See Figure 40

RIGHT

1. Disconnect the negative battery cable. Drain the engine coolant.
2. Remove rocker arm covers.
3. Remove the lower intake and right side exhaust manifolds.
4. Remove engine lift bracket and oil dipstick tube.
5. Reposition AIR bracket.
6. Remove 10 cylinder head bolts.
7. Remove cylinder head.

To install:

➡ Clean sealing surfaces of cylinder head, block and liners. Clean cylinder head bolt holes with an appropriate tap. Ensure that bolt holes are free of shavings, oil and coolant.

8. Install new head gasket over dowels on cylinder block with either side facing up.
9. Install cylinder head.
10. Apply an appropriate lubricant to the threads of the head bolts. Install cylinder head bolts finger-tight.
11. Tighten cylinder head bolts, in sequence, to 38 ft. lbs. (50 Nm).

12. Tighten cylinder head bolts, in sequence, to 68 ft. lbs. (90 Nm).
13. Tighten No. 1, 3 and 4 cylinder head bolts to 90 ft. lbs. (120 Nm).
14. Install engine lift bracket and AIR bracket.
15. Install lower intake and right side exhaust manifolds.
16. Install rocker arm covers.
17. Fill cooling system.
18. Connect negative battery cable.
19. Start engine and check for coolant, oil and fuel leaks. Allow engine to come to normal operating temperature and recheck for leaks.

LEFT

1. Disconnect the negative battery cable.
2. Drain the cooling system.
3. Remove the rocker arm covers.
4. Remove the intake manifold-to-engine bolts and intake manifold.

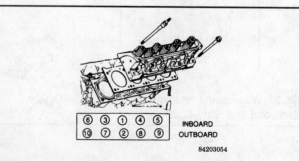

INBOARD
OUTBOARD

84203054

Fig. 40 Cylinder torque sequence — 4.5L and 4.9L engines

5. Disconnect the exhaust manifold crossover pipe, the exhaust pipe-to-exhaust manifold bolts, the exhaust manifold-to-cylinder head bolts and the exhaust manifold.

6. Remove the engine lifting bracket and the dipstick tube.

7. Remove the AIR bracket-to-engine bolts and move the bracket aside.

8. Remove the cylinder head-to-engine bolts and the cylinder head.

To install:

9. Clean the gasket mounting surfaces.

10. Install new head gasket over dowels on cylinder block with either side facing up.

11. Install cylinder head.

12. Apply a suitable lubricant to the cylinder head bolt threads.

13. Install cylinder head bolts finger-tight.

14. Tighten bolts, in sequence, to 38 ft. lbs. (50 Nm).

15. Tighten cylinder head bolts, in sequence, to 68 ft. lbs. (90 Nm).

16. Tighten No. 1, 3 and 4 cylinder head bolts to 90 ft. lbs. (120 Nm).

17. Install AIR bracket. Install dipstick tube and engine lift bracket.

18. Install exhaust manifold. Install lower intake manifold.

19. Install rocker arm covers.

20. Fill cooling system.

21. Connect negative battery cable.

22. Start engine and check for coolant, oil and fuel leaks. Allow engine to come to normal operating temperature and recheck for leaks.

4.6L Northstar Engine

♦ **See Figure 41**

➡ **Because of the bulk and complexity of the 4.6L Northstar engine, cylinder head removal may best be accomplished with the engine out of the vehicle. For this procedure it may be most economical to remove the entire powertrain and cradle out the bottom of the body and to utilize the cradle as an engine stand. 'Powertrain' removal and installation procedures are outlined at the beginning of this Section.**

1. Remove the powertrain assembly as outlined earlier in this Section.

2. Remove the intake manifold, camshaft covers, harmonic balancer, front cover and oil pump as outlined in this Section.

3. Remove the chain tensioner from the timing chain for the cylinder head being removed.

4. Remove the cam sprockets from the head being removed. The timing chain remains in the chain case.

5. Removing the timing chain guides. Access to the retaining screws is through the plugs at the front of the cylinder head.

6. Remove the water crossover.

7. Remove the exhaust manifold as outlined in this Section.

8. Remove the cylinder head bolts.

9. Remove the cylinder head and gasket.

✴✴WARNING

With the camshafts remaining in the cylinder head some valves will be open at all times. Do not rest the cylinder head on a flat service with the cylinder face down, or valve damage will result.

To install:

10. Clean the gasket services and combustion chamber.

✴✴WARNING

When cleaning aluminum gasket services, use only plastic or wood scrapers and/or an appropriate chemical dissolving agent to avoid damaging the sealing surfaces.

11. Using a new cylinder head gasket, install the cylinder head and the 10 M11 and 3 M6 head bolts. Lube the washer and the underside of the bolt head with engine oil prior to installation. Tighten the 10 M11 bolts in sequence to 22 ft. lbs. (30 Nm) plus 90 °, plus an additional 90 ° for a total of 180 °. Tighten the 3 M6 bolts to 10 ft. lbs. (12 Nm).

12. Install the camshafts as outlined in this Section.

13. Set the camshaft timing as outlined in this Section.

14. Install the camshaft guide bolt access hole plugs in the cylinder heads. The plugs should be seated and snug.

15. Install the intake manifold, camshaft covers, harmonic balancer, front cover and oil pump as outlined in this Section.

16. Install the water crossover.

17. Install the exhaust manifold.

18. Install the powertrain assembly as outlined earlier in this Section.

CLEANING & INSPECTION

Once the complete valve train has been removed from the cylinder head(s), the head itself can be inspected, cleaned and machined (if necessary). Set the head(s) on a clean work space, so the combustion chambers are facing up. Begin cleaning the chambers and ports with a hardwood chisel or other non-metallic tool (to avoid nicking gouging the chamber, ports and especially the valve seats). Chip away the major carbon deposits, then remove the remainder of carbon with a wire brush fitted to an electric drill.

➡ **Be sure that the carbon is actually removed, rather than just brushed.**

After decarbonizing is completed, take the head(s) to a machine shop and have the head hot tanked. In this process, the head is lowered into a hot chemical bath that very effectively cleans all grease, corrosion, and scale from all internal and external head surfaces. Also have the machinist check the valve seats and re-cut them if necessary. When you bring the clean head(s) home, place them on a clean surface. Completely clean the entire valve train with solvent.

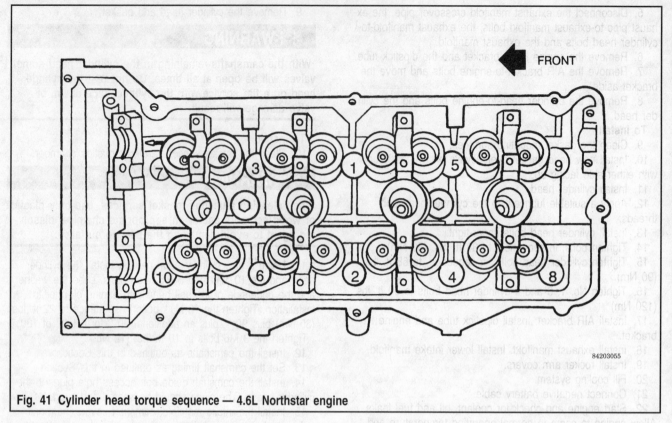

FRONT

84203055

Fig. 41 Cylinder head torque sequence — 4.6L Northstar engine

CHECKING HEAD FOR WARPAGE

▶ See Figure 42

Lay the head down with the combustion chambers facing up. Place a straight edge across the gasket surface of the head, both diagonally and straight across the center. Using a flat feeler gauge, determine the clearance at the center of the straightedge. If warpage exceeds 0.002 inches (0.05mm) in a 6 inch (152mm) span, or 0.0006 inch (0.15) over the total length, the cylinder head must be resurfaced (which is akin to planning a piece of wood). Resurfacing can be performed at most machine shops.

➡When resurfacing the cylinder head(s), the intake manifold mounting position is altered, and must be corrected by machining a proportionate amount from the intake manifold flange.

Valves and Springs

REMOVAL

4.5L and 4.9L Engines

▶ See Figures 43 and 44

1. Remove the head(s), and place on a clean surface.
2. Using a suitable spring compressor (for pushrod type overhead valve engines), compress the valve spring and remove the valve spring cap key. Release the spring compressor

and remove the valve spring and cap (and valve rotator on some engines).

➡Use care in removing the keys; they are easily lost.

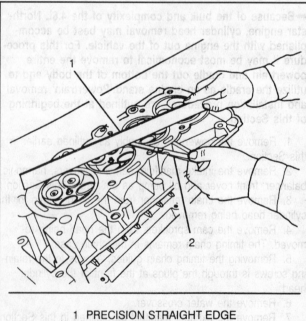

1 PRECISION STRAIGHT EDGE
2 FEELER GAGE

84203056

Fig. 42 Measuring cylinder head flatness

3. Remove the valve seals from the intake valve guides. Throw these old seals away, as you'll be installing new seals during reassembly.

4. Slide the valves out of the head from the combustion chamber side.

5. Make a holder for the valves out of a piece of wood or cardboard, as outlined for the pushrods in Cylinder Head Removal. Make sure you number each hole in the cardboard to keep the valves in proper order. Slide the valves out of the head from the combustion chamber side; they MUST be installed as they were removed.

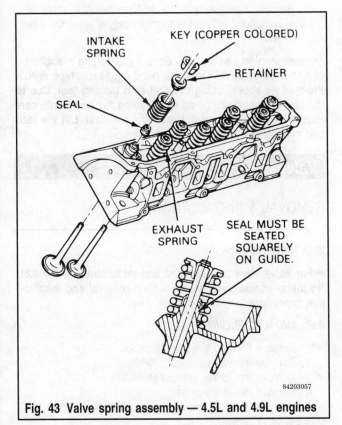

Fig. 43 Valve spring assembly — 4.5L and 4.9L engines

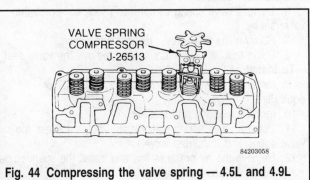

Fig. 44 Compressing the valve spring — 4.5L and 4.9L engines

4.6L Northstar Engine
▶ See Figures 45, 46, 47 and 48

1. Remove the cylinder head as outlined in this Section.

※※WARNING

With the camshafts remaining in the cylinder head some valves will be open at all times. Do not rest the cylinder head on a flat service with the cylinder face down, or valve damage will result.

2. Remove the intake and exhaust camshaft by alternately loosening each cam bearing cap bolt 2 turns at a time until the valve spring pressure is completely released. Note the positions on the bearing cap.

※※WARNING

Do not mix cam bearing caps between positions or between heads. The arrow points toward the front of the engine.

3. Remove the valve lifters and arrange them so they may be installed in their original position. Store the lifters with the cam face down to prevent draining oil from the lifter.

4. Using a suitable deep socket and a plastic hammer, lightly tap on the valve spring retainer to loosen the valve keepers.

5. Using a valve spring compressor J 8062 and adapter J 38823 or their equivalent, compress the valve spring. Using the magnetic end of keeper remover/installer J 38819 or equivalent, remove the valve keepers.

6. Remove the valve.

7. Install J 38820-2 sleeve or equivalent, into the lifter bore to protect the surface.

8. Using J 38820 valve stem seal remover/installer or equivalent, remove the valve stem seal by exerting a twist/pull motion. Discard the stem/seal spring seat.

INSPECTION

Inspect the valve faces and seats (in the head) for pits, burned spots and other evidence of poor seating. If a valve face is in such bad shape that the head of the valve must be ground in order to true up the face, discard the valve because the sharp edge will run too hot. The correct angle for valve

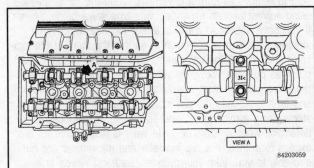

Fig. 45 Cam bearing cap orientation — 4.6L Northstar engine

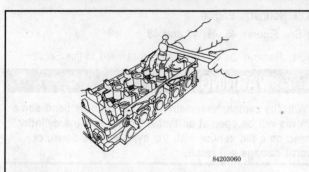

Fig. 46 Loosening valve keepers — 4.6L Northstar engine

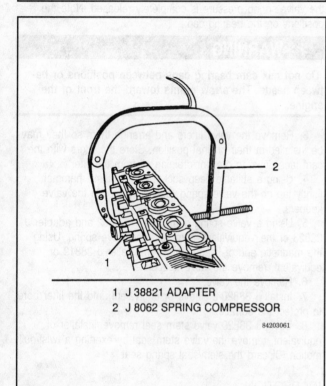

1 J 38821 ADAPTER
2 J 8062 SPRING COMPRESSOR

Fig. 47 Compressing the valve spring — 4.6L Northstar engine

faces is 45°. We recommend the re-facing be done at a reputable machine shop.

Check the valve stem for scoring and burned spots. If not noticeably scored or damaged, clean the valve stem with solvent to remove all gum and varnish. Clean the valve guides using solvent and an expanding wire-type valve guide cleaner. If you have access to a dial indicator for measuring valve stem-to-guide clearance, mount it so that the stem of the indicator is at 90° to the valve stem, and as close to the valve guide as possible. Move the valve off its seat, and measure the valve guide-to-stem clearance by rocking the stem back and forth to actuate the dial indicator. Measure the valve stems using a micrometer, and compare the specifications to determine whether stem or guide wear is responsible for the excess clearance. If a dial indicator and micrometer are not available to you, take your cylinder head and valves to a reputable machine shop for inspection.

REFACING THE VALVES

When valve faces and seats have been re-faced and re-cut, or if they are determined to be in good condition, the valves must be lapped in to ensure efficient sealing when the valve closes against the seat.

1. Invert the cylinder head so that the combustion chambers are facing up.
2. Lightly lubricate the valve stems with clean oil, and coat the valve seats with valve grinding compound. Install the valves in the head as numbered.
3. Attach the suction cup of a valve lapping tool to a valve head. You'll probably have to moisten the cup to securely attach the tool to the valve.
4. Rotate the tool between the palms, changing position and lifting the tool often to prevent grooving. Lap the valve until a smooth, polished seat is evident (you may have to add a bit more compound after some lapping is done).
5. Remove the valve and tool, and remove ALL traces of grinding compound with solvent-soaked rag, or rinse the head with solvent.

➡Valve lapping can also be done by fastening a suction cup to a piece of drill rod in a hand eggbeater type drill. Proceed as above, using the drill as a lapping tool. Due to the higher speeds involved when using the hand drill, care must be exercised to avoid grooving the seat. Lift the tool and change direction of rotation often.

Valve Stem Seals

REMOVAL & INSTALLATION

With Head On Engine

➡For valve stem seal removal and installation on the 4.6L Northstar engine, refer to the 'Valve' removal and installation procedure in this Section.

4.5L AND 4.9L ENGINES

1. Remove the negative battery cable.
2. Remove the valve cover.
3. Remove the rocker arm assemblies.
4. Remove the spark plugs.
5. Using an adaptor apply air pressure to the cylinder to hold the valve closed.
6. Using a valve spring compressing tool, compress the valve spring.
7. Remove the valve keys, retainer and spring.
8. Using tool J36017 or equivalent, remove the valve seal.
To install:
9. Install the new valve seal, using tool J36007 or equivalent.
10. Install the spring and retainer.
11. Using a valve spring compressing tool, compress the valve spring and install the valve keys.
12. Remove the air pressure line and install the spark plugs.
13. Install the spark plugs.
14. Install the rocker arm assemblies and the valve cover.
15. Connect the negative battery cable.

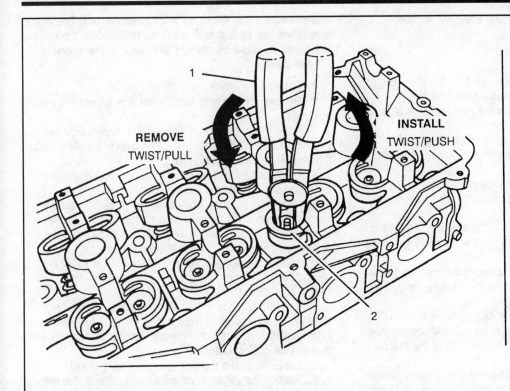

REMOVE
TWIST/PULL

INSTALL
TWIST/PUSH

1 J 38820 SEAL
REMOVE / INSTALLER
2 J 38820−2 LIFTER BORE
PROTECTOR

84203062

Fig. 48 Removing or installing valve stem seals — 4.6L Northstar engine

With Head Off Engine

4.5L AND 4.9L ENGINES

1. Using a valve spring compressing tool, compress the valve spring and remove the valve keys.
2. Remove the retainer and spring.
3. Remove the valve seal, using tool J36017 or equivalent.
4. Remove the rotator.

To install:

5. Install the rotator and install the valve seal, using tool J36007 or equivalent.
6. Install the spring and the retainer.
7. Using a valve spring compressing tool, compress the valve spring and install the valve keys.

Valve Springs

HEIGHT AND PRESSURE CHECK

1. Place the valve spring on a flat, clean surface next to a square.
2. Measure the height of the spring, and rotate it against the edge of the square to measure distortion (out-of-roundness). If spring height varies between springs by more than 1/16 inch (1.5mm) or if the distortion exceeds 1/16 inch (1.5mm), replace the spring.

A valve spring tester is needed to test spring test pressure, so the valve springs must usually be taken to a professional machine shop for this test. Spring pressure at the installed and compressed heights is checked, and a tolerance of plus or minus 5 lbs. is permissible on the springs covered in this guide.

VALVE INSTALLATION

4.5L and 4.9L Engine

New valve seals must be installed when the valve train is put back together. Certain seals slip over the valve stem and guide boss, while others require that the boss be machined. In some applications Teflon guide seals are available. Check with a machinist and/or automotive parts store for a suggestion on the proper seals to use.

➡Remember that when installing valve seals, a small amount of oil is able to pass the seal to lubricate the valve guides; otherwise, excessive wear will result.

To install the valves and rocker assembly:
1. Lubricate the valve stems with clean engine oil.
2. Install the valves in the cylinder head, one at a time, as numbered.
3. Lubricate and position the seals and valve springs, again a valve at a time.
4. Install the spring retainers, and compress the springs.
5. With the valve key groove exposed above the compressed valve spring, wipe some wheel bearing grease around the groove. This will retain the keys as you release the spring compressor.
6. Using needlenose pliers (or your fingers), place the keys in the key grooves. The grease should hold the keys in place. Slowly release the spring compressor; the valve cap or rotator will raise up as the compressor is released, retaining the keys.

7. Install the rocker assembly, and install the cylinder head(s).

4.6L Northstar Engine

1. With J 38820-2 sleeve or equivalent, in the lifter bore to protect the surface, use J 38820 valve stem seal remover/installer or equivalent, and install the new valve stem seal by applying a twist/pushing motion.

2. Flood the stem seal inner diameter with engine oil.

3. Lubricate the valve stem with engine oil and install the valve.

4. Position the valve spring and retainer and using the spring compressor J 8062 and adapter J 38823 or equivalent, compress the valve spring.

5. Install the valve keepers into installation tool J 38819 or equivalent, and put the keeper into position by pushing the tool downward.

6. Release the tension on the spring compressor and remove the adapter J 38823. Verify the valve keepers are in the installed position.

7. Install the valve lifters in their original position.

8. Lubricate the camshaft bearing journals with engine oil and position the intake and exhaust camshafts to the cylinder head.

9. Install the camshaft bearing caps in their original position with the arrows pointing towards the front of the engine. Finger start all camshaft bearing cap bolts.

10. Alternately tighten each pair of bearing cap bolts one turn at a time until the caps are snug with the cylinder head to 9 ft. lbs. (12 Nm).

Valve Guides

The engines covered in this guide use integral valve guides; that is, they are a part of the cylinder head and cannot be replaced. The guides can, however, be reamed oversize if they are found to be worn past an acceptable limit. Occasionally, a valve guide bore will be oversize as manufactured. These are marked on the inboard side of the cylinder heads on the machined surface just above the intake manifold.

If the guides must be reamed (this service is available at most machine shops), then valves with oversize stems must be fitted. Valves are usually available in 0.001 inch, 0.003 inch, and 0.005 inch stem oversizes. Valve guides which are not excessively worn or distorted may, in some cases, be knurled rather than reamed. Knurling is a process in which the metal on the valve guide bore is displaced and raised, thereby reducing clearance. Knurling also provides excellent oil control. The option of knurling rather than reaming valve guides should be discussed with a reputable machinist or engine specialist.

Valve Lifters

REMOVAL & INSTALLATION

4.5L and 4.9L Engines

➡Valve lifters and pushrods should be kept in order so they can be reinstalled in their original position. Some engines will have both standard size 0.010 inch (0.25mm)

and oversize valve lifters as original equipment. The oversize lifters are etched with an O on their sides; the cylinder block will also be marked with an O if the oversize lifter is used.

1. Remove the intake manifold and gasket.

2. Remove the valve covers, rocker arm assemblies and pushrods.

3. If the lifters are coated with varnish, apply carburetor cleaning solvent to the lifter body. The solvent should dissolve the varnish in about 10 minutes.

4. Remove the lifters. A special tool for removing lifters is available, and is helpful for this procedure.

5. New lifters must be primed before installation, as dry lifters will seize when the engine is started. Submerge the lifters in SAE 10 oil, which is very thin. Carefully insert the end of a ⅛inch (3mm) drift into the lifter and push down on the plunger. Hold the plunger down while the lifter is still submerged; do not pump the plunger. Release the plunger. The lifter is now primed.

6. Coat the bottoms of the lifters, and the rollers with Molykote or an equivalent molybdenum-disulfide lubricant before installation. Install the lifters and pushrods into the engine in their original order.

7. Install the intake manifold gaskets and manifold.

8. Position the rocker arms, pivots and bolts on the cylinder head. Position and install the rockers and rocker shaft.

9. Install the valve covers, connect the spark plug wires and install the air cleaner assembly.

➡An additive containing EP lube, such as EOS, should always be added to crankcase oil for break-in when new lifters or a new camshaft is installed. This additive is generally available in automotive parts stores.

4.6L Northstar Engine

1. Remove the camshaft cover as outlined in this Section.

2. Remove the camshafts for the head being worked on as outlined in this Section.

3. Remove the valve lifters in order, and store on their camshaft face so that the residual oil is retained.

➡Retain the lifters in order so that they can be reinstalled in their original bores.

To install:

4. Install the valve lifters in their original bores.

5. Install the camshafts as outlined in this Section.

6. Install the camshaft cover as outlined in this Section.

OVERHAUL

4.5L and 4.9L Engines

1. Remove the push rod seat retainer by holding the plunger down and removing the retainer with a small screwdriver.

2. Remove the push rod seat and the metering valve.

3. Remove the plunger. If plunger is stuck, tap the lifter upside down on a flat surface, if still stuck, soak in parts cleaning solvent.

4. Remove the ball check valve assembly.

5. Remove the plunger spring.

6. Clean lifter of all sludge and varnish build-up.

7. Inspect for excessive wear and scuffing. Replace if excessively worn or scuffed.

8. Inspect for flat spots on the bottom. If worn flat, replace the lifter.

9. If equipped with roller, inspect for freedom of movement, looseness, flat spots or pitting. If any detected, replace the lifter.

10. Install the check ball to the small hole in the bottom of the plunger.

11. Place ball retainer and spring over check ball and press into place using a small screwdriver.

12. Install the plunger spring over the ball retainer.

13. Install the lifter body over the spring and plunger. Make sure the oil holes in the lifter body and in the plunger line up.

14. Using a 1/8inch (3mm) drift pin, push the plunger down until the oil holes in the lifter body and plunger are aligned.

15. Insert a 1/16 inch (1.6mm) pin through the oil holes to lock the plunger down.

16. Remove the 1/8inch (3mm) pin and fill the lifter with engine oil.

17. Install the metering valve, push rod seat and push rod seat retainer.

18. Push down on the push rod seat to relieve the spring pressure and remove the 1/16 inch (1.6mm) pin.

Oil Pan

REMOVAL & INSTALLATION

4.5L and 4.9L Engines
▶ See Figure 49

1. Disconnect the negative battery cable. Raise and safely support the vehicle. Drain the crankcase.

2. Remove the 2 torque converter/flywheel covers from the lower side of the transaxle.

3. On the Eldorado and Seville, remove the exhaust crossunder pipe and reposition.

4. Remove the oil pan-to-engine bolts and the oil pan.
To install:
5. Clean the gasket mounting surfaces.

➡**Apply a 1/4 inch bead of RTV at the rear main bearing cap and front cover to block joints.**

6. Install the oil pan and oil pan-to-engine bolts. Tighten to 14 ft. lbs. (18 Nm).

7. Install the exhaust crossunder pipe.

8. Install the 2 torque converter/flywheel covers.

9. Lower the vehicle.

10. Fill the crankcase.

11. Connect the negative battery cable.

4.6L Northstar Engine
▶ See Figures 50 and 51

1. Remove the engine as outlined in this Section and place on a stand.

2. Drain the engine oil.

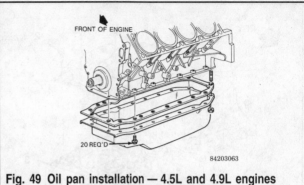

FRONT OF ENGINE

20 REQ'D

84203063

Fig. 49 Oil pan installation — 4.5L and 4.9L engines

3. Remove the 13 oil pan bolts and remove the oil pan.

➡**The oil pan gasket is reusable unless damaged. Do not remove the gasket from the oil pan groove unless replacement is required.**

To install:
4. Install a new oil pan seal, if required by starting the seal into the pan groove and working the seal into the groove in both directions.

✳✳WARNING

Once the seal is exposed to oil it will expand and no longer stay in the groove without wrinkles. If this happens, replace with a new seal.

5. Position the oil pan to the crankcase and install the 13 retaining bolts. Tighten the bolts to 9 ft. lbs. (10 Nm) in the sequence shown.

6. Install the engine as outlined in this Section and fill the crankcase with oil.

Oil Pump

REMOVAL

4.5L and 4.9L Engine
▶ See Figure 52

1. Jack up the car and support on jackstands.

2. Remove the oil pan following the procedures outlined earlier in this chapter.

3. Remove the two screws and one nut securing the oil pump to the engine.

✳✳CAUTION

The EPA warns that prolonged contact with used engine oil may cause a number of skin disorders, including cancer! You should make every effort to minimize your exposure to used engine oil. Protective gloves should be worn when changing the oil. Wash your hands and any other exposed skin areas as soon as possible after exposure to used engine oil. Soap and water, or waterless hand cleaner should be used.

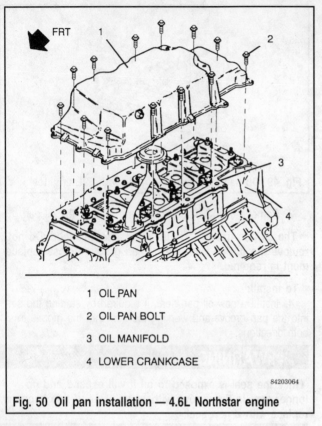

1 OIL PAN

2 OIL PAN BOLT

3 OIL MANIFOLD

4 LOWER CRANKCASE

84203064

Fig. 50 Oil pan installation — 4.6L Northstar engine

4.6L Northstar Engine

▶ **See Figure 53**

1. Remove the front cover as outlined in this Section.

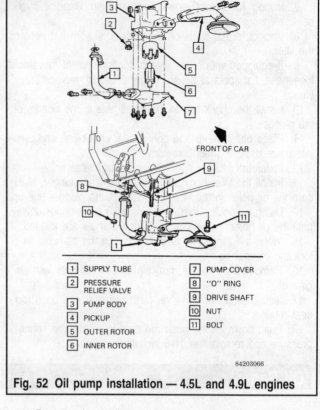

1	SUPPLY TUBE	7	PUMP COVER
2	PRESSURE RELIEF VALVE	8	"O" RING
3	PUMP BODY	9	DRIVE SHAFT
4	PICKUP	10	NUT
5	OUTER ROTOR	11	BOLT
6	INNER ROTOR		

84203066

Fig. 52 Oil pump installation — 4.5L and 4.9L engines

2. Remove the 3 oil pump mounting bolts.

3. Remove the pump and drive spacer.

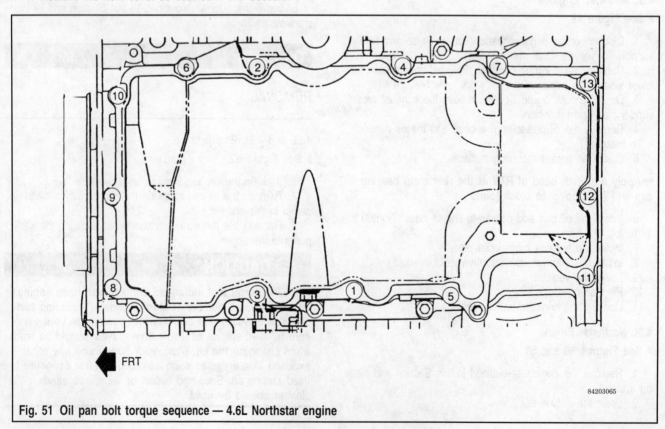

84203065

Fig. 51 Oil pan bolt torque sequence — 4.6L Northstar engine

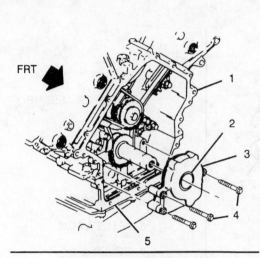

FRT

1 ENGINE UPPER CRANKCASE
2 OIL PUMP DRIVE SPACER
3 OIL PUMP
4 BOLT (3)
5 LOWER CRANKCASE

84203067

Fig. 53 Oil pump installation — 4.6L Northstar engine

INSPECTION

1. Inspect all components carefully for physical damage of any type and replace worn parts.
2. Check the pump housing for cracks, scoring, damaged threads or casting flaws.
3. Check the oil pump gears for chipping, galling or wear and replace if necessary.

OVERHAUL

4.5L and 4.9L Engines

1. Remove the drive shaft extension from the oil pump. DO NOT attempt to remove the washers from the shaft. The shaft extension and washers must be replaced as an assembly if the washers are not $1^{11}/_{32}$ inch (34mm) from the end of the shaft.
2. Remove the cotter pin, spring and the pressure regulator valve.

➡**Place your thumb over the pressure regulator bore before removing the cotter pin to contain the spring.**

3. Remove the oil pump cover attaching screws and remove the cover and gasket. Clean the pump in solvent or kerosene, and wash out the pick-up screen.
4. Remove the idler gear and drive gear from the pump body.
5. Check the gears for burrs and scoring. Install new gears, if necessary. Check the gear end clearance by placing a

straight edge over the gears and measure the clearance between the straight edge and the gasket surface with a feeler gauge. End clearance is 0.0015-0.0085 inches (0.038-0.216mm). If end clearance is excessive, check for scores in the cover that would bring the total clearance over the specs.

6. Check the side clearance by inserting the feeler gauge between the gear teeth and the side wall of the pump body. Clearance should be 0.002-0.005 inches 0.05-0.13mm).
7. Pack the inside of the pump body with petroleum jelly. DO NOT use engine oil. The pump MUST be primed this way or it won't produce any oil pressure when the engine is started.
8. Install the cover screws and tighten alternately and evenly to 8 ft. lbs.
9. Position the pressure regulator valve into the pump cover, closed end first, then install the spring and retaining pin.

➡**When assembling the drive shaft extension to the drive shaft, the end of the extension nearest the washers must be inserted into the drive shaft.**

10. Insert the drive shaft extension through the opening in the main bearing cap and block until the shaft mates into the distributor drive gear.

4.6L Northstar Engine

▶ See Figure 54

1. Remove the drive spacer from the pump housing.
2. Remove the 2 screws holding the pump housing halves together
3. Remove the inner (drive) and outer (driven) rotors out of the housing and mark the mating services.
4. Remove the pressure relief valve.
5. Install the inner (drive) and outer (driven) rotors, matching the marks made during disassembly.
6. Install the pressure relief valve seat, spring and pilot in the pump housing.
7. Assemble housing and cover over the locating dowel.
8. Insert a $^3/_8$ inch (9.5 mm) drill in the pump mounting hole on the opposite side to aid alignment of the housing and cover. Install the 2 screws and tighten to 9 ft. lbs. (12 Nm).

INSTALLATION

4.5L and 4.9L Engine

1. Assemble the oil pump
2. Replace the O-ring at the oil pump outlet pipe.
3. Position the oil pump to the engine block, engaging the drive rod to the distributor gear. Install the 2 screws and 1 nut. Tighten the nut to 22 ft. lbs.(30 Nm.) and screws to 15 ft. lbs.(20 Nm).
4. Install the oil pan.
5. Lower the vehicle.
6. Refill the crankcase with oil.

4.6L Northstar Engine

1. Install the pump drive spacer into the oil pump from the rear so the drive flat engages the pump rotor.

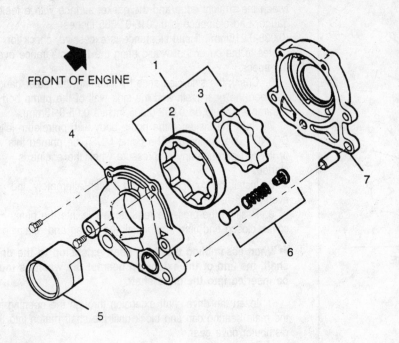

FRONT OF ENGINE

1 GEROTOR ASSEMBLY

2 OUTER GEAR

3 INNER GEAR

4 HOUSING

5 DRIVE SPACER

6 RELIEF VALVE

7 COVER

84203068

Fig. 54 Oil Pump and components — 4.6L Northstar engine

2. Position the oil pump over the crankshaft and loosely install the screws. Hold the pump in the furthest up position while tightening the screws to 7 ft. lbs. (10Nm) plus 35 °.

3. Install the front cover as outlined in this Section.

Crankshaft Damper

REMOVAL & INSTALLATION

4.5L Engine

▶ See Figures 55 and 56

1. Disconnect the negative battery cable.
2. Remove the serpentine belt.
3. Raise and support the vehicle.
4. Remove the right front wheel and tire.
5. Remove the right front air deflector.
6. Support the body of the car and the right side of the engine cradle.
7. Remove the right side cradle body bolts and lower the right side of the cradle.
8. Remove the crankshaft damper bolt and washer.
9. Install a puller and remove the damper.

To install:

10. Lubricate the bore of the hub and seal with EP lubricant.
11. Position the damper on the crankshaft lining up the key slot in the hub with the key on the crankshaft.
12. Use installer J 29774 or equivalent, and bottom the hub out on the crankshaft.
13. Install the crankshaft damper bolt and washer and tighten to 60 ft. lbs. (80 Nm).

14. Raise the right side of the cradle.

➡**Position the ball joint to the steering knuckle while raising.**

15. Support the body of the car and the right side of the engine cradle.
16. Install the right side engine cradle body bolts.
17. Install the right front air deflector.
18. Install the right front wheel and tire.
19. Lower the vehicle.
20. Connect the negative battery cable.

4.9L Engine

▶ See Figures 55 and 56

1. Disconnect the negative battery cable.
2. Remove the serpentine belt.
3. Raise and support the vehicle.
4. Remove the right front wheel and tire.
5. Remove the right front air deflector.

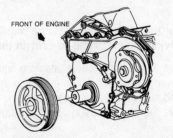

FRONT OF ENGINE

84203069

Fig. 55 Crankshaft and damper — 4.5L and 4.9L engines

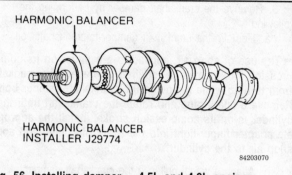

HARMONIC BALANCER

HARMONIC BALANCER
INSTALLER J29774

84203070

Fig. 56 Installing damper — 4.5L and 4.9L engines

6. Loosen and reposition the heater by-pass line.
7. Remove the crankshaft damper bolt and washer.
8. Install a puller and remove the damper.

To install:

9. Lubricate the bore of the hub and seal with EP lubricant.
10. Position the damper on the crankshaft lining up the key slot in the hub with the key on the crankshaft.
11. Use installer J 29774 or equivalent, and bottom the hub out on the crankshaft.
12. Install the crankshaft damper bolt and washer and tighten to 70 ft. lbs. (95 Nm).
13. Install the right front air deflector.
14. Install the right front wheel and tire.
15. Lower the vehicle.
16. Connect the negative battery cable.

Harmonic Balancer

REMOVAL& INSTALLATION

4.6L Northstar Engine

▶ **See Figures 57, 58 and 59**

1. Disconnect the negative battery cable.
2. Release tension from the accessory drive belt.
3. Raise and safely support the vehicle, remove the right front wheel.
4. Remove the splash shields from the wheelhouse and remove the brace between the oil pan and the transmission case.
5. Install the flywheel holder tool J 39411 or equivalent and remove the balancer bolt.
6. Support the engine cradle and remove the 3 bolts from the right side of the cradle.
7. Disconnect the RSS sensor from the right lower control arm.
8. Lower the engine cradle enough for clearance of puller tool.
9. Install pilot tool J39344-2 into the end of the crankshaft.
10. Remove the harmonic balancer using puller tool J38416 or equivalent.

To install:

11. Position the balancer to the crankshaft and using tool J39344 or equivalent install the balancer.

12. Clean the balancer bolt threads and apply oil to the threads. Tighten the balancer bolt to 105 ft. lbs. (145 Nm) + 120 degrees.
13. Raise the engine cradle into place and install the 3 bolts. Tighten the 3 bolts to 75 ft. lbs. (100 Nm).
14. Reconnect the suspension position sensors to the lower control arms.
15. Remove the flywheel holder tool and install the oil pan-to-trans brace. Tighten the 4 bolts to 35 ft. lbs. (50 Nm).
16. Install the wheel house splash shields and the right front wheel.
17. Lower the vehicle and install the accessory drive belt.
18. Connect the negative battery cable.

Engine Front Cover

REMOVAL & INSTALLATION

▶ **See Figure 60**

4.5L and 4.9L Engines

1. Disconnect the negative battery cable.
2. Drain the cooling system. Remove the air cleaner.
3. Remove the serpentine belt.
4. Remove the cross-car brace and coolant reservoir.
5. Remove the AIR air filter and bracket, if equipped.
6. Remove the water pump pulley bolts and the pulley. Remove the water pump from the vehicle.
7. Raise and safely support the vehicle.

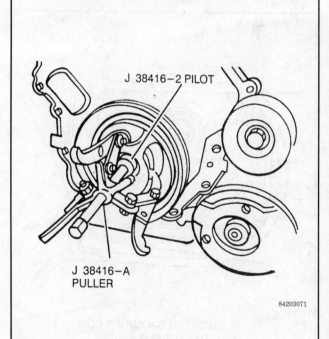

J 38416−2 PILOT

J 38416−A
PULLER

84203071

Fig. 57 Removing the harmonic balancer — 4.6L Northstar engine

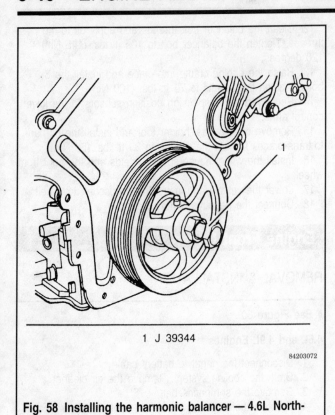

Fig. 58 Installing the harmonic balancer — 4.6L Northstar engine

8. Remove the crankshaft damper by performing the following:

a. Remove the crankshaft damper-to-crankshaft bolt.

➡The use of shop air, applied to a cylinder on its compression stroke, may be required to prevent the crankshaft from turning while removing the crankshaft damper bolt. Remove a spark plug and rotate the crankshaft until that cylinder is on its compression stroke. Install the appropriate adapter finger-tight into the spark plug hole and apply shop air to the cylinder.

b. Attach a wheel puller to the crankshaft damper.

c. Using a pilot between the crankshaft and the center bolt, press the crankshaft damper from the crankshaft.

d. Remove the Woodruff® key from the crankshaft.

9. Remove the timing case cover-to-engine bolts, the oil pan-to-timing case cover bolts and the cover.

To install:

10. Clean the gasket mounting surfaces.

11. To avoid oil leakage, apply RTV sealer according to the following:

a. Apply a bead of RTV on the front cover lip on the oil pan sealing surface. Ensure that this bead is placed along the front cover lip behind the 2 oil pan-to-front cover bolts.

b. Apply a ¼ inch bead of RTV on the oil pan where the oil pan, block and front cover join.

c. Remove any excess RTV that is squeezed out of the sealing area.

12. Install the front cover.

13. Install the crankshaft damper by performing the following:

a. Lubricate the bore of the hub and the inside diameter of the seal with EP lubricant.

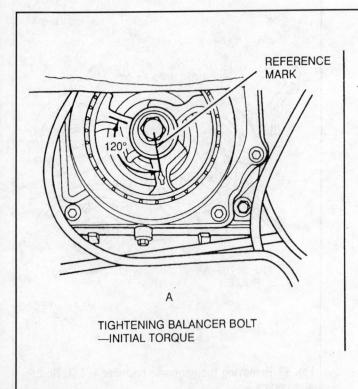

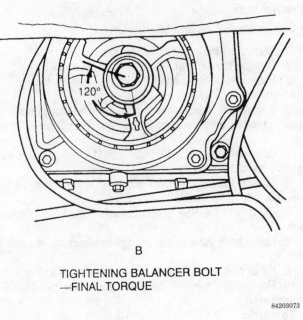

Fig. 59 Tightening the harmonic balancer bolt — 4.6L Northstar engine

b. Install the Woodruff® key in the key slot in the crankshaft.

c. Position the damper on the crankshaft, lining up the key slot with the key.

d. Thread the installer into the end of the crankshaft. Position the thrust bearing with the inner race forward, washer next and installer nut last.

e. Install the damper on the crankshaft by tightening the installer nut.

➡**The use of compressed air, applied to a cylinder on its compression stroke, may be required to prevent the crankshaft from turning while installing the crankshaft damper bolt. Remove a spark plug and rotate the crankshaft until that cylinder is on its compression stroke. Install an adapter finger-tight into the spark plug hole and apply shop air to the cylinder.**

f. Tighten nut until the hub bottoms out on the crankshaft. Tighten the nut to 60-65 ft. lbs. (80-90 Nm) to fully seat the balancer and timing gear. Remove the installer and reinstall the bolt and washer into the crankshaft. Tighten to 60-65 ft. lbs. (80-90 Nm).

g. Exhaust the compressed air to the cylinder, remove the adapter and reinstall the spark plug.

14. Lower the vehicle.
15. Install the water pump.
16. Install the water pump pulley.
17. Install the serpentine belt.
18. Install the coolant reservoir and cross-car brace.
19. Connect the negative battery cable.
20. Fill cooling system and check for leaks. Start the engine and allow to come to normal operating temperature. Recheck for leaks. Top-up coolant.

4.6L Engine
♦ **See Figure 61**

1. Disconnect the negative battery cable.
2. Remove the serpentine belt and the bolt securing the power steering hose.
3. Remove the harmonic balancer as described below:

a. Release tension from the accessory drive belt.

b. Raise and safely support the vehicle, remove the right front wheel.

c. Remove the splash shields from the wheelhouse and remove the brace between the oil pan and the transmission case.

d. Install the flywheel holder tool J39411 or equivalent and remove the balancer bolt.

e. Support the engine cradle and remove the 3 bolts from the right side of the cradle.

f. Disconnect the RSS sensor from the right lower control arm.

g. Lower the engine cradle enough for clearance of puller tool.

h. Install pilot tool J39344-2 into the end of the crankshaft.

i. Remove the harmonic balancer using puller tool J38416 or equivalent.

4. Remove the belt tensioner and the belt idler pulley.
5. Remove the front cover bolts and remove the cover with the gasket.

To install:
6. Install the cover gasket over the dowel pins.
7. Install the front cover over the dowel pins and tighten the cover screws to 7 ft. lbs. (10 Nm).
8. Install the idler pulley and the belt tensioner. Tighten both to 35 ft. lbs. (50 Nm).
9. Install the harmonic balancer as described below:

a. Position the balancer to the crankshaft and using tool J39344 or equivalent install the balancer.

b. Clean the balancer bolt threads and apply oil to the threads. Tighten the balancer bolt to 105 ft. lbs. (145 Nm) + 120 degrees.

c. Raise the engine cradle into place and install the 3 bolts. Tighten the 3 bolts to 75 ft. lbs. (100 Nm).

d. Reconnect the suspension position sensors to the lower control arms.

e. Remove the flywheel holder tool and install the oil pan-to-trans brace. Tighten the 4 bolts to 35 ft. lbs. (50 Nm).

f. Install the wheel house splash shields and the right front wheel.

g. Lower the vehicle and install the accessory drive belt.

h. Remove any excess RTV that is squeezed out of the sealing area.

10. Install the serpentine drive belt and connect the negative battery cable.

Front Cover Oil Seal

REPLACEMENT

4.5L and 4.9L Engines
♦ **See Figures 62 and 63**

1. Disconnect the negative battery cable.
2. Remove the serpentine belt.
3. Raise and safely support the vehicle.
4. Remove right front tire. Remove right front air deflector.
5. Loosen and reposition the heater bypass line.
6. Remove the crankshaft pulley-to-crankshaft pulley bolt. Attach a wheel puller to the crankshaft pulley. Using a pilot between the crankshaft and the center bolt, press the crankshaft pulley from the crankshaft. Remove the Woodruff® key from the crankshaft.
7. Using a small prybar, pry the oil seal from the timing case cover, discard it.

To install:
8. Clean the oil seal mounting surface. Lubricate the new seal with engine oil.
9. Using a hammer and the oil seal installation tool, drive the new oil seal into the timing case cover until it seats.
10. Lubricate bore of hub and inside diameter of seal with EP lubricant to prevent seizure to crankshaft and provide lubrication of oil seal lip.
11. Position damper on crankshaft, lining up key slot in hub with key on crankshaft.
12. Position installer on end of crankshaft. Position thrust bearing with inner race forward, then washer and installer nut last. Install damper on crankshaft by tightening installer nut.
13. Hub will bottom out on crankshaft. Tighten installer nut to 65 ft. lbs. (90 Nm) to ensure balancer and timing gear are

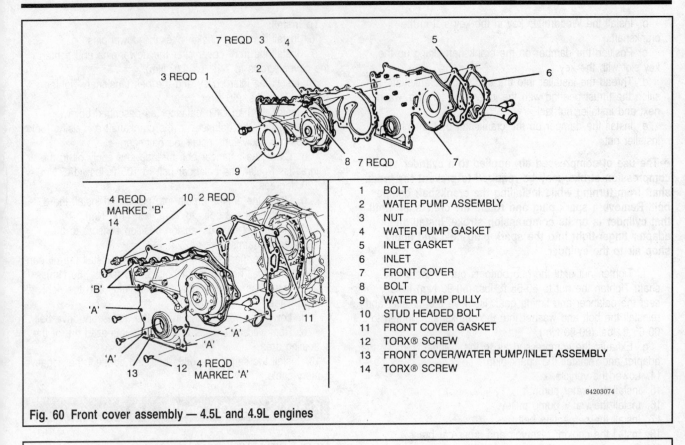

1 BOLT
2 WATER PUMP ASSEMBLY
3 NUT
4 WATER PUMP GASKET
5 INLET GASKET
6 INLET
7 FRONT COVER
8 BOLT
9 WATER PUMP PULLY
10 STUD HEADED BOLT
11 FRONT COVER GASKET
12 TORX® SCREW
13 FRONT COVER/WATER PUMP/INLET ASSEMBLY
14 TORX® SCREW

84203074

Fig. 60 Front cover assembly — 4.5L and 4.9L engines

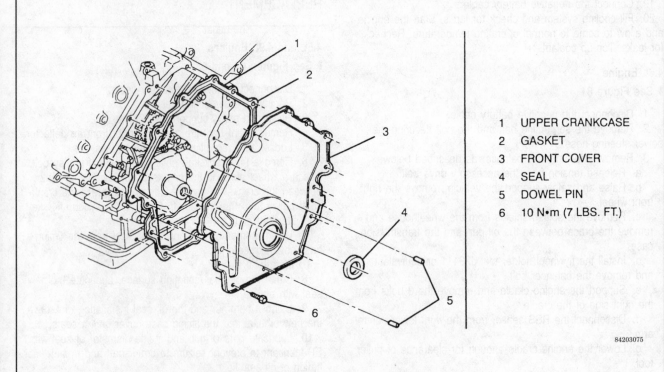

1 UPPER CRANKCASE
2 GASKET
3 FRONT COVER
4 SEAL
5 DOWEL PIN
6 10 N•m (7 LBS. FT.)

84203075

Fig. 61 Front cover assembly — 4.6L Northstar engine

fully seated. Remove installer and reinstall bolt/washer in crankshaft. Tighten to 65 ft. lbs. (90 Nm).

14. Install heater bypass line.

15. Install right front air deflector. Install right front tire.
16. Install serpentine belt.
17. Connect negative battery cable.

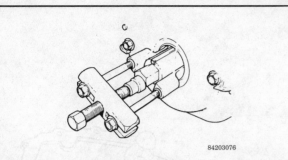

Fig. 62 Front cover oil seal removal — 4.5L and 4.9L engines

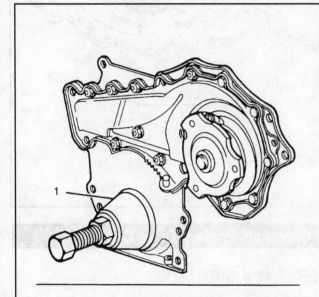

1 FRONT COVER OIL SEAL INSTALLER J29662

Fig. 63 Front cover oil seal installation — 4.5L and 4.9L engines

4.6L Engine

▶ See Figures 64 and 65

1. Disconnect the negative battery cable.
2. Remove the harmonic balancer as described below:

a. Release tension from the accessory drive belt.

b. Raise and safely support the vehicle, remove the right front wheel.

c. Remove the splash shields from the wheelhouse and remove the brace between the oil pan and the transmission case.

d. Install the flywheel holder tool J39411 or equivalent, and remove the balancer bolt.

e. Support the engine cradle and remove the 3 bolts from the right side of the cradle.

f. Disconnect the RSS sensor from the right lower control arm.

g. Lower the engine cradle enough for clearance of puller tool.

h. Install pilot tool J39344-2 into the end of the crankshaft.

i. Remove the harmonic balancer using puller tool J38416 or equivalent.

3. Using a small prybar, pry the oil seal out of the bore. Use caution not to damage the bore. Discard the old oil seal.

To install:

4. Clean the oil seal mounting surface. Lubricate the new seal with engine oil.

5. Install the new seal to the front cover, using seal installer tool J38818 and harmonic balancer installation tool J39344 or equivalents.

6. Install the harmonic balancer as described below:

a. Position the balancer to the crankshaft and using tool J39344 or equivalent install the balancer.

b. Clean the balancer bolt threads and apply oil to the threads. Tighten the balancer bolt to 105 ft. lbs. (145 Nm) + 120 degrees.

c. Raise the engine cradle into place and install the 3 bolts. Tighten the 3 bolts to 75 ft. lbs. (100 Nm).

d. Reconnect the suspension position sensors to the lower control arms.

e. Remove the flywheel holder tool and install the oil pan-to-trans brace. Tighten the 4 bolts to 35 ft. lbs. (50 Nm).

f. Install the wheel house splash shields and the right front wheel.

g. Lower the vehicle and install the accessory drive belt.

h. Remove any excess RTV that is squeezed out of the sealing area.

7. Connect the negative battery cable.

Timing Chain and Sprockets

REMOVAL & INSTALLATION

▶ See Figure 66

1. Disconnect the negative battery cable. Remove the front cover.

2. Remove the oil slinger from the crankshaft. Rotate the Engine to align the sprocket timing marks; the No. 1 cylinder will be on the TDC of its compression stroke.

3. From the camshaft, remove the camshaft thrust button and screw. Discard the camshaft thrust button. Slide the

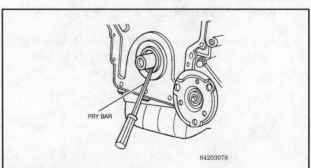

PRY BAR

Fig. 64 Front cover oil seal removal — 4.6L Northstar engine

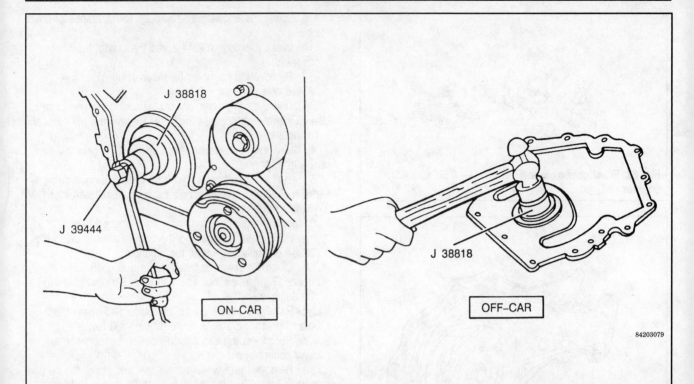

Fig. 65 Front cover oil seal installation — 4.6L Northstar engine

camshaft sprocket, the crankshaft sprocket and timing chain from the Engine as an assembly.

To install:

4. Clean the gasket mounting surfaces. Inspect the parts for wear and/or damage; if necessary, replace the parts.

5. Install the timing chain and sprockets by performing the following:

   a. Assemble the timing chain on the camshaft sprocket and crankshaft sprockets.

   b. Align the timing marks on the sprockets; they must face each other.

   c. Align the dowel pin in the camshaft with the index hole in the sprocket.

   d. Slide the assembly onto the camshaft and crankshaft. Install the camshaft sprocket-to-camshaft bolts. Torque the camshaft sprocket-to-camshaft sprocket bolt to 37 ft. lbs. (50 Nm).

6. Install the new thrust button and install the oil slinger to the crankshaft.

7. Install the front cover. Connect the negative battery cable.

8. Refill the cooling system. Start the engine, allow it to reach normal operating temperatures and check for leaks.

Camshaft Primary Drive Chain

REMOVAL & INSTALLATION

4.6L Engine

▶ **See Figure 67**

1. Remove the engine assembly and put on a engine stand or remove the powertrain assembly. Both procedures are outlined earlier in this Section.

2. Remove the serpentine drive belt, idler pulley and belt tensioner, if not done previously.

3. Remove the front cover and oil pump as outlined in this Section.

4. Remove the cam covers as outlined in this Section.

5. Remove the 3 timing chain tensioners.

6. Remove the camshaft sprocket bolt from all 4 camshafts and remove the sprockets.

7. Remove the secondary drive chains from around the intermediate shaft sprocket.

8. Remove the 1 bolt the intermediate shaft sprocket and slide the gears and the primary drive chain off the crankshaft and intermediate shaft.

➡**The intermediate shaft need not be removed unless wear is evident.**

To install:

9. Retime the camshafts as outlined under 'Resetting Camshaft Timing' in this Section.

10. Install the oil pump as outlined in this Section.

11. Install the cam covers as outlined in this Section.

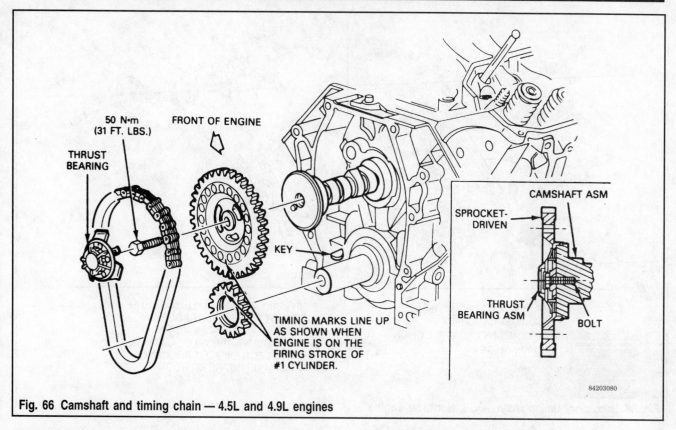

Fig. 66 Camshaft and timing chain — 4.5L and 4.9L engines

12. Install the serpentine drive belt, idler pulley and belt tensioner.

13. Install the engine assembly or the powertrain assembly. Both procedures are outlined earlier in this Section.

Camshaft Secondary Drive Chain

REMOVAL & INSTALLATION

4.6L Engine

▶ See Figure 68

1. Remove the front cover as outlined in this Section.
2. Remove the left side cam covers as outlined in this Section.
3. Remove the left side secondary chain tesioner.
4. Remove the left side chain guide. Access the upper chain guide mounting bolt thru the hole in the cylinder head covered with the plastic plug.
5. Remove the left side cam sprocket bolts and sprockets.
6. Remove the secondary drive chain.
7. Repeat Steps 2 thru 6 if the right side chain is being replaced.

To install:

8. Retime the camshafts as outlined under 'Resetting Camshaft Timing' in this Section.
9. Install the front cover as outlined in this Section.
10. Install the cam cover(s) as outlined in this Section.

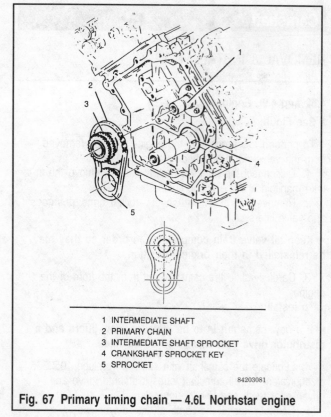

1 INTERMEDIATE SHAFT
2 PRIMARY CHAIN
3 INTERMEDIATE SHAFT SPROCKET
4 CRANKSHAFT SPROCKET KEY
5 SPROCKET

84203081

Fig. 67 Primary timing chain — 4.6L Northstar engine

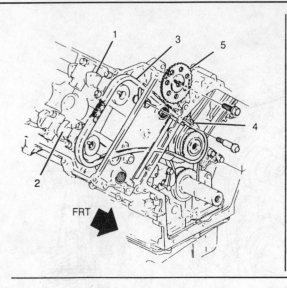

1 INTAKE CAMSHAFT
2 EXHAUST CAMSHAFT
3 SECONDARY CAM DRIVE CHAIN
4 CHAIN GUIDE

5 RH SPROCKET – INSTALL CAM PIN IN
RE SLOT FOR EXHAUST POSITION;
RI SLOT FOR INTAKE POSITION
6 LH SPROCKET – INSTALL CAM PIN IN
LE SLOT FOR EXHAUST POSITION;
LI SLOT FOR INTAKE POSITION

84203082

Fig. 68 Secondary timing chain — 4.6L Northstar engine

Camshaft

REMOVAL & INSTALLATION

4.5L and 4.9L Engines

▶ **See Figure 66**

To perform this procedure, the engine must be removed from the vehicle and attached to an engine stand.
1. Disconnect the negative battery cable. Remove the intake manifold and the timing chain.
2. Remove the rocker arm covers, rocker arms, pushrods and valve lifters.

➡**Keep all valve train components in order so they may be reinstalled in their original positions.**

3. Carefully slide the camshaft out from the front of the engine.
To install:

➡**If a new camshaft is to be installed, new lifters and a distributor drive gear must also be installed.**

4. Lubricate the camshaft with camshaft prelube 1052365 or equivalent, on all camshaft lobes, distributor drive and driven gear teeth and bearing journals.
5. Carefully, install the camshaft into the engine.
6. Install the camshaft sprocket-to-camshaft bolt and tighten to 31 ft. lbs. (50 Nm).
7. Install the lifters, pushrods and rocker arms in their original positions. Install the rocker arm covers.

8. Install the timing chain and intake manifold.
9. Connect the negative battery cable.

4.6L Northstar Engine

▶ **See Figures 69 and 70**

1. Remove the cam cover as outlined in this Section.
2. Secure the cam sprocket to the timing chain by installing tie straps through the cam sprocket holes.

➡**The sprocket/chain relationship must be maintained throughout this procedure or camshaft timing will be lost and require further engine disassembly to retime.**

3. Working from behind the sprockets, install the cam chain holder J 38815 so that it is positioned between the chain tensioner and chain guide. Apply tension to the tool by tightening the tension adjusting screw.
4. Remove both cam sprocket bolts. Note the relative location of the cam drive pins in the end of the camshafts.
5. Work the sprockets off the cams using play in the chain.
6. Alternately loosen the cam bearing cap screws a few turns at a time until all valve spring pressure has been released. Remove the bolts and caps.
7. Remove the camshaft.
8. Inspect the camshaft for excessive lobe wear such as the evidence of grooves, scoring or flaking and replace as necessary.
To install:
9. Lubricate the camshaft with camshaft prelube 1052365 or equivalent, on all camshaft lobes.
10. Install the camshaft.

11. Position the cam bearing caps to the cylinder head.

➡Each cap is identified for position and direction. The arrow points towards the front of the engine. An 'E' indicates a cap for the exhaust cam. An 'I' indicates a cap for the intake cam. Position No. 1 is towards the front of the engine.

12. Loosely install the cam bearing bolts.

13. Alternately tighten the cam bearing cap screws a few turns at a time until against valve spring pressure until the bolts are snug. Tighten the bolts to 9 ft. lbs. (12 Nm).

14. Using the hex cast into the camshaft, rotate the cams until the drive pins are in position to engage the cam sprockets over the cams and install the retaining bolts.

15. Work the cam sprockets over cams and install the retaining bolts. Tighten the bolts to 90 ft. lbs. (120 Nm).

16. Remove the chain holder J 38815.

17. Remove the tie straps from the cam sprockets.

18. Install the cam cover as outlined in this Section.

SETTING CAMSHAFT TIMING

4.6L Northstar Engine

▶ See Figures 71, 72 and 73

Setting camshaft timing is necessary whenever the cam drive system has been disturbed such that the relationship between any chain and sprocket has been lost. Correct timing exist when the crank sprocket and the intermediate shaft sprocket have their timing marks aligned and all 4 camshaft

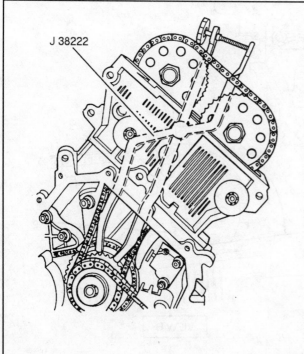

Fig. 69 Holding the drive chain tension — 4.6L Northstar engine

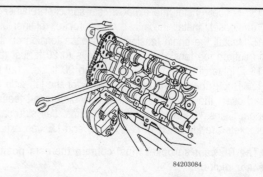

Fig. 70 Rotating the camshaft — 4.6L Northstar engine

drive pins are perpendicular (90 °) to the cylinder head surface.

1. To allow access the following components must be removed:
   a. Both cam covers.
   b. Front cover
   c. The 3 chain tensioners. The tensioners may be in their installed positions but must be fully retracted.
   d. The oil pump.

2. The primary and secondary chain guides should be reinstalled if previously removed.

3. Rotate the crankshaft until the sprocket drive key is at approximately the 1 o'clock position. Use J 39946 to rotate the crankshaft.

4. Install the crankshaft and intermediate shaft sprockets to the primary drive chain with their timing marks adjacent to each other.

5. Install the crank and intermediate sprockets over their respective shafts.

6. Rotate the crankshaft as necessary to engage the crankshaft key in the sprocket without changing the relationship of the timing marks to each other. Use J 39946 to rotate the crankshaft.

7. Install the intermediate sprocket retainer bolt and tighten to 45 ft. lbs. (60 Nm).

8. Install the primary chain tensioner or release tensioner shoe. Tighten the 2 tensioner mounting bolts to 20 ft. lbs. (25 Nm).

9. Install flywheel holder J 39411 to lock the crankshaft in this position. If the engine is on a stand an alternate method should be devised.

10. Route the secondary drive chain for the right side cylinder head over the inner row of the intermediate shaft teeth.

11. Route the secondary drive chain over the chain guide and install the exhaust cam sprocket to the chain such that the camshaft drive pin engages the sprocket notch RE (right head exhaust). There should be no slack in the lower section of the chain and the cam drive pin must be perpendicular to the cylinder head face.

➡The RE cam sprocket must contain the cam position sensor pick-up.

12. Install the intake cam sprocket into the chain so that the sprocket notch RI (right head intake) engages the camshaft drive pin remains perpendicular to the cylinder head face. A hex is cast into the camshafts behind the lobes for cylinder No. 1 (or No. 2, LH) so that an open end wrench may be used to provide minor repositioning of the cams.

13. Loosely install the exhaust cam sprocket retainer bolt.

14. Loosely install the intake cam sprocket retainer bolt.

15. Install the chain tensioner or release tension on the shoe and tighten the tensioner mounting bolts to 20 ft. lbs. (25 Nm).

16. Tighten the cam sprocket bolts to 90 ft lbs. (120 Nm).

17. Route the secondary drive chain for the left side cylinder head over the inner row of the intermediate shaft teeth and repeat Steps 11 thru 16 for left side cams. Left side cam sprockets are identified **LI** (left intake) and **LE** (left exhaust).

➡**The RE cam sprocket must contain the cam position sensor pick-up.**

Pistons and Connecting Rods

REMOVAL & INSTALLATION

Before removing the pistons, the top of the cylinder bore must be examined for a ridge. A ridge at the top of the bore is the result of normal cylinder wear, caused by the piston rings only travelling so far up the bore in the course of the piston stroke. The ridge can be felt by hand; it must be removed before the pistons are removed.

A ridge reamer is necessary for this operation. Place the piston at the bottom of its stroke, and cover it with a rag. Cut the ridge away with the ridge reamer, using extreme care to avoid cutting too deeply. Remove the rag, and remove the cuttings that remain on the piston with a magnet and a rag

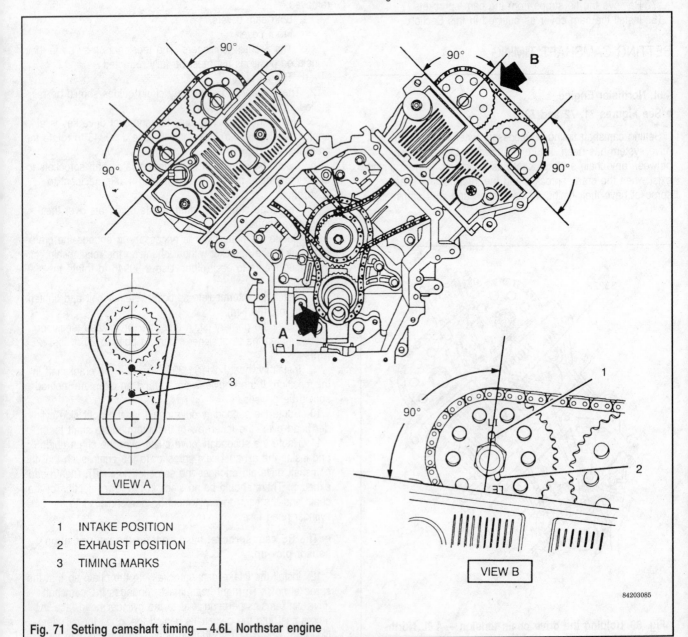

1. INTAKE POSITION
2. EXHAUST POSITION
3. TIMING MARKS

VIEW A

VIEW B

84203085

Fig. 71 Setting camshaft timing — 4.6L Northstar engine

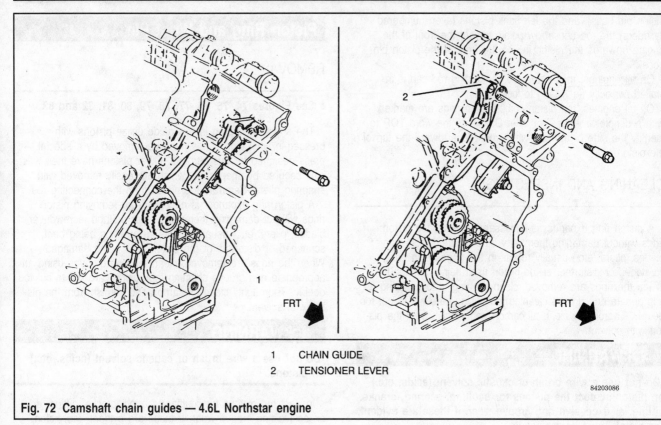

1	CHAIN GUIDE
2	TENSIONER LEVER

84203086

Fig. 72 Camshaft chain guides — 4.6L Northstar engine

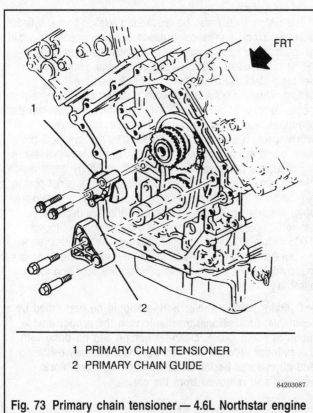

1	PRIMARY CHAIN TENSIONER
2	PRIMARY CHAIN GUIDE

84203087

Fig. 73 Primary chain tensioner — 4.6L Northstar engine

soaked in clean oil. Make sure the piston top and cylinder bore are absolutely clean before moving the piston.

1. Remove intake manifold and cylinder head or heads.

2. Remove oil pan.

3. Remove oil pump assembly if necessary.

4. Matchmark the connecting rod cap to the connecting rod with a scribe; each cap must be reinstalled on its proper rod in the proper direction. Remove the connecting rod bearing cap and the rod bearing. Number the top of each piston with silver paint or a felt-tip pen for later assembly.

5. Cut lengths of ⅜-inch diameter hose to use as rod bolt guides. Install the hose over the threads of the rod bolts, to prevent the bolt threads from damaging the crankshaft journals and cylinder walls when the piston is removed.

6. Squirt some clean engine oil onto the cylinder wall from above, until the wall is coated. Carefully push the piston and rod assembly up and out of the cylinder by tapping on the bottom of the connecting rod with a wooden hammer handle.

7. Place the rod bearing and cap back on the connecting rod, and install the nuts temporarily. Using a number stamp or punch, stamp the cylinder number on the side of the connecting rod and cap this will help keep the proper piston and rod assembly on the proper cylinder.

8. Remove remaining pistons in similar manner.

On all engines, the notch or arrow on the piston will face the front of the engine for assembly.

On the 4.5L and 4.9L engines the connecting rods can be installed in either direction, there is no front or back to the connecting rods since the offset for the assembly is located in the piston.

On the 4.6L Northstar engine, make sure the arrows on the bearing caps face each other for each pair of rods on the crank throw.

On the 4.6L Northstar engine, the right bank pistons (odd numbered cylinders) the rod cap arrow points toward the rear of the engine (away from the piston lug on the front of the piston pin boss), and the left bank pistons (even numbered cylinders) the rod cap arrow points toward the front of the engine (towards the piston lug on the front of the piston pin boss).

On all engines, make sure the connecting rod cap is installed correctly (lock tang to lock tang.

On all engines, the piston compression rings are marked with a dimple, a letter **T**, a letter **O**, **GM** or the word **TOP** to identify the side of the ring which must face toward the top of the piston.

CLEANING AND INSPECTING

A piston ring expander is necessary for removing piston rings without damaging them; any other method (screwdriver blades, pliers, etc.) usually results in the rings being bent, scratched or distorted, or the piston itself being damaged. When the rings are removed, clean the ring grooves using an appropriate ring groove cleaning tool, using care not to cut too deeply. Thoroughly clean all carbon and varnish from the piston with solvent.

✳✳WARNING

Do not use a wire brush or caustic solvent (acids, etc.) on piston!Inspect the pistons for scuffing, scoring, cranks, pitting, or excessive ring groove wear. If these are evident, the piston must be replaced.

The piston should also be checked in relation to the cylinder diameter. Using a telescoping gauge and micrometer, or a dial gauge, measure the cylinder bore diameter perpendicular (90%) to the piston pin, 2½ inches (63.5mm) below the cylinder block deck (surface where the block mates with the heads). Then, with the micrometer, measure the piston perpendicular to its wrist pin on the skirt. The difference between the two measurements is the piston clearance.

If the clearance is within specifications or slightly below (after the cylinders have been bored or honed), finish honing is all that is necessary. If the clearance is excessive try to obtain a slightly larger piston to being clearance to within specifications. If this is not possible obtain the first oversize piston and hone (or if necessary, bore) the cylinder to size. Generally, if the cylinder bore is tapered 0.005 inches (0.13mm) or more or is out-of-round 0.003 inches (0.08mm) or more, it is advisable to rebore for the smallest possible oversize piston and rings. After measuring, mark pistons with a felt-tip pen for reference and for assembly.

➡Cylinder block boring should be performed by a reputable machine shop with the proper equipment. In some cases, cleanup honing can be done with the cylinder block in the car, but most excessive honing and all cylinder boring must be done with the block stripped and removed from the car.

Piston Ring and Wrist Pin

REMOVAL

▶ **See Figures 74, 75, 76, 77, 78, 79, 80, 81, 82 and 83**

The engines covered in this guide utilize pistons with pressed-in wrist pins; these must be removed by a special press designed for this purpose. Other pistons have their wrist pins secured by snap rings, which are easily removed with snapring pliers. Separate the piston from the connecting rod.

A piston ring expander is necessary for removing piston rings without damaging them; any other method (screwdriver blades, pliers, etc.) usually results in the rings being bent, scratched or distorted, or the piston itself being damaged. When the rings are removed, clean the ring grooves using an appropriate ring groove cleaning tool, using care not to cut too deeply. Thoroughly clean all carbon and varnish from the piston with solvent.

✳✳WARNING

Do not use a wire brush or caustic solvent (acids, etc.) on pistons.

Inspect the pistons for scuffing, scoring, cracks, pitting, or excessive ring groove wear. If these are evident, the piston must be replaced.

The piston should also be checked in relation to the cylinder diameter. Using a telescoping gauge and micrometer, or a dial gauge, measure the cylinder bore diameter perpendicular (90%) to the piston pin, 2½ inches (63.5mm) below the cylinder block deck (surface where the block mates with the heads). Then, with the micrometer, measure the piston perpendicular to its wrist pin on the skirt. The difference between the two measurements is the piston clearance. If the clearance is within specifications or slightly below (after the cylinders have been bored or honed), finish honing is all that is necessary. If the clearance is excessive, try to obtain a slightly larger piston to bring clearance to within specifications. If this is not possible, obtain the first oversize piston and hone (or if necessary, bore) the cylinder to size. Generally, if the cylinder bore is tapered 0.005 inches (0.13mm) or more or is out-of-round 0.003 inches (0.08mm) or more, it is advisable to rebore for the smallest possible oversize piston and rings. After measuring, mark pistons with a felt-tip pen for reference and for assembly.

➡Cylinder honing and/or boring should be performed by a reputable, professional mechanic with the proper equipment. In some cases, clean-up honing can be done with the cylinder block in the car, but most excessive honing and all cylinder boring must be done with the block stripped and removed from the car.

CONNECTING ROD BEARINGS

Connecting rod bearings for the engines covered in this guide consist of two halves or shells which are interchangeable in the rod and cap. When the shells are placed in position, the

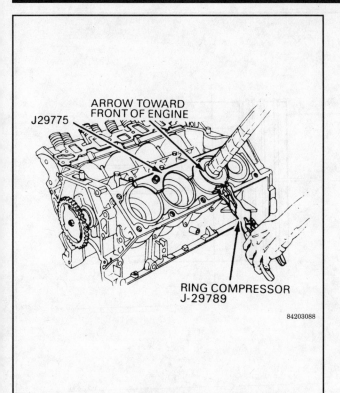

Fig. 74 Installing the piston using the piston ring compressor — 4.5L and 4.9L engines

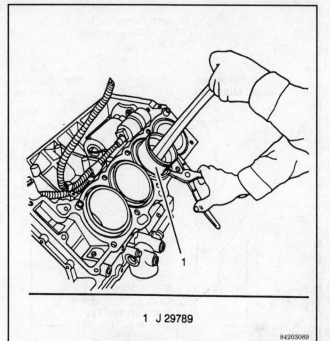

Fig. 75 Installing the piston using the piston ring compressor — 4.6L Northstar engine

ends extend slightly beyond the rod and cap surfaces so that when the rod bolts are torqued the shells will be clamped

tightly in place to insure positive seating and to prevent turning. A tang holds the shells in place.

➡**The ends of the bearing shells must never be filed flush with the mating surface of the rod and cap.**

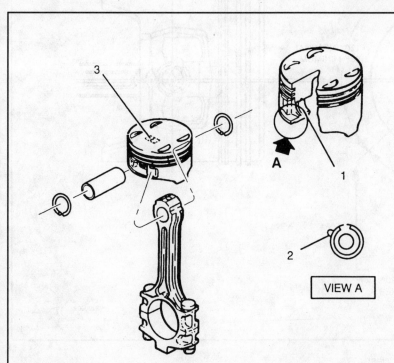

1	RETAINER GROOVE
2	REMOVAL ACCESS SLOT
3	ORIENTATION ARROW

Fig. 76 Piston and rod assembly — 4.6L Northstar engine

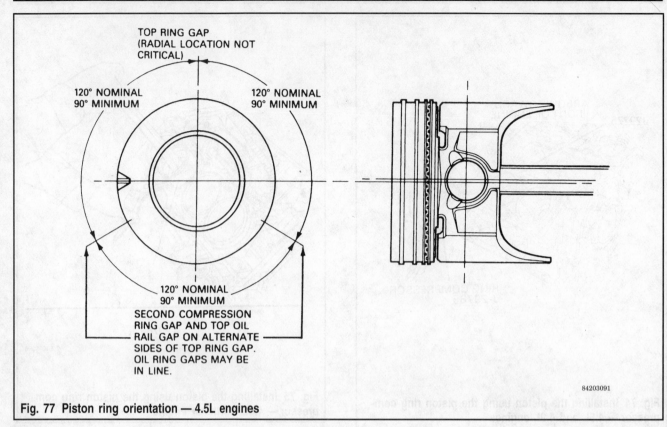

Fig. 77 Piston ring orientation — 4.5L engines

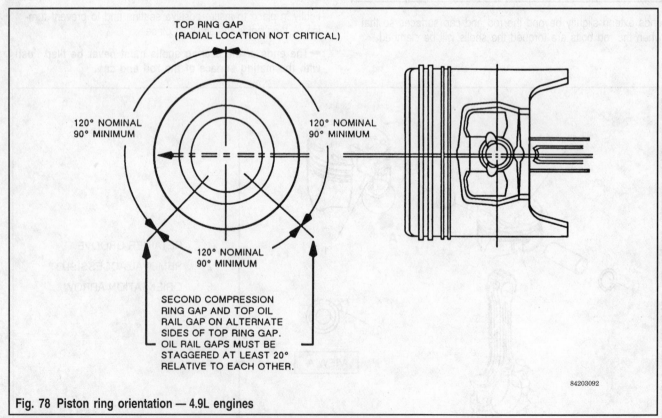

Fig. 78 Piston ring orientation — 4.9L engines

If a rod bearing becomes noisy or is worn so that its clearance on the crank journal is sloppy, a new bearing of the

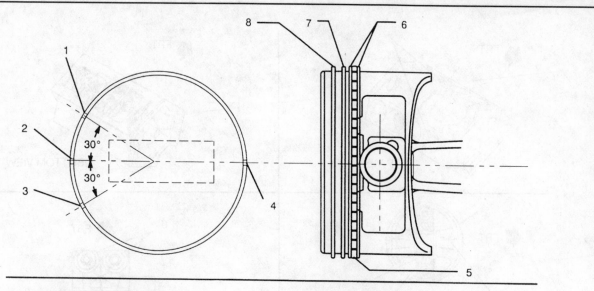

1	OIL RING SEGMENT GAP	5	EXPANDER RING
2	UPPER COMPRESSION RING GAP	6	OIL SEGMENT RINGS
3	OIL RING SEGMENT GAP	7	LOWER COMPRESSION RING
4	EXPANDER & LOWER COMPRESSION RING GAPS	8	UPPER COMPRESSION RING

Fig. 79 Piston ring orientation — 4.6L Northstar engine

correct undersize must be selected and installed since there is no provision for adjustment.

> **✷✷WARNING**
>
> Under no circumstances should the rod end or cap be filed to adjust the bearing clearance, nor should shims of any kind be used.

Inspect the rod bearings while the rod assemblies are out of the engine. If the shells are scored or show flaking, they should be replaced. If they are in good shape check for proper clearance on the crank journal (see below). Any scoring or ridges on the crank journal means the crankshaft must be replaced, or reground and fitted with undersized bearings.

CHECKING BEARING CLEARANCE AND REPLACING BEARINGS

➡️**Make sure connecting rods and their caps are kept together, and that the caps are installed in the proper direction.**

Replacement bearings are available in standard size, and in undersizes for reground crankshafts. Connecting rod-to-crankshaft bearing clearance is checked using Plastigage at either the top or bottom of each crank journal. The Plastigage has a range of 0.001-0.003 inches (0.025-0.080mm).

1. Remove the rod cap with the bearing shell. Completely clean the bearing shell and the crank journal, and blow any oil from the oil hole in the crankshaft; Plastigage is soluble in oil.

2. Place a piece of Plastigage lengthwise along the bottom center of the lower bearing shell, then install the cap with shell and torque the bolt or nuts to specification. DO NOT turn the crankshaft with Plastigage in the bearing.

3. Remove the bearing cap with the shell. The flattened Plastigage will be found sticking to either the bearing shell or crank journal. Do not remove it yet.

4. Use the scale printed on the Plastigage envelope to measure the flattened material at its widest point. The number within the scale which most closely corresponds to the width of the Plastigage indicates bearing clearance in thousandths of an inch.

5. Check the specifications chart in this chapter for the desired clearance. It is advisable to install a new bearing if clearance exceeds 0.003 inches (0.08mm); however, if the bearing is in good condition and is not being checked because of bearing noise, bearing replacement is not necessary.

6. If you are installing new bearings, try a standard size, then each undersize in order until one is found that is within the specified limits when checked for clearance with Plastigage. Each undersize shell has its size stamped on it.

7. When the proper size shell is found, clean off the Plastigage, oil the bearing thoroughly, reinstall the cap with its shell and torque the rod bolt units to specification.

➡️**With the proper bearing selected and the nuts torqued, it should be possible to move the connecting rod back and forth freely on the crank journal as allowed by the specified connecting rod end clearance. If the rod cannot be moved, either the rod bearing is too far undersize or the rod is misaligned.**

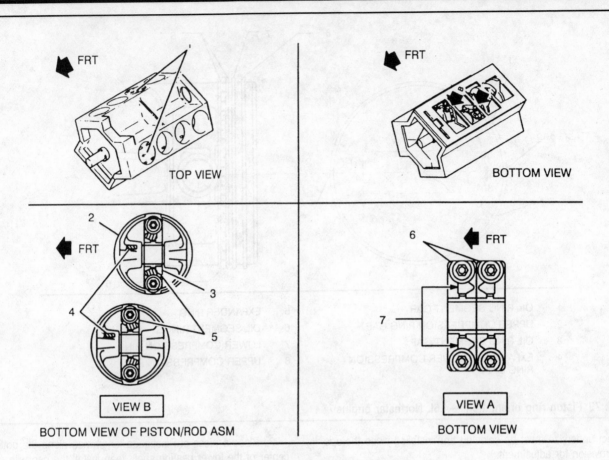

1 PISTON ARROW TOWARD CHAIN CASE ON BOTH SIDES
2 PISTON
3 ROD CAP
4 LOCATER LUGS INDICATE PISTON FRONT TOWARDS ENGINE FRONT
5 BEARING CAP ARROWS POINT TOWARD EACH OTHER ON PAIRED RODS
6 ROD CAPS
7 BEARING CAP ARROWS POINT TOWARD EACH OTHER ON PAIRED RODS

84203094

Fig. 80 Piston and rod orientation — 4.6L Northstar engine

PISTON AND CONNECTING ROD ASSEMBLY AND INSTALLATION

Install the connecting rod to the piston, making sure piston installation notches and any marks on the rod are in proper relation to one another. Lubricate the wrist pin with clean engine oil, and install the pin into the rod and piston assembly, either by hand or by using a wrist pin press as required. Install snap rings if equipped, and rotate them in their grooves to make sure they are seated. To install the piston and connecting rod assembly:

1. Make sure connecting rod big-end bearings (including end cap) are of the correct size and properly installed.

2. Fit rubber hoses over the connecting rod bolts to protect the crankshaft journals, as in the Piston Removal procedure. Coat the rod bearings with clean oil.

3. Using the proper ring compressor, insert the piston assembly into the cylinder so that the notch in the top of the piston faces the front of the engine (this assumes that the dimple(s) or other markings on the connecting rods are in correct relation to the piston notch(s).

4. From beneath the engine, coat each crank journal with clean oil. Pull the connecting rod, with the bearing shell in place, into position against the crank journal.

5. Remove the rubber hoses. Install the bearing cap and cap nuts and torque to specification.

➡ **When more than one rod and piston assembly is being installed, the connecting rod cap attaching nuts should only be tightened enough to keep each rod in position until all have been installed. This will ease the installation of the remaining piston assemblies.**

6. Check the clearance between the sides of the connecting rods and the crankshaft using a feeler gauge. Spread the

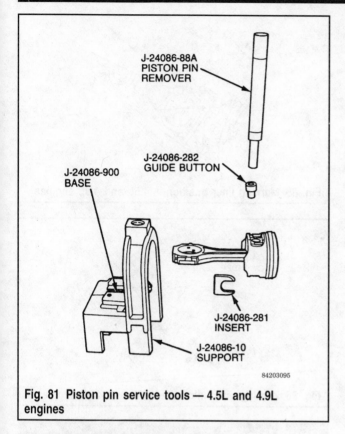

Fig. 81 Piston pin service tools — 4.5L and 4.9L engines

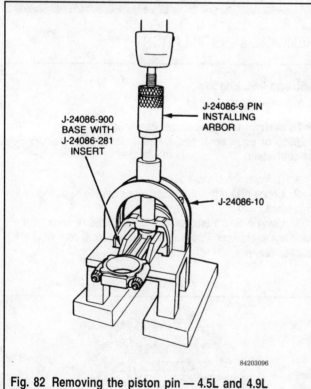

Fig. 82 Removing the piston pin — 4.5L and 4.9L engines

rods slightly with a screwdriver to insert the gauge. If clearance is below the minimum tolerance, the rod may be

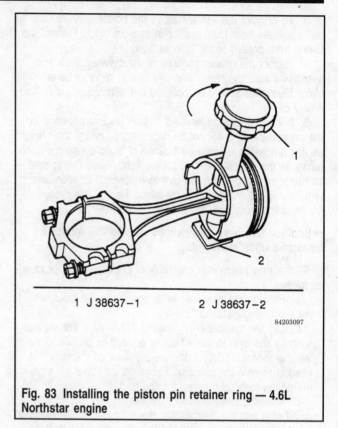

1 J 38637−1   2 J 38637−2

Fig. 83 Installing the piston pin retainer ring — 4.6L Northstar engine

machined to provide adequate clearance. If clearance is excessive, substitute an unworn rod, and recheck. If clearance is still outside specifications, the crankshaft must be welded and reground, or replaced.

7. Replace the oil pump if removed and the oil pan.
8. Install the cylinder head(s) and intake manifold.

Cylinder Liners

REMOVAL & INSTALLATION

4.5L and 4.9L Engines
▶ See Figures 84, 85, 86, 87 and 88

➡This procedure requires special tools; J-29775 cylinder liner holder, and J-29776 cylinder liner gauge. Also this is a complex procedure and is not recommended for the novice mechanic.

1. Remove the cylinder heads and install the cylinder liner holders J-29789.
2. Remove the oil pan and then remove the pistons as previously described.

➡Since the cylinder liners are removable it is necessary to keep the liner matched with the appropriate piston. Ink mark these assemblies as they are removed. Do not stamp liners with a punch stamp. Since it is possible to install the liners without regard to orientation, liners which will be replaced should be ink marked with their original position so that this orientation may be maintained during installation.

3. To remove the liners, remove the holder J-29775 and pull the liners from their position in cylinder block. Discard the O-ring from bottom of the cylinder liner.

4. Inspect the mating surfaces of the cylinder block and liner to be sure they are clean and free of nicks or burrs. Minor blemishes should be polished out with crocus cloth (fine emery cloth).

5. If liners are being installed in their original positions in the original block, it will not be necessary to gauge their height as this process was done on a select-fit basis during manufacturing. In this situation, install a new, lightly oiled O-ring seal on the liner and position the liner in its original position and with its original orientation in the block. Repeat this procedure for each liner removed. Install liner clamp J-29775.

➡**Engines that have experienced overheating must be measured upon reassembly.**

6. If a new piston/liner assembly is to be installed, proceed as follows:

a. Position the new liner in its position in the block without the O-ring installed.

b. Lay the cylinder liner gauge J-29776 on a flat surface such as the cylinder deck face or a piece of glass and zero the dial indicator. Only moderate pressure on the gauge is needed to zero the indicator. Excessive pressure will cause the gauge to bend creating a false zero.

c. Measure the liner height by inserting the spring loaded guide pins into the liner so that the machined pads rest on the edge of the liner and the dial indicator pointer contacts the block's deck face. Apply moderate pressure to the gauge until the pointer stops moving.

d. Read and record the dial reading. If this reading is on the + side of the dial, the cylinder liner is higher that the block face by the indicated amount. If this reading is on the - side of the dial, the cylinder liner is below the block face.

e. Repeat steps C and D at two more locations as shown.

f. Take the average of the three readings as the actual value for liner height. Example: Reading #1 + 5 (0.05mm). Reading #2 + 7 (0.07mm). Reading #3 + 3 (0.03mm). Total 15 divided by 3 = + 5

g. Correct liner height is +0.01mm to +008mm above cylinder deck face. If any liner is below +0.01mm (0.00 or a - value) or above +0.08mm, the liner must be replaced with another new assembly. Liners may be rotated in the block to obtain proper liner height. This orientation must be noted and re-established for final assembly.

h. If liner height is within the range of +0.01mm to +0.08mm, the liner-to-liner dimension must also be established before assembly is attempted.

i. To gauge liner-to-liner height, install the adjacent liner(s) in their original position and orientation without the O-ring. Using gauge J-29776 gauge between the liners while holding the second liner firmly in place with your free hand. This reading must be within ± 0.05mm (± on gauge). Ink mark the liner orientation once it is established.

7. Once the gauging operation is completed on all the new liner assemblies, liners should be installed in their respective positions using a new, lightly oiled, O-ring on each liner. Liners must be installed in the position and orientation in the block for which they have been gauged.

8. Install liner holders J-29775.

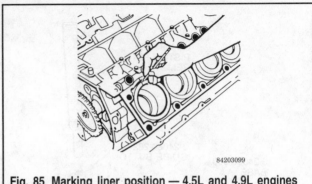

Fig. 85 Marking liner position — 4.5L and 4.9L engines

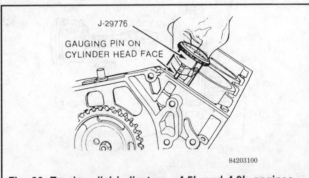

Fig. 86 Zeroing dial indicator — 4.5L and 4.9L engines

Rear Main Seal

REMOVAL & INSTALLATION

4.5L and 4.9L Engines

▶ See Figures 89 and 90

➡**To perform this procedure, use a Seal Removal tool No. J-26868 or equivalent, and a Seal Installer tool No. J-34604 or equivalent.**

1. Remove the transaxle.

2. Unbolt and remove the flexplate from the rear end of the crankshaft.

3. Using a Seal Removal tool No. J-26868 or equivalent, remove the old seal. Thoroughly clean the seal bore of any leftover seal material with a clean rag.

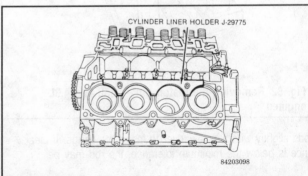

Fig. 84 Cylinder liner holders — 4.5L and 4.9L engines

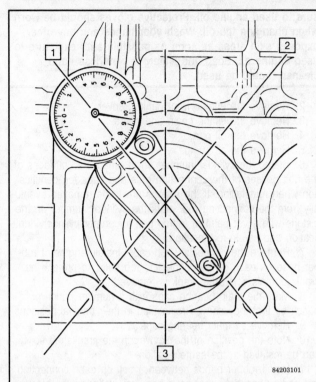

Fig. 87 Gaging cylinder liner height — 4.5L and 4.9L engines

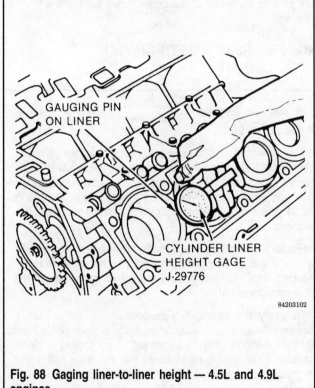

Fig. 88 Gaging liner-to-liner height — 4.5L and 4.9L engines

4. Lubricate the lip of a new seal with wheel bearing grease. Position it over the crankshaft and into the seal bore with the spring facing inside the engine.

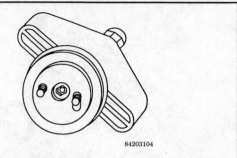

Fig. 90 Rear main seal installer tool — 4.5L and 4.9L engines

5. Using a Seal Installer tool No. J-34604 or equivalent, press the seal into place. The seal must be square (this is the purpose of the installer) and flush with the block to 1mm indented.

6. To complete the installation, reverse the removal procedures. Torque the flexplate-to-crankshaft bolts to 37 ft. lbs. Refill the crankshaft. Operate the engine and check for leaks.

4.6L Northstar Engine

▶ See Figures 91 and 92

1. Remove the transaxle assembly as outlined in Section 7.
2. Remove the flywheel as outlined in this Section.
3. Use a suitable prying tool between the seal lips and the crankshaft and remove the seal.

✳✳WARNING

Use extreme care to avoid damage to the crankshaft sealing surface. NOTE: The preferred method for removing the seal by drilling a 1/8 inch hole in the metal seal body and removing with a body dent puller (slide hammer).

To install

4. Place a small amount of RTV sealant at the crankshaft split line across the end of the upper/lower crankshaft seal.

5. Lubricate the rear main seal sealing lips with engine oil and slide the seal over the arbor of the seal installer J 38817. The garter spring faces in.

6. Thread the seal installer J 38818 into the crankshaft flange and install the seal by turning the handle until it bottoms against the crankcase..

7. Install the flywheel as outlined in this Section.
8. Install the transaxle assembly as outlined in Section 7.

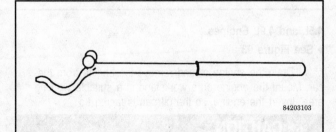

Fig. 89 Rear main seal removal tool — 4.5L and 4.9L engines

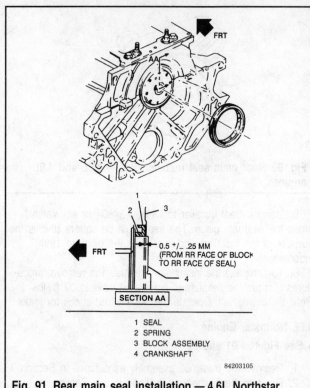

1 SEAL
2 SPRING
3 BLOCK ASSEMBLY
4 CRANKSHAFT

84203105

Fig. 91 Rear main seal installation — 4.6L Northstar engine

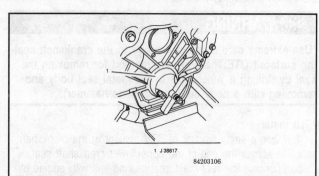

1 J 38817

84203106

Fig. 92 Installing the rear main seal — 4.6L Northstar engine

Crankshaft and Main Bearings

CRANKSHAFT REMOVAL

4.5L and 4.9L Engines
▶ See Figure 93

1. Drain the engine oil and remove the engine from the car. Mount the engine on a workstand in a suitable working area. Invert the engine, so the oil pan is facing up.

✳✳CAUTION

The EPA warns that prolonged contact with used engine oil may cause a number of skin disorders, including cancer! You should make every effort to minimize your expo- sure to used engine oil. Protective gloves should be worn when changing the oil. Wash your hands and any other exposed skin areas as soon as possible after exposure to used engine oil. Soap and water, or waterless hand cleaner should be used.

2. Remove the engine front (timing) cover.
3. Remove the timing chain and gears.
4. Remove the oil pan.
5. Remove the oil pump.
6. Stamp the cylinder number on the machined surfaces of the bolt bosses of the connecting rods and caps for identification when reinstalling. If the pistons are to be removed eventually from the connecting rod, mark the cylinder number on the pistons with silver paint or felt-tip pen for proper cylinder identification and cap-to-rod location.
7. Remove the connecting rod caps. Install lengths of rubber hose on each of the connecting rod bolts, to protect the crank journals when the crank is removed.
8. Mark the main bearing caps with a number punch or punch so that they can be reinstalled in their original positions.
9. Remove all main bearing caps.
10. Note the position of the keyway in the crankshaft so it can be installed in the same position.
11. Install rubber bands between a bolt on each connecting rod and oil pan bolts that have been reinstalled in the block (see illustration). This will keep the rods from banging on the block when the crank is removed.
12. Carefully lift the crankshaft out of the block. The rods will pivot to the center of the engine when the crank is removed.

MAIN BEARING INSPECTION AND REPLACEMENT

4.5L and 4.9L Engines
▶ See Figure 94

Like connecting rod big-end bearings, the crankshaft main bearings are shell-type inserts that do not utilize shims and cannot be adjusted. The bearings are available in various standard and undersizes; if main bearing clearance is found to be too sloppy, a new bearing (both upper and lower halves) is required.

➡**Factory-undersized crankshafts are marked, sometimes with a 9 and/or a large spot of light green paint; the bearing caps also will have the paint on each side of the undersized journal.**

Generally, the lower half of the bearing shell (except No. 1 bearing) shows greater wear and fatigue. If the lower half only shows the effects of normal wear (no heavy scoring or discoloration), it can usually be assumed that the upper half is also in good shape conversely, if the lower half is heavily worn or damaged, both halves should be replaced. Never replace one bearing half without replacing the other.

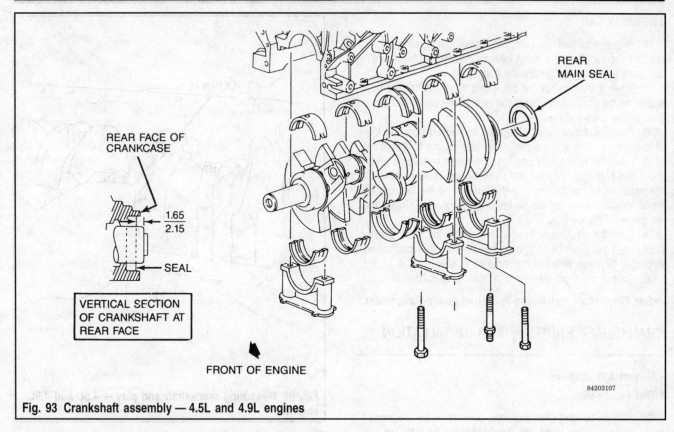

Fig. 93 Crankshaft assembly — 4.5L and 4.9L engines

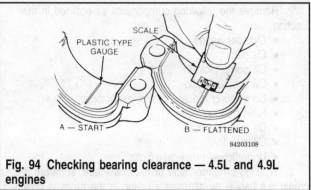

Fig. 94 Checking bearing clearance — 4.5L and 4.9L engines

MAIN BEARING REPLACEMENT

4.5L and 4.9L Engines

▶ See Figure 95

ENGINE OUT OF CAR

1. Remove and inspect the crankshaft.
2. Remove the main bearings from the bearing saddles in the cylinder block and main bearing caps.
3. Coat the bearing surfaces of the new, correct size main bearings with clean engine oil and install them in the bearing saddles in the block and in the main bearing caps.
4. Install the crankshaft. See Crankshaft Installation.

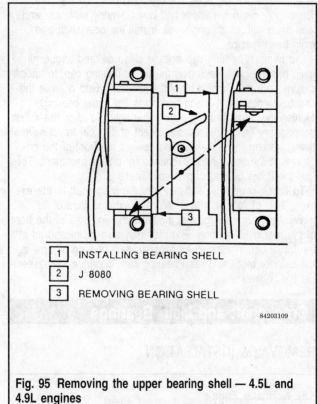

1	INSTALLING BEARING SHELL
2	J 8080
3	REMOVING BEARING SHELL

Fig. 95 Removing the upper bearing shell — 4.5L and 4.9L engines

ENGINE IN CAR

1. With the oil pan, oil pump and spark plugs removed, remove the cap from the main bearing needing replacement and remove the bearing from the cap.

2. Make a bearing roll-out pin, using a bent cotter pin as shown in the illustration. Install the end of the pin in the oil hole in the crankshaft journal.

3. Rotate the crankshaft clockwise as viewed from the front of the engine. This will roll the upper bearing out of the block.

4. Lube the new upper bearing with clean engine oil and insert the plain (unnotched) end between the crankshaft and the indented or notched side of the block. Roll the bearing into place, making sure that the oil holes are aligned. Remove the roll pin from the oil hole.

5. Lube the new lower bearing and install the main bearing cap. Install the main bearing cap, making sure it is positioned in proper direction with the matchmarks in alignment.

6. Torque the main bearing cap bolts to specification.

➥See Crankshaft Installation for thrust bearing alignment.

CRANKSHAFT END PLAY AND INSTALLATION

4.5L and 4.9L Engines

▶ See Figure 96

When main bearing clearance has been checked, bearings examined and/or replaced, the crankshaft can be installed. Thoroughly clean the upper and lower bearing surfaces, and lube them with clean engine oil. Install the crankshaft and main bearing caps.

Dip all main bearing cap bolts in clean oil, and torque all main bearing caps, excluding the thrust bearing cap, to specifications (see the Crankshaft and Connecting Rod chart in this chapter to determine which bearing is the thrust bearing). Tighten the thrust bearing bolts finger tight. To align the thrust bearing, pry the crankshaft the extent of its axial travel several times, holding the last movement toward the front of the engine. Add thrust washers if required for proper alignment. Torque the thrust bearing cap to specifications.

To check crankshaft end-play, pry the crankshaft to the extreme rear of its axial travel, then the extreme front of its travel. Using a feeler gauge, measure the end-play at the front of the rear main bearing. End play may also be measured at the thrust bearing. Install a new rear main bearing oil seal in the cylinder block and main bearing cap. Continue to reassemble the engine.

Crankshaft and Main Bearings

REMOVAL & INSTALLATION

4.6L Northstar Engine

▶ See Figures 97, 98, 99, 100, 101, 102, 103 and 104

1. Remove the engine and place on an engine stand.

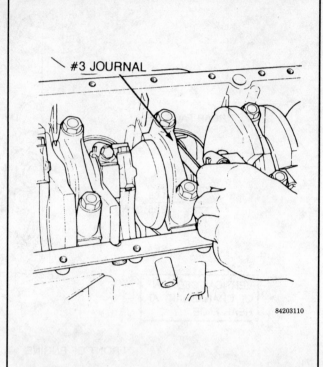

Fig. 96 Measuring crankshaft end play — 4.5L and 4.9L engines

2. Remove the following components as outlined in this Section.
- Cylinder heads
- Oil pan
- Oil pump pick-up
- Oil scraper/baffle
- Connecting rod and piston assemblies
- Main bearing bolts
- Oil manifold bolts
- Oil manifold
- Upper/lower crankcase bolts

3. Working on either side of the crankcase, separate the crankcase halves by alternately prying in the grooves provided until the lower crankcase is free of the dowel pins.

4. Remove the lower crankcase.

➥The upper and lower crankcase seal may be reused unless it is damaged or comes out of its groove in the upper crankcase.

5. Remove the rear main seal and discard.

6. Remove the crankshaft.

7. Inspect each bearing journal and bearing for damage and wear. Refer the the Specification chart at the end of this section and replace as necessary.

To install:

8. Install the main bearings to the upper and lower crankcases.

9. Install the crankshaft.

10. Using plastic gauge material, measure the main bearing clearance. Refer the the Specification chart at the end of this section and replace the bearings as necessary. If bearing clearance is greater than 0.003 inch (0.070 mm) and new

bearings do not reduce the clearance to 0.0005-0.002 inches (0.015-0.055 mm) a new crankshaft will be required.

➡**Undersized bearings are not available and no crankshaft grinding is allowed.**

11. Lubricate the bearing surfaces with engine oil and inspect the upper and lower crankcase seal position prior to installation.

> ✳✳**WARNING**
>
> **The seal must not be nicked, torn or out of the groove over its entire length on both sides of the crankcase.**

12. Replace the seal as follows:
   a. Clean the block groove.
   b. Start the seal at both ends and work the seal into the groove towards the center.
13. Install the crankshaft.
14. Lower the crankcase over the dowel pins.
15. Install the oil manifold.
16. Install the 20 main bearing bolts. The inboard bolts have a stud head. Tighten the bolts to 15 ft. lbs. (20 Nm) plus an additional 65 ° turn. Refer to the main bearing bolt torque sequence
17. Install the 10 oil manifold bolts. Tighten the bolts to 7 ft. lbs. (10 Nm).
18. Install the upper to lower crankcase bolts. Tighten the bolts to 25 ft. lbs. (30 Nm).
19. Measure the crankcase end play. Gently force the crankshaft to the extreme front and rear position. Monitor movement of the dial indicator on the nose of the crankshaft. End play should not exceed 0.019 inches (0.50 mm).
20. Install the connecting rod and piston assemblies.
21. Install the oil scraper/baffle and tighten the 10 retaining nuts to 20 ft. lbs. (25 nm).
22. Use a new O-ring, install the oil pump pick-up and tighten the retaining bolt to 7 ft. lbs. (10 Nm).
23. Install the following components as outlined in this Section.
   - Oil pan
   - Rear main seal
   - Cylinder heads

Flywheel/Flexplate

REMOVAL & INSTALLATION

▶ **See Figures 105 and 106**

1. Remove the transaxle.
2. Remove the 6 bolts (4.5L and 4.9L engine) or 8 bolts (4.6L engine) attaching the flywheel to the crankshaft flange. Remove the flywheel.
3. Inspect the flywheel for cracks, and inspect the ring gear for burrs or worn teeth. Replace the flywheel if any damage is apparent. Remove burrs with a mill file.
4. Install the flywheel. The flywheel will only attach to the crankshaft in one position, as the bolt holes are unevenly

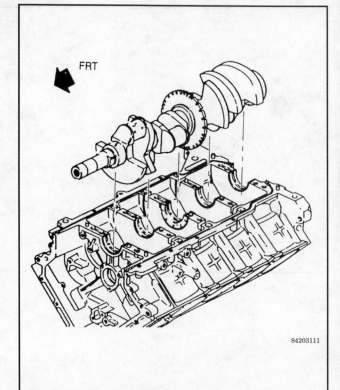

FRT

84203111

Fig. 97 Crankshaft assembly — 4.6L Northstar engine

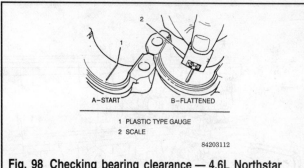

A—START   B—FLATTENED

1 PLASTIC TYPE GAUGE
2 SCALE

84203112

Fig. 98 Checking bearing clearance — 4.6L Northstar engine

spaced. Install the bolts and torque to 70 ft. lbs. (95 Nm) for the 4.5L and 4.9L engines, and 11 ft. lbs. (15 Nm) plus an additional 50 ° turn for the 4.6L Northstar engine.

Exhaust System

▶ **See Figures 107, 108 and 109**

The exhaust system incorporates (in order from front to rear) an exhaust manifold pipe (also called a cross-under pipe), an exhaust manifold rear pipe (or Y-pipe), catalytic converter, intermediate pipe, muffler and tail pipe.

The exhaust system is supported at the rear of the converter, the rear of the intermediate pipe, and the tailpipe by rubber isolated hangers to provide proper alignment.

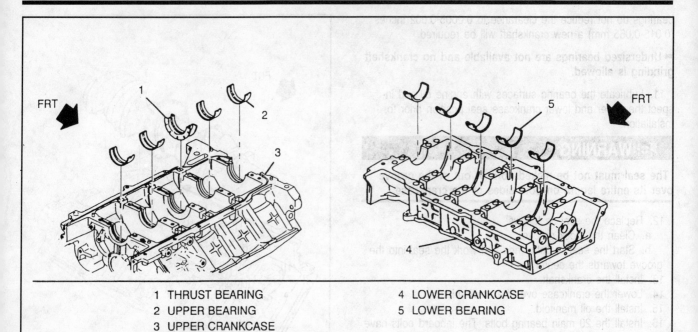

1 THRUST BEARING	4 LOWER CRANKCASE
2 UPPER BEARING	5 LOWER BEARING
3 UPPER CRANKCASE	

84203113

Fig. 99 Main bearings — 4.6L Northstar engine

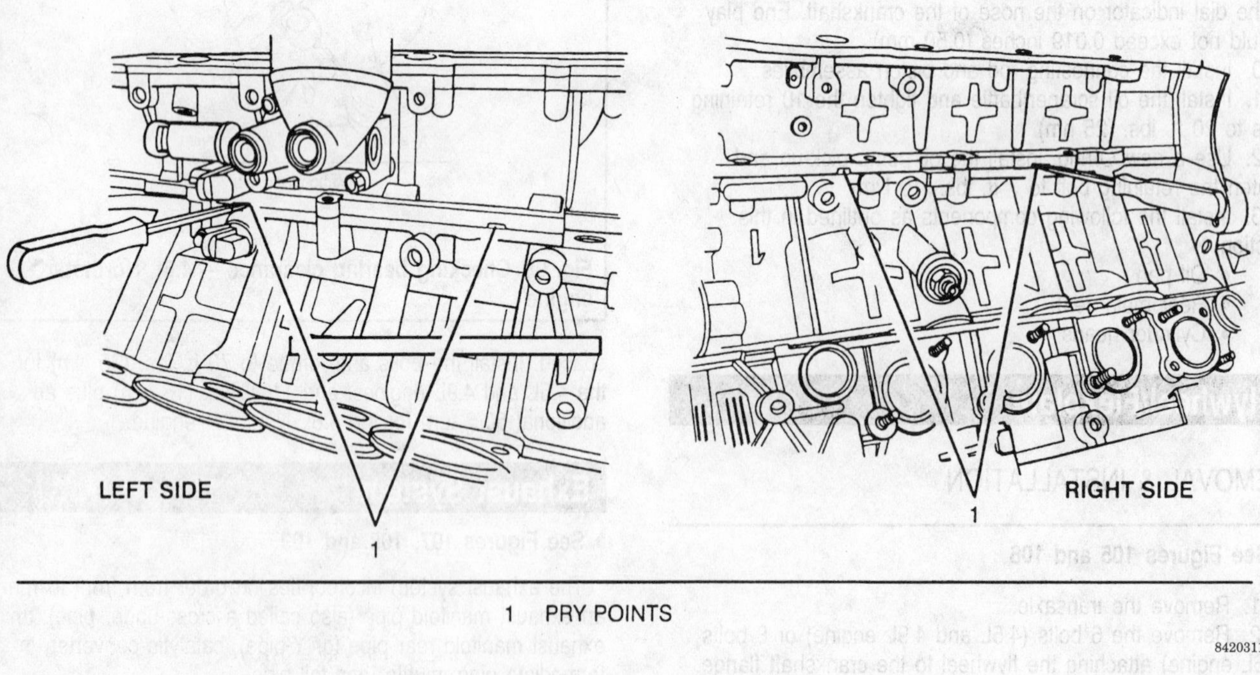

LEFT SIDE

RIGHT SIDE

1 PRY POINTS

84203114

Fig. 100 Separating crankcase halves — 4.6L Northstar engine

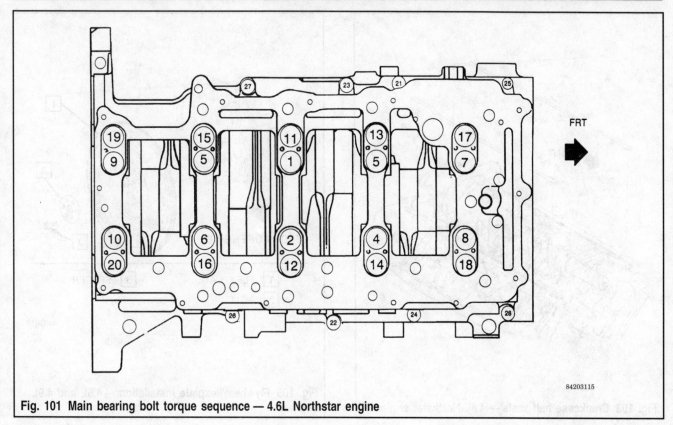

Fig. 101 Main bearing bolt torque sequence — 4.6L Northstar engine

84203115

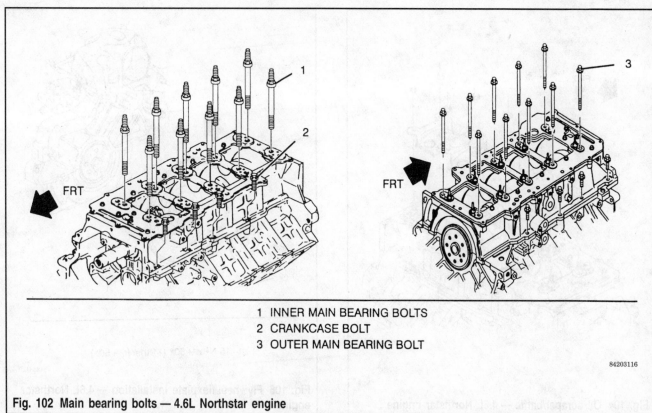

1   INNER MAIN BEARING BOLTS
2   CRANKCASE BOLT
3   OUTER MAIN BEARING BOLT

84203116

Fig. 102 Main bearing bolts — 4.6L Northstar engine

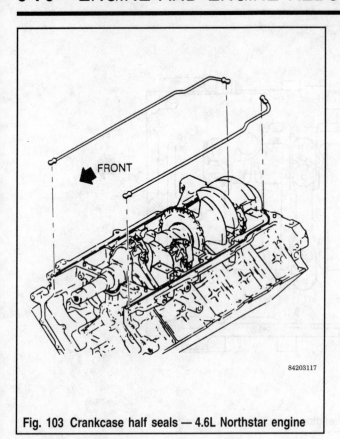

Fig. 103 Crankcase half seals — 4.6L Northstar engine

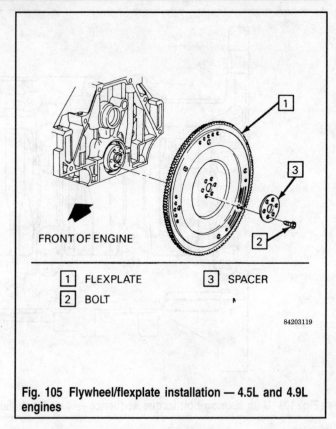

| 1 | FLEXPLATE | 3 | SPACER |
| 2 | BOLT | | |

84203119

Fig. 105 Flywheel/flexplate installation — 4.5L and 4.9L engines

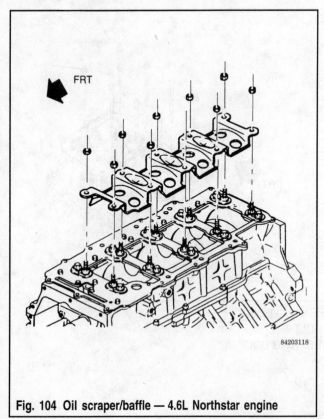

Fig. 104 Oil scraper/baffle — 4.6L Northstar engine

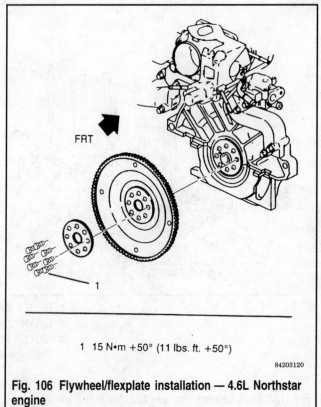

1   15 N•m +50° (11 lbs. ft. +50°)

84203120

Fig. 106 Flywheel/flexplate installation — 4.6L Northstar engine

Heat shields are attached to the underside of the body to reflect the heat of the gasoline engine exhaust system.

✳✳WARNING

Always replace any heat shield that is removed. Failure to do so could cause damage to other components.

The exhaust front pipe attaches to the left hand exhaust manifold. The exhaust rear pipe attaches to the front pipe and right hand exhaust manifold. A flex joint coupling, using a round graphite impregnated seal, connects the exhaust rear pipe to the inlet of the monolithic catalytic converter. The intermediate pipe assembly is welded to the converter outlet.

The exhaust system is completely welded from the converter outlet back, and can be serviced by five components.

1. Exhaust manifold front pipe.
2. Exhaust manifold rear pipe (Eldorado and Seville).
3. Catalytic converter.
4. Intermediate pipe.
5. Muffler and tail pipe.

SAFETY PRECAUTIONS

For a number of reasons, exhaust system work can be the most dangerous type of work you can do on your car. Always observe the following precautions:

• Support the car extra securely. Not only will you often be working directly under it, but you'll frequently be using a lot of force, say, heavy hammer blows, to dislodge rusted parts. This can cause a car that's improperly supported to shift and possibly fall.

• Wear goggles. Exhaust system parts are always rusty. Metal chips can be dislodged, even when you're only turning rusted bolts. Attempting to pry pipes apart with a chisel makes the chips fly even more frequently.

• If you're using a cutting torch, keep it a great distance from either the fuel tank or lines. Stop what you're doing and feel the temperature of the fuel bearing pipes on the tank frequently. Even slight heat can expand and/or vaporize fuel, resulting in accumulated vapor, or even a liquid leak, near your torch.

• Watch where your hammer blows fall and make sure you hit squarely. You could easily tap a brake or fuel line when you hit an exhaust system part with a glancing blow. Inspect all lines and hoses in the area where you've been working.

✳✳CAUTION

Be very careful when working on or near the catalytic converter. External temperatures can reach 1,500°F (816°C) and more, causing severe burns. Removal or installation should be performed only on a cold exhaust system.

A number of special exhaust system tools can be rented from auto supply houses or local stores that rent special equipment. A common one is a tail pipe expander, designed to enable you to join pipes of identical diameter.

It may also be quite helpful to use solvents designed to loosen rusted bolts or flanges. Soaking rusted parts the night before you do the job can speed the work of freeing rusted parts considerably. Remember that these solvents are often flammable. Apply only to parts after they are cool!

COMPONENT REPLACEMENT

System components may be welded or clamped together. The system consists of a head pipe, catalytic converter, intermediate pipe, muffler and tail pipe, in that order from the engine to the back of the car.

The head pipe is bolted to the exhaust manifold. Various hangers suspend the system from the floor pan. When assembling exhaust system parts, the relative clearances around all system parts is extremely critical. In the event that the system is welded, the various parts will have to be cut apart for removal. In these cases, the cut parts may not be reused. To cut the parts, a hacksaw is the best choice. An oxy-acetylene cutting torch may be faster but the sparks are DANGEROUS near the fuel tank, and, at the very least, accidents could happen, resulting in damage to other under-car parts, not to mention yourself!

The following replacement steps relate to clamped parts:

1. Raise and support the car on jackstands. It's much easier on you if you can get the car up on 4 stands. Some pipes need lots of clearance for removal and installation. If the system has been in the car for a long time, spray the clamped joints with a rust dissolving solutions such as WD-40® or Liquid Wrench®, and let it set according to the instructions on the can.

2. Remove the nuts from the U-bolts; don't be surprised if the U-bolts break while removing the nuts. Age and rust account for this. Besides, you shouldn't't reuse old U-bolts. When unbolting the headpipe from the exhaust manifold, make sure that the bolts are free before trying to remove them. If you snap a stud in the exhaust manifold, the stud will have to be removed with a bolt extractor, which often necessitates the removal of the manifold itself. The headpipe uses a necked collar for sealing purposes at the manifold, eliminating the need for a gasket.

3. After the clamps are removed from the joints, first twist the parts at the joints to break loose rust and scale, then pull the components apart with a twisting motion. If the parts twist freely but won't pull apart, check the joint. The clamp may have been installed so tightly that it has caused a slight crushing of the joint. In this event, the best thing to do is secure a chisel designed for the purpose and, using the chisel and a hammer, peel back the female pipe end until the parts are freed.

4. Once the parts are freed, check the condition of the pipes which you had intended keeping. If their condition is at all in doubt, replace them too. You went to a lot of work to get one or more components out. You don't want to have to go through that again in the near future. If you are retaining a pipe, check the pipe end. If it was crushed by a clamp, it can be restored to its original diameter using a pipe expander, which can be rented at most good auto parts stores. Check, also, the condition of the exhaust system hangers. If ANY deterioration is noted, replace them. Oh, and one note about parts: use only parts designed for your car. Don't use fits-all parts or flex pipes. The fits-all parts never fit and the flex pipes don't last very long.

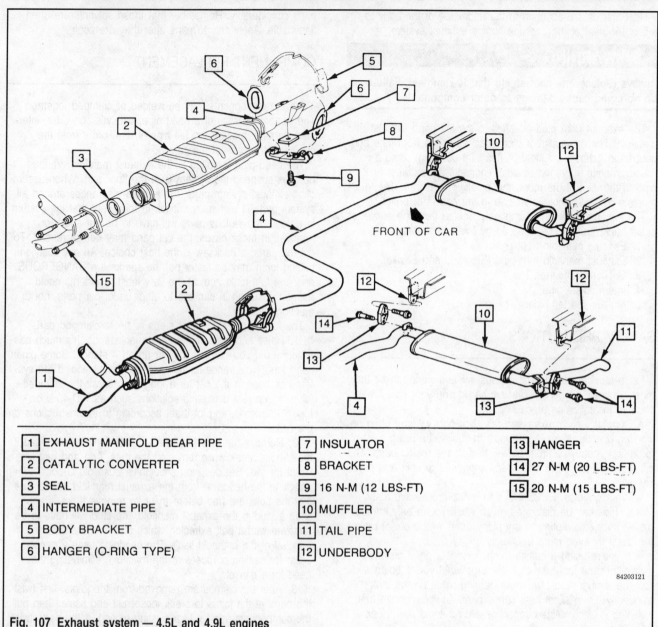

1	EXHAUST MANIFOLD REAR PIPE	**7** INSULATOR	**13**	HANGER
2	CATALYTIC CONVERTER	**8** BRACKET	**14**	27 N-M (20 LBS-FT)
3	SEAL	**9** 16 N-M (12 LBS-FT)	**15**	20 N-M (15 LBS-FT)
4	INTERMEDIATE PIPE	**10** MUFFLER		
5	BODY BRACKET	**11** TAIL PIPE		
6	HANGER (O-RING TYPE)	**12** UNDERBODY		

84203121

Fig. 107 Exhaust system — 4.5L and 4.9L engines

5. When installing the new parts, coat the pipe ends with exhaust system lubricant. It makes fitting the parts much easier. It's also a good idea to assemble all the parts in position before clamping them. This will ensure a good fit, detect any problems and allow you to check all clearances between the parts and surrounding frame and floor members. See the accompanying illustrations for the proper clearances.

6. When you are satisfied with all fits and clearances, install the clamps. The headpipe-to-manifold nuts should be torqued to 20 ft. lbs. If the studs were rusty, wire-brush them clean and spray them with WD-40® or Liquid Wrench®. This will ensure a proper torque reading. Position the clamps on the slip points as illustrated. The slits in the female pipe ends should be under the U-bolts, not under the clamp end. Tighten the U-bolt nuts securely, without crushing the pipe. The pipe fit should be tight, so that you can't swivel the pipe by hand.

Don't forget: always use new clamps. When the system is tight, recheck all clearances. Start the engine and check the joints for leaks. A leak can be felt by hand. MAKE CERTAIN THAT THE CAR IS SECURE ON THE JACKSTANDS BEFORE GETTING UNDER IT WITH THE ENGINE RUNNING!! If any leaks are detected, tighten the clamp until the leak stops. If the pipe starts to deform before the leak stops, reposition the clamp and tighten it. If that still doesn't't stop the lea k, it may be that you don't have enough overlap on the pipe fit. Shut off the engine and try pushing the pipe together further. Be careful; the pipe gets hot quickly.

7. When everything is tight and secure, lower the car and take it for a road test. Make sure there are no unusual sounds or vibration. Most new pipes are coated with a preservative, so the system will be pretty smelly for a day or two while the coating burns off.

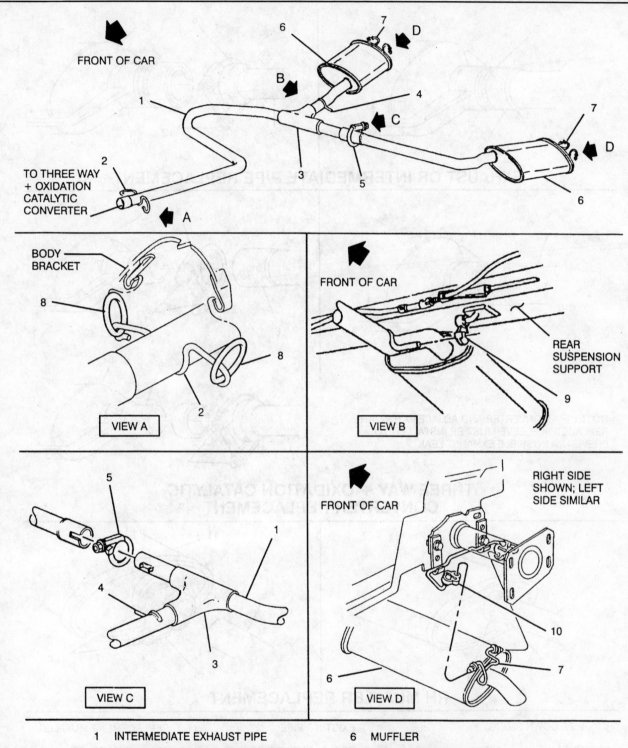

1	INTERMEDIATE EXHAUST PIPE	6	MUFFLER
2	FRONT EXHAUST HANGER BRACKET	7	REAR HANGER BRACKET
3	INTERMEDIATE EXHAUST 'Y' JOINT (DUAL EXHAUST ONLY)	8	FRONT EXHAUST HANGER (O-RING TYPE)
4	INTERMEDIATE EXHAUST HANGER	9	INTERMEDIATE EXHAUST HANGER
5	LEFT MUFFLER EXHAUST CLAMP (DUAL EXHAUST ONLY)	10	REAR MUFFLER HANGER

84203122

Fig. 108 Exhaust system — 4.6L Northstar engine

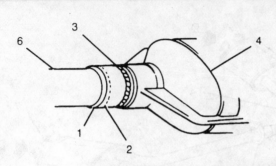

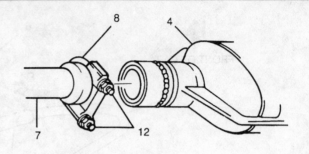

EXHAUST OR INTERMEDIATE PIPE REPLACEMENT

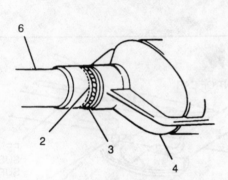

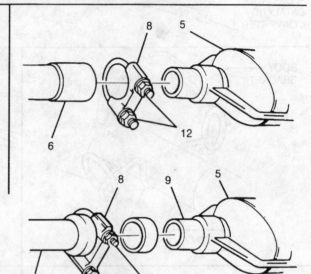

NOTE: IF A CONVERTER AND ADJACENT PIPE ARE REPLACED, A SLEEVE MUST BE INSTALLED TO PREVENT A POSSIBLE EXHAUST LEAK

THREE WAY + OXIDATION CATALYTIC CONVERTER REPLACEMENT

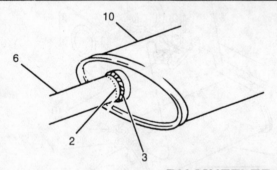

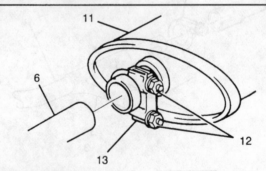

RH MUFFLER REPLACEMENT

1	PIPE DOWN SIZING	6	EXISTING PIPE	11	REPLACEMENT MUFFLER
2	CUT LINE	7	REPLACEMENT PIPE	12	50 N•m (37 LBS. FT.)
3	WELD	8	GUILLOTINE CLAMP	13	SADDLE CLAMP
4	EXISTING THREE WAY + OXIDATION CATALYTIC CONVERTER	9	SLEEVE		
5	REPLACEMENT CONVERTER	10	EXISTING MUFFLER		

84203123

Fig. 109 Exhaust component installation — all models

ENGINE MECHANICAL SPECIFICATIONS

Component	U.S.	Metric
4.6L NORTHSTAR ENGINE		
Camshaft		
Bearing Clearance		
New limits:	0.002–0.004 in.	0.04–0.09mm
Worn limits (not over):	0.006 in.	0.152mm
Out-of-round (not over):	0.0009 in.	0.022mm
Bearing journal diameter:	1.061–1.062 in.	26.948–26.972mm
Valve lift (VIN code 9)		
Intake:	0.370 in.	9.4mm
Exhaust:	0.339 in.	8.6mm
Crankshaft and main bearings		
Clearance		
New limit:	0.0005–0.002 in.	0.015–0.055mm
Worn limit:	0.003 in.	0.070mm
Main bearing journal diameter:	2.52 in.	64.358mm
Main bearing journals, out-of-round		
Not over:	0.0005 in.	0.013mm
Main bearing journal length		
No.1:	0.969 in.	24.6mm
No.2:	1.001 in.	25.6mm
No.3:	0.992 in.	25.2mm
No.4:	0.969 in.	24.6mm
No.5:	0.969 in.	24.6mm
Crankpin diameter:	0.069 in.	53.955mm
Crankpin out-of-round		
Not over:	0.0005 in.	0.013mm
End play in crankshaft		
New limits:	0.002–0.019 in.	0.05–0.5mm
Worn limits:	0.019 in.	0.5mm
Connecting rod bearing clearance (between bearing and shaft)		
New limits:	0.001–0.003 in.	0.025–0.076mm
Worn limits (not over):	0.003 in.	0.076mm
Connecting rod diameter		
Lower end (without bearing):	2.249 in.	57.144mm
Length, center to center:	5.94 in.	151mm
End play of rods on crank pin		
All engines:	0.008–0.020 in.	0.20–0.50mm
Piston and Cylinders		
Cylinder bore out-of-round (new limit):	0.0008 in.	0.020mm
Piston taper, not over:	0.0004 in.	0.01mm.
Piston skirt to cylinder bore:	0.0004–0.0020	0.010–0.050mm.

84203130

ENGINE MECHANICAL SPECIFICATIONS

Component	U.S.	Metric
Piston Rings		
Clearance between rings & sides of groove in piston		
Compression ring:	0.002–0.004 in.	0.040–0.095mm
Oil rings:	None-side sealing	
Gap between ends		
Top compression ring:	0.010–0.016 in.	0.025–0.040mm
2nd Compression rings:	0.014–0.020 in.	0.35–0.50mm
Oil rings:	0.010–0.030 in.	0.25–0.76mm
Width of compression ring groove		
Top ring:	0.060–0.061 in.	1.530–1.555mm
2nd ring:	0.060–0.061 in.	1.530–1.555mm
Width of oil ring		
Groove:	0.119–0.120 in.	3.030–3.055mm
Valves		
Clearance between stem and guide		
New limits (intake):	0.001–0.003 in.	0.03–0.07mm
New limits (exhaust):	0.002–0.004 in.	0.05–0.10mm
Worn limits (not over):	0.005	0.12mm
Valve face angle:	45 degrees	
Valve seat angle (in head):	46 degrees	
Valve lifter clearance:	0.001–0.003 in.	0.025–0.026mm
Valve stem diameter:	0.2331–0.2339 in.	5.9207–5.9411mm
Valve guide diameter in head:	0.235 in.	5.979mm
Valve head diameter over all		
Intake:	1.30 in.	33mm
Exhaust:	1.14 in.	29mm
Valve Springs		
Free length		
VIN code 9 engine:	1.575 in.	40.0mm
VIN code Y engine:	1.591 in.	40.4mm
Installed height:	1.19 in.	30.3mm
4.5L AND 4.9L ENGINES		
Camshaft		
Bearing clearance		
All engines		
New limits:	0.0018–0.0037 in.	0.045–0.095mm
Worn limits (not over):	0.004 in.	0.10mm
Out-of-round (not over):	0.0009 in.	0.022mm
Valve lift		
Intake:	.384 in.	9.75mm
Exhaust:	.396 in.	10.06mm
Connecting rod bearing clearance (between bearing and shaft)		
New limits:	0.0005–0.0028 in.	0.012–0.071mm
Worn limits (not over):	0.0035 in.	0.090mm
Connecting rod diameter, lower end (without bearing)		
All engines:	2.052–2.053 in.	52.132–52.150mm
Length, center to center:	5.7 in.	145mm
End play of rods on crank pin		
All engines:	0.008–0.020 in.	0.20–0.50mm
Crankshaft and main bearings		
Clearance, #1 main bearing		
New limit:	.0008–.0031 in.	0.020–0.079mm

84203131

ENGINE MECHANICAL SPECIFICATIONS

Component	U.S.	Metric
Worn limit:	0.0045 in.	0.115mm
Clearance, #2,3,4,5 main bearings		
New limits:	0.0016–0.0039 in.	0.040–0.100mm
Worn limit:	0.0045 in.	0.115mm
Main bearing caps		
Screw thread diameter:	0.00473 in.	12mm
Main bearing journal diameter:	2.635–2.636 in.	66.940–66.965mm
Main bearing journals, out-of-round		
Not over:	0.0003 in.	0.008mm
Main bearing journal length		
No.1:	0.984 in.	24.99mm
No.2:	1.023 in.	25.98mm
No.3:	1.098 in.	27.88mm
No.4:	1.023 in.	25.98mm
No.5:	1.495 in.	37.98mm
Crankpin diameter:	1.927–1.928 in.	48.945–48.970mm
Crankpin out-of-round		
Not over:	0.0003 in.	0.008mm
End play in crankshaft		
New limits:	0.0010–0.008 in.	0.026–0.206mm
Worn limits:	0.015 in.	0.38mm
Oil Pump		
Minimum pressure at normal operating temperature		
At Idle:	11 psi	80 kPa
At 2000 RPM :	53 psi	365 kPa
Piston and Cylinders		
Cylinder bore out-of-round (new limit):	0.0008 in.	0.020mm
Piston taper, not over:	0.0248 in.	0.61–0.65mm.
Piston skirt to cylinder bore:	0.0004–0.0020	0.010–0.050mm.
Piston Rings		
Clearance between rings & sides of groove in piston		
Compression ring:	0.002–0.004 in.	0.040–0.095mm
Oil rings:	None-side sealing	
Gap between ends		
Compression rings:	0.012–0.022 in.	0.030–0.055mm
Oil rings:	0.004–0.020 in.	0.10–0.50mm
Width of compression ring groove		
Top ring:	0.060–0.061 in.	1.530–1.555mm
2nd ring:	0.060–0.061 in.	1.530–1.555mm
Width of oil ring		
Groove:	0.119–0.120 in.	3.030–3.055mm
Valves		
Clearance between stem and guide		
New limits (intake):	0.001–0.003 in.	0.03–0.07mm
New limits (exhaust):	0.002–0.004 in.	0.05–0.10mm
Worn limits (not over):	0.005	0.12mm
Clearance between lifter body and lifter		
Carrier:	0.0007–0.0027 in.	0.017–0.068mm
Head diameter over all		
Intake:	1.77 in.	45mm
Exhaust:	1.50 in.	38mm
Valve face angle:	44 degrees	
Valve seat angle (in head):	45 degrees	
Rocker arm ratio:	1.60:1	
Valve Springs		
Free length:	1.95 in.	49.5mm

84203132

TORQUE SPECIFICATIONS

Component	U.S.	Metric
4.6L NORTHSTAR ENGINE		
Air conditioner compressor		
To block and bracket:	20 ft. lbs.	25 Nm
Alternator		
All bolts:	35 ft. lbs.	50 Nm
Belt tensioner:	35 ft. lbs.	50 Nm
Camshaft bearing cap:	9 ft. lbs.	12 Nm
Camshaft cover:	7 ft. lbs.	10 Nm
Camshaft chain tensioner to block:	20 ft. lbs.	25 Nm
Camshaft sprocket:	90 ft. lbs.	120 Nm
Connecting rod nut:	20 ft. lbs. plus 90°	25 Nm plus 90°
Coolant drain plug (in block):	6 ft. lbs.	8 Nm
Cylinder head bolts:	(See Text)	
Exhaust manifold		
Bolts:	20 ft. lbs.	25 Nm
Lock nuts:	20 ft. lbs.	25 Nm
Engine lift bracket		
Right rear:	35 ft. lbs.	50 Nm
Engine oil manifold to--lower crankcase:	7 ft. lbs.	10 Nm
EGR valve:	20 ft. lbs.	25 Nm
Flywheel:	11 ft. lbs. plus 50°	15 Nm plus 50°
Front cover:	7 ft. lbs.	10 Nm
Intake manifold:	(See text)	
Ignition module to cam cover:	9 ft. lbs.	12 Nm
Intermediate shaft sprocket:	45 ft. lbs.	60 Nm
Knock sensor:	15 ft. lbs.	20 Nm
Main bearing bolts/studs:	(See text)	
Oil pan:	7 ft. lbs.	10 Nm
Oil pump to lower crankcase:	7 ft. lbs. plus 35°	10 Nm plus 35°
Oil pump suction pipe:	7 ft. lbs.	10 Nm
Oil scraper lock nut:	20 ft. lbs.	25 Nm
Oxygen sensor:	30 ft. lbs.	40 Nm
Power steering pump bracket-to-block:	35 ft. lbs.	50 Nm
Power steering pump to-bracket:	20 ft. lbs.	25 Nm
Starter motor to block:	25 ft. lbs.	30 Nm
Starter motor (brass) locknut:	7 ft. lbs.	10 Nm

84203133

TORQUE SPECIFICATIONS

Component	U.S.	Metric
Thermostat housing		
Upper to lower:	7ft. lbs.	10 Nm
To water pump housing:	7ft. lbs.	10 Nm
Torsioner damper:	145 ft. lbs. plus 120°	105 Nm plus 120°
Torque strut bracket		
To cylinder head:	35 lbs.	50 Nm
To cylinder head (stud):	35 lbs.	50 Nm
To water manifold:	20 lbs.	25 Nm
Torque converter to flywheel	45 ft. lbs.	60 Nm
Transaxle to engine		
Long:	55 lbs.	75 Nm
Short:	35 lbs.	50 Nm
Transaxle brace		
To oil pan:	35 lbs.	50 Nm
To block:	35 lbs.	50 Nm
To transaxle:	35 lbs.	50 Nm
Water pump assembly:	75 ft. lbs.	100 Nm
Water pump housing		
To head:	20 lbs.	25 Nm
To block:	20 lbs.	25 Nm
Water pump outlet		
To head:	20 lbs.	25 Nm
Water outlet fitting:	50 ft. lbs.	35 Nm
4.5L AND 4.9L ENGINES		
Cylinder head bolts		
All engines:	(See Text)	
Connecting rod bolts		
All engines:	25 ft. lbs.	33 Nm
Damper to crankshaft		
All engines:	70 ft. lbs.	95 Nm
Exhaust manifold bolts		
All engines:	16 ft. lbs.	21 Nm
Exhaust outlet flange studs		
All engines:	15 ft. lbs.	20 Nm
Flywheel to crankshaft		
All engines:	70 ft. lbs.	95 Nm
Front cover screws		
All engines:	15 ft. lbs.	20 Nm
Intake manifold bolts		
All engines:	(See Text)	
Lift bracket to cylinder head		
All engines:	29 ft. lbs.	39 Nm
Lower thermostat housing to intake		
All engines:	23 ft. lbs.	31 Nm
Main bearing cap bolts		
All engines:	85 ft. lbs.	115 Nm

84203134

TORQUE SPECIFICATIONS

Component	U.S.	Metric
Oil pan drain plug All engines:	22 ft. lbs.	30 Nm
Oil pan bolts All engines:	14 ft. lbs.	18 Nm
Oil pump mounting nut to main bearing cap All engines:	22 ft. lbs.	29 Nm
Rocker arm cover screws and studs All engines:	8 ft. lbs.	10 Nm
Rocker arm pivot to support screws All engines:	22 ft. lbs.	29 Nm
Rocker arm support to head bolt nuts All engines:	36 ft. lbs.	48 Nm
Spark plugs All engines:	23 ft. lbs.	31 Nm
Timing sprocket to camshaft All engines:	36 ft. lbs.	48 Nm

84203135

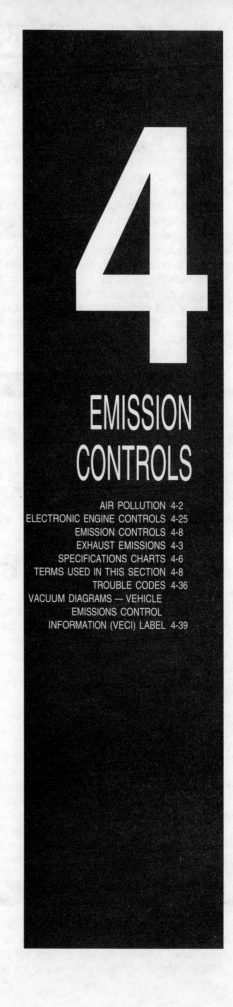

4

EMISSION CONTROLS

AIR POLLUTION

The earth's atmosphere, at or near sea level, consists of 78 percent nitrogen, 21 percent oxygen and 1 percent other gases, approximately. If it were possible to remain in this state, 100 percent clean air would result. However, many varied causes allow other gases and particulates to mix with the clean air, causing the air to become unclean or polluted.

Certain of these pollutants are visible while others are invisible, with each having the capability of causing distress to the eyes, ears, throat, skin and respiratory system. Should these pollutants be concentrated in a specific area and under the right conditions, death could result due to the displacement or chemical change of the oxygen content in the air. These pollutants can cause much damage to the environment and to the many man made objects that are exposed to the elements.

To better understand the causes of air pollution, the pollutants can be categorized into 3 separate types, natural, industrial and automotive.

Natural Pollutants

Natural pollution has been present on earth before man appeared and is still a factor to be considered when discussing air pollution, although it causes only a small percentage of the present overall pollution problem existing in our country. It is the direct result of decaying organic matter, wind born smoke and particulates from such natural events as plains and forest fires (ignited by heat or lightning), volcanic ash, sand and dust which can spread over a large area of the countryside.

Industrial Pollution

Industrial pollution is caused primarily by industrial processes, the burning of coal, oil and natural gas, which in turn produces smoke and fumes. Because the burning fuels contain much sulfur, the principal ingredients of smoke and fumes are sulfur dioxide (SO_2) and particulate matter. This type of pollutant occurs most severely during still, damp and cool weather, such as at night. Even in its less severe form, this pollutant is not confined to just cities. Because of air movements, the pollutants move for miles over the surrounding countryside, leaving in its path a barren and unhealthy environment for all living things.

Working with Federal, State and Local mandated rules, regulations and by carefully monitoring the emissions, industries have greatly reduced the amount of pollutant emitted from their industrial sources, striving to obtain an acceptable level. Because of the mandated industrial emission clean up, many land areas and streams in and around the cities that were formerly barren of vegetation and life, have now begun to move back in the direction of nature's intended balance.

Automotive Pollutants

The third major source of air pollution is the automotive emissions. The emissions from the internal combustion engine were not an appreciable problem years ago because of the small number of registered vehicles and the nation's small highway system. However, during the early 1950's, the trend of the American people was to move from the cities to the surrounding suburbs. This caused an immediate problem in the transportation areas because the majority of the suburbs were not afforded mass transit conveniences. This lack of transportation created an attractive market for the automobile manufacturers, which resulted in a dramatic increase in the number of vehicles produced and sold, along with a marked increase in highway construction between cities and the suburbs. Multi-vehicle families emerged with much emphasis placed on the individual vehicle per family member. As the increase in vehicle ownership and usage occurred, so did the pollutant levels in and around the cities, as the suburbanites drov e daily to their businesses and employment in the city and its fringe area, returning at the end of the day to their homes in the suburbs.

It was noted that a fog and smoke type haze was being formed and at times, remained in suspension over the cities and did not quickly dissipate. At first this 'smog', derived from the words 'smoke' and 'fog', was thought to result from industrial pollution but it was determined that the automobile emissions were largely to blame. It was discovered that as normal automobile emissions were exposed to sunlight for a period of time, complex chemical reactions would take place.

It was found the smog was a photo chemical layer and was developed when certain oxides of nitrogen (NOx) and unburned hydrocarbons (HC) from the automobile emissions were exposed to sunlight and was more severe when the smog would remain stagnant over an area in which a warm layer of air would settle over the top of a cooler air mass at ground level, trapping and holding the automobile emissions, instead of the emissions being dispersed and diluted through normal air flows. This type of air stagnation was given the name 'Temperature Inversion'.

Temperature Inversion

In normal weather situations, the surface air is warmed by the heat radiating from the earth's surface and the sun's rays and will rise upward, into the atmosphere, to be cooled through a convection type heat expands with the cooler upper air. As the warm air rises, the surface pollutants are carried upward and dissipated into the atmosphere.

When a temperature inversion occurs, we find the higher air is no longer cooler but warmer than the surface air, causing the cooler surface air to become trapped and unable to move. This warm air blanket can extend from above ground level to a few hundred or even a few thousand feet into the air. As the surface air is trapped, so are the pollutants, causing a severe smog condition. Should this stagnant air mass extend to a few thousand feet high, enough air movement with the inversion takes place to allow the smog layer to rise above ground level but the pollutants still cannot dissipate. This inversion can remain for days over an area, with only the smog level rising or lowering from ground level to a few hundred feet high. Meanwhile, the pollutant levels increases, causing eye irritation, respirator problems, reduced visibility, plant damage and in some cases, cancer type diseases.

This inversion phenomenon was first noted in the Los Angeles, California area. The city lies in a basin type of terrain and during certain weather conditions, a cold air mass is held in the basin while a warmer air mass covers it like a lid.

Because this type of condition was first documented as prevalent in the Los Angeles area, this type of smog was named Los Angeles Smog, although it occurs in other areas where a large concentration of automobiles are used and the air remains stagnant for any length of time.

Internal Combustion Engine Pollutants

Consider the internal combustion engine as a machine in which raw materials must be placed so a finished product comes out. As in any machine operation, a certain amount of wasted material is formed. When we relate this to the internal combustion engine, we find that by putting in air and fuel, we obtain power from this mixture during the combustion process to drive the vehicle. The by-product or waste of this power is, in part, heat and exhaust gases with which we must concern ourselves.

HEAT TRANSFER

The heat from the combustion process can rise to over 4000°F. The dissipation of this heat is controlled by a ram air

EXHAUST EMISSIONS

Composition Of The Exhaust Gases

The exhaust gases emitted into the atmosphere are a combination of burned and unburned fuel. To understand the exhaust emission and its composition review some basic chemistry.

When the air/fuel mixture is introduced into the engine, we are mixing air, composed of nitrogen (78 percent), oxygen (21 percent) and other gases (1 percent) with the fuel, which is 100 percent hydrocarbons (HC), in a semi-controlled ratio. As the combustion process is accomplished, power is produced to move the vehicle while the heat of combustion is transferred to the cooling system. The exhaust gases are then composed of nitrogen, a diatomic gas (N_2), the same as was introduced in the engine, carbon dioxide (CO_2), the same gas that is used in beverage carbonation and water vapor (H_2O). The nitrogen (N_2), for the most part passes through the engine unchanged, while the oxygen (O_2) reacts (burns) with the hydrocarbons (HC) and produces the carbon dioxide (CO_2) and the water vapors (H_2O). If this chemical process would be the only process to take place, the exhaust emissions would be harmless. However, during the combustion process, other pollutants are formed and are considered dangerous. These pollutants are carbon monoxide (CO), hydrocarbons (HC), oxides of nitrogen (NOx) oxides of sulfur (SOx) and engine particulates.

Lead (Pb), is considered 1 of the particulates and is present in the exhaust gases whenever leaded fuels are used. Lead (Pb) does not dissipate easily. Levels can be high along roadways when it is emitted from vehicles and can pose a

effect, the use of cooling fans to cause air flow and having a liquid coolant solution surrounding the combustion area and transferring the heat of combustion through the cylinder walls and into the coolant. The coolant is then directed to a thin-finned, multi-tubed radiator, from which the excess heat is transferred to the outside air by 1 or all of the 3 heat transfer methods, conduction, convection or radiation.

The cooling of the combustion area is an important part in the control of exhaust emissions. To understand the behavior of the combustion and transfer of its heat, consider the air/fuel charge. It is ignited and the flame front burns progressively across the combustion chamber until the burning charge reaches the cylinder walls. Some of the fuel in contact with the walls is not hot enough to burn, thereby snuffing out or Quenching the combustion process. This leaves unburned fuel in the combustion chamber. This unburned fuel is then forced out of the cylinder along with the exhaust gases and into the exhaust system.

Many attempts have been made to minimize the amount of unburned fuel in the combustion chambers due to the snuffing out or 'Quenching', by increasing the coolant temperature and lessening the contact area of the coolant around the combustion area. Design limitations within the combustion chambers prevent the complete burning of the air/fuel charge, so a certain amount of the unburned fuel is still expelled into the exhaust system, regardless of modifications to the engine.

health threat. Since the increased usage of unleaded gasoline and the phasing out of leaded gasoline for fuel, this pollutant is gradually diminishing. While not considered a major threat lead is still considered a dangerous pollutant.

HYDROCARBONS

Hydrocarbons (HC) are essentially unburned fuel that have not been successfully burned during the combustion process or have escaped into the atmosphere through fuel evaporation. The main sources of incomplete combustion are rich air/fuel mixtures, low engine temperatures and improper spark timing. The main sources of hydrocarbon emission through fuel evaporation come from the vehicle's fuel tank and carburetor bowl.

To reduce combustion hydrocarbon emission, engine modifications were made to minimize dead space and surface area in the combustion chamber. In addition the air/fuel mixture was made more lean through improved carburetion, fuel injection and by the addition of external controls to aid in further combustion of the hydrocarbons outside the engine. Two such methods were the addition of an air injection system, to inject fresh air into the exhaust manifolds and the installation of a catalytic converter, a unit that is able to burn traces of hydrocarbons without affecting the internal combustion process or fuel economy.

To control hydrocarbon emissions through fuel evaporation, modifications were made to the fuel tank and carburetor bowl to allow storage of the fuel vapors during periods of engine shut-down, and at specific times during engine operation, to purge and burn these same vapors by blending them with the air/fuel mixture.

CARBON MONOXIDE

Carbon monoxide is formed when not enough oxygen is present during the combustion process to convert carbon (C) to carbon dioxide (CO_2). An increase in the carbon monoxide (CO) emission is normally accompanied by an increase in the hydrocarbon (HC) emission because of the lack of oxygen to completely burn all of the fuel mixture.

Carbon monoxide (CO) also increases the rate at which the photo chemical smog is formed by speeding up the conversion of nitric oxide (NO) to nitrogen dioxide (NO_2). To accomplish this, carbon monoxide (CO) combines with oxygen (O_2) and nitrogen dioxide (NO_2) to produce carbon dioxide (CO_2) and nitrogen dioxide (NO_2). ($CO + O_2 + NO = CO_2 + NO_2$).

The dangers of carbon monoxide, which is an odorless, colorless toxic gas are many. When carbon monoxide is inhaled into the lungs and passed into the blood stream, oxygen is replaced by the carbon monoxide in the red blood cells, causing a reduction in the amount of oxygen being supplied to the many parts of the body. This lack of oxygen causes headaches, lack of coordination, reduced mental alertness and should the carbon monoxide concentration be high enough, death could result.

NITROGEN

Normally, nitrogen is an inert gas. When heated to approximately 2500°F. through the combustion process, this gas becomes active and causes an increase in the nitric oxide (NOx) emission.

Oxides of nitrogen (NOx) are composed of approximately 97-98 percent nitric oxide (NO_2). Nitric oxide is a colorless gas but when it is passed into the atmosphere, it combines with oxygen and forms nitrogen dioxide (NO_2). The nitrogen dioxide then combines with chemically active hydrocarbons (HC) and when in the presence of sunlight, causes the formation of photo chemical smog.

OZONE

To further complicate matters, some of the nitrogen dioxide (NO_2) is broken apart by the sunlight to form nitric oxide and oxygen. ($NO_2 + sunlight = NO + O$). This single atom of oxygen then combines with diatomic (meaning 2 atoms) oxygen (O_2) to form ozone (O_3). Ozone is 1 of the smells associated with smog. It has a pungent and offensive odor, irritates the eyes and lung tissues, affects the growth of plant life and causes rapid deterioration of rubber products. Ozone can be formed by sunlight as well as electrical discharge into the air.

The most common discharge area on the automobile engine is the secondary ignition electrical system, especially when inferior quality spark plug cables are used. As the surge of high voltage is routed through the secondary cable, the circuit builds up an electrical field around the wire, acting upon the oxygen in the surrounding air to form the ozone. The faint glow along the cable with the engine running that may be visible on a dark night, is called the 'corona discharge.' It is the result of the electrical field passing from a high along the cable, to a low in the surrounding air, which forms the ozone gas. The combination of corona and ozone has been a major cause of cable deterioration. Recently, different types and better quality insulating materials have lengthened the life of the electrical cables.

Although ozone at ground level can be harmful, ozone is beneficial to the earth's inhabitants. By having a concentrated ozone layer called the 'ozonosphere', between 10 and 20 miles up in the atmosphere much of the ultra violet radiation from the sun's rays are absorbed and screened. If this ozone layer were not present, much of the earth's surface would be burned, dried and unfit for human life.

There is much discussion concerning the ozone layer and its density. A feeling exists that this protective layer of ozone is slowly diminishing and corrective action must be directed to this problem. Much experimenting is presently being conducted to determine if a problem exists and if so, the short and long term effects of the problem and how it can be remedied.

OXIDES OF SULFUR

Oxides of sulfur (SOx) were initially ignored in the exhaust system emissions, since the sulfur content of gasoline as a fuel is less than 1/10 of 1 percent. Because of this small amount, it was felt that it contributed very little to the overall pollution problem. However, because of the difficulty in solving the sulfur emissions in industrial pollutions and the introduction of catalytic converter to the automobile exhaust systems, a change was mandated. The automobile exhaust system, when equipped with a catalytic converter, changes the sulfur dioxide (SO_2) into the sulfur trioxide (SO_3).

When this combines with water vapors (H_2O), a sulfuric acid mist (H_2SO_4) is formed and is a very difficult pollutant to handle and is extremely corrosive. This sulfuric acid mist that is formed, is the same mist that rises from the vents of an automobile storage battery when an active chemical reaction takes place within the battery cells.

When a large concentration of vehicles equipped with catalytic converters are operating in an area, this acid mist will rise and be distributed over a large ground area causing land, plant, crop, paints and building damage.

PARTICULATE MATTER

A certain amount of particulate matter is present in the burning of any fuel, with carbon constituting the largest percentage of the particulates. In gasoline, the remaining percentage of particulates is the burned remains of the various other compounds used in its manufacture. When a gasoline engine is in good internal condition, the particulate emissions are low but as the engine wears internally, the particulate emissions increase. By visually inspecting the tail pipe emissions, a determination can be made as to where an engine defect may exist. An engine with light gray smoke emitting from the tail pipe normally indicates an increase in the oil consumption through burning due to internal engine wear. Black smoke would indicate a defective fuel delivery system, causing the engine to operate in a rich mode. Regardless of the color of the smoke, the internal part of the engine or the fuel delivery system should be repaired to a 'like new' condition to prevent excess particulate emissions.

Good grades of engine lubricating oils should be used, meeting the manufacturers specification. 'Cut-rate' oils can contribute to the particulate emission problem because of their low 'flash' or ignition temperature point. Such oils burn prematurely during the combustion process causing emissions of particulate matter.

The cooling system is an important factor in the reduction of particulate matter. With the cooling system operating at a temperature specified by the manufacturer, the optimum of combustion will occur. The cooling system must be maintained in the same manner as the engine oiling system, as each system is required to perform properly in order for the engine to operate efficiently for a long time.

Other Automobile Emission Sources

Before emission controls were mandated on the internal combustion engines, other sources of engine pollutants were discovered, along with the exhaust emission. It was determined the engine combustion exhaust produced 60 percent of the total emission pollutants, fuel evaporation from the fuel tank and carburetor vents produced 20 percent, with the another 20 percent being produced through the crankcase as a by-product of the combustion process.

CRANKCASE EMISSIONS

Crankcase emissions are made up of water, acids, unburned fuel, oil fumes and particulates. The emissions are classified as hydrocarbons (HC) and are formed by the small amount of unburned, compressed air/fuel mixture entering the crankcase from the combustion area during the compression and power strokes, between the cylinder walls and piston rings. The head of the compression and combustion help to form the remaining crankcase emissions.

Since the first engines, crankcase emissions were allowed to go into the air through a road draft tube, mounted on the lower side of the engine block. Fresh air came in through an open oil filler cap or breather. The air passed through the crankcase mixing with blow-by gases. The motion of the vehicle and the air blowing past the open end of the road draft tube caused a low pressure area at the end of the tube. Crankcase emissions were simply drawn out of the road draft tube into the air.

To control the crankcase emission, the road draft tube was deleted. A hose and/or tubing was routed from the crankcase to the intake manifold so the blow-by emission could be burned with the air/fuel mixture. However, it was found that intake manifold vacuum, used to draw the crankcase emissions

into the manifold, would vary in strength at the wrong time and not allow the proper emission flow. A regulating type valve was needed to control the flow of air through the crankcase.

Testing, showed the removal of the blow-by gases from the crankcase as quickly as possible, was most important to the longevity of the engine. Should large accumulations of blow-by gases remain and condense, dilution of the engine oil would occur to form water, soots, resins, acids and lead salts, resulting in the formation of sludge and varnishes. This condensation of the blow-by gases occur more frequently on vehicles used in numerous starting and stopping conditions, excessive idling and when the engine is not allowed to attain normal operating temperature through short runs. The crankcase purge control or PCV system will be described in detail later in this section.

FUEL EVAPORATIVE EMISSIONS

Gasoline fuel is a major source of pollution, before and after it is burned in the automobile engine. From the time the fuel is refined, stored, pumped and transported, again stored until it is pumped into the fuel tank of the vehicle, the gasoline gives off unburned hydrocarbons (HC) into the atmosphere. Through redesigning of the storage areas and venting systems, the pollution factor has been diminished but not eliminated, from the refinery standpoint. However, the automobile still remained the primary source of vaporized, unburned hydrocarbon (HC) emissions.

Fuel pumped form an underground storage tank is cool but when exposed to a warmer ambient temperature, will expand. Before controls were mandated, an owner would fill the fuel tank with fuel from an underground storage tank and park the vehicle for some time in warm area, such as a parking lot. As the fuel would warm, it would expand and should no provisions or area be provided for the expansion, the fuel would spill out the filler neck and onto the ground, causing hydrocarbon (HC) pollution and creating a severe fire hazard. To correct this condition, the vehicle manufacturers added overflow plumbing and/or gasoline tanks with built in expansion areas or domes.

However, this did not control the fuel vapor emission from the fuel tank and the carburetor bowl. It was determined that most of the fuel evaporation occurred when the vehicle was stationary and the engine not operating. Most vehicles carry 5-25 gallons of gasoline. Should a large concentration of vehicles be parked in 1 area, such as a large parking lot, excessive fuel vapor emissions would take place, increasing as the temperature increases.

To prevent the vapor emission from escaping into the atmosphere, the fuel system is designed to trap the fuel vapors while the vehicle is stationary, by sealing the fuel system from the atmosphere. A storage system is used to collect and hold the fuel vapors from the carburetor and the fuel tank when the engine is not operating. When the engine is started, the storage system is then purged of the fuel vapors, which are drawn into the engine and burned with the air/fuel mixture.

EMISSION COMPONENTS MAINTENANCE INTERVALS—TYPE A: NORMAL SERVICE
MODEL: ALL

TO BE SERVICED	TYPE OF SERVICE	VEHICLE MILEAGE INTERVAL							
		7500	15,000	22,500	30,000	37,500	45,000	52,500	60,000
Oxygen Sensor	I								✔
Ignition Timing	I				✔				✔
Vacuum Lines and Hoses	I				✔				✔
Ignition Wires	I				✔				✔
Spark Plugs ①	R				✔				✔
Engine Oil and Filter ②	R	✔	✔	✔	✔	✔	✔	✔	✔
Engine Air Cleaner Element	I				✔				✔
Crankcase Emission Filter	I				✔				✔
PCV Valve	I				✔				✔
Fuel Filter	R				✔				✔
Charcoal Canister	I				✔				✔
Fuel/Vapor Return Lines	I				✔				✔
Fuel Tank Cap and Restrictor	I				✔				✔
Coolant System	R				✔				✔
Exhaust Pipe and Muffler	I				✔				✔
Catalytic Converter and Shield	I				✔				✔
EGR System	I				✔				✔
Timing Belt	I				✔				✔
Throttle Body	I				✔				✔
Drive Belts	I				✔				✔

FOR COMPLETE EMISSION WARRANTY COVERAGE CONSULT INDIVIDUAL VEHICLE MANUFACTURER'S WARRANTY MAINTENANCE GUIDE.

NOTE: Normal driving conditions:
- Normal driving with little Stop/Go driving
- No prolonged idling (vehicle NOT used in police, taxi or delivery service)
- Most trips at least 10 miles or more
- No driving in excessively dusty conditions
- No short trips in severe cold weather
- No sustained high speed driving in hot weather
- No driving in areas using road salt or other corrosive materials
- No driving on rough and/or muddy roads
- No towing a trailer
- No using rooftop carrier or camper

I—Inspect
R—Replace
① 4.6L engine spark plugs should be replaced every 100,000 miles
② Replace engine oil and filter every 7500 miles or 12 months

84204001

EMISSION COMPONENTS MAINTENANCE INTERVALS—TYPE B: SEVERE SERVICE
MODEL: ALL

TO BE SERVICED	TYPE OF SERVICE	VEHICLE MILEAGE INTERVAL					
		3000	6000	12,000	30,000	45,000	60,000
Oxygen Sensor	I				✓		✓
Ignition Timing	I				✓		✓
Vacuum Lines and Hoses	I				✓		✓
Ignition Wires	I			✓	✓	✓	✓
Spark Plugs ①	R				✓		✓
Engine Oil and Filter ②	R	✓	✓	✓	✓	✓	✓
Engine Air Cleaner Element	I				✓		✓
Crankcase Emission Filter	I				✓		✓
PCV Valve	I				✓		✓
Fuel Filter	R				✓		✓
Charcoal Canister	I				✓		✓
Fuel/Vapor Return Lines	I				✓		✓
Fuel Tank Cap and Restrictor	I				✓		✓
Coolant System	R				✓		✓
Exhaust Pipe and Muffler	I				✓		✓
Catalytic Converter and Shield	I				✓		✓
EGR System	I				✓		✓
Timing Belt	I				✓		✓
Throttle Body	I				✓		✓
Drive Belts	I				✓		✓

FOR COMPLETE EMISSION WARRANTY COVERAGE CONSULT INDIVIDUAL VEHICLE MANUFACTURER'S WARRANTY MAINTENANCE GUIDE.

NOTE: Severe driving conditions:
- Stop/Go driving
- Prolonged idling (vehicle used in police, taxi or delivery service)
- Most trips less than 10 miles
- Driving in excessively dusty conditions
- Short trips in severe cold weather
- Sustained high speed driving in hot weather
- Driving in areas using road salt or other corrosive materials
- Driving on rough and/or muddy roads
- Towing a trailer
- Using rooftop carrier or camper

I—Inspect
R—Replace
① 4.6L engine spark plugs should be replaced every 100,000 miles
② Replace engine oil and filter every 3000 miles or 6 months

84204002

TERMS USED IN THIS SECTION

The following is a list of the abbreviations used in this section and their meaning.

ALDL: Assembly Line Data Link
AIR: Air Injection Reaction
BCM: Body Computer Module
CCDIC: Climate Control Driver Information Center
CCV: Canister Control Valve
CO: Carbon Monoxide
DLC: Data Link Connector
DTC: Diagnostic Trouble Code
EAC: Electric Air Control Valve
EAS: Electric Air Switching Valve
ECCP: Electronic Climate Control
ECM: Electronic Control Module
ECT: Electric Air Control Valve with Relief Tube
ECTS: Engine Coolant Temperature Sensor
EDV: Electric Divert Valve
EEC: Electronic Climate Control
EGR: Exhaust Gas Recirculation

ESC: Electronic Spark Control
EVAP: Evaporative Emission System
FDC: Fuel Data Center
HC: Hydrocarbon
HEI: High Energy Ignition
IAC: Idle Air Control Valve
IAT: Intake Air Temperature Sensor
MAP: Manifold Absolute Pressure Sensor
NOx: Oxides of Nitrogen
PCM: Powertrain Control Module (previously called ECM)
PCV: Positive Crankcase Ventilation
PROM: Programmable Read Only Memory
SES: Service Engine Soon Light
SFI: Sequential Multiport Fuel Injection
TPS: Throttle Position Switch
TVV: Thermal Vacuum Valve
VSS: Vehicle Speed Sensor
WOT: Wide Open Throttle

EMISSION CONTROLS

Crankcase Ventilation System

All vehicles covered in this manual are equipped with a Positive Crankcase Ventilation (PCV) system. The PCV system vents crankcase gases into the engine air intake where they are burned with the fuel and air mixture. The PCV system keeps pollutants from being released into the atmosphere, and also helps to keep the engine oil clean, by ridding the crankcase of moisture and corrosive fumes. Fresh air from the air cleaner is pulled into the crankcase, mixed with crankcase gases and then purged into the intake manifold.

OPERATION

▶ **See Figures 1, 2, 3 and 4**

The primary control is through the PCV valve, which meters the flow rate dependent on intake manifold vacuum.

When intake manifold vacuum is high, during deceleration, low speed driving or idle, the PCV valve controls a low flow rate. This is because during these modes of operation, the crankcase gas levels, including cylinder blow-by, are low.

When intake manifold vacuum is low, such as during acceleration or high load operation, the PCV valve controls flow to a higher rate to accommodate increased engine crankcase gases.

Under full throttle operation or abnormal conditions, such as a worn or damaged engine, or during high speed light load operation, the system allows excess blow-by gases to flow through the fresh air tube into the inlet duct to be combined with incoming air from the air cleaner.

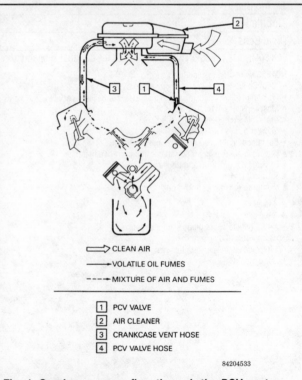

⟹ CLEAN AIR
⟶ VOLATILE OIL FUMES
----⟶ MIXTURE OF AIR AND FUMES

1 PCV VALVE
2 AIR CLEANER
3 CRANKCASE VENT HOSE
4 PCV VALVE HOSE

84204533

Fig. 1 Crankcase vapor flow through the PCV system — 4.9L engine shown

A plugged PCV valve or hose may cause the following conditions:
- Rough idle
- Stalling or slow idle speed
- Oil leaks
- Oil in the air cleaner
- Sludge in the engine

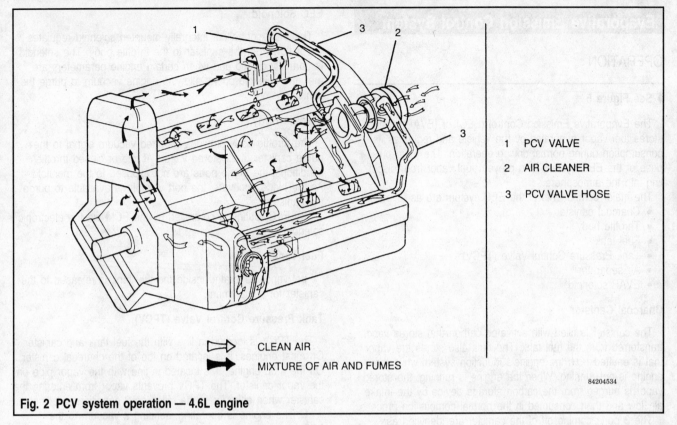

1 PCV VALVE
2 AIR CLEANER
3 PCV VALVE HOSE

84204534

Fig. 2 PCV system operation — 4.6L engine

⇨ CLEAN AIR
⬛➤ MIXTURE OF AIR AND FUMES

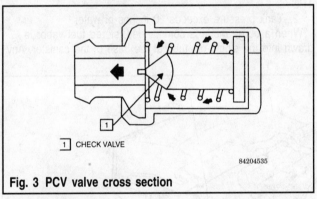

1 CHECK VALVE

84204535

Fig. 3 PCV valve cross section

A leaking valve or hose could cause the following conditions:
- Erratic idle speed
- Rough idle
- Stalling

PCV SYSTEM TESTING

If an engine is idling rough, check for a clogged PCV valve or plugged hose. Replace system components as required.

1. Remove the PCV valve from the rocker cover.
2. Run the engine at idle.
3. Place your thumb over the end of the valve to check for vacuum. If there is no vacuum at the valve, check for plugged hoses, intake manifold port or PCV valve. Replace plugged or deteriorated hoses.

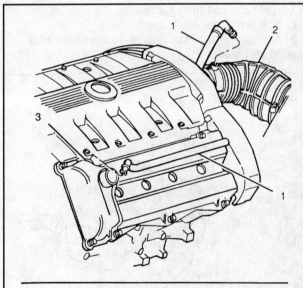

1 PCV FRESH AIR TUBE
2 AIR CLEANER
3 GROMMET

84204536

Fig. 4 PCV hose, air cleaner and grommet on left cam cover — 4.6L engine

4. Turn the engine OFF and remove the PCV valve. Shake the valve and listen for the rattle of the check needle inside the valve. If the valve does not rattle, replace it.

Evaporative Emission Control System

OPERATION

▶ **See Figure 5**

The Evaporative Emission Control (EEC) or (EVAP) system stores fuel vapor generated by the vehicle and regulates its consumption during normal driving operation. The main purpose of the EEC system is to prevent fuel vapor from dispelling into the atmosphere.

The major components of the EEC system are as follows:

- Charcoal canister
- Throttle body
- Fuel tank
- Tank Pressure Control Valve (TPCV)
- Air separator
- EVAP solenoid

Charcoal Canister

The canister is filled with activated carbon that stores vapor transferred from the fuel tank. The tank also stores the vapor that is emitted from the engine's induction system while the engine is not running. When the engine is running, the stored vapor is purged from the carbon storage device by the intake air flow and then consumed in the normal combustion process.

The 3 ports coming off of the canister are identified as:

1. Fuel vapor port (from fuel tank)
2. EEC port (purge line to throttle body)
3. Atmospheric port (from fresh air source via the body mounted vent hose)

EEC Solenoid

The PCM controlled, integrally mounted solenoid regulates vapor flow from the canister to the throttle body. The solenoid is normally closed and when certain engine parameters are met, the solenoid opens allowing engine vacuum to purge the canister.

Throttle Body

The throttle body provides a ported vacuum signal to the purge canister of its stored vapor. At idle or closed throttle conditions, the purge ports are not exposed to the manifold. As the blade uncovers, the port vacuum is available to purge the canister.

The EEC routine is controlled by the PCM via the electronic solenoid.

Fuel Tank

Fuel vapor generated inside the fuel tank is released to the canister for containment.

Tank Pressure Control Valve (TPCV)

The TPCV is located in line with the fuel tank and canister. On most engines, it is located on top of the charcoal canister. On the 4.6L engine, it is located in line with the vapor pipe on the vapor canister. The TPCV prevents vapor from entering the canister when either/or of the following 2 conditions are met:

1. The engine is operating, sending a vacuum to the TPCV.

2. Tank pressure exceeds 20 inches of water

When a purge mode is commanded, stored fuel vapor is drawn into the single dip tube at the base of the canister. Any

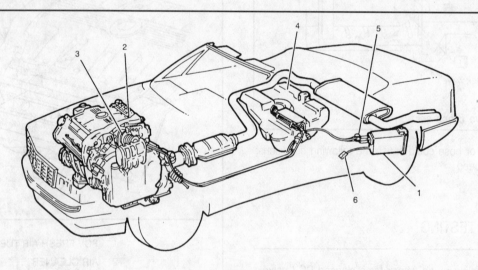

1	EVAP CHARCOAL CANISTER
2	EVAP SOLENOID
3	THROTTLE BODY
4	FUEL TANK
5	TANK PRESSURE CONTROL VALVE (TPCV)
6	AIR SEPARATOR

84204538

Fig. 5 EVAP system component layout — 4.6L engine

liquid trapped in the well is also drawn into the tube. Fresh air is drawn into the canister through the remote vent hose.

The PCM operates a solenoid valve which purges the canister with ported vacuum at the throttle body. Under cold engine operation 'OPEN LOOP', or idle conditions the solenoid de-energized by the PCM, which does not allow vacuum to the canister through the normally closed solenoid.

The canister will be enabled, the PCM will energize the solenoid when:

- Coolant temperature is above 80°C
- Closed loop has been achieved for at least 30 seconds
- Throttle switch open
- Vehicle speed greater than 10 mph
- Codes E013, E017, E042, E044 or E045 is present

When the solenoid is closed (is not receiving voltage or has a stuck plunger) the canister will not purge to the intake manifold. This will prevent the canister from purging vapors and could result in a saturated canister.

FUNCTIONAL TEST OF CHARCOAL CANISTER

4.5L and 4.9L Engines

1. Connect a clean length of hose to the fuel tank vapor line connection on the canister and attempt to blow through the purge control valve. It should be difficult or impossible to blow through the valve. If air passes easily, the valve is stuck open and should be replaced.

2. Connect a hand-held vacuum pump to the top vacuum line fitting of the purge control valve. Apply a vacuum of 15 in. Hg (51 kPa) to the purge valve diaphragm. If the vacuum reading is less than 10 inches after 10 seconds, the diaphragm is leaking and the TPCV must be replaced. If the diaphragm holds vacuum, try to blow through the hose connected to the lower tube while vacuum is still being applied. An increase flow of air should be observed. If not, replace the TPCV.

3. Attach a hose to the lower port of the canister and attempt to blow through it. Air should pass through and into the canister. If not, replace the canister.

4. Disconnect the electrical connector at the canister purge solenoid. Attach a hose to the upper port on the canister and attempt to blow air through it. Air should not pass through into the canister. If air passes, replace the purge solenoid.

5. Measure the resistance of the purge control solenoid. The resistance should be greater than 20 ohms and less than 100 ohms. If the solenoid resistance is not in this range, replace the solenoid.

6. Reconnect all purge hoses and the solenoid electrical connector.

REMOVAL & INSTALLATION

Charcoal Canister

▶ See Figure 6

1. Tag and disconnect the hoses from the canister. During installation, they must be installed in their original locations.
2. Disconnect the purge solenoid electrical connectors.
3. Remove the charcoal canister retainers.
4. Remove the canister from the vehicle.
5. Installation is the reverse of the removal procedure. Torque the retainers to 25 inch lbs. (2.8 Nm). If necessary, refer to the Vehicle Emission Control Information label, located in the engine compartment for proper routing of the vacuum hoses.

EVAP Solenoid

4.5L AND 4.9L ENGINES

The EVAP solenoid is normally mounted on top of the canister assembly. Label all vacuum hoses at the solenoid prior to removal from the solenoid.

1. Tag and disconnect the hoses from the canister. During installation, they must be installed in their original locations.
2. Disconnect the purge solenoid electrical connectors.
3. Remove the charcoal canister retainers.
4. Remove the canister from the vehicle.
5. Remove the solenoid from the top of the canister.
6. Installation is the reverse of the removal procedure.

4.6L ENGINE

▶ See Figure 7

1. Remove the spark plug wires and conduit channel.
2. Release the fuel system pressure and disconnect the fuel lines, if required.
3. Disconnect the EVAP solenoid electrical connector.
4. Remove the retainer bolt and the EVAP solenoid from the engine.
5. Installation is the reverse of the removal procedure. Tighten the solenoid mounting bolt to 106 inch lbs. (12 Nm).

Tank Pressure Control Valve

1. Disconnect the hoses from the control valve.
2. Raise and safely support the vehicle.
3. Remove the mounting hardware.
4. Remove the control valve from the vehicle.
5. Installation is the reverse of the removal procedure.

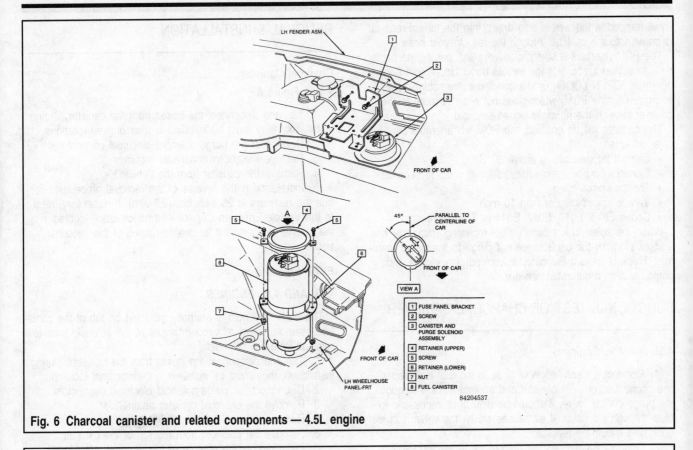

Fig. 6 Charcoal canister and related components — 4.5L engine

1	FUSE PANEL BRACKET
2	SCREW
3	CANISTER AND PURGE SOLENOID ASSEMBLY
4	RETAINER (UPPER)
5	SCREW
6	RETAINER (LOWER)
7	NUT
8	FUEL CANISTER

84204537

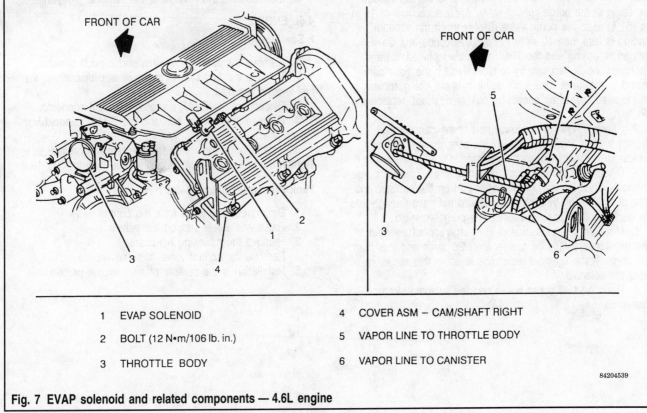

1	EVAP SOLENOID	4	COVER ASM – CAM/SHAFT RIGHT
2	BOLT (12 N•m/106 lb. in.)	5	VAPOR LINE TO THROTTLE BODY
3	THROTTLE BODY	6	VAPOR LINE TO CANISTER

84204539

Fig. 7 EVAP solenoid and related components — 4.6L engine

Exhaust Gas Recirculation (EGR) System

PURPOSE

The Exhaust Gas Recirculation (EGR) system is used in an automotive engine to decrease the emission levels of oxides of nitrogen (NOx). NOx defines a group of chemical compounds containing nitrogen and varying amounts of oxygen that can have harmful environmental effects in large quantities.

NOx forms during the combustion process in amounts that is dependent on the concentration of oxygen in the combustion chamber and the duration that the combustion process temperatures exceed 1500°F. Decreased NOx levels are accomplished by reducing the peak combustion temperature through dilution of the incoming air/fuel charge with exhaust. During combustion, exhaust gas (largely non-reactive carbon dioxide and water vapor) acts to absorb a portion of the combustion energy, resulting in lower temperatures throughout the combustion process yielding lower amounts of NOx.

Desired amounts of EGR depend upon geometry of the combustion chamber and the operating condition of the engine. Extensive laboratory and vehicle tests are used to determine optimal EGR rates for all operating conditions. Too little EGR can yield high NOx, while too much EGR can disrupt combustion events.

OPERATION AND TESTING

4.5L and 4.9L Engines
▶ See Figures 8, 9, 10 and 11

As mentioned earlier, the EGR valve is opened by vacuum to allow exhaust gases to flow into the intake manifold. The exhaust gas then moves with the air/fuel mixture into the combustion chamber. The Powertrain Control Module (PCM) controls the vacuum to the EGR valve with a solenoid valve. A constant 12 volts is supplied to the positive terminal on the EGR valve. The vacuum supply to the EGR valve is regulated by the PCM controlling the EGR solenoid ground. The percentage that the PCM grounds the EGR solenoid is called the duty cycle. The duty cycle is the time the solenoid is on divided by the time it is off. A de-energized solenoid allows vacuum to pass to the EGR valve. A duty cycle of 100 percent will turn the EGR full off since the solenoid will be energized and not allow vacuum to pass to the valve. The EGR pulse width is regulated by the PCM depending on engine load conditions. When the engine is cold, within specified load range and above a specified rpm, the PCM sends 100 percent duty cycle to the solenoid and blocks vacuum to the EGR valve. When the engine is warm, the PCM sends a duty cycle to the solenoid to allow EGR.

These engine use a positive backpressure EGR valve, which requires exhaust backpressure (proportional to engine flow) to open and allow exhaust gas to flow into the intake manifold.

The PCM uses the following sensors to control the EGR solenoid:
- Coolant Temperature (CTS)
- Throttle Position (TPS)
- Manifold Pressure (MAP)
- Manifold Air Temperature (MAT)
- Throttle Switch (ISC)
- RPM data from the distributor reference pulses
- Vehicle Speed Sensor (VSS)

Too much EGR flow tends to weaken combustion, causing the engine to run roughly or stall. With too much EGR flow at idle, cruise speed or cold operation, any of the following conditions may occur:
- Engine stalls after cold start
- Engine stalls at idle after deceleration
- Car surges during cruise
- Rough idle

If the EGR valve should stay open due to a stuck open valve, the engine may not run.

Too little or no EGR flow allows combustion temperatures to get too high during acceleration and load conditions. Any of the following conditions may occur:
- Spark knock
- Emission test failure

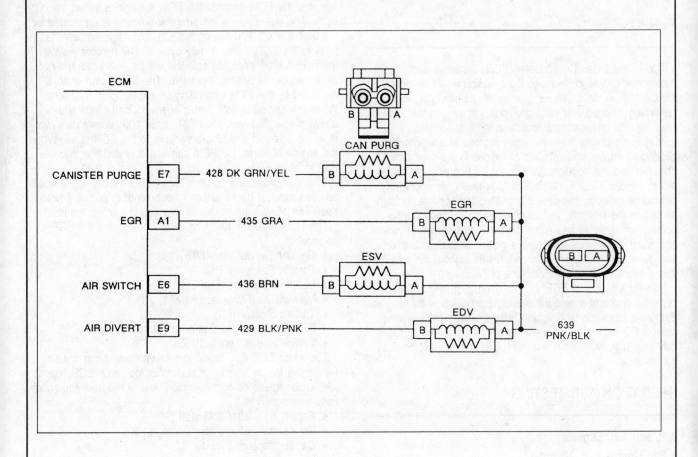

PFI CHART C-7

EGR DIAGNOSIS

Before Staring

- Check 10 amp fuse (# 3) in underhood relay center.

- Measure EGR solenoid resistance – should be 20 – 100 ohms.

  The 4.5L DLPFI engine uses a positive backpressure EGR valve which limits EGR flow with low exhaust backpressure (idle, decel, etc.). It is very important that exhaust tubes which decrease backpressure (pull air through) are **not** hooked to the vehicle when diagnosing the EGR system.

VACUUM TEST

1. Connect a vacuum gage to the source side of the EGR solenoid. Start the engine, manifold vacuum should be present. If it is not, repair leaks or obstruction between the EGR solenoid and throttle body.

2. Connect a vacuum gage to the EGR valve vacuum supply. There should be no vacuum with the engine idling. If there is, follow Chart C-7

3. With the gage hooked to the EGR valve vacuum supply, disconnect the EGR solenoid connector. There should be more than 8 inches of vacuum available. If not, repair leak or obstruction in EGR valve vacuum hose.

84204007

Fig. 8 Exhaust Gas Recirculation (EGR) system check — 4.5L engine

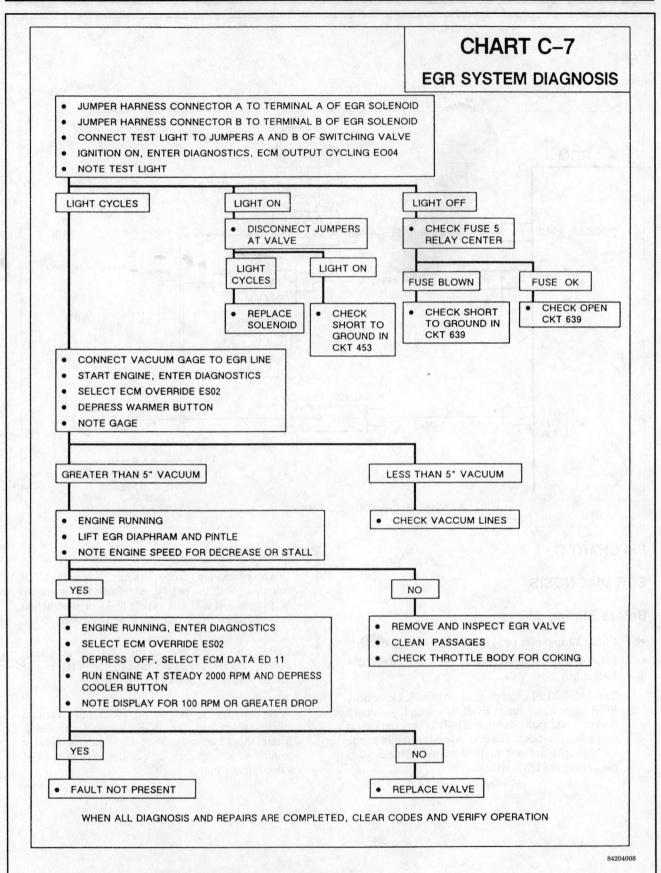

CHART C-7
EGR SYSTEM DIAGNOSIS

- JUMPER HARNESS CONNECTOR A TO TERMINAL A OF EGR SOLENOID
- JUMPER HARNESS CONNECTOR B TO TERMINAL B OF EGR SOLENOID
- CONNECT TEST LIGHT TO JUMPERS A AND B OF SWITCHING VALVE
- IGNITION ON, ENTER DIAGNOSTICS, ECM OUTPUT CYCLING EO04
- NOTE TEST LIGHT

LIGHT CYCLES

LIGHT ON
- DISCONNECT JUMPERS AT VALVE

  LIGHT CYCLES
  - REPLACE SOLENOID

  LIGHT ON
  - CHECK SHORT TO GROUND IN CKT 453

LIGHT OFF
- CHECK FUSE 5 RELAY CENTER

  FUSE BLOWN
  - CHECK SHORT TO GROUND IN CKT 639

  FUSE OK
  - CHECK OPEN CKT 639

- CONNECT VACUUM GAGE TO EGR LINE
- START ENGINE, ENTER DIAGNOSTICS
- SELECT ECM OVERRIDE ES02
- DEPRESS WARMER BUTTON
- NOTE GAGE

GREATER THAN 5" VACUUM

- ENGINE RUNNING
- LIFT EGR DIAPHRAM AND PINTLE
- NOTE ENGINE SPEED FOR DECREASE OR STALL

LESS THAN 5" VACUUM

- CHECK VACCUM LINES

YES

- ENGINE RUNNING, ENTER DIAGNOSTICS
- SELECT ECM OVERRIDE ES02
- DEPRESS OFF, SELECT ECM DATA ED 11
- RUN ENGINE AT STEADY 2000 RPM AND DEPRESS COOLER BUTTON
- NOTE DISPLAY FOR 100 RPM OR GREATER DROP

NO

- REMOVE AND INSPECT EGR VALVE
- CLEAN PASSAGES
- CHECK THROTTLE BODY FOR COKING

YES
- FAULT NOT PRESENT

NO
- REPLACE VALVE

WHEN ALL DIAGNOSIS AND REPAIRS ARE COMPLETED, CLEAR CODES AND VERIFY OPERATION

84204008

Fig. 9 Exhaust Gas Recirculation (EGR) system check — 4.5L engine

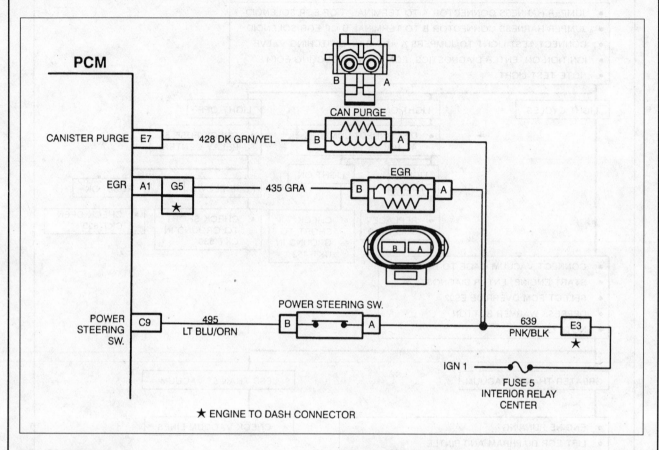

★ ENGINE TO DASH CONNECTOR

PFI CHART C-7

EGR DIAGNOSIS

Before Staring

- Check 10 amp fuse (#5) in underhood relay center.
- Measure EGR solenoid resistance – should be 20 – 100 ohms.

  The 4.9L DLPFI engine uses a positive backpressure EGR valve which limits EGR flow with low exhaust backpressure (idle, decel, etc.). It is very important that exhaust tubes which decrease backpressure (pull air through) are **not** hooked to the vehicle when diagnosing the EGR system.

VACUUM TEST

1. Connect a vacuum gage to the source side of the EGR solenoid. Start the engine, manifold vacuum should be present. If it is not, repair leaks or obstruction between the EGR solenoid and throttle body.

2. Connect a vacuum gage to the EGR valve vacuum supply. There should be no vacuum with the engine idling. If there is, follow Chart C-7.

3. With the gage hooked to the EGR valve vacuum supply, disconnect the EGR solenoid connector. There should be more than 15 inches of vacuum available. If not, repair leak or obstruction in EGR valve vacuum hose.

84204005

Fig. 10 Exhaust Gas Recirculation (EGR) system check — 4.9L engine

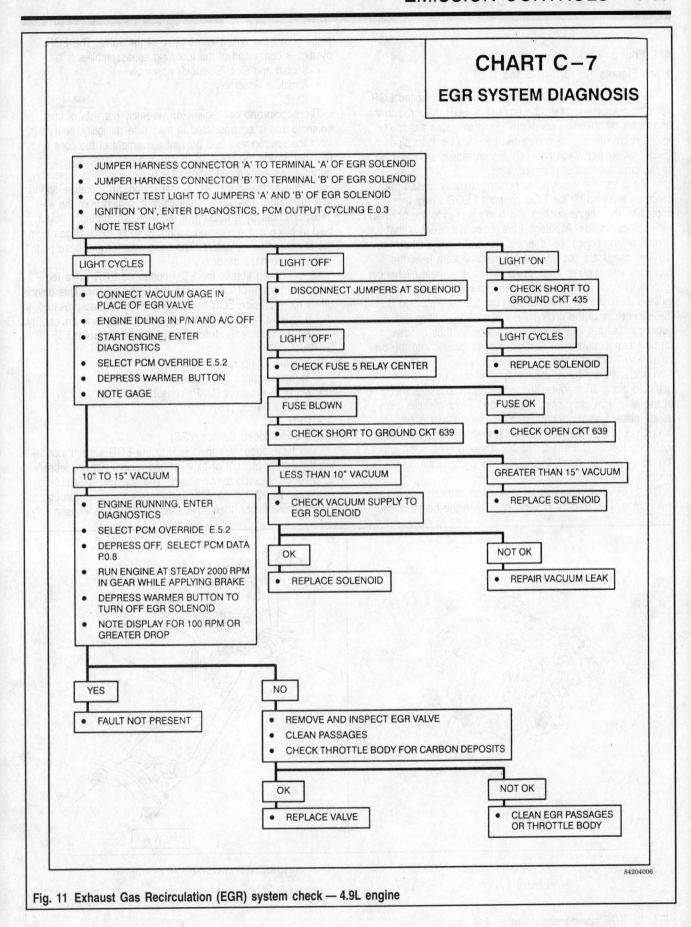

CHART C-7
EGR SYSTEM DIAGNOSIS

- JUMPER HARNESS CONNECTOR 'A' TO TERMINAL 'A' OF EGR SOLENOID
- JUMPER HARNESS CONNECTOR 'B' TO TERMINAL 'B' OF EGR SOLENOID
- CONNECT TEST LIGHT TO JUMPERS 'A' AND 'B' OF EGR SOLENOID
- IGNITION 'ON', ENTER DIAGNOSTICS, PCM OUTPUT CYCLING E.0.3
- NOTE TEST LIGHT

LIGHT CYCLES
- CONNECT VACUUM GAGE IN PLACE OF EGR VALVE
- ENGINE IDLING IN P/N AND A/C OFF
- START ENGINE, ENTER DIAGNOSTICS
- SELECT PCM OVERRIDE E.5.2
- DEPRESS WARMER BUTTON
- NOTE GAGE

LIGHT 'OFF'
- DISCONNECT JUMPERS AT SOLENOID

LIGHT 'ON'
- CHECK SHORT TO GROUND CKT 435

LIGHT 'OFF'
- CHECK FUSE 5 RELAY CENTER

LIGHT CYCLES
- REPLACE SOLENOID

FUSE BLOWN
- CHECK SHORT TO GROUND CKT 639

FUSE OK
- CHECK OPEN CKT 639

10" TO 15" VACUUM
- ENGINE RUNNING, ENTER DIAGNOSTICS
- SELECT PCM OVERRIDE E.5.2
- DEPRESS OFF, SELECT PCM DATA P.0.8
- RUN ENGINE AT STEADY 2000 RPM IN GEAR WHILE APPLYING BRAKE
- DEPRESS WARMER BUTTON TO TURN OFF EGR SOLENOID
- NOTE DISPLAY FOR 100 RPM OR GREATER DROP

LESS THAN 10" VACUUM
- CHECK VACUUM SUPPLY TO EGR SOLENOID

GREATER THAN 15" VACUUM
- REPLACE SOLENOID

OK
- REPLACE SOLENOID

NOT OK
- REPAIR VACUUM LEAK

YES
- FAULT NOT PRESENT

NO
- REMOVE AND INSPECT EGR VALVE
- CLEAN PASSAGES
- CHECK THROTTLE BODY FOR CARBON DEPOSITS

OK
- REPLACE VALVE

NOT OK
- CLEAN EGR PASSAGES OR THROTTLE BODY

84204006

Fig. 11 Exhaust Gas Recirculation (EGR) system check — 4.9L engine

4.6L Engine

▶ **See Figures 12, 13, 14, 15 and 16**

The Northstar 4.6L engine uses a computer controlled EGR valve to precisely regulate the amount of EGR delivered to the engine for all operating conditions. Exhaust gases are routed to the engine through a corrugated semi-flexible feed pipe (EGR valve pipe) which connects the crossover exhaust pipe to the crossover water pump housing.

In the crossover water pump housing, exhaust gases are precisely metered by the PCM controlled EGR valve, then cooled by the engine coolant and finally routed to the front and rear cylinder heads. A potential drawback with EGR is that for certain driving schedules, deposits can accumulate when hot exhaust gases are cooled. The Northstar system uses the crossover water pump housing as a cross-flow heat exchanger to cool exhaust gases in large easily cleaned passages to virtually eliminate any concern with deposit accumulation during the service life of the engine. This is done by having the cooling passages reduce EGR gasses below their deposit forming temperature prior to routing these gasses into the cylinder distribution channels.

In each cylinder bank, exhaust gases travel under the intake manifold along an irregular shaped sandwich passage made up of the aluminum alloy cylinder head and a non-metallic distribution plate. Engine vacuum acts to draw exhaust gases through outlets in the distribution plate where mixing with the incoming fuel/air charges for each cylinder occurs. Although the openings look small, the EGR valve pintle is the flow limiter in the system.

The EGR valve regulates the amount of exhaust gas fed to the engine. This mixture is dependent upon the height of the pintle above the orifice in the base of the valve. The EGR system is comprised of the following subassemblies:

- Bobbin and Coil (Solenoid) assembly
- Armature Assembly
- Base

The bobbin and coil (solenoid) assembly consists of one solenoid that is encapsulated to maximize reliability, seal coils from the environment and prevent movement of the coils and terminal. Inside the solenoid (bobin and coil) assembly is an armature assembly, consisting of a pintle and valve assembly, two seals, retaining washer, a seal spring, an armature spring and a bearing. The valve pintle shaft is sealed from the exhaust chamber by a bearing. In addition, an armature shield, held in place a compression spring, deflects exhaust gas from the shaft and the armature. The base adapter and base plate make up the base assembly.

As mentioned above, the PCM controlled EGR valve regulates the amount of exhaust gas fed to the engine. This device offers more precise EGR flow metering than a backpressure or digital type valve and superior emission control and driveability. The PCM monitors the following sensors to control the linear EGR valve:

- Coolant Temperature (CT) sensor
- Throttle position (TP) sensor
- Manifold Pressure (MAP) sensor
- Throttle Switch (TS)
- RPM data
- Vehicle Speed Sensor (VSS)

Output messages are then sent to the EGR system indicating the proper amount of exhaust gas recirculation necessary to lower combustion temperatures. The solenoid assembly is energized by 12 volt current which enters the valve through an electrical connector, then flows through the solenoid assembly

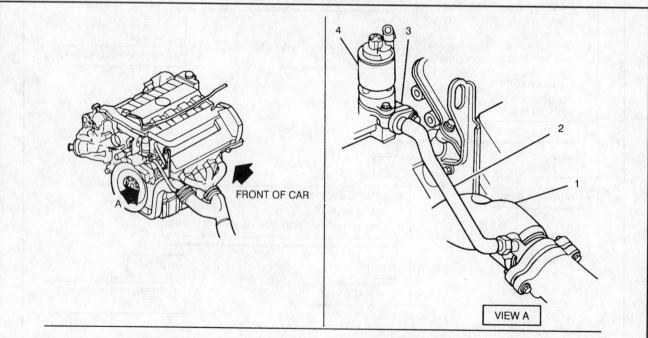

FRONT OF CAR

VIEW A

1	CROSSOVER EXHAUST PIPE	3	CROSSOVER WATER PUMP HOUSING
2	EGR VALVE PIPE	4	EGR VALVE

84204546

Fig. 12 EGR component layout — 4.6L engine

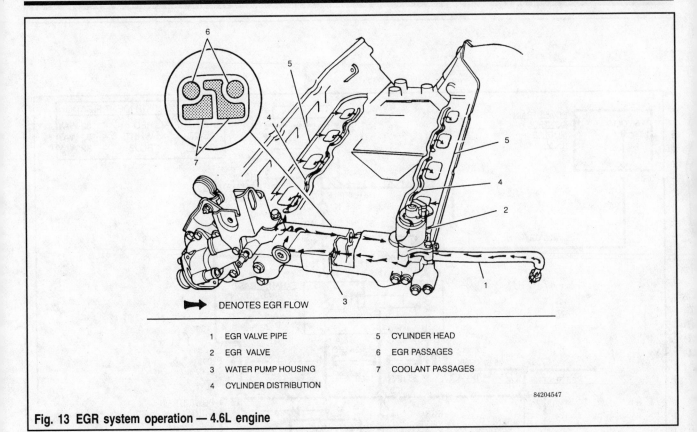

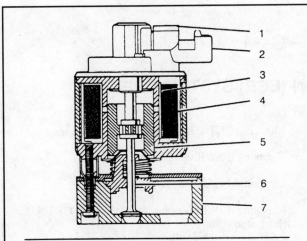

1	EGR VALVE PIPE	5	CYLINDER HEAD
2	EGR VALVE	6	EGR PASSAGES
3	WATER PUMP HOUSING	7	COOLANT PASSAGES
4	CYLINDER DISTRIBUTION		

➤ DENOTES EGR FLOW

84204547

Fig. 13 EGR system operation — 4.6L engine

to the PCM and creates an electromagnetic field. This field causes the armature assembly to be pulled upward, lifting the pintle a variable amount off the base. The exhaust gas then flows from the exhaust manifold (through the orifice) to the

1	CAP – SENSOR
2	SENSOR – EGR PINTLE POSITION
3	POLE PIECE – PRIMARY
4	BOBBIN AND COIL ASSEMBLY
5	SLEEVE – ARMATURE
6	VALVE – PINTLE
7	ARMATURE AND BASE ASSEMBLY

84204548

Fig. 14 Computer controlled EGR valve assembly

cylinder distribution channels. The height of the pintle is read by the pintle position sensor, and the PCM closes the loop on desired position versus actual position read, changing the pulse width modulated command to the solenoid accordingly, until the actual pintle position equals the desired pintle position. This results in improved flow accuracy. The EGR valve is unique in that the PCM continuously monitors pintle height and continuously corrects it in order to obtain accurate flow in a closed loop system. When the solenoid is de-energized (PCM breaks the circuit), the pintle is sealed against the orifice, blocking exhaust flow to the cylinder distribution channels.

To regulate EGR flow to the engine, the PCM controls the solenoid to directly vary the pintle position relative to the closed valve position. The EGR valve contains a potentiometer type position sensor that provides a voltage proportional to pintle position. Pintle position is used by the PCM for closed loop control of the valve pintle position to follow commanded position, for diagnostics, and to correct fuel spark for EGR.

Too much EGR flow tends to weaken combustion, causing the engine to run roughly or stall. With too much EGR flow at idle, cruise speed or cold operation, any of the following conditions may occur:
- Engine stalls after cold start
- Engine stalls at idle after deceleration
- Car surges during cruise

If the EGR valve should stay open due to a stuck open valve, the engine may not run.

Too little or no EGR flow allows combustion temperatures to get too high during acceleration and load conditions. Any of the following conditions may occur:
- Spark knock
- Emission test failure

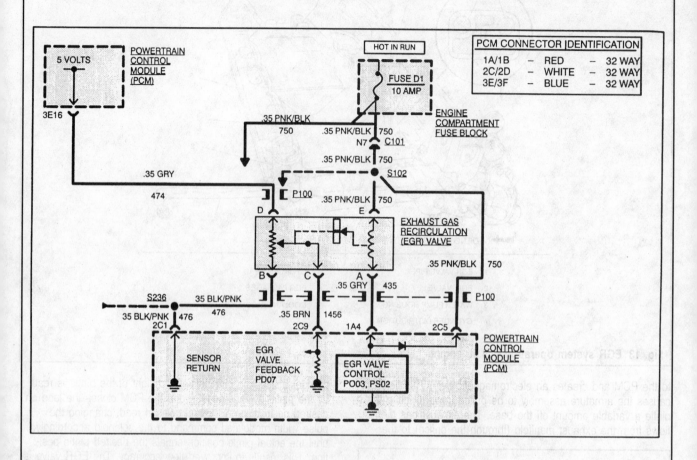

CHART 6E–C–1

EXHAUST GAS RECIRCULATION (EGR) SYSTEM CHECK

CIRCUIT DESCRIPTION:

This procedure tests the EGR system's ability to functionally regulate the amount of exhaust gas fed to the engine.

NOTES ON FAULT TREE:

1. Checking if by using PCM overrides the EGR valve can be shut off (less than 103 counts).

2. Checking if by using PCM overrides the EGR valve can return to full on (greater then 200 counts).

3. Checking CKT 750 and fuse 'D1' for an open.

4. Checking if EGR valve is open circuited.

5. Checking if CKT 435 is open.

6. Checking if PCM is open internally or if CKT 435 is shorted to voltage.

7. EGR valve control circuits are OK. Checking to see if the EGR valve can respond correctly to the signal being sent to it from the PCM.

84204003

Fig. 15 Exhaust Gas Recirculation (EGRr) system check — 4.6L engine

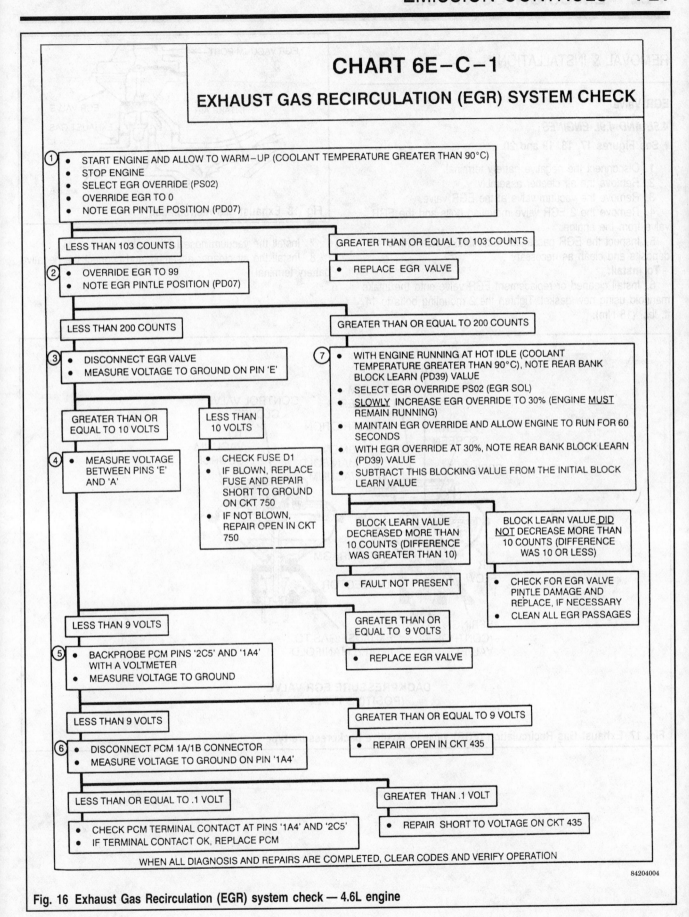

CHART 6E–C–1

EXHAUST GAS RECIRCULATION (EGR) SYSTEM CHECK

1.
- START ENGINE AND ALLOW TO WARM–UP (COOLANT TEMPERATURE GREATER THAN 90°C)
- STOP ENGINE
- SELECT EGR OVERRIDE (PS02)
- OVERRIDE EGR TO 0
- NOTE EGR PINTLE POSITION (PD07)

LESS THAN 103 COUNTS

GREATER THAN OR EQUAL TO 103 COUNTS
- REPLACE EGR VALVE

2.
- OVERRIDE EGR TO 99
- NOTE EGR PINTLE POSITION (PD07)

LESS THAN 200 COUNTS

GREATER THAN OR EQUAL TO 200 COUNTS

3.
- DISCONNECT EGR VALVE
- MEASURE VOLTAGE TO GROUND ON PIN 'E'

7.
- WITH ENGINE RUNNING AT HOT IDLE (COOLANT TEMPERATURE GREATER THAN 90°C), NOTE REAR BANK BLOCK LEARN (PD39) VALUE
- SELECT EGR OVERRIDE PS02 (EGR SOL)
- SLOWLY INCREASE EGR OVERRIDE TO 30% (ENGINE MUST REMAIN RUNNING)
- MAINTAIN EGR OVERRIDE AND ALLOW ENGINE TO RUN FOR 60 SECONDS
- WITH EGR OVERRIDE AT 30%, NOTE REAR BANK BLOCK LEARN (PD39) VALUE
- SUBTRACT THIS BLOCKING VALUE FROM THE INITIAL BLOCK LEARN VALUE

GREATER THAN OR EQUAL TO 10 VOLTS

LESS THAN 10 VOLTS

4.
- MEASURE VOLTAGE BETWEEN PINS 'E' AND 'A'

- CHECK FUSE D1
- IF BLOWN, REPLACE FUSE AND REPAIR SHORT TO GROUND ON CKT 750
- IF NOT BLOWN, REPAIR OPEN IN CKT 750

BLOCK LEARN VALUE DECREASED MORE THAN 10 COUNTS (DIFFERENCE WAS GREATER THAN 10)

BLOCK LEARN VALUE DID NOT DECREASE MORE THAN 10 COUNTS (DIFFERENCE WAS 10 OR LESS)

- FAULT NOT PRESENT

- CHECK FOR EGR VALVE PINTLE DAMAGE AND REPLACE, IF NECESSARY
- CLEAN ALL EGR PASSAGES

LESS THAN 9 VOLTS

GREATER THAN OR EQUAL TO 9 VOLTS

5.
- BACKPROBE PCM PINS '2C5' AND '1A4' WITH A VOLTMETER
- MEASURE VOLTAGE TO GROUND

- REPLACE EGR VALVE

LESS THAN 9 VOLTS

GREATER THAN OR EQUAL TO 9 VOLTS

6.
- DISCONNECT PCM 1A/1B CONNECTOR
- MEASURE VOLTAGE TO GROUND ON PIN '1A4'

- REPAIR OPEN IN CKT 435

LESS THAN OR EQUAL TO .1 VOLT

GREATER THAN .1 VOLT

- CHECK PCM TERMINAL CONTACT AT PINS '1A4' AND '2C5'
- IF TERMINAL CONTACT OK, REPLACE PCM

- REPAIR SHORT TO VOLTAGE ON CKT 435

WHEN ALL DIAGNOSIS AND REPAIRS ARE COMPLETED, CLEAR CODES AND VERIFY OPERATION

84204004

Fig. 16 Exhaust Gas Recirculation (EGR) system check — 4.6L engine

REMOVAL & INSTALLATION

EGR Valve

4.5L AND 4.9L ENGINES

▶ See Figures 17, 18, 19 and 20

1. Disconnect the negative battery terminal.
2. Remove the air cleaner assembly.
3. Remove the vacuum valve at the EGR valve.
4. Remove the 2 EGR valve mounting bolts and the EGR valve from the engine.
5. Inspect the EGR passages in the intake manifold for deposits and clean as necessary.

To install:

6. Install cleaned or replacement EGR valve onto the intake manifold using new gasket. Tighten the 2 mounting bolts to 14 ft. lbs. (18 Nm).

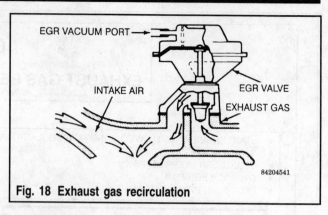

Fig. 18 Exhaust gas recirculation

7. Install the vacuum hose to the valve.
8. Install the air cleaner assembly and connect the negative battery terminal.

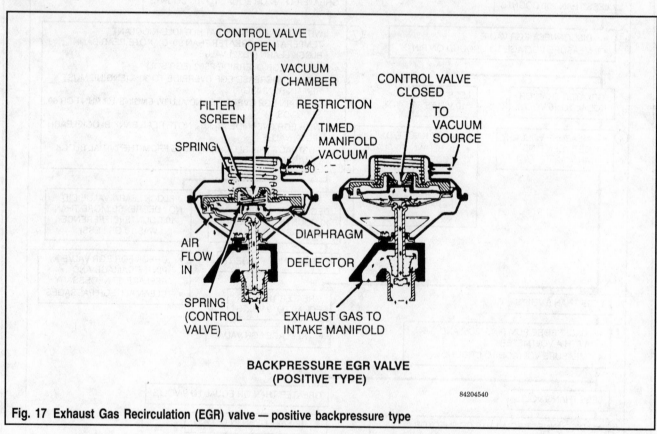

Fig. 17 Exhaust Gas Recirculation (EGR) valve — positive backpressure type

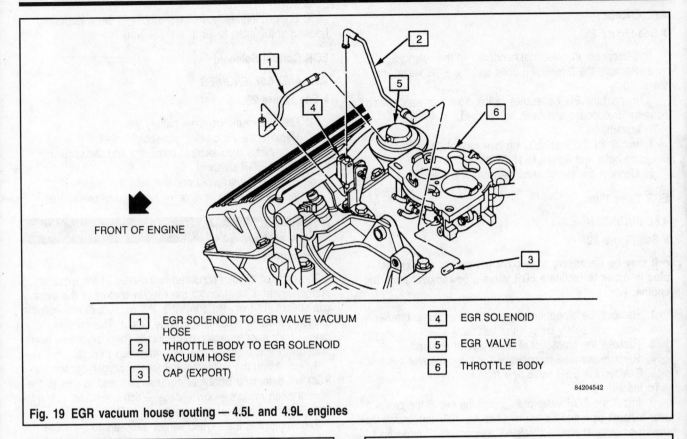

1	EGR SOLENOID TO EGR VALVE VACUUM HOSE
2	THROTTLE BODY TO EGR SOLENOID VACUUM HOSE
3	CAP (EXPORT)
4	EGR SOLENOID
5	EGR VALVE
6	THROTTLE BODY

84204542

Fig. 19 EGR vacuum house routing — 4.5L and 4.9L engines

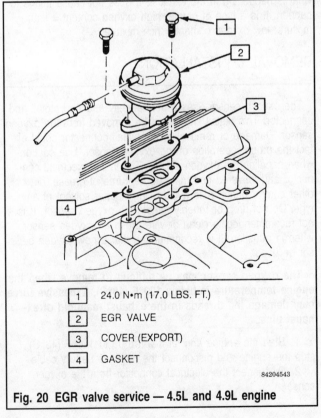

1	24.0 N•m (17.0 LBS. FT.)
2	EGR VALVE
3	COVER (EXPORT)
4	GASKET

84204543

Fig. 20 EGR valve service — 4.5L and 4.9L engine

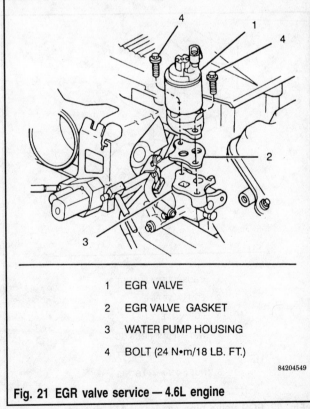

1	EGR VALVE
2	EGR VALVE GASKET
3	WATER PUMP HOUSING
4	BOLT (24 N•m/18 LB. FT.)

84204549

Fig. 21 EGR valve service — 4.6L engine

4.6L ENGINE

▶ **See Figure 21**

1. Disconnect the electrical connector at the solenoid.
2. Remove the 2 mounting bolts and the EGR valve from the stand.
3. Inspect the EGR passages in the crossover water pump housing for deposits and clean as required.

To install:

4. Install the EGR valve using new gasket. Install the 2 mounting bolts and tighten to 18 ft. lbs. (24 Nm).
5. Connect the electrical connector at the solenoid.

EGR Valve Pipe

4.6L ENGINE

▶ **See Figure 22**

➡**It may be necessary to remove the crossover exhaust pipe in order to facilitate EGR valve pipe removal from the engine.**

1. Remove the pipe mounting bolt at water pump bracket.
2. Raise and safely support the vehicle.
3. Remove the crossover exhaust pipe, if required.
4. Remove the pipe mounting nut at the crossover exhaust pipe. Remove the EGR valve pipe from the vehicle.

To install:

5. Install the EGR valve pipe. Install the nut at the crossover exhaust pipe and tighten to 44 ft. lbs. (60 Nm). Install the crossover exhaust pipe and related components, if removed.

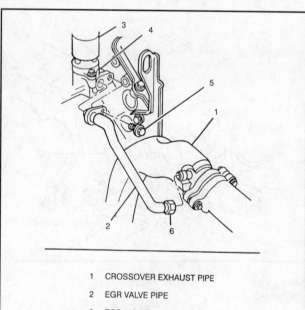

1	CROSSOVER EXHAUST PIPE
2	EGR VALVE PIPE
3	EGR VALVE
4	WATER PUMP HOUSING
5	BOLT (24 N•m/18 LB. FT.)
6	NUT (60 N•m/44 LB. FT.)

84204550

Fig. 22 EGR valve pipe service — 4.6L engine

6. Lower the vehicle. Install the bolts at the water pump housing and tighten to 18 ft. lbs. (24 Nm).

EGR Control Solenoid

4.5L AND 4.9L ENGINES

▶ **See Figure 23**

1. Disconnect the negative battery terminal.
2. Remove the air cleaner assembly.
3. Disconnect the electrical connector and the vacuum hoses at the EGR solenoid.
4. Remove the solenoid and nut from the engine.
5. Installation is the reverse of the removal procedure.

Oxygen Sensor

▶ **See Figure 24**

The exhaust oxygen sensor(s) is mounted in the exhaust system where it can monitor the oxygen content of the exhaust gas stream. The oxygen content in the exhaust reacts with the oxygen sensor to produce a voltage output. This voltage ranges from approximately 100 millivolts (high oxygen — lean mixture) to 900 millivolts (low oxygen — rich mixture).

By monitoring the voltage output of the oxygen sensor, the PCM will determine what fuel mixture command to give to the injector (lean mixture — low voltage — rich command, rich mixture — high voltage — lean command).

Remember that the oxygen sensor indicates to the ECM what is happening in the exhaust. It does not cause things to happen. It is a type of gauge: high oxygen content = lean mixture; low oxygen content = rich mixture.

REMOVAL & INSTALLATION

The oxygen sensor uses a permanently attached pigtail and connector. This pigtail should not be removed from the oxygen sensor. Damage or removal of the pigtail connector could effect the proper operation of the oxygen sensor. Use caution when handling the oxygen sensor. The in-line electrical connector and louvered end must be kept free of grease, dirt or other contaminants. Also avoid using cleaner solvent of any type. Do not drop or roughly handle the oxygen sensor. It is not recommended to clean or wire brush an oxygen sensor when in question, it is recommended that a new oxygen sensor be used.

➡**The oxygen sensor may be difficult to remove when the engine temperature is below 120°F (48°C). Excessive force may damage the threads in the exhaust manifold of exhaust pipe.**

1. Start the engine and let it warm up to 120°F (48°C), stop the engine and disconnect the negative battery cable.
2. Disconnect the electrical connector from the oxygen sensor.

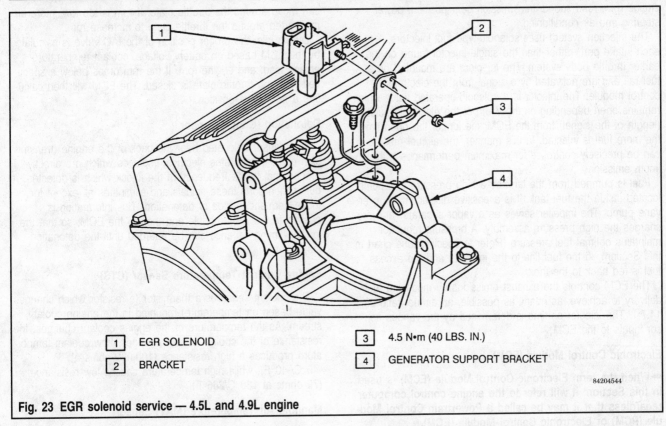

1	EGR SOLENOID	3	4.5 N•m (40 LBS. IN.)
2	BRACKET	4	GENERATOR SUPPORT BRACKET

84204544

Fig. 23 EGR solenoid service — 4.5L and 4.9L engine

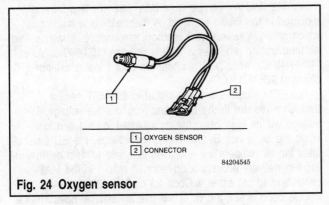

1	OXYGEN SENSOR
2	CONNECTOR

84204545

Fig. 24 Oxygen sensor

3. Using a special oxygen sensor socket, remove the oxygen sensor from the exhaust manifold or exhaust pipe.

➡**A special anti-seize compound is used on the oxygen sensor threads. The compound consists of a liquid graphite and glass beads. The graphite will burn away, but the glass beads will remain, making the sensor easier to remove. New or service sensors will already have the compound applied to the threads. If an oxygen sensor is removed from the engine and if for any reason it is to be reinstalled, the threads must have this anti-seize compound applied before installation.**

4. Coat the threads of the oxygen sensor with anti-seize compound 5613695 or equivalent.
5. Install the sensor and torque it to 30 ft. lbs (41 Nm).
6. Reconnect the electrical connector to the sensor and the negative battery cable.

ELECTRONIC ENGINE CONTROLS

Fuel Injection System

The majority of fuel injection and emission related items are warranted by the manufacturer for an extended mileage and time. Before replacing any fuel or emission related components, check with the manufacturer for possible component replacement under warranty.

GENERAL DESCRIPTION

The Sequential Port Fuel Injection (SPFI) system is controlled by an Electronic Control Module (ECM) or Powertrain Control Module (PCM), which monitors engine operations and generates output signals to provide the correct air/fuel mixture, ignition timing and engine idle speed control. Input to the control unit is provided by an oxygen sensor, coolant temperature sensor, detonation sensor, hot film air mass sensor and throttle position sensor. The ECM also receives information concerning engine rpm, road speed, transmission gear position, power steering and air conditioning.

The injection system uses solenoid-type fuel injectors, 1 at each intake port, rather than the single injector found on the earlier throttle body system. The injectors are mounted on a fuel rail and are activated by a signal from the electronic control module. The injector is a solenoid-operated valve which remains open depending on the width of the electronic pulses (length of the signal) from the ECM; the longer the open time, the more fuel is injected. In this manner, the air/fuel mixture can be precisely controlled for maximum performance with minimum emissions.

Fuel is pumped from the tank by a high pressure fuel pump, located inside the fuel tank. It is a positive displacement roller vane pump. The impeller serves as a vapor separator and precharges the high pressure assembly. A pressure regulator maintains optimal fuel pressure (Refer to specifications chart in this Section), in the fuel line to the injectors and the excess fuel is fed back to the tank.

The ECM controls the exhaust emissions by modifying fuel delivery to achieve, as nearly as possible, an air/fuel ratio of 14.7:1. The injector on-time is determined by the various sensor inputs to the ECM.

Electronic Control Module (ECM)

➡**When the term Electronic Control Module (ECM) is used in this Section, it will refer to the engine control computer regardless that it may be called a Powertrain Control Module (PCM) or Electronic Control Module (ECM).**

The fuel injection system is controlled by an on-board computer, the Electronic Control Module (ECM), usually located in the passenger compartment. The ECM monitors engine operations and environmental conditions (ambient temperature, barometric pressure, etc.) needed to calculate the fuel delivery time (pulse width/injector on-time) of the fuel injector. The fuel pulse may be modified by the ECM to account for special operating conditions, such as cranking, cold starting, altitude, acceleration and deceleration.

The ECM constantly monitors the input information, processes this information from various sensors, and generates output commands to the various systems that affect vehicle performance.

The ability of the ECM to recognize and adjust for vehicle variations (engine transmission, vehicle weight, axle ratio, etc.) is provided by a removable calibration unit (PROM) that is programmed to tailor the ECM for the particular vehicle. There is a specific ECM/PROM combination for each specific vehicle, and the combinations are not interchangeable with those of other vehicles.

The ECM also performs the diagnostic function of the system. It can recognize operational problems, alert the driver through the SERVICE ENGINE SOON light, and store a code or codes which identify the problem areas to aid the technician in making repairs.

Idle Air Control (IAC)

The purpose of the Idle Air Control (IAC) system is to control engine idle speeds while preventing stalls due to changes in engine load. The IAC assembly, mounted on the throttle body, controls bypass air around the throttle plate. By extending or retracting a conical valve, a controlled amount of air

can move around the throttle plate. If rpm is too low, more air is diverted around the throttle plate to increase rpm.

During idle, the proper position of the IAC valve is calculated by the ECM based on battery voltage, coolant temperature, engine load, and engine rpm. If the rpm drops below a specified rate, the throttle plate is closed. The ECM will then calculate a new valve position.

Detonation (Knock) Sensor

This sensor is located near the back of the engine (transmission end). It generates electrical impulses which are directly proportional to the frequency of the knock which is detected. A buffer then sorts these signals and eliminates all except for those frequency range of detonation. This information is passed to the ESC module and then to the ECM, so that the ignition timing advance can be retarded until the detonation stops.

Engine Coolant Temperature Sensor (CTS)

The coolant sensor is a thermistor (a resistor which changes value based on temperature) mounted in the engine coolant stream. As the temperature of the engine coolant changes, the resistance of the coolant sensor changes. Low coolant temperature produces a high resistance (100,000 ohms at -40°C/-40°F), while high temperature causes low resistance (70 ohms at 130°C/266°F).

Manifold Air Temperature (MAT) Sensor

The Manifold Air Temperature (MAT) sensor is a thermistor mounted in the intake manifold. A thermistor is a resistor which changes resistance based on temperature. Low manifold air temperature produces a high resistance (100,000 ohms at -40°F/-40°C), while high temperature cause low resistance (70 ohms at 266°F/130°C).

The ECM supplies a 5 volt signal to the MAT sensor through a resistor in the ECM and monitors the voltage. The voltage will be high when the manifold air is cold and low when the air is hot. By monitoring the voltage, the ECM calculates the air temperature and uses this data to help determine the fuel delivery and spark advance. A failure in the MAT circuit should set either a Code 23 or Code 25. Once the trouble code is set, the ECM will use an artificial default value for the MAT and some vehicle performance will return.

Intake Air Temperature Sensor (IAT)

The Intake Air Temperature sensor (IAT) is the same sensor as the Manifold Air Temperature (MAT) Sensor, the name has been changed. It operates in the same manner and performs the same function.

Manifold Absolute Pressure (MAP) Sensor

The Manifold Absolute Pressure (MAP) sensor measures the changes in the intake manifold pressure which result from engine load and speed changes. The pressure measured by the MAP sensor is the difference between barometric pressure (outside air) and manifold pressure (vacuum). A closed throttle engine coastdown would produce a relatively low MAP value (approximately 20-35 kPa), while wide-open throttle would produce a high value (100 kPa). This high value is produced when the pressure inside the manifold is the same as outside the manifold, and 100% of outside air (or 100 kPa) is being measured. This MAP output is the opposite of what you would measure on a vacuum gauge. The use of this sensor also allows the ECM to adjust automatically for different altitude.

The ECM sends a 5 volt reference signal to the MAP sensor. As the MAP changes, the electrical resistance of the sensor also changes. By monitoring the sensor output voltage the ECM can determine the manifold pressure. A higher pressure, lower vacuum (high voltage) requires more fuel, while a lower pressure, higher vacuum (low voltage) requires less fuel. The ECM uses the MAP sensor to control fuel delivery and ignition timing. A failure in the MAP sensor circuit should set a Code 33 or Code 34.

Throttle Position Sensor (TPS)

The Throttle Position Sensor (TPS) is connected to the throttle shaft and is controlled by the throttle mechanism. A 5 volt reference signal is sent to the TPS from the ECM. As the throttle valve angle is changed (accelerator pedal moved), the resistance of the TPS also changes. At a closed throttle position, the resistance of the TPS is high, so the output voltage to the ECM will be low (approximately 0.5 volt). As the throttle plate opens, the resistance decreases so that, at wide open throttle, the output voltage should be approximately 5 volts. At closed throttle position, the voltage at the TPS should be less than 1.25 volts.

By monitoring the output voltage from the TPS, the ECM can determine fuel delivery based on throttle valve angle (driver demand). The TPS can either be misadjusted, shorted, open or loose. Misadjustment might result in poor idle or poor wide-open throttle performance. An open TPS signals the ECM that the throttle is always closed, resulting in poor performance. A loose TPS indicates to the ECM that the throttle is moving. This causes intermittent bursts of fuel from the injector and an unstable idle. A shorted TPS gives the ECM a constant wide-open throttle signal.

DIAGNOSIS AND TESTING

Service Precautions

When working around any part of the fuel system, take precautionary steps to prevent fire and/or explosion:
- Disconnect negative terminal from battery (except when testing with battery voltage is required).
- When possible, use a flashlight instead of a drop light.
- Keep all open flame and smoking material out of the area.
- Use a shop cloth or similar to catch fuel when opening a fuel system.
- Relieve fuel system pressure before servicing.
- Use eye protection.
- Always keep a dry chemical (class B) fire extinguisher near the area.

➡ **Due to the amount of fuel pressure in the fuel lines, before doing any work to the fuel system, the fuel system should be depressurized. Failure to depressurize the fuel system prior to opening to the environment may result in damage to the vehicle or personal injury. Refer to Section 5 of this manual for the appropriate procedure.**

Electrostatic Discharge Damage

Electronic components used in the control system are often design to carry very low voltage and are very susceptible to damage caused by electrostatic discharge. It is possible for less than 100 volts of static electricity to cause damage to some electronic components. By comparison it takes as much as 4000 volts for a person to even feel the zap of a static discharge.

There are several ways for a person to become statically charged. The most common methods of charging are by friction and induction. An example of charging by friction is a person sliding across a car seat, in which a charge as much as 25000 volts can build up. Charging by induction occurs when a person with well insulated shoes stands near a highly charged object and momentarily touches ground. Charges of the same polarity are drained off, leaving the person highly charged with the opposite polarity. Static charges of either type can cause damage, therefore, it is important to use care when handling and testing electronic components.

➡ **To prevent possible electrostatic discharge damage to the ECM, do not touch the connector pins or soldered components on the circuit board. When handling a PROM, do not touch the component leads and remove the integrated circuit from the carrier.**

Malfunction Indicator Lamp

The Deville, Fleetwood and Sixty Special use two service telltale lights located on the instrument cluster. These are; 'SERVICE ENGINE SOON' AND 'SERVICE VEHICLE SOON.' On the Eldorado and Seville, the 'SERVICE ENGINE SOON' tell-tale is used on the instrument cluster, while 'SERVICE VEHICLE SOON' appears as a message on the Driver Information Center (DIC) display.

Service Telltale Function and Operation

The 'SES' telltale will turn 'ON' whenever the ECM detects a fault in the engine control system. The 'SVS' telltale will turn 'ON' whenever the ECM detects a fault in the following circuits only:
- Generator
- Fuel Pump
- VCC Brake Switch
- PRNDL Switch
- Heated Windshield, (if equipped)

A display message on the Driver Information Center of Eldorado and Seville, which reads 'SERVICE VEHICLE SOON,' replaces the function of the 'SVS' telltale. The 'SERVICE VEHICLE SOON' message on Eldorado and Seville has the same function as the 'SVS' telltale, but does not operate during the following sequence unless a specific code is set.

1. KEY ON: 'SES' and 'SVS' lights will be 'ON' for two seconds.
2. CRANKING: Both indicator lights turn 'OFF.'
3. START: Both indicator lights will will turn 'ON' for two seconds after the engine starts.
4. DIAGNOSTIC MODE: Both indicator lights will turn 'ON.'
5. CODE SET: Depending on the malfunctioning circuit(s) either one or both indicator lights will turn 'ON.'

Current and History Codes

Current codes represent those malfunctions that are present during the present key cycle. History codes represent a malfunction that has occurred during the last 50 cycles of the ignition, but is not occurring during the present key cycle. History codes will automatically be erased after the 51st key 'ON' cycle period.

Set Timing Mode/DLC

The Data Link Connector on these vehicles is used for adjusting the base timing setting. The 'Set Timing Mode' is requested by following the procedure below.

1. Allow engine to reach operating temperature, approximately 85°C. Verify that the RPM is less than 900.
2. Place the shift indicator in Park.
3. If in the diagnostic mode, exit diagnostics. Insert a jumper between terminals A and B of the DLC.

With this procedure completed the ECM will command timing at 10 degrees BTDC. This setting can now be checked with a standard timing light. After checking or adjusting timing, remove the jumper in the DLC. On 1993 4.6L Northstar system, timing adjustment is not possible.

Segment Check

ELDORADO AND SEVILLE

The segment check is the illumination of the IPC, CCP, and DIC to verify that all segments of the liquid crystal displays are working. Only the turn signal indicators do not light during this check. Diagnosis should not be attempted unless all segments appear, as this could lead to misdiagnosis. If any portions or segments are inoperative, the faulty component will need to be replaced .

Entering Diagnostic Mode

EXCEPT ELDORADO AND SEVILLE

With the ignition in the ON position, press the 'OFF' and 'WARMER' buttons on the Electronic Climate Control (ECC) panel simultaneously and hold until all display panel segments illuminate. This indicates the beginning of the diagnostic readout. The purpose of this panel illumination is to verify that all segments of the displays are working. Do not attempt diagnosis if all segments do not appear as this will lead to misdiagnosis by making it difficult to interpret the readout. If any of the segments are inoperative, the affected display panel will need to be replaced.

ELDORADO AND SEVILLE

To enter diagnostics turn the ignition 'ON', then press the 'OFF' and 'WARMER' buttons simultaneously and hold until the segment check appears on the IPC, or combo panel. On 1991-92 models a separate combination panel was used that housed both the ECC and the DIC. For 1993 models the DIC is part of the instrument panel cluster.

Trouble Code Display

EXCEPT ELDORADO AND SEVILLE

If fault codes are present in the system, they will be displayed on the Fuel Data Center (FDC) as follows:

1. Trouble code display will begin with a '8.8.8" display on the FDC for approximately 1 second. Following this an '..E' will be displayed which indicates the beginning of the ECM history codes. The initial pass of ECM codes will include all detected malfunctions, whether they are present or not. If no ECM history codes are present, the '..E' display will be bypassed. Following the display of '..E', the lowest numbered ECM history code will be shown for approximately two seconds. All ECM codes will be prefixed with an 'E' (i.e. E13, E14, etc.). Progressively higher numbered ECM codes if present, will be displayed for two second intervals, until all codes have been displayed.

2. '.E.E' will then be displayed which indicates that the second pass of fault codes will begin. This second pass will include only those codes which are current, or presently exist. Codes which are displayed during the first pass but not the second are history codes. If all the codes displayed are history codes, the '.E.E' display will then be bypassed.

3. At the conclusion of the ECM code display, the BCM fault codes will be shown in a similar fashion. The differences between ECM and BCM code display are as follows:

- BCM codes are prefixed with an 'F'
- '..F' precedes the first pass.
- '.F.F' precedes the second pass.

4. After all ECM and BCM codes have been displayed, or if no fault codes are present at all, .7.0 will be displayed indicating system readiness for the selection of the next diagnostic feature.

ELDORADO AND SEVILLE

After diagnostics is entered, any fault codes stored in computer memory will be displayed. For 1990-92 systems codes may be stored for the ECM, BCM, or SIR systems. For 1993 the system has been expanded to include codes for the PCM, IPC, ACP, SIR, TCS, and RTD systems. The IPC (Instrument Panel Cluster) replaces the BCM for 1993, but serves the same purpose. ACP, SIR, TCS, and RTD stand for Air Conditioning Programmer, Supplemental Inflatable Restraint, Traction Control System, and Real Time Dampening respectively. We will only deal with engine control malfunctions here.

Each trouble code consists of the system identifier (E for ECM, or P for PCM), a three digit code identifier, and the letter 'C' or 'H' to indicate current or history codes. If no codes are present for a system a 'NO X CODE' message will be displayed, with 'X' representing the system. If the communication line to a component is not operating a 'NO X DATA' message will appear indicating that the BCM/IPC could not communicate with that system.

Status Light Display

▶ See Figures 25, 26, 27, 28 and 29

While in the diagnostic mode the ECC mode indicator lights are used to determine the activity of certain operating circuits within the system. These lights will either be turned on or off; for example, loop status will be shown by the 'AUTO' indicator

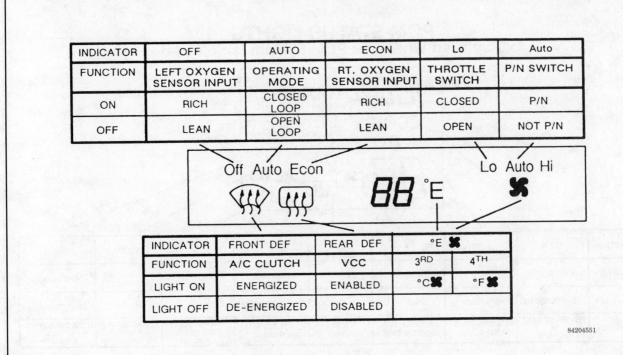

INDICATOR	OFF	AUTO	ECON	Lo	Auto
FUNCTION	LEFT OXYGEN SENSOR INPUT	OPERATING MODE	RT. OXYGEN SENSOR INPUT	THROTTLE SWITCH	P/N SWITCH
ON	RICH	CLOSED LOOP	RICH	CLOSED	P/N
OFF	LEAN	OPEN LOOP	LEAN	OPEN	NOT P/N

INDICATOR	FRONT DEF	REAR DEF	°E	
FUNCTION	A/C CLUTCH	VCC	3RD	4TH
LIGHT ON	ENERGIZED	ENABLED	°C	°F
LIGHT OFF	DE-ENERGIZED	DISABLED		

84204551

Fig. 25 PCM status indicators — 1990-91 Eldorado and Seville

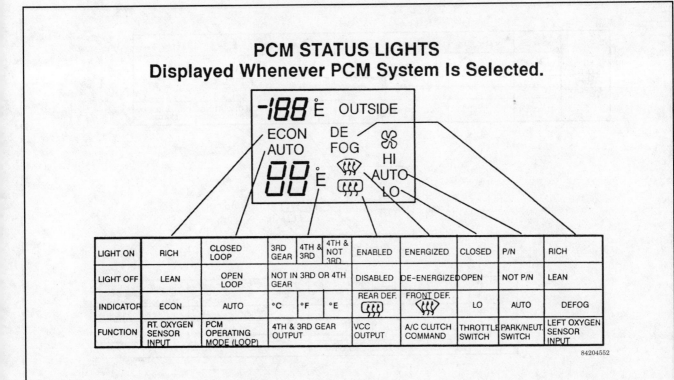

PCM STATUS LIGHTS
Displayed Whenever PCM System Is Selected.

LIGHT ON	RICH	CLOSED LOOP	3RD GEAR	4TH & 3RD	4TH & NOT 3RD	ENABLED	ENERGIZED	CLOSED	P/N	RICH
LIGHT OFF	LEAN	OPEN LOOP	NOT IN 3RD OR 4TH GEAR			DISABLED	DE-ENERGIZED	OPEN	NOT P/N	LEAN
INDICATOR	ECON	AUTO	°C	°F	°E	REAR DEF.	FRONT DEF.	LO	AUTO	DEFOG
FUNCTION	RT. OXYGEN SENSOR INPUT	PCM OPERATING MODE (LOOP)	4TH & 3RD GEAR OUTPUT			VCC OUTPUT	A/C CLUTCH COMMAND	THROTTLE SWITCH	PARK/NEUT. SWITCH	LEFT OXYGEN SENSOR INPUT

84204552

Fig. 26 PCM status indicators — 1992-93 Eldorado and Seville with 4.9L engine

on the ECC. The 'AUTO' indicator will be turned ON to indicate closed loop, and turned OFF to indicate open loop.

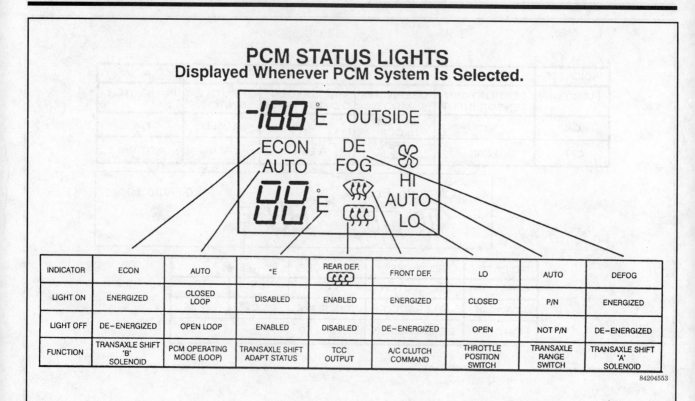

PCM STATUS LIGHTS
Displayed Whenever PCM System Is Selected.

INDICATOR	ECON	AUTO	°E	REAR DEF.	FRONT DEF.	LO	AUTO	DEFOG
LIGHT ON	ENERGIZED	CLOSED LOOP	DISABLED	ENABLED	ENERGIZED	CLOSED	P/N	ENERGIZED
LIGHT OFF	DE-ENERGIZED	OPEN LOOP	ENABLED	DISABLED	DE-ENERGIZED	OPEN	NOT P/N	DE-ENERGIZED
FUNCTION	TRANSAXLE SHIFT 'B' SOLENOID	PCM OPERATING MODE (LOOP)	TRANSAXLE SHIFT ADAPT STATUS	TCC OUTPUT	A/C CLUTCH COMMAND	THROTTLE POSITION SWITCH	TRANSAXLE RANGE SWITCH	TRANSAXLE SHIFT 'A' SOLENOID

84204553

Fig. 27 PCM status display — 1993 Eldorado and Seville with 4.6L engine

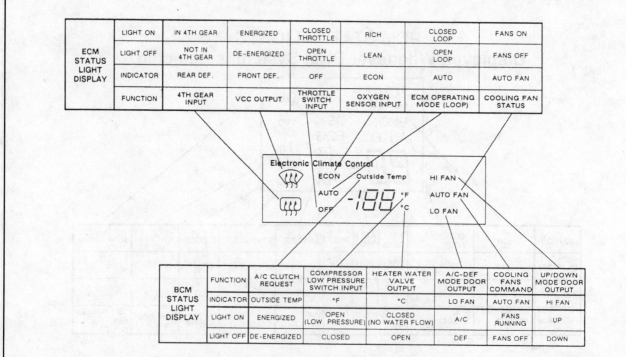

ECM STATUS LIGHT DISPLAY	LIGHT ON	IN 4TH GEAR	ENERGIZED	CLOSED THROTTLE	RICH	CLOSED LOOP	FANS ON
	LIGHT OFF	NOT IN 4TH GEAR	DE-ENERGIZED	OPEN THROTTLE	LEAN	OPEN LOOP	FANS OFF
	INDICATOR	REAR DEF.	FRONT DEF.	OFF	ECON	AUTO	AUTO FAN
	FUNCTION	4TH GEAR INPUT	VCC OUTPUT	THROTTLE SWITCH INPUT	OXYGEN SENSOR INPUT	ECM OPERATING MODE (LOOP)	COOLING FAN STATUS

BCM STATUS LIGHT DISPLAY	FUNCTION	A/C CLUTCH REQUEST	COMPRESSOR LOW PRESSURE SWITCH INPUT	HEATER WATER VALVE OUTPUT	A/C-DEF MODE DOOR OUTPUT	COOLING FANS COMMAND	UP/DOWN MODE DOOR OUTPUT
	INDICATOR	OUTSIDE TEMP	°F	°C	LO FAN	AUTO FAN	HI FAN
	LIGHT ON	ENERGIZED	OPEN (LOW PRESSURE)	CLOSED (NO WATER FLOW)	A/C	FANS RUNNING	UP
	LIGHT OFF	DE-ENERGIZED	CLOSED	OPEN	DEF	FANS OFF	DOWN

84204554

Fig. 28 PCM status display — 1990 Deville and Fleetwood

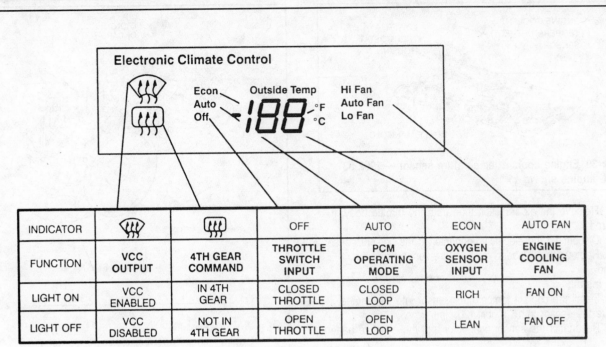

Fig. 29 PCM status display — 1991-93 Deville, Sixty Special and Fleetwood

ECM/PCM Data Display

The ECM/PCM data are similar to the information that is available on other vehicles, through the use of a scan tool. The data displayed is used for monitoring sensors, input switches and other system components, as seen by the ECM or PCM.

ECM/PCM Inputs

The ECM/PCM inputs selection provide testing of inputs to the ECM or PCM. The input status is shown on the display as 'HI' or 'LO'. The input test status is shown as 0 until the ECM/PCM sees a transition in the state of the switch, then 0 will change to an X to indicate that the test 'passed'.

ECM/PCM Outputs

The PCM OUTPUTS option provides the ability to cycle the ECM/PCM controlled outputs. The DIC display identifies the solenoid or relay that is being operated, as well as the state the ECR or PCM is commanding that device. 'HI' indicates that the solenoid or relay is de-energized, and 'LO' indicates that the solenoid or relay is energized. The ECM/PCM outputs tests can only be done with the key in the ON position, and the engine OFF.

ECM/PCM Override

The ECM/PCM override feature allows testing of certain system functions regardless of normal program instructions, provided test conditions are met. Upon selecting a test, the current mode of that function will be displayed as a percentage on the ECCP panel.

Pressing the WARMER or COOLER buttons on the ECCP panel initiates the override. Depressing the 'WARMER' button increases the override value. Upon release of the button, the display may either remain at the override value or automatically return to normal program control. This depends on which function is being overridden at the time. Selection of another override test will cancel the current override.

Engine Coolant Temperature Sensor (CTS)

The engine coolant temperature sensor is located on the intake manifold water jacket or near the thermostat housing. On the 4.6L engine, the coolant temperature sensor is located on the rear cylinder head, at the cruise control servo bracket. It is necessary to drain coolant from the cooling system to a level below the sensor, prior to sensor removal.

REMOVAL & INSTALLATION

4.5L and 4.9L Engines
▶ See Figure 30

> ✴✴**CAUTION**
>
> **Allow sufficient time for the engine to cool before removing the coolant temperature sensor. Excessive coolant loss or personal injury may result if the engine is hot**

1. Disconnect the negative battery cable. Partially drain the engine cooling system to a level below the coolant temperature sensor.

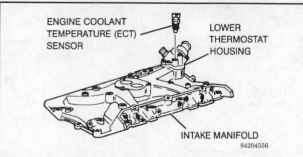

Fig. 30 Engine coolant temperature sensor — 1992-93 4.9L engine shown

2. Remove the air induction tube from the throttle body, if required.

3. Disconnect the electrical connector at the coolant sensor.

4. Remove the threaded temperature sensor from the engine.

To install:

5. Install the coolant temperature sensor into the engine. Torque the sensor to 15 ft. lbs. (20 Nm).

6. Reconnect the sensor connector and the negative battery cable.

7. Refill the cooling system.

4.6L Engine

▶ See Figure 31

✳✳CAUTION

Allow sufficient time for the engine to cool before removing the coolant temperature sensor. Excessive coolant loss or personal injury may result if the engine is hot

1. Disconnect the negative battery cable.

2. Partially drain the engine cooling system to a level below the coolant temperature sensor.

3. Remove the throttle cable from the cruise control servo bracket.

4. Remove the cruise control servo and bracket from the engine.

5. Disconnect the electrical harness connector at the sensor. Remove the threaded sensor from the engine.

To install:

6. Lightly coat the threads of the coolant temperature sensor with a non-hardening sealer to prevent coolant leaks. Install the sensor into the engine and tighten to 106 inch lbs. (12 Nm).

7. Connect the harness connector at the sensor.

8. Install the cruise control servo and bracket.

9. Install the throttle cable to the servo bracket.

10. Refill the cooling system and connect the negative battery terminal.

Idle Air Control (IAC) Valve

For IAC valve removal and installation procedure, please refer to Section 5 of this manual.

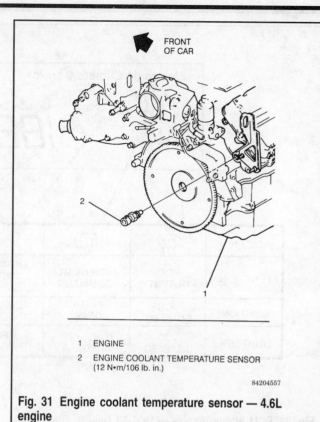

1 ENGINE
2 ENGINE COOLANT TEMPERATURE SENSOR
   (12 N•m/106 lb. in.)

84204557

Fig. 31 Engine coolant temperature sensor — 4.6L engine

Manifold Absolute Pressure (MAP) Sensor

REMOVAL & INSTALLATION

4.5L and 4.9L Engines

▶ See Figures 32 and 33

1. Disconnect the negative battery cable.

2. Remove the intake manifold cover, if required.

3. Disconnect the electrical and vacuum connectors from the sensor.

4. Remove the screws securing the MAP sensor to its mounting bracket. Remove the sensor from the engine.

To install:

5. Install the sensor to the mounting bracket and tighten the retainers to 15 inch lbs. (1.7 Nm).

6. Connect the vacuum and electrical harness connectors at the sensor.

7. Connect the negative battery cable, if disconnected.

4.6L Engine

1. Disconnect the negative battery cable.

2. Remove the intake manifold cover.

3. Remove the MAP sensor from the fuel rail.

4. Disconnect the MAP sensor connectors.

To install:

5. Connect the MAP sensor connectors and install sensor onto the fuel rail.

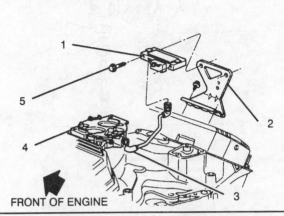

Fig. 32 Manifold Absolute Pressure (MAP) sensor —
1992-93 4.9L engine shown

1	MAP SENSOR	4	THROTTLE BODY
2	SENSOR BRACKET	5	1.6 N•m (14 LBS. IN.)
3	MAP VACUUM TUBE		

FRONT OF ENGINE

84204558

Fig. 33 MAP sensor mounting and location

84204559

6. Install the intake manifold cove and tighten the bolts to 106 inch lbs. (12 NM).

7. Connect the negative battery cable, if disconnected.

Manifold Air Temperature (MAT) Sensor

REMOVAL & INSTALLATION

▶ See Figure 34

➡When servicing the MAT sensor, be careful not to damage the tip of the sensor. Damage to the MAT sensor tip will affect proper operation of the fuel injection system.

1. Disconnect the negative battery cable.
2. Disconnect the electrical connector to the MAT sensor.
3. Unscrew the MAT sensor from the intake manifold.
4. Installation is the reverse order of the removal procedure. Prior to installing the sensor, coat threads with and non-hardening sealant.

Intake Air Temperature (IAT) Sensor

REMOVAL & INSTALLATION

4.6L Engine

The IAT was formerly called the MAT sensor. They are both the same sensor.
1. Disconnect the negative battery cable.
2. Remove the intake manifold cover.
3. Remove the Intake Air Temperature (IAT) sensor from the fuel rail.
4. Installation is the reverse of the removal procedure. Tighten the intake manifold cover bolts to 106 inch lbs. (12 Nm).

Vehicle Speed Sensor (VSS)

REMOVAL & INSTALLATION

▶ See Figures 35 and 36

The Vehicle Speed Sensor (VSS) is located on the side of the transaxle assembly. The speed sensor is serviced as an assembly and includes the housing, coil magnet, washers,

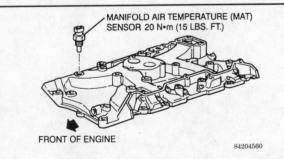

MANIFOLD AIR TEMPERATURE (MAT)
SENSOR 20 N•m (15 LBS. FT.)

FRONT OF ENGINE

84204560

Fig. 34 Intake Air Temperature (IAT) sensor — 1992-93 4.9L engine shown

wave spring washer and housing cover. The VSS rotor is serviced with the transmission governor assembly.

1. Disconnect the electrical connector at the VSS.
2. Remove the 2 speed sensor housing cap screws.
3. Remove the speed sensor assembly.

To install:

4. Install a new O-ring onto the speed sensor housing.
5. Install the speed sensor assembly into the transmission housing. Install the speed sensor housing cap screws and tighten to 20 ft. lbs. (27 Nm).
6. Reconnect the electrical harness connector at the transmission.

Throttle Position Sensor (TPS)

For TPS removal and installation as well as adjustment procedures, please refer to Section 5 of this manual.

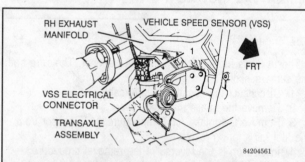

Fig. 35 Vehicle Speed Sensor (VSS) — 1992-93 Deville, Fleetwood and Sixty Special

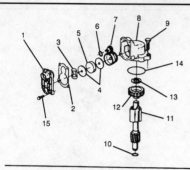

1	COVER, HOUSING
2	GASKET, COVER
3	WASHER, WAVE SPRING
4	WASHER
5	MAGNET
6	SEAL, "O" RING
7	COIL ASSEMBLY
8	HOUSING, SPEED SENSOR
9	CREW, GOVERNOR COVER/CASE
10	RING, OIL SEAL (GOVERNOR SHAFT)
11	GOVERNOR ASSEMBLY
12	ROTOR, SPEED SENSOR
13	BEARING ASM., THRUST (SPEEDO GEAR)
14	SEAL, "O" RING (GOVERNOR COVER)
15	BOLT

84204562

Fig. 36 Vehicle Speed Sensor (VSS) service — 1992-93 Deville, Fleetwood and Sixty Special

Powertrain Control Module (PCM)

REMOVAL & INSTALLATION

▶ **See Figures 37, 38 and 39**

1. Disconnect the negative battery cable.

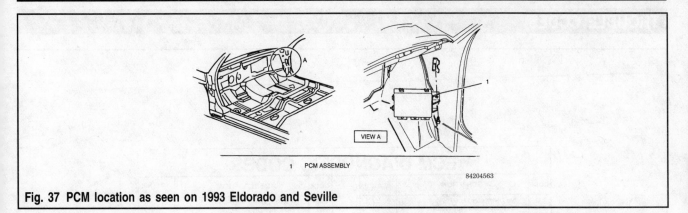

1 PCM ASSEMBLY

84204563

Fig. 37 PCM location as seen on 1993 Eldorado and Seville

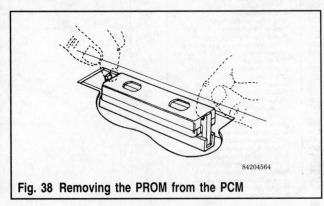

84204564

Fig. 38 Removing the PROM from the PCM

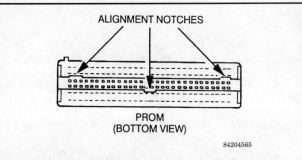

ALIGNMENT NOTCHES

PROM
(BOTTOM VIEW)

84204565

Fig. 39 Correct PROM alignment is required to complete installation into PCM

2. Remove the glove box assembly, if necessary. Remove the right lower dash panel and kick panel to gain access to the PCM.

3. Disconnect the connectors from the PCM.

4. Remove the ECM mounting hardware and remove the ECM from the passenger compartment.

5. Remove the PROM access cover from the old PCM. Using 2 fingers, push both retaining tabs back away from the PROM at the same time. Grasp the PROM at both ends and lift the up out of the PROM socket.

To install:

6. Install the old PROM into the socket of the PCM. The small notches in the PROM must align with the small notches in the socket on the PCM. Press on the ends of the PROM unit until the retaining clips snap into the ends of the PROM. Press the clips into the sides of the PROM until they snap into place.Do not press on the middle of the PROM; only on the ends.

7. Install the PROM accesories cover cover.

8. Install the ECM and mounting hardware into the passenger compartment of the vehicle. Secure te ECM in place.

9. Reconnect the harness connectors at the ECM.

10. Install the kick panel and glove box, as required.

11. Reconnect the negative battery cable.

TROUBLE CODES

ECM DIAGNOSTIC CODES

CODE	DESCRIPTION	TELLTALE STATUS	CODE	DESCRIPTION	TELLTALE STATUS
E12	No Distributor Signal	Ⓐ	E49	A.I.R. Control Problem	Ⓐ
E13	Oxygen Sensor Not Ready	Ⓐ	E52	ECM Memory Reset	Ⓒ
E14	Shorted Coolant Sensor Circuit	Ⓐ	E53	Distributor Signal Interrupt	Ⓒ
E15	Open Coolant Sensor Circuit	Ⓐ	E55	TPS Misadjusted	Ⓒ
E16	Generator Voltage Out Of Range	Ⓑ	E58	PASS Control Problem	Ⓐ
E19	Shorted Fuel Pump Circuit	Ⓑ	E60	Cruise–Transmission Not In Drive	Ⓒ
E20	Open Fuel Pump Circuit	Ⓑ	E61	Cruise–Vent Solenoid Problem	Ⓒ
E21	Shorted TPS Circuit	Ⓐ	E62	Cruise–Vacuum Solenoid Problem	Ⓒ
E22	Open TPS Circuit	Ⓐ	E63	Cruise–Vehicle Speed vs Set Speed Out Of Range	Ⓒ
E23	EST Signal Problem	Ⓐ			
E24	VSS Circuit Problem	Ⓐ	E64	Cruise–Vehicle Acceleration Out Of Range	Ⓒ
E26	Shorted Throttle Switch Circuit	Ⓐ			
E27	Open Throttle Switch Circuit	Ⓐ	E65	Cruise–Servo Position Sensor Failure	Ⓒ
E28	Shorted 3rd Or 4th Gear Switch	Ⓐ			
E30	ISC RPM Out Of Range	Ⓐ	E66	Cruise–Engine RPM Out Of Range	Ⓒ Ⓐ
E31	Shorted MAP Sensor Circuit	Ⓐ	E67	Cruise–Switch Shorted During Enable	Ⓐ
E32	Open MAP Sensor Circuit	Ⓐ			
E34	MAP Sensor Signal Out Of Range	Ⓐ	E68	Cruise Control Command Problem	Ⓐ
E37	Shorted MAT Sensor Circuit	Ⓐ	E74	MAT Signal Interrupt	Ⓒ
E38	Open MAT Sensor Circuit	Ⓐ	E75	VSS Signal Interrupt	Ⓐ
E39	VCC Engagement Problem	Ⓐ	E85	Throttle Body Service Required	Ⓐ
E40	Power Steering Pressure Switch Problem	Ⓐ	E90	VCC Brake Switch Input Problem	Ⓑ
E41	Cam Sensor Circuit Problem	Ⓐ	E91	Park Neutral Switch Problem	Ⓑ
E44	Oxygen Sensor Signal Lean	Ⓐ	E92	Heated W/S Request Problem	Ⓒ
E45	Oxygen Sensor Signal Rich	Ⓐ	E96	Torque Converter Overstress	Ⓒ
E47	BCM—ECM Data Problem	Ⓐ	E97	P/N To D/R Engagement Problem	Ⓒ
E48	EGR Control Problem	Ⓐ	E98	P/N To D/R ISC Engaged Problem	Ⓒ
			E99	Cruise Servo Apply Problem	Ⓒ

TELLTALE STATUS

Ⓐ	"SERVICE ENGINE SOON" Light ON.
Ⓑ	"SERVICE VEHICLE SOON" Light ON.
Ⓒ	NO TELLTALE ON.

Fig. 40 Diagnostic trouble codes — 4.5L engine

84204010

PCM DIAGNOSTIC CODES

CODE	DESCRIPTION	TELLTALE STATUS	CODE	DESCRIPTION	TELLTALE STATUS
E012	No Distributor Signal	A	E048	EGR Control Problem	A
E013	Right Oxygen Sensor Not Read	A,P	E051	MEM-CAL Error	A
E014	Shorted Coolant Sensor Circuit	A	E052	PCM Memory Reset	C
E015	Open Coolant Sensor Circuit	A	E053	Distributor Signal Interrupt	C
E016	Voltage Out Of Range [ALL SOL.]	B	E055	TPS Misadjusted	C
E017	Left Oxygen Sensor Not Ready	A	E058	PASS Control Problem	C
E019	Shorted Fuel Pump Circuit	B	E060	Cruise-Transmission Not In Drive [C/C]	C
E020	Open Fuel Pump Circuit	B	E061	Cruise-Vent Solenoid Problem [C/C]	C
E021	Shorted TPS Circuit [VCC]	A	E062	Cruise-Vacuum Solenoid Problem [C/C]	C
E022	Open TPS Circuit [VCC]	A	E063	Cruise-Speed vs Set Speed [C/C]	C
E023	EST Signal Problem [EGR]	A	E064	Cruise-Vehicle Acceleration [C/C]	C
E024	VSS Circuit Problem [C/C, VCC]	A,Q	E065	Cruise-S P S Failure [C/C]	C
E026	Shorted Throttle Switch Circuit [EGR]	A	E066	Cruise-RPM Out Of Range [C/C]	C
E027	Open Throttle Switch Circuit [EGR]	A	E067	Cruise-Switch Shorted At Enable [C/C]	C
E030	ISC RPM Out Of Range	A	E068	Cruise Command Problem [C/C]	C,Q
E031	Shorted MAP Sensor Circuit	A	E070	Intermittent TPS	C
E032	Open MAP Sensor Circuit	A	E071	Intermittent MAP	C
E034	MAP Sensor Signal Out Of Range	A	E073	Intermittent Coolant Sensor	C
E037	Shorted MAT Sensor Circuit	A	E074	Intermittent MAT	C
E038	Open MAT Sensor Circuit	A	E075	Intermittent VSS	C
E039	VCC Engagement Problem [VCC]	A,F	E080	Fuel System Rich	A
E040	Power Steering Pressure Switch	A	E085	Throttle Body Service Required	A
E041	Cam Sensor Circuit Problem	A	E090	VCC Brake Switch Input Problem [C/C]	B
E042	Left Oxygen Sensor Lean	A,P	E091	PRNDL Switch Problem [C/C]	B
E043	Left Oxygen Sensor Rich	A,P	E092	Heated Windshield Problem	B
E044	Right Oxygen Sensor Signal Lean	A,P	E096	Torque Converter Overstress	A
E045	Right Oxygen Sensor Signal Rich	A,P	E097	High RPM P/N to D/R Shift	C
E046	Right To Left Bank Fueling Problem	A	E098	High RPM P/N To D/R Shift Under ISC	C
E047	BCM—PCM Data Problem	A	E099	Cruise Servo Apply Problem [C/C]	C

TELLTALE STATUS

A = "SERVICE ENGINE SOON" Light ON.
B = "SERVICE CAR SOON" Message On DIC.
C = NO TELLTALE or Message.
F = DISENGAGES VCC FOR IGNITION CYCLE

P = ENABLES CANISTER PURGE
Q = DISABLES CRUISE FOR IGNITION CYCLE
[ ] = BRACKETED SYSTEMS ARE DISABLED WHEN CODE IS CURRENT

DIAGNOSTICS – BASIC OPERATION

- ENTER DIAGNOSTICS BY SIMULTANEOUSLY PRESSING ECCP OFF AND WARMER BUTTONS UNTIL ALL DISPLAYS ARE LIT.

- DIAGNOSTIC CODE LEVEL DISPLAYS PCM CODES FOLLOWED BY BCM and SIR CODES.

- TO PROCEED TO THE DESIRED LEVEL, PRESS AND RELEASE THE INDICATED BUTTON.

- PRESS OFF TO RETURN TO THE NEXT SELECTION IN THE PREVIOUS LEVEL.

- EXIT DIAGNOSTICS BY PRESSING RESET ON THE DRIVER INFORMATION CENTER.

84204277

Fig. 41 Diagnostic trouble codes — 1991-93 vehicles with 4.9L engine

PCM DIAGNOSTIC CODES

CODE	DESCRIPTION	TELLTALE STATUS
P012	No 4X Reference Signal From Ignition Control Module	A
P013	Rear Heated Oxygen Sensor Not Ready	A
P014	Shorted Engine Coolant Temperature Sensor	A
P015	Open Engine Coolant Temperature Sensor	A
P016	Generator Voltage Out Of Range [EVAP, EGR, CRUISE, TCC, Transaxle Pressure Control, Long Term Fuel Trim]	B
P017	Front Heated Oxygen Sensor Not Ready	A
P019	Shorted Fuel Pump Circuit	B
P020	Open Fuel Pump Circuit	B
P021	Shorted Throttle Position (TP) Sensor [TCC, Transaxle Pressure Control]	A
P022	Open Throttle Position (TP) Sensor [TCC, EGR]	A
P023	Ignition Control Circuit Problem [Ignition Control]	A
P024	Vehicle Speed Sensor Circuit Problem [TCC]	A
P025	24X Reference Signal Low	B
P026	Shorted Throttle Position (TP) Switch Circuit [EGR]	A
P027	Open Throttle Position (TP) Switch Circuit [EGR]	A
P028	Transaxle Pressure Switch/Circuit Problem	A
P029	Transaxle Shift 'B' Solenoid Problem [1st, 3rd, 4th Gear]	A
P030	Idle Speed Control (ISC) RPM Out Of Range	A
P031	Shorted Manifold Absolute Pressure (MAP) Sensor [Long Term Fuel Trim]	A
P032	Open Manifold Absolute Pressure (MAP) Sensor [Long Term Fuel Trim]	A
P033	Extended Travel Brake Switch Input Circuit Problem [Cruise]	B
P034	Manifold Absolute Pressure (MAP) Signal Too High [Long Term Fuel Trim]	A
P035	Ignition Ground Voltage Out of Range	C
P036	Exhaust Gas Recirculation (EGR) Valve Pintle Position Out Of Range [EGR]	A
P037	Shorted Intake Air Temperature (IAT) Sensor	A
P038	Open Intake Air Temperature (IAT) Sensor	A
P039	Torque Converter Clutch (TCC) Engagement Problem [4th Gear, TCC for Ignition Cycle]	A
P040	Power Steering Pressure Switch Open	A
P041	No Cam Reference Signal From Ignition Control Module	A
P042	Front Heated Oxygen Sensor Lean Exhaust Signal	A
P043	Front Heated Oxygen Sensor Rich Exhaust Signal	A
P044	Rear Heated Oxygen Sensor Lean Exhaust Signal	A
P045	Rear Heated Oxygen Sensor Rich Exhaust Signal	A
P046	Left To Right Bank Fueling Difference	A
P047	PCM/BCM Data Link Problem	B
P048	Exhaust Gas Recirculation (EGR) System Malfunction [EGR]	A
P051	PROM Checksum Mismatch	A
P052	PCM Keep Alive Memory Reset	C
P053	4X Reference Signal Interrupt From Ignition Control Module	C
P055	Closed Throttle Angle Out-Of-Range [TP Sensor Learn]	A
P056	Transaxle Input Speed Sensor Circuit Problem	A
P057	Shorted Transaxle Temperature Sensor Circuit	B
P058	PASS-Key® Fuel Enable Problem [PASS-Key® Fuel Inhibit]	D
P059	Open Transaxle Temperature Sensor Circuit	B
P060	Cruise Control – Transaxle Not In Drive [Cruise]	C
P061	Cruise Control – Vent Solenoid Problem [Cruise]	C
P062	Cruise Control – Vacuum Solenoid Problem [Cruise]	C
P063	Set vs Vehicle Speed Difference [Cruise]	C
P064	Vehicle Acceleration Too High [Cruise]	C
P065	Cruise Control Servo Position Sensor Failure [Cruise]	C
P066	Cruise Control – Engine RPM Too High [Cruise]	C
P067	Set/Coast Or Resume/Accel Input Shorted [Cruise]	C
P068	Cruise Control Servo Position Out Of Range [Cruise]	C
P069	Traction Control Active While In Cruise [Cruise]	C
P070	Intermittent Throttle Position (TP) Sensor	C
P071	Intermittent Manifold Absolute Pressure (MAP) Sensor	C
P073	Intermittent Engine Coolant Temperature Sensor	C
P074	Intermittent Intake Air Temperature (IAT) Sensor	C
P075	Vehicle Speed Sensor Signal Interrupt [TCC]	C
P076	Transaxle Pressure Control Solenoid Circuit Malfunction [Trans. Pressure Control]	A
P080	TP Sensor/Idle Learn Not Complete	A
P081	CAM To 4X Reference Correlation Problem	C
P083	24X Reference Signal High	A
P085	Idle Throttle Angle Too High	A
P086	Undefined Gear Ratio [Trans. Pressure Control]	A
P088	Torque Converter Clutch (TCC) Not Disengaging [Trans. Adapts]	A
P089	Long Shift and Maximum Adapt [Trans. Pressure Control]	A
P090	TCC Brake Switch Input Circuit Problem [Cruise]	E
P091	Transaxle Range Switch Problem [Cruise]	B
P092	Heated Windshield Request Problem	B
P093	Traction Control System PWM Link Failure	A
P094	Transaxle Shift 'A' Solenoid Problem [1st, 3rd, 4th Gear]	A
P095	Engine Stall Detected	C
P096	Torque Converter Overstress	A
P097	P/N To D/R At High Throttle Angle	E
P099	Cruise Control Servo Applied Not In Cruise	E
P102	Shorted Brake Booster Vacuum (BBV) Sensor [EVAP, Solenoid, EGR, Cruise, TCC, Lt Fuel Trim, Transaxle Adapts]	B
P103	Open Brake Booster Vacuum (BBV) Sensor [EVAP, EGR, Cruise, TCC, Lt Fuel Trim, Transaxle Adapts]	B
P105	Brake Booster Vacuum (BBV) Too Low	B
P106	Stop Lamp Switch Input Circuit Problem	E
P107	PCM/BCM Data Link Problem	C
P108	PROM Checksum Mismatch	A
P109	PCM Keep Alive Memory Reset	C
P110	Generator L–Terminal Circuit Problem	F
P112	Total EEPROM Failure	C
P117	Shift 'A'/Shift 'B' Circuit Output Open Or Shorted	C
P131	Active Knock Sensor Failure	A
P132	Knock Sensor Circuitry Failure	A
P137	Loss Of ABS/TCS Data	E

TELLTALE STATUS

A = 'SERVICE ENGINE SOON' Malfunction Indicator Lamp (MIL) ON.
B = 'SERVICE VEHICLE SOON' message On DIC.
C = No telltale or message.
D = 'THEFT SYSTEM PROBLEM – CAR MAY NOT RESTART' message.
E = 'REDUCED ENGINE POWER' message.
F = 'BATTERY NO CHARGE' message.
[ ] = BRACKETED SYSTEMS ARE DISABLED WHEN CODE IS CURRENT

84204442

Fig. 42 Diagnostic trouble codes — 4.6L engine

VACUUM DIAGRAMS — VEHICLE EMISSIONS CONTROL INFORMATION (VECI) LABEL

➡The following is an assortment of vehicle emission control information labels. If the label on your vehicle differs from what is lisited here, always follow what is on your underhood sticker, as it is most likely the accurate label for your particular engine application.

84204566

Fig. 43 Example of underhood Vehicle Emissions Control Information (VECI) label in the engine compartment

84204567

Fig. 44 Label code MDA — 4.6L engine — California

Fig. 45 Label code MDB — 4.6L engine — California

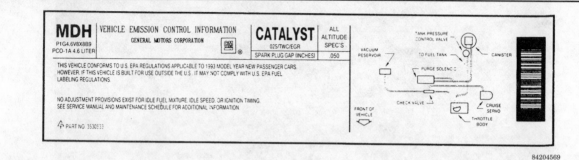

Fig. 46 Label code MDH — 4.6L engine — Federal

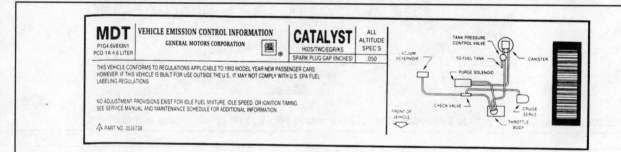

Fig. 47 Label code MDT — 4.6L engine — Federal

Fig. 48 Label code MDW — 4.6L engine — California

Fig. 49 Label code MDL — 4.9L engine — California

Fig. 50 Label code MDM — 4.9L engine — California

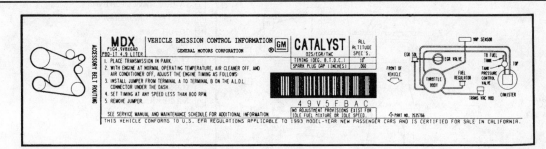

Fig. 51 Label code MDX — 4.9L engine — California

Fig. 52 Label code MDZ — 4.9L engine — Federal

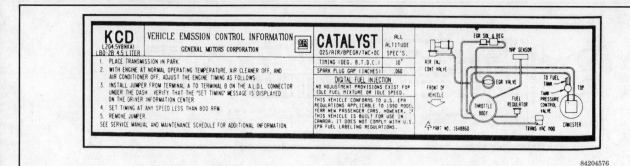

Fig. 53 Label code KCD — 4.5L engine

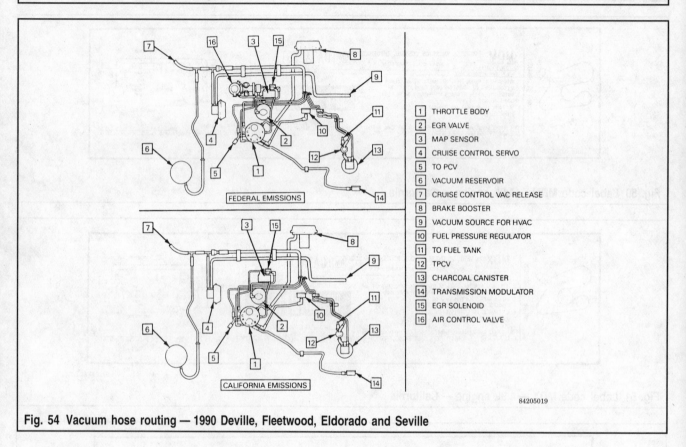

1	THROTTLE BODY
2	EGR VALVE
3	MAP SENSOR
4	CRUISE CONTROL SERVO
5	TO PCV
6	VACUUM RESERVOIR
7	CRUISE CONTROL VAC RELEASE
8	BRAKE BOOSTER
9	VACUUM SOURCE FOR HVAC
10	FUEL PRESSURE REGULATOR
11	TO FUEL TANK
12	TPCV
13	CHARCOAL CANISTER
14	TRANSMISSION MODULATOR
15	EGR SOLENOID
16	AIR CONTROL VALVE

Fig. 54 Vacuum hose routing — 1990 Deville, Fleetwood, Eldorado and Seville

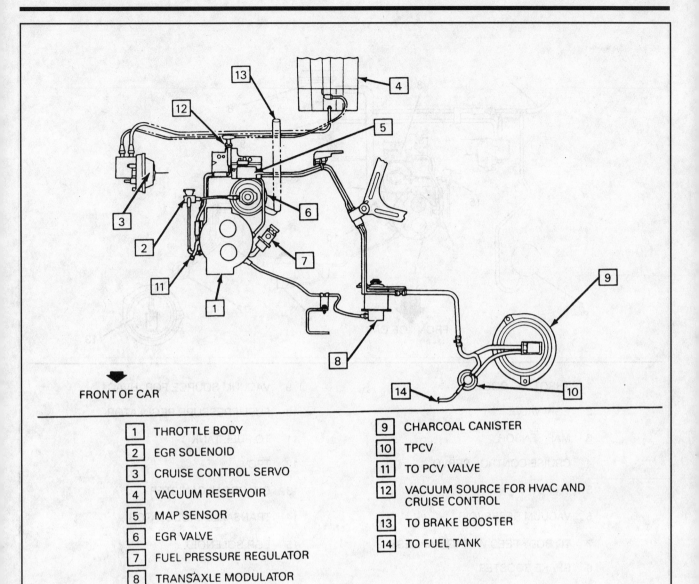

FRONT OF CAR

1	THROTTLE BODY	9	CHARCOAL CANISTER
2	EGR SOLENOID	10	TPCV
3	CRUISE CONTROL SERVO	11	TO PCV VALVE
4	VACUUM RESERVOIR	12	VACUUM SOURCE FOR HVAC AND CRUISE CONTROL
5	MAP SENSOR	13	TO BRAKE BOOSTER
6	EGR VALVE	14	TO FUEL TANK
7	FUEL PRESSURE REGULATOR		
8	TRANSAXLE MODULATOR		

84205020

Fig. 55 Vacuum hose routing — 1991-93 Deville, Fleetwood and Sixty Special

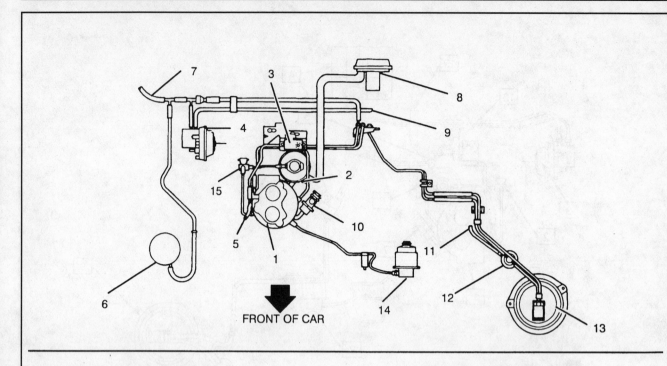

FRONT OF CAR

1	THROTTLE BODY	9	VACUUM SOURCE FOR HVAC
2	EGR VALVE	10	FUEL PRESSURE REGULATOR
3	MAP SENSOR	11	TO FUEL TANK
4	CRUISE CONTROL SERVO	12	TPCV
5	TO PCV	13	CHARCOAL CANISTER
6	VACUUM RESERVOIR	14	TRANSAXLE MODULATOR
7	TO BODY FEED WIRING HARNESS	15	EGR SOLENOID
8	BRAKE BOOSTER		

84205021

Fig. 56 Vacuum hose routing — 1991-93 Eldorado and Seville with 4.9L engine

5

FUEL SYSTEM

SEQUENTIAL PORT FUEL INJECTION (SPFI) SYSTEM

General Information

The Sequential Port Fuel Injection (SPFI) system is controlled by an Electronic Control Module (ECM) which monitors engine operations and generates output signals to provide the correct air/fuel mixture, ignition timing and engine idle speed control. Input to the control unit is provided by an oxygen sensor, coolant temperature sensor, detonation sensor, hot film air mass sensor and throttle position sensor. The ECM also receives information concerning engine rpm, road speed, transmission gear position, power steering and air conditioning.

An Electronic Spark Control (ESC) is used to adjust the spark timing. On V8 engines, the conventional High Energy Ignition (HEI) system is used.

The injection system uses solenoid-type fuel injectors, 1 at each intake port, rather than the single injector found on the earlier throttle body system. The injectors are mounted on a fuel rail and are activated by a signal from the electronic control module. The injector is a solenoid-operated valve which remains open depending on the width of the electronic pulses (length of the signal) from the ECM; the longer the open time, the more fuel is injected.In this manner, the air/fuel mixture can be precisely controlled for maximum performance with minimum emissions.

Fuel is pumped from the tank by a high pressure fuel pump, located inside the fuel tank. It is a positive displacement roller vane pump. The impeller serves as a vapor separator and pre-charges the high pressure assembly. A pressure r regulator maintains 34-47 psi (240-315 kPa) in the fuel line to the injectors and the excess fuel is fed back to the tank.

Engine idle is controlled by an Idle Speed Control (ISC) solenoid. The Idle Speed Control (ISC) assembly consists of a motor, gear reduction section, plunger and throttle contact switch. It is mounted on the throttle body and is used to control engine idle speed. The ISC plunger acts as a movable throttle stop, which changes the primary throttle valve angle. The ECM monitors engine idle speed and causes the motor to move the ISC plunger to maintain the desired idle speed for operating condition. The position of the throttle contact switch determines whether or not the ISC controls idle speed. When the throttle lever rests against the ISC plunger, the contacts in the switch close. This causes the ECM to move the plunger to the programmed idle speed position. When the throttle lever breaks with the ISC plunger, the switch contacts open and the ECM stops sending idle speed commands. Speed is then controlled by the accelerator pedal.

Relieving Fuel System Pressure

1. Disconnect the negative battery cable to avoid possible fuel discharge if an accidental attempt is made to start the engine.

2. Loosen fuel filler cap to relieve tank vapor pressure. Do not tighten until service has been completed.

3. Connect a suitable fuel pressure gauge such as J 34730-1 or equivalent, to fuel pressure connection on fuel rail assembly. Wrap a shop towel around fitting while connecting gauge to avoid spillage.

4. Install bleed hose into an approved container and open valve to bleed system pressure. Fuel connections are now safe for servicing.

5. Drain any fuel into an approved container.

➡**When repairs to the fuel system have been completed, start the engine and check all connections that were loosened for possible leaks. Perform the appropriate TP Sensor/Idle Learn procedure as necessary.**

MINIMUM IDLE (AIR),THROTTLE POSITION SENSOR AND ISC MOTOR ADJUSTMENTS

Minimum Idle (Air) and Throttle Position Sensor

FLEETWOOD, DEVILLE AND SIXTY SPECIAL

1. Preliminary checks:

a. Enter diagnostic and record all the trouble codes displayed. If current or history codes are found, refer to the diagnostic charts. When all the trouble codes are checked and repaired, proceed to the next Step.

b. Start the engine. Enter the diagnostics. Select ECM data P.O.4, Coolant Temperature. Operate the engine until the coolant temperature is greater than 95°C.

c. Exit diagnostics. Select the **OFF** mode on the ECC. This will turn the air conditioning compressor off. Place the transmission in **P**.

d. Enter set timing mode by jumping pin **A** to pin **B** of the ALDL connector. Check for timing at 10 degrees BTDC and adjust as necessary. Disconnect the jumper at the ALDL after the timing is verified as correct.

e. Visually check all vacuum hoses for splits, leaks, or cuts and assure that there are no vacuum leaks.

2. Check minimum idle speed:

a. Retract the ISC motor by selecting the ECM override E.5.3 for ISC Motor. Press the **COOLER** button to retract the ISC motor. The ISC motor will slowly retract (about 20 seconds). Once the ISC has fully retracted, make sure that the throttle lever is resetting on the minimum idle speed screw.

b. With the ISC plunger fully retracted, the plunger should not be touching the throttle lever. Make sure that the throttle lever is not being bound by the throttle, cruise or throttle valve cables. The throttle lever must be resting on the minimum idle speed screw. If contact is noted, adjust the ISC plunger, turn in with a suitable pair of pliers or tool J-29607 so that it is not touching the throttle lever.

c. Connect a tachometer and check the minimum idle speed. Vehicles under 500 miles, rpm should be 450-500 rpm. Vehicles over 500 miles, should be 500-550 rpm.

➡**If the engine speed in not within specifications, check for a vacuum leak at the throttle body, intake manifold vacuum fittings, tees and hoses. If the minimum air setting is made with a vacuum leak present, fuel control can be adversely affected throughout the driving range. If the engine stalled at minimum air (ISC) retracted), check the primary throttle blades for deposits that might restrict air flow. If there are deposits, clean the primary throttle bore and the area behind and around the throttle plate, using a clean shop towel with top engine cleaner or equivalent. Do not use any solvent that contains methyl ethyl ketone. Recheck minimum idle speed after cleaning the throttle body.**

d. If the minimum idle speed is out of limit, connect a tachometer to the engine and adjust the minimum idle speed screw to 475 rpm, for vehicles up to 500 miles and 525 rpm for vehicles over 500 miles. Remove and discard the minimum idle speed screw plug. Use a T-20 Torx® driver to adjust the minimum idle speed screw.

e. If the engine speed cannot be corrected, check that the throttle is not held off the minimum idle speed screw because of the linkage binding or interference with the ISC motor plunger. Also check vacuum hoses for leaks, for air leaks at the throttle body mounting and intake manifold. After making adjustments, go on to Step 3.

3. Check Throttle Position Sensor (TPS) setting by running the engine and selecting ECM override E.5.3, ISC Motor and press the COOLER button to retract the ISC motor, minimum air setting.

4. Adjust the Throttle Position Switch (TPS):

a. Loosen the TPS screws just enough to permit the sensor to be rotated. Use T-25 Torx driver should be used for the TPS adjustment. Open the throttle and allow the throttle lever to shut against the minimum air screw.

b. Adjust the TPS so that the voltmeter reads 0.475-0.525 volts.

c. Tighten the TPS mounting screws with the sensor in the adjusted position. Recheck the voltage reading to be sure it is 0.475-0.525 volts.

➡**Do not use excessive force to adjust the TPS or damage to the TPS may occur. The TPS mounting screws must be loosened to perform the adjustment.**

5. Check and adjust the ISC maximum extension.

ELDORADO AND SEVILLE 1990-93

1. Preliminary checks:

a. Enter diagnostic and record all the trouble codes displayed. If current or history codes are found, refer to the diagnostic charts. When all the trouble codes are checked and repaired, proceed to the next Step.

b. Start the engine. Enter the diagnostics. Select ECM data ED04, Coolant Temperature. Operate the engine until the coolant temperature is greater than 95°C.

c. Exit diagnostics. Select the OFF mode on the ECC. This will turn the air conditioning compressor off. Place the transmission in P. Also on 1992 vehicles, disable the alternator by grounding the green harness connector plug adjacent to the alternator.

d. Enter set timing mode by jumping pin A to pin B of the ALDL connector while not in diagnostic display. Check for timing at 10 degrees BTDC and adjust as necessary. Disconnect the jumper at the ALDL after the timing is verified as correct.

e. Visually check all vacuum hoses for splits, leaks, or cuts and assure that there are no vacuum leaks.

2. Check minimum idle speed:

a. Retract the ISC motor by selecting the ECM override E.S.3 for 1990, ES03 for 1991-92 and PS03 for 1993 for 'ISC Motor'. Press the COOLER button to retract the ISC motor. The ISC motor will slowly retract (about 20 seconds). Once the ISC has fully retracted, make sure that the throttle lever is resetting on the minimum idle speed screw.

b. With the ISC plunger fully retracted, the plunger should not be touching the throttle lever. Make sure that the throttle lever is not being bound by the throttle, cruise or throttle valve cables. The throttle lever must be resting on the minimum idle speed screw. If contact is noted, adjust the ISC plunger, turn in with a suitable pair of pliers or tool J-29607 so that it is not touching the throttle lever.

c. Connect a tachometer and check the minimum idle speed. Vehicles under 500 miles, rpm should be 450-500 rpm. Vehicles over 500 miles, should be 500-550 rpm.

➡**If the engine speed in not within specifications, check for a vacuum leak at the throttle body, intake manifold vacuum fittings, tees and hoses. If the minimum air setting is made with a vacuum leak present, fuel control can be adversely affected throughout the driving range. If the engine stalled at minimum air (ISC) retracted), check the primary throttle blades for deposits that might restrict air flow. If there are deposits, clean the primary throttle bore and the area behind and around the throttle plate, using a clean shop towel with top engine cleaner or equivalent. Do not use any solvent that contains methyl ethyl ketone. Recheck minimum idle speed after cleaning the throttle body.**

d. If the minimum idle speed is out of limit, connect a tachometer to the engine and adjust the minimum idle speed screw to 475 rpm, for vehicles up to 500 miles and 525 rpm for vehicles over 500 miles. Remove and discard the minimum idle speed screw plug. Use a T-20 Torx® L-shaped driver to adjust the minimum idle speed screw.

e. If the engine speed cannot be corrected, check that the throttle is not held off the minimum idle speed screw because of the linkage binding or interference with the ISC motor plunger. Also check vacuum hoses for leaks, for air leaks at the throttle body mounting and intake manifold. After making adjustments, go on to Step 3.

3. Check Throttle Position Sensor (TPS) setting by running the engine and selecting ECM override E.S.3 for 1990, ES03 for 1991-92 and PS03 for 1993, 'ISC Motor' and press the COOLER button to retract the ISC motor, minimum air setting.

4. Adjust the Throttle Position Switch (TPS):

a. Loosen the TPS screws just enough to permit the sensor to be rotated. Use T-25 Torx driver should be used for the TPS adjustment. Open the throttle and allow the throttle lever to shut against the minimum air screw.

b. Adjust the TPS so that the voltmeter reads -0.5°-+0.5°.

c. Tighten the TPS mounting screws with the sensor in the adjusted position. Recheck to be sure it is -0.5°-+0.5°.

➡️**Do not use excessive force to adjust the TPS or damage to the TPS may occur. The TPS mounting screws must be loosened to perform the adjustment.**

5. Check and adjust the ISC maximum extension.

ISC Maximum Extension

FLEETWOOD, DEVILLE AND SIXTY SPECIAL

1. With the ignition **ON**, engine **OFF**, extend the ISC motor override E.5.3. Press the **WARMER** button on the ECC. The fuel data center should display E.5.3 and **99** alternately indicating the override function has started. The ISC will extend to the maximum extend position.

2. With the ISC motor at maximum extension the TPS voltage should be between 1.15-1.20 volts. If the TPS is not within this range, adjust the ISC plunger by turning the plunger in to lower the voltage or out to raise the voltage. An ideal setting is 1.18 volts.

3. Recheck the maximum extension voltage by again pressing the COOLER button to retract the ESC plunger. Wait 5 seconds. Press the WARMER button and read the TPS voltage. Readjust the ISC plunger, as required.

4. After all adjustments and checks are complete, remain in the diagnostic mode, turn the ignition **OFF**. Allow approximately 20 seconds for the ISC motor to retract and perform a TPS learn procedure.

1990-92 ELDORADO AND SEVILLE

1. With the ignition **ON**, engine **OFF**, extend the ISC motor override E.S.3. for 1990 and ES03 for 1991-92. Press the **WARMER** button on the ECC. The fuel data center should change from '50" or '00" to '99" indicating the override function has started. The ISC will extend to the maximum extend position.

2. With the ISC motor at maximum extension the TPS voltage should be between 13.0-13.8 degrees. If the TPS is not within this range, adjust the ISC plunger by turning the plunger in or out. An ideal setting is 13.4 degrees.

3. Recheck the maximum extension voltage by again pressing the COOLER button to retract the ESC plunger. Wait

5 seconds. Press the WARMER button and read the TPS value displayed. Readjust the ISC plunger, as required.

4. After all adjustments and checks are complete, remain in the diagnostic mode, turn the ignition **OFF**. Allow approximately 20 seconds for the ISC motor to retract and perform a TPS learn procedure.

1990-93 ELDORADO AND SEVILLE WITH 4.6L NORTHSTAR ENGINES

▶ See Figures 1 and 2

For idle speed control (ISC) checking on these engines, please refer to Chart 6C-6 IDLE SPEED CONTROL (ISC) CHECK, which follows.

TP SENSOR/IDLE LEARN PROCEDURE

4.5L Engines

The 'TP Sensor/Idle Learn' routine provides a particular idle throttle angle offset, determined by throttle body condition, that is added to all coastdown throttle angles. Whenever the battery is disconnected, the idle throttle angle offset is set to a specific, calibrated value. When the battery is reconnected, and the vehicle driven, this initial idle offset could result in too high or too low of a coastdown throttle angle. Improper throttle angle can result in a coastdown sail-on condition or an engine stall. Performing the 'TP Sensor/Idle Learn' procedure lets the ECM learn the proper throttle angle offset for the particular throttle body.

1. After all service procedures are complete, reset the minimum air, TPS and max ISC extend, if necessary.

2. Warm the engine until normal operating temperature is reached.

3. Allow the engine to idle in **PARK** with the wheels straight ahead for 10 minutes.

4. With the brake applied and the Climate Control in the **OFF** position, place the transaxle in the **DRIVE** position and allow the engine to idle (foot off of the accelerator) for at least 3 minutes.

5. Place the transaxle in **PARK** and turn the engine **OFF**.

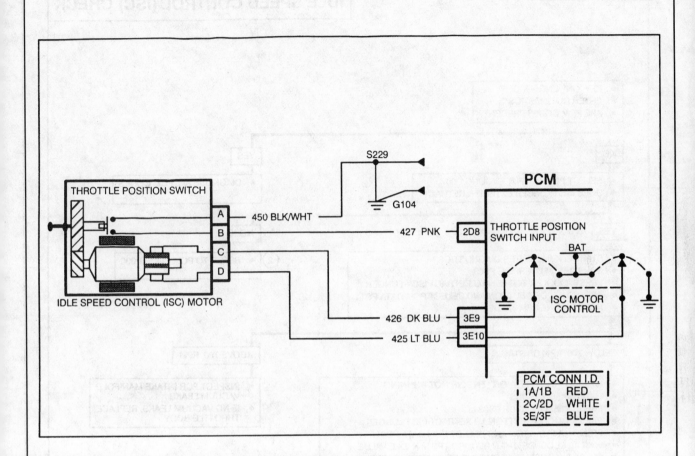

CHART 6C-6

IDLE SPEED CONTROL (ISC) CHECK

CIRCUIT DESCRIPTION:

The Idle Speed Control Check verifies proper ISC motor operation and checks ISC plunger adjustment. This check requires ISC adjusting wrench J 29607.

NOTES ON FAULT TREE:

1. This procedure checks for a high minimum air idle which could cause a sail-on condition. It is OK if engine cannot stay running at minimum air idle.

2. Follow PCM Trouble Code P030 diagnosis to identify the cause of a faulty ISC motor.

3. This procedure determines ISC authority. This is determined by comparing the minimum air TPS value to the maximum ISC extend value. ISC authority should be adjusted to $10° - 11°$ of throttle angle.

4. IDLE LEARN procedure must be performed after ISC plunger adjustment.

84205022

Fig. 1 Idle speed control (ISC) check — 4.6L engine

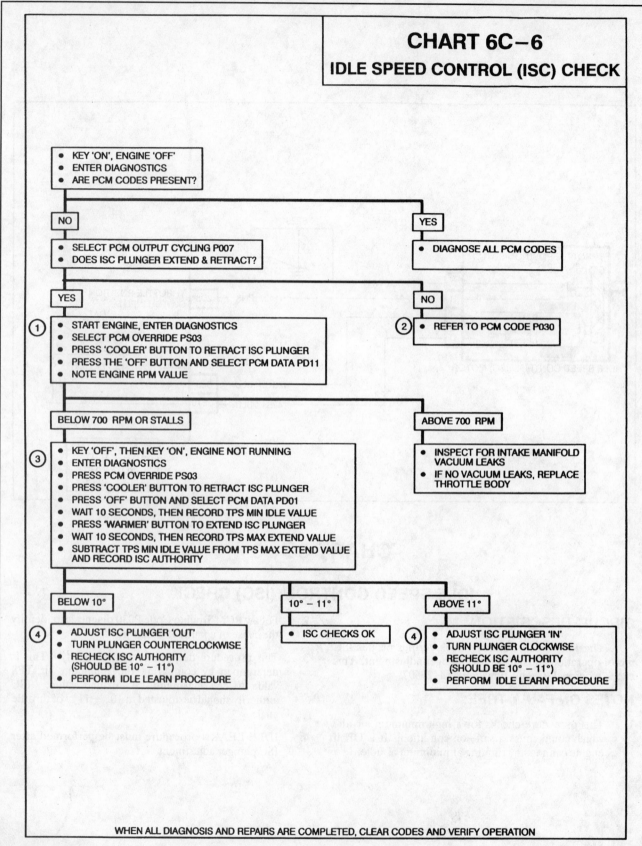

CHART 6C–6
IDLE SPEED CONTROL (ISC) CHECK

- KEY 'ON', ENGINE 'OFF'
- ENTER DIAGNOSTICS
- ARE PCM CODES PRESENT?

NO

- SELECT PCM OUTPUT CYCLING P007
- DOES ISC PLUNGER EXTEND & RETRACT?

YES

- DIAGNOSE ALL PCM CODES

YES

(1)
- START ENGINE, ENTER DIAGNOSTICS
- SELECT PCM OVERRIDE PS03
- PRESS 'COOLER' BUTTON TO RETRACT ISC PLUNGER
- PRESS THE 'OFF' BUTTON AND SELECT PCM DATA PD11
- NOTE ENGINE RPM VALUE

NO

(2)
- REFER TO PCM CODE P030

BELOW 700 RPM OR STALLS

(3)
- KEY 'OFF', THEN KEY 'ON', ENGINE NOT RUNNING
- ENTER DIAGNOSTICS
- PRESS PCM OVERRIDE PS03
- PRESS 'COOLER' BUTTON TO RETRACT ISC PLUNGER
- PRESS 'OFF' BUTTON AND SELECT PCM DATA PD01
- WAIT 10 SECONDS, THEN RECORD TPS MIN IDLE VALUE
- PRESS 'WARMER' BUTTON TO EXTEND ISC PLUNGER
- WAIT 10 SECONDS, THEN RECORD TPS MAX EXTEND VALUE
- SUBTRACT TPS MIN IDLE VALUE FROM TPS MAX EXTEND VALUE AND RECORD ISC AUTHORITY

ABOVE 700 RPM

- INSPECT FOR INTAKE MANIFOLD VACUUM LEAKS
- IF NO VACUUM LEAKS, REPLACE THROTTLE BODY

BELOW 10°

(4)
- ADJUST ISC PLUNGER 'OUT'
- TURN PLUNGER COUNTERCLOCKWISE
- RECHECK ISC AUTHORITY (SHOULD BE 10° – 11°)
- PERFORM IDLE LEARN PROCEDURE

10° – 11°

- ISC CHECKS OK

ABOVE 11°

(4)
- ADJUST ISC PLUNGER 'IN'
- TURN PLUNGER CLOCKWISE
- RECHECK ISC AUTHORITY (SHOULD BE 10° – 11°)
- PERFORM IDLE LEARN PROCEDURE

WHEN ALL DIAGNOSIS AND REPAIRS ARE COMPLETED, CLEAR CODES AND VERIFY OPERATION

84205023

Fig. 2 Idle speed control (ISC) check — 4.6L engine

4.6L Northstar Engine

The TP Sensor/Idle Learn routine of the PCM calculates a throttle angle or offset that is used during closed throttle idle control. If an improper throttle angle offset is maintained by the PCM, a closed throttle engine sail-on or stall condition may occur. Performing the TP Sensor/Idle Learn procedure lets the PCM learn the correct throttle angle.

The TP Sensor/Idle Learn procedure should be performed when:

- The throttle position sensor is replaced.
- The ISC motor is adjusted or replaced.
- The throttle body is replaced.
- The PCM is replaced.
- The PCM EEPROM is replaced.
- The TP SENSOR/IDLE LEARN is reset using PCM override PS13.

Perform the TP Sensor/Idle Learn procedure as follows:

1. Make sure the outside temperature is at least 50 °F so that the A/C compressor will turn **ON**.
2. Start the engine.
3. Allow the vehicle to idle continuously until the coolant temperature is 80 °C, then idle an additional 5 minutes.
4. At the end of 5 minutes, enter diagnostics (engine still running).
5. Turn the ignition to **OFF**.
6. Wait a minimum of 20 seconds.
7. Turn the ignition to **ON** (engine not running).
8. Enter diagnostics.
9. Turn the ignition to **OFF**.
10. Wait a minimum of 20 seconds.
11. Start the engine.
12. Apply the brakes and place the transaxle in **DRIVE**
13. With the brakes applied and the Climate Control Center in the **OFF** position, allow the engine to idle for 30 seconds.
14. Place the transaxle in **PARK** and turn the engine **OFF**.

4.9L Engine

The TP Sensor/Idle Learn routine of the PCM calculates a throttle angle or offset that is used during closed throttle idle control. If an improper throttle angle offset is maintained by the PCM, a closed throttle engine sail-on or stall condition may occur. Performing the TP Sensor/Idle Learn procedure lets the PCM learn the correct throttle angle.

The TP Sensor/Idle Learn procedure should be performed when:

- The throttle position sensor is replaced.
- The ISC motor is adjusted or replaced.
- The throttle body is replaced.
- The PCM is replaced.
- The PCM Code PO52 was set.
- The TP Sensor adjustment procedure has been performed.
- The minimum idle speed adjustment procedure has been performed.

Perform the TP Sensor/Idle Learn procedure as follows:

1. Make sure the outside temperature is at least 50 °F so that the A/C compressor will turn **ON**.
2. Start the engine and allow to idle for 13 minutes.
3. At the end of 13 minutes, enter diagnostics (engine still running).

4. Turn the ignition to **OFF**.
5. Wait a minimum of 20 seconds.
6. Turn the ignition to **ON** (engine not running).
7. Enter diagnostics.
8. Turn the ignition to **OFF**.
9. Wait a minimum of 20 seconds.
10. Start the engine.
11. Apply the brakes and place the transaxle in **DRIVE**
12. With the brakes applied and the Climate Control Panel (CCP) in the **OFF** position, allow the engine to idle for 60 seconds.
13. Turn the Climate Control Panel (CCP) to **AUTO**, and verify that the A/C compressor engagement occurs. Allow the engine to idle for at least 60 seconds.
14. Place the transaxle in **PARK** and turn the engine **OFF**.

Electric Fuel Pump

The fuel pump is a roller vane type, high pressure electric pump mounted in the fuel tank. Fuel is pumped at a positive pressure through an in-line fuel filter to the fuel rail assembly. Excess fuel is returned to the fuel tank through the fuel return line. The electric fuel pump is connected in parallel to the ECU/ECM and is activated by the ECU/ECM when the ignition is turned on and the engine is cranking or operating. If the engine stalls or if the starter is not engaged, the fuel pumps will stop in about one second.

REMOVAL & INSTALLATION

▶ See Figures 3 and 4

4.5L and 4.9L Engine

1. Disconnect the negative battery cable.
2. Relieve the fuel system pressure.
3. Raise and safely support the vehicle with jackstands.
4. Safely drain and remove the fuel tank assembly as outlined in the 'Fuel tank' removal procedures in this Section.
5. Turn the fuel pump cam lock ring counterclockwise and lift the assembly out of the tank.
6. Remove the fuel pump from the level sensor unit as follows:

   a. Pull the pump up into the attaching hose or pulsator while pulling outward away from the bottom support.

   b. Take care to prevent damage to the rubber insulator and strainer during removal.

   c. When the pump assembly is clear of the bottom support, pull the pump out of the rubber connector for removal.

To install:

7. Replace any attaching hoses or rubber sound insulator that show signs of deterioration.
8. Push the fuel pump into the attaching hoses and install the pump/sensor assembly into the tank. Always use a new O-ring seal. Be careful not to fold over or twist the strainer when installing the sensor unit. Also, make sure the strainer does not block full travel of the float arm.
9. Install the cam lock and turn clockwise to lock.
10. Install the fuel tank as outlined in this Section.
11. Fill the tank with four gallons of gas and check for fuel leaks.

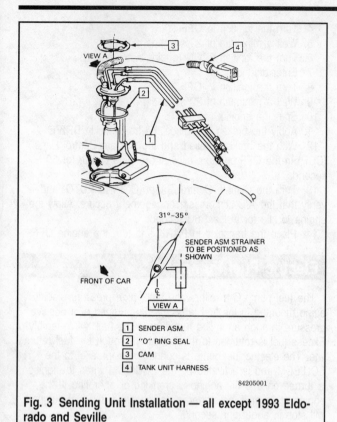

1 SENDER ASM.
2 "O" RING SEAL
3 CAM
4 TANK UNIT HARNESS

84205001

Fig. 3 Sending Unit Installation — all except 1993 Eldorado and Seville

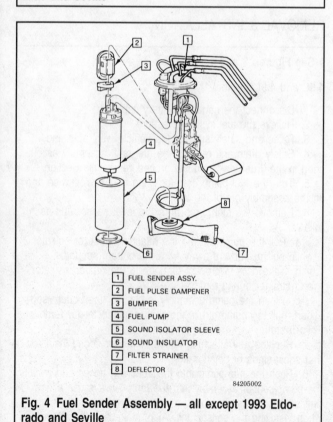

1 FUEL SENDER ASSY.
2 FUEL PULSE DAMPENER
3 BUMPER
4 FUEL PUMP
5 SOUND ISOLATOR SLEEVE
6 SOUND INSULATOR
7 FILTER STRAINER
8 DEFLECTOR

84205002

Fig. 4 Fuel Sender Assembly — all except 1993 Eldorado and Seville

4.6L Northstar Engine

▶ See Figures 5, 6 and 7

The high pressure rollervane fuel pump used in this system is part of the fuel sender assembly. On these engines a modular fuel sender assembly mounts to the threaded opening of the plastic fuel tank with a multi-lipped seal and threaded retainer nut. The spring loaded reservoir, containing the exterior inlet strainer, electric fuel pump, pump strainer and reservoir replenishing jet pump, maintains contact with the tank bottom.

1. Disconnect the negative battery cable.
2. Relieve the fuel system pressure.
3. Raise and safely support the vehicle with jackstands.
4. Safely drain and remove the fuel tank assembly as outlined in the 'Fuel tank' removal procedures in this Section.
5. Remove the modular fuel sender assembly by turning the locking nut counterclockwise and lifting the assembly out of the tank.

✸✸CAUTION

The modular fuel sender assembly may spring out from its position. Be aware that the reservoir is full of fuel. Tip the modular assembly slightly during removal to avoid damage to the float. Have a shop towel ready to absorb any leakage.

6. Carefully slide the fuel sender lip seal downward past the reservoir and over the float arm assembly and discard.
7. Carefully discard the reservoir fuel into a proper container.
8. Disconnect the under cover wire harness from the cover.
9. Disconnect the wire connector to the fuel pump by depressing with a screwdriver.
10. Disconnect the drain pipe from the retainer and bumper pad.
11. Remove the reservoir from the retainer at the locking tabs.

✸✸WARNING

It is important to follow the exact order when disassembling the modular unit to service the fuel pump or damage to the unit may result.

12. Locate the curved side of the modular unit's reservoir.
13. Begin a locking Tab 1 and squeeze the reservoir to release the first locking tab.
14. Moving clockwise to the locking Tab 2 location, apply gentle pressure to the guide rod to release the second locking tab.
15. At locking Tab 3 gently twist and squeeze to release the reservoir from the retainer.
16. Remove the cover and the retainer from the reservoir.

✸✸WARNING

Be careful not to damage the crossover tube.

17. Use a suitable tool and carefully pry the strainer ferrule off of the reservoir and remove the external strainer. Note strainer position for later reinstallation.
18. Remove the rubber pad (bumper) and discard.

19. Remove the fuel pump from the reservoir assembly.

a. The fuel pump and fuel pump sleeve assembly are attached to the retainer when pulled from the reservoir.

b. Depress the flex member on the pump sleeve and rotate the sleeve counterclockwise to remove the fuel pump from the retainer.

20. Slide the lower connector assembly out of the retainer and remove the fuel pulse dampener and discard.

To install:

21. Install a new fuel pulse dampener and slide the lower connector assembly into the retainer.

22. Install the fuel pump as follows:

a. Push the pump outlet tube into the fuel pulse dampener and rotate the flex member back to the original position.

b. Line up the pump tube outlet into the retainer opening. All 3 sleeve tabs should protrude through the retainer before rotating.

c. Rotate clockwise in place (will click). Be sure the fit is snug before rotating.

d. Place the fuel pump back into the reservoir. The crossover tube must be placed in the proper slot.

23. Install a new rubber pad (bumper) as noted in disassembly.

24. Install the drain tube into the proper retainer and bumper pad slots.

25. Install a new external strainer.

✳✳WARNING

Do not use excessive force or the jet pump could be dislodged.

26. Connect the fuel pump wiring connector.

27. Connect the undercover wire harness connector.

28. Install the modular fuel sender unit assembly as follows:

a. Lightly lubricate the inside diameter of a NEW lip seal with engine oil and install it on the modular sending unit. The lip seal should be carefully positioned over the float arm assembly, moved up over the reservoir and half way up the guide post.

b. Install the modular fuel sender assembly into the tank with the seat lip seal into the tank opening.

c. Align the arrow on the top of the fuel sender cover to the arrow on the fuel tank.

d. Slowly apply pressure to the top of the spring loaded sender until the lip seal is flush between the fuel tank and the fuel sender cover.

e. Attach the locking nut and tighten to 37 ft. lbs. (50 Nm).

➡**Make sure the lip seal provides a snug seal between the modular unit and the fuel tank.**

29. Install the fuel tank.

FUEL SYSTEM DIAGNOSIS

For fuel system testing, please see the Fuel System Diagnosis Charts at the end of this Section. Refer to the Electronic Engine Controls part of Section 4 for information on entering the diagnostic system and determining engine codes.

Throttle Body

REMOVAL & INSTALLATION

4.5 and 4.9L Engines

▶ **See Figures 8, 9 and 10**

1. Relieve the fuel system pressure. Raise the hood, install fender covers and remove the air cleaner assembly. Disconnect the negative battery cable.

2. Disconnect the electrical connectors for the idle speed control motor, the throttle position sensor, fuel injectors, EFE and any other component necessary in order to remove the throttle body.

3. Remove the throttle return spring, cruise control, throttle linkage and downshift cable.

4. Disconnect all necessary vacuum lines, the fuel inlet line, fuel return line, brake booster line, MAP sensor hose and the AIR hose. Be sure to use a back-up wrench on all metal lines.

5. Remove the PCV, EVAP and/or EGR hoses from the front of the throttle body.

6. Remove the 3 throttle body mounting screws and remove the throttle body and gasket.

7. The installation is the reverse order of the removal procedure.

8. Torque the throttle body retaining bolts to 14 ft. lbs. (19 Nm). Always use new gaskets and O-rings.

9. Make certain cruise and shift cables do not hold the throttle above the idle stop. Reset the IAC by depressing the accelerator slightly, run engine for 3-4 seconds and turn ignition **OFF** for 10 seconds.

4.6L Northstar Engine

▶ **See Figures 11, 12, 13, 14 and 15**

1. Disconnect the negative battery cable.

2. Refer to Section 3 and remove the intake manifold along with the throttle body.

3. Disconnect the vacuum manifold at the throttle body and the vacuum hoses at the cruise control servo.

4. Disconnect the cruise control cable at the servo. The cable can be removed at the servo without removing the plastic retainer.

5. Remove the cruise control servo and bracket at the throttle body.

6. Disconnect the cruise control cable at the throttle body.

7. Disconnect the TP sensor at the throttle body.

8. Disconnect the fuel pipe retainer at the ISC bracket.

9. Remove the throttle body from the intake manifold.

10. Remove the ISC motor and bracket from the throttle body.

To install:

11. Install the ISC motor and bracket to the throttle body.

12. Position a NEW throttle body O-ring seal on the throttle body with petroleum jelly.

➡**Do not reuse the old throttle body O-ring seal. The seal swells when exposed to fuel and oil and will not seat properly.**

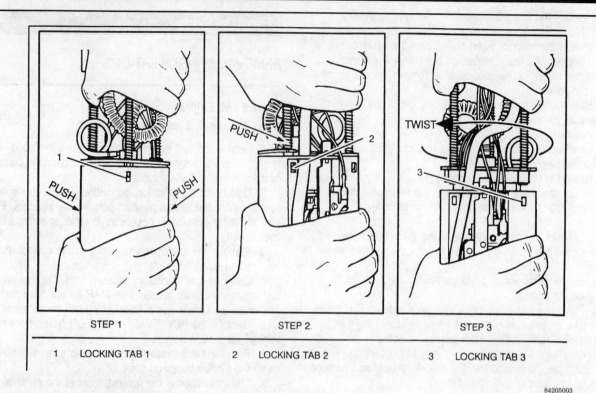

STEP 1   STEP 2   STEP 3

1   LOCKING TAB 1   2   LOCKING TAB 2   3   LOCKING TAB 3

84205003

Fig. 5 Modular fuel sender disassembly to remove the fuel pump — 1993 Eldorado and Seville

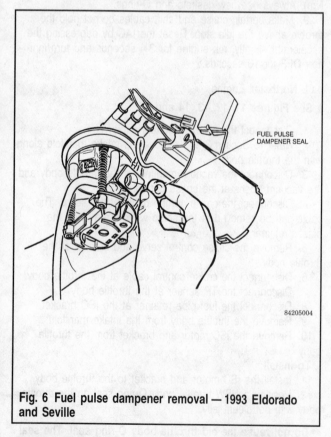

FUEL PULSE
DAMPENER SEAL

84205004

Fig. 6 Fuel pulse dampener removal — 1993 Eldorado and Seville

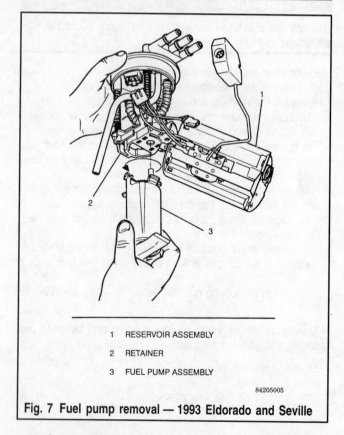

1   RESERVOIR ASSEMBLY

2   RETAINER

3   FUEL PUMP ASSEMBLY

84205005

Fig. 7 Fuel pump removal — 1993 Eldorado and Seville

13. Install the throttle body to the intake manifold and tighten to 106 inch lbs. (12 Nm).

14. Connect the fuel pipe retainer to the ISC bracket.

15. Connect the TP sensor to the throttle body and tighten the retaining bolts to 106 inch lbs. (12 Nm).

16. Connect the cruise control cable to the throttle body.

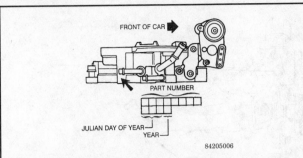

Fig. 8 Throttle body identification — 4.5L and 4.9L engines

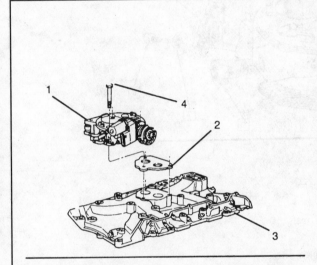

| 1 | THROTTLE BODY ASSEMBLY | 3 | INTAKE MANIFOLD |
| 2 | THROTTLE BODY GASKET | 4 | 19 N•m (14 LBS. FT.) |

84205007

Fig. 9 Throttle body assembly — 4.5L and 4.9L engines

17. Connect the cruise control servo and bracket to the throttle body and tighten the retaining bolts to 106 inch lbs. (12 Nm).

18. Connect the cruise control cable at the servo.

19. Connect the vacuum manifold to the throttle body and the vacuum hoses to the cruise control servo.

20. Refer to Section 3 and install the intake manifold along with the throttle body.

21. Perform the TP Sensor/Idle Learn procedure outlined earlier in this Section.

Fuel Injector

REMOVAL & INSTALLATION

4.5L and 4.9L Engines
▶ See Figures 16 and 17

1. Relieve the fuel system pressure. Raise the hood, install fender covers and remove the air cleaner assembly. Disconnect the negative battery cable.

2. Remove the fuel rail assembly as outlined in this Section. With the fuel rail inverted, disconnect electrical connector to injector by pushing in on the connector clip while pulling the connector body away from the injector. Spread open the clip slightly and slide the clip away from the fuel rail.

3. Remove the injector by twisting back and forth.

4. Disassemble the injector O-ring seals from the injector and discard.

To install:

5. Lubricate the new injector O-ring seals with a petroleum base grease and install on the injector assembly.

6. Install a new injector clip on the injector assembly.

7. Install the fuel injector assembly into the fuel rail socket as follows:

a. Push in to engage the retainer clip with the fuel rail cup.

b. The electrical connectors should be facing the engine front for injectors 1 thru 4. The electrical connectors should be facing the engine rear for injectors 5 thru 8.

8. Connect the electrical connector to the injector assembly.

9. Install the fuel rail assembly.

10. Energize the fuel pump and check for leaks.

11. Perform the Idle Learn procedure outlined earlier in this Section.

4.6L Northstar Engine
▶ See Figure 11

1. Remove the fuel pump relay in the engine compartment micro relay center.

2. Relieve the fuel system pressure as outlined earlier in this Section.

3. Remove the intake manifold top cover.

4. Disconnect the 2 intake manifold electrical connectors.

5. Remove the fuel rail along with the injectors out of the intakemanifold.

6. Remove the injectors from the fuel rail.

To install:

7. Install the injectors to the fuel rail.

8. Install the fuel rail along with the injectors into the intakemanifold housing.

9. Install the intake manifold top cover and torque the retaining bolts to 106 inch lbs. (12 Nm).

10. Connect the 2 intake manifold electrical connectors.

11. Install the fuel pump relay in the engine compartment micro relay center.

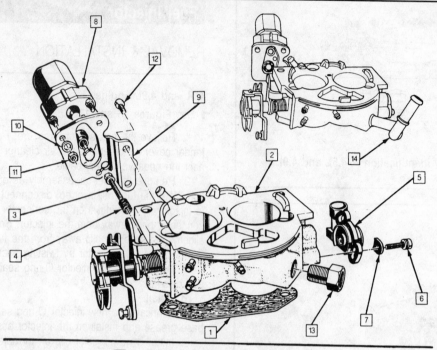

1	THROTTLE BODY GASKET
2	THROTTLE BODY ASSEMBLY
3	MINIMUM AIR (IDLE SPEED) SCREW
4	MINIMUM AIR SPRING
5	THROTTLE POSITION SENSOR (TPS)
6	TPS ATTACHING SCREW
7	TPS ATTACHING SCREW RETAINER
8	IDLE SPEED CONTROL MOTOR (ISC)
9	ISC ASSEMBLY BRACKET
10	ISC ASSEMBLY LOCKWASHER
11	ISC ASSEMBLY NUT
12	ISC BRACKET MOUNTING SCREW
13	BRAKE BOOSTER VACUUM PIPE FITTING (DESIGN 1)
14	BRAKE BOOSTER VACUUM PIPE FITTING (DESIGN 2)

84205008

Fig. 10 Throttle Body Unit — 4.5L and 4.9L engines

Fuel Rail Assembly

Before removal, the fuel rail assembly may be cleaned with a spray type engine cleaner, such as AC-DELCO X-30A or equivalent, following the package directions. Do not immerse fuel rails in liquid cleaning solvents.

When servicing the fuel rail assembly, be careful to prevent dirt or other contaminants from entering the fuel passages. Fittings should be capped and hoses plugged during servicing.

Whenever the fuel system is opened for service, the O-ring seals used with related components should be replaced.

REMOVAL & INSTALLATION

4.5L Engine
▶ See Figure 18

1. Disconnect the negative battery terminal.
2. Loosen the power steering pump bracket bolts and remove the serpentine drive belt. Remove the power steering pump and relocate as necessary.
3. Relieve the fuel pressure.
4. Disconnect the vacuum line from the pressure regulator and base assembly.
5. Remove the inlet fitting screw assemblies and bracket from the rear fuel rail and pressure regulator assemblies.
6. Disconnect the fuel feed line and O-ring from the rear fuel rail assembly.

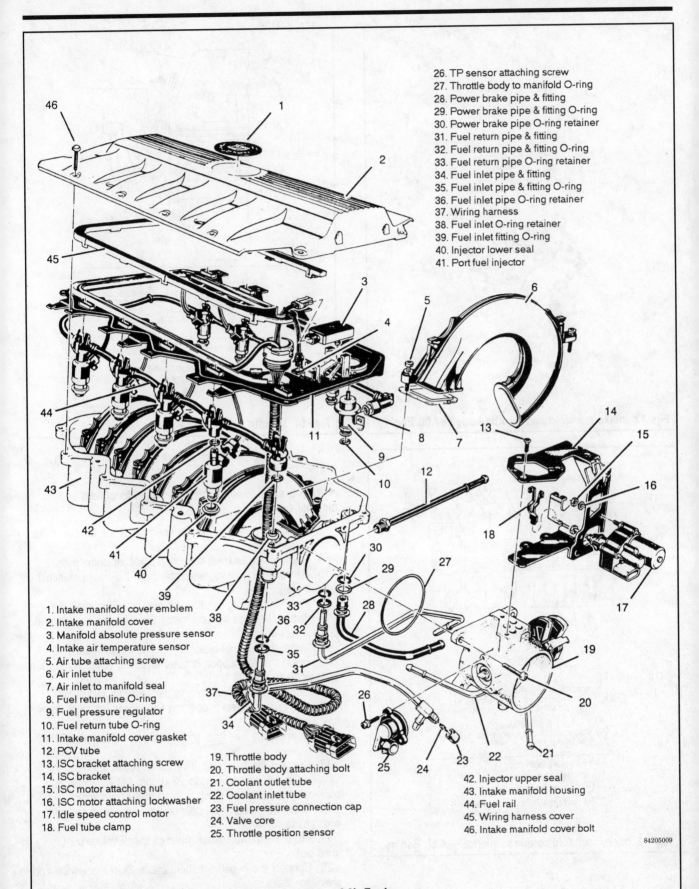

26. TP sensor attaching screw
27. Throttle body to manifold O-ring
28. Power brake pipe & fitting
29. Power brake pipe & fitting O-ring
30. Power brake pipe O-ring retainer
31. Fuel return pipe & fitting
32. Fuel return pipe & fitting O-ring
33. Fuel return pipe O-ring retainer
34. Fuel inlet pipe & fitting
35. Fuel inlet pipe & fitting O-ring
36. Fuel inlet pipe O-ring retainer
37. Wiring harness
38. Fuel inlet O-ring retainer
39. Fuel inlet fitting O-ring
40. Injector lower seal
41. Port fuel injector

1. Intake manifold cover emblem
2. Intake manifold cover
3. Manifold absolute pressure sensor
4. Intake air temperature sensor
5. Air tube attaching screw
6. Air inlet tube
7. Air inlet to manifold seal
8. Fuel return line O-ring
9. Fuel pressure regulator
10. Fuel return tube O-ring
11. Intake manifold cover gasket
12. PCV tube
13. ISC bracket attaching screw
14. ISC bracket
15. ISC motor attaching nut
16. ISC motor attaching lockwasher
17. Idle speed control motor
18. Fuel tube clamp

19. Throttle body
20. Throttle body attaching bolt
21. Coolant outlet tube
22. Coolant inlet tube
23. Fuel pressure connection cap
24. Valve core
25. Throttle position sensor

42. Injector upper seal
43. Intake manifold housing
44. Fuel rail
45. Wiring harness cover
46. Intake manifold cover bolt

84205009

Fig. 11 Intake manifold and throttle body components — 4.6L Engine

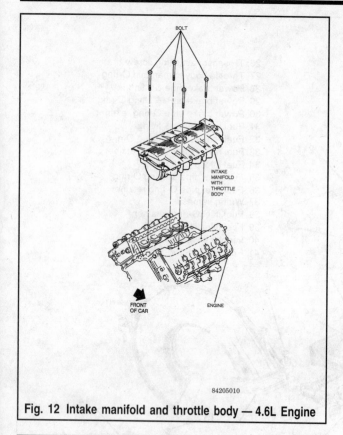

Fig. 12 Intake manifold and throttle body — 4.6L Engine

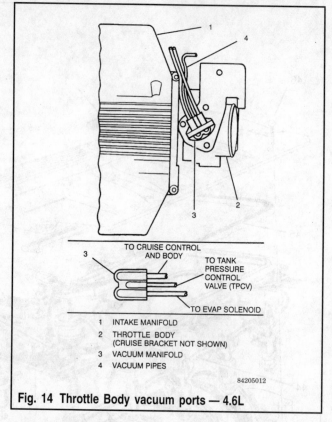

1 INTAKE MANIFOLD
2 THROTTLE BODY
  (CRUISE BRACKET NOT SHOWN)
3 VACUUM MANIFOLD
4 VACUUM PIPES

84205012

Fig. 14 Throttle Body vacuum ports — 4.6L

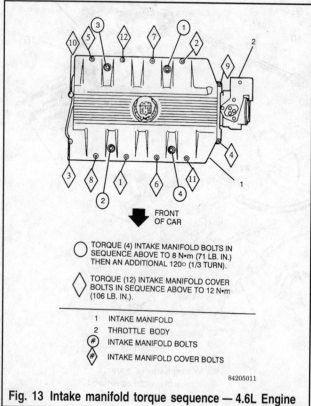

○ TORQUE (4) INTAKE MANIFOLD BOLTS IN
  SEQUENCE ABOVE TO 8 N•m (71 LB. IN.)
  THEN AN ADDITIONAL 120○ (1/3 TURN).

◇ TORQUE (12) INTAKE MANIFOLD COVER
  BOLTS IN SEQUENCE ABOVE TO 12 N•m
  (106 LB. IN.).

1 INTAKE MANIFOLD
2 THROTTLE BODY
(#) INTAKE MANIFOLD BOLTS
(#) INTAKE MANIFOLD COVER BOLTS

84205011

Fig. 13 Intake manifold torque sequence — 4.6L Engine

7. Disconnect the fuel return line from the return fitting. Discard the O-ring.

➡ **Wrap a shop towel around fuel lines to collect any residual fuel.**

8. Disconnect the electrical connectors at the front and rear wiring assemblies.

9. Remove the fuel rail support bracket attaching bolts.

10. Remove the fuel rail assembly from the intake manifold.

To install:

11. Prior to installing the fuel rail assembly, lubricate the new injector O-ring seals, and install them on the spray tip end of each fuel injector.

12. Install the fuel rail assembly on the intake manifold.

13. Install the rail support bracket attaching bolts. Torque the bolts to 18 ft. lbs. (24 Nm).

14. Connect the vacuum line to the pressure regulator.

15. Lubricate the new inlet fitting O-ring and install on the fuel feed line.

16. Connect the fuel feed line into the rear fuel rail inlet port.

17. Connect the fuel return line to the return line fitting. Tighten the fuel return fitting to 22 ft. lbs. (30 Nm). Use a back-up wrench on the fitting to prevent it from turning.

18. Connect the electrical connectors at the front and rear wiring assemblies.

19. Install the power steering pump. Install the serpentine drive belt.

20. Connect the negative battery cable. Start the engine and check for leaks.

21. Perform the Idle Learn procedure as outlined earlier in this Section.

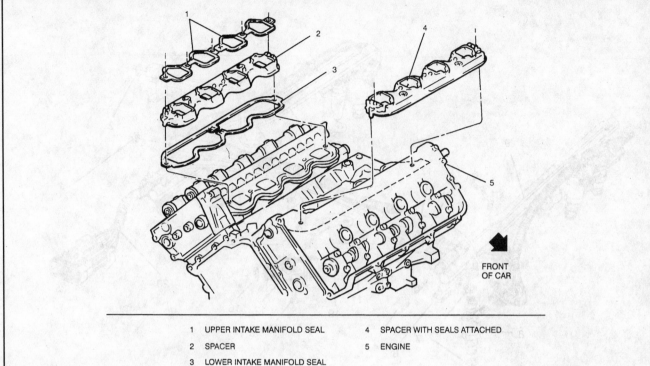

1	UPPER INTAKE MANIFOLD SEAL	4	SPACER WITH SEALS ATTACHED
2	SPACER	5	ENGINE
3	LOWER INTAKE MANIFOLD SEAL		

84205013

Fig. 15 Intake manifold seals — 4.6L Engine

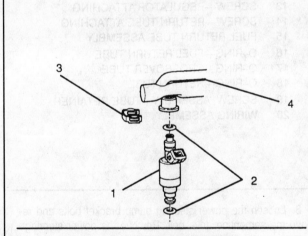

1	INJECTOR ASSEMBLY
2	SEAL–O–RING–INJECTOR
3	CLIP–INJECTOR RETAINER
4	FUEL RAIL

84205014

Fig. 16 Injector assembly and retainer — 4.5L and 4.9L engines

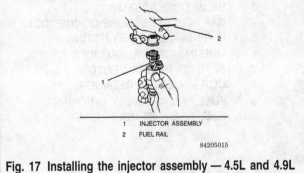

1	INJECTOR ASSEMBLY
2	FUEL RAIL

84205015

Fig. 17 Installing the injector assembly — 4.5L and 4.9L engines

4.6L Northstar Engine

▶ See Figure 11

➡The fuel rail/wiring harness is serviced as an assembly. If wiring repairs are necessary, replace the entire fuel rail/wiring harness.

1. Remove the fuel pump relay in the engine compartment micro relay center.
2. Relieve the fuel system pressure as outlined earlier in this Section.
3. Remove the intake manifold top cover.
4. Disconnect the 2 intake manifold electrical connectors.
5. Remove the fuel rail along with the injectors out of the intakemanifold.
6. Remove the IAT sensor, MAP sensor, fuel pressure regulator and injectors from the fuel rail.

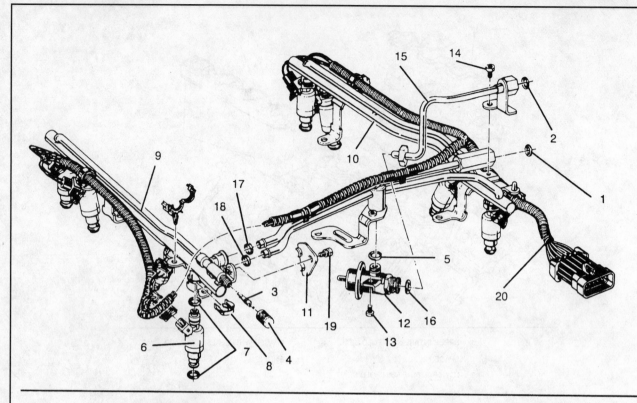

1	O–RING—FUEL INLET LINE	11	RETAINER—CROSSOVER TUBE
2	O–RING—FUEL RETURN LINE	12	PRESSURE REGULATOR ASSEMBLY
3	VALVE CORE ASSEMBLY	13	SCREW—REGULATOR ATTACHING
4	CAP—FUEL PRESSURE CONNECTION	14	SCREW—RETURN TUBE ATTACHING
5	O–RING—FUEL INLET FITTING	15	FUEL RETURN TUBE ASSEMBLY
6	MPFI INJECTOR ASSEMBLY	16	O–RING—FUEL RETURN TUBE
7	SEAL—O–RING—INJECTOR	17	O–RING—CROSSOVER TUBE
8	CLIP—INJECTOR RETAINER	18	O–RING—RETURN TUBE
9	FUEL RAIL ASSEMBLY—FRONT	19	SCREW ASSEMBLY—TUBE RETAINER
10	FUEL RAIL ASSEMBLY—REAR	20	WIRING ASSEMBLY

84205016

Fig. 18 Exploded view of the fuel rail — 4.5L and 4.9L engines

To install:

7. Install the IAT sensor, MAP sensor, fuel pressure regulator and injectors to the fuel rail.the injectors to the fuel rail.

8. Install the fuel rail along with the injectors into the intakemanifold housing.

9. Install the intake manifold top cover and torque the retaining bolts to 106 inch lbs. (12 Nm).

10. Connect the 2 intake manifold electrical connectors.

11. Install the fuel pump relay in the engine compartment micro relay center.

4.9L Engine

▶ See Figure 18

1. Disconnect the negative battery terminal.

2. Remove the air cleaner.

3. Loosen the power steering pump bracket bolts and remove the serpentine drive belt. Remove the power steering pump and relocate as necessary.

4. Relieve the fuel pressure.

5. Disconnect the vacuum line from the pressure regulator and base assembly.

6. Disconnect the accelerator cable, cruise control cable and bracket.

7. Disconnect the electrical connectors at the TPS, ISC, coolant and MAT sensors.

8. Disconnect the coolant hose to the thermostat housing.

9. Disconnect the fuel feed line and O-ring from the rear fuel rail assembly.

10. Disconnect the fuel return line from the return fitting. Discard the O-ring.

➡ **Wrap a shop towel around fuel lines to collect any residual fuel.**

11. Disconnect the EGR vacuum lines and remove the EGR valve.

12. Disconnect the electrical connectors at the front and rear wiring assemblies.

13. Remove the 5 fuel rail support bracket attaching bolts.

14. Remove the fuel rail assembly from the intake manifold.

To install:

15. Prior to installing the fuel rail assembly, lubricate the new injector O-ring seals, and install them on the spray tip end of each fuel injector.

16. Install the fuel rail assembly on the intake manifold.

17. Install the 5 rail support bracket attaching bolts. Torque the bolts to 18 ft. lbs. (24 Nm).

18. Install the EGR valve and connect the vacuum lines.

19. Lubricate the new inlet fitting O-ring and install on the fuel feed line.

20. Connect the fuel feed line into the rear fuel rail inlet port.

21. Connect the fuel return line to the return line fitting. Tighten the fuel return fitting to 22 ft. lbs. (30 Nm). Use a back-up wrench on the fitting to prevent it from turning.

22. Connect the coolant hose to the thermostat housing.

23. Connect the electrical connectors at the TPS, ISC, coolant and MAT sensors.

24. Connect the accelerator cable, cruise control cable and bracket.

25. Connect the vacuum line to the pressure regulator and base assembly.

26. Install the power steering pump and serpentine drive belt.

27. Install the air cleaner.

28. Connect the negative battery terminal.

29. Start the engine and check for leaks.

30. Perform the Idle Learn procedure as outlined earlier in this Section.

Fuel Pressure Regulator

REMOVAL & INSTALLATION

4.5L and 4.9L Engines

▶ **See Figure 18**

1. Disconnect the negative battery cable. Remove the air cleaner upper housing assembly.

2. Relieve the fuel system pressure.

3. Disconnect the fuel return line from rear rail attachment.

4. Remove the pressure regulator-to-rail bracket mounting screws.

5. Remove the pressure regulator and fuel return line as an assembly, from the fuel rail.

6. Disconnect the fuel return line from the pressure regulator. Cover all openings with masking tape to prevent dirt entry.

To install:

7. Prior to assembling the pressure regulator to the fuel return line and rail assembly, lubricate the new O-ring seals with petroleum base grease.

8. Place the O-ring on the fuel return line and assemble the pressure regulator to it.

9. Place a new O-ring seal on the pressure regulator and install the regulator and fuel return line assembly to the fuel rail.

10. Secure the pressure regulator in place with retaining screws. Torque the retaining screws to 9 ft. lbs. (12 Nm).

11. Connect the fuel return line at the rear of the rail assembly, use a backup wrench on the inlet fitting to prevent turning.

12. Connect the negative battery cable.

13. Turn the ignition switch **ON** and **OFF** to allow fuel pressure back into system. Check for leaks.

14. Install the air cleaner assembly. Perform an idle learn procedure.

4.6L Northstar Engine

▶ **See Figure 11**

1. Remove the fuel pump relay in the engine compartment micro relay center.

2. Relieve the fuel system pressure as outlined earlier in this Section.

3. Remove the intake manifold top cover.

4. Lift the fuel rail along with the injectors out of the intakemanifold housing enough to remove the pressure regulator from the rail.

5. Remove the pressure regulator from the fuel rail.

To install:

6. Install the pressure regulator to the fuel rail.

7. Install the fuel rail along with the injectors into the intakemanifold housing.

8. Install the intake manifold top cover and tighten to 106 inch lbs. (12 Nm).

9. Install the fuel pump relay in the engine compartment micro relay center.

Idle Speed Control (ISC) Motor

REMOVAL & INSTALLATION

4.5L and 4.9L Engines

▶ **See Figure 10**

1. Disconnect the negative battery cable.

2. Disconnect the electric connector from the harness connection.

3. Remove the retaining screws attaching the ISC motor to the throttle body and remove the ISC motor.

4. Remove the harness from the ISC motor.

➡**The ISC motor is calibrated at the factory. It is and nonservicable unit. Do not attempt to disassemble it. Do not immerse the ISC motor in any type of cleaning solvent and always remove it prior to cleaning or servicing the throttle body. Immersing in cleaner will damage the ISC unit.**

5. Installation is the reverse of the removal procedure. After the ISC motor is installed, perform Minimum Air, Throttle Position Sensor (TPS) and Idle Learn adjustments, outlined earlier in this Section.

4.6L Northstar Engine

▶ See Figure 11

1. Disconnect the air intake duct.
2. Remove the cruise control servo and bracket as outlined in Section 6.
3. Disconnect the ISC electrical connector.
4. Remove the ISC motor.

To install:

5. Install the ISC motor and tighten the retaining nuts to 53 inch lbs. (6 Nm).
6. Connect the ISC electrical connector.
7. Install the cruise control servo and bracket as outlined in Section 6.
8. Connect the air intake duct.
9. Perform the ISC check as outlined in the chart earlier in this Section.
10. Perform the TP Sensor/Idle Learn procedure outlined earlier in this Section, if necessary.

Throttle Position Sensor

REMOVAL & INSTALLATION

4.5L Engine

▶ See Figure 10

1. Disconnect the negative battery cable.
2. Disconnect the electrical connector from the TPS.
3. Remove the EGR valve assembly.
4. Remove the attaching screws and retainers.
5. Remove the TPS.

To install:

6. Position both throttle valves in the closed position, install the TPS on the throttle body assembly, making sure the throttle shaft flats engage with the TPS lever drive tongs.

7. Install the attaching screws and retainers finger tight.
8. See the Minimum Air, Throttle Position Sensor and ISC Motor adjustment procedure earlier in this Section and adjust as necessary.
9. Tighten the TPS attaching screws after the TPS is adjusted properly.
10. Connect the negative battery cable.
11. Perform the Idle Learn procedure as outlined earlier in this Section.

4.9L Engine

▶ See Figure 10

1. Remove the air cleaner assembly.
2. Disconnect the TP sensor electrical connector.
3. Remove the 2 TP sensor attaching screws and retainers.
4. Remove the TP sensor.

To install:

5. With the throttle valve in the normal closed position, install the TP sensor on the throttle body assembly and install the 2 TP sensor attaching screws and retainers. Do not tighten until after TP sensor adjustment.
6. Adjust the TP sensor as outlined earlier in this Section.
7. Perform the TP Sensor/Idle Learn procedure, outlined earlier in this Section.

4.6L Northstar Engine

▶ See Figure 11

1. Disconnect the TP sensor electrical connector.
2. Remove the TP sensor attaching bolts.
3. Remove the TP sensor from the throttle body.

To install:

4. Install the TP sensor on the throttle body assembly and tighten attaching bolts to 106 inch lbs. (12 Nm).
5. Perform the ISC check as outlined in the chart earlier in this Section.
6. Perform the TP Sensor/Idle Learn procedure outlined earlier in this Section.

FUEL TANK

DRAINING

✳✳CAUTION

Never drain or store fuel in an open container due to the possibility of fire or explosion.

1990-92

1. Disconnect the negative battery cable.

✳✳CAUTION

To reduce the risk of fire and personal injury, always keep a dry chemical (Class B) fire extinguisher near the work area.

2. Remove the fuel cap.
3. Raise the vehicle and support with jackstands.

4. Disconnect the filler vent hose from the tank.
5. Use a hand operated pump approved for gasoline to drain as much fuel as possible through the filler vent hose.
6. Reconnect the filler vent hose and tighten the clamp.
7. Install any removed lines, hoses and cap. Connect the negative battery cable.

1993

▶ See Figure 19

1. Disconnect the negative battery cable.

✳✳CAUTION

To reduce the risk of fire and personal injury, always keep a dry chemical (Class B) fire extinguisher near the work area.

2. Remove the fuel cap.
3. Raise the vehicle and support with jackstands.
4. Locate the fuel tank drain pipe and remove the plug.

5. Install a fuel tank drain adapter J 39581 or equivalent to the drain pipe and fabricate a suitable length of fuel hose and clamp   to the drain adapter.

6. Connect the fuel drain hose to a hand operated pump, approved for gasoline, and remove the fuel.

REMOVAL & INSTALLATION

1990-92

▶ See Figure 20

1. Disconnect the negative battery cable and relieve the fuel system pressure as outlined earlier in this Section.

2. Drain the fuel tank.

3. Remove the fuel filler door assembly and disconnect the screw retaining the filler pipe-to-body bracket.

4. Raise the vehicle and support with jackstands.

5. Disconnect the tank level sender lead connector.

6. Support the tank with a transmission jack or equivalent. Remove the two tank retaining straps.

7. Lower the tank far enough to disconnect the ground lead and fuel hoses from the pump assembly.

8. Remove the tank from the vehicle slowly to ensure all connections and hoses have been disconnected.

9. Remove the fuel pump/level sender assembly using a locking cam tool J-24187 or equivalent. Refer to the Electric Fuel Pump removal and installation procedure earlier in this Section.

To install:

10. Using a new fuel pump O-ring gasket, install the pump/sender assembly into the tank.

✳✳CAUTION

Do not twist the strainer when installing the pump/sender assembly. Make sure the strainer does not block the full travel of the float arm.

11. Place the tank on the jack.

12. Position the tank sound insulators in their original positions and raise the tank far enough to connect the electrical and hose connectors.

13. Raise the tank to the proper position and loosely install the retaining straps. Make sure the tank is in the proper position before tightening the retaining straps.

14. Torque the straps to 26 ft. lbs. (35 Nm).

15. Connect the grounding strap and negative battery cable.

16. With the engine OFF, turn the ignition key to the ON position and check for fuel leaks at the tank.

1993

▶ See Figure 20

1. Disconnect the negative battery cable.

2. Relieve the fuel system pressure as outlined earlier in this Section.

3. Raise the vehicle and support with jackstands.

4. Drain the fuel tank as outlined earlier in this Section.

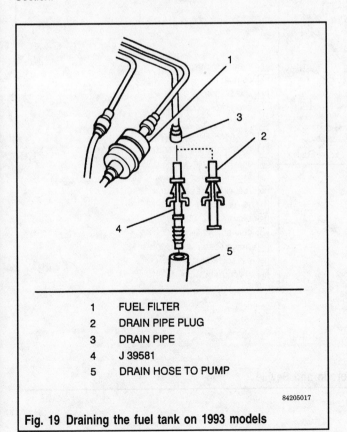

1	FUEL FILTER
2	DRAIN PIPE PLUG
3	DRAIN PIPE
4	J 39581
5	DRAIN HOSE TO PUMP

84205017

Fig. 19 Draining the fuel tank on 1993 models

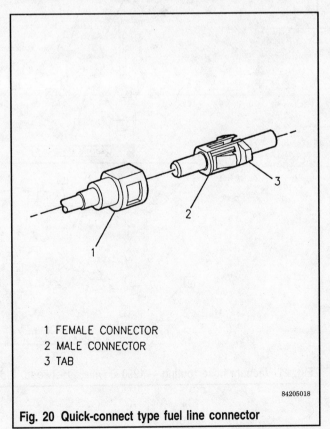

1	FEMALE CONNECTOR
2	MALE CONNECTOR
3	TAB

84205018

Fig. 20 Quick-connect type fuel line connector

5. Disconnect the fuel feed and return quick-connect fittings at the fuel tank as follows:

a. Grasp both ends of one fuel pipe connection and twist ¼ turn in each direction to loosen the dirt in the connection.

b. If compressed air is available, blow out the dirt within the connection.

c. Squeeze the plastic tabs of the male end connector, then pull the connection apart.

d. Repeat for the fuel return pipe fitting.

❋❋WARNING

If the nylon fuel or feed lines become kinked or damaged in any way they must be replaced. Do not try to straighten.

6. Disconnect the fuel sender electrical connector.

7. With the aid of an assistant, support the tank and remove the fuel tank strap retaining nuts and bolts and place the tank in a suitable work area.

8. Remove the modular fuel sender assembly from the fuel tank as outlined under Electric Fuel Pump removal and installation, outlined earlier in this Section.

To install:

9. Install the modular fuel sender assembly to the fuel tank as outlined under Electric Fuel Pump removal and installation, outlined earlier in this Section.

10. With the aid of an assistant, position and support the tank and install the fuel tank straps and retaining nuts and bolts. Tighten to 26 ft. lbs. (34 Nm).

11. Install the vapor pipe.

12. Connect the fuel sender electrical connector.

13. Connect the fuel feed and return quick-connect fittings at the fuel tank as follows:

a. Apply a few drops of clean engine oil to the male connector pipe ends.

❋❋CAUTION

Applying a few drops of clean engine oil to the male connector pipe ends will ensure proper reconnecting and prevent a possible fuel leak.

b. Push the connectors together to cause the retaining tabs to snap into place.

c. Once installed, pull on both ends of each connection to make sure they are secure.

14. Lower the car.

15. Turn the ignition switch to the **ON** position for 2 seconds, then turn to **OFF** for 5 seconds. Again turn to **ON** and check for leaks.

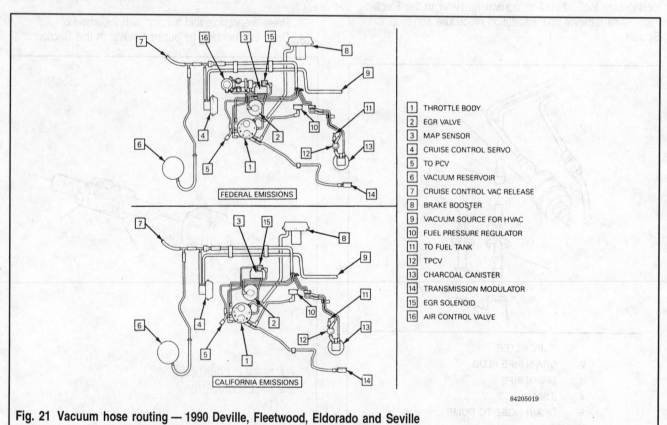

1	THROTTLE BODY
2	EGR VALVE
3	MAP SENSOR
4	CRUISE CONTROL SERVO
5	TO PCV
6	VACUUM RESERVOIR
7	CRUISE CONTROL VAC RELEASE
8	BRAKE BOOSTER
9	VACUUM SOURCE FOR HVAC
10	FUEL PRESSURE REGULATOR
11	TO FUEL TANK
12	TPCV
13	CHARCOAL CANISTER
14	TRANSMISSION MODULATOR
15	EGR SOLENOID
16	AIR CONTROL VALVE

84205019

Fig. 21 Vacuum hose routing — 1990 Deville, Fleetwood, Eldorado and Seville

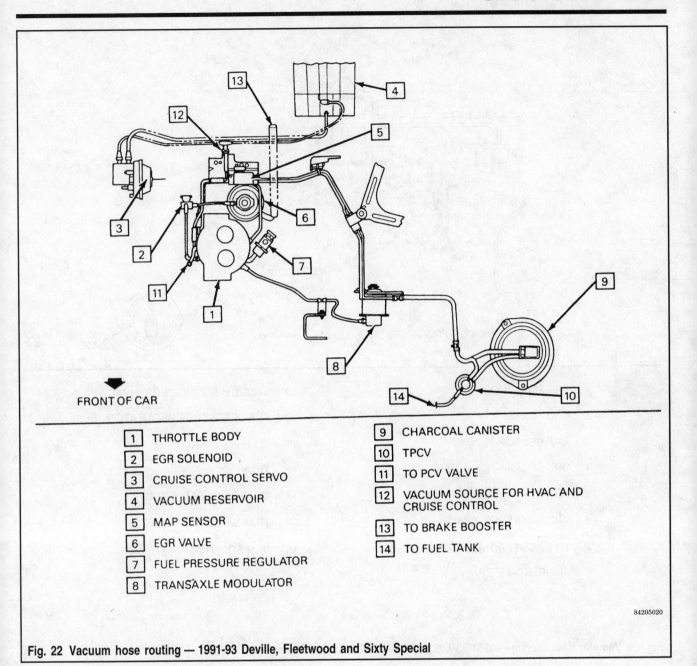

FRONT OF CAR

1	THROTTLE BODY		9	CHARCOAL CANISTER
2	EGR SOLENOID		10	TPCV
3	CRUISE CONTROL SERVO		11	TO PCV VALVE
4	VACUUM RESERVOIR		12	VACUUM SOURCE FOR HVAC AND CRUISE CONTROL
5	MAP SENSOR		13	TO BRAKE BOOSTER
6	EGR VALVE		14	TO FUEL TANK
7	FUEL PRESSURE REGULATOR			
8	TRANSAXLE MODULATOR			

84205020

Fig. 22 Vacuum hose routing — 1991-93 Deville, Fleetwood and Sixty Special

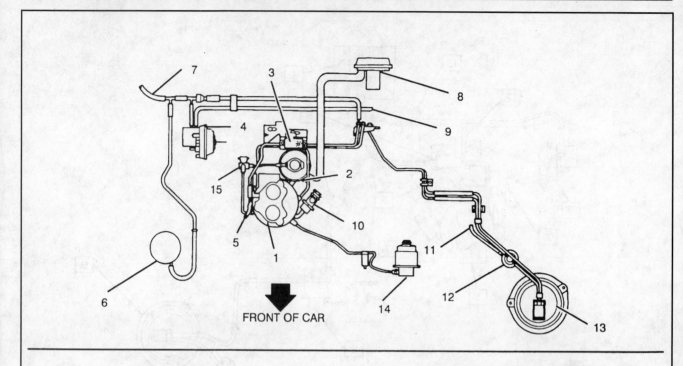

FRONT OF CAR

1	THROTTLE BODY	9	VACUUM SOURCE FOR HVAC
2	EGR VALVE	10	FUEL PRESSURE REGULATOR
3	MAP SENSOR	11	TO FUEL TANK
4	CRUISE CONTROL SERVO	12	TPCV
5	TO PCV	13	CHARCOAL CANISTER
6	VACUUM RESERVOIR	14	TRANSAXLE MODULATOR
7	TO BODY FEED WIRING HARNESS	15	EGR SOLENOID
8	BRAKE BOOSTER		

84205021

Fig. 23 Vacuum hose routing — 1991-93 Eldorado and Seville with 4.9L engine

Fuel System Diagnosis

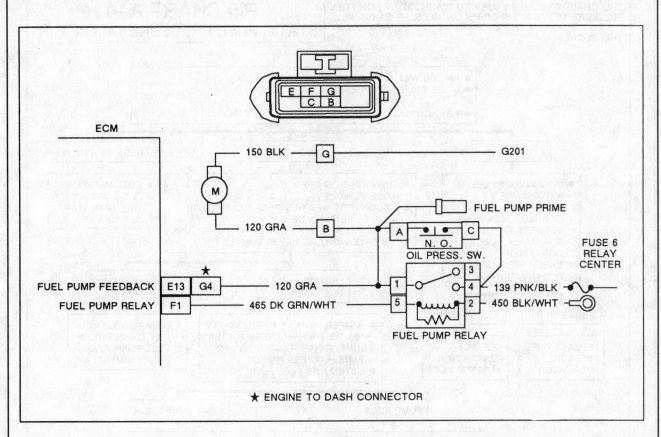

PFI Fuel Pump Circuit

STATIC FUEL PRESSURE DIAGNOSIS

DESCRIPTION:

This procedure tests for fuel supply system problems that can cause incorrect fuel pressure or incorrect fuel pump operation.

Notes On Chart A–4A:

1. Fuel pressure above 50 PSI is caused either by a malfunction of the pressure regulator or by a restriction in the fuel return line. It should be noted that secondary conditions of spark plug fouling, code E45, or oxygen sensor contamination resulting in codes E13 and E45 may result from the too rich fuel flow. To isolate the cause of the high fuel pressure, disconnect the return line at the fuel rail and connect a suitable fitting to the fuel rail which will accept a length of flexible rubber fuel hose. Insert the other end of the hose into a suitable fuel container and observe the fuel pressure as the ignition switch is turned on. If the fuel pressure remains above 50 PSI, replace the fuel pressure regulator—it is unable to control pressure properly.

If the fuel pressure drops below 50 PSI, with the fuel return line bypassed, then the fuel return line is restricted. A restricted fuel return line can be diagnosed by visually inspecting the line for kinks, damage, etc. A kink in the Teflon fuel line (braided stainless steel clad) may not be visually obvious.

2. If the fuel pump relay or ECM were the cause of a low fuel pressure, there would be an ECM code E20 set. This step is to check for voltage supply to the fuel tank five-way connector.

3. If the voltage signal to the fuel tank connector is OK, then an open may exist between the five-way fuel tank connector and the fuel pump. If fuel pump runs with an alternative power source connected, the fuel tank unit is OK; check fuel pressure regulator for cause of low pressure.

4. Checking for fuel supply system (tank, filter, pump, sender, supply line) able to deliver at least 40 PSI pressure or for fuel pressure regulator fault.

84205033

Fig. 24 Fuel system diagnosis — 1990 Deville/Fleetwood with 4.5L engine

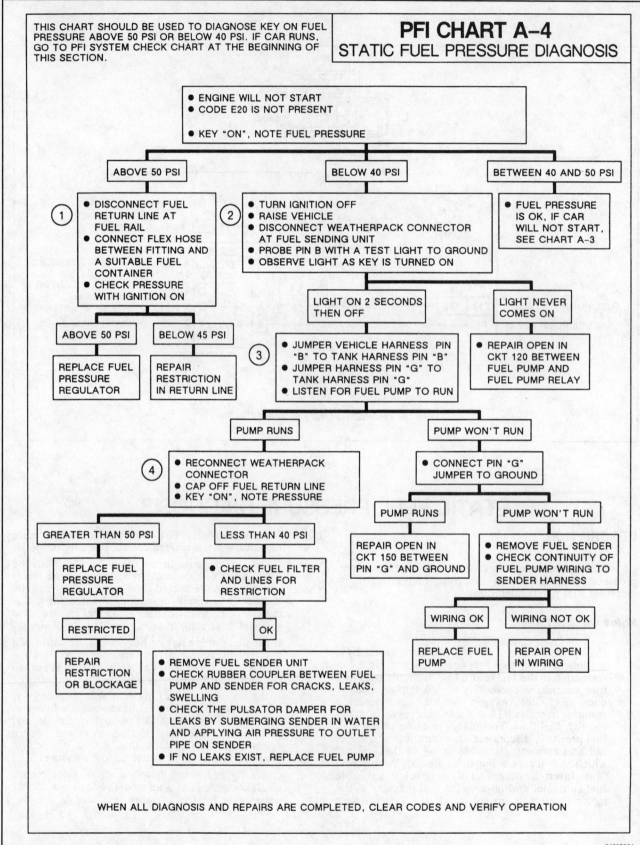

THIS CHART SHOULD BE USED TO DIAGNOSE KEY ON FUEL PRESSURE ABOVE 50 PSI OR BELOW 40 PSI. IF CAR RUNS, GO TO PFI SYSTEM CHECK CHART AT THE BEGINNING OF THIS SECTION.

PFI CHART A–4
STATIC FUEL PRESSURE DIAGNOSIS

- ENGINE WILL NOT START
- CODE E20 IS NOT PRESENT

- KEY "ON", NOTE FUEL PRESSURE

ABOVE 50 PSI

(1)
- DISCONNECT FUEL RETURN LINE AT FUEL RAIL
- CONNECT FLEX HOSE BETWEEN FITTING AND A SUITABLE FUEL CONTAINER
- CHECK PRESSURE WITH IGNITION ON

BELOW 40 PSI

(2)
- TURN IGNITION OFF
- RAISE VEHICLE
- DISCONNECT WEATHERPACK CONNECTOR AT FUEL SENDING UNIT
- PROBE PIN B WITH A TEST LIGHT TO GROUND
- OBSERVE LIGHT AS KEY IS TURNED ON

BETWEEN 40 AND 50 PSI

- FUEL PRESSURE IS OK, IF CAR WILL NOT START, SEE CHART A–3

ABOVE 50 PSI

REPLACE FUEL PRESSURE REGULATOR

BELOW 45 PSI

REPAIR RESTRICTION IN RETURN LINE

LIGHT ON 2 SECONDS THEN OFF

(3)
- JUMPER VEHICLE HARNESS PIN "B" TO TANK HARNESS PIN "B"
- JUMPER HARNESS PIN "G" TO TANK HARNESS PIN "G"
- LISTEN FOR FUEL PUMP TO RUN

LIGHT NEVER COMES ON

- REPAIR OPEN IN CKT 120 BETWEEN FUEL PUMP AND FUEL PUMP RELAY

PUMP RUNS

(4)
- RECONNECT WEATHERPACK CONNECTOR
- CAP OFF FUEL RETURN LINE
- KEY "ON", NOTE PRESSURE

PUMP WON'T RUN

- CONNECT PIN "G" JUMPER TO GROUND

GREATER THAN 50 PSI

REPLACE FUEL PRESSURE REGULATOR

LESS THAN 40 PSI

- CHECK FUEL FILTER AND LINES FOR RESTRICTION

PUMP RUNS

REPAIR OPEN IN CKT 150 BETWEEN PIN "G" AND GROUND

PUMP WON'T RUN

- REMOVE FUEL SENDER
- CHECK CONTINUITY OF FUEL PUMP WIRING TO SENDER HARNESS

RESTRICTED

REPAIR RESTRICTION OR BLOCKAGE

OK

- REMOVE FUEL SENDER UNIT
- CHECK RUBBER COUPLER BETWEEN FUEL PUMP AND SENDER FOR CRACKS, LEAKS, SWELLING
- CHECK THE PULSATOR DAMPER FOR LEAKS BY SUBMERGING SENDER IN WATER AND APPLYING AIR PRESSURE TO OUTLET PIPE ON SENDER
- IF NO LEAKS EXIST, REPLACE FUEL PUMP

WIRING OK

REPLACE FUEL PUMP

WIRING NOT OK

REPAIR OPEN IN WIRING

WHEN ALL DIAGNOSIS AND REPAIRS ARE COMPLETED, CLEAR CODES AND VERIFY OPERATION

84205034

Fig. 25 Fuel system diagnosis — 1990 Deville/Fleetwood with 4.5L engine

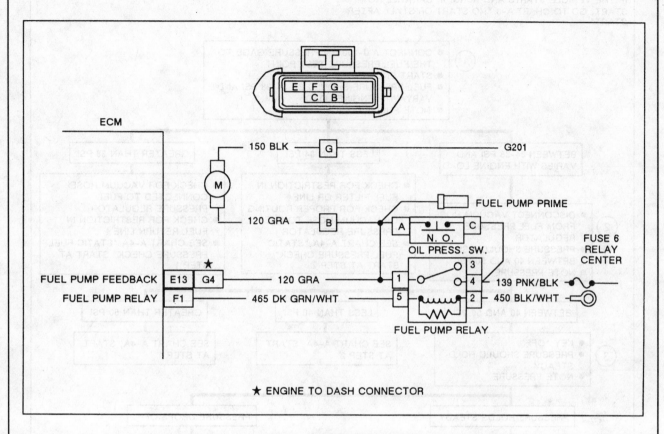

PFI Fuel Pump Circuit

DYNAMIC FUEL PRESSURE DIAGNOSIS

DESCRIPTION:

This procedure tests for proper operation of the fuel delivery system while the engine is running and for the ability of the fuel system to maintain pressure at key off.

Notes On Chart A–4B:

1. Fuel pressure should be 32 – 38 psi depending on engine load and altitude.

2. By disconnecting the vacuum hose, engine load compensation is taken away from the fuel pressure regulator. Pressure should rise to approximately 45 psi. If fuel pressure is higher than 50 or lower than 40 psi, go to Chart A–4 to diagnose fuel delivery problems.

3. Fuel pressure should hold steady at key off. If pressure bleeds down the vehicle may exhibit extended cranking time upon restart. Pressure bleed down means that either the pressure regulator can't hold pressure, the fuel pump check ball is not seating, or an injector is sticking open.

4. At this point the fuel system has checked out OK. If any oxygen sensor codes were set, go to the appropriate chart listed.

84205035

Fig. 26 Fuel system diagnosis — 1990 Deville/Fleetwood with 4.5L engine

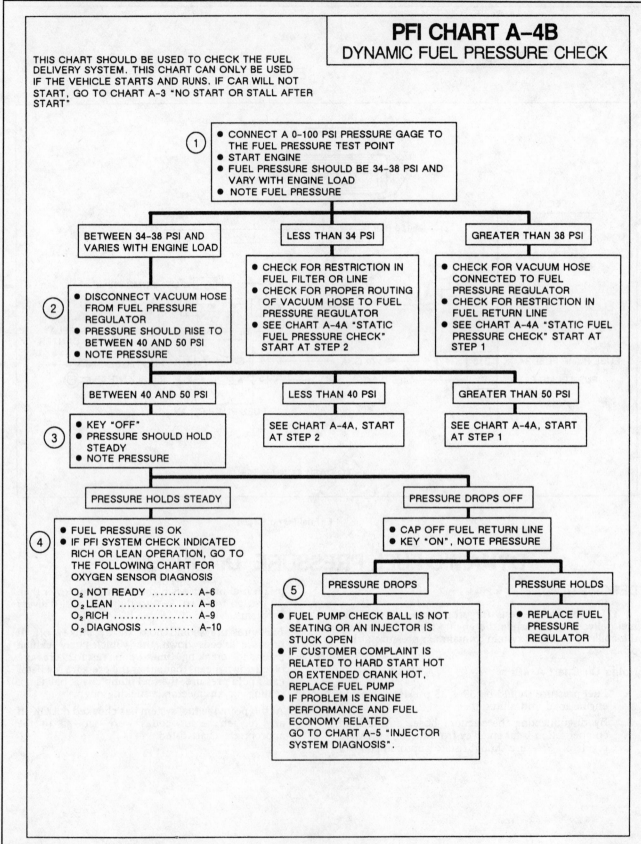

PFI CHART A–4B
DYNAMIC FUEL PRESSURE CHECK

THIS CHART SHOULD BE USED TO CHECK THE FUEL DELIVERY SYSTEM. THIS CHART CAN ONLY BE USED IF THE VEHICLE STARTS AND RUNS. IF CAR WILL NOT START, GO TO CHART A-3 "NO START OR STALL AFTER START"

1
- CONNECT A 0-100 PSI PRESSURE GAGE TO THE FUEL PRESSURE TEST POINT
- START ENGINE
- FUEL PRESSURE SHOULD BE 34-38 PSI AND VARY WITH ENGINE LOAD
- NOTE FUEL PRESSURE

BETWEEN 34-38 PSI AND VARIES WITH ENGINE LOAD

LESS THAN 34 PSI
- CHECK FOR RESTRICTION IN FUEL FILTER OR LINE
- CHECK FOR PROPER ROUTING OF VACUUM HOSE TO FUEL PRESSURE REGULATOR
- SEE CHART A-4A "STATIC FUEL PRESSURE CHECK" START AT STEP 2

GREATER THAN 38 PSI
- CHECK FOR VACUUM HOSE CONNECTED TO FUEL PRESSURE REGULATOR
- CHECK FOR RESTRICTION IN FUEL RETURN LINE
- SEE CHART A-4A "STATIC FUEL PRESSURE CHECK" START AT STEP 1

2
- DISCONNECT VACUUM HOSE FROM FUEL PRESSURE REGULATOR
- PRESSURE SHOULD RISE TO BETWEEN 40 AND 50 PSI
- NOTE PRESSURE

BETWEEN 40 AND 50 PSI

LESS THAN 40 PSI

SEE CHART A-4A, START AT STEP 2

GREATER THAN 50 PSI

SEE CHART A-4A, START AT STEP 1

3
- KEY "OFF"
- PRESSURE SHOULD HOLD STEADY
- NOTE PRESSURE

PRESSURE HOLDS STEADY

PRESSURE DROPS OFF
- CAP OFF FUEL RETURN LINE
- KEY "ON", NOTE PRESSURE

4
- FUEL PRESSURE IS OK
- IF PFI SYSTEM CHECK INDICATED RICH OR LEAN OPERATION, GO TO THE FOLLOWING CHART FOR OXYGEN SENSOR DIAGNOSIS

  O_2 NOT READY A-6
  O_2 LEAN A-8
  O_2 RICH A-9
  O_2 DIAGNOSIS A-10

5

PRESSURE DROPS
- FUEL PUMP CHECK BALL IS NOT SEATING OR AN INJECTOR IS STUCK OPEN
- IF CUSTOMER COMPLAINT IS RELATED TO HARD START HOT OR EXTENDED CRANK HOT, REPLACE FUEL PUMP
- IF PROBLEM IS ENGINE PERFORMANCE AND FUEL ECONOMY RELATED GO TO CHART A-5 "INJECTOR SYSTEM DIAGNOSIS".

PRESSURE HOLDS
- REPLACE FUEL PRESSURE REGULATOR

84205036

Fig. 27 Fuel system diagnosis — 1990 Deville/Fleetwood with 4.5L engine

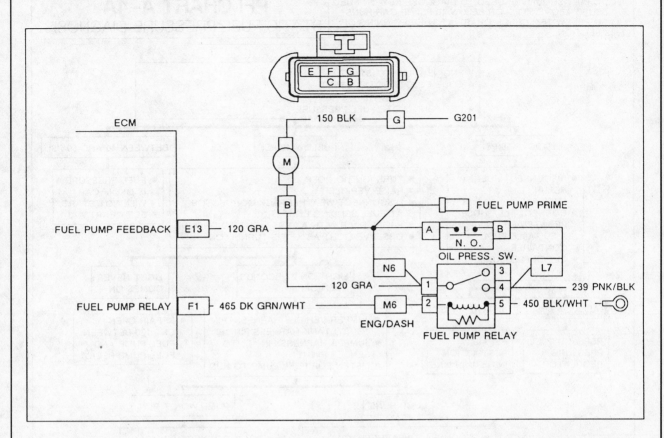

PFI Fuel Pump Circuit

STATIC FUEL PRESSURE DIAGNOSIS

DESCRIPTION:

This procedure tests for fuel supply system problems that can cause incorrect fuel pressure or incorrect fuel pump operation.

Notes On Chart A–4A:

1. Fuel pressure above 50 PSI is caused either by a malfunction of the pressure regulator or by a restriction in the fuel return line. It should be noted that secondary conditions of spark plug fouling, codes E043 and E045, or oxygen sensor contamination resulting in codes E013, E017, E043, and E045 may result from the too rich fuel flow. To isolate the cause of the high fuel pressure, disconnect the return line at the fuel rail and connect a suitable fitting to the fuel rail which will accept a length of flexible rubber fuel hose. Insert the other end of the hose into a suitable fuel container and observe the fuel pressure as the ignition switch is turned on. If the fuel pressure remains above 50 PSI, replace the fuel pressure regulator—it is unable to control pressure properly.

If the fuel pressure drops below 50 PSI, with the fuel return line bypassed, then the fuel return line is restricted. A restricted fuel return line can be diagnosed by visually inspecting the line for kinks, damage, etc.

2. If the fuel pump relay or ECM were the cause of a low fuel pressure, there would be an ECM code E20 set. This step is to check for voltage supply to the fuel tank five-way connector.

3. If the voltage signal to the fuel tank connector is OK, then an open may exist between the five-way fuel tank connector and the fuel pump. If fuel pump runs with an alternative power source connected, the fuel tank unit is OK; check fuel pressure regulator for cause of low pressure.

4. Checking for fuel supply system (tank, filter, pump, sender, supply line) able to deliver at least 40 PSI pressure or for fuel pressure regulator fault.

84205098

Fig. 28 Fuel system diagnosis — 1990 Eldorado/Seville with 4.5L engine

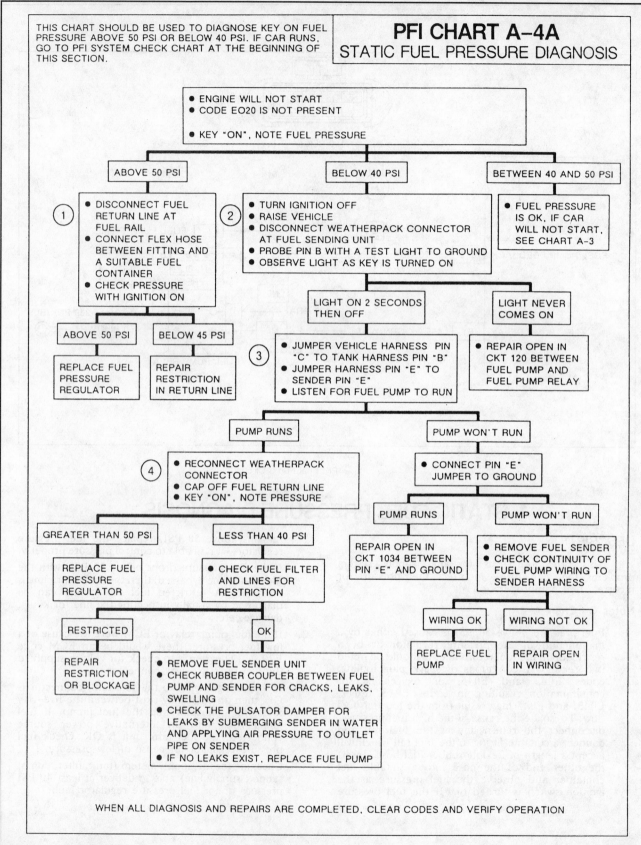

THIS CHART SHOULD BE USED TO DIAGNOSE KEY ON FUEL PRESSURE ABOVE 50 PSI OR BELOW 40 PSI. IF CAR RUNS, GO TO PFI SYSTEM CHECK CHART AT THE BEGINNING OF THIS SECTION.

PFI CHART A-4A
STATIC FUEL PRESSURE DIAGNOSIS

- ENGINE WILL NOT START
- CODE EO20 IS NOT PRESENT

- KEY "ON", NOTE FUEL PRESSURE

ABOVE 50 PSI

BELOW 40 PSI

BETWEEN 40 AND 50 PSI

1
- DISCONNECT FUEL RETURN LINE AT FUEL RAIL
- CONNECT FLEX HOSE BETWEEN FITTING AND A SUITABLE FUEL CONTAINER
- CHECK PRESSURE WITH IGNITION ON

2
- TURN IGNITION OFF
- RAISE VEHICLE
- DISCONNECT WEATHERPACK CONNECTOR AT FUEL SENDING UNIT
- PROBE PIN B WITH A TEST LIGHT TO GROUND
- OBSERVE LIGHT AS KEY IS TURNED ON

- FUEL PRESSURE IS OK, IF CAR WILL NOT START, SEE CHART A-3

ABOVE 50 PSI

BELOW 45 PSI

LIGHT ON 2 SECONDS THEN OFF

LIGHT NEVER COMES ON

REPLACE FUEL PRESSURE REGULATOR

REPAIR RESTRICTION IN RETURN LINE

3
- JUMPER VEHICLE HARNESS PIN "C" TO TANK HARNESS PIN "B"
- JUMPER HARNESS PIN "E" TO SENDER PIN "E"
- LISTEN FOR FUEL PUMP TO RUN

- REPAIR OPEN IN CKT 120 BETWEEN FUEL PUMP AND FUEL PUMP RELAY

PUMP RUNS

PUMP WON'T RUN

4
- RECONNECT WEATHERPACK CONNECTOR
- CAP OFF FUEL RETURN LINE
- KEY "ON", NOTE PRESSURE

- CONNECT PIN "E" JUMPER TO GROUND

PUMP RUNS

PUMP WON'T RUN

GREATER THAN 50 PSI

LESS THAN 40 PSI

REPAIR OPEN IN CKT 1034 BETWEEN PIN "E" AND GROUND

- REMOVE FUEL SENDER
- CHECK CONTINUITY OF FUEL PUMP WIRING TO SENDER HARNESS

REPLACE FUEL PRESSURE REGULATOR

- CHECK FUEL FILTER AND LINES FOR RESTRICTION

WIRING OK

WIRING NOT OK

RESTRICTED

OK

REPLACE FUEL PUMP

REPAIR OPEN IN WIRING

REPAIR RESTRICTION OR BLOCKAGE

- REMOVE FUEL SENDER UNIT
- CHECK RUBBER COUPLER BETWEEN FUEL PUMP AND SENDER FOR CRACKS, LEAKS, SWELLING
- CHECK THE PULSATOR DAMPER FOR LEAKS BY SUBMERGING SENDER IN WATER AND APPLYING AIR PRESSURE TO OUTLET PIPE ON SENDER
- IF NO LEAKS EXIST, REPLACE FUEL PUMP

WHEN ALL DIAGNOSIS AND REPAIRS ARE COMPLETED, CLEAR CODES AND VERIFY OPERATION

84205099

Fig. 29 Fuel system diagnosis — 1990 Eldorado/Seville with 4.5L engine

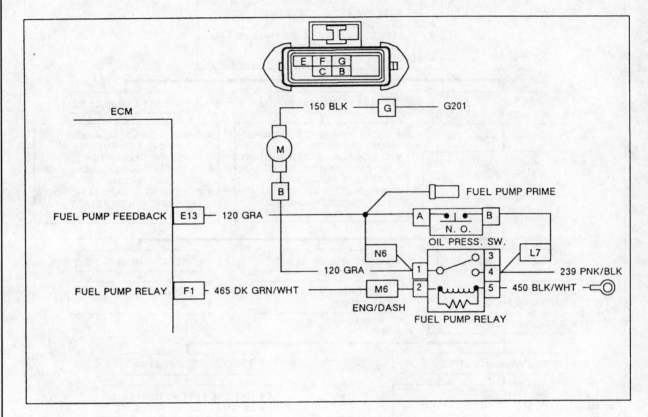

PFI Fuel Pump Circuit

DYNAMIC FUEL PRESSURE DIAGNOSIS

DESCRIPTION:

This procedure tests for proper operation of the fuel delivery system while the engine is running and for the ability of the fuel system to maintain pressure at key off.

Notes On Chart A–4B:

1. Fuel pressure should be 34 – 38 PSI depending on engine load and altitude.

2. By disconnecting the vacuum hose, engine load compensation is taken away from the fuel pressure regulator. Pressure should rise to approximately 45 PSI. If fuel pressure is higher than 50 or lower than 40 PSI, go to Chart A-4A to diagnose fuel delivery problems.

3. Fuel pressure should hold steady at key off. If pressure bleeds down the vehicle may exhibit extended cranking time upon restart. Pressure bleed down means that either the pressure regulator can't hold pressure, the fuel pump check ball is not seating, or an injector is sticking open.

4. At this point the fuel system has checked out OK. If any oxygen sensor codes were set, go to the appropriate chart listed.

84205100

Fig. 30 Fuel system diagnosis — 1990 Eldorado/Seville with 4.5L engine

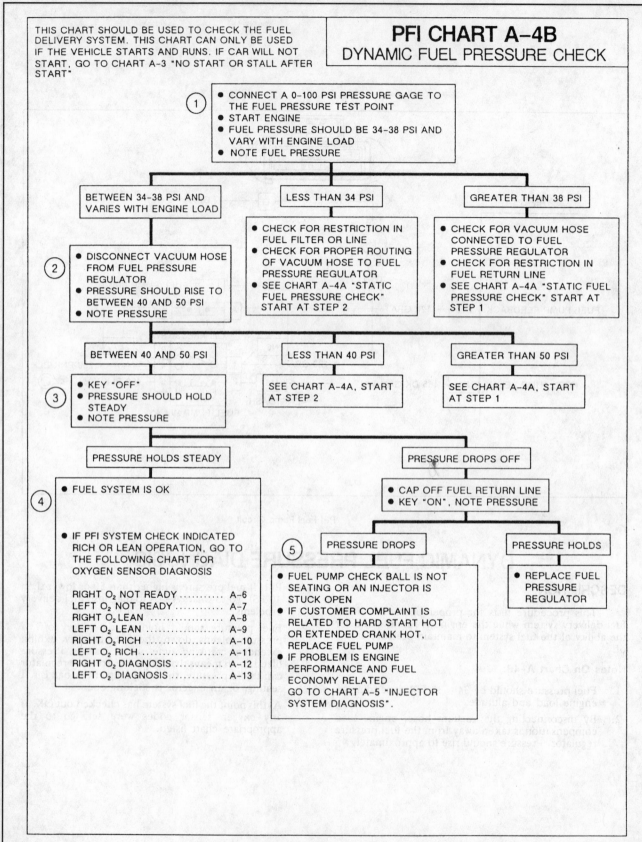

Fig. 31 Fuel system diagnosis — 1990 Eldorado/Seville with 4.5L engine

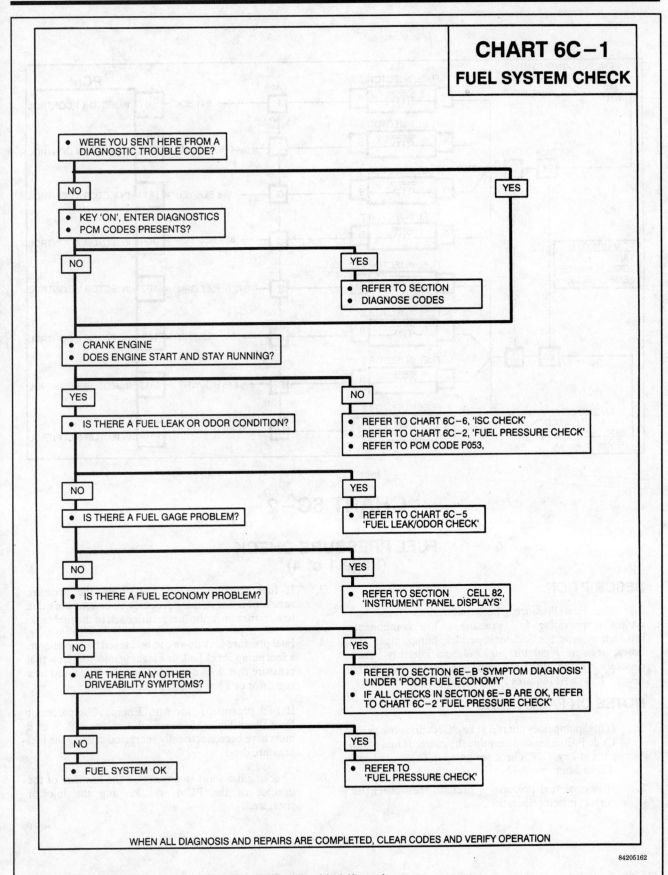

CHART 6C-1
FUEL SYSTEM CHECK

- WERE YOU SENT HERE FROM A DIAGNOSTIC TROUBLE CODE?

NO   YES

- KEY 'ON', ENTER DIAGNOSTICS
- PCM CODES PRESENTS?

NO   YES

- REFER TO SECTION
- DIAGNOSE CODES

- CRANK ENGINE
- DOES ENGINE START AND STAY RUNNING?

YES   NO

- IS THERE A FUEL LEAK OR ODOR CONDITION?

- REFER TO CHART 6C-6, 'ISC CHECK'
- REFER TO CHART 6C-2, 'FUEL PRESSURE CHECK'
- REFER TO PCM CODE P053,

NO   YES

- IS THERE A FUEL GAGE PROBLEM?

- REFER TO CHART 6C-5 'FUEL LEAK/ODOR CHECK'

NO   YES

- IS THERE A FUEL ECONOMY PROBLEM?

- REFER TO SECTION   CELL 82, 'INSTRUMENT PANEL DISPLAYS'

NO   YES

- ARE THERE ANY OTHER DRIVEABILITY SYMPTOMS?

- REFER TO SECTION 6E-B 'SYMPTOM DIAGNOSIS' UNDER 'POOR FUEL ECONOMY'
- IF ALL CHECKS IN SECTION 6E-B ARE OK, REFER TO CHART 6C-2 'FUEL PRESSURE CHECK'

NO   YES

- FUEL SYSTEM OK

- REFER TO 'FUEL PRESSURE CHECK'

WHEN ALL DIAGNOSIS AND REPAIRS ARE COMPLETED, CLEAR CODES AND VERIFY OPERATION

84205162

Fig. 32 Fuel system diagnosis — 1993 Eldorado/Seville with 4.6L engine

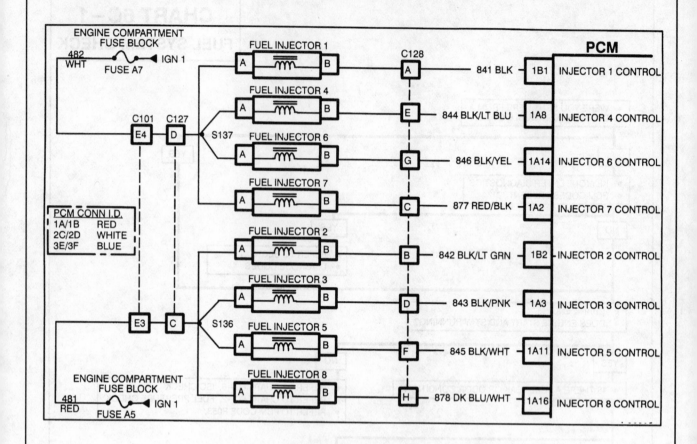

CHART 6C-2

FUEL PRESSURE CHECK
(Page 1 of 4)

DESCRIPTION:

The Fuel Pressure Check determines if the fuel system is providing fuel pressure. The components involved include the fuel tank, sender, pump, pipes and hoses, pressure regulator, fuel rail, and injectors. Also checked are the electrical operation of the fuel pump relays. This chart requires J 34730-1 Fuel Pressure Gage.

NOTES ON FAULT TREE:

1. If fuel pump does not run at key 'ON', diagnose as if a Code P020 is set to determine the cause. If fuel pump runs at key 'ON', check for an open or clogged fuel line or filter.

2. If normal fuel pressure is present, then check for correct injector operation.

3. If fuel pressure is too high, then the pressure regulator is not working properly, or cannot work due to a restriction in the fuel return back to the fuel tank.

4. Fuel pressure leak down can be caused by a regulator, a fuel pump check ball, or a leaking injector. Low fuel pressure that does not leak down can be caused by a regulator or a low output pump.

5. If fuel pressure holds with Engine Compartment Fuse Block Fuse 'A5' removed, injector 2, 3, 5, or 8 must have been electrically energized causing the fuel pressure drop.

6. Checking if a short to ground on the low side of the injector or the PCM was keeping the injector energized.

84205163

Fig. 33 Fuel system diagnosis — 1993 Eldorado/Seville with 4.6L engine

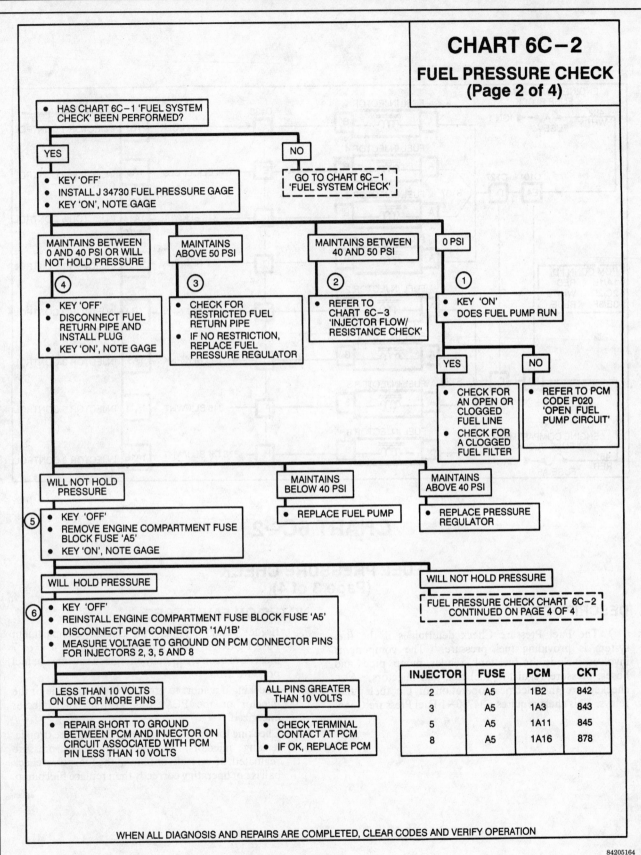

CHART 6C-2
FUEL PRESSURE CHECK
(Page 2 of 4)

- HAS CHART 6C-1 'FUEL SYSTEM CHECK' BEEN PERFORMED?

YES → **NO** → GO TO CHART 6C-1 'FUEL SYSTEM CHECK'

YES branch:
- KEY 'OFF'
- INSTALL J 34730 FUEL PRESSURE GAGE
- KEY 'ON', NOTE GAGE

Results:
- **MAINTAINS BETWEEN 0 AND 40 PSI OR WILL NOT HOLD PRESSURE** ④
- **MAINTAINS ABOVE 50 PSI** ③
- **MAINTAINS BETWEEN 40 AND 50 PSI** ②
- **0 PSI** ①

④
- KEY 'OFF'
- DISCONNECT FUEL RETURN PIPE AND INSTALL PLUG
- KEY 'ON', NOTE GAGE

③
- CHECK FOR RESTRICTED FUEL RETURN PIPE
- IF NO RESTRICTION, REPLACE FUEL PRESSURE REGULATOR

②
- REFER TO CHART 6C-3 'INJECTOR FLOW/RESISTANCE CHECK'

①
- KEY 'ON'
- DOES FUEL PUMP RUN

YES →
- CHECK FOR AN OPEN OR CLOGGED FUEL LINE
- CHECK FOR A CLOGGED FUEL FILTER

NO →
- REFER TO PCM CODE P020 'OPEN FUEL PUMP CIRCUIT'

WILL NOT HOLD PRESSURE

MAINTAINS BELOW 40 PSI →
- REPLACE FUEL PUMP

MAINTAINS ABOVE 40 PSI →
- REPLACE PRESSURE REGULATOR

⑤
- KEY 'OFF'
- REMOVE ENGINE COMPARTMENT FUSE BLOCK FUSE 'A5'
- KEY 'ON', NOTE GAGE

WILL HOLD PRESSURE

WILL NOT HOLD PRESSURE

FUEL PRESSURE CHECK CHART 6C-2 CONTINUED ON PAGE 4 OF 4

⑥
- KEY 'OFF'
- REINSTALL ENGINE COMPARTMENT FUSE BLOCK FUSE 'A5'
- DISCONNECT PCM CONNECTOR '1A/1B'
- MEASURE VOLTAGE TO GROUND ON PCM CONNECTOR PINS FOR INJECTORS 2, 3, 5 AND 8

LESS THAN 10 VOLTS ON ONE OR MORE PINS →
- REPAIR SHORT TO GROUND BETWEEN PCM AND INJECTOR ON CIRCUIT ASSOCIATED WITH PCM PIN LESS THAN 10 VOLTS

ALL PINS GREATER THAN 10 VOLTS →
- CHECK TERMINAL CONTACT AT PCM
- IF OK, REPLACE PCM

INJECTOR	FUSE	PCM	CKT
2	A5	1B2	842
3	A5	1A3	843
5	A5	1A11	845
8	A5	1A16	878

WHEN ALL DIAGNOSIS AND REPAIRS ARE COMPLETED, CLEAR CODES AND VERIFY OPERATION

84205164

Fig. 34 Fuel system diagnosis — 1993 Eldorado/Seville with 4.6L engine

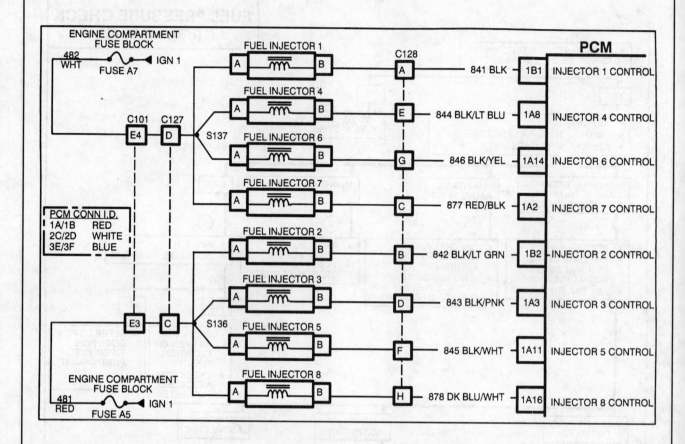

CHART 6C–2

FUEL PRESSURE CHECK
(Page 3 of 4)

DESCRIPTION:

The Fuel Pressure Check determines if the fuel system is providing fuel pressure. The components involved include the fuel tank, sender, pump, pipes and hoses, pressure regulator, fuel rail, and injectors. Also checked are the electrical operation of the fuel pump relays. This chart requires J 34730–1 Fuel Pressure Gage.

NOTES ON FAULT TREE:

7. If fuel pressure holds with Engine Compartment Fuse Block Fuse 'A7' removed, injector 1, 4, 6 or 7 must have been electrically energized causing the fuel pressure drop.

8. Checking if a short to ground on the low side of the injector or the PCM was keeping the injector energized.

9. Checking for a physical cause of the pressure drop ie. leaking injectors, leaking fuel railer pressure regulated. If no leaks are found the fuel pump check ball is not operating correctly then replace fuel pump.

84205165

Fig. 35 Fuel system diagnosis — 1993 Eldorado/Seville with 4.6L engine

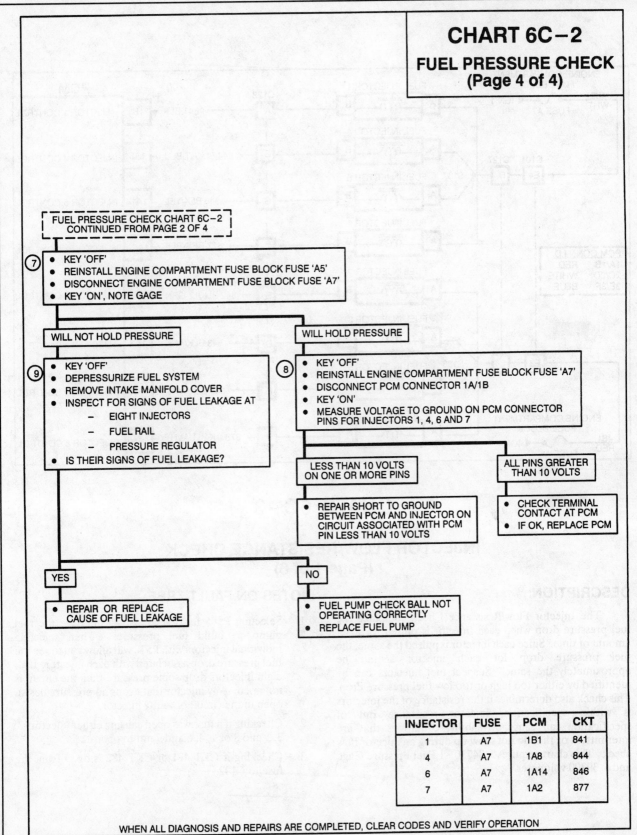

CHART 6C-2
FUEL PRESSURE CHECK
(Page 4 of 4)

FUEL PRESSURE CHECK CHART 6C-2
CONTINUED FROM PAGE 2 OF 4

⑦
- KEY 'OFF'
- REINSTALL ENGINE COMPARTMENT FUSE BLOCK FUSE 'A5'
- DISCONNECT ENGINE COMPARTMENT FUSE BLOCK FUSE 'A7'
- KEY 'ON', NOTE GAGE

WILL NOT HOLD PRESSURE

WILL HOLD PRESSURE

⑨
- KEY 'OFF'
- DEPRESSURIZE FUEL SYSTEM
- REMOVE INTAKE MANIFOLD COVER
- INSPECT FOR SIGNS OF FUEL LEAKAGE AT
    - EIGHT INJECTORS
    - FUEL RAIL
    - PRESSURE REGULATOR
- IS THEIR SIGNS OF FUEL LEAKAGE?

⑧
- KEY 'OFF'
- REINSTALL ENGINE COMPARTMENT FUSE BLOCK FUSE 'A7'
- DISCONNECT PCM CONNECTOR 1A/1B
- KEY 'ON'
- MEASURE VOLTAGE TO GROUND ON PCM CONNECTOR PINS FOR INJECTORS 1, 4, 6 AND 7

LESS THAN 10 VOLTS ON ONE OR MORE PINS

ALL PINS GREATER THAN 10 VOLTS

- REPAIR SHORT TO GROUND BETWEEN PCM AND INJECTOR ON CIRCUIT ASSOCIATED WITH PCM PIN LESS THAN 10 VOLTS

- CHECK TERMINAL CONTACT AT PCM
- IF OK, REPLACE PCM

YES

NO

- REPAIR OR REPLACE CAUSE OF FUEL LEAKAGE

- FUEL PUMP CHECK BALL NOT OPERATING CORRECTLY
- REPLACE FUEL PUMP

INJECTOR	FUSE	PCM	CKT
1	A7	1B1	841
4	A7	1A8	844
6	A7	1A14	846
7	A7	1A2	877

WHEN ALL DIAGNOSIS AND REPAIRS ARE COMPLETED, CLEAR CODES AND VERIFY OPERATION

84205166

Fig. 36 Fuel system diagnosis — 1993 Eldorado/Seville with 4.6L engine

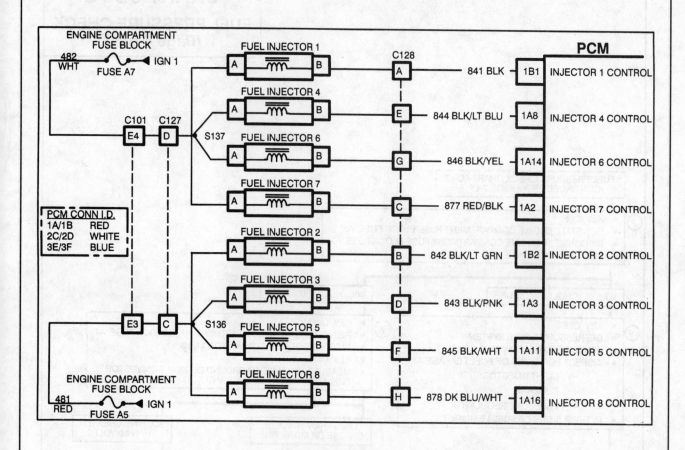

CHART 6C-3

INJECTOR FLOW/RESISTANCE CHECK
(Page 1 of 6)

DESCRIPTION:

The Injector Flow/Resistance Check compares the fuel pressure drop when each injector is pulsed for a set amount of time. Since each injector is pulsed the same, the fuel pressure drop for each injector should be approximately the same. Suspect fuel injectors can be identified by either too high or too low fuel pressure drop. This check also determines if the resistance of the injectors is within specification. Injector resistance out of specification can cause driveability conditions that are intermittent or that do not show up during an injector flow check. This chart requires J 34730-1 Fuel Pressure Gage and J 39200 voltmeter

NOTES ON FAULT TREE:

1. Selecting PS05 for 5 seconds will energize the fuel pump to build fuel pressure. Then selecting individual injectors with PS10 will allow you to see the fuel pressure drop associated with each injector. If all eight injectors drop some pressure then the circuit is not open. Any injector that drops no pressure has an open in the circuit or faulty injector.

2. Checking if a fuse was open causing either injectors 2, 3, 5 and 8 or 1, 4, 6 and 7 not to operate.

3. Checking if CKT 481 or CKT 482 is open from the fuse to C102.

84205167

Fig. 37 Fuel system diagnosis — 1993 Eldorado/Seville with 4.6L engine

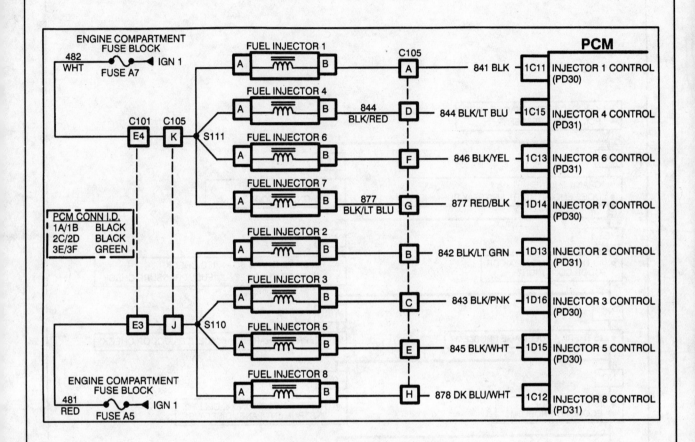

CHART 6C-1

FUEL SYSTEM CHECK

CIRCUIT DESCRIPTION:

The Fuel System Check provides a quick analysis of the fuel system. This chart then identifies more detailed diagnosis required based on the symptoms present.

84205180

Fig. 40 Fuel system diagnosis — 1993 Eldorado/Seville with 4.9L engine

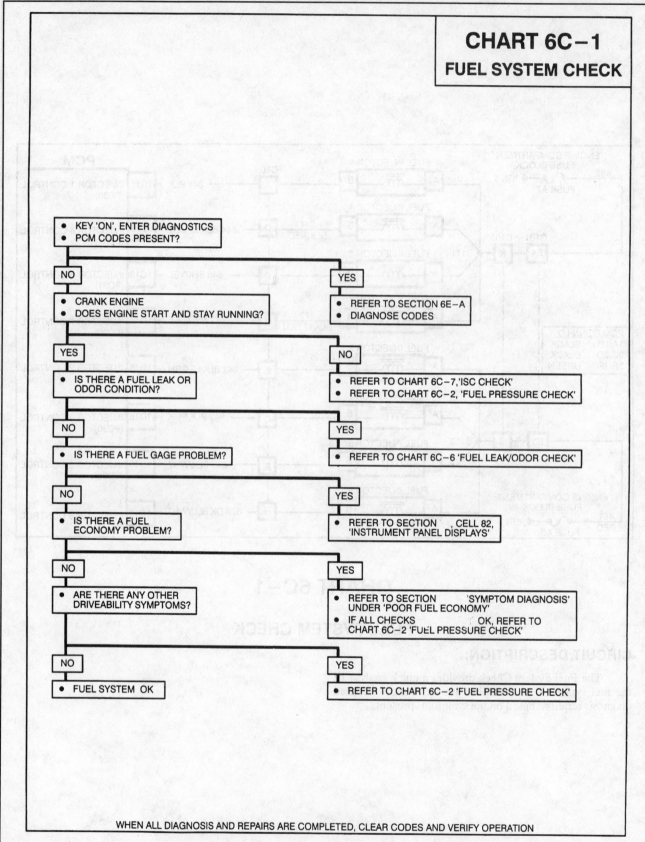

CHART 6C-1
FUEL SYSTEM CHECK

- KEY 'ON', ENTER DIAGNOSTICS
- PCM CODES PRESENT?

NO

- CRANK ENGINE
- DOES ENGINE START AND STAY RUNNING?

YES
- REFER TO SECTION 6E–A
- DIAGNOSE CODES

YES

- IS THERE A FUEL LEAK OR ODOR CONDITION?

NO
- REFER TO CHART 6C–7,'ISC CHECK'
- REFER TO CHART 6C–2, 'FUEL PRESSURE CHECK'

NO

- IS THERE A FUEL GAGE PROBLEM?

YES
- REFER TO CHART 6C–6 'FUEL LEAK/ODOR CHECK'

NO

- IS THERE A FUEL ECONOMY PROBLEM?

YES
- REFER TO SECTION , CELL 82, 'INSTRUMENT PANEL DISPLAYS'

NO

- ARE THERE ANY OTHER DRIVEABILITY SYMPTOMS?

YES
- REFER TO SECTION 'SYMPTOM DIAGNOSIS' UNDER 'POOR FUEL ECONOMY'
- IF ALL CHECKS OK, REFER TO CHART 6C–2 'FUEL PRESSURE CHECK'

NO
- FUEL SYSTEM OK

YES
- REFER TO CHART 6C–2 'FUEL PRESSURE CHECK'

WHEN ALL DIAGNOSIS AND REPAIRS ARE COMPLETED, CLEAR CODES AND VERIFY OPERATION

84205181

Fig. 41 Fuel system diagnosis — 1993 Eldorado/Seville with 4.9L engine

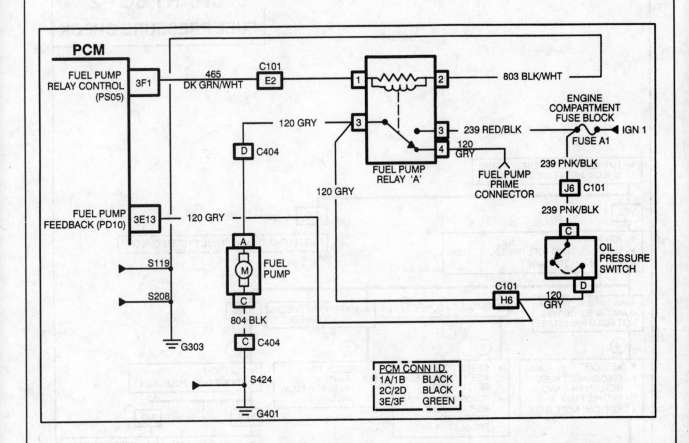

CHART 6C-2

FUEL PRESSURE CHECK

CIRCUIT DESCRIPTION:

The Fuel Pressure Check determines if the fuel system is providing fuel pressure. The components involved include the fuel tank, sender, pump, pipes and hoses, pressure regulator, fuel rail, and injectors. Also checked are the electrical operation of the fuel pump relay. This chart requires J 34730–1 Fuel Pressure Gage.

NOTES ON FAULT TREE:

1. If fuel pump does not run at key 'ON', diagnose as if a Code P020 is set to determine the cause. If fuel pump runs at key 'ON', check for an open or clogged fuel line or filter.

2. If normal fuel pressure is present, then check for correct injector operation.

3. If fuel pressure is too high, then the pressure regulator is not working properly, or cannot work due to a restriction in the fuel return back to the fuel tank.

4. Fuel pressure leak down can be caused by a regulator, a fuel pump check ball, or a leaking injector. Low fuel pressure that does not leak down can be caused by a regulator or a low output pump.

84205183

Fig. 42 Fuel system diagnosis — 1993 Eldorado/Seville with 4.9L engine

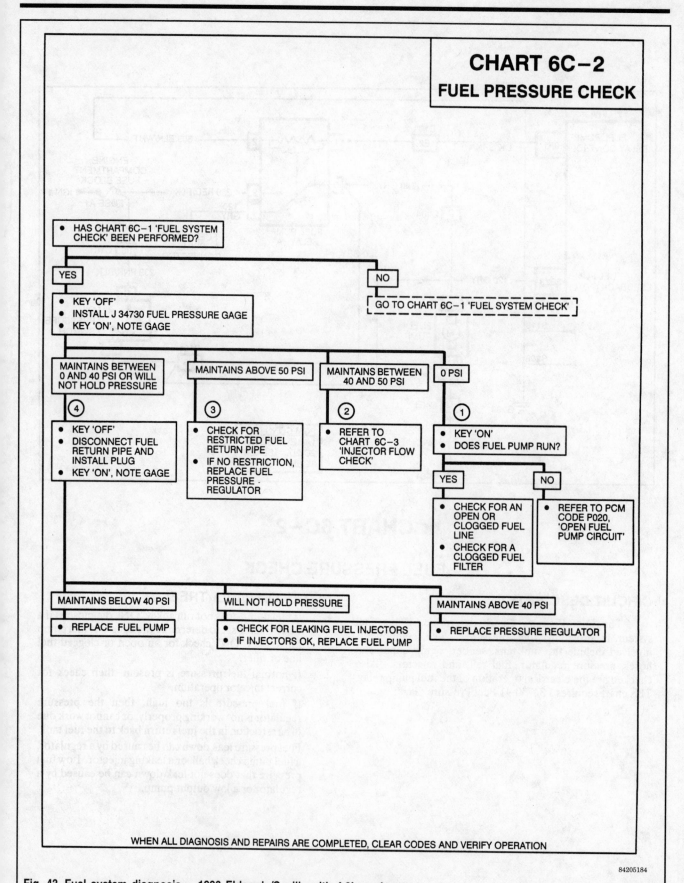

CHART 6C-2
FUEL PRESSURE CHECK

- HAS CHART 6C-1 'FUEL SYSTEM CHECK' BEEN PERFORMED?

YES

NO

GO TO CHART 6C-1 'FUEL SYSTEM CHECK'

- KEY 'OFF'
- INSTALL J 34730 FUEL PRESSURE GAGE
- KEY 'ON', NOTE GAGE

MAINTAINS BETWEEN 0 AND 40 PSI OR WILL NOT HOLD PRESSURE

④

MAINTAINS ABOVE 50 PSI

③

MAINTAINS BETWEEN 40 AND 50 PSI

②

0 PSI

①

- KEY 'OFF'
- DISCONNECT FUEL RETURN PIPE AND INSTALL PLUG
- KEY 'ON', NOTE GAGE

- CHECK FOR RESTRICTED FUEL RETURN PIPE
- IF NO RESTRICTION, REPLACE FUEL PRESSURE REGULATOR

- REFER TO CHART 6C-3 'INJECTOR FLOW CHECK'

- KEY 'ON'
- DOES FUEL PUMP RUN?

YES

NO

- CHECK FOR AN OPEN OR CLOGGED FUEL LINE
- CHECK FOR A CLOGGED FUEL FILTER

- REFER TO PCM CODE P020, 'OPEN FUEL PUMP CIRCUIT'

MAINTAINS BELOW 40 PSI

- REPLACE FUEL PUMP

WILL NOT HOLD PRESSURE

- CHECK FOR LEAKING FUEL INJECTORS
- IF INJECTORS OK, REPLACE FUEL PUMP

MAINTAINS ABOVE 40 PSI

- REPLACE PRESSURE REGULATOR

WHEN ALL DIAGNOSIS AND REPAIRS ARE COMPLETED, CLEAR CODES AND VERIFY OPERATION

84205184

Fig. 43 Fuel system diagnosis — 1993 Eldorado/Seville with 4.9L engine

HARD START

DEFINITION: Engine cranks OK, but does not start quickly. Engine cranks for more than 2 seconds before starting in ambient temperatures above 0° F. Engine cranks for more than 4 seconds before starting in ambient temperatures between −20° F and 0° F.

Perform 'Powertrain System Check', if not already completed

Perform 'Fuel System Check' in Section looking in particular for:

- Fuel Quality
  - Alcohol Content
  - Contaminants
  - Water Content
  - Sour Fuel
- Low Fuel Pressure
  - Fuel Pump Circuit problem
- Plugged or dirty Fuel Filter
- Fuel Injectors
  - Not Operating
  - Low Flow Rate
- Idle Speed Control
  - Faulty ISC Motor
  - TP Sensor/Idle Learn Not Complete

Perform 'Ignition System Check'

- High Resistance, Open, Shorted, or Arcing Spark Plug Wires, crossfire between spark plug wires
- Contaminated or Damaged Spark Plugs
- Distributor Grounding Points Clean and Tight
- Correct Ignition Timing
- Faulty Ignition Coil or IC Module
- Distributor Cap, Rotor, Brush and Button for Moisture, Cracks, Dust or Carbon Tracking
- Worn or Loose Distributor Shaft Gear
- Bent Distributor Shaft or Worn Distributor Shaft Bushing

Check for the following mechanical causes:

- Air induction restrictions
- Low engine compression
- Throttle linkage sticking or binding

Check for possible driver−induced causes:

- Improper starting procedure. Refer to Starting Instructions described in owner's manual.

HESITATION, SAG, STUMBLE

DEFINITION: Momentary lack of response as the accelerator is depressed. The problem can occur at all vehicle speeds. Usually most severe when accelerating from a stop, and may cause the engine to stall. Usually caused by a lean condition (not enough fuel).

Perform 'Powertrain System Check', if not already completed

Perform 'Fuel System Check' in Section looking in particular for:

- Fuel Quality
  - Alcohol Content
  - Contaminants
  - Water Content
  - Sour Fuel
- Low Fuel Pressure
- Fuel Injectors
  - Not Operating
  - Low Flow Rate
- Plugged or dirty Fuel Filter

- Idle Speed Control
  - Binding ISC Motor
  - Sticking TP Switch

Perform 'Ignition System Check'

- High Resistance, Open, Shorted, or Arcing Spark Plug Wires, crossfire between spark plug wires
- Contaminated or Damaged Spark Plugs
- Distributor Grounding Points Clean and Tight
- Correct Ignition Timing
- Faulty Ignition Coil or IC Module
- Distributor Cap, Rotor, Brush and Button for Moisture, Cracks, Dust or Carbon Tracking
- Worn or Loose Distributor Shaft Gear
- Bent Distributor Shaft or Worn Distributor Shaft Bushing

84205199

Fig. 44 Powertrain symptom diagnosis

Perform 'EGR System Check'

Check for the following mechanical causes:

- Binding or Sticking Throttle Linkage

- Intake Valve Deposits
- Valves Sticking in Guides
- Vacuum Leaks in Intake Manifold
- Bent Push Rods
- Worn Rocker Arms

SURGES, CHUGGLE

DEFINITION: Engine power variation under steady throttle. Vehicle speeds up and slows down with no change to the accelerator pedal position. Usually caused by rich operation (too much fuel).

Perform 'Powertrain System Check', if not already completed

Check for possible driver–induced causes:

- Owner Complaining About Normal Operation of the Torque Converter Clutch(TCC) and/or A/C Compressor Clutch

Perform 'Ignition System Check'

- High Resistance, Open, Shorted, or Arcing Spark Plug Wires, crossfire between spark plug wires
- Contaminated or Damaged Spark Plugs
- Distributor Grounding Points Clean and Tight
- Correct Ignition Timing
- Faulty Ignition Coil or IC Module
- Distributor Cap, Rotor, Brush and Button for Moisture, Cracks, Dust or Carbon Tracking
- Worn or Loose Distributor Shaft Gear
- Bent Distributor Shaft or Worn Distributor Shaft Bushing

Perform 'Fuel System Check' looking in particular for:

- Fuel Quality
  - Alcohol Content
  - Contaminants
  - Water Content
  - Sour Fuel

- Incorrect Fuel Pressure
- Fuel Injectors
  - Leaking
  - Incorrect Flow Rate

Perform '4T60–E Functional Test'

- Intermittent Torque Converter Clutch(TCC) Operation

Perform 'Exhaust Diagnosis' looking in particular for:

- Restricted Catalytic Converter or Exhaust

Perform 'EGR System Check'

Perform 'Functional Test of EVAP Components' in Section 6E–C.

Perform 'PCV System Check'

Check for the following mechanical causes:

- Valves Sticking in Guides
- Excessive Oil Consumption
- Erratic VSS Readings
- Bent Push Rods
- Worn Rocker Arms

BACKFIRE

DEFINITION: Fuel ignites in intake manifold, or in exhaust system, making a loud popping noise.

Perform 'Powertrain System Check', if not already completed

Perform 'Ignition System Check'

- Spark Plug Wires
  - Crossfire Between Cylinders
  - Wrong Firing Order

- Distributor Grounding Points Clean and Tight
- Correct Ignition Timing
- Distributor Cap, Rotor, Brush and Button for Moisture, Cracks, Dust or Carbon Tracking
- Worn or Loose Distributor Shaft Gear
- Bent Distributor Shaft or Worn Distributor Shaft Bushing

84205200

Fig. 45 Powertrain symptom diagnosis

Perform 'Fuel System Check' in Section 6C, looking in particular for:

- Fuel Quality
  - Low Octane Level
  - Contaminants
- Low Fuel Pressure
- Low Flow Rate Injector

Perform 'Exhaust Diagnosis' in Section 6F, looking in particular for:

- Restricted Catalytic Converter or Exhaust

Check for the following mechanical causes:

- Valves Sticking in Guides
- Worn Camshaft Lobes
- Broken/Weak Valve Springs
- Bent Push Rods
- Worn Rocker Arms

DETONATION, SPARK KNOCK

DEFINITION: A mild to severe knock, that usually occurs under acceleration. The engine produces sharp metallic sounds that change with throttle opening. Generally higher pitched than an engine knock. May be described as a ticking or clatter noise. Occurs when fuel/air charge is ignited by something other than the spark plug.

Perform 'Powertrain System Check', if not already completed

Perform 'EGR System Check'

Perform 'Fuel System Check' in Section 6C, looking in particular for:

- Fuel Quality
  - Low Octane Level
  - Contaminants
- Low Fuel Pressure
- Low Flow Rate Injector

Perform 'Ignition System Check' in Section 6D4, looking in particular for:

- Correct Ignition Timing
- Correct Spark Plug Type and Heat Range

Refer to 'Symptom Diagnosis'

- Overheating Engine
  - Depressurized Engine Cooling System
  - Restricted Engine Coolant Flow
  - Engine Coolant Fans Inoperative

Check for the following mechanical causes:

- Throttle body deposits
- Excessive Oil Consumption
- Intake Valve Deposits
- Engine Knock

POOR FUEL ECONOMY

DEFINITION: Fuel economy as measured by an actual road test, is noticeably lower than expected. Or, economy is noticeably lower than it was on this vehicle at one time, as previously shown by an actual road test.

Perform 'Powertrain System Check', if not already completed

Check for the following mechanical causes:

- Dragging Brakes
- Low Engine Compression
- Low Tire Pressure
- Air Induction Restrictions
- Vacuum Leaks in Intake Manifold

Check for possible driver-induced causes:

- A/C ON at All Times
- Vehicle Used Only for Short Trips (Engine Never Warms Up)
- Fuel Economy Calculated Incorrectly
- Vehicle Regularly Carries a Heavy Load
- Driving Habits (Lead Foot)
- Driving in D3, D2, or D1

Perform 'EGR System Check'

84205201

Fig. 46 Powertrain symptom diagnosis

Perform 'Exhaust Diagnosis' looking in particular for:

- Restricted Catalytic Converter or Exhaust

Perform 'Ignition System Check'

- High Resistance, Open, Shorted, or Arcing Spark Plug Wires, crossfire between spark plug wires
- Contaminated or Damaged Spark Plugs
- Correct Ignition Timing

Perform 'Fuel System Check' looking in particular for:

- Fuel Quality
  - Alcohol Content
  - Contaminants
  - Water Content
  - Sour Fuel
- Incorrect Fuel Pressure
- Fuel Injectors
  - Leaking
  - High Flow Rate

LACK OF POWER, SLUGGISH, SPONGY

DEFINITION: Engine delivers less than expected power. Little or no increase in speed when accelerator pedal is DEPRESSED part way.

Perform 'Powertrain System Check', if not already completed

Perform 'Fuel System Check'

- Fuel Quality
  - Alcohol Content
  - Low Octane Level
  - Contaminants
- Incorrect Fuel Pressure
- Plugged or Dirty Fuel Filter
- Fuel Injectors
  - Incorrect Flow Rate

Perform 'Ignition System Check' in Section 6D4, looking in particular for:

- High Resistance, Open, Shorted, or Arcing Spark Plug Wires, crossfire between spark plug wires
- Contaminated or Damaged Spark Plugs
- Distributor Grounding Points Clean and Tight
- Correct Ignition Timing
- Faulty Ignition Coil or IC Module
- Distributor Cap, Rotor, Brush and Button for Moisture, Cracks, Dust or Carbon Tracking
- Worn or Loose Distributor Shaft Gear
- Bent Distributor Shaft or Worn Distributor Shaft Bushing

Perform 'Exhaust Diagnosis' in Section 6F, looking in particular for:

- Restricted Catalytic Converter or Exhaust

Perform 'EGR System Check'

Check for the following mechanical causes:

- Worn Camshaft Lobes
- Bent Push Rods
- Low Engine Compression
- Broken/Weak Valve Springs
- Throttle not Opening Fully
- Worn Rocker Arms
- Restricted Air Induction Flow
- Vacuum Leaks in Intake Manifold
- Erratic VSS Readings
- Erratic Engine RPM Readings

Check for possible driver-induced causes:

- Vehicle Displaying Normal Power

84205202

Fig. 47 Powertrain symptom diagnosis

EXCESSIVE EXHAUST EMISSIONS (ODORS)

DEFINITION: Vehicle fails an emission test. May also have excessive 'rotten egg' smell (hydrogen sulfide).

Perform 'Powertrain System Check', if not already completed

Check for the following mechanical causes:

- Throttle Body Deposits
- Fuel in Crankcase
- Worn Piston Rings
- Vacuum Leaks in Intake Manifold
- Engine Overheating
- Carbon Build–Up
- Air Restrictions to Intake Manifold

Perform 'PCV System Check'

Perform 'Functional Test of EVAP Components'

Perform 'EGR System Check'

Perform 'Exhaust Diagnosis' looking in particular for:

- Restricted Exhaust

Perform 'Fuel System Check' looking in particular for:

- Fuel Quality
  - Water Content
  - Sour Fuel
- Leaking Fuel Injectors
- Incorrect Fuel Pressure

Perform 'Ignition System Check'

- High Resistance, Open, Shorted, or Arcing Spark Plug Wires, crossfire between spark plug wires
- Contaminated or Damaged Spark Plugs
- Distributor Grounding Points Clean and Tight
- Correct Ignition Timing
- Faulty Ignition Coil or IC Module
- Distributor Cap, Rotor, Brush and Button for Moisture, Cracks, Dust or Carbon Tracking
- Worn or Loose Distributor Shaft Gear
- Bent Distributor Shaft or Worn Distributor Shaft Bushing

ROUGH, UNSTABLE, INCORRECT IDLE

DEFINITION: The engine runs unevenly at idle. If bad enough, the car may shake. Also, the idle may vary in RPM (called 'hunting' or 'surging'). Either condition may be bad enough to cause stalling. Engine idles at incorrect speed.

Perform 'Powertrain System Check', if not already completed

Perform 'Ignition System Check'

- High Resistance, Open, Shorted, or Arcing Spark Plug Wires, crossfire between spark plug wires
- Contaminated or Damaged Spark Plugs
- Distributor Grounding Points Clean and Tight
- Correct Ignition Timing
- Faulty Ignition Coil or IC Module
- Distributor Cap, Rotor, Brush and Button for Moisture, Cracks, Dust or Carbon Tracking
- Worn or Loose Distributor Shaft Gear
- Bent Distributor Shaft or Worn Distributor Shaft Bushing

Perform 'Fuel System Check' looking in particular for:

- Fuel Quality
  - Alcohol Content
  - Contaminants
  - Water Content
  - Sour Fuel
- Low Fuel Pressure
- Fuel Injectors
  - Not Operating
  - Low Flow Rate
- Idle Speed Control
  - Binding ISC Motor
  - Sticking TP Switch
  - TP Sensor/Idle Learn Not Complete

84205203

Fig. 48 Powertrain symptom diagnosis

Check for the following mechanical causes:

- Throttle Body Deposits
- Intake Valve Deposits
- Valves Sticking in Guides
- Vacuum Leaks in Intake Manifold
- Loose Timing Chain (Timing Gear Wear)
- Broken/Weak Valve Springs
- Collapsed Lifter
- Bent Push Rods
- Worn Camshaft Lobes
- Worn Rocker Arms
- Low Engine Compression

- Binding or Sticking Throttle/TV and/or Cruise Cables
- Erratic A/C Compressor Clutch operation
- Erratic VSS Readings
- Erratic Engine RPM Readings

Perform 'PCV System Check'

Perform 'EGR System Check'

Perform 'Functional Test of EVAP Components'

CUTS OUT, MISSES

DEFINITION: Pulsation or jerking that follows engine speed, usually more pronounced as engine load increases. The exhaust has a steady spitting sound at idle or low speed.

Perform 'Powertrain System Check', if not already completed

Perform 'Fuel System Check' looking in particular for:

- Fuel Injectors
  - Not Operating
  - Low Flow Rate

Perform 'Ignition System Check' in Section 6D4, looking in particular for:

- High Resistance, Open, Shorted, or Arcing Spark Plug Wires, crossfire between spark plug wires
- Contaminated or Damaged Spark Plugs
- Distributor Grounding Points Clean and Tight
- Correct Ignition Timing
- Faulty Ignition Coil or IC Module

- Distributor Cap, Rotor, Brush and Button for Moisture, Cracks, Dust or Carbon Tracking
- Worn or Loose Distributor Shaft Gear
- Bent Distributor Shaft or Worn Distributor Shaft Bushing

Check for the following mechanical causes:

- Valves Sticking in Guides
- Broken or Weak Valve Spring
- Collapsed Lifter
- Worn Rocker Arms
- Camshaft Worn
- Bent Push Rods
- Erratic VSS Readings
- Erratic Engine RPM Readings

Check Park/Neutral input using code P091 diagnosis

INTERMITTENT ENGINE STALL, NO CODES

DEFINITION: Engine stalls, no PCM or BCM trouble codes are set, engine will restart immediatey.

Perform 'Powertrain System Check', if not already completed

Perform 'Fuel System Check' looking in particular for:

- Low Fuel Pressure
  - Fuel Pump Circuit Problem
  - Fuel Pickup Problem at Low Fuel Levels (during deceleration or corning maneuvers)

- Plugged or Dirty Fuel Filter
- Fuel Injectors
  - Not Operating
  - Low Flow Rate
- Idle Speed Control
  - Binding or Slow ISC Motor
  - Sticking TP Switch
  - TP Sensor/Idle Learn Not Complete
  - Minimun Idle Air Adjustment

84205204

Fig. 49 Powertrain symptom diagnosis

Perform 'Ignition System Check'

- Faulty Ignition Coil or IC Module
- Distributor and PCM grounding Points Clean and Tight

Perform 'EGR System Check'

- Cause of EGR Valve Open

Perform 'Functional Test of EVAP Components'
particular for:

- EVAP Canister Loaded with Fuel
- EVAP Solenoid Proper Operation

Check for the following mechanical causes:

- Intermittent Ignition Switch or Out of Adjustment
- Erratic A/C Compressor Clutch Operation
- Erratic Power Steering Loads (Intermittent Power Steering Pressure Switch)
- Intermittent PARK/NEUTRAL Inputs to the PCM, when Transaxle not in PARK/NEUTRAL

STARTER DOES NOT CLICK, ENGINE DOES NOT CRANK

DEFINITION: Starter solenoid does not energize and engine does not turn over.

Perform 'Powertrain System Check', if not already completed

Perform 'Cranking System Electrical Diagnosis'

STARTER CLICKS, ENGINE DOES NOT CRANK

DEFINITION: Starter solenoid energizes but engine does not crank.

Perform 'Powertrain System Check', if not already completed

Perform 'Cranking System Electrical Diagnosis'

Check for the following mechanical causes:

- Engine seized

ENGINE CRANKS, BUT DOES NOT START

DEFINITION: Engine cranks normally but does not start and run.

Perform 'Powertrain System Check', if not already completed

Perform 'Fuel System Check'
looking in particular for:

- Fuel Quality
  - Alcohol Content
  - Contaminants
  - Water Content
- No Fuel Pressure
- Plugged fuel lines or fuel filter

- Fuel Injectors
  - Not Operating
  - Low Flow Rate

Perform 'Ignition System Check'

- Faulty Ignition Coil or IC Module

Check for the following mechanical causes:

- No Compression
- Severely Restricted Air Induction Flow

84205205

Fig. 50 Powertrain symptom diagnosis

TORQUE SPECIFICATIONS

Component	U.S.	Metric
Fuel pump sending unit locking nut		
4.6L Northstar engine:	37 ft. lbs.	50 Nm
Throttle body retaining bolts		
4.5L and 4.9L engines:	14 ft. lbs.	19 Nm
4.6L Northstar engine:	106 inch lbs.	12 Nm
Intake manifold top cover retaining bolts		
4.6L Northstar engine:	106 inch lbs.	12 Nm
Fuel rail support bracket attaching bolts		
4.5L and 4.9L engines:	18 ft. lbs.	24 Nm
Fuel return line to the return line fitting		
4.5L and 4.9L engines:	22 ft. lbs.	30 Nm
Fuel pressure regulator retaining screws		
4.5L and 4.9L engines:	9 ft. lbs.	12 Nm
ISC motor retaining nuts		
4.6L Northstar engine:	53 inch lbs.	6 Nm
TPS attaching screws		
4.6L Northstar engine:	106 inch lbs.	12 Nm
4.9L engine:	106 inch lbs.	12 Nm
Fuel tank retaining straps:	26 ft. lbs.	35 Nm

84205206

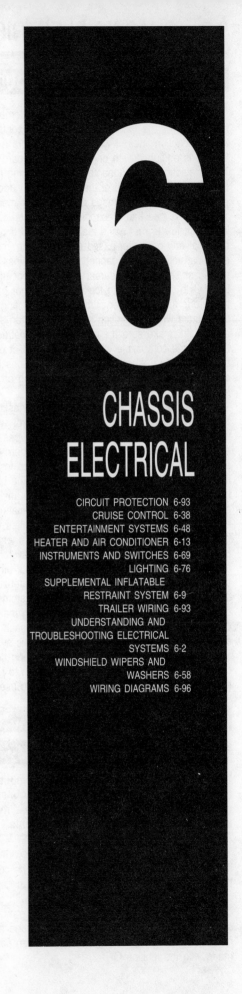

6

CHASSIS
ELECTRICAL

UNDERSTANDING AND TROUBLESHOOTING ELECTRICAL SYSTEMS

With the rate at which both import and domestic manufacturers are incorporating electronic control systems into their production lines, it won't be long before every new vehicle is equipped with one or more on-board computer. These electronic components (with no moving parts) should theoretically last the life of the vehicle, provided nothing external happens to damage the circuits or memory chips.

While it is true that electronic components should never wear out, in the real world malfunctions do occur. It is also true that any computer-based system is extremely sensitive to electrical voltages and cannot tolerate careless or haphazard testing or service procedures. An inexperienced individual can literally do major damage looking for a minor problem by using the wrong kind of test equipment or connecting test leads or connectors with the ignition switch ON. When selecting test equipment, make sure the manufacturers instructions state that the tester is compatible with whatever type of electronic control system is being serviced. Read all instructions carefully and double check all test points before installing probes or making any test connections.

The following section outlines basic diagnosis techniques for dealing with computerized automotive control systems. Along with a general explanation of the various types of test equipment available to aid in servicing modern electronic automotive systems, basic repair techniques for wiring harnesses and connectors is given. Read the basic information before attempting any repairs or testing on any computerized system, to provide the background of information necessary to avoid the most common and obvious mistakes that can cost both time and money. Although the replacement and testing procedures are simple in themselves, the systems are not, and unless one has a thorough understanding of all components and their function within a particular computerized control system, the logical test sequence these systems demand cannot be followed. Minor malfunctions can make a big difference, so it is important to know how each component affects the operation of the overall electronic system to find the ultimate cause of a problem without replacing good components unnecessarily. It is not enough to use the correct test equipment; the test equipment must be used correctly.

Safety Precautions

❄❄CAUTION

Whenever working on or around any computer based microprocessor control system, always observe these general precautions to prevent the possibility of personal injury or damage to electronic components.

• Never install or remove battery cables with the key ON or the engine running. Jumper cables should be connected with the key OFF to avoid power surges that can damage electronic control units. Engines equipped with computer controlled systems should avoid both giving and getting jump starts due to the possibility of serious damage to components from arcing in the engine compartment when connections are made with the ignition ON.

• Always remove the battery cables before charging the battery. Never use a high output charger on an installed battery or attempt to use any type of "hot shot" (24 volt) starting aid.

• Exercise care when inserting test probes into connectors to insure good connections without damaging the connector or spreading the pins. Always probe connectors from the rear (wire) side, NOT the pin side, to avoid accidental shorting of terminals during test procedures.

• Never remove or attach wiring harness connectors with the ignition switch ON, especially to an electronic control unit.

• Do not drop any components during service procedures and never apply 12 volts directly to any component (like a solenoid or relay) unless instructed specifically to do so. Some component electrical windings are designed to safely handle only 4 or 5 volts and can be destroyed in seconds if 12 volts are applied directly to the connector.

• Remove the electronic control unit if the vehicle is to be placed in an environment where temperatures exceed approximately 176°F (80°C), such as a paint spray booth or when arc or gas welding near the control unit location in the car.

ORGANIZED TROUBLESHOOTING

When diagnosing a specific problem, organized troubleshooting is a must. The complexity of a modern automobile demands that you approach any problem in a logical, organized manner. There are certain troubleshooting techniques that are standard:

1. Establish when the problem occurs. Does the problem appear only under certain conditions? Were there any noises, odors, or other unusual symptoms?

2. Isolate the problem area. To do this, make some simple tests and observations; then eliminate the systems that are working properly. Check for obvious problems such as broken wires, dirty connections or split or disconnected vacuum hoses. Always check the obvious before assuming something complicated is the cause.

3. Test for problems systematically to determine the cause once the problem area is isolated. Are all the components functioning properly? Is there power going to electrical switches and motors? Is there vacuum at vacuum switches and/or actuators? Is there a mechanical problem such as bent linkage or loose mounting screws? Doing careful, systematic checks will often turn up most causes on the first inspection without wasting time checking components that have little or no relationship to the problem.

4. Test all repairs after the work is done to make sure that the problem is fixed. Some causes can be traced to more than one component, so a careful verification of repair work is important to pick up additional malfunctions that may cause a problem to reappear or a different problem to arise. A blown fuse, for example, is a simple problem that may require more than another fuse to repair. If you don't look for a problem that caused a fuse to blow, for example, a shorted wire may go undetected.

Experience has shown that most problems tend to be the result of a fairly simple and obvious cause, such as loose or corroded connectors or air leaks in the intake system; making careful inspection of components during testing is essential to quick and accurate troubleshooting. Special, hand held computerized testers designed specifically for diagnosing the engine control system are available from a variety of aftermarket sources, as well as from the vehicle manufacturer, but care should be taken that any test equipment being used is designed to diagnose that particular computer controlled system accurately without damaging the control unit or components being tested.

➡Pinpointing the exact cause of trouble in an electrical system can sometimes only be accomplished by the use of special test equipment. The following describes commonly used test equipment and explains how to put it to best use in diagnosis. In addition to the information covered below, the manufacturer's instructions booklet provided with the tester should be read and clearly understood before attempting any test procedures.

TEST EQUIPMENT

Jumper Wires

Jumper wires are simple, yet extremely valuable, pieces of test equipment. Jumper wires are merely wires that are used to bypass sections of a circuit. The simplest type of jumper wire is merely a length of multistrand wire with an alligator clip at each end. Jumper wires are usually fabricated from lengths of standard automotive wire and whatever type of connector (alligator clip, spade connector or pin connector) that is required for the particular vehicle being tested. The well equipped tool box will have several different styles of jumper wires in several different lengths. Some jumper wires are made with three or more terminals coming from a common splice for special purpose testing. In cramped, hard-to-reach areas it is advisable to have insulated boots over the jumper wire terminals in order to prevent accidental grounding, sparks, and possible fire, especially when testing fuel system components.

Jumper wires are used primarily to locate open electrical circuits, on either the ground (-) side of the circuit or on the hot (+) side. If an electrical component fails to operate, connect the jumper wire between the component and a good ground. If the component operates only with the jumper installed, the ground circuit is open. If the ground circuit is good, but the component does not operate, the circuit between the power feed and component is open. You can sometimes connect the jumper wire directly from the battery to the hot terminal of the component, but first make sure the component uses 12 volts in operation. Some electrical components, such as fuel injectors, are designed to operate on about 4 volts and running 12 volts directly to the injector terminals can burn out the wiring. By inserting an inline fuseholder between a set of test leads, a fused jumper wire can be used for bypassing open circuits. Use a 5 amp fuse to provide protection against voltage spikes. When in doubt, use a volt meter to check the voltage input to the component and measure how much voltage is being applied normally. By moving the jumper wire

successively back from the lamp toward the power source, you can isolate the area of the circuit where the open is located. When the component stops functioning, or the power is cut off, the open is in the segment of wire between the jumper and the point previously tested.

✳✳CAUTION

Never use jumpers made from wire that is of lighter gauge than used in the circuit under test. If the jumper wire is of too small gauge, it may overheat and possibly melt. Never use jumpers to bypass high resistance loads (such as motors) in a circuit. Bypassing resistances, in effect, creates a short circuit which may, in turn, cause damage and fire. Never use a jumper for anything other than temporary bypassing of components in a circuit.

12 Volt Test Light

The 12 volt test light is used to check circuits and components while electrical current is flowing through them. It is used for voltage and ground tests. Twelve volt test lights come in different styles but all have three main parts; a ground clip, a probe, and a light. The most commonly used 12 volt test lights have pick-type probes. To use a 12 volt test light, connect the ground clip to a good ground and probe wherever necessary with the pick. The pick should be sharp so that it can penetrate wire insulation to make contact with the wire, without making a large hole in the insulation. The wrap-around light is handy in hard to reach areas or where it is difficult to support a wire to push a probe pick into it. To use the wrap around light, hook the wire to probed with the hook and pull the trigger. A small pick will be forced through the wire insulation into the wire core.

✳✳CAUTION

Do not use a test light to probe electronic ignition spark plug or coil wires. Never use a pick-type test light to probe wiring on computer controlled systems unless specifically instructed to do so. Any wire insulation that is pierced by the test light probe should be taped and sealed with silicone after testing.

Like the jumper wire, the 12 volt test light is used to isolate opens in circuits. But, whereas the jumper wire is used to bypass the open to operate the load, the 12 volt test light is used to locate the presence of voltage in a circuit. If the test light glows, you know that there is power up to that point; if the 12 volt test light does not glow when its probe is inserted into the wire or connector, you know that there is an open circuit (no power). Move the test light in successive steps back toward the power source until the light in the handle does glow. When it does glow, the open is between the probe and point previously probed.

➡The test light does not detect that 12 volts (or any particular amount of voltage) is present; it only detects that some voltage is present. It is advisable before using the test light to touch its terminals across the battery posts to make sure the light is operating properly.

Self-Powered Test Light

The self-powered test light usually contains a 1.5 volt penlight battery. One type of self-powered test light is similar in design to the 12 volt test light. This type has both the battery and the light in the handle and pick-type probe tip. The second type has the light toward the open tip, so that the light illuminates the contact point. The self-powered test light is dual purpose piece of test equipment. It can be used to test for either open or short circuits when power is isolated from the circuit (continuity test). A powered test light should not be used on any computer controlled system or component unless specifically instructed to do so. Many engine sensors can be destroyed by even this small amount of voltage applied directly to the terminals.

Open Circuit Testing

To use the self-powered test light to check for open circuits, first isolate the circuit from the vehicle's 12 volt power source by disconnecting the battery or wiring harness connector. Connect the test light ground clip to a good ground and probe sections of the circuit sequentially with the test light (start from either end of the circuit). If the light is out, the open is between the probe and the circuit ground. If the light is on, the open is between the probe and end of the circuit toward the power source.

Short Circuit Testing

By isolating the circuit both from power and from ground, and using a self-powered test light, you can check for shorts to ground in the circuit. Isolate the circuit from power and ground. Connect the test light ground clip to a good ground and probe any easy-to-reach test point in the circuit. If the light comes on, there is a short somewhere in the circuit. To isolate the short, probe a test point at either end of the isolated circuit (the light should be on). Leave the test light probe connected and open connectors, switches, remove parts, etc., sequentially, until the light goes out. When the light goes out, the short is between the last circuit component opened and the previous circuit opened.

➡**The 1.5 volt battery in the test light does not provide much current. A weak battery may not provide enough power to illuminate the test light even when a complete circuit is made (especially if there are high resistances in the circuit). Always make sure that the test battery is strong. To check the battery, briefly touch the ground clip to the probe; if the light glows brightly the battery is strong enough for testing. Never use a self-powered test light to perform checks for opens or shorts when power is applied to the electrical system under test. The 12 volt vehicle power will quickly burn out the 1.5 volt light bulb in the test light.**

Voltmeter

A voltmeter is used to measure voltage at any point in a circuit, or to measure the voltage drop across any part of a circuit. It can also be used to check continuity in a wire or circuit by indicating current flow from one end to the other. Voltmeters usually have various scales on the meter dial and a selector switch to allow the selection of different voltages. The voltmeter has a positive and a negative lead. To avoid damage to the meter, always connect the negative lead to the negative (-) side of circuit (to ground or nearest the ground side of the circuit) and connect the positive lead to the positive (+) side of the circuit (to the power source or the nearest power source). Note that the negative voltmeter lead will always be black and that the positive voltmeter will always be some color other than black (usually red). Depending on how the voltmeter is connected into the circuit, it has several uses.

A voltmeter can be connected either in parallel or in series with a circuit and it has a very high resistance to current flow. When connected in parallel, only a small amount of current will flow through the voltmeter current path; the rest will flow through the normal circuit current path and the circuit will work normally. When the voltmeter is connected in series with a circuit, only a small amount of current can flow through the circuit. The circuit will not work properly, but the voltmeter reading will show if the circuit is complete or not.

Available Voltage Measurement

Set the voltmeter selector switch to the 20V position and connect the meter negative lead to the negative post of the battery. Connect the positive meter lead to the positive post of the battery and turn the ignition switch ON to provide a load. Read the voltage on the meter or digital display. A well charged battery should register over 12 volts. If the meter reads below 11.5 volts, the battery power may be insufficient to operate the electrical system properly. This test determines voltage available from the battery and should be the first step in any electrical trouble diagnosis procedure. Many electrical problems, especially on computer controlled systems, can be caused by a low state of charge in the battery. Excessive corrosion at the battery cable terminals can cause a poor contact that will prevent proper charging and full battery current flow.

Normal battery voltage is 12 volts when fully charged. When the battery is supplying current to one or more circuits it is said to be "under load". When everything is off the electrical system is under a "no-load" condition. A fully charged battery may show about 12.5 volts at no load; will drop to 12 volts under medium load; and will drop even lower under heavy load. If the battery is partially discharged the voltage decrease under heavy load may be excessive, even though the battery shows 12 volts or more at no load. When allowed to discharge further, the battery's available voltage under load will decrease more severely. For this reason, it is important that the battery be fully charged during all testing procedures to avoid errors in diagnosis and incorrect test results.

Voltage Drop

When current flows through a resistance, the voltage beyond the resistance is reduced (the larger the current, the greater the reduction in voltage). When no current is flowing, there is no voltage drop because there is no current flow. All points in the circuit which are connected to the power source are at the same voltage as the power source. The total voltage drop always equals the total source voltage. In a long circuit with many connectors, a series of small, unwanted voltage drops due to corrosion at the connectors can add up to a total loss of voltage which impairs the operation of the normal loads in the circuit.

INDIRECT COMPUTATION OF VOLTAGE DROPS

1. Set the voltmeter selector switch to the 20 volt position.
2. Connect the meter negative lead to a good ground.
3. Probe all resistances in the circuit with the positive meter lead.
4. Operate the circuit in all modes and observe the voltage readings.

DIRECT MEASUREMENT OF VOLTAGE DROPS

1. Set the voltmeter switch to the 20 volt position.
2. Connect the voltmeter negative lead to the ground side of the resistance load to be measured.
3. Connect the positive lead to the positive side of the resistance or load to be measured.
4. Read the voltage drop directly on the 20 volt scale.

Too high a voltage indicates too high a resistance. If, for example, a blower motor runs too slowly, you can determine if there is too high a resistance in the resistor pack. By taking voltage drop readings in all parts of the circuit, you can isolate the problem. Too low a voltage drop indicates too low a resistance. If, for example, a blower motor runs too fast in the MED and/or LOW position, the problem can be isolated in the resistor pack by taking voltage drop readings in all parts of the circuit to locate a possibly shorted resistor. The maximum allowable voltage drop under load is critical, especially if there is more than one high resistance problem in a circuit because all voltage drops are cumulative. A small drop is normal due to the resistance of the conductors.

HIGH RESISTANCE TESTING

1. Set the voltmeter selector switch to the 4 volt position.
2. Connect the voltmeter positive lead to the positive post of the battery.
3. Turn on the headlights and heater blower to provide a load.
4. Probe various points in the circuit with the negative voltmeter lead.
5. Read the voltage drop on the 4 volt scale. Some average maximum allowable voltage drops are:
   - FUSE PANEL — 7 volts
   - IGNITION SWITCH — 5 volts
   - HEADLIGHT SWITCH — 7 volts
   - IGNITION COIL (+) — 5 volts
   - ANY OTHER LOAD — 1.3 volts

➡**Voltage drops are all measured while a load is operating; without current flow, there will be no voltage drop.**

Ohmmeter

The ohmmeter is designed to read resistance (ohms) in a circuit or component. Although there are several different styles of ohmmeters, all will usually have a selector switch which permits the measurement of different ranges of resistance (usually the selector switch allows the multiplication of the meter reading by 10, 100, 1000, and 10,000). A calibration knob allows the meter to be set at zero for accurate measurement. Since all ohmmeters are powered by an internal battery (usually 9 volts), the ohmmeter can be used as a self-powered test light. When the ohmmeter is connected, current from the ohmmeter flows through the circuit or component

being tested. Since the ohmmeter's internal resistance and voltage are known values, the amount of current flow through the meter depends on the resistance of the circuit or component being tested.

The ohmmeter can be used to perform continuity test for opens or shorts (either by observation of the meter needle or as a self-powered test light), and to read actual resistance in a circuit. It should be noted that the ohmmeter is used to check the resistance of a component or wire while there is no voltage applied to the circuit. Current flow from an outside voltage source (such as the vehicle battery) can damage the ohmmeter, so the circuit or component should be isolated from the vehicle electrical system before any testing is done. Since the ohmmeter uses its own voltage source, either lead can be connected to any test point.

➡**When checking diodes or other solid state components, the ohmmeter leads can only be connected one way in order to measure current flow in a single direction. Make sure the positive (+) and negative (-) terminal connections are as described in the test procedures to verify the one-way diode operation.**

In using the meter for making continuity checks, do not be concerned with the actual resistance readings. Zero resistance, or any resistance readings, indicate continuity in the circuit. Infinite resistance indicates an open in the circuit. A high resistance reading where there should be none indicates a problem in the circuit. Checks for short circuits are made in the same manner as checks for open circuits except that the circuit must be isolated from both power and normal ground. Infinite resistance indicates no continuity to ground, while zero resistance indicates a dead short to ground.

RESISTANCE MEASUREMENT

The batteries in an ohmmeter will weaken with age and temperature, so the ohmmeter must be calibrated or "zeroed" before taking measurements. To zero the meter, place the selector switch in its lowest range and touch the two ohmmeter leads together. Turn the calibration knob until the meter needle is exactly on zero.

➡**All analog (needle) type ohmmeters must be zeroed before use, but some digital ohmmeter models are automatically calibrated when the switch is turned on. Self-calibrating digital ohmmeters do not have an adjusting knob, but its a good idea to check for a zero readout before use by touching the leads together. All computer controlled systems require the use of a digital ohmmeter with at least 10 megohms impedance for testing. Before any test procedures are attempted, make sure the ohmmeter used is compatible with the electrical system or damage to the on-board computer could result.**

To measure resistance, first isolate the circuit from the vehicle power source by disconnecting the battery cables or the harness connector. Make sure the key is OFF when disconnecting any components or the battery. Where necessary, also isolate at least one side of the circuit to be checked to avoid reading parallel resistances. Parallel circuit resistances will always give a lower reading than the actual resistance of either of the branches. When measuring the resistance of parallel circuits, the total resistance will always be lower than the smallest resistance in the circuit. Connect the meter leads to both sides of the circuit (wire or component) and read the actual measured ohms on the meter scale. Make sure the selector switch is set to the proper ohm scale for the circuit being tested to avoid misreading the ohmmeter test value.

✳✳CAUTION

Never use an ohmmeter with power applied to the circuit. Like the self-powered test light, the ohmmeter is designed to operate on its own power supply. The normal 12 volt automotive electrical system current could damage the meter.

Ammeters

An ammeter measures the amount of current flowing through a circuit in units called amperes or amps. Amperes are units of electron flow which indicate how fast the electrons are flowing through the circuit. Since Ohms Law dictates that current flow in a circuit is equal to the circuit voltage divided by the total circuit resistance, increasing voltage also increases the current level (amps). Likewise, any decrease in resistance will increase the amount of amps in a circuit. At normal operating voltage, most circuits have a characteristic amount of amperes, called 'current draw" which can be measured using an ammeter. By referring to a specified current draw rating, measuring the amperes, and comparing the two values, one can determine what is happening within the circuit to aid in diagnosis. An open circuit, for example, will not allow any current to flow so the ammeter reading will be zero. More current flows through a heavily loaded circuit or when the charging system is operating.

An ammeter is always connected in series with the circuit being tested. All of the current that normally flows through the circuit must also flow through the ammeter; if there is any other path for the current to follow, the ammeter reading will not be accurate. The ammeter itself has very little resistance to current flow and therefore will not affect the circuit, but it will measure current draw only when the circuit is closed and electricity is flowing. Excessive current draw can blow fuses and drain the battery, while a reduced current draw can cause motors to run slowly, lights to dim and other components to not operate properly. The ammeter can help diagnose these conditions by locating the cause of the high or low reading.

Multimeters

Different combinations of test meters can be built into a single unit designed for specific tests. Some of the more common combination test devices are known as Volt/Amp testers, Tach/Dwell meters, or Digital Multimeters. The Volt/Amp tester is used for charging system, starting system or battery tests and consists of a voltmeter, an ammeter and a variable resistance carbon pile. The voltmeter will usually have at least two ranges for use with 6, 12 and 24 volt systems. The ammeter also has more than one range for testing various levels of battery loads and starter current draw and the carbon pile can be adjusted to offer different amounts of resistance. The Volt/Amp tester has heavy leads to carry large amounts of current and many later models have an inductive ammeter pickup that clamps around the wire to simplify test

connections. On some models, the ammeter also has a zero-center scale to allow testing of charging and starting systems without switching leads or polarity. A digital multimeter is a voltmeter, ammeter and ohmmeter combined in an instrument which gives a digital readout. These are often used when testing solid state circuits because of their high input impedance (usually 10 megohms or more).

The tach/dwell meter combines a tachometer and a dwell (cam angle) meter and is a specialized kind of voltmeter. The tachometer scale is marked to show engine speed in rpm and the dwell scale is marked to show degrees of distributor shaft rotation. In most electronic ignition systems, dwell is determined by the control unit, but the dwell meter can also be used to check the duty cycle (operation) of some electronic engine control systems. Some tach/dwell meters are powered by an internal battery, while others take their power from the car battery in use. The battery powered testers usually require calibration much like an ohmmeter before testing.

Special Test Equipment

A variety of diagnostic tools are available to help troubleshoot and repair computerized engine control systems. The most sophisticated of these devices are the console type engine analyzers that usually occupy a garage service bay, but there are several types of aftermarket electronic testers available that will allow quick circuit tests of the engine control system by plugging directly into a special connector located in the engine compartment or under the dashboard. Several tool and equipment manufacturers offer simple, hand held testers that measure various circuit voltage levels on command to check all system components for proper operation. Although these testers usually cost about $300-$500, consider that the average computer control unit can cost just as much and the money saved by not replacing perfectly good sensors or components in an attempt to correct a problem could justify the purchase price of a special diagnostic tester the first time it's used.

These computerized testers can allow quick and easy test measurements while the engine is operating or while the car is being driven. In addition, the on-board computer memory can be read to access any stored trouble codes; in effect allowing the computer to tell you where it hurts and aid trouble diagnosis by pinpointing exactly which circuit or component is malfunctioning. In the same manner, repairs can be tested to make sure the problem has been corrected. The biggest advantage these special testers have is their relatively easy hookups that minimize or eliminate the chances of making the wrong connections and getting false voltage readings or damaging the computer accidentally.

➡**It should be remembered that these testers check voltage levels in circuits; they don't detect mechanical problems or failed components if the circuit voltage falls within the preprogrammed limits stored in the tester PROM unit. Also, most of the hand held testers are designed to work only on one or two systems made by a specific manufacturer.**

A variety of aftermarket testers are available to help diagnose different computerized control systems. Owatonna Tool Company (OTC), for example, markets a device called the OTC Monitor which plugs directly into the Assembly Line

Diagnostic Link (ALDL). The OTC tester makes diagnosis a simple matter of pressing the correct buttons and, by changing the internal PROM or inserting a different diagnosis cartridge, it will work on any model from full size to subcompact, over a wide range of years. An adapter is supplied with the tester to allow connection to all types of ALDL links, regardless of the number of pin terminals used. By inserting an updated PROM into the OTC tester, it can be easily updated to diagnose any new modifications of computerized control systems.

Wiring Harnesses

The average automobile contains about ½ mile of wiring, with hundreds of individual connections. To protect the many wires from damage and to keep them from becoming a confusing tangle, they are organized into bundles, enclosed in plastic or taped together and called wire harnesses. Different wiring harnesses serve different parts of the vehicle. Individual wires are color coded to help trace them through a harness where sections are hidden from view.

A loose or corroded connection or a replacement wire that is too small for the circuit will add extra resistance and an additional voltage drop to the circuit. A ten percent voltage drop can result in slow or erratic motor operation, for example, even though the circuit is complete. Automotive wiring or circuit conductors can be in any one of three forms:

1. Single strand wire
2. Multistrand wire
3. Printed circuitry

Single strand wire has a solid metal core and is usually used inside such components as alternators, motors, relays and other devices. Multistrand wire has a core made of many small strands of wire twisted together into a single conductor. Most of the wiring in an automotive electrical system is made up of multistrand wire, either as a single conductor or grouped together in a harness. All wiring is color coded on the insulator, either as a solid color or as a colored wire with an identification stripe. A printed circuit is a thin film of copper or other conductor that is printed on an insulator backing. Occasionally, a printed circuit is sandwiched between two sheets of plastic for more protection and flexibility. A complete printed circuit, consisting of conductors, insulating material and connectors for lamps or other components is called a printed circuit board. Printed circuitry is used in place of individual wires or harnesses in places where space is limited, such as behind instrument panels.

WIRE GAUGE

Since computer controlled automotive electrical systems are very sensitive to changes in resistance, the selection of properly sized wires is critical when systems are repaired. The wire gauge number is an expression of the cross section area of the conductor. The most common system for expressing wire size is the American Wire Gauge (AWG) system.

Wire cross section area is measured in circular mils. A mil is 0.001 in.; a circular mil is the area of a circle one mil in diameter. For example, a conductor ¼ inch in diameter is 0.250 in. or 250 mils. The circular mil cross section area of the wire is 250 squared, or 62,500 circular mils. Imported car models usually use metric wire gauge designations, which is simply the cross section area of the conductor in square millimeters.

Gauge numbers are assigned to conductors of various cross section areas. As gauge number increases, area decreases and the conductor becomes smaller. A 5 gauge conductor is smaller than a 1 gauge conductor and a 10 gauge is smaller than a 5 gauge. As the cross section area of a conductor decreases, resistance increases and so does the gauge number. A conductor with a higher gauge number will carry less current than a conductor with a lower gauge number.

➡Gauge wire size refers to the size of the conductor, not the size of the complete wire. It is possible to have two wires of the same gauge with different diameters because one may have thicker insulation than the other.

12 volt automotive electrical systems generally use 10, 12, 14, 16 and 18 gauge wire. Main power distribution circuits and larger accessories usually use 10 and 12 gauge wire. Battery cables are usually 4 or 6 gauge, although 1 and 2 gauge wires are occasionally used. Wire length must also be considered when making repairs to a circuit. As conductor length increases, so does resistance. An 18 gauge wire, for example, can carry a 10 amp load for 10 feet without excessive voltage drop; however if a 15 foot wire is required for the same 10 amp load, it must be a 16 gauge wire.

An electrical schematic shows the electrical current paths when a circuit is operating properly. It is essential to understand how a circuit works before trying to figure out why it does not work. Schematics break the entire electrical system down into individual circuits and show only one particular circuit. In a schematic, no attempt is made to represent wiring and components as they physically appear on the vehicle; switches and other components are shown as simply as possible. Face views of harness connectors show the cavity or terminal locations in all multi-pin connectors to help locate test points.

If you need to backprobe a connector while it is on the component, the order of the terminals must be mentally reversed. The wire color code can help in this situation, as well as a keyway, lock tab or other reference mark.

WIRING REPAIR

Soldering is a quick, efficient method of joining metals permanently. Everyone who has the occasion to make wiring repairs should know how to solder. Electrical connections that are soldered are far less likely to come apart and will conduct electricity much better than connections that are only "pig-tailed" together. The most popular (and preferred) method of soldering is with an electrical soldering gun. Soldering irons are available in many sizes and wattage ratings. Irons with higher wattage ratings deliver higher temperatures and recover lost heat faster. A small soldering iron rated for no more than 50 watts is recommended, especially on electrical systems where excess heat can damage the components being soldered.

There are three ingredients necessary for successful soldering; proper flux, good solder and sufficient heat. A soldering flux is necessary to clean the metal of tarnish, prepare it for soldering and to enable the solder to spread into tiny crevices. When soldering, always use a resin flux or resin core solder which is non-corrosive and will not attract moisture once the job is finished. Other types of flux (acid core) will leave a residue that will attract moisture and cause the wires to corrode. Tin is a unique metal with a low melting point. In a molten state, it dissolves and alloys easily with many metals. Solder is made by mixing tin with lead. The most common proportions are 40/60, 50/50 and 60/40, with the percentage of tin listed first. Low priced solders usually contain less tin, making them very difficult for a beginner to use because more heat is required to melt the solder. A common solder is 40/60 which is well suited for all-around general use, but 60/40 melts easier, has more tin for a better joint and is preferred for electrical work.

Soldering Techniques

Successful soldering requires that the metals to be joined be heated to a temperature that will melt the solder — usually 360-460°F (182-238°C). Contrary to popular belief, the purpose of the soldering iron is not to melt the solder itself, but to heat the parts being soldered to a temperature high enough to melt the solder when it is touched to the work. Melting flux-cored solder on the soldering iron will usually destroy the effectiveness of the flux.

➡**Soldering tips are made of copper for good heat conductivity, but must be 'tinned" regularly for quick transference of heat to the project and to prevent the solder from sticking to the iron. To 'tin" the iron, simply heat it and touch the flux-cored solder to the tip; the solder will flow over the hot tip. Wipe the excess off with a clean rag, but be careful as the iron will be hot.**

After some use, the tip may become pitted. If so, simply dress the tip smooth with a smooth file and "tin" the tip again. An old saying holds that "metals well cleaned are half soldered." Flux-cored solder will remove oxides but rust, bits of insulation and oil or grease must be removed with a wire brush or emery cloth. For maximum strength in soldered parts, the joint must start off clean and tight. Weak joints will result in gaps too wide for the solder to bridge.

If a separate soldering flux is used, it should be brushed or swabbed on only those areas that are to be soldered. Most solders contain a core of flux and separate fluxing is unnecessary. Hold the work to be soldered firmly. It is best to solder on a wooden board, because a metal vise will only rob the piece to be soldered of heat and make it difficult to melt the solder. Hold the soldering tip with the broadest face against the work to be soldered. Apply solder under the tip close to the work, using enough solder to give a heavy film between the iron and the piece being soldered, while moving slowly and making sure the solder melts properly. Keep the work level or the solder will run to the lowest part and favor the thicker parts, because these require more heat to melt the solder. If the soldering tip overheats (the solder coating on the face of the tip burns up), it should be retinned. Once the soldering is completed, let the soldered joint stand until cool. Tape and seal all soldered wire splices after the repair has cooled.

Wire Harness and Connectors

The on-board computer wire harness electrically connects the control unit to the various solenoids, switches and sensors used by the control system. Most connectors in the engine compartment or otherwise exposed to the elements are protected against moisture and dirt which could create oxidation and deposits on the terminals. This protection is important because of the very low voltage and current levels used by the computer and sensors. All connectors have a lock which secures the male and female terminals together, with a secondary lock holding the seal and terminal into the connector. Both terminal locks must be released when disconnecting the connectors.

These special connectors are weather-proof and all repairs require the use of a special terminal and the tool required to service it. This tool is used to remove the pin and sleeve terminals. If removal is attempted with an ordinary pick, there is a good chance that the terminal will be bent or deformed. Unlike standard blade type terminals, these terminals cannot be straightened once they are bent. Make certain that the connectors are properly seated and all of the sealing rings in place when connecting leads. On some models, a hinge-type flap provides a backup or secondary locking feature for the terminals. Most secondary locks are used to improve the connector reliability by retaining the terminals if the small terminal lock tangs are not positioned properly.

Molded-on connectors require complete replacement of the connection. This means splicing a new connector assembly into the harness. All splices in on-board computer systems should be soldered to insure proper contact. Use care when probing the connections or replacing terminals in them as it is possible to short between opposite terminals. If this happens to the wrong terminal pair, it is possible to damage certain components. Always use jumper wires between connectors for circuit checking and never probe through weatherproof seals.

Open circuits are often difficult to locate by sight because corrosion or terminal misalignment are hidden by the connectors. Merely wiggling a connector on a sensor or in the wiring harness may correct the open circuit condition. This should always be considered when an open circuit or a failed sensor is indicated. Intermittent problems may also be caused by oxidized or loose connections. When using a circuit tester for diagnosis, always probe connections from the wire side. Be careful not to damage sealed connectors with test probes.

All wiring harnesses should be replaced with identical parts, using the same gauge wire and connectors. When signal wires are spliced into a harness, use wire with high temperature insulation only. With the low voltage and current levels found in the system, it is important that the best possible connection at all wire splices be made by soldering the splices together. It is seldom necessary to replace a complete harness. If replacement is necessary, pay close attention to insure proper harness routing. Secure the harness with suitable plastic wire clamps to prevent vibrations from causing the harness to wear in spots or contact any hot components.

➡**Weatherproof connectors cannot be replaced with standard connectors. Instructions are provided with replacement connector and terminal packages. Some wire harnesses have mounting indicators (usually pieces of colored tape) to mark where the harness is to be secured.**

In making wiring repairs, it's important that you always replace damaged wires with wires that are the same gauge as the wire being replaced. The heavier the wire, the smaller the gauge number. Wires are color-coded to aid in identification and whenever possible the same color coded wire should be used for replacement. A wire stripping and crimping tool is necessary to install terminal connectors. Test all crimps by pulling on the wires; it should not be possible to pull the wires out of a good crimp.

Wires which are open, exposed or otherwise damaged are repaired by simple splicing. Where possible, if the wiring harness is accessible and the damaged place in the wire can be located, it is best to open the harness and check for all possible damage. In an inaccessible harness, the wire must be bypassed with a new insert, usually taped to the outside of the old harness.

When replacing fusible links, be sure to use fusible link wire, NOT ordinary automotive wire. Make sure the fusible segment is of the same gauge and construction as the one being replaced and double the stripped end when crimping the terminal connector for a good contact. The melted (open) fusible link segment of the wiring harness should be cut off as close to the harness as possible, then a new segment spliced in as described. In the case of a damaged fusible link that feeds two harness wires, the harness connections should be replaced with two fusible link wires so that each circuit will have its own separate protection.

➡Most of the problems caused in the wiring harness are due to bad ground connections. Always check all vehicle ground connections for corrosion or looseness before performing any power feed checks to eliminate the chance of a bad ground affecting the circuit.

Repairing Hard Shell Connectors

Unlike molded connectors, the terminal contacts in hard shell connectors can be replaced. Weatherproof hard-shell connectors with the leads molded into the shell have non-replaceable terminal ends. Replacement usually involves the use of a special terminal removal tool that depress the locking tangs (barbs) on the connector terminal and allow the connector to be removed from the rear of the shell. The connector shell should be replaced if it shows any evidence of burning, melting, cracks, or breaks. Replace individual terminals that are burnt, corroded, distorted or loose.

➡The insulation crimp must be tight to prevent the insulation from sliding back on the wire when the wire is pulled. The insulation must be visibly compressed under the crimp tabs, and the ends of the crimp should be turned in for a firm grip on the insulation.

The wire crimp must be made with all wire strands inside the crimp. The terminal must be fully compressed on the wire strands with the ends of the crimp tabs turned in to make a firm grip on the wire. Check all connections with an ohmmeter to insure a good contact. There should be no measurable resistance between the wire and the terminal when connected.

Mechanical Test Equipment

VACUUM GAUGE

Most gauges are graduated in inches of mercury (in. Hg), although a device called a manometer reads vacuum in inches of water (in. H_2O). The normal vacuum reading usually varies between 18 and 22 in. Hg at sea level. To test engine vacuum, the vacuum gauge must be connected to a source of manifold vacuum. Many engines have a plug in the intake manifold which can be removed and replaced with an adapter fitting. Connect the vacuum gauge to the fitting with a suitable rubber hose or, if no manifold plug is available, connect the vacuum gauge to any device using manifold vacuum, such as EGR valves, etc. The vacuum gauge can be used to determine if enough vacuum is reaching a component to allow its actuation.

HAND VACUUM PUMP

Small, hand-held vacuum pumps come in a variety of designs. Most have a built-in vacuum gauge and allow the component to be tested without removing it from the vehicle. Operate the pump lever or plunger to apply the correct amount of vacuum required for the test specified in the diagnosis routines. The level of vacuum in inches of Mercury (in. Hg) is indicated on the pump gauge. For some testing, an additional vacuum gauge may be necessary.

Intake manifold vacuum is used to operate various systems and devices on late model vehicles. To correctly diagnose and solve problems in vacuum control systems, a vacuum source is necessary for testing. In some cases, vacuum can be taken from the intake manifold when the engine is running, but vacuum is normally provided by a hand vacuum pump. These hand vacuum pumps have a built-in vacuum gauge that allow testing while the device is still attached to the component. For some tests, an additional vacuum gauge may be necessary.

SUPPLEMENTAL INFLATABLE RESTRAINT SYSTEM

General Information

The Supplemental Inflatable Restraint (SIR) system offers protection in addition to that provided by the seat belt by deploying an air bag from the center of the steering wheel and (if equipped with passenger side air bag) from the top of the right side of the instrument panel. The air bag(s) deploy when the vehicle is involved in a frontal crash of sufficient force up to 30° off the centerline of the vehicle.

The system has an energy reserve, which can store a large enough electrical charge to deploy the air bag(s) for up to 10 minutes after the battery has been disconnected or damaged. The system **MUST** be disabled before any service is performed on or around SIR components or SIR wiring.

SYSTEM OPERATION

The SIR system contains a deployment loop for each air bag and a Diagnostic Energy Reserve Module (DERM). The deployment loop supplies current through the inflator module which will cause air bag deployment in the event of a frontal collision of sufficient force. The DERM supplies the necessary power, even if the battery has been damaged.

The deployment loop is made up of the arming sensors, coil assembly (driver's side only), inflator module and the discriminating sensors. The inflator module is only supplied sufficient current to deploy the air bag when the arming sensor and at least one of the discriminating sensors close simultaneously. The function of the DERM is to supply the deployment loop a 36 Volt Loop Reserve (36VLR) to assure sufficient voltage to deploy the air bag if ignition voltage is lost in a frontal crash.

The DERM, in conjunction with the sensor resistors, make it possible to detect circuit and component malfunctions within the deployment loop. If the voltages monitored by the DERM fall outside expected limits, the DERM will indicate a malfunction by storing a diagnostic trouble code and illuminating the INFLATABLE RESTRAINT lamp.

SYSTEM COMPONENTS

▶ **See Figures 1 and 2**

Diagnostic Energy Reserve Module (DERM)

The DERM is designed to perform 5 main functions: energy reserve, malfunction detection, malfunction recording, driver notification and frontal crash recording.

The DERM maintains a reserve voltage supply to provide deployment energy for a few seconds when the vehicle voltage is low or lost in a frontal crash. The DERM performs diagnostic monitoring of the SIR system and records malfunctions in the form of diagnostic trouble codes, which can be obtained from a hand scan tool and/or on-board diagnostics. The DERM warns the driver of SIR system malfunctions by controlling the INFLATABLE RESTRAINT warning lamp and records SIR system status during a frontal crash.

Inflatable Restraint Indicator

The INFLATABLE RESTRAINT indicator lamp is used to verify lamp and DERM operation by flashing 7-9 times when the ignition is first turned **ON**. It is also used to warn the driver of an SIR system malfunction.

Discriminating Sensors

Vehicles equipped with driver's side air bag only, have 2 discriminating sensors; the forward discriminating sensor and the passenger compartment discriminating sensor. The forward discriminating sensor is located in front of the radiator. The passenger compartment discriminating sensor is located behind the right side of the instrument panel.

There are 3 discriminating sensors used on vehicles with both driver's and passenger's side air bags; the forward discriminating sensor, the right-hand discriminating sensor and the

left-hand discriminating sensor. The forward sensor is located in front of the radiator while the left and right sensors are located in the engine compartment, on the left and right siderails, inboard of the wheelwells and forward of the strut towers.

The discriminating sensor consists of a sensing element, diagnostic resistor (except left-hand sensor) and normally open switch contacts. The sensing element closes the switch contacts when vehicle velocity changes are severe enough to warrant air bag deployment.

Arming Sensor

The arming sensor in single air bag vehicles is contained in the same housing as the passenger compartment discriminating sensor and is referred to as the dual sensor. The arming sensor in a dual air bag vehicle is known as the dual pole arming sensor and is located behind the right side of the instrument panel.

The arming sensor is a switch located in the power side of the deployment loop. It is calibrated to close at low level velocity changes (lower than the discriminating sensors), assuring that the inflator module(s) is connected directly to the 36VLR output of the DERM or Ignition 1 voltage when any discriminating sensor closes.

SIR Coil Assembly

The SIR coil assembly consists of 2 current carrying coils. They are attached to the steering column and allow rotation of the steering wheel while maintaining continuous deployment loop contact through the inflator module.

There is a shorting bar on the lower steering column connector that connects the SIR coil to the SIR wiring harness. The shorting bar shorts the circuit when the connector is disconnected. The circuit to the inflator module is shorted in this way to prevent unwanted air bag deployment when servicing the steering column or other SIR components.

Inflator Module

The inflator module consists of an inflatable bag and an inflator (a canister of gas-generating material and an initiating device). When the vehicle is in a frontal crash of sufficient force to close the arming sensor and at least one discriminating sensor simultaneously, current flows through the deployment loop(s). Current passing through the initiator ignites the material in the inflator module(s), causing a reaction which produces a gas that rapidly inflates the air bag(s).

All vehicles are equipped with an inflator module located in the steering wheel. Vehicles with dual air bags are also equipped with an inflator module located at the top of the right side of the instrument panel.

SERVICE PRECAUTIONS

• When performing service around SIR system components or wiring, the SIR system must be disabled. Failure to do so could result in possible air bag deployment, personal injury or unneeded SIR system repairs.

• When carrying a live inflator module, make sure that the bag and trim cover are pointed away from you. Never carry the inflator module by the wires or connector on the underside

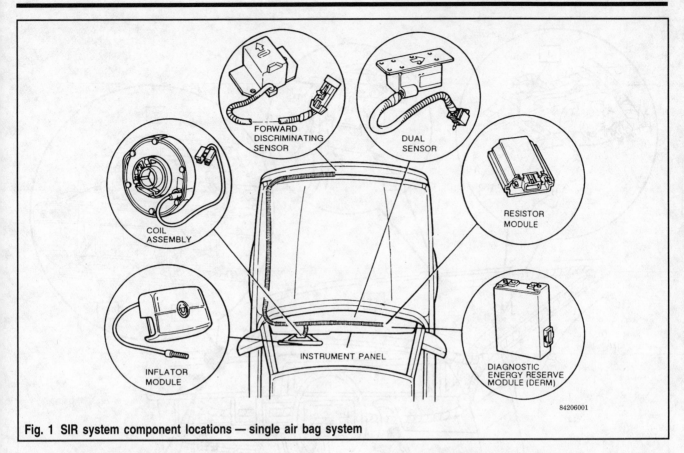

Fig. 1 SIR system component locations — single air bag system

of the module. In case of accidental deployment, the bag will then deploy with minimal chance of injury.

• When placing a live inflator module on a bench or other surface, always face the bag and trim cover up, away from the surface.

DISARMING THE SYSTEM

▶ **See Figures 3, 4 and 5**

1. Disconnect the negative battery cable.
2. Make sure the ignition switch is **OFF**.
3. Remove the SIR fuse. On 1990 Deville and Fleetwood, remove SIR fuse No. 3 from the fuse panel. On 1991-93 Deville, Fleetwood and Sixty Special, remove SIR fuse No. 18 from the fuse panel. On 1990-91 Eldorado and Seville, remove SIR fuse No. 19 from the fuse panel. On 1992-93 Eldorado and Seville, remove SIR fuse No. A11 from the engine compartment fuse panel.
4. On Deville, Fleetwood and Sixty Special, remove the left lower sound insulator. On Eldorado and Seville, remove the left side sound insulator.
5. Remove the Connector Position Assurance (CPA) and disconnect the yellow 2-way connector at the base of the steering column.
6. If equipped with a passenger side air bag, access the passenger inflator module connector through the "trap" door in

the instrument panel glove box. Remove the CPA and disconnect the yellow 2-way connector.
7. Connect the negative battery cable.

ENABLING THE SYSTEM

▶ **See Figures 3, 4 and 5**

1. Disconnect the negative battery cable.
2. Make sure the ignition switch is **OFF**.
3. If equipped with a passenger's side air bag, connect the yellow 2-way inflator module connector and install the CPA. Reposition the connector through the "trap" door in the glove box.
4. Connect the yellow 2-way connector at the base of the steering column and install the CPA.
5. On Deville, Fleetwood and Sixty Special, install the left lower sound insulator. On Eldorado and Seville, install the left side sound insulator.
6. Install the SIR fuse.
7. Connect the negative battery cable.
8. Turn the ignition switch to **RUN**. Verify that the INFLATABLE RESTRAINT indicator lamp flashes 7-9 times and then remains OFF. If the lamp does not function as specified, there is a malfunction in the SIR system.

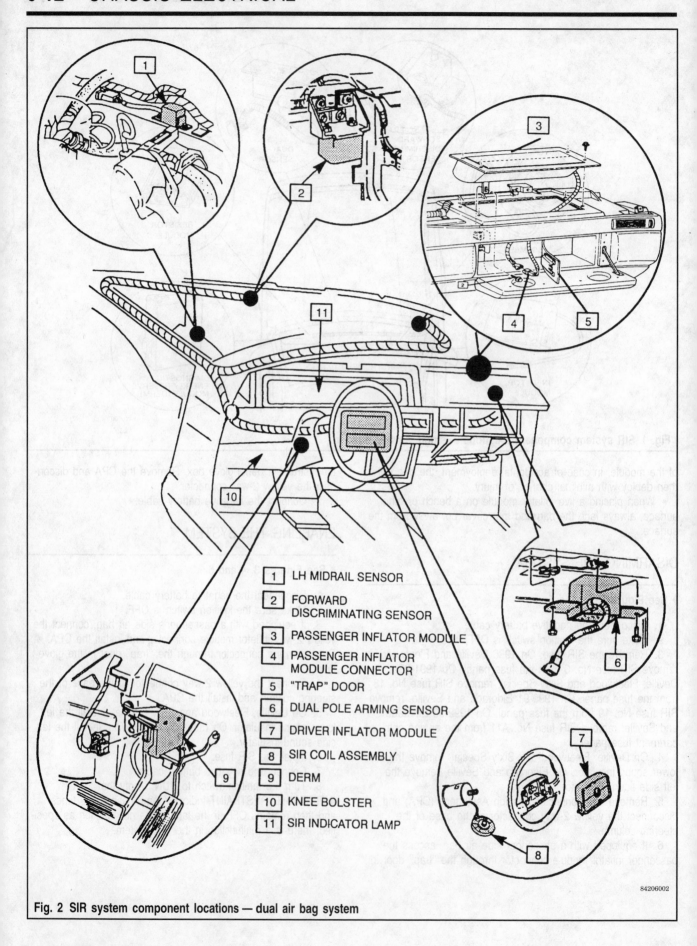

1	LH MIDRAIL SENSOR
2	FORWARD DISCRIMINATING SENSOR
3	PASSENGER INFLATOR MODULE
4	PASSENGER INFLATOR MODULE CONNECTOR
5	"TRAP" DOOR
6	DUAL POLE ARMING SENSOR
7	DRIVER INFLATOR MODULE
8	SIR COIL ASSEMBLY
9	DERM
10	KNEE BOLSTER
11	SIR INDICATOR LAMP

84206002

Fig. 2 SIR system component locations — dual air bag system

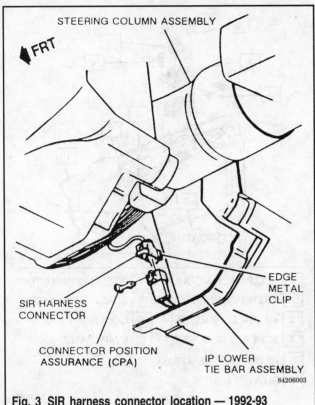

Fig. 3 SIR harness connector location — 1992-93 Deville, Fleetwood and Sixty Special

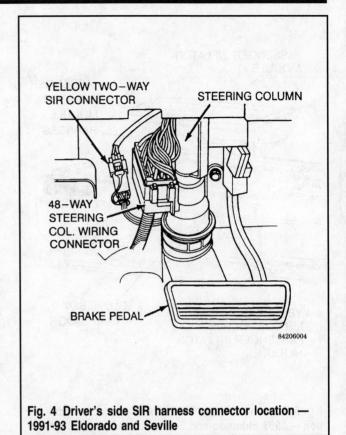

Fig. 4 Driver's side SIR harness connector location — 1991-93 Eldorado and Seville

HEATER AND AIR CONDITIONER

Blower Motor

REMOVAL & INSTALLATION

Deville, Fleetwood and Sixty Special

▶ See Figure 6

1. Disconnect the negative battery cable.
2. On 1992-93 vehicles, remove the nuts and the cross brace bar.
3. Disconnect the wiring connector and the cooling tube from the blower motor.
4. Remove the blower motor mounting screws and remove the blower motor and fan assembly.

To install:

5. Position the blower motor and fan assembly and install the mounting screws. Tighten to 5 inch lbs. (0.6 Nm).
6. Connect the cooling tube and wiring connector to the blower motor.
7. If equipped, install the cross brace bar and nuts and tighten to 18 ft. lbs. (25 Nm).
8. Connect the negative battery cable.

Eldorado and Seville

1990-92

▶ See Figure 7

1. Disconnect the negative battery cable.
2. Remove 2 nuts from each side and remove the cowl cross-tower brace.
3. Remove the 2 cowl relay center bracket mounting nuts and position the cowl relay center aside.
4. Disconnect the wiring connector and the cooling tube from the blower motor and remove the blower motor mounting screws.
5. Remove the MAP sensor mounting bracket and position aside.
6. Tilt the blower motor in the case and remove the fan from the blower motor.
7. Remove the blower motor from the case.
8. Remove the fan from the case.

To install:

9. Install the fan into the case.
10. Position the blower motor into the case, then install the fan onto the blower motor.
11. Install the MAP sensor mounting bracket.
12. Install the blower motor mounting screws and connect the cooling hose and wiring connector.
13. Position the cowl relay center and install the cowl relay center bracket nuts.

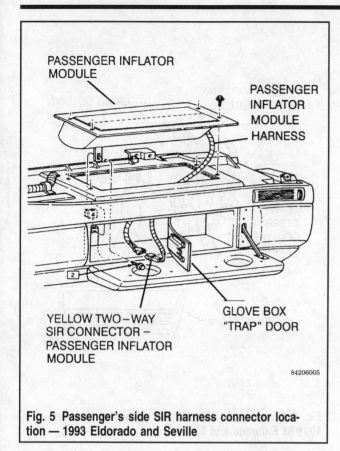

Fig. 5 Passenger's side SIR harness connector location — 1993 Eldorado and Seville

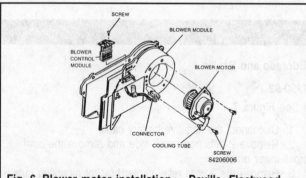

Fig. 6 Blower motor installation — Deville, Fleetwood and Sixty Special

14. Install the cowl cross-tower brace and secure with 2 nuts on each side.

15. Connect the negative battery cable.

1993

▶ **See Figure 7**

1. Disconnect the negative battery cable.

2. Remove 2 nuts from each side and remove the cowl cross-tower brace.

3. Using a utility knife, cut the rubber insulator at the guide lines and remove the metal patch plate beneath.

4. Disconnect the wiring connector and the cooling tube from the blower motor.

5. Remove the blower motor mounting screws and remove the blower motor and fan assembly.

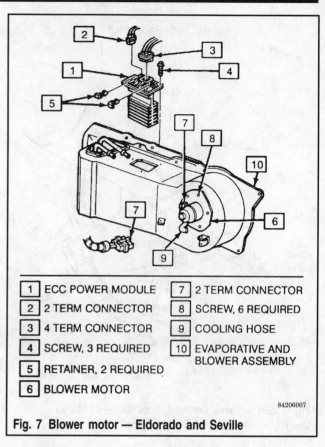

1	ECC POWER MODULE	7	2 TERM CONNECTOR
2	2 TERM CONNECTOR	8	SCREW, 6 REQUIRED
3	4 TERM CONNECTOR	9	COOLING HOSE
4	SCREW, 3 REQUIRED	10	EVAPORATIVE AND BLOWER ASSEMBLY
5	RETAINER, 2 REQUIRED		
6	BLOWER MOTOR		

Fig. 7 Blower motor — Eldorado and Seville

To install:

6. Install the blower motor and fan assembly and secure with the mounting screws.

7. Connect the cooling hose and wiring connector.

8. Install the patch plate and seal the insulator.

9. Install the cowl cross-tower brace and secure with 2 nuts on each side.

10. Connect the negative battery cable.

Heater Core

REMOVAL & INSTALLATION

Deville, Fleetwood and Sixty Special

▶ **See Figure 8**

1. Disconnect the negative battery cable.

2. Drain the cooling system.

✳✳CAUTION

When draining the coolant, keep in mind that cats and dogs are attracted by the ethylene glycol antifreeze, and are quite likely to drink any that is left in an uncovered container or in puddles on the ground. This will prove fatal in sufficient quantity. Always drain the coolant into a sealable container.

3. Disconnect the heater core hoses using tool J-37097 or equivalent.

4. Remove the right side sound insulator and the glove box module. If necessary, refer to the instrument panel removal and installation procedure in Section 10.

5. Remove the programmer shield, if equipped, and disconnect the air mix valve link.

6. Disconnect the programmer vacuum and electrical connectors.

7. Remove the heater core cover, leaving the programmer attached.

8. Remove the heater core retaining screws and the heater core.

To install:

9. Position the heater core and secure with the retaining screws.

10. Install the heater core cover.

11. Connect the programmer vacuum and electrical connectors.

12. Connect the air mix valve link and, if equipped, install the programmer shield.

13. Connect the heater core hoses.

14. Connect the negative battery cable and fill the cooling system.

15. Adjust the air mix valve as follows:

a. Set the temperature on the heater and A/C control panel to 90°F (32°C). Allow 1-2 minutes for the programmer arm to travel to the maximum heat position.

b. Unsnap the threaded rod from the plastic retainer on the programmer output arm.

c. Check the air mix valve for free travel. Push the valve to the maximum A/C position and check for binding.

d. Preload the air mix valve in the maximum heat position by pulling the threaded rod to ensure the valve is sealing. The programmer output arm should be in the maximum heat position.

e. Snap the threaded rod into the plastic retainer on the programmer arm. Avoid moving the programmer arm or air mix valve.

f. Set the temperature on the control panel to 60°F (16°C). Verify that the programmer arm and the air mix valve travel to the maximum cold position.

16. Install the right side sound insulator and the glove box module.

Eldorado and Seville

♦ **See Figures 9, 10 and 11**

1. Disconnect the negative battery cable.

2. Partially drain the cooling system.

✳✳CAUTION

When draining the coolant, keep in mind that cats and dogs are attracted by the ethylene glycol antifreeze, and are quite likely to drink any that is left in an uncovered container or in puddles on the ground. This will prove fatal in sufficient quantity. Always drain the coolant into a sealable container.

3. Remove the glove box unit and right side lower sound insulator. If necessary, refer to the instrument panel removal and installation procedure in Section 10.

4. Remove the programmer as follows:

a. Remove the 2 PCM bracket screws. Position the PCM aside to gain access to the rear programmer mounting screw.

b. Disconnect the threaded rod from the programmer.

c. Remove the vacuum connector retaining nut.

d. Disconnect the vacuum and wiring connectors from the programmer.

e. Remove the 3 screws and the programmer.

5. On 1990-91 vehicles, proceed as follows:

a. Disconnect the wiring connectors from the BCM and remove the BCM and mounting bracket.

b. Disconnect the wiring connectors from the PCM and remove the PCM and mounting bracket.

6. Remove the heater core cover.

7. Disconnect the heater hoses from the heater core.

8. Remove the 2 heater core retaining screws and remove the heater core.

To install:

9. Install the heater core to the heater case and secure with the 2 screws.

10. Connect the heater hoses to the heater core.

11. Install the heater core cover.

12. On 1990-91 vehicles, proceed as follows:

a. Install the PCM mounting bracket and PCM. Connect the wiring connectors to the PCM.

b. Install the BCM mounting bracket and BCM. Connect the wiring connectors to the BCM.

13. Install the programmer as follows:

a. Install the programmer in the vehicle and connect the vacuum and wiring connectors.

b. Install the vacuum connector retaining nut.

c. Connect the threaded rod to the programmer.

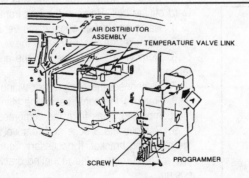
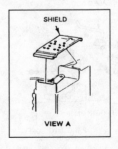

84206008

Fig. 8 Programmer assembly and temperature valve linkage — Deville, Fleetwood and Sixty Special

d. Return the PCM to its original position and secure with the 2 bracket screws.

14. Connect the negative battery cable and fill the cooling system.

15. Adjust the air mix valve as follows:

a. Set the temperature on the heater and A/C control panel to 90°F (32°C). Allow 1-2 minutes for the programmer arm to travel to the maximum heat position.

b. Unsnap the threaded rod from the plastic retainer on the programmer output arm.

c. Check the air mix valve for free travel. Push the valve to the maximum A/C position and check for binding.

d. Preload the air mix valve in the maximum heat position by pulling the threaded rod to ensure the valve is sealing. The programmer output arm should be in the maximum heat position.

e. Snap the threaded rod into the plastic retainer on the programmer arm. Avoid moving the programmer arm or air mix valve.

f. Set the temperature on the control panel to 60°F (16°C). Verify that the programmer arm and the air mix valve travel to the maximum cold position.

16. Install the right side lower sound insulator and the glove box unit.

Compressor

REMOVAL & INSTALLATION

Deville, Fleetwood and Sixty Special
▶ See Figures 12, 13 and 14

1. Disconnect the negative battery cable.
2. Discharge the refrigerant from the system according to the proper procedure.
3. Remove the serpentine belt.
4. Raise and safely support the vehicle.
5. Remove the 3 compressor splash shield screws and the splash shield.
6. Remove the 4 right engine splash shield retainers and the splash shield.
7. Disconnect the compressor wiring connectors.
8. Remove the compressor hose assembly bolt and the hose assembly. Cap the openings to prevent the entrance of air, dirt or moisture into the system.

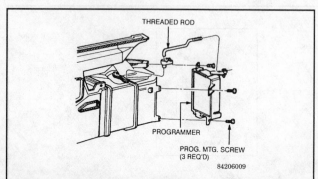

THREADED ROD

PROGRAMMER

PROG. MTG. SCREW
(3 REQ'D)

84206009

Fig. 9 Air conditioning programmer — Eldorado and Seville

9. Loosen the AIR pump-to-compressor brace bolt one turn.
10. Remove the compressor mounting bolts and the compressor.
11. Remove the compressor port O-rings.
12. Drain the oil from the compressor into a clean measuring container.
13. Remove the compressor mounting bracket bolts and brackets, as necessary.

To install:

14. If the compressor is to be replaced, drain the oil from the new compressor.
15. If removed, install the necessary brackets to the compressor. Tighten the front compressor-to-mounting bracket bolts to 32 ft. lbs. (44 Nm) and the rear compressor-to-mounting bracket bolts to 23 ft. lbs. (31 Nm). Tighten the mounting brace-to-compressor bolts to 29 ft. lbs. (39 Nm).
16. Install new compressor port O-rings.
17. Install the compressor. Tighten the front compressor mounting bracket bolts to 32 ft. lbs. (44 Nm) and the rear compressor mounting bracket bolts to 23 ft. lbs. (31 Nm).
18. Tighten the AIR pump-to-compressor brace bolt.
19. Connect the compressor hose assembly and tighten the hose assembly bolt to 24 ft. lbs. (33 Nm).
20. Connect the compressor wiring connectors.
21. Install the right engine splash shield with the 4 right engine splash shield retainers.
22. Install the compressor splash shield with the 3 compressor splash shield screws.
23. Lower the vehicle.
24. Install the serpentine belt.
25. Disconnect the suction line from the accumulator. If more than one fl. oz. (30ml) of refrigerant oil was drained from the compressor during the removal procedure, add the same amount of new refrigerant oil to the suction line. If less than one fl. oz. (30ml) of refrigerant oil was drained from the compressor during the removal procedure, add 2 fl. oz. (60ml) of new refrigerant oil to the suction line.
26. Reconnect the suction line to the accumulator.
27. Connect the negative battery cable. Leak test, evacuate and charge the system according to the proper procedure.

Eldorado and Seville
▶ See Figures 15, 16, 17 and 18

1. Disconnect the negative battery cable.
2. Discharge the refrigerant from the system according to the proper procedure.
3. Using a wrench, rotate the serpentine belt tensioner upward off the belt. Remove the belt from all components.
4. Raise and safely support the vehicle.
5. Remove the 3 screws and the compressor splash shield.
6. Remove the 3 screws and the engine splash shield and retainer.
7. Disconnect the compressor wiring connector.
8. Remove the compressor line fitting bolt and disconnect the compressor lines from the compressor.
9. Remove the 3 bolts and remove the compressor from the mounting bracket. If necessary, remove the 3 bolts and one nut and remove the mounting bracket and brace from the engine.
10. Drain the oil from the compressor into a clean measuring container.

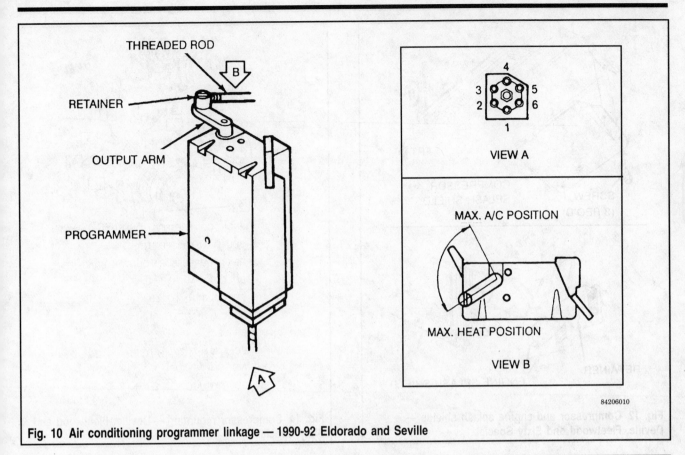

THREADED ROD

RETAINER

OUTPUT ARM

PROGRAMMER

B

VIEW A

MAX. A/C POSITION

MAX. HEAT POSITION

VIEW B

84206010

Fig. 10 Air conditioning programmer linkage — 1990-92 Eldorado and Seville

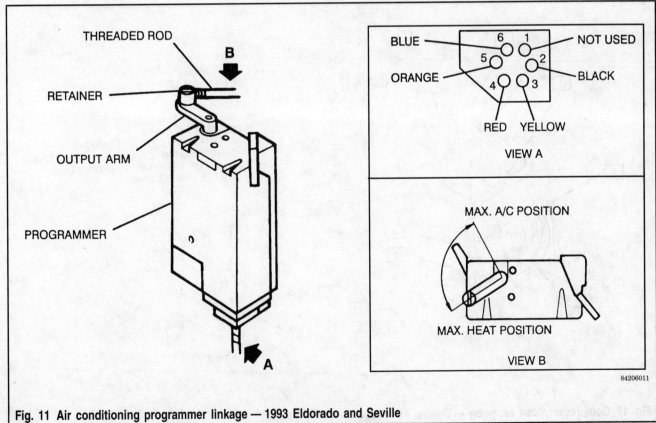

THREADED ROD

RETAINER

OUTPUT ARM

PROGRAMMER

B

A

BLUE

NOT USED

ORANGE

BLACK

RED   YELLOW

VIEW A

MAX. A/C POSITION

MAX. HEAT POSITION

VIEW B

84206011

Fig. 11 Air conditioning programmer linkage — 1993 Eldorado and Seville

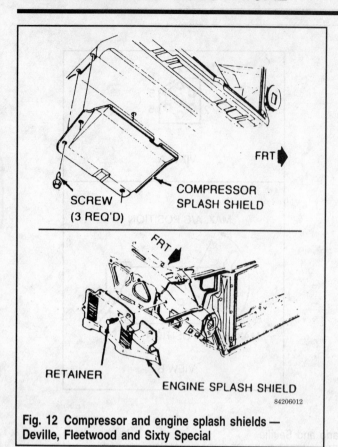

SCREW
(3 REQ'D)

COMPRESSOR
SPLASH SHIELD

FRT

RETAINER

ENGINE SPLASH SHIELD

84206012

Fig. 12 Compressor and engine splash shields — Deville, Fleetwood and Sixty Special

FRT

1. FRONT COMPRESSOR MOUNTING BRACKET
2. BOLT: 44 N•M (32 LB-FT)
3. REAR COMPRESSOR MOUNTING BRACKET
4. BOLT: 31 N•M (23 LB-FT)
5. BOLT (2): 31 N•M (23 LB-FT)
6. BOLT: 31 N•M (23 LB-FT)
7. BRACE
8. BOLT: 39 N•M (29 LB-FT)
9. A/C COMPRESSOR
10. BOLT: 4 N•M (32 LB-FT)

84206014

Fig. 14 Compressor mounting — Deville, Fleetwood and Sixty Special

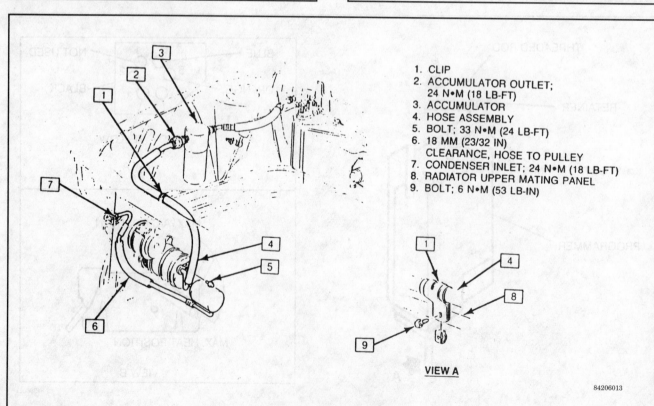

1. CLIP
2. ACCUMULATOR OUTLET;
   24 N•M (18 LB-FT)
3. ACCUMULATOR
4. HOSE ASSEMBLY
5. BOLT; 33 N•M (24 LB-FT)
6. 18 MM (23/32 IN)
   CLEARANCE, HOSE TO PULLEY
7. CONDENSER INLET; 24 N•M (18 LB-FT)
8. RADIATOR UPPER MATING PANEL
9. BOLT; 6 N•M (53 LB-IN)

VIEW A

84206013

Fig. 13 Compressor hose assembly — Deville, Fleetwood and Sixty Special

To install:

11. If the compressor is to be replaced, drain the oil from the new compressor.

12. If removed, install the compressor mounting bracket and brace to the engine. Tighten the brace bolts and nut to 25 ft. lbs. (34 Nm) and the bracket-to-engine bolts to 33 ft. lbs. (45 Nm).

13. Install the compressor. Tighten the lower rear compressor mounting bolt to 25 ft. lbs. (34 Nm) and the upper and front mounting bolts to 33 ft. lbs. (45 Nm).

14. Install a new O-ring/sealing washer and connect the compressor hoses. Tighten the compressor line fitting bolt to 24 ft. lbs. (33 Nm).

15. Connect the compressor wiring connector.

16. Install the compressor and engine splash shields and lower the vehicle.

17. Loosely install the serpentine drive belt, making sure it is properly aligned into the grooves of the accessory pulleys. Using a wrench, rotate the belt tensioner upward and thread the belt under the tensioner pulley. Return the tensioner to the normal position.

18. Disconnect the suction line from the accumulator. If more than one fl. oz. (30ml) of refrigerant oil was drained from the compressor during the removal procedure, add the same amount of new refrigerant oil to the suction line. If less than one fl. oz. (30ml) of refrigerant oil was drained from the compressor during the removal procedure, add 2 fl. oz. (60ml) of new refrigerant oil to the suction line.

19. Reconnect the suction line to the accumulator.

20. Connect the negative battery cable. Leak test, evacuate and charge the system according to the proper procedure.

Condenser

REMOVAL & INSTALLATION

Deville, Fleetwood and Sixty Special

1990

▶ See Figure 19

1. Disconnect the negative battery cable.

2. Discharge the refrigerant from the system according to the proper procedure.

3. Remove the cooling fans.

4. Remove the upper radiator mounting panel.

5. Remove the bolt that holds the transmission cooler lines to the lower radiator tie bar.

6. Move the radiator toward the engine, being careful not to damage the radiator.

7. Separate the transmission cooler lines at the rubber hoses near the radiator cap.

8. Disconnect the refrigerant lines from the condenser. Cap the openings to prevent the entrance of air, dirt or moisture into the system.

9. Remove the condenser mounting brackets and insulators. Tip the condenser toward the engine and remove it from the vehicle.

To install:

10. Position the condenser in the vehicle and install the insulators and mounting brackets. Tighten the mounting bracket bolts to 53 inch lbs. (6 Nm).

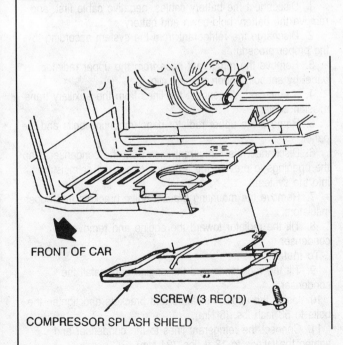

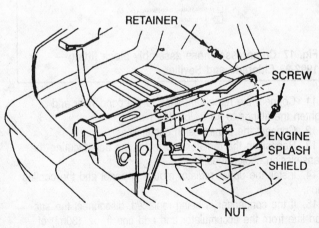

84206015

Fig. 15 Compressor and engine splash shields — Eldorado and Seville

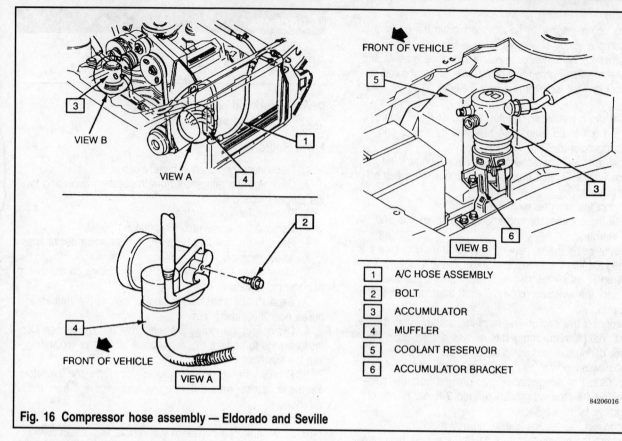

Fig. 16 Compressor hose assembly — Eldorado and Seville

1	A/C HOSE ASSEMBLY
2	BOLT
3	ACCUMULATOR
4	MUFFLER
5	COOLANT RESERVOIR
6	ACCUMULATOR BRACKET

84206016

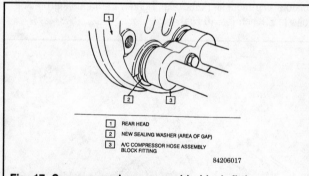

1	REAR HEAD
2	NEW SEALING WASHER (AREA OF GAP)
3	A/C COMPRESSOR HOSE ASSEMBLY BLOCK FITTING

84206017

Fig. 17 Compressor hose assembly block fitting — 1992-93 Eldorado and Seville

11. Connect the refrigerant lines to the condenser and tighten the fittings to 18 ft. lbs. (24 Nm).

12. Connect the transmission cooler lines.

13. Reposition the radiator and install the bolt securing the transmission cooler lines.

14. Install the upper radiator mounting panel and the cooling fans.

15. If the condenser is being replaced, disconnect the suction line from the accumulator and add one fl. oz. (30ml) of new refrigerant oil to the suction line. Reconnect the suction line to the accumulator.

16. Connect the negative battery cable. Leak test, evacuate and charge the system according to the proper procedure.

1991-93

▶ See Figure 20

1. Disconnect the battery cables, negative cable first, and remove the battery hold-down and battery.

2. Discharge the refrigerant from the system according to the proper procedure.

3. Remove the refrigerant hose from the upper radiator panel by snapping open the line clip.

4. If equipped, disconnect the lines from the auxiliary transmission cooler.

5. Remove the upper radiator panel mounting bolts and the panel.

6. Disconnect the refrigerant lines from the condenser. Cap the openings to prevent the entrance of air, dirt or moisture into the system.

7. Remove the mounting bracket bolts, brackets and upper insulators.

8. Tilt the radiator toward the engine and remove the condenser.

To install:

9. Tilt the radiator toward the engine and install the condenser.

10. Install the upper insulators and brackets and tighten the bolts to 53 inch lbs. (6 Nm).

11. Connect the refrigerant lines to the condenser and tighten the fittings to 18 ft. lbs. (24 Nm).

12. Install the upper radiator panel and tighten the bolts to 89 inch lbs. (10 Nm).

13. If equipped, connect the lines to the auxiliary transmission cooler.

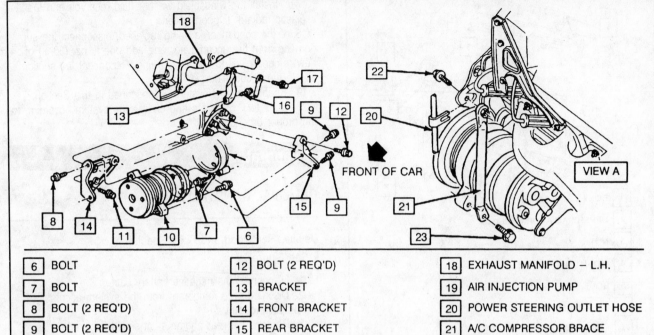

6	BOLT	12	BOLT (2 REQ'D)	18	EXHAUST MANIFOLD – L.H.
7	BOLT	13	BRACKET	19	AIR INJECTION PUMP
8	BOLT (2 REQ'D)	14	FRONT BRACKET	20	POWER STEERING OUTLET HOSE
9	BOLT (2 REQ'D)	15	REAR BRACKET	21	A/C COMPRESSOR BRACE
10	A/C COMPRESSOR ASSEMBLY	16	BOLT	22	BOLT
11	SCREW ASSEMBLY (2 REQ'D)	17	BOLT – EXHAUST MANIFOLD	23	BOLT

84206018

Fig. 18 Compressor installation — Eldorado and Seville

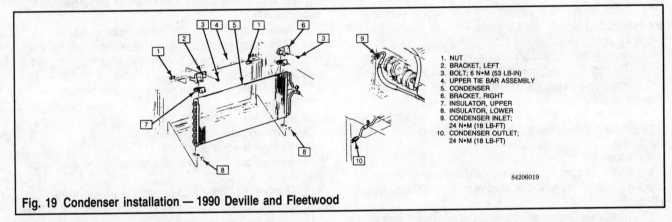

1. NUT
2. BRACKET, LEFT
3. BOLT; 6 N•M (53 LB-IN)
4. UPPER TIE BAR ASSEMBLY
5. CONDENSER
6. BRACKET, RIGHT
7. INSULATOR, UPPER
8. INSULATOR, LOWER
9. CONDENSER INLET;
   24 N•M (18 LB-FT)
10. CONDENSER OUTLET;
   24 N•M (18 LB-FT)

84206019

Fig. 19 Condenser installation — 1990 Deville and Fleetwood

14. Position the refrigerant line in the clip on the upper radiator panel and snap the clip closed.

15. If the condenser is being replaced, disconnect the suction line from the accumulator and add one fl. oz. (30ml) of new refrigerant oil to the suction line. Reconnect the suction line to the accumulator.

16. Install the battery and battery hold-down and connect the battery cables.

17. Leak test, evacuate and charge the system according to the proper procedure.

Eldorado and Seville

▶ See Figure 21

1. Disconnect the negative battery cable.

2. On 1993 vehicles, disable the Supplemental Inflatable Restraint (SIR) system as described in this Section.

3. Discharge the refrigerant from the system according to the proper procedure.

4. On 1993 vehicles with 4.6L engine, remove the SIR forward discriminating sensor as follows:

   a. Remove the plastic radiator support cover.

   b. Remove the windshield washer fluid reservoir.

   c. Remove the Connector Position Assurance (CPA) clip and disconnect the sensor wiring connector located along the left fender. Pull the harness through the radiator support brace.

   d. Use tool J-38597 or equivalent, to remove the 4 tamper resistant sensor retaining bolts, and remove the sensor from the bracket.

5. Remove the front engine torque struts.

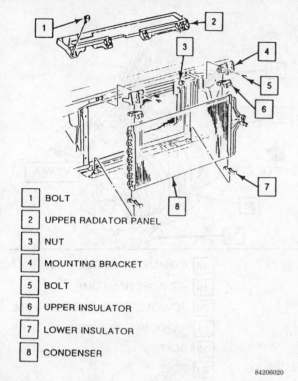

1	BOLT
2	UPPER RADIATOR PANEL
3	NUT
4	MOUNTING BRACKET
5	BOLT
6	UPPER INSULATOR
7	LOWER INSULATOR
8	CONDENSER

84206020

Fig. 20 Condenser installation — 1991-93 Deville, Fleetwood and Sixty Special

6. On all except 1993 vehicles with 4.6L engine, remove the rear cooling fan. On 1993 vehicles with 4.6L engine, remove the right and left cooling fans.

7. Remove the radiator upper support.

8. Disconnect the refrigerant lines from the condenser. Cap the openings to prevent the entrance of air, dirt or moisture into the system.

9. Remove the 2 screws and the refrigerant hose bracket.

10. Remove the condenser mounting brackets and the condenser.

To install:

11. Install the condenser in the vehicle with the mounting brackets. Tighten the mounting bracket bolts to 106 inch lbs. (12 Nm).

12. Install new O-rings and connect the refrigerant lines to the condenser, being careful not to nick the O-rings or cross-thread the connections. Tighten the fittings to 18 ft. lbs. (24 Nm).

13. Install the refrigerant hose bracket with the 2 screws.

14. Install the radiator upper support.

15. Install the cooling fan(s).

16. Install the front engine torque struts.

17. On 1993 vehicles with 4.6L engine, install the SIR forward discriminating sensor as follows:

a. Route the harness through the radiator support bracket and along the engine compartment rail.

b. Align the sensor to the vehicle bracket with the arrow pointing to the front of the vehicle.

c. Use tool J-38597 or equivalent, to install the 4 tamper resistant sensor retaining bolts, and tighten to 98 inch lbs. (11 Nm).

d. Connect the wiring connector and install the CPA.

e. Install the windshield washer fluid reservoir and the plastic radiator support cover.

18. If the condenser is being replaced, disconnect the suction line from the accumulator and add one fl. oz. (30ml) of new refrigerant oil to the suction line. Reconnect the suction line to the accumulator.

19. Enable the SIR system as described in this Section.

20. Leak test, evacuate and charge the system according to the proper procedure.

Evaporator

REMOVAL & INSTALLATION

Deville, Fleetwood and Sixty Special

▶ **See Figure 22**

1. Disconnect the negative battery cable.

2. Discharge the refrigerant from the system according to the proper procedure.

3. Remove the rear engine sight shield.

4. Remove the vacuum tank.

5. Disconnect the relay bracket and position aside.

6. Disconnect the accumulator refrigerant line from the evaporator. Cap the openings to prevent the entrance of air, dirt or moisture into the system.

7. Label and disconnect the wiring connectors from the A/C low side temperature sensor, blower motor and blower motor control module.

8. Remove the A/C low side temperature sensor.

9. Disconnect the condenser refrigerant line from the evaporator. Cap the openings to prevent the entrance of air, dirt or moisture into the system.

10. Remove the evaporator refrigerant lines bracket.

11. Remove the 4 bolts from the top of the evaporator module.

12. Raise and safely support the vehicle.

13. Remove the heat shield.

14. Remove the 3 bolts from the bottom of the evaporator module.

15. Remove the power module and the blower motor.

16. Cut the barrier insulator on the marked line and remove.

17. Lower the vehicle.

18. Remove the 4 screws retaining the evaporator shield and remove the shield.

19. Remove the evaporator.

To install:

20. Install the evaporator.

21. Install the evaporator shield and secure with the 4 screws.

22. Raise and safely support the vehicle.

23. Install the power module and blower motor.

24. Install the 3 bolts at the bottom of the evaporator module.

25. Install the heat shield and lower the vehicle.

26. Install the 4 bolts at the top of the evaporator module.

27. Install the evaporator refrigerant lines bracket.

28. Connect the condenser refrigerant line to the evaporator and tighten the fitting to 18 ft. lbs. (24 Nm).

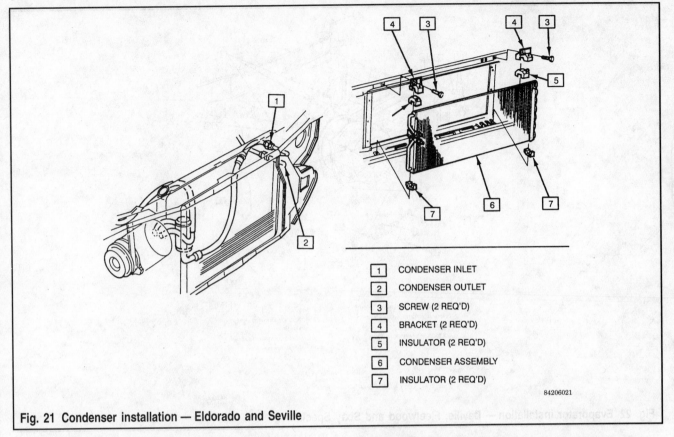

1	CONDENSER INLET
2	CONDENSER OUTLET
3	SCREW (2 REQ'D)
4	BRACKET (2 REQ'D)
5	INSULATOR (2 REQ'D)
6	CONDENSER ASSEMBLY
7	INSULATOR (2 REQ'D)

84206021

Fig. 21 Condenser installation — Eldorado and Seville

29. Install the A/C low side temperature sensor and tighten to 18 ft. lbs. (24 Nm).

30. Connect the wiring connectors to the A/C low side temperature sensor, blower motor and blower motor control module.

31. Connect the accumulator refrigerant line to the evaporator and tighten the fitting to 18 ft. lbs. (24 Nm).

32. Install the relay bracket, vacuum tank and rear engine sight shield.

33. If the evaporator is being replaced, disconnect the suction line from the accumulator and add 3 fl. oz. (90ml) of new refrigerant oil to the suction line. Reconnect the suction line to the accumulator.

34. Connect the negative battery cable. Leak test, evacuate and charge the system according to the proper procedure.

Eldorado and Seville

EXCEPT 1993 VEHICLES WITH 4.6L ENGINE

▶ See Figures 23 and 24

1. Disconnect the negative battery cable.
2. Discharge the refrigerant from the system according to the proper procedure.
3. Drain the cooling system.

✳✳CAUTION

When draining the coolant, keep in mind that cats and dogs are attracted by the ethylene glycol antifreeze, and are quite likely to drink any that is left in an uncovered

container or in puddles on the ground. This will prove fatal in sufficient quantity. Always drain the coolant into a sealable container.

4. Remove the 2 bolts from each side and remove the cross-tower support bracket.

5. Remove the 2 nuts securing the cowl relay center bracket and position the relay center aside.

6. Label and disconnect the wiring connectors from the power module, blower motor and blower motor resistor.

7. Disconnect the heater hoses from the heater core.

8. Remove the evaporator line retaining bracket. Disconnect the refrigerant lines from the evaporator and cap the openings to prevent the entrance of air, dirt or moisture into the system.

9. Remove the heater hose T-connector.

10. Remove the heat shield as follows:
    a. Remove the 2 screws in the engine compartment.
    b. Raise and safely support the vehicle.
    c. Remove the 2 screws from beneath the vehicle and remove the heat shield.

11. Remove the 2 A/C module retaining screws and lower the vehicle.

12. Remove the MAP sensor bracket.

13. Remove the valve from the right valve cover. Remove the 2 harness hold-down brackets from the valve cover.

14. Remove the retaining clips from the sound insulator.

15. Remove the power module and blower motor.

16. Remove the sound insulator.

17. Remove the A/C module cover screws and remove the module cover, sound insulator and seal.

18. Remove the evaporator retaining clamp and pull the evaporator from the case.

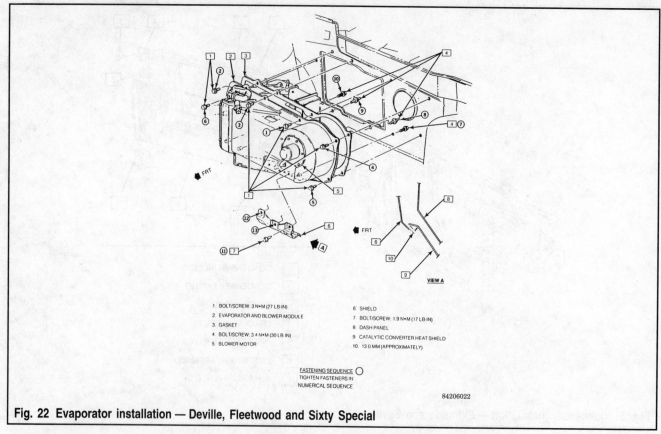

1. BOLT/SCREW: 3 N•M (27 LB-IN)
2. EVAPORATOR AND BLOWER MODULE
3. GASKET
4. BOLT/SCREW: 3.4 N•M (30 LB-IN)
5. BLOWER MOTOR

6. SHIELD
7. BOLT/SCREW: 1.9 N•M (17 LB-IN)
8. DASH PANEL
9. CATALYTIC CONVERTER HEAT SHIELD
10. 13.0 MM (APPROXIMATELY)

FASTENING SEQUENCE ○
TIGHTEN FASTENERS IN
NUMERICAL SEQUENCE

84206022

Fig. 22 Evaporator installation — Deville, Fleetwood and Sixty Special

To install:

19. Position the evaporator in the case and install the retaining clamp.

20. Install the module cover, retaining screws and seal. Tighten the module cover retaining screws to 27 inch lbs. (3 Nm).

21. Install the sound insulator.

22. Install the power module and blower motor.

23. Install the retaining clips to the sound insulator.

24. Install the 2 harness hold-down brackets to the valve cover. Install the valve to the right valve cover.

25. Install the MAP sensor bracket.

26. Install the heat shield as follows:

   a. Raise and safely support the vehicle.

   b. Install the 2 A/C module retaining screws.

   c. Install the 2 heat shield retaining screws from beneath the vehicle.

   d. Lower the vehicle.

   e. Install the 2 screws in the engine compartment.

27. Install the heater hose T-connector.

28. Install new O-rings and connect the refrigerant lines. Tighten the fittings to 18 ft. lbs. (24 Nm).

❋❋WARNING

When connecting the refrigerant lines, be careful not to nick the O-rings or cross-thread the connections.

29. Install the evaporator line retaining bracket.

30. Connect the heater hoses to the heater core.

31. Install the cowl relay center bracket and secure with the 2 nuts.

32. Install the cross-tower support bracket and secure with 2 bolts on each side.

33. If the evaporator is being replaced, disconnect the suction line from the accumulator and add 3 fl. oz. (90ml) of new refrigerant oil to the suction line. Reconnect the suction line to the accumulator.

34. Fill the cooling system.

35. Connect the negative battery cable. Leak test, evacuate and charge the system according to the proper procedure.

1993 VEHICLES WITH 4.6L ENGINE

1. Disconnect the negative battery cable.

2. Discharge the refrigerant from the system according to the proper procedure.

3. Remove the right side sound insulator.

4. Label and disconnect the wiring connectors from the power module and blower motor.

5. Disconnect the wiring connectors and vacuum connector and remove the Powertrain Control Module (PCM).

6. Remove the evaporator housing-to-dash bolt, located above the carpet directly behind the left side of the console.

7. Remove the 2 bolts securing the harness pass-through to the front of the dash.

8. Remove the cross-car brace.

9. Label and disconnect the wiring connectors at the ignition control module, rear heated oxygen sensor, A/C high and low side temperature sensors, HVAC power module and A/C low pressure switch.

10. Remove the ignition control module.

11. Remove the air cleaner.

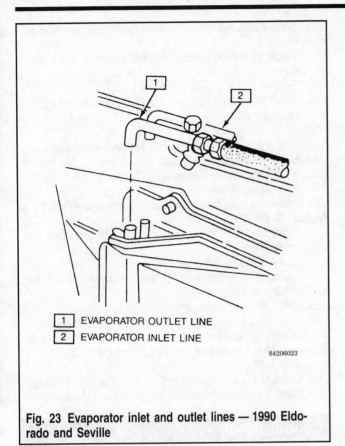

Fig. 23 Evaporator inlet and outlet lines — 1990 Eldorado and Seville

| 1 | EVAPORATOR OUTLET LINE |
| 2 | EVAPORATOR INLET LINE |

84206023

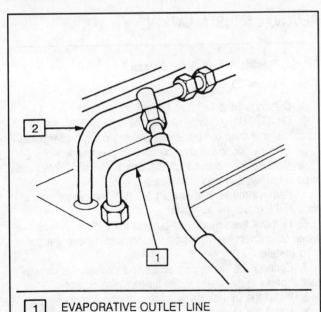

Fig. 24 Evaporator inlet and outlet lines — 1991-93 Eldorado and Seville with 4.9L engine

| 1 | EVAPORATIVE OUTLET LINE |
| 2 | EVAPORATOR INLET LINE |

84206024

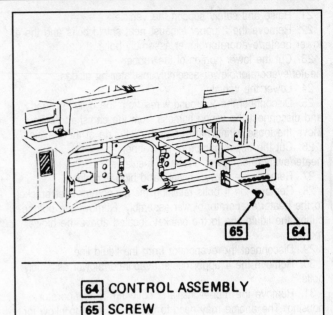

| 64 | CONTROL ASSEMBLY |
| 65 | SCREW |

84206025

Fig. 25 Climate control panel — Deville, Fleetwood and Sixty Special

12. Disconnect the accumulator refrigerant line from the evaporator. Cap the openings to prevent the entrance of air, dirt or moisture into the system.

13. Install a suitable engine support tool, then raise and safely support the vehicle.

14. Remove the left front wheel and tire assembly.

15. Remove the intermediate shaft pinch bolt from the rack and pinion gear.

✳✳CAUTION

Failure to disconnect the intermediate shaft from the rack and pinion stub shaft can result in damage to the steering gear and/or intermediate shaft. This damage can cause loss of steering control which could result in vehicle crash with possible bodily injury.

16. Disconnect the left and right Road Sensing Suspension position sensors.

17. Disconnect the exhaust Y-pipe at the catalytic converter and remove the 2 lower heat shield bolts.

18. Label and disconnect the wiring connectors at the power steering pressure switch, vehicle speed sensor and knock sensor.

19. Remove the 4 rear bolts securing the frame to the body, then lower the vehicle.

20. Lower the engine/transaxle assembly.

➡The engine support tool may not be designed to raise or lower the engine/transaxle assembly, but rather only support it in position. If necessary, use a suitable jack to lower the engine/transaxle assembly.

21. Raise and safely support the vehicle.

22. Remove the 2 upper exhaust heat shield bolts and the 4 lower heater/evaporator/blower assembly bolts.

23. Cut the lower portion of the rubber heater/evaporator/blower assembly insulator bit guides.

24. Lower the vehicle.

25. Disconnect the 2 ground wires from the cylinder head and disconnect the wiring harness from the camshaft cover. Move the loose wiring harness to the left side of the vehicle.

26. Cut the upper portion of the rubber heater/evaporator/blower assembly insulator.

27. Remove the power module and blower motor.

28. Remove the 4 bolts retaining the evaporator inlet bracket to the heater/evaporator/blower assembly. Remove the bolt securing the liquid line to the bracket, located above the blower motor.

29. Disconnect the evaporator from the liquid line.

30. Remove the 4 upper heater/evaporator/blower assembly bolts.

31. Remove the rubber insulator covering the evaporator housing. The engine may need to be repositioned to allow for removal of the evaporator housing.

32. Remove the 3 bolts securing the evaporator housing to the front of the dash and remove the housing. The engine may need to be repositioned to allow for removal of the evaporator housing.

33. Remove the evaporator from the housing.

To install:

34. Install the evaporator in the evaporator housing.

35. Install the evaporator housing in the vehicle.

36. Install the rubber insulator covering the evaporator housing.

37. Install the 4 upper heater/evaporator/blower assembly insulator bolts.

38. Install the blower motor and power module.

39. Connect the evaporator inlet bracket to the heater/evaporator/blower assembly.

40. Seal the upper portion of the rubber heater/evaporator/blower assembly insulator.

41. Reposition the loose wiring harness along the rear of the engine/transaxle assembly.

42. Raise and safely support the vehicle.

43. Connect the 2 ground wires attached to the cylinder head. Route the power steering pressure switch, vehicle speed sensor and knock sensor wires behind the heater pipes but do not connect at this time.

44. Install the 4 lower heater/evaporator/blower assembly insulator bolts.

45. Seal the lower portion of the rubber heater/evaporator/blower assembly insulator.

46. Install the 2 upper exhaust heat shield bolts, then lower the vehicle.

47. Raise the engine/transaxle assembly into position.

48. Raise and safely support the vehicle.

49. Install the 4 rear frame-to-body bolts.

50. Install the 2 lower bolts on the exhaust heat shield and connect the exhaust Y-pipe.

51. Connect the wiring connectors at the power steering pressure switch, vehicle speed sensor and knock sensor.

52. Install the intermediate shaft pinch bolt to the rack and pinion gear.

53. Connect the left and right Road Sensing Suspension position sensors.

54. Install the left front wheel and tire assembly and lower the vehicle.

55. Remove the engine support tool.

56. Install the 2 bolts securing the harness pass-through to the front of the dash.

57. Install the ignition control module.

58. Connect the wiring connectors at the ignition control module, blower motor, rear heated oxygen sensor, A/C high and low side temperature sensors, HVAC power module and A/C low pressure switch.

59. Install the interior bolt securing the evaporator housing to the front of the dash.

60. Install the PCM and connect the vacuum connector and wiring connectors.

61. Install the right side sound insulator.

62. Connect the refrigerant lines and install the bolt securing the liquid line to the bracket.

63. Install the air cleaner and the cross car brace.

64. If the evaporator is being replaced, disconnect the suction line from the accumulator and add 3 fl. oz. (90ml) of new refrigerant oil to the suction line. Reconnect the suction line to the accumulator.

65. Connect the negative battery cable. Leak test, evacuate and charge the system according to the proper procedure.

Control Panel

REMOVAL & INSTALLATION

Deville, Fleetwood and Sixty Special
▶ See Figures 25 and 26

1. Disconnect the negative battery cable.

2. On 1990-91 vehicles, remove the right and left sound insulators and snap out the upper steering column filler panel.

3. Remove the lower steering column filler panel.

4. Remove the screws from the tops of the trim plates and remove the left and right trim plates.

5. Remove the screws at the bottom of the center trim plate and remove the trim plate.

6. Remove the screws and pull out the climate control panel. Disconnect the wiring connectors and remove the panel.

To install:

7. Connect the wiring connectors and position the climate control panel in the dash. Install the retaining screws.

8. Install the trim plates with the retaining screws.

9. Install the steering column filler panel(s) and the left and right sound insulators, if removed.

10. Connect the negative battery cable.

Eldorado and Seville

1990-91

▶ See Figure 27

1. Disconnect the negative battery cable.

2. Remove the 2 center trim plate retaining screws and remove the center trim plate.

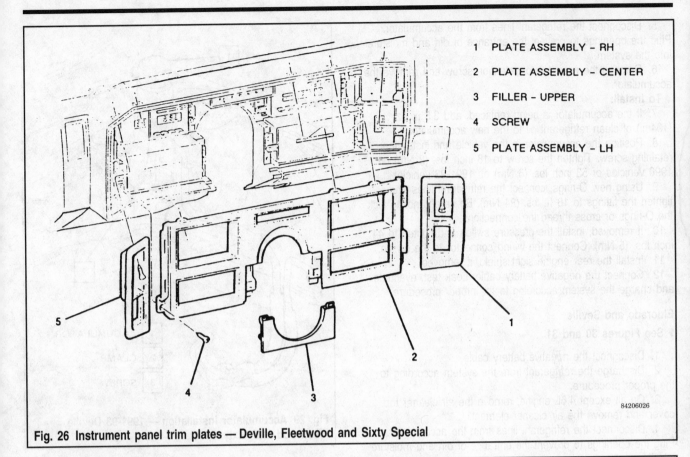

1 PLATE ASSEMBLY – RH

2 PLATE ASSEMBLY – CENTER

3 FILLER – UPPER

4 SCREW

5 PLATE ASSEMBLY – LH

84206026

Fig. 26 Instrument panel trim plates — Deville, Fleetwood and Sixty Special

3. Remove the 3 control panel retaining screws and pull out the control panel.

4. Disconnect the wiring connector and remove the control panel.

To install:

5. Connect the wiring connectors and position the control panel in the dash. Install the retaining screws.

6. Install the center trim plate and secure with the screws.

7. Connect the negative battery cable.

1992-93

The climate control panel is contained within the instrument cluster on 1992-93 Eldorado and Seville. Refer to the instrument cluster removal and installation procedure in this Section.

Accumulator

REMOVAL & INSTALLATION

Deville, Fleetwood and Sixty Special

▶ See Figures 28 and 29

1. Disconnect the negative battery cable.

2. Discharge the refrigerant from the system according to the proper procedure.

3. On 1991-93 vehicles, remove the rear engine sight shield.

4. Disconnect the wiring connector from the low pressure switch. On 1990 vehicles, remove the switch.

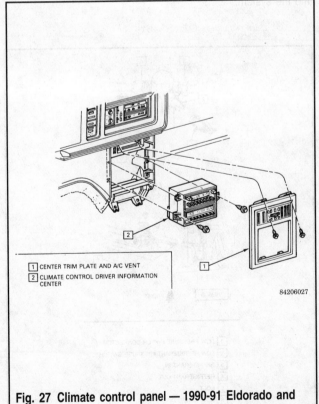

1 CENTER TRIM PLATE AND A/C VENT
2 CLIMATE CONTROL DRIVER INFORMATION CENTER

84206027

Fig. 27 Climate control panel — 1990-91 Eldorado and Seville

5. Disconnect the refrigerant lines from the accumulator. Plug the openings to prevent the entrance of dirt and moisture into the system.

6. Remove the accumulator retention screw and remove the accumulator.

To install:

7. If the accumulator is being replaced, add 3.5 fl. oz. (104ml) of clean refrigerant oil to the new accumulator.

8. Position the accumulator in the vehicle and install the retaining screw. Tighten the screw to 18 inch lbs. (2 Nm) on 1990 vehicles or 53 inch lbs. (6 Nm) on 1991-93 vehicles.

9. Using new O-rings, connect the refrigerant lines and tighten the fittings to 18 ft. lbs. (24 Nm). Be careful not to nick the O-rings or cross thread the connections.

10. If removed, install the pressure switch and tighten to 44 inch lbs. (5 Nm). Connect the wiring connector to the switch.

11. Install the rear engine sight shield, if removed.

12. Connect the negative battery cable. Leak test, evacuate and charge the system according to the proper procedure.

Eldorado and Seville

▶ **See Figures 30 and 31**

1. Disconnect the negative battery cable.

2. Discharge the refrigerant from the system according to the proper procedure.

3. On all except 4.6L engine, remove the air cleaner top cover and remove the air cleaner element.

4. Disconnect the refrigerant lines from the accumulator. Plug the openings to prevent the entrance of dirt and moisture into the system.

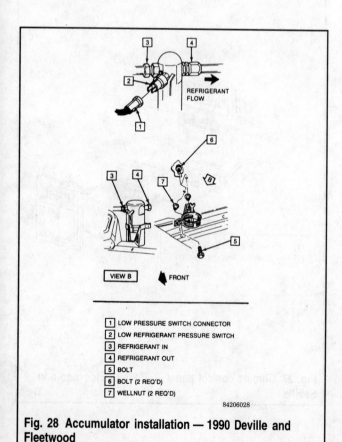

1	LOW PRESSURE SWITCH CONNECTOR
2	LOW REFRIGERANT PRESSURE SWITCH
3	REFRIGERANT IN
4	REFRIGERANT OUT
5	BOLT
6	BOLT (2 REQ'D)
7	WELLNUT (2 REQ'D)

84206028

Fig. 28 Accumulator installation — 1990 Deville and Fleetwood

1	ACCUMULATOR
2	CLAMP
3	SCREW

84206029

Fig. 29 Accumulator installation — 1991-93 Deville, Fleetwood and Sixty Special

5. Remove the accumulator retention screws and remove the accumulator.

To install:

6. If the accumulator is being replaced, add 3.5 fl. oz. (104ml) of clean refrigerant oil to the new accumulator.

7. Position the accumulator in the vehicle and install the retaining screws. Tighten the screws to 35 inch lbs. (4 Nm).

8. Using new O-rings, connect the refrigerant lines and tighten the fittings to 18 ft. lbs. (24 Nm). Be careful not to nick the O-rings or cross thread the connections.

9. If removed, install the air cleaner element and the air cleaner top cover.

10. Connect the negative battery cable. Leak test, evacuate and charge the system according to the proper procedure.

Refrigerant Lines

DISCONNECT & CONNECT

▶ **See Figures 32, 33, 34 and 35**

1. Disconnect the negative battery cable.

2. Discharge the refrigerant from the system according to the proper procedure.

3. Place tool J-38042 or equivalent, on the refrigerant line directly behind the dual O-ring joint female nut.

4. Back off the female nut until the dual O-ring joint seal is broken.

5. Once the seal is broken, slightly tighten the female nut to facilitate tool removal.

6. Remove the female nut and separate the connection.

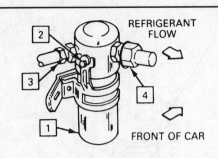

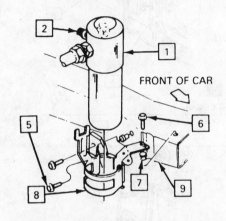

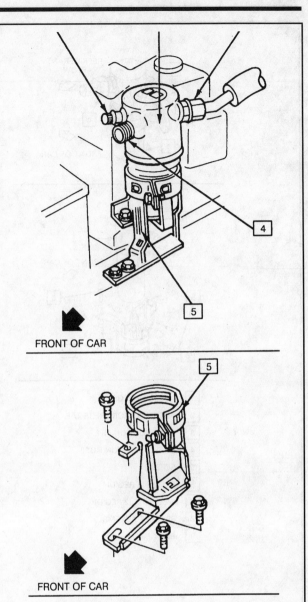

1	ACCUMULATOR
2	ACCUMULATOR PRESS TAP
3	INLET SUCTION PIPE
4	OUTLET SUCTION HOSE
5	SCREW
6	SCREW (2 REQ'D)
7	WELL NUT (2 REQ'D)
8	BRACKET ASSEMBLY
9	BODY FRAME RAIL

84206030

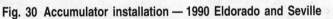

Fig. 30 Accumulator installation — 1990 Eldorado and Seville

7. Use a non-metallic pick (to minimize the chance of damaging the seal surface) or similar tool to remove the O-rings.

8. Inspect the refrigerant line for kinks and dents and the connection for burrs and nicks. Repair or replace parts as necessary.

To install:

9. Lubricate new O-rings with clean refrigerant oil and install them on the refrigerant line.

10. Lubricate the inside of the refrigerant line bore with clean refrigerant oil, then align the end forms for pilot-to-bore insertion.

11. Tighten the female nut to 18 ft. lbs. (24 Nm).

❊❊WARNING

Excessive torque may distort the bore, damaging the line and possibly causing a leak.

12. Connect the negative battery cable. Leak test, evacuate and charge the system according to the proper procedure.

Vacuum Motors

REMOVAL & INSTALLATION

1990 Deville and Fleetwood

1. Disconnect the negative battery cable.

2. Remove the air distributor assembly; refer to the procedure under Heater/AC Ducts and Outlets in Section 10.

3. Disengage the motor from the air distributor assembly and the valve.

4. Installation is the reverse of the removal procedure.

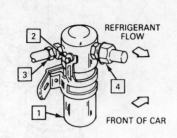

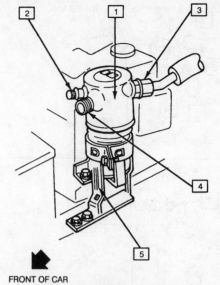

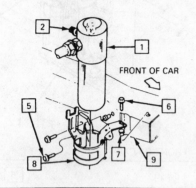

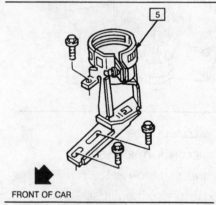

1	ACCUMULATOR
2	ACCUMULATOR PRESS TAP
3	INLET SUCTION PIPE
4	OUTLET SUCTION HOSE
5	SCREW
6	SCREW (2 REQ'D)
7	WELL NUT (2 REQ'D)
8	BRACKET ASSEMBLY
9	BODY FRAME RAIL

1	ACCUMULATOR
2	ACCUMULATOR PRESS TAP
3	INLET SUCTION PIPE
4	OUTLET SUCTION HOSE
5	BRACKET ASSEMBLY

84206031

Fig. 31 Accumulator installation — 1991-93 Eldorado and Seville

1991-93 Deville, Fleetwood and Sixty Special

OUTSIDE AIR RECIRCULATION VALVE MOTOR

▶ See Figure 36

1. Remove the left sound insulator.
2. Disconnect the vacuum hose from the motor.
3. Unclip the motor from the air inlet assembly and disengage from the valve.
4. Installation is the reverse of the removal procedure.

AIR CONDITIONING DEFROST VALVE MOTOR

▶ See Figure 36

✳✳CAUTION

When performing service around Supplemental Inflatable Restraint (SIR) system components or wiring, the SIR system must be disabled. Failure to do so could result in possible air bag deployment, personal injury or unneeded SIR system repairs.

1. Disconnect the negative battery cable.
2. Disable the SIR system; refer to the procedure in this Section.
3. Remove the air distributor assembly; refer to the procedure under Heater/AC Ducts and Outlets in Section 10.

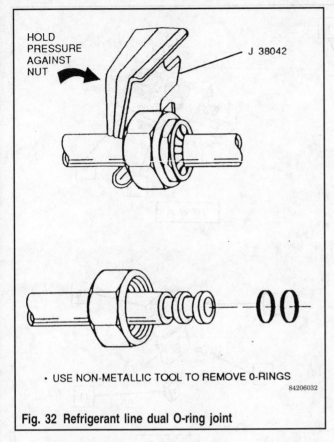

HOLD PRESSURE AGAINST NUT

J 38042

• USE NON-METALLIC TOOL TO REMOVE O-RINGS

84206032

Fig. 32 Refrigerant line dual O-ring joint

4. Unclip the motor from the air distributor assembly and disengage from the valve.

5. Installation is the reverse of the removal procedure. After installation is completed, properly enable the SIR system; refer to the procedure in this Section.

HEATER-AIR CONDITIONER BI-LEVEL VALVE MOTOR
▶ See Figure 36

✳✳CAUTION

When performing service around Supplemental Inflatable Restraint (SIR) system components or wiring, the SIR system must be disabled. Failure to do so could result in possible air bag deployment, personal injury or unneeded SIR system repairs.

1. Disconnect the negative battery cable.
2. Disable the SIR system; refer to the procedure in this Section.
3. Remove the air distributor assembly; refer to the procedure under Heater/AC Ducts and Outlets in Section 10.
4. Remove the clips and screws attaching the air distributor assembly halves and separate the assembly.
5. Rotate the motor and disengage it from the valve.
6. Installation is the reverse of the removal procedure. After installation is completed, properly enable the SIR system; refer to the procedure in this Section.

Eldorado and Seville
▶ See Figures 37 and 38

1. Disconnect the negative battery cable.

2. Remove the air distributor assembly; refer to the procedure under Heater/AC Ducts and Outlets in Section 10.
3. Disengage the motor from the air distributor assembly and the valve.
4. Installation is the reverse of the removal procedure.

Low Pressure Switch

REMOVAL & INSTALLATION

Deville, Fleetwood and Sixty Special
▶ See Figure 39

1. Disconnect the negative battery cable.
2. Disconnect the wiring connector from the switch, which is located on the accumulator.
3. Unscrew and remove the switch. The switch is mounted on a Schrader valve; it is not necessary to discharge the refrigerant from the system.
4. Installation is the reverse of the removal procedure. Tighten the switch to 44 inch lbs. (5 Nm).

Eldorado and Seville
▶ See Figures 34 and 35

1. Disconnect the negative battery cable.
2. Disconnect the wiring connector from the switch, which is located on the low-side refrigerant line.
3. Unscrew and remove the switch. The switch is mounted on a Schrader valve; it is not necessary to discharge the refrigerant from the system.
4. Installation is the reverse of the removal procedure.

Orifice Tube

REMOVAL & INSTALLATION

Deville, Fleetwood and Sixty Special
1990
▶ See Figures 40 and 41

1. Disconnect the negative battery cable.
2. Discharge the refrigerant from the system according to the proper procedure.
3. Disconnect the high pressure liquid line from the evaporator inlet line.
4. Grip the plastic tip of the orifice tube using needle nose pliers or tool J-26549-D or equivalent. Using a turning, push-pull motion, remove the tube.

➡**If orifice tube removal is difficult, use a suitable tool (heat gun, hair dryer, epoxy dryer, etc.) to apply heat to the refrigerant line, approximately ¼ in. from the dimples on the inlet line. Do not overheat the line.**

5. Cap the inlet line.
To install:
6. Uncap the inlet line and swab the inside of the line with R-11 refrigerant or equivalent.

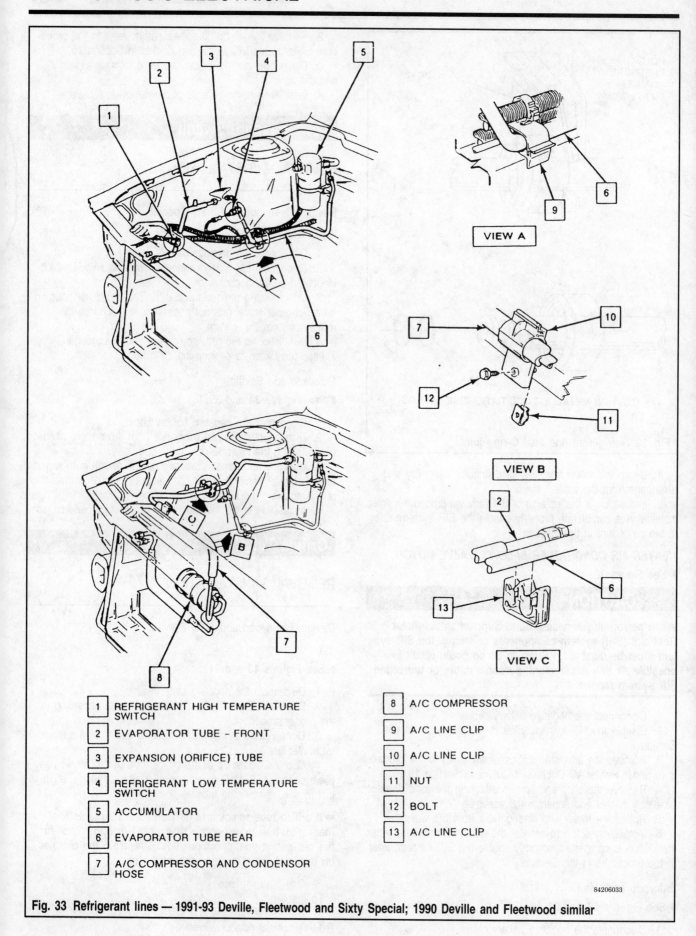

1	REFRIGERANT HIGH TEMPERATURE SWITCH	8	A/C COMPRESSOR
2	EVAPORATOR TUBE - FRONT	9	A/C LINE CLIP
3	EXPANSION (ORIFICE) TUBE	10	A/C LINE CLIP
4	REFRIGERANT LOW TEMPERATURE SWITCH	11	NUT
5	ACCUMULATOR	12	BOLT
6	EVAPORATOR TUBE REAR	13	A/C LINE CLIP
7	A/C COMPRESSOR AND CONDENSOR HOSE		

84206033

Fig. 33 Refrigerant lines — 1991-93 Deville, Fleetwood and Sixty Special; 1990 Deville and Fleetwood similar

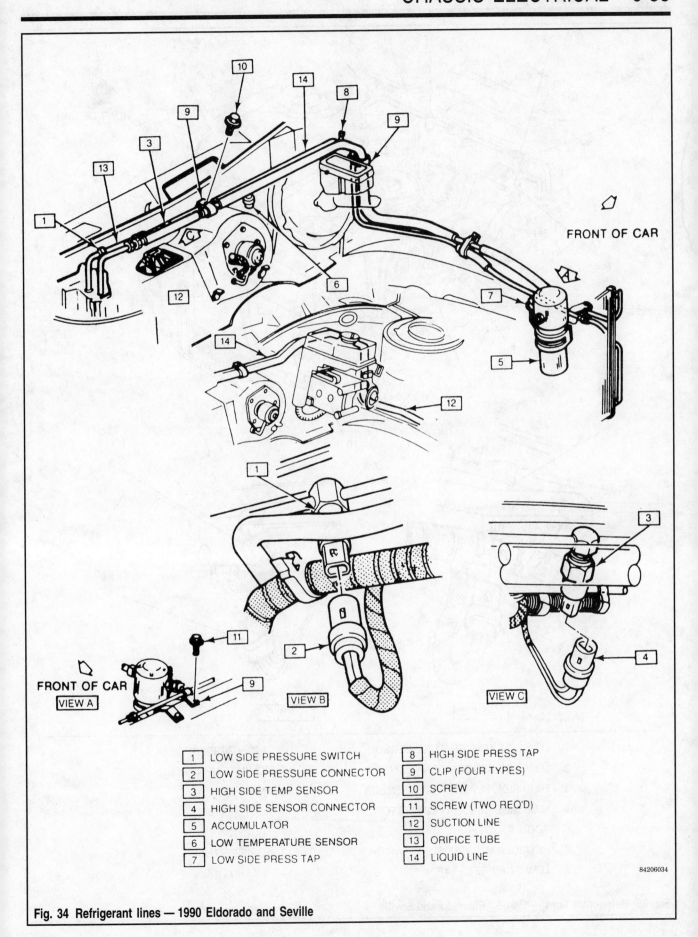

1	LOW SIDE PRESSURE SWITCH	8	HIGH SIDE PRESS TAP
2	LOW SIDE PRESSURE CONNECTOR	9	CLIP (FOUR TYPES)
3	HIGH SIDE TEMP SENSOR	10	SCREW
4	HIGH SIDE SENSOR CONNECTOR	11	SCREW (TWO REQ'D)
5	ACCUMULATOR	12	SUCTION LINE
6	LOW TEMPERATURE SENSOR	13	ORIFICE TUBE
7	LOW SIDE PRESS TAP	14	LIQUID LINE

84206034

Fig. 34 Refrigerant lines — 1990 Eldorado and Seville

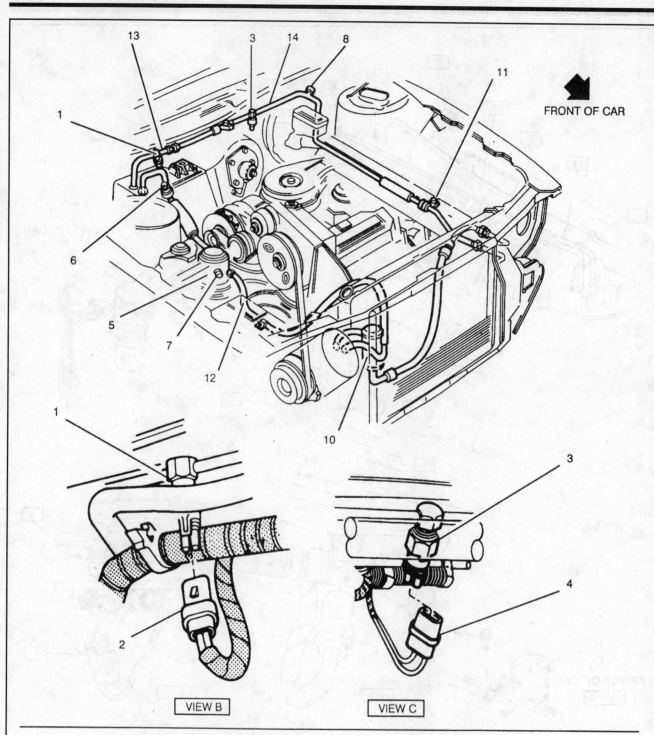

FRONT OF CAR

VIEW B

VIEW C

1	LOW SIDE TEMPERATURE SENSOR	8	HIGH SIDE PRESS TAP
2	LOW SIDE SENSOR CONNECTOR	9	CLIP (FOUR TYPES)
3	HIGH SIDE TEMPERATURE SENSOR	10	MUFFLER
4	HIGH SIDE SENSOR CONNECTOR	11	CLIP (1 SCREW)
5	ACCUMULATOR	12	SUCTION LINE
6	REFRIGERANT PRESSURE SWITCH	13	ORIFICE TUBE
7	LOW SIDE PRESS TAP	14	LIQUID LINE

84206035

Fig. 35 Refrigerant lines — 1991-93 Eldorado and Seville

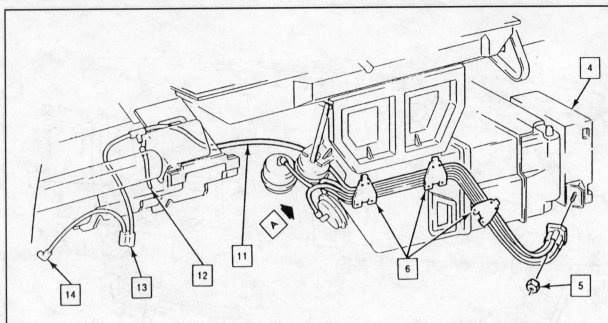

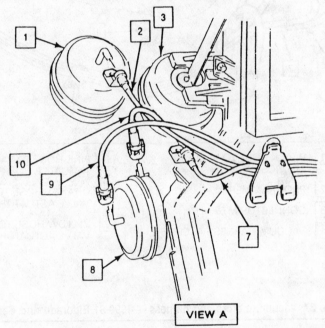

VIEW A

1	O/S AIR RECIRC. VALVE VACUUM ACTUATOR
2	ORANGE; TO O/S AIR RECIRC. VALVE VACUUM ACTUATOR
3	A/C-DEFROST VALVE VACUUM ACTUATOR
4	PROGRAMMER
5	NUT
6	VACUUM HARNESS RETAINER
7	BLUE; TO A/C-DEFROST VALVE VACUUM ACTUATOR
8	HEATER-A/C BI-LEVEL VALVE VACUUM ACTUATOR
9	YELLOW; TO HEATER-A/C BI-LEVEL VALVE VACUUM ACTUATOR
10	RED; TO HEATER-A/C BI-LEVEL VALVE VACUUM ACTUATOR
11	BLACK; TO SOURCE VACUUM
12	BLACK; SOURCE VACUUM
13	PARK BRAKE RELEASE SWITCH VACUUM CONNECTOR
14	PINK; TO PARK BRAKE RELEASE LEVER

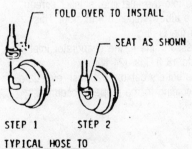

FOLD OVER TO INSTALL

SEAT AS SHOWN

STEP 1   STEP 2

TYPICAL HOSE TO
ACTUATOR INSTALLATION

84206036

Fig. 36 Vacuum motors and harness — 1991-93 Deville, Fleetwood and Sixty Special

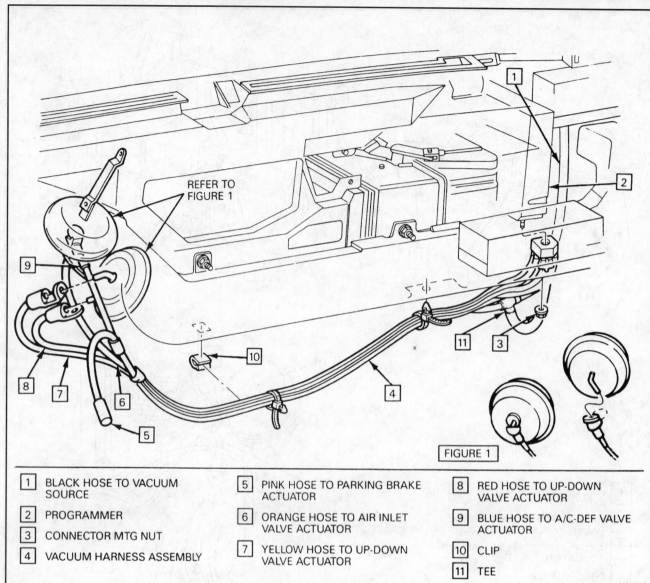

1	BLACK HOSE TO VACUUM SOURCE	5	PINK HOSE TO PARKING BRAKE ACTUATOR	8	RED HOSE TO UP-DOWN VALVE ACTUATOR
2	PROGRAMMER	6	ORANGE HOSE TO AIR INLET VALVE ACTUATOR	9	BLUE HOSE TO A/C-DEF VALVE ACTUATOR
3	CONNECTOR MTG NUT	7	YELLOW HOSE TO UP-DOWN VALVE ACTUATOR	10	CLIP
4	VACUUM HARNESS ASSEMBLY			11	TEE

84206037

Fig. 37 Vacuum motors and harness — 1990-91 Eldorado and Seville

7. Coat the new orifice tube O-ring with clean refrigerant oil.

8. Insert the orifice tube into the inlet line, smaller screen end first, and push until the tube reaches a firm stop. This indicates proper seating of the O-ring.

9. Connect the high pressure line to the evaporator inlet line and tighten the fitting to 18 ft. lbs. (24 Nm).

10. Connect the negative battery cable. Leak test, evacuate and charge the system according to the proper procedure.

1991-93

▶ See Figures 33 and 41

1. Disconnect the negative battery cable.
2. Discharge the refrigerant from the system according to the proper procedure.
3. Remove the engine coolant reservoir.

4. Disconnect the refrigerant line clip attaching the evaporator line to the compressor and condenser hose.

5. Disconnect the front evaporator line fittings at the condenser outlet and evaporator line midpoint. Remove the front evaporator line.

6. Grip the plastic tip of the orifice tube using needle nose pliers or tool J-26549-D or equivalent. Using a turning, push-pull motion, remove the tube.

➡**If orifice tube removal is difficult, use a suitable tool (heat gun, hair dryer, epoxy dryer, etc.) to apply heat to the refrigerant line. Do not overheat the line.**

7. Cap the refrigerant lines to prevent the entrance of dirt and moisture into the system.
To install:
8. Swab the inside of the front evaporator line with R-11 refrigerant or equivalent.

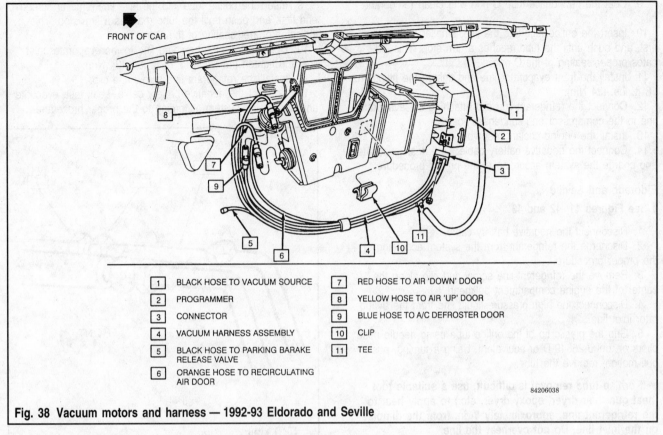

Fig. 38 Vacuum motors and harness — 1992-93 Eldorado and Seville

1	BLACK HOSE TO VACUUM SOURCE
2	PROGRAMMER
3	CONNECTOR
4	VACUUM HARNESS ASSEMBLY
5	BLACK HOSE TO PARKING BARAKE RELEASE VALVE
6	ORANGE HOSE TO RECIRCULATING AIR DOOR
7	RED HOSE TO AIR 'DOWN' DOOR
8	YELLOW HOSE TO AIR 'UP' DOOR
9	BLUE HOSE TO A/C DEFROSTER DOOR
10	CLIP
11	TEE

84206038

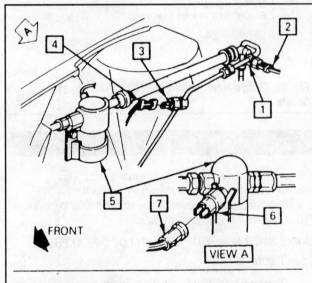

1 LOW SIDE TEMP SENSOR
2 LOW SIDE SENSOR CONNECTOR
3 HIGH SIDE TEMP SENSOR
4 HIGH SIDE SENSOR CONNECTOR
5 ACCUMULATOR
6 LOW PRESSURE SWITCH
7 PRESSURE SWITCH CONNECTOR

84206039

Fig. 39 Refrigerant sensors and switch — Deville, Fleetwood and Sixty Special

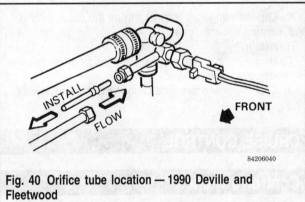

84206040

Fig. 40 Orifice tube location — 1990 Deville and Fleetwood

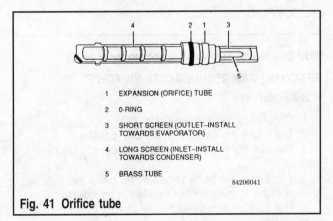

1 EXPANSION (ORIFICE) TUBE
2 O-RING
3 SHORT SCREEN (OUTLET–INSTALL TOWARDS EVAPORATOR)
4 LONG SCREEN (INLET–INSTALL TOWARDS CONDENSER)
5 BRASS TUBE

84206041

Fig. 41 Orifice tube

9. Coat the new orifice tube O-ring with clean refrigerant oil.

10. Insert the orifice tube into the line, smaller screen first, and push until the tube reaches a firm stop. This indicates proper seating of the O-ring.

11. Install the front evaporator line and tighten the fittings to 18 ft. lbs. (24 Nm).

12. Connect the refrigerant line clip attaching the evaporator line to the compressor and condenser hose.

13. Install the engine coolant reservoir.

14. Connect the negative battery cable. Leak test, evacuate and charge the system according to the proper procedure.

Eldorado and Seville

▶ See Figures 41, 42 and 43

1. Disconnect the negative battery cable.

2. Discharge the refrigerant from the system according to the proper procedure.

3. Remove the refrigerant line screw and clip along the center of the engine compartment bulkhead.

4. Disconnect the high pressure liquid line from the evaporator inlet line.

5. Grip the plastic tip of the orifice tube using needle nose pliers or tool J-26549-D or equivalent. Using a turning, push-pull motion, remove the tube.

➡If orifice tube removal is difficult, use a suitable tool (heat gun, hair dryer, epoxy dryer, etc.) to apply heat to the refrigerant line, approximately ¼ in. from the dimples on the inlet line. Do not overheat the line.

6. Cap the refrigerant lines to prevent the entrance of dirt and moisture into the system.

To install:

7. Uncap the inlet line and swab the inside of the line with R-11 refrigerant or equivalent.

8. Coat the new orifice tube O-ring with clean refrigerant oil.

9. Insert the orifice tube into the inlet line, smaller screen end first, and push until the tube reaches a firm stop. This indicates proper seating of the O-ring.

10. Connect the high pressure line to the evaporator inlet line and tighten the fitting to 18 ft. lbs. (24 Nm).

11. Install the refrigerant line screw and clip.

12. Connect the negative battery cable. Leak test, evacuate and charge the system according to the proper procedure.

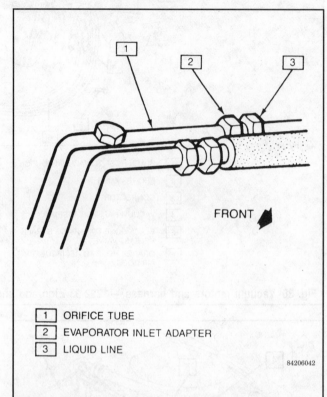

1	ORIFICE TUBE
2	EVAPORATOR INLET ADAPTER
3	LIQUID LINE

84206042

Fig. 42 Orifice tube location — 1990 Eldorado and Seville

CRUISE CONTROL

Control Switches

REMOVAL & INSTALLATION

1990 Deville and Fleetwood

SET/COAST AND RESUME/ACCEL SWITCHES

▶ See Figure 44

1. Disconnect the negative battery cable.

2. Make sure the switch is in the **OFF** position.

3. Remove the access cover from the steering column housing.

4. Disconnect the cruise control wiring connector. Note the position of the connector when installed in the column.

5. Pull the turn signal switch lever straight out of the turn signal switch.

To install:

6. Make sure the lever is in the **OFF** position.

7. Push the lever into the turn signal switch.

8. Connect the cruise control wiring connector.

9. Install the access cover to the steering column housing.

10. Connect the negative battery cable.

BRAKE SWITCH — WITHOUT ANTI-LOCK BRAKES

▶ See Figure 45

1. Disconnect the negative battery cable.

2. Remove the left sound insulator.

3. Label and disconnect the wiring connector(s).

4. Disconnect the vacuum hose, if equipped.

5. Remove the switch by carefully pulling rearward.

To install:

6. Hold the brake pedal depressed, away from the pedal stop.

7. Install the switch into the tubular retainer until the switch body seats on the retainer.

➡As the switch is installed, audible clicks can be heard when the switch is pressed toward the brake pedal.

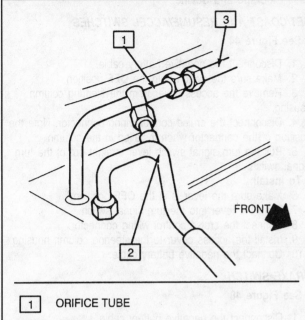

1 ORIFICE TUBE

2 EVAPORATOR OUTLET ADAPTER

3 LIQUID LINE

84206043

Fig. 43 Orifice tube location — 1991-93 Eldorado and Seville

8. Pull the brake pedal fully rearward against the pedal stop until audible clicks can no longer be heard. The switch will move in the tubular retainer, providing adjustment.

9. Release the brake pedal and repeat Step 8 to assure no audible clicks can be heard.

10. Connect the wiring connector(s) and vacuum hose, if equipped.

11. Install the left sound insulator.

12. Connect the negative battery cable.

BRAKE SWITCH — WITH ANTI-LOCK BRAKES

▶ See Figure 45

1. Disconnect the negative battery cable.
2. Remove the left sound insulator.
3. Label and disconnect the wiring connector(s).
4. Disconnect the vacuum hose, if equipped.
5. Remove the switch by carefully pulling rearward.

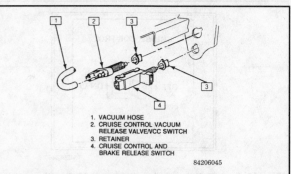

1. VACUUM HOSE
2. CRUISE CONTROL VACUUM RELEASE VALVE/VCC SWITCH
3. RETAINER
4. CRUISE CONTROL AND BRAKE RELEASE SWITCH

84206045

Fig. 45 Brake switch/vacuum dump valve — 1990 Deville and Fleetwood

To install:

6. Hold the brake pedal depressed, away from the pedal stop.

7. Install the switch into the retainer, approximately 4 threads from the end of the barrel.

➡ **As the switch is installed, audible clicks can be heard when the switch is pressed toward the brake pedal.**

8. Release the brake pedal and allow it to come to rest.

9. Slowly push the switch further into the retainer until the barrel is seated against the brake pedal arm. Inspect the switch for proper seating against the brake pedal arm.

10. Connect the wiring connector(s) and vacuum hose, if equipped.

11. Install the left sound insulator.

12. Connect the negative battery cable.

INSTRUMENT PANEL SWITCH

▶ See Figures 26 and 46

1. Disconnect the negative battery cable.

2. Remove the right and left sound insulators and snap out the upper steering column filler panel.

3. Remove the lower steering column filler panel.

4. Remove the screws from the tops of the trim plates and remove the left and right trim plates.

5. Remove the screws at the bottom of the center trim plate and remove the trim plate.

6. Remove the 2 retaining screws and the switch.

7. Disconnect the wiring connector and remove the switch from the vehicle.

8. Installation is the reverse of the removal procedure.

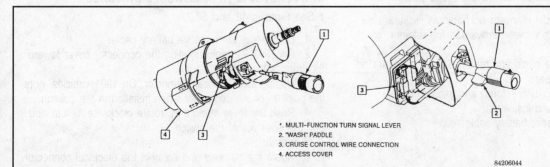

1. MULTI-FUNCTION TURN SIGNAL LEVER
2. "WASH" PADDLE
3. CRUISE CONTROL WIRE CONNECTION
4. ACCESS COVER

84206044

Fig. 44 Set/Coast and Resume/Accel switches (turn signal switch lever) installation — Deville, Fleetwood and Sixty Special and 1990 Eldorado and Seville

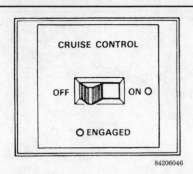

Fig. 46 Instrument panel switch — 1990 Deville and Fleetwood

1991-93 Deville, Fleetwood and Sixty Special

SET/COAST AND RESUME/ACCEL SWITCHES

▶ See Figure 44

1. Disconnect the negative battery cable.
2. Make sure the switch is in the **OFF** position.
3. Remove the access cover from the steering column housing.
4. Disconnect the cruise control wiring connector. Note the position of the connector when installed in the column.
5. Pull the turn signal switch lever straight out of the turn signal switch.

To install:

6. Make sure the lever is in the **OFF** position.
7. Push the lever into the turn signal switch.
8. Connect the cruise control wiring connector.
9. Install the access cover to the steering column housing.
10. Connect the negative battery cable.

CRUISE CONTROL/SHIFT INTERLOCK/BRAKE SWITCH

▶ See Figure 47

1. Disconnect the negative battery cable.
2. Remove the left sound insulator.
3. Label and disconnect the wiring connector(s).
4. Disconnect the vacuum hose.
5. Remove the switch by carefully pulling rearward.

To install:

6. Fully depress the brake pedal and hold.
7. Install the switch into the mounting bracket, then press the switch until it is firmly seated against the mounting bracket.

➡**As the switch is installed, audible clicks can be heard when the switch is pressed toward the brake pedal.**

8. Pull the brake pedal rearward until audible clicks are no longer heard. The switch moves rearward in the retainer, providing adjustment.
9. Release the brake pedal and repeat Step 8 to assure no audible clicks can be heard.
10. Connect the wiring connector(s) and vacuum hose.
11. Install the left sound insulator.
12. Connect the negative battery cable.

1990 Eldorado and Seville

SET/COAST AND RESUME/ACCEL SWITCHES

▶ See Figure 44

1. Disconnect the negative battery cable.
2. Make sure the switch is in the **OFF** position.
3. Remove the access cover from the steering column housing.
4. Disconnect the cruise control wiring connector. Note the position of the connector when installed in the column.
5. Pull the turn signal switch lever straight out of the turn signal switch.

To install:

6. Make sure the lever is in the **OFF** position.
7. Push the lever into the turn signal switch.
8. Connect the cruise control wiring connector.
9. Install the access cover to the steering column housing.
10. Connect the negative battery cable.

BRAKE SWITCH

▶ See Figure 48

1. Disconnect the negative battery cable.
2. Remove the left-hand hush panel.
3. Label and disconnect the wiring connector(s).
4. Disconnect the vacuum hose, if equipped.
5. Remove the switch.

To install:

6. Hold the brake pedal depressed and install the switch into the retainer. The switch should bottom on the retainer.

➡**Audible clicks can be heard as the threaded portion of the switch is pushed through the retainer.**

7. Slowly pull the brake pedal fully rearward against the pedal stop moving the switch rearward.
8. Release the brake pedal and pull back again to assure proper adjustment of the switch.

➡**The cruise control switch contacts must open at $1/8$-$1/2$ in. pedal travel measured at the centerline of the brake pedal pad.**

9. Connect the wiring connector(s) and vacuum hose, if equipped.
10. Install the left-hand hush panel.
11. Connect the negative battery cable.

1991-93 Eldorado and Seville

SET/COAST AND RESUME/ACCEL SWITCHES

▶ See Figures 49 and 50

1. Disconnect the negative battery cable.
2. On 1992-93 vehicles, slide the connector cover toward the front of the vehicle.
3. Unplug the electrical connector. On 1991 vehicles, note the position of the connector when installed in the column.
4. Push the lever straight in, rotate clockwise $1/4$ turn and pull the lever out of the switch.

To install:

5. Route the harness and connect the electrical connector.
6. Push the lever straight in and rotate counterclockwise $1/4$ turn to lock into position.
7. On 1992-93 vehicles, reposition the connector cover.

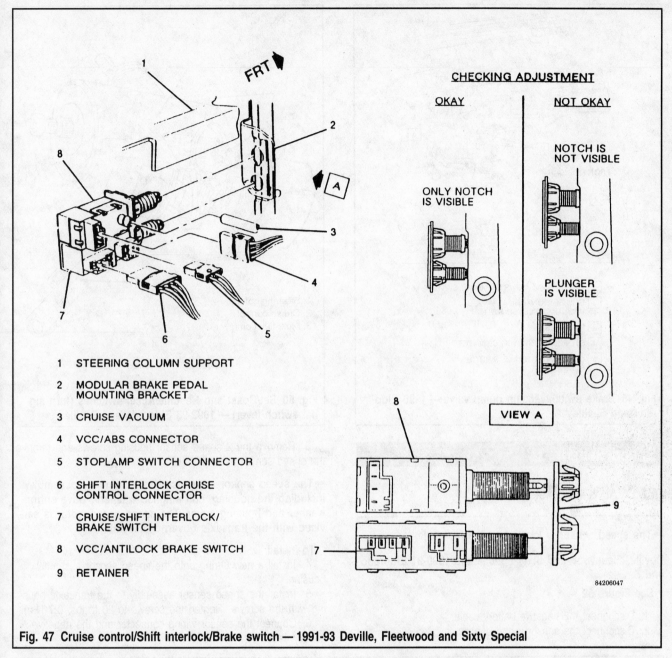

CHECKING ADJUSTMENT

OKAY | NOT OKAY

ONLY NOTCH IS VISIBLE

NOTCH IS NOT VISIBLE

PLUNGER IS VISIBLE

VIEW A

1 STEERING COLUMN SUPPORT

2 MODULAR BRAKE PEDAL MOUNTING BRACKET

3 CRUISE VACUUM

4 VCC/ABS CONNECTOR

5 STOPLAMP SWITCH CONNECTOR

6 SHIFT INTERLOCK CRUISE CONTROL CONNECTOR

7 CRUISE/SHIFT INTERLOCK/ BRAKE SWITCH

8 VCC/ANTILOCK BRAKE SWITCH

9 RETAINER

84206047

Fig. 47 Cruise control/Shift interlock/Brake switch — 1991-93 Deville, Fleetwood and Sixty Special

8. Connect the negative battery cable.

BRAKE SWITCH
▶ See Figure 51

1. Disconnect the negative battery cable.
2. Remove the left-hand hush panel.
3. Label and disconnect the wiring connector(s).
4. Disconnect the vacuum hose, if equipped.
5. Remove the switch.

To install:

6. Hold the brake pedal depressed and install the switch into the retainer. The switch should bottom on the retainer.

➡**Audible clicks can be heard as the threaded portion of the switch is pushed through the retainer.**

7. Slowly pull the brake pedal fully rearward against the pedal stop moving the switch rearward.

8. Release the brake pedal and pull back again to assure proper adjustment of the switch.

➡**The cruise control switch contacts must open at 0.95-1.2 in. pedal travel measured at the centerline of the brake pedal pad.**

9. Connect the wiring connector(s) and vacuum hose, if equipped.

10. Install the left-hand hush panel.

11. Connect the negative battery cable.

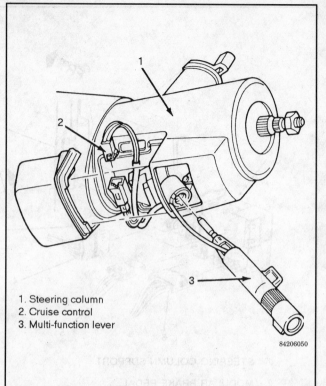

1. CRUISE/VCC AND STOP LAMP SWITCH
2. CRUISE CONTROL VACUUM RELEASE SWITCH
3. RETAINER
4. STOP LAMP SWITCH CONNECTOR
5. CRUISE/VCC BRAKE SWITCH CONNECTOR

84206048

Fig. 48 Brake switch/vacuum dump valve — 1990 Eldorado and Seville

Speed Sensor

REMOVAL & INSTALLATION

➡️The speed sensor is located on the transaxle.

Deville, Fleetwood and Sixty Special and 1990-91 Eldorado and Seville

▶ See Figure 52

1. Disconnect the negative battery cable.
2. Disconnect the sensor wiring connector.

1. Steering column
2. Cruise control
3. Multi-function lever

84206050

Fig. 50 Set/Coast and Resume/Accel switches (turn signal switch lever) — 1992-93 Eldorado and Seville

3. Remove the 2 speed sensor housing screws and remove the speed sensor assembly.

➡️**The speed sensor is serviced as a complete assembly, including the housing, coil magnet, washers, wave spring washer and housing cover. The speed sensor rotor is serviced with the transaxle governor assembly.**

To install:

4. Install a new O-ring onto the speed sensor assembly housing.
5. Install the speed sensor assembly to the transaxle housing with the screws. Tighten the screws to 20 ft. lbs. (27 Nm).
6. Connect the sensor wiring connector and the negative battery cable.

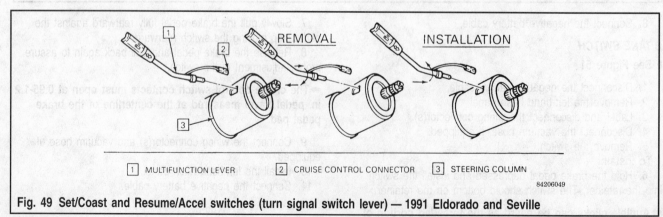

REMOVAL   INSTALLATION

1 MULTIFUNCTION LEVER   2 CRUISE CONTROL CONNECTOR   3 STEERING COLUMN

84206049

Fig. 49 Set/Coast and Resume/Accel switches (turn signal switch lever) — 1991 Eldorado and Seville

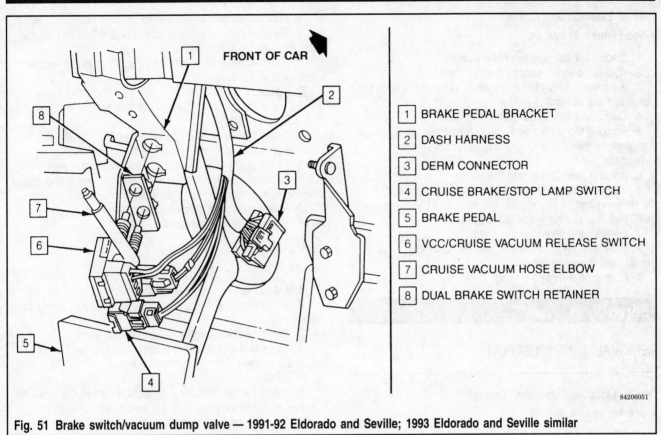

1	BRAKE PEDAL BRACKET
2	DASH HARNESS
3	DERM CONNECTOR
4	CRUISE BRAKE/STOP LAMP SWITCH
5	BRAKE PEDAL
6	VCC/CRUISE VACUUM RELEASE SWITCH
7	CRUISE VACUUM HOSE ELBOW
8	DUAL BRAKE SWITCH RETAINER

84206051

Fig. 51 Brake switch/vacuum dump valve — 1991-92 Eldorado and Seville; 1993 Eldorado and Seville similar

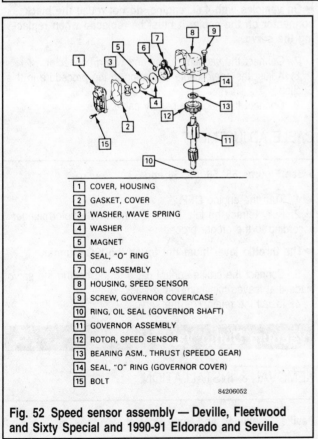

1	COVER, HOUSING
2	GASKET, COVER
3	WASHER, WAVE SPRING
4	WASHER
5	MAGNET
6	SEAL, "O" RING
7	COIL ASSEMBLY
8	HOUSING, SPEED SENSOR
9	SCREW, GOVERNOR COVER/CASE
10	RING, OIL SEAL (GOVERNOR SHAFT)
11	GOVERNOR ASSEMBLY
12	ROTOR, SPEED SENSOR
13	BEARING ASM., THRUST (SPEEDO GEAR)
14	SEAL, "O" RING (GOVERNOR COVER)
15	BOLT

84206052

Fig. 52 Speed sensor assembly — Deville, Fleetwood and Sixty Special and 1990-91 Eldorado and Seville

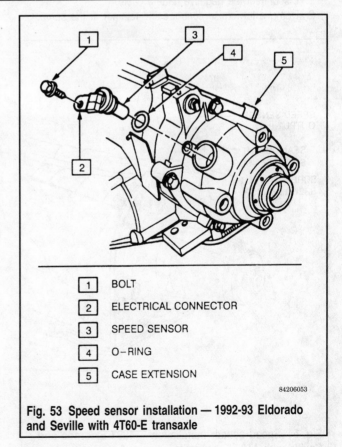

1	BOLT
2	ELECTRICAL CONNECTOR
3	SPEED SENSOR
4	O-RING
5	CASE EXTENSION

84206053

Fig. 53 Speed sensor installation — 1992-93 Eldorado and Seville with 4T60-E transaxle

1992-93 Eldorado and Seville

▶ **See Figures 53 and 54**

1. Disconnect the negative battery cable.
2. Raise and safely support the vehicle.
3. If equipped with 4T80-E transaxle, remove the right front wheel and tire assembly.
4. Disconnect the sensor wiring connector.
5. Remove the sensor retaining bolt and remove the sensor. Remove the sensor O-ring and discard.

To install:

6. Install a new O-ring onto the sensor.
7. Install the speed sensor into the transaxle case. Tighten the retaining bolt to 97 inch lbs. (11 Nm) on 4T60-E transaxle or 89 inch lbs. (10 Nm) on 4T80-E transaxle.
8. Connect the sensor wiring connector.
9. Install the right front wheel and tire assembly, if removed, and lower the vehicle.
10. Connect the negative battery cable.

Servo

REMOVAL & INSTALLATION

Deville, Fleetwood and Sixty Special

▶ **See Figures 55 and 56**

1. Disconnect the negative battery cable.
2. Remove the cruise control cable retainer at the servo.

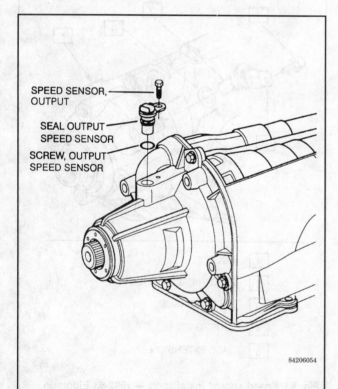

SPEED SENSOR, OUTPUT

SEAL OUTPUT SPEED SENSOR

SCREW, OUTPUT SPEED SENSOR

84206054

Fig. 54 Speed sensor installation — 1993 Eldorado and Seville with 4T80-E transaxle

3. Disconnect the vacuum hoses and the wiring connector.
4. Remove the mounting bracket nut and bolt and remove the servo and bracket assembly.
5. Remove the screws retaining the servo to the bracket and remove the servo.

To install:

6. Install the servo to the bracket and tighten the screws to 12 inch lbs. (1.4 Nm).
7. Install the servo and bracket assembly. Tighten the mounting bracket nut and bolt to 13 ft. lbs. (17 Nm).
8. Connect the wiring connector and vacuum hoses.
9. Connect the cruise control cable to the servo and adjust the cable according to the procedure in this Section.
10. Install the cruise control cable retainer.
11. Connect the negative battery cable.

Eldorado and Seville

▶ **See Figures 57, 58 and 59**

1. Disconnect the negative battery cable.
2. Disconnect the wiring connector and vacuum hoses from the servo.
3. Disconnect the throttle cable from the servo.
4. Remove the 3 retaining screws and remove the servo from the bracket.

To install:

5. Install the servo to the bracket and tighten the retaining screws to 11-15 inch lbs. (1.2-1.8 Nm).
6. Connect the throttle cable to the servo.

➡**On vehicles with 4.6L engine, do not reuse the black connector on the cable; it must be replaced when replacing the servo.**

7. Connect the vacuum hoses and wiring connector.
8. Adjust the servo cable according to the procedure in this Section.
9. Connect the negative battery cable.

CABLE ADJUSTMENT

▶ **See Figures 55, 56, 57, 58 and 59**

1. Turn the engine **OFF**.
2. Fully retract the Idle Speed Control (ISC) motor plunger according to the proper procedure.

➡**The throttle lever must not touch the ISC plunger.**

3. Connect the cruise control cable to the hole in the servo blade that leaves minimum cable slack.
4. Install the retainer at the servo.

Vacuum Dump Valve

REMOVAL & INSTALLATION

Deville, Fleetwood and Sixty Special

Refer to the Brake Switch removal and installation procedures in this Section.

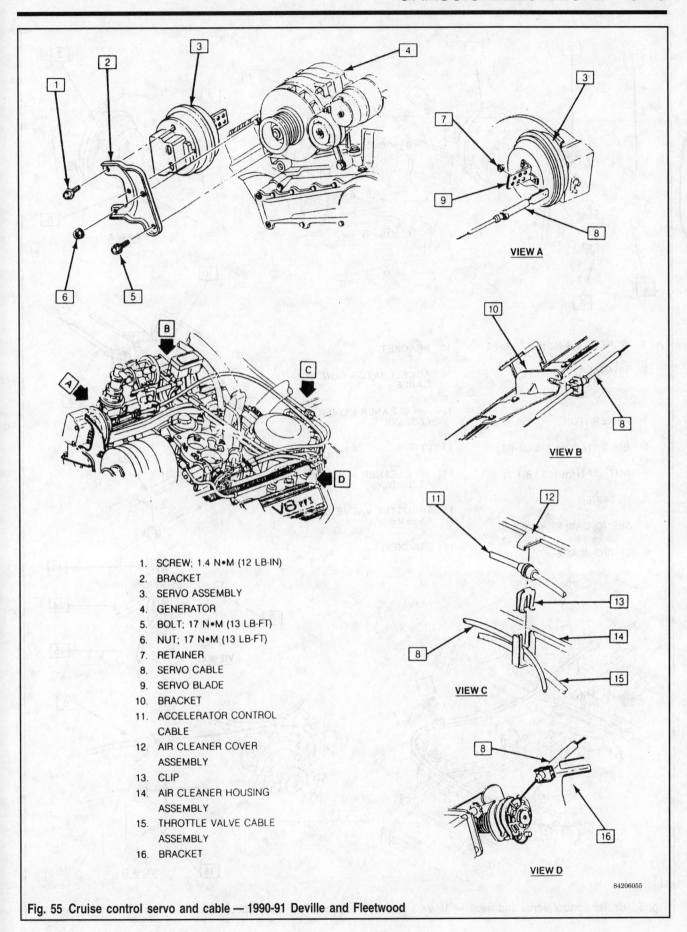

1. SCREW; 1.4 N•M (12 LB-IN)
2. BRACKET
3. SERVO ASSEMBLY
4. GENERATOR
5. BOLT; 17 N•M (13 LB-FT)
6. NUT; 17 N•M (13 LB-FT)
7. RETAINER
8. SERVO CABLE
9. SERVO BLADE
10. BRACKET
11. ACCELERATOR CONTROL
    CABLE
12. AIR CLEANER COVER
    ASSEMBLY
13. CLIP
14. AIR CLEANER HOUSING
    ASSEMBLY
15. THROTTLE VALVE CABLE
    ASSEMBLY
16. BRACKET

VIEW A

VIEW B

VIEW C

VIEW D

84206055

Fig. 55 Cruise control servo and cable — 1990-91 Deville and Fleetwood

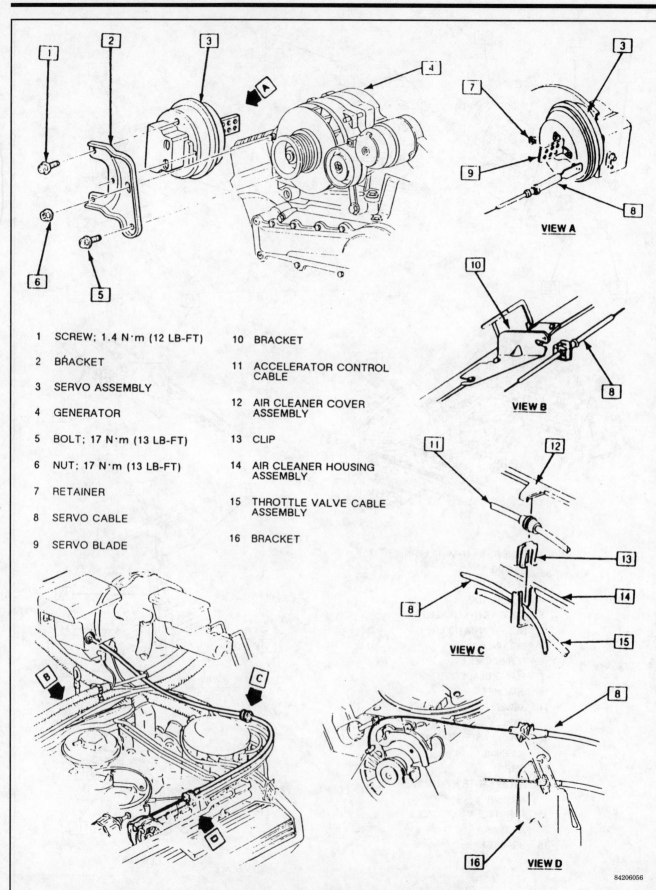

1 SCREW; 1.4 N·m (12 LB-FT)
2 BRACKET
3 SERVO ASSEMBLY
4 GENERATOR
5 BOLT; 17 N·m (13 LB-FT)
6 NUT; 17 N·m (13 LB-FT)
7 RETAINER
8 SERVO CABLE
9 SERVO BLADE

10 BRACKET
11 ACCELERATOR CONTROL CABLE
12 AIR CLEANER COVER ASSEMBLY
13 CLIP
14 AIR CLEANER HOUSING ASSEMBLY
15 THROTTLE VALVE CABLE ASSEMBLY
16 BRACKET

VIEW A

VIEW B

VIEW C

VIEW D

84206056

Fig. 56 Cruise control servo and cable — 1992-93 Deville, Fleetwood and Sixty Special

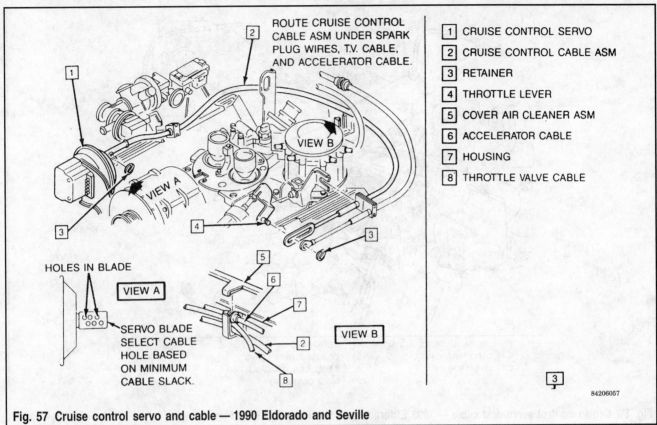

ROUTE CRUISE CONTROL
CABLE ASM UNDER SPARK
PLUG WIRES, T.V. CABLE,
AND ACCELERATOR CABLE.

1	CRUISE CONTROL SERVO
2	CRUISE CONTROL CABLE ASM
3	RETAINER
4	THROTTLE LEVER
5	COVER AIR CLEANER ASM
6	ACCELERATOR CABLE
7	HOUSING
8	THROTTLE VALVE CABLE

HOLES IN BLADE

VIEW A

SERVO BLADE
SELECT CABLE
HOLE BASED
ON MINIMUM
CABLE SLACK.

VIEW B

84206057

Fig. 57 Cruise control servo and cable — 1990 Eldorado and Seville

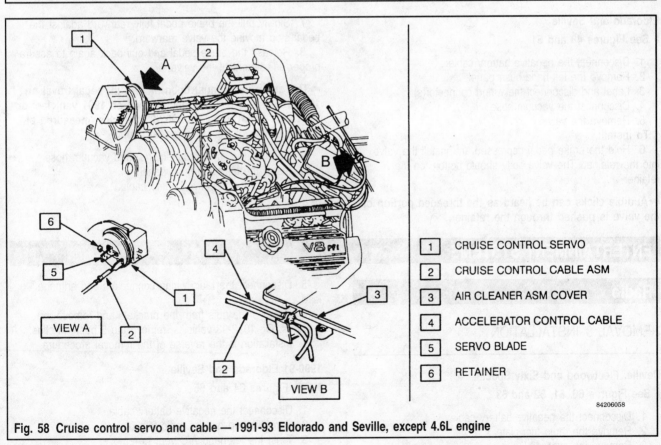

V8 PFI

1	CRUISE CONTROL SERVO
2	CRUISE CONTROL CABLE ASM
3	AIR CLEANER ASM COVER
4	ACCELERATOR CONTROL CABLE
5	SERVO BLADE
6	RETAINER

VIEW A

VIEW B

84206058

Fig. 58 Cruise control servo and cable — 1991-93 Eldorado and Seville, except 4.6L engine

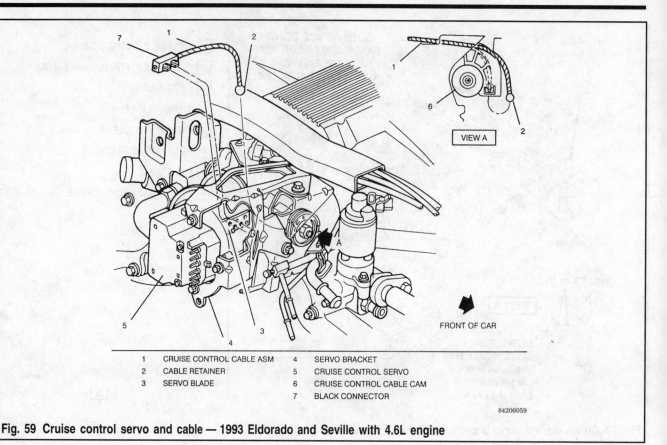

1	CRUISE CONTROL CABLE ASM	4	SERVO BRACKET
2	CABLE RETAINER	5	CRUISE CONTROL SERVO
3	SERVO BLADE	6	CRUISE CONTROL CABLE CAM
		7	BLACK CONNECTOR

84206059

Fig. 59 Cruise control servo and cable — 1993 Eldorado and Seville with 4.6L engine

Eldorado and Seville

▶ **See Figures 48 and 51**

1. Disconnect the negative battery cable.
2. Remove the left-hand hush panel.
3. Label and disconnect the wiring connector(s).
4. Disconnect the vacuum hose.
5. Remove the valve.

To install:

6. Hold the brake pedal depressed and install the valve into the retainer. The valve body should bottom on the retainer.

➡**Audible clicks can be heard as the threaded portion of the valve is pushed through the retainer.**

7. Slowly pull the brake pedal fully rearward against the pedal stop moving the valve rearward.
8. Release the brake pedal and pull back again to assure proper adjustment of the valve.

➡**The dump valve must open at 1-1/16 in. pedal travel on 1990 vehicles, 0.6-0.8 in. pedal travel on 1991 vehicles, or 1.2-1.4 in. pedal travel on 1992-93 vehicles, measured at the centerline of the brake pedal pad.**

9. Connect the wiring connector(s) and vacuum hose.
10. Install the left-hand hush panel.
11. Connect the negative battery cable.

ENTERTAINMENT SYSTEMS

Radio

REMOVAL & INSTALLATION

Deville, Fleetwood and Sixty Special

▶ **See Figures 60, 61, 62 and 63**

1. Disconnect the negative battery cable.
2. Remove the radio trim plate.
3. Remove the ashtray.
4. Remove one screw from the rear radio support bracket and 2 screws from the front of the radio.

5. Disconnect the radio wiring connectors and antenna lead.
6. Remove the nuts from the brackets and remove the brackets. On 1992-93 vehicles, remove the 5 push-on clips.
7. Installation is the reverse of the removal procedure.

1990-91 Eldorado and Seville

▶ **See Figures 64 and 65**

1. Disconnect the negative battery cable.
2. Carefully pop out the radio trim plate.
3. Twist the left-hand A/C vent to remove.
4. Remove the 7 instrument panel trim plate retaining screws and remove the trim plate.

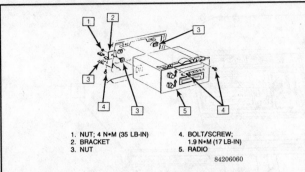

1. NUT; 4 N•M (35 LB-IN)
2. BRACKET
3. NUT
4. BOLT/SCREW; 1.9 N•M (17 LB-IN)
5. RADIO

84206060

Fig. 60 Radio installation — 1990-91 Deville and Fleetwood

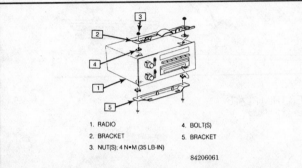

1. RADIO
2. BRACKET
3. NUT(S); 4 N•M (35 LB-IN)
4. BOLT(S)
5. BRACKET

84206061

Fig. 61 Radio bracket installation — 1990-91 Deville and Fleetwood

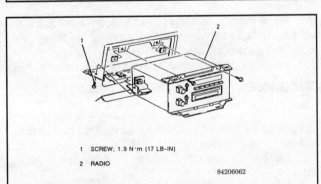

1 SCREW; 1.9 N·m (17 LB-IN)
2 RADIO

84206062

Fig. 62 Radio installation — 1992-93 Deville, Fleetwood and Sixty Special

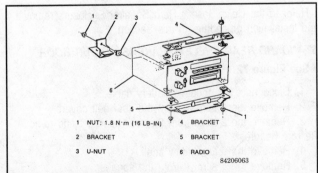

1 NUT; 1.8 N·m (16 LB-IN)
2 BRACKET
3 U-NUT
4 BRACKET
5 BRACKET
6 RADIO

84206063

Fig. 63 Radio bracket installation — 1992-93 Deville, Fleetwood and Sixty Special

5. Loosen the lower 2 mounting nuts under the radio.
6. Slide the radio forward and disconnect the wiring connectors and antenna lead. Remove the radio.
7. Installation is the reverse of the removal procedure.

1992-93 Eldorado and Seville

RADIO CONTROL HEAD WITH CONSOLE SHIFT

▶ **See Figure 66**

1. Disconnect the negative battery cable.
2. Remove the radio trim plate.
3. Remove the console trim plate; it pulls up first from the upper edge.
4. Remove the 2 nuts from the bottom of the control head.
5. Twist the control head so the right side exits first from the dash to clear the connectors on the left side.
6. Disconnect the wiring connectors and remove the radio control head.
7. Installation is the reverse of the removal procedure.

RADIO CONTROL HEAD WITH COLUMN SHIFT

▶ **See Figure 67**

1. Disconnect the negative battery cable.
2. Remove the radio trim plate.
3. Remove the 4 screws from the side brackets.
4. Pull out the control head and disconnect the wiring connectors. Remove the radio control head.
5. Installation is the reverse of the removal procedure.

REMOTE RADIO RECEIVER

▶ **See Figures 68 and 69**

1. Disconnect the negative battery cable.
2. Open the trunk.
3. On 1992 vehicles, remove the close out panel from the trunk electronics bay. On 1993 vehicles, remove the right hand trunk trim.
4. Disconnect the wiring connectors and antenna lead.
5. Remove the receiver attaching nuts and remove the receiver.
6. Installation is the reverse of the removal procedure.

Speakers

REMOVAL & INSTALLATION

1990-91 Deville and Fleetwood

STANDARD FRONT SPEAKER

▶ **See Figure 70**

1. Disconnect the negative battery cable.
2. Remove the 3 screws from the defroster grille.
3. Remove the 4 A/C outlets, then remove the 4 screws from behind the outlets.
4. Remove the instrument panel upper trim pad; refer to the instrument panel removal and installation procedure in Section 10.
5. Remove the aspirator tube and wiring connector from the in-vehicle temperature sensor.

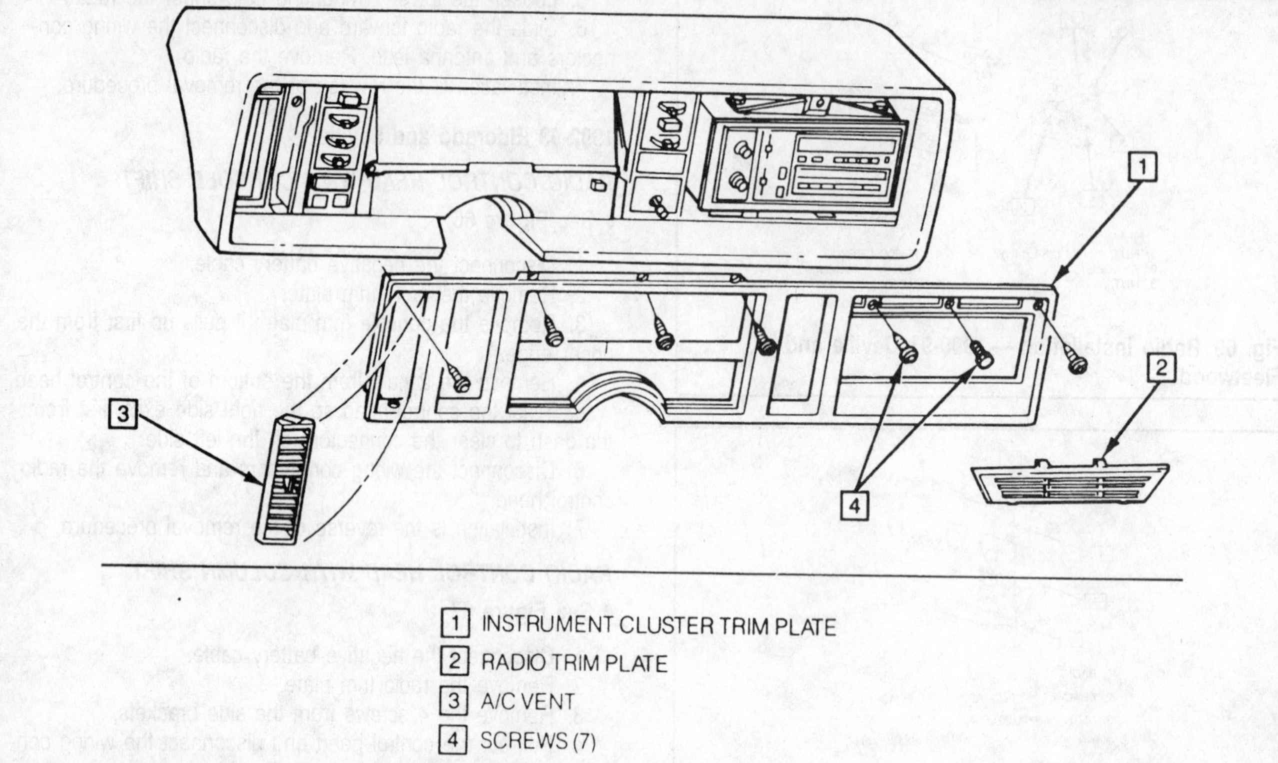

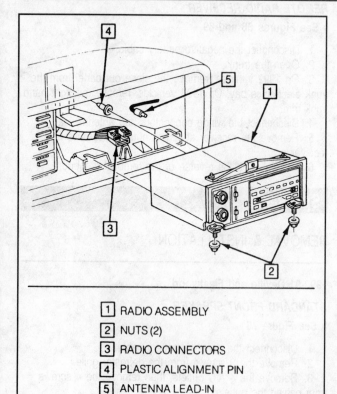

1 INSTRUMENT CLUSTER TRIM PLATE
2 RADIO TRIM PLATE
3 A/C VENT
4 SCREWS (7)

84206064

Fig. 64 Instrument panel trim plate removal — 1990-91 Eldorado and Seville

1 RADIO ASSEMBLY
2 NUTS (2)
3 RADIO CONNECTORS
4 PLASTIC ALIGNMENT PIN
5 ANTENNA LEAD-IN

84206065

Fig. 65 Radio removal — 1990-91 Eldorado and Seville

6. Remove the 2 mounting screws from the speaker flange and pull out the speaker assembly. Disconnect the wiring connector and remove the speaker.

7. Installation is the reverse of the removal procedure.

DELCO/BOSE® FRONT SPEAKER ENCLOSURE

▶ **See Figure 71**

1. Raise the door glass to the full-up position, then disconnect the negative battery cable.

2. Remove the door panel; refer to the procedure in Section 10.

3. Remove the speaker enclosure retaining screws.

4. Disconnect the wiring connector and remove the speaker.

5. Installation is the reverse of the removal procedure.

STANDARD REAR SHELF SPEAKERS — TWO DOOR

Refer to the Delco/Bose® Rear Speaker Enclosure removal and installation procedure, in this Section.

STANDARD REAR SHELF SPEAKERS — FOUR DOOR

▶ **See Figure 72**

1. Disconnect the negative battery cable.

2. Remove the 2 screws from the seat belt covers.

3. Remove the 2 bolts from the rear headrest and remove the rear headrest.

4. Remove the rear window shelf.

5. Remove the 4 screws from the speaker.

6. Disconnect the wiring connector and remove the speaker.

7. Installation is the reverse of the removal procedure.

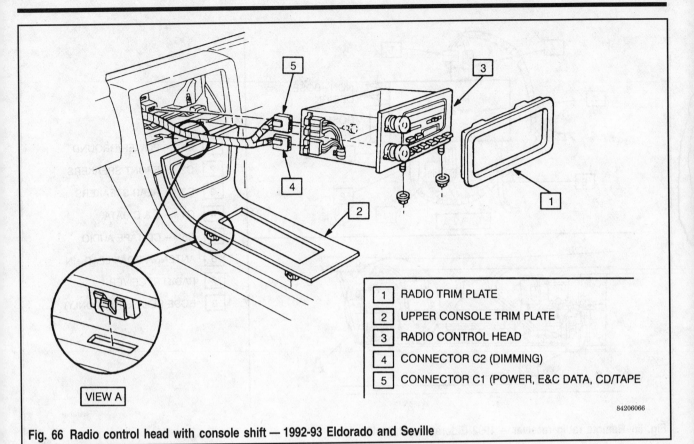

VIEW A

1	RADIO TRIM PLATE
2	UPPER CONSOLE TRIM PLATE
3	RADIO CONTROL HEAD
4	CONNECTOR C2 (DIMMING)
5	CONNECTOR C1 (POWER, E&C DATA, CD/TAPE

84206066

Fig. 66 Radio control head with console shift — 1992-93 Eldorado and Seville

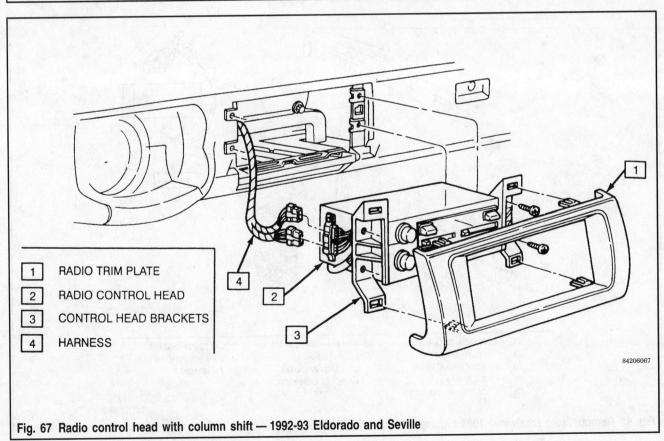

1	RADIO TRIM PLATE
2	RADIO CONTROL HEAD
3	CONTROL HEAD BRACKETS
4	HARNESS

84206067

Fig. 67 Radio control head with column shift — 1992-93 Eldorado and Seville

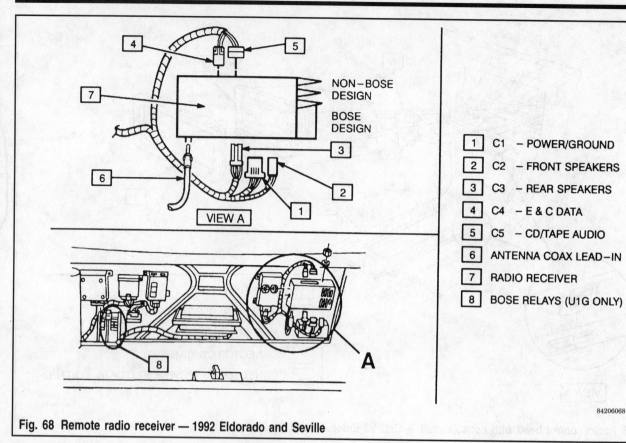

1	C1	– POWER/GROUND
2	C2	– FRONT SPEAKERS
3	C3	– REAR SPEAKERS
4	C4	– E & C DATA
5	C5	– CD/TAPE AUDIO
6	ANTENNA COAX LEAD–IN	
7	RADIO RECEIVER	
8	BOSE RELAYS (U1G ONLY)	

84206068

Fig. 68 Remote radio receiver — 1992 Eldorado and Seville

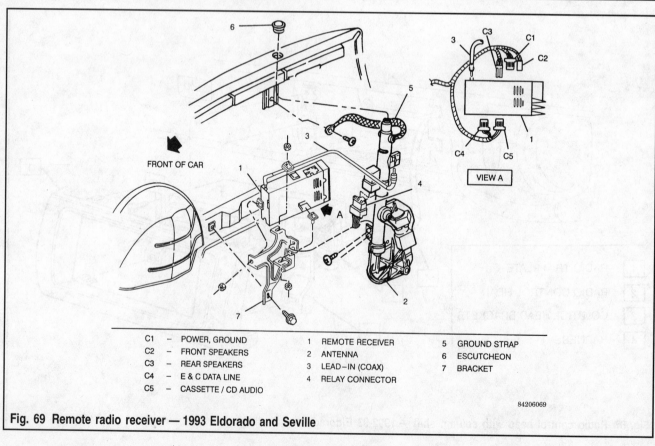

C1	– POWER, GROUND	1	REMOTE RECEIVER	5	GROUND STRAP
C2	– FRONT SPEAKERS	2	ANTENNA	6	ESCUTCHEON
C3	– REAR SPEAKERS	3	LEAD–IN (COAX)	7	BRACKET
C4	– E & C DATA LINE	4	RELAY CONNECTOR		
C5	– CASSETTE / CD AUDIO				

84206069

Fig. 69 Remote radio receiver — 1993 Eldorado and Seville

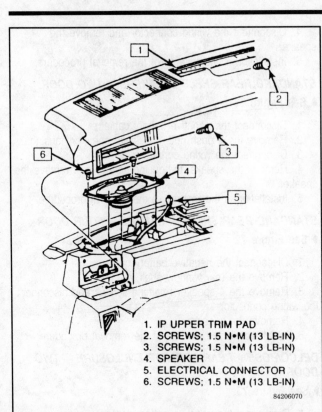

1. IP UPPER TRIM PAD
2. SCREWS; 1.5 N•M (13 LB-IN)
3. SCREWS; 1.5 N•M (13 LB-IN)
4. SPEAKER
5. ELECTRICAL CONNECTOR
6. SCREWS; 1.5 N•M (13 LB-IN)

84206070

Fig. 70 Standard front speaker installation — 1990-91 Deville and Fleetwood

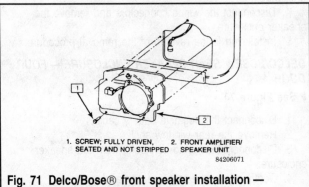

1. SCREW; FULLY DRIVEN, SEATED AND NOT STRIPPED
2. FRONT AMPLIFIER/ SPEAKER UNIT

84206071

Fig. 71 Delco/Bose® front speaker installation — Deville, Fleetwood and Sixty Special

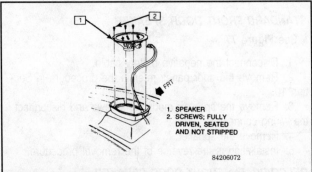

1. SPEAKER
2. SCREWS; FULLY DRIVEN, SEATED AND NOT STRIPPED

84206072

Fig. 72 Standard rear shelf speaker — Deville, Fleetwood and Sixty Special

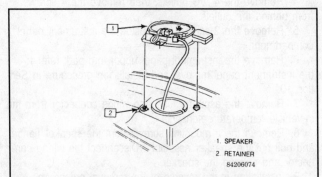

1. SPEAKER ASSEMBLY
2. NUT
3. SCREW/BOLT. 1 4 N•M (12 LB-IN)

84206073

Fig. 73 Rear speaker installation, two door vehicles — Deville, Fleetwood and Sixty Special

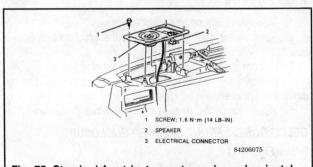

1. SPEAKER
2. RETAINER

84206074

Fig. 74 Delco/Bose® rear speaker installation, four door vehicles — Deville, Fleetwood and Sixty Special

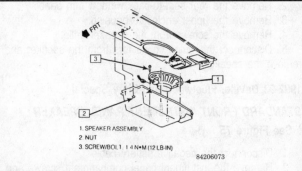

1. SCREW; 1.6 N·m (14 LB-IN)
2. SPEAKER
3. ELECTRICAL CONNECTOR

84206075

Fig. 75 Standard front instrument panel speaker installation — 1992-93 Deville, Fleetwood and Sixty Special

DELCO/BOSE® REAR SPEAKER ENCLOSURE — TWO DOOR

▶ See Figure 73

1. Disconnect the negative battery cable.
2. Open the trunk.
3. Remove the 2 speed nuts and lower the speaker enclosure.
4. Disconnect the wiring connectors and remove the speaker enclosure.
5. Installation is the reverse of the removal procedure.

DELCO/BOSE® REAR SPEAKER ENCLOSURE — FOUR DOOR

▶ See Figure 74

1. Disconnect the negative battery cable.

2. Remove the rear seat-to-back window trim panel.
3. Remove the upper enclosure housing.
4. Remove the screws from the speaker grille.
5. Disconnect the wiring connectors from the speaker and remove the speaker.

1992-93 Deville, Fleetwood and Sixty Special

STANDARD FRONT INSTRUMENT PANEL SPEAKER

▶ See Figure 75

1. Disconnect the negative battery cable.
2. Remove the instrument panel compartment screws and compartment.
3. Remove the 3 screws from the defroster grille.
4. Remove the 4 A/C outlets, then remove the 4 screws from behind the outlets.
5. Remove the 2 screws from inside the instrument panel compartment.
6. Remove the instrument panel upper trim pad; refer to the instrument panel removal and installation procedure in Section 10.
7. Remove the aspirator tube and wiring connector from the in-vehicle temperature sensor.
8. Remove the 2 mounting screws from the speaker flange and pull out the speaker assembly. Disconnect the wiring connector and remove the speaker.
9. Installation is the reverse of the removal procedure.

STANDARD FRONT DOOR SPEAKER

▶ See Figure 76

1. Disconnect the negative battery cable.
2. Remove the door panel; refer to the procedure in Section 10.
3. Disconnect the speaker wiring connector.
4. Remove the speaker-to-housing retaining screws and remove the speaker.
5. Installation is the reverse of the removal procedure.

DELCO/BOSE® FRONT SPEAKER ENCLOSURE

▶ See Figure 71

1. Raise the door glass to the full-up position, then disconnect the negative battery cable.
2. Remove the door panel; refer to the procedure in Section 10.
3. Remove the speaker enclosure retaining screws.

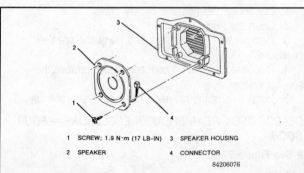

1 SCREW: 1.9 N·m (17 LB-IN)   3 SPEAKER HOUSING
2 SPEAKER   4 CONNECTOR
84206076

Fig. 76 Standard front door speaker — 1992-93 Deville, Fleetwood and Sixty Special

4. Disconnect the wiring connector and remove the speaker.
5. Installation is the reverse of the removal procedure.

STANDARD REAR SHELF SPEAKERS — TWO DOOR

▶ See Figure 73

1. Disconnect the negative battery cable.
2. Remove the 2 push nuts and lower speaker housing.
3. Disconnect the wiring connector.
4. Remove the speaker-to-housing screws and remove the speaker.
5. Installation is the reverse of the removal procedure.

STANDARD REAR SHELF SPEAKERS — FOUR DOOR

▶ See Figure 72

1. Disconnect the negative battery cable.
2. Remove the rear window shelf.
3. Remove the 4 speaker retaining screws and disconnect the wiring connector.
4. Remove the speaker.
5. Installation is the reverse of the removal procedure.

DELCO/BOSE® REAR SPEAKER ENCLOSURE — TWO DOOR

▶ See Figure 73

1. Disconnect the negative battery cable.
2. Open the trunk.
3. Remove the 2 push nuts and lower the speaker enclosure.
4. Disconnect the wiring connectors and remove the speaker enclosure.
5. Installation is the reverse of the removal procedure.

DELCO/BOSE® REAR SPEAKER ENCLOSURE — FOUR DOOR

▶ See Figure 74

1. Disconnect the negative battery cable.
2. Remove the rear window shelf.
3. Disconnect the wiring connector from the speaker enclosure.
4. Gently pry up the rear speaker enclosure.
5. Installation is the reverse of the removal procedure.

1990-91 Eldorado and Seville

STANDARD FRONT DOOR SPEAKER

▶ See Figure 77

1. Disconnect the negative battery cable.
2. Remove the door panel; refer to the procedure in Section 10.
3. Remove the speaker mounting screws and disconnect the wiring connector.
4. Remove the speaker.
5. Installation is the reverse of the removal procedure.

DELCO/BOSE® FRONT DOOR SPEAKER

▶ See Figures 78 and 79

1. Disconnect the negative battery cable.
2. Remove the door panel; refer to the procedure in Section 10.

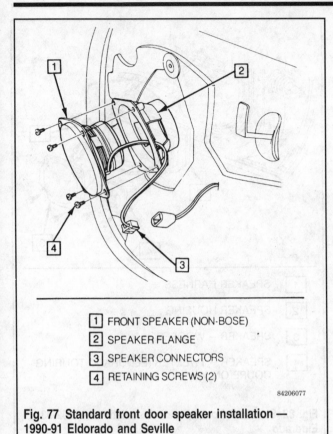

1 FRONT SPEAKER (NON-BOSE)
2 SPEAKER FLANGE
3 SPEAKER CONNECTORS
4 RETAINING SCREWS (2)

84206077

**Fig. 77 Standard front door speaker installation —
1990-91 Eldorado and Seville**

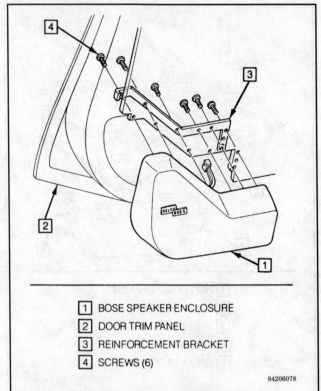

1 BOSE SPEAKER ENCLOSURE
2 DOOR TRIM PANEL
3 REINFORCEMENT BRACKET
4 SCREWS (6)

84206078

**Fig. 78 Delco/Bose® front door speaker enclosure re-
moval — 1990-91 Eldorado and Seville**

3. Disconnect the speaker wiring connector.

4. Remove the screws retaining the speaker enclosure to
the door panel through the metal support strip and remove the
speaker enclosure.

5. Carefully peel back the carpet from the enclosure lip.

6. Remove the screws retaining the rear enclosure cover.

7. Remove the screws retaining the speaker and disconnect
the speaker wiring connector.

8. Remove the speaker.

9. Installation is the reverse of the removal procedure.

REAR SPEAKERS

♦ See Figures 80 and 81

1. Disconnect the negative battery cable.

2. Open the trunk.

3. Remove the 2 plastic speed nuts attaching the speaker
enclosure, then swing the enclosure down. The other side is
held up by the flange only.

4. Remove the speaker bracket spring clip, then swing the
bracket down. The other side is held up by the flange only.

5. Disconnect the speaker wiring connector.

6. If equipped with the standard speakers, lift the speaker
out of the bracket.

7. If equipped with Delco/Bose® speakers, remove the
screws accessed through the bottom of the amplifier. Remove
the screw through the bracket into the speaker magnet and
remove the speaker.

8. Installation is the reverse of the removal procedure.

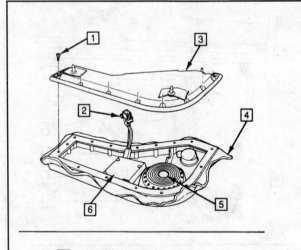

1 RETAINING SCREWS (12)
2 SPEAKER CONNECTOR
3 BOSE ENCLOSURE COVER
4 ENCLOSURE CARPET TRIM COVER
5 SPEAKER
6 BOSE AMPLIFIER

84206079

**Fig. 79 Delco/Bose® front door speaker removal —
1990-91 Eldorado and Seville**

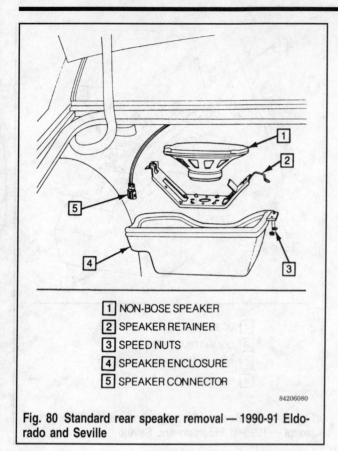

1 NON-BOSE SPEAKER
2 SPEAKER RETAINER
3 SPEED NUTS
4 SPEAKER ENCLOSURE
5 SPEAKER CONNECTOR

84206080

Fig. 80 Standard rear speaker removal — 1990-91 Eldorado and Seville

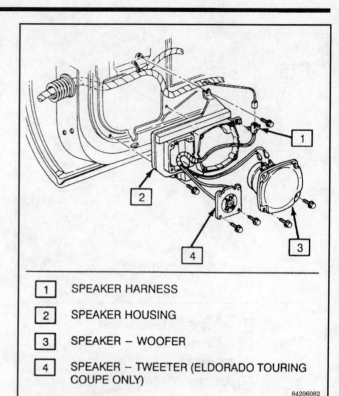

1 SPEAKER HARNESS
2 SPEAKER HOUSING
3 SPEAKER – WOOFER
4 SPEAKER – TWEETER (ELDORADO TOURING COUPE ONLY)

84206082

Fig. 82 Standard front speaker installation — 1992-93 Eldorado

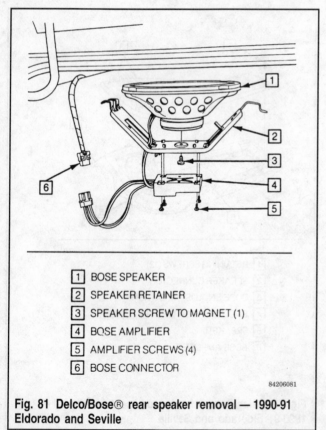

1 BOSE SPEAKER
2 SPEAKER RETAINER
3 SPEAKER SCREW TO MAGNET (1)
4 BOSE AMPLIFIER
5 AMPLIFIER SCREWS (4)
6 BOSE CONNECTOR

84206081

Fig. 81 Delco/Bose® rear speaker removal — 1990-91 Eldorado and Seville

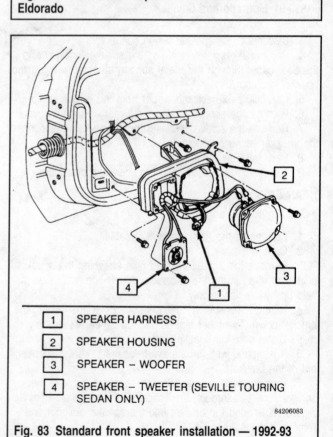

1 SPEAKER HARNESS
2 SPEAKER HOUSING
3 SPEAKER – WOOFER
4 SPEAKER – TWEETER (SEVILLE TOURING SEDAN ONLY)

84206083

Fig. 83 Standard front speaker installation — 1992-93 Seville

1992-93 Eldorado and Seville

FRONT DOOR SPEAKER

▶ **See Figures 82, 83, 84 and 85**

1. Disconnect the negative battery cable.
2. Remove the door panel; refer to the procedure in Section 10.
3. Disconnect the speaker wiring connector.
4. Remove the screws to release the speaker unit.
5. If equipped with standard speakers, remove the retaining screws and disconnect the wiring connector. Remove the speaker.
6. If equipped with Delco/Bose® speakers, remove the amplifier cover and gasket and remove the amplifier. Disconnect the wiring connector and remove the speaker.
7. Installation is the reverse of the removal procedure.

REAR SPEAKER

▶ **See Figures 86 and 87**

1. Disconnect the negative battery cable.
2. Remove the rear seat cushion, seat back and quarter trim panel; refer to Section 10.
3. Remove the rear shelf trim panel.
4. Disconnect the wiring connector and pry the speaker from the retaining clips.
5. Installation is the reverse of the removal procedure.

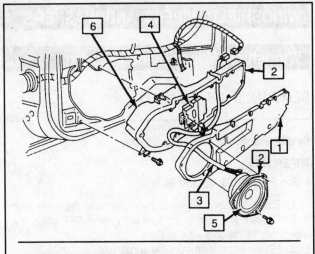

1	SPEAKER/AMPLIFIER ASSEMBLY COVER
2	GASKET
3	SPEAKER/AMPLIFIER HARNESS
4	AMPLIFIER
5	SPEAKER
6	SPEAKER/AMPLIFIER ASSEMBLY

84206085

Fig. 85 Delco/Bose® front speaker installation — 1992-93 Seville

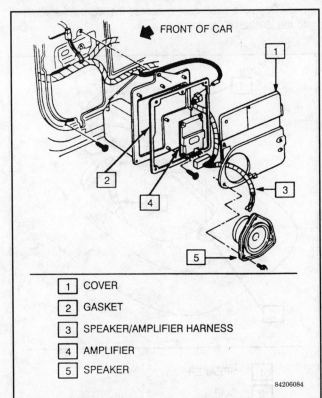

FRONT OF CAR

1	COVER
2	GASKET
3	SPEAKER/AMPLIFIER HARNESS
4	AMPLIFIER
5	SPEAKER

84206084

Fig. 84 Delco/Bose® front speaker installation — 1992-93 Eldorado

WINDSHIELD WIPERS AND WASHERS

Windshield Wiper Blade and Arm

REMOVAL & INSTALLATION

Deville, Fleetwood and Sixty Special

WIPER ARM

▶ **See Figures 88, 89 and 90**

1. Raise the hood as needed for access to the wiper arms.
2. Operate the wipers and turn the ignition **OFF** when the wipers are at the mid-wipe position.
3. Lift the wiper arm from the windshield.
4. On 1990 vehicles, pull the retaining latch and remove the arm from the transmission shaft.
5. On 1991-93 vehicles, disengage the retaining latch using a suitable tool and remove the arm from the transmission shaft.

To install:

6. Install the wiper arm onto the transmission shaft.
7. Push the retaining latch in and return the arm assembly to the windshield.
8. Park the wipers. If adjustment is necessary, proceed as follows:

   a. Remove the right wiper arm.

   b. Open the small door to access the wiper linkage; refer to the illustration for details.

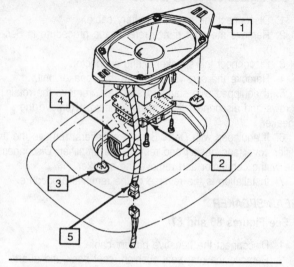

1	SPEAKER ASSEMBLY
2	AMPLIFIER
3	CLIP
4	AMPLIFIER HARNESS
5	SPEAKER/AMPLIFIER ASSEMBLY HARNESS

84206087

Fig. 87 Delco/Bose® rear speaker installation — 1992-93 Eldorado and Seville

   c. Loosen, but do not remove the transmission linkage adjustment nuts.

   d. Rotate the left arm and blade assembly to slightly below the blade stops.

   e. On 1990 vehicles, tighten the transmission adjustment screws to 64 inch lbs. (7 Nm). On 1991 vehicles, tighten the transmission linkage adjustment nuts to 44 inch lbs. (5 Nm). On 1992-93 vehicles, tighten the transmission linkage adjustment nuts to 71 inch lbs. (8 Nm).

   f. Position the right wiper arm and blade assembly slightly below the blade stops, then install the arm onto the transmission shaft.

   g. Lift both arm and blade assemblies over the stops.

   h. Check the wiper pattern and park position with the windshield wet and the wipers operating at low speed. Dimension A in figure '84206090' should be $^{11}/_{16}$ from the top of the driver's blade assembly on the outwipe to the edge of the glass.

WIPER BLADE

▶ **See Figures 91 and 92**

1. Operate the wipers and turn the ignition **OFF** when the wipers are at the mid-wipe position.
2. If equipped with Anco® blades, lift the blade retainer.
3. If equipped with Trico® blades, use a suitable tool to disengage the blade retainer.
4. Remove the wiper blade.

To install:

5. Install the wiper blade onto the wiper arm by pushing.

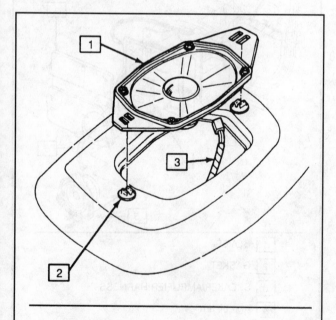

1	SPEAKER
2	CLIP
3	SPEAKER HARNESS

84206086

Fig. 86 Standard rear speaker installation — 1992-93 Eldorado and Seville

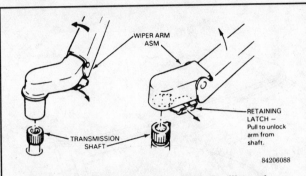

Fig. 88 Wiper arm attachment — 1990 Deville and Fleetwood

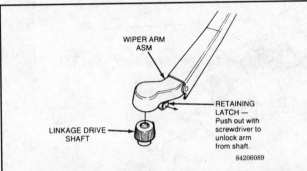

Fig. 89 Wiper arm attachment — 1991-93 Deville, Fleetwood and Sixty Special

6. Park the wipers.

1990-91 Eldorado and Seville

WIPER ARM

▶ See Figures 93, 94 and 95

1. Operate the wipers and turn the ignition **OFF** when the wipers are at the mid-wipe position.
2. Disconnect the hose on the wiper arm from the hose connector.
3. Lift the wiper arm from the windshield and pull the retaining latch.
4. Remove the arm from the transmission shaft.

To install:

5. Install the arm on the transmission shaft.
6. Push the retaining latch in and return the arm to the windshield.
7. Connect the hose on the wiper arm to the hose connector.
8. Park the wipers. If adjustment is necessary, proceed as follows:
   a. Raise the hood and remove the wiper arms.
   b. Open the transmission adjustment window on the left side of the cowl vent screen.
   c. Loosen, but do not remove the transmission drive link-to-motor crank arm attaching screws.
   d. Position the left arm and blade assembly to the transmission shaft. Align the slot in the arm to the keyway and push the arm down. Engage the slide latch.
   e. Rotate the left arm assembly to a position one inch below the ramp stop.

f. Tighten the attaching screws on the transmission link-to-motor crank arm to 4 ft. lbs. (6 Nm).

g. While the left arm assembly is still below the ramp stop, position the right arm and blade assembly to the transmission shaft approximately one inch below the ramp stop. Push the arm down and engage the slide latch.

h. Close the adjustment window and place the arm assemblies on the ramp stop on the vent screen.

i. Check the wiper pattern and park position as shown in Figures '84206094' and '84206095'. The outwipe dimensions are determined with the wipers operating at low speed on wet glass.

WIPER BLADE

▶ See Figure 93

1. Operate the wipers and turn the ignition **OFF** when the wipers are at the mid-wipe position.
2. Use a suitable tool to disengage the blade retainer.
3. Remove the wiper blade.

To install:

4. Install the wiper blade onto the wiper arm by pushing.
5. Park the wipers.

1992-93 Eldorado and Seville

WIPER ARM

▶ See Figures 96, 97, 98, 99 and 100

1. Turn the ignition **ON**, place the wipers in the park position, then turn the ignition **OFF**.
2. Disconnect the washer hose from the hose connector.
3. Remove the protective cap.
4. Lift the wiper arm and insert a suitable pin or pop rivet completely through the 2 holes located next to the pivot of the arm.
5. Remove the wiper arm retaining nut.
6. Lift the arm from the shaft using a rocking motion.

➡If the arm will not lift off the shaft using a rocking motion, use a battery terminal remover or similar tool to aid removal. Clean the knurls of the shaft with a suitable wire brush.

To install:

7. Connect the washer hose.
8. Install the wiper arm (without the blade) one inch below the park ramp.
9. Remove the pivot prevention pin from the wiper arm.
10. Install a new wiper arm retaining nut.
11. Lift the wiper arm over the park ramp and install the wiper blade.
12. Tighten the nut to 15-19 ft. lbs. (20-26 Nm).
13. Operate the wipers and check for correct wipe pattern. The left-hand blade tip should wipe from 1 3/16 to 3 3/16 from the inner edge of the windshield molding. The right-hand blade should overlap the left-hand wipe pattern.
14. Install the protective cap.

WIPER BLADE

▶ See Figure 92

1. Operate the wipers and turn the ignition **OFF** when the wipers are at the mid-wipe position.
2. Lift the blade release latch.

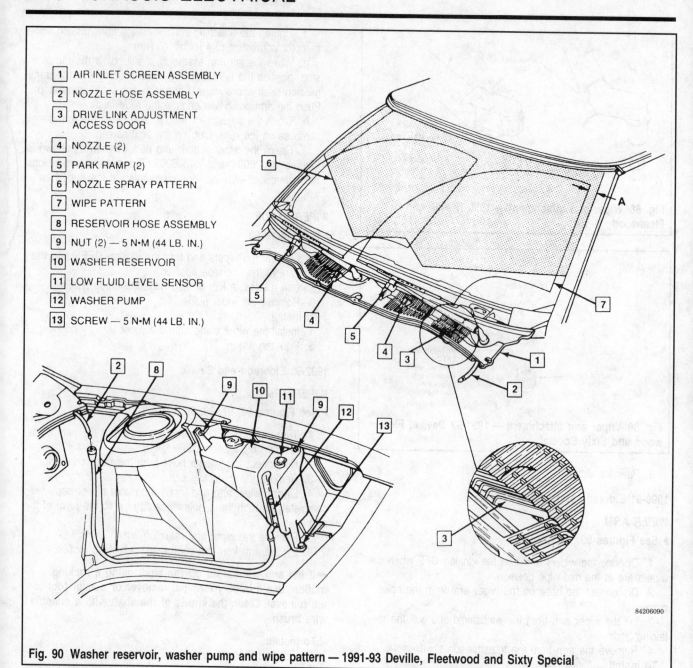

1. AIR INLET SCREEN ASSEMBLY
2. NOZZLE HOSE ASSEMBLY
3. DRIVE LINK ADJUSTMENT ACCESS DOOR
4. NOZZLE (2)
5. PARK RAMP (2)
6. NOZZLE SPRAY PATTERN
7. WIPE PATTERN
8. RESERVOIR HOSE ASSEMBLY
9. NUT (2) — 5 N•M (44 LB. IN.)
10. WASHER RESERVOIR
11. LOW FLUID LEVEL SENSOR
12. WASHER PUMP
13. SCREW — 5 N•M (44 LB. IN.)

Fig. 90 Washer reservoir, washer pump and wipe pattern — 1991-93 Deville, Fleetwood and Sixty Special

3. Remove the wiper blade.
To install:
4. Install the wiper blade onto the wiper arm.
5. Park the wipers.

Windshield Wiper Motor

REMOVAL & INSTALLATION

Deville, Fleetwood and Sixty Special
▶ **See Figures 101 and 102**

1. On 1991-93 vehicles, disconnect the washer hoses.
2. Remove the wiper arm and blade assemblies.

3. Remove the cowl screen.
4. Disconnect the motor drive link from the motor crank arm by loosening the nuts.
5. Disconnect the wiring connectors.
6. Remove the wiper motor mounting bolts and remove the wiper motor, guiding the crank arm through the hole.
To install:
7. Guide the wiper motor crank arm through the hole and position the wiper motor. Install the mounting bolts and tighten to 80 inch lbs. (9 Nm).
8. Connect the wiring connectors.
9. Attach the motor drive link to the motor crank arm and tighten the nuts.
10. Install the cowl screen.
11. Install the wiper arm and blade assemblies.
12. Connect the washer hoses.

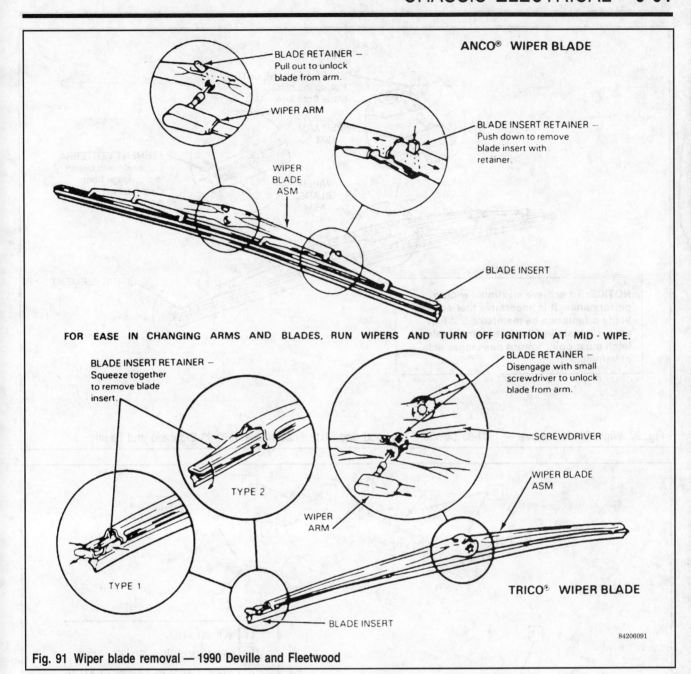

Fig. 91 Wiper blade removal — 1990 Deville and Fleetwood

Eldorado and Seville

▶ **See Figures 103 and 104**

1. On 1992-93 vehicles, remove the A/C pipe shroud.
2. Remove the wiper arms.
3. On 1990-91 vehicles, remove the windshield reveal molding.
4. Remove the cowl vent.
5. Disconnect the wiper arm drive link from the wiper motor.
6. Disconnect the wiring connectors.
7. On 1992-93 vehicles, remove the A/C pipe shroud bracket from the wheelwell.

8. Remove the wiper motor mounting bolts and remove the wiper motor.

To install:

9. Position the wiper motor and install the mounting bolts. Tighten to 80 inch lbs. (9 Nm).
10. On 1992-93 vehicles, install the A/C pipe shroud bracket to the wheelwell.
11. Connect the wiring connectors.
12. Connect the wiper arm drive link to the wiper motor.
13. Install the cowl vent.
14. On 1990-91 vehicles, install the windshield reveal molding.
15. Install the wiper arms.
16. On 1992-93 vehicles, install the A/C pipe shroud.

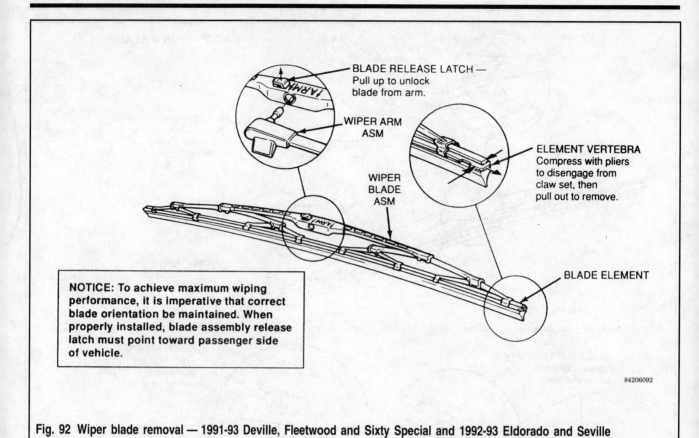

BLADE RELEASE LATCH —
Pull up to unlock
blade from arm.

WIPER ARM
ASM

WIPER
BLADE
ASM

ELEMENT VERTEBRA
Compress with pliers
to disengage from
claw set, then
pull out to remove.

BLADE ELEMENT

NOTICE: To achieve maximum wiping
performance, it is imperative that correct
blade orientation be maintained. When
properly installed, blade assembly release
latch must point toward passenger side
of vehicle.

84206092

Fig. 92 Wiper blade removal — 1991-93 Deville, Fleetwood and Sixty Special and 1992-93 Eldorado and Seville

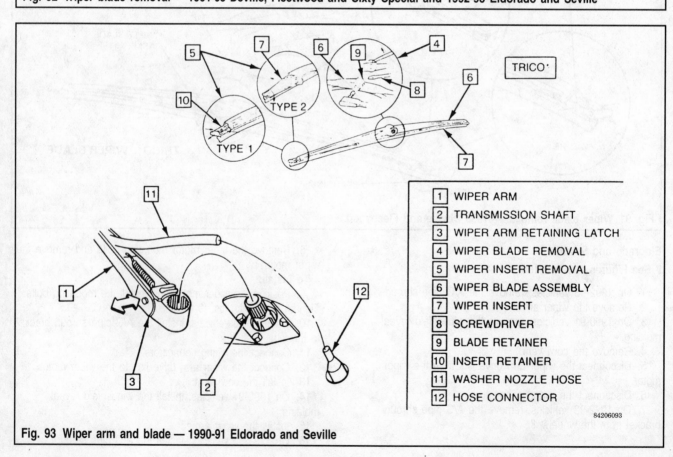

TRICO

1	WIPER ARM
2	TRANSMISSION SHAFT
3	WIPER ARM RETAINING LATCH
4	WIPER BLADE REMOVAL
5	WIPER INSERT REMOVAL
6	WIPER BLADE ASSEMBLY
7	WIPER INSERT
8	SCREWDRIVER
9	BLADE RETAINER
10	INSERT RETAINER
11	WASHER NOZZLE HOSE
12	HOSE CONNECTOR

84206093

Fig. 93 Wiper arm and blade — 1990-91 Eldorado and Seville

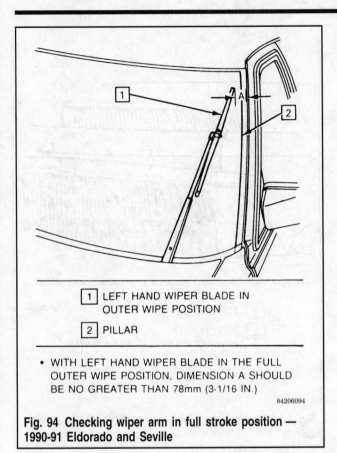

1. LEFT HAND WIPER BLADE IN OUTER WIPE POSITION

2. PILLAR

- WITH LEFT HAND WIPER BLADE IN THE FULL OUTER WIPE POSITION, DIMENSION A SHOULD BE NO GREATER THAN 78mm (3-1/16 IN.)

84206094

Fig. 94 Checking wiper arm in full stroke position — 1990-91 Eldorado and Seville

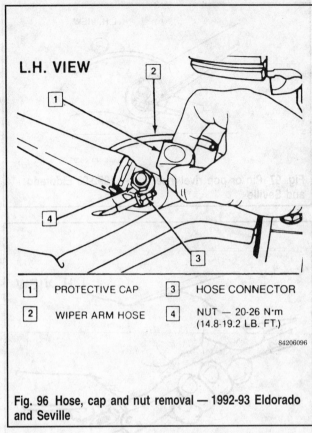

L.H. VIEW

| 1 | PROTECTIVE CAP | 3 | HOSE CONNECTOR |
| 2 | WIPER ARM HOSE | 4 | NUT — 20-26 N·m (14.8-19.2 LB. FT.) |

84206096

Fig. 96 Hose, cap and nut removal — 1992-93 Eldorado and Seville

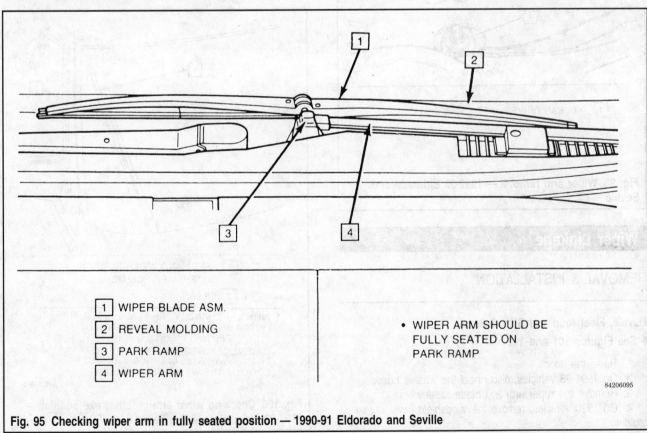

1. WIPER BLADE ASM.

2. REVEAL MOLDING

3. PARK RAMP

4. WIPER ARM

- WIPER ARM SHOULD BE FULLY SEATED ON PARK RAMP

84206095

Fig. 95 Checking wiper arm in fully seated position — 1990-91 Eldorado and Seville

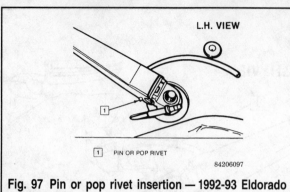

Fig. 97 Pin or pop rivet insertion — 1992-93 Eldorado and Seville

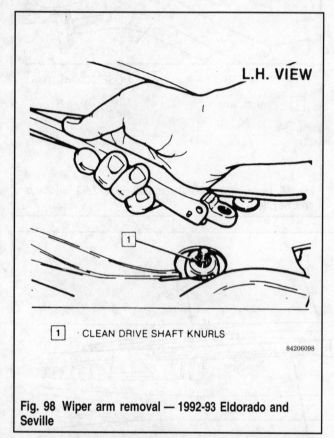

Fig. 98 Wiper arm removal — 1992-93 Eldorado and Seville

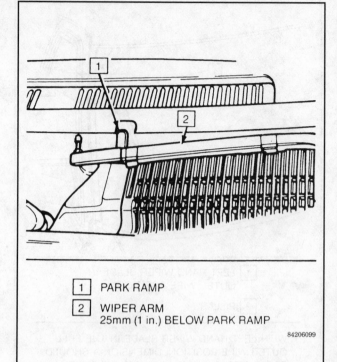

| 1 | PARK RAMP |
| 2 | WIPER ARM
25mm (1 in.) BELOW PARK RAMP |

Fig. 99 Wiper arm installation — 1992-93 Eldorado and Seville

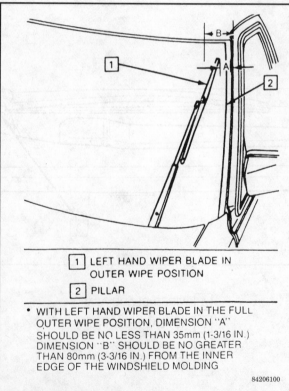

| 1 | LEFT HAND WIPER BLADE IN
OUTER WIPE POSITION |
| 2 | PILLAR |

* WITH LEFT HAND WIPER BLADE IN THE FULL
OUTER WIPE POSITION, DIMENSION ''A''
SHOULD BE NO LESS THAN 35mm (1-3/16 IN.)
DIMENSION ''B'' SHOULD BE NO GREATER
THAN 80mm (3-3/16 IN.) FROM THE INNER
EDGE OF THE WINDSHIELD MOLDING

Fig. 100 Checking wiper arm in full stroke position — 1992-93 Eldorado and Seville

Wiper Linkage

REMOVAL & INSTALLATION

Deville, Fleetwood and Sixty Special

▶ **See Figures 101 and 102**

1. Raise the hood.
2. On 1991-93 vehicles, disconnect the washer hoses.
3. Remove the wiper arm and blade assemblies.
4. On 1990 vehicles, remove the windshield lower reveal molding.
5. Remove the cowl screen.

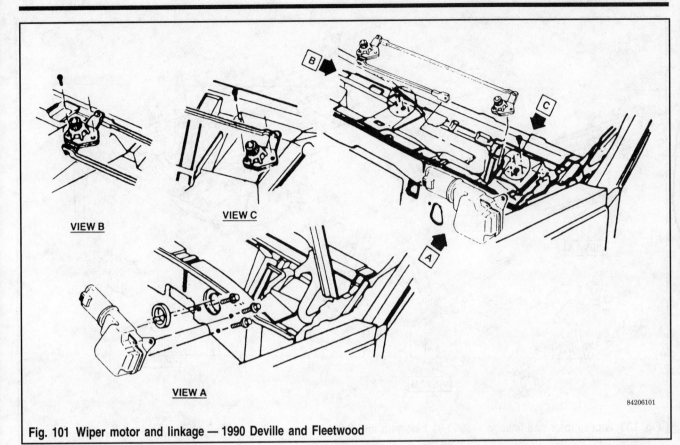

Fig. 101 Wiper motor and linkage — 1990 Deville and Fleetwood

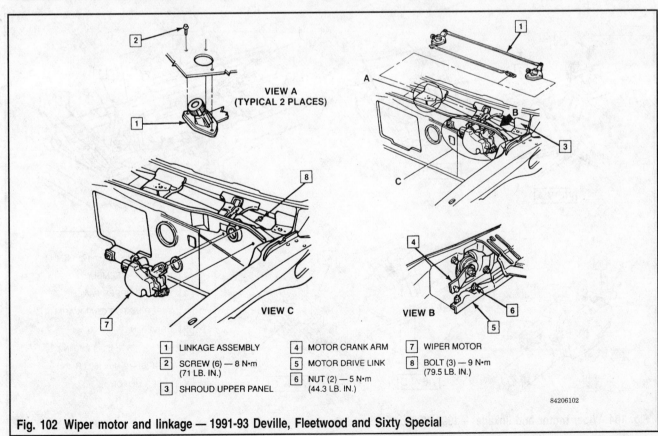

1	LINKAGE ASSEMBLY	4	MOTOR CRANK ARM	7	WIPER MOTOR
2	SCREW (6) — 8 N•m (71 LB. IN.)	5	MOTOR DRIVE LINK	8	BOLT (3) — 9 N•m (79.5 LB. IN.)
3	SHROUD UPPER PANEL	6	NUT (2) — 5 N•m (44.3 LB. IN.)		

Fig. 102 Wiper motor and linkage — 1991-93 Deville, Fleetwood and Sixty Special

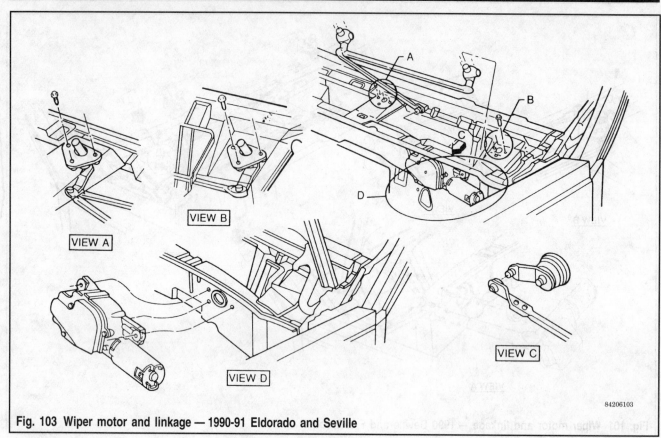

Fig. 103 Wiper motor and linkage — 1990-91 Eldorado and Seville

84206103

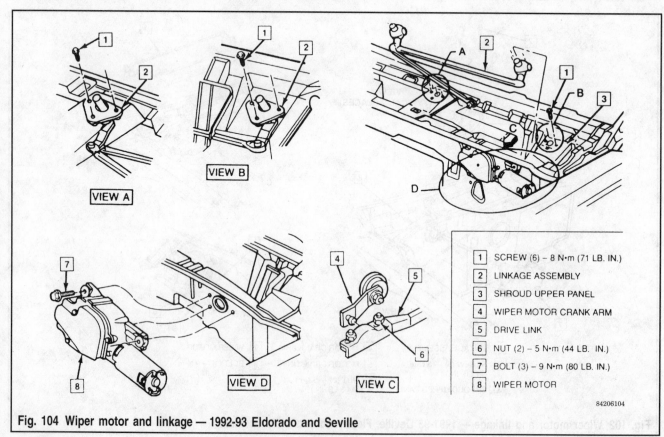

1	SCREW (6) – 8 N•m (71 LB. IN.)
2	LINKAGE ASSEMBLY
3	SHROUD UPPER PANEL
4	WIPER MOTOR CRANK ARM
5	DRIVE LINK
6	NUT (2) – 5 N•m (44 LB. IN.)
7	BOLT (3) – 9 N•m (80 LB. IN.)
8	WIPER MOTOR

Fig. 104 Wiper motor and linkage — 1992-93 Eldorado and Seville

84206104

6. Disconnect the motor drive link from the motor crank arm by loosening the nuts.

7. Remove the linkage-to-body attaching screws.

8. Remove the linkage assembly by guiding it through the access hole in the shroud upper panel.

To install:

9. Guide the linkage assembly through the access hole and position it in the vehicle. Install the linkage attaching screws but do not tighten yet.

10. Connect the drive link to the wiper motor crank arm.

11. Align the linkage and tighten the attaching screws to 66 inch lbs. (7.5 Nm).

12. Install the cowl screen. On 1990 vehicles, install the lower reveal molding.

13. Install the wiper arm and blade assemblies.

14. Connect the washer hoses.

15. Check wiper operation, wiper pattern and park position. If adjustment is needed, refer to the Wiper Arm removal and installation procedures.

Eldorado and Seville

▶ **See Figures 103 and 104**

1. Raise the hood.

2. Remove the wiper arms.

3. On 1990-91 vehicles, remove the windshield reveal molding.

4. Remove the cowl vent.

5. Disconnect the wiper arm drive link from the wiper motor crank arm.

6. Remove the linkage-to-body attaching screws.

7. Remove the linkage assembly by guiding it through the access hole in the shroud upper panel.

To install:

8. Guide the linkage assembly through the access hole and position it in the vehicle. Install the linkage attaching screws but do not tighten yet.

9. Connect the drive link to the wiper motor crank arm.

10. Align the linkage and tighten the attaching screws to 71 inch lbs. (8 Nm).

11. Install the cowl screen. On 1990-91 vehicles, install the lower reveal molding.

12. Install the wiper arms.

13. Check wiper operation, wiper pattern and park position. If adjustment is needed, refer to the Wiper Arm removal and installation procedures.

Windshield Washer Fluid Reservoir

REMOVAL & INSTALLATION

▶ **See Figures 90, 105, 106 and 107**

1. Disconnect the negative battery cable.

2. On 1992-93 Eldorado and Seville, proceed as follows:
   a. Remove the headlamp access cover.
   b. Remove the radiator support-to-wheelwell brace.
   c. Remove the relay center and position aside.

3. Use a syringe or similar tool to remove the washer fluid from the reservoir.

4. Disconnect the wiring connectors and washer hose.

5. Remove the mounting screws/nuts and remove the reservoir.

6. Installation is the reverse of the removal procedure.

Windshield Washer Pump

REMOVAL & INSTALLATION

▶ **See Figures 90, 105, 106 and 107**

1. Remove the windshield washer fluid reservoir.

2. Remove the pump from the reservoir.

3. Installation is the reverse of the removal procedure. Make sure the new pump is pushed all the way into the reservoir gasket.

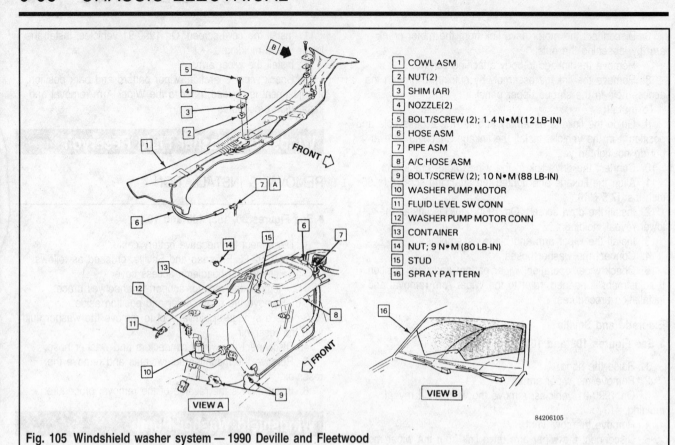

1 COWL ASM
2 NUT(2)
3 SHIM (AR)
4 NOZZLE(2)
5 BOLT/SCREW (2); 1.4 N•M (12 LB-IN)
6 HOSE ASM
7 PIPE ASM
8 A/C HOSE ASM
9 BOLT/SCREW (2); 10 N•M (88 LB-IN)
10 WASHER PUMP MOTOR
11 FLUID LEVEL SW CONN
12 WASHER PUMP MOTOR CONN
13 CONTAINER
14 NUT; 9 N•M (80 LB-IN)
15 STUD
16 SPRAY PATTERN

VIEW A

VIEW B

84206105

Fig. 105 Windshield washer system — 1990 Deville and Fleetwood

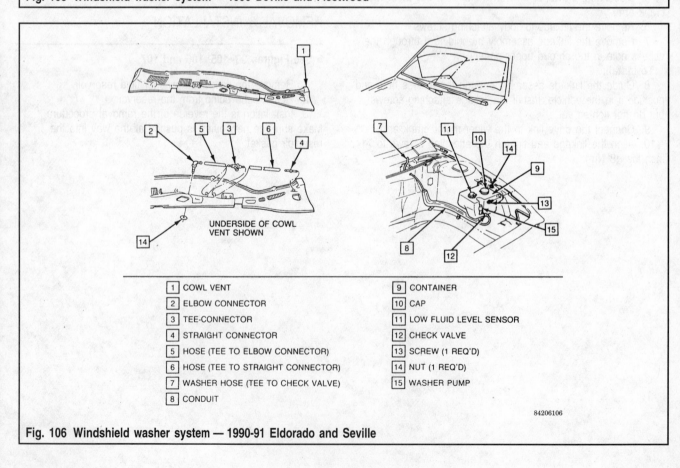

UNDERSIDE OF COWL VENT SHOWN

1 COWL VENT	9 CONTAINER
2 ELBOW CONNECTOR	10 CAP
3 TEE-CONNECTOR	11 LOW FLUID LEVEL SENSOR
4 STRAIGHT CONNECTOR	12 CHECK VALVE
5 HOSE (TEE TO ELBOW CONNECTOR)	13 SCREW (1 REQ'D)
6 HOSE (TEE TO STRAIGHT CONNECTOR)	14 NUT (1 REQ'D)
7 WASHER HOSE (TEE TO CHECK VALVE)	15 WASHER PUMP
8 CONDUIT	

84206106

Fig. 106 Windshield washer system — 1990-91 Eldorado and Seville

INSTRUMENTS AND SWITCHES

Instrument Cluster

REMOVAL & INSTALLATION

Deville, Fleetwood and Sixty Special
▶ See Figures 108, 109 and 110

1. Disconnect the negative battery cable.
2. Remove the upper trim pad as follows:
   a. Carefully pry out the A/C outlets.
   b. Remove one screw from behind each outlet and 3 screws through the defroster outlet.
   c. Remove the glove box module retaining screws. Disconnect the wiring connectors from the switches and light and remove the glove box module.
   d. Remove 2 screws working through the glove box opening.
   e. Disconnect the in-vehicle temperature sensor electrical connector and aspirator tube.
   f. If equipped, remove the solar sensor from the trim pad.
   g. Remove the upper trim pad.
3. Remove the 2 screws and the plate.
4. Remove the instrument cluster attaching screws.
5. Label and disconnect the wiring connectors.
6. Remove the shift indicator cable clip and remove the instrument cluster.

To install:

7. Position the instrument cluster and connect the electrical connectors.
8. Install the attaching screws and tighten to 13 inch lbs. (1.5 Nm).
9. Install the plate with the 2 screws.
10. Install the upper trim pad in the reverse order of removal.
11. Install the shift indicator cable clip and adjust the shift indicator as follows:
    a. Position and release the shift lever in the **N** gate notch.
    b. Move the clip on the edge of the shift bowl to center the pointer on **N**.
    c. Push the clip onto the bowl. Make sure the cable rests on the bowl, not on the column jacket. Make sure the clip is tight on the bowl and does not slip.
    d. Move the shift lever through all positions and then back to **N** to check adjustment. Make sure the pointer covers a portion of each graphic.

Eldorado and Seville

1990-91
▶ See Figures 111 and 112

1. Disconnect the negative battery cable.
2. Remove the instrument cluster trim plate as follows:
   a. Remove the left side A/C vent.
   b. Remove the radio trim plate.
   c. Remove the retaining screws and the trim plate.

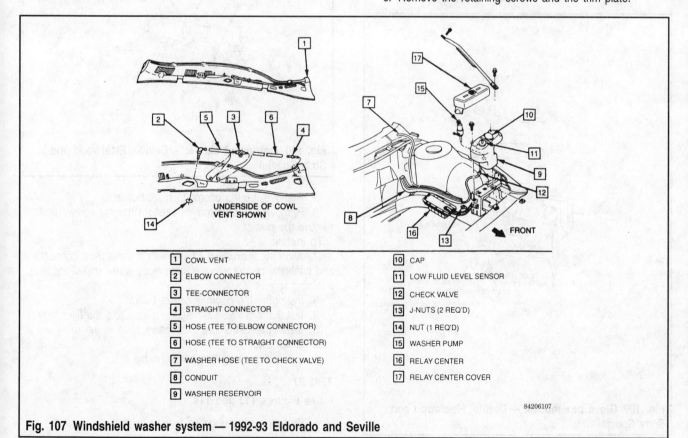

1 COWL VENT	10 CAP
2 ELBOW CONNECTOR	11 LOW FLUID LEVEL SENSOR
3 TEE-CONNECTOR	12 CHECK VALVE
4 STRAIGHT CONNECTOR	13 J-NUTS (2 REQ'D)
5 HOSE (TEE TO ELBOW CONNECTOR)	14 NUT (1 REQ'D)
6 HOSE (TEE TO STRAIGHT CONNECTOR)	15 WASHER PUMP
7 WASHER HOSE (TEE TO CHECK VALVE)	16 RELAY CENTER
8 CONDUIT	17 RELAY CENTER COVER
9 WASHER RESERVOIR	

UNDERSIDE OF COWL VENT SHOWN

FRONT

84206107

Fig. 107 Windshield washer system — 1992-93 Eldorado and Seville

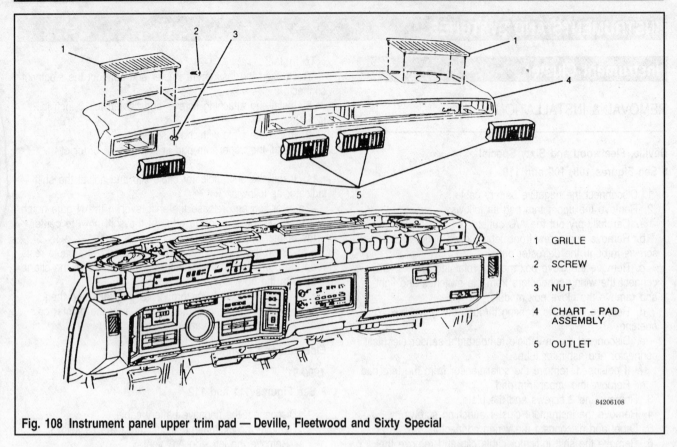

Fig. 108 Instrument panel upper trim pad — Deville, Fleetwood and Sixty Special

1	GRILLE
2	SCREW
3	NUT
4	CHART – PAD ASSEMBLY
5	OUTLET

84206108

3. Remove the screws and the filter lens.
4. Remove the 2 screws and the telltale warning lamp lens.

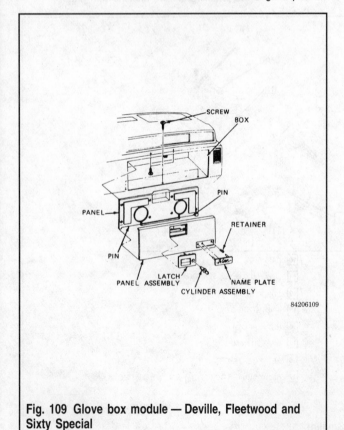

Fig. 109 Glove box module — Deville, Fleetwood and Sixty Special

84206109

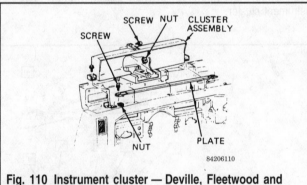

Fig. 110 Instrument cluster — Deville, Fleetwood and Sixty Special

84206110

5. Remove the trip odometer reset button.
6. Remove the 2 instrument cluster retaining screws and remove the cluster.
To install:
7. Align the instrument cluster with the electrical connectors and push the cluster into the instrument panel. Install the 2 retaining screws.
8. Install the trip odometer reset button.
9. Install the telltale warning lamp lens and the filter lens.
10. Install the instrument cluster trim plate in the reverse order of removal.
11. Connect the negative battery cable.

1992-93

▶ See Figures 113 and 114

1. Disconnect the negative battery cable.

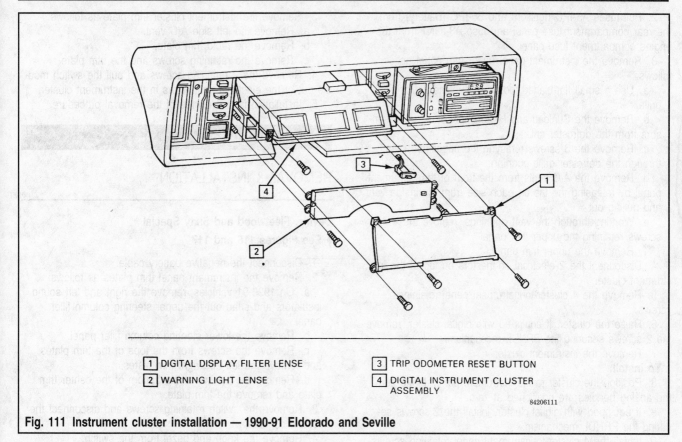

| 1 | DIGITAL DISPLAY FILTER LENSE | 3 | TRIP ODOMETER RESET BUTTON |
| 2 | WARNING LIGHT LENSE | 4 | DIGITAL INSTRUMENT CLUSTER ASSEMBLY |

84206111

Fig. 111 Instrument cluster installation — 1990-91 Eldorado and Seville

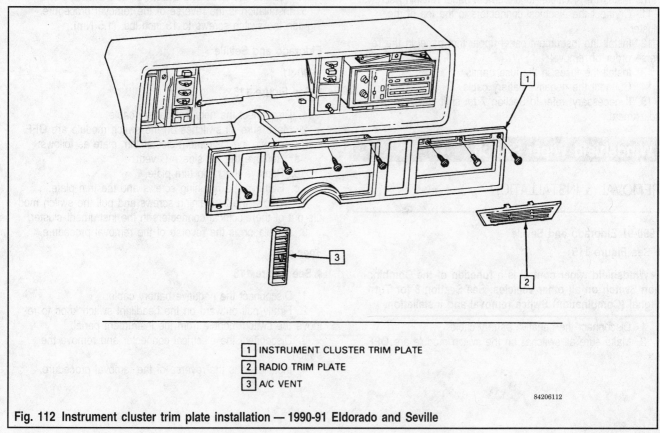

1	INSTRUMENT CLUSTER TRIM PLATE
2	RADIO TRIM PLATE
3	A/C VENT

84206112

Fig. 112 Instrument cluster trim plate installation — 1990-91 Eldorado and Seville

2. Pull fuses A5-IPC (Ignition) and B5-IPC (Battery) from the rear compartment fuse panel and fuse A3-IGN1 from the engine compartment fuse panel.

3. Remove the instrument panel upper trim panel as follows:

a. Use a small flat-bladed tool to pry up the defroster grille.

b. Remove the Sunload and Headlamp Auto Control sensors from the defroster grille.

c. Remove the 3 screws retaining the upper trim panel through the defroster grille opening.

d. Remove the A/C vents from the front of the instrument panel by releasing the tab on each side from the inside vent and pulling out.

e. Working through the vent openings, remove the 4 screws retaining the upper trim panel.

f. Remove the upper trim panel.

4. Disconnect the 2 electrical connectors on top of the instrument cluster.

5. Remove the 4 cluster-to-instrument panel retaining screws.

6. Raise the cluster. If equipped with digital cluster, remove the 2 screws securing the PRNDL mechanism.

7. Remove the instrument cluster.

To install:

8. Position the cluster to the instrument panel. Make sure the analog needles are positioned at zero.

9. If equipped with digital cluster, install the 2 screws securing the PRNDL mechanism.

10. Install the 4 cluster-to-instrument panel retaining screws.

11. Connect the electrical connectors to the top of the cluster.

12. Install the instrument panel upper trim panel in the reverse order of removal.

13. Install the fuses in the fuse panel.

14. Connect the negative battery cable.

15. If necessary, refer to Section 7 for shift indicator adjustment.

Windshield Wiper Switch

REMOVAL & INSTALLATION

1990-91 Eldorado and Seville

▶ See Figure 115

➡Windshield wiper control is a function of the Combination Switch on all other vehicles. See Section 8 for Turn Signal (Combination) Switch removal and installation.

1. Disconnect the negative battery cable.

2. Make sure all switches on the switch module are **OFF**.

3. Remove the instrument cluster trim plate as follows:

a. Remove the left side A/C vent.

b. Remove the radio trim plate.

c. Remove the retaining screws and the trim plate.

4. Remove the 2 retaining screws and pull the switch module out of the electrical connectors in the instrument cluster.

5. Installation is the reverse of the removal procedure.

Headlight Switch

REMOVAL & INSTALLATION

Deville, Fleetwood and Sixty Special

▶ See Figures 116 and 117

1. Disconnect the negative battery cable.

2. Remove the instrument panel trim plates as follows:

a. On 1990-91 vehicles, remove the right and left sound insulators and snap out the upper steering column filler panel.

b. Remove the lower steering column filler panel.

c. Remove the screws from the tops of the trim plates and remove the left and right trim plates.

d. Remove the screws at the bottom of the center trim plate and remove the trim plate.

3. Remove the switch retaining screws and disconnect the electrical connector.

4. Remove the knob and bezel from the switch.

5. Installation is the reverse of the removal procedure. Tighten the switch screws to 13 inch lbs. (1.5 Nm).

Eldorado and Seville

1990-91

▶ See Figure 115

1. Disconnect the negative battery cable.

2. Make sure all switches on the switch module are **OFF**.

3. Remove the instrument cluster trim plate as follows:

a. Remove the left side A/C vent.

b. Remove the radio trim plate.

c. Remove the retaining screws and the trim plate.

4. Remove the 2 retaining screws and pull the switch module out of the electrical connectors in the instrument cluster.

5. Installation is the reverse of the removal procedure.

1992-93

▶ See Figure 118

1. Disconnect the negative battery cable.

2. Firmly pull outward on the headlight switch knob to remove the switch module from the instrument panel.

3. Disconnect the electrical connector and remove the switch.

4. Installation is the reverse of the removal procedure.

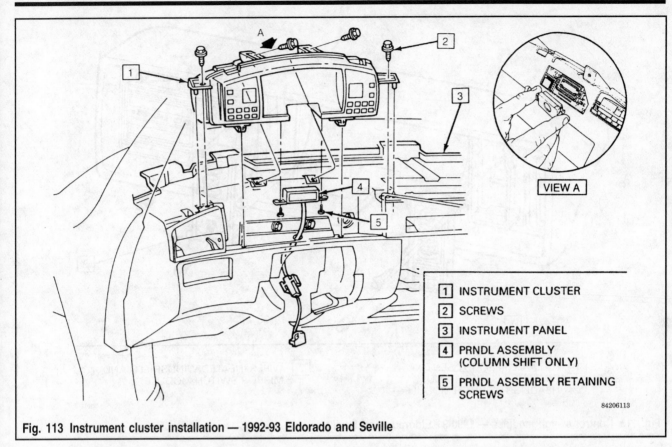

1	INSTRUMENT CLUSTER
2	SCREWS
3	INSTRUMENT PANEL
4	PRNDL ASSEMBLY (COLUMN SHIFT ONLY)
5	PRNDL ASSEMBLY RETAINING SCREWS

84206113

Fig. 113 Instrument cluster installation — 1992-93 Eldorado and Seville

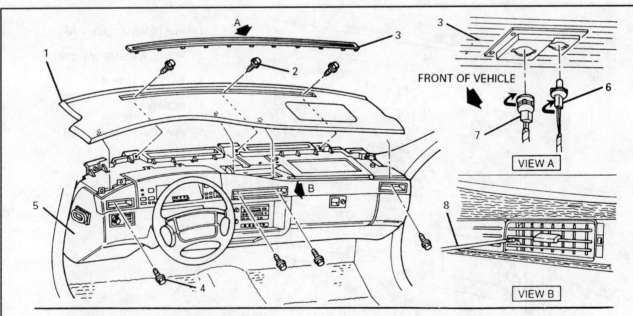

1	INSTRUMENT PANEL UPPER TRIM PANEL	5	INSTRUMENT PANEL CARRIER
2	SCREWS	6	SUNLOAD SENSOR
3	WINDSHIELD DEFROSTER GRILLE	7	HEADLAMP AUTO CONTROL AMBIENT LIGHT SENSOR
4	SCREWS	8	SMALL FLAT-BLADED TOOL

84206114

Fig. 114 Instrument panel upper trim panel installation — 1992-93 Eldorado and Seville

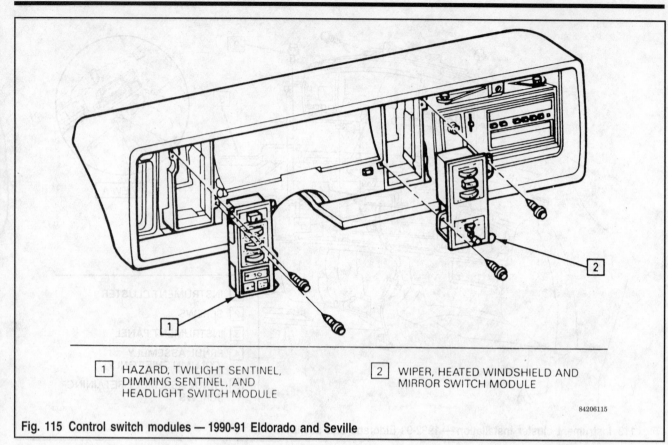

| 1 | HAZARD, TWILIGHT SENTINEL, DIMMING SENTINEL, AND HEADLIGHT SWITCH MODULE | 2 | WIPER, HEATED WINDSHIELD AND MIRROR SWITCH MODULE |

84206115

Fig. 115 Control switch modules — 1990-91 Eldorado and Seville

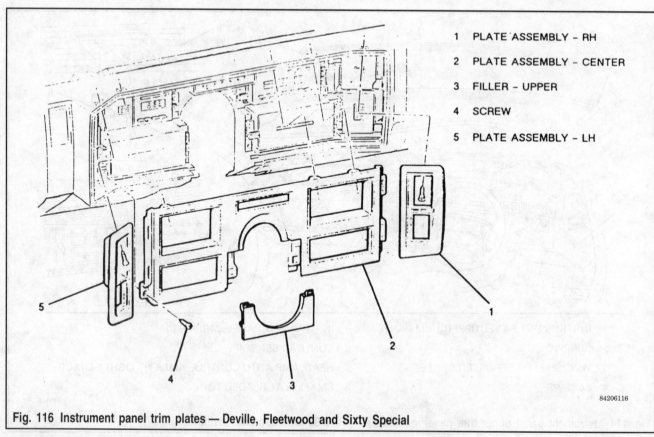

1 PLATE ASSEMBLY – RH

2 PLATE ASSEMBLY – CENTER

3 FILLER – UPPER

4 SCREW

5 PLATE ASSEMBLY – LH

84206116

Fig. 116 Instrument panel trim plates — Deville, Fleetwood and Sixty Special

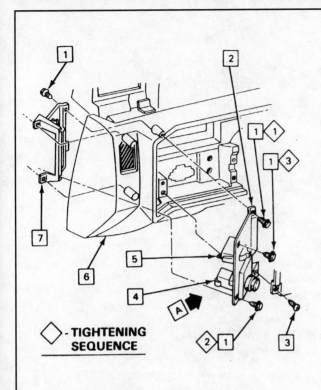

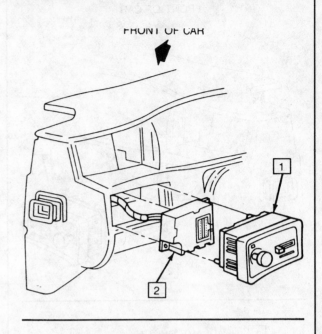

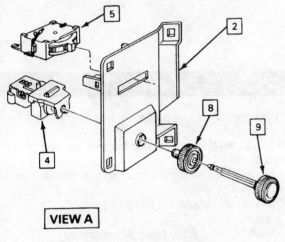

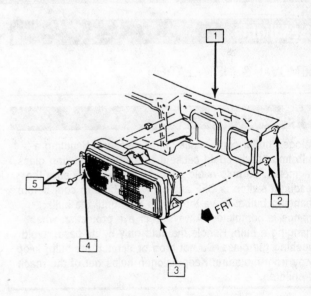

◇ - **TIGHTENING SEQUENCE**

VIEW A

1. HEADLAMP SWITCH
2. TWILIGHT SENTINEL/DRL MODULE

1. BOLT/SCREW; 1.5 N•M (13 LB-IN)
2. HOUSING ASSEMBLY
3. TRIM PLATE SCREW
4. SWITCH ASM (HEADLAMP)
5. SWITCH ASM (SENTINEL)
6. IP ASSEMBLY
7. BRACKET
8. BEZEL
9. KNOB ASM; 5 N•M (44 LB-IN)

1. HEADLAMP AND RADIATOR GRILLE MOUNTING PANEL
2. NUT: 1.5 N•M (13 LB-IN)
3. HEADLAMP ASSEMBLY

84206117

Fig. 117 Headlight switch installation — Deville, Fleetwood and Sixty Special

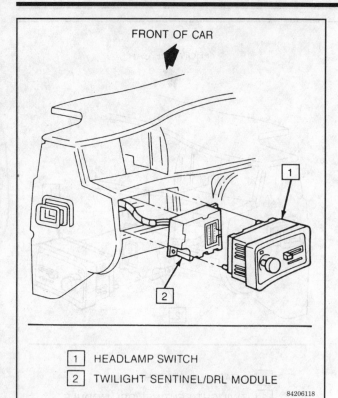

FRONT OF CAR

1 HEADLAMP SWITCH
2 TWILIGHT SENTINEL/DRL MODULE

84206118

Fig. 118 Headlight switch — 1992-93 Eldorado and Seville

LIGHTING

Headlights

REMOVAL & INSTALLATION

✳✳CAUTION

Halogen bulbs contain gas under pressure. Handling a bulb improperly could cause it to shatter into flying glass fragments. To help avoid personal injury: Make sure the headlight switch is OFF and allow the bulb to cool before changing bulbs; leave the switch OFF until the bulb change is completed. Always wear eye protection when changing a bulb. Handle the bulb only by its base; avoid touching the glass. Do not drop or scratch the bulb; keep away from moisture. Keep halogen bulbs out of the reach of children.

Deville, Fleetwood and Sixty Special

1990

▶ **See Figure 119**

1. Make sure the headlight switch is **OFF**.
2. Remove the front cornering/side marker lamps; refer to the procedure in this Section.
3. Remove the 2 rear headlight assembly nuts.

4. Disconnect the wiring connectors from the headlight bulbs.
5. Remove the 2 screws through the grille and remove the headlight assembly.
6. Disconnect the lamp monitor connections from the headlight assembly.
7. If necessary, remove the headlight bulbs.
   To install:
8. Install the bulbs in the headlight assembly.
9. Connect the lamp monitor connections.
10. Position the headlight assembly and install the 2 screws through the grille. Tighten to 13 inch lbs. (1.5 Nm).
11. Connect the wiring connectors to the headlight bulbs.
12. Install the 2 headlight assembly nuts and tighten to 13 inch lbs. (1.5 Nm).
13. Install the front cornering/side marker lamps.
14. Check the headlight aim.

1991-93

▶ **See Figures 120, 121, 122 and 123**

1. Make sure the headlight switch is **OFF**.
2. Remove the thumbscrews.
3. Pull out the headlight assembly and disconnect the wiring connectors from the headlight bulbs.
4. If necessary, remove the bulbs from the headlight assembly.
5. Disconnect the lamp monitor fiber optic cable.

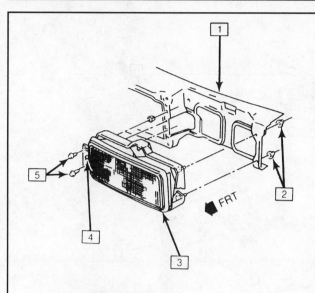

1. HEADLAMP AND RADIATOR
   GRILLE MOUNTING PANEL
2. NUT: 1.5 N•M (13 LB-IN)
3. HEADLAMP ASSEMBLY
4. GUIDE PIN HOLE
5. BOLT/SCREW: 1.5 N•M (13 LB-IN)

84206119

Fig. 119 Headlight installation — 1990 Deville and Fleetwood

To install:

6. Connect the lamp monitor fiber optic cable.
7. Install the bulbs in the headlight assembly.
8. Connect the wiring connectors to the headlight bulbs.
9. Position the headlight assembly and install the thumbscrews.
10. Check the headlight aim.

Eldorado and Seville

1990-91

▶ See Figure 124

1. Make sure the headlight switch is **OFF**.
2. Remove the 4 plastic radiator cover retaining clips and remove the cover.
3. Remove the 4 grille retaining clips and remove the grille.

84206120

Fig. 120 Remove the thumbscrew from the headlight assembly — 1991-93 Deville, Fleetwood and Sixty Special

84206121

Fig. 121 Pull the headlight assembly outward — 1991-93 Deville, Fleetwood and Sixty Special

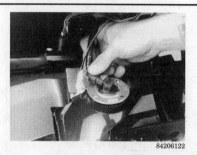

84206122

Fig. 122 Disconnect the wiring connector from the headlight bulb — 1991-93 Deville, Fleetwood and Sixty Special

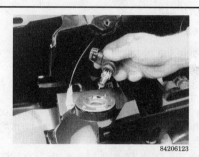

84206123

Fig. 123 Remove the bulb from the headlight assembly — 1991-93 Deville, Fleetwood and Sixty Special

4. Remove the 4 headlight assembly retaining screws.
5. Disconnect the headlight bulb wiring connectors and if necessary, remove the bulbs.
6. On all except Seville STS, disconnect the fiber optic connectors.
7. Remove the headlight assembly.

To install:

8. Position the headlight assembly to the vehicle.
9. If equipped, connect the fiber optic connectors.
10. Install the bulbs in the headlight assembly and connect the wiring connectors.
11. Install the 4 headlight assembly retaining screws.
12. Install the grille and the plastic radiator cover.
13. Check the headlight aim.

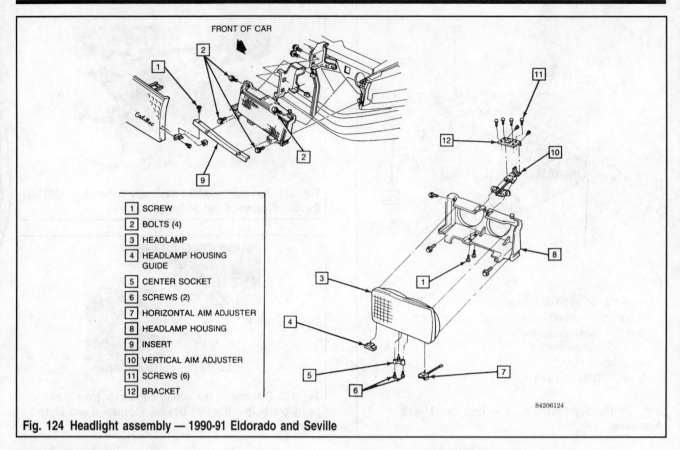

FRONT OF CAR

1	SCREW
2	BOLTS (4)
3	HEADLAMP
4	HEADLAMP HOUSING GUIDE
5	CENTER SOCKET
6	SCREWS (2)
7	HORIZONTAL AIM ADJUSTER
8	HEADLAMP HOUSING
9	INSERT
10	VERTICAL AIM ADJUSTER
11	SCREWS (6)
12	BRACKET

84206124

Fig. 124 Headlight assembly — 1990-91 Eldorado and Seville

1992-93 ELDORADO

▶ **See Figures 125 and 126**

1. Make sure the headlight switch is **OFF**.
2. Remove the upper filler panel.
3. Remove the bolt retaining the cornering lamp housing and remove the cornering lamp sockets.
4. Remove the 2 nuts retaining the headlight housing to the fender and the 2 bolts retaining the headlight housing to the rail.
5. Remove the lower headlight housing-to-body bolt.
6. Disconnect the headlight housing wiring connector and remove the headlight housing.
7. If necessary, remove the headlight bulbs.
   To install:
8. Install the headlight bulbs.
9. Position the headlight housing assembly to the body and connect the wiring connector.
10. Install the lower headlight housing-to-body bolt.
11. Install the 2 bolts retaining the headlight housing to the rail and the 2 nuts retaining the headlight housing to the fender.
12. Install the cornering lamp sockets and the retaining bolt.
13. Install the upper filler panel.
14. Check the headlight aim.

1992-93 SEVILLE

▶ **See Figure 127**

1. Make sure the headlight switch is **OFF**.
2. Remove the upper filler panel.
3. Remove the one screw retaining the headlight to the headlight housing.

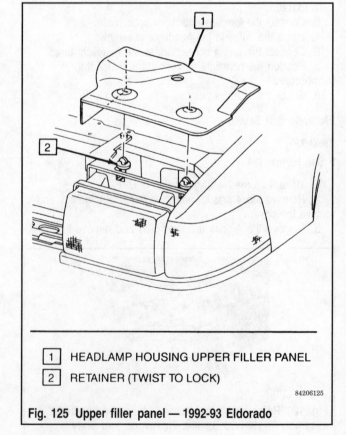

1	HEADLAMP HOUSING UPPER FILLER PANEL
2	RETAINER (TWIST TO LOCK)

84206125

Fig. 125 Upper filler panel — 1992-93 Eldorado

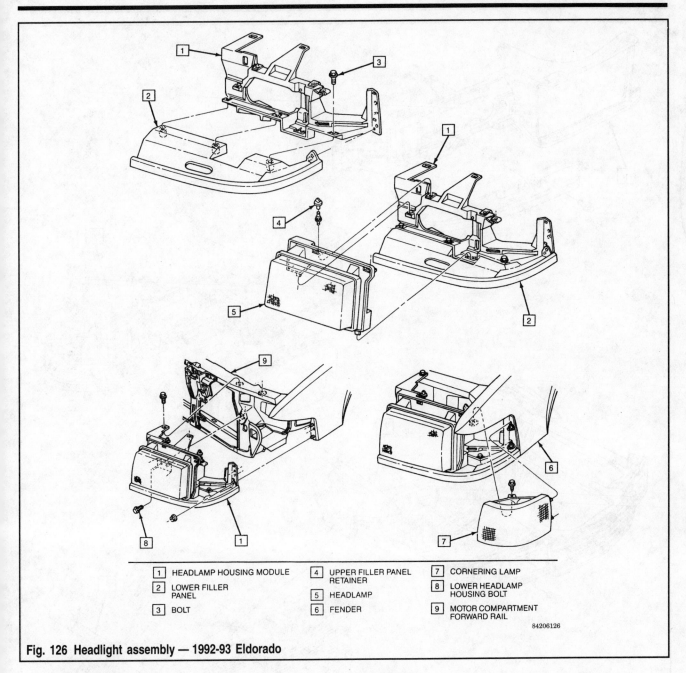

1	HEADLAMP HOUSING MODULE	4	UPPER FILLER PANEL RETAINER	7	CORNERING LAMP
2	LOWER FILLER PANEL	5	HEADLAMP	8	LOWER HEADLAMP HOUSING BOLT
3	BOLT	6	FENDER	9	MOTOR COMPARTMENT FORWARD RAIL

84206126

Fig. 126 Headlight assembly — 1992-93 Eldorado

4. Disconnect the headlight bulb wiring connectors and re-move the headlight assembly.

5. If necessary, remove the headlight bulbs.

To install:

6. Install the headlight bulbs and connect the wiring connectors.

7. Engage the 2 headlight assembly tabs into the slots on the housing and retain the headlight with the screw.

8. Install the upper filler panel.

9. Check the headlight aim.

AIMING

Headlight aiming kit J-25300 or equivalent, is required for headlight adjustment. Aim the headlights according to the instructions in the kit.

When checking headlight aim, the vehicle must be at normal height, with fuel, oil water and spare tire. The tires must be inflated to the proper pressure. If the vehicle will regularly carry a heavy load in the rear compartment, or pull a trailer, these loads should be on the vehicle when the headlights are checked.

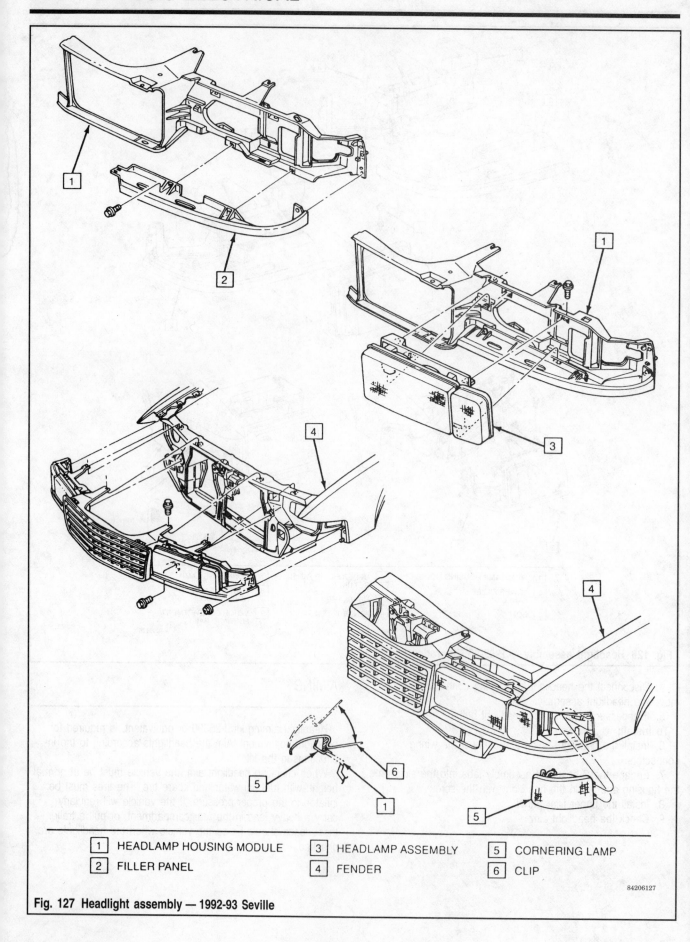

1	HEADLAMP HOUSING MODULE	3	HEADLAMP ASSEMBLY	5	CORNERING LAMP
2	FILLER PANEL	4	FENDER	6	CLIP

84206127

Fig. 127 Headlight assembly — 1992-93 Seville

Signal and Marker Lights

REMOVAL & INSTALLATION

Front Turn Signal and Parking Lights

DEVILLE, FLEETWOOD AND SIXTY SPECIAL

▶ See Figure 128

1. Raise and safely support the vehicle.
2. Disconnect the lamp monitor fiber optic cable.
3. Remove the retaining nut, then pry the inner release tab upward and push the assembly forward.
4. Remove the bulb and socket from the lamp assembly.
5. If replacing the bulb, remove the bulb from the socket.
6. Installation is the reverse of the removal procedure. Tighten the nut to 13 inch lbs. (1.5 Nm).

1990-91 ELDORADO AND SEVILLE

▶ See Figure 129

1. Remove the bumper fascia; refer to Section 10.
2. Remove the lamp assembly retaining nuts.
3. On all except Seville STS, disconnect the fiber optic connector.
4. Remove the lamp assembly from the bumper fascia.
5. Remove the socket and bulb from the lamp assembly.
6. Installation is the reverse of the removal procedure.

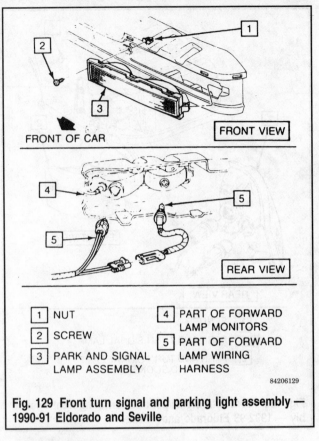

1	NUT	4	PART OF FORWARD LAMP MONITORS
2	SCREW	5	PART OF FORWARD LAMP WIRING HARNESS
3	PARK AND SIGNAL LAMP ASSEMBLY		

84206129

Fig. 129 Front turn signal and parking light assembly — 1990-91 Eldorado and Seville

1992-93 ELDORADO AND SEVILLE

▶ See Figure 130

1. On Eldorado, remove the upper filler panel.
2. Remove the bolt on Eldorado or the clip on Seville, that retains the lamp assembly.
3. Remove the lamp assembly.
4. Remove the socket and bulb from the lamp assembly.
5. Installation is the reverse of the removal procedure.

Front Cornering and Side Marker Lights

DEVILLE, FLEETWOOD AND SIXTY SPECIAL

▶ See Figure 131

1. Remove the lamp assembly retaining screws and the lamp assembly.
2. Remove the bulbs and sockets from the assembly.
3. Remove the bulb from the side marker socket and disconnect the connector from the cornering lamp bulb.
4. Installation is the reverse of the removal procedure. Tighten the screws to 13 inch lbs. (1.5 Nm).

1990-91 ELDORADO AND SEVILLE

▶ See Figure 132

1. On Eldorado and Seville STS, remove the bumper fascia; refer to Section 10.
2. On Eldorado and Seville STS, remove the lamp assembly retaining nuts and remove the lamp assembly from the bumper fascia.
3. On Seville, remove the lamp assembly retaining nut and remove the lamp assembly.
4. Remove the socket and bulb from the lamp assembly.

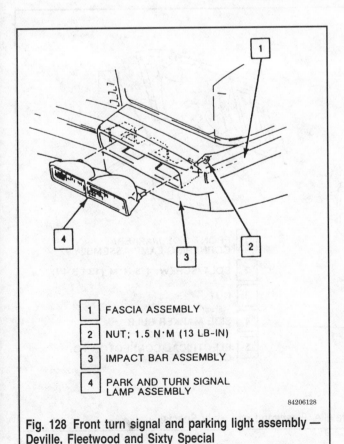

1	FASCIA ASSEMBLY
2	NUT; 1.5 N·M (13 LB-IN)
3	IMPACT BAR ASSEMBLY
4	PARK AND TURN SIGNAL LAMP ASSEMBLY

84206128

Fig. 128 Front turn signal and parking light assembly — Deville, Fleetwood and Sixty Special

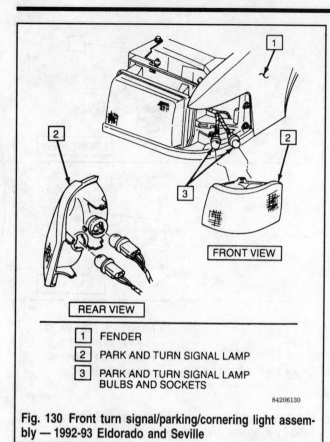

1	FENDER
2	PARK AND TURN SIGNAL LAMP
3	PARK AND TURN SIGNAL LAMP BULBS AND SOCKETS

84206130

Fig. 130 Front turn signal/parking/cornering light assembly — 1992-93 Eldorado and Seville

5. Installation is the reverse of the removal procedure.

1992-93 ELDORADO AND SEVILLE

▶ See Figure 133

➡The following procedure is for the front side marker light. The cornering light on these vehicles is part of the front turn signal and parking light assembly.

1. Remove the lamp assembly retaining screws and remove the lamp assembly from the bumper fascia.
2. Remove the socket and bulb from the lamp assembly.
3. Installation is the reverse of the removal procedure.

Rear Side Marker Lights

DEVILLE, FLEETWOOD AND SIXTY SPECIAL

▶ See Figure 134

1. Remove the inner trunk panel.
2. Remove the bulb and socket assembly and remove the bulb from the socket.
3. Remove the lamp assembly retaining nuts and remove the rear side marker lamp assembly.
4. Installation is the reverse of the removal procedure.

1992-93 ELDORADO

▶ See Figure 135

1. Remove the lamp assembly retaining screws.
2. Remove the socket from the lamp assembly and remove the bulb from the socket.
3. Remove the lamp assembly.
4. Installation is the reverse of the removal procedure.

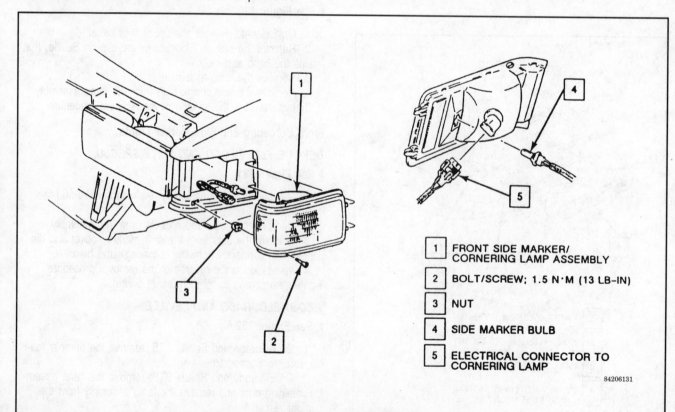

1	FRONT SIDE MARKER/ CORNERING LAMP ASSEMBLY
2	BOLT/SCREW; 1.5 N·M (13 LB–IN)
3	NUT
4	SIDE MARKER BULB
5	ELECTRICAL CONNECTOR TO CORNERING LAMP

84206131

Fig. 131 Front cornering and side marker light assembly — Deville, Fleetwood and Sixty Special

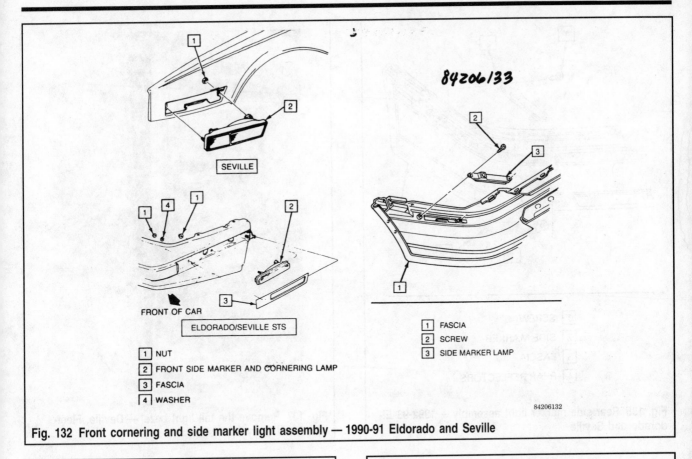

84206133

84206132

Fig. 132 Front cornering and side marker light assembly — 1990-91 Eldorado and Seville

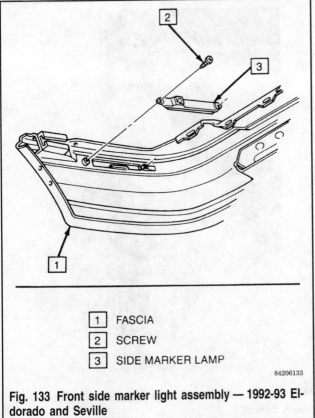

1	FASCIA
2	SCREW
3	SIDE MARKER LAMP

84206133

Fig. 133 Front side marker light assembly — 1992-93 Eldorado and Seville

| 1 | REAR SIDE MARKER LAMP ASSEMBLY |
| 2 | NUT; 3 N·M (27 LB-IN) |

84206134

Fig. 134 Rear side marker light assembly — Deville, Fleetwood and Sixty Special

Rear Turn Signal, Brake and Parking Lights

DEVILLE, FLEETWOOD AND SIXTY SPECIAL

▶ See Figures 136, 137, 138, 139 and 140

1. Remove the retaining screws and the bezel.
2. Remove the lamp assembly.
3. Remove the socket from the lamp assembly and remove the bulb from the socket.
4. Disconnect the lamp monitor fiber optic cable and remove the lamp assembly.
5. Installation is the reverse of the removal procedure. Tighten the screws to 13 inch lbs. (1.5 Nm).

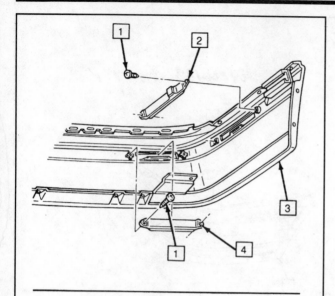

1 SCREW
2 SIDE MARKER
3 FASCIA
4 REAR REFLECTORS

84206135

Fig. 135 Rear side marker light assembly — 1992-93 Eldorado and Seville

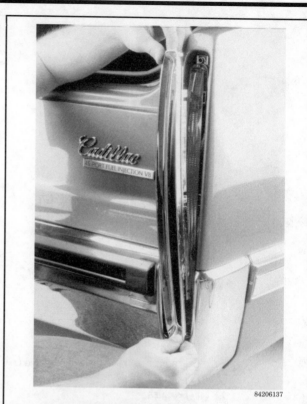

84206137

Fig. 137 Remove the tail light bezel — Deville, Fleetwood and Sixty Special

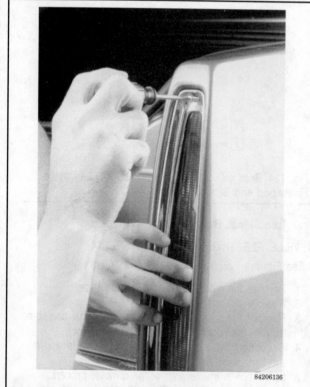

84206136

Fig. 136 Remove the tail light retaining screws — Deville, Fleetwood and Sixty Special

84206138

Fig. 138 Remove the tail light — Deville, Fleetwood and Sixty Special

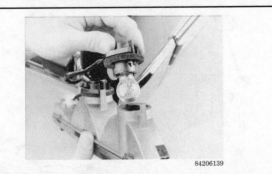

Fig. 139 Remove the bulb and socket assembly from the tail light — Deville, Fleetwood and Sixty Special

Fig. 140 Remove the bulb from the socket — Deville, Fleetwood and Sixty Special

1990-91 ELDORADO

▶ See Figure 141

1. Remove the lamp assembly retaining screw.
2. Pull the bottom of the lamp assembly out and down.
3. Remove the bulb sockets from the lamp and remove the bulbs from the sockets.
4. If equipped, disconnect the fiber optic connector.
5. Remove the lamp assembly.
6. Installation is the reverse of the removal procedure.

1990-91 SEVILLE

▶ See Figures 142 and 143

1. Open the trunk lid and remove the rear compartment trim to gain access to the lamp assembly retaining nuts.
2. Remove the retaining nuts and pull the lamp assembly out.
3. Remove the bulb sockets and disconnect the fiber optic connector.
4. Remove the bulbs from the sockets.
5. Remove the lamp assembly.
6. Installation is the reverse of the removal procedure.

1992-93 ELDORADO

▶ See Figure 144

1. Remove the rear compartment trim.
2. Remove the lamp assembly retaining nuts.
3. Remove the bulb sockets from the lamp assembly and remove the bulbs from the sockets.
4. Remove the lamp assembly.

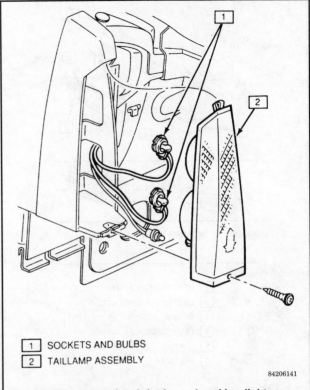

| 1 | SOCKETS AND BULBS |
| 2 | TAILLAMP ASSEMBLY |

Fig. 141 Rear turn signal, brake and parking light assembly — 1990-91 Eldorado

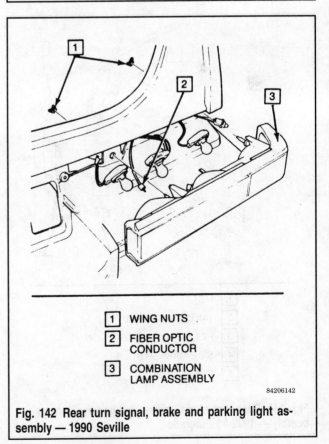

1	WING NUTS
2	FIBER OPTIC CONDUCTOR
3	COMBINATION LAMP ASSEMBLY

Fig. 142 Rear turn signal, brake and parking light assembly — 1990 Seville

5. Installation is the reverse of the removal procedure.

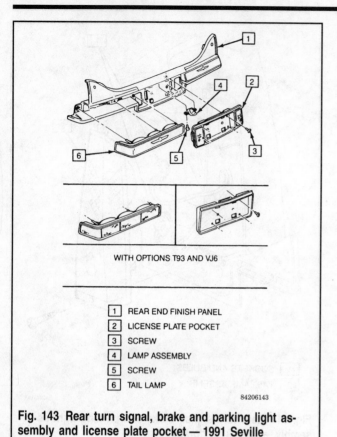

WITH OPTIONS T93 AND VJ6

1	REAR END FINISH PANEL
2	LICENSE PLATE POCKET
3	SCREW
4	LAMP ASSEMBLY
5	SCREW
6	TAIL LAMP

84206143

Fig. 143 Rear turn signal, brake and parking light assembly and license plate pocket — 1991 Seville

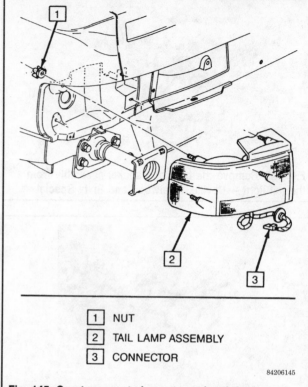

1	NUT
2	TAIL LAMP ASSEMBLY
3	CONNECTOR

84206145

Fig. 145 Quarter mounted rear turn signal, brake and parking light assembly — 1992-93 Seville

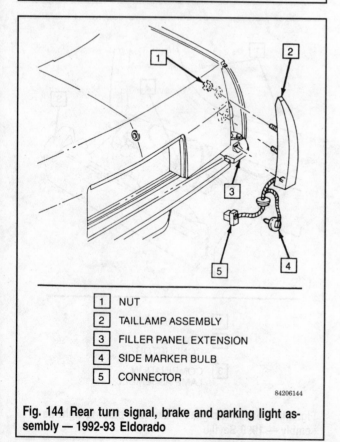

1	NUT
2	TAILLAMP ASSEMBLY
3	FILLER PANEL EXTENSION
4	SIDE MARKER BULB
5	CONNECTOR

84206144

Fig. 144 Rear turn signal, brake and parking light assembly — 1992-93 Eldorado

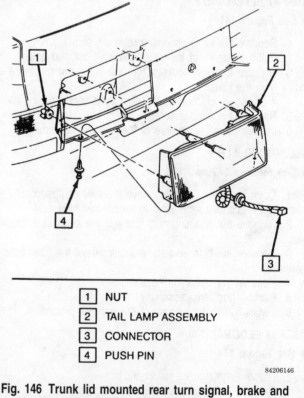

1	NUT
2	TAIL LAMP ASSEMBLY
3	CONNECTOR
4	PUSH PIN

84206146

Fig. 146 Trunk lid mounted rear turn signal, brake and parking light assembly — 1992-93 Seville

1992-93 SEVILLE

▶ **See Figures 145 and 146**

1. Open the trunk lid.
2. Remove the rear compartment trim to gain access to the quarter mounted lamp assembly retaining nuts.
3. Remove the lamp assembly-to-quarter panel nuts and the lamp assembly-to-trunk lid nuts and push pins.
4. Remove the bulb sockets from the lamp assemblies and remove the bulbs from the sockets.
5. Remove the lamp assemblies.
6. Installation is the reverse of the removal procedure.

High-Mount Brake Light

DEVILLE, FLEETWOOD AND SIXTY SPECIAL SEDAN

1. Remove the rear shelf compartment door.
2. Grasp the rear compartment vertical panel and pull down.
3. Remove the socket from the assembly and remove the bulb from the socket.
4. Installation is the reverse of the removal procedure.

DEVILLE, FLEETWOOD AND SIXTY SPECIAL COUPE

1. Remove the 2 screws from the base of the assembly.
2. Remove the bulb and socket assembly and remove the bulb.
3. Remove the lamp assembly.
4. Installation is the reverse of the removal procedure.

1990-91 ELDORADO AND SEVILLE

▶ **See Figure 147**

1. Remove the 2 lamp assembly retaining screws.
2. Disconnect the wiring connector and remove the lamp assembly.
3. Remove the bulb from the lamp assembly.
4. Installation is the reverse of the removal procedure.

1992-93 ELDORADO

▶ **See Figure 148**

1. Pry up the carpet trimmed cover from the lamp assembly.
2. Pull the lamp assembly toward the front of the vehicle and up to disengage the retainers.
3. Disconnect the wiring connectors and remove the lamp assembly.
4. Installation is the reverse of the removal procedure.

1992-93 SEVILLE

▶ **See Figure 148**

1. Open the trunk lid.
2. Remove the trunk lid carpet trim.
3. Remove the lamp assembly retaining nuts.
4. Disconnect the wiring connector and remove the lamp assembly.
5. Installation is the reverse of the removal procedure.

License Plate Lights

▶ **See Figures 149, 150 and 151**

1. Remove the lamp assembly retaining screws or nuts.

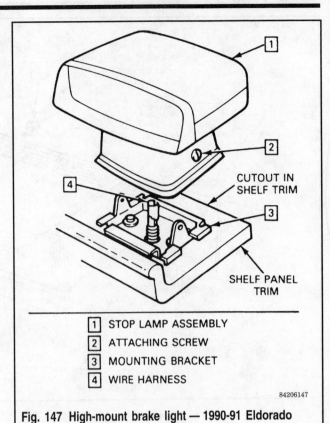

1	STOP LAMP ASSEMBLY
2	ATTACHING SCREW
3	MOUNTING BRACKET
4	WIRE HARNESS

84206147

Fig. 147 High-mount brake light — 1990-91 Eldorado and Seville

2. Remove the bulb sockets from the lamp assembly and remove the bulbs from the sockets.
3. Remove the lamp assembly.
4. Installation is the reverse of the removal procedure.

Fog Lights

REMOVAL & INSTALLATION

1992-93 Eldorado and Seville

▶ **See Figure 152**

1. Disconnect the the fog light socket connector.
2. Remove the 2 lamp assembly-to-bracket bolts.

➡**It may be necessary to loosen the mounting bracket bolts to remove the lamp assembly.**

3. Remove the fog light.
4. Installation is the reverse of the removal procedure. Check the fog light aim.

AIMING

1992-93 Eldorado and Seville

▶ **See Figure 153**

1. Position the vehicle on a level surface 25 ft. from a wall or other flat surface.

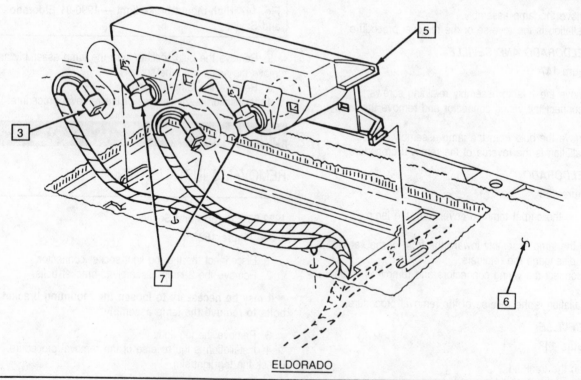

SEVILLE

ELDORADO

1	NUT	5	LAMP HOUSING
2	REAR COMPARTMENT LID	6	REAR SHELF
3	CONNECTOR	7	LAMPS
4	LAMP ASSEMBLY		

84206148

Fig. 148 High-mount brake light — 1992-93 Eldorado and Seville

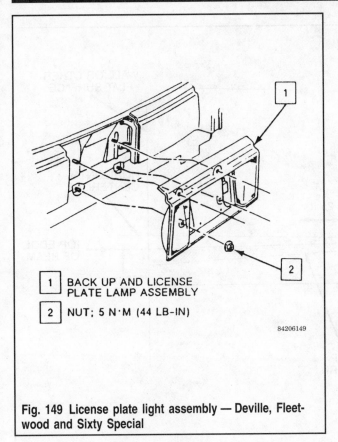

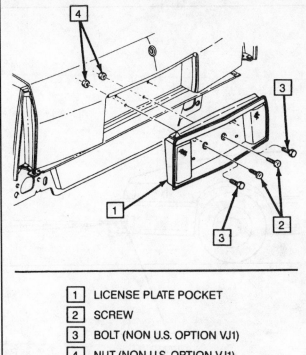

| 1 | BACK UP AND LICENSE PLATE LAMP ASSEMBLY |
| 2 | NUT; 5 N·M (44 LB-IN) |

84206149

Fig. 149 License plate light assembly — Deville, Fleetwood and Sixty Special

1	LICENSE PLATE POCKET
2	SCREW
3	BOLT (NON U.S. OPTION VJ1)
4	NUT (NON U.S. OPTION VJ1)

84206151

Fig. 151 License plate light assembly — 1992-93 Eldorado

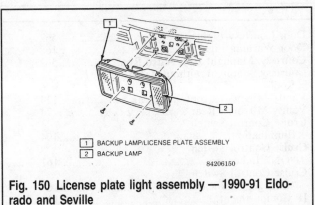

| 1 | BACKUP LAMP/LICENSE PLATE ASSEMBLY |
| 2 | BACKUP LAMP |

84206150

Fig. 150 License plate light assembly — 1990-91 Eldorado and Seville

2. Mark the horizontal centerline of the fog light on the flat surface directly in front of the vehicle, by measuring from the floor to the centerline on the fog light and transferring the measurement to the flat aiming surface.

3. Turn on the fog lights and adjust them so that the top edge of the beam pattern is 4 in. below the horizontal centerline.

4. Repeat the procedure for the other fog light.

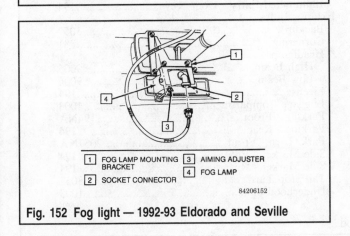

| 1 | FOG LAMP MOUNTING BRACKET | 3 | AIMING ADJUSTER |
| 2 | SOCKET CONNECTOR | 4 | FOG LAMP |

84206152

Fig. 152 Fog light — 1992-93 Eldorado and Seville

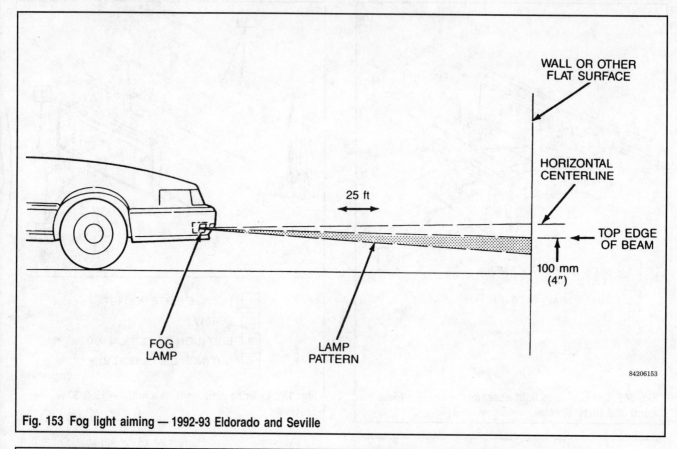

Fig. 153 Fog light aiming — 1992-93 Eldorado and Seville

Instrument Cluster Bulbs		Door Courtesy Lights	562
Anti-Lock	194	Door Warning Lights	168
Brake	194	Courtesy/Maplight with Astro Roof	562
Coolant Temp	194	Courtesy/Maplight without Astro	
Fasten Belts	194	Roof	906
Inflatable Restraint	194	Vanity Mirrors - Front	124
Charge	194	Vanity Mirrors - Rear	74
Service Vehicle Soon	194	Cruise Control Switch	
Service Engine Soon	194	Illumination	194
Oil	194	Cruise Control Switch	
Stop Engine Temp	194	"ON" Indicator	161
Turn Signal	194	Cruise Control Switch	
PRNDL Illumination	161	"Engaged" Indicator	161
Cluster Illumination	161	IP Compartment	194
Fuel Data Center Illumination	194	Illuminated Entry - Door Key	194
High Beam	161	**Exterior Bulbs**	
Right Information Center Bulbs		Backup	3057
Service Air Cond	PC168	Cornering	881
Trunk	PC168	Headlamps	
Left Information Center Bulbs		High Beam	9005
Washer Fluid	PC161	Low Beam	9006
Security	PC194	License	194
Interior Bulbs		Luggage Compartment	1003
Ash Tray	1445	Parking - Front	194NA
Center High-Mounted Stop Lamp		Parking - Rear	194
2 Door	1156	Park/Turn - Front	2057NA
Center High-Mounted Stop Lamp		Side Marker - Front	194
4 Door	1141	Side Marker - Rear	194
Courtesy - Rear Sail Panel	562	Tail Stop Turn	3057
Reading - Rear Sail Panel	561	Underhood	1003

Fig. 154 Light bulb usage chart — 1990 Deville and Fleetwood

Instrument Cluster Bulbs
Antilock 194
Brake 194
Coolant Temp 194
Fasten Belts 194
Inflatable Restraint 194
Charge 194
Service Vehicle Soon 194
Service Engine Soon 194
Oil 194
Stop Engine Temp 194
Turn Signal 194
PRNDL Illumination 161
Cluster Illumination 161
Fuel Data Center Illumination . . . 194
High Beam 161
Right Information Center Bulbs
Service Air Cond PC168
Trunk PC168
Left Information Center Bulbs
Washer Fluid PC161
Security PC194
Interior Bulbs
Ash Tray 1445
Center High-Mounted Stoplamp 2 Door 1156
Center High-Mounted Stoplamp 4 Door 1141
Courtesy - Rear Sail Panel 562

Reading - Rear Sail Panel 561
Door Courtesy Lights 12864
Door Warning Lights 12864
Courtesy/Map Light with Astro Roof 562
Courtesy/Map Light without Astro Roof 906
Vanity Mirrors - Front 124
Vanity Mirrors - Rear 74
Cruise Control Switch Illumination 194
Cruise Control Switch ON" Indicator 161
Cruise Control Switch "Engaged" Indicator . . . 161
IP Compartment 194
Illuminated Entry - Door Key 194
Exterior Bulbs
Backup 3057
Cornering 881
Headlamps
High Beam 9005
Low Beam 9006
License 194
Luggage Compartment 93
Parking - Front 194NA
Parking - Rear 194
Park/Turn - Front 2057NA
Side Marker - Front 194
Side Marker - Rear T24
Tail Stop Turn 3057
Underhood 561

84206155

Fig. 155 Light bulb usage chart — 1991-93 Deville, Fleetwood and Sixty Special

BULB	TRADE #
ASHTRAY ILLUMINATION	161
BACKUP LAMP	1156
CCDIC ILLUMINATION	74
CENTER HIGH MOUNT STOPLAMP	1156
CORNERING LAMP	880H
COURTESY LAMPS	
–FLOOR - LH	168
–FLOOR - RH	89
–DOOR COURTESY (WHT)	563
–DOOR WARNING (RED)	168(K)
	214-2(E)
–REAR COURTESY READ	562
CRUISE CONTROL ILLUM.	194
DOME LAMP	
–WITHOUT SUNROOF	906
–WITH SUNROOF	562
GLOVE BOX ILLUMINATION	194
HEADLAMP	9004H
HEADLAMP SWITCH ILLUMINATION	74/194
ILLUM. ENTRY LOCK CYLINDER	192
INSTRUMENT PANEL TELTALLES	74/194
INSTRUMENT PANEL ILLUMINATION	194
LICENSE PANEL ILLUMINATION	194
MIRROR CONTROL SWITCH ILLUM.	194
PARK/STOP/TURN LAMPS	
–DOUBLE FILAMENT	2057NA
–SINGLE FILAMENT	1156
SIDE MARKER LAMP	194NA
TRIP RESET BUTTON ILLUM.	74
TRUNK ILLUMINATION	1003
UNDERHOOD LAMP	93
VANITY MIRROR ILLUM.	124
WINDS. WIPER SWITCH ILLUM.	194

84206156

Fig. 156 Light bulb usage chart — 1990 Eldorado and Seville

BULB	TRADE #	TO ACCESS BULB
ASHTRAY ILLUMINATION	161	REMOVE FRONT CONSOLE (SEE SECTION 8C)
BACKUP LAMP	2057	REMOVE LICENSE PLATE ASSEMBLY (SEE SECTION 10)
CCDIC ILLUMINATION	74	REMOVE CCDIC (SEE SECTION 8C)
CENTER HIGH MOUNT STOPLAMP (CHMSL)	1156	REMOVE CHMSL (SEE SECTION 10)
CORNERING LAMP	880H	REACH BEHIND BUMPER
COURTESY LAMPS		
– FLOOR – LH	168	PULL FROM SOCKET IN LOWER SOUND INSULATOR
– FLOOR – RH	89	(SEE SECTION 8C)
– DOOR COURTESY (WHT)	563	REMOVE LENS FROM BRACKET
	214-2(E)	
– DOOR WARNING (RED)	168(K)	REMOVE LENS AND BRACKET
	214-2(E)	
– REAR COURTESY/READ	212-2(E)	REMOVE LENS FROM BRACKET
	562	
DOME LAMP		
– WITHOUT SUNROOF	906	REMOVE LENS FROM BRACKET
– WITH SUNROOF	562	REMOVE LENS FROM BRACKET
	212-2(E)	
GLOVE BOX ILLUMINATION	194	REMOVE GLOVE BOX DOOR INNER PANEL (SEE SECTION 8C)
HEADLAMP	9004(H)	REMOVE HEADLAMP ASSEMBLY (SEE SECTION 10)
HEADLAMP INDICATOR	194	REMOVE LEFT SWITCH POD (SEE SECTION 8C)
ILLUMINATION ENTRY LOCK CYLINDER	192	REMOVE DOOR LOCK CYLINDER (SEE SECTION 10)
INSTRUMENT PANEL TELLTALES	76/161	REMOVE INSTRUMENT PANEL CLUSTER (SEE SECTION 8C)
LICENSE PLATE ILLUMINATION	194	REMOVE LICENSE PLATE ASSEMBLY (SEE SECTION 10)
LIGHTS OFF INDICATOR	194	REMOVE LEFT SWITCH POD (SEE SECTION 8C)
MIRROR CONTROL SWITCH ILLUMINATION	194	REMOVE RIGHT SWITCH POD (SEE SECTION 8C)
PARK INDICATOR	194	REMOVE LEFT SWITCH POD (SEE SECTION 8C)
PARK/STOP/TURN LAMP	2057NA	REMOVE LAMP ASSEMBLY (SEE SECTION 10)
PRNDL ILLUMINATION	103	REMOVE FRONT CONSOLE (SEE SECTION 8C)
SIDE MARKER LAMP	194	REACH BEHIND BUMPER
TRIP RESET BUTTON ILLUMINATION	76	REMOVE INSTRUMENT PANEL CLUSTER (SEE SECTION 8C)
TRUNK ILLUMINATION	1004	OPEN TRUNK LID
UNDERHOOD LAMP	93	RAISE HOOD
VANITY MIRROR ILLUMINATION	7065	REMOVE LENS FROM BRACKET
WINDSHIELD WIPER SWITCH ILLUMINATION	194	REMOVE RIGHT SWITCH POD (SEE SECTION 8C)

84206157

Fig. 157 Light bulb usage chart — 1991 Eldorado and Seville

BULB	TRADE #	TO ACCESS BULB
ASHTRAY ILLUMINATION	1445	REMOVE FRONT CONSOLE/ASHTRAY
BACKUP LAMP	2057	REMOVE LICENSE PLATE ASSEMBLY (SEE SECTION 10)
CENTER HIGH MOUNT STOPLAMP (CHMSL)	1141	REMOVE CHMSL (SEE SECTION 10)
CORNERING LAMP	1156	REMOVE COVER OVER HEADLAMP AND REMOVE SOCKET
COURTESY LAMPS		
FLOOR – LH	564	PULL FROM SOCKET IN LOWER SOUND INSULATOR
FLOOR – RH	564	(SEE SECTION 8C)
REAR COURTESY/ READ	168	REMOVE SCREW BY COAT HOOK COVER, SLIDE ASSEMBLY FROM HEADLINER
FRONT COURTESY/ READ	168	REMOVE TRIM PLATE
FRONT FOG LAMP	886	REACH INSIDE BUMPER
GLOVE BOX ILLUMINATION	194	OPEN GLOVE BOX, REMOVE LENS
HEADLAMP COMPOSITE	9005HB3	REMOVE HEADLAMP ASSEMBLY (SEE SECTION 10)
– HI BEAM	9005HB3	REMOVE HEADLAMP ASSEMBLY (SEE SECTION 10)
– LO BEAM	9006HB4	REMOVE HEADLAMP ASSEMBLY (SEE SECTION 10)
– EXPORT	H4	REMOVE HEADLAMP ASSEMBLY (SEE SECTION 10)
HEADLAMP SWITCH	194	REMOVE HEADLAMP ASSEMBLY (SEE SECTION 10)
HEADLAMP SWITCH	BQ245-36210A	REMOVE HEADLAMP SWITCH FROM IP, (SEE SECTION 8C)
ILLUMINATION ENTRY LOCK CYLINDER	192	REMOVE DOOR LOCK CYLINDER (SEE SECTION 10)
INSTRUMENT PANEL TELLTALES	194	REMOVE INSTRUMENT PANEL CLUSTER (SEE SECTION 8C)
LICENSE PLATE ILLUMINATION	194	REMOVE LICENSE PLATE ASSEMBLY (SEE SECTION 10)
PARK /TURN/ LAMP (FRONT)	2057	REMOVE LAMP ASSEMBLY (SEE SECTION 10)
PARK/STOP/TURN (REAR)	2057	PULL BACK TRUNK TRIM, REMOVE LAMP ASSEMBLY
PRNDL ILLUMINATION	194	REMOVE FRONT CONSOLE (SEE SECTION 8C)
REAR BLOWER SWITCH	BQ245-35003A	REMOVE SWITCH LEVER HANDLE AND COVER PLATE
REAR FOG/ BACK-UP LIGHT (EXPORT)	P21/5W	(SEE SECTION 10)
STOP/TAIL/TURN SIGNAL (EXPORT)	P21/5W	(SEE SECTION 10)
SIDE MARKER LAMP	194	REACH BEHIND BUMPER
TRUNK ILLUMINATION	561	OPEN TRUNK LID
UNDERHOOD LAMP	561	RAISE HOOD
VANITY MIRROR ILLUMINATION	7065	REMOVE LENS FROM BRACKET

84206158

Fig. 158 Light bulb usage chart — 1992-93 Eldorado and Seville

TRAILER WIRING

Wiring the car for towing is fairly easy. There are a number of good wiring kits available and these should be used, rather than trying to design your own. All trailers will need brake lights and turn signals as well as tail lights and side marker lights. Most states require extra marker lights for overly wide trailers. Also, most states have recently required back-up lights for trailers, and most trailer manufacturers have been building trailers with back-up lights for several years.

Additionally, some Class I, most Class II and just about all Class III trailers will have electric brakes.

Add to this number an accessories wire, to operate trailer internal equipment or to charge the trailer's battery, and you can have as many as seven wires in the harness.

Determine the equipment on your trailer and buy the wiring kit necessary. The kit will contain all the wires needed, plus a plug adapter set which included the female plug, mounted on the bumper or hitch, and the male plug, wired into, or plugged into the trailer harness.

When installing the kit, follow the manufacturer's instructions. The color coding of the wires is standard throughout the industry.

One point to note, some domestic vehicles, and most imported vehicles, have separate turn signals. On most domestic vehicles, the brake lights and rear turn signals operate with the same bulb. For those vehicles with separate turn signals, you can purchase an isolation unit so that the brake lights won't blink whenever the turn signals are operated, or, you can go to your local electronics supply house and buy four diodes to wire in series with the brake and turn signal bulbs. Diodes will isolate the brake and turn signals. The choice is yours. The isolation units are simple and quick to install, but far more expensive than the diodes. The diodes, however, require more work to install properly, since they require the cutting of each bulb's wire and soldering in place of the diode.

One final point, the best kits are those with a spring loaded cover on the vehicle mounted socket. This cover prevents dirt and moisture from corroding the terminals. Never let the vehicle socket hang loosely. Always mount it securely to the bumper or hitch.

CIRCUIT PROTECTION

Fuses

▶ **See Figures 159, 160, 161, 162 and 163**

Fuses are used to protect the electrical circuits in the vehicle. If there is an excessive amount of current flowing through a circuit, the element within the fuse will melt, stopping the current flow.

To determine if a fuse is blown, remove it from the fuse block and examine the fuse element for a break. If the element is broken, replace the fuse with one of equal current rating.

✳✳CAUTION

Always replace a fuse with one that is the same type and current rating. Replacing a fuse with a fuse of a higher current rating may cause a vehicle fire and result in personal injury and vehicle damage.

All Devilles, Fleetwoods and Sixty Specials are equipped with a fuse block located under the left-hand side of the instrument panel. In addition, 1991-93 Deville, Fleetwood and Sixty Special are equipped with a fuse block located in the rear of the engine compartment. The fuse block is located in the glove box behind an access panel on 1990-91 Eldorado and Seville. There are 2 fuse blocks on 1992-93 Eldorado and Seville, one located in the left-hand side of the engine compartment, on the wheelwell and the other located in the side of the trunk.

Fig. 160 Squeeze the 2 tabs together on the passenger compartment fuse block, then pull it toward you. The fuse block will drop down to access the fuses — Deville, Fleetwood and Sixty Special

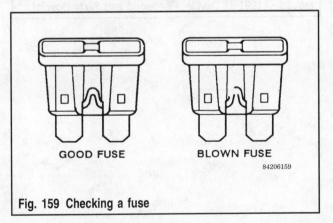

GOOD FUSE   BLOWN FUSE

84206159

Fig. 159 Checking a fuse

Fig. 161 Passenger compartment fuse block with cover removed — Deville, Fleetwood and Sixty Special

Fig. 162 Remove the engine compartment fuse block cover to access the fuses — 1991-93 Deville, Fleetwood and Sixty Special

Fig. 163 Engine compartment fuse block with cover removed — 1991-93 Deville, Fleetwood and Sixty Special

Fusible Links

▶ See Figures 164, 165 and 166

Fusible links are used instead of a fuse in circuits that are not normally fused, such as the ignition circuit. The fusible link is a smaller gauge than the cable it is designed to protect. Fusible links are marked on the insulation with wire gauge size because the heavy insulation makes the link appear to be a heavier gage than it actually is. The same wire size fusible link must be used when replacing a blown fusible link.

Some vehicles have replaced fusible links with very large plug-in fuses, sometimes called Maxi fuses. These fuses do not require repair like a fusible link, but simply replacement.

To replace a damaged fusible link, cut it off beyond the splice and replace with a repair link. When connecting the repair link, strip the wire and use crimping pliers to crimp the splice securely in 2 places. To replace a damaged fusible link that feeds 2 harness wires, cut them both off beyond the splice and use 2 repair links, one spliced to each harness wire.

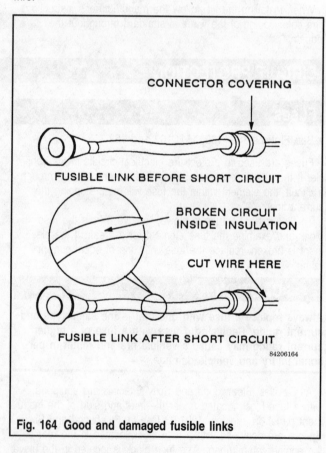

Fig. 164 Good and damaged fusible links

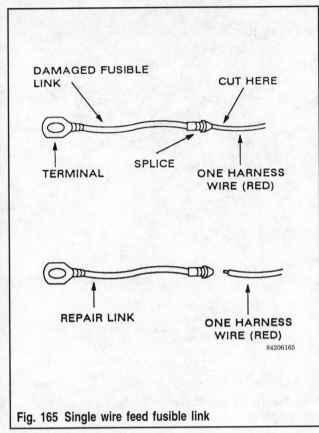

Fig. 165 Single wire feed fusible link

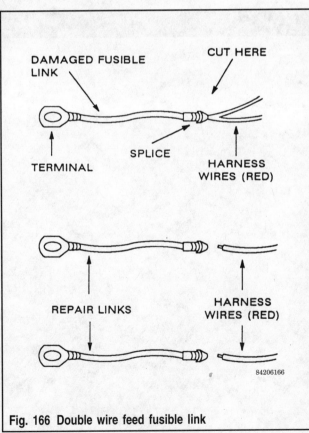

Fig. 166 Double wire feed fusible link

Circuit Breakers

A circuit breaker is a protective device designed to open the circuit when a current load is in excess of the circuit breaker's rating. If there is a short or other type of overload in the circuit, the excessive current will open the circuit between the circuit breaker terminals.

The headlights are protected by a circuit breaker in the headlight switch. If the circuit breaker opens, the headlights will either flash on and off, or stay off altogether. The circuit breaker resets automatically after the overload is removed.

The windshield wipers are protected by a circuit breaker. If the motor overheats, the circuit breaker will open, remaining off until the motor cools or the overload is removed. A common cause of wiper motor overheating is wiper operation in heavy snow.

Circuit breakers in the fuse block are used to protect the power windows and other power accessories.

Flashers

REPLACEMENT

▶ See Figures 167 and 168

➡ All vehicles except 1990-91 Eldorado and Seville are equipped with separate turn signal and hazard flashers, which are located under the instrument panel in the steering column area. 1990-91 Eldorado and Seville are equipped with a turn signal/hazard module located behind the center of the instrument panel.

1. Remove the necessary sound insulator panel(s) from under the instrument panel.
2. Remove the flasher from the retaining clip and disconnect the wiring connector.
3. Connect the wiring connector to the new flasher and install the flasher in the retaining clip.
4. Install the sound insulator panel(s).

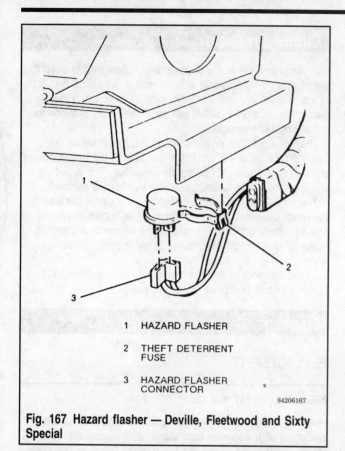

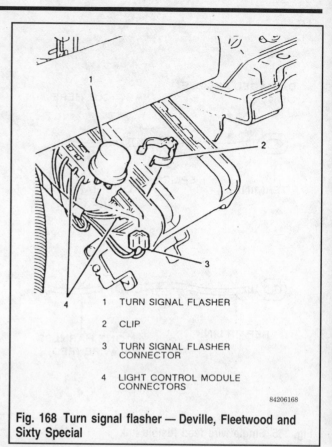

1 HAZARD FLASHER

2 THEFT DETERRENT FUSE

3 HAZARD FLASHER CONNECTOR

84206167

Fig. 167 Hazard flasher — Deville, Fleetwood and Sixty Special

1 TURN SIGNAL FLASHER

2 CLIP

3 TURN SIGNAL FLASHER CONNECTOR

4 LIGHT CONTROL MODULE CONNECTORS

84206168

Fig. 168 Turn signal flasher — Deville, Fleetwood and Sixty Special

WIRING DIAGRAMS

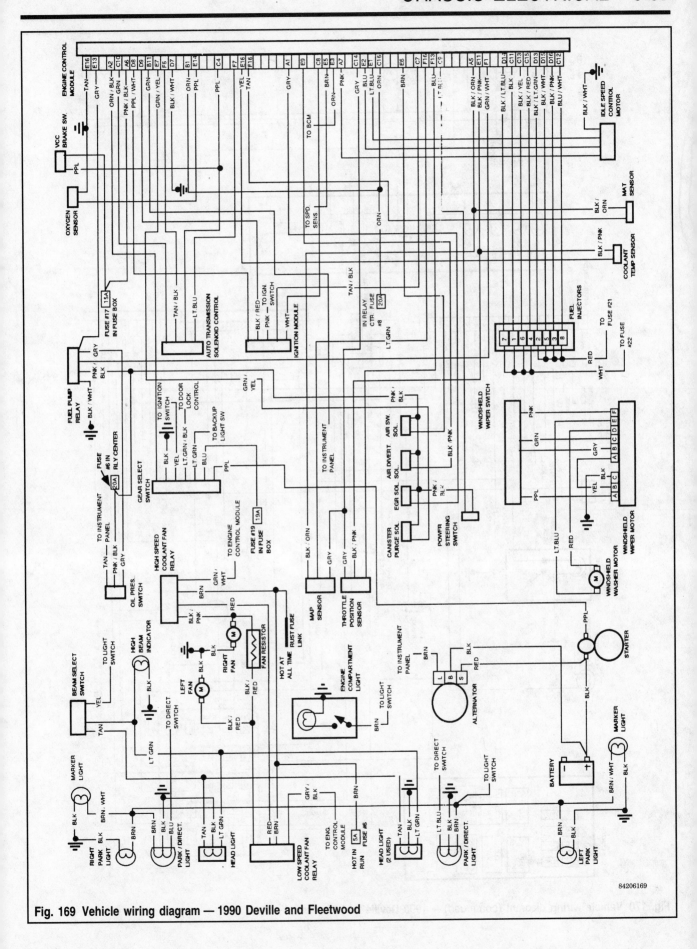

Fig. 169 Vehicle wiring diagram — 1990 Deville and Fleetwood

84206169

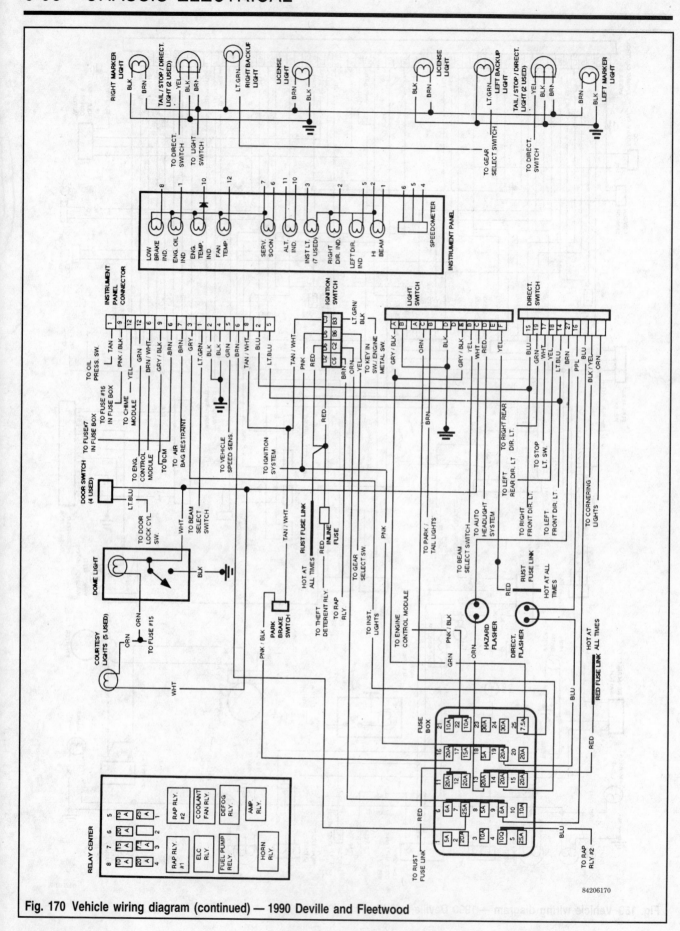

Fig. 170 Vehicle wiring diagram (continued) — 1990 Deville and Fleetwood

84206170

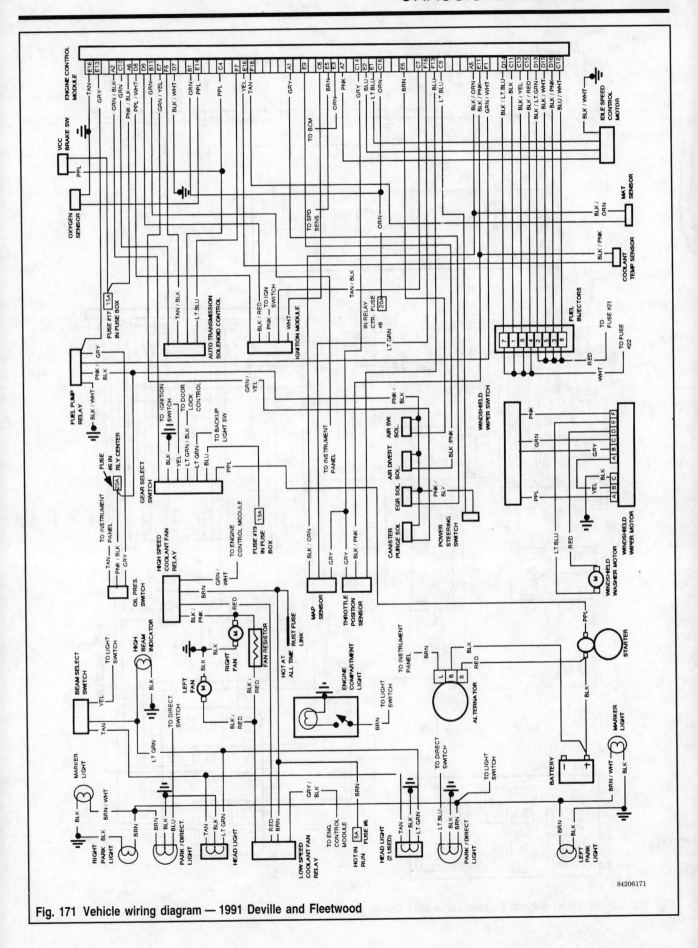

Fig. 171 Vehicle wiring diagram — 1991 Deville and Fleetwood

84206171

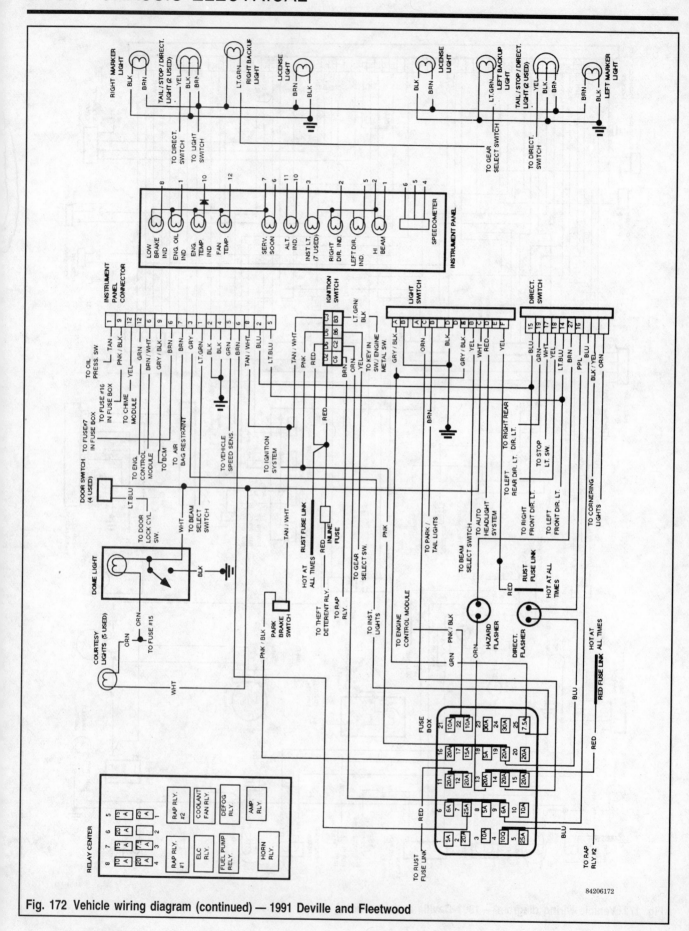

Fig. 172 Vehicle wiring diagram (continued) — 1991 Deville and Fleetwood

84206172

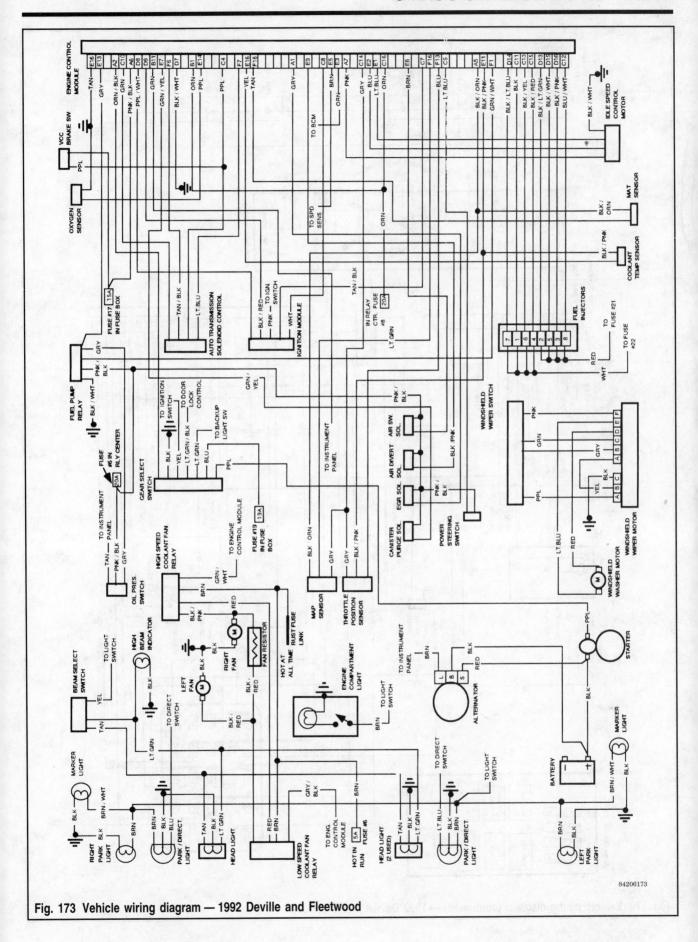

Fig. 173 Vehicle wiring diagram — 1992 Deville and Fleetwood

84206173

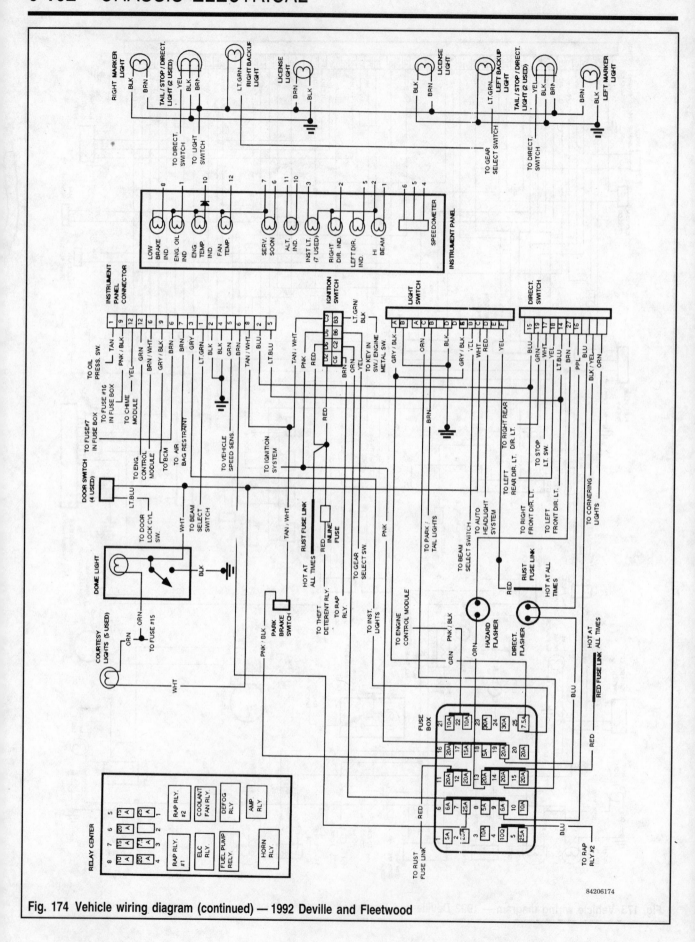

Fig. 174 Vehicle wiring diagram (continued) — 1992 Deville and Fleetwood

84206174

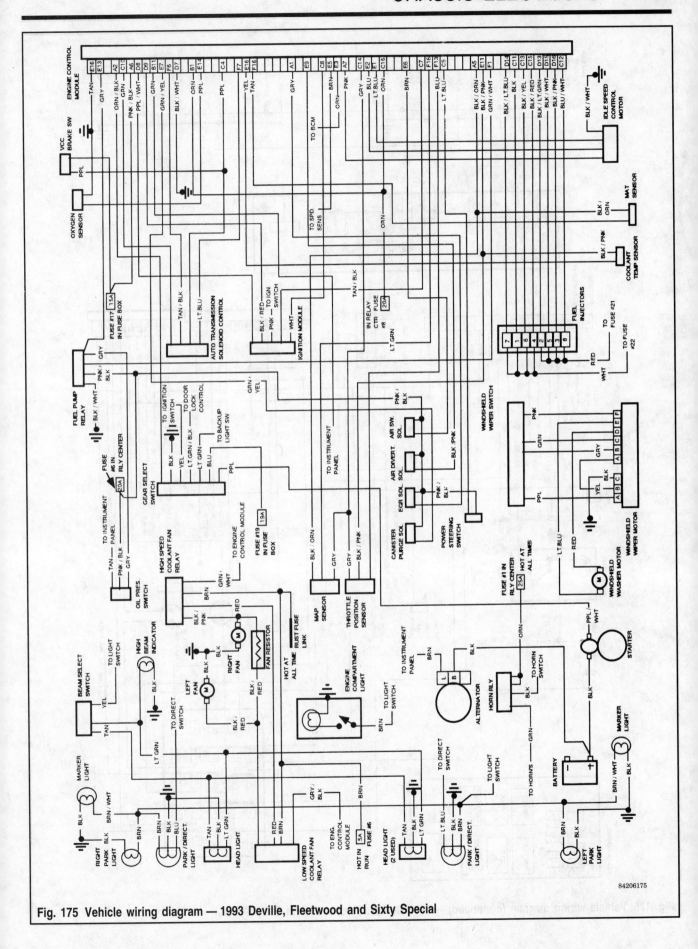

Fig. 175 Vehicle wiring diagram — 1993 Deville, Fleetwood and Sixty Special

84206175

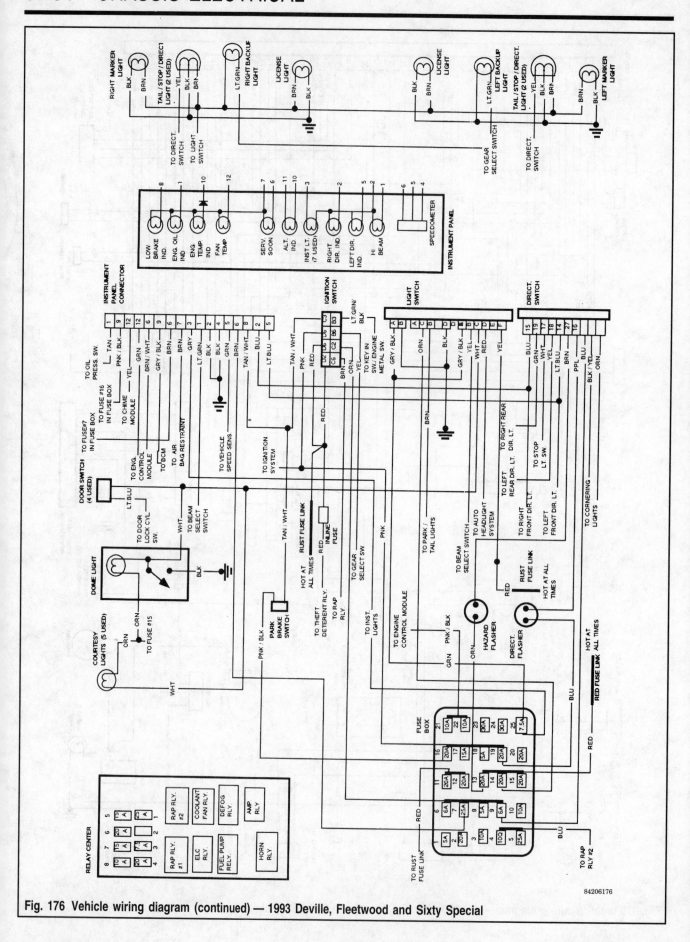

Fig. 176 Vehicle wiring diagram (continued) — 1993 Deville, Fleetwood and Sixty Special

84206176

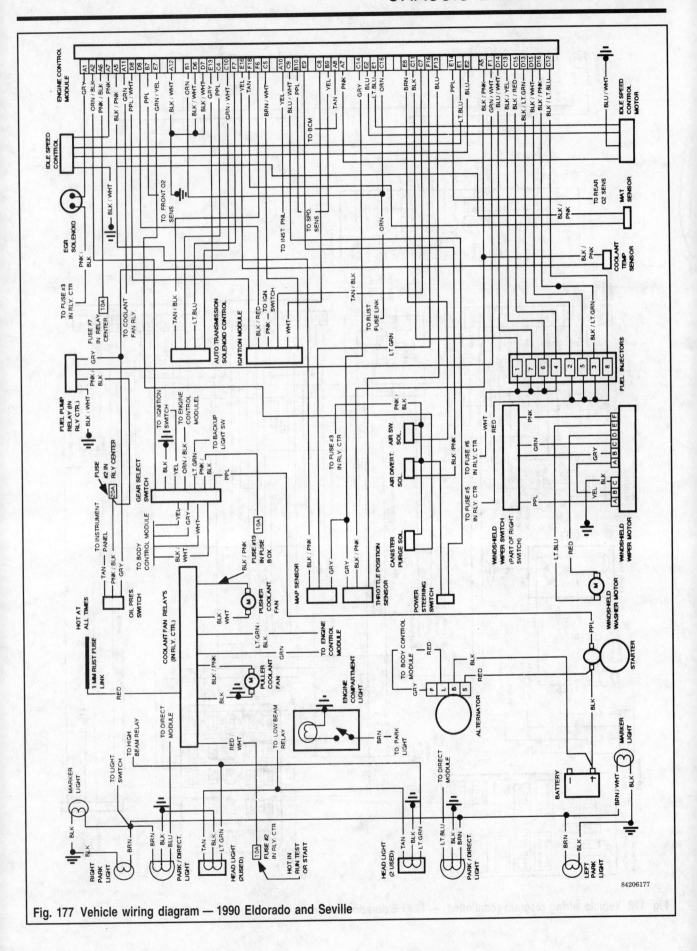

Fig. 177 Vehicle wiring diagram — 1990 Eldorado and Seville

84206177

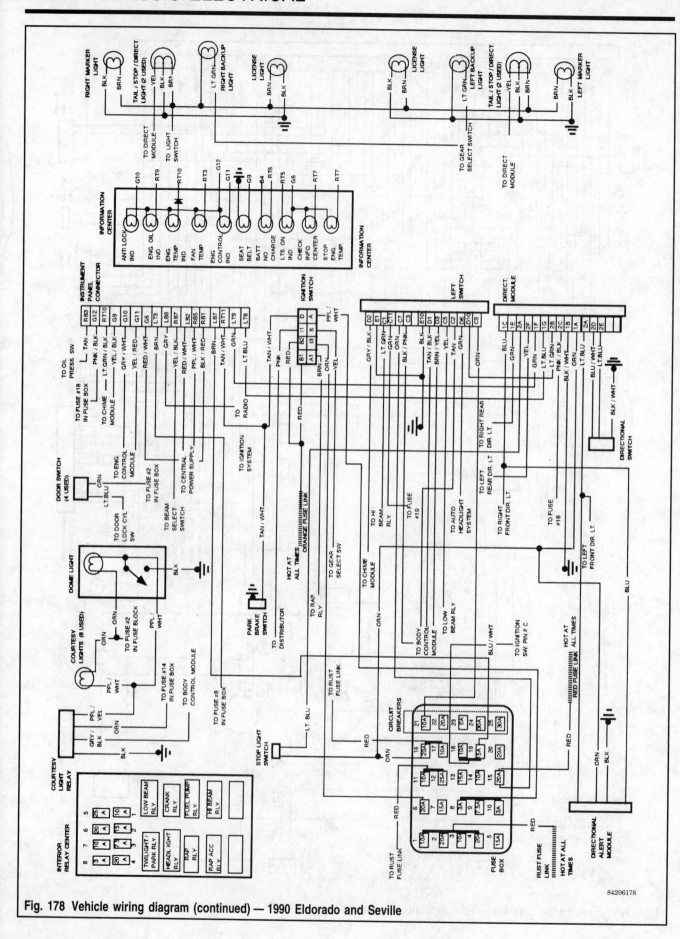

Fig. 178 Vehicle wiring diagram (continued) — 1990 Eldorado and Seville

84206178

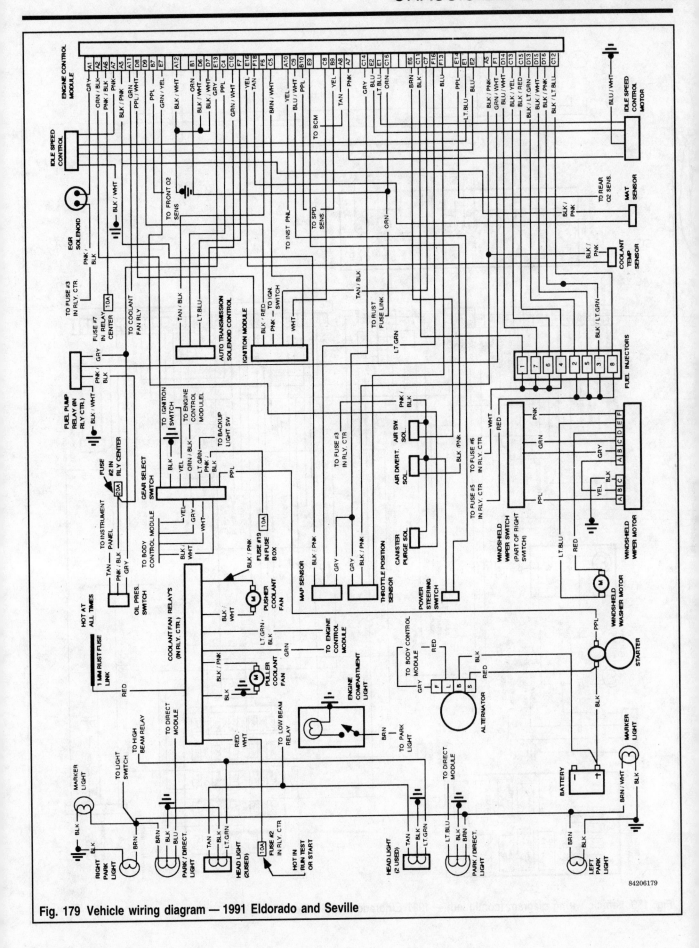

Fig. 179 Vehicle wiring diagram — 1991 Eldorado and Seville

84206179

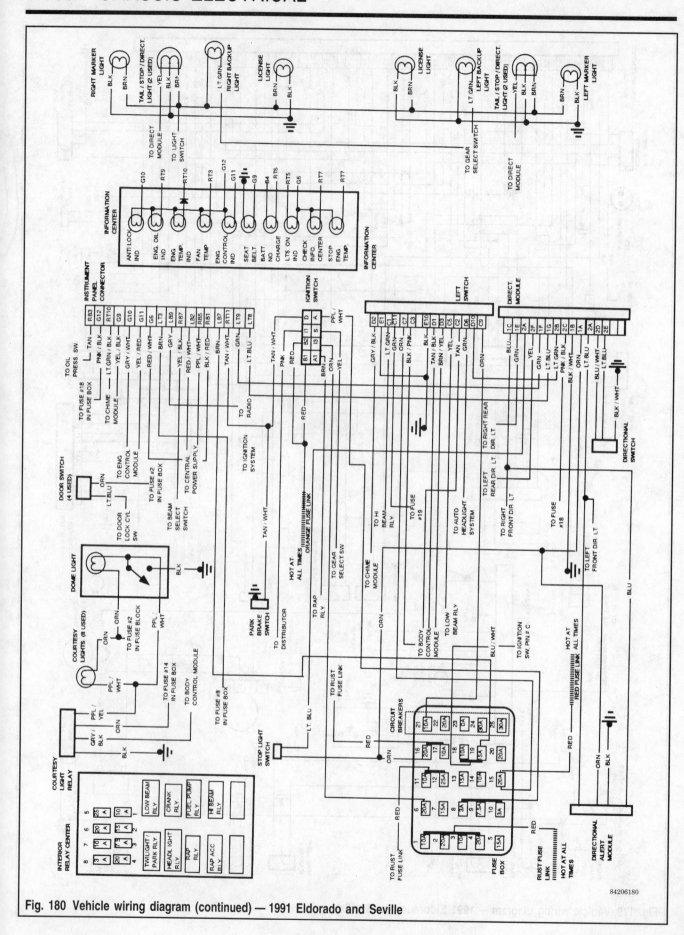

Fig. 180 Vehicle wiring diagram (continued) — 1991 Eldorado and Seville

84206180

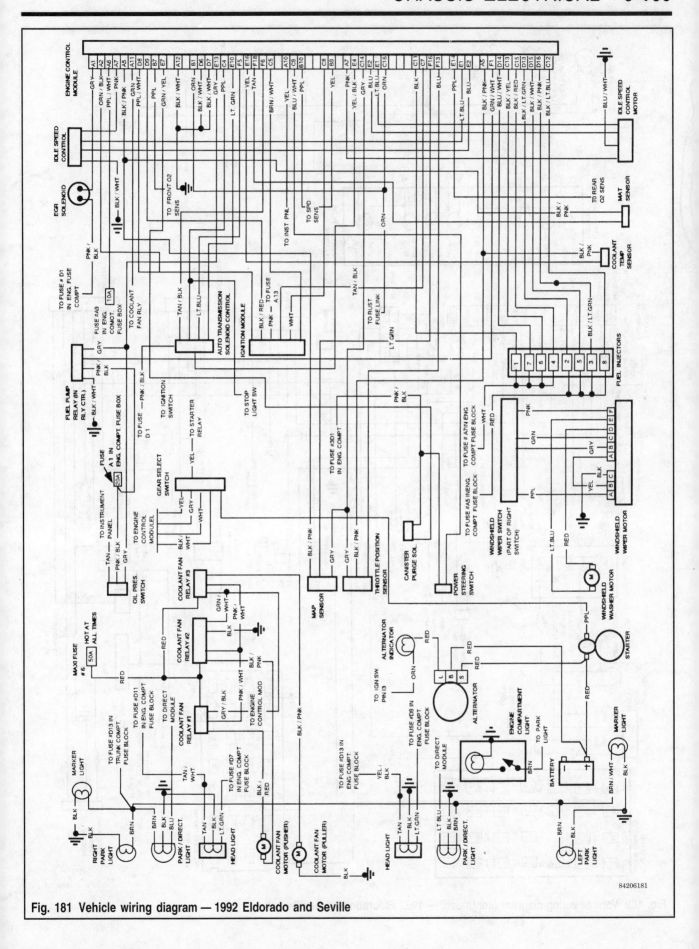

Fig. 181 Vehicle wiring diagram — 1992 Eldorado and Seville

84206181

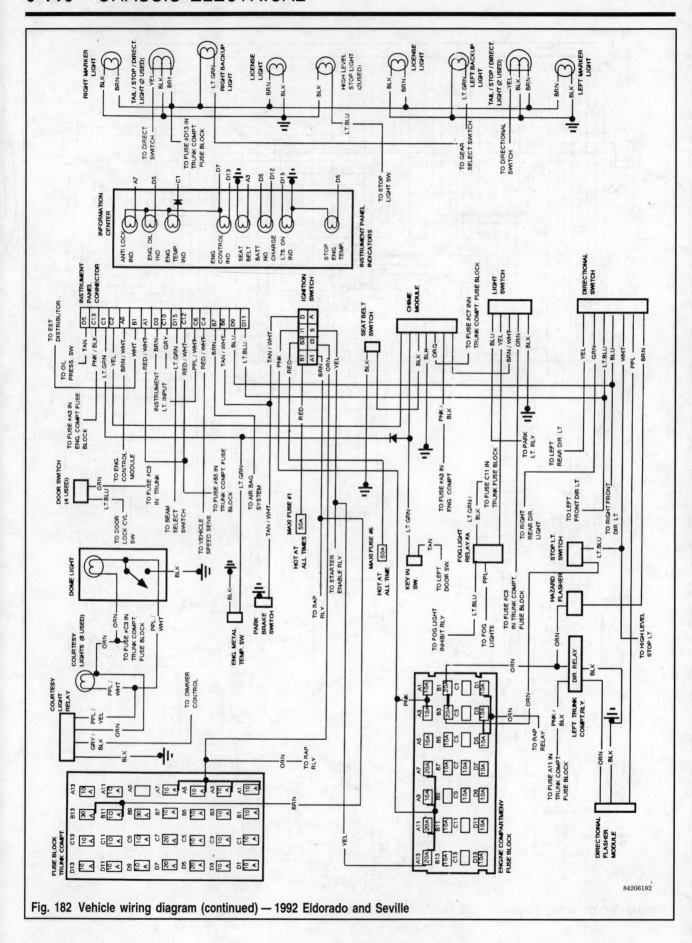

Fig. 182 Vehicle wiring diagram (continued) — 1992 Eldorado and Seville

7

DRIVE TRAIN

AUTOMATIC TRANSAXLE 7-2

AUTOMATIC TRANSAXLE

Identification

All 1990 vehicles are equipped with the 4T60 four-speed automatic overdrive transaxle. All 1991-93 vehicles with the 4.9L engine are equipped with the 4T60-E four-speed automatic overdive transaxle. The 4T60-E is a more advanced version of the 4T60, and features electronic shift control timing by the Powertrain Control Module (PCM). All 1993 Eldorados and Sevilles with the 4.6L Northstar engine are equipped with the 4T80-E four-speed automatic overdrive transaxle. The 4T80-E was developed as an integral part of the Northstar powertrain, and features an electronically controlled torque converter as well as electronic shift control.

For automatic transaxle serial number identification information, see Section 1.

Fluid Pan and Filter

REMOVAL & INSTALLATION

4T60 and 4T60-E Transaxle

▶ **See Figures 1, 2 and 3**

1. Raise and safely support the vehicle.
2. Place a suitable drain pan under the transaxle fluid pan.
3. Remove the retaining bolts at the front and sides of the fluid pan.
4. Loosen the rear fluid pan bolts approximately 4 turns.
5. Pry the fluid pan loose with a small prybar and allow the fluid to drain.

✳✳WARNING

Be careful not to damage the fluid pan and transaxle case mating surfaces, as damage may result in fluid leaks.

6. Remove the remaining bolts and the fluid pan and gasket.
7. Remove the transaxle screen/filter. The lip ring seal pressed into the case should be removed only if replacement is necessary.
8. Inspect the fluid pan and screen for foreign material, such as metal particles, clutch facing material, rubber particles or engine coolant. If necessary, determine and correct the source of the contamination.

To install:
9. Clean all gasket mating surfaces. Clean the fluid pan and screen in solvent and allow to dry. Inspect the fluid pan flange for distortion and straighten, if necessary.

➡The transaxle case and fluid pan flanges must be clean, dry and free of any oil film prior to fluid pan and gasket installation, or leakage may result. Inspect the washers on the fluid pan bolts before reuse, as shown in Fig. 3.

10. Install the screen, using a new filter. The filter uses a lip ring seal pressed into the case. The seal should be removed only if replacement is necessary.

11. Install the fluid pan, using a new gasket. Tighten the bolts to 10 ft. lbs. (13 Nm) on 1990 vehicles or 12-13 ft. lbs. (16-17 Nm) on 1991-93 vehicles.
12. Lower the vehicle.
13. Fill the transaxle with 6 qts. of Dexron®II-E transmission fluid.
14. Place the gearshift lever in **P**. Start the engine and let it idle; do not race the engine.
15. Check the fluid level and correct as required. Check the fluid pan for leaks.

4T80-E Transaxle

➡The 4T80-E transaxle has a filter under the side cover that requires service only during a complete transaxle overhaul. However, the scavenging screens under the bottom pan must be cleaned whenever the transaxle fluid is changed.

▶ **See Figures 4, 5 and 6**

1. Raise and safely support the vehicle.
2. Place a suitable drain pan under the transaxle fluid pan.
3. Loosen the bottom fluid pan bolts in the reverse order of the torque sequence and drain the fluid from the pan.
4. Remove the drain plug in the case.

➡Removing the bottom fluid pan will only partially drain the transaxle fluid. The remaining fluid is held in the side cover and torque converter. Removing the drain plug in the case after bottom fluid pan removal will drain the fluid from the side cover.

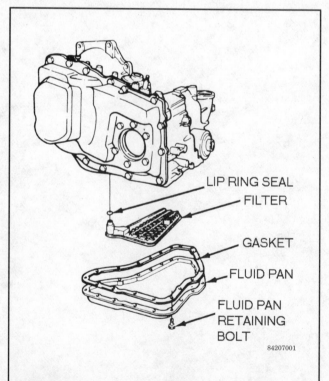

LIP RING SEAL
FILTER
GASKET
FLUID PAN
FLUID PAN RETAINING BOLT

84207001

Fig. 1 Transaxle fluid pan and filter — 1990 4T60 transaxle

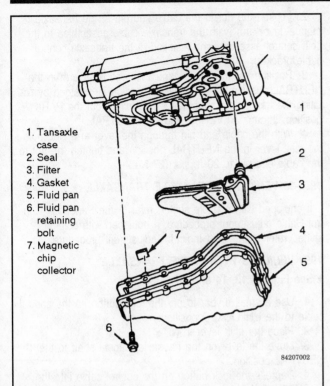

1. Tansaxle case
2. Seal
3. Filter
4. Gasket
5. Fluid pan
6. Fluid pan retaining bolt
7. Magnetic chip collector

84207002

Fig. 2 Transaxle fluid pan and filter — 1991-93 vehicles with 4T60-E transaxle

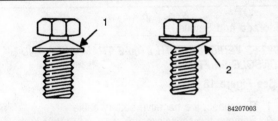

84207003

Fig. 3 If the washers on the fluid pan bolts look the same as on bolt No. 1, the bolts can be reused. If the washers look like the one on bolt No. 2, the bolts should not be reused

5. Remove the retaining bolts, fluid pan and seal. Discard the seal.

6. Remove the left and right scavenger screens.

7. Inspect the scavenger screen lip seals in the transaxle case for nicks or cuts and replace, if damaged. Inspect the scavenger screens for cuts in the screen or a cracked housing; replace if necessary.

8. Check the fluid pan and transaxle case for dents or nicks in the sealing surface that could cause leaks. Inspect the fluid pan bolts for damaged threads and replace, if necessary.

To install:

9. Clean the scavenger screens and fluid pan in solvent and allow to dry. Clean the fluid pan retaining bolts and the tapped holes in the transaxle case.

➡**The fluid pan and case sealing surfaces must be clean and dry for proper sealing. The retaining bolts and tapped holes must be clean and dry to maintain proper bolt torque.**

10. Install the drain plug in the case and tighten to 6-10 ft. lbs. (8-14 Nm).

11. Install the left and right scavenger screens.

12. Install the bottom fluid pan using a new seal. Install the fluid pan retaining bolts finger-tight.

13. Tighten the fluid pan bolts in 3 steps. First tighten the bolts, in sequence, to 27 inch lbs. (3 Nm). Then tighten the bolts, in sequence, to 53 inch lbs. (6 Nm). Finally, tighten the bolts, in sequence, to 106 inch lbs. (12 Nm).

14. Lower the vehicle. Add the proper quantity of Dexron®II-E transmission fluid to the transaxle.

15. Make sure the transaxle is in **P**, then start the engine. With a cold powertrain, engine coolant temperature below 90°F (32°C), the fluid level should be in the 'Cold' range on the dipstick.

16. When the powertrain is at normal operating temperature, engine coolant temperature 180-200°F (82-93°C), the fluid level should be in the 'Hot' crosshatched range on the dipstick.

17. Shut off the engine. To reset the transaxle fluid change indicator, press and hold the 'off' and 'rear defog' buttons for 5-20 seconds on the climate control simultaneously until the 'TRANS FLUID RESET' message appears in the information center.

Adjustments

SHIFT LINKAGE

Deville, Fleetwood and Sixty Special
▶ See Figures 7, 8 and 9

The shift linkage should be adjusted so that the engine will start in **P** and **N** only. Incorrect shift linkage adjustment can cause clutch and/or band failure.

1. Place the column shift lever in **N**.

2. Loosely assemble the nut on the cable through the transaxle lever with the transaxle cable assembled to the steering column bracket and installed at the transaxle control cable bracket.

3. Tighten the nut to 20 ft. lbs. (27 Nm). The lever must be held out of park when torquing.

Eldorado and Seville

1990-91

▶ See Figures 10, 11 and 12

The shift control cable and manual linkage should be adjusted so that the transaxle manual linkage lever is positioned in NEUTRAL when the shift control **N** detent position is selected.

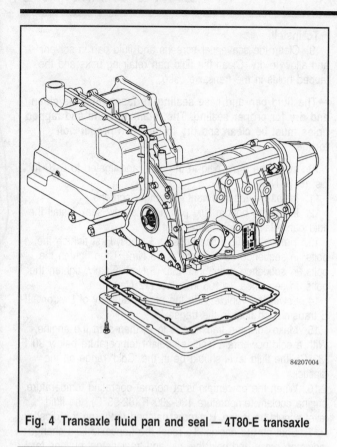

Fig. 4 Transaxle fluid pan and seal — 4T80-E transaxle

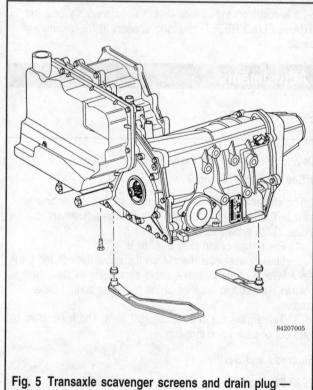

Fig. 5 Transaxle scavenger screens and drain plug — 4T80-E transaxle

Incorrect shift linkage adjustment can cause clutch and/or band failure.

1. Place the console shift lever in **N**.

2. Loosen the nut to the cable end pin at the transaxle manual lever arm (with the transaxle cable assembled to the shift control assembly and installed at the transaxle control cable bracket).

3. Position the transaxle manual linkage lever arm in the NEUTRAL position. The NEUTRAL position is obtained by rotating the transaxle manual lever clockwise from the PARK position, through REVERSE and into NEUTRAL.

4. With the cable end pin through the lever arm slot, hold the shift lever in the NEUTRAL position and tighten the nut to the cable end pin to 20 ft. lbs. (27 Nm).

1992-93 VEHICLES WITH 4T60-E TRANSAXLE

If equipped with console shifter, refer to the Park/Lock Control Cable adjustment procedure. If equipped with column shifter, refer to the Shift Indicator adjustment procedure.

1993 VEHICLES WITH 4T80-E TRANSAXLE

▶ See Figures 13, 14 and 15

1. Use a small prybar to pry the lock button on the control cable to the UNLOCKED position.
2. Place the shift lever in **N**.
3. Move the lever on the transaxle manual shaft to the NEUTRAL position.
4. Depress the lock button on the control cable into the LOCKED position.

PARK/LOCK CONTROL CABLE

Eldorado and Seville

1992-93 VEHICLES WITH 4T60-E TRANSAXLE AND CONSOLE SHIFTER

▶ See Figure 16

1. Disconnect the negative battery cable.
2. Remove the console cover.
3. Place the shift lever in **P** and turn the ignition key to **RUN**. Do not proceed further with the ignition key in any other position.
4. Remove the left hush panel and loosen the driver's side carpet to allow access to the cable routing, if necessary.
5. Remove the steering column reinforcement plates. Remove the steering column retaining bolts and lower the steering column.
6. Slip a screwdriver blade into the slot provided in the ignition switch inhibitor, depress the cable latch and pull the cable from the inhibitor.
7. Pull the cable connector lock button at the shifter base to the up position.
8. Snap the cable from the shifter assembly park lock lever pin.
9. Depress the 2 cable connector latches and remove the shifter base.
10. Remove the cable, if replacement is necessary.
11. If removed, reinstall the cable, making sure the routing is correct.
12. With the cable lock button in the up position and the shift lever in the **P** position, snap the cable connector into the shifter base.

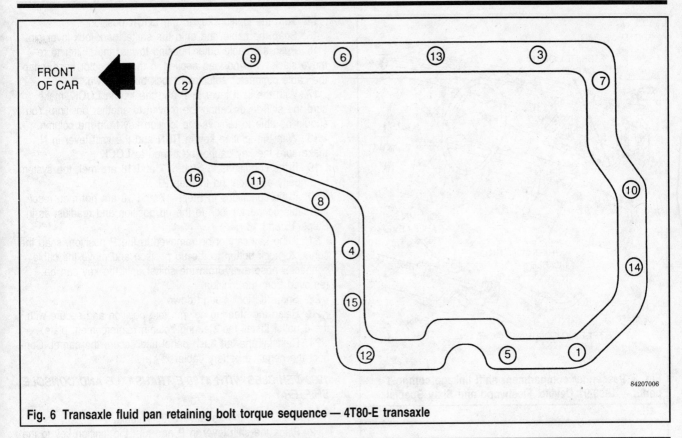

FRONT
OF CAR

84207006

Fig. 6 Transaxle fluid pan retaining bolt torque sequence — 4T80-E transaxle

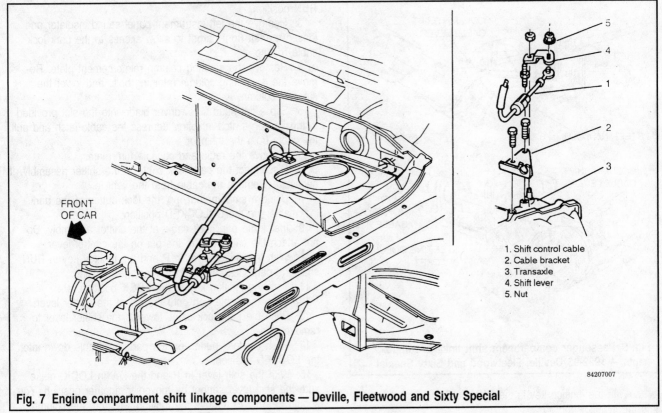

FRONT
OF CAR

1. Shift control cable
2. Cable bracket
3. Transaxle
4. Shift lever
5. Nut

84207007

Fig. 7 Engine compartment shift linkage components — Deville, Fleetwood and Sixty Special

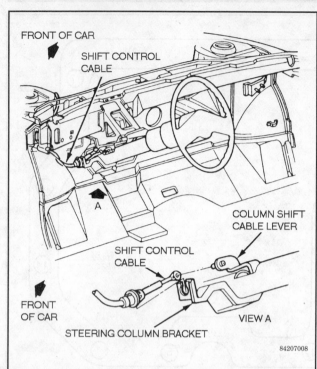

Fig. 8 Passenger compartment shift linkage components — 1990-91 Deville, Fleetwood and Sixty Special

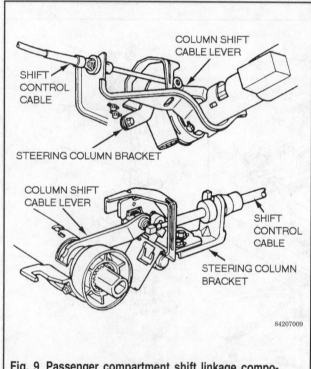

Fig. 9 Passenger compartment shift linkage components — 1992-93 Deville, Fleetwood and Sixty Special

13. With the ignition key in the **RUN** position, snap the cable into the inhibitor housing.

➡ **Do not attempt to insert the cable with the key in any other position.**

14. Turn the ignition key to the **LOCK** position.

15. Snap the cable end onto the shifter park lock lever pin.

16. Push the cable outer housing toward the shifter to remove slack. With no load applied to the connector nose, snap the cable connector adjustment lock button down.

17. With the shift lever in **P** and the key in **LOCK**, make sure the shift lever cannot be moved to another position. You should be able to remove the ignition key from the column.

18. With the ignition key in **RUN** and the shift lever in **N**, make sure the key cannot be turned to **LOCK**.

19. If the conditions in Steps 17 and 18 are met, the system is properly adjusted; go to Step 21.

20. If the conditions in Steps 17 and 18 are not met, reset the cable connector lock to the up position and readjust as in Steps 15 and 16.

21. If the key cannot be removed in the **P** position, snap the connector lock button to the up position and move the cable connector nose away from the shifter until the key can be removed from the ignition.

22. Snap the lock button down.

23. Raise the steering column into position and secure with the 4 bolts. Install the steering column reinforcement plate.

24. Reinstall the left hush panel and secure the carpet. Connect the negative battery cable.

1993 VEHICLES WITH 4T80-E TRANSAXLE AND CONSOLE SHIFTER

1. Disconnect the negative battery cable.

2. Place the shift lever in **P** and turn the ignition key to the **RUN** position.

3. Remove the left instrument panel sound insulator and loosen the left front carpet to allow access to the park lock cable routing.

4. Remove the steering column reinforcement plate. Remove the 4 steering column retaining bolts and lower the steering column.

5. Slip a flat head screwdriver blade into the slot provided in the ignition switch inhibitor, depress the cable latch and pull the cable from the inhibitor.

6. Remove the radio and console trim plates.

7. Disconnect the park lock cable at the shifter assembly. If necessary, remove the cable from the vehicle.

8. Using a small prybar, pry the lock button of the park lock cable into the UNLOCKED position.

9. Install the park lock cable at the shifter assembly. Do not attach the cable end to the pin on the control lever.

10. With the shifter lever in **P** and the ignition key in **RUN**, snap the park lock cable into the inhibitor housing.

11. Turn the ignition key to the **LOCK** position.

12. Snap the cable end onto the pin of the shifter lever.

13. Push the park lock cable towards the shifter lever to remove slack.

14. Push the lock button on the park lock cable down into the LOCKED position.

15. With the shift lever in **P** and the key in **LOCK**, make sure the shift lever cannot be moved to another position. You should be able to remove the ignition key from the column.

16. With the ignition key in **RUN** and the shift lever in **N**, make sure the key cannot be turned to **LOCK**.

17. If the conditions in Steps 15 and 16 are met, go to Step 18. If the conditions are not met, readjust the park lock cable beginning at Step 8.

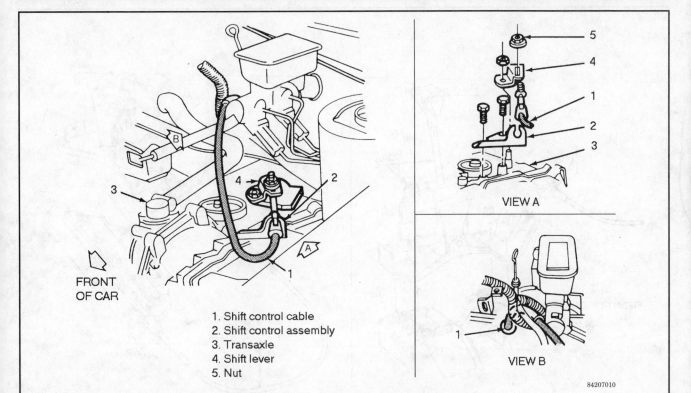

1. Shift control cable
2. Shift control assembly
3. Transaxle
4. Shift lever
5. Nut

84207010

Fig. 10 Engine compartment shift linkage components — 1990-91 Eldorado and Seville

18. Raise the steering column into position and secure with the 4 bolts. Install the steering column reinforcement plate.
19. Install the console and radio trim plates.
20. Secure the left front carpet and install the left instrument panel sound insulator. Connect the negative battery cable.

SHIFT INDICATOR

Deville, Fleetwood and Sixty Special
▶ See Figure 17

1. Place the shift lever in the NEUTRAL gate notch.
2. Guide the clip on the edge of the shift bowl to position the pointer on **N**.
3. Push the clip onto the bowl.
4. Make sure the cable rests on the bowl, not on the column jacket.

Eldorado and Seville

1992-93 VEHICLES WITH COLUMN SHIFTER
▶ See Figure 18

1. Remove the left-hand sound insulator panel to gain access to the steering column.
2. Move the shift lever to the NEUTRAL position.
3. Loosen the shift indicator cable adjustment nut on the steering column.
4. Slide the adjustment mechanism until the shift indicator in the instrument panel is centered in the NEUTRAL position.
5. Tighten the adjustment nut.

6. Install the left-hand sound insulator panel.

THROTTLE VALVE (TV) CABLE

4T60 Transaxle
▶ See Figures 19, 20, 21 and 22

1. After installation of the cable to the transaxle, engine bracket and cable actuating lever, check to make sure that the cable slider is in the 'zero' or fully retracted position. If it is not, proceed as follows:
    a. Make sure the engine is **OFF**.
    b. Depress and hold down the metal readjust tab at the engine end of the TV cable.
    c. Move the slider until it stops against the fitting.
    d. Release the readjustment tab.
2. Rotate the throttle lever to its 'full travel' position (wide-open throttle).

➡Adjustment of the TV cable must be made by rotating the throttle lever at the throttle body. Do not use the accelerator pedal to rotate the throttle lever.

3. The slider must move (ratchet) toward the lever when the lever is rotated to its 'full travel' position.

Neutral Safety Switch

➡The neutral safety switch incorporates the back-up light switch.

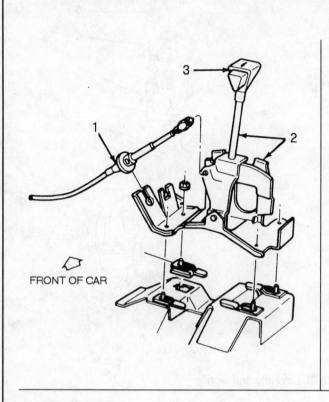

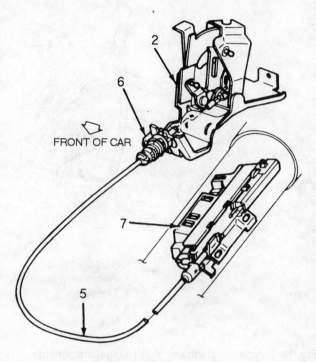

FRONT OF CAR

FRONT OF CAR

1. Shift control cable
2. Control cable
   retaining clip
3. Shift handle
4. Handle retainer clip
5. Park lock cable
6. Park lock adjuster
7. Steering column unit

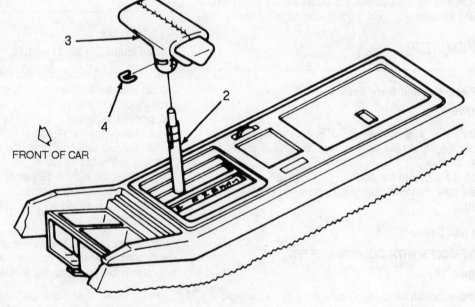

FRONT OF CAR

84207011

Fig. 11 Passenger compartment shift linkage components — 1990 Eldorado and Seville

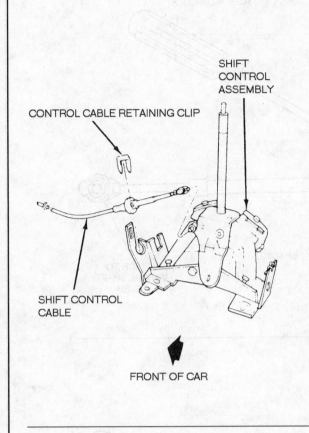

CONTROL CABLE RETAINING CLIP

SHIFT
CONTROL
ASSEMBLY

SHIFT CONTROL
CABLE

FRONT OF CAR

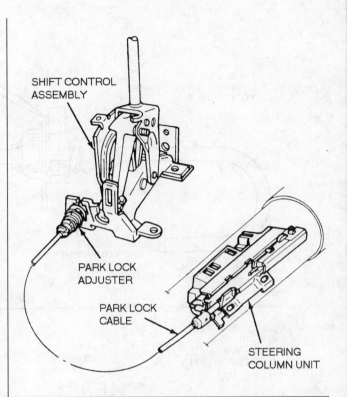

SHIFT CONTROL
ASSEMBLY

PARK LOCK
ADJUSTER

PARK LOCK
CABLE

STEERING
COLUMN UNIT

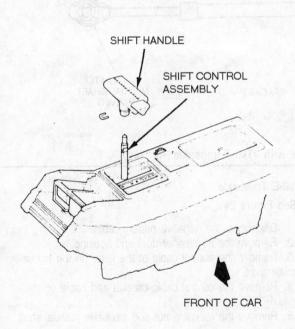

SHIFT HANDLE

SHIFT CONTROL
ASSEMBLY

FRONT OF CAR

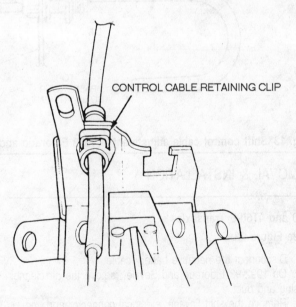

CONTROL CABLE RETAINING CLIP

84207012

Fig. 12 Passenger compartment shift linkage components — 1991 Eldorado and Seville

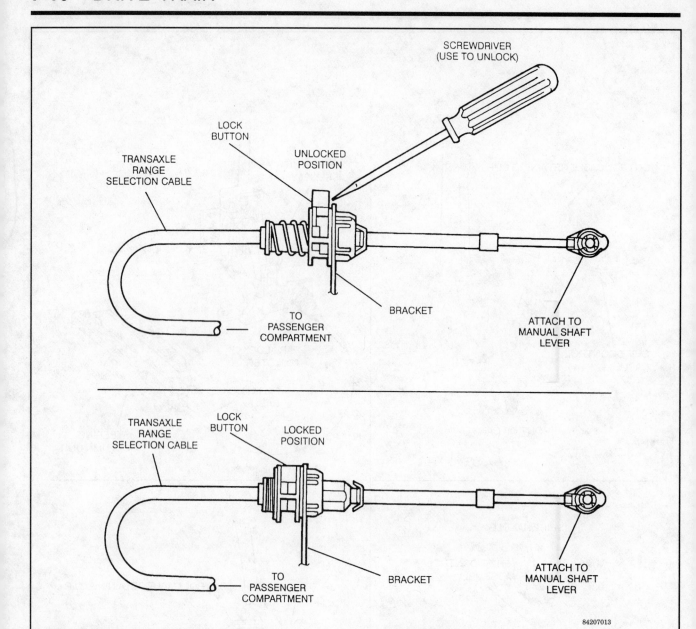

Fig. 13 Shift control cable adjustment — 1993 Eldorado and Seville with 4T80-E transaxle

REMOVAL & INSTALLATION

4T60 and 4T60-E Transaxles

▶ See Figure 23

1. Disconnect the negative battery cable.
2. On 1992-93 Eldorado and Seville, remove the air cleaner housing and duct.
3. Remove the shift linkage, electrical connector and vacuum hose.
4. Remove the attaching nut and the shift lever.
5. Remove the fuel line bracket and bolt.
6. Remove the retaining bolts and the switch.
7. Installation is the reverse of the removal procedure. Adjust the switch and tighten the retaining bolts to 20 ft. lbs. (27 Nm).

4T80-E Transaxle

▶ See Figure 24

1. Disconnect the negative battery cable.
2. Remove the air cleaner duct and housing.
3. Remove the control cable at the lever on the transaxle manual shaft.
4. Remove the control cable bracket and cable on the transaxle.
5. Remove the retaining nut and transaxle manual shaft lever.
6. Disconnect the electrical connector and hose.
7. Remove the retaining bolts and the neutral safety switch.
8. Installation is the reverse of the removal procedure. Adjust the switch and tighten the retaining bolts to 106 inch lbs. (12 Nm). Tighten the manual shaft lever retaining nut to 15 ft. lbs. (20 Nm).

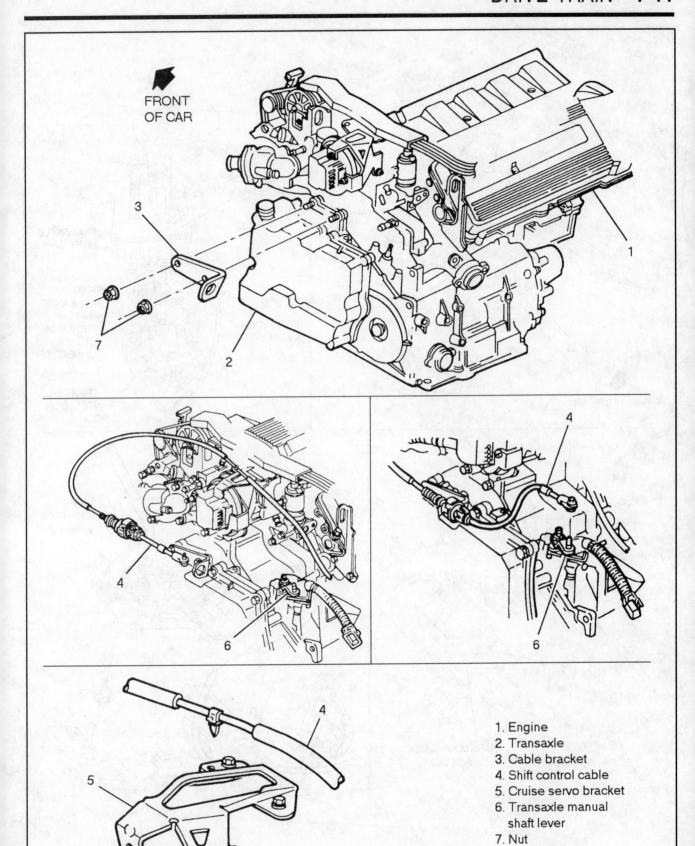

FRONT OF CAR

1. Engine
2. Transaxle
3. Cable bracket
4. Shift control cable
5. Cruise servo bracket
6. Transaxle manual shaft lever
7. Nut

84207014

Fig. 14 Engine compartment shift linkage components — 1993 Eldorado and Seville with 4T80-E transaxle

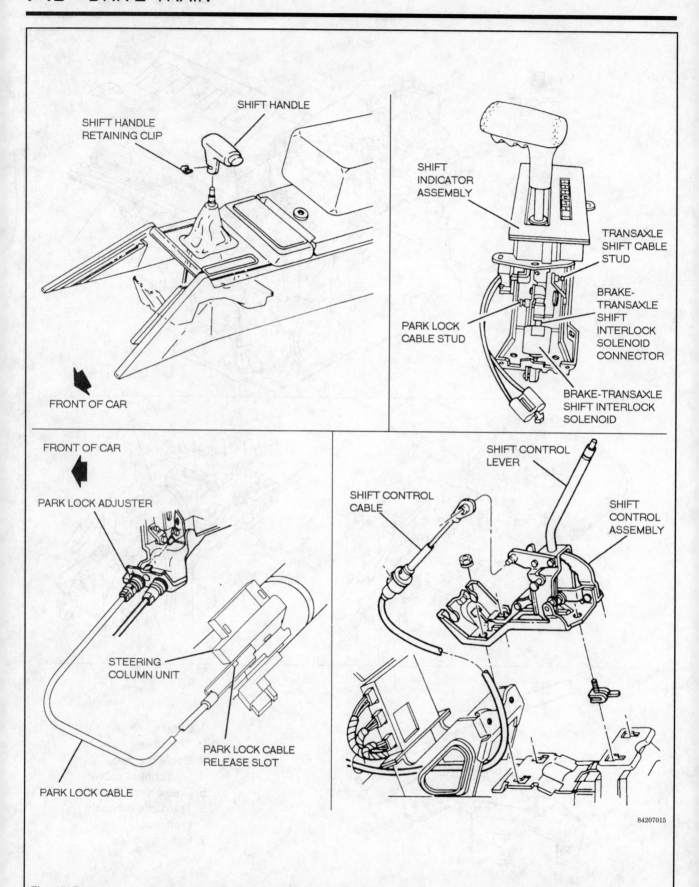

SHIFT HANDLE

SHIFT HANDLE RETAINING CLIP

FRONT OF CAR

SHIFT INDICATOR ASSEMBLY

TRANSAXLE SHIFT CABLE STUD

BRAKE-TRANSAXLE SHIFT INTERLOCK SOLENOID CONNECTOR

PARK LOCK CABLE STUD

BRAKE-TRANSAXLE SHIFT INTERLOCK SOLENOID

FRONT OF CAR

PARK LOCK ADJUSTER

STEERING COLUMN UNIT

PARK LOCK CABLE RELEASE SLOT

PARK LOCK CABLE

SHIFT CONTROL LEVER

SHIFT CONTROL CABLE

SHIFT CONTROL ASSEMBLY

84207015

Fig. 15 Passenger compartment shift linkage components — 1993 Eldorado and Seville with 4T80-E transaxle

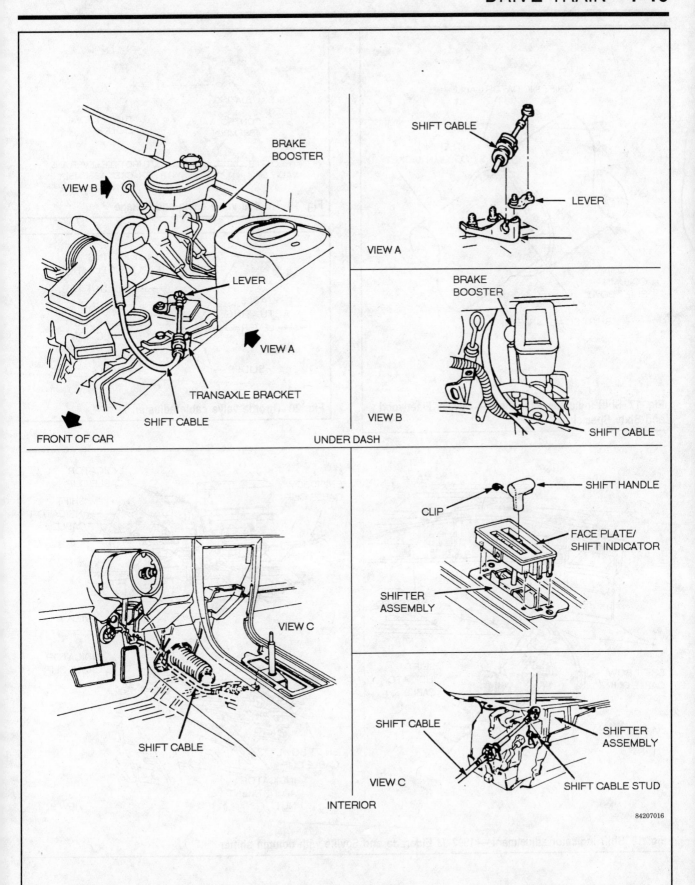

Fig. 16 Shift control system — 1992-93 Eldorado and Seville with 4T60-E transaxle and console shifter

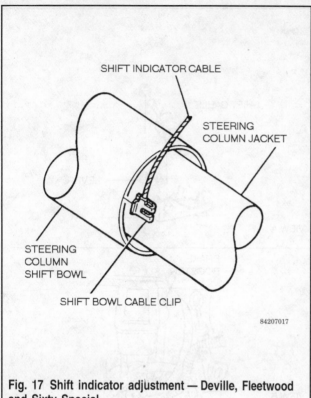

Fig. 17 Shift indicator adjustment — Deville, Fleetwood and Sixty Special

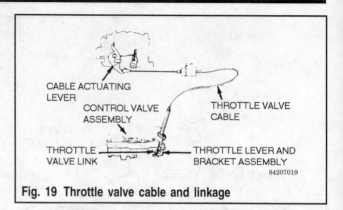

Fig. 19 Throttle valve cable and linkage

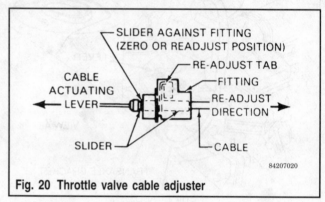

Fig. 20 Throttle valve cable adjuster

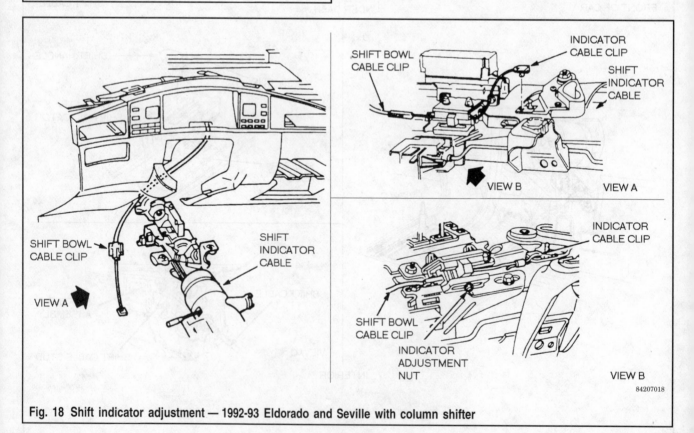

Fig. 18 Shift indicator adjustment — 1992-93 Eldorado and Seville with column shifter

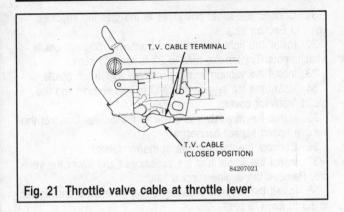

Fig. 21 Throttle valve cable at throttle lever

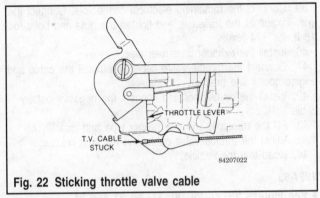

Fig. 22 Sticking throttle valve cable

ADJUSTMENT

❋❋CAUTION

The neutral safety switch must be adjusted so that the engine will start in PARK or NEUTRAL only. Personal injury may result if the engine can be started in a drive position.

1. Loosen the neutral safety switch retaining bolts.
2. Rotate the transaxle manual shaft to the NEUTRAL position.
3. Rotate the switch until a 3/32 in. (2.34mm) gauge pin can be inserted in the adjustment hole.
4. Tighten the switch retaining bolts to 20 ft. lbs. (27 Nm) on 4T60 and 4T60-E transaxles or 106 inch lbs. (12 Nm) on 4T80-E transaxles.

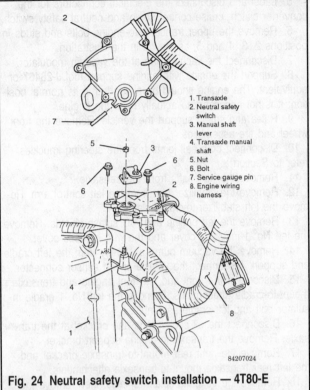

1. Transaxle
2. Neutral safety switch
3. Manual shaft lever
4. Transaxle manual shaft
5. Nut
6. Bolt
7. Service gauge pin
8. Engine wiring harness

Fig. 24 Neutral safety switch installation — 4T80-E transaxle

Transaxle

REMOVAL & INSTALLATION

Deville, Fleetwood and Sixty Special

1990

▶ **See Figures 25, 26, 27, 28, 29, 30 and 31**

1. Disconnect the negative battery cable.
2. Remove the air cleaner. Disconnect the throttle valve cable and remove the throttle valve cable/engine cooler line bracket.
3. Remove the exhaust crossover pipe.
4. Disconnect the shift linkage, shift cable and bracket. It is not necessary to remove the cable from the bracket.

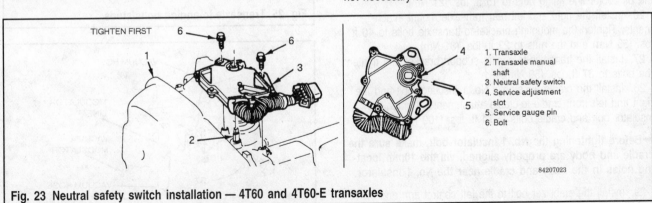

TIGHTEN FIRST

1. Transaxle
2. Transaxle manual shaft
3. Neutral safety switch
4. Service adjustment slot
5. Service gauge pin
6. Bolt

Fig. 23 Neutral safety switch installation — 4T60 and 4T60-E transaxles

5. Label and disconnect the electrical connectors for the converter clutch, cruise control servo and neutral safety switch.

6. Remove the upper transaxle-to-engine bolts and studs in positions 2, 3, 4 and 5, as shown in the illustration.

7. Disconnect the vacuum line at the vacuum modulator.

8. Support the engine with engine support tool J-28467 or equivalent. The engine should be supported in its normal position; it is not necessary to actually raise the engine.

9. Raise and safely support the vehicle. Remove the front wheel and tire assemblies.

10. Disconnect both ball joints from the steering knuckles; refer to Section 8.

11. Remove the halfshafts from the transaxle.

12. Remove the stabilizer bolt from the left control arm. Remove the left stabilizer-to-cradle clamp.

13. Remove the left engine and A/C splash shields. Remove the left No. 1 insulator cover and the wire harness cover.

14. Remove the vacuum pump assembly from the left cradle and support. Disconnect the vehicle speed sensor connector.

15. Disconnect the right and left front engine and transaxle mount-to-cradle attachments. Remove the left No. 1 cradle insulator bolt and left cradle assembly.

16. Disconnect the oil cooler lines and bracket at the transaxle. Remove the transaxle-to-engine support bracket.

17. Remove the right rear mount-to-transaxle bracket and the left rear transaxle mount-to-transaxle attachments.

18. Remove the flexplate splash shields, then remove the torque converter-to-flexplate bolts.

19. Position a suitable jack under the transaxle.

20. Remove the transaxle-to-engine bolt from position 1.

21. Working through the right wheelwell, use a 3 foot extension and socket to remove the transaxle-to-engine bolt from position 6.

22. Remove the transaxle from the vehicle.

To install:

23. Position the transaxle in the vehicle and install the lower transaxle-to-engine bolts/studs. Tighten the bolts/studs to 55 ft. lbs. (75 Nm).

➡ **Studs must be installed in positions 2 and 3. Bolts must be installed in positions 1, 4, 5 and 6. Refer to the proper illustration for positions.**

24. Install the torque converter-to-flexplate bolts and tighten to 46 ft. lbs. (63 Nm). Install the flexplate splash shields.

25. Connect the oil cooler lines and bracket at the transaxle. Tighten the bracket mounting bolts to 40 ft. lbs. (55 Nm) and the oil cooler line fitting nuts to 15 ft. lbs. (21 Nm).

26. Install the right and left rear transaxle mount attachments. Tighten the mounting bracket-to-transaxle bolts to 40 ft. lbs. (55 Nm) and the nuts to 23 ft. lbs. (31 Nm).

27. Install the transaxle-to-engine support bracket and tighten the bolts to 37 ft. lbs. (50 Nm).

28. Install the cradle assembly, No. 1 insulator bolt and the right and left front cradle-to-cradle attachments. Tighten the insulator bolt and cradle bolts to 74 ft. lbs. (100 Nm).

➡ **Before tightening the No. 1 insulator bolt, make sure the cradle and body are properly aligned, via the 10mm locating holes in the body and cradle near the No. 1 insulator.**

29. Install the stabilizer bolt to the left control arm and the stabilizer cradle clamp.

30. Install the halfshafts.

31. Connect the lower ball joints to the steering knuckles; refer to Section 8.

32. Install the right and left front transaxle mount-to-cradle attachments. Tighten the nuts to 23 ft. lbs. (31 Nm).

33. Install the vacuum pump assembly to the left cradle.

34. Install the left engine and A/C splash shields and the No. 1 insulator cover.

35. Install the wire harness cover to the cradle. Connect the vehicle speed sensor connector.

36. Connect the vacuum line at the modulator.

37. Install the wheel and tire assemblies and lower the vehicle. Remove the engine support fixture.

38. Install the remaining transaxle-to-engine bolts and tighten to 55 ft. lbs. (75 Nm).

39. Connect the remaining electrical connectors. Connect the shift linkage at the transaxle and tighten the nuts and bolts to 18 ft. lbs. (24 Nm).

40. Install the exhaust crossover pipe.

41. Connect the throttle valve cable and install the cable and engine cooler line bracket.

42. Install the air cleaner and connect the negative battery cable.

43. Fill the transaxle with the proper type and quantity of fluid. Adjust the throttle valve cable and the shift linkage.

44. Road test the vehicle.

1991-93

▶ **See Figures 25, 27, 28, 30, 31, 32, 33 and 34**

1. Disconnect the negative battery cable.
2. Remove the air cleaner assembly.
3. Label and disconnect the necessary electrical connectors.

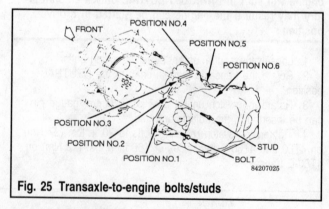

Fig. 25 Transaxle-to-engine bolts/studs

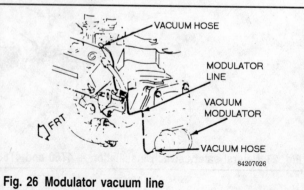

Fig. 26 Modulator vacuum line

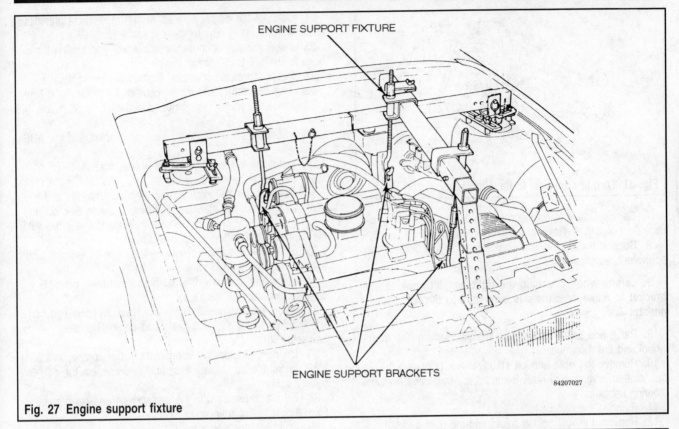

Fig. 27 Engine support fixture

4. Remove the engine harness and shift cable brackets.
5. Remove the engine oil cooler line, vacuum hose and fuel line bracket.

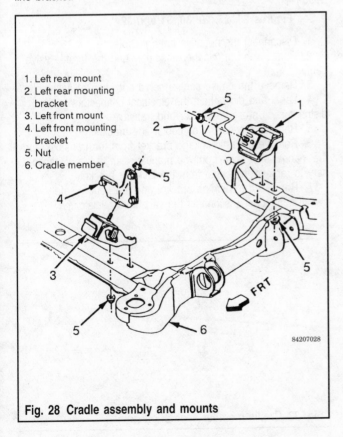

1. Left rear mount
2. Left rear mounting bracket
3. Left front mount
4. Left front mounting bracket
5. Nut
6. Cradle member

Fig. 28 Cradle assembly and mounts

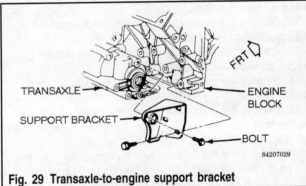

Fig. 29 Transaxle-to-engine support bracket

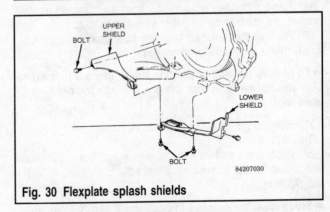

Fig. 30 Flexplate splash shields

6. Disconnect the vacuum modulator. Remove the transaxle filler tube and transaxle mounting bracket.

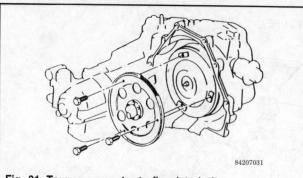

84207031

Fig. 31 Torque converter-to-flexplate bolts

7. Remove the 4 transaxle-to-engine bolts/studs from positions 2, 3, 4 and 5. Refer to the proper illustration.

8. Support the engine with engine support tool J-28467 or equivalent, as shown in Fig. 27.

➡**Be careful when attaching the right rear lift hook to the bracket to make sure there is clearance to the A/C accumulator line.**

9. Raise and safely support the vehicle. Remove the front wheel and tire assemblies.

10. Remove the right and left stabilizer link bolts and the ball joint cotter pins and nuts. Separate the ball joints from the steering knuckles.

11. Remove the halfshafts.

12. Remove the A/C splash shield and the right and left wheelwell splash shields.

13. Remove the power steering return line bracket and the ABS pump from the bracket.

14. Remove the flexplate splash shields, then remove the torque converter-to-flexplate bolts.

15. Remove the power steering line and the transaxle oil cooler lines.

16. Remove the cradle mount bolts and motor mount nuts on the right side, then remove the cradle mount bolts on the left side.

17. Remove the No. 1 cradle mount insulator bolt and the left cradle member, separating the right front corner first.

18. Support the transaxle with a suitable jack.

19. Remove the bracket assembly from the transaxle mount bracket and remove the engine-to-transaxle bracket.

20. Remove the transaxle-to-engine bolts from positions 1 and 6. Refer to the proper illustration.

➡**To remove the bolt at position No. 6, use a 3 foot extension and socket to access the bolt through the right wheelwell.**

21. Remove the transaxle from the vehicle.

To install:

22. Position the transaxle in the vehicle and install the lower transaxle-to-engine bolts/studs. Tighten the bolts/studs to 55 ft. lbs. (75 Nm).

➡**Studs must be installed in positions 2 and 3. Bolts must be installed in positions 1, 4, 5 and 6. Refer to the proper illustration.**

23. Install the torque converter-to-flexplate bolts and tighten to 46 ft. lbs. (63 Nm). Install the flexplate splash shields.

24. Connect the oil cooler lines at the transaxle. Tighten the oil cooler line fitting nuts to 15 ft. lbs. (21 Nm).

25. Install the engine-to-transaxle bracket and tighten the bolts to 37 ft. lbs. (50 Nm).

26. Install the cradle member. Tighten the No. 1 insulator mount bolt and the cradle mount bolts to 74 ft. lbs. (100 Nm).

27. Install the motor mount nuts and tighten to 35 ft. lbs. (45 Nm).

28. Install the power steering line and bracket and the ABS pump.

29. Install the wheelwell and A/C splash shields.

30. Install the halfshafts.

31. Connect the ball joints to the steering knuckles and install the right and left stabilizer link bolts; refer to Section 8.

32. Install the wheel and tire assemblies and lower the vehicle. Remove the engine support fixture.

33. Install the remaining transaxle-to-engine bolts/studs and tighten to 55 ft. lbs. (75 Nm).

34. Install the transaxle filler tube and mounting bracket. Connect the vacuum modulator.

35. Install the engine oil cooler line, vacuum hose and fuel line bracket. Install the shift cable and engine harness brackets.

36. Connect all electrical connectors in their proper locations.

37. Install the air cleaner assembly and connect the negative battery cable.

38. Fill the transaxle with the proper type and quantity of fluid. Adjust the shift linkage.

39. Road test the vehicle.

Eldorado and Seville

1990

▶ **See Figures 25, 27, 29, 30, 31 and 32**

1. Disconnect the negative battery cable.

2. Remove the air cleaner assembly and the throttle valve cable.

3. Remove the cruise control servo and bracket assembly.

4. Label and disconnect the electrical connectors to the distributor, oil pressure sender and transaxle.

5. Remove the engine oil cooler line bracket.

6. Remove the shift linkage bracket from the transaxle and the manual shift lever from the manual shaft. It is not necessary to remove the cable from the lever or bracket.

7. Remove the fuel line bracket and the neutral safety switch connector. Disconnect the vacuum modulator.

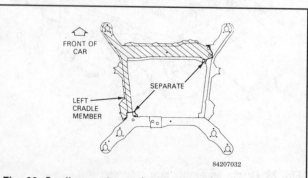

84207032

Fig. 32 Cradle member separation points

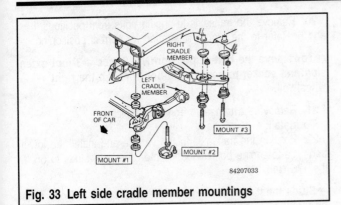

Fig. 33 Left side cradle member mountings

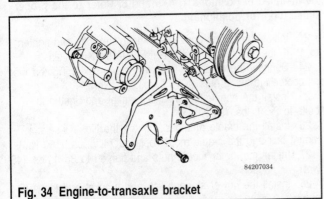

Fig. 34 Engine-to-transaxle bracket

8. Remove the throttle valve cable support bracket and the engine oil cooler line bracket. Remove the transaxle-to-engine bolts/studs in positions 2, 3, 4 and 5; refer to illustration.

9. Disconnect the air injection system crossover pipe fitting and reposition the pipe. Remove the radiator hose bracket and the transaxle mount-to-bracket nuts.

10. Support the engine with engine support tool J-28467 or equivalent, as shown in the illustration.

11. Raise and safely support the vehicle. Remove the front wheel and tire assemblies.

12. Remove the right and left stabilizer link bolts and the ball joint cotter pins and nuts. Separate the ball joints from the steering knuckles.

13. Remove the A/C splash shield and the No. 1 cradle insulator mount cover.

14. Disconnect the air injection system pipe end hose connections and rear mounting clip. Remove the vacuum hoses and wire loom from the clips on the front of the cradle.

15. Remove the engine mount and dampener-to-cradle attachments, the transaxle mount-to-cradle attachments and the wire loom clip-to-transaxle mount bracket.

16. Lower the vehicle.

17. Raise the transaxle 2 in. using the support hooks on the engine support tool.

18. Raise and safely support the vehicle.

19. Remove the right front and left rear cradle-to-cradle bolts and the left stabilizer mount bolts.

20. Remove the No. 1 cradle mount insulator bolt and the left cradle member, separating the right front corner first.

21. Remove the air injection system management valve and bracket assembly from the transaxle mount bracket and reposition.

22. Lower the vehicle.

23. Lower the transaxle to its original position. Remove the transaxle mounting bracket.

24. Raise and safely support the vehicle.

25. Remove the right rear transaxle mount-to-transaxle bracket. Disconnect the vehicle speed sensor connector.

26. Remove the flexplate splash shields, then remove the torque converter-to-flexplate bolts.

27. Support the transaxle with a suitable jack.

28. Remove the transaxle-to-engine bolts from positions 1 and 6. Refer to the proper illustration.

➡**To remove the bolt at position No. 6, use a 3 foot extension and socket to access the bolt through the right wheelwell.**

29. Disconnect the oil cooler lines from the transaxle.

30. Remove the halfshafts.

31. Remove the transaxle from the vehicle.

To install:

32. Position the transaxle in the vehicle and install the lower transaxle-to-engine bolts/studs. Tighten the bolts/studs to 55 ft. lbs. (75 Nm).

➡**Studs must be installed in positions 2 and 3. Bolts must be installed in positions 1, 4, 5 and 6. Refer to the proper illustration.**

33. Install the torque converter-to-flexplate bolts and tighten to 46 ft. lbs. (63 Nm). Install the flexplate splash shields.

34. Connect the oil cooler lines at the transaxle. Tighten the oil cooler line fitting nuts to 15 ft. lbs. (21 Nm).

35. Install the halfshafts.

36. Connect the vehicle speed sensor connector.

37. Install the right rear transaxle mount-to-transaxle bracket. Tighten the bolts to 50 ft. lbs. (70 Nm).

38. Install the air injection system management valve and bracket assembly.

39. Install the left cradle member. Tighten the No. 1 insulator mount bolts and the cradle-to-cradle mounting bolts to 74 ft. lbs. (100 Nm).

40. Install the engine mount-to-cradle and transaxle mount-to-cradle attachments. Tighten as follows:

    Upper transaxle mount stud bolts: 74 ft. lbs. (100 Nm)

    Side transaxle mount bracket stud bolts: 50 ft. lbs. (70 Nm)

    Rear (left) transaxle mount nuts: 35 ft. lbs. (45 Nm)

    Engine mount-to-cradle attachments: 35 ft. lbs. (45 Nm)

    Right rear mount bracket nuts: 35 ft. lbs. (45 Nm)

41. Install the wire loom clip to the transaxle mount bracket. Install the vacuum hoses and wire loom to the clip on the front of the cradle.

42. Connect the air injection system pipe end hose connections and rear mounting clip. Install the No. 1 cradle insulator mount cover and A/C splash shield.

43. Connect the ball joints to the steering knuckles. Tighten the ball joint nuts to 81 ft. lbs. (110 Nm) and install new cotter pins.

44. Install the stabilizer link bolts and tighten to 13 ft. lbs. (17 Nm).

45. Install the wheel and tire assemblies and lower the vehicle. Remove the engine support fixture.

46. Install the radiator hose bracket. Reposition the air injection system crossover pipe and connect the fitting.

47. Install the remaining transaxle-to-engine bolts and tighten to 55 ft. lbs. (75 Nm).

48. Install the engine oil cooler line bracket and the throttle valve cable support bracket.

49. Connect the vacuum modulator and the neutral safety switch connector. Install the fuel line bracket.

50. Install the manual shift lever on the manual shaft and install the shift linkage bracket on the transaxle.

51. Connect all remaining electrical connectors in their proper locations.

52. Install the cruise control servo and bracket assembly. Install the throttle valve cable and the air cleaner assembly.

53. Connect the negative battery cable. Fill the transaxle with the proper type and quantity of fluid. Adjust the throttle valve cable and the shift linkage.

54. Road test the vehicle.

1991

▶ **See Figures 25, 27, 28, 30, 31, 32, 33 and 34**

1. Disconnect the negative battery cable.
2. Remove the air cleaner assembly.
3. Label and disconnect the necessary electrical connectors.
4. Remove the engine harness and shift cable brackets.
5. Remove the engine oil cooler line, vacuum hose and fuel line bracket.
6. Disconnect the vacuum modulator. Remove the transaxle filler tube and transaxle mounting bracket.
7. Remove the 4 transaxle-to-engine bolts/studs from positions 2, 3, 4 and 5. Refer to the proper illustration.
8. Support the engine with engine support tool J-28467 or equivalent.

➡ **Be careful when attaching the right rear lift hook to the bracket to make sure there is clearance to the A/C accumulator line.**

9. Raise and safely support the vehicle. Remove the front wheel and tire assemblies.

10. Remove the right and left stabilizer link bolts and the ball joint cotter pins and nuts. Separate the ball joints from the steering knuckles.

11. Remove the halfshafts.

12. Remove the A/C splash shield and the right and left wheelwell splash shields.

13. Remove the power steering return line bracket and the ABS pump from the bracket.

14. Remove the flexplate splash shields, then remove the torque converter-to-flexplate bolts.

15. Remove the power steering line and the transaxle oil cooler lines.

16. Remove the cradle mount bolts and motor mount nuts on the right side, then remove the cradle mount bolts on the left side.

17. Remove the No. 1 cradle mount insulator bolt and the left cradle member, separating the right front corner first.

18. Support the transaxle with a suitable jack.

19. Remove the bracket assembly from the transaxle mount bracket and remove the engine-to-transaxle bracket.

20. Remove the transaxle-to-engine bolts from positions 1 and 6. Refer to the proper illustration for correct positioning.

➡ **To remove the bolt at position No. 6, use a 3 foot extension and socket to access the bolt through the right wheelwell.**

21. Remove the transaxle from the vehicle.

To install:

22. Position the transaxle in the vehicle and install the lower transaxle-to-engine bolts/studs. Tighten the bolts/studs to 55 ft. lbs. (75 Nm).

➡ **Studs must be installed in positions 2 and 3. Bolts must be installed in positions 1, 4, 5 and 6. Refer to the proper illustration for positioning.**

23. Install the torque converter-to-flexplate bolts and tighten to 46 ft. lbs. (63 Nm). Install the flexplate splash shields.

24. Connect the oil cooler lines at the transaxle. Tighten the oil cooler line fitting nuts to 15 ft. lbs. (21 Nm).

25. Install the engine-to-transaxle bracket and tighten the bolts to 37 ft. lbs. (50 Nm).

26. Install the cradle member. Tighten the No. 1 insulator mount bolt and the cradle mount bolts to 74 ft. lbs. (100 Nm).

27. Install the motor mount nuts and tighten to 35 ft. lbs. (45 Nm).

28. Install the power steering line and bracket and the ABS pump.

29. Install the wheelwell and A/C splash shields.

30. Install the halfshafts.

31. Connect the ball joints to the steering knuckles and install the right and left stabilizer link bolts; refer to Section 8.

32. Install the wheel and tire assemblies and lower the vehicle. Remove the engine support fixture.

33. Install the remaining transaxle-to-engine bolts/studs and tighten to 55 ft. lbs. (75 Nm).

34. Install the transaxle filler tube and mounting bracket. Connect the vacuum modulator.

35. Install the engine oil cooler line, vacuum hose and fuel line bracket. Install the shift cable and engine harness brackets.

36. Connect all electrical connectors in their proper locations.

37. Install the air cleaner assembly and connect the negative battery cable.

38. Fill the transaxle with the proper type and quantity of fluid. Adjust the shift linkage.

39. Road test the vehicle.

1992

▶ **See Figures 25, 27, 30, 31, 35 and 36**

1. Disconnect the negative battery cable.
2. Remove the air cleaner assembly.
3. Label and disconnect the following electrical connectors: transaxle connector, speed sensor connector, neutral safety switch and power steering pressure switch.
4. Remove the shift cable and bracket and the neutral safety switch. Disconnect the vacuum modulator.
5. Remove the transaxle filler tube.
6. Disconnect the power steering pressure hose at the power steering pump and the engine. Disconnect the power steering return line at the auxiliary cooler.

7. Support the engine with engine support tool J-28467 or equivalent, as shown in Fig. 27.

8. Raise and safely support the vehicle. Remove the front wheel and tire assemblies.

9. Remove the splash shields from both front wheelwells.

10. Rotate the intermediate steering shaft until the steering gear stub shaft clamp bolt is accessible from the left wheelwell. Remove the clamp bolt and disconnect the intermediate steering shaft from the steering gear.

✳✳CAUTION

If the intermediate steering shaft is not disconnected from the steering gear stub shaft, damage to the steering gear and/or intermediate shaft may result. This damage can cause loss of steering control which could result in personal injury.

11. Remove the stabilizer links from the steering knuckles.

12. Remove the tie rod end cotter pins and nuts. Separate the tie rod ends from the steering knuckles.

13. Remove the lower ball joint cotter pins and nuts. Separate the lower ball joints from the steering knuckles.

14. Remove the halfshafts.

15. Remove the A/C splash shield from the frame. Remove the ABS modulator from the bracket and support.

16. Remove the flexplate splash shields, then remove the torque converter-to-flexplate bolts.

17. Disconnect the transaxle oil cooler lines from the transaxle.

18. Remove the left and right transaxle mount nuts and the right engine mount nuts at the frame.

19. Disconnect the exhaust pipe at the exhaust manifolds and catalytic converter. Remove the exhaust pipe.

20. Support the frame and remove the 6 frame mount bolts. Lower the frame with the steering gear attached.

21. Remove the left transaxle mount and right rear transaxle mount and bracket from the transaxle. Remove the engine-to-transaxle bracket.

22. Support the transaxle with a suitable jack. Remove the transaxle-to-engine bolts and lower the transaxle.

To install:

23. Raise the transaxle into position and install the transaxle-to-engine bolts. Tighten to 55 ft. lbs. (75 Nm).

24. Install the engine-to-transaxle bracket.

25. Install the right rear transaxle mount and bracket and left transaxle mount and bracket to the transaxle.

26. Support the frame and raise into place, with the steering gear attached. Install the 6 frame mount bolts and tighten to 83 ft. lbs. (112 Nm).

27. On the right rear transaxle mount and bracket, tighten the mount-to-cradle nut to 75 ft. lbs. (100 Nm), the mount-to-bracket nuts to 35 ft. lbs. (45 Nm), the bracket-to-transaxle bolts to 50 ft. lbs. (70 Nm) and the bracket-to-brace bolt to 15 ft. lbs. (20 Nm).

28. On the left transaxle mount and bracket, tighten the mount-to-cradle nuts to 35 ft. lbs. (45 Nm) and the transaxle mount-to-bracket nuts to 35 ft. lbs. (45 Nm).

29. Connect the transaxle oil cooler lines to the transaxle.

30. Install the torque converter-to-flexplate bolts and tighten to 46 ft. lbs. (63 Nm). Install the flexplate splash shields.

31. Install the ABS modulator to the bracket and support. Install the A/C splash shield to the frame.

32. Install the halfshafts.

33. Connect the lower ball joints, tie rod ends and stabilizer links to the steering knuckles. See Section 8.

34. Install the intermediate steering shaft to the steering gear. See Section 8.

35. Install the splash shields in the front wheelwells.

36. Install the exhaust pipe.

37. Install the wheel and tire assemblies and lower the vehicle. Remove the engine support fixture.

38. Connect the power steering return line at the auxiliary cooler. Connect the power steering pressure hose at the power steering pump and the engine.

39. Install the transaxle filler tube and connect the vacuum modulator.

40. Install the neutral safety switch and the shift cable and bracket.

41. Connect the power steering pressure switch, neutral safety switch, speed sensor and transaxle connectors.

42. Install the air cleaner assembly and connect the negative battery cable.

43. Fill the transaxle with the proper type and quantity of fluid. Adjust the shift linkage.

44. Road test the vehicle.

1993 4T60-E TRANSAXLE

▶ **See Figures 25, 27, 30, 31, 35 and 36**

1. Disconnect the negative battery cable.

2. Remove the air cleaner assembly.

3. Label and disconnect the following electrical connectors: transaxle connector, distributor connectors, neutral safety switch and vacuum connection.

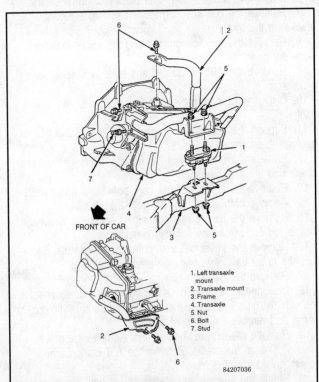

FRONT OF CAR

1. Left transaxle mount
2. Transaxle mount
3. Frame
4. Transaxle
5. Nut
6. Bolt
7. Stud

84207036

Fig. 35 Left transaxle mount and bracket — 1992-93 Eldorado and Seville with 4T60-E transaxle

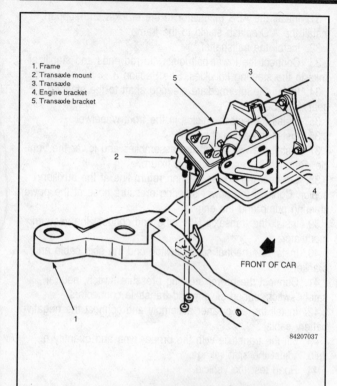

1. Frame
2. Transaxle mount
3. Transaxle
4. Engine bracket
5. Transaxle bracket

FRONT OF CAR

84207037

Fig. 36 Right rear transaxle mount and bracket — 1992-93 Eldorado and Seville with 4T60-E transaxle

4. Remove the shift cable and bracket.

5. Disconnect the vacuum modulator. Disconnect the oil cooler lines from the engine and bracket from the transaxle.

6. Remove the 4 transaxle-to-engine bolts/studs from positions 2, 3, 4 and 5. Refer to proper illustration for positions.

7. Remove the bolt securing the left transaxle mount bracket to the transaxle.

8. Remove the fuel line bracket and the upper radiator close-out panel.

9. Remove the ABS modulator and support it aside, using a tie strap.

10. Disconnect the power steering return line at the auxiliary cooler.

11. Support the engine with engine support tool J-28467 or equivalent, as shown in Fig. 27.

12. Raise and safely support the vehicle. Remove the front wheel and tire assemblies.

13. Remove the splash shields from both front wheelwells.

14. Remove both stabilizer links from the struts.

15. Remove the tie rod end cotter pins and nuts. Separate the tie rod ends from the steering knuckles.

16. Remove the lower ball joint cotter pins and nuts. Separate the lower ball joints from the steering knuckles.

17. Remove the halfshafts.

18. Disconnect the oxygen sensor connectors. Disconnect the exhaust pipe at the exhaust manifolds and catalytic converter and remove the exhaust pipe.

19. Remove the exhaust heat shield. Remove the power steering filter at the cradle. Remove the A/C compressor splash shield from the frame.

20. Rotate the intermediate steering shaft until the steering gear stub shaft clamp bolt is accessible from the left wheel-

well. Remove the clamp bolt and disconnect the intermediate steering shaft from the steering gear.

✳✳CAUTION

If the intermediate steering shaft is not disconnected from the steering gear stub shaft, damage to the steering gear and/or intermediate shaft may result. This damage can cause loss of steering control which could result in personal injury.

21. Remove the wiring harness from the cradle. Label and disconnect the harness electrical connectors.

22. Remove the left and right transaxle mount nuts and the right engine mount nuts at the cradle.

23. Place a suitable jack under the rear of the cradle and remove the 4 rear cradle bolts.

24. Lower the rear of the cradle using the jack to gain access to the power steering pressure line fitting. Disconnect the power steering pressure line and the power steering electrical connector. Remove the power steering pressure line retainer.

25. Lower the cradle.

26. Remove the flexplate splash shields, then remove the torque converter-to-flexplate bolts.

27. Disconnect the transaxle oil cooler lines from the transaxle.

28. Remove the left transaxle mount bracket nuts and the harness retainer from the transaxle.

29. Support the transaxle with a suitable jack.

30. Disconnect the vehicle speed sensor connector.

31. Remove the right rear transaxle mount and bracket from the transaxle. Remove the engine-to-transaxle bracket.

32. Remove the remaining transaxle-to-engine bolts/studs and lower the transaxle.

To install:

33. Raise the transaxle into position with the left transaxle mount bracket in place but not bolted down.

34. Install the transaxle-to-engine bolts in positions 1 and 6 and tighten to 55 ft. lbs. (75 Nm). Refer to illustration for proper position.

35. Install the engine-to-transaxle bracket.

36. Install the right rear transaxle mount and bracket to the transaxle. Tighten the mount-to-bracket nuts to 35 ft. lbs. (45 Nm).

37. Connect the vehicle speed sensor connector. Remove the support jack from the transaxle.

38. Install the left transaxle mount and bracket to the transaxle, making sure the harness is positioned between the side cover and bracket. Tighten the mount-to-bracket nuts to 35 ft. lbs. (45 Nm).

39. Connect the oil cooler lines to the transaxle.

40. Raise the cradle into position with the steering gear attached. Install the 4 cradle mount bolts, one in each corner.

41. Support the rear of the cradle with a jack and remove the 2 rear bolts. Lower the jack enough to gain access to the power steering pressure line fitting.

42. Connect the power steering pressure line and the power steering electrical connector. Install the power steering pressure line retainer.

43. Raise the rear of the cradle and install the 4 rear cradle bolts. Tighten all 6 bolts to 76 ft. lbs. (103 Nm). Remove the jack.

44. Install the left and right transaxle mount nuts and the right engine mount nuts at the cradle. Tighten the left mount-to-cradle nuts to 35 ft. lbs. (70 Nm) and the right rear mount-to-cradle nut to 75 ft. lbs. (100 Nm).

45. Install the torque converter-to-flexplate bolts and tighten to 46 ft. lbs. (63 Nm). Install the flexplate splash shields.

46. Install the wiring harness to the cradle and connect the electrical connectors. Install the A/C splash shield to the frame.

47. Install the intermediate steering shaft to the steering gear. See Section 8.

48. Install the power steering filter at the cradle. Install the halfshafts.

49. Connect the lower ball joints and tie rod ends to the steering knuckles. Install the stabilizer links into the struts. See Section 8.

50. Install the exhaust heat shield and the exhaust pipe. Connect the oxygen sensor connectors.

51. Install the splash shields in the front wheelwells.

52. Install the wheel and tire assemblies and lower the vehicle. Remove the engine support fixture.

53. Connect the power steering return line at the auxiliary cooler.

54. Install the ABS modulator and the upper radiator hose close-out panel.

55. Install the left transaxle mount bracket upper bolts and tighten to 50 ft. lbs. (70 Nm).

56. Install the fuel line bracket to the transaxle.

57. Install the remaining transaxle-to-engine bolts/studs and tighten to 55 ft. lbs. (75 Nm).

58. Install the engine oil cooler lines and bracket. Connect the vacuum modulator.

59. Connect the neutral safety switch electrical connector and vacuum line. Connect the distributor and transaxle electrical connectors.

60. Install the shift cable and bracket and the air cleaner assembly.

61. Connect the negative battery cable. Fill the transaxle with the proper type and quantity of fluid. Adjust the shift linkage.

62. Road test the vehicle.

1993 4T80-E TRANSAXLE

▶ See Figures 37, 38, 39, 40, 41, 42, 43 and 44

1. Disconnect the negative battery cable.

2. Remove the headlight housing upper filler panel and diagonal brace.

3. Remove the air cleaner assembly.

4. Disconnect the shift control cable and bracket at the transaxle.

5. Remove the torque struts.

6. Disconnect the oil cooler lines at the cooler and the oil sending line at the transaxle.

7. Remove the 2 upper transaxle-to-engine bolts.

8. Disconnect the power steering return hose at the auxiliary cooler. Plug the cooler and return hose to prevent leakage.

9. Support the engine with engine support fixture J-28467 or equivalent, as shown. Tighten the wing nuts several turns to take the weight of the powertrain off of the mounts and frame.

10. Raise and safely support the vehicle. Remove the front wheel and tire assemblies.

11. Remove the splash shields from both front wheelwells.

12. Disconnect both front suspension position sensors from the lower control arms and position aside.

13. Remove both stabilizer links from the struts.

14. Remove the tie rod end cotter pins and nuts. Separate the tie rod ends from the steering knuckles.

15. Remove the lower ball joint cotter pins and nuts. Separate the lower ball joints from the steering knuckles.

16. Remove the halfshafts.

17. Remove the power steering filter at the cradle and the A/C splash shield from the frame.

18. Remove the ABS modulator from the bracket and support. Remove the engine oil pan-to-transaxle bracket.

19. Remove the torque converter cover, then remove the torque converter-to-flexplate bolts. Prior to bolt removal, mark the torque converter position in relation to the flexplate so they can be reassembled in the same position.

20. Remove the powertrain mount nuts from the cradle.

21. Rotate the intermediate steering shaft until the steering gear stub shaft clamp bolt is accessible from the left wheelwell. Remove the clamp bolt and disconnect the intermediate steering shaft from the steering gear.

❋❋CAUTION

If the intermediate steering shaft is not disconnected from the steering gear stub shaft, damage to the steering gear and/or intermediate shaft may result. This damage can cause loss of steering control which could result in personal injury.

❋❋WARNING

Do not turn the steering wheel or move the position of the steering gear once the intermediate steering shaft is disconnected as this will uncenter the air bag coil in the steering column. If the air bag coil becomes uncentered, it may be damaged during vehicle operation.

22. Remove the electrical harness and connector from the front of the cradle.

23. Support the rear of the cradle with a suitable jack, then remove the 4 rear cradle bolts.

24. Lower the jack a few inches to gain access to the power steering gear heat shield and return line fitting. Remove the heat shield and disconnect the return line. Plug the line and the opening in the gear to prevent fluid leakage.

25. Disconnect the power steering electrical connector.

26. Raise the jack and reinstall one rear cradle bolt on each side finger tight to support the cradle. Remove the jack.

27. Support the frame with a suitable jack and remove the 6 frame mount bolts. Lower the frame and/or raise the vehicle with the steering gear attached.

28. Label and disconnect the electrical connectors to the transaxle, vehicle speed sensor and ground. Remove the transaxle harness from the transaxle clip.

29. Remove the fuel line bundle from the transaxle.

30. Remove the left and right transaxle mount and bracket from the transaxle.

31. Support the transaxle with a suitable jack.

32. Remove the engine-to-transaxle heat shield and bracket and the remaining transaxle-to-engine bolts. Lower the transaxle.

33. Remove the manual shaft linkage and neutral safety switch. Remove the vehicle speed sensor and oil return line.

To install:

34. Install the oil return line and the vehicle speed sensor.

35. Install the neutral safety switch and tighten the bolts to 106 inch lbs. (12 Nm).

36. Install the manual shaft linkage and tighten the manual shaft nut to 15 ft. lbs. (20 Nm).

37. Raise the transaxle into position and install the 2 lower transaxle-to-engine bolts. Tighten to 35 ft. lbs. (47 Nm).

38. Install the engine-to-transaxle bracket and heat shield. Tighten the bolts to 35 ft. lbs. (47 Nm).

39. Remove the transaxle jack.

40. Install the right and left transaxle bracket and mount to the transaxle. Tighten the bolts and nuts to 35 ft. lbs. (47 Nm).

41. Install the fuel line bundle to the transaxle.

42. Connect the electrical connectors to the transaxle, vehicle speed sensor and ground. Install the transaxle harness to the transaxle clip.

43. Raise the frame and/or lower the vehicle while locating the engine and transaxle mount studs into the frame, harnesses at the cradle, and frame mount bolt holes to the underbody.

44. Install 2 front and 2 rear cradle bolts finger-tight to support the cradle, then remove the cradle support.

45. Support the rear of the cradle with a suitable jack and remove the 2 rear cradle bolts.

46. Lower the jack a few inches to gain access to the power steering gear. Connect the hose at the steering gear and tighten the fitting to 20 ft. lbs. (27 Nm). Connect the power steering gear electrical connector and install the steering gear heat shield.

47. Raise the cradle with the jack. Install the 6 frame mount bolts beginning with the No. 2 mount bolt into the body, followed by the No. 1 mount bolt into the body, followed by the remaining frame mount bolts. Tighten the bolts to 74 ft. lbs. (100 Nm).

48. Install the electrical harness to the front of the cradle.

49. Connect the intermediate steering shaft to the steering gear and install the clamp bolt. Tighten the bolt to 35 ft. lbs. (47 Nm).

✳✳WARNING

Do not turn the steering wheel or move the position of the steering gear while the intermediate steering shaft is disconnected as this will uncenter the air bag coil in the steering column. If the air bag coil becomes uncentered, it may be damaged during vehicle operation.

50. Install the left and right transaxle mount nuts and right engine mount nuts at the frame. Tighten the nuts to 35 ft. lbs. (47 Nm).

51. Align the flexplate and torque converter using the marks made during the removal procedure. Install the flexplate-to-converter bolts and tighten to 35 ft. lbs. (47 Nm).

52. Install the torque converter cover and tighten the bolts to 106 inch lbs. (12 Nm).

53. Install the engine oil pan-to-transaxle bracket and tighten the bolts to 35 ft. lbs. (47 Nm).

54. Install the ABS modulator to the bracket and install the A/C splash shield at the frame.

55. Install the halfshafts. Tighten the halfshaft nuts to 110 ft. lbs. (145 Nm).

56. Install the lower ball joints into the steering knuckles and install the nuts. Tighten the ball joint nuts to 84 inch lbs. (10 Nm), then an additional 120 degrees.

➡**A minimum torque of 37 ft. lbs. (50 Nm) must be obtained when tightening the nuts. If the minimum torque is not obtained, inspect for stripped threads. If the threads are okay, replace the ball joint and knuckle.**

57. Install new cotter pins after the ball joint nuts have been torqued. If necessary, turn the nuts up to an additional 60° to allow for installation of the cotter pins. NEVER loosen the nut to allow for cotter pin installation.

58. Install the tie rod ends into the steering knuckles and install the nuts. Tighten the nuts to 7.5 ft. lbs. (10 Nm), then an additional 1/3 turn (2 flats).

➡**A minimum torque of 33 ft. lbs. (45 Nm) must be obtained when tightening the nuts. If the minimum torque is not obtained, inspect for stripped threads. If the threads are okay, replace the tie rod end and knuckle.**

59. Install new cotter pins after the tie rod ends have been torqued. If necessary, align the slots in the nuts to the cotter pin holes by tightening the nuts. NEVER loosen the nut to allow for cotter pin installation.

60. Connect the stabilizer links to the struts and tighten the nuts to 49 ft. lbs. (65 Nm).

61. Install both front suspension position sensors to the lower control arms.

62. Install the power steering filter to the cradle and install the splash shields in the wheelwells.

63. Install the wheel and tire assemblies and lower the vehicle. Remove the engine support fixture.

64. Connect the power steering hose at the auxiliary cooler.

65. Install the remaining transaxle-to-engine bolts and tighten to 35 ft. lbs. (47 Nm).

66. Flush the transaxle oil cooler using flushing tool J-35944 and flushing solution J-35944-20. The transaxle oil cooler and lines should be flushed before the oil cooler lines are connected to the transaxle.

67. Connect the transaxle oil cooler lines to the transaxle. Start the fittings by hand and tighten them finger-tight, then torque the fittings to 16 ft. lbs. (22 Nm).

68. Install the torque struts.

69. Adjust the neutral safety switch.

70. Install the shift control cable and bracket to the transaxle and tighten the bracket bolts to 106 inch lbs. (12 Nm). Adjust the shift control cable.

71. Install the air cleaner assembly. Install the headlight housing upper filler panel and diagonal brace.

72. Connect the negative battery cable.

73. Fill the transaxle with the proper type and quantity of transaxle fluid. Bleed the power steering system.

74. Check the front suspension alignment and adjust as necessary.

75. The Powertrain Control Module (PCM) maintains 3 types of transaxle adapt parameters which are used to modify tran-

saxle line pressure. The line pressure is modified to maintain shift quality regardless of wear or tolerance variations within the transaxle. Whenever the transaxle is replaced, the transaxle adapts must be reset as follows:

    a. Turn the ignition key **ON**. Enter the self-diagnostic system.

    b. Select Powertrain Control Module (PCM) override PS13 (TP SENSOR LEARN).

    c. Press the WARMER button. The Driver Information Center (DIC) should display 09, indicating that the Garage Shift Adapt value has been reset.

    d. Select PCM override PS14 (TRAN ADAPT).

    e. Press the COOLER button. The DIC should display 90, indicating the Upshift Adapt value has been reset.

    f. Press the WARMER button. The DIC should display 09, indicating the Steady State Adapt value has been reset.

76. The PCM maintains a value for transaxle oil life. This value indicates the percentage of oil life remaining and is calculated based on transaxle temperature and speed. When the vehicle is new, the transaxle oil life value is 100%. As the vehicle operates, the percentage will decrease. Whenever the transaxle is replaced, the transaxle oil life indicator should be reset to 100% as follows:

    a. Turn the ignition key **ON**, but leave the engine OFF.

    b. Press and hold the OFF and REAR DEFOG buttons on the DIC until the message TRANSAXLE OIL LIFE RESET is displayed on the DIC.

Halfshafts

REMOVAL&INSTALLATION

▶ See Figures 45, 46, 47, 48, 49 and 50

❊❊WARNING

Be careful not to over-extend the inboard CV-joint. When either end of the halfshaft is disconnected, over-extension of the joint could result in separation of internal components and possible joint failure. Use CV-joint boot protectors any time service is performed on or near the halfshafts. If these precautions are not taken, boot or interior joint damage may result, with possible eventual joint failure.

1. Raise and safely support the vehicle.
2. Remove the wheel and tire assembly.
3. Install modified boot protector J-34754 or equivalent, on the outer CV-joint.
4. Insert a drift into the caliper and rotor to prevent the rotor from turning, then remove the hub nut.
5. Disconnect the stabilizer link, if necessary.
6. Remove the ball joint cotter pin and nut. Loosen the ball joint in the knuckle using a suitable ball joint tool, being careful not to damage the ball joint and grease seal. If removing the right halfshaft, turn the wheel to the left; if removing the left halfshaft, turn the wheel to the right.

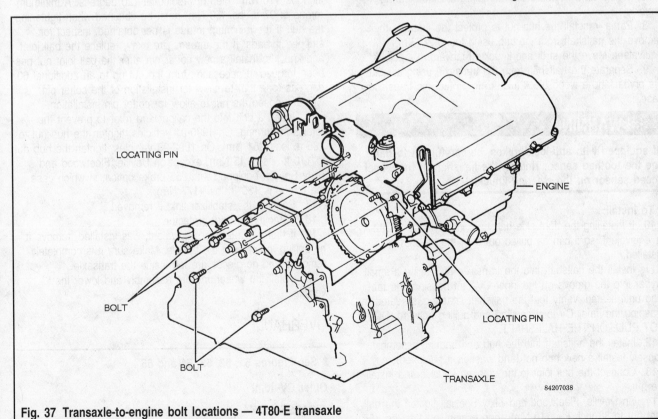

Fig. 37 Transaxle-to-engine bolt locations — 4T80-E transaxle

LOCATING PIN

BOLT

BOLT

ENGINE

LOCATING PIN

TRANSAXLE

84207038

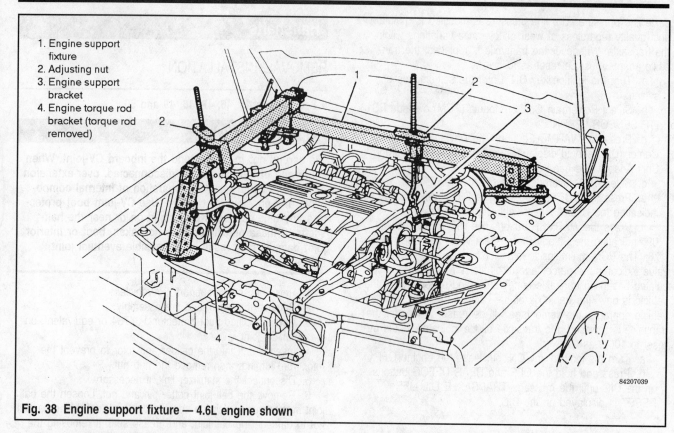

1. Engine support fixture
2. Adjusting nut
3. Engine support bracket
4. Engine torque rod bracket (torque rod removed)

84207039

Fig. 38 Engine support fixture — 4.6L engine shown

7. Using a prybar between the suspension support and the lower control arm, separate the ball joint from the steering knuckle.

8. Partially install the hub nut to protect the threads, then remove the halfshaft from the hub using tool J-28733 or equivalent. Move the strut and knuckle rearward.

9. Separate the halfshaft from the transaxle using a suitable prybar and a wood block fulcrum to protect the transaxle case.

✳✳WARNING

If equipped with anti-lock brakes, be careful not to damage the toothed sensor ring on the halfshaft or the wheel speed sensor on the steering knuckle.

To install:

10. If installing the right side halfshaft, install tool J-37292-A or equivalent, so it can be pulled out after the halfshaft is installed.

11. Install the halfshaft into the transaxle by placing a small prybar into the groove on the inner CV-joint housing and tapping until seated. verify that the halfshaft snapring is seated by grasping the inner CV-joint housing and pulling outward. DO NOT PULL ON THE HALFSHAFT.

12. Install the halfshaft into the hub and bearing assembly. Loosely install a new hub nut (and washer, if equipped).

13. Connect the ball joint to the steering knuckle and install the nut.

14. On Deville, Fleetwood and Sixty Special, tighten the ball joint nut to 88 inch lbs. (10 Nm), then tighten to 41 ft. lbs. (55 Nm) minimum. Install a new cotter pin. If it is necessary to align the slot in the nut, tighten the nut (up to one more flat).

15. On Eldorado and Seville, tighten the ball joint nut to 84 inch lbs. (10 Nm), then an additional 120 degrees. A minimum torque of 37 ft. lbs. (50 Nm) must be obtained when tightening the nut. If the minimum torque is not obtained, inspect for stripped threads. If the threads are okay, replace the ball joint and knuckle. Install a new cotter pin after the ball joint nut has been torqued. If necessary, turn the nut up to an additional 60 degrees (one flat) to allow for installation of the cotter pin. NEVER loosen the nut to allow for cotter pin installation.

16. Insert a drift into the caliper and rotor to prevent the rotor from turning. On 1990-91 vehicles, tighten the hub nut to 185 ft. lbs. (251 Nm). On 1992-93 vehicles, tighten the hub nut to 110 ft. lbs. (145 Nm), except on Deville, Fleetwood and Sixty Special equipped with J55 brake option, in which case the torque is 130 ft. lbs. (177 Nm).

17. Connect the stabilizer link, if removed.

18. Remove the boot protector.

19. If tool J-37292-A or equivalent, was installed, remove it by pulling in line with the handle. Make sure it is completely removed and no pieces are left inside the transaxle.

20. Install the wheel and tire assembly and lower the vehicle.

OVERHAUL

▶ See Figures 51, 52, 53, 54 and 55

Outer CV-Joint

DISASSEMBLY

1. Cut the boot retaining clamps from the CV-joint with side cutters and discard.

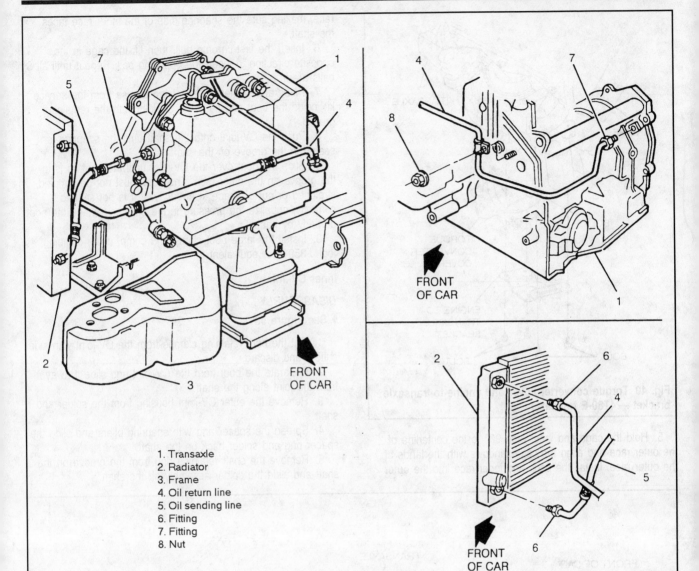

1. Transaxle
2. Radiator
3. Frame
4. Oil return line
5. Oil sending line
6. Fitting
7. Fitting
8. Nut

Fig. 39 Transaxle cooler lines and fittings — 4T80-E transaxle

2. Separate the boot from the CV-joint and slide it away from the joint along the shaft.

3. Wipe the grease from the face of the CV-joint inner race. Spread the retaining snapring with snapring pliers and remove the CV-joint from the shaft.

4. Remove the boot from the shaft.

5. Using a brass drift and hammer, gently tap on the CV-joint cage until it is tilted enough to remove the first chrome ball. Tilt the cage in the opposite direction to remove the opposing ball.

6. Repeat Step 5 until all 6 balls are removed.

7. Position the cage and inner race 90° to the centerline of the outer race and align the cage windows with the lands of the outer race. Remove the cage and inner race from the outer race.

8. Rotate the inner race 90° to the centerline of the cage with the lands of the inner race aligned with the windows of the cage. Pivot the inner race into the cage window and remove the inner race.

9. Thoroughly clean the inner and outer races and the cage and balls with clean solvent and allow to dry. Inspect all parts for damage and replace the CV-joint, if necessary.

ASSEMBLY
▶ **See Figures 56 and 57**

1. Install a new small boot clamp on the neck of a new boot, but do not crimp yet.

2. Slide the boot onto the shaft and position the boot neck in the groove on the shaft. Crimp the boot clamp with crimping tool J-35910 or equivalent.

3. Put a light coat of grease from the CV-joint service kit on the ball grooves of the inner and outer races.

4. Hold the inner race 90° to the centerline of the cage with the lands of the inner race aligned with the windows of the cage. Insert the inner race into the cage.

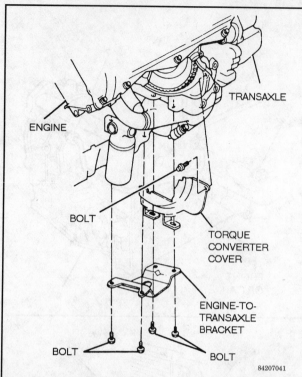

Fig. 40 Torque converter cover and engine-to-transaxle bracket — 4T80-E transaxle

5. Hold the cage and inner race 90° to the centerline of the outer race and align the cage windows with the lands of the outer race. Install the cage and inner race into the outer race, making sure the snapring side of the inner race faces the shaft.

6. Insert the first chrome ball, then tilt the cage in the opposite direction to insert the opposing ball. Repeat until all 6 balls are in place.

7. Place approximately half of the grease from the service kit inside the boot and pack the CV-joint with the remaining grease.

8. Push the CV-joint onto the shaft until the snapring is seated in the groove on the shaft.

9. Slide the boot over the CV-joint until the boot lip is in the groove on the outer race. The boot must not be dimpled, stretched or out of shape in any way. If it is not shaped correctly, equalize the pressure in the boot and shape the boot properly by hand.

10. Install the large boot clamp and crimp, using crimping tool J-35910 or equivalent.

Inner CV-Joint

DISASSEMBLY

▶ See Figure 58

1. Cut the boot retaining clamps from the CV-joint with side cutters and discard.

2. Separate the boot from the CV-joint and slide it away from the joint along the shaft.

3. Remove the outer CV-joint housing from the spider and shaft.

4. Spread the spacer ring with snapring pliers and slide the spacer ring and spider back on the shaft.

5. Remove the shaft retaining ring from the groove on the shaft and slide the spider assembly off the shaft.

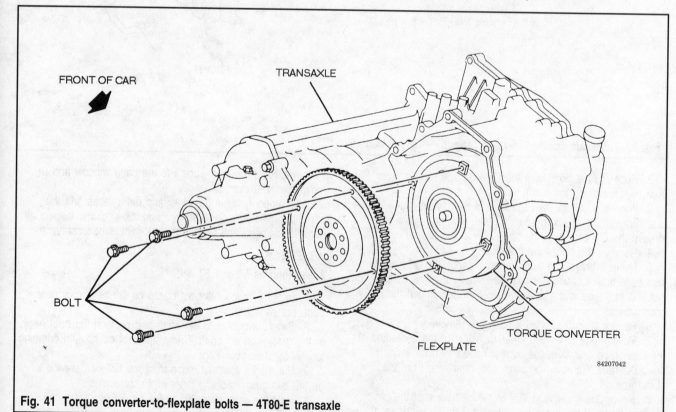

Fig. 41 Torque converter-to-flexplate bolts — 4T80-E transaxle

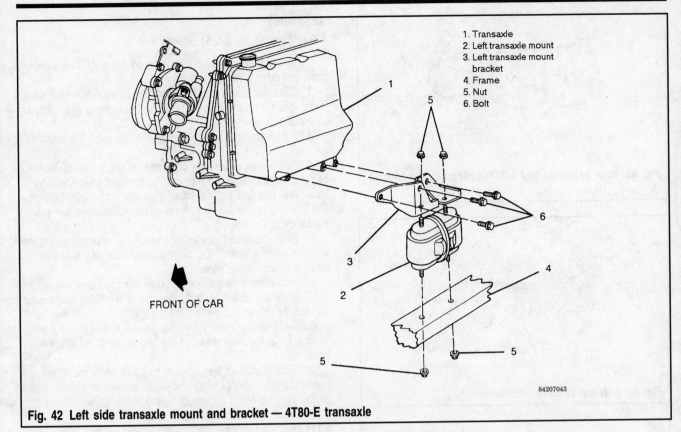

1. Transaxle
2. Left transaxle mount
3. Left transaxle mount bracket
4. Frame
5. Nut
6. Bolt

FRONT OF CAR

84207043

Fig. 42 Left side transaxle mount and bracket — 4T80-E transaxle

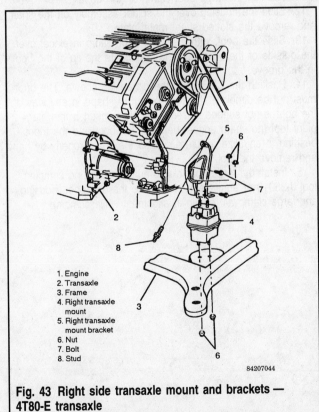

1. Engine
2. Transaxle
3. Frame
4. Right transaxle mount
5. Right transaxle mount bracket
6. Nut
7. Bolt
8. Stud

84207044

Fig. 43 Right side transaxle mount and brackets — 4T80-E transaxle

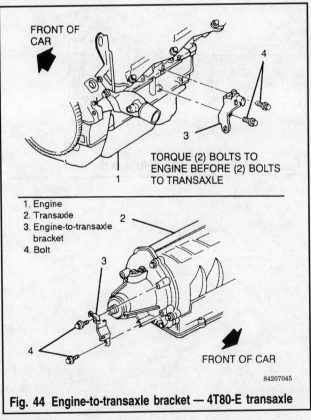

FRONT OF CAR

TORQUE (2) BOLTS TO ENGINE BEFORE (2) BOLTS TO TRANSAXLE

1. Engine
2. Transaxle
3. Engine-to-transaxle bracket
4. Bolt

FRONT OF CAR

84207045

Fig. 44 Engine-to-transaxle bracket — 4T80-E transaxle

6. Thoroughly clean the bearing blocks, spider and housing with clean solvent and allow to dry.

7. Remove the tripot bushing from the housing.

8. Remove the spacer ring and boot from the shaft.

9. Inspect the spider, housing, bearing blocks and tripot bushing for damage. Replace the CV-joint, if necessary.

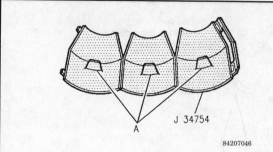

Fig. 45 Boot protector tool J-34754. Remove the tabs at 'A'

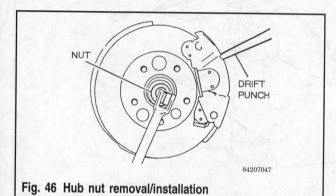

Fig. 46 Hub nut removal/installation

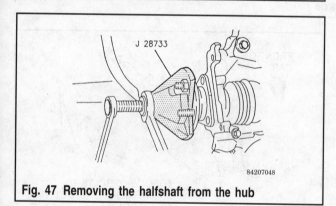

Fig. 47 Removing the halfshaft from the hub

ASSEMBLY

▶ See Figures 59, 60, 61, 62, 63 and 64

1. Install a new small boot clamp on the neck of a new boot, but do not crimp yet.

2. Slide the boot onto the shaft and position the boot neck in the groove on the shaft. Crimp the boot clamp with crimping tool J-35910 or equivalent.

3. Install the spacer ring on the shaft beyond the second groove.

4. Apply a small amount of grease to the inside of the bearing blocks. Align the flats on the opening in the bearing block with the flats on the spider trunnion. Attach the bearing block to the spider trunnion, then rotate 90 degrees to secure the block to the spider.

5. Slide the spider assembly against the spacer ring on the shaft, making sure that the counterbored face of the spider faces the end of the shaft.

6. Install the shaft retaining ring in the groove of the shaft.

7. Slide the spider towards the end of the shaft and reseat the spacer ring in the groove on the shaft.

8. Place approximately half the grease from the CV-joint service kit in the boot and use the remainder to repack the housing.

9. Place a slotted 6 in. square piece of sheet metal between the boot and bearing blocks, as shown, to maintain proper bearing block alignment during reassembly.

10. Install the tripot bushing to the housing.

11. Position the large boot clamp on the boot.

12. Slide the housing over the spider assembly on the shaft and remove the slotted sheet metal plate.

13. Slide the boot, with the large boot clamp in place, over the outside of the tripot bushing and locate the lip of the boot in the groove.

14. Position the CV-joint to the dimension shown. The boot must not be dimpled, stretched or out of shape in any way. If the boot is not shaped correctly, carefully insert a thin, flat, blunt tool (no sharp edges) between the boot and the tripot bushing to equalize pressure. Shape the boot properly by hand and remove the tool.

15. Install the large boot clamp and crimp, using crimping tool J-35910 or equivalent. Make sure that the boot, housing and large clamp all remain in alignment while crimping.

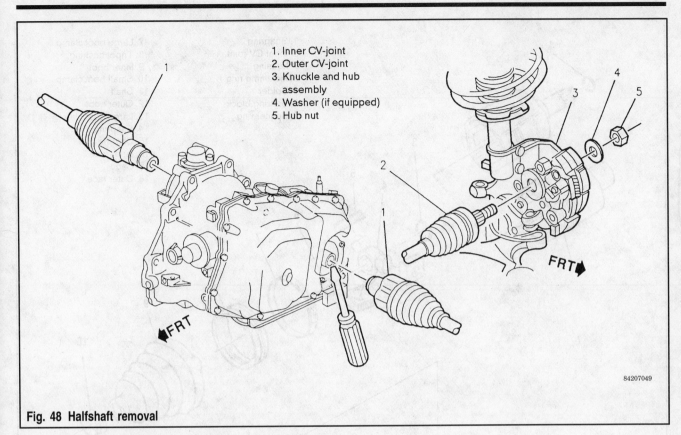

1. Inner CV-joint
2. Outer CV-joint
3. Knuckle and hub assembly
4. Washer (if equipped)
5. Hub nut

84207049

Fig. 48 Halfshaft removal

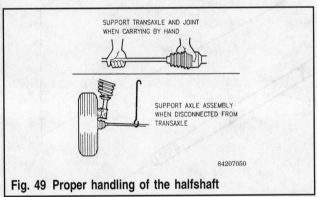

SUPPORT TRANSAXLE AND JOINT WHEN CARRYING BY HAND

SUPPORT AXLE ASSEMBLY WHEN DISCONNECTED FROM TRANSAXLE

84207050

Fig. 49 Proper handling of the halfshaft

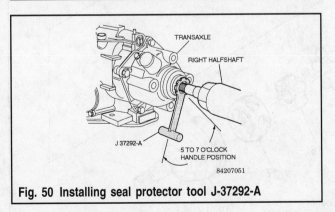

TRANSAXLE

RIGHT HALFSHAFT

J 37292-A

5 TO 7 O'CLOCK HANDLE POSITION

84207051

Fig. 50 Installing seal protector tool J-37292-A

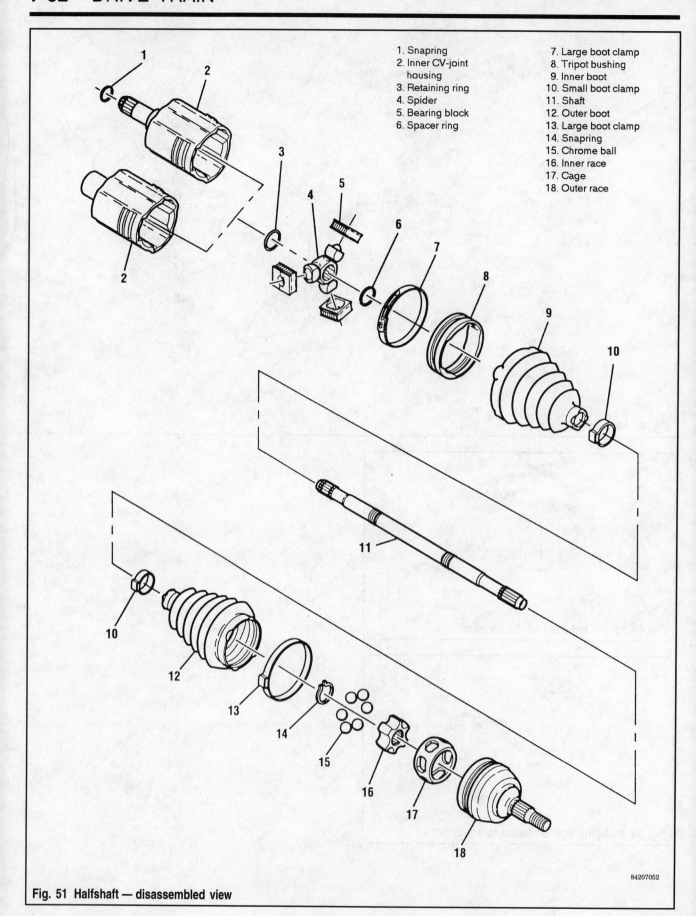

1. Snapring
2. Inner CV-joint housing
3. Retaining ring
4. Spider
5. Bearing block
6. Spacer ring
7. Large boot clamp
8. Tripot bushing
9. Inner boot
10. Small boot clamp
11. Shaft
12. Outer boot
13. Large boot clamp
14. Snapring
15. Chrome ball
16. Inner race
17. Cage
18. Outer race

84207052

Fig. 51 Halfshaft — disassembled view

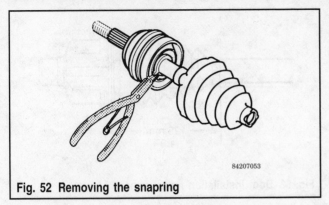

Fig. 52 Removing the snapring

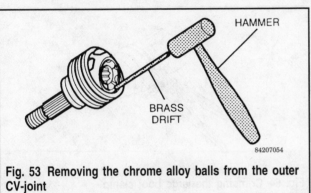

Fig. 53 Removing the chrome alloy balls from the outer CV-joint

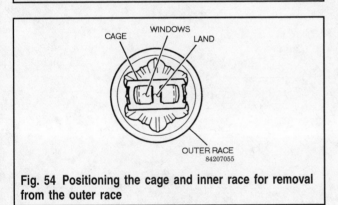

Fig. 54 Positioning the cage and inner race for removal from the outer race

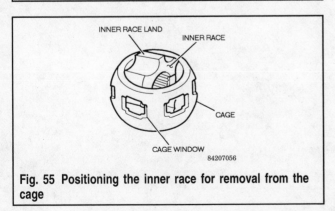

Fig. 55 Positioning the inner race for removal from the cage

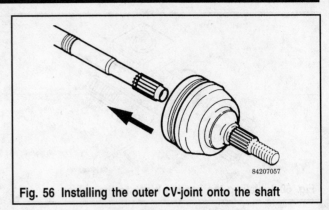

Fig. 56 Installing the outer CV-joint onto the shaft

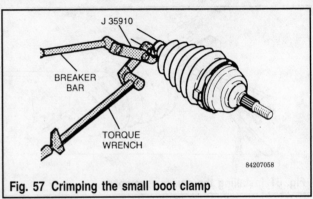

Fig. 57 Crimping the small boot clamp

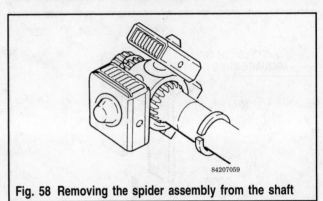

Fig. 58 Removing the spider assembly from the shaft

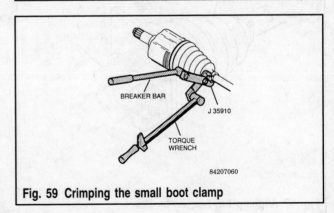

Fig. 59 Crimping the small boot clamp

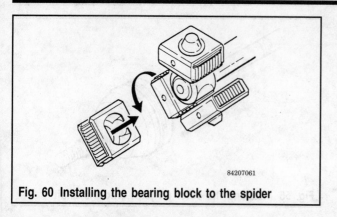

84207061

Fig. 60 Installing the bearing block to the spider

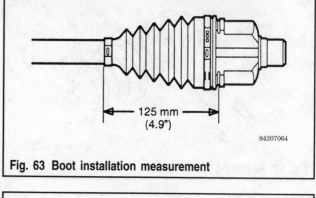

125 mm
(4.9")

84207064

Fig. 63 Boot installation measurement

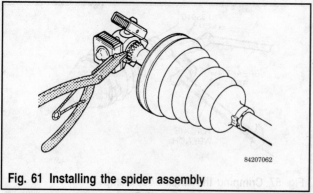

84207062

Fig. 61 Installing the spider assembly

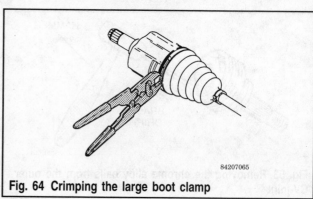

84207065

Fig. 64 Crimping the large boot clamp

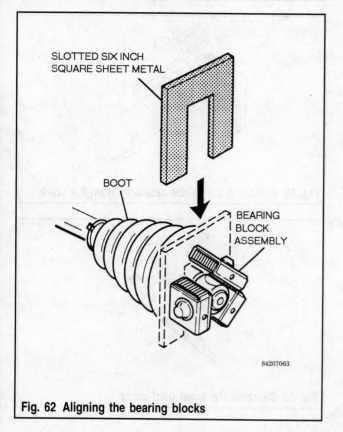

SLOTTED SIX INCH
SQUARE SHEET METAL

BOOT

BEARING
BLOCK
ASSEMBLY

84207063

Fig. 62 Aligning the bearing blocks

TORQUE SPECIFICATIONS

Component	U.S.	Metric
Ball joint nut		
Deville, Fleetwood and Sixty Special		
Step 1	88 inch lbs.	10 Nm
Step 2	41 ft. lbs.	55 Nm
Eldorado and Seville		
Step 1	84 inch lbs.	10 Nm
Step 2	+ 120°	+ 120°
Drain plug		
4T80-E transaxle	6–10 ft. lbs.	8–14 Nm
Fluid pan bolts		
4T60 transaxle	10 ft. lbs.	13 Nm
4T60-E transaxle	12–13 ft. lbs.	16–17 Nm
4T80-E transaxle		
Step 1	27 inch lbs.	3 Nm
Step 2	53 inch lbs.	6 Nm
Step 3	106 inch lbs.	12 Nm
Hub nut		
1990–91	185 ft. lbs.	251 Nm
1992–93		
Deville, Fleetwood and Sixty Special		
Except with J55 brake option	110 ft. lbs.	145 Nm
With J55 brake option	130 ft. lbs.	177 Nm
Eldorado and Seville	110 ft. lbs.	145 Nm
Manual lever nut		
4T60 and 4T60-E transaxles	20 ft. lbs.	27 Nm
4T80-E transaxle	15 ft. lbs.	20 Nm
Neutral safety switch bolts		
4T60 and 4T60-E transaxles	20 ft. lbs.	27 Nm
4T80-E transaxle	106 inch lbs.	12 Nm
Oil cooler line fittings	15 ft. lbs.	20 Nm
Torque converter-to-flexplate bolts		
4T60 and 4T60-E transaxles	46 ft. lbs.	63 Nm
4T80-E transaxle	35 ft. lbs.	47 Nm
Transaxle mounting		
Deville, Fleetwood and Sixty Special		
1990		
Cradle bolts	74 ft. lbs.	100 Nm
Insulator bolt	74 ft. lbs.	100 Nm
Mounting bracket-to-transaxle bolts	40 ft. lbs.	55 Nm
Mounting bracket-to-transaxle nuts	23 ft. lbs.	31 Nm
Transaxle mount-to-cradle nuts	23 ft. lbs.	31 Nm
Transaxle-to-engine bracket bolts	37 ft. lbs.	50 Nm
1991–93		
Cradle bolts	74 ft. lbs.	100 Nm
Insulator bolt	74 ft. lbs.	100 Nm
Mount nuts	35 ft. lbs.	45 Nm
Transaxle-to-engine bracket bolts	37 ft. lbs.	50 Nm
Eldorado and Seville		
1990		
Cradle bolts	74 ft. lbs.	100 Nm
Mount-to-cradle attachments	35 ft. lbs.	45 Nm
Insulator bolt	74 ft. lbs.	100 Nm
Rear (left) transaxle mount nuts	35 ft. lbs.	45 Nm
Right rear mount bracket nuts	35 ft. lbs.	45 Nm
Rear mount-to-trans bracket bolts	50 ft. lbs.	70 Nm
Side transaxle mount bracket bolts	50 ft. lbs.	70 Nm
Upper transaxle mount stud bolts	74 ft. lbs.	100 Nm

84207066

TORQUE SPECIFICATIONS

Component	U.S.	Metric
1991		
Cradle bolts	74 ft. lbs.	100 Nm
Insulator bolt	74 ft. lbs.	100 Nm
Mount nuts	35 ft. lbs.	45 Nm
Transaxle-to-engine bracket bolts	37 ft. lbs.	50 Nm
1992		
Frame mount bolts	83 ft. lbs.	112 Nm
Left mount-to-cradle nuts	35 ft. lbs.	45 Nm
Left mount-to-bracket nuts	35 ft. lbs.	45 Nm
Right rear mount-to-cradle nut	75 ft. lbs.	100 Nm
Right rear mount-to-bracket nuts	35 ft. lbs.	45 Nm
Rear mount bracket-to-trans bolts	50 ft. lbs.	70 Nm
Rear mount bracket-to-brace bolt	15 ft. lbs.	20 Nm
1993		
4T60-E transaxle		
Cradle bolts	76 ft. lbs.	103 Nm
Left mount bracket upper bolts	50 ft. lbs.	70 Nm
Left mount-to-cradle nuts	35 ft. lbs.	45 Nm
Right rear mount-to-cradle nut	75 ft. lbs.	100 Nm
Transaxle mount-to-bracket nuts	35 ft. lbs.	45 Nm
4T80-E transaxle		
Engine-to-transaxle bracket	35 ft. lbs.	47 Nm
Frame mount bolts	74 ft. lbs.	100 Nm
Mount-to-transaxle bolts/nuts	35 ft. lbs.	47 Nm
Oil pan-to-transaxle bracket bolts	35 ft. lbs.	47 Nm
Transaxle mount-to-frame nuts	35 ft. lbs.	47 Nm
Transaxle-to-engine bolts/studs		
4T60 and 4T60-E transaxles	55 ft. lbs.	75 Nm
4T80-E transaxle	35 ft. lbs.	47 Nm

84207067

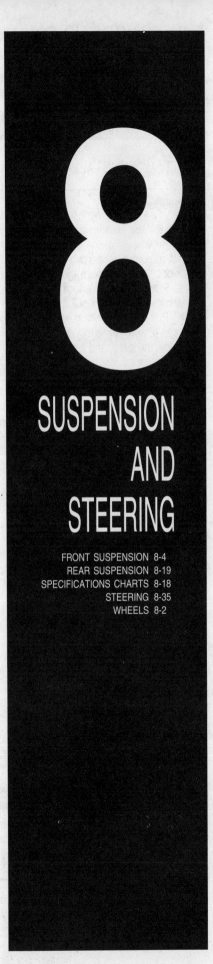

8

SUSPENSION AND STEERING

WHEELS

Wheels

REMOVAL & INSTALLATION

▶ See Figure 1

1. Place the shift lever in **P** and apply the parking brake. Chock the wheels at the opposite end of the vehicle.

2. If removing a rear wheel and the vehicle is equipped with fender skirts, remove the fender skirt as follows:

   a. Push the handle, located inside the fender skirt, up and inward, and then pull it down.

   b. Pull the fender skirt toward you and remove it from the vehicle. Place the fender skirt aside, being careful not to damage the paint and trim.

3. If equipped with wheel covers, use the special wrench supplied with the car to pry off the small center cover and remove the anti-theft wheel nut. Remove the wheel cover.

4. If equipped with aluminum wheels, use the flat end of the lug wrench supplied with the car to carefully pry off the center cover. Be careful not to damage the wheel or cover.

5. Loosen, but do not remove the wheel lug nuts.

6. Raise and safely support the vehicle. Refer to the Jacking procedure in Section 1. If any service other than wheel REMOVAL & installation is to be performed, if the wheel will be removed from the vehicle for any length of time, or if you are going to crawl under the vehicle for any reason, the vehicle must be supported with jackstands.

7. Remove the lug nuts and remove the wheel. If the wheel is difficult to remove because of corrosion or a tight fit between the wheel center hole and hub or rotor, proceed as follows:

   a. Reinstall the lug nuts finger-tight, then loosen each nut 2 turns.

   b. Lower the vehicle.

   c. Rock the vehicle from side to side as hard as possible, using your body weight (and that of an assistants, if necessary) to loosen the wheel.

   d. If the wheel will still not come loose, start the engine and rock the vehicle from **D** to **R**, moving the vehicle several feet in each direction. Apply quick, hard jabs on the brake pedal to loosen the wheel.

   e. Stop the engine. Raise and safely support the vehicle. Remove the lug nuts and the wheel.

❊❊WARNING

Never use heat to loosen a tight wheel, as the wheel and/or wheel bearings may become damaged. Never hammer on the wheel to loosen it, however, slight tapping on the tire sidewall with a rubber mallet is acceptable.

8. Inspect the wheel and hub mating surfaces. If necessary, use a scraper or wire brush to remove any dirt or corrosion.

To install:

9. Install the wheel on the hub. Install the lug nuts, tightening them until the wheel is fully seated.

10. Lower the vehicle. Tighten the lug nuts to 100 ft. lbs. (140 Nm), using the sequence shown in Fig. 1.

11. If equipped with aluminum wheels, carefully install the center cover.

12. If equipped with wheel covers, install the wheelcover by hand, being careful to line up the tire valve stem with the hole in the wheelcover. Install the anti-theft wheel nut and the center cover.

13. If equipped, install the fender skirt as follows:

   a. Pull the fender skirt handle down.

   b. Align the locator pins and insert them into the holes.

   c. Push the handle up and lock it in place.

   d. Push the bottom part of the fender skirt into place by hand.

INSPECTION

▶ See Figure 2

Inspect the wheels to make sure they are not bent, dented, have excessive lateral or radial runout, leak air, have elongated bolt holes or are heavily rusted.

Wheel runout can be measured with a dial indicator. The wheel must be mounted on an accurate surface, such as a tire balancer, and the tire should be removed. Measure the runout at the locations shown in Fig. 2. On aluminum wheels, radial and lateral runout must not exceed 0.030 in. On steel wheels, radial runout must not exceed 0.040 in. and lateral runout must not exceed 0.045 in.

If wheel replacement is necessary, make sure the load capacity, diameter, rim width, offset, and mounting configuration of the replacement wheel is the same as that of the original equipment wheel. An improper size or type of wheel may affect wheel and bearing life, brake cooling, speedometer/odometer calibration, vehicle ground clearance and tire clearance to the body and chassis.

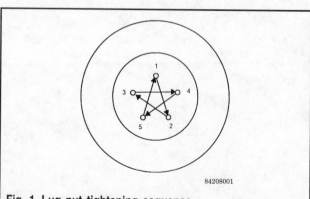

84208001

Fig. 1 Lug nut tightening sequence

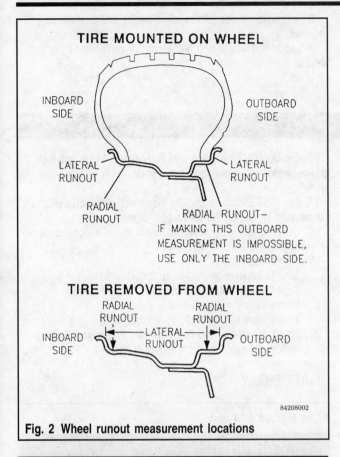

Fig. 2 Wheel runout measurement locations

Wheel Lug Studs

REPLACEMENT

▶ **See Figures 3 and 4**

Front Wheel

EXCEPT 1990-91 DEVILLE AND FLEETWOOD

1. Raise and safely support the vehicle.
2. Remove the wheel and tire assembly.
3. Remove the disc brake caliper and rotor; refer to Section 9. If necessary, remove the dust shield.

➡ **It is not necessary to disconnect the brake hose when removing the caliper. Suspend the caliper aside in the wheel well. Do not let the caliper hang by the brake hose.**

4. Use tool J-6627-A or equivalent, to press the stud from the hub and bearing assembly.
   To install:
5. Place the replacement stud into the hole in the hub and bearing assembly. Insert washers over the stud.
6. Thread an inverted lug nut onto the stud so the flat end of the nut contacts the washers. Tighten the nut to draw the stud into position, then remove the washers and nut.
7. Install the dust shield, rotor and disc brake caliper.
8. Install the wheel and tire assembly and lower the vehicle.

1990-91 DEVILLE AND FLEETWOOD

1. Raise and safely support the vehicle.
2. Remove the wheel and tire assembly.
3. Remove the hub and bearing assembly; refer to the procedure in this Section.
4. Use tool J-6627-A or equivalent, to press the stud from the hub and bearing assembly.
   To install:
5. Place the replacement stud into the hole in the hub and bearing assembly. Insert washers over the stud.
6. Thread an inverted lug nut onto the stud so the flat end of the nut contacts the washers. Tighten the nut to draw the stud into position, then remove the washers and nut.
7. Install the hub and bearing assembly.
8. Install the wheel and tire assembly and lower the vehicle.

Rear Wheel

1. Raise and safely support the vehicle.
2. Remove the wheel and tire assembly.
3. On Deville, Fleetwood and Sixty Special, remove the brake drum.
4. On Eldorado and Seville, remove the disc brake caliper and rotor; refer to Section 9.

➡ **It is not necessary to disconnect the brake hose when removing the caliper. Suspend the caliper aside in the wheel well. Do not let the caliper hang by the brake hose.**

5. Use tool J-6627-A or equivalent, to press the stud from the hub and bearing assembly.

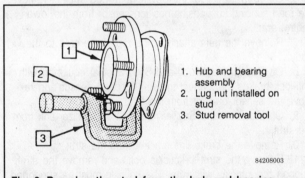

1. Hub and bearing assembly
2. Lug nut installed on stud
3. Stud removal tool

Fig. 3 Pressing the stud from the hub and bearing assembly

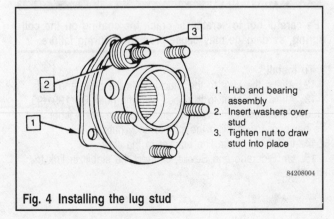

1. Hub and bearing assembly
2. Insert washers over stud
3. Tighten nut to draw stud into place

Fig. 4 Installing the lug stud

To install:

6. Place the replacement stud into the hole in the hub and bearing assembly. Insert washers over the stud.

7. Thread an inverted lug nut onto the stud so the flat end of the nut contacts the washers. Tighten the nut to draw the stud into position, then remove the washers and nut.

FRONT SUSPENSION

MacPherson Struts

REMOVAL & INSTALLATION

▶ See Figures 5, 6 and 7

❊❊WARNING

When working near the halfshafts, be careful not to overextend the inner CV-joints. If the joint is overextended, the internal components may separate resulting in joint failure.

1. Disconnect the negative battery cable.

2. Raise and safely support the vehicle. The vehicle must be supported by the frame with the control arms hanging free.

3. Remove the wheel and tire assembly.

4. On Eldorado and Seville, disconnect the electrical connector from the top of the strut, if equipped.

5. On 1991-93 Deville, Fleetwood and Sixty Special, loosen the strut housing tie bar through bolts at each end of the bar.

6. On 1993 Eldorado and Seville with 4.6L engine, remove the road sensing suspension position sensor from the lower control arm.

7. Remove the nuts attaching the top of the strut to the body.

8. On Deville, Fleetwood and Sixty Special equipped with anti-lock brakes, disconnect the wheel speed sensor and remove the sensor bracket from the strut.

9. On Eldorado and Seville, remove the stabilizer link from the strut.

10. Remove the brake line bracket from the strut.

11. Remove the strut-to-knuckle bolts and remove the strut. Support the knuckle with wire. The knuckle must be supported to prevent damage to the ball joint and/or halfshaft.

❊❊WARNING

Be careful not to scratch or crack the coating on the coil spring, as damage may cause premature spring failure.

To install:

12. Attach the strut to the knuckle with the bolts and nuts.

13. Attach the strut to the body with the nuts. On 1991-93 Deville, Fleetwood and Sixty Special, position the washer and tie bar prior to installing the strut-to-body nuts.

14. Install the brake line bracket to the strut.

15. On Eldorado and Seville, connect the stabilizer link to the strut.

8. Install the brake rotor and caliper or brake drum, as required.

9. Install the wheel and tire assembly and lower the vehicle.

16. On Deville, Fleetwood and Sixty Special with anti-lock brakes, install the wheel speed sensor bracket and connect the sensor.

17. On 1993 Eldorado and Seville, install the road sensing suspension sensor to the lower control arm.

18. On Eldorado and Seville, connect the electrical connector at the top of the strut, if equipped.

19. Tighten as follows:
   Strut-to-knuckle bolts: 140 ft. lbs. (190 Nm)
   Strut-to-body nuts: 18 ft. lbs. (24 Nm)
   Stabilizer link nuts: 48 ft. lbs. (65 Nm)
   Tie bar through bolts: 20 ft. lbs. (27 Nm)

20. Install the wheel and tire assembly and lower the vehicle. Check and adjust the front wheel alignment.

DISASSEMBLY

▶ See Figures 8, 9 and 10

❊❊WARNING

Be careful not to scratch or crack the coating on the coil spring, as damage may cause premature spring failure.

1. Mount the strut assembly in strut compressor tool J-34013 or equivalent.

2. Turn the compressor forcing screw until the spring compresses slightly.

3. Use a T-50 Torx® bit to keep the strut shaft from turning, then remove the nut on the top of the strut shaft.

4. Loosen the compressor screw while guiding the strut shaft out of the assembly. Continue loosening the compressor screw until the strut and spring can be removed.

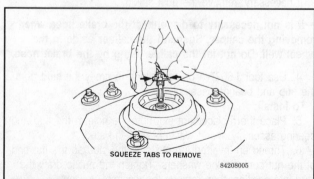

SQUEEZE TABS TO REMOVE

84208005

Fig. 5 Disconnecting the electrical connector at the top of the strut

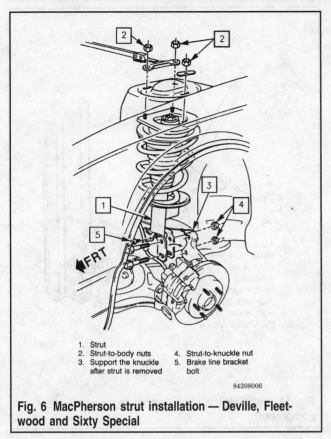

Fig. 6 MacPherson strut installation — Deville, Fleetwood and Sixty Special

1. Strut
2. Strut-to-body nuts
3. Support the knuckle after strut is removed
4. Strut-to-knuckle nut
5. Brake line bracket bolt

84208006

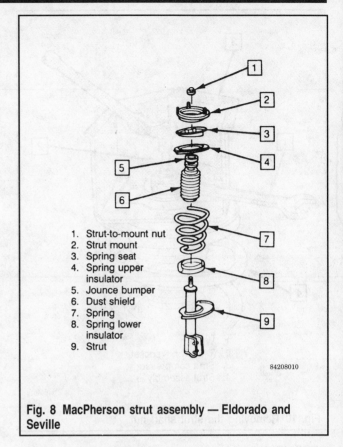

Fig. 8 MacPherson strut assembly — Eldorado and Seville

1. Strut-to-mount nut
2. Strut mount
3. Spring seat
4. Spring upper insulator
5. Jounce bumper
6. Dust shield
7. Spring
8. Spring lower insulator
9. Strut

84208010

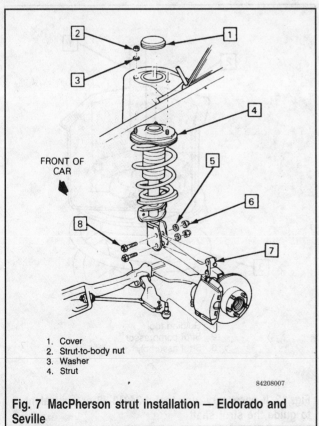

Fig. 7 MacPherson strut installation — Eldorado and Seville

1. Cover
2. Strut-to-body nut
3. Washer
4. Strut

84208007

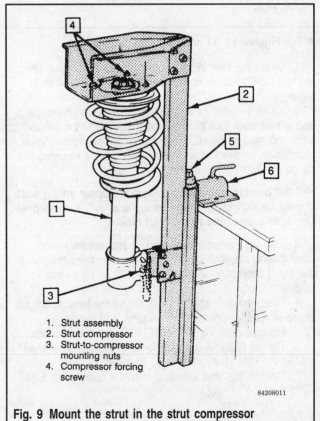

Fig. 9 Mount the strut in the strut compressor

1. Strut assembly
2. Strut compressor
3. Strut-to-compressor mounting nuts
4. Compressor forcing screw

84208011

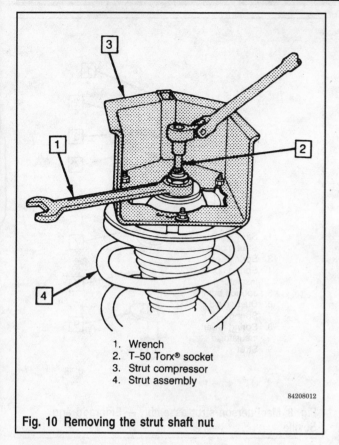

1. Wrench
2. T–50 Torx® socket
3. Strut compressor
4. Strut assembly

84208012

Fig. 10 Removing the strut shaft nut

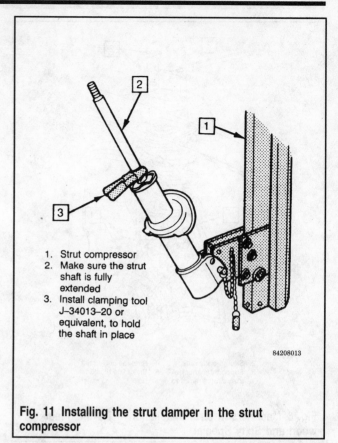

1. Strut compressor
2. Make sure the strut shaft is fully extended
3. Install clamping tool J–34013–20 or equivalent, to hold the shaft in place

84208013

Fig. 11 Installing the strut damper in the strut compressor

ASSEMBLY

▶ **See Figures 11, 12 and 13**

1. Mount the strut in the strut compressor tool. Use clamping tool J-34013-20 or equivalent, to hold the strut shaft in place.

2. Install the spring over the strut. The flat on the upper spring seat must face out from the centerline of the vehicle, or when mounted in the strut compressor, the spring seat must face the same direction as the steering knuckle mounting flange.

➡**If the bearing was removed from the upper spring seat, it must be reinstalled in the spring seat in the same position before attaching to the strut mount.**

3. Turn the compressor screw to compress the spring, while guiding the strut shaft through the top of the strut assembly. If necessary, use tool J-34013-38 or equivalent, to guide the shaft.

4. When the strut shaft threads are visible through the top of the strut assembly, install the washer and nut.

5. Remove clamping tool J-34013-20 from the strut shaft.

6. Tighten the strut shaft nut to 55 ft. lbs. (75 Nm) while holding the strut shaft with a T-50 Torx® bit.

7. Remove the strut assembly from the compressor tool.

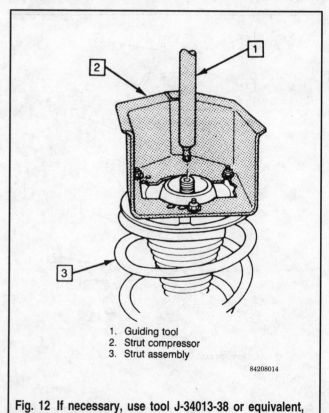

1. Guiding tool
2. Strut compressor
3. Strut assembly

84208014

Fig. 12 If necessary, use tool J-34013-38 or equivalent, to guide the strut shaft

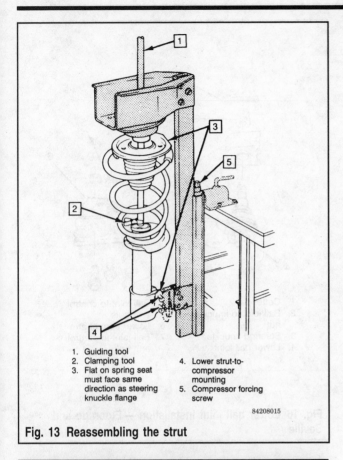

1. Guiding tool
2. Clamping tool
3. Flat on spring seat must face same direction as steering knuckle flange
4. Lower strut-to-compressor mounting
5. Compressor forcing screw

84208015

Fig. 13 Reassembling the strut

Lower Ball Joint

INSPECTION

Replace the lower ball joint if there is any looseness in the joint or if the ball joint seal is damaged. Inspect the ball joint as follows:

1. Raise and safely support the vehicle, allowing the front suspension to hang free.
2. Have an assistant grasp the tire at the top and bottom and move the top of the tire in and out. Check for any horizontal movement of the knuckle relative to the lower control arm. If there is any movement, replace the ball joint.
3. Check the ball stud tightness in the knuckle boss by shaking the wheel and feeling for movement of the stud end or castellated nut at the knuckle boss. Check the torque of the castellated nut — a loose nut can indicate a bent stud or an enlarged hole in the knuckle boss. Replace a worn or damaged ball joint and/or knuckle.
4. If the ball stud is disconnected from the knuckle and looseness is detected, or if the ball stud can be twisted in its socket using finger pressure, replace the ball joint.

REMOVAL & INSTALLATION

▶ **See Figures 14, 15 and 16**

1. Raise and safely support the vehicle, allowing the front suspension to hang free.
2. Remove the wheel and tire assembly.

✳✳WARNING

Be careful when working in the area of the CV-joint boot. Damage to the boot could result in eventual CV-joint failure. If necessary, install CV-joint boot protector tool J-34754 or equivalent, to protect the boot.

3. On 1993 Eldorado and Seville with 4.6L engine, remove the road sensing suspension position sensor from the lower control arm.
4. Remove the cotter pin and nut from the ball joint stud. Use ball joint separator tool J-36226 or equivalent, on Deville, Fleetwood and Sixty Special or ball joint separator tool J-35315 or equivalent, on Eldorado and Seville, to separate the ball joint from the steering knuckle.
5. On Deville, Fleetwood and Sixty Special, loosen the stabilizer bar link nut.
6. Drill out the 3 rivets retaining the ball joint to the lower control arm and remove the ball joint.

To install:
7. Attach the new ball joint to the lower control arm with 3 mounting bolts and nuts. On Deville, Fleetwood and Sixty Special, the bolts must be installed from the top of the control arm. On Eldorado and Seville, the bolts must be installed from the bottom of the control arm. Tighten the nuts to 50 ft. lbs. (68 Nm).
8. On Deville, Fleetwood and Sixty Special, tighten the stabilizer bar link nut to 13 ft. lbs. (17 Nm).
9. Connect the ball joint to the steering knuckle and install the castellated nut.
10. On Deville, Fleetwood and Sixty Special, tighten the ball joint nut to 88 inch lbs. (10 Nm). Then tighten the nut an additional 120°, during which a torque of 41 ft. lbs. (55 Nm) must be obtained.
11. On Eldorado and Seville, tighten the ball joint nut to 84 inch lbs. (10 Nm). Then tighten the nut an additional 120°, during which a minimum torque of 37 ft. lbs. (50 Nm) must be obtained. If the minimum torque is not obtained, check for stripped threads. If the threads are okay, replace the ball joint and knuckle.
12. Install a new cotter pin. If the cotter pin cannot be installed because the hole in the stud does not align with a nut catellation, tighten the nut up to an additional 60° to allow for installation. NEVER loosen the nut to provide for cotter pin installation.
13. On 1993 Eldorado and Seville with 4.6L engine, install the road sensing suspension position sensor to the lower control arm.
14. If necessary, remove the CV-joint boot protector tool.
15. Install the wheel and tire assembly and lower the vehicle.

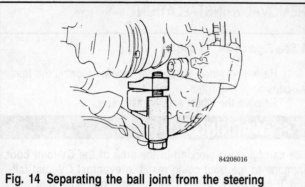

Fig. 14 Separating the ball joint from the steering knuckle

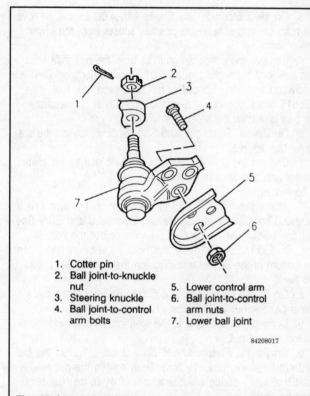

1. Cotter pin
2. Ball joint-to-knuckle nut
3. Steering knuckle
4. Ball joint-to-control arm bolts
5. Lower control arm
6. Ball joint-to-control arm nuts
7. Lower ball joint

84208017

Fig. 15 Lower ball joint installation — Deville, Fleetwood and Sixty Special

Stabilizer Bar

REMOVAL & INSTALLATION

Deville, Fleetwood and Sixty Special
▶ See Figures 17, 18 and 19

1. Raise and safely support the vehicle, allowing the front suspension to hang free.

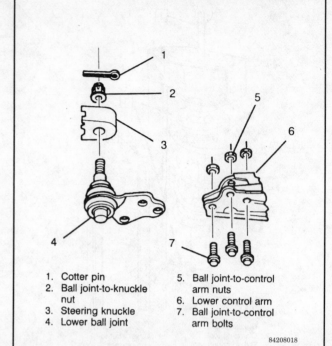

1. Cotter pin
2. Ball joint-to-knuckle nut
3. Steering knuckle
4. Lower ball joint
5. Ball joint-to-control arm nuts
6. Lower control arm
7. Ball joint-to-control arm bolts

84208018

Fig. 16 Lower ball joint installation — Eldorado and Seville

2. Remove the wheel and tire assemblies.

✳✳WARNING

Be careful when working in the area of the CV-joint boots. Damage to the boots could result in eventual CV-joint failure. If necessary, install CV-joint boot protector tools J-34754 or equivalent, to protect the boots.

3. Remove the stabilizer bar link bolts from the lower control arms.
4. Remove the stabilizer bar bushing brackets from the frame.
5. Remove the cotter pins and nuts from the tie rod ends. Use separator tool J-24319-01 or equivalent, to separate the tie rod ends from the steering knuckles.
6. Disconnect the exhaust pipe from the exhaust manifold.
7. Turn the passenger side strut all the way to the right.
8. Slide the stabilizer bar over the steering knuckle and pull down until the stabilizer bar clears the frame. Remove the stabilizer bar.

To install:
9. Slide the stabilizer bar over the steering knuckle, raise it over the frame and slide it into position. Loosely install the mount bushings, brackets and bolts.
10. Loosely install the stabilizer bar link components to the lower control arms.
11. Connect the tie rod ends to the steering knuckles. Install the tie rod end nuts and tighten to 35 ft. lbs. (48 Nm). Install new cotter pins. If a cotter pin cannot be installed because the hole in the stud does not align with a nut castellation, tighten the nut up to a maximum of 52 ft. lbs. (70 Nm) to allow for

installation. NEVER loosen the nut to provide for cotter pin installation.

12. Tighten the stabilizer bar bracket bolts to 35 ft. lbs. (48 Nm). Tighten the stabilizer bar link bolt nuts to 13 ft. lbs. (17 Nm).

13. Connect the exhaust pipe to the manifold. Tighten the bolts to 15 ft. lbs. (20 Nm) on 1990-91 vehicles or 18 ft. lbs. (25 Nm) on 1992-93 vehicles.

14. If necessary, remove the CV-joint boot protector tools.

15. Install the wheel and tire assemblies and lower the vehicle.

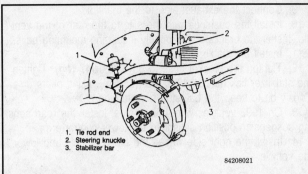

1. Tie rod end
2. Steering knuckle
3. Stabilizer bar

84208021

Fig. 19 Correct position of the stabilizer bar for removal or installation

Eldorado and Seville

▶ See Figure 20

1. Raise and safely support the vehicle, allowing the front suspension to hang free.

2. Remove the wheel and tire assembly from the right side of the vehicle.

3. On 1993 vehicles with 4.6L engine, remove the road sensing suspension position sensor from the lower control arm.

4. Remove the stabilizer links. Use pliers or a Torx® bit, as required, to keep the ball stud from turning while loosening the nut.

5. Remove the bracket bolts, brackets and bushings.

6. Disconnect the exhaust pipe from the manifold.

7. Remove the stabilizer bar.

To install:

8. Position the stabilizer bar in the vehicle.

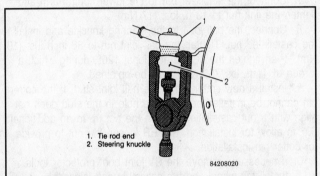

1. Tie rod end
2. Steering knuckle

84208020

Fig. 18 Separating the tie rod end from the steering knuckle

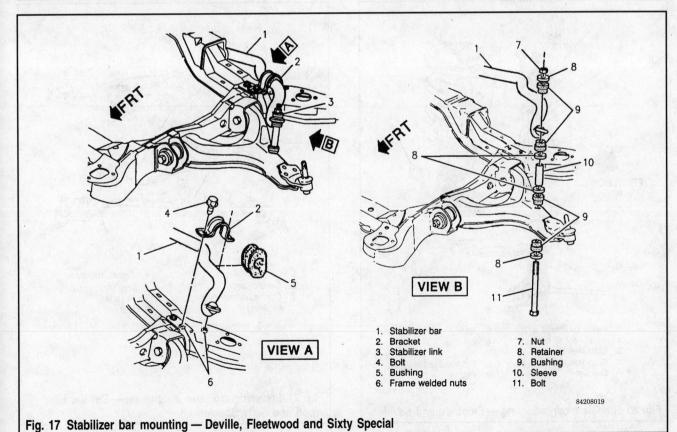

VIEW A

VIEW B

1. Stabilizer bar
2. Bracket
3. Stabilizer link
4. Bolt
5. Bushing
6. Frame welded nuts
7. Nut
8. Retainer
9. Bushing
10. Sleeve
11. Bolt

84208019

Fig. 17 Stabilizer bar mounting — Deville, Fleetwood and Sixty Special

9. Connect the exhaust pipe to the manifold.

10. Install the bushings with the slits to the rear of the vehicle. Install the brackets and loosely install the mounting bolts.

11. Install the stabilizer links.

12. Tighten the bracket bolts to 35 ft. lbs. (47 Nm). Tighten the stabilizer link nuts to 48 ft. lbs. (65 Nm), using pliers or a Torx® bit to keep the ball stud from turning.

13. On 1993 vehicles with 4.6L engine, install the road sensing suspension position sensor to the lower control arm.

14. Install the right side wheel and tire assembly and lower the vehicle.

Lower Control Arm

REMOVAL & INSTALLATION

Deville, Fleetwood and Sixty Special
▶ See Figures 21 and 22

1. Raise and safely support the vehicle, allowing the front suspension to hang free.

2. Remove the wheel and tire assembly.

❊❊WARNING

Be careful when working in the area of the CV-joint boot. Damage to the boot could result in eventual CV-joint failure. If necessary, install CV-joint boot protector tool J-34754 or equivalent, to protect the boot.

3. Remove the stabilizer bar-to-control arm bolt.

4. Remove the cotter pin and nut from the ball joint stud. Use ball joint separator tool J-36226 or equivalent, to separate the ball joint from the steering knuckle.

❊❊WARNING

When working near the halfshafts, be careful not to over-extend the inner CV-joints. If the joint is overextended, the internal components may separate resulting in joint failure.

5. Remove the control arm mounting bolts and remove the control arm from the frame.

To install:

6. Position the control arm to the frame and install the mounting bolts, washers and nuts. Do not tighten the mounting nuts at this time.

7. Connect the stabilizer bar to the lower control arm and tighten the link nut to 13 ft. lbs. (17 Nm).

8. Connect the ball joint to the steering knuckle and install the castellated nut. Tighten the ball joint nut to 88 inch lbs. (10 Nm). Then tighten the nut an additional 120°, during which a torque of 41 ft. lbs. (55 Nm) must be obtained.

9. Install a new cotter pin in the ball joint stud. If the cotter pin cannot be installed because the hole in the stud does not align with a nut castellation, tighten the nut up to an additional 60° to allow for installation. NEVER loosen the nut to provide for cotter pin installation.

10. If necessary, remove the CV-joint boot protector tools.

11. Install the wheel and tire assembly and lower the vehicle.

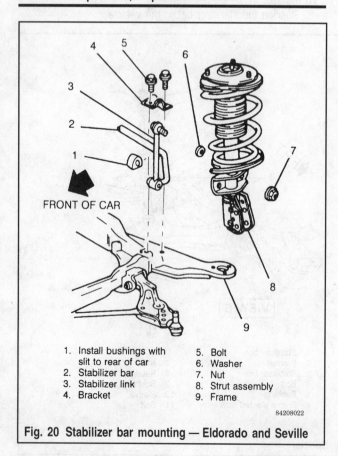

FRONT OF CAR

1. Install bushings with slit to rear of car	5. Bolt
2. Stabilizer bar	6. Washer
3. Stabilizer link	7. Nut
4. Bracket	8. Strut assembly
	9. Frame

84208022

Fig. 20 Stabilizer bar mounting — Eldorado and Seville

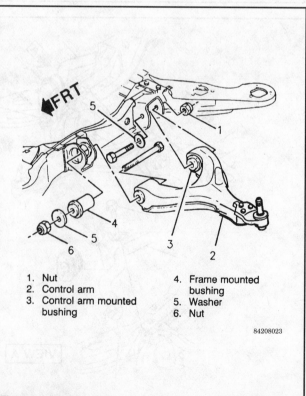

◀FRT

1. Nut	4. Frame mounted bushing
2. Control arm	5. Washer
3. Control arm mounted bushing	6. Nut

84208023

Fig. 21 Lower control arm installation — Deville, Fleetwood and Sixty Special

12. When the weight of the vehicle is supported by the lower control arms, tighten the front mounting nut to 140 ft. lbs. (190 Nm), then the rear mounting nut to 91 ft. lbs. (123 Nm).

13. Check the front wheel alignment.

Eldorado and Seville

▶ See Figure 23

1. Raise and safely support the vehicle, allowing the front suspension to hang free.
2. Remove the wheel and tire assembly.

❋❋WARNING

When working near the halfshafts, be careful not to overextend the inner CV-joints. If the joint is overextended, the internal components may separate resulting in joint failure. Be careful when working in the area of the CV-joint boot. Damage to the boot could result in eventual CV-joint failure. If necessary, install CV-joint boot protector tool J-34754 or equivalent, to protect the boot.

3. On 1993 vehicles with 4.6L engine, remove the road sensing suspension position sensor from the lower control arm.
4. Remove the cotter pin and castellated nut from the lower ball joint stud. Use ball joint separator tool J-35315 or equivalent, to separate the ball joint from the steering knuckle.
5. Remove the control arm bushing bolt and brake reaction rod nut, retainer and insulator. Remove the control arm.

To install:

6. Position the control arm to the frame and install the bushing bolt and brake reaction rod nut, retainer and insulator. Do not tighten at this time.
7. Connect the ball joint to the steering knuckle and install the castellated nut. Tighten the ball joint nut to 84 inch lbs. (10 Nm). Then tighten the nut an additional 120°, during which a minimum torque of 37 ft. lbs. (50 Nm) must be obtained. If the minimum torque is not obtained, check for stripped threads. If the threads are okay, replace the ball joint and knuckle.
8. Install a new cotter pin in the ball joint stud. If the cotter pin cannot be installed because the hole in the stud does not align with a nut castellation, tighten the nut up to an additional 60° to allow for installation. NEVER loosen the nut to provide for cotter pin installation.
9. On 1993 vehicles with 4.6L engine, install the road sensing suspension position sensor to the lower control arm.

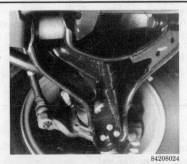
84208024

Fig. 22 View of the lower control arm — Deville, Fleetwood and Sixty Special

10. Install the tire and wheel assembly and lower the vehicle.
11. When the weight of the vehicle is supported by the lower control arms, tighten the control arm bushing bolt to 103 ft. lbs. (140 Nm) or nut to 91 ft. lbs. (123 Nm). Tighten the brake reaction rod nut to 58 ft. lbs. (78 Nm).
12. Check the front wheel alignment.

CONTROL ARM BUSHING REPLACEMENT

Deville, Fleetwood and Sixty Special

FRAME-MOUNTED BUSHING

▶ See Figures 24 and 25

1. Remove the control arm from the vehicle.
2. Insert bolt, washer and bearing assembly J-21474-19 or equivalent, through bushing driver J-21474-13 or equivalent, and position the small end facing the bushing.
3. Place bushing receiver J-21474-5 or equivalent, on the front of the bushing.
4. Tighten the bolt until the bushing is driven out of the frame, then remove the bushing driver tool.

To install:

5. Insert bolt, washer and bearing assembly J-21474-19 or equivalent, through bushing receiver J-21474-5 or equivalent, with the large end facing the bushing.
6. Position the large end of bushing driver J-21474-13 or equivalent, facing the bushing.
7. Thread on nut J-21474-18 or equivalent.
8. Tighten bolt J-21474-19 or equivalent, until the bushing is fully seated.
9. Remove the bushing driver tool and reinstall the control arm.

CONTROL ARM MOUNTED BUSHING

▶ See Figures 26 and 27

1. Remove the control arm from the vehicle.
2. Remove the bushing from the control arm by tapping down the flare with a hammer and punch.

To install:

3. Insert bolt, washer and bearing assembly J-21474-19 or equivalent, through bushing driver J-21474-13 or equivalent, and position the small end facing the bushing.
4. Position flaring tool J-23915 or equivalent, with the small flare facing the bushing.
5. Install nut J-21474-18 and tighten until a 45° flare is obtained and the bushing is secure in the control arm.
6. Install the control arm on the vehicle.

Eldorado and Seville

▶ See Figures 28 and 29

1. Remove the lower control arm.
2. Position the control arm in a press with tools J-35561-1 and J-35561-2 or equivalents, as shown in Fig. 29.
3. Press out the control arm bushing.

To install:

4. Lubricate a new bushing with a suitable rubber lubricant.

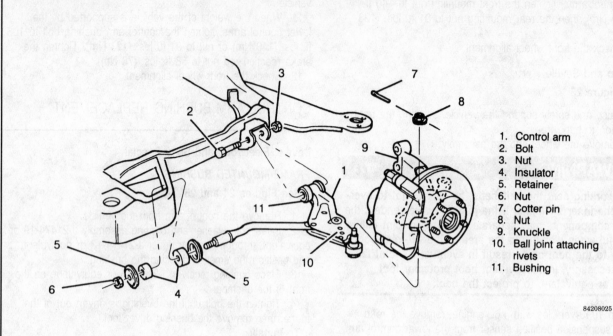

1. Control arm
2. Bolt
3. Nut
4. Insulator
5. Retainer
6. Nut
7. Cotter pin
8. Nut
9. Knuckle
10. Ball joint attaching rivets
11. Bushing

84208025

Fig. 23 Lower control arm installation — Eldorado and Seville

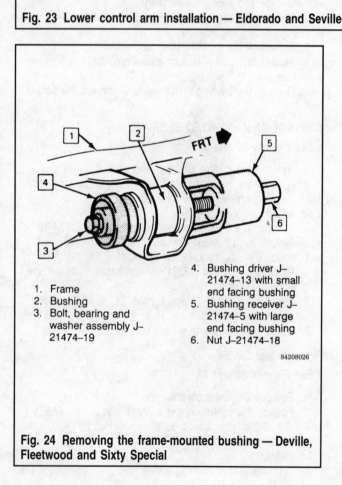

1. Frame
2. Bushing
3. Bolt, bearing and washer assembly J–21474–19
4. Bushing driver J–21474–13 with small end facing bushing
5. Bushing receiver J–21474–5 with large end facing bushing
6. Nut J–21474–18

84208026

Fig. 24 Removing the frame-mounted bushing — Deville, Fleetwood and Sixty Special

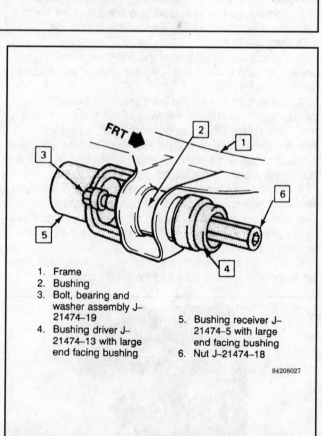

1. Frame
2. Bushing
3. Bolt, bearing and washer assembly J–21474–19
4. Bushing driver J–21474–13 with large end facing bushing
5. Bushing receiver J–21474–5 with large end facing bushing
6. Nut J–21474–18

84208027

Fig. 25 Installing the frame-mounted bushing — Deville, Fleetwood and Sixty Special

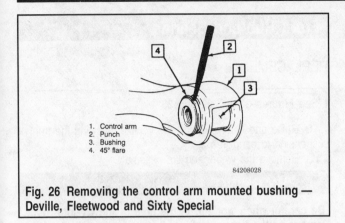

Fig. 26 Removing the control arm mounted bushing —
Deville, Fleetwood and Sixty Special

1. Control arm
2. Punch
3. Bushing
4. 45° flare

84208028

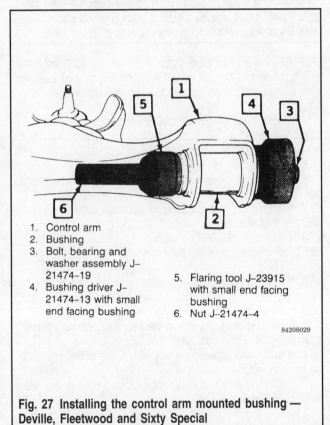

1. Control arm
2. Bushing
3. Bolt, bearing and
   washer assembly J–
   21474–19
4. Bushing driver J–
   21474–13 with small
   end facing bushing
5. Flaring tool J–23915
   with small end facing
   bushing
6. Nut J–21474–4

84208029

Fig. 27 Installing the control arm mounted bushing —
Deville, Fleetwood and Sixty Special

5. Position the control arm and bushing in a press with
tools J-35561-1, J-35561-2 and J-35561-3 or equivalents, as
shown in Fig. 30.
6. Press in the new control arm bushing.
7. Reinstall the control arm.

Knuckle

REMOVAL & INSTALLATION

1. Raise and safely support the vehicle, allowing the front
suspension to hang free.

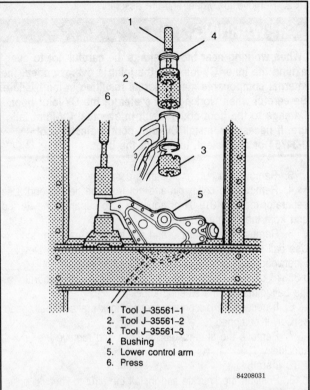

1. Tool J–35561–1
2. Tool J–35561–2
3. Tool J–35561–3
4. Bushing
5. Lower control arm
6. Press

84208031

Fig. 29 Installing the control arm bushing — Eldorado
and Seville

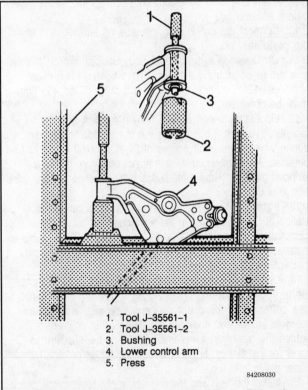

1. Tool J–35561–1
2. Tool J–35561–2
3. Bushing
4. Lower control arm
5. Press

84208030

Fig. 28 Removing the control arm bushing — Eldorado
and Seville

2. Remove the wheel and tire assembly.

✳✳WARNING

When working near the halfshafts, be careful not to over-extend the inner CV-joints. If the joint is overextended, the internal components may separate resulting in joint failure. Be careful when working in the area of the CV-joint boot. Damage to the boot could result in eventual CV-joint fail-ure. If necessary, install CV-joint boot protector tool J-34754 or equivalent, to protect the boot.

3. Remove the hub and bearing assembly.
4. Remove the cotter pin and nut from the tie rod end. Use separator tool J-24319-01 or equivalent, to separate the tie rod end from the steering knuckle.
5. Remove the cotter pin and nut from the ball joint stud. Use ball joint separator tool J-36226 or equivalent, on Deville, Fleetwood and Sixty Special or ball joint separator tool J-35315 or equivalent, on Eldorado and Seville, to separate the ball joint from the steering knuckle.
6. If necessary, disconnect the anti-lock brake wheel speed sensor, if equipped.
7. Remove the strut-to-knuckle bolts and remove the knuckle.

To install:

8. Position the knuckle and install the strut-to-knuckle bolts. Tighten the strut-to-knuckle bolts to 140 ft. lbs. (190 Nm).
9. If necessary, connect the anti-lock brake wheel speed sensor. If the sensor was removed on 1990-91 Eldorado and Seville, anti-corrosion compound must be applied to the sensor before assembly.
10. Connect the ball joint to the steering knuckle and install the castellated nut.
11. On Deville, Fleetwood and Sixty Special, tighten the ball joint nut to 88 inch lbs. (10 Nm). Then tighten the nut an additional 120°, during which a torque of 41 ft. lbs. (55 Nm) must be obtained.
12. On Eldorado and Seville, tighten the ball joint nut to 84 inch lbs. (10 Nm). Then tighten the nut an additional 120°, during which a minimum torque of 37 ft. lbs. (50 Nm) must be obtained. If the minimum torque is not obtained, check for stripped threads. If the threads are okay, replace the ball joint and knuckle.
13. Install a new cotter pin. If the cotter pin cannot be in-stalled because the hole in the stud does not align with a nut castellation, tighten the nut up to an additional 60° to allow for installation. NEVER loosen the nut to provide for cotter pin installation.
14. Connect the tie rod end to the steering knuckle. Install the tie rod end nut and tighten to 35 ft. lbs. (48 Nm). Install a new cotter pin. If the cotter pin cannot be installed because the hole in the stud does not align with a nut castellation, tighten the nut up to a maximum of 52 ft. lbs. (70 Nm) to allow for installation. NEVER loosen the nut to provide for cotter pin installation.
15. Install the hub and bearing assembly; refer to the proce-dure in this Section.
16. Install the wheel and tire assembly and lower the vehi-cle. Check the front wheel alignment.

Front Hub and Bearing

REPLACEMENT

◆ **See Figures 30, 31, 32 and 33**

1. Raise and safely support the vehicle, allowing the front suspension to hang free.
2. Remove the wheel and tire assembly.

✳✳WARNING

Be careful when working in the area of the CV-joint boot. Damage to the boot could result in eventual CV-joint fail-ure. If necessary, install CV-joint boot protector tool J-34754 or equivalent, to protect the boot.

3. Clean the halfshaft threads of all dirt and lubricant. Insert a drift punch through the caliper and into the rotor to keep the rotor from turning, then remove the hub nut and washer, if equipped.
4. Remove the caliper without disconnecting the brake hose. Suspend the caliper from the coil spring with wire; do not let it hang by the brake hose.
5. Remove the disc brake rotor.
6. If equipped, disconnect the anti-lock brake wheel speed sensor connector.
7. Remove the hub and bearing assembly retaining bolts and the dust shield.
8. Use tool J-28733-A or equivalent, to separate the hub and bearing assembly from the halfshaft.

To install:

9. Apply a light coating of grease to the knuckle bore. Install the new hub and bearing assembly. Draw the hub and bearing assembly onto the halfshaft with a new hub nut.
10. Install the dust shield and the hub and bearing assembly retaining bolts. Tighten to 70 ft. lbs. (95 Nm).
11. If equipped, connect the anti-lock brake wheel speed sensor connector.
12. Install the disc brake rotor and caliper; refer to the pro-cedures in Section 9.
13. Insert a drift punch into the caliper and rotor to prevent the rotor from turning. On 1990-91 vehicles, tighten the hub nut to 185 ft. lbs. (251 Nm). On 1992-93 vehicles, tighten the hub nut to 110 ft. lbs. (145 Nm), except on Deville, Fleetwood and Sixty Special equipped with J55 brake option, in which case the torque is 130 ft. lbs. (177 Nm).
14. Install the wheel and tire assembly and lower the vehicle.

Front Wheel Alignment

Wheel alignment is the angular relationship between the wheels and suspension components and the ground. The ac-curate alignment of these components is critical to proper vehi-cle tracking and to tire tread life.

Caster, camber and toe are adjustable on the front suspen-sion. When adjustments are made, the alignment should be precisely set to the specifications shown in the chart.

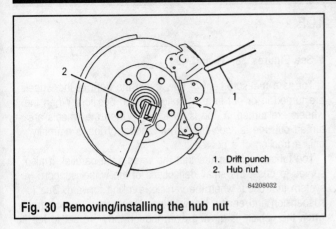

Fig. 30 Removing/installing the hub nut

1. Drift punch
2. Hub nut

84208032

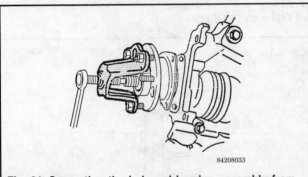

Fig. 31 Separating the hub and bearing assembly from the halfshaft

84208033

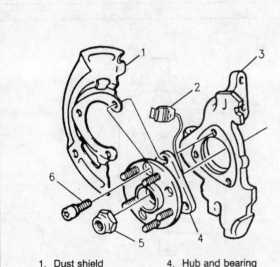

1. Dust shield
2. Wheel speed sensor connector
3. Steering knuckle
4. Hub and bearing assembly
5. Hub nut
6. Retaining bolt

84208034

Fig. 32 Hub and bearing assembly and related components — Deville, Fleetwood and Sixty Special

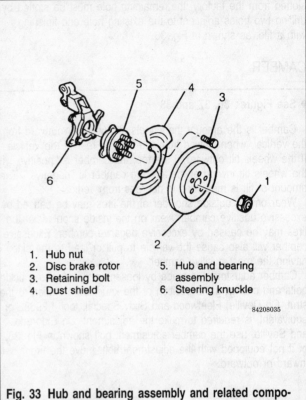

1. Hub nut
2. Disc brake rotor
3. Retaining bolt
4. Dust shield
5. Hub and bearing assembly
6. Steering knuckle

84208035

Fig. 33 Hub and bearing assembly and related components — Eldorado and Seville

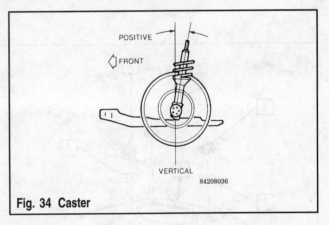

84208036

Fig. 34 Caster

CASTER

▶ **See Figures 34 and 35**

Caster is the amount the top of the strut is tilted forward or backward from the vertical. A backward tilt is "positive" and a forward tilt is "negative". The amount of tilt is measured in degrees from the vertical.

Caster influences directional control of the steering, but does not affect tire wear. If one wheel has more positive caster than the other, it will cause the wheel to pull toward the center of the vehicle, causing the vehicle to move or lead toward the side with the least positive caster.

Caster adjustment is made by loosening the strut top mounting nuts and moving the strut forward or backward in the slotted holes in the strut tower. Only two of the holes are slotted from the factory, the remaining hole must be slotted by drilling two holes adjacent to the existing hole and finishing with a file, as shown in Fig. 36.

CAMBER

▶ See Figures 36, 37 and 38

Camber is the amount the wheels tilt inward or outward from the vertical, when viewed from the front or rear of the vehicle. If the wheels tilt outward at the top, the camber is "positive". If the wheels tilt inward at the top, the camber is "negative". The amount of tilt is measured in degrees from vertical.

Wear on the outside shoulder of the tires may be caused by excessive positive camber; wear on the inside shoulder of the tires may be caused by excessive negative camber. Excessive camber will also cause the vehicle to pull or lead to the side having the most positive camber.

Camber adjustment is made by loosening the strut-to-knuckle bolts and changing the position of the knuckle in relation to the strut. On Deville, Fleetwood and Sixty Special, tool J-29682 or equivalent, is required to make the adjustment. On Eldorado and Seville, use the camber adjustment bolt shown in Fig. 38, or if not equipped with the adjustment bolt, move the tire inward or outward.

TOE

▶ See Figures 38, 39 and 40

Toe is a measurement of how much the front of the wheels are turned in or out from a straight-ahead position. When the wheels are turned in, toe is "positive". When the wheels are turned out, toe is "negative". The amount of toe is normally only a fraction of a degree.

Toe functions to ensure that the wheels roll parallel. It also serves to offset the small deflections of the wheel support system that occur when the vehicle is rolling forward. Due to suspension and engine loading, the wheels tend to roll parallel when the vehicle is moving even though they are set to toe in or out slightly when the vehicle is standing still. Incorrect toe will cause abnormal tire wear.

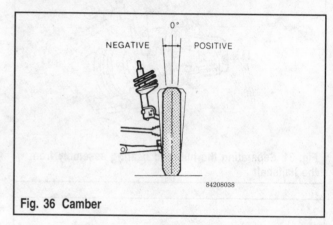

Fig. 36 Camber

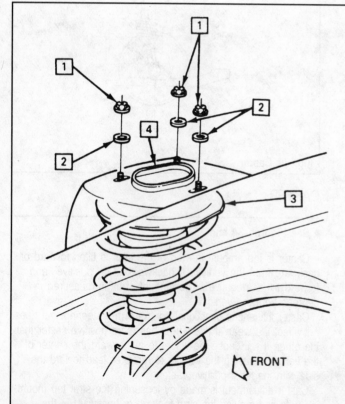

Fig. 35 Caster adjustment

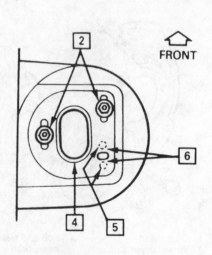

1. Nut
2. Washer
3. Strut
4. Cover
5. Drill $^{11}/_{32}$ in. holes
6. File here

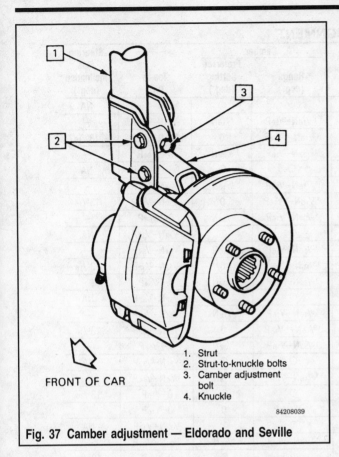

1. Strut
2. Strut-to-knuckle bolts
3. Camber adjustment bolt
4. Knuckle

84208039

Fig. 37 Camber adjustment — Eldorado and Seville

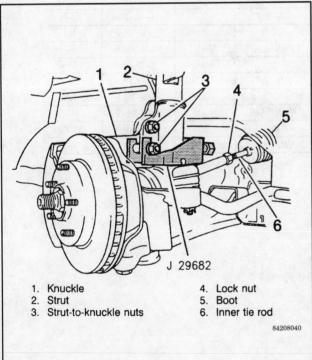

J 29682

1. Knuckle
2. Strut
3. Strut-to-knuckle nuts
4. Lock nut
5. Boot
6. Inner tie rod

84208040

Fig. 38 Camber and toe adjustment — Deville, Fleetwood and Sixty Special

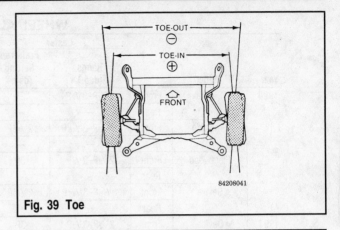

84208041

Fig. 39 Toe

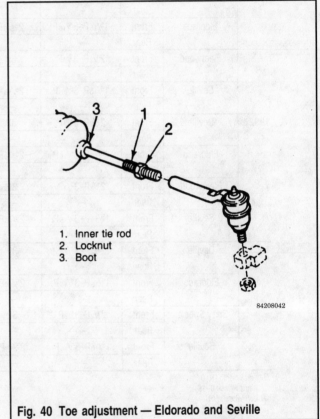

1. Inner tie rod
2. Locknut
3. Boot

84208042

Fig. 40 Toe adjustment — Eldorado and Seville

Toe is adjusted by loosening the locknuts on the inner tie rods and turning the inner tie rods.

WHEEL ALIGNMENT

Year	Model		Caster Range (deg.)	Caster Preferred Setting (deg.)	Camber Range (deg.)	Camber Preferred Setting (deg.)	Toe-in (in.)	Steering Axis Inclination (deg.)
1990	Deville	Front	$2\frac{1}{2}$P–$3\frac{1}{2}$P	3P	①	②	$\frac{5}{32}$N–$\frac{5}{32}$P	NA
		Rear	—	—	$\frac{13}{16}$N–$\frac{3}{16}$P	$\frac{5}{16}$N	$\frac{3}{64}$N–$\frac{9}{64}$P	—
	Eldorado	Front	$1\frac{5}{16}$P–$3\frac{5}{16}$P	$2\frac{5}{16}$P	$\frac{13}{16}$N–$\frac{13}{16}$P	0	$\frac{3}{32}$N–$\frac{3}{32}$P	$13\frac{5}{16}$
		Rear	—	—	$\frac{13}{32}$N–$\frac{3}{16}$P	$\frac{3}{32}$N	0–$\frac{13}{64}$P	—
	Fleetwood	Front	$2\frac{1}{2}$P–$3\frac{1}{2}$P	3P	①	②	$\frac{5}{32}$N–$\frac{5}{32}$P	NA
		Rear	—	—	$\frac{13}{16}$N–$\frac{3}{16}$P	$\frac{5}{16}$N	$\frac{3}{64}$N–$\frac{9}{64}$P	—
	Seville	Front	$1\frac{5}{16}$P–$3\frac{5}{16}$P	$2\frac{5}{16}$P	$\frac{13}{16}$N–$\frac{13}{16}$P	0	$\frac{3}{32}$N–$\frac{3}{32}$P	$13\frac{5}{16}$
		Rear	—	—	$\frac{13}{32}$N–$\frac{3}{16}$P	$\frac{3}{32}$N	0–$\frac{13}{64}$P	—
1991	Deville	Front	$2\frac{1}{2}$P–$3\frac{1}{2}$P	3P	①	②	$\frac{5}{32}$N–$\frac{5}{32}$P	NA
		Rear	—	—	$\frac{13}{16}$N–$\frac{3}{16}$P	$\frac{5}{16}$N	$\frac{3}{64}$N–$\frac{9}{64}$P	—
	Eldorado	Front	$1\frac{5}{16}$P–$3\frac{5}{16}$P	$2\frac{5}{16}$P	$\frac{13}{16}$N–$\frac{13}{16}$P	0	$\frac{3}{32}$N–$\frac{3}{32}$P	$13\frac{5}{16}$
		Rear	—	—	$\frac{13}{32}$N–$\frac{3}{16}$P	$\frac{3}{32}$N	0–$\frac{13}{64}$P	—
	Fleetwood	Front	$2\frac{1}{2}$P–$3\frac{1}{2}$P	3P	①	②	$\frac{5}{32}$N–$\frac{5}{32}$P	NA
		Rear	—	—	$\frac{13}{16}$N–$\frac{3}{16}$P	$\frac{5}{16}$N	$\frac{3}{64}$N–$\frac{9}{64}$P	—
	Seville	Front	$1\frac{5}{16}$P–$3\frac{5}{16}$P	$2\frac{5}{16}$P	$\frac{13}{16}$N–$\frac{13}{16}$P	0	$\frac{3}{32}$N–$\frac{3}{32}$P	$13\frac{5}{16}$
		Rear	—	—	$\frac{13}{32}$N–$\frac{3}{16}$P	$\frac{3}{32}$N	0–$\frac{13}{64}$P	—
1992	Deville	Front	$2\frac{1}{2}$P–$3\frac{1}{2}$P	3P	①	②	$\frac{5}{32}$N–$\frac{5}{32}$P	NA
		Rear	—	—	$\frac{13}{16}$N–$\frac{3}{16}$P	$\frac{5}{16}$N	$\frac{3}{64}$N–$\frac{9}{64}$P	—
	Eldorado	Front	$1\frac{5}{16}$P–$3\frac{5}{16}$P	$2\frac{5}{16}$P	①	②	0–$\frac{3}{16}$P	$13\frac{5}{16}$
		Rear	—	—	$\frac{1}{2}$N–$\frac{1}{2}$P	0	0–$\frac{3}{16}$P	—
	Fleetwood	Front	$2\frac{1}{2}$P–$3\frac{1}{2}$P	3P	①	②	$\frac{5}{32}$N–$\frac{5}{32}$P	NA
		Rear	—	—	$\frac{13}{16}$N–$\frac{3}{16}$P	$\frac{5}{16}$N	$\frac{3}{64}$N–$\frac{9}{64}$P	—
	Seville	Front	$1\frac{5}{16}$P–$3\frac{5}{16}$P	$2\frac{5}{16}$P	①	②	0–$\frac{3}{16}$P	$13\frac{5}{16}$
		Rear	—	—	$\frac{1}{2}$N–$\frac{1}{2}$P	0	0–$\frac{3}{16}$P	—
1993	Deville	Front	$2\frac{1}{2}$P–$3\frac{1}{2}$P	3P	①	②	$\frac{5}{32}$N–$\frac{5}{32}$P	NA
		Rear	—	—	$\frac{13}{16}$N–$\frac{3}{16}$P	$\frac{5}{16}$N	$\frac{3}{64}$N–$\frac{9}{64}$P	—
	Eldorado	Front	$1\frac{5}{16}$P–$3\frac{5}{16}$P	$2\frac{5}{16}$P	①	②	0–$\frac{3}{16}$P	$13\frac{5}{16}$
		Rear	—	—	$\frac{1}{2}$N–$\frac{1}{2}$P	0	0–$\frac{3}{16}$P	—
	Sixty Special	Front	$2\frac{1}{2}$P–$3\frac{1}{2}$P	3P	①	②	$\frac{5}{32}$N–$\frac{5}{32}$P	NA
		Rear	—	—	$\frac{13}{16}$N–$\frac{3}{16}$P	$\frac{5}{16}$N	$\frac{3}{64}$N–$\frac{9}{64}$P	—
	Seville	Front	$1\frac{5}{16}$P–$3\frac{5}{16}$P	$2\frac{5}{16}$P	①	②	0–$\frac{3}{16}$P	$13\frac{5}{16}$
		Rear	—	—	$\frac{1}{2}$N–$\frac{1}{2}$P	0	0–$\frac{3}{16}$P	—

① Left wheel: 1N–0
   Right wheel: 0–1P
② Left wheel: $\frac{1}{2}$N
   Right wheel: $\frac{1}{2}$P

84208130

REAR SUSPENSION

▶ See Figures 41, 42 and 43

Coil Springs

REMOVAL & INSTALLATION

Deville, Fleetwood and Sixty Special

▶ See Figures 44, 45, 46 and 47

1. Raise and safely support the vehicle so that the control arm hangs free.
2. Remove the wheel and tire assembly.
3. Remove the height sensor link from the right control arm and/or the parking brake cable retaining clip from the left control arm.
4. Remove the rear stabilizer bar from the bracket on the knuckle.
5. Position tool J-23028-01 or equivalent, to cradle the control arm bushings. Secure the tool to a suitable jack.

❋❋CAUTION

Tool J-23028-01 must be secured to a jack or personal injury may result.

6. Raise the jack to remove the tension from the control arm bolts.

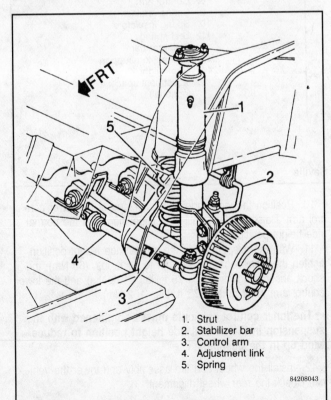

1. Strut
2. Stabilizer bar
3. Control arm
4. Adjustment link
5. Spring

84208043

Fig. 41 Rear suspension components — Fleetwood and Sixty Special

7. As a safety measure, place a chain around the spring and through the control arm.
8. Remove the pivot bolt, nut and washer, if equipped, from the rear of the control arm.
9. Slowly maneuver the jack to relieve tension in the front control arm pivot bolt. Remove the pivot bolt, nut and washer, if equipped, from the front of the control arm.
10. Lower the jack, allowing the control arm to pivot downward. When all compression is removed from the spring, remove the safety chain, spring and insulators.

➡**Do not apply force to the control arm and/or ball joint to remove the spring. The spring can be removed easily with proper maneuvering.**

To install:

11. Inspect the spring insulators and replace them if they are cut or torn. If the vehicle has been driven more than 50,000 miles, replace the insulators regardless of condition.
12. Snap the upper insulator onto the spring. Install the lower insulator and spring in the vehicle; refer to Figs. 47 or 48 for proper spring positioning.
13. Using tool J-23028-01 or equivalent, mounted on a suitable jack, raise the control arm into position.
14. Slowly maneuver the jack until the front and rear control arm pivot bolts and nuts can be installed.
15. Connect the rear stabilizer bar to the knuckle bracket with the link.
16. Install the height sensor link to the right control arm and/or the parking brake cable retaining clip to the left control arm.
17. Install the wheel and tire assembly and lower the vehicle.
18. When the vehicle is resting on its wheels, tighten the control arm nuts to 85 ft. lbs. (115 Nm) and the stabilizer bar link bolt to 13 ft. lbs. (17 Nm).

❋❋WARNING

The control arm nuts must be tightened with the vehicle unsupported and resting on its wheels at normal trim height. If not, ride and handling may be adversely affected.

Eldorado and Seville

1993

1. Raise and safely support the vehicle so that the control arm hangs free.
2. Remove the wheel and tire assembly.
3. Support the inner end of the lower control arm with a suitable jack. Position the jack to securely hold the control arm.
4. Disconnect the stabilizer bar and shock absorber from the lower control arm.
5. Remove the inner lower control arm nuts and bolts, then slowly lower the control arm to relieve the spring pressure.
6. Pull the lower control arm down and remove the coil spring.

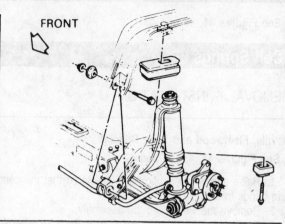

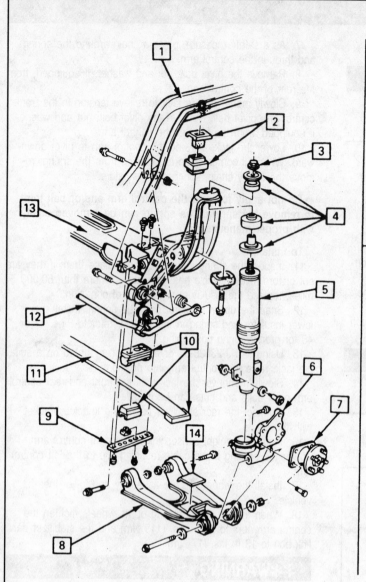

1. Underbody assembly
2. Suspension support insulators
3. Upper strut mounting nut
4. Strut mounting insulators
5. Strut
6. Knuckle
7. Hub and bearing assembly
8. Control arm
9. Spring retainer
10. Spring insulators
11. Leaf spring
12. Stabilizer bar
13. Suspension support
14. Trim height adjustment spacer (optional)

84208044

Fig. 42 Rear suspension components — 1990-92 Eldorado and Seville

To install:
7. Install the coil spring and insulators.

➡**To ensure the spring is installed in the proper position, rest the spring (without insulators) on a flat surface prior to installation. The spring will stand up straight when resting on its lower end, but will lean or tip over when resting on its top end.**

8. Raise the inner end of the lower control arm with the jack to slightly compress the coil spring. Install the inner lower control arm nuts and bolts.

9. Connect the shock absorber and stabilizer link to the lower control arm.

10. Position the jack under the outer end of the lower control arm. Raise the jack until the suspension is in the normal ride height position.

11. With the suspension in the normal ride height position, tighten the stabilizer link lower nut to 44 ft. lbs. (60 Nm), the shock absorber lower nut to 75 ft. lbs. (102 Nm) and the lower control arm inner nuts to 75 ft. lbs. (102 Nm).

➡**The inner control arm nuts must be tightened with the suspension in the normal ride height position to reduce wind up in the bushings.**

12. Install the wheel and tire assembly and lower the vehicle. Check the rear wheel alignment.

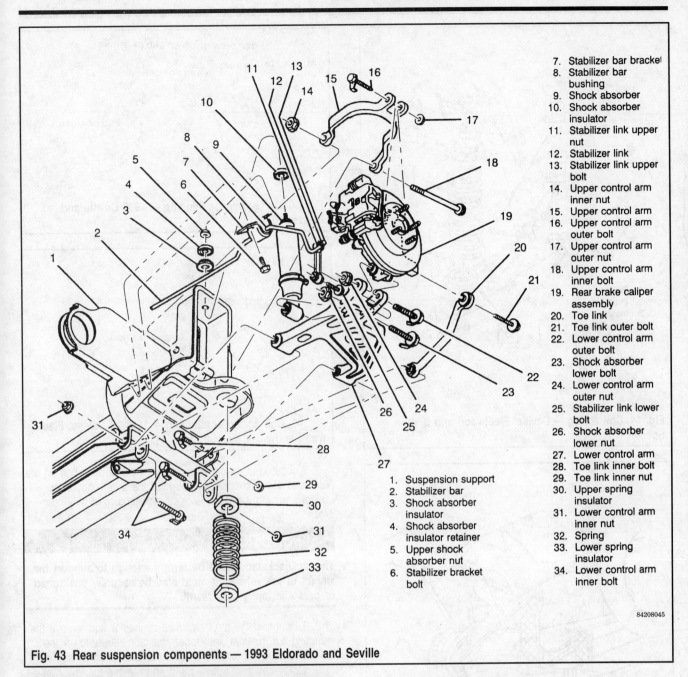

7. Stabilizer bar bracket
8. Stabilizer bar bushing
9. Shock absorber
10. Shock absorber insulator
11. Stabilizer link upper nut
12. Stabilizer link
13. Stabilizer link upper bolt
14. Upper control arm inner nut
15. Upper control arm
16. Upper control arm outer bolt
17. Upper control arm outer nut
18. Upper control arm inner bolt
19. Rear brake caliper assembly
20. Toe link
21. Toe link outer bolt
22. Lower control arm outer bolt
23. Shock absorber lower bolt
24. Lower control arm outer nut
25. Stabilizer link lower bolt
26. Shock absorber lower nut
27. Lower control arm
28. Toe link inner bolt
29. Toe link inner nut
30. Upper spring insulator
31. Lower control arm inner nut
32. Spring
33. Lower spring insulator
34. Lower control arm inner bolt

1. Suspension support
2. Stabilizer bar
3. Shock absorber insulator
4. Shock absorber insulator retainer
5. Upper shock absorber nut
6. Stabilizer bracket bolt

84208045

Fig. 43 Rear suspension components — 1993 Eldorado and Seville

Leaf Spring

REMOVAL & INSTALLATION

Eldorado and Seville

1990-92

▶ See Figures 48 and 49

➡Leaf spring removal requires disassembly of either the left or right suspension while leaving the other side intact. The spring can be removed from either side of the vehicle.

1. Raise and safely support the vehicle.
2. Remove the wheel and tire assembly.

3. If disassembling the left control arm, disconnect the electronic level control height sensor link.

4. If equipped with a stabilizer bar, remove the stabilizer bar mounting bolt at the strut.

5. Reinstall 2 lug nuts to hold the disc brake rotor on the hub and bearing assembly.

6. Remove the rear brake caliper as follows:

   a. Loosen the parking brake cable at the adjuster.

   b. Lift up on the end of the cable spring to free the end of the cable from the lever.

   c. Remove the bolt and washer attaching the cable support bracket to the caliper.

   d. Remove the caliper mounting bracket bolts and suspend the caliper in the wheelwell with wire. Do not disconnect the brake hose or allow the caliper to hang by the brake hose.

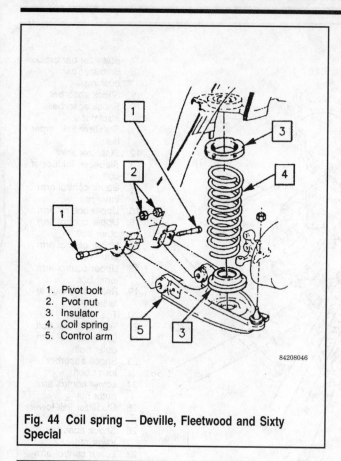

1. Pivot bolt
2. Pivot nut
3. Insulator
4. Coil spring
5. Control arm

84208046

Fig. 44 Coil spring — Deville, Fleetwood and Sixty Special

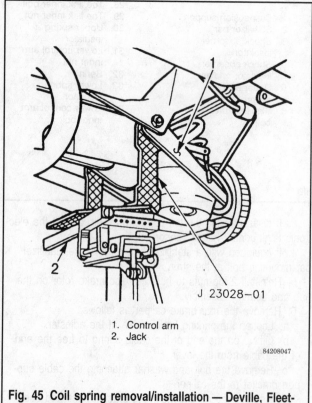

1. Control arm
2. Jack

J 23028-01

84208047

Fig. 45 Coil spring removal/installation — Deville, Fleetwood and Sixty Special

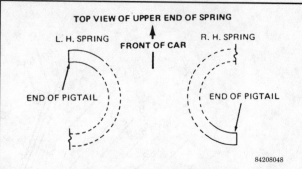

Fig. 46 Coil spring positioning — 1990 Deville and Fleetwood

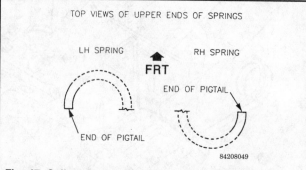

Fig. 47 Coil spring positioning — 1991-93 Deville, Fleetwood and Sixty Special

7. Loosen, but do not remove, the knuckle pivot bolt on the outer end of the control arm. Support the outer end of the control arm with a suitable jack or jackstand to slightly compress the spring.

✳✳CAUTION

The jack/jackstand must be strong enough to support the weight of the vehicle. It must also be securely positioned or personal injury may result.

8. Disconnect the strut electrical connector and remove the mounting nut, retainer and upper insulator. Slowly lower the jack or remove the jackstand to relieve the spring pressure.
9. Compress the strut by hand and remove the lower insulator. Disconnect the wheel speed sensor connector.
10. Remove the inner control arm nuts. Support the knuckle and control arm, then remove the inner control arm bolts and remove the control arm, knuckle, strut, hub and bearing and rotor from the vehicle as an assembly.
11. Place a jackstand under the outer end of the spring.

✳✳CAUTION

The jackstand must be strong enough to support the weight of the vehicle. It must also be securely positioned or personal injury may result.

12. Lower the vehicle so that the vehicle weight loads the spring downward on the jackstand. Remove the 3 spring retainer bolts, retainer and lower insulator from the retainer nearest the supported end of the spring.

13. Slowly raise the vehicle, allowing the spring to deflect downward until the spring no longer exerts force on the jackstand. Remove the jackstand.

14. Remove the spring retainer bolts, retainer and lower insulator from the retainer on the other side of the vehicle.

15. Remove the spring from the rear suspension support on the disassembled side of the vehicle. Remove the upper spring insulators, as required.

To install:

16. Inspect the spring insulators, insulator locating pads, retainers and the control arm contact pads on the ends of the spring for cuts, cracks, tears or other damage and replace as necessary.

17. Install the previously removed spring insulators. When installing the upper inner insulators, the molded arrow on the insulator must point toward the centerline of the car. Tighten the upper outer insulator nuts to 21 ft. lbs. (28 Nm).

18. Install the spring in the suspension support through the disassembled side of the vehicle.

✷✷WARNING

The outer insulator locating bands must be centered on the spring insulators when the spring is positioned in the suspension support. Vehicle handling may be impaired if the spring is not positioned correctly.

19. Install the lower insulator and spring retainer on the side of the vehicle that was not disassembled. Place a jackstand under the free end of the spring.

20. Lower the vehicle, allowing the vehicle weight to load the spring and deflect the free end of the spring into position in the suspension support.

21. Install the lower insulator and spring retainer on the disassembled side of the vehicle. Tighten the spring retainer bolts to 21 ft. lbs. (28 Nm).

22. Raise the vehicle and remove the jackstand.

23. Position the control arm, knuckle, strut, hub and bearing and rotor assembly in the suspension support. Install the inner control arm bolts and nuts but do not tighten at this time.

24. Connect the wheel speed sensor connector.

25. Install the lower strut insulator and position the strut in the suspension support assembly.

26. Position a jack or jackstand under the outer end of the lower control arm to slightly compress the spring.

✷✷CAUTION

The jack/jackstand must be strong enough to support the weight of the vehicle. It must also be securely positioned or personal injury may result.

27. Install the upper strut insulator, retainer and nut. Tighten the upper strut nut to 65 ft. lbs. (88 Nm), the knuckle pivot bolt to 59 ft. lbs. (80 Nm) and the inner control arm bolts to 66 ft. lbs. (90 Nm).

28. Connect the electrical connector at the top of the strut. Remove the jack or jackstand.

29. If equipped, install the stabilizer bar mounting bolt and tighten to 43 ft. lbs. (58 Nm).

30. Remove the 2 lug nuts that were installed to retain the rotor.

31. Install the caliper with new mounting bracket bolts. Tighten the mounting bracket bolts to 83 ft. lbs. (113 Nm). Install the parking brake cable support bracket and tighten the bolt to 32 ft. lbs. (43 Nm).

32. Lift up on the end of the cable spring clip and work the end of the parking brake cable into the notch on the lever. Adjust the parking brake as described in Section 9.

33. If assembling the left side of the suspension, connect the electronic level control height sensor link.

34. Install the wheel and tire assembly and lower the vehicle. Check the rear wheel alignment.

Shock Absorbers

REMOVAL & INSTALLATION

Eldorado and Seville

1993

▶ **See Figures 50 and 51**

1. Raise and safely support the vehicle.
2. Remove the wheel and tire assembly.
3. If equipped with 4.6L engine, disconnect the shock absorber electrical connector from the rear suspension support.
4. Support the lower control arm with a suitable jack to relieve the spring load.
5. Remove the shock absorber lower mounting nut and bolt.
6. If equipped with 4.9L engine, disconnect the electrical connector from the top of the shock absorber.

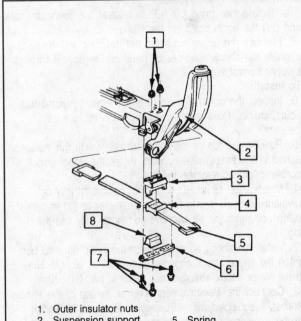

1. Outer insulator nuts
2. Suspension support
3. Upper outer insulator
4. Outer insulator locating band
5. Spring
6. Spring retainer
7. Retainer bolts
8. Lower outer insulator

84208050

Fig. 48 Leaf spring — 1990-92 Eldorado and Seville

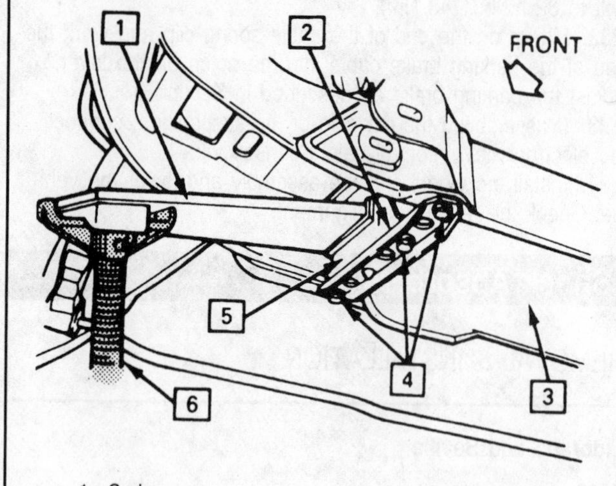

1. Spring
2. Spring retainer
3. Suspension support
4. Retainer bolts
5. Lower outer insulator
6. Jackstand

84208051

Fig. 49 Removing the leaf spring — 1990-92 Eldorado and Seville

7. Disconnect the air line from the shock absorber as follows:

a. Clean the connector and surrounding area to prevent dirt from entering the system.

b. Rotate the spring clip 90° to release the connector lock and pull the connector from the fitting.

8. Remove the upper mounting nut, retainer and insulator. Compress the shock absorber by hand and remove it through the upper control arm.

To install:

9. Inspect the upper and lower shock absorber insulators for cuts, cracks, tears or other damage and replace as necessary.

10. Position the top of the shock absorber with the insulator attached in the suspension support. Install the upper shock absorber insulator, retainer and nut.

11. Moisten the air line O-rings with petroleum jelly or equivalent lubricant, rotate the spring retainer to the engaged position and push the air line and connector fully into the fitting.

12. Install the shock absorber lower mounting nut and bolt. Tighten the upper shock absorber nut to 55 ft. lbs. (75 Nm) and the lower shock absorber nut to 75 ft. lbs. (102 Nm).

13. Connect the electrical connector at the top of the shock absorber, if equipped with 4.9L engine. Connect the shock absorber electrical connector to the rear suspension support, if equipped with 4.6L engine.

14. Install the wheel and tire assembly and lower the vehicle.

TESTING

Air-adjustable shock absorbers should be stroked before testing. When stored horizontally, an air pocket can form in the pressure chamber. An air pocket can also form when the shock is off the vehicle if it is not continuously held with the top end up.

To remove air from the pressure chamber, extend the shock absorber in a vertical position with the top end up, then collapse the shock absorber in a vertical position with the top end down. Repeat this procedure 5 times to make sure the air is purged from the pressure chamber.

Test the shock absorber as follows:

1. Clamp the shock absorber in a vise with the shock absorber upright, top end up. Do not clamp on the reservoir tube.

2. Pump the shock absorber by hand at various rates of speed and note the resistance.

3. Rebound resistance normally is stronger than compression resistance by about 2 to 1. The resistance should be smooth and constant for each stroking rate.

4. Compare the shock absorber with one that is known to be good.

5. It is normal to hear a hissing noise from the shock absorber. The following symptoms are abnormal and indicate replacement is necessary:

a. A skip or lag at reversal near mid-stroke.

b. A seize, except at either extreme end of travel.

c. A noise, such as a grunt or squeal, after completing one full stroke in both directions.

d. A clicking noise at fast reversal.

e. Fluid leakage.

MacPherson Struts

REMOVAL & INSTALLATION

Deville, Fleetwood and Sixty Special
▶ See Figures 51, 52 and 53

❈❈CAUTION

The control arm must be supported with a suitable jack to prevent the coil spring from forcing the control arm downward, causing component damage and possible bodily injury.

❈❈WARNING

To prevent ball joint damage, the knuckle must be restrained after the strut-to-knuckle bolts have been removed.

1. Raise and safely support the vehicle.
2. Remove the wheel and tire assembly.
3. Remove the trunk side cover.
4. Disconnect the electronic level control air line from the strut as follows:

a. Clean the connector and surrounding area to prevent dirt from entering the system.

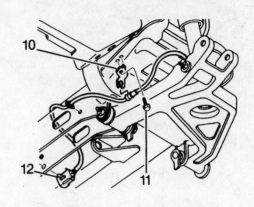

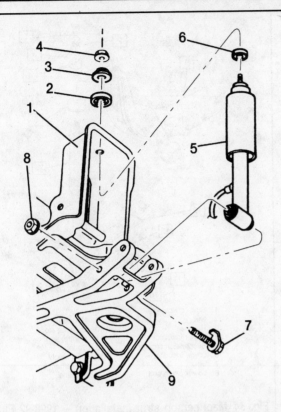

1. Suspension support
2. Upper shock absorber insulator
3. Shock absorber insulator retainer
4. Upper shock absorber nut
5. Shock absorber
6. Lower shock absorber insulator
7. Lower shock absorber bolt
8. Lower shock absorber nut
9. Lower control arm
10. Shock absorber wiring bracket
11. Shock absorber wiring bracket screw
12. Shock absorber wiring connector

84208052

Fig. 50 Shock absorber installation — 1993 Eldorado and Seville

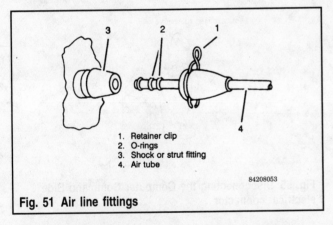

1. Retainer clip
2. O-rings
3. Shock or strut fitting
4. Air tube

84208053

Fig. 51 Air line fittings

b. Squeeze the spring clip to release the connector.

5. If equipped, disconnect the Computer Command Ride electrical connector.

6. Remove the strut tower mounting nuts from inside the trunk.

7. Remove the bolts, washers and nuts from the knuckle and stabilizer bar bracket and remove the strut.

To install:

8. Position the strut in the vehicle and install the upper mounting nuts.

➡ **If equipped with Computer Command Ride, make sure the strut wiring is upright and centered on the strut mount when positioning the strut. After the strut is installed, make sure the wiring is upright and clear of the spacer plate to tower interface.**

9. Install the strut-to-knuckle and stabilizer bar bracket bolts, washers and nuts. On 1992-93 vehicles, the bolts must be installed in the direction shown in Fig. 54.

10. Moisten the air line O-rings with petroleum jelly or equivalent lubricant, and push the air line and connector fully into the fitting.

11. If equipped with Computer Command Ride, connect the electrical connector to the harness.

12. Tighten the strut tower mounting nuts to 19 ft. lbs. (25 Nm) and the strut-to-knuckle nuts to 140 ft. lbs. (190 Nm).

13. Install the trunk side cover.

14. Lightly pressurize the electronic level control system by momentarily grounding the compressor test lead in the engine compartment. This must be done before lowering the vehicle.

15. Install the wheel and tire assembly and lower the vehicle. Check the rear wheel alignment.

Eldorado and Seville

1990-92

▶ **See Figures 51, 54 and 55**

1. Raise and safely support the vehicle.

2. Remove the wheel and tire assembly.

3. Disconnect the electronic level control height sensor link if removing the left strut.

4. Install 2 lug nuts to hold the rotor on the hub and bearing assembly.

5. If equipped with a stabilizer bar, remove the mounting bolt at the strut.

6. Remove the rear brake caliper as follows:

   a. Loosen the parking brake cable at the adjuster.

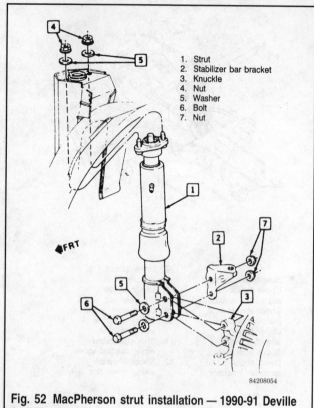

1. Strut
2. Stabilizer bar bracket
3. Knuckle
4. Nut
5. Washer
6. Bolt
7. Nut

◀FRT

84208054

Fig. 52 MacPherson strut installation — 1990-91 Deville and Fleetwood

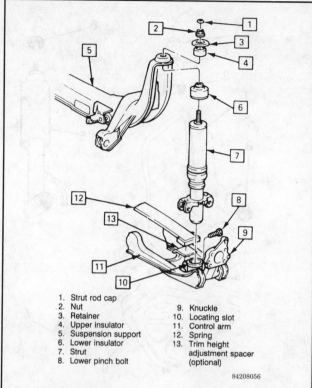

1. Strut rod cap
2. Nut
3. Retainer
4. Upper insulator
5. Suspension support
6. Lower insulator
7. Strut
8. Lower pinch bolt
9. Knuckle
10. Locating slot
11. Control arm
12. Spring
13. Trim height adjustment spacer (optional)

84208056

Fig. 54 MacPherson strut installation — 1990-92 Eldorado and Seville

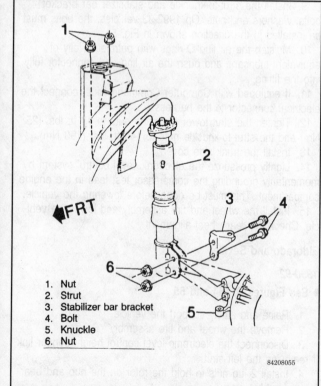

◀FRT

1. Nut
2. Strut
3. Stabilizer bar bracket
4. Bolt
5. Knuckle
6. Nut

84208055

Fig. 53 MacPherson strut installation — 1992-93 Deville, Fleetwood and Sixty Special

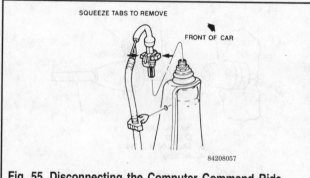

SQUEEZE TABS TO REMOVE

FRONT OF CAR

84208057

Fig. 55 Disconnecting the Computer Command Ride electrical connector

b. Lift up on the end of the cable spring to free the end of the cable from the lever.

c. Remove the bolt and washer attaching the cable support bracket to the caliper.

d. Remove the caliper mounting bracket bolts and suspend the caliper in the wheelwell with wire. Do not disconnect the brake hose or allow the caliper to hang by the brake hose.

7. Loosen, but do not remove, the knuckle pivot bolt on the outer end of the control arm. Support the outer end of the

control arm with a suitable jack or jackstand to slightly compress the spring.

❋❋CAUTION

The jack/jackstand must be strong enough to support the weight of the vehicle. It must also be securely positioned or personal injury may result.

8. If equipped, disconnect the Computer Command Ride electrical connector at the top of the strut.

9. Disconnect the air line from the strut as follows:

a. Clean the connector and surrounding area to prevent dirt from entering the system.

b. Rotate the spring clip 90° to release the connector lock and pull the connector from the fitting.

10. Remove the upper strut rod cap, mounting nut, retainer and insulator. Slowly lower the jack or remove the jackstand to relieve the spring pressure.

11. Compress the strut by hand and remove the lower insulator. Rotate the strut and knuckle assembly outward by pivoting on the knuckle pivot bolt.

12. Remove the knuckle pinch bolt and remove the strut from the knuckle.

To install:

13. Inspect the upper and lower strut insulators for cuts, cracks, tears or other damage and replace as necessary.

14. Position the strut so it is fully seated in the knuckle with the tang on the strut bottomed in the knuckle slot. Install the knuckle pinch bolt and tighten to 40 ft. lbs. (55 Nm).

15. Install the lower insulator on the strut and position the strut rod in the suspension support.

16. Position a jack or jackstand under the outer end of the lower control arm to slightly compress the spring.

❋❋CAUTION

The jack/jackstand must be strong enough to support the weight of the vehicle. It must also be securely positioned or personal injury may result.

17. Install the upper strut insulator, retainer and nut. Tighten the upper strut nut to 65 ft. lbs. (88 Nm) and the knuckle pivot bolt to 59 ft. lbs. (80 Nm). Remove the jack or jackstand.

18. Moisten the air line O-rings with petroleum jelly or equivalent lubricant, rotate the spring retainer to the engaged position and push the air line and connector fully into the fitting.

19. If equipped, connect the Computer Command Ride electrical connector at the top of the strut.

20. If equipped with a stabilizer bar, install the mounting bolt and tighten to 43 ft. lbs. (58 Nm).

21. Install the caliper with new mounting bracket bolts. Tighten the mounting bracket bolts to 83 ft. lbs. (113 Nm). Install the parking brake cable support bracket and tighten the bolt to 32 ft. lbs. (43 Nm).

22. Lift up on the end of the cable spring clip and work the end of the parking brake cable into the notch on the lever. Adjust the parking brake as described in Section 9.

23. If installing the left strut, connect the electronic level control height sensor link.

24. Remove the 2 lug nuts that were installed to retain the rotor.

25. Install the wheel and tire assembly and lower the vehicle.

Control Arms/Links

REMOVAL & INSTALLATION

Deville, Fleetwood and Sixty Special

CONTROL ARM

▶ See Figure 56

1. Raise and safely support the vehicle.

2. Remove the wheel and tire assembly.

3. Remove the height sensor link from the right control arm and/or the parking brake cable retaining clip from the left control arm.

4. Remove the suspension adjustment link retaining nut and separate the link assembly from the control arm.

5. Remove the coil spring as described in this Section.

6. Remove the cotter pin and nut from the ball joint stud. Turn the nut over and install with the flat portion facing upward. Do not tighten the nut.

7. Use tool J-34505 or equivalent, on 1990 vehicles or tool J-36226 or equivalent, on 1991-93 vehicles, to separate the knuckle from the ball joint. Remove the nut from the ball joint stud.

8. Remove the control arm.

To install:

9. Position the control arm ball joint stud in the knuckle and install a new nut.

10. On 1990-91 vehicles, tighten the nut to 88 inch lbs. (10 Nm), then tighten an additional 2/3 turn.

11. On 1992-93 vehicles, tighten the nut to 88 inch lbs. (10 Nm), then tighten an additional 4 flats of the nut; the torque should be 40 ft. lbs. (55 Nm) minimum. On 1992-93 vehicles with heavy duty chassis and RPO J55 brake option, tighten the nut 2½ flats; the torque should be 99 ft. lbs. (135 Nm) minimum.

➡**It may be necessary to partially load the ball joint to keep the ball stud from rotating while the nut is tightened.**

12. Install a new cotter pin. If the hole in the ball stud does not align with the slot in the nut, tighten the nut to allow cotter pin installation. NEVER loosen the nut to align the hole and the slot.

13. Install the coil spring as described in this Section.

14. Attach the adjustment link to the control arm with the nut. Tighten the nut to 63 ft. lbs. (85 Nm).

15. Install the height sensor link to the right control arm and/or the parking brake cable retaining clip to the left control arm.

16. Install the wheel and tire assembly and lower the vehicle.

17. After the vehicle has been lowered and is resting on the wheels at normal trim height, tighten the control arm nuts to

85 ft. lbs. (115 Nm) and the stabilizer bar link bolt to 13 ft. lbs. (17 Nm).

> ## ❋❋WARNING
>
> The control arm nuts must be tightened with the wheels on the ground and the vehicle at normal trim height. Failure to do so may adversely affect ride and handling.

18. Lubricate the ball joint and inner link joint with suitable chassis lubricant.

ADJUSTMENT LINK

▶ See Figure 57

1. Raise and safely support the vehicle.
2. Remove the wheel and tire assembly.
3. Remove the cotter pin and nut, then separate the link from the knuckle using tool J-24319-01 or equivalent.

> ## ❋❋WARNING
>
> Do not try to disengage the link by driving a wedge between the joint and the attached part, as seal damage may result.

4. Remove the link retaining nut and remove the link from the control arm.

To install:

5. Attach the link to the control arm with the retaining nut.
6. Attach the link to the knuckle and install the nut. On the left side link, position the boot towards the front of the vehicle.

7. Tighten the link-to-control arm nut to 63 ft. lbs. (85 Nm) and the link-to-knuckle nut to 33 ft. lbs. (45 Nm).
8. After tightening the link-to-knuckle nut, install a new cotter pin. If the hole in the ball stud does not align with the slot in the nut, tighten the nut to allow cotter pin installation. NEVER loosen the nut to align the hole and the slot.
9. Lubricate the inner and outer link joints with a suitable chassis lubricant.
10. Install the wheel and tire assembly and lower the vehicle. Check the rear wheel alignment.

1990-92 Eldorado and Seville

CONTROL ARM

▶ See Figure 58

1. Raise and safely support the vehicle.
2. Remove the wheel and tire assembly.
3. If disassembling the left control arm, disconnect the electronic level control height sensor link.
4. If equipped with a stabilizer bar, remove the stabilizer bar mounting bolt at the strut.
5. Reinstall 2 lug nuts to hold the disc brake rotor on the hub and bearing assembly.
6. Remove the rear brake caliper as follows:

   a. Loosen the parking brake cable at the adjuster.

   b. Lift up on the end of the cable spring to free the end of the cable from the lever.

   c. Remove the bolt and washer attaching the cable support bracket to the caliper.

   d. Remove the caliper mounting bracket bolts and suspend the caliper in the wheelwell with wire. Do not discon-

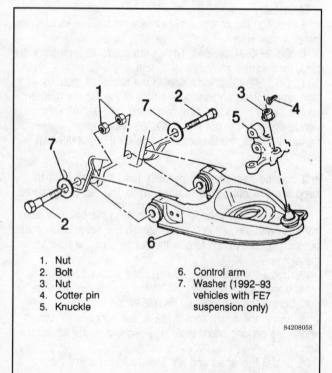

1. Nut	6. Control arm
2. Bolt	7. Washer (1992-93
3. Nut	vehicles with FE7
4. Cotter pin	suspension only)
5. Knuckle	

84208058

Fig. 56 Control arm installation — Deville, Fleetwood and Sixty Special

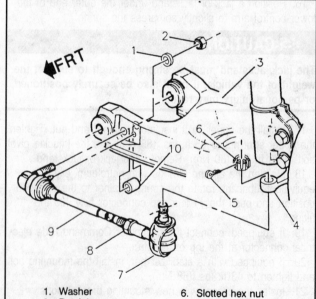

1. Washer	6. Slotted hex nut
2. Retaining nut	7. Boot, left side only
3. Control arm	8. Nut
4. Knuckle	9. Adjustment link
5. Cotter pin	10. Spacer

84208059

Fig. 57 Adjustment link installation — Deville, Fleetwood and Sixty Special

nect the brake hose or allow the caliper to hang by the brake hose.

7. Loosen, but do not remove, the knuckle pivot bolt on the outer end of the control arm. Support the outer end of the control arm with a suitable jack or jackstand to slightly compress the spring.

❋❋CAUTION

The jack/jackstand must be strong enough to support the weight of the vehicle. It must also be securely positioned or personal injury may result.

8. Disconnect the strut electrical connector and remove the mounting nut, retainer and upper insulator. Slowly lower the jack or remove the jackstand to relieve the spring pressure.

9. Compress the strut by hand and remove the lower insulator. Disconnect the wheel speed sensor connector.

10. While supporting the knuckle, remove the knuckle pivot bolt and remove the knuckle, strut, hub and bearing and rotor from the vehicle as an assembly.

11. Remove both inner control arm bolts and remove the control arm from the vehicle.

To install:

12. Position the control arm in the vehicle and install both inner control arm bolts. Do not tighten the bolts at this time.

13. Position the assembled knuckle, strut, hub and bearing and rotor assembly in the control arm and install the knuckle pivot bolt. Do not tighten the bolt at this time.

14. Connect the wheel speed sensor connector.

15. Install the lower strut insulator and position the strut in the suspension support assembly.

16. Position a jack or jackstand under the outer end of the lower control arm to slightly compress the spring.

❋❋CAUTION

The jack/jackstand must be strong enough to support the weight of the vehicle. It must also be securely positioned or personal injury may result.

17. Install the upper strut insulator, retainer and nut. Tighten the upper strut nut to 65 ft. lbs. (88 Nm), the knuckle pivot bolt to 59 ft. lbs. (80 Nm) and the inner control arm bolts to 66 ft. lbs. (90 Nm).

18. Connect the electrical connector at the top of the strut. Remove the jack or jackstand.

19. If equipped, install the stabilizer bar mounting bolt and tighten to 43 ft. lbs. (58 Nm).

20. Remove the 2 lug nuts that were installed to retain the rotor.

21. Install the caliper with new mounting bracket bolts. Tighten the mounting bracket bolts to 83 ft. lbs. (113 Nm). Install the parking brake cable support bracket and tighten the bolt to 32 ft. lbs. (43 Nm).

22. Lift up on the end of the cable spring clip and work the end of the parking brake cable into the notch on the lever. Adjust the parking brake as described in Section 9.

23. If installing the left control arm, connect the electronic level control height sensor link.

24. Install the wheel and tire assembly and lower the vehicle. Check the rear wheel alignment.

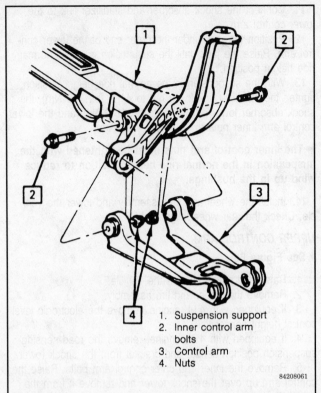

1. Suspension support
2. Inner control arm bolts
3. Control arm
4. Nuts

84208061

Fig. 58 Control arm installation — 1990-92 Eldorado and Seville

1993 Eldorado and Seville

LOWER CONTROL ARM

▶ See Figure 59

1. Raise and safely support the vehicle so that the control arm hangs free.

2. Remove the wheel and tire assembly.

3. Support the inner end of the lower control arm with a suitable jack. Position the jack to securely hold the control arm.

4. Disconnect the stabilizer bar and shock absorber from the lower control arm.

5. Remove the inner lower control arm nuts and bolts, then slowly lower the control arm to relieve the spring pressure.

6. Pull the lower control arm down and remove the coil spring.

7. Remove the lower control arm outer bolt and remove the lower control arm.

To install:

8. Position the lower control arm in the vehicle and install the outer bolt and nut. Tighten the nut to 75 ft. lbs. (102 Nm).

9. Install the coil spring and insulators.

➡**To ensure the spring is installed in the proper position, rest the spring (without insulators) on a flat surface prior to installation. The spring will stand up straight when resting on its lower end, but will lean or tip over when resting on its top end.**

10. Raise the inner end of the lower control arm with the jack to slightly compress the coil spring. Install the inner lower control arm nuts and bolts.

11. Connect the shock absorber and stabilizer link to the lower control arm.

12. Position the jack under the outer end of the lower control arm. Raise the jack until the suspension is in the normal ride height position.

13. With the suspension in the normal ride height position, tighten the stabilizer link lower nut to 44 ft. lbs. (60 Nm), the shock absorber lower nut to 75 ft. lbs. (102 Nm) and the lower control arm inner nuts to 75 ft. lbs. (102 Nm).

➡**The inner control arm nuts must be tightened with the suspension in the normal ride height position to reduce wind up in the bushings.**

14. Install the wheel and tire assembly and lower the vehicle. Check the rear wheel alignment.

UPPER CONTROL ARM

▶ **See Figure 60**

1. Raise and safely support the vehicle.
2. Remove the wheel and tire assembly.
3. If equipped with 4.9L engine, remove the electronic level control height sensor link.
4. If equipped with 4.6L engine, remove the road sensing suspension position sensor and bracket from the shock tower.
5. Remove the inner and outer control arm bolts. Raise the control arm up over the shock tower and remove it from the vehicle.

To install:

6. Lower the control arm over the shock tower and position it in the vehicle. Install the inner and outer control arm bolts.

7. Position a suitable jack under the outer end of the lower control arm. Raise the suspension with the jack until it is in the normal ride height position, then tighten the upper control arm inner and outer nuts to 42 ft. lbs. (57 Nm).

✳✳WARNING

The inner control arm nuts must be tightened with the suspension in the normal ride height position to reduce wind up in the bushings.

8. If equipped with 4.6L engine, install the road sensing suspension position sensor and bracket to the shock tower.
9. If equipped with 4.9L engine, install the electronic level control height sensor link.
10. Install the wheel and tire assembly and lower the vehicle.

TOE LINK

▶ **See Figure 61**

1. Raise and safely support the vehicle.
2. Remove the wheel and tire assembly.
3. Remove and discard the toe link bolt from the knuckle. Do not reuse the bolt.
4. Remove the toe link-to-suspension support bolt and nut and the toe link.

To install:

5. Position the toe link and install the toe link-to-suspension support bolt and nut. Do not tighten at this time.
6. Install a new toe link outer bolt, but do not tighten at this time.

1. Suspension support
2. Lower control arm
3. Inner nut
4. Inner bolt

84208062

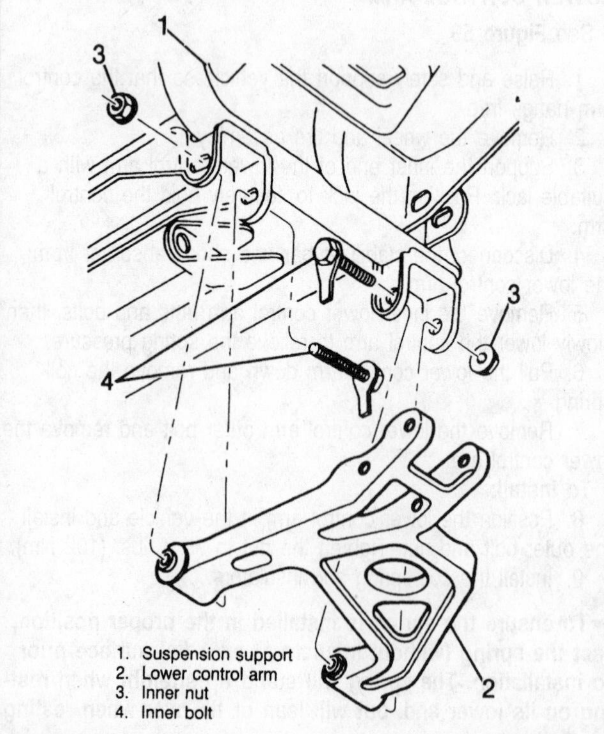

Fig. 59 Lower control arm installation — 1993 Eldorado and Seville

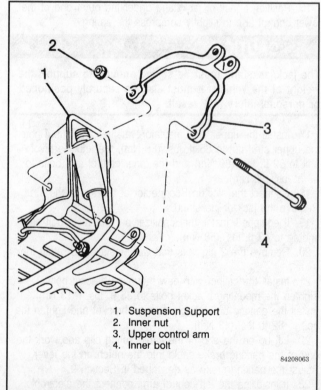

1. Suspension Support
2. Inner nut
3. Upper control arm
4. Inner bolt

84208063

Fig. 60 Upper control arm installation — 1993 Eldorado and Seville

7. Position a suitable jack under the outer end of the lower control arm. Raise the suspension with the jack until it is in the normal ride height position, then tighten the outer toe link bolt to 55 ft. lbs. (75 Nm) and the inner toe link nut to 42 ft. lbs. (57 Nm).

✳✳WARNING

The toe link must be tightened with the suspension in the normal ride height position to reduce wind up in the bushings.

8. Install the wheel and tire assembly and lower the vehicle. Check the rear wheel alignment.

Stabilizer Bar

REMOVAL & INSTALLATION

Deville, Fleetwood and Sixty Special
▶ See Figure 62

1. Raise and safely support the vehicle.
2. Remove the rear wheel and tire assemblies.
3. Remove the stabilizer bar link bolt, nut, retainer and bushings from the stabilizer bar bracket.
4. Remove the link bolt and bend the open end of the link downward.
5. Remove the stabilizer bar and bushings.

To install:
6. Install the stabilizer bar and bushings. Install the bushing into the link with the slit facing the rear of the vehicle.
7. Bend the link upward to close around the bushing and install the link bolt.
8. Install the link bushings, retainers, support bolt and nut.
9. Tighten the link nut to 13 ft. lbs. (17 Nm) and the link bolt to 37 ft. lbs. (50 Nm) on 1990-91 vehicles or 17 ft. lbs. (23 Nm) on 1992-93 vehicles.

Eldorado and Seville

1990-92

▶ See Figure 63

➡It is easier to remove and install the stabilizer bar with the vehicle on the ground and supported by the wheels. If it is necessary to raise the vehicle for stabilizer bar REMOVAL & installation, use drive-on ramps or support the control arms as far outboard as possible with jacks.

1. Raise and safely support the vehicle.
2. Remove the stabilizer bar attaching nut and bolt at the strut.
3. Remove the stabilizer link bolt and nut at the suspension support.
4. Remove the stabilizer bar from the vehicle. Remove the stabilizer link and bushings, if required.

To install:
5. Inspect the bushings for cuts, cracks or tears and replace as necessary.
6. Install the bushings and links on the stabilizer bar.

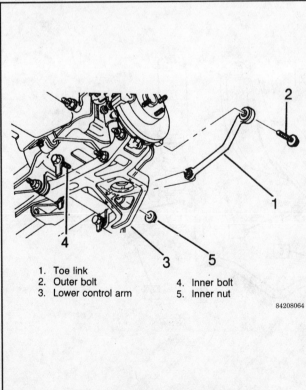

1. Toe link
2. Outer bolt
3. Lower control arm
4. Inner bolt
5. Inner nut

84208064

Fig. 61 Toe link installation — 1993 Eldorado and Seville

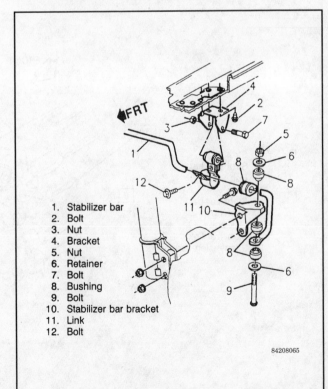

1. Stabilizer bar
2. Bolt
3. Nut
4. Bracket
5. Nut
6. Retainer
7. Bolt
8. Bushing
9. Bolt
10. Stabilizer bar bracket
11. Link
12. Bolt

84208065

Fig. 62 Stabilizer bar installation — Deville, Fleetwood and Sixty Special

7. Position the stabilizer bar in the vehicle and install the bolts and nuts at the suspension support and strut.

8. Tighten the link bolt and stabilizer mounting nuts to 43 ft. lbs. (58 Nm).

1993

▶ See Figure 64

1. Raise and safely support the vehicle.

2. Remove the rear wheel and tire assemblies.

3. Remove the stabilizer link lower bolt and upper nut on both sides of the vehicle.

4. Remove the stabilizer brackets and remove the bushings from the stabilizer bar.

5. Lower and support the exhaust system at the rear of the vehicle.

6. Remove the stabilizer bar.

To install:

7. Position the stabilizer bar in the vehicle.

8. Raise the exhaust system into position and secure.

9. Position the bushings on the stabilizer bar and install the brackets.

10. Install the link upper nuts and lower bolts. Tighten the upper link nut to 38 ft. lbs. (52 Nm) and the lower link bolt to 44 ft. lbs. (60 Nm).

11. Tighten the stabilizer bracket bolt to 44 ft. lbs. (60 Nm).

12. Install the wheel and tire assembly and lower the vehicle.

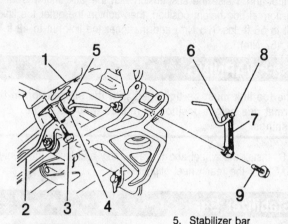

1. Suspension support
2. Stabilizer bar
3. Stabilizer bracket bolt
4. Stabilizer bar bracket
5. Stabilizer bar bushing
6. Link upper nut
7. Stabilizer link
8. Link upper bolt
9. Link lower bolt

84208067

Fig. 64 Stabilizer bar installation — 1993 Eldorado and Seville

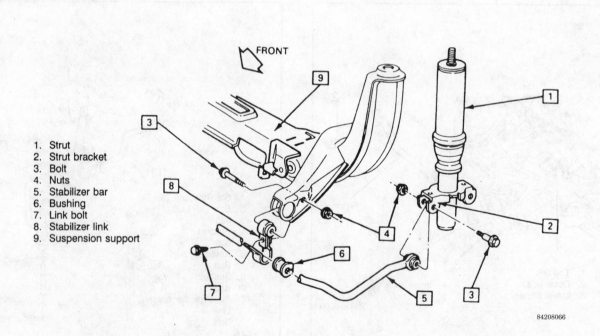

FRONT

1. Strut
2. Strut bracket
3. Bolt
4. Nuts
5. Stabilizer bar
6. Bushing
7. Link bolt
8. Stabilizer link
9. Suspension support

84208066

Fig. 63 Stabilizer bar installation — 1990-92 Eldorado and Seville

Rear Hub and Bearing

REMOVAL & INSTALLATION

Deville, Fleetwood and Sixty Special

▶ See Figure 65

1. Raise and safely support the vehicle.
2. Remove the wheel and tire assembly.
3. Remove the brake drum.
4. Remove the retaining bolts and remove the hub and bearing assembly from the axle. If equipped with anti-lock brakes, be careful working around the sensor wires; disconnect them as needed.

✳✳WARNING

The bolts that attach the hub and bearing also support the brake assembly. When the bolts are removed, the brake assembly must be supported with wire or other means. Do not let the brake assembly hang by the brake line or anti-lock brake electrical wire.

To install:

5. Install the hub and bearing assembly with the retaining bolts. Tighten the bolts to 52 ft. lbs. (70 Nm).
6. Reconnect the anti-lock brake sensor wire, as necessary.
7. Install the brake drum.
8. Install the wheel and tire assembly and lower the vehicle.

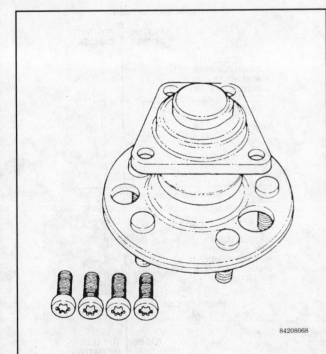

84208068

Fig. 65 Hub and bearing assembly — Deville, Fleetwood and Sixty Special

Eldorado and Seville

1990-92

▶ See Figure 66

1. Raise and safely support the vehicle.
2. Remove the wheel and tire assembly.
3. Remove the rear brake caliper as follows:
   a. Loosen the parking brake cable at the adjuster.
   b. Lift up on the end of the cable spring to free the end of the cable from the lever.
   c. Remove the bolt and washer attaching the cable support bracket to the caliper.
   d. Remove the caliper mounting bracket bolts and suspend the caliper in the wheelwell with wire. Do not disconnect the brake hose or allow the caliper to hang by the brake hose.
4. If equipped, remove and discard the disc brake rotor retainers. Remove the disc brake rotor.
5. Remove the hub mounting bolts and remove the hub and bearing assembly.

To install:

6. Position the hub and bearing assembly on the knuckle and install the mounting bolts. Tighten to 52 ft. lbs. (70 Nm).
7. Install the disc brake rotor.
8. Install the caliper with new mounting bracket bolts. Tighten the mounting bracket bolts to 83 ft. lbs. (113 Nm). Install the parking brake cable support bracket and tighten the bolt to 32 ft. lbs. (43 Nm).
9. Lift up on the end of the cable spring clip and work the end of the parking brake cable into the notch on the lever. Adjust the parking brake as described in Section 9.
10. Install the wheel and tire assembly and lower the vehicle.

1993

1. Raise and safely support the vehicle.
2. Remove the wheel and tire assembly.
3. Remove the parking brake cable bracket from the knuckle.
4. Remove and discard the caliper mounting bracket bolts. Remove the caliper and suspend it in the wheelwell with wire. Do not disconnect the brake hose or allow the caliper to hang by the brake hose.
5. Remove the disc brake rotor.
6. Remove the hub mounting bolts and remove the hub and bearing assembly.

To install:

7. Install the hub and bearing assembly and tighten the mounting bolts to 52 ft. lbs. (70 Nm).
8. Install the disc brake rotor.
9. Install the caliper with new mounting bracket bolts. Tighten the mounting bracket bolts to 83 ft. lbs. (113 Nm). Install the parking brake cable bracket and tighten the bolt to 32 ft. lbs. (43 Nm).
10. Install the wheel and tire assembly and lower the vehicle.

Rear Wheel Alignment

Wheel alignment is the angular relationship between the wheels and suspension components and the ground. The ac-

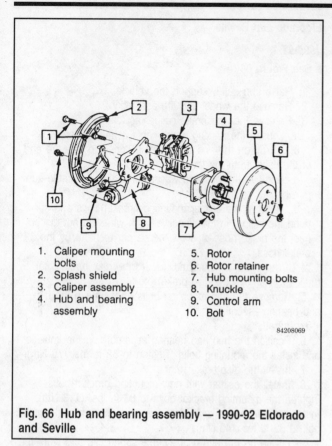

1. Caliper mounting bolts
2. Splash shield
3. Caliper assembly
4. Hub and bearing assembly
5. Rotor
6. Rotor retainer
7. Hub mounting bolts
8. Knuckle
9. Control arm
10. Bolt

84208069

Fig. 66 Hub and bearing assembly — 1990-92 Eldorado and Seville

curate alignment of these components is critical to proper vehicle tracking and to tire tread life.

Camber and toe adjustments can be made to the rear suspension on Deville, Fleetwood, Sixty Special and 1993 Eldorado and Seville. Only the toe is adjustable on 1990-92 Eldorado and Seville rear suspensions. When adjustments are made, the alignment should be precisely set to the specifications shown in the chart in this Section.

CAMBER

▶ **See Figures 67 and 68**

Camber is the amount the wheels tilt inward or outward from the vertical, when viewed from the front or rear of the vehicle. If the wheels tilt outward at the top, the camber is "positive". If the wheels tilt inward at the top, the camber is "negative". The amount of tilt is measured in degrees from vertical.

On Deville, Fleetwood and Sixty Special, the camber adjustment is made by loosening the strut-to-knuckle bolts and changing the position of the knuckle in relation to the strut; tool J-29682 or equivalent, is required to make the adjustment. On 1993 Eldorado and Seville, the camber adjustment is made by loosening the lower control arm inner bolts and moving the lower control arm.

TOE

▶ **See Figures 67, 68 and 69**

Toe is a measurement of how much the front of the wheels are turned in or out from a straight-ahead position. When the wheels are turned in, toe is "positive". When the wheels are turned out, toe is "negative". The amount of toe is normally only a fraction of a degree.

Toe functions to ensure that the wheels roll parallel. It also serves to offset the small deflections of the wheel support system that occur when the vehicle is rolling forward. Due to suspension and engine loading, the wheels tend to roll parallel when the vehicle is moving even though they are set to toe in or out slightly when the vehicle is standing still. Incorrect toe will cause abnormal tire wear.

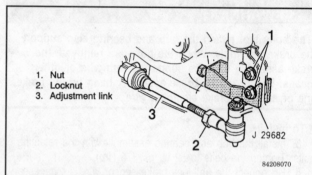

1. Nut
2. Locknut
3. Adjustment link

J 29682

84208070

Fig. 67 Rear camber and toe adjustment — Deville, Fleetwood and Sixty Special

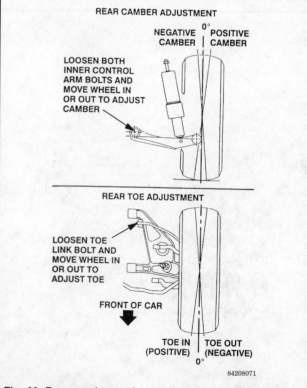

REAR CAMBER ADJUSTMENT

NEGATIVE CAMBER   0°   POSITIVE CAMBER

LOOSEN BOTH INNER CONTROL ARM BOLTS AND MOVE WHEEL IN OR OUT TO ADJUST CAMBER

REAR TOE ADJUSTMENT

LOOSEN TOE LINK BOLT AND MOVE WHEEL IN OR OUT TO ADJUST TOE

FRONT OF CAR

TOE IN (POSITIVE)   0°   TOE OUT (NEGATIVE)

84208071

Fig. 68 Rear camber and toe adjustment — 1993 Eldorado and Seville

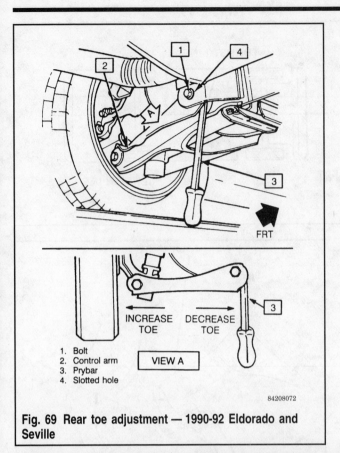

INCREASE TOE   DECREASE TOE

1. Bolt
2. Control arm
3. Prybar
4. Slotted hole

VIEW A

84208072

Fig. 69 Rear toe adjustment — 1990-92 Eldorado and Seville

On Deville, Fleetwood and Sixty Special, toe is adjusted by loosening the locknuts on the adjustment links and turning the inner link. On 1990-92 Eldorado and Seville, toe is adjusted by loosening the inner control arm bolts and prying between the rear inner bolt and the rear support assembly, to move the control arm. On 1993 Eldorado and Seville, the toe adjustment is made by loosening the inner toe link bolts and prying between the inner rear toe link bolt and the rear support assembly.

THRUST ANGLE

▶ See Figure 70

The thrust angle is the path the rear wheels will take. If the rear wheel path is the same as the path of the vehicle, the thrust angle is zero. Ideally, the thrust angle should be aligned perfectly with the centerline of the vehicle.

STEERING

Steering Wheel

REMOVAL & INSTALLATION

▶ See Figures 71, 72 and 73

> ❊❊CAUTION
>
> **When performing service around Supplemental Inflatable Restraint (SIR) system components or wiring, the SIR system must be disabled. Failure to do so could result in possible air bag deployment, personal injury or unneeded SIR system repairs.**

1. Disable the SIR system as follows:
   a. Disconnect the negative battery cable.
   b. Turn the ignition switch **OFF**.
   c. Remove the SIR fuse. On 1990 Deville and Fleetwood, remove SIR fuse No. 3 from the fuse panel. On 1991-93 Deville, Fleetwood and Sixty Special, remove SIR fuse No. 18 from the fuse panel. On 1990-91 Eldorado and Seville, remove SIR fuse No. 19 from the fuse panel. On 1992-93 Eldorado and Seville, remove SIR fuse No. A11 from the engine compartment fuse panel.

   d. On Deville, Fleetwood and Sixty Special, remove the left lower sound insulator. On Eldorado and Seville, remove the left side sound insulator.
   e. Remove the Connector Position Assurance (CPA) and disconnect the yellow 2-way connector at the base of the steering column.
2. Remove the bolts/screws from the back of the steering wheel and remove the inflator module.
3. Remove the horn contact by pushing slightly and twisting counterclockwise. Disconnect the electrical connectors from the inflator module.

> ❊❊CAUTION
>
> **When carrying a live inflator module, make sure that the bag and trim cover are pointed away from you. Never carry the inflator module by the wires or connector on the underside of the module. In case of accidental deployment, the bag will then deploy with minimal chance of injury. When placing a live inflator module on a bench or other surface, always face the bag and trim cover up, away from the surface.**

4. Remove the steering column shaft nut. If not already marked, mark the steering wheel and steering column shaft to ensure proper alignment during installation.
5. Remove the steering wheel using steering wheel puller J-1859-03 or equivalent.

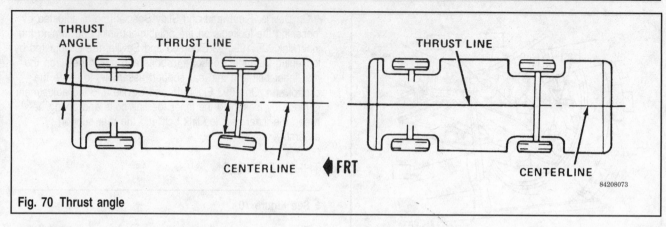

Fig. 70 Thrust angle

To install:

6. Feed the SIR coil assembly lead through the slot in the steering wheel. Align the mark on the steering wheel with the mark on the steering column shaft and install the steering wheel.

7. Install the steering column shaft nut and tighten to 30 ft. lbs. (41 Nm).

8. Install the horn contact to the steering column.

9. Connect the electrical connectors to the inflator module. Position the inflator module on the steering wheel taking care to ensure no wires are pinched.

10. Install the inflator module retaining bolts/screws and tighten to 27 inch lbs. (3 Nm).

11. Enable the SIR system as follows:

a. Connect the yellow 2-way connector at the base of the steering column and install the CPA.

b. On Deville, Fleetwood and Sixty Special, install the left lower sound insulator. On Eldorado and Seville, install the left side sound insulator.

c. Install the SIR fuse.

d. Connect the negative battery cable.

e. Turn the ignition switch to **RUN**. Verify that the "INFLATABLE RESTRAINT" indicator light flashes 7-9 and then remains OFF. If the light does not function as specified, there is a fault in the SIR system.

Turn Signal (Combination) Switch

▶ See Figures 74, 75, 76, 77, 78, 79, 80, 81 and 82

REMOVAL & INSTALLATION

❋❋CAUTION

When performing service around Supplemental Inflatable Restraint (SIR) system components or wiring, the SIR system must be disabled. Failure to do so could result in possible air bag deployment, personal injury or unneeded SIR system repairs.

1. Disable the SIR system as follows:

a. Disconnect the negative battery cable.

b. Turn the ignition switch **OFF**.

c. Remove the SIR fuse. On 1990 Deville and Fleetwood, remove SIR fuse No. 3 from the fuse panel. On 1991-93

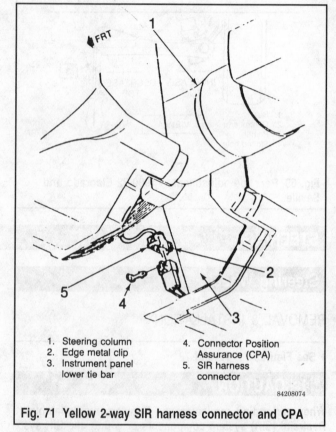

1. Steering column
2. Edge metal clip
3. Instrument panel lower tie bar
4. Connector Position Assurance (CPA)
5. SIR harness connector

Fig. 71 Yellow 2-way SIR harness connector and CPA

Deville, Fleetwood and Sixty Special, remove SIR fuse No. 18 from the fuse panel. On 1990-91 Eldorado and Seville, remove SIR fuse No. 19 from the fuse panel. On 1992-93 Eldorado and Seville, remove SIR fuse No. A11 from the engine compartment fuse panel.

d. On Deville, Fleetwood and Sixty Special, remove the left lower sound insulator. On Eldorado and Seville, remove the left side sound insulator.

e. Remove the Connector Position Assurance (CPA) and disconnect the yellow 2-way connector at the base of the steering column.

2. Remove the steering wheel as described in this Section.

3. Make sure the ignition switch is in the **LOCK** position to prevent uncentering the SIR coil assembly.

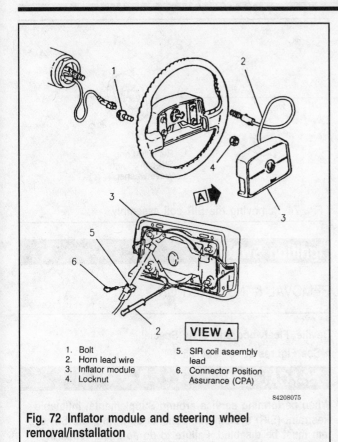

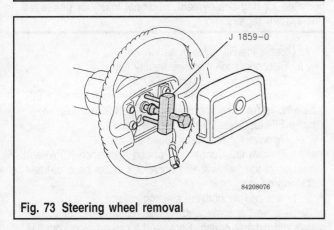

1. Bolt
2. Horn lead wire
3. Inflator module
4. Locknut
5. SIR coil assembly lead
6. Connector Position Assurance (CPA)

VIEW A

84208075

Fig. 72 Inflator module and steering wheel removal/installation

J 1859-0

84208076

Fig. 73 Steering wheel removal

4. Remove the SIR coil assembly retaining ring and the coil assembly. Allow the coil to hang freely.

❊❊WARNING

The SIR coil assembly will become uncentered if the steering column is separated from the steering gear and is allowed to rotate or if the centering spring is pushed down, letting the hub rotate while the coil is removed from the column.

5. Remove the wave washer.
6. Use tool J-23653-C or equivalent, to depress the shaft lock, then remove and discard the shaft lock retaining ring.
7. Remove the shaft lock.
8. Remove the turn signal cancelling cam assembly.

9. Remove the upper bearing spring, upper bearing inner race seat and inner race.
10. Move the turn signal switch to the RIGHT TURN position.
11. On Deville, Fleetwood, Sixty Special and 1990 Eldorado and Seville, remove the multi-function turn signal lever as follows:
   a. Make sure the lever is in the **OFF** position.
   b. Remove the access cover from the steering column housing.
   c. Disconnect the cruise control wiring connector. Note the position of the connector when installed in the column.
   d. Pull the lever straight out of the turn signal switch.
12. On 1991-93 Eldorado and Seville, remove the multi-function turn signal lever as follows:
   a. On 1992-93 vehicles, slide the connector cover toward the front of the vehicle.
   b. Unplug the electrical connector. On 1991 vehicles, note the position of the connector when installed in the column.
   c. Push the lever straight in, rotate clockwise ¼ turn and pull the lever out of the switch.
13. On Deville, Fleetwood, Sixty Special and 1992-93 Eldorado and Seville, remove the screw, button, spring and hazard warning switch knob.
14. On Deville, Fleetwood and Sixty Special, remove the one signal switch arm retaining screw. On 1992-93 Eldorado and Seville, remove the 2 signal switch arm retaining screws. Remove the signal switch arm.
15. Remove the turn signal switch retaining screws.
16. Remove the wiring protector and disconnect the turn signal switch connector.
17. Gently pull the wire harness through the column and remove the turn signal switch.

To install:
18. Route the turn signal switch wire harness through the column and connect the electrical connector. Install the wiring connector.
19. Position the turn signal switch and install the retaining screws. Tighten the screws to 30 inch lbs. (3.4 Nm).
20. If equipped, install the signal switch arm and tighten the retaining screw(s) to 20 inch lbs. (2.3 Nm).
21. If removed, install the hazard warning switch knob, spring, button and screw.
22. On 1991-93 Eldorado and Seville, install the multi-function turn signal lever as follows:
   a. Route the harness and connect the electrical connector.
   b. Push the lever straight in and rotate counterclockwise ¼ turn to lock into position.
   c. On 1992-93 vehicles, reposition the connector cover.
23. On Deville, Fleetwood, Sixty Special and 1990 Eldorado and Seville, install the multi-function turn signal lever as follows:
   a. Make sure the lever is in the **OFF** position.
   b. Push the lever into the turn signal switch.
   c. Connect the cruise control wiring connector.
   d. Install the access cover to the steering column housing.
24. Install the inner race, upper bearing inner race seat and upper bearing spring.
25. Install the turn signal cancelling cam assembly and lubricate with suitable grease.

26. Position the shaft lock. Use tool J-23653-C or equivalent, to depress the shaft lock, then install a new shaft lock retaining ring. The ring must be firmly seated in the groove on the shaft.

27. Install the wave washer.

28. If the SIR coil has become uncentered, proceed as follows:

a. On 1990 Deville and Fleetwood and 1990-91 Eldorado and Seville, set the steering shaft so that the block teeth on the upper steering shaft are at the 12 o'clock and 6 o'clock positions. The alignment mark at the end of the shaft should be at the 12 o'clock position and the vehicle wheels straight ahead. Turn the ignition switch to the **LOCK** position.

b. On 1991-93 Deville, Fleetwood and Sixty Special and 1992-93 Eldorado and Seville, set the steering shaft so that the block tooth on the upper steering shaft is at the 12 o'clock position. The vehicle wheels should be straight ahead. Turn the ignition switch to the **LOCK** position.

c. Remove the SIR coil assembly.

d. Hold the coil assembly with the clear bottom up to see the coil ribbon. There are 2 different types of coils: one rotates clockwise and the other rotates counterclockwise.

e. While holding the coil assembly, depress the spring lock to rotate the hub in the direction of the arrow until it stops. The coil ribbon should be wound up snug against the center hub.

f. Rotate the coil hub in the opposite direction approximately 2½ turns. Release the spring lock between the locking tabs in front of the arrow.

➡If a new SIR coil assembly is being installed, assemble the pre-centered coil assembly to the steering column. Remove the centering tab and dispose.

29. Install the SIR coil assembly, using the horn tower on the cancelling cam assembly and the projection on the housing cover for alignment.

30. Install the coil assembly retaining ring. The ring must be firmly seated in the groove on the shaft.

✳✳WARNING

Gently pull the coil assembly and turn signal harness wires to remove any slack or kinks that may be inside the steering column. Failure to do so may cause damage to the wire harness.

31. Install the steering wheel as described in this Section.

32. Enable the SIR system as follows:

a. Connect the yellow 2-way connector at the base of the steering column and install the CPA.

b. On Deville, Fleetwood and Sixty Special, install the left lower sound insulator. On Eldorado and Seville, install the left side sound insulator.

c. Install the SIR fuse.

d. Connect the negative battery cable.

e. Turn the ignition switch to **RUN**. Verify that the "INFLATABLE RESTRAINT" indicator light flashes 7-9 and then remains OFF. If the light does not function as specified, there is a fault in the SIR system.

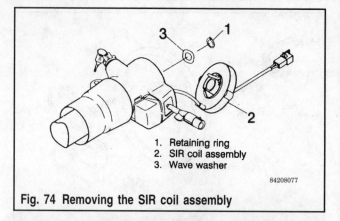

1. Retaining ring
2. SIR coil assembly
3. Wave washer

84208077

Fig. 74 Removing the SIR coil assembly

Ignition Switch

REMOVAL & INSTALLATION

Deville, Fleetwood and Sixty Special
▶ See Figures 83, 84 and 85

✳✳CAUTION

When performing service around Supplemental Inflatable Restraint (SIR) system components or wiring, the SIR system must be disabled. Failure to do so could result in possible air bag deployment, personal injury or unneeded SIR system repairs.

1. Disable the SIR system as follows:

a. Disconnect the negative battery cable.

b. Turn the ignition switch **OFF**.

c. Remove the SIR fuse. On 1990 vehicles, remove SIR fuse No. 3 from the fuse panel. On 1991-93 vehicles, remove SIR fuse No. 18 from the fuse panel.

d. Remove the left lower sound insulator.

e. Remove the Connector Position Assurance (CPA) and disconnect the yellow 2-way connector at the base of the steering column.

2. Lower and support the steering column.

3. Remove the screw and washer retaining the ignition switch and dimmer switch. Remove the ground wire from the mounting stud.

4. Remove the dimmer switch from the rod.

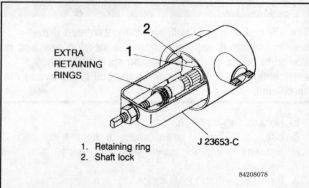

EXTRA RETAINING RINGS

J 23653-C

1. Retaining ring
2. Shaft lock

84208078

Fig. 75 Removing the shaft lock retaining ring

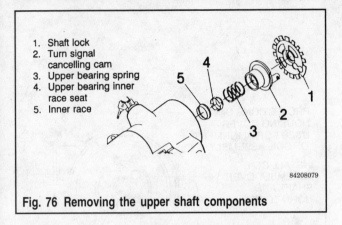

1. Shaft lock
2. Turn signal cancelling cam
3. Upper bearing spring
4. Upper bearing inner race seat
5. Inner race

84208079

Fig. 76 Removing the upper shaft components

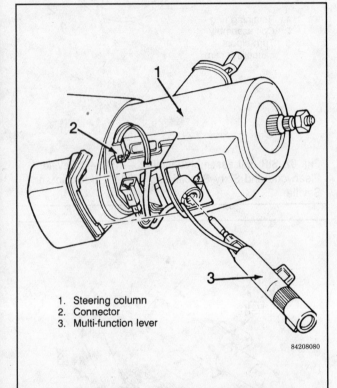

1. Steering column
2. Connector
3. Multi-function lever

84208080

Fig. 77 Removing the multi-function turn signal lever — 1992-93 Eldorado and Seville shown, others similar

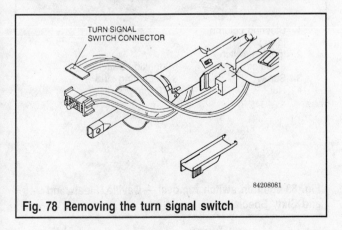

TURN SIGNAL SWITCH CONNECTOR

84208081

Fig. 78 Removing the turn signal switch

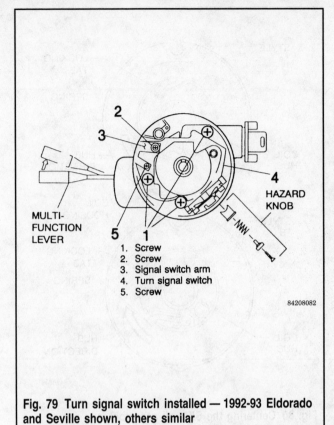

MULTI-FUNCTION LEVER

HAZARD KNOB

1. Screw
2. Screw
3. Signal switch arm
4. Turn signal switch
5. Screw

84208082

Fig. 79 Turn signal switch installed — 1992-93 Eldorado and Seville shown, others similar

5. Remove the dimmer and ignition switch mounting stud.
6. Remove the ignition switch from the ignition switch actuator.
7. Remove the wire harness strap, if equipped.
8. Disconnect the necessary electrical connectors.

To install:

9. Connect the electrical connectors.
10. Move the ignition switch slider to the extreme right position, then move it one detent to the left to the **OFF-LOCK** position.

➡The ignition switch must be installed with the switch in the OFF-LOCK position. A new ignition switch will be pinned in the OFF-LOCK position. Remove the plastic pin after the switch is installed on the column. Failure to do so may cause switch damage.

11. Install the ignition switch with the mounting stud. Tighten the stud to 35 inch lbs. (4 Nm).
12. Install the dimmer switch and install the ground wire to the stud. Install the nut and screw finger-tight.
13. Adjust the dimmer switch as follows:

a. Place a $9/32$ in. drill bit in the hole on the switch to limit travel.

b. Position the switch on the column and push against the dimmer switch rod to remove all lash.

c. Remove the drill bit and tighten the nut and screw to 35 inch lbs. (4 Nm).

14. Raise the column into position and secure; refer to the steering column removal & installation procedure in this Section.

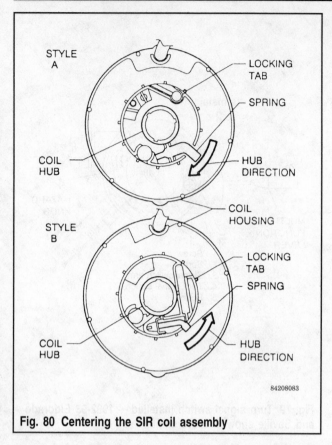

Fig. 80 Centering the SIR coil assembly

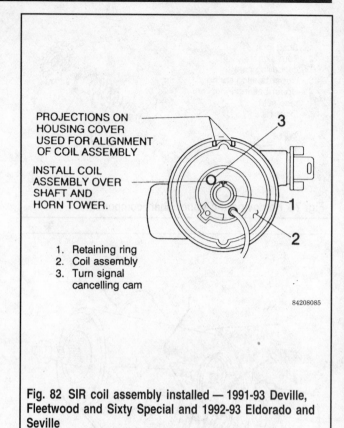

Fig. 82 SIR coil assembly installed — 1991-93 Deville, Fleetwood and Sixty Special and 1992-93 Eldorado and Seville

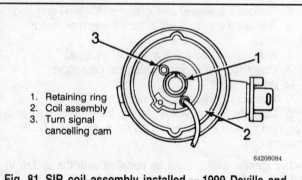

1. Retaining ring
2. Coil assembly
3. Turn signal cancelling cam

Fig. 81 SIR coil assembly installed — 1990 Deville and Fleetwood and 1990-91 Eldorado and Seville

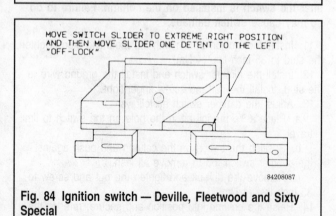

MOVE SWITCH SLIDER TO EXTREME RIGHT POSITION AND THEN MOVE SLIDER ONE DETENT TO THE LEFT "OFF-LOCK"

Fig. 84 Ignition switch — Deville, Fleetwood and Sixty Special

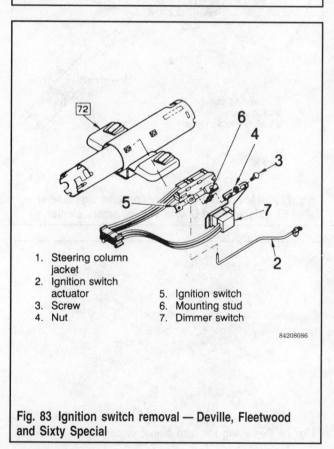

1. Steering column jacket
2. Ignition switch actuator
3. Screw
4. Nut
5. Ignition switch
6. Mounting stud
7. Dimmer switch

Fig. 83 Ignition switch removal — Deville, Fleetwood and Sixty Special

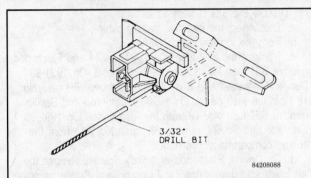

Fig. 85 Adjusting the dimmer switch — Deville, Fleetwood and Sixty Special

15. Enable the SIR system as follows:
   a. Connect the yellow 2-way connector at the base of the steering column and install the CPA.
   b. Install the left lower sound insulator.
   c. Install the SIR fuse.
   d. Connect the negative battery cable.
   e. Turn the ignition switch to **RUN**. Verify that the "INFLATABLE RESTRAINT" indicator light flashes 7-9 and then remains OFF. If the light does not function as specified, there is a fault in the SIR system.

Eldorado and Seville

1990

▶ See Figure 84

❋❋CAUTION

When performing service around Supplemental Inflatable Restraint (SIR) system components or wiring, the SIR system must be disabled. Failure to do so could result in possible air bag deployment, personal injury or unneeded SIR system repairs.

1. Disable the SIR system as follows:
   a. Disconnect the negative battery cable.
   b. Turn the ignition switch **OFF**.
   c. Remove SIR fuse No. 19 from the fuse panel.
   d. Remove the left side sound insulator.
   e. Remove the Connector Position Assurance (CPA) and disconnect the yellow 2-way connector at the base of the steering column.
2. Remove the 2 screws and the center trim plate.
3. Remove the 5 screws and the knee bolster.
4. Remove the 4 screws and the instrument panel steering column reinforcement plate.
5. Remove the ignition switch wiring protector and the ignition switch retaining screws.
6. Disconnect the ignition and turn signal switch column harness connectors from the instrument panel harness.
7. Disconnect the turn signal switch connector from the column harness. Remove the ignition switch.
   To install:
8. Move the ignition switch slider to the extreme right position, then move it one detent to the left to the **OFF-LOCK**

position. Install the ignition switch and secure with the retaining screws.

➡**The ignition switch must be installed with the switch in the OFF-LOCK position. A new ignition switch will be pinned in the OFF-LOCK position. Remove the plastic pin after the switch is installed on the column. Failure to do so may cause switch damage.**

9. Connect the turn signal switch connector to the column harness and connect the ignition and turn signal switch column harness connectors to the instrument panel harness.
10. Install the ignition switch wiring protector.
11. Install the steering column reinforcement plate and secure with the 4 screws.
12. Install the knee bolster and secure with the 5 screws.
13. Install the center trim plate and secure with the 2 screws.
14. Enable the SIR system as follows:
   a. Connect the yellow 2-way connector at the base of the steering column and install the CPA.
   b. Install the left side sound insulator.
   c. Install the SIR fuse.
   d. Connect the negative battery cable.
   e. Turn the ignition switch to **RUN**. Verify that the "INFLATABLE RESTRAINT" indicator light flashes 7-9 and then remains OFF. If the light does not function as specified, there is a fault in the SIR system.

1991-93

▶ See Figure 84

❋❋CAUTION

When performing service around Supplemental Inflatable Restraint (SIR) system components or wiring, the SIR system must be disabled. Failure to do so could result in possible air bag deployment, personal injury or unneeded SIR system repairs.

1. Disable the SIR system as follows:
   a. Disconnect the negative battery cable.
   b. Turn the ignition switch **OFF**.
   c. On 1991 Eldorado and Seville, remove SIR fuse No. 19 from the fuse panel. On 1992-93 Eldorado and Seville, remove SIR fuse No. A11 from the engine compartment fuse panel.
   d. Remove the left side sound insulator.
   e. Remove the Connector Position Assurance (CPA) and disconnect the yellow 2-way connector at the base of the steering column.
2. Remove the knee bolster and instrument panel steering column reinforcement plate.

❋❋WARNING

The steering column should never be supported by only the lower support bracket alone. Damage to the column lower bearing adapter could result.

3. Remove the 2 bolts or bolt and nut and the lower support bracket. Remove the 2 bolts and the upper column support from the instrument panel. Lower the steering column and let it rest on the driver seat.

4. Remove the ignition switch wiring protector and the ignition switch retaining screw and nut.

5. Disconnect the ignition and turn signal switch column harness connectors from the instrument panel harness.

6. Disconnect the turn signal switch connector from the column harness. Remove the ignition switch.

To install:

7. Move the ignition switch slider to the extreme right position, then move it one detent to the left to the **OFF-LOCK** position. Install the ignition switch and secure with the retaining screws.

➡**The ignition switch must be installed with the switch in the OFF-LOCK position. A new ignition switch will be pinned in the OFF-LOCK position. Remove the plastic pin after the switch is installed on the column. Failure to do so may cause switch damage.**

8. Connect the turn signal switch connector to the column harness and connect the ignition and turn signal switch column harness connectors to the instrument panel harness.

9. Install the ignition switch wiring protector.

10. Raise the steering column to the support bracket. Install the 2 bolts to the upper support bracket and the bolt and nut or 2 bolts to the lower support bracket. Do not tighten at this time.

11. Align the steering column to the instrument panel opening. A small shim (wedge) placed between the instrument panel column support bracket and the column can be used to hold the column in place while tightening the support bolts. Tighten the upper and lower column support bolts (and nut, if equipped) to 20 ft. lbs. (27 Nm).

12. Install the instrument panel steering column reinforcement plate and knee bolster.

13. Enable the SIR system as follows:

a. Connect the yellow 2-way connector at the base of the steering column and install the CPA.

b. Install the left side sound insulator.

c. Install the SIR fuse.

d. Connect the negative battery cable.

e. Turn the ignition switch to **RUN**. Verify that the "INFLATABLE RESTRAINT" indicator light flashes 7-9 and then remains OFF. If the light does not function as specified, there is a fault in the SIR system.

Ignition Lock Cylinder

REMOVAL & INSTALLATION

▶ See Figures 86, 87, 88, 89, 90 and 91

✳✳CAUTION

When performing service around Supplemental Inflatable Restraint (SIR) system components or wiring, the SIR system must be disabled. Failure to do so could result in possible air bag deployment, personal injury or unneeded SIR system repairs.

1. Disable the SIR system as follows:

a. Disconnect the negative battery cable.

b. Turn the ignition switch **OFF**.

c. Remove the SIR fuse. On 1990 Deville and Fleetwood, remove SIR fuse No. 3 from the fuse panel. On 1991-93 Deville, Fleetwood and Sixty Special, remove SIR fuse No. 18 from the fuse panel. On 1990-91 Eldorado and Seville, remove SIR fuse No. 19 from the fuse panel. On 1992-93 Eldorado and Seville, remove SIR fuse No. A11 from the engine compartment fuse panel.

d. On Deville, Fleetwood and Sixty Special, remove the left lower sound insulator. On Eldorado and Seville, remove the left side sound insulator.

e. Remove the Connector Position Assurance (CPA) and disconnect the yellow 2-way connector at the base of the steering column.

2. Remove the steering wheel and the turn signal switch as described in this Section. When removing the turn signal switch, allow the switch to hang freely; do not disconnect the electric connectors.

3. Remove the key from the lock cylinder.

4. Remove the buzzer switch assembly.

5. Reinsert the key in the lock cylinder and turn the key to the **LOCK** position.

6. Remove the lock retaining screw. If not equipped with pass key lock cylinder, remove the lock cylinder.

7. On 1990-91 Eldorado and Seville equipped with pass key lock cylinder, remove the lock cylinder as follows:

a. Disconnect the terminal connector.

b. Remove the retaining clip from the housing cover and the wiring protector.

c. Attach a length of mechanics wire to the terminal connector to aid in reassembly.

d. Gently pull the wire through the bracket and column housing and remove the lock cylinder.

8. On 1991-93 Deville, Fleetwood and Sixty Special and 1992-93 Eldorado and Seville equipped with pass key lock cylinder, remove the lock cylinder as follows:

a. Disconnect the pivot and pulse switch connector from the bulkhead connector and remove the 13-way secondary lock.

b. Remove the 2 terminals of the pass key wire harness from cavities 12 and 13 of the switch connector.

c. Remove the wiring protector.

d. Attach a length of mechanics wire to the terminal to aid in reassembly.

e. Remove the retaining clip from the housing cover and gently pull the wire harness through the column. Remove the lock cylinder.

To install:

✳✳WARNING

If equipped with pass key lock cylinder, route the wire from the lock cylinder as shown in Figs. 92 or 93, and snap the retaining clip in the hole in the housing. Failure to route the wire properly may result in component damage or malfunction of the pass key lock cylinder.

9. Install the lock cylinder.

10. On 1990-91 Eldorado and Seville equipped with pass key lock cylinder, proceed as follows:

a. Connect the mechanics wire to the terminal connector and gently feed the lock cylinder wire through the column housing.

b. Snap the clip into the hole in the housing.

c. Make sure the wires are not interfered with by the normal travel of the switch actuator rack and lock cylinder sector gear.

d. Gently pull the lock cylinder wire at the base of the column to remove any wire kinks that may be inside the column assembly.

e. Connect the pass key connector to the vehicle harness.

11. On 1991-93 Deville, Fleetwood and Sixty Special and 1992-93 Eldorado and Seville equipped with pass key lock cylinder, proceed as follows:

a. Route the wire terminal through the column and snap the retaining clip into the hole in the housing.

b. Connect the 2 terminal of the pass key wire harness to cavities 12 and 13 of the pivot and pulse switch connector.

c. Install the 13-way secondary lock.

d. Connect the switch connector to the bulkhead connector.

12. Install the lock retaining screw and tighten to 22 inch lbs. (2.5 Nm).

13. On 1990 Deville and Fleetwood and 1990-91 Eldorado and Seville, turn the ignition key to the **RUN** position. On all other vehicles, remove the key.

14. Install the buzzer switch assembly.

15. If the key was removed in Step 13, reinstall it and make sure it is in the **LOCK** position.

16. Install the turn signal switch and steering wheel according to the procedures in this Section.

17. Enable the SIR system as follows:

a. Connect the yellow 2-way connector at the base of the steering column and install the CPA.

b. On Deville, Fleetwood and Sixty Special, install the left lower sound insulator. On Eldorado and Seville, install the left side sound insulator.

c. Install the SIR fuse.

d. Connect the negative battery cable.

e. Turn the ignition switch to **RUN**. Verify that the "INFLATABLE RESTRAINT" indicator light flashes 7-9 and then remains OFF. If the light does not function as specified, there is a fault in the SIR system.

Steering Column

REMOVAL & INSTALLATION

✳✳WARNING

The steering column is extremely susceptible to damage once it has been removed from the vehicle. If the column assembly is dropped on its end, the steering shaft could collapse or the plastic injectors that maintain column rigid-

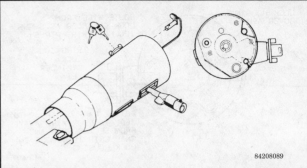

Fig. 86 Removing the buzzer switch — 1990-91 Eldorado and Seville shown, others similar

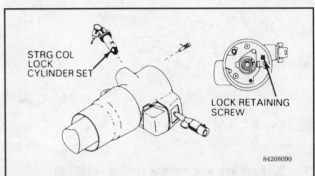

Fig. 87 Ignition lock cylinder removal — without pass key lock cylinder

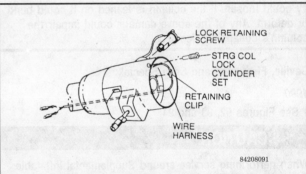

Fig. 88 Ignition lock cylinder removal — with pass key lock cylinder

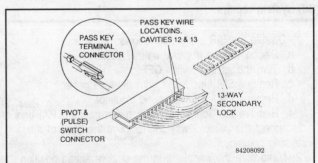

Fig. 89 Pass key wire connection locations — 1991-93 Deville, Fleetwood and Sixty Special and 1992-93 Eldorado and Seville

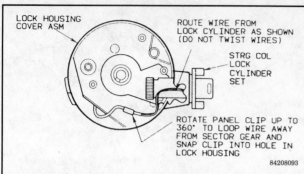

LOCK HOUSING COVER ASM

ROUTE WIRE FROM LOCK CYLINDER AS SHOWN (DO NOT TWIST WIRES)

STRG COL LOCK CYLINDER SET

ROTATE PANEL CLIP UP TO 360° TO LOOP WIRE AWAY FROM SECTOR GEAR AND SNAP CLIP INTO HOLE IN LOCK HOUSING

84208093

Fig. 90 Pass key wire harness routing — 1990-91 Eldorado and Seville

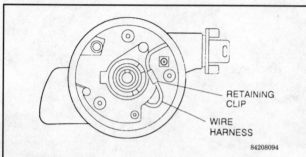

RETAINING CLIP

WIRE HARNESS

84208094

Fig. 91 Pass key wire harness routing — 1991-93 Deville, Fleetwood and Sixty Special and 1992-93 Eldorado and Seville

ity could loosen. If the column is leaned on it could bend or deform. Any of the above damage could impair the column's collapsible design.

Deville, Fleetwood and Sixty Special

1990

♦ See Figures 92, 93 and 94

✳✳CAUTION

When performing service around Supplemental Inflatable Restraint (SIR) system components or wiring, the SIR system must be disabled. Failure to do so could result in possible air bag deployment, personal injury or unneeded SIR system repairs.

1. Disable the SIR system as follows:
   a. Disconnect the negative battery cable.
   b. Turn the ignition switch **OFF**.
   c. Remove SIR fuse No. 3 from the fuse panel.
   d. Remove the left lower sound insulator.
   e. Remove the Connector Position Assurance (CPA) and disconnect the yellow 2-way connector at the base of the steering column.
2. Make sure the wheel are in the straight ahead position and the steering column is in the **LOCK** position.
3. Remove the steering wheel; refer to the procedure in this Section.
4. Snap out the steering column trim plate.

5. Remove the 2 screws retaining the filler and remove the filler.
6. Remove the 4 bolts/screws from the steering column reinforcement plate and remove the reinforcement plate.
7. Label and disconnect the necessary electrical connectors.
8. Remove the shift cable from the actuator.
9. Remove the 4 bolts/screws securing the seal assembly.
10. Remove the bolt from the upper knuckle of the intermediate steering shaft.
11. Remove the nut and bolt securing the lower brace assembly and remove the lower brace assembly.

✳✳WARNING

The steering column should never be supported only by the lower support bracket as damage to the column lower bearing will result.

12. Remove the 3 remaining bolts/screws and remove the lower support bracket.
13. Remove the 2 bolts/screws securing the column to the upper support and remove the steering column.
   To install:
14. Install the lower support bracket to the steering column but do not tighten the fasteners at this time.
15. Install the 2 bolts/screws into the upper support assembly several turns but leave them loose.
16. Place the steering column in position, sliding the lower support bracket slots over the fasteners installed in Step 15. Do not let the steering column hang freely but do not tighten the fasteners at this time.
17. Install the 2 bolts through the steering column into the upper support assembly but do not tighten at this time.
18. Connect the upper knuckle of the intermediate shaft to the upper steering shaft. Install the bolt and tighten to 35 ft. lbs. (47 Nm).
19. Install the seal assembly and tighten the 4 bolts/screws to 21 inch lbs. (2.4 Nm).
20. Remove the left bolt/screw that was installed in Step 14 and install the lower brace assembly. Tighten the 2 bolts/screws through the lower support bracket and lower brace assembly to 84 inch lbs. (9.5 Nm). Tighten the nut to the lower brace assembly to 84 inch lbs. (9.5 Nm).
21. Tighten the 2 bolts/screws to the upper support assembly to 20 ft. lbs. (27 Nm). Tighten the 2 bolts/screws through the lower support bracket to 20 ft. lbs. (27 Nm).
22. Connect the shift cable to the actuator and connect the electrical connectors.
23. Install the steering wheel; refer to the procedure in this Section.
24. Install the reinforcement plate and tighten the 4 bolts/screws to 17 inch lbs. (1.9 Nm).
25. Install the steering column filler and trim plate.
26. Enable the SIR system as follows:
   a. Connect the yellow 2-way connector at the base of the steering column and install the CPA.
   b. Install the left lower sound insulator.
   c. Install the SIR fuse.
   d. Connect the negative battery cable.
   e. Turn the ignition switch to **RUN**. Verify that the "INFLATABLE RESTRAINT" indicator light flashes 7-9 and

then remains OFF. If the light does not function as specified, there is a fault in the SIR system.

1991

▶ **See Figures 95 and 96**

✳✳CAUTION

When performing service around Supplemental Inflatable Restraint (SIR) system components or wiring, the SIR system must be disabled. Failure to do so could result in possible air bag deployment, personal injury or unneeded SIR system repairs.

1. Disable the SIR system as follows:
  a. Disconnect the negative battery cable.
  b. Turn the ignition switch **OFF**.
  c. Remove SIR fuse No. 18 from the fuse panel.
  d. Remove the left lower sound insulator.
  e. Remove the Connector Position Assurance (CPA) and disconnect the yellow 2-way connector at the base of the steering column.
2. Make sure the wheel are in the straight ahead position and the steering column is in the **LOCK** position.
3. If the column is to be disassembled, remove the steering wheel. Refer to the procedure in this Section.
4. Snap out the steering column trim plate.
5. Remove the 2 screws retaining the filler and remove the filler.
6. Remove the 4 bolts/screws from the steering column reinforcement plate and remove the reinforcement plate.

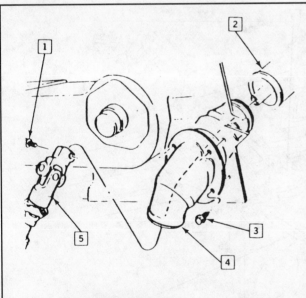

1. BOLT; 47 N•M (35 LB-FT)
2. STEERING COLUMN
3. SCREW (4); 2.4 N•M (21 LB-IN)
4. SEAL ASSEMBLY
5. INTERMEDIATE SHAFT ASSEMBLY

84208095

Fig. 92 Steering column intermediate shaft — 1990 Deville, Fleetwood, Eldorado and Seville

7. Label and disconnect the necessary electrical connectors.
8. Remove the shift indicator cable by removing the shift indicator clip. Remove the shift cable at the actuator.
9. Disconnect the steering column shaft from the intermediate shaft by positioning the seal assembly as needed and loosening or removing the upper intermediate shaft pinch bolt.
10. Remove the lower support brace assembly and the lower support bracket.
11. Remove the 2 bolts/screws securing the column to the upper support.
12. Disconnect the parking brake release vacuum harness connector from the switch on the steering column.
13. Remove the steering column.

To install:

➡**During the installation procedure, install the fasteners needed for completing each Step, but do not tighten them until instructed to do so.**

14. Install the lower support bracket to the steering column.
15. Connect the parking brake release vacuum harness connector to the switch on the steering column.
16. Install the 2 bolts/screws into the upper support assembly. Tighten them several turns, still leaving them loose.
17. Place the steering column in position, sliding the lower support bracket slots over the fasteners installed in Step 16. Do not let the steering column hang freely.
18. Install the 2 bolts through the steering column into the upper support assembly.
19. Connect the intermediate shaft to the steering column with the pinch bolt. Tighten to 35 ft. lbs. (47 Nm).
20. Position the seal assembly and tighten the fasteners to 21 inch lbs. (2.4 Nm).
21. Remove the left bolt/screw that was installed in Step 14 and install the lower brace assembly. Tighten the 2 bolts/screws through the lower support bracket and lower brace assembly to 84 inch lbs. (9.5 Nm). Tighten the nut to the lower brace assembly to 84 inch lbs. (9.5 Nm).
22. Tighten the 2 bolts/screws to the upper support assembly to 20 ft. lbs. (27 Nm). Tighten the 2 bolts/screws through the lower support bracket to 20 ft. lbs. (27 Nm).
23. Connect the shift cable to the actuator and connect the shift indicator cable. Refer to Section 7 for the adjustment procedure.
24. Connect the electrical connectors.
25. Install the steering wheel, if removed.
26. Install the reinforcement plate and tighten the bolts/screws to 17 inch lbs. (1.9 Nm).
27. Install the steering column filler and trim plate.
28. Enable the SIR system as follows:
  a. Connect the yellow 2-way connector at the base of the steering column and install the CPA.
  b. Install the left lower sound insulator.
  c. Install the SIR fuse.
  d. Connect the negative battery cable.
  e. Turn the ignition switch to **RUN**. Verify that the "INFLATABLE RESTRAINT" indicator light flashes 7-9 and then remains OFF. If the light does not function as specified, there is a fault in the SIR system.

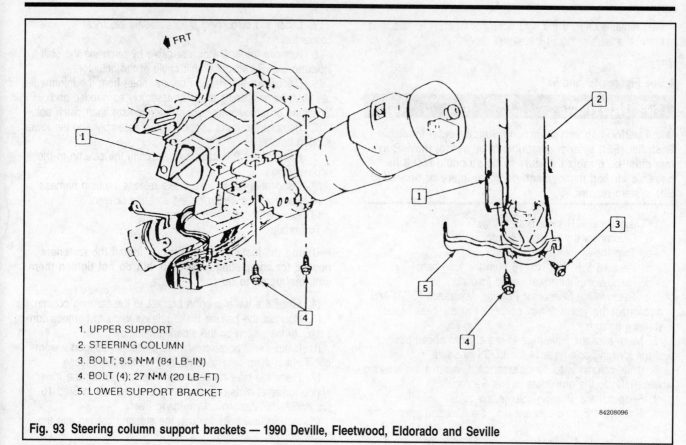

1. UPPER SUPPORT
2. STEERING COLUMN
3. BOLT; 9.5 N•M (84 LB-IN)
4. BOLT (4); 27 N•M (20 LB-FT)
5. LOWER SUPPORT BRACKET

84208096

Fig. 93 Steering column support brackets — 1990 Deville, Fleetwood, Eldorado and Seville

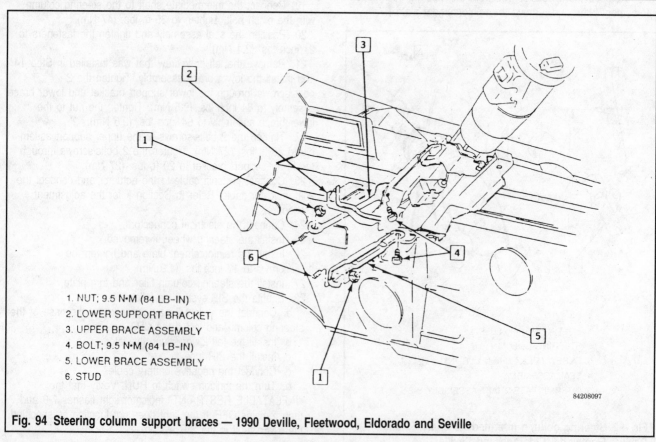

1. NUT; 9.5 N•M (84 LB-IN)
2. LOWER SUPPORT BRACKET
3. UPPER BRACE ASSEMBLY
4. BOLT; 9.5 N•M (84 LB-IN)
5. LOWER BRACE ASSEMBLY
6. STUD

84208097

Fig. 94 Steering column support braces — 1990 Deville, Fleetwood, Eldorado and Seville

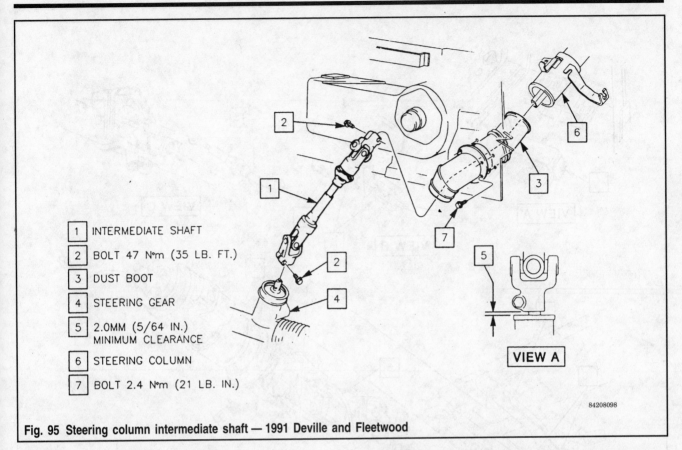

1 | INTERMEDIATE SHAFT
2 | BOLT 47 N·m (35 LB. FT.)
3 | DUST BOOT
4 | STEERING GEAR
5 | 2.0MM (5/64 IN.) MINIMUM CLEARANCE
6 | STEERING COLUMN
7 | BOLT 2.4 N·m (21 LB. IN.)

VIEW A

84208098

Fig. 95 Steering column intermediate shaft — 1991 Deville and Fleetwood

1992-93

▶ **See Figures 97 and 98**

✻✻CAUTION

When performing service around Supplemental Inflatable Restraint (SIR) system components or wiring, the SIR system must be disabled. Failure to do so could result in possible air bag deployment, personal injury or unneeded SIR system repairs.

1. Disable the SIR system as follows:
   a. Disconnect the negative battery cable.
   b. Turn the ignition switch **OFF**.
   c. Remove SIR fuse No. 18 from the fuse panel.
   d. Remove the left lower sound insulator.
   e. Remove the Connector Position Assurance (CPA) and disconnect the yellow 2-way connector at the base of the steering column.
2. Make sure the wheel are in the straight ahead position and the steering column is in the **LOCK** position.
3. If the column is to be disassembled, remove the steering wheel. Refer to the procedure in this Section.
4. Remove the steering column trim plate, filler, reinforcement plate and side window defog hose.
5. Disconnect the shift indicator cable.
6. Loosen the steering column support bracket and upper support bracket bolts/screws.
7. Remove the lower support brace screw and the brace.

8. Disconnect the steering column wiring harness connector from the main harness.

✻✻WARNING

The steering column should never be supported only by the lower support bracket as damage to the column lower bearing will result.

9. Support the column and remove the 2 bolts/screws.
10. Disconnect the shift cable from the actuator and, if necessary, from the slot in the lower column bracket.
11. Remove the bolt and disconnect the intermediate steering shaft from the steering column.
12. Disconnect the parking brake release vacuum harness connector from the valve switch on the steering column.
13. Remove the steering column from the vehicle.
   To install:

➡**During the installation procedure, install the fasteners needed for completing each Step, but do not tighten them until instructed to do so.**

14. Hand start one bolt/screw into the steering column support bracket at the lower right position.
15. Position the steering column in the vehicle.
16. Support the column and insert the intermediate steering shaft through the seal from the front. Connect the shaft with the pinch bolt and tighten to 35 ft. lbs. (47 Nm).
17. Connect the parking brake release vacuum harness connector to the valve switch on the steering column.
18. Connect the shift cable at the actuator, snapping it onto the range selector pin on the column. Make sure the cable

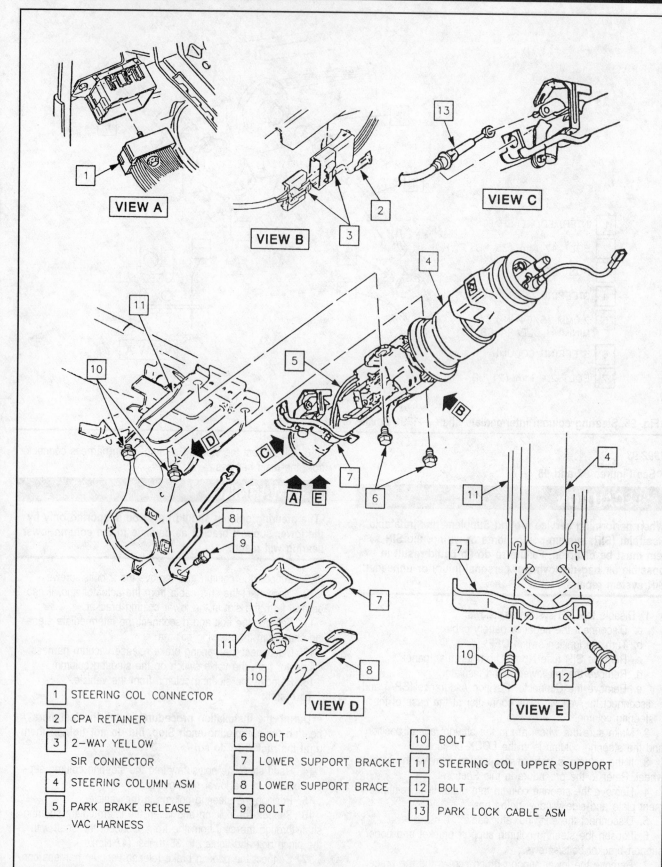

1 | STEERING COL CONNECTOR

2 | CPA RETAINER

3 | 2-WAY YELLOW SIR CONNECTOR

4 | STEERING COLUMN ASM

5 | PARK BRAKE RELEASE VAC HARNESS

6 | BOLT

7 | LOWER SUPPORT BRACKET

8 | LOWER SUPPORT BRACE

9 | BOLT

10 | BOLT

11 | STEERING COL UPPER SUPPORT

12 | BOLT

13 | PARK LOCK CABLE ASM

Fig. 96 Steering column assembly — 1991 Deville and Fleetwood

84208099

fitting is secured in the slot in the lower column bracket so that both fitting ears are fully expanded to retain the cable in the bracket.

☀☀WARNING

The steering column should never be supported only by the lower support bracket as damage to the column lower bearing will result.

19. Support the column and guide the lower support slotted hole onto the bolt/screw.

20. Install the 2 bolts/screws through the upper support bracket into the steering column support bracket but do not tighten at this time.

21. Install the bolt/screw into the steering column support bracket.

22. Install the brace onto the bolt/screw, as shown in Fig. 100. Install bolt/screw through the brace into the bulkhead.

23. Move the seal into position and tighten the brace-to-bulkhead bolt/screw to 84 inch lbs. (9.5 Nm). Tighten the seal bolt/screw to 21 inch lbs. (2.4 Nm).

24. Center the column in the steering column opening and tighten the lower right support bolt/screw to 20 ft. lbs. (27 Nm).

25. Connect the steering column wiring harness connector to the main harness and tighten the bolt/screw to 42 inch lbs. (4.8 Nm).

26. Center the column in the steering column opening and tighten the remaining lower support bolt/screw and the upper bracket bolts/screws to 20 ft. lbs. (27 Nm).

27. Connect the shift indicator cable.

28. Install the reinforcement plate and tighten the bolts/screws to 17 inch lbs. (1.9 Nm).

29. Install the steering column filler, trim plate, side window defog hose and sound insulator.

30. Install the steering wheel, if removed.

31. Enable the SIR system as follows:
   a. Connect the yellow 2-way connector at the base of the steering column and install the CPA.
   b. Install the left lower sound insulator.
   c. Install the SIR fuse.
   d. Connect the negative battery cable.
   e. Turn the ignition switch to **RUN**. Verify that the "INFLATABLE RESTRAINT" indicator light flashes 7-9 and then remains OFF. If the light does not function as specified, there is a fault in the SIR system.

Eldorado and Seville

1990

▶ See Figures 92, 93 and 94

☀☀CAUTION

When performing service around Supplemental Inflatable Restraint (SIR) system components or wiring, the SIR system must be disabled. Failure to do so could result in possible air bag deployment, personal injury or unneeded SIR system repairs.

1. Disable the SIR system as follows:
   a. Disconnect the negative battery cable.

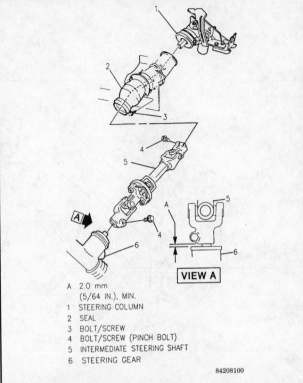

Fig. 97 Steering column intermediate shaft — 1992-93 Deville, Fleetwood and Sixty Special

A 2.0 mm (5/64 IN.), MIN.
1 STEERING COLUMN
2 SEAL
3 BOLT/SCREW
4 BOLT/SCREW (PINCH BOLT)
5 INTERMEDIATE STEERING SHAFT
6 STEERING GEAR

84208100

   b. Turn the ignition switch **OFF**.
   c. Remove SIR fuse No. 19 from the fuse panel.
   d. Remove the left side sound insulator.
   e. Remove the Connector Position Assurance (CPA) and disconnect the yellow 2-way connector at the base of the steering column.

2. Make sure the wheel are in the straight ahead position and the steering column is in the **LOCK** position.

3. Remove the inflator module from the steering wheel. Refer to the steering wheel REMOVAL & installation procedure in this Section.

4. Remove the 2 screws and the center trim plate.

5. Remove the 5 screws and the knee bolster.

6. Remove the 4 screws and the instrument panel steering column reinforcement plate.

7. Label and disconnect the ignition wiring connector and the combination switch connector.

8. Remove the pinch bolt from the intermediate shaft.

9. Remove the bolt and nut and remove the lower support bracket.

10. Remove the 2 bolts retaining the upper column support and remove the steering column.

To install:

11. Position the steering column in the vehicle and support it at the upper bracket with the 2 bolts. Do not tighten the bolts at this time.

12. Install the lower column support bracket but do not tighten the bolts at this time.

13. Connect the steering column intermediate shaft and install the pinch bolt. Tighten the pinch bolt and nut to 35 ft. lbs. (47 Nm).

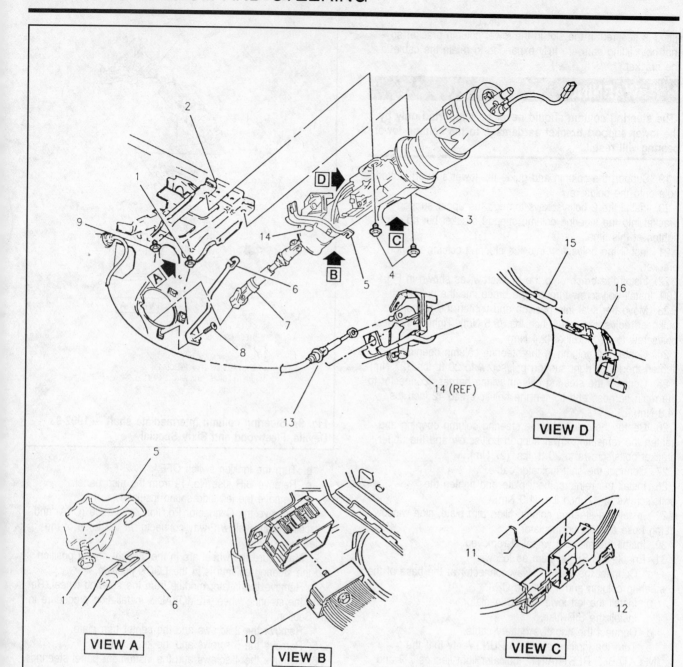

1 BOLT/SCREW, STEERING
  COLUMN SUPPORT BRACKET
2 BRACKET, STEERING COLUMN
  SUPPORT
3 BRACKET, UPPER SUPPORT
4 BOLT/SCREW
5 LOWER SUPPORT
6 BRACE, STEERING COLUMN
  LOWER SUPPORT

7 SHAFT, INTERMEDIATE STEERING
8 BOLT/SCREW
9 BOLT/SCREW
10 CONNECTOR, STEERING
   COLUMN WIRING HARNESS
11 CONNECTOR, SIR (YELLOW)
12 RETAINER
13 CABLE, SHIFT CONTROL

14 SOLENOID, BRAKE
   TRANSMISSION SHIFT
   INTERLOCK
15 PARK BRAKE RELEASE
   VACUUM HARNESS
16 VALVE, PARK BRAKE
   RELEASE VACUUM

84208101

Fig. 98 Steering column mounting components — 1992-93 Deville, Fleetwood and Sixty Special

14. Tighten the upper and lower column support nut and bolts to 20 ft. lbs. (27 Nm). Tighten the lower support bracket-to-column screws to 12 ft. lbs. (16 Nm).

15. Connect the combination and ignition wiring connectors.

16. Install the steering column reinforcement plate and secure with the 4 screws.

17. Install the knee bolster and secure with the 5 screws.

18. Install the center trim plate and secure with the 2 screws.

19. Install the inflator module to the steering wheel. Refer to the steering wheel REMOVAL & installation procedure in this Section.

20. Enable the SIR system as follows:

   a. Connect the yellow 2-way connector at the base of the steering column and install the CPA.

   b. Install the left side sound insulator.

   c. Install the SIR fuse.

   d. Connect the negative battery cable.

   e. Turn the ignition switch to **RUN**. Verify that the 'INFLATABLE RESTRAINT" indicator light flashes 7-9 and then remains OFF. If the light does not function as specified, there is a fault in the SIR system.

1991-93

▶ See Figure 99

❊❊CAUTION

When performing service around Supplemental Inflatable Restraint (SIR) system components or wiring, the SIR system must be disabled. Failure to do so could result in possible air bag deployment, personal injury or unneeded SIR system repairs.

1. Disable the SIR system as follows:

   a. Disconnect the negative battery cable.

   b. Turn the ignition switch **OFF**.

   c. Remove the SIR fuse. On 1991 vehicles, remove SIR fuse No. 19 from the fuse panel. On 1992-93 vehicles, remove SIR fuse No. A11 from the engine compartment fuse panel.

   d. Remove the left side sound insulator.

   e. Remove the Connector Position Assurance (CPA) and disconnect the yellow 2-way connector at the base of the steering column.

2. Make sure the wheel are in the straight ahead position and the steering column is in the **LOCK** position.

3. Remove the inflator module from the steering wheel. Refer to the steering wheel REMOVAL & installation procedure in this Section.

4. Remove the knee bolster and steering column reinforcement plate.

5. Label and disconnect the ignition, pass key and 48-way wiring connectors.

6. Remove the pinch bolt from the intermediate shaft.

7. Remove the 2 bolts and the lower support bracket.

8. Remove the 2 bolts retaining the upper column support and remove the steering column.

To install:

9. Position the steering column in the vehicle and support it at the upper bracket with the 2 bolts. Do not tighten the bolts at this time.

10. Install the bolt and nut to the lower support bracket but do not tighten at this time.

11. Connect the steering column intermediate shaft and install the pinch bolt. Tighten to 35 ft. lbs. (47 Nm).

12. Align the steering column to the instrument panel opening. A small shim (wedge) placed between the instrument panel column support bracket and the column can be used to hold the column in place while tightening the support bolts. Tighten the upper and lower column support bolts and nut to 20 ft. lbs. (27 Nm).

13. Tighten the lower bracket-to-column screws to 12 ft. lbs. (16 Nm).

14. Connect the electrical connectors.

15. Install the steering column reinforcement plate and knee bolster.

16. Install the inflator module to the steering wheel. Refer to the steering wheel REMOVAL & installation procedure in this Section.

17. Enable the SIR system as follows:

   a. Connect the yellow 2-way connector at the base of the steering column and install the CPA.

   b. Install the left side sound insulator.

   c. Install the SIR fuse.

   d. Connect the negative battery cable.

   e. Turn the ignition switch to **RUN**. Verify that the "INFLATABLE RESTRAINT" indicator light flashes 7-9 and then remains OFF. If the light does not function as specified, there is a fault in the SIR system.

Steering Linkage

REMOVAL & INSTALLATION

Outer Tie Rod

▶ See Figures 100 and 101

1. Raise and safely support the vehicle.

2. Remove the wheel and tire assembly.

3. Remove the cotter pin and nut from the tie rod ball stud.

4. Loosen the jam nut on the inner tie rod.

5. Separate the outer tie rod from the steering knuckle using tool J-24319-01 or equivalent.

6. Mark the position of the outer tie rod on the inner tie rod. Remove the outer tie rod from the inner tie rod.

To install:

7. Thread the outer tie rod onto the inner tie rod to the position marked during the removal procedure. This will approximate the original toe setting.

8. Connect the outer tie rod to the steering knuckle and install the nut. Tighten the nut to 35 ft. lbs. (47 Nm).

9. Install a new cotter pin. If the cotter pin cannot be installed because the hole in the stud does not align with a nut castellation, tighten the nut up to a maximum of 52 ft. lbs. (70 Nm) to allow for installation. NEVER loosen the nut to provide for cotter pin installation.

10. Install the wheel and tire assembly and lower the vehicle. Adjust the toe setting by turning the inner tie rod.

➡**Make sure the rack and pinion boot is not twisted during toe adjustment.**

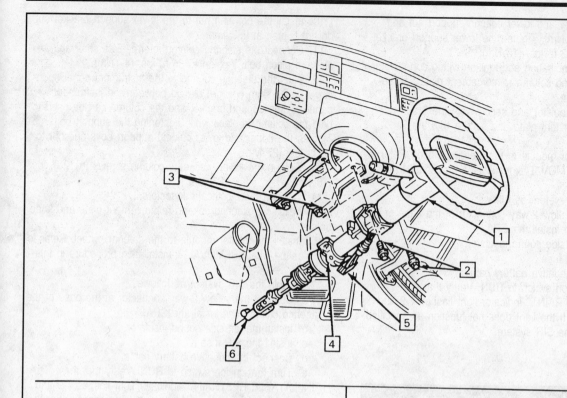

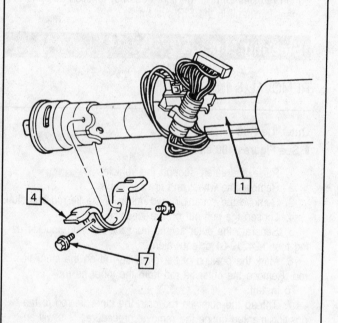

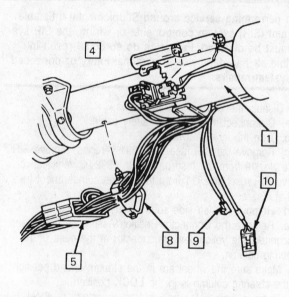

[1]	STEERING COLUMN	[6]	INTERMEDIATE SHAFT
[2]	UPPER MOUNTING BOLTS (20–27 N·m/15–20 ft. lbs.)	[7]	LOWER BRACKET BOLTS (13–19 N·m/10–14 ft. lbs.)
[3]	LOWER MOUNTING BOLTS (20–27 N·m/15–20 ft. lbs.)	[8]	WIRING CUP
[4]	LOWER BRACKET	[9]	PASS-KEY CONNECTOR (ORANGE)
[5]	COLUMN CONNECTOR	[10]	SIR CONNECTOR (YELLOW)

84208103

Fig. 99 Steering column mounting — 1991-93 Eldorado and Seville

11. After the toe is set, tighten the jam nut against the outer tie rod to 40 ft. lbs. (54 Nm).

Inner Tie Rod
▶ **See Figures 102, 103, 104, 105, 106 and 107**

1. Remove the rack and pinion assembly from the vehicle.
2. Remove the outer tie rod as described in this Section.
3. Remove the jam nut from the inner tie rod.
4. Remove the tie rod end clamp. Remove the boot clamp using side cutters.
5. Mark the location of the breather tube on the steering gear before removing the tube or rack and pinion boot.
6. Remove the rack and pinion boot and breather tube.
7. Remove the shock dampener from the inner tie rod and slide it back on the rack.

❊❊WARNING

The rack must be held during removal of the inner tie rod to prevent rack damage.

8. Place a wrench on the flat of the rack assembly and another wrench on the flats of the inner tie rod housing. Rotate the housing counterclockwise until the inner tie rod separates from the rack.

To install:

❊❊WARNING

The rack must be held during inner tie rod installation to prevent internal gear damage.

Fig. 101 View of the outer tie rod

9. Install the shock dampener onto the rack.
10. Position the inner tie rod on the rack. Place a wrench on the flat of the rack assembly and another wrench on the flats of the inner tie rod housing. Tighten the inner tie rod to 74 ft. lbs. (100 Nm).

➡**Make sure the tie rod rocks freely in the housing before staking the inner tie rod assembly to the rack.**

11. Support the rack and housing of the inner tie rod and stake both sides of the inner tie rod housing to the flats on the rack, as shown in Fig. 108. Check both stakes by inserting a 0.010 in. (0.25mm) feeler gauge between the rack and tie rod housing. The feeler gauge must not pass between the rack and housing stake.
12. Slide the shock dampener over the inner tie rod housing until it engages.
13. Install a new boot clamp onto the rack and pinion boot.
14. Apply grease to the inner tie rod and gear assembly prior to boot installation, as shown in Fig. 109, then install the boot onto the inner tie rod assembly.
15. Make sure the breather tube is aligned with the mark made during REMOVAL & the molded nipple of the boot is aligned with the tube.
16. Install the boot onto the gear assembly until it is seated in the gear assembly groove.

➡**The boot must not be twisted or out of shape in any way. If the boot is not shaped properly, adjust by hand before installing the boot clamp.**

17. Install the boot clamp onto the boot using tool J-22610 or equivalent, and crimp as shown in Fig. 110. Install the tie rod end clamp on the boot using pliers.

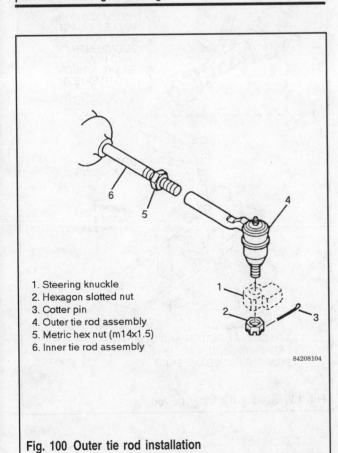

1. Steering knuckle
2. Hexagon slotted nut
3. Cotter pin
4. Outer tie rod assembly
5. Metric hex nut (m14x1.5)
6. Inner tie rod assembly

Fig. 100 Outer tie rod installation

18. Install the outer tie rod and install the rack and pinion assembly in the vehicle; refer to the procedures in this Section.

Power Rack and Pinion

ADJUSTMENT

Rack Bearing Preload
▶ See Figure 108

1. Raise and safely support the front of the vehicle. Center the steering wheel.

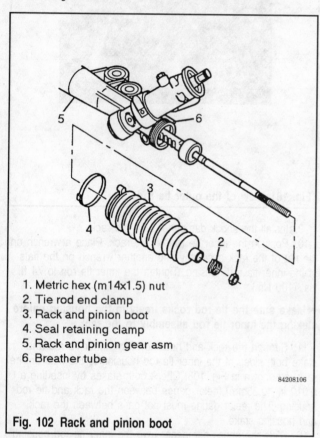

1. Metric hex (m14x1.5) nut
2. Tie rod end clamp
3. Rack and pinion boot
4. Seal retaining clamp
5. Rack and pinion gear asm
6. Breather tube

84208106

Fig. 102 Rack and pinion boot

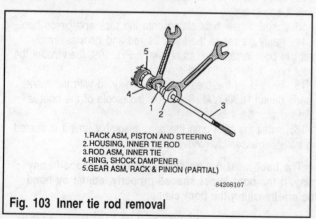

1. RACK ASM, PISTON AND STEERING
2. HOUSING, INNER TIE ROD
3. ROD ASM, INNER TIE
4. RING, SHOCK DAMPENER
5. GEAR ASM, RACK & PINION (PARTIAL)

84208107

Fig. 103 Inner tie rod removal

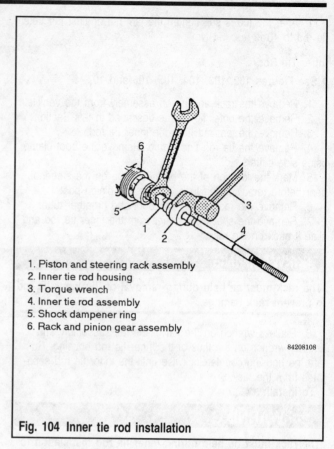

1. Piston and steering rack assembly
2. Inner tie rod housing
3. Torque wrench
4. Inner tie rod assembly
5. Shock dampener ring
6. Rack and pinion gear assembly

84208108

Fig. 104 Inner tie rod installation

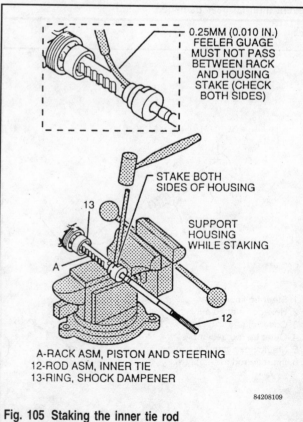

0.25MM (0.010 IN.) FEELER GUAGE MUST NOT PASS BETWEEN RACK AND HOUSING STAKE (CHECK BOTH SIDES)

STAKE BOTH SIDES OF HOUSING

SUPPORT HOUSING WHILE STAKING

A-RACK ASM, PISTON AND STEERING
12-ROD ASM, INNER TIE
13-RING, SHOCK DAMPENER

84208109

Fig. 105 Staking the inner tie rod

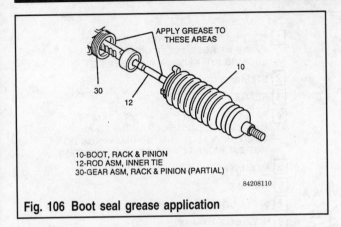

10-BOOT, RACK & PINION
12-ROD ASM, INNER TIE
30-GEAR ASM, RACK & PINION (PARTIAL)

84208110

Fig. 106 Boot seal grease application

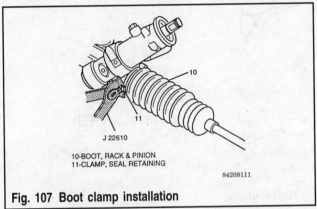

J 22610

10-BOOT, RACK & PINION
11-CLAMP, SEAL RETAINING

84208111

Fig. 107 Boot clamp installation

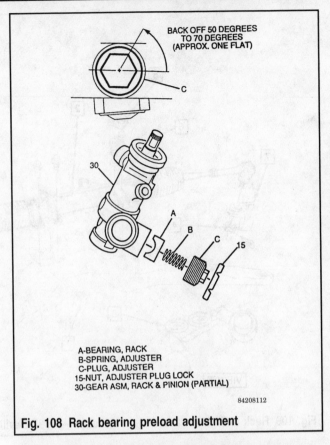

A-BEARING, RACK
B-SPRING, ADJUSTER
C-PLUG, ADJUSTER
15-NUT, ADJUSTER PLUG LOCK
30-GEAR ASM, RACK & PINION (PARTIAL)

84208112

Fig. 108 Rack bearing preload adjustment

2. Loosen the adjuster plug locknut and turn the adjuster plug clockwise until it bottoms in the gear assembly, then back off 50-70 degrees (about one flat).

3. Tighten the lock nut to 55 ft. lbs. (75 Nm) while holding the adjuster plug stationary.

4. Check the returnability of the steering wheel to center after adjustment.

REMOVAL & INSTALLATION

Deville, Fleetwood and Sixty Special

1990

▶ **See Figure 109**

1. Raise and safely support the vehicle.
2. Remove both front wheel and tire assemblies.

✳✳WARNING

The front wheels must be in the straight-ahead position and the steering column in the LOCK position before disconnecting the steering column or intermediate shaft from the steering gear. Failure to do so will cause the coil assembly in the steering column to become uncentered which will cause damage to the coil assembly.

3. Disconnect the intermediate shaft lower connection.

✳✳CAUTION

Failure to disconnect the intermediate shaft from the rack and pinion stub shaft can result in damage to the steering gear and/or intermediate shaft. This damage can cause loss of steering control which could result in personal injury.

4. Disconnect both tie rod ends from the steering knuckles; refer to the procedure in this Section.
5. Remove the line retainer.
6. Disconnect the outlet and pressure lines.
7. Remove the 5 rack and pinion mounting bolts and remove the rack and pinion assembly by sliding it out to the side.

To install:

8. Position the rack and pinion assembly and install the 5 mounting bolts. Tighten to 50 ft. lbs. (68 Nm).
9. Connect the outlet and pressure lines to the rack and pinion assembly and tighten the fittings to 20 ft. lbs. (27 Nm).
10. Install the line retainer.
11. Connect the tie rod ends to the steering knuckles; refer to the procedure in this Section.
12. Connect the intermediate shaft coupling and tighten the bolt to 30 ft. lbs. (50 Nm).
13. Install the wheel and tire assemblies and lower the vehicle.
14. Fill and bleed the power steering system as described in this Section.

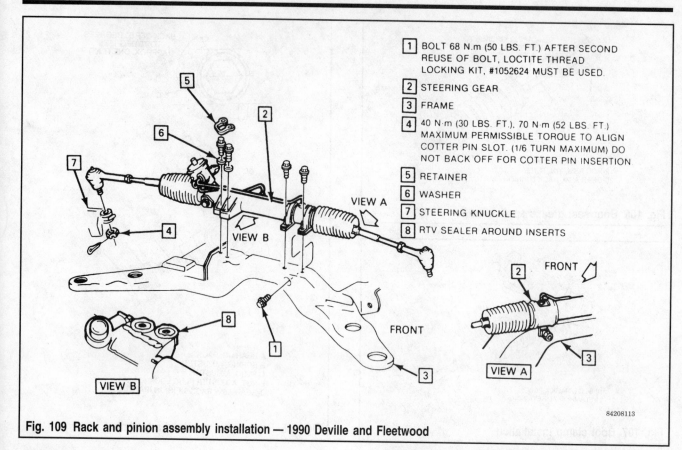

BOLT 68 N.m (50 LBS. FT.) AFTER SECOND
REUSE OF BOLT, LOCTITE THREAD
LOCKING KIT, #1052624 MUST BE USED.

2 STEERING GEAR

3 FRAME

4 40 N·m (30 LBS. FT.), 70 N·m (52 LBS. FT.)
MAXIMUM PERMISSIBLE TORQUE TO ALIGN
COTTER PIN SLOT. (1/6 TURN MAXIMUM) DO
NOT BACK OFF FOR COTTER PIN INSERTION

5 RETAINER

6 WASHER

7 STEERING KNUCKLE

8 RTV SEALER AROUND INSERTS

Fig. 109 Rack and pinion assembly installation — 1990 Deville and Fleetwood

1991-93

▶ See Figure 110

1. Raise and safely support the vehicle.
2. Remove the left front wheel and tire assembly.

✳✳CAUTION

Failure to disconnect the intermediate shaft from the rack and pinion stub shaft can result in damage to the steering gear and/or intermediate shaft. This damage can cause loss of steering control which could result in personal injury.

✳✳WARNING

The front wheels must be in the straight-ahead position and the steering column in the LOCK position before disconnecting the steering column or intermediate shaft from the steering gear. Failure to do so will cause the coil assembly in the steering column to become uncentered which will cause damage to the coil assembly.

3. Disconnect the intermediate shaft lower connection.
4. Disconnect both tie rod ends from the steering knuckles; refer to the procedure in this Section.
5. Remove the line retainer.
6. Disconnect the pressure switch electrical connection. If equipped with speed sensitive steering, disconnect the electrical connection at the control valve and manifold.

7. Disconnect the power steering pressure and return lines. If equipped with speed sensitive steering, remove the filter as needed for access.
8. Support the body with jackstands to allow lowering of the frame.
9. Loosen the front frame bolts. Remove the rear frame bolts and lower the rear of the frame about 3 in. (76mm).

✳✳WARNING

Do not lower the rear of the frame too far, as damage to the engine components nearest to the cowl may result.

10. Remove the rack and pinion mounting bolts and remove the rack and pinion assembly through the left wheel opening.
   To install:
11. Install the rack and pinion assembly through the left wheel opening and position it in the vehicle.
12. Raise the rear of the frame and tighten the frame bolts to 76 ft. lbs. (103 Nm). Remove the jackstands.
13. Install the 2 washers and 5 rack and pinion mounting bolts. Loctite® thread locking kit No. 1052624 or equivalent, must be used. Tighten the bolts to 50 ft. lbs. (68 Nm), in the sequence shown.
14. Connect the power steering pressure and return lines (including the filter on speed sensitive steering systems, if removed) and tighten the connections to 20 ft. lbs. (27 Nm).
15. Connect the pressure switch electrical connector. If equipped with speed sensitive steering, also make the electrical connections at the control valve and manifold.
16. Install the line retainer.

17. Connect the tie rod ends to the steering knuckles; refer to the procedure in this Section.

18. Connect the intermediate shaft lower coupling and tighten the bolt to 35 ft. lbs. (47 Nm).

19. Install the left front wheel and tire assembly and lower the vehicle.

20. Fill and bleed the power steering system as described in this Section.

Eldorado and Seville

1990-92

▶ See Figure 111

1. Raise and safely support the vehicle.
2. Remove the left front wheel and tire assembly.

✱✱CAUTION

Failure to disconnect the intermediate shaft from the rack and pinion stub shaft can result in damage to the steering gear and/or intermediate shaft. This damage can cause loss of steering control which could result in personal injury.

✱✱WARNING

The front wheels must be in the straight-ahead position and the steering column in the LOCK position before disconnecting the steering column or intermediate shaft from the steering gear. Failure to do so will cause the coil assembly in the steering column to become uncentered which will cause damage to the coil assembly.

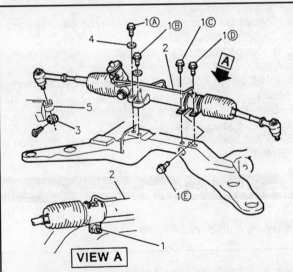

VIEW A

1 BOLT; 68 N•m (50 LB. FT.).
   TIGHTEN IN SEQUENCE A THRU E.

2 STEERING GEAR

3 NUT; 47 N•m (35 LB. FT.). MAXIMUM
   PERMISSIBLE TORQUE TO ALIGN COTTER
   PIN SLOT IS 70 N•m (52 LB. FT.).

4 WASHER

5 STEERING KNUCKLE

84208114

**Fig. 110 Rack and pinion assembly installation —
1991-93 Deville, Fleetwood and Sixty Special**

3. Disconnect the intermediate shaft lower coupling.
4. Remove the heat shield.
5. Disconnect both tie rod ends from the steering knuckles; refer to the procedure in this Section.
6. Support the rear of the frame with a jack.

✱✱WARNING

The frame must be properly supported before partial lowering. The frame should not be lowered any further than needed to gain access to the steering gear.

7. Loosen the rear body mount bolts and slowly lower the rear of the frame.
8. Remove the line retainer.
9. Disconnect the power steering pressure and return lines.
10. Disconnect the pressure switch connector.
11. Remove the 5 rack and pinion mounting bolts and remove the rack and pinion assembly by sliding it out to the side.

To install:

12. Position the rack and pinion assembly and install the 5 mounting bolts. Tighten to 50 ft. lbs. (68 Nm).

13. Connect the return and pressure lines to the rack and pinion assembly and tighten the fittings to 20 ft. lbs. (27 Nm).

14. Install the line retainer.

15. Raise the frame into position and tighten the body mount bolts to 76 ft. lbs. (103 Nm).

16. Connect the tie rod ends to the steering knuckles; refer to the procedure in this Section.

17. Connect the intermediate shaft lower coupling and tighten the bolt to 35 ft. lbs. (47 Nm).

18. Connect the pressure switch connector and install the heat shield.

19. Install the left front wheel and tire assembly and lower the vehicle.

20. Fill and bleed the power steering system as described in this Section.

1993

▶ See Figure 112

✱✱CAUTION

Failure to disconnect the intermediate shaft from the rack and pinion stub shaft can result in damage to the steering gear and/or intermediate shaft. This damage can cause loss of steering control which could result in personal injury.

✱✱WARNING

The front wheels must be in the straight-ahead position and the steering column in the LOCK position before disconnecting the steering column or intermediate shaft from the steering gear. Failure to do so will cause the coil assembly in the steering column to become uncentered which will cause damage to the coil assembly.

1. Disconnect the intermediate shaft lower coupling.
2. Raise and safely support the vehicle.
3. Remove the left front wheel and tire assembly.

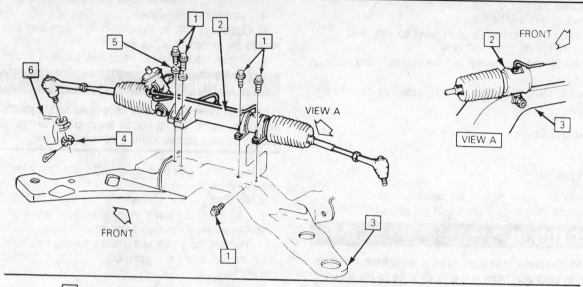

1 BOLTS (68 N·m/50 FT. LBS.) AFTER SECOND REUSE OF BOLT, LOCTITE THREAD LOCKING KIT. #1052624 MUST BE USED.

2 STEERING GEAR

3 FRAME

4 NUT. SEE INSTALLATION PROCEDURE FOR TORQUE SPECIFICATION.

5 WASHER

6 STEERING KNUCKLE

84208115

Fig. 111 Rack and pinion assembly installation — 1990-92 Eldorado and Seville

4. If equipped with 4.6L engine, disconnect the road sensing suspension position sensor.

5. Disconnect both tie rod ends from the steering knuckles; refer to the procedure in this Section.

6. If equipped with 4.6L engine, disconnect the exhaust pipe at the catalytic converter.

7. Support the rear of the frame with a jack.

✳✳WARNING

The frame must be properly supported before partial lowering. The frame should not be lowered any further than needed to gain access to the steering gear.

8. Loosen the rear body mount bolts and slowly lower the rear of the frame.

9. Remove the heat shield and the plastic line retainer.

10. Disconnect the power steering pressure and return lines.

11. Disconnect the speed sensitive steering solenoid valve connector.

12. Remove the 5 rack and pinion mounting bolts and remove the rack and pinion assembly by sliding it out to the side.

To install:

13. Position the rack and pinion assembly and install the 5 mounting bolts. Tighten to 50 ft. lbs. (68 Nm).

14. Connect the speed sensitive steering solenoid valve connector.

15. Connect the return and pressure lines to the rack and pinion assembly and tighten the fittings to 20 ft. lbs. (27 Nm).

16. Install the plastic line retainer and the heat shield.

17. Raise the frame into position and tighten the body mount bolts to 76 ft. lbs. (103 Nm).

18. If equipped with 4.6L engine, connect the exhaust pipe at the catalytic converter.

19. Connect the tie rod ends to the steering knuckles; refer to the procedure in this Section.

20. If equipped, connect the road sensing suspension position sensor.

21. Install the left front wheel and tire assembly and lower the vehicle.

22. Connect the intermediate shaft lower coupling and tighten the bolt to 35 ft. lbs. (47 Nm).

23. Fill and bleed the power steering system as described in this Section.

Power Steering Pump

REMOVAL & INSTALLATION

Deville, Fleetwood and Sixty Special

1990

▶ **See Figures 113, 114 and 115**

1. Remove the serpentine drive belt.

2. Remove the power steering fluid from the reservoir.

3. Remove the reservoir mounting bolts and remove the reservoir from the vehicle by disengaging the reservoir tubes from the adapter.

4. Remove the belt tensioner.

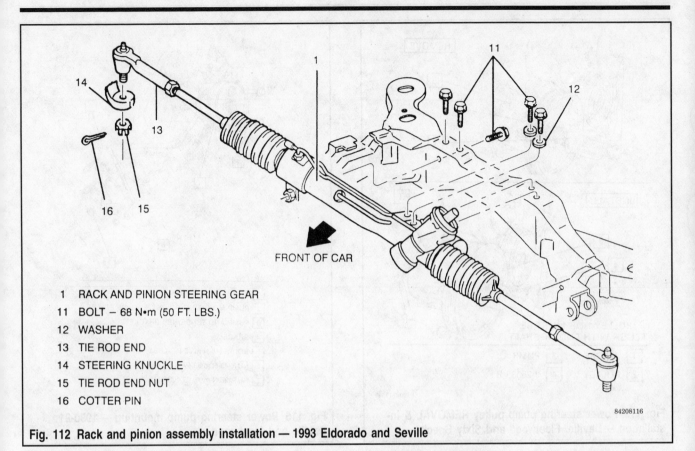

1   RACK AND PINION STEERING GEAR
11 BOLT – 68 N•m (50 FT. LBS.)
12 WASHER
13 TIE ROD END
14 STEERING KNUCKLE
15 TIE ROD END NUT
16 COTTER PIN

84208116

Fig. 112 Rack and pinion assembly installation — 1993 Eldorado and Seville

5. Remove the power steering pump pulley using tool J-29785-A or equivalent. Hold the body of the tool with a wrench and turn the bolt into the body of the tool to remove the pulley from the shaft.

6. Remove the pressure line fitting from the pump.

7. Remove the pump mounting bolts.

8. Use a small prybar to disengage the return line adapter clip from the adapter.

9. Disengage the adapter from the pump inlet. Make sure the O-ring is removed from the inlet port.

10. Remove the adapter from the return line.

To install:

11. Inspect all adapter O-rings for proper positioning or damage. Replace any cut or damaged O-rings.

12. Insert the return line adapter clip on the adapter at the return line port. Make sure that the beveled edges of the clip are facing outward.

13. Position the adapter on the pump, inserting the pump inlet tube until fully seated.

14. Position the pump in the vehicle while inserting the return line into the adapter port. Make sure that the line is fully seated and is retained by the adapter clip.

15. Install the pump mounting bolts but do not tighten at this time.

16. Install the pressure line fitting to the pump.

17. Tighten the pump mounting bolts to 18 ft. lbs. (25 Nm) and the pressure line fitting to 20 ft. lbs. (27 Nm).

18. Press the pulley onto the pump shaft using tool J-25033-B or equivalent. The face of the pulley hub must be flush with the pump shaft.

19. Position the belt tensioner mounting bolt in the vehicle.

20. Install the reservoir by carefully inserting the reservoir tubes into the adapter ports. Use a rocking motion to fully seat the tubes in the adapter. Install the reservoir mounting bolts.

21. Install the belt tensioner and tighten the mounting nut to 55 ft. lbs. (75 Nm).

22. Install the serpentine drive belt.

23. Fill and bleed the power steering system as described in this Section.

1991

▶ **See Figures 113, 115 and 117**

1. Remove the pump drive belt.

2. Remove the belt tensioner, if necessary for access.

3. Remove the power steering pump pulley using tool J-29785-A or equivalent. Hold the body of the tool with a wrench and turn the bolt into the body of the tool to remove the pulley from the shaft.

4. Remove the pressure line fitting from the pump. Remove the return line from the adapter using tool J-36391 or equivalent.

5. Remove the pump mounting bolts and the pump adapter assembly.

6. Disengage the adapter from the pump inlet. Make sure the pump O-ring is removed from the inlet port.

To install:

7. Inspect all adapter O-rings for proper positioning or damage. Replace any cut or damaged O-rings.

8. Position the adapter on the pump, inserting the pump inlet tube until fully seated.

9. Position the pump on the vehicle while inserting the adapter into the reservoir. The reservoir tubes do not need to be fully seated.

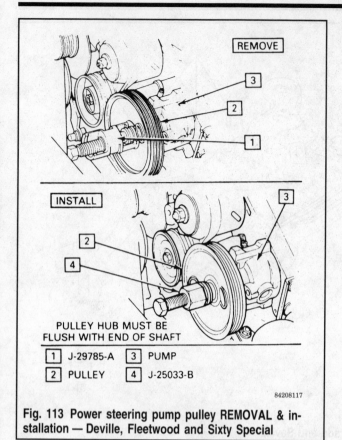

Fig. 113 Power steering pump pulley REMOVAL & installation — Deville, Fleetwood and Sixty Special

PULLEY HUB MUST BE FLUSH WITH END OF SHAFT

| 1 | J-29785-A | 3 | PUMP |
| 2 | PULLEY | 4 | J-25033-B |

84208117

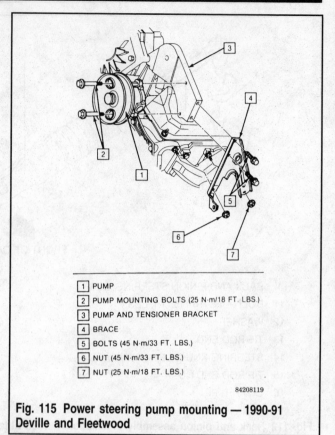

1	PUMP
2	PUMP MOUNTING BOLTS (25 N·m/18 FT. LBS.)
3	PUMP AND TENSIONER BRACKET
4	BRACE
5	BOLTS (45 N·m/33 FT. LBS.)
6	NUT (45 N·m/33 FT. LBS.)
7	NUT (25 N·m/18 FT. LBS.)

84208119

Fig. 115 Power steering pump mounting — 1990-91 Deville and Fleetwood

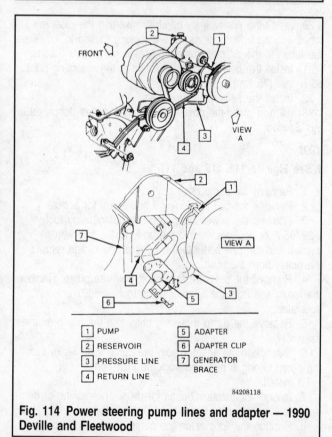

1	PUMP	5	ADAPTER
2	RESERVOIR	6	ADAPTER CLIP
3	PRESSURE LINE	7	GENERATOR BRACE
4	RETURN LINE		

84208118

Fig. 114 Power steering pump lines and adapter — 1990 Deville and Fleetwood

10. Insert the return pipe into the adapter port, making sure it is fully seated.

11. Install the pump mounting bolts but do not tighten at this time.

12. Install the pressure line fitting to the pump.

13. Tighten the pump mounting bolts to 18 ft. lbs. (25 Nm) and the pressure line fitting to 20 ft. lbs. (27 Nm).

14. Press the pulley onto the pump shaft using tool J-25033-B or equivalent. The face of the pulley hub must be flush with the pump shaft.

15. Install the belt tensioner, if removed, and tighten the mounting nut to 55 ft. lbs. (75 Nm).

16. Install the pump drive belt.

17. Fill and bleed the power steering system as described in this Section.

1992-93

▶ See Figures 113, 116, 117 and 118

1. Remove the pump drive belt.

2. Remove the belt tensioner, if necessary for access.

3. Remove the pump mounting bolts, then move the pump just enough for the pulley remover to access the shaft.

4. Remove the power steering pump pulley using tool J-29785-A or equivalent. Hold the body of the tool with a wrench and turn the bolt into the body of the tool to remove the pulley from the shaft.

5. Reinstall the pump and mounting bolts. Tighten the bolts just enough to hold the pump in place for disconnecting the power steering pressure hose from the pump.

6. Remove the pressure hose from the pump.

7. Remove the pump adapter, if necessary. Remove the return line from the adapter using tool J-36391 or equivalent. If

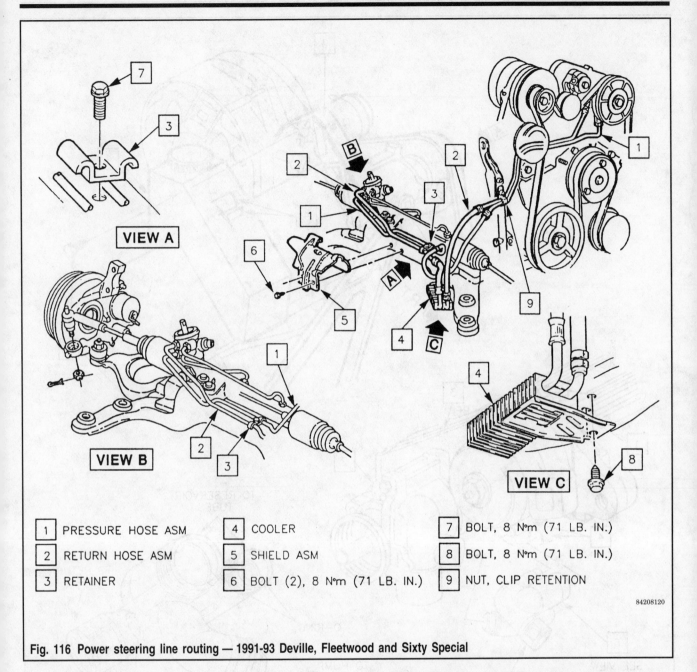

VIEW A

VIEW B

VIEW C

1	PRESSURE HOSE ASM	4	COOLER	7	BOLT, 8 N•m (71 LB. IN.)	
2	RETURN HOSE ASM	5	SHIELD ASM	8	BOLT, 8 N•m (71 LB. IN.)	
3	RETAINER	6	BOLT (2), 8 N•m (71 LB. IN.)	9	NUT, CLIP RETENTION	

84208120

Fig. 116 Power steering line routing — 1991-93 Deville, Fleetwood and Sixty Special

the adapter is removed from the pump, make sure the pump O-ring is removed from the inlet port.

To install:

8. Inspect all adapter O-rings for proper positioning or damage. Replace any cut or damaged O-rings.

9. With a new O-ring in place, position the adapter on the pump, inserting the pump inlet tube until fully seated.

10. Loosely connect the pressure hose to the pump, but do not tighten the fitting at this time.

11. Press the pulley onto the pump shaft using tool J-25033-B or equivalent. The face of the pulley hub must be flush with the pump shaft.

12. Position the pump on the vehicle, mating adapter to reservoir. The reservoir tubes do not need to be fully seated. Insert the return pipe into the adapter port, making sure it is fully seated.

13. Install the pump mounting bolts and tighten to 18 ft. lbs. (25 Nm). Tighten the pressure line fitting to 20 ft. lbs. (27 Nm).

14. Install the belt tensioner and the pump drive belt.

15. Fill and bleed the power steering system as described in this Section.

Eldorado and Seville

4.6L ENGINE

▶ **See Figure 119**

1. Remove the serpentine drive belt.

2. Remove the power steering fluid from the reservoir.

3. Disconnect the return line from the reservoir and the pressure line from the pump.

4. Remove the pump mounting bolt and remove the pump, reservoir, pulley and bracket assembly from the vehicle.

5. Remove the pump and reservoir from the bracket.

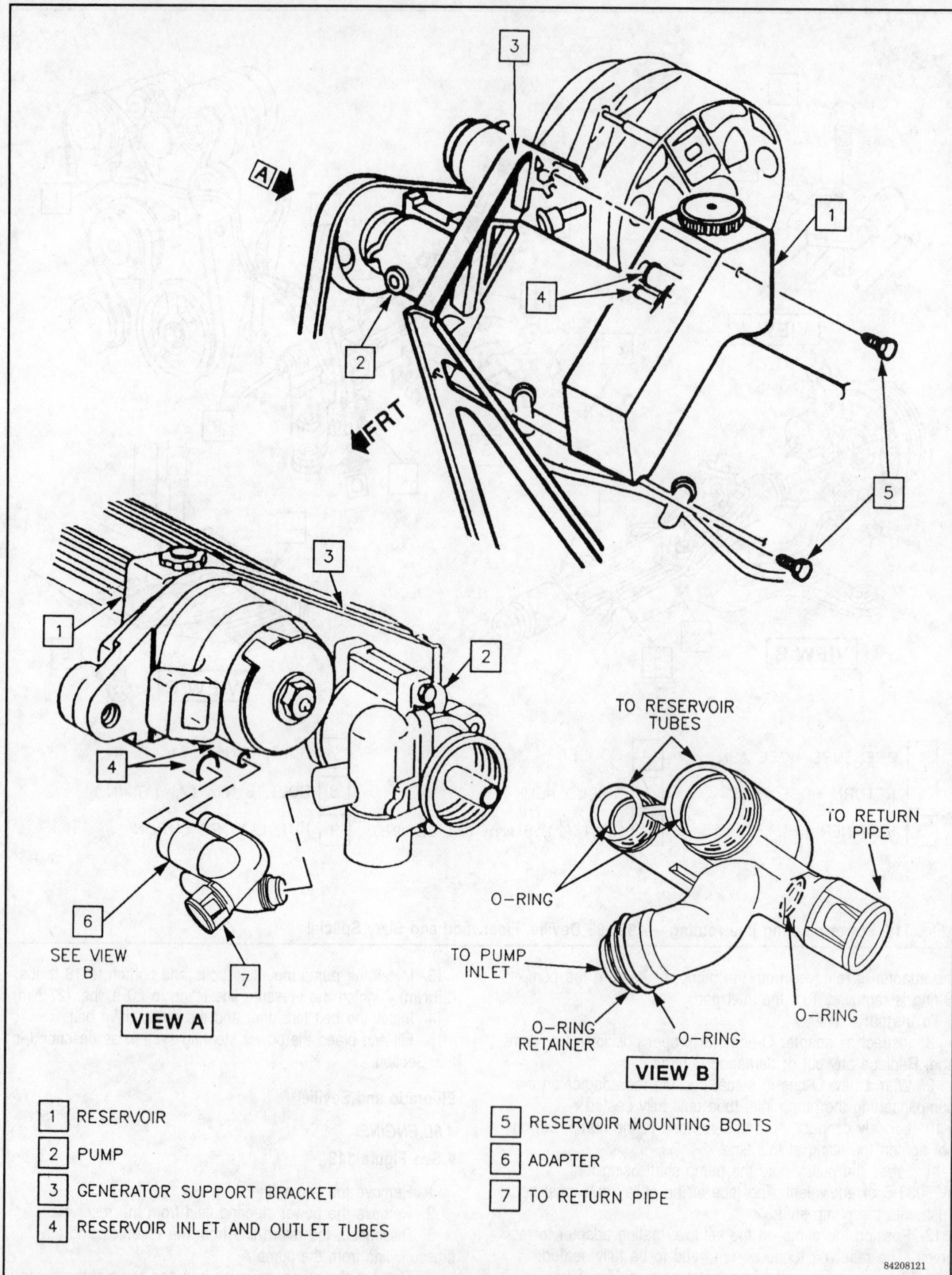

3

A

FRT

1

2

4

5

TO RESERVOIR
TUBES

TO RETURN
PIPE

O-RING

O-RING

TO PUMP
INLET

O-RING
RETAINER

O-RING

VIEW B

3

1

2

4

6

SEE VIEW
B

7

VIEW A

1	RESERVOIR	5	RESERVOIR MOUNTING BOLTS
2	PUMP	6	ADAPTER
3	GENERATOR SUPPORT BRACKET	7	TO RETURN PIPE
4	RESERVOIR INLET AND OUTLET TUBES		

84208121

Fig. 117 Power steering reservoir and adapter — 1991-93 Deville, Fleetwood and Sixty Special

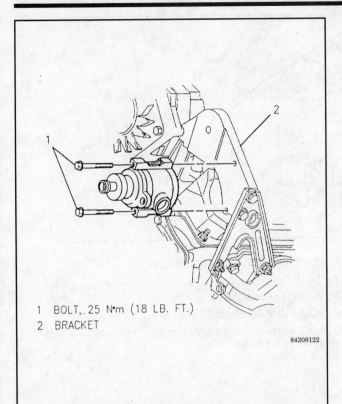

1 BOLT, 25 N•m (18 LB. FT.)
2 BRACKET

84208122

Fig. 118 Power steering pump installation — 1992-93 Deville, Fleetwood and Sixty Special

6. Remove the retaining clips that attach the reservoir to the pump.

7. Remove the pulley from the pump as follows:

   a. If not equipped with center hub, remove the pulley using 3-jaw puller J-25031 and tool J-38343-4 or equivalents. Make sure that the puller is properly aligned to the pump shaft.

   b. If equipped with center hub, remove the pulley using tool J-25034-B or equivalent. Hold the body of the tool with a wrench and turn the bolt into the body of the tool to remove the pulley from the shaft.

To install:

8. Install the pulley to the pump as follows:

   a. If not equipped with center hub, install the pulley using tools J-36015 and J-39391 or equivalents. The face of the pulley hub must be flush with the pump shaft.

❋❋WARNING

Do not use an arbor press to install the pulley.

   b. If equipped with center hub, use installation tool J-25033-B or equivalent, to install the pulley.

9. Attach the reservoir to the pump with the retaining clips.

10. Install the pump and reservoir to the bracket and tighten the pump-to-bracket bolts to 18 ft. lbs. (24 Nm).

11. Position the pump, reservoir, pulley and bracket assembly in the vehicle. Install the pump-to-engine mounting bolt and tighten to 35 ft. lbs. (47 Nm).

12. Connect the pressure line to the pump and tighten the fitting to 20 ft. lbs. (27 Nm).

13. Connect the return line to the reservoir.

14. Install the serpentine drive belt.

15. Fill and bleed the power steering system as described in this Section.

4.9L ENGINE

▶ **See Figures 120 and 121**

1. Disconnect the negative battery cable.

2. Remove the serpentine drive belt.

3. Remove the pump pulley using removal tool J-25034-B or equivalent.

4. Disconnect the pressure line at the pump.

5. Remove the pump mounting bolts.

6. Remove the adapter from the pump as follows:

   a. Remove the power steering fluid from the reservoir.

   b. Remove the pressure line retainer nut on the engine block to ease removal of the return line.

   c. Remove the return line from the adapter using tool J-36391 or equivalent.

   d. Reposition the pump to disengage the adapter from the pump inlet.

   e. Disengage the return line from the adapter and remove the adapter from the reservoir tubes.

To install:

7. Inspect all adapter O-rings for proper positioning or damage. Replace any cut or damaged O-rings.

8. Make sure that all O-rings are properly positioned on the adapter, including the pump port O-ring and seal protector.

9. Lubricate all adapter ports with petroleum jelly.

10. Install the adapter on the return line.

11. Position the pump so the adapter pump inlet tube is positioned in the pump inlet. Be extremely careful to prevent seal damage.

12. Install the adapter on the reservoir tubes.

13. Install the pump mounting bolts and tighten to 18 ft. lbs. (24 Nm).

14. Install the retainer nut on the block.

15. Connect the pressure line at the pump.

16. Install the pulley using installation tool J-25033-B.

➡ **On 1990 vehicles the pulley hub must be flush with the end of the shaft. On 1991-93 vehicles, the pulley hub is installed until it contacts the internal stop.**

17. Install the serpentine drive belt.

18. Fill and bleed the power steering system as described in this Section.

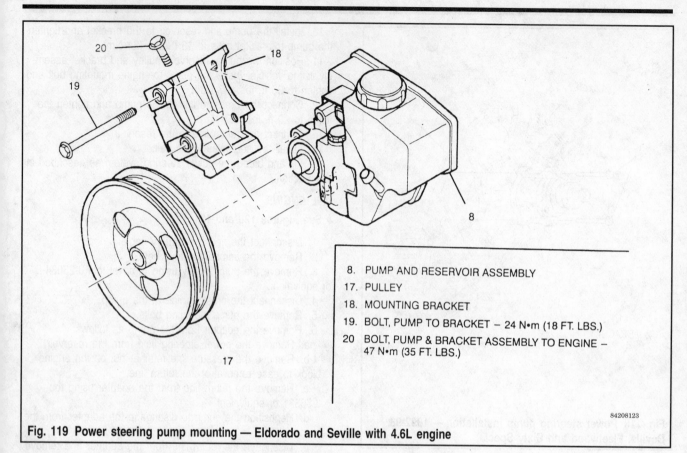

8. PUMP AND RESERVOIR ASSEMBLY
17. PULLEY
18. MOUNTING BRACKET
19. BOLT, PUMP TO BRACKET — 24 N•m (18 FT. LBS.)
20. BOLT, PUMP & BRACKET ASSEMBLY TO ENGINE — 47 N•m (35 FT. LBS.)

84208123

Fig. 119 Power steering pump mounting — Eldorado and Seville with 4.6L engine

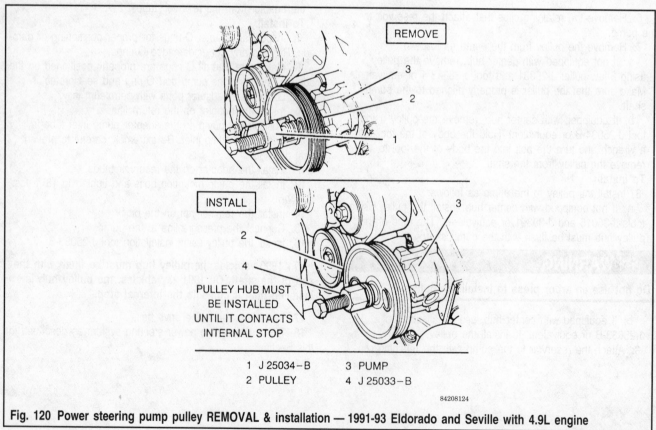

REMOVE

INSTALL

PULLEY HUB MUST
BE INSTALLED
UNTIL IT CONTACTS
INTERNAL STOP

1 J 25034–B   3 PUMP
2 PULLEY   4 J 25033–B

84208124

Fig. 120 Power steering pump pulley REMOVAL & installation — 1991-93 Eldorado and Seville with 4.9L engine

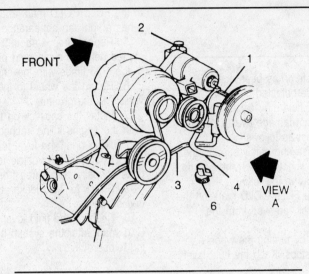

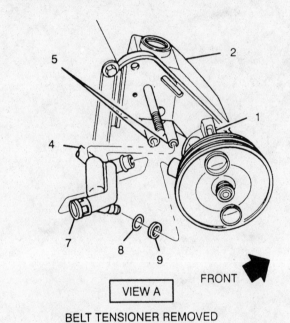

VIEW A

BELT TENSIONER REMOVED

1	PUMP
2	RESERVOIR
3	PRESSURE PIPE (TO GEAR)
4	RETURN PIPE (FROM COOLER)
5	RESERVOIR TUBES
6	J 36391 QUICK DISCONNECT TOOL
7	ADAPTER
8	$5/8$" O–RING
9	SEAL PROTECTOR

84208126

Fig. 121 Power steering pump mounting — Eldorado and Seville with 4.9L engine

BLEEDING

If the power steering hydraulic system has been serviced, an accurate fluid level reading cannot be obtained unless air is bled from the system. The air in the fluid may cause pump cavitation noise and may cause pump damage over a period of time. Bleed the air from the system as follows:

1. The engine must be OFF. Raise and safely support the front of the vehicle just so the front wheels are off the ground.

2. Turn the front wheel all the way to the left.

3. Add power steering fluid to the FULL COLD mark on the fluid level indicator. Leave the capstick removed from the reservoir.

4. Bleed the air from the system by turning the wheels from side-to-side without hitting the stops. Keep the fluid level at the FULL COLD mark and check its color. Fluid with air in it has a light tan appearance.

5. Repeat Step 4 about 12 times. If the engine had been started before the bleeding procedure was begun, repeat Step 4 about 20 times with the engine OFF.

6. Return the wheel to the center position and lower the vehicle to the ground.

7. Install the capstick on the reservoir and start the engine. With the engine idling, recheck the fluid level. If necessary, add fluid to bring the level to the FULL COLD mark.

8. Road test the vehicle to make sure the steering functions normally and is free from noise.

9. Check for fluid leaks at all power steering system connection points.

10. Recheck the fluid level. The fluid level should be at the HOT mark after the system has stabilized at its normal operating temperature.

TORQUE SPECIFICATIONS

Component	U.S.	Metric
Ball joint nut*		
Deville, Fleetwood and Sixty Special		
Step 1:	88 inch lbs.	10 Nm
Step 2:	+ 120°	+ 120°
Eldorado and Seville		
Step 1:	84 inch lbs.	10 Nm
Step 2:	+ 120°	+ 120°
* See Text		
Ball joint-to-lower control arm nuts	50 ft. lbs.	68 Nm
Front hub nut		
1990–91:	185 ft. lbs.	251 Nm
1992–93*:	110 ft. lbs.	145 Nm
* See Text		
Front hub retaining bolts:	70 ft. lbs.	95 Nm
Front lower control arm		
Deville, Fleetwood and Sixty Special		
Front mounting nut:	140 ft. lbs.	190 Nm
Rear mounting nut:	91 ft. lbs.	123 Nm
Eldorado and Seville		
Brake reaction rod nut:	58 ft. lbs.	78 Nm
Bushing bolt:	103 ft. lbs.	140 Nm
Bushing nut:	91 ft. lbs.	123 Nm
Front stabilizer bar bracket bolts:	35 ft. lbs.	48 Nm
Front stabilizer bar link nuts		
Deville, Fleetwood and Sixty Special:	13 ft. lbs.	17 Nm
Eldorado and Seville:	48 ft. lbs.	65 Nm
Front strut shaft nut:	55 ft. lbs.	75 Nm
Front strut-to-body nuts:	18 ft. lbs.	24 Nm
Front strut-to-knuckle bolts:	140 ft. lbs.	190 Nm
Front tie bar through bolts:	20 ft. lbs.	27 Nm
Ignition lock cylinder retaining screw:	22 inch lbs.	2.5 Nm
Ignition switch mounting stud		
Deville, Fleetwood and Sixty Special:	35 inch lbs.	4 Nm
Ignition/dimmer switch nut and screw		
Deville, Fleetwood and Sixty Special:	35 inch lbs.	4 Nm
Inflator module bolts/screws:	27 inch lbs.	3 Nm
Inner tie rod housing:	74 ft. lbs.	100 Nm
Inner tie rod jam nut:	40 ft. lbs.	54 Nm
Leaf spring insulator nuts:	21 ft. lbs.	28 Nm
Leaf spring retainer bolts:	21 ft. lbs.	28 Nm
Outer tie rod nut:	35 ft. lbs.	47 Nm
Power steering line fittings:	20 ft. lbs.	27 Nm
Power steering pump mounting bolts:	18 ft. lbs.	24 Nm
Rack and pinion mounting bolts:	50 ft. lbs.	68 Nm
Rear control arms/links		
Deville Fleetwood and Sixty Special		
Adjustment link-to-control arm nut:	63 ft. lbs.	85 Nm
Adjustment link-to-knuckle nut:	33 ft. lbs.	45 Nm
Control arm ball joint nut		
1990–91		
Step 1:	88 inch lbs.	10 Nm
Step 2:	+ ⅔ turn	+ ⅔ turn

84208127

TORQUE SPECIFICATIONS

Component	U.S.	Metric
1992–93		
Except HD chassis and J55		
Step 1:	88 inch lbs.	10 Nm
Step 2:	+ 4 flats	+ 4 flats
With HD chassis and J55		
Step 1:	88 inch lbs.	10 Nm
Step 2:	+ 2½ flats	+ 2½ flats
Control arm nut:	85 ft. lbs.	115 Nm
Eldorado and Seville		
1990–92		
Inner control arm bolts:	66 ft. lbs.	90 Nm
Knuckle pivot bolt:	59 ft. lbs.	80 Nm
1993		
Lower control arm inner nuts:	75 ft. lbs.	102 Nm
Lower control arm outer nut:	75 ft. lbs.	102 Nm
Upper control arm inner nuts:	42 ft. lbs.	57 Nm
Upper control arm outer nuts:	42 ft. lbs.	57 Nm
Toe link inner nut:	42 ft. lbs.	57 Nm
Toe link outer bolt:	55 ft. lbs.	75 Nm
Rear hub retaining bolts:	52 ft. lbs.	70 Nm
Rear shock absorber lower nut		
1993 Eldorado and Seville:	75 ft. lbs.	102 Nm
Rear shock absorber upper nut		
1993 Eldorado and Seville:	55 ft. lbs.	75 Nm
Rear stabilizer bar		
Deville, Fleetwood and Sixty Special		
Link bolt		
1990–91:	37 ft. lbs.	50 Nm
1992–93:	17 ft. lbs.	23 Nm
Link nut:	13 ft. lbs.	17 Nm
Eldorado and Seville		
1990–92		
Link bolts:	43 ft. lbs.	58 Nm
Mounting nuts:	43 ft. lbs.	58 Nm
1993		
Bracket bolt:	44 ft. lbs.	60 Nm
Lower link bolt:	44 ft. lbs.	60 Nm
Upper link nut:	38 ft. lbs.	52 Nm
Rear strut		
Deville, Fleetwood and Sixty Special		
Strut-to-knuckle nuts:	140 ft. lbs.	190 Nm
Strut tower nuts:	19 ft. lbs.	25 Nm
Eldorado and Seville		
Knuckle pinch bolt:	40 ft. lbs.	55 Nm
Upper strut nut:	65 ft. lbs.	88 Nm
Steering column		
Deville, Fleetwood and Sixty Special		
Brace-to-bulkhead bolt/screw:	84 inch lbs.	9.5 Nm
Intermediate shaft pinch bolt:	35 ft. lbs.	47 Nm
Lower support bolt/screw:	20 ft. lbs.	27 Nm
Reinforcement plate bolts/screws:	17 inch lbs.	1.9 Nm
Seal bolt/screw:	21 inch lbs.	2.4 Nm
Shaft nut:	30 ft. lbs.	41 Nm
Upper bracket bolt/screw:	20 ft. lbs.	27 Nm
Eldorado and Seville		
Intermediate shaft pinch bolt:	35 ft. lbs.	47 Nm
Lower column support bolts/nuts:	20 ft. lbs.	27 Nm
Lower bracket-to-column screws:	12 ft. lbs.	16 Nm
Shaft nut:	30 ft. lbs.	41 Nm
Upper column support bolts/nuts:	20 ft. lbs.	27 Nm

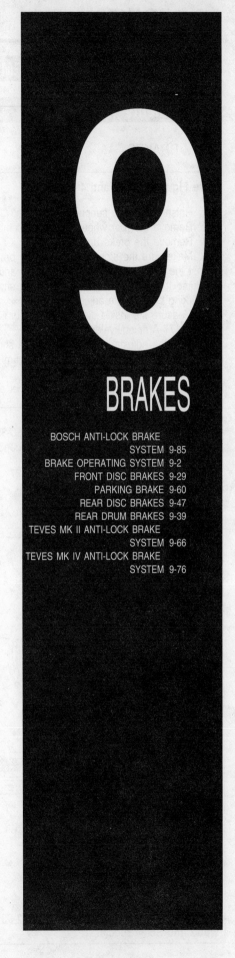

9

BRAKES

BRAKE OPERATING SYSTEM

Adjustments

DRUM BRAKES

▶ See Figures 1, 2, 3 and 4

1. Raise and safely support the vehicle.
2. Remove the rear wheel and tire assemblies.
3. Remove the brake drums.
4. Make sure the stops on the parking brake levers are against the edge of the shoe web. If the parking brake cable is holding the stops off of the edge of the shoe web, loosen the parking brake cable adjustment.
5. Measure the inside diameter of the brake drum using tool J-21177-A or equivalent.
6. Turn the adjuster nut until the brake shoe diameter is 0.050 in. (1.27mm) less than the inside drum diameter for each rear wheel.
7. Install the brake drums and the wheel and tire assemblies.
8. Lower the vehicle.
9. Apply and release the brake pedal 30-35 times using normal pedal force, pausing about one second between applications.

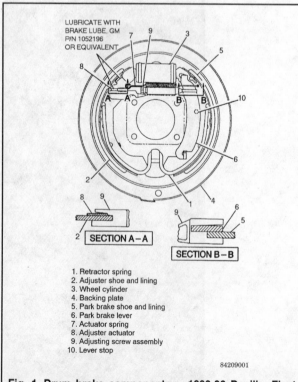

LUBRICATE WITH BRAKE LUBE, GM P/N 1052196 OR EQUIVALENT

SECTION A–A

SECTION B–B

1. Retractor spring
2. Adjuster shoe and lining
3. Wheel cylinder
4. Backing plate
5. Park brake shoe and lining
6. Park brake lever
7. Actuator spring
8. Adjuster actuator
9. Adjusting screw assembly
10. Lever stop

84209001

Fig. 1 Drum brake components — 1992-93 Deville, Fleetwood and Sixty Special

Brake Light Switch

REMOVAL & INSTALLATION

▶ See Figures 5, 6 and 7

1. Disconnect the negative battery cable.
2. Remove the necessary instrument panel sound insulators, to gain access to the switch.
3. Disconnect the electrical connector(s) from the switch.
4. If equipped, disconnect the vacuum hose from the switch.
5. Remove the brake light switch.
6. Installation is the reverse of the removal procedure. Adjust the switch.

ADJUSTMENT

▶ See Figures 5, ?, 6 and 7

Eldorado, Seville and 1990 Deville and Fleetwood

1. Hold the brake pedal in the applied position.
2. Insert the switch into the retainer until the switch body seats on the tube clip.
3. Pull the brake pedal upward against the internal pedal stop. The switch will be moved in the retainer providing proper adjustment.

1991-93 Deville, Fleetwood and Sixty Special

1. Fully depress and hold the brake pedal.
2. Insert the switch, with all connections made, into the mounting bracket until no more audible clicks are heard and all retaining tabs are seated.
3. Pull the brake pedal rearward until no audible clicks are heard, then release the pedal. Repeat to make sure no audible clicks remain.
4. Check the adjustment of the switch, comparing the installation to the example shown in the figure. Only the notch should be visible; if the plunger is visible or the notch is not, repeat the adjustment.

Brake Pedal

REMOVAL & INSTALLATION

Deville, Fleetwood and Sixty Special

1990

▶ See Figure 8

1. Remove the necessary sound insulator panel(s) to gain access to the pedal assembly.
2. Remove the upper pivot bolt, bushings and spacer.
3. Remove the retainer and washer from the pedal stud.

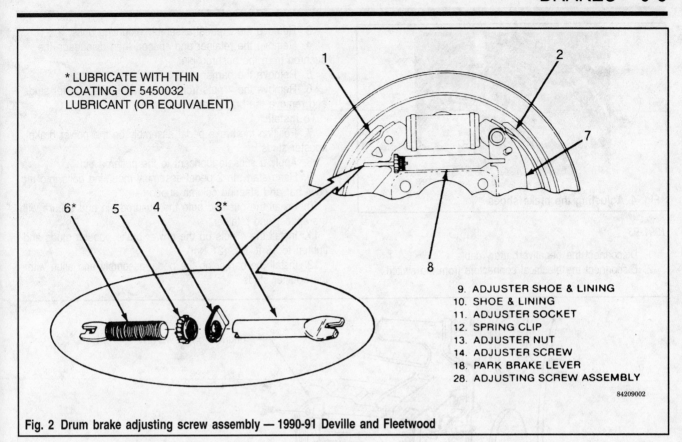

* LUBRICATE WITH THIN
COATING OF 5450032
LUBRICANT (OR EQUIVALENT)

9. ADJUSTER SHOE & LINING
10. SHOE & LINING
11. ADJUSTER SOCKET
12. SPRING CLIP
13. ADJUSTER NUT
14. ADJUSTER SCREW
18. PARK BRAKE LEVER
28. ADJUSTING SCREW ASSEMBLY

84209002

Fig. 2 Drum brake adjusting screw assembly — 1990-91 Deville and Fleetwood

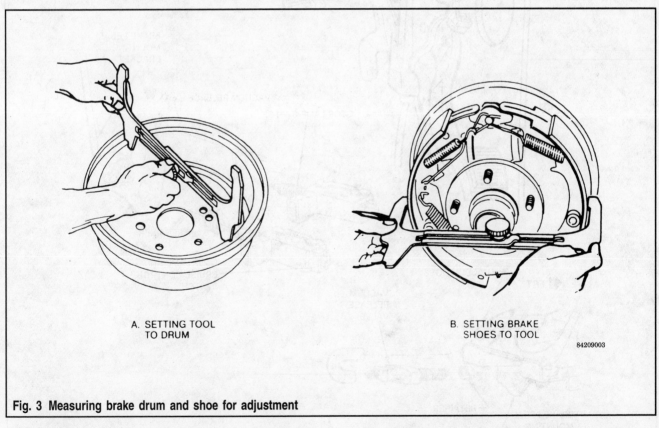

A. SETTING TOOL
TO DRUM

B. SETTING BRAKE
SHOES TO TOOL

84209003

Fig. 3 Measuring brake drum and shoe for adjustment

4. Disengage the booster pushrod from the pedal stud and remove the pedal from the vehicle.

5. Installation is the reverse of the removal procedure. Tighten the pivot bolt to 25 ft. lbs. (34 Nm).

Fig. 4 Adjusting the brake shoes

1991-93

1. Disconnect the negative battery cable.
2. Disconnect the electrical connectors from the switch.

3. Remove the 2 pedal assembly mounting bolts.
4. Remove the retainer and spacer, then disengage the pushrod from the pushrod pin.
5. Remove the barrier.
6. Remove the 4 nuts from the power brake booster studs and remove the brake pedal assembly.

To install:

7. Position the brake pedal assembly on the power brake booster studs.
8. Apply a suitable lubricant to the pushrod pin.
9. Hand start the 2 pedal assembly mounting bolts into the cowl bar and steering column support.
10. Install the pushrod onto the pushrod pin and secure with the spacer and retainer.
11. Install the 4 nuts on the power brake booster studs and tighten to 15 ft. lbs. (21 Nm).
12. Install the barrier on the pedal assembly and align with the booster studs.

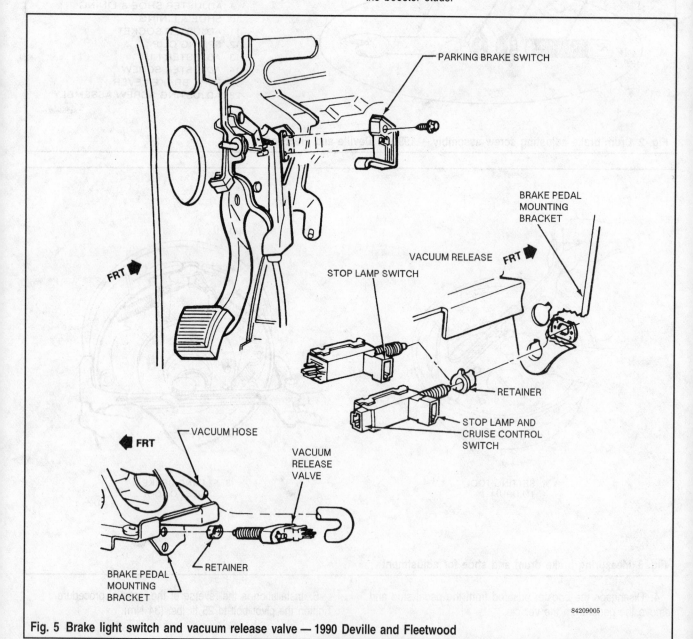

Fig. 5 Brake light switch and vacuum release valve — 1990 Deville and Fleetwood

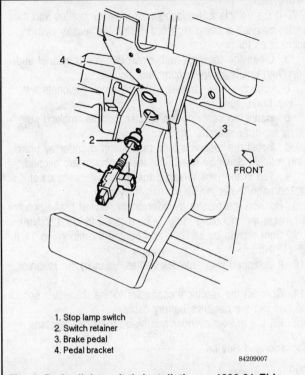

1. Stop lamp switch
2. Switch retainer
3. Brake pedal
4. Pedal bracket

84209007

Fig. 6 Brake light switch installation — 1990-91 Eldorado and Seville

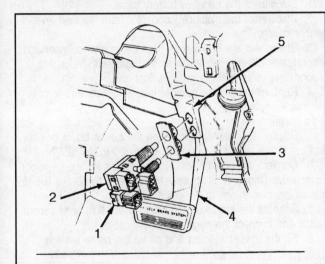

1. Stop lamp switch
2. TCC switch
3. Switch retainer
4. Brake pedal
5. Pedal bracket

84209008

Fig. 7 Brake light switch installation — 1992-93 Eldorado and Seville

13. Tighten bolt 1 to 18 ft. lbs. (24 Nm), then tighten bolt 2 to the same specification; refer to the figure.

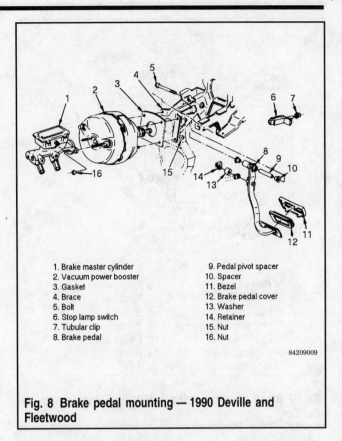

1. Brake master cylinder	9. Pedal pivot spacer
2. Vacuum power booster	10. Spacer
3. Gasket	11. Bezel
4. Brace	12. Brake pedal cover
5. Bolt	13. Washer
6. Stop lamp switch	14. Retainer
7. Tubular clip	15. Nut
8. Brake pedal	16. Nut

84209009

Fig. 8 Brake pedal mounting — 1990 Deville and Fleetwood

14. Connect the electrical connectors to the switch and connect the negative battery cable.

Eldorado and Seville

▶ See Figures 9 and 10

1. Remove the left-hand sound insulator panel.
2. Remove the central power supply and mounting bracket.
3. Remove the upper pivot bolt, bushings and spacer.
4. Remove the retainer and washer from the pedal stud.
5. Disengage the booster pushrod from the pedal stud and remove the pedal from the vehicle.
6. Installation is the reverse of the removal procedure. Tighten the pivot bolt to 33 ft. lbs. (45 Nm).

Master Cylinder

REMOVAL & INSTALLATION

Deville, Fleetwood and Sixty Special

1990

▶ See Figure 11

1. Disconnect the negative battery cable.
2. Disconnect the electrical connector from the fluid level sensor switch.
3. Disconnect the brake lines from the master cylinder and proportioner valves. Plug the lines and master cylinder and proportioner valve ports to prevent fluid loss.
4. Remove the master cylinder mounting nuts and remove the master cylinder.

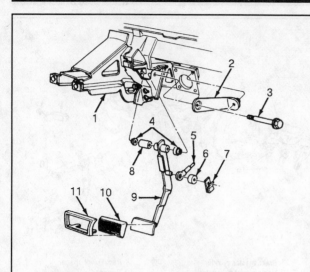

1. Pedal bracket
2. Brace
3. Pivot bolt
   (45 N·m/33 ft.lbs.)
4. Bushings
5. Pushrod (part
   of hydraulic unit)
6. Foam washer
7. Retainer
8. Spacer
9. Pedal assembly
10. Pedal cover
11. Bezel

84209011

Fig. 9 Brake pedal mounting — 1990-91 Eldorado and Seville

To install:

5. Position the master cylinder on the power brake booster and install the mounting nuts. Tighten to 20 ft. lbs. (27 Nm).

6. Connect the brake lines and tighten the fittings to 11 ft. lbs. (15 Nm).

7. Connect the electrical connector to the fluid level sensor switch and connect the negative battery cable.

8. Fill the master cylinder and bleed the brake system.

1991-93

▶ See Figures 12, 13 and 14

1. Disconnect the negative battery cable.

2. Disconnect the electrical connector from the fluid level sensor.

3. If equipped with anti-lock brakes, drain the brake fluid from the master cylinder reservoir, then disconnect and plug the reservoir hose.

4. Disconnect the brake lines from the master cylinder. Plug the lines and master cylinder ports to prevent fluid loss.

5. Remove the master cylinder mounting nuts and remove the master cylinder.

6. If the vehicle is equipped with anti-lock brakes and the master cylinder is being replaced, remove the master cylinder reservoir as follows:

   a. Clamp the mounting flange on the master cylinder body in a vise. Do not clamp on the master cylinder body.

   b. Tap back the spring pins until they are clear of the reservoir. Be careful not to damage the reservoir or master cylinder.

   c. Remove the reservoir and the reservoir seals. Inspect the reservoir for cracks or deformities and replace as necessary.

To install:

7. If the vehicle is equipped with anti-lock brakes and the master cylinder is being replaced, install the master cylinder reservoir as follows:

   a. Clean the reservoir with clean denatured alcohol and dry with unlubricated compressed air.

   b. Lubricate new seals and the reservoir bayonets with clean brake fluid.

   c. Install the seals on the master cylinder, making sure they are fully seated.

   d. Install the reservoir onto the master cylinder by pressing straight down by hand until the pin holes are aligned.

   e. Tap in the pins to retain the reservoir, being careful not to damage the reservoir or master cylinder.

8. Position the master cylinder on the power brake booster and install the mounting nuts. Tighten to 20 ft. lbs. (27 Nm).

9. Connect the brake lines and tighten the fittings to 11 ft. lbs. (15 Nm).

10. If equipped with anti-lock brakes, connect the reservoir hose.

11. Connect the electrical connector to the fluid level sensor and connect the negative battery cable.

12. Fill the master cylinder and bleed the brake system.

Eldorado and Seville

1990

▶ See Figure 11

1. Disconnect the negative battery cable.

2. Disconnect the electrical connector from the fluid level sensor switch.

3. Disconnect the brake lines from the master cylinder and proportioner valves. Plug the lines and master cylinder and proportioner valve ports to prevent fluid loss.

4. Remove the master cylinder mounting nuts and remove the master cylinder.

To install:

5. Position the master cylinder on the power brake booster and install the mounting nuts. Tighten to 20 ft. lbs. (27 Nm).

6. Connect the brake lines. Tighten the brake line-to-proportioner valve fittings to 11 ft. lbs. (15 Nm) and the brake line-to-master cylinder fittings to 24 ft. lbs. (32 Nm).

7. Connect the electrical connector to the fluid level sensor switch and connect the negative battery cable.

8. Fill the master cylinder and bleed the brake system.

1991-92

▶ See Figure 15

1. Disconnect the negative battery cable.

2. Disconnect the electrical connector from the fluid level sensor switch.

3. Disconnect the brake lines from the master cylinder. Plug the lines and master cylinder ports to prevent fluid loss.

4. Remove the master cylinder mounting nuts and remove the master cylinder.

To install:

5. Position the master cylinder on the power brake booster and install the mounting nuts. Tighten to 20 ft. lbs. (27 Nm).

6. Connect the brake lines and tighten the fittings to 24 ft. lbs. (32 Nm).

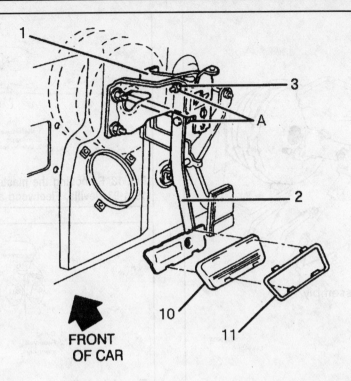

FRONT OF CAR

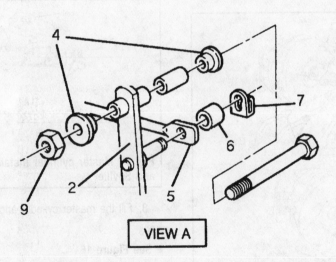

VIEW A

1. Pedal bracket
2. Pedal assembly
3. Pivot bolt
4. Bushings
5. Pushrod (part of hydraulic unit)
6. Washer
7. Retainer
8. Spacer
9. Nut (45 N m/ 33 ft.lbs.)
10. Pedal cover
11. Bezel

84209012

Fig. 10 Brake pedal mounting — 1992-93 Eldorado and Seville

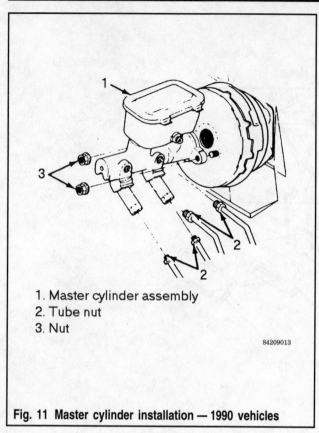

1. Master cylinder assembly
2. Tube nut
3. Nut

84209013

Fig. 11 Master cylinder installation — 1990 vehicles

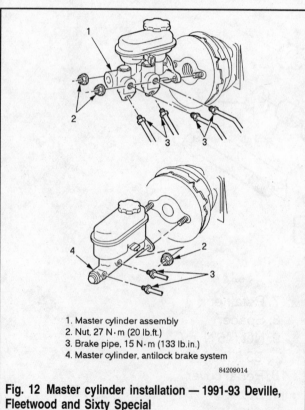

1. Master cylinder assembly
2. Nut, 27 N·m (20 lb.ft.)
3. Brake pipe, 15 N·m (133 lb.in.)
4. Master cylinder, antilock brake system

84209014

Fig. 12 Master cylinder installation — 1991-93 Deville, Fleetwood and Sixty Special

7. Connect the electrical connector to the fluid level sensor switch and connect the negative battery cable.

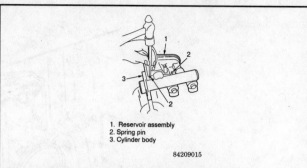

1. Reservoir assembly
2. Spring pin
3. Cylinder body

84209015

Fig. 13 Removing the master cylinder reservoir — 1991-93 Deville, Fleetwood and Sixty Special

1. O-ring
2. Reservoir assembly
3. O-ring
4. Cylinder body

84209016

Fig. 14 Installing the master cylinder reservoir — 1991-93 Deville, Fleetwood and Sixty Special

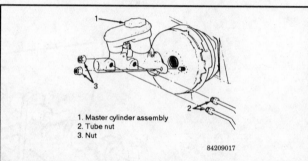

1. Master cylinder assembly
2. Tube nut
3. Nut

84209017

Fig. 15 Master cylinder installation — 1991-92 Eldorado and Seville

8. Fill the master cylinder and bleed the brake system.

1993

▶ See Figure 16

1. Disconnect the negative battery cable.

2. Remove the master cylinder reservoir cap and diaphragm. Use a syringe to remove as much brake fluid as possible from the master cylinder. Reinstall the diaphragm and cap.

3. Disconnect the electrical connector from the fluid level sensor switch.

4. Disconnect the brake lines from the master cylinder. Plug the lines and master cylinder ports to prevent fluid loss.

5. Remove the master cylinder mounting nuts.

6. Being careful not to damage the rubber hose or reservoir nozzle, pinch off the hose as close to the nozzle as possible, using clamp-type pliers.

7. Move the master cylinder forward off the booster studs and lower the flange end of the master cylinder so that the reservoir nozzle points up.

✴✴WARNING

Use shop cloths to prevent any brake fluid that may leak from the master cylinder or rubber hose from contacting the vehicle body or electrical connections.

8. Remove the hose clamp and rubber hose from the reservoir nozzle and remove the master cylinder from the vehicle.

To install:

9. Position the master cylinder on the power brake booster and install the mounting nuts. Tighten to 20 ft. lbs. (27 Nm).

10. Connect the brake lines and tighten the fittings to 24 ft. lbs. (32 Nm).

11. Connect the rubber hose to the reservoir nozzle and secure with a new hose clamp.

12. Connect the electrical connector to the fluid level sensor switch and connect the negative battery cable.

13. Fill the master cylinder and bleed the brake system.

OVERHAUL

1990 Vehicles

▶ See Figure 17

DISASSEMBLY

1. Remove the master cylinder from the vehicle.

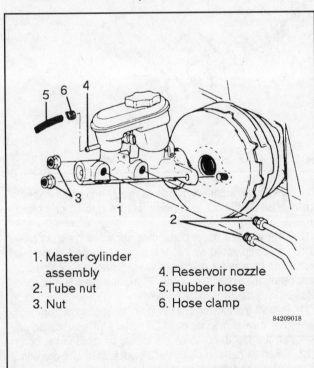

1. Master cylinder
   assembly
2. Tube nut
3. Nut
4. Reservoir nozzle
5. Rubber hose
6. Hose clamp

84209018

Fig. 16 Master cylinder installation — 1993 Eldorado and Seville

2. Wipe the reservoir cover clean and remove the cover and diaphragm. Empty the brake fluid from the master cylinder. Properly dispose the fluid.

3. Inspect the reservoir cover and diaphragm for cuts, cracks, nicks or deformation and replace as necessary.

4. Use needle nose pliers to compress the switch locking tabs at the inboard side of the master cylinder and remove the fluid level switch.

5. Remove the proportioner valves and O-rings.

6. Depress the primary piston assembly and remove the retainer. Be careful not to damage the piston, bore or retainer groove.

7. Plug all other outlet ports, then apply low pressure unlubricated compressed air into the upper outlet port at the blind end of the bore to remove the primary piston assembly, secondary piston assembly and spring. Remove the seals and spring retainer from the secondary piston.

8. Inspect the master cylinder bore for scoring or corrosion. The entire master cylinder must be replaced if any scoring or corrosion are found; no abrasives should be used in the bore.

9. Clean all parts in clean denatured alcohol and dry with unlubricated compressed air.

ASSEMBLY

1. Lubricate the primary and secondary seals with clean brake fluid. Install the seals and spring retainer onto the secondary piston.

2. Lubricate the master cylinder bore and secondary piston assembly with clean brake fluid. Install the spring and secondary piston assembly into the master cylinder bore.

3. Lubricate the primary piston assembly with clean brake fluid and install it into the master cylinder bore.

4. Depress the primary piston assembly and install the retainer.

5. Lubricate new O-rings and the external proportioner valve threads with clean brake fluid. Install the O-rings on the proportioner valves.

6. Install the proportioner valves into the master cylinder and tighten to 24 ft. lbs. (31 Nm).

7. Install the fluid level sensor switch until the locking tabs snap into place.

8. Install the diaphragm into the reservoir cover and install on the reservoir.

9. Install the master cylinder on the vehicle.

1991-93 Deville, Fleetwood and Sixty Special

▶ See Figure 18

➡The following procedure applies only to vehicles without anti-lock brakes. The master cylinder on vehicles equipped with anti-lock brakes cannot be overhauled; service is by replacement only.

DISASSEMBLY

1. Remove the master cylinder from the vehicle.

2. Wipe the reservoir cap clean and remove the cap and diaphragm. Empty the brake fluid from the master cylinder. Properly dispose the fluid.

3. Inspect the reservoir cap and diaphragm for cuts, cracks, nicks or deformation and replace as necessary.

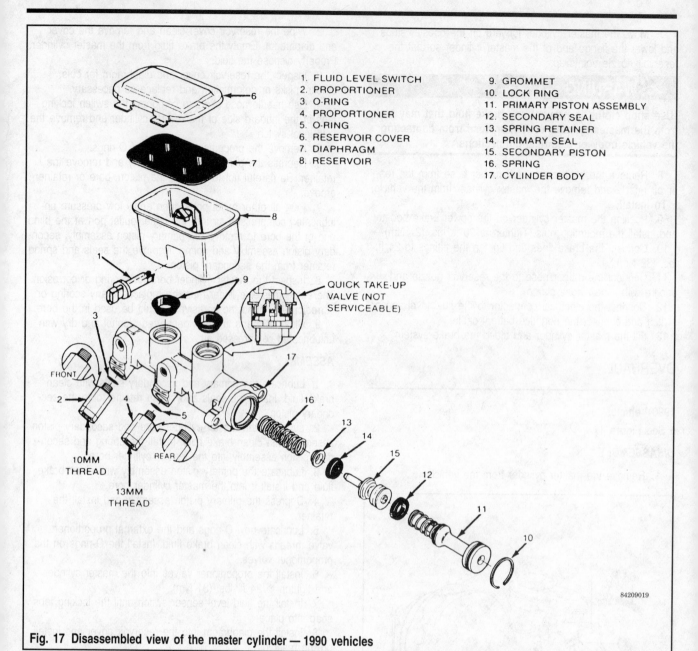

1. FLUID LEVEL SWITCH
2. PROPORTIONER
3. O-RING
4. PROPORTIONER
5. O-RING
6. RESERVOIR COVER
7. DIAPHRAGM
8. RESERVOIR
9. GROMMET
10. LOCK RING
11. PRIMARY PISTON ASSEMBLY
12. SECONDARY SEAL
13. SPRING RETAINER
14. PRIMARY SEAL
15. SECONDARY PISTON
16. SPRING
17. CYLINDER BODY

QUICK TAKE-UP VALVE (NOT SERVICEABLE)

FRONT

10MM THREAD

13MM THREAD

REAR

84209019

Fig. 17 Disassembled view of the master cylinder — 1990 vehicles

4. Use needle nose pliers to compress the switch locking tabs at the inboard side of the master cylinder and remove the fluid level switch.

5. Clamp the mounting flange on the master cylinder body in a vise. Do not clamp on the master cylinder body.

6. Tap back the spring pins until they are clear of the master cylinder reservoir. Be careful not to damage the reservoir or master cylinder.

7. Remove the reservoir and the reservoir seals. Inspect the reservoir for cracks or deformities and replace as necessary.

8. Remove the proportioner valve caps, O-rings and springs. Using needle nose pliers, remove the proportioner valve pistons. Remove the seals from the pistons. Inspect the proportioner valve pistons for corrosion and deformities and replace as necessary.

9. Depress the primary piston assembly and remove the retainer. Be careful not to damage the piston, bore or retainer groove.

10. Plug all other outlet ports, then apply low pressure un-lubricated compressed air into the upper outlet port at the blind end of the bore to remove the primary piston assembly, secondary piston assembly and spring. Remove the seals and spring retainer from the secondary piston.

11. Inspect the master cylinder bore for scoring or corrosion. The entire master cylinder must be replaced if any scoring or corrosion are found; no abrasives should be used in the bore.

12. Clean all parts in clean denatured alcohol and dry with unlubricated compressed air.

ASSEMBLY

1. Lubricate the primary and secondary seals with clean brake fluid. Install the seals and spring retainer onto the secondary piston.

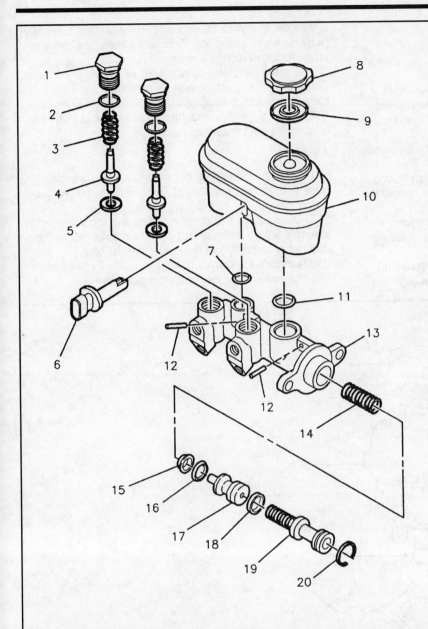

1 PROPORTIONER VALVE CAP
2 O-RING
3 SPRING
4 PROPORTIONER VALVE PISTON
5 PROPORTIONER VALVE SEAL
6 FLUID LEVEL SENSOR
7 O-RING
8 RESERVOIR CAP
9 DIAPHRAGM
10 RESERVOIR
11 O-RING
12 SPRING PIN
13 CYLINDER BODY
14 SPRING
15 SPRING RETAINER
16 PRIMARY SEAL
17 SECONDARY PISTON
18 SECONDARY SEAL
19 PRIMARY PISTON
20 RETAINER

84209020

Fig. 18 Disassembled view of the master cylinder — 1991-93 Deville, Fleetwood and Sixty Special

2. Lubricate the master cylinder bore and secondary piston assembly with clean brake fluid. Install the spring and secondary piston assembly into the master cylinder bore.

3. Lubricate the primary piston assembly with clean brake fluid and install it into the master cylinder bore.

4. Depress the primary piston assembly and install the retainer.

5. Lubricate new O-rings and proportioner valve seals as well as the stems of the proportioner valve pistons with silicone grease.

6. Install the new seals (seal lips facing upward toward the cap) on the proportioner valve pistons.

7. Install the proportioner valve pistons, seals and springs into the master cylinder body.

8. Install the new O-rings in the grooves in the proportioner valve caps. Install the proportioner valve caps in the master cylinder and tighten to 20 ft. lbs. (27 Nm).

9. Lubricate new O-rings and the master cylinder reservoir bayonets with clean brake fluid.

10. Install the O-rings on the master cylinder, making sure they are fully seated.

11. Install the reservoir onto the master cylinder by pressing straight down by hand until the pin holes are aligned.

12. Tap in the pins to retain the reservoir, being careful not to damage the reservoir or master cylinder.

13. Install the fluid level sensor switch until the locking tabs snap into place.

14. Install the diaphragm into the reservoir cap and install on the reservoir.

15. Install the master cylinder on the vehicle.

1991-93 Eldorado and Seville

▶ **See Figures 19 and 20**

DISASSEMBLY

1. Remove the master cylinder from the vehicle.
2. Wipe the reservoir cap clean and remove the cap and diaphragm. Empty the brake fluid from the master cylinder. Properly dispose the fluid.
3. Inspect the reservoir cap and diaphragm for cuts, cracks, nicks or deformation and replace as necessary.
4. Use needle nose pliers to compress the switch locking tabs at the inboard side of the master cylinder and remove the fluid level switch.
5. Depress the primary piston assembly and remove the retainer. Be careful not to damage the piston, bore or retainer groove.
6. Plug all other outlet ports, then apply low pressure unlubricated compressed air into the outlet port at the blind end of the bore to remove the primary piston assembly, secondary piston assembly and spring. Remove the seals and spring retainer from the secondary piston.
7. Inspect the master cylinder bore for scoring or corrosion. The entire master cylinder must be replaced if any scoring or corrosion are found; no abrasives should be used in the bore.
8. Clean all parts in clean denatured alcohol and dry with unlubricated compressed air.

ASSEMBLY

1. Lubricate the primary and secondary seals with clean brake fluid. Install the seals and spring retainer onto the secondary piston.
2. Lubricate the master cylinder bore and secondary piston assembly with clean brake fluid. Install the spring and secondary piston assembly into the master cylinder bore.
3. Lubricate the primary piston assembly with clean brake fluid and install it into the master cylinder bore.

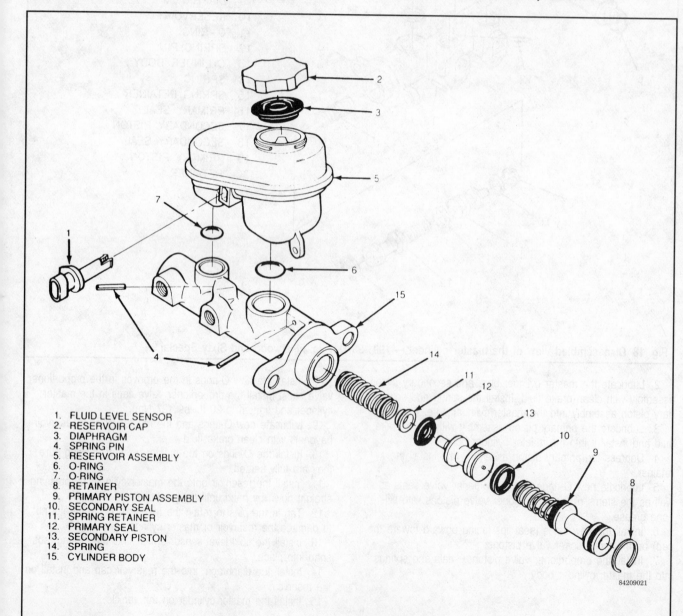

1. FLUID LEVEL SENSOR
2. RESERVOIR CAP
3. DIAPHRAGM
4. SPRING PIN
5. RESERVOIR ASSEMBLY
6. O-RING
7. O-RING
8. RETAINER
9. PRIMARY PISTON ASSEMBLY
10. SECONDARY SEAL
11. SPRING RETAINER
12. PRIMARY SEAL
13. SECONDARY PISTON
14. SPRING
15. CYLINDER BODY

84209021

Fig. 19 Disassembled view of the master cylinder — 1991-92 Eldorado and Seville

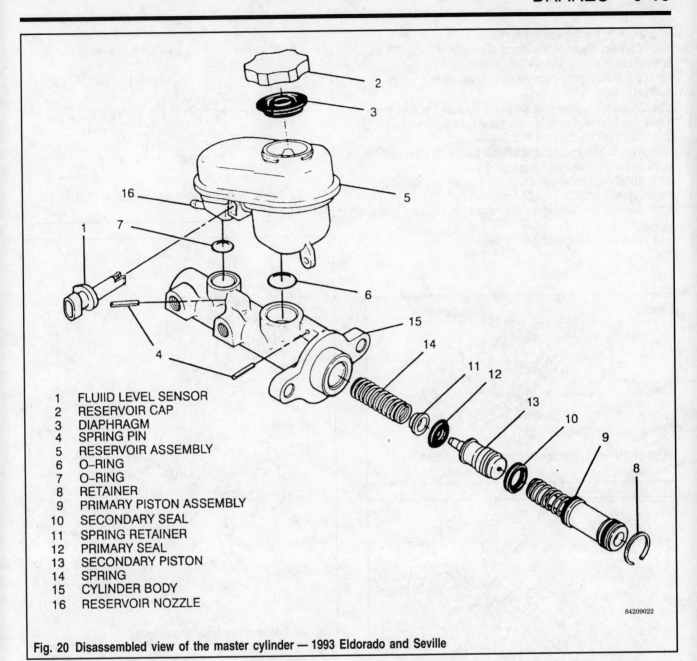

1	FLUIID LEVEL SENSOR
2	RESERVOIR CAP
3	DIAPHRAGM
4	SPRING PIN
5	RESERVOIR ASSEMBLY
6	O–RING
7	O–RING
8	RETAINER
9	PRIMARY PISTON ASSEMBLY
10	SECONDARY SEAL
11	SPRING RETAINER
12	PRIMARY SEAL
13	SECONDARY PISTON
14	SPRING
15	CYLINDER BODY
16	RESERVOIR NOZZLE

84209022

Fig. 20 Disassembled view of the master cylinder — 1993 Eldorado and Seville

4. Depress the primary piston assembly and install the retainer.

5. Install the fluid level sensor switch until the locking tabs snap into place.

6. Install the diaphragm into the reservoir cap and install on the reservoir.

7. Install the master cylinder on the vehicle.

Power Brake Booster

REMOVAL & INSTALLATION

▶ **See Figures 21, 22, 23 and 24**

1. Disconnect the negative battery cable.

2. Disconnect the booster vacuum hose from the vacuum check valve.

3. Remove the master cylinder mounting nuts. Remove the master cylinder from the booster without disconnecting the brake lines.

➡**Move the master cylinder forward just enough to clear the studs on the booster. This will flex the brake lines slightly; be careful not to bend or distort the brake lines.**

4. Working under the instrument panel, remove the acoustical barrier from the booster studs, if equipped.

5. Remove the booster mounting nuts.

6. Disengage the booster pushrod from the brake pedal. Tilt the entire booster slightly to work the pushrod off the pedal clevis pin without putting unnecessary side pressure on the pushrod.

7. Remove the booster assembly from the vehicle. Remove the gasket if necessary.

To install:

8. If necessary, install the gasket to the booster.

9. Position the booster in the vehicle.

10. Connect the booster pushrod to the brake pedal. Tilt the entire booster slightly to work the pushrod onto the pedal clevis pin without putting unnecessary side pressure on the pushrod.

11. Install the booster mounting nuts. Tighten the nuts to 15 ft. lbs. (21 Nm) on Deville, Fleetwood and Sixty Special or 20 ft. lbs. (27 Nm) on Eldorado and Seville.

12. If equipped, install the acoustical barrier onto the booster studs under the instrument panel.

13. Install the master cylinder to the booster and tighten the mounting nuts to 20 ft. lbs. (27 Nm).

14. Connect the booster vacuum hose to the vacuum check valve.

15. Connect the negative battery cable.

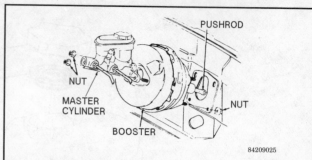

Fig. 23 Power brake booster installation — 1991-93 Eldorado and Seville

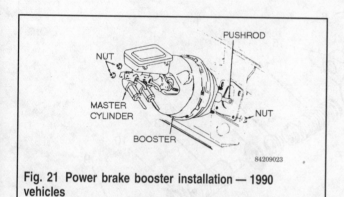

Fig. 21 Power brake booster installation — 1990 vehicles

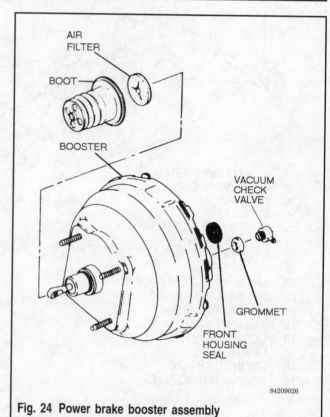

Fig. 24 Power brake booster assembly

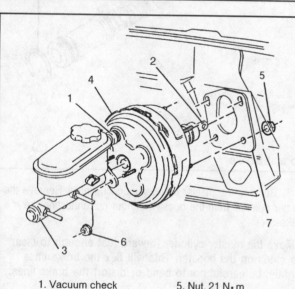

1. Vacuum check valve	5. Nut, 21 N•m (15 lb.ft.)
2. Pushrood	6. Nut, 27 N•m (20 lb.ft.)
3. Master cylinder	7. Gasket
4. Booster	

Fig. 22 Power brake booster installation — 1991-93 Deville, Fleetwood and Sixty Special

ADJUSTMENT

▶ **See Figure 25**

1. Remove the master cylinder from the booster.

➡**The booster piston rod length can be checked with the booster removed from the vehicle if 25 in. Hg vacuum is available from a suitable vacuum source.**

2. Start the engine. Make sure maximum engine vacuum is available to the booster.

3. Position gage tool J-37839 or equivalent, over the booster piston rod. Check both the maximum and minimum rod length using the tool.

4. If the piston rod length does not fall between the maximum and minimum dimensions, use a service-adjustable piston rod to obtain the correct length.

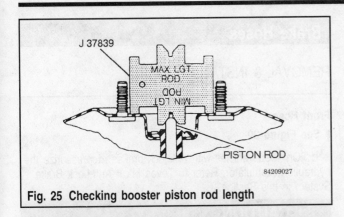

Fig. 25 Checking booster piston rod length

Proportioner Valves

All vehicles without anti-lock brakes are equipped with proportioner valves that are attached to the master cylinder. All vehicles with anti-lock brakes are equipped with proportioner valves that are mounted under the rear of the vehicle, in series with the rear brake lines.

REMOVAL & INSTALLATION

Without Anti-Lock Brakes

1990 VEHICLES

▶ See Figure 26

1. Disconnect the negative battery cable.
2. Disconnect the brake lines from the proportioner valves. Plug the lines to prevent fluid loss.
3. Remove the proportioner valves and O-rings from the master cylinder.
   To install:
4. Lubricate new O-rings and the external proportioner valve threads with clean brake fluid. Install the new O-rings on the proportioner valves.
5. Install the proportioner valves on the master cylinder and tighten to 24 ft. lbs. (31 Nm).
6. Connect the brake lines to the proportioner valves and tighten the fittings to 11 ft. lbs. (15 Nm).
7. Connect the negative battery cable. Bleed the brake system.

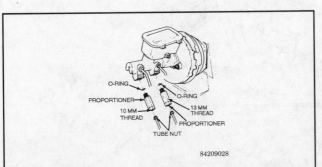

Fig. 26 Proportioner valve installation — 1990 vehicles without anti-lock brakes

1991-93 DEVILLE, FLEETWOOD AND SIXTY SPECIAL

▶ See Figure 18

1. Remove the master cylinder from the vehicle.
2. Clamp the mounting flange on the master cylinder body in a vise. Do not clamp on the master cylinder body.
3. Tap back the spring pins until they are clear of the master cylinder reservoir. Be careful not to damage the reservoir or master cylinder.
4. Remove the reservoir and the reservoir seals. Inspect the reservoir for cracks or deformities and replace as necessary.
5. Remove the proportioner valve caps, O-rings and springs.
6. Using needle nose pliers, remove the proportioner valve pistons.
7. Remove the seals from the pistons. Inspect the proportioner valve pistons for corrosion and deformities and replace as necessary.
8. Clean all parts in clean denatured alcohol and dry with unlubricated compressed air.
   To install:
9. Lubricate new O-rings and proportioner valve seals as well as the stems of the proportioner valve pistons with silicone grease.
10. Install the new seals (seal lips facing upward toward the cap) on the proportioner valve pistons.
11. Install the proportioner valve pistons, seals and springs into the master cylinder body.
12. Install the new O-rings in the grooves in the proportioner valve caps. Install the proportioner valve caps in the master cylinder and tighten to 20 ft. lbs. (27 Nm).
13. Lubricate new O-rings and the master cylinder reservoir bayonets with clean brake fluid.
14. Install the O-rings on the master cylinder, making sure they are fully seated.
15. Install the reservoir onto the master cylinder by pressing straight down by hand until the pin holes are aligned.
16. Tap in the pins to retain the reservoir, being careful not to damage the reservoir or master cylinder.
17. Install the master cylinder on the vehicle and bleed the brake system.

With Anti-Lock Brakes

1990 VEHICLES

▶ See Figure 27

1. Depressurize the hydraulic accumulator. Refer to Teves Mk II Anti-Lock Brake System in this Section.

✳✳CAUTION

The hydraulic system contains brake fluid at extremely high pressure. It is mandatory that the system be depressurized before disconnecting any hoses, lines or fittings, or personal injury may result.

2. Raise and safely support the vehicle.
3. Disconnect the brake lines from the proportioner valve. Plug the lines to prevent fluid loss.
4. Remove the proportioner valve.

To install:

5. Install the proportioner valve and connect the brake lines. Observe the brake line clearances as shown in the figure.

6. Tighten the brake line fittings to 11 ft. lbs. (15 Nm).

7. Lower the vehicle.

8. Fill the fluid reservoir and bleed the brake system.

1991-93 VEHICLES

▶ **See Figures 28 and 29**

1. Raise and safely support the vehicle.

2. Clean the proportioner valve and brake line connections to make sure the system will not be contaminated during servicing.

3. Disconnect the brake lines from the proportioner valve. Plug the lines to prevent fluid loss.

4. Remove the proportioner valve.

To install:

5. Install the proportioner valve and connect the brake lines. Tighten the brake line fittings to 11 ft. lbs. (15 Nm).

6. Lower the vehicle.

7. Fill the fluid reservoir and bleed the brake system.

Brake Hoses

REMOVAL & INSTALLATION

Front Hose

▶ **See Figure 30**

1. On 1990 vehicles with anti-lock brakes, depressurize the hydraulic accumulator. Refer to Teves Mk II Anti-Lock Brake System in this Section.

❊❊CAUTION

The hydraulic system contains brake fluid at extremely high pressure. It is mandatory that the system be depressurized before disconnecting any hoses, lines or fittings, or personal injury may result.

2. Raise and safely support the vehicle.

3. Remove the wheel and tire assembly.

4. Loosen the brake line fitting at the line-to-brake hose junction. Remove the hose retainer at the bracket and disconnect the hose from the line. Plug the line to prevent fluid loss.

5. Remove the brake hose attaching bolt at the disc brake caliper and disconnect the hose from the caliper. Discard the gaskets.

6. Remove the hose retainer bracket bolt from the strut and remove the brake hose.

To install:

7. Position the brake hose and retainer bracket on the strut and install the mounting bolt. Tighten to 13 ft. lbs. (17 Nm).

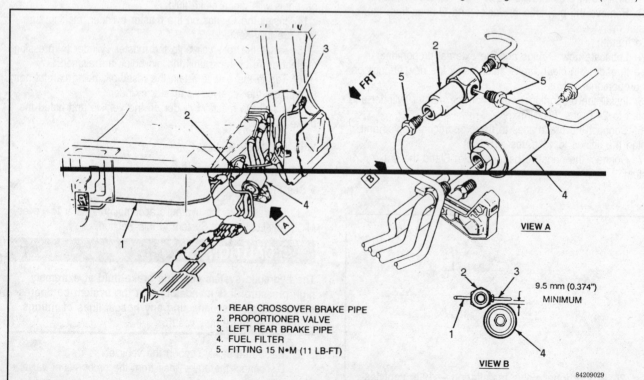

1. REAR CROSSOVER BRAKE PIPE
2. PROPORTIONER VALVE
3. LEFT REAR BRAKE PIPE
4. FUEL FILTER
5. FITTING 15 N•M (11 LB-FT)

VIEW A

9.5 mm (0.374") MINIMUM

VIEW B

84209029

Fig. 27 Proportioner valve — 1990 Deville and Fleetwood with anti-lock brakes, 1990 Eldorado and Seville with anti-lock brakes similar

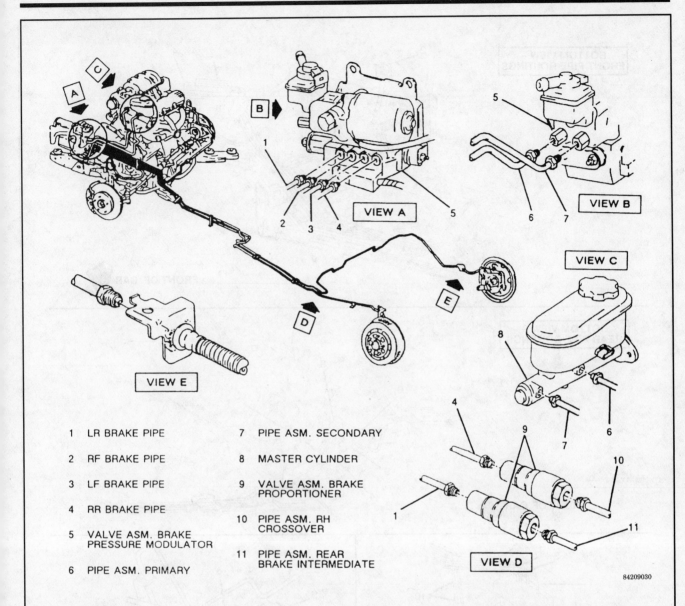

1   LR BRAKE PIPE

2   RF BRAKE PIPE

3   LF BRAKE PIPE

4   RR BRAKE PIPE

5   VALVE ASM. BRAKE
    PRESSURE MODULATOR

6   PIPE ASM. PRIMARY

7   PIPE ASM. SECONDARY

8   MASTER CYLINDER

9   VALVE ASM. BRAKE
    PROPORTIONER

10 PIPE ASM. RH
    CROSSOVER

11 PIPE ASM. REAR
    BRAKE INTERMEDIATE

84209030

Fig. 28 Proportioner valve and brake line connections — 1991-93 Deville, Fleetwood and Sixty Special with anti-lock brakes

8. Position the brake hose on the disc brake caliper. Connect the hose to the caliper using the attaching bolt and 2 new gaskets. Tighten the bolt to 32 ft. lbs. (44 Nm).

9. Insert the brake hose through the body bracket. Unplug the brake line and thread the fitting into the hose.

10. Install the retainer at the bracket, making sure the brake hose is not twisted. Tighten the brake line fitting to 11 ft. lbs. (15 Nm).

11. Bleed the brake system.

12. Install the wheel and tire assembly and lower the vehicle.

Rear Hose

DEVILLE, FLEETWOOD AND SIXTY SPECIAL

▶ See Figure 31

1. On 1990 vehicles with anti-lock brakes, depressurize the hydraulic accumulator. Refer to Teves Mk II Anti-Lock Brake System in this Section.

❋❋CAUTION

The hydraulic system contains brake fluid at extremely high pressure. It is mandatory that the system be depressurized before disconnecting any hoses, lines or fittings, or personal injury may result.

2. Raise and safely support the vehicle.

3. Remove the wheel and tire assembly.

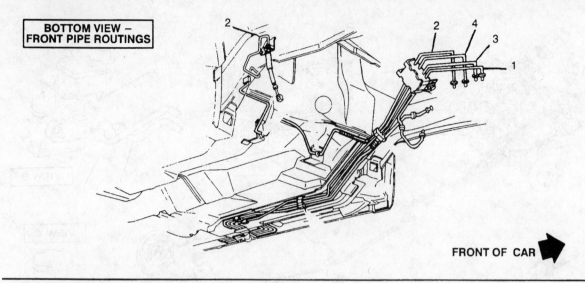

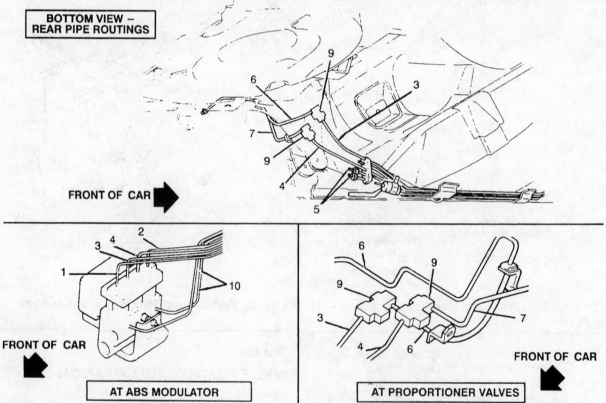

BOTTOM VIEW – FRONT PIPE ROUTINGS

FRONT OF CAR

BOTTOM VIEW – REAR PIPE ROUTINGS

FRONT OF CAR

FRONT OF CAR

AT ABS MODULATOR

FRONT OF CAR

AT PROPORTIONER VALVES

1 LEFT FRONT BRAKE PIPE
2 RIGHT FRONT BRAKE PIPE
3 RIGHT REAR BRAKE PIPE (MOD TO PROP)
4 LEFT REAR BRAKE PIPE (MOD TO PROP)
5 FUEL PIPES

6 RIGHT REAR BRAKE PIPE
7 LEFT REAR BRAKE PIPE
8 ABS MODULATOR
9 PROPORTIONER VALVE
10 MASTER CYLINDER TO MODULATOR

84209031

Fig. 29 Proportioner valve location and brake line routing — 1991-93 Eldorado and Seville

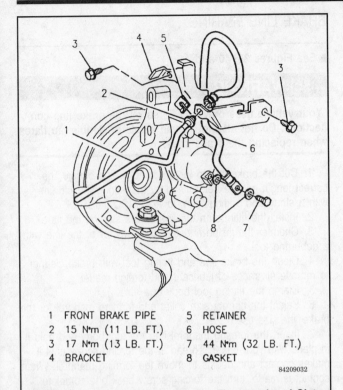

1	FRONT BRAKE PIPE	5	RETAINER
2	15 N•m (11 LB. FT.)	6	HOSE
3	17 N•m (13 LB. FT.)	7	44 N•m (32 LB. FT.)
4	BRACKET	8	GASKET

84209032

Fig. 30 Front brake hose — Deville, Fleetwood and Sixty Special

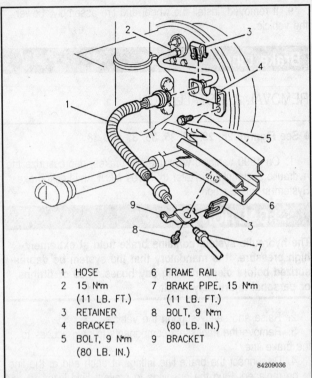

1	HOSE	6	FRAME RAIL
2	15 N•m	7	BRAKE PIPE, 15 N•m
	(11 LB. FT.)		(11 LB. FT.)
3	RETAINER	8	BOLT, 9 N•m
4	BRACKET		(80 LB. IN.)
5	BOLT, 9 N•m	9	BRACKET
	(80 LB. IN.)		

84209036

Fig. 31 Rear brake hose — Deville, Fleetwood and Sixty Special

4. Loosen the brake line fittings at the line-to-brake hose junctions. Remove the hose retainers at the brackets and disconnect the hose from the lines. Plug the lines to prevent fluid loss.

To install:

5. Position the brake hose in the brackets. Unplug the brake lines and thread the fittings into the hose.

6. Install the retainers at the brackets, making sure the brake hose is not twisted. Tighten the brake line fittings to 11 ft. lbs. (15 Nm).

7. Bleed the brake system.

8. Install the wheel and tire assembly and lower the vehicle.

ELDORADO AND SEVILLE

▶ See Figures 32 and 33

1. On 1990 vehicles with anti-lock brakes, depressurize the hydraulic accumulator. Refer to Teves Mk II Anti-Lock Brake System in this Section.

❋❋CAUTION

The hydraulic system contains brake fluid at extremely high pressure. It is mandatory that the system be depressurized before disconnecting any hoses, lines or fittings, or personal injury may result.

2. Raise and safely support the vehicle.

3. Remove the wheel and tire assembly, as necessary.

4. If removing the crossover hose on 1990-92 vehicles or intermediate hose on 1993 vehicles, proceed as follows:

a. Loosen the brake line fittings at the line-to-brake hose junctions.

b. Remove the hose retainers at the brackets and disconnect the hose from the lines. Plug the lines to prevent fluid loss.

5. If removing the right or left rear hoses, proceed as follows:

a. Loosen the brake line fitting at the line-to-brake hose junction.

b. Remove the hose retainer at the bracket and disconnect the hose from the line. Plug the line to prevent fluid loss.

c. Remove the brake hose attaching bolt at the disc brake caliper and disconnect the hose from the caliper. Discard the gaskets.

To install:

6. If installing the crossover hose on 1990-92 vehicles or intermediate hose on 1993 vehicles, proceed as follows:

a. Position the brake hose in the brackets. Unplug the brake lines and thread the fittings into the hose.

b. Install the retainers at the brackets, making sure the brake hose is not twisted. Tighten the brake line fittings to 11 ft. lbs. (15 Nm).

7. If installing the right or left rear hoses, proceed as follows:

a. Position the brake hose on the disc brake caliper. Connect the hose to the caliper using the attaching bolt and 2 new gaskets. Tighten the bolt to 32 ft. lbs. (44 Nm).

b. Insert the brake hose through the bracket. Unplug the brake line and thread the fitting into the hose.

c. Install the retainer at the bracket, making sure the brake hose is not twisted. Tighten the brake line fitting to 11 ft. lbs. (15 Nm).

8. Bleed the brake system.

9. If removed, install the wheel and tire assembly. Lower the vehicle.

Brake Lines

REMOVAL & INSTALLATION

▶ See Figures 28, 29, 34, 35, 36, 37 and 38

1. On 1990 vehicles with anti-lock brakes, depressurize the hydraulic accumulator. Refer to Teves Mk II Anti-Lock Brake System in this Section.

✳✳CAUTION

The hydraulic system contains brake fluid at extremely high pressure. It is mandatory that the system be depressurized before disconnecting any hoses, lines or fittings, or personal injury may result.

2. Raise and safely support the vehicle.
3. Remove the necessary components to gain access to the brake line.
4. Disconnect the brake line fittings at each end of the line to be replaced. Plug the openings to prevent fluid loss.
5. Disconnect the brake line from any retainers and remove the line from the vehicle.

To install:
6. Try to obtain a replacement line that is the same length as the line that was removed. If the line is longer, you will have to cut it and flare the end.

✳✳CAUTION

Use only double walled steel tubing specified for use in hydraulic brake systems. Using any other type of tubing may cause brake system failure.

7. Use a suitable tubing bender to make the necessary bends in the line. Work slowly and carefully; try to make the bends look as close as possible to those on the line being replaced.

✳✳WARNING

When bending the brake line, be careful not to kink or crack the line. If the brake line becomes kinked or cracked, it must be replaced.

8. Before installing the brake line, flush it with brake cleaner to remove any dirt or foreign material.
9. Install the line into the vehicle. Be sure to attach the line to the retainers, as necessary. Make sure the replacement brake line does not contact any components that could rub the line and cause a leak. Clearance of ¾ in. must be maintained to all moving or vibrating parts.
10. Connect the brake line fittings and tighten to 11 ft. lbs. (15 Nm).
11. Bleed the brake system.
12. Install any removed components and lower the vehicle.

BRAKE LINE FLARING

▶ See Figures 39, 40 and 41

✳✳WARNING

Your vehicle uses only ISO flares on the brake line connections. Do not attempt to use single or double lap flares when replacing the brake lines.

1. Cut the brake line to length using a pipe cutter. The correct length can be determined by measuring the old line with a string and adding ⅛ in. for each ISO flare.
2. Install the fittings on the line before starting the flare.
3. Chamfer the inside and outside diameter of the line with a deburring tool.
4. Clean the brake line and flaring tool with brake cleaner to remove all traces of lubricant and foreign matter.
5. Clamp the flaring tool body in a vise.
6. Select the correct size collet and forming mandrel for the brake line size used.
7. Insert the forming mandrel into the tool body and hold it in place with your finger. Thread in the forcing screw until it makes contact and begins to move the forming mandrel. When contact is made, turn the forcing screw back one complete turn.
8. Slide the clamping nut over the brake line and insert the brake line into the collet. Leave approximately ¾ in. of tubing extending out the collet. Insert the assembly into the tool body. The brake line end must contact the face of the forming mandrel.
9. Tighten the clamping nut into the tool body very tightly, or the line may push out.
10. Wrench tighten the forcing screw until it bottoms. Do not over-tighten the forcing screw, or the flare may become oversized.
11. Back the clamping nut out of the tool body and disassemble the clamping nut and collet assembly. The flare is now completed and ready for use.

Bleeding

▶ See Figures 42, 43 and 44

Whenever air gets into the brake hydraulic system, the system must be bled to remove it. If air has entered the system due to low fluid level, or from brake lines having been disconnected at the master cylinder, you might have to bleed the hydraulic system at all 4 wheels. If a brake line is disconnected at one wheel, only that wheel cylinder or caliper needs to be bled. If lines are disconnected at any fitting located between the master cylinder and the wheels, then the brake system served by the disconnected line must be bled.

The following procedure applies to all vehicles without anti-lock brakes and 1991-93 vehicles with anti-lock brakes. To bleed the brake system on 1990 vehicles with anti-lock brakes, refer to Teves Mk II Anti-Lock Brake System in this Section.

The proper fluid level in the master cylinder reservoir must be maintained during bleeding. Periodically check the fluid level in the reservoir throughout the bleeding procedure, however, be sure the reservoir cap is installed before the brake pedal is

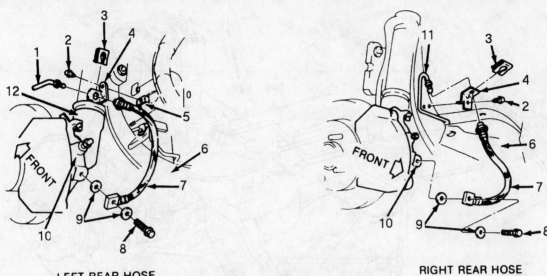

LEFT REAR HOSE

RIGHT REAR HOSE

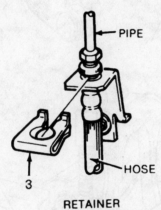

PIPE

HOSE

RETAINER
INSTALLATION

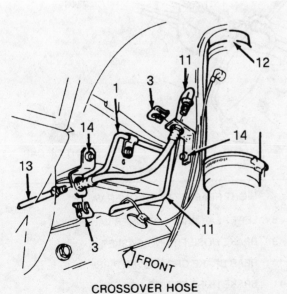

CROSSOVER HOSE

1. Left rear brake pipe
2. Bracket bolt (10 N m/7.5 ft.lbs.)
3. Retainer
4. Bracket
5. Nut
6. Rear suspension crossmember
7. Brake hose
8. Caliper inlet fitting (44 N m/
   32 ft.lbs.)
9. Copper gaskets
10. Caliper assembly
11. Rear crossover pipe
12. Strut
13. Right rear brake pipe
14. Bracket screws (6 N m/
    53 in.lbs. maximum)

84209037

Fig. 32 Rear brake hoses — 1990-92 Eldorado and Seville

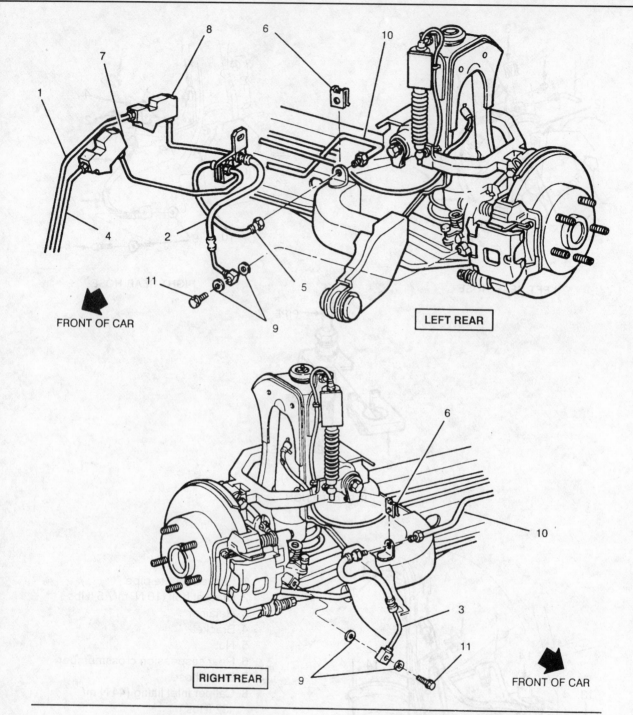

1 LEFT REAR PIPE
2 LEFT REAR BRAKE HOSE
3 RIGHT REAR BRAKE HOSE
4 RIGHT REAR PIPE
5 INTERMEDIATE BRAKE HOSE
6 RETAINER

7 RIGHT REAR PROPORTIONER VALVE
8 LEFT REAR PROPORTIONER VALVE
9 BRAKE HOSE FITTING GASKET
10 REAR BRAKE CROSSOVER PIPE
11 BRAKE HOSE FITTING

84209038

Fig. 33 Rear brake hoses — 1993 Eldorado and Seville

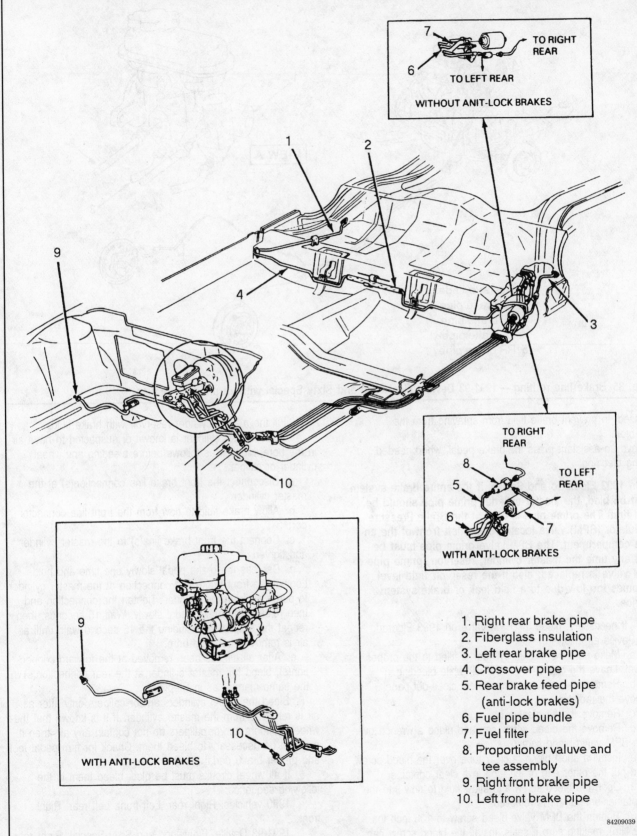

WITHOUT ANIT-LOCK BRAKES

WITH ANTI-LOCK BRAKES

WITH ANTI-LOCK BRAKES

1. Right rear brake pipe
2. Fiberglass insulation
3. Left rear brake pipe
4. Crossover pipe
5. Rear brake feed pipe
   (anti-lock brakes)
6. Fuel pipe bundle
7. Fuel filter
8. Proportioner valuve and
   tee assembly
9. Right front brake pipe
10. Left front brake pipe

84209039

Fig. 34 Brake line routing — 1990 Deville and Fleetwood

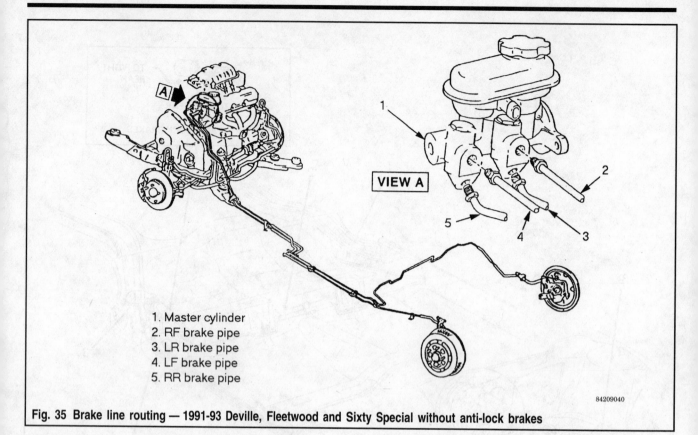

1. Master cylinder
2. RF brake pipe
3. LR brake pipe
4. LF brake pipe
5. RR brake pipe

84209040

Fig. 35 Brake line routing — 1991-93 Deville, Fleetwood and Sixty Special without anti-lock brakes

pressed, to prevent brake fluid from spraying from the reservoir.

Have an assistant press the brake pedal, when needed, during bleeding.

➡On 1993 Eldorado and Seville, if the entire brake system must be bled, the master cylinder prime pipe should be bled first. The prime pipe is bled at the Brake Pressure Modulator (BPM) valve located in the left front of the engine compartment. The BPM valve prime pipe must be bled any time the master cylinder, reservoir, prime pipe or BPM valve is replaced; also if the reservoir fluid level becomes too low due to a fluid leak or brake system service.

1. If necessary, bleed the BPM valve on 1993 Eldorado and Seville as follows:

a. Make sure the master cylinder is filled to the proper level. Leave the cap off the reservoir while bleeding.

b. Remove the engine compartment close-out panel above the radiator.

c. Remove the air cleaner box.

d. Remove the bleed screw cap and place a wrench over the BPM valve bleed screw.

e. Install a short piece of clear tube over the bleed screw and put the other end of the tube in a clear container.

f. Open the bleed screw and allow fluid to flow into the container until all air is removed.

g. Tighten the BPM valve bleed screw to 106 inch lbs. (12 Nm), making sure it seals. Install the bleed screw cap.

h. Install the air cleaner box and the close-out panel.

2. Deplete the power brake booster vacuum reserve by applying the brakes several times with the ignition **OFF**.

3. Fill the master cylinder reservoir with brake fluid.

4. If the master cylinder is known or suspected to have air in the bore, bleed it as follows before bleeding any wheel cylinder or caliper.

a. Disconnect the front brake line connection(s) at the master cylinder.

b. Allow brake fluid to flow from the front line connector port.

c. Connect the front brake line(s) to the master cylinder and tighten.

d. Depress the brake pedal slowly one time and hold. Loosen the front brake line connection at the master cylinder to purge air from the cylinder. Tighten the connection and then release the brake pedal slowly. Wait 15 seconds, then repeat the sequence, including the 15 second wait, until all air is removed from the bore.

e. After all air has been removed at the forward connection(s), bleed the master cylinder at the rear connection(s) in the same manner as in Step d.

5. Bleed the wheel cylinders and/or calipers only after all air is removed from the master cylinder. If it is known that the wheel cylinders and/or calipers do not contain any air, then it may not be necessary to bleed them. Check for firm pedal feel and proper brake pedal travel.

6. If all wheel circuits must be bled, bleed them in the following sequence:

1990 vehicles: Right rear, Left front, Left rear, Right front.

1991-93 Deville, Fleetwood and Sixty Special: Right rear, Left rear, Right front, Left front.

1991-93 Eldorado and Seville: Left front, Right front, Left rear, Right rear.

7. Raise and safely support the vehicle.

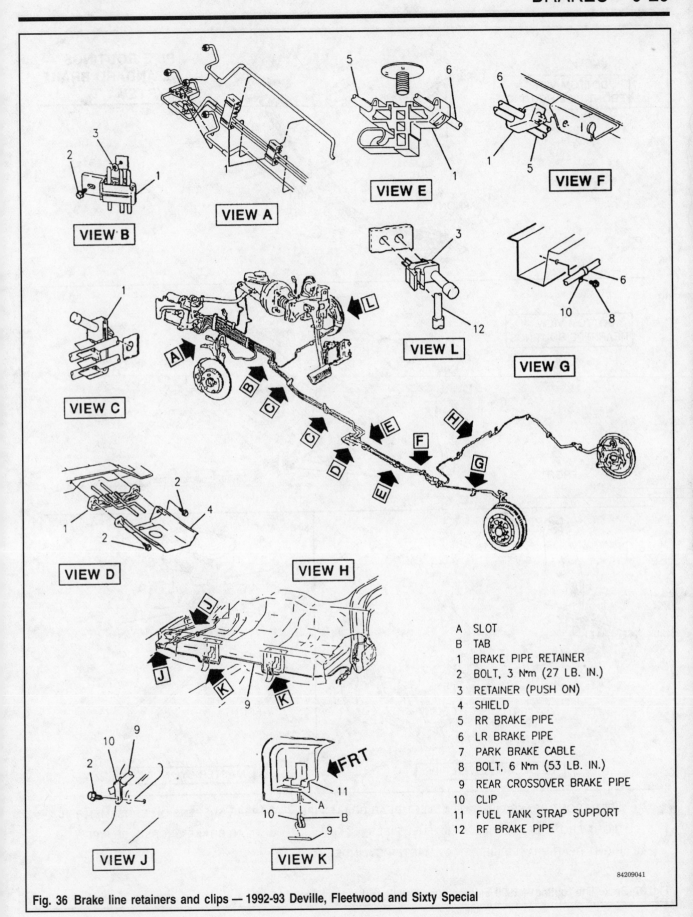

VIEW A

VIEW B

VIEW E

VIEW F

VIEW C

VIEW L

VIEW G

VIEW D

VIEW H

A SLOT
B TAB
1 BRAKE PIPE RETAINER
2 BOLT, 3 N·m (27 LB. IN.)
3 RETAINER (PUSH ON)
4 SHIELD
5 RR BRAKE PIPE
6 LR BRAKE PIPE
7 PARK BRAKE CABLE
8 BOLT, 6 N·m (53 LB. IN.)
9 REAR CROSSOVER BRAKE PIPE
10 CLIP
11 FUEL TANK STRAP SUPPORT
12 RF BRAKE PIPE

VIEW J

VIEW K

FRT

84209041

Fig. 36 Brake line retainers and clips — 1992-93 Deville, Fleetwood and Sixty Special

PIPE ROUTINGS — STANDARD BRAKE SYSTEM

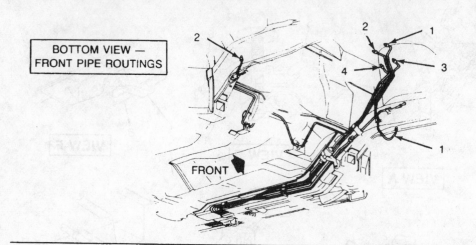

BOTTOM VIEW — FRONT PIPE ROUTINGS

FRONT

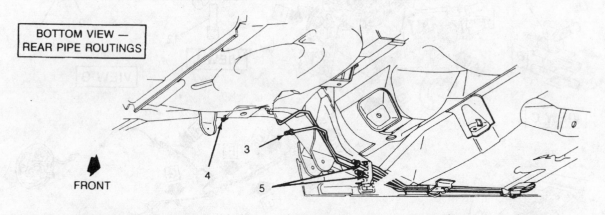

BOTTOM VIEW — REAR PIPE ROUTINGS

FRONT

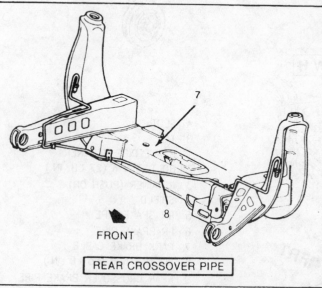

REAR CROSSOVER PIPE

MASTER CYLINDER

FRONT

1 LEFT FRONT BRAKE PIPE 4 LEFT REAR BRAKE PIPE 7 REAR SUSPENSION CROSSMEMBER

2 RIGHT FRONT BRAKE PIPE 5 FUEL PIPES 8 REAR BRAKE CROSSOVER PIPE

3 RIGHT REAR BRAKE PIPE 6 MASTER CYLINDER

84209042

Fig. 37 Brake line routing — 1990 Eldorado and Seville without anti-lock brakes

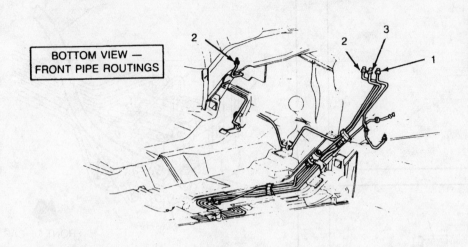

PIPE ROUTINGS — ANTI-LOCK BRAKE SYSTEM

BOTTOM VIEW — FRONT PIPE ROUTINGS

BOTTOM VIEW — REAR PIPE ROUTINGS

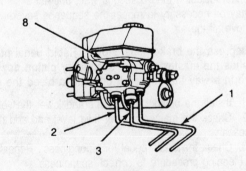

AT HYDRAULIC UNIT

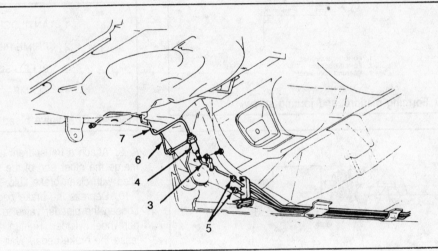

AT PROPORTIONER VALVE

1 LEFT FRONT BRAKE PIPE	5 FUEL PIPES
2 RIGHT FRONT BRAKE PIPE	6 RIGHT REAR BRAKE PIPE
3 REAR BRAKE PIPE (M/C TO PROP)	7 LEFT REAR BRAKE PIPE
4 PROPORTIONER VALVE	8 ABS HYDRAULIC UNIT

84209043

Fig. 38 Brake line routing — 1990 Eldorado and Seville with anti-lock brakes

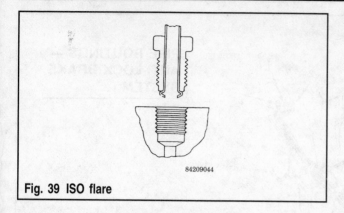

Fig. 39 ISO flare

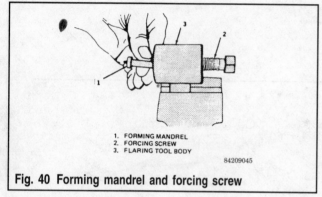

1. FORMING MANDREL
2. FORCING SCREW
3. FLARING TOOL BODY

84209045

Fig. 40 Forming mandrel and forcing screw

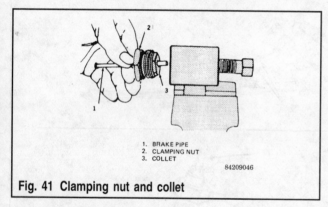

1. BRAKE PIPE
2. CLAMPING NUT
3. COLLET

84209046

Fig. 41 Clamping nut and collet

8. Remove the bleeder valve cap and place the proper size box-end wrench over the bleeder valve.

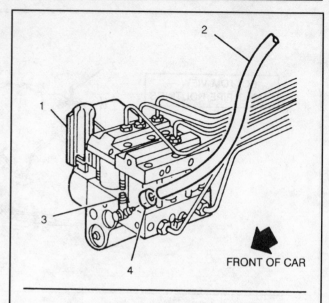

FRONT OF CAR

1   ANTILOCK BRAKE PRESSURE VALVE
2   PRIME PIPE
3   BLEED SCREW — 12 N•m (106 lb. in.)
4   CLAMP

84209047

Fig. 42 BPM valve bleed screw

9. Attach a transparent tube to the bleeder valve. Submerge the other end of the tube in a clear container, partially filled with clean brake fluid.

10. Depress the brake pedal slowly one time and hold. Loosen the bleeder valve to purge the air from the caliper/wheel cylinder. Tighten the bleeder valve and slowly release the brake pedal. Wait 15 seconds, then repeat the sequence, including the 15 second wait, until all air is removed. It may be necessary to repeat the sequence several times to remove all the air.

➡ **Depress the brake pedal slowly. Rapid pedal pumping pushes the master cylinder secondary piston down the bore in a way that makes it difficult to bleed the system.**

11. Install the bleeder valve caps and lower the vehicle.
12. Check the master cylinder fluid level and add fluid as necessary.
13. Check the brake pedal for 'sponginess'. Repeat the entire bleeding procedure to correct 'sponginess'.

FRONT DISC BRAKES

✳✳CAUTION

Brake pads contain asbestos, which has been determined to be a cancer causing agent. Never clean the brake surfaces with compressed air! Avoid inhaling any dust from any brake surface! When cleaning brake surfaces, use a commercially available brake cleaning fluid.

Fig. 43 Bleeding the disc brake caliper

Fig. 44 Bleeding the wheel cylinder

Brake Pads

REMOVAL & INSTALLATION

▶ See Figures 45, 46, 47, 48, 49, 50 and 51

➡Disc brake pads must be replaced in axle sets only.

1. Use a syringe or similar tool to remove ⅔ of the brake fluid from the master cylinder reservoir.
2. Raise and safely support the vehicle.
3. Remove the wheel and tire assembly, then reinstall 2 lug nuts to retain the disc brake rotor.
4. Remove the disc brake caliper from the mounting bracket (refer to the procedure in this Section), but do not disconnect the brake hose from the caliper. Suspend the caliper with wire from the coil spring.

✳✳WARNING

Do not let the caliper hang from the brake hose. The hose may become damaged, causing possible brake failure.

5. Use a small prybar to disengage the buttons on the outboard disc brake pad from the holes in the caliper housing. Remove the outboard disc brake pad.
6. Remove the inboard disc brake pad.
7. Inspect the disc brake rotor and machine or replace, as necessary.
   To install:
8. Wipe the outside surface of the caliper piston boot clean using denatured alcohol.
9. Using a C-clamp, bottom the caliper piston into the caliper bore. Tighten the clamp slowly, and be careful not to damage the piston or piston boot. After bottoming the piston, use a small plastic or wood tool to lift the inner edge of the boot next to the piston and press out any trapped air; the boot must lay flat.
10. Install the inboard disc brake pad by snapping the retainer spring into the piston. Make sure the pad lays flat against the piston and does not touch the boot. If the pad contacts the boot, remove the pad and reseat or reposition the boot.
11. Install the outboard disc brake pad. Position the pad so that the wear sensor is at the trailing edge of the pad during forward wheel rotation on all except 1990 Deville and Fleetwood. On 1990 Deville and Fleetwood, position the pad so that the wear sensor is at the leading edge of the pad during forward wheel rotation. The back of the pad must lay flat against the caliper.
12. Install the disc brake caliper as described in this Section.
13. Install the wheel and tire assembly and lower the vehicle.
14. Apply the brake pedal several times to position the caliper piston and seat the brake pads in the caliper.
15. Check the brake fluid level in the master cylinder and add fluid as necessary.

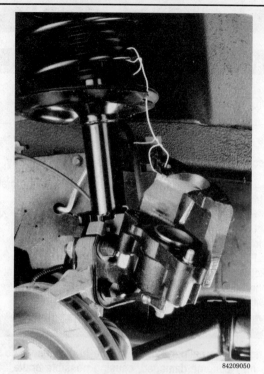

Fig. 45 Suspend the caliper with wire from the coil spring; do not let the caliper hang by the brake hose

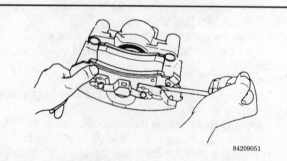

Fig. 46 Disengaging the buttons on the outboard disc brake pad from the holes in the caliper housing

Fig. 47 Removing the outboard disc brake pad from the caliper

Fig. 48 Removing the inboard disc brake pad from the caliper

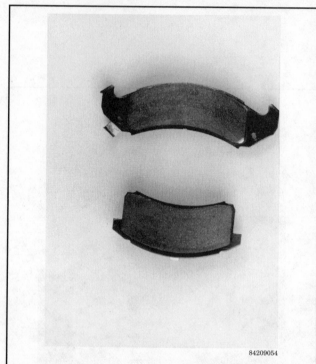

Fig. 49 View of the disc brake pads from a 1992 Deville. Note the wear sensor on the trailing edge of the outboard pad

INSPECTION

▶ See Figures 49, 52 and 53

Inspect the disc brake pads every 6000 miles and any time the wheels are removed. Check both ends of the outer pad by looking in at each end of the caliper. These points are where the highest rate of wear normally occurs. Check the inner pad by looking down through the hole in the top of the caliper. When any lining thickness is worn to within 1/32 in. (0.76mm) of the backing plate or rivet, the pads must be replaced in axle sets. Some inner pads have a thermal layer against the backing plate, integrally molded with the lining; don't confuse this extra layer with uneven inboard-outboard lining wear.

The outer disc brake pad is also equipped with a wear sensor. When the lining is worn, the sensor contacts the disc brake rotor and produces a warning noise, indicating that disc brake pad replacement is necessary.

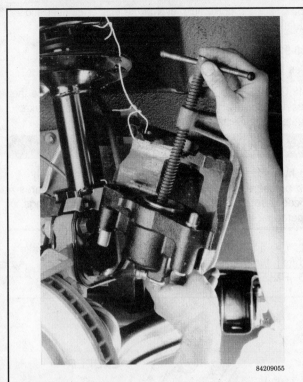

Fig. 50 Using a C-clamp to bottom the piston in the caliper bore

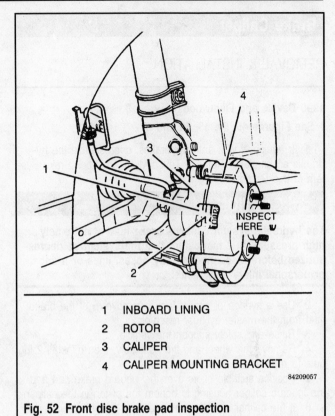

1	INBOARD LINING
2	ROTOR
3	CALIPER
4	CALIPER MOUNTING BRACKET

Fig. 52 Front disc brake pad inspection

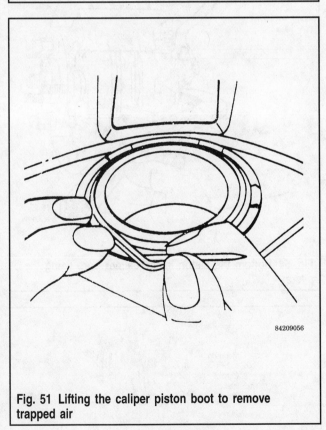

Fig. 51 Lifting the caliper piston boot to remove trapped air

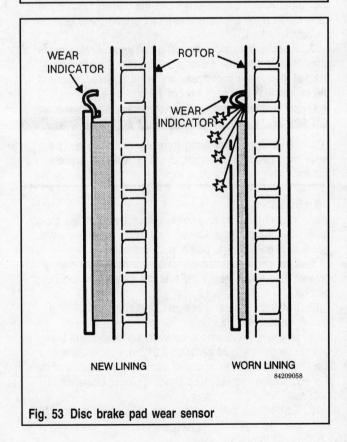

Fig. 53 Disc brake pad wear sensor

Brake Caliper

REMOVAL & INSTALLATION

1990 Deville and Fleetwood
▶ See Figures 45, 54, 55, 56 and 57

1. If equipped with anti-lock brakes, depressurize the hydraulic accumulator. Refer to Teves Mk II Anti-Lock Brake System in this Section.

❊❊CAUTION

The hydraulic system contains brake fluid at extremely high pressure. It is mandatory that the system be depressurized before disconnecting any hoses, lines or fittings, or personal injury may result.

2. Use a syringe or similar tool to remove ⅔ of the brake fluid from the master cylinder reservoir.
3. Raise and safely support the vehicle.
4. Remove the wheel and tire assembly, then reinstall 2 lug nuts to retain the disc brake rotor.
5. Position suitable pliers over the inboard brake pad and the inboard caliper housing to bottom the piston in the caliper.
6. If the caliper is to be removed from the vehicle, remove the bolt attaching the brake hose to the caliper. Discard the gaskets. Plug the openings in the caliper and brake hose to prevent fluid loss.
7. Remove the caliper mounting bolt and sleeve assemblies, then remove the caliper from the rotor and mounting bracket. If only the brake pads are being replaced, suspend the caliper with wire from the coil spring.

❊❊WARNING

Do not let the caliper hang from the brake hose. The hose may become damaged, causing possible brake failure.

To install:

8. Inspect the mounting bolt and sleeve assemblies for corrosion and the bushings for cuts and nicks. Replace parts as necessary; do not try to polish away corrosion.
9. Coat the inside diameter of the bushings with silicone grease, then install the caliper over the rotor in the mounting bracket.
10. Install the mounting bolt and sleeve assemblies and tighten to 38 ft. lbs. (51 Nm).
11. Measure the clearance between the caliper and the bracket stops, it should be 0.005-0.012 in. (0.13-0.30mm). If the clearance is not as specified, remove the caliper and file the ends of the bracket stops until the proper clearance is obtained.
12. Connect the brake hose to the caliper with the attaching bolt, using new gaskets. Tighten the bolt to 33 ft. lbs. (45 Nm).
13. Bleed the brake system.
14. Install the wheel and tire assembly and lower the vehicle.

15. Check the brake fluid level in the master cylinder and add fluid as necessary.

1990-91 Eldorado and Seville
▶ See Figures 58, 59 and 60

1. On 1990 vehicles with anti-lock brakes, depressurize the hydraulic accumulator. Refer to Teves Mk II Anti-Lock Brake System in this Section.

❊❊CAUTION

The hydraulic system contains brake fluid at extremely high pressure. It is mandatory that the system be depressurized before disconnecting any hoses, lines or fittings, or personal injury may result.

2. Use a syringe or similar tool to remove ⅔ of the brake fluid from the master cylinder reservoir.
3. Raise and safely support the vehicle.

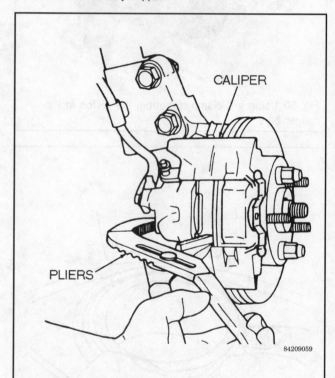

Fig. 54 Bottom the piston in the caliper bore using pliers

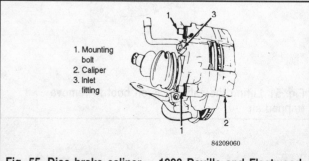

Fig. 55 Disc brake caliper — 1990 Deville and Fleetwood

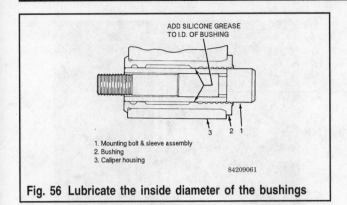

Fig. 56 Lubricate the inside diameter of the bushings

1. Mounting bolt & sleeve assembly
2. Bushing
3. Caliper housing

84209061

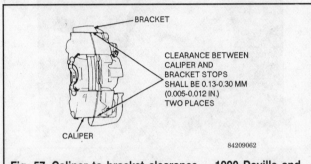

Fig. 57 Caliper to bracket clearance — 1990 Deville and Fleetwood

BRACKET

CLEARANCE BETWEEN CALIPER AND BRACKET STOPS SHALL BE 0.13-0.30 MM (0.005-0.012 IN.) TWO PLACES

CALIPER

84209062

4. Remove the wheel and tire assembly, then reinstall 2 lug nuts to retain the disc brake rotor.

5. If the caliper is to be removed from the vehicle, remove the bolt attaching the brake hose to the caliper. Discard the gaskets. Plug the openings in the caliper and brake hose to prevent fluid loss.

6. Remove the caliper mounting bolts, then remove the caliper from the rotor and mounting bracket. If only the brake pads are being replaced, suspend the caliper with wire from the coil spring.

✳✳WARNING

Do not let the caliper hang from the brake hose. The hose may become damaged, causing possible brake failure.

To install:

7. Inspect the bolt boots and mounting bracket support bushings for cuts, tears or deterioration and replace as necessary. Inspect the mounting bolts for corrosion and replace them and the bushings if any is found; do not try to polish away corrosion.

8. Position the caliper over the rotor in the mounting bracket, making sure the bolt boots are in place.

9. Lubricate the shaft of the mounting bolts with silicone grease. Install the bolts and tighten to 63 ft. lbs. (85 Nm).

10. Position the brake hose on the disc brake caliper. Connect the hose to the caliper using the attaching bolt and 2 new gaskets. Tighten the bolt to 32 ft. lbs. (44 Nm).

11. Bleed the brake system.

12. Install the wheel and tire assembly and lower the vehicle.

13. Check the brake fluid level in the master cylinder and add fluid as necessary.

1991-93 Deville, Fleetwood and Sixty Special1992-93 Eldorado and Seville

▶ **See Figures 45, 56, 61, 62, 63 and 64**

1. Use a syringe or similar tool to remove ⅔ of the brake fluid from the master cylinder reservoir.

2. Raise and safely support the vehicle.

3. Remove the wheel and tire assembly, then reinstall 2 lug nuts to retain the disc brake rotor.

4. If the caliper is to be removed from the vehicle, remove the bolt attaching the brake hose to the caliper. Discard the gaskets. Plug the openings in the caliper and brake hose to prevent fluid loss.

5. Install a large C-clamp over the top of the caliper housing and against the back of the outboard pad. Slowly tighten

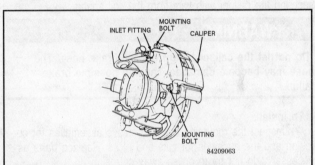

Fig. 58 Disc brake caliper — 1990-91 Eldorado and Seville

INLET FITTING

MOUNTING BOLT

CALIPER

MOUNTING BOLT

84209063

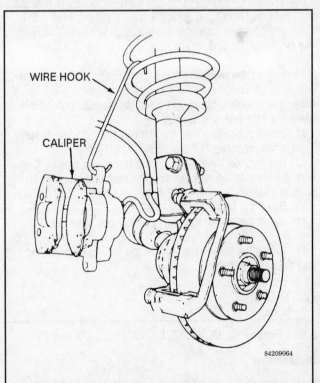

Fig. 59 Suspending the caliper with wire — 1990-91 Eldorado and Seville

WIRE HOOK

CALIPER

84209064

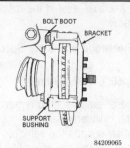

Fig. 60 Bolt boot and support bushing — 1990-91 Eldorado and Seville

the C-clamp until the piston is pushed into the caliper far enough to slide the caliper off the rotor.

6. Remove the caliper mounting bolts and sleeves, then remove the caliper. If only the brake pads are being replaced, suspend the caliper with wire from the coil spring.

✳✳WARNING

Do not let the caliper hang from the brake hose. The hose may become damaged, causing possible brake failure.

To install:

7. Inspect the mounting bolt and sleeve assemblies for corrosion and the bushings for cuts and nicks. Replace parts as necessary; do not try to polish away corrosion.

8. Coat the inside diameter of the bushings with silicone grease.

9. Install the mounting bolt and sleeve assemblies through the bushings using hand pressure only. If greater than hand force is required or mechanical assistance is needed, remove the mounting bolt and sleeve assemblies along with the bushings.

10. Inspect the mounting bores for corrosion. If there is any corrosion, remove it using a 1 in. wheel cylinder honing brush. Clean the mounting bores with clean denatured alcohol, replace the bushings and lubricate.

11. Install the caliper over the rotor in the mounting bracket. Tighten the mounting bolts to 38 ft. lbs. (51 Nm).

12. Position the brake hose on the disc brake caliper. Connect the hose to the caliper using the attaching bolt and 2 new gaskets. Tighten the bolt to 32 ft. lbs. (44 Nm).

13. Bleed the brake system.

14. Install the wheel and tire assembly and lower the vehicle.

15. Check the brake fluid level in the master cylinder and add fluid as necessary.

OVERHAUL

▶ See Figures 65, 66, 67, 68, 69, 70, 71, 72, 73 and 74

Disassembly

1. Remove the caliper from the vehicle and place on a clean workbench.

2. On all except 1990-91 Eldorado and Seville, inspect the caliper bushings for nicks or cuts and replace them if damage

Fig. 61 Disc brake assembly — 1992 Deville

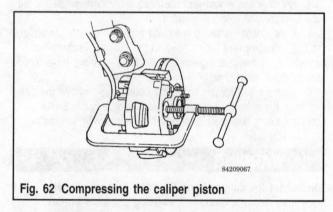

Fig. 62 Compressing the caliper piston

is found. Inspect the mounting bores for corrosion. If there is any corrosion, remove it using a 1 in. wheel cylinder honing brush. Clean the mounting bores with clean denatured alcohol.

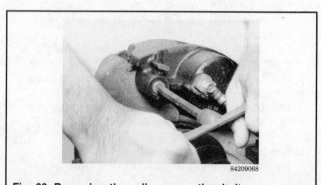

Fig. 63 Removing the caliper mounting bolt

Fig. 64 Removing the disc brake caliper

3. On 1990-91 Eldorado and Seville, inspect the bolt boots and support bushings on the caliper mounting bracket for cuts, tears or deterioration. If replacement is necessary, remove the mounting bracket. Remove the boots and pry out the support bushings, then use a paper clip with the end bent over to remove the bushings.

4. Pad the interior of the caliper with shop towels, then use compressed air through the caliper fluid inlet to remove the piston from the caliper.

✳✳CAUTION

Do not place your fingers in front of the piston in an attempt to catch or protect it when applying compressed air. This could result in serious injury.

5. Inspect the caliper piston for scoring, nicks, corrosion and worn or damaged chrome plating. Replace the piston if any damage is found.

6. Remove the boot, being careful not to scratch the housing bore.

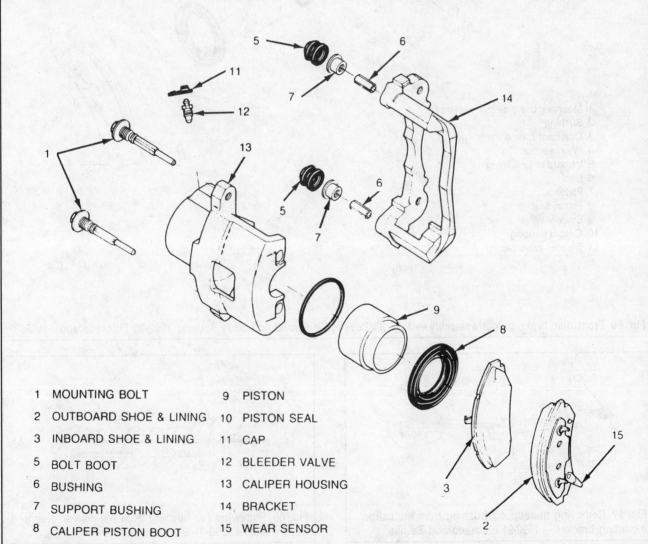

1	MOUNTING BOLT	9	PISTON
2	OUTBOARD SHOE & LINING	10	PISTON SEAL
3	INBOARD SHOE & LINING	11	CAP
5	BOLT BOOT	12	BLEEDER VALVE
6	BUSHING	13	CALIPER HOUSING
7	SUPPORT BUSHING	14	BRACKET
8	CALIPER PISTON BOOT	15	WEAR SENSOR

Fig. 65 Front disc brake caliper assembly — 1990-91 Eldorado and Seville

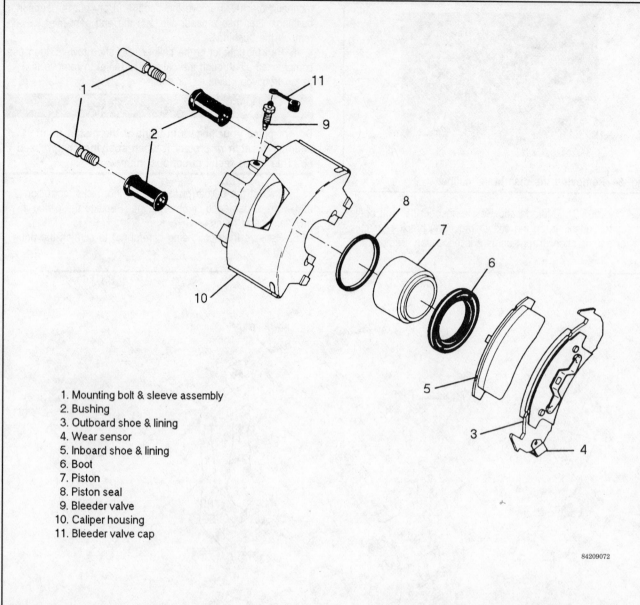

1. Mounting bolt & sleeve assembly
2. Bushing
3. Outboard shoe & lining
4. Wear sensor
5. Inboard shoe & lining
6. Boot
7. Piston
8. Piston seal
9. Bleeder valve
10. Caliper housing
11. Bleeder valve cap

84209072

Fig. 66 Front disc brake caliper assembly — 1991-93 Deville, Fleetwood and Sixty Special, 1992-93 Eldorado and Seville

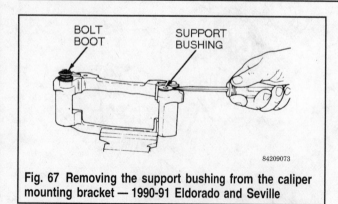

BOLT
BOOT

SUPPORT
BUSHING

84209073

Fig. 67 Removing the support bushing from the caliper mounting bracket — 1990-91 Eldorado and Seville

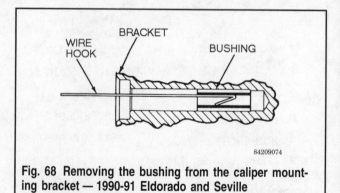

WIRE
HOOK

BRACKET

BUSHING

84209074

Fig. 68 Removing the bushing from the caliper mounting bracket — 1990-91 Eldorado and Seville

7. Use a small plastic or wood tool to remove the piston seal from the groove in the caliper. Do not use a metal tool as this may damage the seal groove or caliper bore.

8. Inspect the caliper bore and seal groove for scoring, nicks, corrosion and wear. Use crocus cloth to polish out light

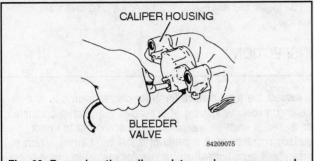

Fig. 69 Removing the caliper piston using compressed air

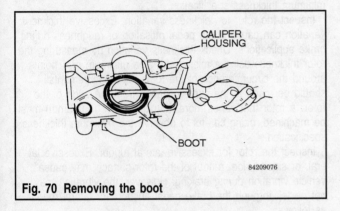

Fig. 70 Removing the boot

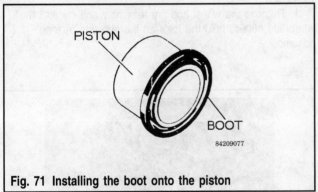

Fig. 71 Installing the boot onto the piston

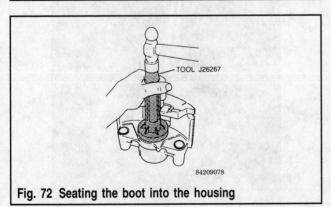

Fig. 72 Seating the boot into the housing

corrosion. If corrosion in and around the seal groove will not clean off with crocus cloth, replace the caliper housing.

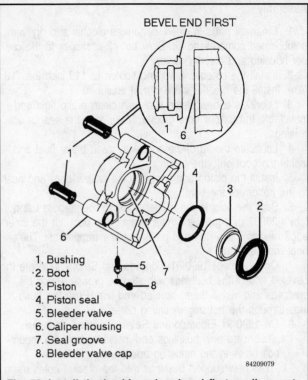

1. Bushing
2. Boot
3. Piston
4. Piston seal
5. Bleeder valve
6. Caliper housing
7. Seal groove
8. Bleeder valve cap

Fig. 73 Install the bushings bevel end first — all except 1990-91 Eldorado and Seville

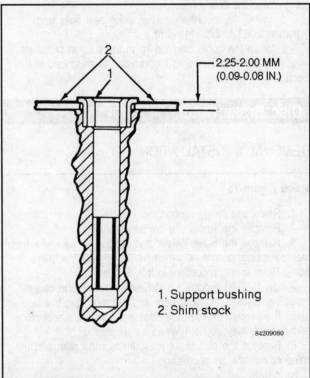

1. Support bushing
2. Shim stock

2.25-2.00 MM (0.09-0.08 IN.)

Fig. 74 Installing the support bushing in the caliper mounting bracket — 1990-91 Eldorado and Seville

9. Remove the bleeder valve cap, if equipped, and remove the bleeder valve from the caliper.

Assembly

1. Clean all parts in clean, denatured alcohol and dry with unlubricated compressed air. Blow out all passages in the caliper housing and bleeder valve.

2. Install the bleeder valve and tighten to 110 inch lbs. (13 Nm). Install the bleeder valve cap, if equipped.

3. Lubricate a new piston seal with clean brake fluid and install into the caliper bore groove. Make sure the seal is not twisted.

4. Lubricate the lip of the boot with clean brake fluid and install the boot onto the piston.

5. Install the piston and boot into the caliper bore and push to the bottom of the bore.

6. Seat the boot in the caliper housing counterbore using tool J-26267 or equivalent. After seating the boot, lift the inner edge next to the piston and press out any trapped air. The boot must lay flat.

7. On all except 1990-91 Eldorado and Seville, lubricate the beveled end of the bushings with silicone grease. Pinch the bushings and install them, beveled end first. Push the bushings through the housing mounting bores.

8. On 1990-91 Eldorado and Seville, proceed as follows:

   a. Lubricate new bushings and install them in the mounting bolt holes in the mounting bracket.

   b. Tap new support bushings into the bracket holes using a plastic mallet. Use 0.08-0.09 in. (2-2.25mm) shim stock on either side of the support bushing (or a U-shaped tool made from shim stock) to maintain the proper height of the bushing above the bracket face.

   c. Install the mounting bracket using new bolts and tighten to 83 ft. lbs. (112 Nm).

   d. Snap the boots over the lip of the support bushings.

9. Install the caliper onto the vehicle, as described in this Section.

Disc Brake Rotor

REMOVAL & INSTALLATION

▶ **See Figure 75**

1. Raise and safely support the vehicle.
2. Remove the wheel and tire assembly.
3. Remove the brake caliper and suspend it with wire from the coil spring; do not let the caliper hang from the brake hose. Refer to the procedure in this Section.
4. On 1990-91 Eldorado and Seville, remove the caliper mounting bracket mounting bolts and the mounting bracket.
5. If equipped, remove the retainers from the wheel studs and discard; they do not have to be reinstalled.
6. Remove the disc brake rotor. Inspect the rotor and machine or replace, as necessary.

To install:

7. Install the disc brake rotor over the wheel studs and hub assembly.

8. On 1990-91 Eldorado and Seville, install the caliper mounting bracket using new mounting bolts. Tighten the bolts to 83 ft. lbs. (112 Nm).

9. Install the brake caliper; refer to the procedure in this Section.

10. Install the wheel and tire assembly and lower the vehicle.

INSPECTION

Inspect the rotor surface finish for discoloration due to overheating, excessive glazing or scoring. If the rotor is discolored or glazed, it must be machined. Light scoring of the rotor surface not exceeding a depth of 0.050 in. (1.2mm), which may result from normal use, is not detrimental to brake operation and refinishing is usually not necessary. Heavier scoring must be removed by refinishing, being careful to observe the minimum thickness specification.

Inspect the rotor for thickness variation. Excessive thickness variation can cause brake pedal pulsation or roughness during brake applications. Check thickness variation by measuring the rotor thickness using a micrometer at a minimum of 4 points around the circumference of the rotor. All measurements should be made at the same distance from the edge of the rotor. A rotor that varies more than 0.0005 in. (0.013mm) must be machined, being careful to observe the minimum thickness specification.

Inspect the rotor for excessive lateral runout. Excessive lateral, or side-to-side, runout of the rotor surface may cause vehicle vibration during braking. However, the vibration may not be felt through the brake pedal. Inspect for lateral runout as follows:

1. Remove the wheel and tire assembly and reinstall the wheel lug nuts to hold the rotor on the hub and bearing assembly.

84209081

Fig. 75 View of the disc brake rotor showing retainers at 2 of the wheel studs. The retainers do not have to be reinstalled

2. Attach a dial indicator to the steering knuckle or caliper mounting bracket. Position the indicator foot so it contacts the rotor surface approximately 1/2-1 in. from the rotor edge.

3. Zero the dial indicator. Move the rotor one complete revolution and check the total indicated runout. Compare the reading with the specifications in the chart at the end of this Section.

4. If runout is excessive, in some instances it can be corrected by indexing the rotor on the hub one or two wheel stud positions from the original position.

5. If the lateral runout cannot be corrected by indexing, check the hub and bearing assembly for excessive lateral runout or looseness. If the hub and bearing lateral runout exceeds 0.0015 in. (0.040mm) on Deville, Fleetwood and Sixty Special, 0.004 in. (0.10mm) on 1990-91 Eldorado and Seville, or 0.002 in. (0.06mm) on 1992-93 Eldorado and Seville, replace the hub and bearing assembly and recheck rotor lateral runout.

6. If the lateral runout still exceeds specification, machine the rotor, being careful to observe the minimum thickness specification.

REAR DRUM BRAKES

✳✳CAUTION

Brake shoes contain asbestos, which has been determined to be a cancer causing agent. Never clean the brake surfaces with compressed air! Avoid inhaling any dust from any brake surface! When cleaning brake surfaces, use a commercially available brake cleaning fluid.

Brake Drums

REMOVAL & INSTALLATION

▶ **See Figures 76, 77 and 78**

1. Raise and safely support the vehicle.
2. Remove the wheel and tire assembly.
3. If equipped, remove the retainers from the wheel studs and discard; they do not have to be reinstalled.
4. Remove the brake drum. If the drum is difficult to remove, proceed as follows:

   a. Make sure the parking brake is released.

   b. Back off the parking brake cable adjustment.

   c. On 1990 through early 1992 vehicles, remove the access hole plug from the backing plate. On 1992-93 vehicles equipped with a knockout slug in the drum, use a hammer and a metal punch to bend in the backing plate knockout slug.

   d. Insert a suitable tool through the hole and press in to push the parking brake lever off its stop. This will allow the brake shoes to retract slightly.

   e. Apply a small amount of penetrating oil around the drum pilot hole. Use a rubber mallet to tap gently on the outer rim of the drum and/or around the inner drum diameter by the spindle. Be careful not to deform the drum through the use of excessive force.

➡**After a drum having a metal knockout slug has been removed from the vehicle, remove the slug using pliers or vise grips. Install a rubber access hole plug into the hole to prevent dirt or contamination from entering the drum brake assembly.**

5. Inspect the brake drum and machine or replace, as necessary.

To install:

6. Adjust the brake shoes and install the brake drum.

7. Install the wheel and tire assembly and lower the vehicle.

INSPECTION

Inspect the brake drums for cracks, scores, deep grooves, out-of-round and taper. Replace any drum that is cracked; it is unsafe for further use. Do not attempt to weld a cracked drum.

Smooth up any light scores. Normal, light scoring of drum surfaces not exceeding a depth of 1/16 in. (1.5mm) is not detrimental to brake operation. Heavy or extensive scoring will cause excessive brake shoe wear, and it may be necessary to machine the drum. When machining the drum, observe the maximum machine diameter specification.

If the brake shoes are slightly worn (but still usable) and the drum is grooved, polish the drum with fine emery cloth; do not machine it. Eliminating all drum grooves and smoothing the

84209082

Fig. 76 If equipped, remove the retainers from the wheel studs and discard; they do not have to be reinstalled

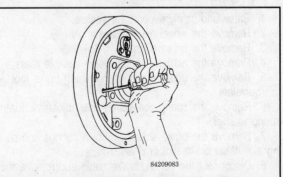

84209083

Fig. 77 Moving the parking brake lever off its stop

84209084

Fig. 78 Removing the brake drum

lining ridges would require removing too much metal and lining, while if left alone, the grooves and ridges match and satisfactory service can be obtained. However, if the brake shoes are to be replaced, a grooved drum must be machined. A grooved drum will wear a new brake shoe, resulting in improper brake performance.

An out-of-round or tapered drum prevents accurate brake shoe adjustment, and could possibly wear other brake parts due to its eccentric action. An out-of-round drum can also cause severe and irregular tire tread wear, as well as a pulsating brake pedal. Check for out-of-round and taper by measuring the inside diameter of the drum at several points using an inside micrometer. Take measurements at the open and closed edges of the machined surface and at right angles to each other. Machine the drum to correct out-of-round and taper, being careful to observe the maximum machine diameter specification.

Brake Shoes

INSPECTION

Inspect the brake shoes every 6000 miles and any time the wheels are removed. When any lining thickness is worn to within 1/32 in. (0.76mm) of the backing plate or rivet, the shoes must be replaced in axle sets.

REMOVAL & INSTALLATION

1990-91 Deville and Fleetwood

▶ See Figures 79, 80 and 81

1. Raise and safely support the vehicle.
2. Remove the wheel and tire assembly.
3. Remove the brake drum.
4. Remove the actuator spring, using suitable pliers.
5. Remove the upper return spring, using brake tool J-8057 or equivalent.
6. Remove the spring connecting link, adjuster actuator and spring washer.
7. Remove the brake shoe hold-down springs and pins using a suitable brake tool or pliers.
8. Disconnect the parking brake cable and remove the brake shoes.

9. Remove the adjusting screw assembly and lower return spring.
10. Remove the retaining ring, pin, spring washer and parking brake lever from the brake shoe.
11. Inspect all parts for wear, over-stress and discoloration from heat and replace as necessary. Inspect the wheel cylinder for leakage and the wheel cylinder dust boots for cuts or tears; replace the entire wheel cylinder if any damage is found.
12. Disassemble the adjuster screw assembly and clean the threads with a wire brush. Wash all components in clean denatured alcohol and allow to dry. Apply suitable brake lubricant to the adjuster screw threads, inside diameter of the socket and the socket face. Inspect the adjuster screw threads for smooth rotation over the full length.

To install:

13. Install the parking brake lever on the brake shoe with the spring washer (concave side against the lever), pin and retaining ring.
14. Install the adjuster pin in the other brake shoe so that the pin projects 0.275-0.283 in. (7.0-7.2mm) from the side of the shoe web where the adjuster actuator is installed.
15. Assemble the adjuster screw assembly, making sure the spring clip is installed in the same position from where it was removed.
16. Install the lower return spring between the brake shoes.

✱✱WARNING

Do not over-stretch the lower return spring; it will be damaged if the extended length is greater than 3.88 in. (98.6mm).

17. Connect the parking brake cable and install the brake shoes with the hold pins and springs. The lower return spring should be positioned under the anchor plate.

➡**The adjuster brake shoe is the one in which the adjuster pin was installed in the shoe web. The adjuster brake shoe is to the front of the vehicle on the left-hand brake assembly and to the rear of the vehicle on the right-hand brake assembly.**

18. Install the adjuster screw assembly between the brake shoes on the backing plate. Make sure the adjuster screw engages the notch in the adjuster shoe and the spring clip points towards the backing plate.
19. Install the spring washer with the concave side against the web of the adjuster brake shoe.
20. Install the adjuster actuator so its top leg engages the notch in the adjuster screw.
21. Install the spring connecting link and hold in place.
22. Insert the angled hook end of the upper return spring through the parking brake lever and brake shoe. Grasp the long, straight section of the spring using brake tool J-8057 or equivalent, pull the spring straight across, then down to hook into the crook on the spring connecting link.

✱✱WARNING

Do not over-stretch the upper return spring. The spring will be damaged if extended greater than 5.49 in. (139.5mm).

23. Install the actuator spring, using suitable pliers.

✳✳WARNING

Do not over-stretch the actuator spring. The spring will be damaged if extended greater than 3.27 in. (83mm).

24. Make sure the parking brake lever is on its stop and the brake shoes are properly centered on the wheel cylinder pistons.
25. Adjust the brakes and install the brake drum.
26. Install the wheel and tire assembly and lower the vehicle. Check the parking brake adjustment.

1992-93 Deville, Fleetwood and Sixty Special

▶ **See Figures 82, 83, 84, 85, 86, 87, 88, 89, 90, 91 and 92**

1. Raise and safely support the vehicle.
2. Remove the wheel and tire assembly.
3. Remove the brake drum.
4. Remove the loop end of the actuator spring from the adjuster actuator, then disconnect the other end of the spring from the parking brake shoe web.
5. Pry the end of the retractor spring from the hole in the adjuster brake shoe web.

✳✳CAUTION

Keep your fingers away from the retractor spring to prevent them from being pinched between the spring and shoe web or spring and backing plate.

✳✳WARNING

When removing the retractor spring from either brake shoe, do not overstretch it. Overstretching reduces the spring's effectiveness.

6. Pry the end of the retractor spring toward the axle until the spring snaps down off the shoe web onto the backing plate.
7. Remove the adjuster brake shoe, adjuster actuator and adjusting screw assembly.
8. Remove the parking brake lever from the parking brake shoe. Do not remove the parking brake cable from the lever unless the lever is to be replaced.
9. Pry the end of the retractor spring from the hole in the parking brake shoe web.

✳✳CAUTION

Keep your fingers away from the retractor spring to prevent them from being pinched between the spring and shoe web or spring and backing plate.

10. Pry the end of the retractor spring toward the axle until the spring snaps down off the shoe web onto the backing plate.
11. Remove the parking brake shoe.

12. Remove the retractor spring from the backing plate. If only the brake shoes are being replaced, the retractor spring does not have to be removed.
13. Clean all parts in clean denatured alcohol.
14. Inspect all parts for wear, over-stress and discoloration from heat and replace as necessary. Inspect the wheel cylinder for leakage and wheel cylinder dust boots for cuts or tears; replace the entire wheel cylinder if any damage is found.
15. Disassemble the adjuster screw assembly and clean the threads with a wire brush. Wash all components in clean denatured alcohol and allow to dry. Apply suitable brake lubricant to the adjuster screw threads, inside diameter of the socket and the socket face. Inspect the adjuster screw threads for smooth rotation over the full length.

To install:

16. Lubricate the 6 raised brake shoe pads on the backing plate and the anchor surfaces on the backing plate that contact the lower ends of the brake shoes with suitable brake lubricant.
17. If the retractor spring was removed, reinstall it, hooking the center spring section under the tab on the anchor.
18. Position the parking brake shoe on the backing plate. Using a suitable brake tool, pull the end of the retractor spring up to rest on the web of the brake shoe. Pull the end of the spring over until it snaps into the slot in the brake shoe.
19. Install the parking brake lever to the parking brake shoe. Connect the parking brake cable to the lever, if disconnected.
20. Assemble the adjusting screw assembly.
21. Engage the pivot nut of the adjusting screw assembly with the web of the parking brake shoe and the parking brake lever. Position the adjuster brake shoe so that the shoe web engages the deep slot in the adjuster socket.
22. Using a suitable brake tool, pull the end of the retractor spring up to rest on the web of the adjuster brake shoe. Pull the end of the spring over until it snaps into the slot in the brake shoe.
23. Lubricate the tab and pivot point on the adjuster actuator with suitable brake lubricant. Using a suitable tool, spread the brake shoes while working the adjuster actuator into position.
24. Engage the U-shaped end of the actuator spring in the hole in the web of the parking brake shoe. Using a suitable tool, stretch the spring and engage the loop end over the tab on the adjuster actuator.
25. Check the following to make sure the adjuster actuator is positioned and functioning properly:
  a. Adjuster actuator pivot in shoe web slot.
  b. Notch in adjuster actuator is on step in adjusting screw notch (View B-B in the figure).
  c. Arm of adjuster actuator is resting freely on star wheel teeth of adjuster screw, not trapped under teeth in a downward angle.
  d. Position a suitable brake tool between the upper ends of the brake shoes. Spread the shoes and watch for proper operation of the star wheel.
26. Adjust the brakes and install the brake drum.
27. Install the wheel and tire assembly and lower the vehicle. Check the parking brake adjustment.

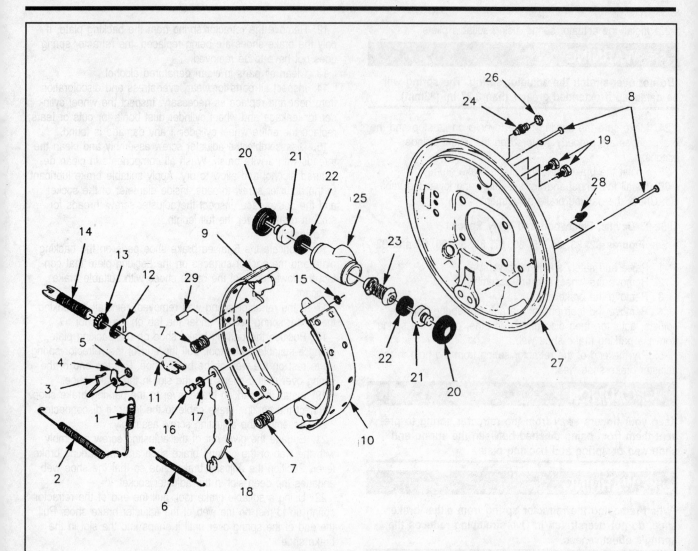

	10 SHOE AND LINING	20 BOOT
1 ACTUATOR SPRING	11 ADJUSTER SOCKET	21 PISTON
2 UPPER RETURN SPRING	12 SPRING CLIP	22 SEAL
3 SPRING CONNECTING LINK	13 ADJUSTER NUT	23 SPRING ASSEMBLY
4 ADJUSTER ACTUATOR	14 ADJUSTER SCREW	24 BLEEDER VALVE
5 SPRING WASHER	15 RETAINING RING	25 WHEEL CYLINDER
6 LOWER RETURN SPRING	16 PIN	26 BLEEDER VALVE CAP
7 HOLD–DOWN SPRING ASSEMBLY	17 SPRING WASHER	27 BACKING PLATE ASSEMBLY
8 HOLD–DOWN PIN	18 PARK BRAKE LEVER	28 ACCESS HOLE PLUG
9 ADJUSTER SHOE AND LINING	19 SCREW AND LOCKWASHER	29 ADJUSTER PIN

84209085

Fig. 79 Drum brake assembly — 1990-91 Deville and Fleetwood

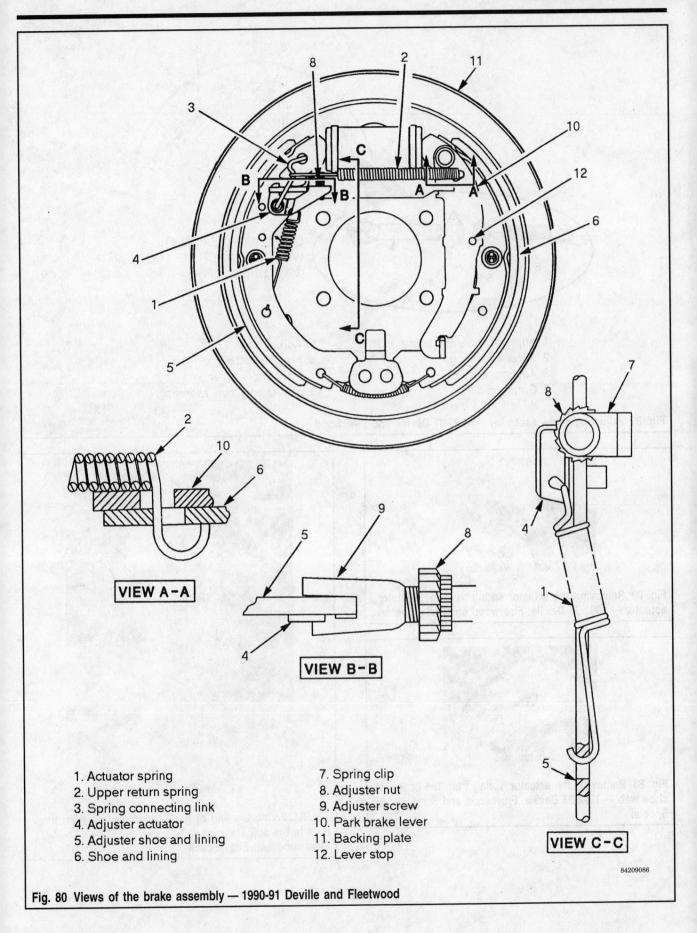

1. Actuator spring
2. Upper return spring
3. Spring connecting link
4. Adjuster actuator
5. Adjuster shoe and lining
6. Shoe and lining
7. Spring clip
8. Adjuster nut
9. Adjuster screw
10. Park brake lever
11. Backing plate
12. Lever stop

VIEW A-A

VIEW B-B

VIEW C-C

84209086

Fig. 80 Views of the brake assembly — 1990-91 Deville and Fleetwood

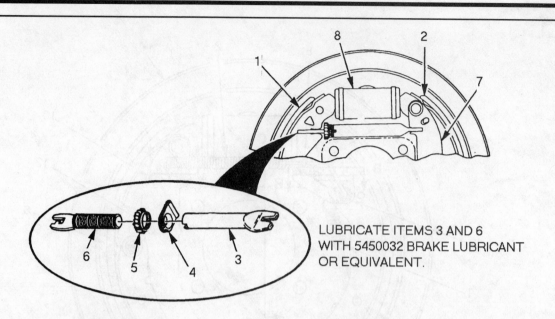

LUBRICATE ITEMS 3 AND 6
WITH 5450032 BRAKE LUBRICANT
OR EQUIVALENT.

1. Adjuster shoe and lining
2. Shoe and lining
3. Adjuster socket
4. Spring clip
5. Adjuster nut
6. Adjuster screw
7. Park brake lever
8. Adjusting screw assembly

84209087

Fig. 81 Adjusting screw assembly — 1990-91 Deville and Fleetwood

84209088

Fig. 82 Removing the actuator spring from the adjuster actuator — 1992-93 Deville, Fleetwood and Sixty Special

84209089

Fig. 83 Removing the actuator spring from the brake shoe web — 1992-93 Deville, Fleetwood and Sixty Special

84209090

Fig. 84 Prying the end of the retractor spring from the hole in the adjuster brake shoe web — 1992-93 Deville, Fleetwood and Sixty Special

Fig. 85 Removing the adjuster brake shoe and adjuster actuator — 1992-93 Deville, Fleetwood and Sixty Special

Fig. 86 Removing the adjusting screw assembly — 1992-93 Deville, Fleetwood and Sixty Special

Wheel Cylinder

REMOVAL & INSTALLATION

▶ See Figure 93

1. On 1990 vehicles with anti-lock brakes, depressurize the hydraulic accumulator. Refer to Teves Mk II Anti-Lock Brake System in this Section.

✳✳CAUTION

The hydraulic system contains brake fluid at extremely high pressure. It is mandatory that the system be depressurized before disconnecting any hoses, lines or fittings, or personal injury may result.

2. Raise and safely support the vehicle.

Fig. 87 Prying the end of the retractor spring from the hole in the parking brake shoe web — 1992-93 Deville, Fleetwood and Sixty Special

3. Remove the wheel and tire assembly and the brake drum.

4. Clean the area around the wheel cylinder inlet, pilot and bleeder valve.

Fig. 88 Removing the retractor spring — 1992-93 Deville, Fleetwood and Sixty Special

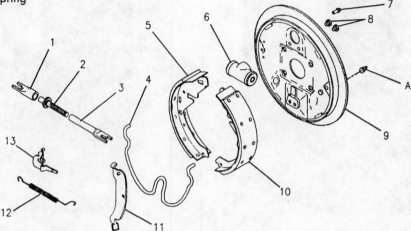

A. Access hole plug.
   Not part of assembly
   on 1993 vehicles.
   Service only item.
1. Adjuster socket
2. Adjuster screw
3. Pivot nut
4. Retractor spring

5. Adjuster shoe and lining
6. Wheel cylinder
7. Bleeder valve
8. Bolt
9. Backing plate

10. Park brake shoe and lining
11. Park brake lever
12. Actuator Spring
13. Adjuster actuator

84209095

Fig. 89 Drum brake assembly — 1992-93 Deville, Fleetwood and Sixty Special

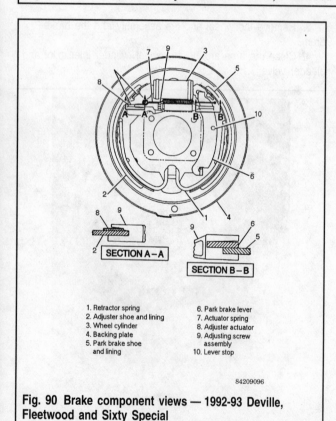

1. Retractor spring
2. Adjuster shoe and lining
3. Wheel cylinder
4. Backing plate
5. Park brake shoe
   and lining
6. Park brake lever
7. Actuator spring
8. Adjuster actuator
9. Adjusting screw
   assembly
10. Lever stop

84209096

Fig. 90 Brake component views — 1992-93 Deville, Fleetwood and Sixty Special

5. Remove the brake shoes; refer to the procedure in this Section.

6. Remove the bleeder valve.

LUBRICATE WITH BRAKE LUBE,
GM P/N 1052196, OR EQUIVALENT

ADJUSTER
SOCKET

ADJUSTER
SCREW

PIVOT
NUT

84209097

Fig. 91 Adjusting screw assembly components — 1992-93 Deville, Fleetwood and Sixty Special

7. Disconnect the brake line from the wheel cylinder. Plug the opening in the line to prevent fluid loss.

8. Remove the wheel cylinder mounting bolts and the wheel cylinder.

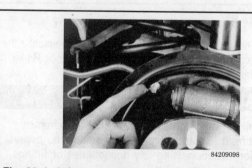

84209098

Fig. 92 Lubricate the 6 raised brake shoe pads on the backing plate with suitable brake lubricant

9. Clean the old sealant from the backing plate where the wheel cylinder was removed. Clean the sealant from the wheel cylinder if it is to be reinstalled.

To install:

10. Apply Loctite® Master Gasket or equivalent, to the wheel cylinder shoulder face that contacts the backing plate.

11. Position the wheel cylinder and install the mounting bolts. Tighten the mounting bolts to 106 inch lbs. (12 Nm).

12. Connect the brake line to the wheel cylinder and tighten the fitting to 11 ft. lbs. (15 Nm).

13. Install the bleeder valve and tighten to 88 inch lbs. (10 Nm).

14. Install the brake shoes. Adjust the brake shoes and install the brake drum. Refer to the procedures in this Section.

15. Bleed the brake system.

16. Install the wheel and tire assembly and lower the vehicle. Check the parking brake adjustment.

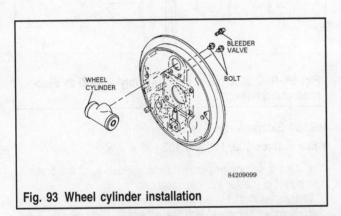

Fig. 93 Wheel cylinder installation

REAR DISC BRAKES

✳✳CAUTION

Brake pads contain asbestos, which has been determined to be a cancer causing agent. Never clean the brake surfaces with compressed air! Avoid inhaling any dust from any brake surface! When cleaning brake surfaces, use a commercially available brake cleaning fluid.

Brake Pads

REMOVAL & INSTALLATION

➡Disc brake pads must be replaced in axle sets only.

1990-91 Eldorado and Seville

▶ See Figures 94, 95, 96, 97, 98 and 99

1. Use a syringe or similar tool to remove ⅔ of the brake fluid from the master cylinder reservoir.

Brake Backing Plate

REMOVAL & INSTALLATION

1. On 1990 vehicles with anti-lock brakes, depressurize the hydraulic accumulator. Refer to Teves Mk II Anti-Lock Brake System in this Section.

✳✳CAUTION

The hydraulic system contains brake fluid at extremely high pressure. It is mandatory that the system be depressurized before disconnecting any hoses, lines or fittings, or personal injury may result.

2. Raise and safely support the vehicle.

3. Remove the wheel and tire assembly.

4. Remove the brake drum, brake shoes and the wheel cylinder; refer to the procedures in this Section.

5. Disconnect the parking brake cable from the backing plate.

6. Remove the hub and bearing bolts and remove the backing plate.

To install:

7. Position the backing plate and install the hub and bearing with the bolts. Tighten the bolts to 52 ft. lbs. (70 Nm).

8. Connect the parking brake cable to the backing plate.

9. Install the wheel cylinder and brake shoes. Adjust the brake shoes and install the brake drum. Refer to the procedures in this Section.

10. Bleed the brake system.

11. Install the wheel and tire assembly and lower the vehicle. Check the parking brake adjustment.

2. Raise and safely support the vehicle.

3. Remove the wheel and tire assembly, then reinstall 2 lug nuts to retain the disc brake rotor.

4. Remove the disc brake caliper from the rotor and mounting bracket (refer to the procedure in this Section), but do not disconnect the brake hose from the caliper. Suspend the caliper with wire from the strut.

✳✳WARNING

Do not let the caliper hang from the brake hose. The hose may become damaged, causing possible brake failure.

5. Remove the outboard disc brake pad by unsnapping the springs from the caliper holes.

6. Press in on the edge of the inboard disc brake pad from the open side of the caliper, and tilt outward to release the pad from the retainer.

7. Remove the bushings from the mounting bolt holes in the caliper mounting bracket.

8. Remove the 2-way check valve from the end of the caliper piston using a small prybar.

→If evidence of leakage can be seen at the piston hole after the check valve is removed, replace the actuator and overhaul the caliper.

To install:

9. Position suitable adjustable pliers over the caliper housing and piston surface, and bottom the caliper piston in the caliper bore. After the piston is bottomed, lift the inner edge of the boot next to the piston and press out any trapped air. The boot must lay flat.

✳✳WARNING

Do not let the pliers contact the actuator screw. Protect the piston so the surface will not be damaged.

10. Lubricate new bushings with silicone grease and install them in the mounting bolt holes in the caliper mounting bracket.

11. Lubricate a new 2-way check valve and install it into the end of the caliper piston.

12. Install the inboard disc brake pad as follows:

a. Engage the inboard pad edge in the straight tabs on the retainer, press down and snap the pad under the S-shaped tabs. The back of the pad must lay flat against the caliper piston.

b. Make sure the pad retainer and piston are properly positioned. The tabs on the pad retainer are different; rotate the retainer if necessary.

c. The buttons on the back of the pad must engage the D-shaped notches in the piston. The piston will be properly aligned when the D-shaped notches are aligned with the caliper mounting bolt holes. Turn the piston with spanner wrench J-7624 or equivalent, if necessary.

13. Install the outboard disc brake pad with the wear sensor at the trailing edge of the pad during forward wheel rotation. Snap the pad springs fully into the caliper holes. The back of the pad must lay flat against the caliper.

14. Install the disc brake caliper as described in this Section.

15. Install the wheel and tire assembly and lower the vehicle.

16. Apply the brake pedal several times to seat the brake pads in the caliper.

17. Check the brake fluid level in the master cylinder and add fluid as necessary.

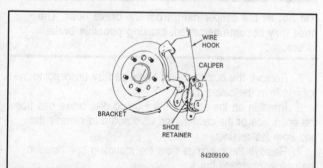

Fig. 94 Suspend the caliper with wire from the strut; do not let the caliper hang from the brake hose

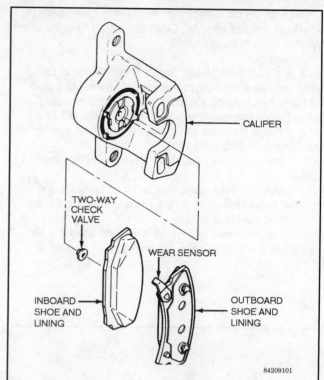

Fig. 95 Rear disc brake pad assembly — 1990-91 Eldorado and Seville

1992-93 Eldorado and Seville

▶ See Figures 100, 101 and 102

1. Use a syringe or similar tool to remove ⅔ of the brake fluid from the master cylinder reservoir.

2. Raise and safely support the vehicle.

3. Remove the wheel and tire assembly, then reinstall 2 lug nuts to retain the disc brake rotor.

4. Remove the bolt and washer attaching the cable support bracket to the caliper.

→It is not necessary to disconnect the parking brake cable from the caliper parking brake lever or disconnect the brake hose unless the caliper is to be completely removed from the vehicle. Freeing the cable support bracket provides enough flexibility in the cable to pivot the caliper up and remove the disc brake pads.

5. Remove the sleeve bolt.

6. Pivot the caliper upward; do not completely remove the caliper.

7. Remove the disc brake pads and clips from the caliper mounting bracket.

To install:

8. Use a suitable tool in the caliper piston slots to turn the piston and thread it into the caliper. After bottoming the piston, lift the inner edge of the boot next to the piston and press out any trapped air. The boot must lay flat.

→Make sure the slots in the end of the caliper piston are positioned as shown in the figure before pivoting the caliper down over the brake pads in the caliper support. Use a suitable tool in the piston slots to turn the piston as necessary.

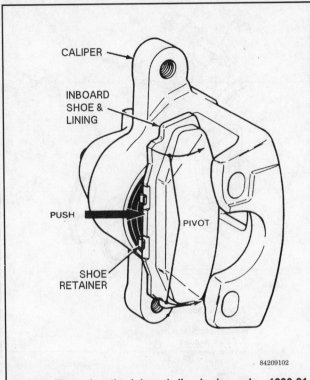

Fig. 96 Removing the inboard disc brake pad — 1990-91 Eldorado and Seville

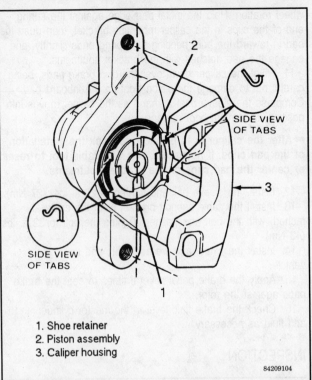

1. Shoe retainer
2. Piston assembly
3. Caliper housing

Fig. 98 Positioning of the caliper piston and disc brake pad retainer — 1990-91 Eldorado and Seville

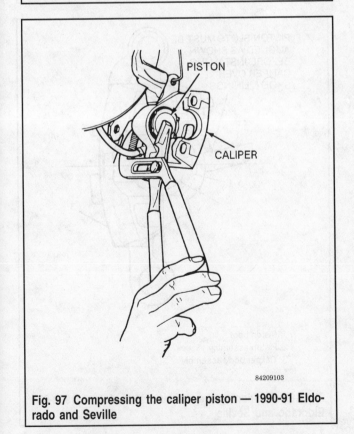

Fig. 97 Compressing the caliper piston — 1990-91 Eldorado and Seville

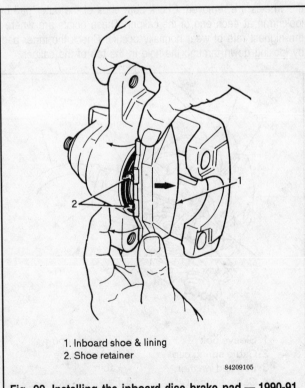

1. Inboard shoe & lining
2. Shoe retainer

Fig. 99 Installing the inboard disc brake pad — 1990-91 Eldorado and Seville

9. Install 2 new pad clips in the caliper mounting bracket. New clips should always be used when replacing the disc brake pads.

10. Install the disc brake pads in the caliper mounting bracket with the wear sensor on the outboard pad positioned downward at the leading edge of the rotor during forward

wheel rotation. Hold the metal pad edge against the spring end of the clips in the caliper mounting bracket, then push the pad in toward the hub, bending the spring ends slightly, and engage the pad notches with the bracket abutments.

11. Pivot the caliper down over the disc brake pads, being careful not to damage the piston boot on the inboard pad. Compress the sleeve boot by hand as the caliper moves into position, to prevent boot damage.

➡**After the caliper is in position, recheck the installation of the pad clips. If necessary, use a suitable tool to reseat or center the pad clips on the bracket abutments.**

12. Install the sleeve bolt and tighten to 20 ft. lbs. (27 Nm).

13. Install the cable support bracket (with the cable attached) with the bolt and washer. Tighten the bolt to 32 ft. lbs. (43 Nm).

14. Install the wheel and tire assembly and lower the vehicle.

15. Apply the brake pedal several times to seat the brake pads against the rotor.

16. Check the brake fluid level in the master cylinder and add fluid as necessary.

INSPECTION

▸ **See Figures 53 and 103**

Inspect the disc brake pads every 6000 miles and any time the wheels are removed. Check both ends of the outer pad by looking in at each end of the caliper. These points are where the highest rate of wear normally occurs. Check the inner pad by looking down through the hole in the top of the caliper.

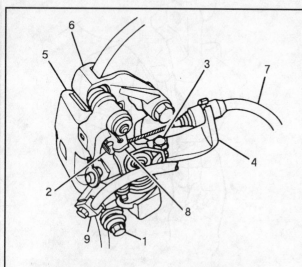

1. Sleeve bolt
2. Cable spring cup
3. Bolt and washer
4. Cable support bracket
5. Caliper body assembly
6. Caliper support
7. Parking brake cable
8. Parking brake lever
9. Brake hose

84209106

Fig. 100 Rear disc brake caliper — 1992-93 Eldorado and Seville

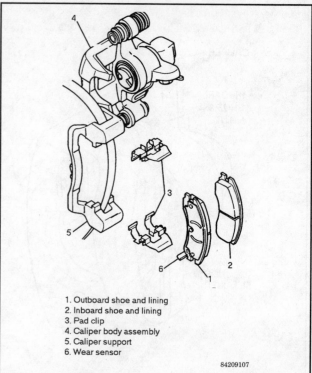

1. Outboard shoe and lining
2. Inboard shoe and lining
3. Pad clip
4. Caliper body assembly
5. Caliper support
6. Wear sensor

84209107

Fig. 101 Rear disc brake pad assembly — 1992-93 Eldorado and Seville

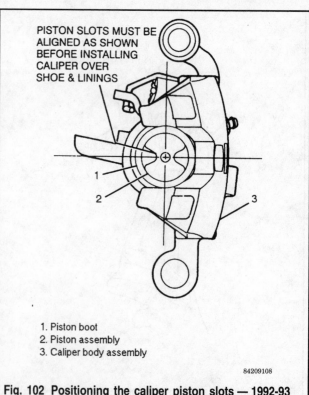

PISTON SLOTS MUST BE ALIGNED AS SHOWN BEFORE INSTALLING CALIPER OVER SHOE & LININGS

1. Piston boot
2. Piston assembly
3. Caliper body assembly

84209108

Fig. 102 Positioning the caliper piston slots — 1992-93 Eldorado and Seville

When any lining thickness is worn to within 1/32 in. (0.76mm) of the backing plate or rivet, the pads must be replaced in axle sets. Some inner pads have a thermal layer against the backing plate, integrally molded with the lining; don't confuse this extra layer with uneven inboard-outboard lining wear.

The outer disc brake pad is also equipped with a wear sensor. When the lining is worn, the sensor contacts the disc brake rotor and produces a warning noise, indicating that disc brake pad replacement is necessary.

Brake Caliper

REMOVAL & INSTALLATION

1990-91 Eldorado and Seville
▶ **See Figures 104, 105, 106 and 107**

1. On 1990 vehicles with anti-lock brakes, depressurize the hydraulic accumulator. Refer to Teves Mk II Anti-Lock Brake System in this Section.

❋❋CAUTION

The hydraulic system contains brake fluid at extremely high pressure. It is mandatory that the system be depressurized before disconnecting any hoses, lines or fittings, or personal injury may result.

2. Use a syringe or similar tool to remove ⅔ of the brake fluid from the master cylinder reservoir.
3. Raise and safely support the vehicle.
4. Remove the wheel and tire assembly, then reinstall 2 lug nuts to retain the disc brake rotor.
5. Loosen the tension on the parking brake cable at the equalizer.
6. Remove the retaining clip from the parking brake lever.
7. Remove the parking brake cable and return spring, then remove the damper from the return spring.
8. Hold the parking brake lever and remove the locknut.
9. Remove the parking brake lever, lever seal and anti-friction washer, and check them for cuts, nicks and excessive wear. Replace any worn or damaged parts.
10. Bottom the piston into the caliper bore to provide clearance between the disc brake pads and rotor.
11. Reinstall the anti-friction washer, lever seal (sealing bead against housing), lever and nut.
12. If the caliper is to be removed from the vehicle, remove the bolt attaching the brake hose to the caliper. Discard the

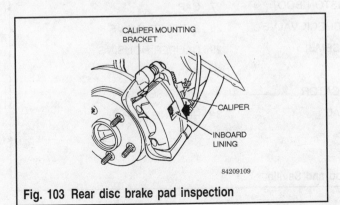

CALIPER MOUNTING BRACKET
CALIPER
INBOARD LINING
84209109
Fig. 103 Rear disc brake pad inspection

gaskets. Plug the openings in the caliper and brake hose to prevent fluid loss.
13. Remove the mounting bolts and remove the caliper from the rotor and mounting bracket. If only the disc brake pads are being replaced, suspend the caliper with wire from the strut.

❋❋WARNING

Do not let the caliper hang from the brake hose. The hose may become damaged, causing possible brake failure.

To install:
14. Inspect the bolt boots and mounting bracket support bushings for cuts, tears or deterioration and replace as necessary. Inspect the mounting bolts for corrosion and replace them and the bushings if any is found; do not try to polish away corrosion.
15. Position the caliper over the rotor in the mounting bracket, making sure the bolt boots are in place.
16. Lubricate the shaft of the mounting bolts with silicone grease. Install the bolts and tighten to 63 ft. lbs. (85 Nm).
17. Position the brake hose on the disc brake caliper. Connect the hose to the caliper using the attaching bolt and 2 new gaskets. Tighten the bolt to 32 ft. lbs. (44 Nm).
18. Disconnect the nut, parking brake lever, lever seal and anti-friction washer. Clean any contamination from the caliper surface in the area of the lever seal and around the actuator screw.
19. Install the anti-friction washer.
20. Lubricate the lever seal and install it with the sealing bead against the caliper housing.
21. Install the parking brake lever on the actuator screw hex with the lever pointing down.
22. Rotate the parking brake lever toward the front of the vehicle and hold in position. Install the nut and tighten to 35 ft. lbs. (48 Nm), then rotate the lever back against the stop on the caliper.
23. Install the damper and return spring.
24. Connect the parking brake cable. Install the retaining clip on the lever to keep the cable from sliding out of the slot in the lever.
25. Bleed the brake system.
26. Install the wheel and tire assembly and lower the vehicle. Check the parking brake adjustment.

1992-93 Eldorado and Seville
▶ **See Figures 100, 108 and 109**

1. Raise and safely support the vehicle.
2. Remove the wheel and tire assembly.
3. If the caliper is to be removed from the vehicle, remove the bolt attaching the brake hose to the caliper. Discard the gaskets. Plug the openings in the caliper and brake hose to prevent fluid loss.
4. If the caliper is to be removed from the vehicle, lift up on the end of the parking brake cable spring to free the end of the cable from the parking brake lever.
5. Remove the bolt and washer attaching the cable support bracket to the caliper.
6. Remove the sleeve bolt, pivot the caliper up to clear the rotor and then slide it inboard off the pin sleeve.

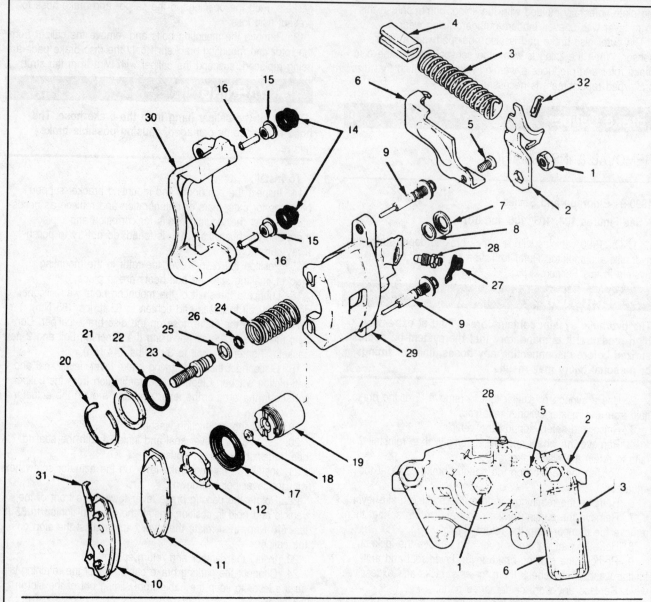

1 NUT	12 SHOE RETAINER	23 ACTUATOR SCREW
2 PARK BRAKE LEVER	14 BOLT BOOT	24 BALANCE SPRING & RETAINER
3 RETURN SPRING	15 SUPPORT BUSHING	25 THRUST WASHER
4 DAMPER	16 BUSHING	26 SHAFT SEAL
5 BOLT	17 CALIPER PISTON BOOT	27 CAP
6 BRACKET	18 TWO-WAY CHECK VALVE	28 BLEEDER VALVE
7 LEVER SEAL	19 PISTON ASSEMBLY	29 CALIPER HOUSING
8 ANTI-FRICTION WASHER	20 RETAINER	30 BRACKET
9 MOUNTING BOLT	21 PISTON LOCATOR	31 WEAR SENSOR
10 OUTBOARD SHOE & LINING	22 PISTON SEAL	32 RETAING CLIP
11 INBOARD SHOE & LINING		

84209110

Fig. 104 Rear disc brake caliper assembly — 1990-91 Eldorado and Seville

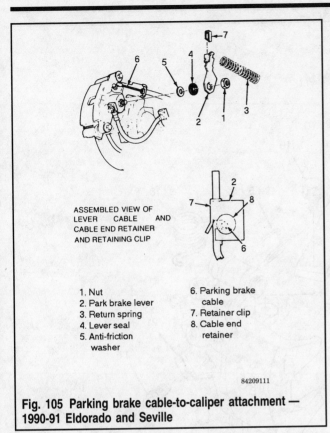

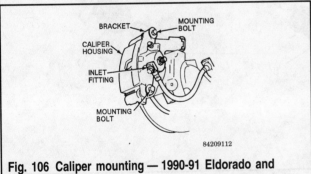

1. Nut
2. Park brake lever
3. Return spring
4. Lever seal
5. Anti-friction washer
6. Parking brake cable
7. Retainer clip
8. Cable end retainer

ASSEMBLED VIEW OF LEVER CABLE AND CABLE END RETAINER AND RETAINING CLIP

84209111

Fig. 105 Parking brake cable-to-caliper attachment — 1990-91 Eldorado and Seville

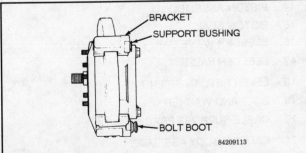

84209112

Fig. 106 Caliper mounting — 1990-91 Eldorado and Seville

84209113

Fig. 107 Bolt boot and support bushing — 1990-91 Eldorado and Seville

7. If the caliper is being removed only for brake pad replacement or to provide access to the mounting bracket, rotor

or other components, suspend the caliper with wire from the strut.

✱✱WARNING

Do not let the caliper hang from the brake hose. The hose may become damaged, causing possible brake failure.

To install:

8. Inspect the pin boot, bolt boot and sleeve boot for cuts, tears or deterioration and replace as necessary.

9. Inspect the bolt sleeve and pin sleeve for corrosion or damage. Pull the boots to gain access to the sleeves for inspection or replacement. Replace corroded or damaged sleeves; do not try to polish away corrosion.

10. If not replaced, remove the pin boot from the caliper and install the small end over the pin sleeve (installed on caliper support) until the boot seats in the pin groove. This prevents cutting the pin boot when sliding the caliper onto the pin sleeve.

11. Hold the caliper in the position it was removed and start it over the end of the pin sleeve. As the caliper approaches the pin boot, work the large end of the pin boot in the caliper groove, then push the caliper fully onto the pin.

12. Pivot the caliper down, being careful not to damage the piston boot on the inboard disc brake pad. Compress the sleeve boot by hand as the caliper moves into position to prevent boot damage.

13. After the caliper is in position, recheck the position of the pad clips. If necessary, use a small prybar to reseat or center the pad clips on the bracket abutments.

14. Install the sleeve bolt and tighten to 20 ft. lbs. (27 Nm).

15. Install the cable support bracket (with cable attached) with the bolt and washer and tighten to 32 ft. lbs. (43 Nm).

16. Lift up on the end of the cable spring clip and work the end of the parking brake cable into the notch in the lever.

17. Position the brake hose on the disc brake caliper. Connect the hose to the caliper using the attaching bolt and 2 new gaskets. Tighten the bolt to 32 ft. lbs. (44 Nm).

18. Bleed the brake system.

19. Install the wheel and tire assembly and lower the vehicle. Check the parking brake adjustment.

OVERHAUL

1990-91 Eldorado and Seville

▶ See Figures 104, 110, 111, 112, 113, 114, 115, 116, 117 and 118

DISASSEMBLY

1. Remove the caliper from the vehicle and place on a clean work bench.

2. Inspect the bolt boots and support bushings on the caliper mounting bracket for cuts, tears or deterioration. If replacement is necessary, remove the mounting bracket. Remove the boots and pry out the support bushings, then use a paper clip with the end bent over to remove the bushings.

3. Remove the disc brake retainer from the end of the caliper piston by rotating the retainer until the inside tabs line up with the notches in the piston.

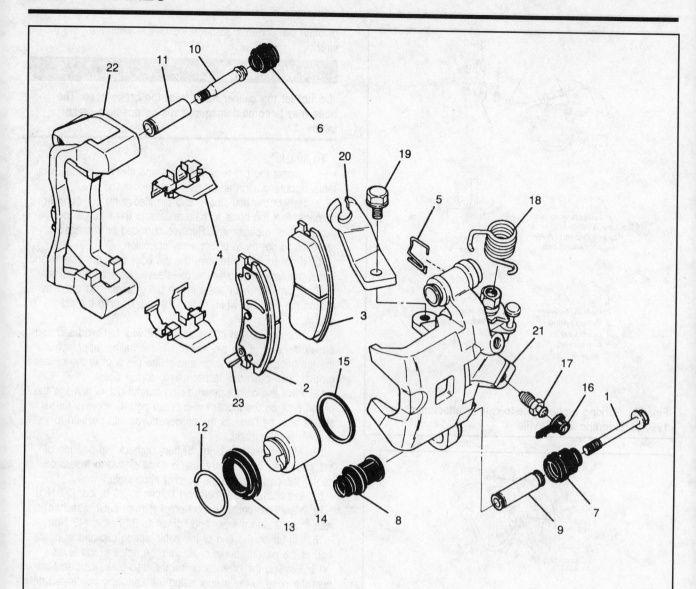

1	SLEEVE BOLT	13	PISTON BOOT	
2	OUTBOARD SHOE & LINING	14	PISTON ASSEMBLY	
3	INBOARD SHOE & LINING	15	PISTON SEAL	
4	PAD CLIP	16	BLEEDER VALVE CAP	
5	CABLE SPRING CLIP	17	BLEEDER VALVE	
6	PIN BOOT	18	LEVER RETURN SPRING	
7	BOLT BOOT	19	BOLT AND WASHER	
8	SLEEVE BOLT	20	CABLE SUPPORT BRACKET	
9	BOLT SLEEVE	21	CALIPER BODY ASSEMBLY	
10	PIN BOLT	22	CALIPER SUPPORT	
11	PIN SLEEVE	23	WEAR SENSOR	
12	BOOT RING			

84209114

Fig. 108 Rear disc brake caliper assembly — 1992-93 Eldorado and Seville

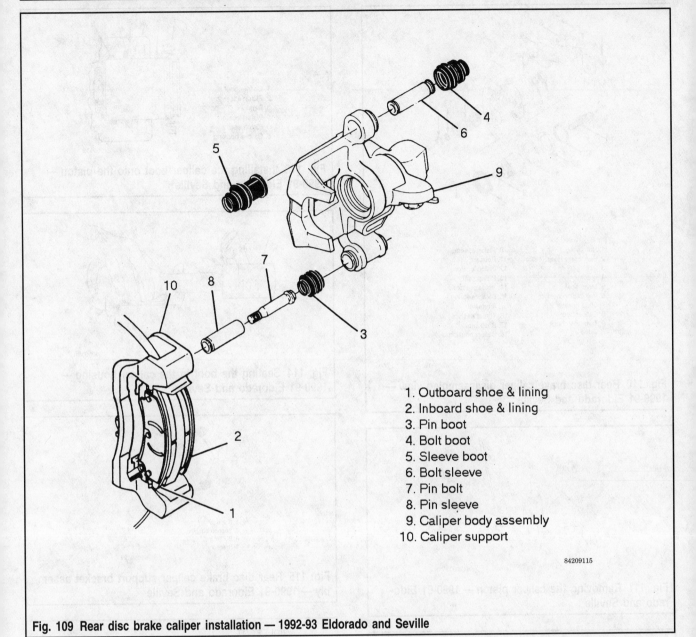

1. Outboard shoe & lining
2. Inboard shoe & lining
3. Pin boot
4. Bolt boot
5. Sleeve boot
6. Bolt sleeve
7. Pin bolt
8. Pin sleeve
9. Caliper body assembly
10. Caliper support

84209115

Fig. 109 Rear disc brake caliper installation — 1992-93 Eldorado and Seville

4. If installed, remove the nut, parking brake lever, lever seal and anti-friction washer.

5. Pad the interior of the caliper with clean shop towels. Use a wrench to rotate the actuator screw in the parking brake apply direction, to work the piston out of the caliper bore.

6. Inspect the piston for scoring, nicks, corrosion and worn or damaged chrome plating. Replace the piston if worn or damaged.

7. Remove the balance spring.

8. Press on the thread end to remove the actuator screw. Remove the shaft seal and thrust washer from the actuator screw.

9. Remove the boot, being careful not to scratch the housing bore.

10. Use retaining ring pliers to remove the retainer ring, then remove the piston locator.

11. Remove the piston seal using a wooden or plastic tool to prevent damage to the caliper bore.

12. Remove the bleeder screw. If damaged, remove the bracket.

13. Inspect the caliper bore and seal groove for scoring, nicks, corrosion and wear. Use crocus cloth to polish out light corrosion. If corrosion in and around the seal groove will not clean up with crocus cloth, replace the caliper housing.

ASSEMBLY

1. Clean all parts in clean, denatured alcohol and dry with unlubricated compressed air. Blow out all passages in the caliper housing and bleeder valve.

2. Install the bleeder valve and tighten to 110 inch lbs. (13 Nm). If removed, install the bracket and tighten the bolt to 31 ft. lbs. (43 Nm).

3. Lubricate a new caliper piston seal with clean brake fluid and install it in the caliper bore groove. Make sure the seal is not twisted.

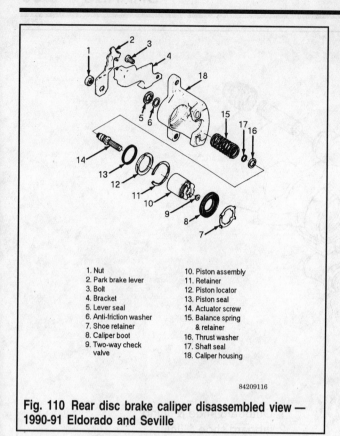

1. Nut
2. Park brake lever
3. Bolt
4. Bracket
5. Lever seal
6. Anti-friction washer
7. Shoe retainer
8. Caliper boot
9. Two-way check valve
10. Piston assembly
11. Retainer
12. Piston locator
13. Piston seal
14. Actuator screw
15. Balance spring & retainer
16. Thrust washer
17. Shaft seal
18. Caliper housing

84209116

Fig. 110 Rear disc brake caliper disassembled view — 1990-91 Eldorado and Seville

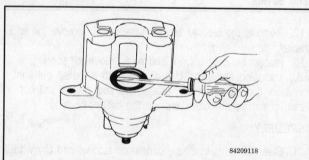

84209117

Fig. 111 Removing the caliper piston — 1990-91 Eldorado and Seville

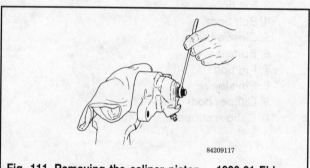

84209118

Fig. 112 Removing the caliper boot — 1990-91 Eldorado and Seville

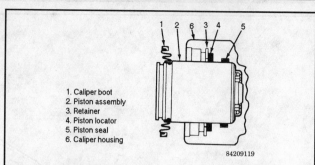

1. Caliper boot
2. Piston assembly
3. Retainer
4. Piston locator
5. Piston seal
6. Caliper housing

84209119

Fig. 113 Installing the caliper boot onto the piston — 1990-91 Eldorado and Seville

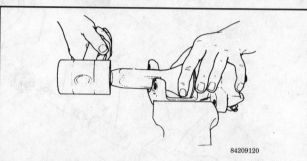

84209120

Fig. 114 Seating the boot in the caliper housing — 1990-91 Eldorado and Seville

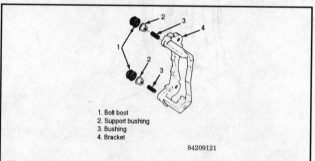

1. Bolt boot
2. Support bushing
3. Bushing
4. Bracket

84209121

Fig. 115 Rear disc brake caliper support bracket assembly — 1990-91 Eldorado and Seville

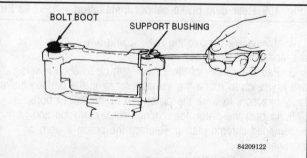

BOLT BOOT   SUPPORT BUSHING

84209122

Fig. 116 Removing the caliper mounting bracket support bushing — 1990-91 Eldorado and Seville

4. Lubricate a new piston locator with clean brake fluid and install it on the piston using tools J-35588-2 and J-35588-1 or equivalents.

5. Install the thrust washer on the actuator screw with the copper side of the washer towards the piston and the grayish side towards the caliper housing.

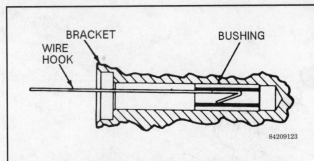

Fig. 117 Removing the caliper mounting bracket bushing — 1990-91 Eldorado and Seville

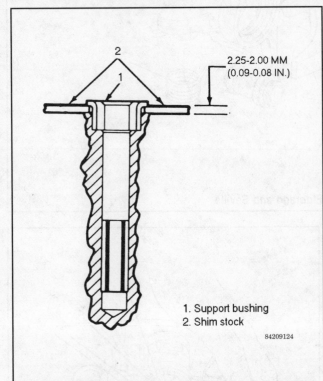

1. Support bushing
2. Shim stock

Fig. 118 Installing the caliper mounting bracket support bushing — 1990-91 Eldorado and Seville

6. Lubricate a new shaft seal with clean brake fluid and install it on the actuator screw.

7. Install the actuator screw along with the thrust washer and shaft seal into the caliper housing.

8. Install the balance spring into the piston recess.

9. Lubricate the piston and caliper bore with clean brake fluid. Push the piston with the balance spring into the caliper bore so that the locator is past the retainer groove in the caliper bore. Turn the actuator screw, as necessary, to allow the piston to move to the bottom of the caliper bore.

10. Use retaining ring pliers to install the retainer.

11. Lubricate the lip of the boot with clean brake fluid and install it onto the piston, with the inside lip of the boot in the piston groove and the boot fold toward the end of the piston that contacts the inboard brake pad. Push the piston to the bottom of the caliper bore.

12. Lubricate the anti-friction washer and install it and the lever seal over the end of the actuator screw. The sealing bead on the lever seal should be against the housing.

13. Position the parking brake lever on the actuator screw. Rotate the lever away from the stop slightly and hold in position while installing the nut. Tighten the nut to 35 ft. lbs. (48 Nm), then rotate the lever back to contact the stop.

14. Seat the boot in the caliper housing counterbore using tool J-35587 or equivalent. After seating the boot, lift the inner edge next to the piston and press out any trapped air. The boot must lay flat.

15. Install the brake pad retainer in the groove in the end of the piston. Align the inside of the retainer tabs with the piston notches. Rotate the retainer so that the tabs enter the piston groove.

16. If the caliper mounting bracket boots and bushings were removed, proceed as follows:

    a. Lubricate new bushings and install them in the mounting bolt holes in the mounting bracket.

    b. Tap new support bushings into the bracket holes using a plastic mallet. Use 0.08-0.09 in. (2-2.25mm) shim stock on either side of the support bushing (or a U-shaped tool made from shim stock) to maintain the proper height of the bushing above the bracket face.

    c. Install the mounting bracket using new bolts and tighten to 83 ft. lbs. (112 Nm).

    d. Snap the boots over the lip of the support bushings.

17. Install the caliper onto the vehicle, as described in this Section.

1992-93 Eldorado and Seville

▶ See Figures 108, 119, 120, 121, 122 and 123

DISASSEMBLY

1. Remove the caliper from the vehicle and place on a clean work bench.

2. Pad the interior of the caliper with shop towels to protect the piston, then use compressed air through the caliper fluid inlet to remove the piston from the caliper.

✴✴CAUTION

Do not place your fingers in front of the piston in an attempt to catch or protect it when applying compressed air. This could result in serious injury.

➡**The piston can also be threaded out of the caliper using a spanner tool in the slots in the end of the piston.**

3. Use a small prybar to pry up one end of the piston boot ring, then work the boot ring out of the caliper groove. Remove the boot ring and piston boot.

4. Use a small wooden or plastic tool (not metal) to remove the piston seal from the caliper bore groove.

5. Remove the bleeder valve cap and bleeder valve.

6. Remove the lever return spring from the caliper only if it is to be replaced. Remove it using a small prybar to disengage the spring from the parking brake lever, then unhook the spring from the stopper pin.

7. Remove the pin boot, bolt boot, bolt sleeve and sleeve boot from the caliper. Remove the pin bolt and pin sleeve from the caliper support.

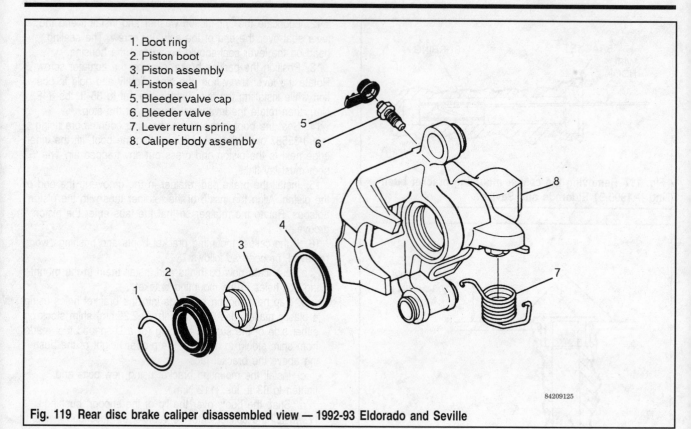

1. Boot ring
2. Piston boot
3. Piston assembly
4. Piston seal
5. Bleeder valve cap
6. Bleeder valve
7. Lever return spring
8. Caliper body assembly

Fig. 119 Rear disc brake caliper disassembled view — 1992-93 Eldorado and Seville

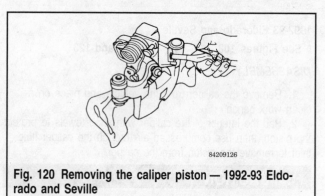

Fig. 120 Removing the caliper piston — 1992-93 Eldorado and Seville

8. Clean all parts in clean denatured alcohol and dry with unlubricated compressed air. Blow out all passages in the caliper and the bleeder valve.

9. Inspect the caliper piston for scoring, nicks, cracks, wear or corrosion and replace if any damage is found.

10. Inspect the caliper piston bore for scoring, nicks, wear or corrosion. Use crocus cloth to polish out light corrosion. If there is any damage to the caliper or corrosion that will not polish out, the caliper must be replaced; do not attempt to hone the caliper bore.

11. Inspect the seal groove in the caliper bore for nicks or burrs and replace the caliper if any are found.

12. Inspect the piston boot for cuts, tears or deterioration and replace if damaged.

13. Inspect the bolt sleeve and pin sleeve for corrosion or damage. Damaged or corroded sleeves must be replaced; do not attempt to polish away corrosion.

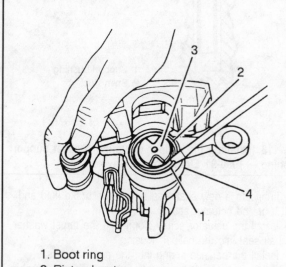

1. Boot ring
2. Piston boot
3. Piston assembly
4. Caliper body assembly

Fig. 121 Removing the boot ring — 1992-93 Eldorado and Seville

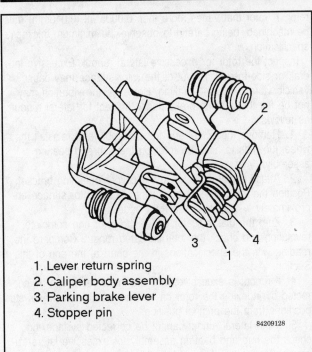

1. Lever return spring
2. Caliper body assembly
3. Parking brake lever
4. Stopper pin

84209128

Fig. 122 Removing/installing the lever return spring — 1992-93 Eldorado and Seville

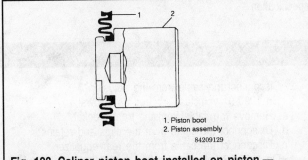

1. Piston boot
2. Piston assembly

84209129

Fig. 123 Caliper piston boot installed on piston — 1992-93 Eldorado and Seville

ASSEMBLY

1. Install the pin bolt to the caliper support and tighten to 20 ft. lbs. (27 Nm). Lubricate the outside diameter of the pin sleeve with silicone grease and install on the caliper support.

2. Lubricate the sleeve boot with silicone grease. Compress the lip on the sleeve boot and push it all the way through the caliper until the lip emerges and seats on the inboard face of the caliper ear.

3. Lubricate the outside diameter of the sleeve. Push the bolt sleeve in through the lip end of the boot until the boot seats in the sleeve groove at the other end.

4. Install the bolt boot onto the caliper.

5. Install the small end of the pin boot over the pin sleeve (installed on caliper support) until the boot seats in the pin groove.

6. If removed, install a new lever return spring. Position the spring with the hook end around the stopper pin, then pry the other end of the spring over the lever.

7. Install the bleeder valve and tighten to 8 ft. lbs. (11 Nm). Install the bleeder valve cap.

8. Lubricate a new piston seal with clean brake fluid and install it in the groove in the caliper bore. Make sure the seal is not twisted.

9. Install the piston boot onto the caliper piston. Lubricate the outside diameter of the piston with clean brake fluid.

10. Start the piston into the caliper bore by hand, then thread it into the bottom of the caliper bore using a spanner tool in the slots in the end of the piston.

11. Make sure the outside edge of the piston boot is smoothly seated in the counterbore of the caliper. Work the boot ring into the groove near the open end of the caliper bore, being careful not to pinch the piston boot between the boot ring and caliper.

12. After installing the boot ring, lift the inner edge of the boot next to the piston and press out any trapped air. The boot must lay flat.

13. Install the caliper onto the vehicle, as described in this Section.

Disc Brake Rotor

REMOVAL & INSTALLATION

▶ **See Figure 124**

1. Raise and safely support the vehicle.
2. Remove the wheel and tire assembly.
3. Remove the brake caliper and suspend it with wire from the strut; do not let the caliper hang from the brake hose. Refer to the procedure in this Section.
4. On 1992-93 vehicles, remove the disc brake pads from the caliper mounting bracket. Refer to the procedure in this Section.
5. Remove the caliper mounting bracket mounting bolts and the mounting bracket.
6. If equipped, remove the retainers from the wheel studs and discard; they do not have to be reinstalled.
7. Remove the disc brake rotor. Inspect the rotor and machine or replace, as necessary.

To install:

8. Install the disc brake rotor over the wheel studs and hub assembly.
9. Install the caliper mounting bracket using new mounting bolts. Tighten the bolts to 83 ft. lbs. (112 Nm).
10. On 1992-93 vehicles, install the disc brake pads in the caliper mounting bracket. Refer to the procedure in this Section.
11. Install the brake caliper; refer to the procedure in this Section.
12. Install the wheel and tire assembly and lower the vehicle.

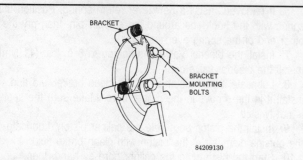

**Fig. 124 Rear disc brake caliper mounting bracket —
1990-91 Eldorado and Seville**

INSPECTION

Inspect the rotor surface finish for discoloration due to overheating, excessive glazing or scoring. If the rotor is discolored or glazed, it must be machined. Light scoring of the rotor surface not exceeding a depth of 0.050 in. (1.2mm), which may result from normal use, is not detrimental to brake operation and refinishing is usually not necessary. Heavier scoring must be removed by refinishing, being careful to observe the minimum thickness specification.

Inspect the rotor for thickness variation. Excessive thickness variation can cause brake pedal pulsation or roughness during brake applications. Check thickness variation by measuring the rotor thickness using a micrometer at a minimum of 4 points around the circumference of the rotor. All measurements should be made at the same distance from the edge of the rotor. A rotor that varies more than 0.0005 in. (0.013mm) must be machined, being careful to observe the minimum thickness specification.

Inspect the rotor for excessive lateral runout. Excessive lateral, or side-to-side, runout of the rotor surface may cause vehicle vibration during braking. However, the vibration may not be felt through the brake pedal. Inspect for lateral runout as follows:

1. Remove the wheel and tire assembly and reinstall the wheel lug nuts to hold the rotor on the hub and bearing assembly.
2. Attach a dial indicator to the caliper mounting bracket. Position the indicator foot so it contacts the rotor surface approximately ½-1 in. from the rotor edge.
3. Zero the dial indicator. Move the rotor one complete revolution and check the total indicated runout. Compare the reading with the specifications in the chart at the end of this Section.
4. If runout is excessive, in some instances it can be corrected by indexing the rotor on the hub one or two wheel stud positions from the original position.
5. If the lateral runout cannot be corrected by indexing, check the hub and bearing assembly for excessive lateral runout or looseness. If the hub and bearing lateral runout exceeds 0.004 in. (0.10mm) on 1990-91 Eldorado and Seville, or 0.002 in. (0.06mm) on 1992-93 Eldorado and Seville, replace the hub and bearing assembly and recheck rotor lateral runout.
6. If the lateral runout still exceeds specification, machine the rotor, being careful to observe the minimum thickness specification.

PARKING BRAKE

Cables

REMOVAL & INSTALLATION

Deville, Fleetwood and Sixty Special
▶ **See Figure 125**

FRONT CABLE

1. Raise and safely support the vehicle.
2. Loosen the adjuster.
3. Remove the cable from the adjuster.
4. Remove the cable retaining nut from the underbody of the vehicle.
5. Lower the vehicle and remove the cable from the lever assembly.

To install:

6. Attach the cable to the lever assembly.
7. Raise and safely support the vehicle.
8. Install the cable retaining nut and tighten to 22 ft. lbs. (30 Nm).
9. Attach the cable to the adjuster.
10. Adjust the parking brake cable and lower the vehicle.

INTERMEDIATE CABLE

1. Raise and safely support the vehicle.

2. Disconnect the cable from the adjuster.
3. On 1990-91 vehicles, proceed as follows:
   a. Remove the cable from the front bracket.
   b. Disconnect the cable from the clips and retainers.
   c. Disconnect the cable from the rear equalizer.
4. On 1992-93 vehicles, proceed as follows:
   a. Remove the clip from the brake line retainer and cable.
   b. Disconnect the cable from the rear equalizer.
   c. Remove the cable from the bracket and brake line retainers.

To install:

5. On 1990-91 vehicles, proceed as follows:
   a. Connect the cable to the rear equalizer.
   b. Attach the cable to the clips and retainers.
   c. Install the cable through the front bracket.
   d. Connect the cable to the adjuster.
   e. Adjust the parking brake cable and lower the vehicle.
6. On 1992-93 vehicles, proceed as follows:
   a. Snap the cable into the bracket.
   b. Install the cable through the top support hole in the vehicle underbody.
   c. Connect the cable to the rear equalizer.
   d. Install the clip around the cable and then to the brake line retainer. Tighten the bolt to 17 inch lbs. (3 Nm).
   e. Connect the cable to the adjuster.
   f. Adjust the parking brake cable.

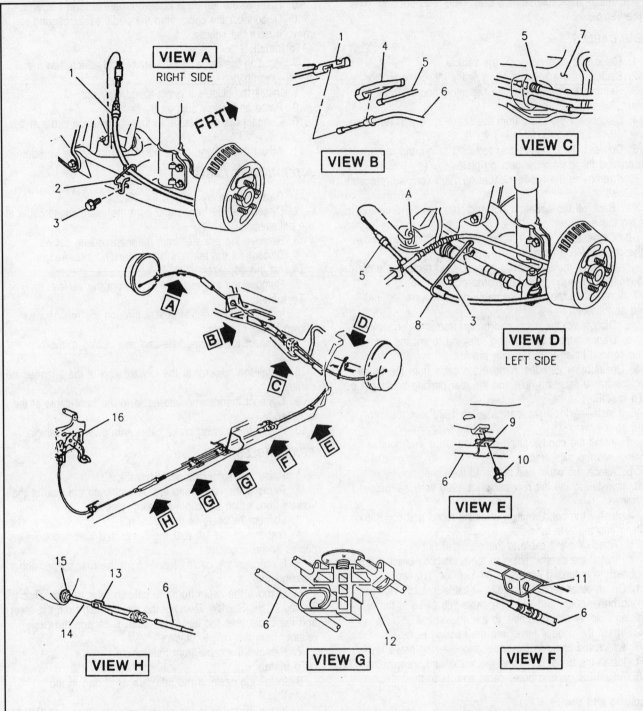

VIEW A
RIGHT SIDE

VIEW B

VIEW C

VIEW D
LEFT SIDE

VIEW E

VIEW H

VIEW G

VIEW F

A	INSTALL CABLE IN TOP HOLE ONLY	5	CABLE ASM, LEFT REAR	11	BRACKET
		6	CABLE ASM, INTERMEDIATE	12	RETAINER, BRAKE PIPE
1	CABLE ASM, RIGHT REAR	7	REAR SUSPENSION SUPPORT	13	ADJUSTER
2	GUIDE, PARK BRAKE REAR CABLE (RH)	8	GUIDE, PARK BRAKE REAR CABLE (LH)	14	CABLE ASM, FRONT
3	8 N•m (71 LB. IN.)	9	CLIP	15	NUT
4	EQUALIZER	10	6 N•m (53 LB. IN.)	16	PARK BRAKE LEVER ASM

84209131

Fig. 125 Parking brake cables — 1992-93 Deville, Fleetwood and Sixty Special; 1990-91 similar

g. Install the cable into the brake line retainers and lower the vehicle.

REAR CABLES

1. Raise and safely support the vehicle.
2. Back off the adjuster nut to release the cable tension.
3. Remove the wheel and tire assembly and the brake drum.
4. Disconnect the cable from the brake shoe parking brake lever.
5. Depress the conduit fitting retaining tangs and remove the conduit fitting from the backing plate.
6. If removing the left rear cable on 1990 vehicles, proceed as follows:

a. Back off the equalizer nut and disconnect the cable from the equalizer.

b. Depress the conduit fitting retaining tangs and remove the conduit fitting from the axle bracket.

c. Remove the 2 attaching screws, then remove the conduit fitting from the underbody bracket.

7. If removing the right rear cable on 1990 vehicles, proceed as follows:

a. Disconnect the cable end button from the connector.

b. Depress the conduit fitting retaining tangs and remove the conduit fitting from the axle bracket.

8. On all other vehicles, remove the cable from the equalizer, the frame retaining hole and the rear parking brake guide.

To install:

9. If installing the right rear cable on 1990 vehicles, proceed as follows:

a. Install the conduit fitting retaining tangs and conduit fitting into the axle bracket.

b. Attach the cable end button to the connector.

10. If installing the left rear cable on 1990 vehicles, proceed as follows:

a. Install the conduit fitting retaining tangs and conduit fitting into the axle bracket.

b. Attach the left cable to the equalizer nut.

c. Install the conduit fitting to the underbody bracket and tighten the mounting screws to 84 inch lbs. (10 Nm).

11. On all other vehicles, install the cable through the rear parking brake guide and snap the cable into place in the retaining hole. Attach the cable to the equalizer.

12. Install the conduit fitting into the backing plate.
13. Attach the cable to the brake shoe parking brake lever.
14. Install the brake drum and the wheel and tire assembly.
15. Adjust the parking brake cable and lower the vehicle.

Eldorado and Seville
▶ **See Figure 126**

FRONT CABLE

1. Raise and safely support the vehicle.
2. Disconnect the front cable from the intermediate cable at the adjuster.
3. Disengage the cable housing retainer/nut at the point where the cable passes through the underbody.
4. Lower the vehicle.

5. Remove the left dash close-out panel/sound insulator.
6. Disconnect the cable from the pedal assembly and remove it from the vehicle.

To install:

7. Position the cable in the vehicle and attach it to the pedal assembly.
8. Install the close-out panel/sound insulator.
9. Raise and safely support the vehicle.
10. Connect the front cable to the intermediate cable at the adjuster.
11. Adjust the parking brake cable and lower the vehicle.

INTERMEDIATE CABLE

1. Raise and safely support the vehicle.
2. Disconnect the front cable from the intermediate cable at the adjuster.
3. Remove the adjuster from the intermediate cable.
4. Disconnect the left rear, right rear and intermediate cables at the equalizer.
5. Remove the intermediate cable from the vehicle.

To install:

6. Install the intermediate cable through the retainers as shown in the illustration.
7. Connect the intermediate and rear cables at the equalizer.
8. Install the adjuster at the forward end of the intermediate cable.
9. Connect the intermediate cable to the front cable at the adjuster.
10. Adjust the parking brake cable and lower the vehicle.

REAR CABLES

1. Raise and safely support the vehicle.
2. Remove the wheel and tire assembly on the side of the vehicle from which the cable is being removed.
3. Loosen the cable at the adjuster.
4. Disconnect the left rear, right rear and intermediate cables at the equalizer.
5. Disengage the cable retainer from the rear suspension crossmember.
6. Remove the cable from the caliper; refer to Rear Disc Brakes in this Section. Remove the retainer clip from the lever and the cable from the lever slot, then disengage the cable retainer from the caliper bracket.
7. Remove the cable from the vehicle.

To install:

8. Install the cable in the retainers as shown in the illustration.
9. Install the cable in the caliper; refer to Rear Disc Brakes in this Section. Install the cable retainer in the caliper bracket. Position the cable in the lever slot and install the retainer clip on the lever.
10. Connect the intermediate and rear cables at the equalizer.
11. Adjust the parking brake cable.
12. Install the wheel and tire assembly and lower the vehicle.

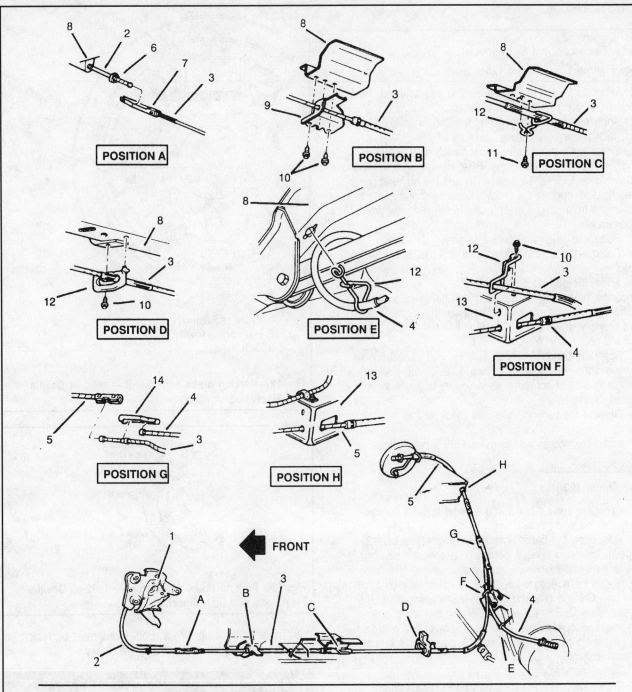

1	PEDAL ASSEMBLY	8	PART OF UNDERBODY
2	FRONT CABLE	9	BRACKET
3	INTERMEDIATE CABLE	10	SCREWS (8 N•m/71 IN. LBS.)
4	LEFT REAR CABLE	11	SCREW (18 N•m/13 FT. LBS.)
5	RIGHT REAR CABLE	12	CABLE GUIDE
6	ADJUSTER NUT	13	REAR SUSPENSION CROSSMEMBER
7	ADJUSTER	14	EQUALIZER

84209132

Fig. 126 Parking brake cables — Eldorado and Seville

ADJUSTMENT

Deville, Fleetwood and Sixty Special

▶ See Figures 125, 127 and 128

1. Make sure the brake shoes are properly adjusted. Refer to Brake Operating System in this Section.
2. Apply and release the parking brake 6 times to 10 clicks, then release the parking brake pedal.
3. Check the parking brake pedal for full release by turning the ignition **ON** and checking the 'BRAKE' warning light. The light should be OFF. If the light is ON and the brake appears to be released, operate the pedal release lever and pull downward on the front parking brake cable to remove slack from the assembly.
4. Raise and safely support the vehicle.
5. Remove the access hole plugs in the rear brake backing plates.
6. Adjust the parking brake cable until a ⅛ in. drill bit can be inserted through the access hole into the space between the shoe web and the parking brake lever. The cable is adjusted properly when a ⅛ in. bit will fit into the space, but a ¼ in. bit will not.
7. Apply the parking brake to 4 clicks. The wheels should not move when you try to rotate them in a forward direction; they should drag or not move when you try to rotate them in a rearward direction.
8. Release the parking brake and check for free wheel rotation.
9. Install the access hole plugs and lower the vehicle.

Eldorado and Seville

▶ See Figure 126

1. Apply the service brake with a pedal force of approximately 150 lbs. and release.
2. Fully apply the parking brake using approximately 125 lbs. pedal force and release. Apply and release the parking brake in the same manner, 2 more times.
3. Check the parking brake pedal for full release by turning the ignition **ON** and checking the 'BRAKE' warning light. The light should be OFF. If the light is ON and the brake appears to be released, operate the pedal release lever and pull downward on the front parking brake cable to remove slack from the pedal assembly.
4. Raise and safely support the vehicle.
5. Check the parking brake levers on the rear calipers. The levers should be against the stops on the caliper. If the levers are not against the stops, check for binding in the rear cables and/or loosen the cables at the adjuster until both levers are against their stops.
6. Tighten the parking brake cable at the adjuster until either the left or right lever begins to move off of stop. Then loosen the adjuster until the lever is again resting on the stop. Both levers should now be resting on the stops.
7. Operate the parking brake several times to check the adjustment. A firm pedal feel should be obtained by pumping the pedal less than 3½ full strokes on 1990-91 vehicles or depressing the pedal less than one full stroke on 1992-93 vehicles.

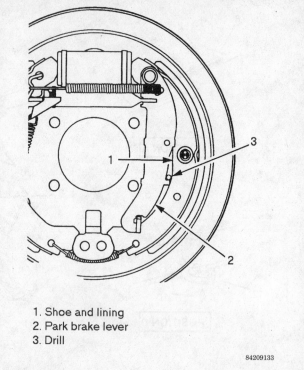

1. Shoe and lining
2. Park brake lever
3. Drill

84209133

Fig. 127 Parking brake adjustment — 1990-91 Deville and Fleetwood

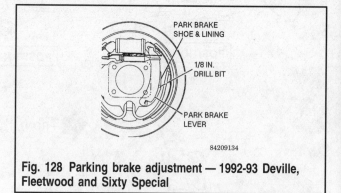

PARK BRAKE
SHOE & LINING

1/8 IN.
DRILL BIT

PARK BRAKE
LEVER

84209134

Fig. 128 Parking brake adjustment — 1992-93 Deville, Fleetwood and Sixty Special

8. Inspect the caliper levers. Both levers must be resting on the stops after adjustment of the parking brake.

Brake Pedal

REMOVAL & INSTALLATION

Deville, Fleetwood and Sixty Special

1990

▶ See Figure 129

1. Disconnect the release handle cable at the pedal assembly.
2. Remove the retaining clip and disconnect the front parking brake cable at the pedal assembly.
3. Remove the mounting screws and the pedal assembly.

To install:

4. Position the pedal assembly and install the mounting screws. Tighten to 15 ft. lbs. (20 Nm).

5. Connect the front parking brake cable and install the retaining clip.

6. Connect the release handle cable.

7. Adjust the parking brake cable.

1991-93

※※CAUTION

When performing service around Supplemental Inflatable Restraint (SIR) system components or wiring, the SIR system must be disabled. Failure to do so could result in possible air bag deployment, personal injury or unneeded SIR system repairs.

1. Disable the SIR system as follows:
   a. Disconnect the negative battery cable.
   b. Turn the ignition switch **OFF**.
   c. Remove SIR fuse No. 18 from the fuse panel.

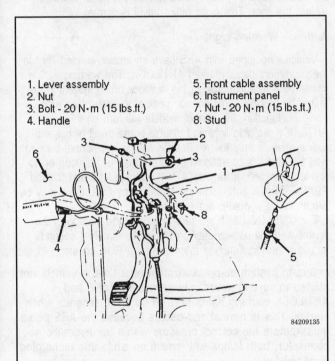

1. Lever assembly
2. Nut
3. Bolt - 20 N·m (15 lbs.ft.)
4. Handle
5. Front cable assembly
6. Instrument panel
7. Nut - 20 N·m (15 lbs.ft.)
8. Stud

84209135

Fig. 129 Parking brake pedal (lever) assembly — 1990 Deville and Fleetwood

d. Remove the left lower sound insulator.

e. Remove the Connector Position Assurance (CPA) and disconnect the yellow 2-way connector at the base of the steering column.

2. Disconnect the vacuum hose from the actuator.

3. Remove the retaining clip and disconnect the front parking brake cable at the pedal assembly.

4. Disconnect the electrical connector from the parking brake switch.

5. Remove the parking brake pedal assembly mounting nuts and the pedal assembly.

To install:

6. Position the pedal assembly onto the dash panel studs and install the mounting nuts. Tighten the nuts to 13 ft. lbs. (18 Nm).

➡**The parking brake cable and pedal assembly should be routed left of the transmission shift cable. Do not place the cable or pedal assembly over the shift cable.**

7. Connect the electrical connector to the parking brake switch.

8. Connect the front parking brake cable and install the retaining clip.

9. Connect the vacuum hose to the actuator.

10. Enable the SIR system as follows:
   a. Connect the yellow 2-way connector at the base of the steering column and install the CPA.
   b. Install the left lower sound insulator.
   c. Install the SIR fuse.
   d. Connect the negative battery cable.
   e. Turn the ignition switch to **RUN**. Verify that the 'INFLATABLE RESTRAINT' indicator light flashes 7-9 times and then remains OFF. If the light does not function as specified, there is a fault in the SIR system.

Eldorado and Seville

▶ **See Figure 130**

1. Loosen the cable at the adjuster.

2. Disconnect the front parking brake cable at the pedal assembly.

3. Disconnect the vacuum hose from the vacuum diaphragm.

4. Remove the 3 mounting nuts and the pedal assembly.

To install:

5. Position the pedal assembly and install the mounting nuts. Tighten to 13 ft. lbs. (18 Nm).

6. Connect the front parking brake cable at the pedal assembly.

7. Connect the vacuum hose to the vacuum diaphragm.

8. Adjust the parking brake cable.

TEVES MK II ANTI-LOCK BRAKE SYSTEM

Description

The Teves Mk II Anti-lock Brake System (ABS) is used on all 1990 vehicles. The system uses a combination of wheel speed sensors and a microprocessor to determine impending wheel lock-up and adjust the brake pressure to maintain the best braking. This system helps the driver maintain control of the vehicle under heavy braking conditions.

SYSTEM OPERATION

Under normal driving conditions, the anti-lock brake system functions the same as a standard brake system. The primary difference is that the power assist for normal braking is provided by the booster portion of the hydraulic unit through the use of pressurized brake fluid.

If a wheel locking tendency is noted during a brake application, the ABS will modulate hydraulic pressure in the individual wheel circuits to prevent any wheel from locking. A separate hydraulic line and 2 specific solenoid valves are provided for each front wheel; both rear wheels share a set of solenoid valves and a single line from the master cylinder to the proportioner valve/tee assembly. The proportioner valve/tee assembly splits the right and left rear brake circuits.

The ABS can increase, decrease or hold pressure in each hydraulic circuit depending on signals from the wheel speed sensors and the electronic brake control module.

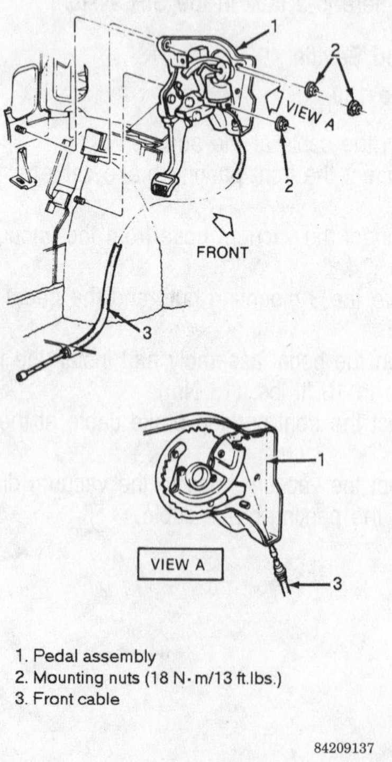

1. Pedal assembly
2. Mounting nuts (18 N·m/13 ft.lbs.)
3. Front cable

84209137

Fig. 130 Parking brake pedal assembly — Eldorado and Seville

During an ABS stop, a slight bump or kick-back will be felt in the brake pedal. This bump will be followed by a series of short pulsations that occur in rapid succession. The brake pedal pulsations will continue until there is no longer a need for the anti-lock function or until the vehicle is stopped. A slight ticking or popping noise may be heard during brake applications with anti-lock. This noise is normal and indicates that the anti-lock system is being used.

During antilock stops on dry pavement, the tires may make intermittent chirping noises as they approach lock-up. These noises are considered normal as long as the wheel does not truly lock or skid. When the anti-lock system is being used, the brake pedal may rise even as the brakes are being applied. This is normal. Maintaining a constant force on the pedal will provide the shortest stopping distance.

Vehicles equipped with ABS may be stopped by applying normal force to the brake pedal. Although there is no need to push the brake pedal beyond the point where it stops or holds the vehicle, applying more force causes the pedal to travel toward the floor. This extra brake travel is normal.

Anti-lock Warning Light

Vehicles equipped with ABS have an amber warning light in the instrument panel marked ANTILOCK. The warning light will illuminate if a malfunction in the anti-lock brake system is detected by the electronic control module. In case of an electronic malfunction, the control module will turn on the ANTILOCK warning light and disable some or all of the anti-lock system. If only the ANTILOCK light is on, normal braking with full assist is operational but there may be reduced or no anti-lock function. If the ANTILOCK warning light and the red BRAKE warning light come on at the same time, there may be a fault in the hydraulic brake system.

The ANTILOCK light will turn on during the starting of the engine and will usually stay on for approximately 4 seconds after the ignition switch is returned to the RUN position.

➡ **Due to system de-pressurization over time, a vehicle not started in several hours may have the BRAKE and ANTILOCK warning lights stay on up to 40 seconds when started. This is normal and occurs because the ABS pump must restore the correct pressure within the hydraulic accumulator; both lamps will remain on while this recharging is completed.**

Brake System Warning Light

The Anti-lock Brake System uses a 2 circuit design so that some braking capacity is still available if hydraulic pressure is lost in 1 circuit. A BRAKE warning light is located on the instrument cluster and is designed to alert the driver of conditions that could result in reduced braking ability.

The BRAKE warning light should turn on briefly during engine starting and should remain on whenever the parking brake is not fully released. Additionally, the BRAKE warning lamp will illuminate if a sensor detects low brake fluid, if the pressure switch detects low accumulator pressure or if certain on-board computers run a self-check of the dashboard and instruments.

If the BRAKE warning light stays on longer than 30 seconds after starting the engine, or comes on and stays on while driving, there may be a malfunction in the brake hydraulic system.

SYSTEM COMPONENTS

▶ **See Figures 131 and 132**

Electronic Brake Control Module (EBCM)

The EBCM monitors the speed of each wheel and the electrical status of the hydraulic unit. The EBCM's primary functions are to detect wheel lockup, control the brake system while in anti-lock mode and monitor the system for proper electrical operation. When one or more wheels approach lockup during a stop, the EBCM will command appropriate valve positions to modulate brake fluid pressure and provide optimum braking. It will continue to command pressure changes in the system until a locking tendency is no longer noted.

The EBCM is a separate computer used exclusively for control of the anti-lock brake system. The unit also controls the retention and display of the ABS trouble codes when in the diagnostic mode. As the EBCM monitors the system or performs a self-check, it can react to a fault by disabling all or part of the ABS system and illuminating the amber ANTILOCK warning light.

On Deville and Fleetwood, the EBCM is located under the lower left dash, between the steering column and the parking brake pedal. Eldorado and Seville have the unit mounted in the trunk on the left wheelhouse.

Wheel Speed Sensors

A wheel speed sensor at each wheel transmits speed information to the EBCM by generating a small AC voltage relative to the wheel speed. The voltage is generated by magnetic induction caused by passing a toothed sensor ring past a stationary sensor. The signals are transmitted through a pair of wires which are shielded against interference. The EBCM then calculates wheel speed for each wheel based on the frequency of the AC voltage received from the sensor.

Hydraulic Components

The Teves Mk II anti-lock brake system uses an integrated hydraulic unit mounted on the firewall or cowl. This unit functions as a brake master cylinder and brake booster. Additionally, the hydraulic unit provides brake fluid pressure modulation for each of the individual wheel circuits as required during braking. The hydraulic unit consists of several individual components.

MASTER CYLINDER/BOOSTER ASSEMBLY

This portion of the hydraulic unit contains the valves and pistons necessary to develop hydraulic pressure within the brake lines. Pressure in the booster servo circuit is controlled by a spool valve which opens in response to the amount of force applied to the brake pedal. The rate at which the vehicle decelerates depends on the type of road surface and the pressure applied to the brake pedal.

The master cylinder portion uses a 3-circuit configuration during normal braking; individual circuits are provided for each front wheel while a shared circuit is used for the rear wheels. The 3 circuits are isolated so that a leak or malfunction in one will allow continued braking on the others.

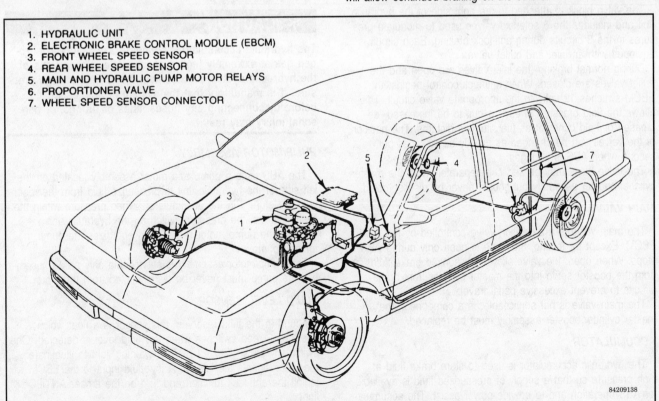

1. HYDRAULIC UNIT
2. ELECTRONIC BRAKE CONTROL MODULE (EBCM)
3. FRONT WHEEL SPEED SENSOR
4. REAR WHEEL SPEED SENSOR
5. MAIN AND HYDRAULIC PUMP MOTOR RELAYS
6. PROPORTIONER VALVE
7. WHEEL SPEED SENSOR CONNECTOR

84209138

Fig. 131 Teves Mk II anti-lock brake system component locations — 1990 Deville and Fleetwood

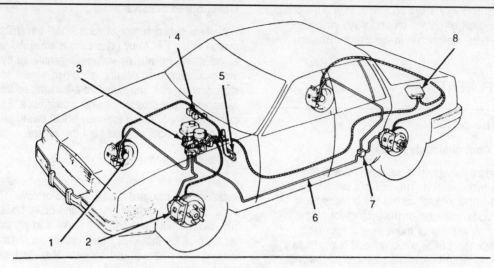

1. WHEEL SPEED SENSOR AND TOOTHED SENSOR RING (ONE AT EACH WHEEL)
2. CALIPER (ONE AT EACH WHEEL)
3. HYDRAULIC UNIT
4. RELAY BRACKET
5. PEDAL
6. REAR BRAKE PIPE
7. PROPORTIONER/TEE
8. ELECTRONIC BRAKE CONTROL MODULE (EBCM)

84209139

Fig. 132 Teves Mk II anti-lock brake system component locations — 1990 Eldorado and Seville

The master cylinder/booster is a non-serviceable component and should never be disassembled.

VALVE BLOCK

The valve block is attached to the right side of the hydraulic unit and includes the 6 solenoid valves used to modulate pressures in the 3 circuits during anti-lock braking. Each circuit is equipped with an inlet and outlet valve.

During normal braking, the inlet valves are open and the outlet valves are closed. When anti-lock control begins, the EBCM switches 12 volts to the appropriate valve circuit. This allows the fluid pressure in each circuit to be increased, decreased or held constant as the situation dictates. The position of the valves can be changed as quickly as 15 times per second when ABS is engaged.

The valve block may be serviced separately from the master cylinder/booster assembly but should never be disassembled.

MAIN VALVE

The main valve is a 2-position valve controlled by the EBCM. Except for testing, the valve is open only during ABS stops. When open, the valve allows pressurized brake fluid from the booster servo into the master cylinder front brake circuits to prevent excessive pedal travel.

The main valve is not serviceable as a component; the master cylinder/booster assembly must be replaced.

ACCUMULATOR

The hydraulic accumulator is used to store brake fluid at high pressure so that a supply of pressurized fluid is available for ABS operation and to provide power assist. The accumulator uses a rubber diaphragm to separate high-pressure nitrogen gas from the brake fluid.

Nitrogen in the accumulator is pre-charged to approximately 870 psi. During normal operation, the pump and motor assembly charges the accumulator with brake fluid to an operation range of 2000-2600 psi.

✳✳CAUTION

The hydraulic accumulator contains brake fluid and nitrogen gas at extremely high pressures. Certain portions of the hydraulic system also contain brake fluid at high pressure. It is mandatory that the system be depressurized before disconnecting any hoses, lines or fittings, or personal injury may result.

PUMP/MOTOR ASSEMBLY

The ABS uses a pump and motor assembly located on the left side of the hydraulic unit to pressurize fluid from the reservoir and store it in the accumulator. When pressure within the system drops, the pressure switch on the hydraulic unit grounds the pump motor relay which energizes the pump motor and pump.

The pump/motor assembly is serviceable only as an assembly; the pump must never be disconnected from the motor.

FLUID LEVEL SENSOR

Found in the fluid reservoir, this sensor is a float which operates 2 reed switches when low fluid level is detected. One switch will cause the red BRAKE warning light to illuminate; the other signals the EBCM. A low fluid input to the EBCM will inhibit the anti-lock function and turn on the amber ANTILOCK light.

PRESSURE SWITCH

The pressure switch is mounted on the pump/motor assembly and serves 2 major functions, controlling the pump/motor and providing low pressure warning to the EBCM.

The switch will allow the pump/motor to run when system pressure drops below approximately 2030 psi and will shut the pump/motor off when pressure in the accumulator is approximately 2610 psi. Should pressure within the accumulator drop below approximately 1500 psi, internal switches will both signal the EBCM and turn on the red BRAKE warning lamp. If the system re-pressurizes and reaches at least 1900 psi, the switches will reset.

PROPORTIONER VALVE

Included in the rear brake circuit is a proportioner valve/tee assembly which limits brake pressure build-up at the rear brake calipers. Since the front brakes do the majority of the braking, less pressure is required for the rear brakes under certain conditions. The proportioner valve improves front-to-rear brake balance during normal braking.

Self-Diagnostic System

The system is equipped with self-diagnostic capability, which can be used to assist in isolation of ABS faults. There are 42 trouble codes which can be displayed by the EBCM through flashing of the amber ANTILOCK warning light. In order to access any trouble code which may be present, it is necessary to enter the ABS diagnostic mode and read the trouble codes using the following procedure.

READING ABS TROUBLE CODES

▶ See Figures 133, 134 and 135

Only certain ABS malfunctions will cause the EBCM to store diagnostic trouble codes. Failures causing a code will generally involve wheel speed sensors, main valve or the inlet and outlet valves. Conditions affecting the pump/motor assembly, the accumulator, pressure switch or fluid level sensor usually do not cause a code to set.

The EBCM will store trouble codes in a non-volatile memory. These codes remain in memory until erased through use of the correct procedure. The codes are NOT erased by disconnecting the EBCM, disconnecting the battery cable or turning off the ignition. Always be sure to clear the codes from the memory after repairs are made. To read stored ABS trouble codes:

1. Turn ignition switch to **ON**. Allow the pump to charge the accumulator; if fully discharged, dash warning lights may stay on up to 30 seconds. If ANTI-LOCK warning light does not go off within 30 seconds, note it and go to Step 2.

2. Turn ignition switch to **OFF**.

3. Remove the cover from the ALDL connector. Enter the diagnostic mode by using a jumper wire to connect pins H and A or to connect pin H to body ground. The ALDL is located on the driver's side of the vehicle under the dash.

4. Turn the ignition switch to **RUN** and count the light flashes for the first digit of the first code. The ANTI-LOCK light should illuminate for 4 seconds before beginning to flash. If,

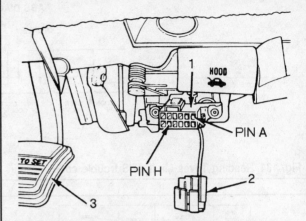

PLACE JUMBER BETWEEN PINS A AND H (OR BETWEEN H AND GROUND) TO ENTER ABS DIAGNOSTIC MODE

1. ALDL connector
2. ALDL connector cover
3. Parking brake pedal

84209140

Fig. 133 ALDL connector location — 1990 Eldorado and Seville, 1990 Deville and Fleetwood similar

after 4 seconds, the light turns off and stays off, no codes are stored.

5. The light will pause for 3 seconds between the first and second digits of the first code and then continue flashing. When counting flashes, count only the ON pulses.

6. When the EBCM is finished transmitting the second digit of the first code, the ANTI-LOCK light will remain on. This last, constant ON should not be counted as a flash. Record the 2-digit code.

7. Without turning the ignition switch **OFF**, disconnect the jumper from pin H and reconnect it. If an additional code is present, it will be displayed in similar fashion to the first. Record the second code.

8. Repeat the disconnection and reconnection of pin H without changing the ignition switch until no more codes are displayed. The system is capable of storing and displaying 7 codes; the ANTI-LOCK warning light will stay on continuously when all codes have been displayed.

9. After recording all codes, remove the jumper from the ALDL and replace the cover.

➡**The ABS trouble codes are not specifically designated current or history codes. If the ANTI-LOCK light is on before entering the ABS diagnostic mode, at least 1 of the stored codes is current. It is impossible to tell which code is current. If the ANTI-LOCK light is off before entering the diagnostic mode, none of the codes are current.**

CLEARING ABS TROUBLE CODES

Stored ABS trouble codes should not be cleared until all repairs are completed. The control module will not allow any

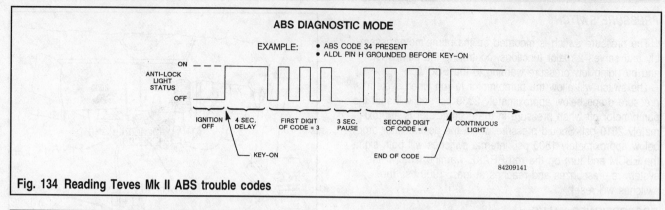

Fig. 134 Reading Teves Mk II ABS trouble codes

ABS CODE	SYSTEM	ABS CODE	SYSTEM
11	EBCM	45	2 SENSOR (LF)
12	EBCM	46	2 SENSORS (RF)
21	MAIN VALVE	47	2 SENSORS (REAR)
22	LF INLET VALVE	48	3 SENSORS
23	LF OUTLET VALVE	51	LF OUTLET VALVE
24	RF INLET VALVE	52	RF OUTLET VALVE
25	RF OUTLET VALVE	53	REAR OUTLET VALVE
26	REAR INLET VALVE	54	REAR OUTLET VALVE
27	REAR OUTLET VALVE	55	LF WSS
31	LF WSS	56	RF WSS
32	RF WSS	57	RR WSS
33	RR WSS	58	LR WSS
34	LR WSS	61	EBCM LOOP CKT
35	LF WSS	71	LF OUTLET VALVE
36	RF WSS	72	RF OUTLET VALVE
37	RR WSS	73	REAR OUTLET VALVE
38	LR WSS	74	REAR OUTLET VALVE
41	LF WSS	75	LF WSS
42	RF WSS	76	RF WSS
43	RR WSS	77	RR WSS
44	LR WSS	78	LR WSS

84209142

Fig. 135 Teves Mk II ABS trouble codes

codes to be cleared until all have been read. Drive the vehicle at a speed greater than 18 mph to clear ABS trouble codes.

Re-read the system; if codes are still present, not all codes were read previously or additional repair is needed.

Depressurizing the Hydraulic Accumulator

The ABS pump/motor assembly will keep the accumulator charged to a pressure between approximately 2000 and 2600 psi any time the ignition is in the **RUN** position. The pump/motor cannot operate if the ignition is **OFF** or if a battery cable is disconnected. Disconnecting the pressure switch connector or the pump motor connector from the hydraulic unit will also prevent the pump from operating.

Unless otherwise specified, the hydraulic accumulator should be depressurized before working on any portion of the hydraulic system. The following procedure should be used:

1. With the ignition **OFF**, pressure switch disconnected, pump motor disconnected or the negative battery cable disconnected, pump the brake pedal a minimum of 25 times using at least 50 lbs. of pedal force each time. A definite change in pedal feel will occur when the accumulator is discharged.

2. When a definite increase in pedal effort is felt, stroke the pedal a few additional times to remove all hydraulic pressure from the system.

Front Wheel Speed Sensor

REMOVAL & INSTALLATION

▶ See Figures 136 and 137

1. Disconnect the negative battery cable.
2. Disconnect the sensor connector. Cut the wire retaining strap, if necessary.
3. Raise and safely support the vehicle. Remove the wheel and tire assembly.
4. On Eldorado and Seville, disengage the sensor cable grommet from the wheelwell pass-through hole.
5. Remove the sensor cable from the brackets/retainers.
6. Remove the sensor mounting bolt and remove the sensor.
7. Inspect the sensor face for accumulation of metallic particles, dirt, grease or other contaminants and clean as necessary. Make sure the sensor face shows no evidence of damage from toothed sensor ring contact.

To install:

8. Coat the sensor with anti-corrosion compound 1052856 or equivalent, where the sensor will contact the knuckle.
9. Install the sensor with the mounting bolt. Tighten the bolt to 84 inch lbs. (9.5 Nm) on Deville and Fleetwood or 106 inch lbs. (12 Nm) on Eldorado and Seville.
10. Position and install the cable in the grommets, brackets and retainers, as necessary. The cable must be secure in the retainers and clear of moving parts. The cable must not be pulled too tight.
11. Connect the sensor to the wiring harness.
12. Install the wheel and tire assembly and lower the vehicle.
13. Connect the negative battery cable.

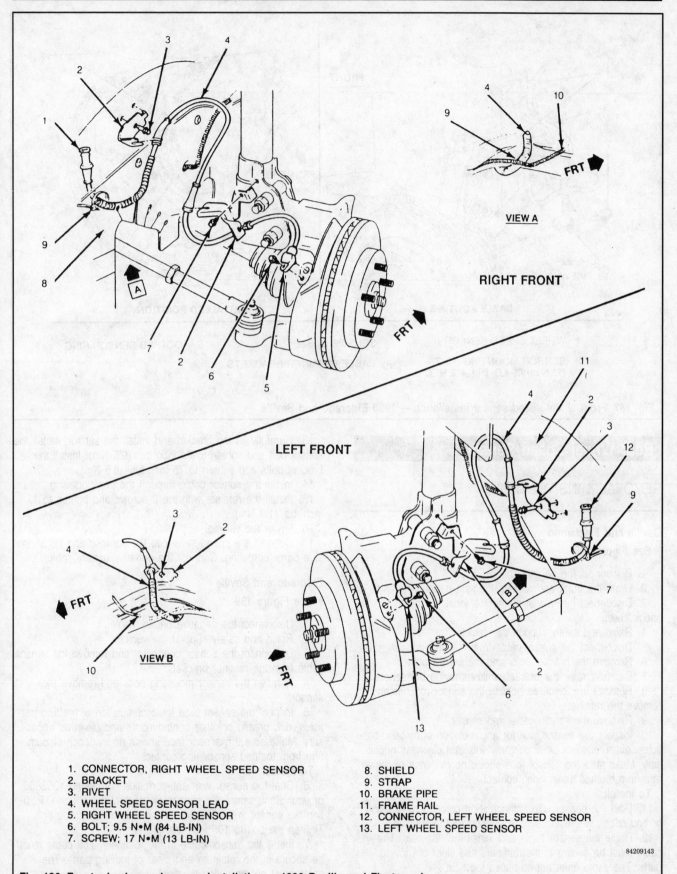

1. CONNECTOR, RIGHT WHEEL SPEED SENSOR
2. BRACKET
3. RIVET
4. WHEEL SPEED SENSOR LEAD
5. RIGHT WHEEL SPEED SENSOR
6. BOLT; 9.5 N•M (84 LB-IN)
7. SCREW; 17 N•M (13 LB-IN)

8. SHIELD
9. STRAP
10. BRAKE PIPE
11. FRAME RAIL
12. CONNECTOR, LEFT WHEEL SPEED SENSOR
13. LEFT WHEEL SPEED SENSOR

84209143

Fig. 136 Front wheel speed sensor installation — 1990 Deville and Fleetwood

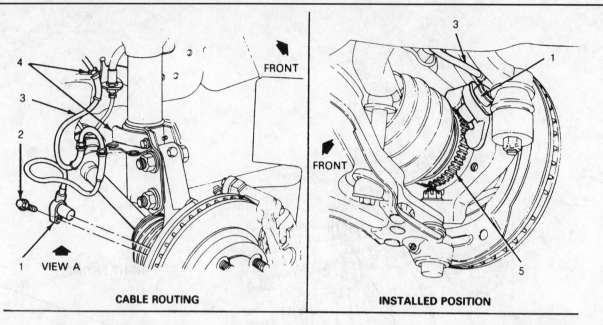

CABLE ROUTING | INSTALLED POSITION

1 WHEEL SPEED SENSOR   3 SENSOR CABLE   5 TOOTHED SENSOR RING

2 SENSOR MOUNTING BOLT   4 CABLE RETAINER BRACKETS
(12 N·m/106 LB. IN.) — 2 REQ'D

84209144

Fig. 137 Front wheel speed sensor installation — 1990 Eldorado and Seville

Rear Wheel Speed Sensor

REMOVAL & INSTALLATION

Deville and Fleetwood

▶ **See Figure 138**

1. Disconnect the negative battery cable.
2. Open the trunk and remove the side panel carpeting.
3. Disconnect the sensor connector, located forward of the shock tower.
4. Raise and safely support the vehicle.
5. Disconnect the sensor cable from the bracket.
6. Remove the bracket bolts and the sensor bolt.
7. Carefully raise the bracket while removing the sensor.
8. Remove the 2 screws holding the sensor retainer and remove the retainer.
9. Remove the sensor cable and sensor.
10. Inspect the sensor face for accumulation of metallic particles, dirt, grease or other contaminants and clean as necessary. Make sure the sensor face shows no evidence of damage from toothed sensor ring contact.

To install:

11. Coat the sensor with anti-corrosion compound 1052856 or equivalent, where the sensor will contact the knuckle.
12. Route the sensor cable and install the retainers. The cable must be secure in the retainers and clear of moving parts. The cable must not be pulled too tight.

13. Carefully lift the bracket and install the sensor. Install the sensor bolt and tighten to 84 inch lbs. (9.5 Nm). Install the bracket bolts and tighten to 75 inch lbs. (8.5 Nm).
14. Install the sensor cable through the trunk opening.
15. Install the retainer with the 2 screws and tighten to 17 inch lbs. (1.9 Nm).
16. Lower the vehicle.
17. Connect the speed sensor to the harness and install the side panel carpeting. Connect the negative battery cable.

Eldorado and Seville

▶ **See Figure 139**

1. Disconnect the negative battery cable.
2. Raise and safely support the vehicle.
3. Disconnect the sensor connector and remove the sensor cable from the retainer brackets.
4. Remove the sensor mounting bolts and remove the sensor.
5. Inspect the sensor face for accumulation of metallic particles, dirt, grease or other contaminants and clean as necessary. Make sure the sensor face shows no evidence of damage from toothed sensor ring contact.

To install:

6. Coat the sensor with anti-corrosion compound 1052856 or equivalent, where the sensor will contact the knuckle. Position the sensor in the knuckle and install the mounting bolt. Tighten the bolt to 106 inch lbs. (12 Nm).
7. Install the sensor cable in the retainers. The cable must be secure in the retainers and clear of moving parts. The cable must not be pulled too tight.
8. Connect the sensor connector and lower the vehicle. Connect the negative battery cable.

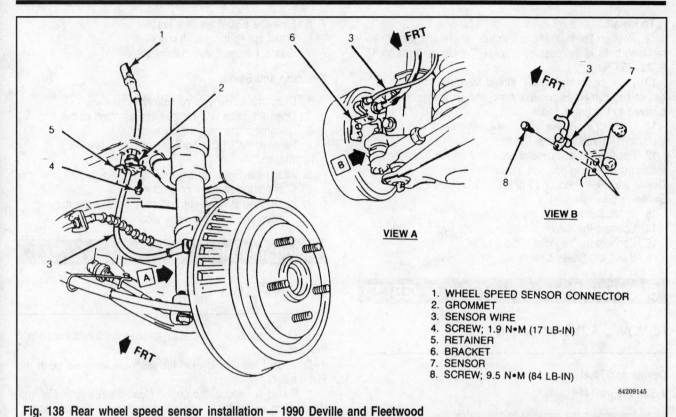

1. WHEEL SPEED SENSOR CONNECTOR
2. GROMMET
3. SENSOR WIRE
4. SCREW; 1.9 N•M (17 LB-IN)
5. RETAINER
6. BRACKET
7. SENSOR
8. SCREW; 9.5 N•M (84 LB-IN)

84209145

Fig. 138 Rear wheel speed sensor installation — 1990 Deville and Fleetwood

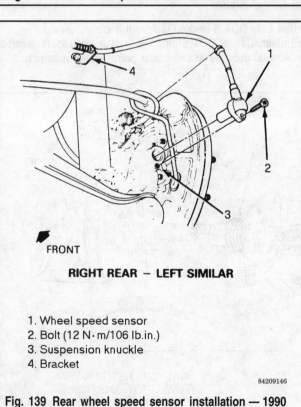

FRONT

RIGHT REAR – LEFT SIMILAR

1. Wheel speed sensor
2. Bolt (12 N·m/106 lb.in.)
3. Suspension knuckle
4. Bracket

84209146

Fig. 139 Rear wheel speed sensor installation — 1990 Eldorado and Seville

Hydraulic Unit

REMOVAL & INSTALLATION

▶ See Figure 140

1. Disconnect the negative battery cable.
2. Depressurize the hydraulic accumulator according to the procedure in this Section.

✳✳CAUTION

The hydraulic accumulator contains brake fluid and nitrogen gas at extremely high pressures. It is mandatory that it be depressurized before disconnecting any brake lines, or personal injury may result.

3. Label and disconnect all electrical connections at the hydraulic unit.
4. On Eldorado and Seville, remove the cross-car brace.
5. Remove the pump mounting bolt and move pump/motor assembly aside to allow access to the brake lines.
6. Using a backup wrench, disconnect the brake lines from the valve block.
7. Working inside the vehicle, disconnect the pushrod from the brake pedal. Push the dust boot forward, past the hex on the pushrod, and separate the pushrod into 2 sections by unscrewing it.
8. Remove the hydraulic unit mounting bolts at the pushrod bracket and remove the hydraulic unit from the vehicle. The front half of the pushrod will remain locked into the hydraulic unit.

To install:

9. Position the hydraulic unit in the vehicle and install new retaining bolts at the pushrod bracket. Tighten the bolts to 37 ft. lbs. (50 Nm).

10. From inside the vehicle, thread the pushrod halves together and tighten. Reposition the dust boot and connect the pushrod to the brake pedal.

11. Connect the brake lines to the valve block and tighten the fittings to 106 inch lbs. (12 Nm).

12. Position the pump/motor assembly on the hydraulic unit. Install the mounting bolt and tighten to 71 inch lbs. (8 Nm) on Deville and Fleetwood or 10 ft. lbs. (13 Nm) on Eldorado and Seville.

13. Install the cross-car brace, if removed.

14. Connect the electrical harness to the hydraulic unit.

15. Connect the negative battery cable.

16. Bleed the brake system.

Electronic Brake Control Module (EBCM)

REMOVAL & INSTALLATION

Deville and Fleetwood

▶ See Figure 141

1. Disconnect the negative battery cable.
2. Remove the right sound insulator.
3. Slide the EBCM from the bracket and disconnect the harness connector.

To install:

4. Connect the harness connector.

5. Slide the EBCM into the bracket.
6. Install the right sound insulator.
7. Connect the negative battery cable.

Eldorado and Seville

1. Disconnect the negative battery cable.
2. Open the trunk and remove the left trunk carpet trim.
3. Disconnect the harness connector.
4. Remove the EBCM from the mounting bracket.

To install:

5. Attach the EBCM to the mounting bracket.
6. Connect the harness connector.
7. Install the left trunk carpet trim and close the trunk.
8. Connect the negative battery cable.

Filling and Bleeding

SYSTEM FILLING

1. Depressurize the hydraulic accumulator as explained in this Section.

2. Inspect the fluid level in the reservoir; it should be at the FULL mark.

3. If fluid is needed, thoroughly clean the reservoir cap and surrounding area prior to cap removal. Remove the cap and add fluid as needed.

➡**Use only DOT 3 brake fluid from a clean, sealed container. Use of DOT 5 silicone fluid is not recommended as internal damage to the pump components may result.**

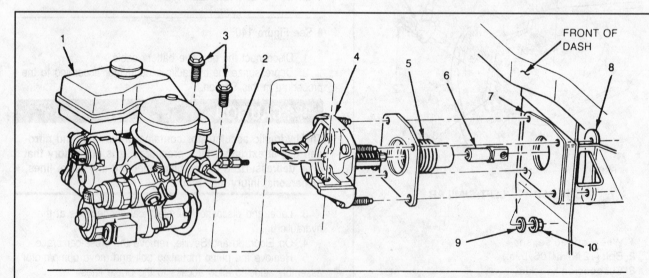

1	HYDRAULIC UNIT	5	RUBBER BOOT	9	WASHER - USED ON LOWER R.H. STUD ONLY
2	FRONT PUSHROD HALF	6	REAR PUSHROD HALF		
3	MOUNTING BOLTS (50 N·m/37 LB.FT.)	7	GASKET	10	NUTS - 4 REQ'D (20 N·m/15 LB.FT.)
4	PUSHROD BRACKET ASM.	8	REINFORCEMENT WASHER		

84209147

Fig. 140 Hydraulic unit installation — 1990 Eldorado and Seville, 1990 Deville and Fleetwood similar

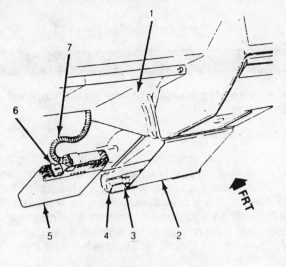

1. RIGHT SOUND INSULATOR
2. EBCM BRACKET
3. LOCKING TAB
4. HVAC OUTLET
5. EBCM
6. LOCKING PLATE
7. EBCM HARNESS

84209148

Fig. 141 EBCM installation — 1990 Deville and Fleetwood

SYSTEM BLEEDING

The front brake circuit should be bled using a standard diaphragm type pressure bleeder. The rear brake circuit can only be bled using system pressure.

➡**If necessary, the front brake circuit can be bled manually; refer to the Bleeding procedure under Brake Operating System in this Section. The rear brakes cannot be bled using conventional methods.**

Front Brake Circuit
▶ **See Figure 142**

> ✳✳CAUTION
>
> **Do not move the vehicle until a firm brake pedal is achieved. Failure to obtain a firm brake pedal may result in personal injury and/or property damage**

1. Disconnect the negative battery cable.
2. Depressurize the hydraulic accumulator as explained in this Section.
3. Remove the reservoir cap.
4. Install pressure bleeder adapter tool J-35798 or equivalent,in place of the cap.
5. Attach the pressure bleeder to the adapter tool. Charge the pressure bleeder to 20 psi (138 kPa).
6. Attach a transparent hose to the bleeder valve on either front caliper and submerge the other end in a container partially filled with clean brake fluid.
7. With the pressure bleeder turned ON, open the bleeder valve.

8. Allow fluid to flow from the bleeder valve until no air bubbles are seen in the brake fluid.
9. Close the bleeder valve.
10. Repeat Steps 6-9 at the other caliper.
11. Check the fluid level and adjust as necessary.
12. Remove the brake bleeding equipment and install the reservoir cap.
13. Connect the negative battery cable, turn the ignition **ON** and allow the pump to charge the accumulator.

Rear Brake Circuit

> ✳✳CAUTION
>
> **Do not move the vehicle until a firm brake pedal is achieved. Failure to obtain a firm brake pedal may result in personal injury and/or property damage**

1. Turn the ignition switch **ON** and allow the system to charge. (Listen for the pump motor; it will stop when the system is charged.)
2. Attach a transparent hose to one rear bleeder valve and submerge the other end in a container partially filled with clean brake fluid.
3. With the ignition **ON**, have an assistant slightly depress the brake pedal and hold.
4. Open the bleeder valve.
5. Allow fluid to flow from the bleeder valve until no air bubbles are seen in the brake fluid.
6. Close the bleeder valve.
7. Check the brake fluid level periodically during the bleeding procedure; do not allow the fluid level to fall below the reservoir seam line.
8. Repeat Steps 2-6 on the other rear bleeder valve.

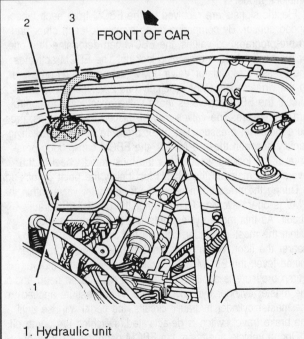

1. Hydraulic unit
2. J-35798 bleeder adapter
3. Hose to bleeder

84209149

Fig. 142 Pressure bleeder adapter tool installation

9. When bleeding is completed, depressurize the hydraulic accumulator as explained in this Section. Check the fluid level in the reservoir.

TEVES MK IV ANTI-LOCK BRAKE SYSTEM

Description

The Teves Mk IV anti-lock brake system is used on 1991-93 Deville, Fleetwood and Sixty Special. The system allows individual modulation of braking force at each wheel as well as providing traction control at the drive wheels if the vehicle is so equipped. The ABS system employs a conventional diagonally-split braking system and additional ABS components. The system allows the operator to maintain directional control during heavy braking situations by preventing locked-wheel skidding.

On vehicles equipped with the Traction Control System (TCS), wheel spin at the drive wheels is reduced by selective application of the brakes if vehicle speed is below 25 mph (40 km/h). The TCS system is designed to improve traction on loose or wet surfaces and aid in getting the vehicle moving from rest.

SYSTEM OPERATION

Anti-Lock System

Braking is performed by the conventional brake system until the Electronic Brake Control Module (EBCM) detects a wheel beginning to lock or the brake pedal has traveled beyond a specified limit. The EBCM will then command the system into anti-lock mode.

Electric signals are received by the EBCM from each wheel speed sensor. By comparing these signals to each other and to pre-programmed values, the EBCM can determine that one or more wheels is approaching lock-up. The EBCM activates the Pressure Modulator Valve (PMV) to control fluid pressure to the wheels. The PMV assembly has 2 valves per hydraulic circuit; the EBCM operates these valves electrically to control brake pressure. The valves may be placed into 3 modes: pressure increase, pressure reduce or pressure hold. By switching rapidly between these 3 modes, the EBCM can reduce pressure at the locking wheel, slow the most rapid wheel to the average or maintain the wheels just below the point of lock-up.

During the pressure increase mode, the inlet valve within the PMV is open, allowing fluid to enter the particular hydraulic circuit. As this mode cycles, pressure and fluid is reduced within the master cylinder, causing the brake pedal to drop nearer the floor. When the pedal travel exceeds a pre-determined level, the EBCM will activate the PMV pump motor. Pump pressure is applied to the wheel circuit(s) in need and/or the master cylinder hydraulic circuits. With pressure applied to the master cylinder hydraulic circuits, the pedal will rise until the brake travel switch is de-activated, switching the pump off.

During vehicle operation, the EBCM performs a series of self-tests, checking both electronic and hydraulic systems for vaults. If detectable problems exist, the EBCM will set a fault code and/or illuminate the ANTILOCK dash warning lamp. The ANTILOCK warning lamp is in addition to the normal BRAKE warning lamp which warns of problems in the conventional brake system.

Traction Control System (TCS)

The traction control system is additional to the ABS system and is not found on all vehicles with ABS. With traction control, brake pressure is increased to reduce wheel spin; with ABS, line pressure is reduced to allow greater wheel spin. The EBCM monitors the speed of the drive wheels through the wheel speed sensors; if wheel slip is detected below 25 mph with the brakes not applied, the EBCM enters the traction control mode.

Once in traction control mode, the EBCM commands two isolation valves in the PMV into operation. The isolation valves close to separate the non-driven wheels and the master cylinder circuits from the drive wheels. Once isolated, brake fluid pressure may be applied to the drive wheels without affecting the other circuits. The EBCM turns on the PMV pump motor and begins cycling the inlet and outlet valves to slow the slipping wheel(s).

Since the pump motor supplies more fluid than required, two pressure relief valves allow excess fluid to return to the master cylinder reservoir. If the brakes are manually applied by the operator during traction control operation, the PMV pressure switch and the brake pedal switch signal the EBCM to disable traction control and allow manual braking. Additionally, manual braking can override the traction control system at any time; the isolation valves act as one-way check valves, allowing manually-applied brake fluid pressure to enter the system.

Vehicles equipped with TCS are also equipped with a manual switch to disable the traction system. When the switch is engaged, cancelling system operation, a TRACTION OFF dashboard warning lamp will be illuminated. Some vehicles also have indicators showing that the TCS is engaged, either by lighting a dashboard lamp or displaying a TRACTION ENGAGED message.

SYSTEM COMPONENTS

▶ See Figure 143

Electronic Brake Control Module (EBCM)

Located on the inner firewall, the EBCM is a solid-state computer which monitors the speed of each wheel as well as the electrical status of the PMV assembly. Once wheel lock or wheel slip (with TCS) is detected, the EBCM operates the inlet and outlet valves in the PMV to control wheel speed. The valves can be cycled very rapidly, allowing control to be maintained in all operating situations.

The EBCM will disable either the TCS or ABS if a fault is detected. In most cases, the system will remain disabled for the remainder of the driving cycle, even if the fault self-corrects before the next key-on cycle. If either low system voltage is detected at the EBCM or low brake fluid level is detected at

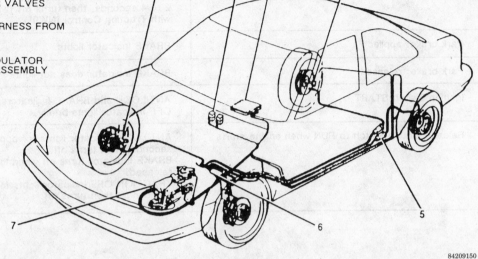

1 FRONT WHEEL SPEED SENSOR

2 ABS RELAYS

3 ELECTRONIC BRAKE CONTROL
   MODULE (EBCM)

4 REAR WHEEL SPEED SENSOR

5 PROPORTIONER VALVES

6 BRAKE PIPE HARNESS FROM
   PMV ASSEMBLY

7 PRESSURE MODULATOR
   VALVE (PMV) ASSEMBLY

84209150

Fig. 143 Teves Mk IV anti-lock brake system component locations — 1991-93 Deville, Fleetwood and Sixty Special

the PMV, the systems(s) will be disabled until the condition is corrected. Once the sensors indicate normal voltage or fluid level, the system(s) are enabled, even if the vehicle has not been shut off and restarted.

If the control unit detects an electrical fault, it will disable the TCS and/or ABS system immediately and illuminate the appropriate dash warning lamp to advise the operator. A fault code will usually be set in memory. Although it is possible for just the TCS system to be disabled, any fault in the ABS system will also cause the TCS system to be disabled.

The fault codes may be retrieved when the EBCM is placed into the diagnostic mode. A bi-directional hand scanner is required to retrieve or clear stored codes; no warning lamp flash outputs are used.

Wheel Speed Sensors

A wheel speed sensor at each wheel transmits speed information to the EBCM by generating a small AC voltage relative to the wheel speed. The voltage is generated by magnetic induction caused by passing a toothed sensor ring past a stationary sensor. the signals are transmitted through a pair of wires which are shielded against interference. The EBCM then calculates wheel speed for each wheel based on the frequency of the AC signal received from the sensor.

WARNING Lamps
▶ See Figure 144

➡Certain models equipped with traction control may cause a pilot lamp to light or a message to be displayed when the system is engaged. These signals are a convenience to the operator but are not system warning lamps.

BRAKE

The red BRAKE warning lamp in the instrument panel illuminates to alert the operator of conditions in the conventional braking system which may affect braking or vehicle operation. The lamp will illuminate when the parking brake is applied, the brake fluid in the master cylinder reservoir is low or when the ignition is switched to **START**, allowing the function of the bulb to be confirmed. Illumination of this lamp during vehicle operation signals a potentially hazardous condition within the brake system.

ANTILOCK

The amber ANTILOCK dashboard warning lamp is lit when the EBCM detects a fault within the ABS system. When this lamp is lit, the ABS system is disabled. If only the ANTILOCK lamp is lit, full power-assisted braking is available without the added benefit of the anti-lock system.

TRACTION or TRACTION OFF

This warning lamp applies specifically to the traction control system. It will light if the EBCM detects a problem specific to the TCS or if the operator has switched the system off manually.

On vehicles equipped with traction control, the EBCM is programmed to prevent brake overheating. During heavy braking conditions, if traction control mode is entered and the controller determines that the brakes are too hot to function properly, the TCS is disabled and the warning lamp is lit. After a period of time, usually 15-20 minutes, the system is enabled and the warning lamp extinguished. This protective behavior is normal operation and should not be mistaken for an intermittent system failure.

ACTION	NORMAL RESULT
Igniton Switch: RUN	ANTILOCK Indicator lights for approximately 2 to 4 seconds, then turns off. TRACTION OFF Indicator lights for approximately 2 to 4 seconds, then turns off (when equipped with Traction Control [NW9]).
Park brake: applied	BRAKE Indicator lights.
Park brake: released	BRAKE Indicator does not light.
Ignition Switch:START	ANTILOCK and BRAKE Indicators light, TRACTION OFF Indicator lights briefly.
Release Igntion Switch to RUN when engine starts	ANTILOCK Indicator lights for approximately 2 to 4 seconds, then turns off. BRAKE Indicator turns off when Ignition Switch is released. TRACTION OFF Indicator lights for approximately 2 to 4 seconds, then turns off.

84209151

Fig. 144 Normal functions of ABS/TCS dashboard warning lamps

Additionally, the EBCM monitors the signal from the transaxle temperature switch. If transaxle temperature exceeds approximately 320°F (160°C), the controller will disable the traction system, allowing both the brakes and the transaxle to cool. When the temperature switch closes again, at approximately 300°F (140°C), the EBCM will keep the system disabled for an additional 3-5 minutes to allow further cooling. The dash warning lamp will be illuminated during the period of disablement.

VCC/ABS Brake Switch

This normally-closed switch is integral to the normal electrical/vacuum-release brake switch. It monitors position of the brake pedal, opening when the pedal exceeds 40 per cent of total travel. The EBCM then turns on the pump in the pressure modulator valve assembly, circulating fluid and forcing the pedal upward until the switch closes.

Fluid Level Sensors

The brake fluid reservoirs on both the master cylinder and pressure modulator valve contain fluid level sensors. If the master cylinder reservoir becomes low on fluid, the red BRAKE warning lamp will be lit, signaling a potential system hazard. If the fluid level in the PMV reservoir becomes too low, the amber ANTILOCK warning lamp is lit and the ABS/TCS system disabled until the level returns to minimum.

Pressure Modulator Valve (PMV) Assembly

The assembly consists of the pump and motor, the valve body and the fluid reservoir. The reservoir provides fluid to the pump while the pump circulates the fluid to the master cylinder and maintains pedal height. The valve block contains the inlet and outlet valves for each wheel circuit.

When equipped with traction control, the PMV contains the isolation valves used to block pressure in the master cylinder and rear wheel circuits. A pressure switch within the PMV detects operator application of the brakes during TCS operation; when this signal is received, the EBCM immediately disables TCS function and allows manual braking.

The PMV is not serviceable except for replacement of the reservoir.

Proportioner Valves

Each rear wheel circuit contains a proportioning valve to limit brake pressure to the non-driven wheels. These valves improve front-to-rear brake balance during normal braking.

Self-Diagnostic System

▶ See Figures 145 and 146

The EBCM monitors operating conditions for possible system malfunctions. Malfunctions are detected by comparing system conditions against standard operating limits. Evidence of a malfunction is stored in the computer memory in the form of a 4-digit numerical Diagnostic Trouble Code (DTC).

Trouble codes are accessed by connecting a bi-directional scan tool to the Assembly Line Diagnostic Link (ALDL) connector. Follow the scan tool manufacturer's instructions to read the trouble codes. After all codes have been read and repairs are completed, use the scan tool to clear the codes, then cycle the ignition switch.

'Current' or 'history' codes are not differentiated in the EBCM, however, if the amber ANTILOCK lamp is illuminated before entering the diagnostic mode, at least one DTC is current. If the amber ANTILOCK lamp is not illuminated before entering the diagnostic mode, no DTC is current. If more than one DTC is stored and the amber ANTILOCK lamp was illuminated before entering the diagnostic mode, it is impossible to determine between current and history trouble codes.

Electronic Brake Control Module (EBCM)

REMOVAL & INSTALLATION

▶ See Figure 147

1. Disconnect the negative battery cable.
2. Remove the right and left sound insulators from the instrument panel.
3. Remove the floor outlet for the heating and cooling system.
4. Remove the EBCM retaining bolt and slide the unit toward the accelerator pedal.
5. Disconnect the harness connector and remove the EBCM.

To install:

6. Connect the wiring harness connector to the EBCM.
7. Slide the EBCM into its mounting bracket and install the retaining bolt. Tighten the bolt to 19 inch lbs. (2.2 Nm) on 1991 vehicles or 42 inch lbs. (4.7 Nm) on 1992-93 vehicles.
8. Install the floor outlet and the sound insulators.
9. Connect the negative battery cable.

Front Wheel Speed Sensor

REMOVAL & INSTALLATION

1991

▶ See Figure 148

1. Disconnect the negative battery cable.
2. Working under the hood, disconnect the wheel speed sensor connector.
3. Cut the strap retaining the sensor cable.
4. Raise and safely support the vehicle.
5. Disconnect the sensor cable from the brackets.
6. Remove the retaining bolt and remove the sensor.
7. Inspect the sensor face for accumulation of metallic particles, dirt, grease or other contaminants and clean as necessary. Make sure the sensor face shows no evidence of damage from toothed sensor ring contact.

To install:

8. Coat the sensor with anti-corrosion compound 1052856 or equivalent, where the sensor will contact the knuckle.
9. Route the sensor cable and install the retainers. The cable must be secure in the retainers and clear of moving parts. The cable must not be pulled too tight.
10. Position the sensor in the knuckle and install the retaining bolt. Tighten the bolt to 84 inch lbs. (9.5 Nm).
11. Lower the vehicle.
12. Connect the sensor connector and install a new retaining strap.
13. Connect the negative battery cable.

CODE	DESCRIPTION	CODE	DESCRIPTION
21	RF speed sensor circuit open	45	LF inlet valve circuit
22	RF speed sensor signal erratic	46	LF outlet valve circuit
23	RF wheel speed is 0 mph	47	LF speed sensor noisy
25	LF speed sensor circuit open	51	RR inlet valve circuit
26	LF speed sensor signal erratic	52	RR outlet valve circuit
27	LF wheel speed is 0 mph	53	RR speed sensor noisy
31	RR speed sensor circuit open	55	LR inlet valve circuit
32	RR speed sensor signal is erratic	56	LR outlet valve circuit
33	RR wheel speed is 0 mph	57	LR speed sensor noisy
35	LR speed sensor circuit open	61	Pump motor test fault
36	LR speed sensor signal erratic	62	Pump motor fault in ABS stop
37	LR wheel speed is 0 mph	71	EBCM problem
41	RF inlet valve circuit	72	VCC/antilock brake switch circuit.
42	RF outlet valve circuit	73	Fluid level switch circuit
43	RF speed sensor noisy		

84209152

Fig. 145 Teves Mk IV ABS trouble codes — 1991 Deville and Fleetwood

DTC	DESCRIPTION	DTC	DESCRIPTION
21	RF speed sensor circuit open	44	LF isolation valve circuit
22	RF speed sensor signal erratic	45	LF inlet valve circuit
23	RF wheel speed is 0 mph	46	LF outlet valve circuit
25	LF speed sensor circuit open	48	RF isolation valve circuit
26	LF speed sensor signal erratic	51	RR inlet valve circuit
27	LF wheel speed is 0 mph	52	RR outlet valve circuit
31	RR speed sensor circuit open	55	LR inlet valve circuit
32	RR speed sensor signal is erratic	56	LR outlet valve circuit
33	RR wheel speed is 0 mph	61	Pump motor test fault
35	LR speed sensor circuit open	62	Pump motor fault in ABS stop
36	LR speed sensor signal erratic	71	EBCM problem
37	LR wheel speed is 0 mph	72	VCC/antilock brake switch circuit
41	RF inlet valve circuit	73	Fluid level switch circuit
42	RF outlet valve circuit	74	PMV pressure switch circuit

84209153

Fig. 146 Teves Mk IV ABS trouble codes — 1992-93 Deville, Fleetwood and Sixty Special

1992-93

◗ See Figures 149 and 150

1. Disconnect the negative battery cable.
2. Disconnect the sensor connector.
3. Remove the hub and bearing assembly; refer to Section 8. Clean all dirt from the sensor housing area.
4. Gently pry the slinger from the speed sensor assembly. Discard the used slinger.
5. Carefully pry the speed sensor from the bearing assembly. Do not allow dirt to enter the bearing when the sensor is removed. Do not add lubricant through the sensor opening; the bearing is permanently lubricated.
6. Inspect the bearing and sensor for any signs of rust or water intrusion; if such damage is found, replace the hub and bearing assembly. Do not clean the grease from the toothed sensor ring; grease does not affect operation of the sensor.
7. Use a clean, lint-free cloth to remove sealant from the outer diameter of the bearing hub.

To install:

8. Apply a sealant, 620 Loctite® or equivalent, to the groove in the outer diameter of the bearing hub.
9. Place the hub and bearing on tool J-38764-4 or equivalent, to prevent damage to the studs.
10. Install the sensor using a press and tool J-38764-1 or equivalent.
11. Install the hub and bearing assembly; refer to Section 8.
12. Connect the sensor wiring connector and connect the negative battery cable.

Rear Wheel Speed Sensor

REMOVAL & INSTALLATION

◗ See Figures 151 and 152

1. Disconnect the negative battery cable.
2. Disconnect the wheel speed sensor connector.
3. Remove the hub and bearing assembly; refer to Section 8.
4. Clean the sensor housing of any dirt or debris.
5. Remove the screws holding the sensor and remove the sensor. Do not allow dirt to enter the bearing when the sensor is removed. Do not add lubricant through the sensor opening; the bearing is permanently lubricated.
6. Inspect the sensor ring and plate for any signs of contact or mechanical wear; if such damage is found, replace the hub and bearing assembly. Do not clean the grease from the toothed sensor ring; grease does not affect operation of the sensor.

To install:

7. Inspect the O-ring for damage and replace if necessary.
8. Install the sensor with the screws. Tighten the screws to 33 inch lbs. (3.7 Nm).
9. Install the hub and bearing assembly; refer to Section 8.
10. Connect the sensor wiring connector and connect the negative battery cable.

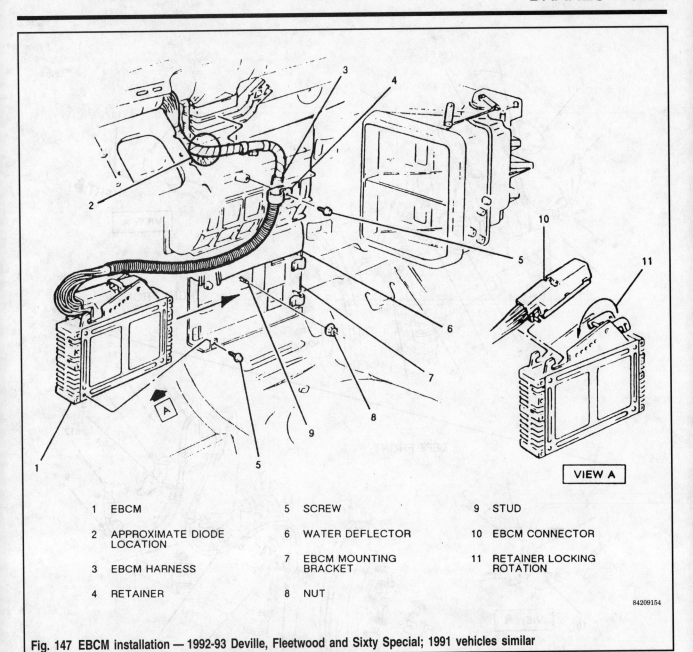

1	EBCM	5	SCREW	9	STUD
2	APPROXIMATE DIODE LOCATION	6	WATER DEFLECTOR	10	EBCM CONNECTOR
3	EBCM HARNESS	7	EBCM MOUNTING BRACKET	11	RETAINER LOCKING ROTATION
4	RETAINER	8	NUT		

84209154

Fig. 147 EBCM installation — 1992-93 Deville, Fleetwood and Sixty Special; 1991 vehicles similar

Pressure Modulator Valve (PMV) Assembly

REMOVAL & INSTALLATION

▶ See Figure 153

1. Disconnect the negative battery cable.
2. Remove the air cleaner assembly.
3. Label and disconnect the wiring connectors at the PMV assembly. The connectors are for the fluid level switch, pump motor and valve block.
4. Loosen or reposition the clamp on the hose at the PMV reservoir.

5. Position a clean pan to catch any spilled fluid from the reservoir. Disconnect the hose from the reservoir and plug the hose with a ⅝-inch (15.5mm) diameter plug.
6. Disconnect the primary and secondary brake lines at the PMV.
7. Disconnect the 4 brake lines from the PMV assembly.
8. Raise and safely support the vehicle.
9. Remove the lower PMV assembly retaining bolt.
10. Lower the vehicle to the ground.
11. Remove the harness strap, if equipped.
12. Support the PMV assembly and remove the upper retaining bolts. Remove the assembly from the vehicle. If the unit is being replaced with another, the reservoir and bracket(s) must be transferred to the new assembly.

➡ **The PMV assembly is not serviceable. Do not attempt to disassemble any part of the unit.**

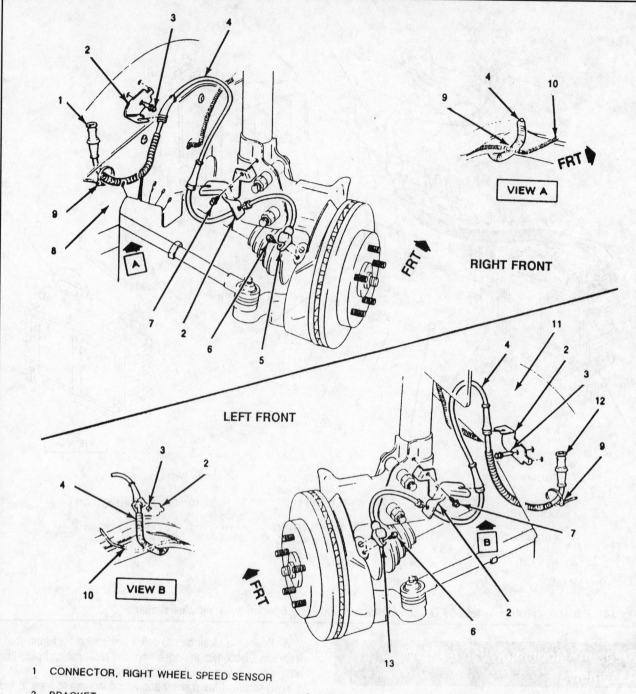

1	CONNECTOR, RIGHT WHEEL SPEED SENSOR		
2	BRACKET	8	SHIELD
3	RIVET	9	STRAP
4	WHEEL SPEED SENSOR LEAD	10	BRAKE PIPE
5	RIGHT WHEEL SPEED SENSOR	11	FRAME RAIL
6	BOLT	12	CONNECTOR, LEFT WHEEL SPEED SENSOR
7	SCREW	13	LEFT WHEEL SPEED SENSOR

84209155

Fig. 148 Front wheel speed sensor installation — 1991 Deville and Fleetwood

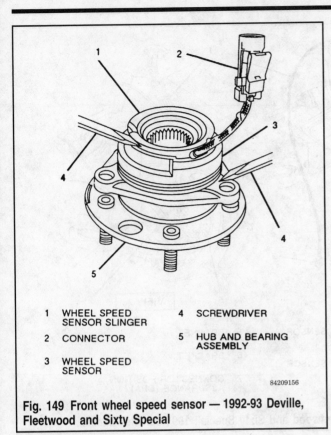

Fig. 149 Front wheel speed sensor — 1992-93 Deville, Fleetwood and Sixty Special

1   WHEEL SPEED
    SENSOR SLINGER

2   CONNECTOR

3   WHEEL SPEED
    SENSOR

4   SCREWDRIVER

5   HUB AND BEARING
    ASSEMBLY

84209156

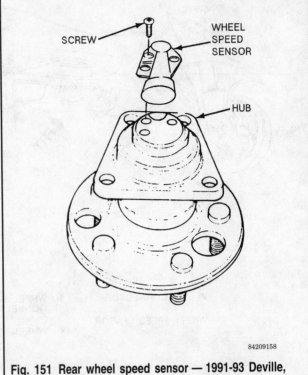

Fig. 151 Rear wheel speed sensor — 1991-93 Deville, Fleetwood and Sixty Special

84209158

To install:

13. Position the PMV assembly and install the upper retaining bolts. Tighten the bolts to 20 ft. lbs. (27 Nm).

14. Raise and safely support the vehicle. Install the lower retaining bolt and tighten it to 20 ft. lbs. (27 Nm). Lower the vehicle.

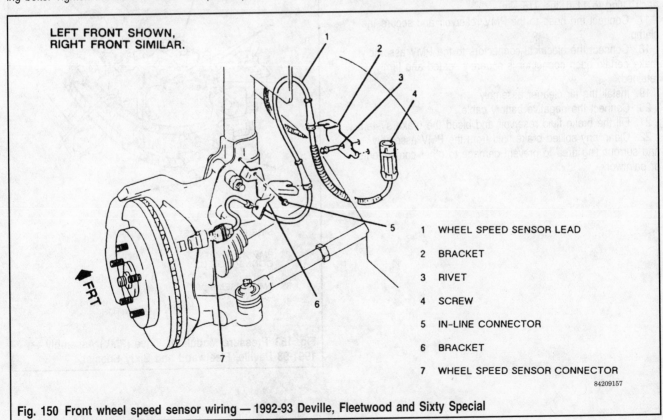

LEFT FRONT SHOWN,
RIGHT FRONT SIMILAR.

1   WHEEL SPEED SENSOR LEAD

2   BRACKET

3   RIVET

4   SCREW

5   IN-LINE CONNECTOR

6   BRACKET

7   WHEEL SPEED SENSOR CONNECTOR

84209157

Fig. 150 Front wheel speed sensor wiring — 1992-93 Deville, Fleetwood and Sixty Special

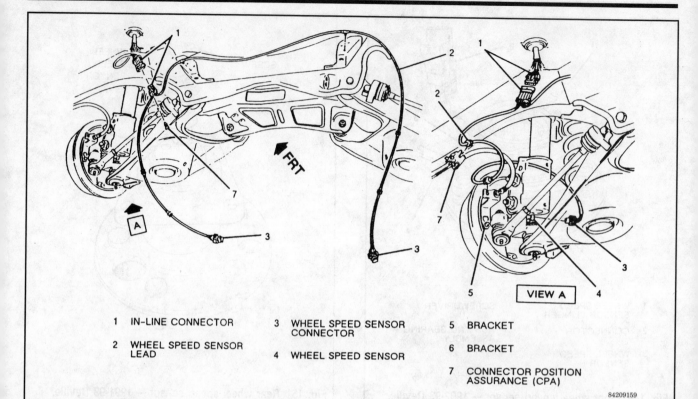

Fig. 152 Rear wheel speed sensor wiring — 1992-93 Deville, Fleetwood and Sixty Special; 1991 vehicles similar

1	IN-LINE CONNECTOR	3	WHEEL SPEED SENSOR CONNECTOR	5	BRACKET
2	WHEEL SPEED SENSOR LEAD	4	WHEEL SPEED SENSOR	6	BRACKET
				7	CONNECTOR POSITION ASSURANCE (CPA)

84209159

15. Connect the 4 brake lines to the PMV. Tighten the fittings to 11 ft. lbs. (15 Nm).

16. Install the primary and secondary brake lines, tightening each fitting to 11 ft. lbs. (15 Nm).

17. Connect the hose to the PMV reservoir and secure the clamp.

18. Connect the electrical connectors to the PMV assembly; make certain each connector is squarely seated and firmly retained.

19. Install the air cleaner assembly.

20. Connect the negative battery cable.

21. Fill the brake fluid reservoir and bleed the brake system.

22. Clean any spilled brake fluid from the PMV assembly and surrounding area to prevent damage to other components or paintwork.

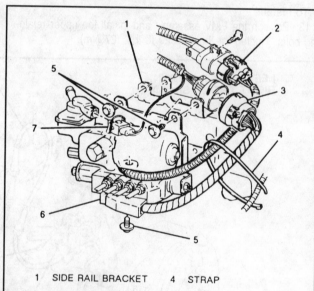

1	SIDE RAIL BRACKET	4	STRAP
2	PMV ASSEMBLY CONNECTOR C2	5	BOLT
3	PMV ASSEMBLY CONNECTOR C1	6	PMV ASSEMBLY
		7	PMV FLUID LEVEL SWITCH

84209160

Fig. 153 Pressure Modulator Valve (PMV) Assembly — 1991-93 Deville, Fleetwood and Sixty Special

BOSCH ANTI-LOCK BRAKE SYSTEM

Description

The Bosch Anti-lock Brake System (ABS) is used on 1991-93 Eldorado and Seville. The system maintains vehicle maneuverability by preventing wheel lock-up under heavy braking conditions, allowing the driver to retain greater control of the vehicle.

Some 1993 vehicles are equipped with a Traction Control System (TCS) in addition to ABS. The TCS prevents the wheels from spinning excessively during acceleration or when turning corners at higher speeds. The TCS also prevents wheel slip on slippery surfaces, allowing improved acceleration ability and vehicle stability. The ABS and TCS are both part of the same hydraulic and electrical system. Both systems use many of the same components; a problem in either system usually will disable the other system until it is repaired.

SYSTEM OPERATION

Anti-Lock Brake System

Under normal braking conditions, the anti-lock brake system functions virtually like a conventional vacuum boost brake system. If a wheel begins to lock under braking, the system enters the anti-lock mode. Hydraulic pressure in the individual wheel circuits is modulated to prevent any wheel from locking. A separate hydraulic line and solenoid valve run from the hydraulic modulator (Brake Pressure Modulator valve on 1993 vehicles) to each wheel on TCS equipped vehicles. On non-TCS vehicles, there is a separate solenoid valve for each front wheel, while the rear wheel share a 3rd solenoid.

The ABS system can apply, reduce or hold hydraulic line pressure to the wheels; it cannot increase pressure above that developed within the master cylinder. During anti-lock braking, a series of rapid pedal pulsations will be felt by the operator. This is caused by the rapid cycling of the solenoids as they control line pressure according to the direction of the Electronic Brake Control Module (EBCM) on non-TCS vehicles or the Electronic Brake and Traction Control Module (EBTCM) on TCS equipped vehicles. The pedal pulsation will stop when normal braking resumes or when the vehicle comes to a stop. Under some conditions, a ticking or popping noise may be heard within the vehicle when ABS is engaged; this is a normal noise and is caused by the solenoids and other components operating.

Pedal operation and feel during normal braking should be no different than conventional vacuum boost systems. During anti-lock braking, the brake pedal may actually rise under the operator's foot as the system functions; this pedal feedback is considered a normal condition during ABS stops. Maintaining constant force on the pedal provides the shortest stopping distance with ABS engaged.

Traction Control System

The TCS uses front brake intervention and torque management to enhance acceleration and vehicle stability. The TCS provides well balanced performance over a variety of road conditions and can function up to maximum vehicle speed. The system enhances directional control, traction and maneuverability through the use of information concerning wheel speed, vehicle speed, speed difference of the non-driven (rear) wheels, vehicle acceleration and throttle position, and brake applied input.

The TCS operates only when the system senses that one or both of the front wheels is slipping or beginning to lose traction. If excessive wheel slip is detected, the EBTCM will activate the TCS pilot valve and will increase, hold or decrease hydraulic pressure to the front brakes by modulating the front ABS solenoid valves, keeping an optimum slip rate on the front wheels.

If applying the brakes does not provide the necessary traction, the Powertrain Control Module (PCM) receives a pulse width modulated signal from the EBTCM requesting the desired torque level for proper traction control system operation. If the duty cycle of the signal is between 10% and 90%, torque reduction will be indicated and one to five cylinders will be disabled. The percent duty cycle indicates the percent torque required. The PCM will selectively disable fuel to certain cylinders to achieve torque reduction.

SYSTEM COMPONENTS

▶ See Figure 154

Electronic Brake Control Module (EBCM) or Electronic Brake and Traction Control Module (EBTCM)

The EBCM (non-TCS vehicles) or EBTCM (TCS equipped vehicles) is a small computer, located in the luggage compartment, that monitors the speed of each wheel as well as the electrical status of the hydraulic modulator (Brake Pressure Modulator on 1993 vehicles).

The primary functions of the EBCM/EBTCM are to detect wheel locking and wheel slip tendencies, control the brake system while in anti-lock or traction control mode, and monitor the system for proper operation.

The EBCM/EBTCM can disable the ABS/TCS system if a fault is detected during monitoring. If this occurs, the amber ANTILOCK warning lamp will illuminate on the dashboard. Once the EBCM/EBTCM has detected a fault, it will generate a fault code and store it for later retrieval. When the ABS is disabled, the vehicle's normal braking system will still function but without anti-lock capability.

Wheel Speed Sensors

Information on wheel speed is transmitted from sensors at each wheel to the control module. A small AC voltage is generated by magnetic induction as a toothed wheel mounted on the hub/bearing assembly turns past a fixed sensor; the voltage varies with the speed. The signal is passed to the EBCM/EBTCM through a pair of wires which are shielded to avoid interference.

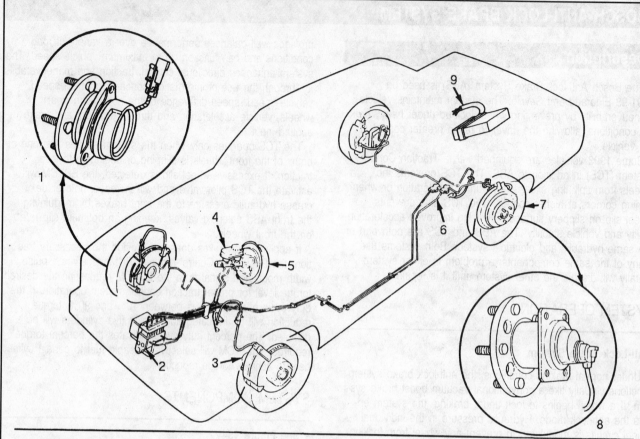

1. **FRONT WHEEL SPEED SENSOR INTEGRAL WITH BEARING**
2. **HYDRAULIC MODULATOR**
3. **CALIPER**
4. **MASTER CYLINDER**
5. **VACUUM ASSIST POWER BRAKE BOOSTER**

6. **REAR BRAKE CIRCUIT PROPORTIONING VALVES**
7. **CALIPER**
8. **REAR WHEEL SPEED SENSOR INTEGRAL WITH BEARING**
9. **ELECTRONIC BRAKE CONTROL MODULE (EBCM)**

84209161

Fig. 154 Bosch anti-lock brake system component locations — 1991-92 Eldorado and Seville; 1993 vehicles similar

Hydraulic Modulator

➡**The hydraulic modulator is referred to as the Brake Pressure Modulator (BPM) valve on 1993 vehicles.**

Mounted in the engine compartment, the hydraulic modulator provides pressure control for each of the wheel circuits as required during anti-lock braking and traction control. During anti-lock mode, the modulator can maintain or reduce brake fluid pressure independent of the pressure generated in the master cylinder.

The hydraulic modulator uses a 4 circuit configuration during normal braking. There are individual circuits for each wheel. The diagonally split circuits are hydraulically isolated so that a leak or malfunction in one circuit will allow continued braking ability on the other.

With the exception of the ABS relay and the pump motor relay (located under the cover) the hydraulic modulator is an integral, non-serviceable unit. It must be replaced as a unit and must never be disassembled.

Additional components contained within the hydraulic modulator are:

SOLENOID VALVES

The solenoid valves within the modulator are non-serviceable. They are controlled electrically by the EBCM/EBTCM and control brake fluid pressure to the wheels. During normal braking, the solenoid valves are open, allowing pressure to increase as called for by the driver. Upon entering anti-lock mode, the EBCM/EBTCM will control the solenoid valve, causing it to either hold or release pressure within the line.

PUMP AND MOTOR

The pump and motor within the hydraulic modulator circulates brake fluid back to the master cylinder circuit during ABS operation. During TCS operation, it transfers fluid from the master cylinder reservoir to the front brake calipers. The pump is located in the bottom of the hydraulic modulator and cannot be serviced.

RELAYS

The ABS valve relay and the pump relay are located under the cover of the hydraulic modulator. Either relay may be replaced if found to be faulty. The ABS valve relay provides power to the solenoid valves within the hydraulic modulator; the pump relay provides power to the pump motor during anti-lock braking and traction control.

Self-Diagnostic System

▶ See Figures 155, 156, 157 and 158

READING CODES

The EBCM/EBTCM can store several fault codes simultaneously. The order in which the codes are displayed may not indicate the order in which they occurred. If the ANTILOCK warning light is on before displaying the trouble codes, at least 1 of the codes is current, having occurred during the present ignition cycle.

If a scanning diagnostic tool is not available, the system may still be put in the diagnostic mode except when any of the current or hard faults involve the solenoid valves or pump motor. If one or more of the codes is/are Code 41, 45, 55, or

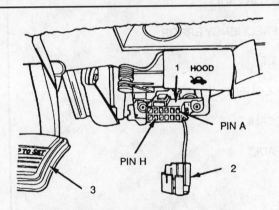

PLACE JUMPER BETWEEN PINS 'A' AND 'H'
(OR BETWEEN 'H' AND GROUND) TO ENTER
ABS DIAGNOSTIC MODE

1	ALDL CONNECTOR
2	ALDL CONNECTOR COVER
3	PARKING BRAKE PEDAL

84209162

Fig. 155 ALDL connector location — 1991-93 Eldorado and Seville

63, diagnostic display of the trouble codes cannot occur until the fault has been repaired. (Use of the scan tool eliminates this problem; all stored codes will display.)

To enter the diagnostic mode and have fault codes transmitted without the use of a scan tool:

1. Turn ignition switch **ON**. If the ANTILOCK warning light does not go out within 4 seconds, make a note of it and continue.

2. Turn ignition switch **OFF**. Remove the cover from the Assembly Line Diagnostic Link (ALDL) connector, located behind the left-hand side of the instrument panel, to the right of the parking brake.

3. Connect a jumper wire between pin H of the ALDL connector and body ground or connect pin H to pin A.

4. Turn the ignition switch **ON** and watch the ANTILOCK warning light. It should illuminate for 4 seconds and switch off, after which it will flash the stored codes.

5. The first code displayed will be Code 12. This is an initialization code and is not a fault code. It will be displayed as one flash followed by 2 flashes and a pause. Code 12 will be displayed 3 times in succession before fault codes are displayed.

6. Count the light flashes for any stored fault codes. Each stored code will be displayed 3 times before the next code is displayed. Record each code in writing. If no codes are stored, the readout of the Code 12 initialization sequence will begin again.

7. The code readout will repeat until the ground or jumper at the ALDL is removed. After recording all stored codes, disconnect the jumper from the ALDL and reinstall the cover.

CLEARING CODES

The control module will not permit codes to be cleared until all have been read. Codes cannot be cleared by by unplugging the module, disconnecting the battery or turning the ignition **OFF**.

If using the Tech I diagnostic tool, codes may be cleared using the Clear Codes function of the tool.

To clear codes via the ALDL connector:

1. Turn the ignition switch **OFF**.
2. Ground pin H on the ALDL connector.
3. Turn the ignition switch **ON**.
4. Wait for codes to begin flashing.
5. Unground pin H for at least 1 second, then reconnect the ground. This must be done 3 times within 10 seconds.
6. Wait at least 15 seconds. Repeat Steps 1-4 of this procedure: confirm that code 12 is the only code being flashed. If not, either codes were not cleared properly or an ABS fault still exists.

Additionally, if the vehicle ignition is cycled a pre-determined number of times without a particular fault reappearing, the related fault code will be erased from the control module memory and the ignition cycle counter will reset to zero. The reset threshold is usually either 50 or 100 cycles, depending on the model and the system fault.

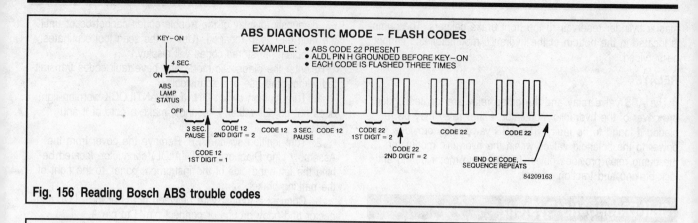

Fig. 156 Reading Bosch ABS trouble codes

ABS CODE	SYSTEM
21	RIGHT FRONT WHEEL SPEED SENSOR FAULT
22	RIGHT FRONT TOOTHED WHEEL FREQUENCY ERROR
25	LEFT FRONT WHEEL SPEED SENSOR FAULT
26	LEFT FRONT TOOTHED WHEEL FREQUENCY ERROR
31	RIGHT REAR WHEEL SPEED SENSOR FAULT
32	RIGHT REAR TOOTHED WHEEL FREQUENCY ERROR
35	LEFT REAR SPEED SENSOR FAULT
36	LEFT REAR TOOTHED WHEEL FREQUENCY ERROR
41	RIGHT FRONT SOLENOID VALVE FAULT
45	LEFT FRONT SOLENOID VALVE FAULT
55	REAR SOLENOID VALVE FAULT
61	MOTOR PUMP CIRCUIT FAULT
63	SOLENOID VALVE RELAY FAULT
71	ELECTRONIC BRAKE CONTROL MODULE FAULT
72	SERIAL DATA LINK FAULT (TECH 1 ERROR)

Fig. 157 Bosch ABS trouble codes — 1991-92 Eldorado and Seville

FAULT CODE	DESCRIPTION
21	RF WHEEL SPEED SENSOR FAULT
22	RF WHEEL SPEED SENSOR FREQUENCY ERROR
23	RF WHEEL SPEED SENSOR CONTINUITY FAULT
25	LF WHEEL SPEED SENSOR FAULT
26	LF WHEEL SPEED SENSOR FREQUENCY ERROR
27	LF WHEEL SPEED SENSOR CONTINUITY FAULT
28	WHEEL SPEED SENSOR FREQUENCY ERROR
31	RR WHEEL SPEED SENSOR FAULT
32	RR WHEEL SPEED SENSOR FREQUENCY ERROR
33	RR WHEEL SPEED SENSOR CONTINUITY FAULT
35	LR WHEEL SPEED SENSOR FAULT
36	LR WHEEL SPEED SENSOR FREQUENCY ERROR
37	LR WHEEL SPEED SENSOR CONTINUITY FAULT
41	RF ABS VALVE SOLENOID FAULT
44	RF TCS PILOT VALVE FAULT
45	LF ABS VALVE SOLENOID FAULT
48	LF TCS PILOT VALVE FAULT
51	RR ABS VALVE SOLENOID FAULT
55	LR VALVE SOLENOID FAULT (TCS)
55	REAR VALVE SOLENOID FAULT (NON–TCS)
61	PUMP MOTOR OR PUMP MOTOR RELAY FAULT
63	VALVE RELAY CIRCUIT FAULT
67	BRAKE LIGHT SWITCH FAULT
71	EBTCM/EBCM INTERNAL FAULT
72	SERIAL DATA LINK FAULT
73	PCM–EBTCM/EBCM PWM SIGNAL FAULT (4.6L)
83	BRAKE FLUID LEVEL LOW

84209165

Fig. 158 Bosch ABS trouble codes — 1993 Eldorado and Seville

Hydraulic Modulator

REMOVAL & INSTALLATION

1991-92

▶ See Figure 159

1. Disconnect the negative battery cable.
2. Use a syringe or similar tool to remove the brake fluid from the master cylinder.
3. Remove the left front radiator brace and air cleaner intake hose.
4. Remove the modulator relay cover and disconnect the 12-way connector and modulator ground strap.
5. Label and disconnect the brake lines from the modulator. Plug the lines to prevent the entry of dirt and debris.
6. Remove the modulator mounting nuts and remove the modulator from the mounting bracket.
7. Remove the modulator mounting insulators and inspect them for damage. Replace as necessary.

To install:

8. Install the insulators on the modulator and install the modulator to the mounting bracket. Install the nuts and tighten to 8 ft. lbs. (11 Nm).
9. Connect the brake lines to the modulator and tighten the fittings to 9 ft. lbs. (12 Nm).
10. Connect the modulator connector and ground strap. Install the relay cover.
11. Install the air intake hose and radiator brace.
12. Fill the master cylinder reservoir with brake fluid and bleed the brake system.

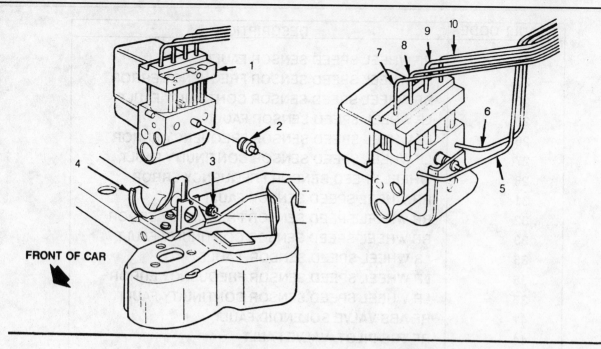

FRONT OF CAR

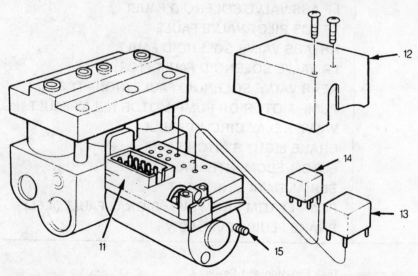

1 HYDRAULIC MODULATOR

2 MOUNTING INSULATOR — 3 REQUIRED

3 NUT — 3 REQUIRED

4 MOUNTING BRACKET

5 FRONT HYDRAULIC CIRCUIT FROM MASTER CYLINDER

6 REAR HYDRAULIC CIRCUIT FROM MASTER CYLINDER

7 LEFT FRONT BRAKE LINE-TO LF WHEEL

8 RIGHT REAR BRAKE LINE-TO-RR WHEEL

9 LEFT REAR BRAKE LINE-TO LR WHEEL

10 RIGHT FRONT BRAKE LINE-TO RF WHEEL

11 MODULATOR CONNECTOR

12 MODULATOR COVER AND SCREWS

13 PUMP RELAY

14 SOLENOID VALVE RELAY

15 MODULATOR GROUND CONNECTION

84209166

Fig. 159 Hydraulic modulator — 1991-92 Eldorado and Seville

Brake Pressure Modulator (BPM)

REMOVAL & INSTALLATION

1993

▶ **See Figure 160**

1. Disconnect the negative battery cable.
2. Raise and safely support the vehicle.
3. Remove the left front wheel and tire assembly.
4. Support the front of the cradle with a suitable jack.
5. Disconnect the exhaust pipe from the catalytic converter.
6. Remove the left front wheelwell splash shields.
7. Label and disconnect the brake lines from the modulator. Plug the lines to prevent the entry of dirt and debris.
8. Disconnect the brake line bundle from the left-hand frame rail.
9. Remove the bolts from the No. 1 and No. 2 body mounts. Loosen the No. 3 body mounts.
10. Using the jack, slowly lower the front cradle about 4-5 inches.
11. Remove the BPM valve cover.
12. Pull out (do not remove) the locking mechanism on the outer side of the ABS/TCS wiring harness connector. When 2 clicks are heard, the connector is completely disengaged and can be removed from the BPM valve.
13. Remove the TCS prime pipe, if equipped.
14. Disconnect the BPM ground strap.
15. Remove the BPM mounting nuts and remove the BPM through the left front wheelwell.

To install:

16. Install the BPM through the left front wheelwell and position it on the mounting bracket. Install the mounting nuts and tighten to 86 inch lbs. (10 Nm).
17. Connect the ground strap.
18. Connect the ABS/TCS wiring harness connector and install the BPM valve cover.
19. Connect the brake lines to the BPM and tighten the fittings to 13 ft. lbs. (18 Nm).

✴✴CAUTION

Make sure the brake lines are connected to their proper locations. If the lines are switched by mistake (inlet vs. outlet), wheel lockup will occur and personal injury may result.

20. Connect the TCS prime pipe, if equipped.
21. Raise the front cradle into position with the jack (do not over raise). Install the body mount bolts and tighten to 50 ft. lbs. (68 Nm).
22. Connect the brake line bundle to the left-hand frame rail.
23. Install the left front wheelwell splash shields.
24. Connect the exhaust pipe to the catalytic converter and tighten the bolts to 9 ft. lbs. (12 Nm).
25. Install the wheel and tire assembly and lower the vehicle.
26. Connect the negative battery cable.
27. Fill the master cylinder reservoir with brake fluid and bleed the brake system.

Electronic Brake Control Module (EBCM) or Electronic Brake and Traction Control Module (EBTCM)

REMOVAL & INSTALLATION

▶ **See Figures 161 and 162**

1. Disconnect the negative battery cable.
2. Open the trunk and remove the necessary carpeting to gain access to the EBCM/EBTCM.
3. Disconnect the harness connector from the EBCM/EBTCM.
4. Remove the EBCM/EBTCM from its mounting bracket.

To install:

5. Secure the EBCM/EBTCM in its mounting bracket.
6. Connect the wiring harness connector. Make sure the connector is securely mated to the EBCM/EBTCM.
7. Reposition the carpet and close the trunk.
8. Connect the negative battery cable.

Front Wheel Speed Sensor

REMOVAL & INSTALLATION

1991

▶ **See Figure 163**

1. Disconnect the negative battery cable.
2. Disconnect the sensor connector at the strut tower.
3. Raise and safely support the vehicle.
4. Disengage the sensor cable grommet from the wheelwell pass-through hole and remove the sensor cable from the retainers.
5. Remove the sensor mounting bolt and remove the sensor from the vehicle.
6. Inspect the sensor face for accumulation of metallic particles, dirt, grease or other contaminants and clean as necessary.

To install:

7. Coat the sensor with anti-corrosion compound 1052856 or equivalent, where the sensor will contact the knuckle.
8. Route the sensor cable and install the retainers. The cable must be secure in the retainers and clear of moving parts. The cable must not be pulled too tight.
9. Position the sensor in the knuckle and install the retaining bolt. Tighten the bolt to 106 inch lbs. (12 Nm).
10. Lower the vehicle.
11. Connect the sensor connector and connect the negative battery cable.

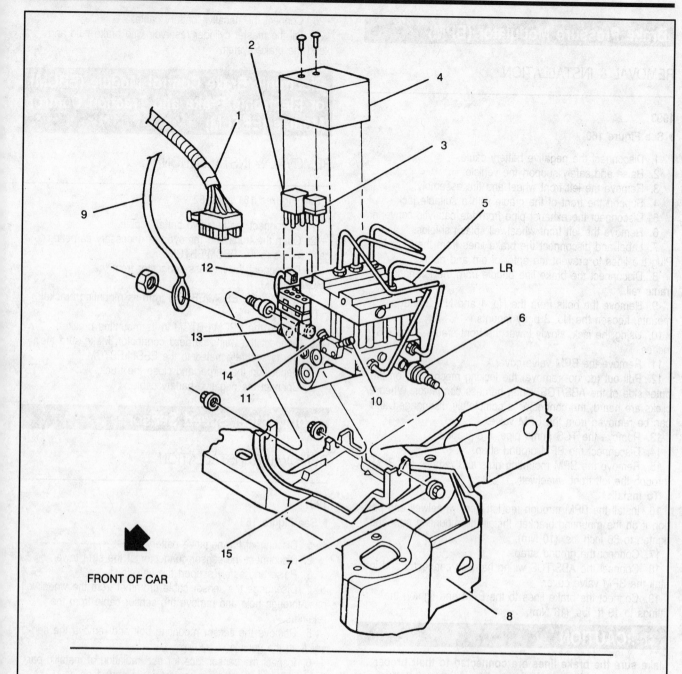

FRONT OF CAR

1	ABS VALVE HARNESS CONNECTOR	9	PUMP/MOTOR GROUND STOP
2	PUMP RELAY	10	TCS PRIME PIPE NOZZLE
3	VALVE RELAY	11	TCS PRIME PIPE BLEED SCREW
4	BPM VALVE COVER	12	PUMP/MOTOR POWER FEED
5	BRAKE PRESSURE MODULATOR VALVE (BPM)	13	PUMP/MOTOR GROUND STUD
6	BUSHING (3)	14	PUMP/MOTOR
7	MOUNTING NUT (3)	15	BPM VALVE MOUNTING BRACKET
8	FRAME		

84209167

Fig. 160 Brake Pressure Modulator — 1993 Eldorado and Seville

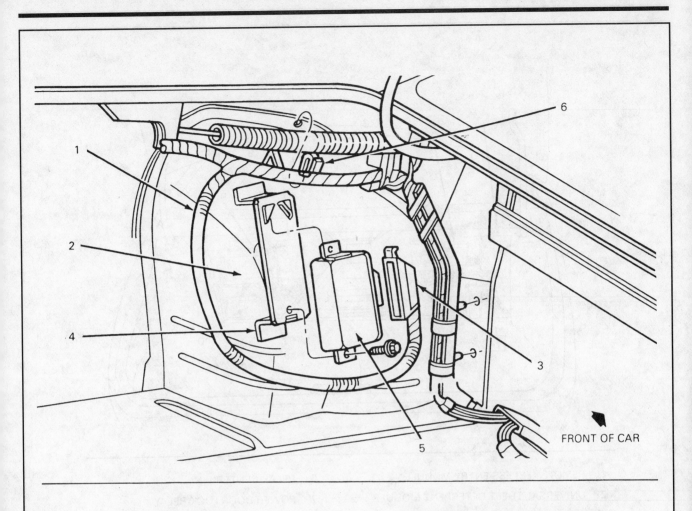

1	ABS HARNESS	4	EBCM WHEEL HOUSE MOUNTING PLATE
2	LEFT REAR WHEEL HOUSE	5	EBCM
3	EBCM CONNECTOR	6	ABS HARNESS CLIP

84209168

Fig. 161 EBCM location — 1991 Eldorado and Seville

1992-93

▶ **See Figure 164**

➡ **The front wheel speed sensors are integrated with the hub and bearing assembly. The sensor may be replaced and is serviced separately from the hub and bearing assembly. The sensor must be replaced whenever it is separated from the hub or bearing. Do not attempt to reuse the sensor once it is removed**

1. Disconnect the negative battery cable.
2. Disconnect the wheel speed sensor connector.
3. Remove the hub and bearing assembly; refer to Section 8. Clean all dirt from the sensor housing area.
4. Gently pry the slinger from the speed sensor assembly. Discard the used slinger.
5. Carefully pry the speed sensor from the bearing assembly. Do not allow dirt to enter the bearing when the sensor is

removed. Do not add lubricant through the sensor opening; the bearing is permanently lubricated.
6. Inspect the bearing and sensor for any signs of rust or water intrusion; if damage is found, replace the hub and bearing assembly. Do not clean the grease from the toothed sensor ring; grease does not affect operation of the sensor.
7. Use a clean, lint-free cloth to remove sealant from the outer diameter of the bearing hub.
   To install:
8. Apply a sealant, 620 Loctite® or equivalent, to the groove in the outer diameter of the bearing hub.
9. Place the hub and bearing on tool J-38764-4 or equivalent, to prevent damage to the studs.
10. Install the sensor using a press and tool J-38764-1 or equivalent.
11. Install the hub and bearing assembly; refer to Section 8.
12. Connect the sensor wiring connector and make sure the connector is clipped to the dust shield on the knuckle.

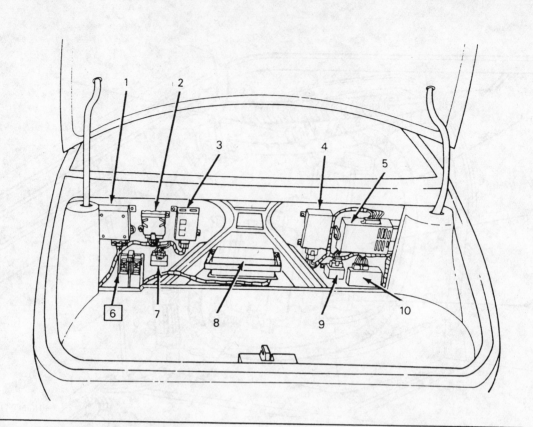

1   REMOTE KEYLESS ENTRY MODULE
2   UNIVERSAL THEFT DETERRENT MODULE
3   HEATED WINDSHIELD CONTROL MODULE
4   PASS KEY MODULE
5   REMOTE RADIO CHASSIS

6   RELAY CENTER
7   POWER DOOR LOCK RELAY
8   ANTI-LOCK BRAKE CONTROL MODULE
9   DELAYED ACCESSORY BUS MODULE
10 COMPUTER COMMAND RIDE MODULE

84209169

Fig. 162 EBCM location — 1992 Eldorado and Seville; 1993 similar

13. Connect the negative battery cable.

Rear Wheel Speed Sensor

REMOVAL & INSTALLATION

The rear wheel speed sensor is an integral part of the rear bearing assembly and cannot be serviced separately. Should a sensor fail, the entire hub and bearing assembly must be replaced. For rear hub and bearing service procedures, see Section 8.

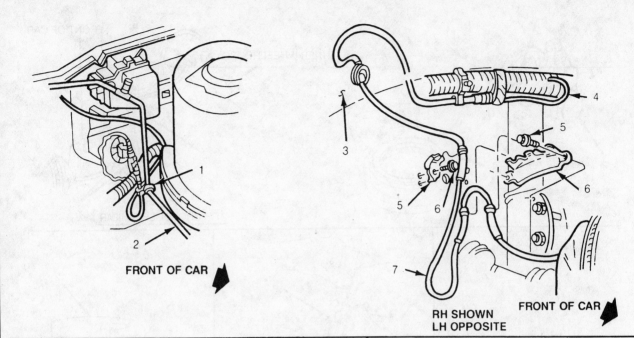

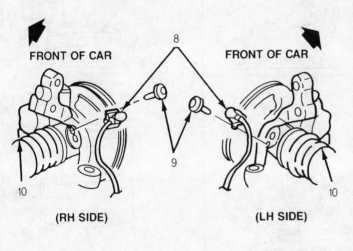

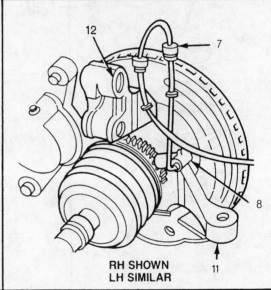

1	WHEEL SPEED SENSOR HARNESS CLIP	7	WHEEL SPEED SENSOR HARNESS
2	A/C TUBE ASSEMBLY	8	WHEEL SPEED SENSOR
3	LH/RH WHEEL HOUSE	9	WHEEL SPEED SENSOR MOUNTING BOLT
4	STRUT	10	DRIVE AXLE ASSEMBLY
5	WHEEL SPEED SENSOR BRACKET BOLT — 4 REQUIRED	11	KNUCKLE ASSEMBLY
6	WHEEL SPEED SENSOR BRACKET	12	TOOTHED WHEEL SPEED SENSOR RING

84209170

Fig. 163 Front wheel speed sensor installation — 1991 Eldorado and Seville

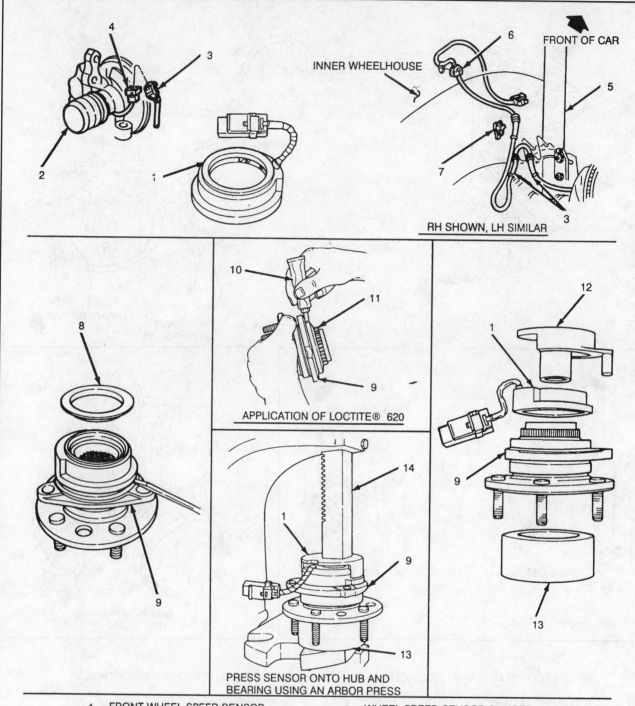

INNER WHEELHOUSE

FRONT OF CAR

RH SHOWN, LH SIMILAR

APPLICATION OF LOCTITE® 620

PRESS SENSOR ONTO HUB AND
BEARING USING AN ARBOR PRESS

1	FRONT WHEEL SPEED SENSOR	8	WHEEL SPEED SENSOR SLINGER
2	KNUCKLE	9	FRONT INTEGRAL HUB BEARING ASSEMBLY
3	WHEEL SPEED SENSOR HARNESS	10	LOCTITE® 620
4	WHEEL SPEED SENSOR CONNECTOR	11	TOOTHED SENSOR RING
5	STRUT	12	J 38764−1
6	WHEEL SPEED SENSOR HARNESS WHEELHOUSE GROMMET	13	J 38764−4
7	WHEEL SPEED SENSOR HARNESS BRACKET	14	ARBOR PRESS

84209171

Fig. 164 Front wheel speed sensor installation — 1992-93 Eldorado and Seville

BRAKE SPECIFICATIONS

All measurements in inches unless noted.

Year	Model	Master Cylinder Bore	Brake Disc Original Thickness	Brake Disc Minimum Thickness	Maximum Runout	Brake Drum Diameter Original Inside Diameter	Brake Drum Diameter Max. Wear Limit	Brake Drum Diameter Maximum Machine Diameter	Minimum Lining Thickness Front	Minimum Lining Thickness Rear
1990	Deville	0.937	1.043	0.957	0.004	8.860	8.909	8.880	0.030	0.030
	Eldorado	①	②	③	④	—	—	—	0.030	0.030
	Fleetwood	0.937	1.043	0.957	0.004	8.860	8.909	8.880	0.030	0.030
	Seville	①	②	③	④	—	—	—	0.030	0.030
1991	Deville	1.000	1.276	1.209	0.004	8.860	8.909	8.880	0.030	0.030
	Eldorado	1.000	②	③	④	—	—	—	0.030	0.030
	Fleetwood	1.000	1.276	1.209	0.004	8.860	8.909	8.880	0.030	0.030
	Seville	1.000	②	③	④	—	—	—	0.030	0.030
1992	Deville	1.000	1.276	1.209	0.004	8.860	8.909	8.880	0.030	0.030
	Eldorado	1.000	⑤	⑥	0.002	—	—	—	0.030	0.030
	Fleetwood	1.000	1.276	1.209	0.004	8.860	8.909	8.880	0.030	0.030
	Seville	1.000	⑤	⑥	0.002	—	—	—	0.030	0.030
1993	Deville	1.000	1.276	1.209	0.004	8.860	8.909	8.880	0.030	0.030
	Eldorado	1.000	⑤	⑥	0.002	—	—	—	0.030	0.030
	Seville	1.000	⑤	⑥	0.002	—	—	—	0.030	0.030
	Sixty Special	1.000	1.276	1.209	0.004	8.860	8.909	8.880	0.030	0.030

① Standard brake system: 1.126
   Anti-lock brake system: 1.000
② Front: 1.035
   Rear: 0.494
③ Front: 0.956
   Rear: 0.429
④ Front: 0.004
   Rear: 0.003
⑤ Front: 1.260
   Rear: 0.433
⑥ Front: 1.209
   Rear: 0.374

84209172

TORQUE SPECIFICATIONS

Component	U.S.	Metric
ABS hydraulic unit mounting bolts		
1990 vehicles	37 ft. lbs.	50 Nm
ABS pump/motor mounting bolt		
1990 Deville and Fleetwod	71 inch lbs.	8 Nm
1990 Eldorado and Seville	10 ft. lbs.	13 Nm
Brake caliper mounting bolt		
Front caliper		
Deville, Fleetwood and Sixty Special	38 ft. lbs.	51 Nm
Eldorado and Seville		
1990–91	63 ft. lbs.	85 Nm
1992–93	38 ft. lbs.	51 Nm
Rear caliper		
Eldorado and Seville		
1990–91	63 ft. lbs.	85 Nm
1992–93	20 ft. lbs.	27 Nm
Brake caliper bracket bolt	83 ft. lbs.	112 Nm
Brake hose-to-caliper bolt	32 ft. lbs.	44 Nm
Brake line fittings	11 ft. lbs.	15 Nm
Brake pedal assembly mounting bolts		
Deville, Fleetwood and Sixty Special		
1991–93	18 ft. lbs.	24 Nm
Brake pedal pivot bolt		
1990 Deville and Fleetwood	25 ft. lbs.	34 Nm
Eldorado and Seville	33 ft. lbs.	45 Nm
Brake pressure modulator		
Eldorado and Seville		
1993	86 inch lbs.	10 Nm
Hydraulic modulator mounting nuts		
Eldorado and Seville		
1991–92	8 ft. lbs.	11 Nm
Master cylinder mounting nuts	20 ft. lbs.	27 Nm
Master cylinder proportioner valves		
1990 vehicles	24 ft. lbs.	31 Nm
Master cylinder proportioner valve caps		
Deville, Fleetwood and Sixty Special		
1991	20 ft. lbs.	27 Nm
Parking brake pedal nuts/screws		
Deville, Fleetwood and Sixty Special		
1990	15 ft. lbs.	20 Nm
1991–93	13 ft. lbs.	18 Nm
Eldorado and Seville	13 ft. lbs.	18 Nm
Power brake booster mounting nuts		
Deville, Fleetwood and Sixty Special	15 ft. lbs.	21 Nm
Eldorado and Seville	20 ft. lbs.	27 Nm
Pressure modulator valve bolts		
Deville, Fleetwood and Sixty Special		
1991–93	20 ft. lbs.	27 Nm
Wheel cylinder mounting bolts	106 inch lbs.	12 Nm
Wheel speed sensor mounting bolt		
Deville, Fleetwood and Sixty Special		
Front		
1990–91	84 inch lbs.	9.5 Nm
Rear		
1990	84 inch lbs.	9.5 Nm
1991–93	33 inch lbs.	3.7 Nm
Eldorado and Seville	106 inch lbs.	12 Nm

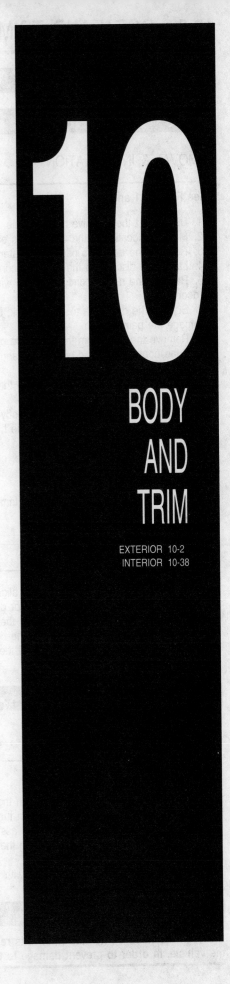

10

BODY
AND
TRIM

EXTERIOR

Doors

REMOVAL & INSTALLATION

▶ See Figures 1 and 2

1. Disconnect the negative battery cable.
2. Mark the location of the door hinges on the door.
3. Remove the door trim panel and water deflector.
4. Label and disconnect the electrical connections.
5. Remove the rubber conduit and the wiring harness from the door.
6. Support the door with a suitable jack, being careful not to damage the paint or trim.
7. Remove the bolts from the door side of the hinges and remove the door with the aid of an assistant.

To install:

8. Position the door to the hinges with the aid of an assistant. Install the bolts.
9. Adjust the door for proper door-to-body alignment and lock-to-striker engagement, then tighten the bolts to 38 ft. lbs. (48 Nm).
10. Attach the wiring harness and rubber conduit to the door.
11. Connect the electrical connectors.
12. Install the water deflector and door trim panel.
13. Connect the negative battery cable.

ADJUSTMENT

Adjust the door for proper door-to-body alignment and lock-to-striker engagement. Move the door up or down or in or out by loosening the nuts on the pillar side of the hinge and repositioning the door as needed. Move the door fore and aft by loosening the bolts on the door side of the hinge and repositioning the door as needed.

Hood

REMOVAL & INSTALLATION

▶ See Figures 3, 4 and 5

1. Scribe the locations of the hinges on the underside of the hood so the hood can be reinstalled in the same position.
2. Support the hood with the aid of an assistant.
3. Remove the nuts and bolts retaining the hood to the hinges and remove the gas spring clips.
4. Remove the hood from the vehicle with the aid of an assistant.

❋❋WARNING

Position the hood on its side when it is removed from the vehicle, in order to prevent damage to the sheet metal.

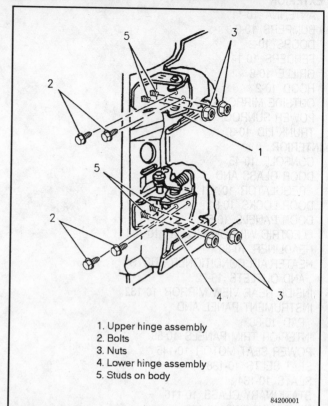

1. Upper hinge assembly
2. Bolts
3. Nuts
4. Lower hinge assembly
5. Studs on body

84200001

Fig. 1 Front door hinge — Deville, Fleetwood and Sixty Special; Eldorado and Seville similar

To install:

5. With the aid of an assistant, position the hood on the hinges, aligning the scribe marks that were made during the removal procedure.
6. Install the nuts, bolts and gas spring clips.
7. Check hood alignment and adjust, if necessary.

ALIGNMENT

▶ See Figure 6

Hood Panel

1. Loosen the hood attaching bolts at each hood hinge. The holes in the hinge are elongated for fore an aft hood adjustment.
2. When the hood is positioned properly, tighten the hinge-to-hood attaching bolts.
3. Adjust the rubber bumpers so the hood is flush with the fenders.
4. Adjust the hood latch mechanism as described in this Section.
5. After hood alignment, there must be sufficient load remaining on the hood stops to eliminate hood flutter. This can be obtained by lowering the primary latch an additional 1/8 inch.

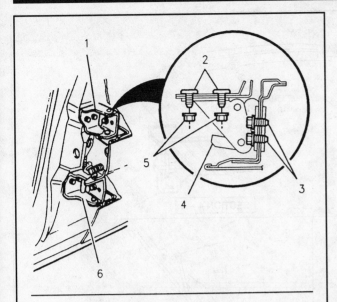

1. Upper hinge assembly
2. Studs
3. Bolts
4. Hinge
5. Nuts
6. Lower hinge assembly

84200002

Fig. 2 Rear door hinge — Deville, Fleetwood and Sixty Special; Eldorado and Seville similar

Hood Latch

The striker plate in the hood panel is large enough to allow normal fore and aft adjustment. Cross vehicle adjustment is provided at the hood lock mounting bracket to radiator support on Deville, Fleetwood and Sixty Special or at the front end sheet metal support-to-radiator support tie bar on Eldorado and Seville. Up and down adjustment is provided by loosening the 2 screws securing the latch to the hood latch bracket or support.

When the hood latch mounting screws have been loosened or the hood adjustment changed, make sure that proper alignment has been obtained before tightening the mounting screws. Proper cross vehicle adjustment of the primary lock is achieved by slowly lowering the hood onto the lock with the attaching screws loose, then raising the hood and tightening the screws.

Trunk Lid

REMOVAL & INSTALLATION

▶ See Figures 7, 8, 9 and 10

1. Disconnect the negative battery cable.
2. Disconnect the electric lock release solenoid connector.
3. If equipped, disconnect the trunk lid courtesy light connector.

4. If equipped, disconnect the connector from the lock cylinder.
5. Tie a string to the wiring harness and pull the harness out of the trunk lid, leaving the string completely through the lid and hanging out.
6. Scribe the locations of the hinges on the trunk lid so the trunk lid can be reinstalled in the same position.
7. Support the trunk lid with the aid of an assistant.
8. Remove the trunk lid mounting bolts, then remove the trunk lid from the vehicle with the aid of an assistant.

To install:
9. With the aid of an assistant, position the trunk lid on the hinges, aligning the scribe marks that were made during the removal procedure.
10. Install the trunk lid mounting bolts.
11. Pull the wiring harness through the trunk lid using the string, then remove the string from the wiring harness.
12. Connect the necessary electrical connectors and connect the negative battery cable.
13. Check the trunk lid alignment and adjust, if necessary.

ALIGNMENT

▶ See Figures 7, 8, 9 and 10

1. Loosen the trunk lid mounting bolts and move the trunk lid, as necessary.
2. When the trunk lid is properly positioned within the body opening, tighten the mounting bolts.
3. To adjust the up and down alignment at the rear corners, turn the rubber bumpers to raise or lower the trunk lid.

Bumpers

REMOVAL & INSTALLATION

➡ **Bumper removal and installation requires the aid of an assistant.**

Deville, Fleetwood and Sixty Special

FRONT

▶ See Figures 11, 12 and 13

1. Disconnect the negative battery cable.
2. Label and disconnect the necessary electrical connectors and bulb sockets.
3. Remove the retaining nuts and remove the bumper from the energy absorber.
4. Slowly slide the bumper and fascia forward and remove it from the vehicle.

To install:
5. Place the fascia onto the rollers and slide the bumper onto the energy absorbers.
6. Install the retaining nuts.
7. Connect the necessary electrical connectors and bulb sockets. Connect the negative battery cable.
8. Adjust the bumper clearances as shown in Figs. 12 and 13, then tighten the bumper-to-energy absorber nuts to 20 ft. lbs. (27 Nm).

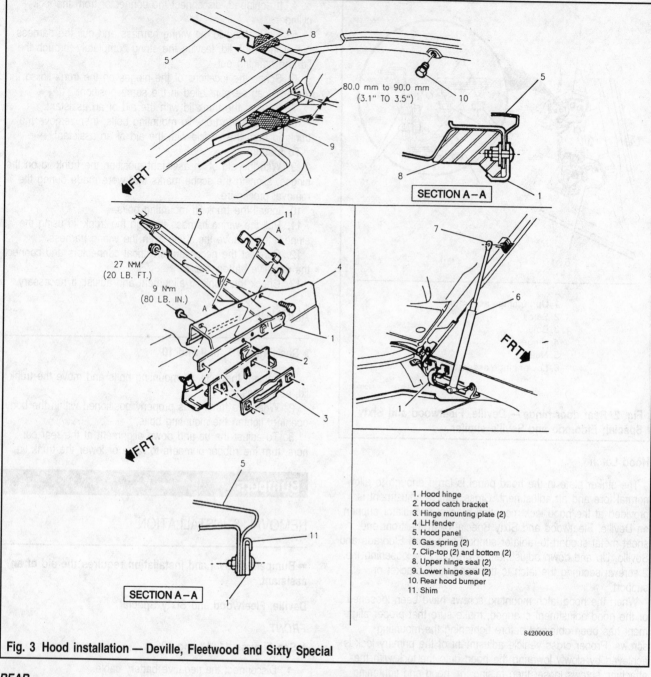

1. Hood hinge
2. Hood catch bracket
3. Hinge mounting plate (2)
4. LH fender
5. Hood panel
6. Gas spring (2)
7. Clip-top (2) and bottom (2)
8. Upper hinge seal (2)
9. Lower hinge seal (2)
10. Rear hood bumper
11. Shim

80.0 mm to 90.0 mm
(3.1" TO 3.5")

SECTION A-A

27 N·M
(20 LB. FT.)

9 N·m
(80 LB. IN.)

SECTION A-A

84200003

Fig. 3 Hood installation — Deville, Fleetwood and Sixty Special

REAR

▶ See Figures 14, 15 and 16

1. Disconnect the negative battery cable.
2. Remove the tail lamp assemblies; refer to Section 6.
3. Label and disconnect the necessary electrical connectors.
4. Remove the bumper-to-energy absorber mounting bolts/nuts and remove the bumper.

To install:

5. Position the bumper assembly and install the bumper-to-energy absorber mounting bolts/nuts.
6. Connect the necessary electrical connectors.
7. Install the tail lamp assemblies; refer to Section 6.
8. Adjust the bumper clearances as shown in Figs. 15 and 16, then tighten the mounting nuts to 20 ft. lbs. (27 Nm).

1990-91 Eldorado and Seville

FRONT

▶ See Figures 17, 18, 19 and 20

1. Disconnect the negative battery cable.
2. Remove the valance panel as follows:
   a. Remove the 2 bolts from each side securing the valance panel to each side of the bumper.
   b. Remove the 8 push tabs securing the valance panel to the bumper and remove the panel.
3. Remove the 2 screws from each side securing the wheel opening moulding to the bumper.
4. Remove one bolt from each side securing the outer fascia bracket to the bumper fascia brace.
5. Remove the side marker lamps from each side.

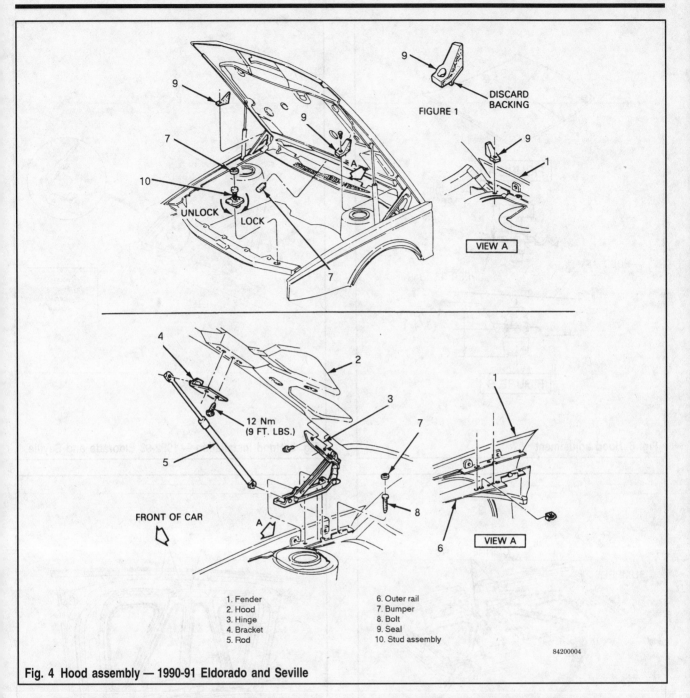

1. Fender
2. Hood
3. Hinge
4. Bracket
5. Rod
6. Outer rail
7. Bumper
8. Bolt
9. Seal
10. Stud assembly

84200004

Fig. 4 Hood assembly — 1990-91 Eldorado and Seville

6. Working through the side marker lamp holes, remove the 2 screws from each side securing the bumper fascia to the fender.

7. Disconnect the bulb sockets and connectors at the turn signal lamps.

8. Remove 4 bumper-to-energy absorber mounting nuts from each side of the vehicle and remove the bumper by pulling straight out.

To install:

9. With the aid of an assistant, position the bumper to obtain the clearances shown in Figs. 19 and 20, then install the bumper-to-energy absorber nuts.

10. Connect the bulb sockets and connectors at the turn signal lamps.

11. Working through the side marker lamp holes, secure the bumper fascia to the fender with the 4 screws.

12. Install the side marker lamps.

13. Secure the outer fascia bracket to the front bumper fascia brace with the 2 bolts.

14. Secure the wheel opening moulding to the bumper with the 4 screws.

15. Install the valance panel in the reverse order of removal.

16. Connect the negative battery cable.

REAR

▶ **See Figures 19, 20 and 21**

1. Open the trunk lid and pull back the trunk carpet to expose the 4 quarter panel-to-fascia plate nuts. Remove the nuts.

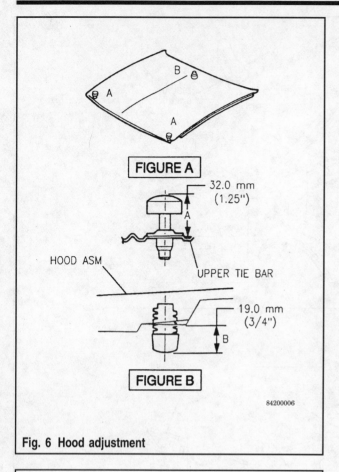

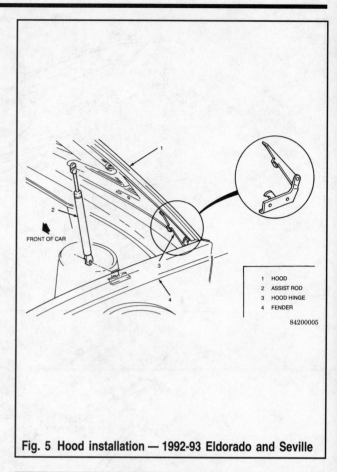

Fig. 6 Hood adjustment

Fig. 5 Hood installation — 1992-93 Eldorado and Seville

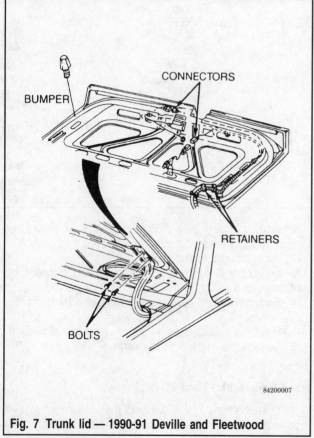

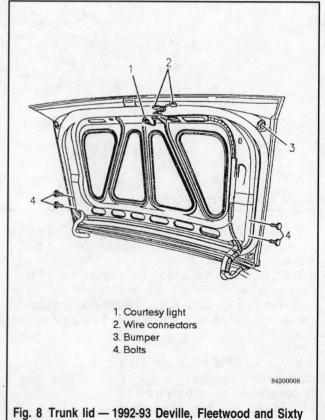

Fig. 7 Trunk lid — 1990-91 Deville and Fleetwood

1. Courtesy light
2. Wire connectors
3. Bumper
4. Bolts

Fig. 8 Trunk lid — 1992-93 Deville, Fleetwood and Sixty Special

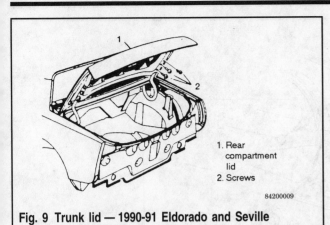

1. Rear compartment lid
2. Screws

84200009

Fig. 9 Trunk lid — 1990-91 Eldorado and Seville

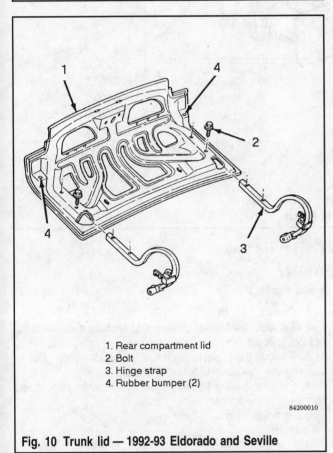

1. Rear compartment lid
2. Bolt
3. Hinge strap
4. Rubber bumper (2)

84200010

Fig. 10 Trunk lid — 1992-93 Eldorado and Seville

2. Raise and safely support the vehicle.
3. Remove the lower valance panel.
4. Remove the lower 3 screws from the wheel opening moulding to fascia.
5. Remove the 8 energy absorber-to-impact bar nuts and remove the bumper.
   To install:
6. With the aid of an assistant, position the bumper to obtain the clearances shown in Figs. 19 and 20, then install the bumper-to-energy absorber nuts. Tighten to 20 ft. lbs. (27 Nm).

7. Install the wheel opening moulding-to-fascia screws.
8. Install the lower valance with the 9 retainers and 2 screws. Tighten the screws to 9 ft. lbs. (12 Nm).
9. Lower the vehicle.
10. Working inside the trunk, install the fascia plate-to-quarter panel nuts and tighten to 9 ft. lbs. (12 Nm).
11. Reposition the trunk carpet and close the trunk lid.

1992-93 Eldorado and Seville

FRONT

▶ **See Figures 22, 23 and 24**

1. Disconnect the negative battery cable.
2. Remove 3 screws securing the fascia panel extension to the front fascia from each side at the wheel opening.
3. On Eldorado, disconnect the side marker lamp sockets at each side of the vehicle.
4. Remove the 6 splash shield-to-bumper fascia fasteners.
5. If equipped, remove the fog lamps from the mounting brackets.
6. Remove one bolt from each side securing the bumper to the energy absorber units.
7. Remove the bumper by pulling it straight out from the vehicle.
   To install:
8. With the aid of an assistant, position the bumper to obtain the clearances shown in Figs. 23 and 24, being sure to engage the sliding retainers on each side. Install the bolts at the energy absorbing units and tighten to 18 ft. lbs. (24 Nm).
9. Install the fog lamps to the mounting brackets, if equipped.
10. Install the 6 splash shield-to-bumper fascia fasteners.
11. On Eldorado, connect the side marker lamp sockets.
12. Install the 3 screws securing the fascia panel extension to the front fascia on each side at the wheel opening.
13. Connect the negative battery cable.

REAR

▶ **See Figures 23, 24 and 25**

1. Disconnect the negative battery cable.
2. Raise and safely support the vehicle.
3. On Eldorado, disconnect the side marker lamp sockets.
4. Remove the 3 fascia extension-to-fascia screws at the wheel opening.
5. Remove the 2 energy absorber-to-impact bar bolts and remove the bumper.
   To install:
6. With the aid of an assistant, position the bumper to obtain the clearances shown in Figs. 23 and 24, being sure to engage the fascia side retainers to the guide on the fender. Install the 2 energy absorber-to-impact bar bolts and tighten to 18 ft. lbs. (24 Nm).
7. Install the fascia extension-to-fascia screws at the wheel opening.
8. On Eldorado, connect the side marker lamp sockets.
9. Lower the vehicle and connect the negative battery cable.

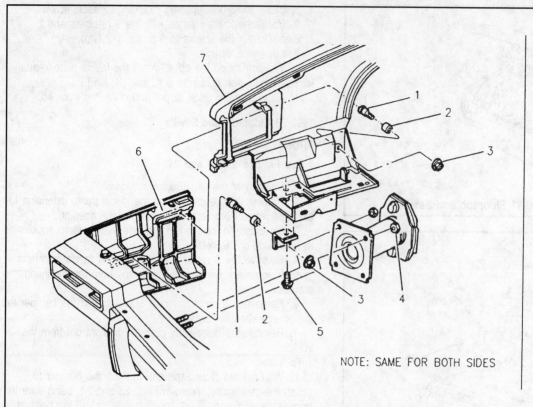

1. Roller
2. Spacer
3. Nut
4. Nut
5. Bolt
6. Fascia
7. Fender

NOTE: SAME FOR BOTH SIDES

84200011

Fig. 11 Front bumper installation — Deville, Fleetwood and Sixty Special

Grille

REMOVAL & INSTALLATION

Deville, Fleetwood and Sixty Special

1990

▶ See Figures 26 and 27

1. Open the hood.
2. Remove the left and right headlamp filler panels.
3. Remove the 6 grille mounting screws and remove the grille.

To install:

4. Position the grille and install the mounting screws.
5. Install the headlamp filler panels.

1991-93

▶ See Figures 28 and 29

1. Open the hood.
2. Remove the 5 screws attaching the grille to the grille support bracket.
3. Remove the 4 nuts attaching the grille to the hood and remove the hood.

To install:

4. Position the grille to the hood and support bracket.
5. Install the nuts to the hood and the screws to the support bracket.

Eldorado and Seville

1990-91

▶ See Figure 30

1. Open the hood.
2. Remove the 4 plastic screws and anchors securing the radiator/grille opening filler and remove the opening filler.
3. Remove the 2 plastic screws at each side of the grille securing the headlamp filler to the bracket.
4. Remove the 4 grille retainers. Pull the center pin out and remove with the anchor.
5. Remove the grille.

To install:

6. Position the grille and secure with the grille retainers. Push in the anchor and the center pin.
7. Install the 2 plastic screws at each side of the grille securing the headlamp filler to the bracket.
8. Position the radiator/grille opening filler and secure with the plastic anchors and screws.

1992-93 ELDORADO

▶ See Figure 31

1. Open the hood.
2. Remove the 2 bolts securing the secondary latch release lever and the 2 nuts securing the grille support brace.
3. Remove the 6 grille-to-hood nuts and remove the grille.

To install:

4. Position the grille and install the 6 nuts.
5. Install the 2 nuts securing the support brace and the 2 bolts securing the secondary latch release lever.

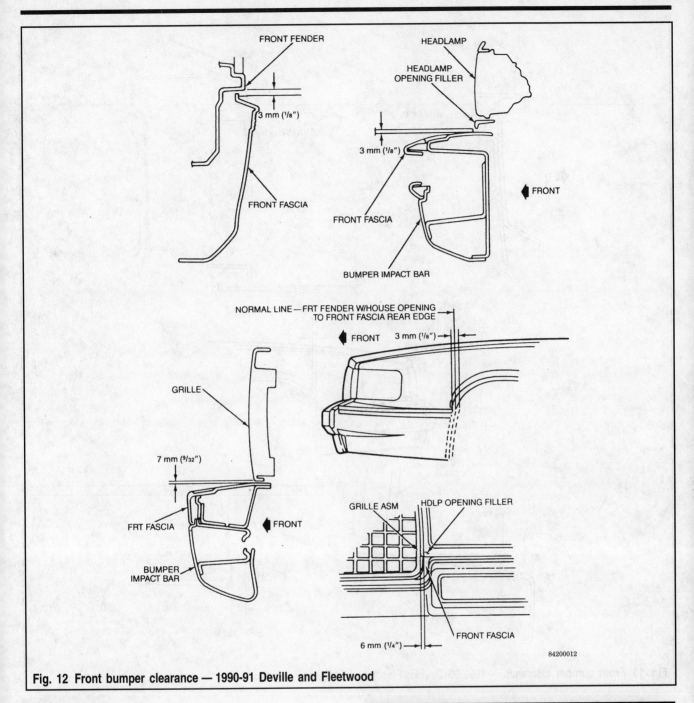

Fig. 12 Front bumper clearance — 1990-91 Deville and Fleetwood

1992-93 SEVILLE

▶ See Figures 32 and 33

1. Open the hood.
2. Remove the 4 plastic rivets and unsnap the 2 clips securing the headlamp housing upper filler panel. Remove the filler panel.
3. Remove the 2 push pins and release the locking tabs.
4. Remove the grille.

To install:

5. Install the grille, making sure the retaining tabs engage the slots in the headlamp housing module.
6. Install the 2 push pins.
7. Install the headlamp housing upper filler panel. Snap the clips and install the plastic rivets.

Outside Mirrors

REMOVAL & INSTALLATION

Deville, Fleetwood and Sixty Special

1990-91

▶ See Figure 34

1. Disconnect the negative battery cable.
2. Remove the door trim panel; refer to the procedure in this Section.
3. Remove the upper trim panel retainer.
4. Label and disconnect the wiring connectors.

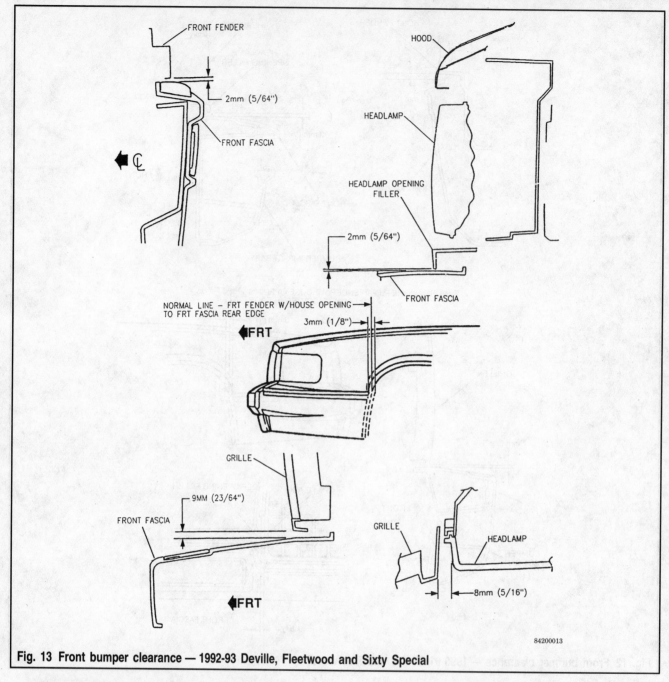

Fig. 13 Front bumper clearance — 1992-93 Deville, Fleetwood and Sixty Special

5. Remove the mounting nuts and remove the mirror.

To install:

6. Position the mirror to the door and install the mounting nuts. Tighten to 54 inch lbs. (6 Nm).

7. Connect the wiring connectors.

8. Install the upper trim panel retainer and the door trim panel.

9. Connect the negative battery cable.

1992-93

▶ See Figure 35

1. Disconnect the negative battery cable.

2. Remove the door trim panel; refer to the procedure in this Section.

3. Remove the 3 screws and the mirror trim plate.

4. Remove the foam sound insulator.

5. Disconnect the wiring connector.

6. Remove the 3 mounting nuts and the mirror. The black plastic cap under the door weatherstrip must be removed to access the forward nut.

To install:

7. Position the mirror to the door and install the mounting nuts. Tighten to 54 inch lbs. (6 Nm).

8. Install the black plastic cap under the weatherstrip.

9. Connect the wiring connector.

10. Install the foam sound insulator.

11. Install the mirror trim plate with the 3 screws.

12. Install the door trim panel.

13. Connect the negative battery cable.

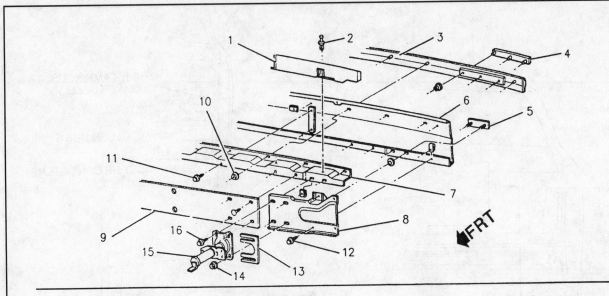

1. Filler support
2. Retainer
3. Rub strip
4. Reflector
5. Impact bar stud plate
6. Impact bar
7. Impact bar reinforcement
8. Impact bar outer reinforcement
9. Splash shield
10. Nut
11. Bolt
12. Bolt
13. Shim
14. Nut
15. Energy absorbing unit
16. Bolt

84200014

Fig. 14 Rear bumper assembly — Deville, Fleetwood and Sixty Special

Eldorado and Seville

1990-91

▶ **See Figure 36**

1. Disconnect the negative battery cable.
2. Remove the door trim panel; refer to the procedure in this Section.
3. On Seville STS, remove the upper trim panel retainer.
4. Remove the sound absorber pad.
5. Label and disconnect the wiring connectors.
6. Remove the mirror mounting nuts and remove the mirror and patch.

To install:

7. Position the patch and mirror to the door. Install the mounting nuts and tighten to 36-72 inch lbs. (4-8 Nm).
8. Connect the wiring connectors.
9. Install the sound absorber pad.
10. On Seville STS, install the upper trim panel retainer.
11. Install the door trim panel.
12. Connect the negative battery cable.

1992-93

▶ **See Figure 37**

1. Disconnect the negative battery cable.
2. Remove the door trim panel; refer to the procedure in this Section.
3. Label and disconnect the wiring connectors.
4. Remove the mirror mounting nuts and remove the mirror and gasket.

To install:

5. Position the gasket and mirror to the door. Install the mounting nuts and tighten to 45-63 inch lbs. (4-8 Nm).
6. Connect the wiring connectors.
7. Install the door trim panel.
8. Connect the negative battery cable.

Antenna

REPLACEMENT

Deville, Fleetwood and Sixty Special

▶ **See Figures 38 and 39**

1. Disconnect the negative battery cable.
2. Open the trunk and pull back the trunk liner.
3. Remove the antenna upper nut and bezel.
4. Remove the antenna bracket bolts.
5. Disconnect the wiring connector from the relay.
6. Disconnect the antenna cable and remove the antenna assembly.

To install:

7. Position the antenna assembly and connect the antenna cable.
8. Install the antenna bracket bolts.
9. Install the antenna bezel and upper nut.
10. Connect the wiring connector to the relay.
11. Reposition the trunk liner.
12. Connect the negative battery cable.

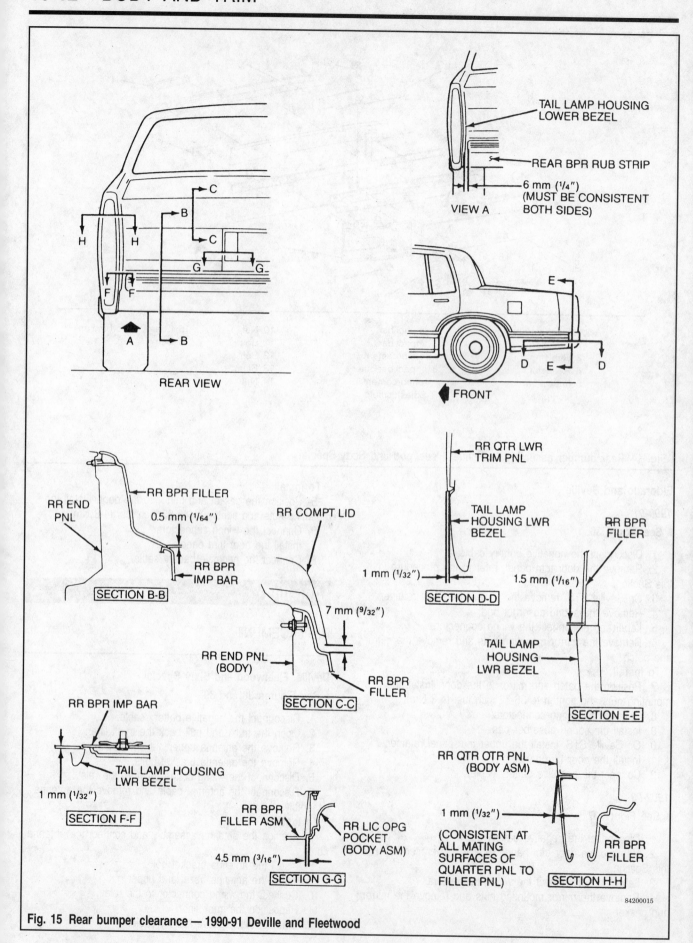

Fig. 15 Rear bumper clearance — 1990-91 Deville and Fleetwood

REAR VIEW

TAIL LAMP HOUSING LOWER BEZEL

REAR BPR RUB STRIP

6 mm (1/4") (MUST BE CONSISTENT BOTH SIDES)

VIEW A

FRONT

RR BPR FILLER

RR END PNL

0.5 mm (1/64")

RR BPR IMP BAR

SECTION B-B

RR COMPT LID

7 mm (9/32")

RR END PNL (BODY)

RR BPR FILLER

SECTION C-C

RR BPR IMP BAR

TAIL LAMP HOUSING LWR BEZEL

1 mm (1/32")

SECTION F-F

RR BPR FILLER ASM

RR LIC OPG POCKET (BODY ASM)

4.5 mm (3/16")

SECTION G-G

RR QTR LWR TRIM PNL

TAIL LAMP HOUSING LWR BEZEL

1 mm (1/32")

SECTION D-D

RR BPR FILLER

1.5 mm (1/16")

TAIL LAMP HOUSING LWR BEZEL

SECTION E-E

RR QTR OTR PNL (BODY ASM)

1 mm (1/32")

(CONSISTENT AT ALL MATING SURFACES OF QUARTER PNL TO FILLER PNL)

RR BPR FILLER

SECTION H-H

84200015

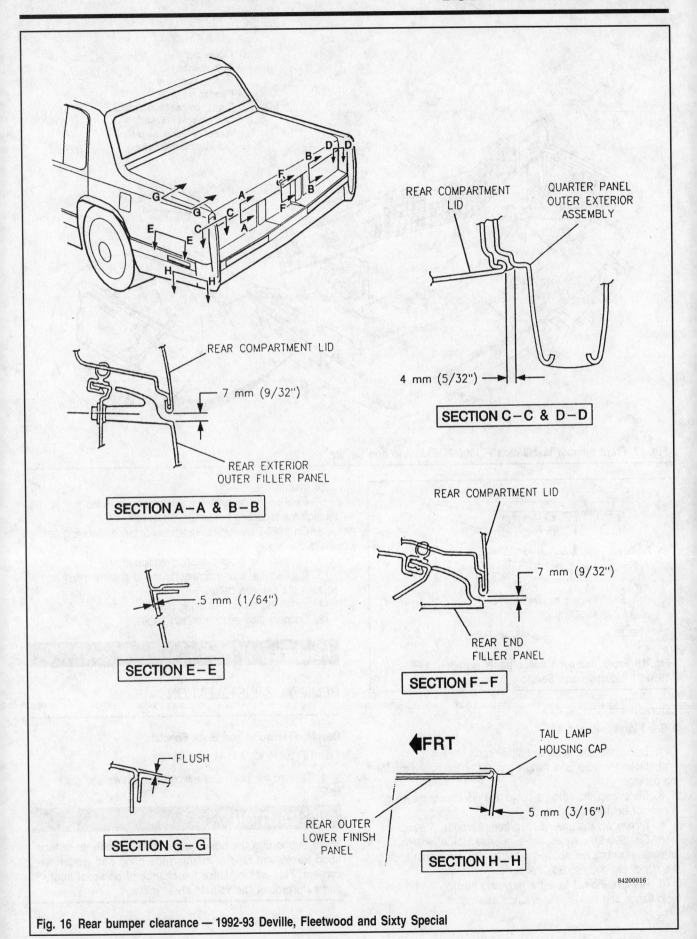

REAR COMPARTMENT LID

QUARTER PANEL OUTER EXTERIOR ASSEMBLY

4 mm (5/32")

SECTION C–C & D–D

REAR COMPARTMENT LID

7 mm (9/32")

REAR EXTERIOR OUTER FILLER PANEL

SECTION A–A & B–B

.5 mm (1/64")

SECTION E–E

REAR COMPARTMENT LID

7 mm (9/32")

REAR END FILLER PANEL

SECTION F–F

FLUSH

SECTION G–G

FRT

TAIL LAMP HOUSING CAP

5 mm (3/16")

REAR OUTER LOWER FINISH PANEL

SECTION H–H

84200016

Fig. 16 Rear bumper clearance — 1992-93 Deville, Fleetwood and Sixty Special

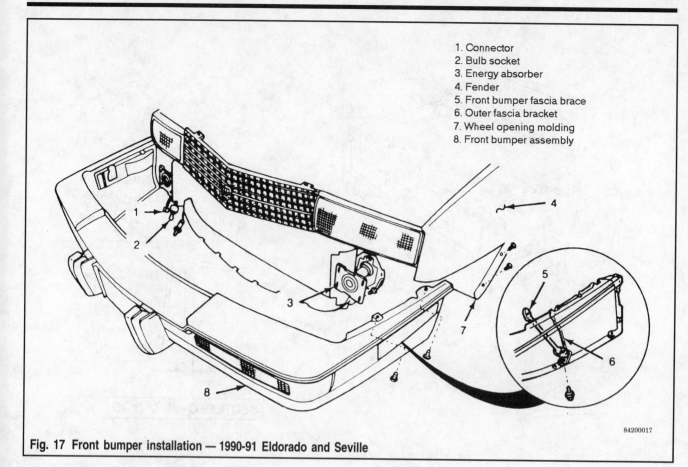

1. Connector
2. Bulb socket
3. Energy absorber
4. Fender
5. Front bumper fascia brace
6. Outer fascia bracket
7. Wheel opening molding
8. Front bumper assembly

84200017

Fig. 17 Front bumper installation — 1990-91 Eldorado and Seville

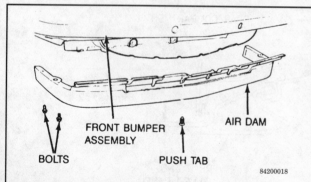

BOLTS

FRONT BUMPER ASSEMBLY

PUSH TAB

AIR DAM

84200018

Fig. 18 Front bumper valance panel installation — 1990-91 Eldorado and Seville

Eldorado and Seville

▶ See Figures 40 and 41

1. Disconnect the negative battery cable.
2. Open the trunk and remove the right-hand sound insulating panel.
3. Disconnect the antenna cable and disconnect the wiring connector from the relay.
4. Disconnect the ground strap from the body, if equipped.
5. On 1990-91 vehicles, use a suitable tool to remove the antenna mounting nut above the fender. Be careful not to strip the nut or slip and damage the paint.
6. Remove the nut from the mounting bracket to wheelwell weld flange and remove the antenna assembly.

To install:

7. Position the antenna assembly and install the nut through the mounting bracket to wheelwell.
8. On 1990-91 vehicles, install the antenna mounting nut above the fender.
9. Connect the ground strap, if equipped.
10. Connect the wiring connector to the antenna relay and connect the antenna cable.
11. Install the sound insulating panel.
12. Connect the negative battery cable.

Fenders

REMOVAL & INSTALLATION

Deville, Fleetwood and Sixty Special

▶ See Figures 42, 43, 44 and 45

1. Support the hood and remove the 2 bolts and gas spring.

❊❊CAUTION

When supporting the hood, place braces evenly to reduce hood travel, and tape or cushion the hood and fender corners. This will minimize the chance of personal injury and help protect the vehicle sheet metal.

2. Remove the cornering lamp and bezel.

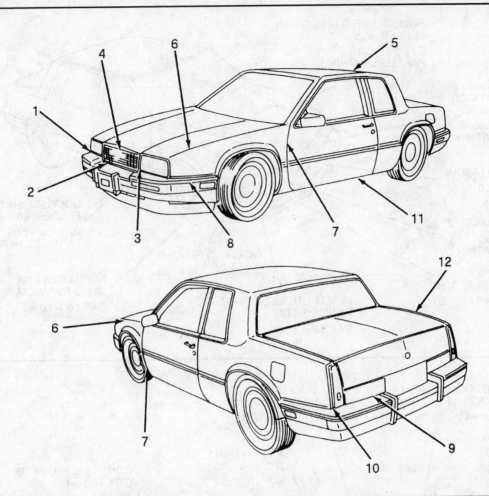

LOCATION	CLEARANCE GAP MM	FLUSHNESS
1 BUMPER FASCIA TO HEAD LAMP FILLER	5.0 mm ± 1 mm	—
2 BUMPER FASCIA TO GRILLE	5.0 mm ± 1 mm	—
3 GRILLE TO HEAD LAMP CAPSULE FILLER	3.0 mm ± 2 mm	—
4 HOOD TO GRILLE	5.0 mm ± 1 mm	-5.5 mm ± 1.5 mm
5 DOOR TO ROOF	6.0 mm ± 1 mm	1.0 mm ± .5 mm
6 HOOD TO FENDER	3.5 mm + 1.5 — 1.0 mm	.5 mm DOWN TO 1.5 mm UP
7 FENDER TO DOOR	5.0 mm ± 1 mm	FLUSH TO 1.5 mm IN
8 BUMPER UPPER FASCIA TO FENDER	3.0 mm + 2. — 1.0 mm	—
9 REAR END PANEL TO BUMPER FASCIA	5.0 mm ± 1 mm	—
10 QUARTER PANEL TO BUMPER FASCIA	3.0 mm + 2. — 1.0 mm	—
11 DOOR TO ROCKER PANEL	6.0 mm + 1.5 — 1.0 mm	—
12 LID TO QUARTER PANEL	4.0 mm ± 1.5 mm	FLUSH TO 1.5 mm DOWN

84200019

Fig. 19 Body panel clearances — 1990-91 Eldorado

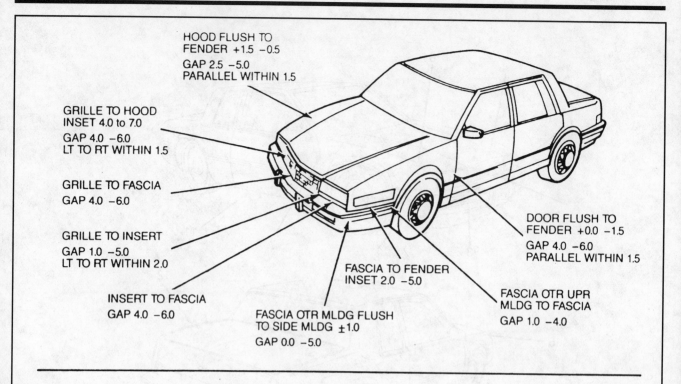

HOOD FLUSH TO
FENDER +1.5 −0.5
GAP 2.5 −5.0
PARALLEL WITHIN 1.5

GRILLE TO HOOD
INSET 4.0 to 7.0
GAP 4.0 −6.0
LT TO RT WITHIN 1.5

GRILLE TO FASCIA
GAP 4.0 −6.0

GRILLE TO INSERT
GAP 1.0 −5.0
LT TO RT WITHIN 2.0

INSERT TO FASCIA
GAP 4.0 −6.0

FASCIA OTR MLDG FLUSH
TO SIDE MLDG ±1.0
GAP 0.0 −5.0

FASCIA TO FENDER
INSET 2.0 −5.0

DOOR FLUSH TO
FENDER +0.0 −1.5
GAP 4.0 −6.0
PARALLEL WITHIN 1.5

FASCIA OTR UPR
MLDG TO FASCIA
GAP 1.0 −4.0

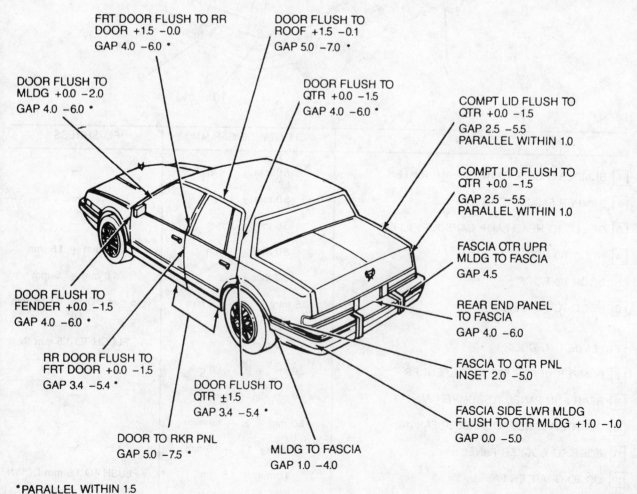

FRT DOOR FLUSH TO RR
DOOR +1.5 −0.0
GAP 4.0 −6.0 *

DOOR FLUSH TO
ROOF +1.5 −0.1
GAP 5.0 −7.0 *

DOOR FLUSH TO
MLDG +0.0 −2.0
GAP 4.0 −6.0 *

DOOR FLUSH TO
QTR +0.0 −1.5
GAP 4.0 −6.0 *

COMPT LID FLUSH TO
QTR +0.0 −1.5
GAP 2.5 −5.5
PARALLEL WITHIN 1.0

COMPT LID FLUSH TO
QTR +0.0 −1.5
GAP 2.5 −5.5
PARALLEL WITHIN 1.0

FASCIA OTR UPR
MLDG TO FASCIA
GAP 4.5

REAR END PANEL
TO FASCIA
GAP 4.0 −6.0

DOOR FLUSH TO
FENDER +0.0 −1.5
GAP 4.0 −6.0 *

RR DOOR FLUSH TO
FRT DOOR +0.0 −1.5
GAP 3.4 −5.4 *

DOOR TO RKR PNL
GAP 5.0 −7.5 *

DOOR FLUSH TO
QTR ±1.5
GAP 3.4 −5.4 *

MLDG TO FASCIA
GAP 1.0 −4.0

FASCIA TO QTR PNL
INSET 2.0 −5.0

FASCIA SIDE LWR MLDG
FLUSH TO OTR MLDG +1.0 −1.0
GAP 0.0 −5.0

*PARALLEL WITHIN 1.5

Fig. 20 Body panel clearances — 1990-91 Seville

84200020

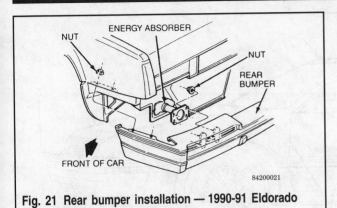

Fig. 21 Rear bumper installation — 1990-91 Eldorado and Seville

3. Remove the screws and the wheel opening moulding.
4. Remove the wheelwell filler panel as follows:
   a. Raise and safely support the vehicle.
   b. Remove the wheel and tire assembly.
   c. Remove the necessary screws, bolts and retainers and remove the filler panel.
5. Remove the fender moulding.
6. Remove the 2 screws and the support bracket.
7. Remove the bolt and nut.
8. Remove the sound filler insulator.
9. Remove the 2 screws and the front bracket.
10. Disconnect the forward lamp monitor.
11. Remove the fender assembly bolts and the fender.

To install:
12. Install the fender assembly. Be careful when positioning the fascia and headlamp mounting.
13. Connect the forward lamp monitor.
14. Install the 2 screws and bracket.
15. Install the sound filler insulator.
16. Install the nut and tighten to 20 ft. lbs. (27 Nm).
17. Install the bolt and tighten to 90 inch lbs. (10 Nm).
18. Install the support bracket and the 2 screws.
19. Install the fender moulding.
20. Install the wheelwell filler panel as follows:
   a. Position the filler panel and install the retainers, bolts and screws.
   b. Install the wheel and tire assembly.
   c. Lower the vehicle.
21. Install the wheel opening moulding and secure with the screws.
22. Install the cornering lamp and bezel.
23. Install the hood bolts and shims.
24. Adjust the sheet metal to the proper tolerances, as shown in the appropriate illustration.

Eldorado and Seville

1990-91

▶ **See Figures 19, 20, 46, 47, 48 and 49**

1. Remove the sill plate insert.
2. Remove the 4 sill plate screws and the sill plate.
3. Remove the 14 front wheelwell panel extension screws and one bolt.
4. Remove the wheelwell inner filler panel.

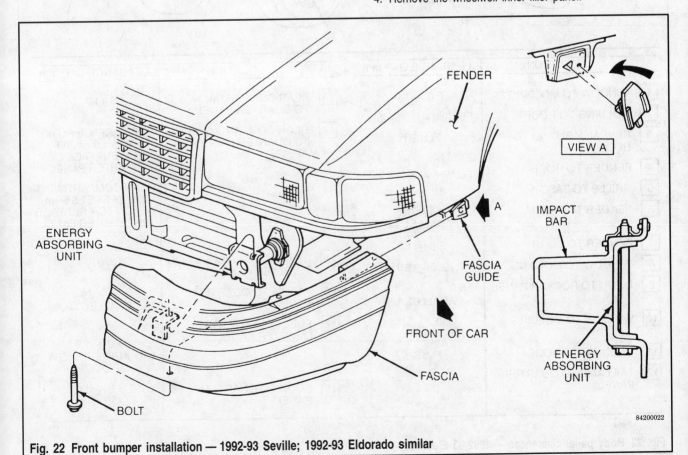

Fig. 22 Front bumper installation — 1992-93 Seville; 1992-93 Eldorado similar

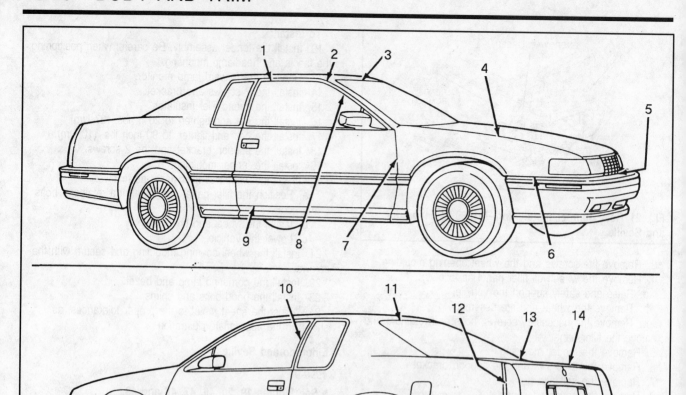

LOCATION		CLEARANCE GAP mm
1	WINDOW TO MOLDING	5.0 ± 1.0
2	MOLDING TO ROOF	FLUSH + 0.0 – 2.0
3	REVEAL MOLDING TO ROOF	FLUSH
4	FENDER TO HOOD	4.0 ± 1.0 FLUSH +2.0 – 1.0
5	GRILLE TO FASCIA	8.0 ± 2.0
6	FENDER TO FASCIA	2.5 – 6.0 PARALLEL 1.0
7	FENDER TO DOOR	5.0 ± 1.0
8	WINDOW TO MOLDING	6.0 ± 1.0
9	DOOR TO ROCKER PANEL	6.0 + 1.5 – 1.0 PARALLEL 1.5
10	WINDOW TO MOLDING	10.0 ± 5.0
11	MOLDING TO ROOF	FLUSH
12	TAILLAMP TO QUARTER PANEL	0.75 ± 0.5

LOCATION		CLEARANCE GAP mm
13	REAR COMPARTMENT LID TO QUARTER PANEL	4.0 ± 1.0
14	REAR COMPARTMENT LID TO QUARTER PANEL AT SIDE	TOP SURFACE FLUSH TO –1.0mm TO TOP SURFACE OF QUARTER PANEL REAR COMPARTMENT LID OFFSET 5.5mm BELOW TOP SURFACE OF QUARTER PANEL
15	REAR COMPARTMENT LID TO FILLER PANEL	5.0
16	FASCIA TO QUARTER PANEL	2.5 – 6.0 PARALLEL 1.0
17	FUEL FILLER DOOR TO QUARTER PANEL	3.0 ± 1.0 AROUND PERIPHERY OF DOOR
18	DOOR TO QUARTER PANEL	5.0 ± 1.0

Fig. 23 Body panel clearances — 1992-93 Eldorado

84200023

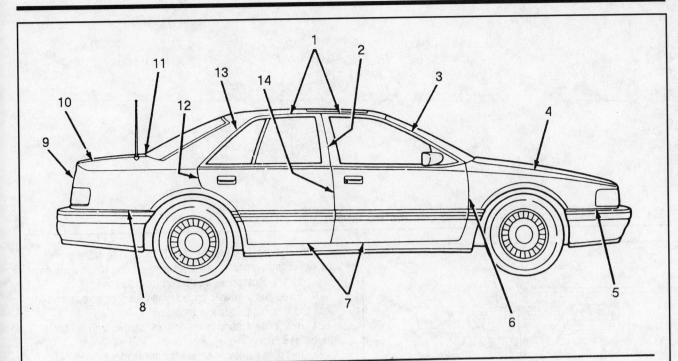

LOCATION		CLEARANCE GAP mm
1	DOOR TO ROOF	6.0 ± 1.0

2	FRONT DOOR TO REAR DOOR
	    WITHOUT MOLDING
	    WITH MOLDING
		
		10.0 ± 1.0
		5.0 ± 1.0

3	DOOR TO MOLDING	5.0 ± 1.0
4	FENDER TO HOOD	4.0 ± 1.0 FLUSH TO −1.0
5	FENDER TO FASCIA	2.5 – 6.0 PARALLEL 1.0
6	DOOR TO FENDER	5.0 ± 1.0
7	DOOR EDGE TO BODY OR MOLDING (STS)	6.0 + 1.5 – 1.0
8	FASCIA TO QUARTER PANEL	2.5 – 6.0 PARALLEL 1.0
9	REAR COMPARTMENT LID TO QUARTER PANEL	4.0 ± 1.0 FLUSH ± 1.0
10	REAR COMPARTMENT LID TO QUARTER PANEL	4.0 ± 1.0 FLUSH +0.0 TO −1.5
11	REAR COMPARTMENT LID TO REAR WINDOW	9.3
12	DOOR TO REAR QUARTER PANEL	5.0 ± 1.0
13	DOOR TO ROOF QUARTER	5.0 ± 1.0
14	FRONT DOOR TO REAR DOOR	5.0 ± 1.0
	FUEL FILLER DOOR (NOT SHOWN)	4.0 ± 1.0 AROUND PERIPHERY OF DOOR TO QUARTER PANEL

84200024

Fig. 24 Body panel clearances — 1992-93 Seville

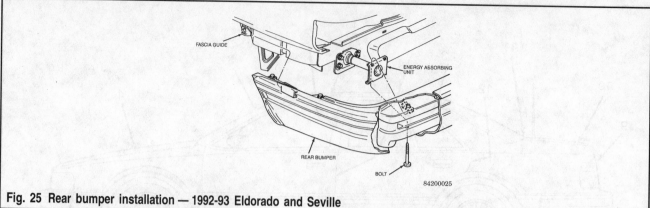

Fig. 25 Rear bumper installation — 1992-93 Eldorado and Seville

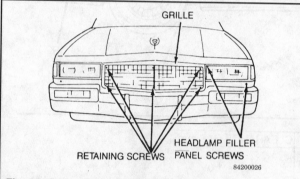

Fig. 26 Grille and headlamp filler panel mounting screw locations — 1990 Deville and Fleetwood

5. Remove the wheel opening moulding screws and the wheel opening moulding.

6. Remove the 2 screws from above the cornering lamp.

7. Remove the rocker panel moulding.

8. Remove the 2 lower screws from the fender.

9. Support the hood and remove the 4 hood hinge-to-body screws.

✳✳CAUTION

When supporting the hood, place braces evenly to reduce hood travel, and tape or cushion the hood and fender corners. This will minimize the chance of personal injury and help protect the vehicle sheet metal.

10. Remove the hood hinge stop bumper.

11. Remove the 4 upper fender-to-body screws.

12. Remove the headlamp-to-fascia moulding screw and the headlamp-to-fascia moulding.

13. Remove the 2 headlamp housing-to-fender screws.

14. Remove the sound filler insulator.

15. Disconnect the fiber optics connector and remove the fender assembly.

To install:

16. Position the fender assembly and connect the fiber optics connector.

17. Install the sound filler insulator.

18. Install the 4 upper fender-to-body screws and tighten to 9 ft. lbs. (12 Nm).

19. Install the hood hinge stop bumper. The bumper must be set at the proper height to eliminate hood hinge damage. Refer to the appropriate illustration for reference.

20. Install the 2 headlamp housing-to-fender screws and install the headlamp-to-fascia moulding.

21. Install the 4 hood hinge-to-body screws and tighten to 9 ft. lbs. (12 Nm).

22. Install the 2 lower screws to the fender.

23. Install the rocker panel moulding.

24. Install the 2 screws above the cornering lamps.

25. Install the wheel opening moulding and the wheelwell inner panel.

26. Install the sill plate and the sill plate insert.

27. Adjust the sheet metal to the proper tolerances, as shown in Figs. 19 and 20.

1992-93

▶ See Figures 23, 24, 50, 51, 52, 53 and 54

1. Disconnect the negative battery cable.

2. Remove the headlamp housing cover and engine compartment fuse and relay center cover.

3. Remove the headlamp housing assembly from Eldorado as follows:

  a. Remove the upper filler panel.

  b. Remove the bolt retaining the cornering lamp housing.

  c. Disconnect the cornering lamp sockets.

  d. Remove the 2 nuts retaining the headlamp housing assembly to the fender and the 2 bolts retaining the headlamp housing to the rail.

  e. Remove the lower headlamp housing-to-body bolt.

  f. Disconnect the wiring harness connector and remove the headlamp housing assembly.

4. Remove the headlamp housing assembly from Seville as follows:

  a. Remove the 4 push pins and the upper filler panel.

  b. Remove the clip retaining the cornering lamp to the headlamp housing module.

  c. Remove the 6 bolts and 4 nuts retaining the headlamp module to the rail.

  d. Disconnect the wiring harness connector and remove the headlamp housing assembly.

5. Remove the wheelwell panel extension and wheelwell panel.

6. Remove the wheel opening moulding.

7. Remove the fender sound insulator.

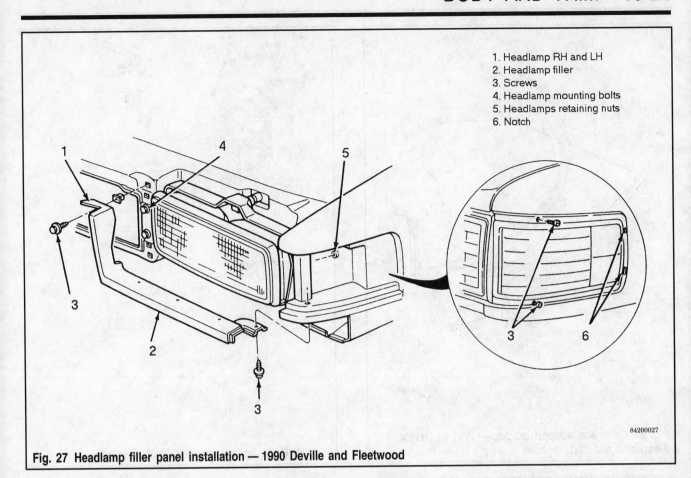

1. Headlamp RH and LH
2. Headlamp filler
3. Screws
4. Headlamp mounting bolts
5. Headlamps retaining nuts
6. Notch

84200027

Fig. 27 Headlamp filler panel installation — 1990 Deville and Fleetwood

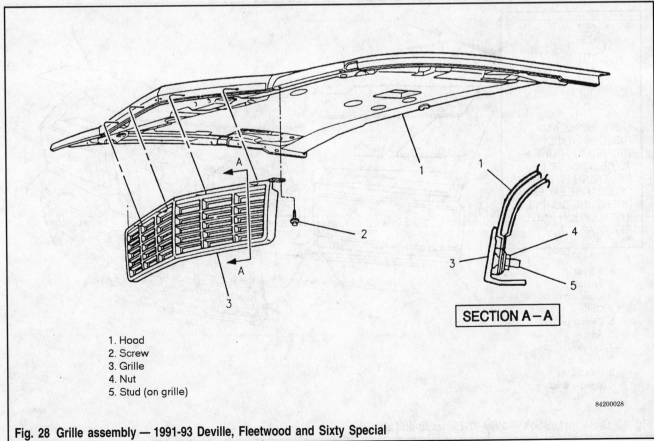

1. Hood
2. Screw
3. Grille
4. Nut
5. Stud (on grille)

SECTION A—A

84200028

Fig. 28 Grille assembly — 1991-93 Deville, Fleetwood and Sixty Special

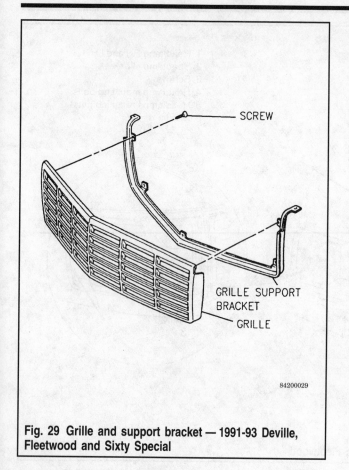

SCREW

GRILLE SUPPORT
BRACKET

GRILLE

84200029

Fig. 29 Grille and support bracket — 1991-93 Deville, Fleetwood and Sixty Special

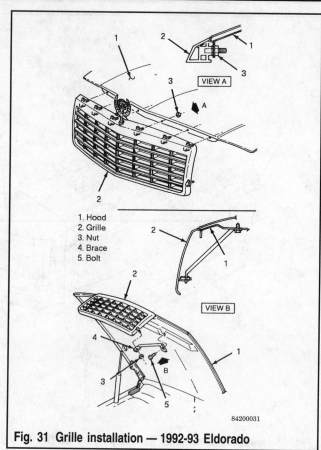

VIEW A

1. Hood
2. Grille
3. Nut
4. Brace
5. Bolt

VIEW B

84200031

Fig. 31 Grille installation — 1992-93 Eldorado

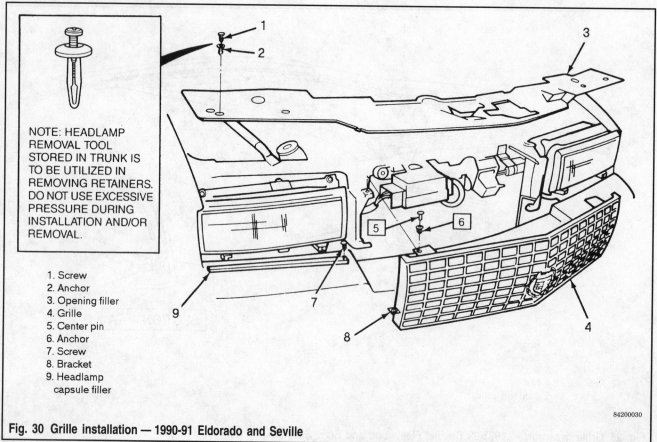

NOTE: HEADLAMP
REMOVAL TOOL
STORED IN TRUNK IS
TO BE UTILIZED IN
REMOVING RETAINERS.
DO NOT USE EXCESSIVE
PRESSURE DURING
INSTALLATION AND/OR
REMOVAL.

1. Screw
2. Anchor
3. Opening filler
4. Grille
5. Center pin
6. Anchor
7. Screw
8. Bracket
9. Headlamp
   capsule filler

84200030

Fig. 30 Grille installation — 1990-91 Eldorado and Seville

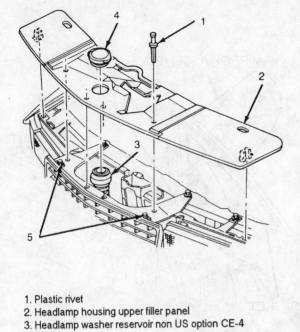

1. Plastic rivet
2. Headlamp housing upper filler panel
3. Headlamp washer reservoir non US option CE-4
4. Headlamp washer reservoir cap (if equipped)
5. Pushpins

84200032

Fig. 32 Headlamp housing upper filler panel installation — 1992-93 Seville

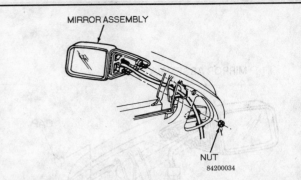

84200034

Fig. 34 Outside mirror installation — 1990-91 Deville and Fleetwood

8. Remove the screws, retaining clip and the front rocker panel moulding.
9. Support the hood and remove the 2 hood hinge-to-fender screws.

❋❋CAUTION

When supporting the hood, place braces evenly to reduce hood travel, and tape or cushion the hood and fender corners. This will minimize the chance of personal injury and help protect the vehicle sheet metal.

10. Remove the 2 bolts retaining the fender at the rocker panel and the 2 bolts retaining the fender to the fascia sliding mount.

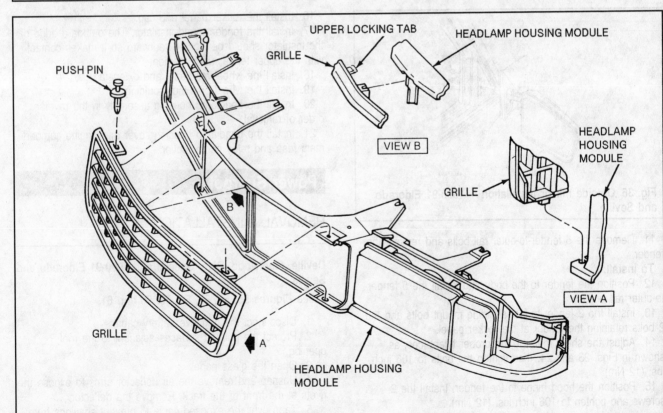

84200033

Fig. 33 Grille installation — 1992-93 Seville

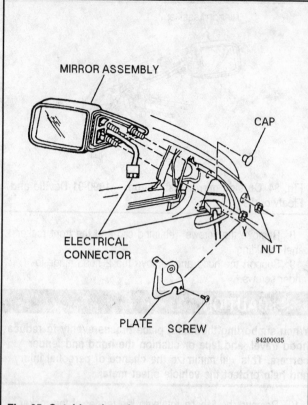

Fig. 35 Outside mirror installation — 1992-93 Deville, Fleetwood and Sixty Special

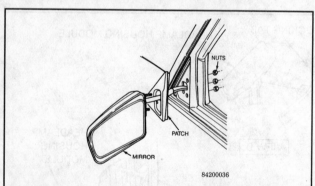

Fig. 36 Outside mirror installation — 1990-91 Eldorado and Seville

11. Remove the 5 fender-to-outer rail bolts and remove the fender.

To install:

12. Position the fender to the body and install the 5 fender-to-outer rail bolts.

13. Install the 2 fender-to-fascia sliding mount bolts and the 2 bolts retaining the fender at the rocker panel.

14. Adjust the sheet metal to the proper tolerances, as shown in Figs. 23 and 24, then tighten the bolts to 106 inch lbs. (12 Nm).

15. Position the hood hinge to the fender. Install the 2 screws and tighten to 106 inch lbs. (12 Nm).

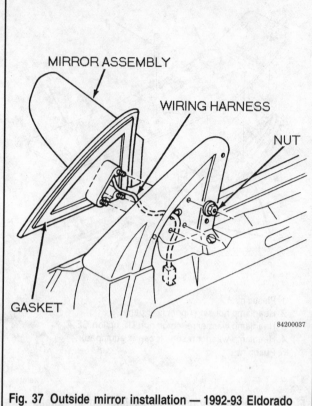

Fig. 37 Outside mirror installation — 1992-93 Eldorado and Seville

16. Install the rocker panel end cap.

17. Install the fender sound insulator. The outboard edge of the insulator should be located rearward so it makes contact with the upper fender reinforcement.

18. Install the wheelwell panel and extension.

19. Install the wheel opening moulding.

20. Install the headlamp housing assembly in the reverse order of removal.

21. Install the headlamp housing cover and engine compartment fuse and relay center cover.

Power Sunroof

REMOVAL & INSTALLATION

Deville, Fleetwood, Sixty Special and 1990-91 Eldorado and Seville

▶ See Figures 55, 56, 57, 58, 59, 60 and 61

1. Disconnect the negative battery cable.

2. Protect the painted surfaces adjacent to the roof opening.

3. Open the glass panel.

4. Unsnap and remove the air deflector arms to expose the rivets at the front of the track. Remove the deflector.

5. Tape over the exposed cable to prevent shavings from entering the track.

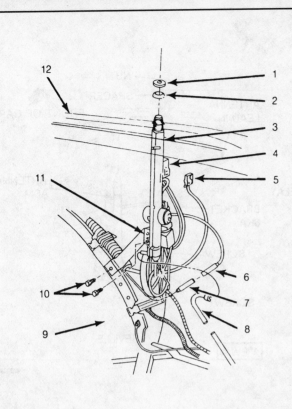

1. NUT; 4 N•M (35 LB-IN)
2. BEZEL
3. POWER ANTENNA ASSEMBLY
4. POWER ANTENNA RELAY
5. RELAY CONNECTOR (BODY HARNESS)
6. LEAD-IN CABLE
7. ANTENNA CABLE
8. DRAIN HOSE
9. RIGHT REAR WHEELHOUSE
10. BOLT/SCREW; 7 N•M (62 LB-IN)
11. BRACKET
12. RIGHT REAR QUARTERPANEL

84200038

Fig. 38 Antenna installation — 1990-91 Deville and Fleetwood

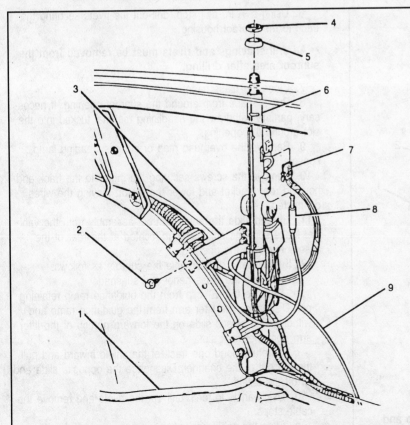

1   RH REAR WHEELHOUSE

2   SCREW; 8 N·m (71 LB-FT)

3   BRACKET

4   NUT; 4 N·m (35 LB-FT)

5   BEZEL

6   POWER ANTENNA

7   RELAY CONNECTOR

8   COAX CABLE LEAD

9   DRAIN HOSE

84200039

Fig. 39 Antenna installation — 1992-93 Deville, Fleetwood and Sixty Special

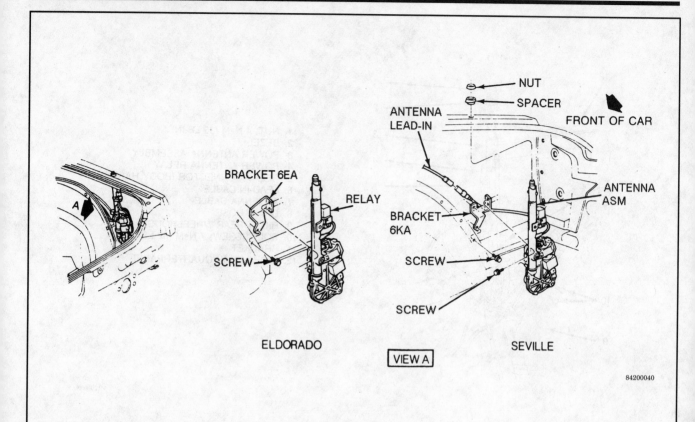

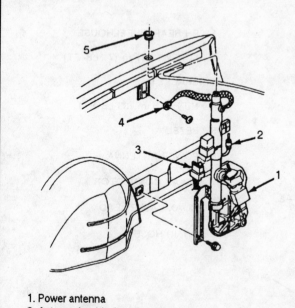

Fig. 40 Antenna installation — 1990-91 Eldorado and Seville

1. Power antenna
2. Antenna lead-in (coax) cable
3. Motor relay connector
4. Ground strap
5. Insulator

84200041

Fig. 41 Antenna installation — 1992-93 Eldorado and Seville

6. Using a ⅜ in. drill stop, drill out the rivets securing the track to the sunroof housing.

➡️ **All drill shavings and rivets must be removed from the sunroof area after drilling.**

7. Close the glass panel.

8. Pull the lace from around the sunroof opening. If necessary, partially withdraw the headlining material tucked into the slot around the opening.

9. Remove the overhead map or courtesy/reading lamp console.

10. Remove the screws securing the motor to the track and housing roof bracket and lower the motor, leaving the wires connected.

11. Lift and slide the entire sunroof assembly from the vehicle. Make sure the shield trough located at the rear of the assembly clears the opening.

12. If necessary, disassemble the sunroof as follows:

   a. Remove the glass panel and sunshade.

   b. Remove the 'E" clip from the guidance ramp retaining pin. Disengage the lifter arm from the guidance ramp and withdraw the plastic slide on the forward portion of the lifter arm from the track slot.

   c. Carefully bend one track of the shield inward and pull the tab out of the channel. Disengage the opposite slide and lift off the shield.

   d. Using an ⅛ in. drill, drill out the rivets and remove the cable stops.

   e. Slide the cable assembly out the rear end of the track.

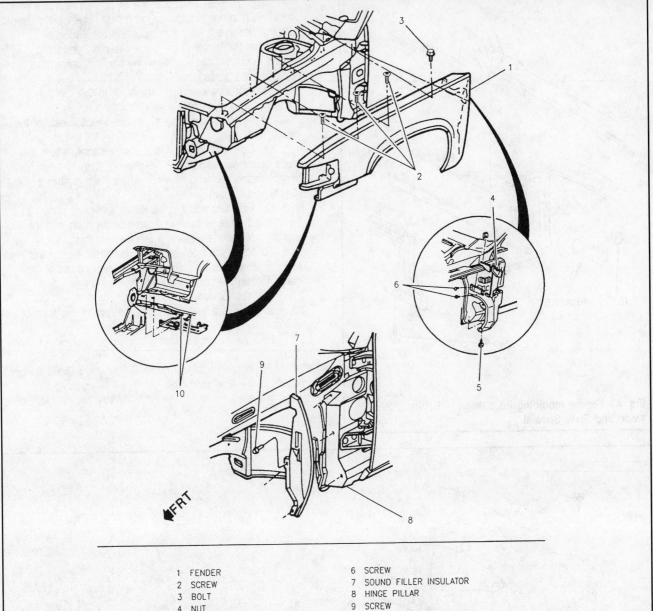

1	FENDER	6	SCREW
2	SCREW	7	SOUND FILLER INSULATOR
3	BOLT	8	HINGE PILLAR
4	NUT	9	SCREW
5	SCREW	10	SCREW

84200042

Fig. 42 Fender installation — Deville, Fleetwood and Sixty Special

To install:

13. If necessary, assemble the sunroof as follows:

   a. Only replace the cables in sets. Sparingly lubricate the cables with Lubriplate #70 or equivalent.

   b. Slide the cable assembly into the track and rivet the cable stops on.

   c. Install the shield.

   d. Install the lifter arms, sunshade and glass panel.

14. Apply a little zinc rich primer to the rivet holes.

15. Lower and slide the sunroof assembly into the roof opening.

➡If the sunroof assembly and motor are removed, both the motor and track must be synchronized for proper system operation.

16. Synchronize the motor and track as follows:

   a. Close the glass, or, if the glass is removed, make sure the lifter arms align with the tracks.

   b. Release the gear synchronizing lever from the notch on the motor casting and rotate the lever in the direction of the arrow on the motor casting. The cams should turn freely when the lever is released. If the cams do not turn freely, make sure the lever is rotated fully upward.

   c. Manually rotate the small cam using a 4mm hex wrench until the aligning mark (hole in large cam) is aligned with centerline drawn through shafts of the large and small cams.

   d. Return the synchronizing lever to the notched position.

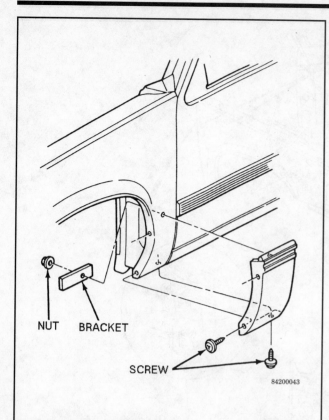

Fig. 43 Fender moulding installation — Deville, Fleetwood and Sixty Special

e. Align the lifter arms with the track slots. Install a 4mm hex wrench into the guidance ramp hole. Line up the wrench with the slot in the lifter arm mounting bracket.

17. Secure the motor to the track assembly and lamp mounting bracket. Connect the wiring harness connectors.

18. Open the glass panel.

19. Install the rivets securing the track to the sunroof.

20. Adjust the glass height as follows:

a. Loosen the 3 adjustment screws on each side of the glass.

b. On Deville, Fleetwood and Sixty Special, adjust the glass height so the front of the glass is flush to 1mm below flush with the roof and the rear of the glass is flush to 1/8 in. (3mm) above flush.

c. On Eldorado and Seville, adjust the glass height so the front of the glass is flush to 1.5mm below flush with the roof and the rear of the glass is 1.5mm above flush.

d. To adjust the front corner of the glass, loosen the front and center screws only. To adjust the rear corner of the glass, loosen the center and rear screws only.

21. Install the air deflector.

22. Install the lace and headlining material to the sunroof opening.

23. Install the overhead maplight or courtesy/reading lamp console.

24. Remove the protective material from the painted surfaces adjacent to the roof opening.

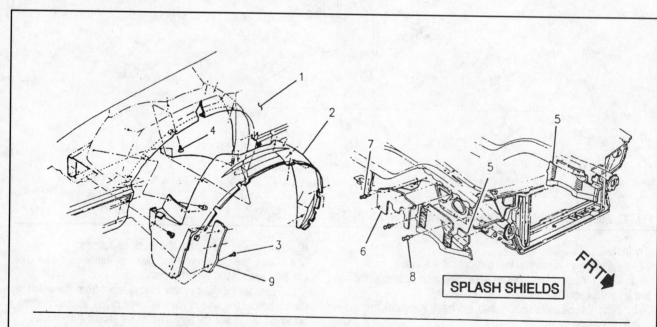

1	LH FENDER	4	SCREW	7	RETAINER
2	WHEELHOUSE FILLER PANEL RH AND LH	5	ENGINE SPLASH SHIELD FRONT	8	RETAINER
3	RETAINER	6	ENGINE SPLASH SHIELD REAR RH	9	DEFLECTOR

Fig. 44 Wheelwell filler panel installation — Deville, Fleetwood and Sixty Special

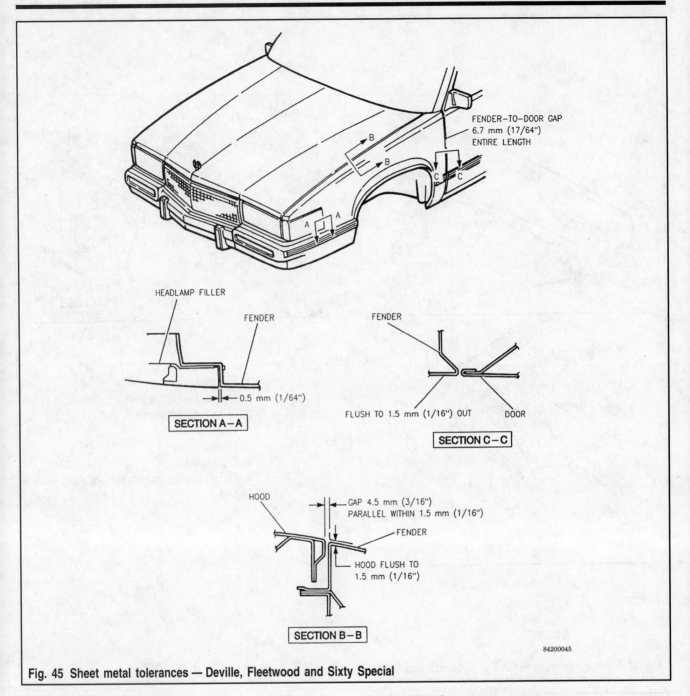

Fig. 45 Sheet metal tolerances — Deville, Fleetwood and Sixty Special

1992-93 Eldorado and Seville

▶ **See Figures 62, 63, 64, 65 and 66**

1. Disconnect the negative battery cable.
2. Protect the painted surfaces adjacent to the roof opening.
3. Open the glass panel.
4. Remove the 12 retaining screws. Do not remove the 4 machine screws retaining the track cover rails.
5. Close the glass panel.
6. Remove the power sunroof motor cover.
7. Remove the 2 screws securing the motor to the track assembly and remove the motor. Before disconnecting the motor wiring connector, perform the following operation to ensure proper track and motor synchronization at reassembly:

   a. Connect the negative battery cable.
   b. Turn the ignition switch **ON**.
   c. Move the sunroof switch to the rear position for several seconds and release the switch.
   d. Push the switch into forward position and hold until the motor stops.
   e. Turn the ignition switch **OFF** and disconnect the negative battery cable. Do not move the sunroof switch until after the motor is reinstalled.

8. Pull the relays from the brackets, disconnect the wiring connector and remove the motor and relays.
9. Lift and slide the entire sunroof assembly from the vehicle.

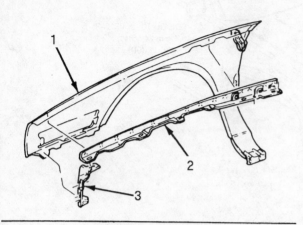

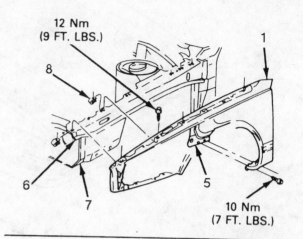

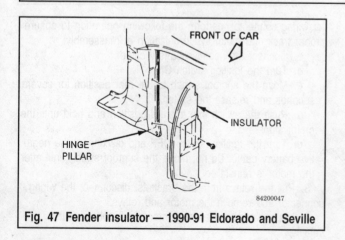

1. Fender
2. Upper reinforcement
3. Front reinforcement
4. Reinforcement
5. Hinge pillar
6. Outer rail
7. Panel motor compartment side
8. Nut

12 Nm
(9 FT. LBS.)

10 Nm
(7 FT. LBS.)

12 Nm
(9 FT. LBS.)

12 Nm
(9 FT. LBS.)

84200046

Fig. 46 Fender assembly — 1990-91 Eldorado and Seville

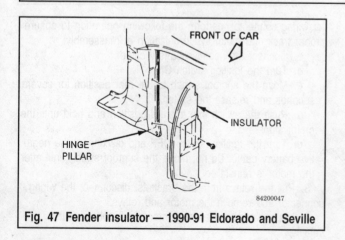

Fig. 47 Fender insulator — 1990-91 Eldorado and Seville

FRONT OF CAR

INSULATOR

HINGE
PILLAR

84200047

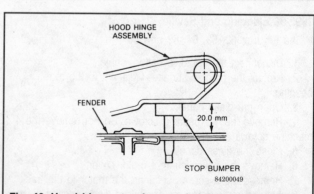

HOOD HINGE
ASSEMBLY

FENDER

20.0 mm

STOP BUMPER

84200049

Fig. 48 Hood hinge stop bumper height — 1990-91 Eldorado and Seville

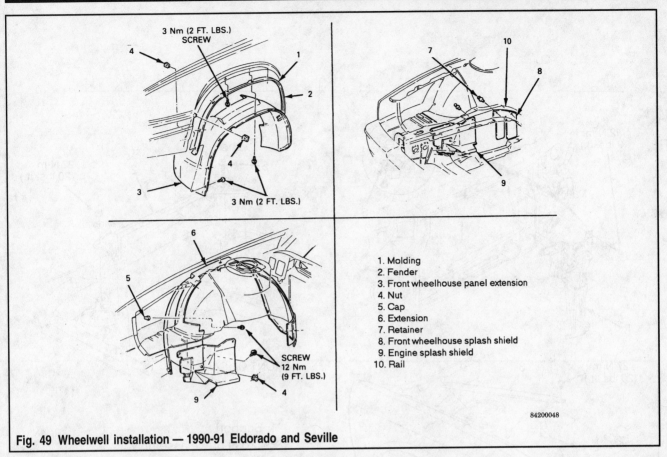

3 Nm (2 FT. LBS.)
SCREW

3 Nm (2 FT. LBS.)

SCREW
12 Nm
(9 FT. LBS.)

1. Molding
2. Fender
3. Front wheelhouse panel extension
4. Nut
5. Cap
6. Extension
7. Retainer
8. Front wheelhouse splash shield
9. Engine splash shield
10. Rail

84200048

Fig. 49 Wheelwell installation — 1990-91 Eldorado and Seville

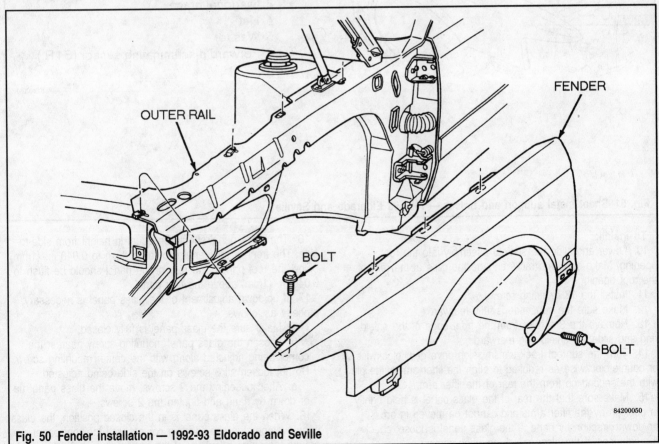

OUTER RAIL

FENDER

BOLT

BOLT

84200050

Fig. 50 Fender installation — 1992-93 Eldorado and Seville

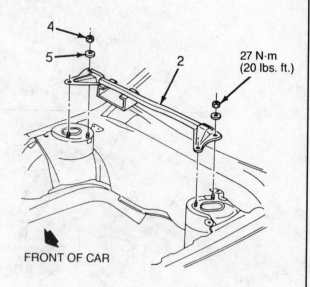
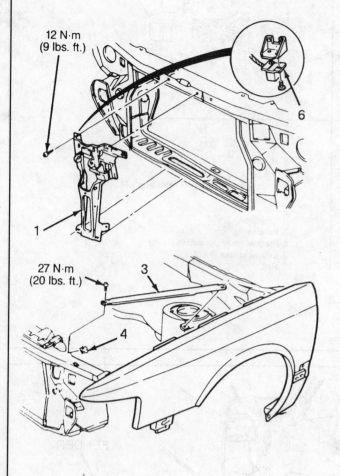

12 N·m
(9 lbs. ft.)

27 N·m
(20 lbs. ft.)

4

5

6

1

3

4

2

27 N·m
(20 lbs. ft.)

FRONT OF CAR

1. Support
2. Cross brace assembly
3. Diagonal brace
4. Nut
5. Washer
6. Forward discriminating sensor (S.I.R.)

84200051

Fig. 51 Sheet metal support and braces — 1992-93 Eldorado and Seville

To install:

10. Lower and slide the sunroof assembly into the roof opening. Make sure the tracks engage the clips at the rear of the roof opening.

11. Install the 12 retaining screws.

12. Make sure the sunshade is fully rearward.

13. Remove the 3 screws from the front edge of the shield ring and slide the shield ring rearward.

14. Turn the sunroof track transmission drive gear clockwise or counterclockwise as required to align the lifter arm guide pin with the second rib from the rear of the lifter arm.

15. Make sure that the rear of the glass panel is held tightly in position by the lifter arms and cannot be moved in an up/down direction by hand. If the glass panel is loose, check the tightness of the glass panel mounting screws.

16. The glass panel should be equal in height from side-to-side. The front of the panel should be flush to 0.040 in. (1mm) below the roof panel. The rear of the panel should be flush to 0.040 in. (1mm) above the roof panel.

17. If up/down adjustment of the glass panel is necessary, proceed as follows:

   a. Make sure the glass panel is fully closed.

   b. Loosen the glass panel mounting screw nearest the corner being adjusted along with the center mounting screw. Do not loosen all 3 screws on the side being adjusted.

   c. After loosening the 2 screws, move the glass panel up or down by hand and tighten the 2 screws.

18. When the glass panel is in the closed position, the glass panel weatherstrip should have contact with the roof panel around the entire periphery of the seal, without being crushed

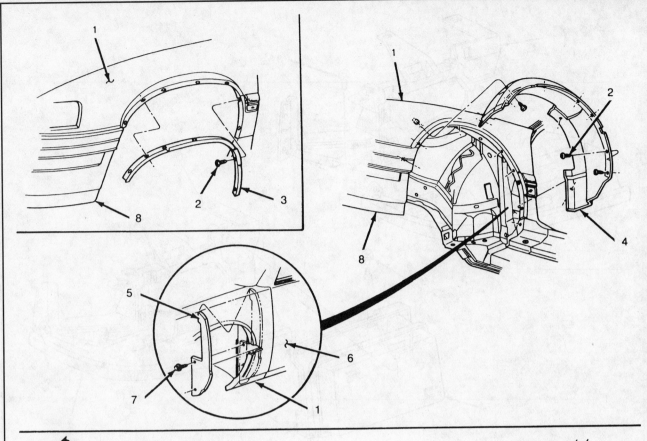

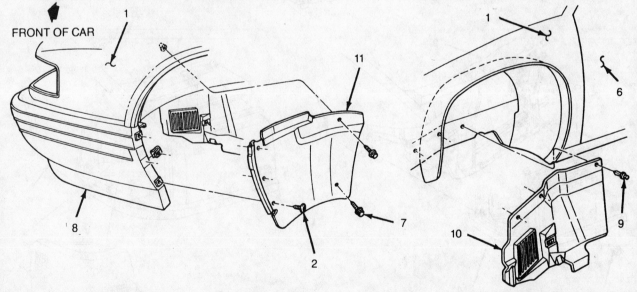

1	FENDER	7	BOLT
2	SCREW	8	FASCIA
3	WHEEL OPENING MOLDING	9	PUSH PIN
4	WHEEL HOUSE PANEL	10	ENGINE SPLASH SHIELD
5	FENDER SOUND INSULATOR	11	FRONT FASCIA PANEL EXTENSION
6	DOOR		

84200052

Fig. 52 Wheelwell attachments — 1992-93 Eldorado and Seville

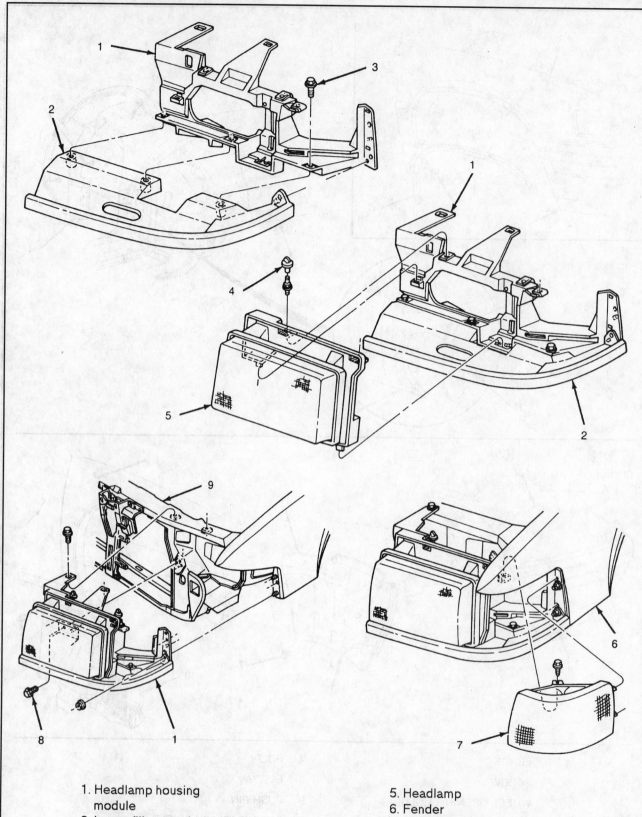

1. Headlamp housing module
2. Lower filler panel
3. Bolt
4. Upper filler panel retainer
5. Headlamp
6. Fender
7. Cornering lamp
8. Lower headlamp housing bolt
9. Motor compartment forward rail

Fig. 53 Headlamp housing assembly installation — 1992-93 Eldorado

84200053

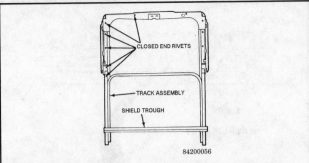

Fig. 55 Power sunroof track assembly — Deville, Fleetwood, Sixty Special and 1990-91 Eldorado and Seville

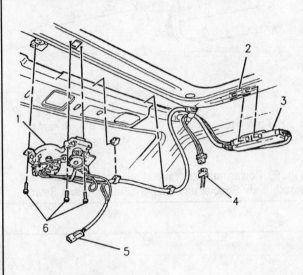

1. Motor
2. Express module bracket
3. Express module
4. Wiring harness connector
5. Sunroof switch connector
6. Screws

Fig. 56 Power sunroof motor and express module — Deville, Fleetwood and Sixty Special

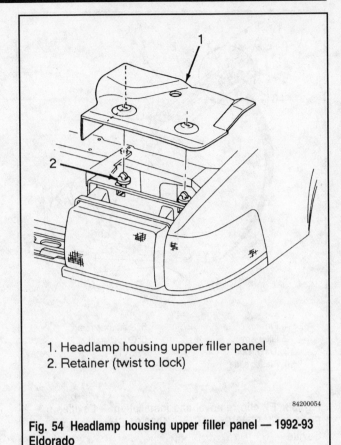

1. Headlamp housing upper filler panel
2. Retainer (twist to lock)

Fig. 54 Headlamp housing upper filler panel — 1992-93 Eldorado

1. Motor
2. Relay
3. Bracket
4. Relay mounting tab
5. Rivet
6. Sunroof switch connector
7. Manual cranking hole (4 mm HEX)

Fig. 57 Power sunroof motor and relay — 1990-91 Eldorado and Seville

at either end. Check for seal contact by inserting a business card or feeler gauge between the seal and roof panel and dragging it around the entire contact area. The card or feeler gauge should make continuous contact with the seal and roof panel.

19. If fore/aft adjustment of the glass panel is necessary, proceed as follows:

    a. Fully open the glass panel.

    b. Working from the top of the vehicle, note the position of the track assembly on the fore/aft adjustment scale.

    c. Loosen the track cover rail screws on both sides of the sunroof module. Loosen only those screws called out in illustration '84200068' for fore/aft adjustment.

    d. Slide the track cover rail on both sides forward or rearward as required (one or two notches on adjustment

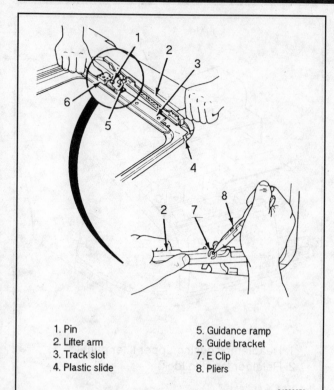

1. Pin
2. Lifter arm
3. Track slot
4. Plastic slide

5. Guidance ramp
6. Guide bracket
7. E Clip
8. Pliers

84200059

Fig. 58 'E" clip removal and installation — Deville, Fleetwood, Sixty Special and 1990-91 Eldorado and Seville

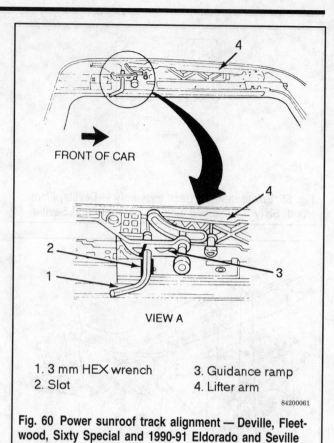

VIEW A

1. 3 mm HEX wrench
2. Slot

3. Guidance ramp
4. Lifter arm

84200061

Fig. 60 Power sunroof track alignment — Deville, Fleetwood, Sixty Special and 1990-91 Eldorado and Seville

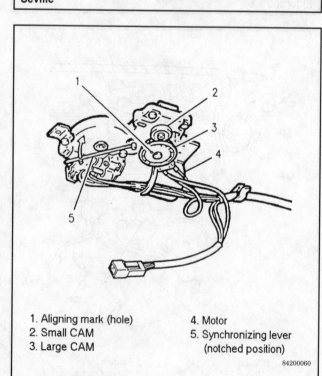

1. Aligning mark (hole)
2. Small CAM
3. Large CAM

4. Motor
5. Synchronizing lever (notched position)

84200060

Fig. 59 Power sunroof motor synchronization — Deville, Fleetwood, Sixty Special and 1990-91 Eldorado and Seville

FRONT OF CAR

1. Shield
2. Sunshade
3. Glass adjustment screws
   0.8-1.5 N m (7-13 in.-lb.)

84200062

Fig. 61 Power sunroof glass adjustment and retaining screws — Deville, Fleetwood, Sixty Special and 1990-91 Eldorado and Seville

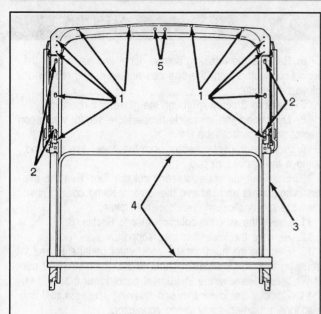

1. Screws (course thread)
2. Cover rail screws (fine thread)
3. Track assembly
4. Shield ring
5. Motor mounting holes

84200063

Fig. 62 Power sunroof track retaining screws — 1992-93 Eldorado and Seville

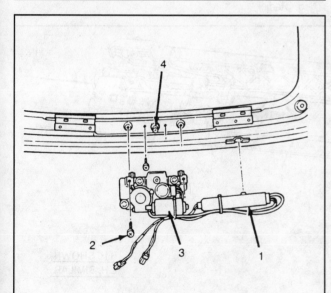

1. Express open module
2. Screws
3. Motor
4. Track transmission drive gear

84200064

Fig. 63 Power sunroof motor and module — 1992-93 Eldorado and Seville

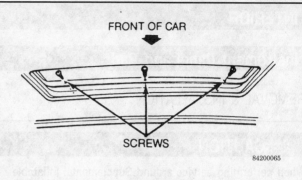

FRONT OF CAR

SCREWS

84200065

Fig. 64 Power sunroof shield ring — 1992-93 Eldorado and Seville

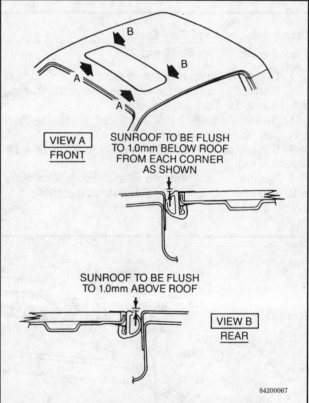

VIEW A
FRONT

SUNROOF TO BE FLUSH TO 1.0mm BELOW ROOF FROM EACH CORNER AS SHOWN

SUNROOF TO BE FLUSH TO 1.0mm ABOVE ROOF

VIEW B
REAR

84200067

Fig. 65 Power sunroof glass panel up/down adjustment — 1992-93 Eldorado and Seville

scale). Tighten the screws. Make sure the left and right tracks are positioned evenly fore/aft.

e. Close the glass panel and inspect the seal position as in Step 18. Repeat adjustment as necessary.

20. Reinstall the shield ring with the 3 screws.

21. Install the relays to the brackets and connect the motor wiring connector. Position the motor to the track assembly and install the retaining screws.

22. Install the sunroof motor cover.

23. Connect the negative battery cable. Turn the ignition **ON** and verify proper operation by cycling the sunroof from closed to vent and fully open positions.

INTERIOR

Instrument Panel and Pad

REMOVAL & INSTALLATION

❋❋CAUTION

When performing service around Supplemental Inflatable Restraint (SIR) system components or wiring, the SIR system must be disabled. Failure to do so could result in possible air bag deployment, personal injury or unneeded SIR system repairs.

Deville, Fleetwood and Sixty Special
▶ See Figures 67, 68, 69, 70 and 71

1. Disconnect the negative battery cable.
2. Disable the Supplemental Inflatable Restraint (SIR) system. Refer to the procedure in Section 6.
3. Remove the push-on nuts and screws and remove the right, then left sound insulators.
4. Carefully pry the heating/air conditioning outlets from the upper trim pad.
5. Remove the upper trim pad retaining screws. One screw is found behind each outlet and 3 screws are accessed through the defroster outlet.

6. Remove the retaining screws, label and disconnect the wiring connectors from the switches and light, and remove the glove box module.
7. Remove 2 screws through the glove box opening.
8. Disconnect the in-vehicle temperature sensor wiring connector and aspirator tube.
9. Remove the solar sensor from the upper trim pad and remove the upper trim pad.
10. Snap out the upper steering column filler. Remove the retaining screws and remove the lower steering column filler, then the steering column reinforcement plate.
11. Lower the steering column; refer to Section 8.
12. Remove the lower trim pad support.
13. Remove the nut from the accelerator pedal stud and the screw(s) from the instrument panel end of the instrument panel lower brace. Remove the instrument panel lower brace.
14. Remove the lower trim pad retaining screws. Label and disconnect the necessary wiring connectors.
15. Remove the lower trim pad with the aid of an assistant.
16. If necessary, disassemble the lower trim pad by removing the following components:
   a. Information centers
   b. Trim plates
   c. Headlamp switch
   d. Fuel data center
   e. Climate control panel
   f. Instrument cluster
   g. Radio

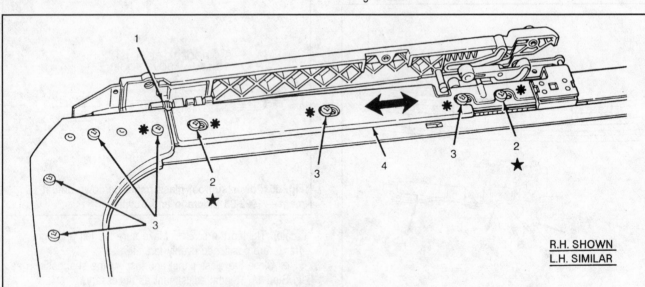

1. For/aft adjustment scale
2. Track cover rail screw (fine thread)
3. Track retaining screw (coarse thread machine screws)
4. Track cover rail

❋ LOOSEN TO ADJUST FOR/AFT

★ DO NOT REMOVE FOR R&R OF MODULE

R.H. SHOWN
L.H. SIMILAR

84200068

Fig. 66 Power sunroof glass panel fore/aft adjustment — 1992-93 Eldorado and Seville

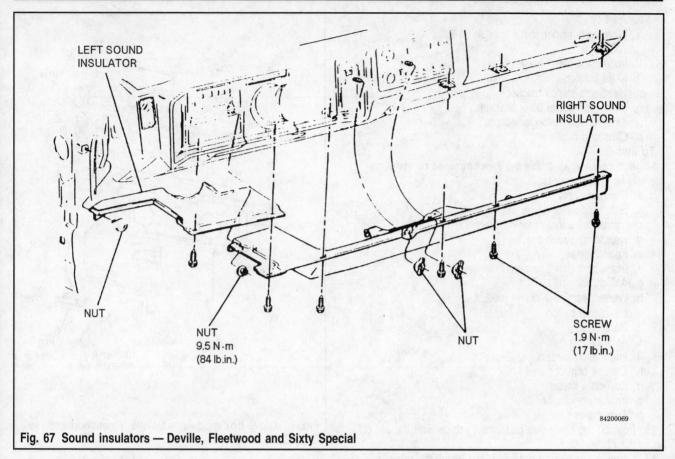

Fig. 67 Sound insulators — Deville, Fleetwood and Sixty Special

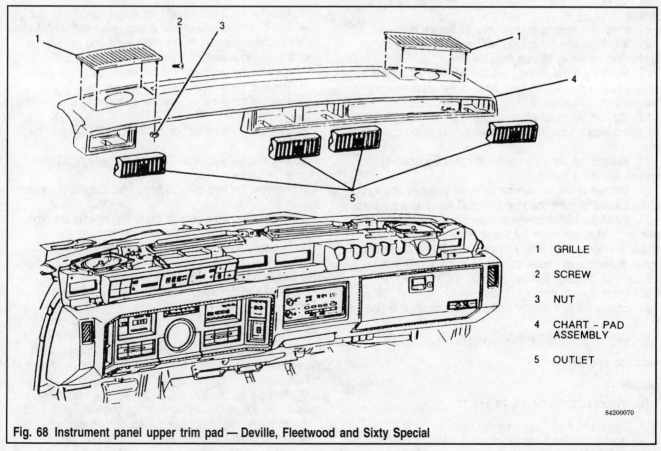

1 GRILLE

2 SCREW

3 NUT

4 CHART – PAD ASSEMBLY

5 OUTLET

Fig. 68 Instrument panel upper trim pad — Deville, Fleetwood and Sixty Special

h. Ashtray
i. Warning/reminder chime module
j. A/C ducts
k. Instrument panel harness
l. Knee bolster
m. Headlamp switch bracket
n. Instrument panel outer brackets
o. Side window defogger outlets
p. Clips and nuts

To install:

17. If necessary, assemble the lower trim pad by installing the following components:
    a. Clips and nuts
    b. Side window defogger outlets
    c. Instrument panel outer brackets
    d. Headlamp switch bracket
    e. Knee bolster
    f. Instrument panel harness
    g. A/C ducts
    h. Warning/reminder chime module
    i. Headlamp switch
    j. Radio
    k. Ashtray
    l. Information centers
    m. Climate control panel
    n. Fuel data center
    o. Instrument cluster
    p. Trim plates

18. Position the lower trim pad in the vehicle with the aid of an assistant.

19. Connect the wiring connectors and install the retaining screws.

20. Install the steering column; refer to Section 8.

21. Install the steering column reinforcement plate and tighten the screws to 17 inch lbs. (1.9 Nm).

22. Install the lower steering column filler and tighten the screws to 13 inch lbs. (1.5 Nm). Snap in the upper steering column filler.

23. Connect the in-vehicle temperature sensor wiring connector and aspirator tube. Install the solar sensor to the upper trim pad.

24. Position the upper trim pad and install the retaining screws. Install the outlets.

25. Connect the wiring connectors to the switches and light and position the glove box module. Install the retaining screws.

26. Install the instrument panel lower brace over the accelerator pedal stud and install the screw at the instrument panel end of the brace. Tighten to 84 inch lbs. (9.5 Nm). Tighten the nut to the accelerator pedal stud to 84 inch lbs. (9.5 Nm).

27. Install the lower trim pad support.

28. Install the left, then right sound insulators.

29. Enable the SIR system. Refer to the procedure in Section 6.

30. Connect the negative battery cable.

Eldorado and Seville

1990-91

▶ **See Figures 72, 73, 74, 75, 76 and 77**

1. Disconnect the negative battery cable.

2. Disable the Supplemental Inflatable Restraint (SIR) system. Refer to the procedure in Section 6.

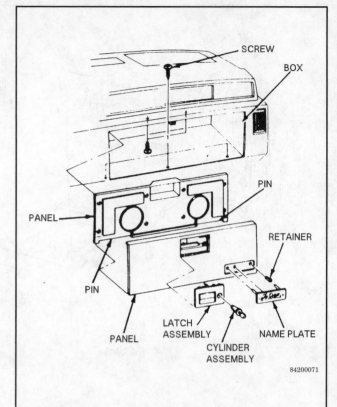

Fig. 69 Glove box module — Deville, Fleetwood and Sixty Special

3. Remove the 3 screws and the center sound insulator.

4. Remove the 3 screws and 2 nuts retaining the right side sound insulator. Remove the courtesy lamp and remove the right side sound insulator.

5. Remove the 2 screws and the center trim plate.

6. Remove the 5 screws and the knee bolster.

7. Remove the 4 screws and the instrument panel steering column reinforcement plate.

8. Remove the steering column; refer to the procedure in Section 8.

9. Remove the 3 screws and the Climate Control/Driver Information Center.

10. Remove the instrument cluster; refer to the procedure in Section 6.

11. Remove the front console assembly; refer to the procedure in this Section.

12. Disconnect the dash-to-instrument panel interconnect.

13. Remove the 4 screws and the glove box unit. Pull the fuse panel up from the dash panel.

14. Label and disconnect the instrument panel wiring connectors.

15. Remove the instrument panel reinforcement brace.

16. Remove the 6 screws retaining the instrument panel. With the aid of an assistant, remove the instrument panel from the vehicle.

To install:

17. With the aid of an assistant, position the instrument panel in the vehicle. Install the retaining screws.

18. Install the instrument panel reinforcement brace.

19. Connect the instrument panel wiring connectors.

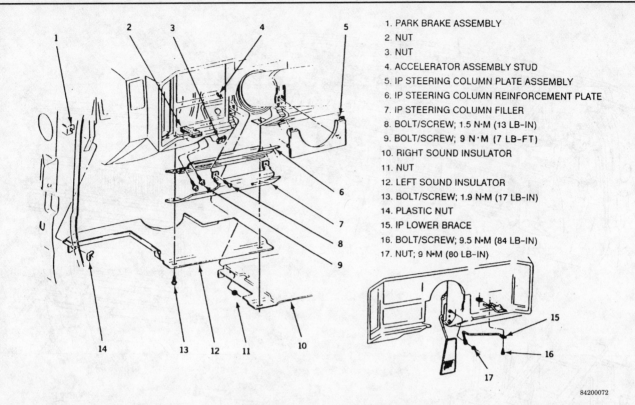

1. PARK BRAKE ASSEMBLY
2. NUT
3. NUT
4. ACCELERATOR ASSEMBLY STUD
5. IP STEERING COLUMN PLATE ASSEMBLY
6. IP STEERING COLUMN REINFORCEMENT PLATE
7. IP STEERING COLUMN FILLER
8. BOLT/SCREW; 1.5 N·M (13 LB-IN)
9. BOLT/SCREW; 9 N·M (7 LB-FT)
10. RIGHT SOUND INSULATOR
11. NUT
12. LEFT SOUND INSULATOR
13. BOLT/SCREW; 1.9 N·M (17 LB-IN)
14. PLASTIC NUT
15. IP LOWER BRACE
16. BOLT/SCREW; 9.5 N·M (84 LB-IN)
17. NUT; 9 N·M (80 LB-IN)

84200072

Fig. 70 Instrument panel steering column reinforcement plate and instrument panel lower brace — Deville, Fleetwood and Sixty Special

20. Push the glove box fuse panel into place in the dash panel. Install the glove box unit with the 4 screws.

21. Connect the dash-to-instrument panel interconnect.

22. Install the front console assembly; refer to the procedure in this Section.

23. Install the instrument cluster; refer to the procedure in Section 6.

24. Install the Climate Control/Driver Information Center with the 3 screws.

25. Install the steering column; refer to the procedure in Section 8.

26. Install the instrument panel steering column reinforcement plate with the 4 screws.

27. Install the knee bolster and the center trim panel.

28. Install the courtesy lamp to the right side sound insulator and install the sound insulator with the nuts and screws.

29. Install the center sound insulator.

30. Enable the SIR system. Refer to the procedure in Section 6.

31. Connect the negative battery cable.

1992-93

▶ **See Figures 78, 79, 80, 81 and 82**

1. Disconnect the negative battery cable.

2. Disable the Supplemental Inflatable Restraint (SIR) system. Refer to the procedure in Section 6.

3. Carefully pry upward, using a small, flat-bladed tool, to remove the defroster grille.

4. Remove the Sunload and Headlamp Auto Control sensors from the defroster grille.

5. Working through the defroster grille opening, remove 3 upper trim panel retaining screws.

6. Remove the heater/air conditioning vents from the front of the instrument panel by releasing the tab on each side from inside the vent and pulling out.

7. Working through the vent openings, remove 4 upper trim panel retaining screws and remove the upper trim panel.

8. Remove the instrument cluster; refer to Section 6.

9. Remove the right and left A/C vent trim panels.

10. Open the trap door in the rear of the glove compartment and remove the the passenger inflatable restraint wiring connector from the retaining clip on the rear of the glove compartment assembly.

11. Remove the 4 glove compartment-to-instrument panel retaining screws.

12. Pull the glove compartment assembly outward enough to access the wiring connectors for the glove compartment switches. Label and disconnect the wiring connectors.

13. Remove the glove compartment assembly from the instrument panel.

14. Remove the retaining screws and courtesy lamps from the right and left sound insulators and remove the sound insulators.

15. Remove the steering column opening filler trim by grasping at the front and rear edges and pulling downward.

16. Remove the 4 retaining bolts and the steering column opening bracket.

17. If equipped with full console, remove the console; refer to the procedure in this Section.

18. If equipped with mini console, remove the radio; refer to Section 6.

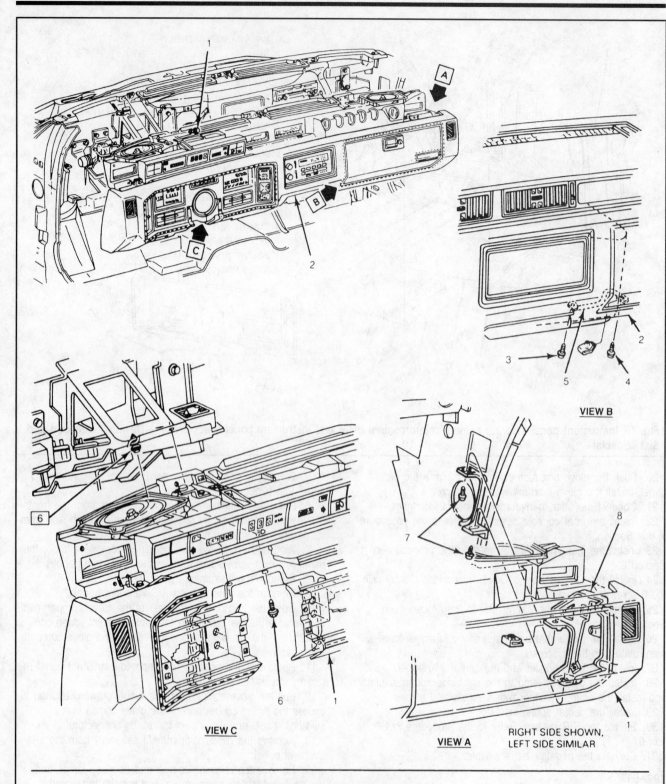

VIEW B

VIEW C

VIEW A

RIGHT SIDE SHOWN,
LEFT SIDE SIMILAR

1. BOLT/SCREW ; 1.9 N•M (17 LB-IN)
2. LOWER TRIM PAD ASSEMBLY
3. BOLT/SCREW; 9 N•M (7 LB-FT)
4. BOLT/SCREW; 12 N•M (9 LB-FT)
5. LOWER TRIM PAD SUPPORT
6. BOLT/SCREW; 12 N•M (106 LB-IN)
7. BOLT/SCREW; 9 N•M (7 LB-FT)
8. I/P OUTER BRACKET

84200073

Fig. 71 Instrument panel lower trim pad — Deville, Fleetwood and Sixty Special

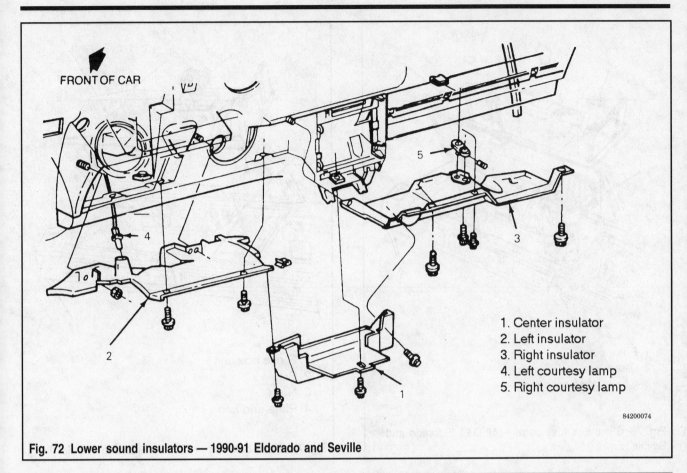

FRONT OF CAR

1. Center insulator
2. Left insulator
3. Right insulator
4. Left courtesy lamp
5. Right courtesy lamp

84200074

Fig. 72 Lower sound insulators — 1990-91 Eldorado and Seville

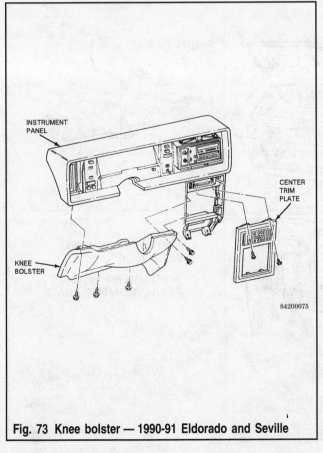

INSTRUMENT PANEL

CENTER TRIM PLATE

KNEE BOLSTER

84200075

Fig. 73 Knee bolster — 1990-91 Eldorado and Seville

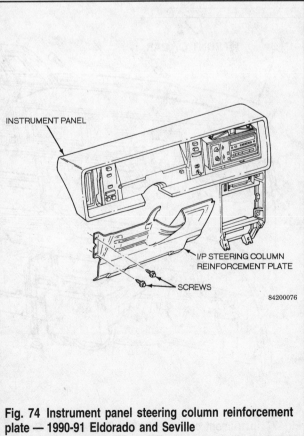

INSTRUMENT PANEL

I/P STEERING COLUMN REINFORCEMENT PLATE

SCREWS

84200076

Fig. 74 Instrument panel steering column reinforcement plate — 1990-91 Eldorado and Seville

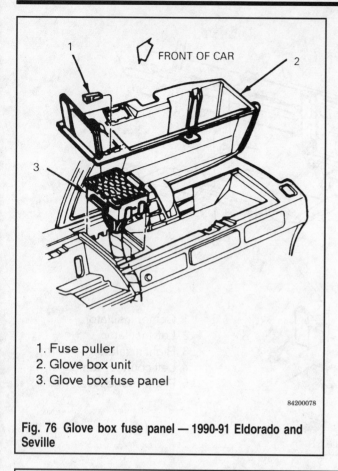

1. Fuse puller
2. Glove box unit
3. Glove box fuse panel

84200078

Fig. 76 Glove box fuse panel — 1990-91 Eldorado and Seville

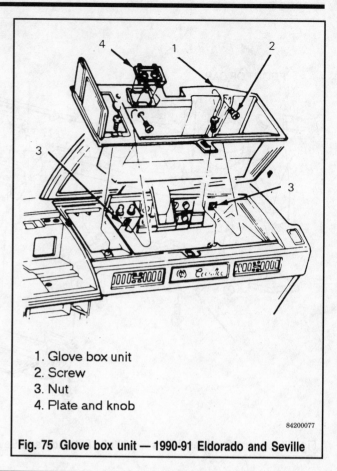

1. Glove box unit
2. Screw
3. Nut
4. Plate and knob

84200077

Fig. 75 Glove box unit — 1990-91 Eldorado and Seville

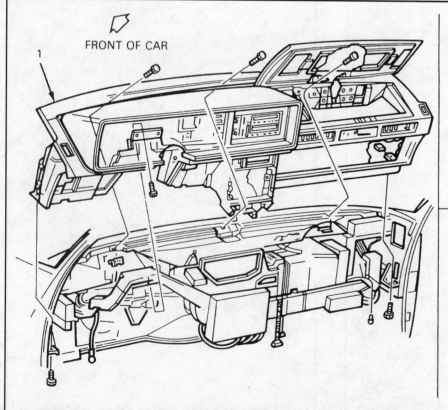
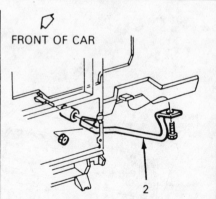

1 INSTRUMENT PANEL
   ASSEMBLY

2 INSTRUMENT PANEL
   REINFORCEMENT BRACE

84200079

Fig. 77 Instrument panel — 1990-91 Eldorado and Seville

19. Remove the headlamp switch module; refer to Section 6.
20. Remove the 2 bolts and the hood latch release.
21. Move the driver's seat to its full rearward position.
22. Remove the steering column; refer to Section 8.
23. Remove the 8 instrument panel retaining screws, disconnect the wiring connector at each side of the instrument panel, and remove the shims at the lower mounting screws.
24. Remove the instrument panel with the aid of an assistant.

To install:

25. With the aid of an assistant, position the instrument panel in the vehicle.
26. Connect the wiring connector at each side of the instrument panel, install the shims and the 8 instrument panel retaining screws.
27. Install the steering column; refer to Section 8.
28. Install the hood latch release with the 2 bolts.
29. Install the headlamp switch module.
30. If equipped with mini console, install the radio.
31. If equipped, install the console.
32. Install the steering column opening bracket and the steering column opening filler trim.
33. Install the right and left sound insulators.
34. Position the glove compartment assembly and connect the wiring connectors to the switches.
35. Push the glove compartment into place and install the retaining screws.
36. Place the passenger inflatable restraint wiring connector on the retaining clip on the rear of the glove compartment assembly and close the trap door.
37. Install the right and left A/C vent trim panels.
38. Install the instrument cluster; refer to Section 6.
39. Position the upper trim panel on top of the instrument panel, making sure the sensors are through the trim panel.
40. Install the upper trim panel retaining screws through the heater/air conditioning vent openings.
41. Gently push the heater/air conditioning vents into place.
42. Install the upper trim panel retaining screws through the defroster grille opening.
43. Install the Sunload and Headlamp Auto Control sensors to the defroster grille.
44. Gently push the defroster grille into place.
45. Enable the SIR system. Refer to the procedure in Section 6.
46. Connect the negative battery cable.

Console

REMOVAL & INSTALLATION

Deville and Fleetwood

1990 VEHICLES WITH 45/55 PNEUMATIC SEAT

▶ **See Figure 83**

1. Disconnect the negative battery cable.
2. Remove the 4 mounting bolts.
3. Disconnect the wiring connector.
4. Remove the console.

To install:

5. Position the console in the vehicle and install the mounting bolts.
6. Connect the wiring connector.
7. Connect the negative battery cable.

Eldorado and Seville

1990-91 FRONT CONSOLE

▶ **See Figures 84, 85, 86, 87 and 88**

1. Disconnect the negative battery cable.
2. Remove the gearshift retaining clip and knob.
3. Remove the 2 retaining screws and remove the storage compartment assembly.
4. Pull the ashtray from the ashtray housing.
5. Disconnect the cigar lighter wiring connector.
6. Remove the retaining screw and the ashtray housing assembly.
7. Remove the 5 upper console retaining screws.
8. Disconnect the illumination bulbs and sockets and remove the upper console assembly.
9. Remove the retaining screw and 2 nuts retaining the lower console to the brackets.
10. Remove the 2 lower console-to-instrument panel retaining screws, the support rod and the lower console.

To install:

11. Install the lower console and support rod.
12. Install the 2 lower console-to-instrument panel retaining screws.
13. Install the screw and 2 nuts securing the lower console to the brackets.
14. Connect the bulbs and sockets to the upper console and install the upper console. Install the 5 upper-to-lower console retaining screws.
15. Install the ashtray housing and connect the cigar lighter wiring connector. Push the ashtray into the housing.
16. Install the storage compartment with the retaining screws.
17. Install the gearshift handle and retaining clip.
18. Connect the negative battery cable.

1990 SEVILLE STS REAR CONSOLE

▶ **See Figures 89 and 90**

1. Disconnect the negative battery cable.
2. Open the upper and lower storage compartment doors. Remove the upper and lower storage compartment boxes by gently prying up and out of the console assembly.
3. Remove the 2 lower retaining bolts and 2 upper retaining screws.
4. Remove the 3 screws retaining the lumbar seat air pump and control assembly from the back of the upper console assembly.
5. Lift and remove the console assembly.

To install:

6. Position the console assembly in the vehicle.
7. Install the lumbar seat air pump and control assembly on the back of the upper console and secure with the 3 screws.
8. Install the console retaining screws and bolts.
9. Snap the upper and lower storage compartment boxes into place.
10. Connect the negative battery cable.

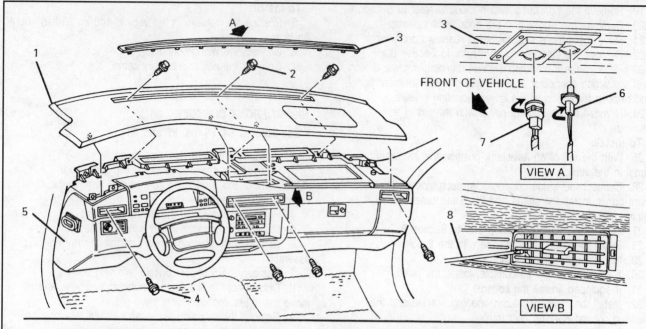

1 INSTRUMENT PANEL UPPER TRIM PANEL
2 SCREWS
3 WINDSHIELD DEFROSTER GRILLE
4 SCREWS

5 INSTRUMENT PANEL CARRIER
6 SUNLOAD SENSOR
7 HEADLAMP AUTO CONTROL AMBIENT LIGHT SENSOR
8 SMALL FLAT-BLADED TOOL

84200080

Fig. 78 Instrument panel upper trim panel — 1992-93 Eldorado and Seville

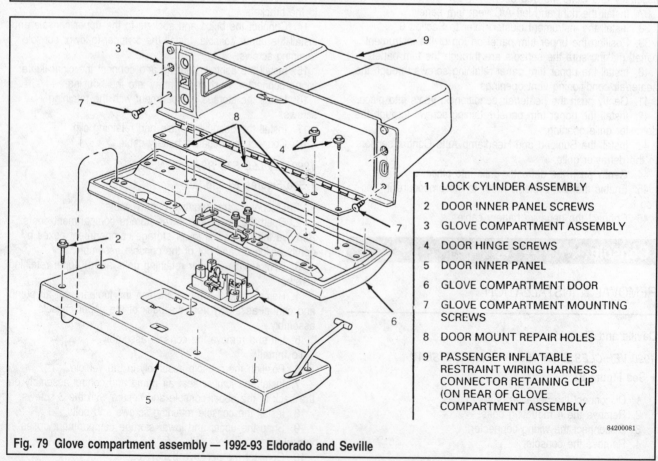

1 LOCK CYLINDER ASSEMBLY
2 DOOR INNER PANEL SCREWS
3 GLOVE COMPARTMENT ASSEMBLY
4 DOOR HINGE SCREWS
5 DOOR INNER PANEL
6 GLOVE COMPARTMENT DOOR
7 GLOVE COMPARTMENT MOUNTING SCREWS
8 DOOR MOUNT REPAIR HOLES
9 PASSENGER INFLATABLE RESTRAINT WIRING HARNESS CONNECTOR RETAINING CLIP (ON REAR OF GLOVE COMPARTMENT ASSEMBLY

84200081

Fig. 79 Glove compartment assembly — 1992-93 Eldorado and Seville

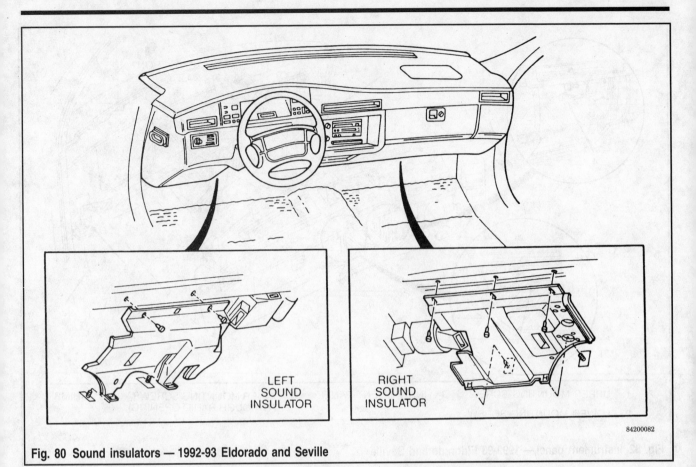

Fig. 80 Sound insulators — 1992-93 Eldorado and Seville

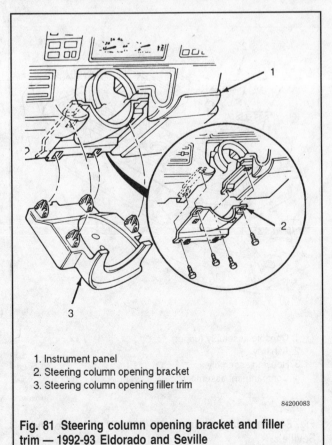

1. Instrument panel
2. Steering column opening bracket
3. Steering column opening filler trim

84200083

Fig. 81 Steering column opening bracket and filler trim — 1992-93 Eldorado and Seville

1992-93 FULL CONSOLE

▶ See Figures 91, 92 and 93

1. Disconnect the negative battery cable.
2. Remove the storage compartment by pulling up and out.
3. Remove the gearshift handle retaining clip and handle.
4. Gently pull the console upper trim plate up and out.
5. Disconnect the wiring connector for the cigar lighter.
6. Remove the radio; refer to Section 6.
7. Remove the 4 console-to-instrument panel retaining screws.
8. Remove the gear selector trim plate, which is retained by clips, and the PRNDL illumination lamp socket.
9. Remove the 2 shifter plate upper mounting bolts and the 2 nuts retaining the shifter assembly to the floor.
10. Working through the storage compartment opening, remove the 2 console-to-floor retaining nuts.
11. Turn to release the console blower air supply duct.
12. Slide the console up, then label and disconnect the wiring connectors.
13. Slide the console back to clear the shifter and remove the console.

To install:

14. Position the console over the shifter and connect the wiring connectors.
15. Turn to push on the console blower air supply duct.
16. Working through the storage compartment opening, install the 2 console-to-floor retaining nuts.
17. Install the 2 shifter assembly-to-floor retaining nuts and the 2 shifter plate upper mounting bolts.

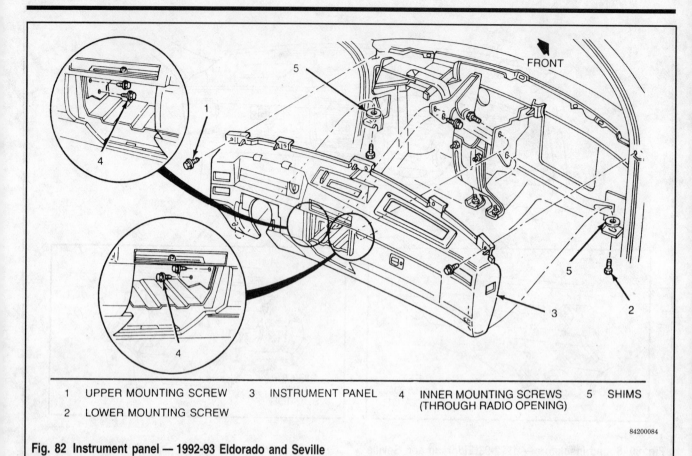

1 UPPER MOUNTING SCREW   3 INSTRUMENT PANEL   4 INNER MOUNTING SCREWS   5 SHIMS
                                                      (THROUGH RADIO OPENING)
2 LOWER MOUNTING SCREW

84200084

Fig. 82 Instrument panel — 1992-93 Eldorado and Seville

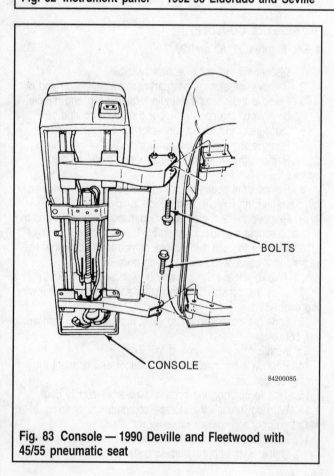

84200085

Fig. 83 Console — 1990 Deville and Fleetwood with 45/55 pneumatic seat

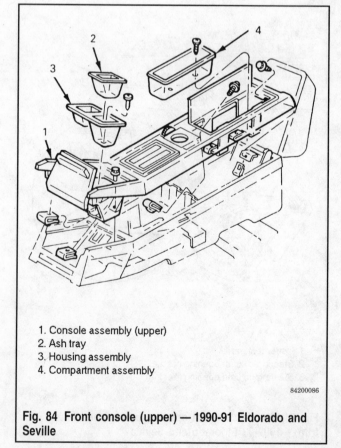

1. Console assembly (upper)
2. Ash tray
3. Housing assembly
4. Compartment assembly

84200086

Fig. 84 Front console (upper) — 1990-91 Eldorado and Seville

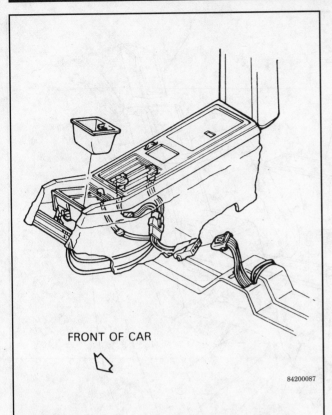

Fig. 85 Front console wiring — 1990-91 Eldorado and Seville

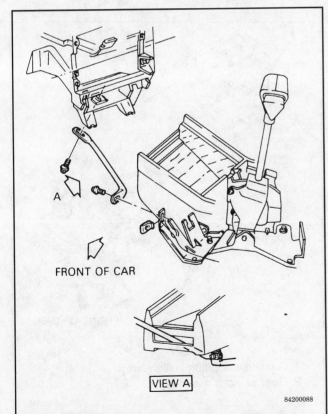

VIEW A

Fig. 86 Instrument panel support rod — 1990-91 Eldorado and Seville

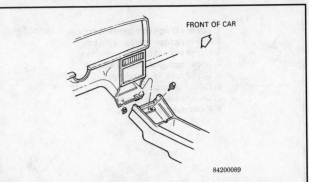

Fig. 87 Front console-to-instrument panel attachment — 1990-91 Eldorado and Seville

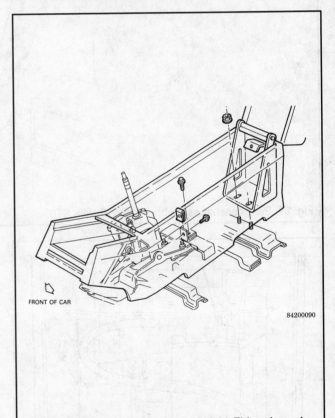

Fig. 88 Front console (lower) — 1990-91 Eldorado and Seville

18. Install the PRNDL illumination lamp socket and gear selector trim plate.
19. Install the 4 console-to-instrument panel retaining screws.
20. Install the radio.
21. Connect the wiring connector for the cigar lighter and install the console upper trim plate.
22. Install the gearshift handle and retaining clip.
23. Install the storage compartment.
24. Connect the negative battery cable.

1992-93 MINI CONSOLE

▶ See Figure 94

1. Disconnect the negative battery cable.
2. Pull the storage compartment up and out.

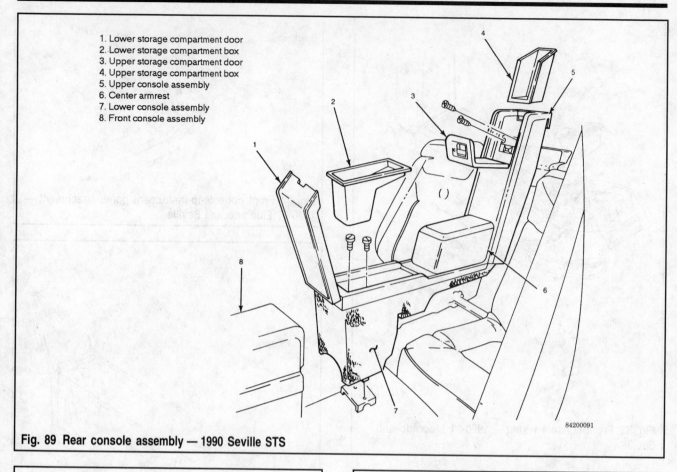

1. Lower storage compartment door
2. Lower storage compartment box
3. Upper storage compartment door
4. Upper storage compartment box
5. Upper console assembly
6. Center armrest
7. Lower console assembly
8. Front console assembly

84200091

Fig. 89 Rear console assembly — 1990 Seville STS

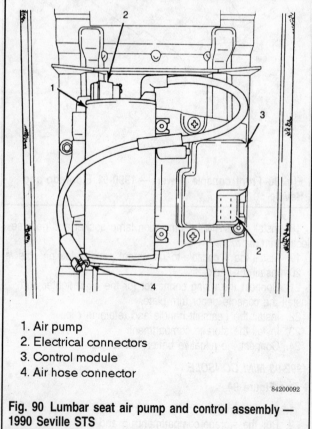

1. Air pump
2. Electrical connectors
3. Control module
4. Air hose connector

84200092

Fig. 90 Lumbar seat air pump and control assembly — 1990 Seville STS

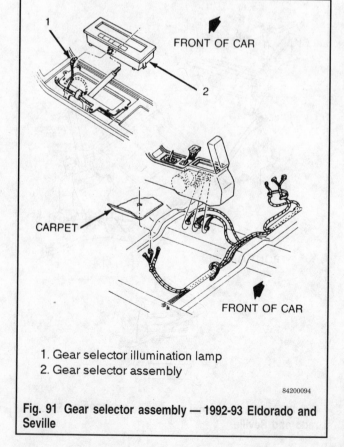

FRONT OF CAR

CARPET

FRONT OF CAR

1. Gear selector illumination lamp
2. Gear selector assembly

84200094

Fig. 91 Gear selector assembly — 1992-93 Eldorado and Seville

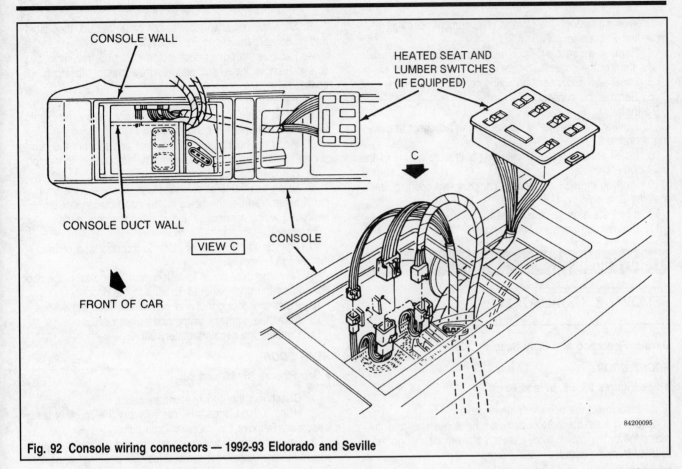

Fig. 92 Console wiring connectors — 1992-93 Eldorado and Seville

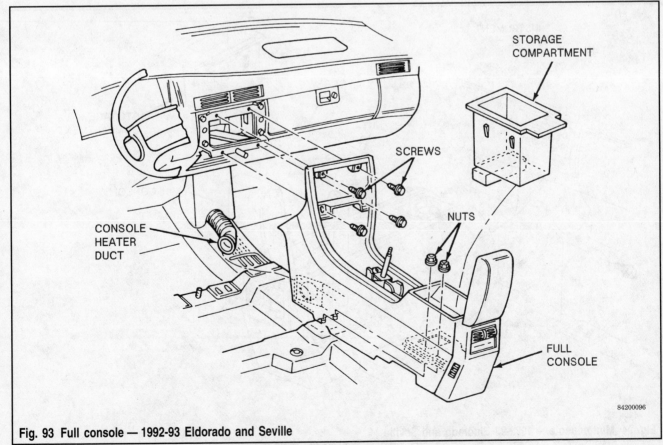

Fig. 93 Full console — 1992-93 Eldorado and Seville

3. Working through the storage compartment opening, remove the 2 retaining nuts.

4. Remove a console-to-floor retaining bolt from each side of the front of the console.

5. Label and disconnect the wiring connectors.

6. Remove the console.

To install:

7. Position the console in the vehicle and connect the wiring connectors.

8. Install a console-to-floor retaining bolt at each side of the front of the console.

9. Working through the storage compartment opening, install the 2 retaining nuts.

10. Install the storage compartment.

11. Connect the negative battery cable.

Door Panels

REMOVAL & INSTALLATION

Deville, Fleetwood and Sixty Special

FRONT DOOR

▶ **See Figures 95, 96, 97 and 98**

1. Disconnect the negative battery cable.

2. Insert a flat-bladed tool between the door panel and the rear edge of the power window switch plate to disengage the retainer from the panel.

3. Slide the power window switch plate forward, then label and disconnect the wiring connectors.

4. Remove the power door lock switch plate retaining screw. Remove the switch plate and disconnect the wiring connector.

5. Remove the pull handle retaining screws.

6. Using a thin-bladed tool, carefully pry the courtesy lamp lenses off. Remove the courtesy lamp bulb.

7. Pinch the courtesy lamp retainers and pull out the lamp socket holder. Disconnect the courtesy lamp wiring connector.

8. Remove the door panel retaining screws.

9. Using tool J-2459B or equivalent, disengage the door panel fasteners from the holes in the door. Disconnect any remaining wiring connectors and remove the door panel.

To install:

10. Position the door panel close to the door and connect the wiring connectors.

11. Align the door panel fasteners with the holes in the door. Push in on the door panel to install it to the door.

12. Install the door panel and pull handle retaining screws.

13. Install the courtesy lamps and switch plates.

14. Connect the negative battery cable.

REAR DOOR

▶ **See Figures 97, 98 and 99**

1. Disconnect the negative battery cable.

2. Using a thin-bladed tool, carefully pry the courtesy lamp lenses off. Remove the courtesy lamp bulb.

3. Pinch the courtesy lamp retainers and pull out the lamp socket holder. Disconnect the courtesy lamp wiring connector.

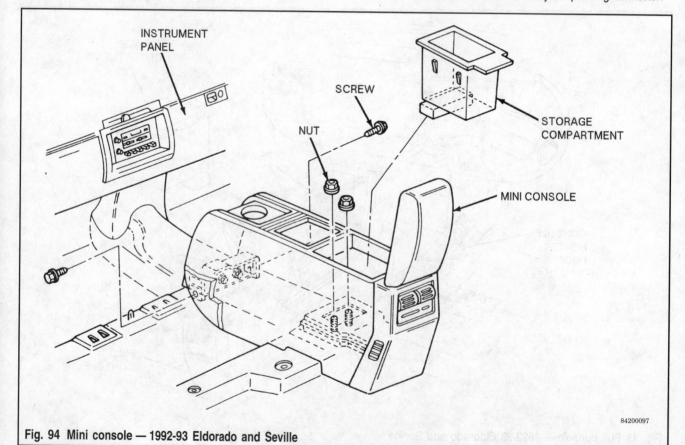

INSTRUMENT PANEL

SCREW

NUT

STORAGE COMPARTMENT

MINI CONSOLE

84200097

Fig. 94 Mini console — 1992-93 Eldorado and Seville

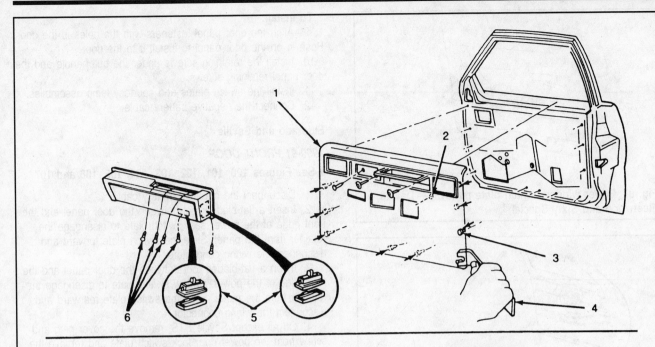

1 TRIM PANEL
2 RETAINER NUTS (ARMREST)
3 TRIM PANEL RETAINERS
4 TOOL J 2459B
5 LENS ASSEMBLIES
6 SCREWS (TRIM PANEL)

84200098

Fig. 95 Front door panel — 1990-91 Deville and Fleetwood

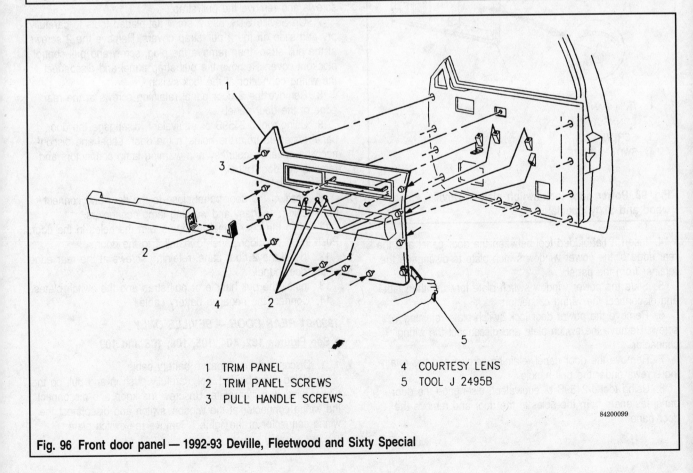

1 TRIM PANEL
2 TRIM PANEL SCREWS
3 PULL HANDLE SCREWS
4 COURTESY LENS
5 TOOL J 2495B

84200099

Fig. 96 Front door panel — 1992-93 Deville, Fleetwood and Sixty Special

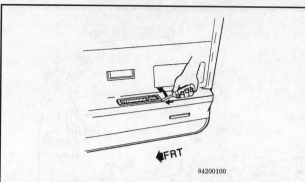

Fig. 97 Power window switch plate removal — Deville, Fleetwood and Sixty Special

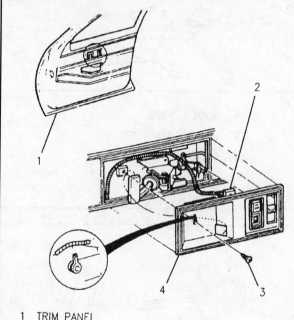

1 TRIM PANEL
2 CONNECTOR
3 SCREW
4 SWITCH PLATE

84200101

Fig. 98 Power door lock switch plate — Deville, Fleetwood and Sixty Special

4. Insert a flat-bladed tool between the door panel and the rear edge of the power window switch plate to disengage the retainer from the panel.

5. Slide the power window switch plate forward, then label and disconnect the wiring connectors.

6. Remove the power door lock switch plate retaining screw. Remove the switch plate and disconnect the wiring connector.

7. Remove the door panel retaining screws and the retaining screws under the pull handle.

8. Using tool J-2459B or equivalent, disengage the door panel fasteners from the holes in the door and remove the door panel.

To install:

9. Align the door panel fasteners with the holes in the door. Push in on the door panel to install it to the door.

10. Install the retaining screws under the pull handle and the door panel retaining screws.

11. Install the switch plates and courtesy lamp assemblies.

12. Connect the negative battery cable.

Eldorado and Seville

1990-91 FRONT DOOR

▶ **See Figures 100, 101, 102, 103, 104, 105, 106 and 107**

1. Disconnect the negative battery cable.

2. Insert a flat-bladed tool between the door panel and the front edge of the power seat switch plate to disengage the retainer from the panel. Slide the switch plate forward and disconnect the wiring connectors.

3. Insert a flat-bladed tool between the door panel and the rear edge of the power window switch plate to disengage the retainer from the panel. Slide the switch plate rearward and disconnect the wiring connector.

4. On all except Seville STS, remove the cover plug and screw from the power door lock switch plate and remove the finishing cup. Remove the door lock switch plate retaining screw and disconnect the switch wiring connector.

5. On Eldorado, lift up on the pull handle and remove the 2 retaining screws. Push down on top of the handle, tip it out and up to remove it from the door panel.

6. On Seville, except STS, remove the pull strap covers by sliding them away from the pull strap. Remove the retaining screws and remove the pull strap.

7. On Seville STS, use 2 small flat-bladed tools to carefully pry and slide off the 2 pull strap covers. Remove the 2 screws at the pull strap, then remove the plug, screw and pull control blockout cover. Remove the pull strap panel and disconnect the wiring connector at the lock switch.

8. Remove the 2 door panel retaining screws at the rear edge of the door panel.

9. Using tool J-2459B or equivalent, disengage the door panel fasteners from the holes in the door. Label and disconnect the speaker, courtesy and warning lamp connectors and remove the door panel.

To install:

10. Position the door panel close to the door and connect the speaker, courtesy and warning lamp connectors.

11. Align the door panel fasteners with the holes in the door. Push in on the door panel to install it to the door.

12. Install the 2 door panel retaining screws at the rear edge of the door panel.

13. Install the pull handle or pull strap and the switch plates.

14. Connect the negative battery cable.

1990-91 REAR DOOR — SEVILLE ONLY

▶ **See Figures 102, 104, 105, 106, 108 and 109**

1. Disconnect the negative battery cable.

2. Using a flat-bladed tool, carefully push in and pull up the power window switch plate. Unscrew the knob and disconnect the wiring connector at the window switch and disconnect the wiring connector at the lighter. Remove the switch plate.

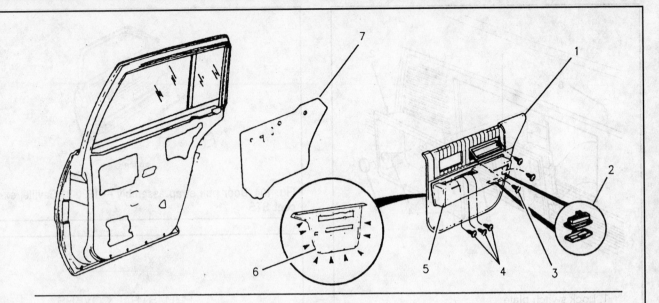

1 TRIM PANEL
2 LENS ASSEMBLIES
3 RETAINING SCREWS (TRIM PANEL)
4 RETAINING SCREWS
5 ARMREST
6 RETAINERS (TRIM PANEL)
7 WATER DEFLECTOR

84200102

Fig. 99 Rear door panel — Deville, Fleetwood and Sixty Special

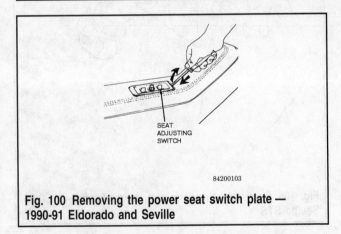

84200103

Fig. 100 Removing the power seat switch plate — 1990-91 Eldorado and Seville

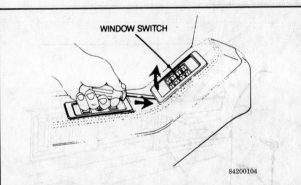

84200104

Fig. 101 Removing the front door power window switch plate — 1990-91 Eldorado and Seville

3. On all except STS, remove the pull strap covers by sliding them away from the pull strap. Remove the retaining screws and remove the pull strap.

4. On STS, use 2 small flat-bladed tools to carefully pry and slide off the 2 pull strap covers. Remove the 2 screws at the pull strap, then remove the plug, screw and pull control blockout cover. Remove the pull strap panel and disconnect the wiring connector at the lock switch.

5. Remove the door panel retaining screw at the rear edge of the door panel.

6. Using tool J-2459B or equivalent, disengage the door panel fasteners from the holes in the door. Disconnect the courtesy and lamp connectors and remove the door panel.

To install:

7. Position the door panel close to the door and connect the courtesy lamp connectors.

8. Align the door panel fasteners with the holes in the door. Push in on the door panel to install it to the door.

9. Install the door panel retaining screw at the rear edge of the door panel.

10. Install the pull strap and the switch plates.

11. Connect the negative battery cable.

1992-93 ELDORADO

▶ **See Figures 110, 111 and 112**

1. Disconnect the negative battery cable.

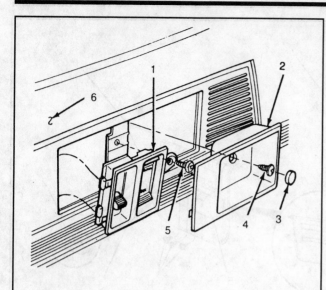

1. Lock switch plate
2. Door handle finishing cup
3. Cover plug
4. Screw
5. Screw

84200105

Fig. 102 Power door lock switch — 1990-91 Eldorado and Seville, except Seville STS

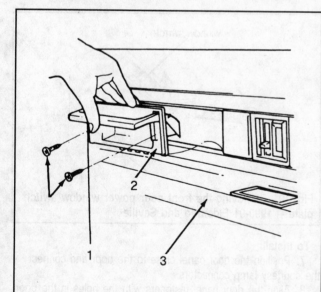

1. Screws
2. Pull handle
3. Trim handle

84200106

Fig. 103 Door pull handle assembly — 1990-91 Eldorado

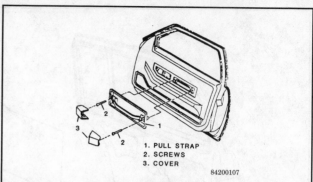

1. PULL STRAP
2. SCREWS
3. COVER

84200107

Fig. 104 Door pull strap assembly — 1990-91 Seville, except STS

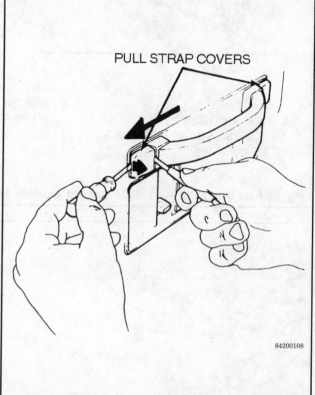

PULL STRAP COVERS

84200108

Fig. 105 Removing the door pull strap covers — 1990-91 Seville STS

2. Remove the power window switch plate as follows:

a. Use a ½ in. wide flat-bladed tool to pry up on the rear edge of the trim plate.

b. Insert the blade ¾ in. into the door trim to engage the retention clip. Press firmly toward the switch plate to disengage the clip.

c. Pull the flat-bladed tool upward while pressing firmly toward the plate to pull the plate from the door panel.

➡ Before lifting the switch plate from the door panel, make sure the flat-bladed tool has fully disengaged the retention clip, or damage to the switch plate or clip may occur.

d. Label and disconnect the wiring connectors and remove the switch plate.

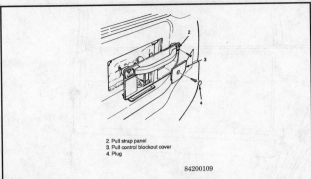

2. Pull strap panel
3. Pull control blockout cover
4. Plug

84200109

Fig. 106 Door pull strap panel assembly — 1990-91 Seville STS

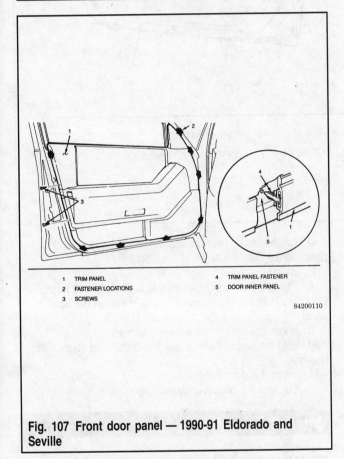

1	TRIM PANEL	4	TRIM PANEL FASTENER
2	FASTENER LOCATIONS	5	DOOR INNER PANEL
3	SCREWS		

84200110

Fig. 107 Front door panel — 1990-91 Eldorado and Seville

3. Carefully pull the power door lock switch trim plate from the door panel. Disconnect the wiring connector for the switch and remove the door lock switch.

4. Working through the switch plate opening, remove the door panel retaining screw.

5. Insert a flat-bladed tool between the upper rear corner of the carpet attached to the door panel. Disengage the fastener and fold back the carpet to expose the door panel retaining screw. Remove the screw.

6. Lift the door panel up and away from the door to disengage the hooks.

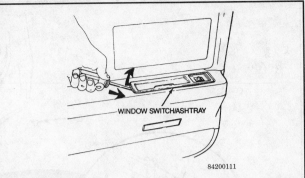

WINDOW SWITCH/ASHTRAY

84200111

Fig. 108 Removing the rear door power window switch plate — 1990-91 Seville

To install:

7. Position the door panel on the door. Align the hooks to the holes in the door and push in and down on the door panel.

8. Install one screw through the switch plate opening and one screw under the carpet.

9. Fold the carpet flush to the trim panel and engage the fastener.

10. Install the door switches.

11. Connect the negative battery cable.

1992-93 SEVILLE

▶ See Figures 110, 111, 113 and 114

1. Disconnect the negative battery cable.

2. If removing the front door panel, remove the power window switch plate as follows:

a. Use a ½ in. wide flat-bladed tool to pry up on the rear edge of the trim plate.

b. Insert the blade ¾ in. into the door trim to engage the retention clip. Press firmly toward the switch plate to disengage the clip.

c. Pull the flat-bladed tool upward while pressing firmly toward the plate to pull the plate from the door panel.

➡ Before lifting the switch plate from the door panel, make sure the flat-bladed tool has fully disengaged the retention clip, or damage to the switch plate or clip may occur.

d. Label and disconnect the wiring connectors and remove the switch plate.

3. If removing the rear door panel, remove the power window switch plate as follows:

a. Using a flat-bladed tool, carefully push in firmly and pull up to disengage the window switch/ash tray clip from the door panel.

b. Label and disconnect the wiring connectors for the window switch and lighter.

c. Remove the window switch/ash tray.

4. Carefully pull the power door lock switch trim plate from the door panel. Disconnect the wiring connectors for the switch and lamp and remove the door lock switch.

5. Remove one door panel retaining screw from the door lock switch plate area.

6. Insert a flat-bladed tool between the upper rear corner of the carpet attached to the door panel. Disengage the fastener and fold back the carpet to expose the door panel retaining screw. Remove the screw.

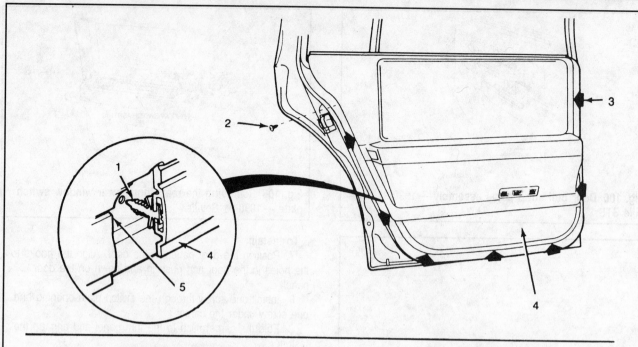

1	TRIM PANEL FASTENER	4	TRIM PANEL
2	SCREW	5	DOOR INNER PANEL
3	FASTENER LOCATION		

84200112

Fig. 109 Rear door panel — 1990-91 Seville

VIEW A

LEFT SIDE

1. Power mirror and window switch
2. Electrical connector
3. Door trim pad
4. Metal clip

84200113

Fig. 110 Front door power window switch plate — 1992-93 Eldorado and Seville

7. Lift the door panel up and out to disengage the door panel hooks from the holes in the door.

To install:

8. Position the door panel on the door. Align the hooks to the holes in the door and push in and down on the door panel.

9. Install the door panel retaining screws.

10. Fold the carpet flush to the trim panel and engage the fastener.

11. Install the door switches.

12. Connect the negative battery cable.

Interior Trim Panels

REMOVAL & INSTALLATION

1990-91 Deville and Fleetwood

QUARTER TRIM PANEL

▶ **See Figures 115, 116 and 117**

1. Disconnect the negative battery cable.

2. Remove the rear seat cushion and seat back; refer to the procedure in this Section.

3. Remove the armrest as follows:

a. Remove the ashtray receiver.

b. Insert a flat-bladed tool between the armrest and the front of the switch plate. Disengage the retainer from the

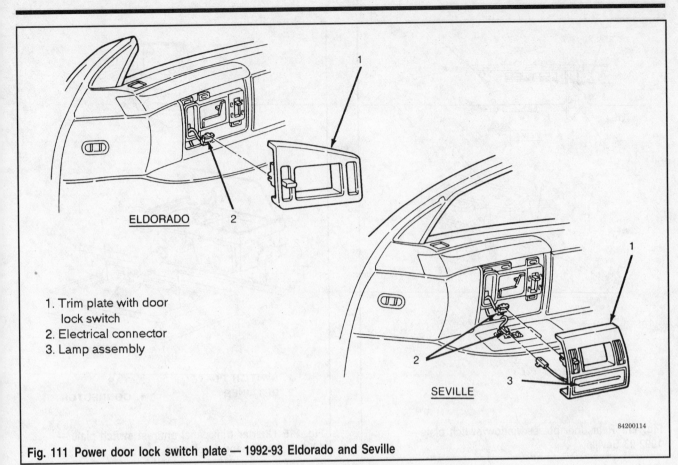

1. Trim plate with door lock switch
2. Electrical connector
3. Lamp assembly

ELDORADO

SEVILLE

84200114

Fig. 111 Power door lock switch plate — 1992-93 Eldorado and Seville

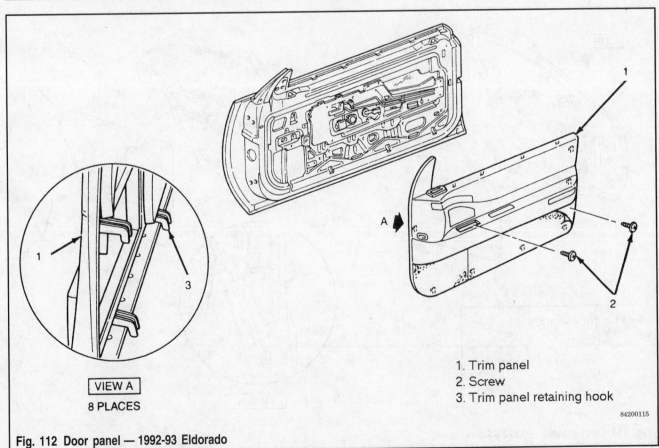

VIEW A

8 PLACES

1. Trim panel
2. Screw
3. Trim panel retaining hook

84200115

Fig. 112 Door panel — 1992-93 Eldorado

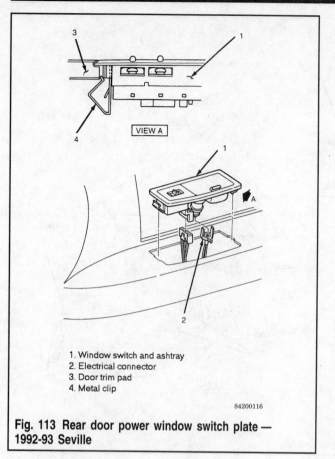

1. Window switch and ashtray
2. Electrical connector
3. Door trim pad
4. Metal clip

84200116

Fig. 113 Rear door power window switch plate — 1992-93 Seville

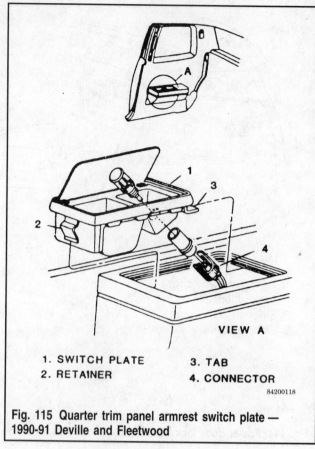

1. **SWITCH PLATE**   3. **TAB**
2. **RETAINER**   4. **CONNECTOR**

84200118

Fig. 115 Quarter trim panel armrest switch plate — 1990-91 Deville and Fleetwood

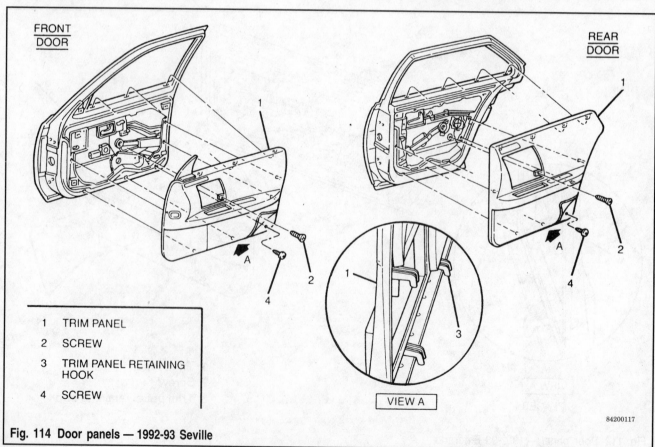

1	TRIM PANEL
2	SCREW
3	TRIM PANEL RETAINING HOOK
4	SCREW

84200117

Fig. 114 Door panels — 1992-93 Seville

armrest and slide the switch plate forward to disengage the tab from the trim panel.

c. Disconnect the wiring connector.

d. Remove the armrest retaining screw.

e. Slide the armrest forward to disengage the tabs on the armrest from the trim panel.

4. Loosen the rear carpet.

5. Remove the quarter trim panel retaining screws.

6. Remove the trim panel by grasping and pulling inboard. Disconnect the wiring connector.

To install:

7. Connect the wiring connector. Align the fasteners on the quarter trim panel with the holes in the body and push the panel outboard to install.

8. Install the trim panel retaining screws and reposition the carpet.

9. Install the armrest as follows:

a. Align the tabs on the armrest with the holes in the trim panel and slide the armrest rearward.

b. Install the armrest retaining screw.

c. Connect the switch wiring connector.

d. Place the rear tab of the switch plate under the armrest. Slide the switch plate rearward and then press down on the front edge of the switch plate to engage the retainer.

e. Install the ashtray receiver.

10. Install the rear seat cushion and seat back.

11. Connect the negative battery cable.

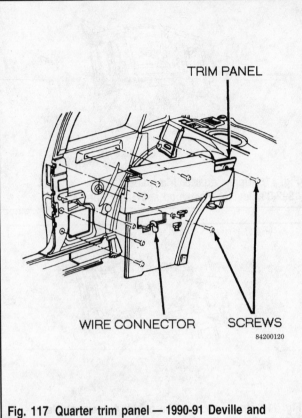

Fig. 117 Quarter trim panel — 1990-91 Deville and Fleetwood

1992-93 Deville, Fleetwood and Sixty Special

UPPER QUARTER TRIM PANEL

▶ See Figures 118 and 119

1. Disconnect the negative battery cable.

2. Remove the upper quarter trim panel by grasping the trim and pulling toward the inside of the vehicle.

3. Disconnect the wiring connector.

To install:

4. Install new fasteners to the upper quarter trim panel if they are broken or damaged.

5. Disconnect the wiring connector.

6. Align the trim panel fasteners to the holes in the body and press the trim in place.

7. Connect the negative battery cable.

LOWER QUARTER TRIM PANEL

▶ See Figures 120, 121 and 122

1. Disconnect the negative battery cable.

2. Remove the rear seat cushion and seat back; refer to the procedure in this Section.

3. Remove the armrest as follows:

a. Remove the ashtray receiver.

b. Insert a flat-bladed tool between the armrest and the front of the ashtray mount plate. Disengage the retainer from the armrest and slide the mount plate forward to disengage the tab from the armrest.

c. Disconnect the wiring connector.

d. Remove the armrest retaining screws.

e. Disengage the tabs on the armrest from the trim panel.

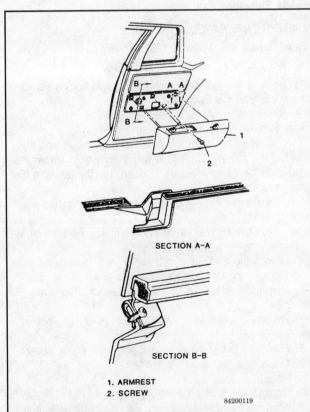

SECTION A-A

SECTION B-B

1. ARMREST
2. SCREW

Fig. 116 Quarter trim panel armrest — 1990-91 Deville and Fleetwood

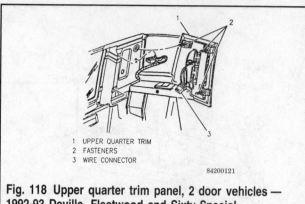

1 UPPER QUARTER TRIM
2 FASTENERS
3 WIRE CONNECTOR

84200121

**Fig. 118 Upper quarter trim panel, 2 door vehicles —
1992-93 Deville, Fleetwood and Sixty Special**

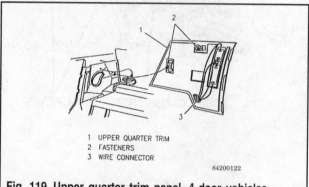

1 UPPER QUARTER TRIM
2 FASTENERS
3 WIRE CONNECTOR

84200122

**Fig. 119 Upper quarter trim panel, 4 door vehicles —
1992-93 Deville, Fleetwood and Sixty Special**

4. Loosen the rear carpet.
5. Remove the lower quarter trim panel by disengaging the fasteners and feeding the wire connector through the access hole.

To install:

6. Feed the wire connector through the access hole.
7. Align the trim panel fasteners with the holes in the body and push outboard to install.
8. Reposition the rear carpet.
9. Install the armrest as follows:
   a. Insert the tabs on the armrest into the holes in the trim panel.
   b. Install the retaining screws.
   c. Connect the wiring connector.
   d. Place the rear tab of the ashtray mount plate under the armrest. Slide the mount plate rearward and then press down on the front edge of the mount plate to engage the retainer.
   e. Install the ashtray receiver.
10. Install the rear seat cushion and seat back.
11. Connect the negative battery cable.

BODY LOCK PILLAR TRIM PANEL

▶ See Figure 123

1. Remove the rear seat cushion and seat back; refer to the procedure in this Section.
2. Remove the retaining screws and the body lock pillar trim panel.
3. Installation is the reverse of the removal procedure.

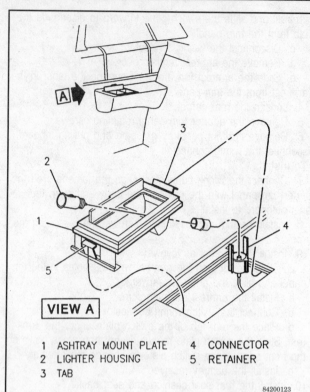

VIEW A

1 ASHTRAY MOUNT PLATE   4 CONNECTOR
2 LIGHTER HOUSING   5 RETAINER
3 TAB

84200123

**Fig. 120 Lower quarter trim panel armrest ashtray
mount plate — 1992-93 Deville, Fleetwood and Sixty
Special**

1990-91 Eldorado

QUARTER TRIM PANEL

▶ See Figures 124, 125 and 126

1. Disconnect the negative battery cable.
2. Remove the rear seat cushion and seat back; refer to the procedure in this Section.
3. Remove the armrest as follows:
   a. Remove the ashtray receiver.
   b. Insert a flat-bladed tool between the armrest and the front of the ashtray. Disengage the retainer from the armrest and slide the ashtray forward to disengage the tab from the trim panel.
   c. Disconnect the wiring connector and remove the armrest retaining screw.
   d. Slide the armrest forward to disengage the tabs on the armrest from the trim panel.
4. Loosen the rear carpet retainer.
5. Remove the trim panel retaining screws.
6. Use a flat-bladed tool to remove the pull strap screw covers.
7. Remove the pull strap retaining screws and the pull strap.
8. Remove the trim panel by grasping and pulling inboard.
9. Disconnect the wiring connector.

To install:

10. Connect the wiring connector.
11. Align the trim panel fasteners with the body holes and push the panel outboard to install, making sure the safety belt is pulled through the opening in the panel.

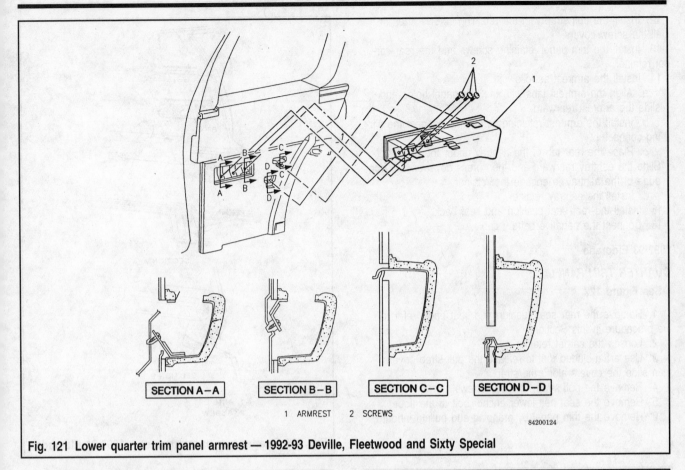

SECTION A–A   SECTION B–B   SECTION C–C   SECTION D–D

1 ARMREST   2 SCREWS

84200124

Fig. 121 Lower quarter trim panel armrest — 1992-93 Deville, Fleetwood and Sixty Special

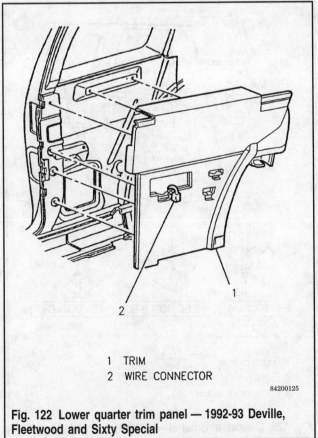

1 TRIM
2 WIRE CONNECTOR

84200125

Fig. 122 Lower quarter trim panel — 1992-93 Deville, Fleetwood and Sixty Special

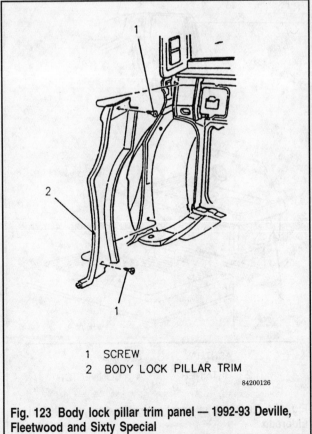

1 SCREW
2 BODY LOCK PILLAR TRIM

84200126

Fig. 123 Body lock pillar trim panel — 1992-93 Deville, Fleetwood and Sixty Special

12. Install the pull strap with the retaining screws, then install the screw covers.

13. Install the trim panel retaining screws and the rear carpet retainer.

14. Install the armrest as follows:

 a. Align the armrest tabs with the trim panel holes and slide the armrest rearward.

 b. Install the armrest retaining screw and connect the wiring connector.

 c. Place the rear tab of the ashtray under the armrest. Slide the ashtray rearward and then press down on the front edge of the ashtray to engage the retainer.

 d. Install the ashtray retainer.

15. Install the rear seat cushion and seat back.

16. Connect the negative battery cable.

1992-93 Eldorado

QUARTER TRIM PANEL

▶ See Figure 127

1. Remove the rear seat cushion and seat back; refer to the procedure in this Section.

2. Loosen the carpet retainer.

3. Use a flat-bladed tool to release the pull strap covers, then slide the covers along the strap.

4. Remove the pull strap retaining screws.

5. Remove the seat belt lower anchor bolt at the floor.

6. Remove the trim panel by grasping and pulling inboard.

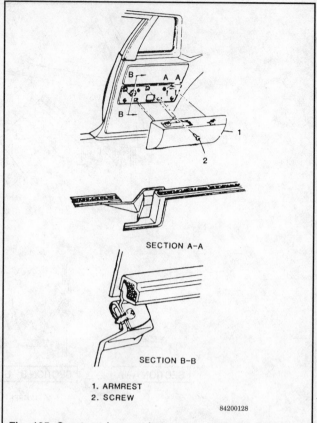

SECTION A-A

SECTION B-B

1. ARMREST
2. SCREW

84200128

Fig. 125 Quarter trim panel armrest — 1990-91 Eldorado

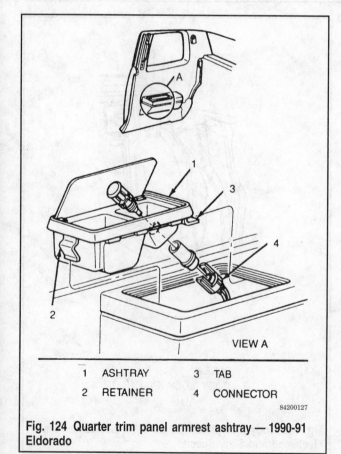

VIEW A

1	ASHTRAY	3	TAB
2	RETAINER	4	CONNECTOR

84200127

Fig. 124 Quarter trim panel armrest ashtray — 1990-91 Eldorado

SECTION A-A   SECTION B-B   SECTION C-C

1. Trim panel
2. Screws
3. Wire connector

84200129

Fig. 126 Quarter trim panel — 1990-91 Eldorado

To install:

7. Align the trim panel fasteners with the body holes and push the panel outboard to install, making sure the seat belt is pulled through the opening in the panel.

8. Install the anchor bolt securing the seat belt to the floor.

9. Install the pull strap retaining screws and covers.

10. Install the carpet retainer.

11. Install the rear seat cushion and seat back.

1990-91 Seville

QUARTER UPPER TRIM PANEL

1. Disconnect the negative battery cable.

2. Remove the rear seat cushion and seat back; refer to the procedure in this Section.

3. Remove the trim panel-to-body retaining screws.

4. Remove the trim panel by pulling outboard to disengage the panel fasteners from the holes in the body.

5. Disconnect the courtesy lamp wiring connector.

To install:

6. Connect the courtesy lamp wiring connector.

7. Align the trim panel fasteners with the body holes and push the panel outboard to install.

8. Install the trim panel retaining screws.

9. Install the rear seat back and seat cushion.

1992-93 Seville

QUARTER TRIM PANEL

▶ **See Figure 128**

1. Remove the rear seat cushion and seat back; refer to the procedure in this Section.

2. Remove the trim panel-to-body retaining screw.

3. Remove the trim panel by pulling outboard to disengage the panel fasteners from the holes in the body.

4. Remove the lower shoulder belt mounting bolt and feed the belt through the trim panel.

To install:

5. Feed the shoulder belt through the trim panel and install the mounting bolt.

6. Align the trim panel fasteners with the body holes and push the panel outboard to install.

7. Install the trim panel retaining screw.

8. Install the rear seat back and seat cushion.

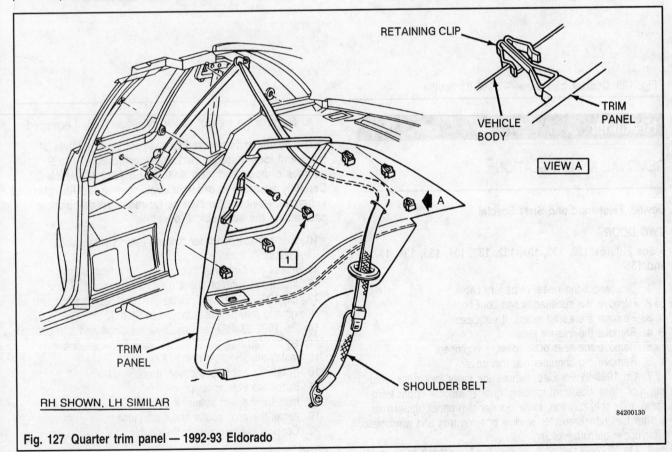

RH SHOWN, LH SIMILAR

Fig. 127 Quarter trim panel — 1992-93 Eldorado

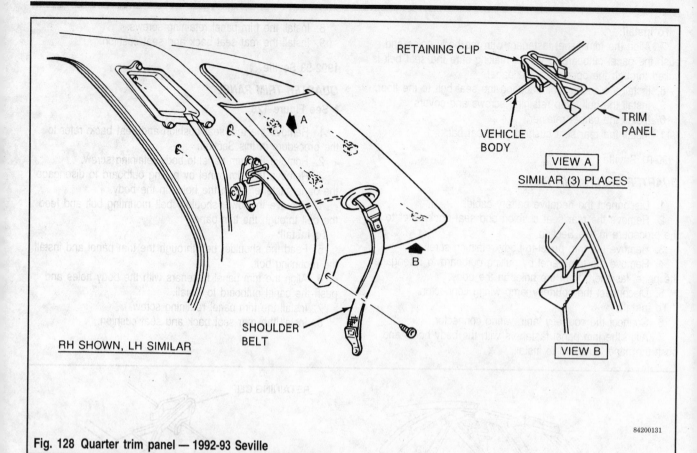

RETAINING CLIP

VEHICLE BODY

TRIM PANEL

VIEW A
SIMILAR (3) PLACES

VIEW B

RH SHOWN, LH SIMILAR

SHOULDER BELT

84200131

Fig. 128 Quarter trim panel — 1992-93 Seville

Headliner

REMOVAL & INSTALLATION

Deville, Fleetwood and Sixty Special

TWO DOOR

▶ See Figures 129, 130, 131, 132, 133, 134, 135, 136, 137 and 138

1. Disconnect the negative battery cable.
2. Remove the sunshades and coat hooks.
3. Remove the assist straps, if equipped.
4. Remove the interior lamps.
5. Remove the fiber optic cover, if equipped.
6. Remove the shoulder belt trim cover.
7. On 1990-91 vehicles, remove the lower lock pillar molding, roof inner side front molding, quarter window upper front panel, rear seat cushion, lower quarter trim panel, upper rear quarter trim panel, quarter window opening trim and windshield pillar upper garnish molding.
8. On 1992-93 vehicles, remove the body lower pillar molding, roof inner side front molding, quarter upper front panel, upper and lower quarter trim panels, quarter window molding, windshield side upper garnish molding and rear window garnish moldings.

9. Remove the sunroof opening closeout lace, if equipped.

➡The headliner is secured to the roof by 7 patches of hook and loop material on 1990-91 vehicles or 3 to 6 patches of hook and loop material on 1992-93 vehicles. Carefully separate in order to avoid tearing the fiberglass substrate. Position the seat as far rearward as possible and recline the seatback, if possible.

10. Remove the headliner through the right front door.
To install:
11. Install the headliner through the right front door.
12. Install the sunroof opening lace, if equipped.
13. On 1990-91 vehicles, install the rear seat cushion and all moldings and trim panels removed in Step 7.
14. On 1992-93 vehicles, install all moldings and trim panels removed in Step 8.
15. Install the shoulder belt trim cover.
16. Install the fiber optic cover, if equipped.
17. Install the interior lamps.
18. Install the assist straps, if equipped.
19. Install the coat hooks and sunshades.
20. Connect the negative battery cable.

FOUR DOOR

▶ See Figures 129, 130, 131, 133, 136, 137, 138, 139, 140 and 141

1. Disconnect the negative battery cable.
2. Remove the sunshades and coat hooks.
3. Remove the assist straps, if equipped.
4. Remove the interior lamps.

1 SUNSHADE
2 SUNSHADE EXTENSION
3 SCREWS
4 SUNSHADE CENTER SUPPORT

84200132

Fig. 129 Sunshade — Deville, Fleetwood and Sixty Special

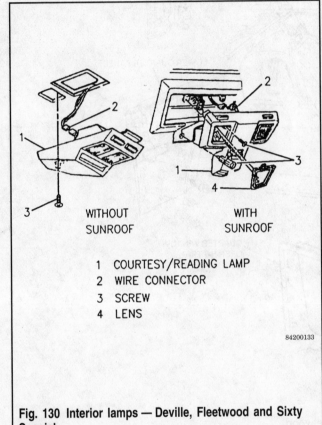

WITHOUT SUNROOF WITH SUNROOF

1 COURTESY/READING LAMP
2 WIRE CONNECTOR
3 SCREW
4 LENS

84200133

Fig. 130 Interior lamps — Deville, Fleetwood and Sixty Special

5. Remove the fiber optic cover, if equipped.
6. On 1990-91 vehicles, remove the front and rear roof inner side moldings, windshield pillar upper garnish molding, lock pillar upper trim panel, rear window garnish molding (if equipped) and upper rear quarter panel.
7. On 1992-93 vehicles, remove the front and rear roof inner side moldings, windshield side upper garnish molding, center pillar upper trim panel and upper quarter trim panel.
8. Remove the sunroof opening closeout lace, if equipped.
9. Remove the rear vanity mirror, if equipped.

➡The headliner is secured to the roof by 7 patches of hook and loop material on 1990-91 vehicles or 3 to 6 patches of hook and loop material on 1992-93 vehicles.

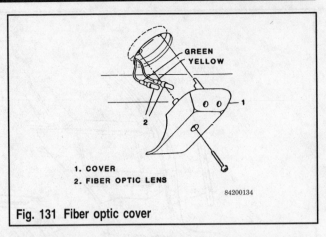

GREEN
YELLOW

1. COVER
2. FIBER OPTIC LENS

84200134

Fig. 131 Fiber optic cover

Carefully separate in order to avoid tearing the fiberglass substrate. Position the seat as far rearward as possible and recline the seatback, if possible.

10. Remove the headliner through the right front door.
To install:
11. Install the headliner through the right front door.
12. Install the sunroof opening lace, if equipped.
13. On 1990-91 vehicles, install all moldings and trim panels removed in Step 6.
14. On 1992-93 vehicles, install all moldings and trim panels removed in Step 7.
15. Install the fiber optic cover, if equipped.
16. Install the interior lamps.
17. Install the rear vanity mirror, if equipped.
18. Install the assist straps, if equipped.
19. Install the coat hooks and sunshades.
20. Connect the negative battery cable.

1990-91 Eldorado

▶ **See Figures 131, 137, 142, 143, 144, 145 and 146**

1. Disconnect the negative battery cable.
2. Remove the rear seat cushion and seat back; refer to the procedure in this Section.
3. Remove both quarter trim panels; refer to the procedure in this Section.
4. Disengage both windshield pillar and side roof rail garnish moldings from the clips and retainers.
5. Remove interior roof mounted lamps, coat hooks, sunshade and support assemblies, fiber optic lens cover and sunroof lace, if equipped.
6. Remove both shoulder belt to headliner escutcheons.

➡The headliner is secured to the roof by patches of hook and loop material. Carefully separate in order to avoid tearing the fiberglass substrate. Position the seat as far rearward as possible and recline the seatback, if possible.

7. Remove the headliner through the right front door.
To install:
8. Position the headliner and press in at the hook and loop locations.
9. Install the shoulder belt-to-headliner escutcheons.
10. Install the interior roof mounted lamps, sunroof lace (if equipped), sunshade and support assemblies, fiber optic lens cover and coat hooks.

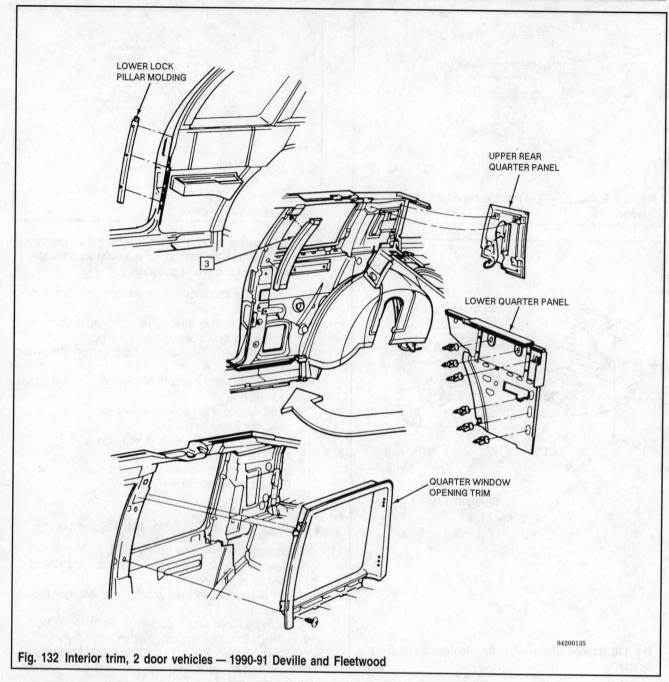

Fig. 132 Interior trim, 2 door vehicles — 1990-91 Deville and Fleetwood

11. Install the windshield pillar and side roof rail garnish moldings as follows:

   a. Position the retainers into the slots of the molding.

   b. Position the molding, aligning the retainers to the holes at the windshield pillar.

   c. Push in on the molding at the front to install.

   d. Align the tabs on the molding to the clips and push in on the molding.

12. Install the quarter trim panels, rear seat cushion and seat back.

13. Connect the negative battery cable.

1990-91 Seville

▶ See Figures 131, 137, 142, 143, 144, 145, 146 and 147

1. Disconnect the negative battery cable.

2. Remove the rear seat cushion; refer to the procedure in this Section.

3. Remove the speakers and back panel of the rear seat (rear compartment side).

4. Remove the rear seat back.

5. Remove the upper quarter and rear lock pillar panel and the center lock pillar panel.

6. Disengage both windshield pillar and side roof rail garnish moldings from the clips and retainers.

7. Remove the fiber optic lens cover.

8. Remove the sunshade and support assembly.

9. Remove the interior roof mounted lamps, coat hooks and assist straps, if equipped.

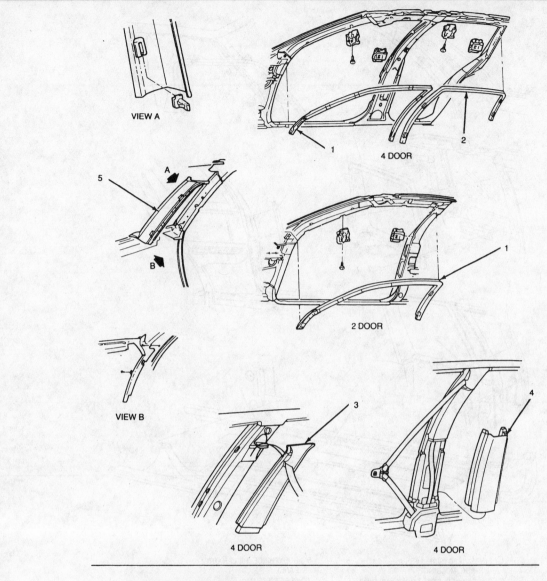

VIEW A

4 DOOR

2 DOOR

VIEW B

4 DOOR

4 DOOR

1	ROOF INNER SIDE FRONT MOLDING	4	LOCK PILLAR LOWER PANEL
2	ROOF INNER SIDE REAR MOLDING	5	WINDSHIELD PILLAR UPPER GARNISH MOLDING
3	LOCK PILLAR UPPER PANEL		

84200136

Fig. 133 Interior trim, 2 and 4 door vehicles — 1990-91 Deville and Fleetwood

10. Remove the sunroof lace, if equipped.

➡**The headliner is secured to the roof by approximately 6 patches of hook and loop material. Carefully separate in order to avoid tearing the fiberglass substrate. Position the seat as far rearward as possible and recline the seatback, if possible.**

11. Remove the headliner through the right front door.
To install:
12. Position the headliner and press in at the hook and loop locations.
13. Install the sunroof lace, if equipped.
14. Install the coat hooks, assist straps, if equipped and interior roof mounted lamps.
15. Install the sunshade and support assembly.

16. Install the fiber optic cover lens cover.
17. Install the windshield pillar and side roof rail garnish moldings as follows:
    a. Position the retainers into the slots of the molding.
    b. Position the molding, aligning the retainers to the holes at the windshield pillar.
    c. Push in on the molding at the front to install.
    d. Align the tabs on the molding to the clips and push in on the molding.
18. Install the center lock pillar panel and upper quarter and rear lock pillar panel.
19. Install the rear seatback.
20. Install the speakers and back panel of the rear seat (rear compartment side).
21. Install the rear seat cushion.

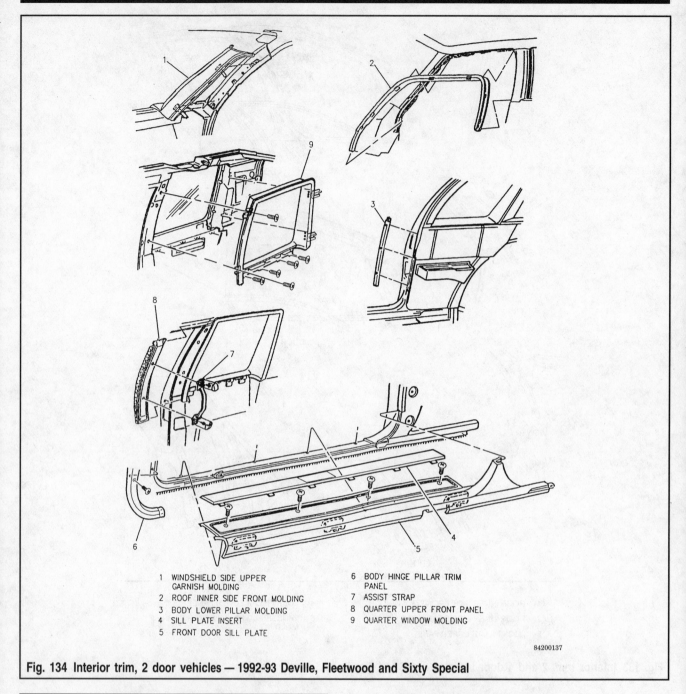

1	WINDSHIELD SIDE UPPER GARNISH MOLDING
2	ROOF INNER SIDE FRONT MOLDING
3	BODY LOWER PILLAR MOLDING
4	SILL PLATE INSERT
5	FRONT DOOR SILL PLATE
6	BODY HINGE PILLAR TRIM PANEL
7	ASSIST STRAP
8	QUARTER UPPER FRONT PANEL
9	QUARTER WINDOW MOLDING

84200137

Fig. 134 Interior trim, 2 door vehicles — 1992-93 Deville, Fleetwood and Sixty Special

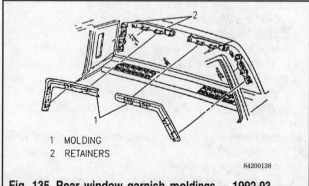

1	MOLDING
2	RETAINERS

84200138

Fig. 135 Rear window garnish moldings — 1992-93 Deville, Fleetwood and Sixty Special

22. Connect the negative battery cable.

1992-93 Eldorado and Seville

▶ See Figures 148, 149, 150, 151, 152 and 153

1. Disconnect the negative battery cable.

2. On Eldorado, remove the rear seat cushion and seat back; refer to the procedure in this Section.

3. Remove both quarter trim panels; refer to the procedure in this Section.

4. Remove both windshield pillar garnish moldings by pulling away from the pillar, disengaging the clips.

5. On Seville, remove the center pillar trim.

6. On Eldorado, remove both shoulder belt-to-headliner escutcheons.

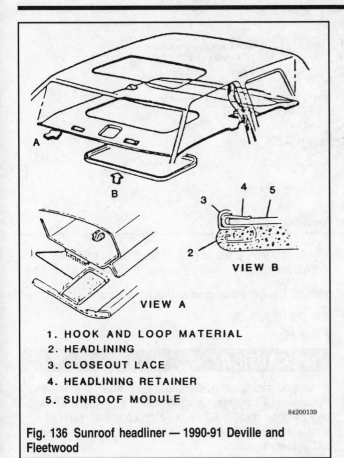

1. HOOK AND LOOP MATERIAL
2. HEADLINING
3. CLOSEOUT LACE
4. HEADLINING RETAINER
5. SUNROOF MODULE

84200139

Fig. 136 Sunroof headliner — 1990-91 Deville and Fleetwood

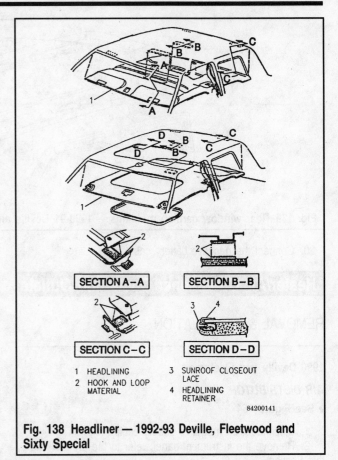

SECTION A–A   SECTION B–B

SECTION C–C   SECTION D–D

1 HEADLINING
2 HOOK AND LOOP MATERIAL

3 SUNROOF CLOSEOUT LACE
4 HEADLINING RETAINER

84200141

Fig. 138 Headliner — 1992-93 Deville, Fleetwood and Sixty Special

7. Disconnect the wiring connectors at the rear quarters. There is one on each side if equipped with a sunroof, one on the left side only without a sunroof.

8. Remove the interior roof mounted lamps, sunshades and supports.

9. Detach 'DUAL LOCK" by pulling firmly down at the attachment locations.

➡The headliner is secured to the roof panel by the sunshades and the locator at the rear. To disengage the locator, pull down directly behind the attachment location at the rear. Recline the seatbacks if possible and position the seat as far back as possible before removing the headliner.

10. Remove the headliner through the right front door.
To install:

11. With the aid of an assistant, engage the locator at the rear, then raise the front and attach the sunshade supports. Be careful not to pinch the vanity mirror wires when installing the sunshade support screws.

12. Install the interior roof mounted lamps and sunshades.

13. Connect the wiring connector(s) at the rear quarter(s).

14. On Eldorado, install both shoulder belt-to-headliner escutcheons.

15. Position the windshield pillar garnish moldings, aligning the retainers to the holes at the windshield pillar. Push in on the moldings to install.

16. On Seville, install the center pillar trim.

17. Install the quarter trim panels.

18. On Eldorado, install the rear seat cushion and seatback.

19. Press the headliner firmly at the 'DUAL LOCK" locations.

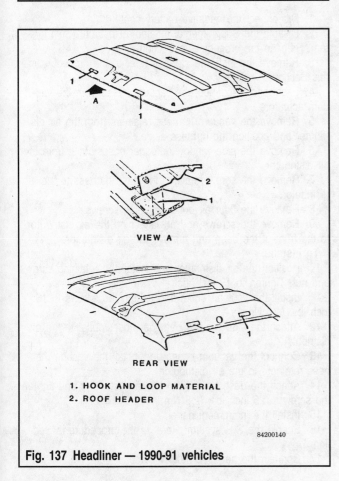

VIEW A

REAR VIEW

1. HOOK AND LOOP MATERIAL
2. ROOF HEADER

84200140

Fig. 137 Headliner — 1990-91 vehicles

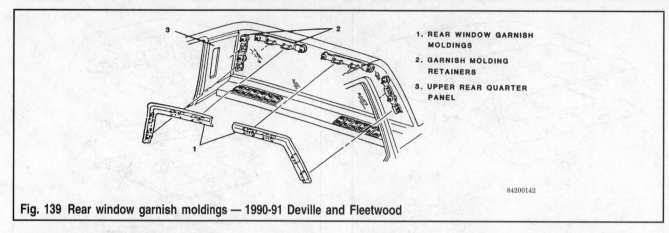

1. REAR WINDOW GARNISH
   MOLDINGS
2. GARNISH MOLDING
   RETAINERS
3. UPPER REAR QUARTER
   PANEL

84200142

Fig. 139 Rear window garnish moldings — 1990-91 Deville and Fleetwood

20. Connect the negative battery cable.

Heater/Air Conditioner Ducts and Outlets

REMOVAL & INSTALLATION

1990 Deville and Fleetwood

AIR DISTRIBUTOR

▶ See Figure 154

1. Disconnect the negative battery cable.
2. Remove the instrument panel; refer to the procedure in this Section.
3. Remove the side window defogger connectors and screws.
4. Label and disconnect the vacuum hoses from the vacuum actuators.
5. Remove the outlet assembly screws.
6. Remove the distributor assembly screws and the distributor assembly.
7. Installation is the reverse of the removal procedure. Tighten the distributor assembly and outlet assembly screws to 13 inch lbs. (1.5 Nm).

DUCTS

▶ See Figures 155, 156 and 157

1. Disconnect the negative battery cable.
2. Remove the instrument panel; refer to the procedure in this Section.
3. Remove the left and right duct assembly mounting screws, ducts and seals.
4. Remove the center duct mounting screws, duct and seals.
5. Installation is the reverse of the removal procedure. Tighten the duct mounting screws to 13 inch lbs. (1.5 Nm).

OUTLETS

▶ See Figures 158 and 159

1. Disconnect the negative battery cable.
2. Remove the instrument panel upper trim pad; refer to the procedure in this Section.
3. Remove the outlet housing mounting screws and the outlet housing.

4. Installation is the reverse of the removal procedure. Tighten the housing mounting screws to 13 inch lbs. (1.5 Nm).

1991-93 Deville, Fleetwood and Sixty Special

AIR DISTRIBUTOR

▶ See Figures 160 and 161

❊❊CAUTION

When performing service around Supplemental Inflatable Restraint (SIR) system components or wiring, the SIR system must be disabled. Failure to do so could result in possible air bag deployment, personal injury or unneeded SIR system repairs.

1. Disconnect the negative battery cable.
2. Disable the Supplemental Inflatable Restraint (SIR) system. Refer to the procedure in Section 6.
3. Remove the instrument panel; refer to the procedure in this Section.
4. Label and disconnect the vacuum hoses from the vacuum actuators.
5. Remove the vacuum harness retainers from the air distributor and position the harness aside.
6. Remove the side window defogger hoses/outlet from the air distributor.
7. Remove the screw retaining the dash harness to the air distributor.
8. Remove the floor air outlet retaining screws.
9. Remove the screws and nut attaching the air distributor to the front of the dash and remove the air distributor.
   To install:
10. Position the sir distributor and install the retaining screws and nut. Tighten to 13 inch lbs. (1.5 Nm).
11. Install the floor air outlet and tighten the screws to 13 inch lbs. (1.5 Nm).
12. Attach the side window defogger hoses/outlet to the air distributor.
13. Connect the vacuum hoses and install the vacuum harness retainers to the air distributor.
14. Attach the dash harness to the air distributor and tighten the screw to 25 inch lbs. (2.8 Nm).
15. Install the instrument panel.
16. Enable the SIR system. Refer to the procedure in Section 6.
17. Connect the negative battery cable.

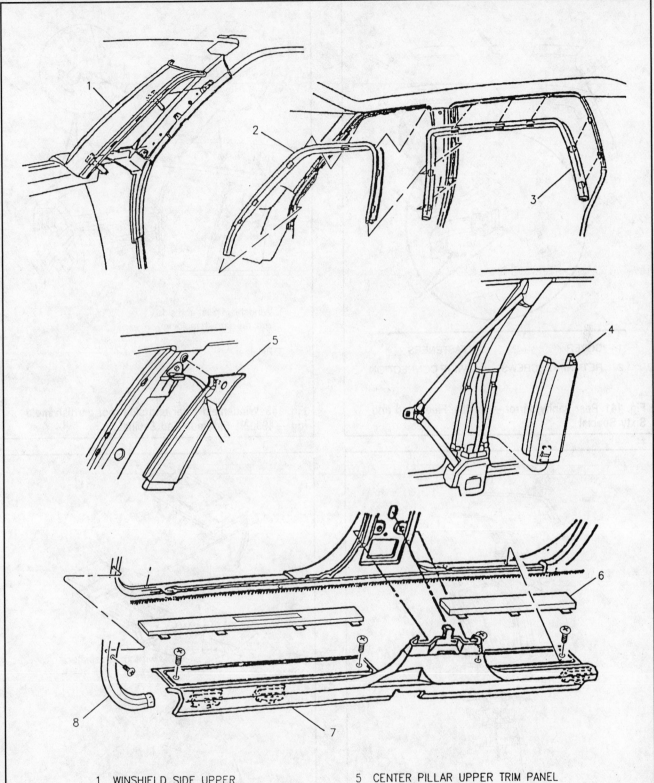

1 WINSHIELD SIDE UPPER
   GARNISH MOLDING
2 ROOF INNER SIDE FRONT MOLDING
3 ROOF INNER SIDE REAR MOLDING
4 CENTER PILLAR CENTER TRIM PANEL

5 CENTER PILLAR UPPER TRIM PANEL
6 SILL PLATE INSERT
7 CENTER PILLAR LOWER TRIM PANEL
8 BODY HINGE PILLAR TRIM PANEL

84200143

Fig. 140 Interior trim, 4 door vehicles — 1992-93 Deville, Fleetwood and Sixty Special

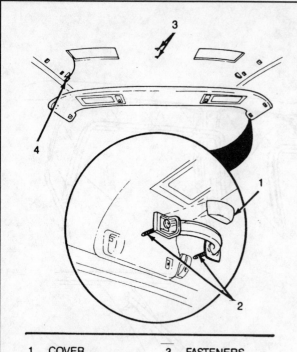

1	COVER	3	FASTENERS
2	RETAINING SCREWS	4	WIRE CONNECTION

84200144

Fig. 141 Rear vanity mirror — Deville, Fleetwood and Sixty Special

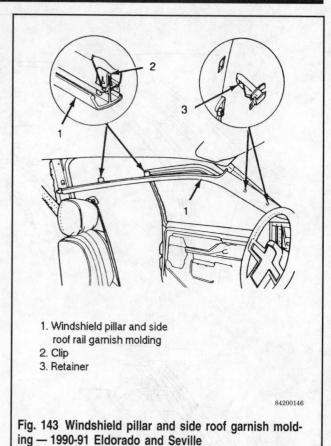

1. Windshield pillar and side roof rail garnish molding
2. Clip
3. Retainer

84200146

Fig. 143 Windshield pillar and side roof garnish molding — 1990-91 Eldorado and Seville

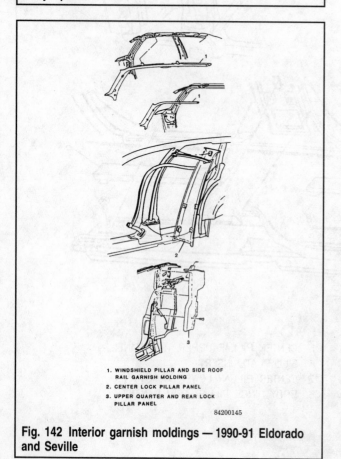

1. WINDSHIELD PILLAR AND SIDE ROOF RAIL GARNISH MOLDING
2. CENTER LOCK PILLAR PANEL
3. UPPER QUARTER AND REAR LOCK PILLAR PANEL

84200145

Fig. 142 Interior garnish moldings — 1990-91 Eldorado and Seville

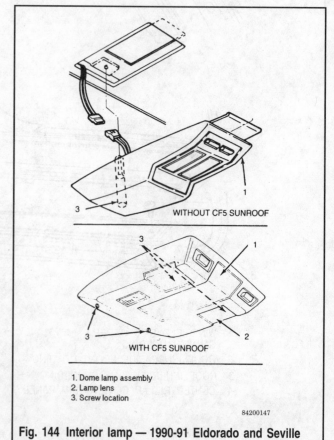

WITHOUT CF5 SUNROOF

WITH CF5 SUNROOF

1. Dome lamp assembly
2. Lamp lens
3. Screw location

84200147

Fig. 144 Interior lamp — 1990-91 Eldorado and Seville

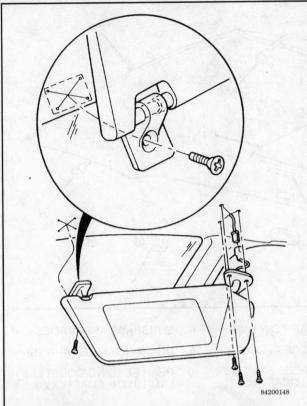

Fig. 145 Sunshade and support assembly — 1990-91 Eldorado and Seville

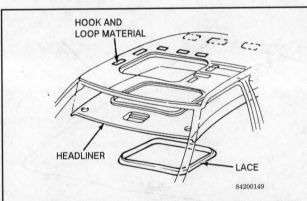

Fig. 146 Sunroof lace — 1990-91 Eldorado and Seville

DUCTS

▶ **See Figures 156, 157 and 162**

✳✳CAUTION

When performing service around Supplemental Inflatable Restraint (SIR) system components or wiring, the SIR system must be disabled. Failure to do so could result in possible air bag deployment, personal injury or unneeded SIR system repairs.

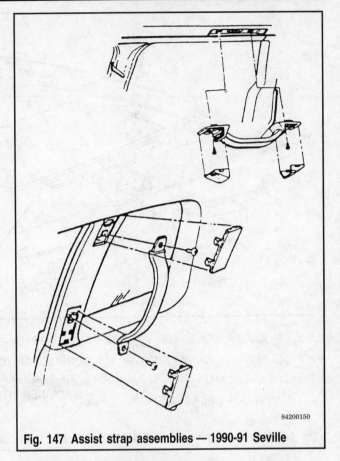

Fig. 147 Assist strap assemblies — 1990-91 Seville

1. Disconnect the negative battery cable.
2. Disable the Supplemental Inflatable Restraint (SIR) system. Refer to the procedure in Section 6.
3. Remove the instrument panel; refer to the procedure in this Section.
4. Remove the left and right duct assembly mounting screws, ducts and seals.
5. Remove the center duct mounting screws, duct and seal.
To install:
6. Install the center duct, seal and screws to the instrument panel. Tighten the duct mounting screws to 13 inch lbs. (1.5 Nm).
7. Install the left and right ducts, seals and screws. Tighten the duct mounting screws to 13 inch lbs. (1.5 Nm).
8. Install the instrument panel.
9. Enable the SIR system. Refer to the procedure in Section 6.
10. Connect the negative battery cable.

OUTLETS

▶ **See Figures 158 and 159**

1. Disconnect the negative battery cable.
2. Remove the instrument panel upper trim pad; refer to the procedure in this Section.
3. Remove the outlet housing mounting screws and the outlet housing.
4. Installation is the reverse of the removal procedure. Tighten the housing mounting screws to 13 inch lbs. (1.5 Nm).

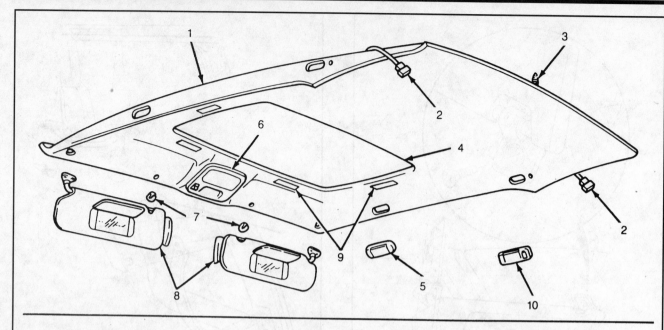

1	MODULAR HEADLINER	5	FRONT READING/COURTESY LAMP	8	SUNSHADE ASSEMBLIES
2	ELECTRICAL CONNECTOR	6	SUNROOF MOTOR ACCESS COVER	9	DUAL-LOCK (4 LOCATIONS)
3	REAR LOCATOR	7	SUNSHADE RECEPTACLE (HEADLINER FRONT LOCATOR)	10	REAR READING/COURTESY LAMP (WITH COAT HOOK)
4	SUNROOF OPENING				

84200151

Fig. 148 Headliner with sunroof — 1992-93 Eldorado; 1992-93 Seville similar

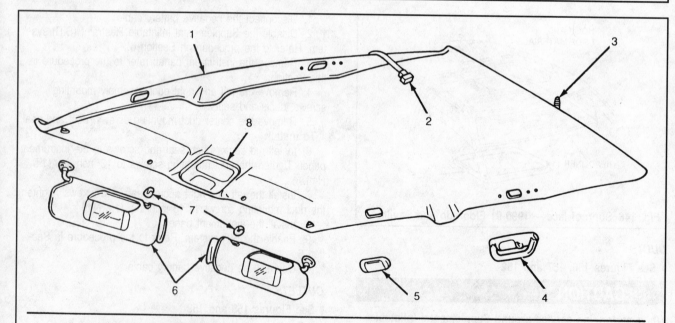

1	MODULAR HEADLINER	5	FRONT COURTESY/READING LAMP
2	ELECTRICAL CONNECTOR	6	SUNSHADE ASSEMBLIES
3	REAR LOCATOR	7	SUNSHADE RECEPTACLE (HEADLINER FRONT LOCATOR)
4	REAR COURTESY/READING LAMP (WITH ASSIST HANDLE)	8	OVERHEAD STORAGE BIN

84200152

Fig. 149 Headliner without sunroof — 1992-93 Seville; 1992-93 Eldorado similar

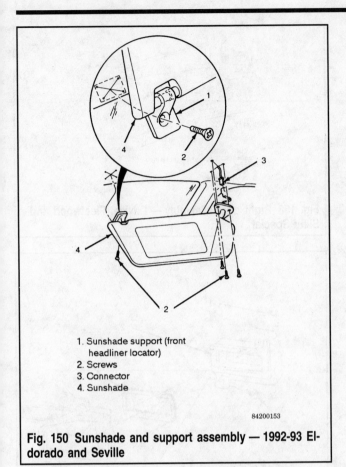

1. Sunshade support (front headliner locator)
2. Screws
3. Connector
4. Sunshade

84200153

Fig. 150 Sunshade and support assembly — 1992-93 Eldorado and Seville

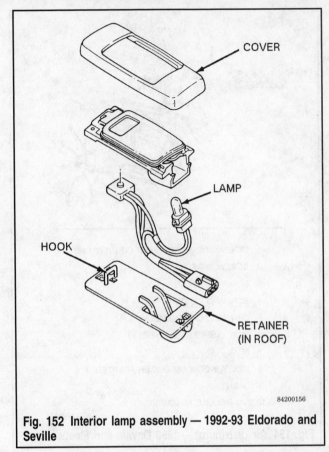

COVER

LAMP

HOOK

RETAINER (IN ROOF)

84200156

Fig. 152 Interior lamp assembly — 1992-93 Eldorado and Seville

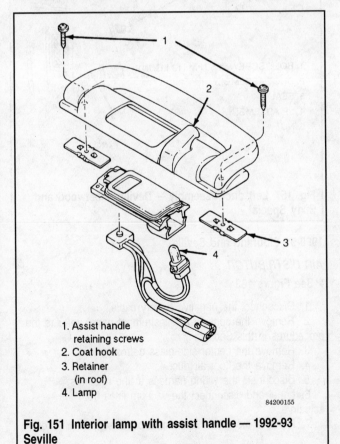

1. Assist handle retaining screws
2. Coat hook
3. Retainer (in roof)
4. Lamp

84200155

Fig. 151 Interior lamp with assist handle — 1992-93 Seville

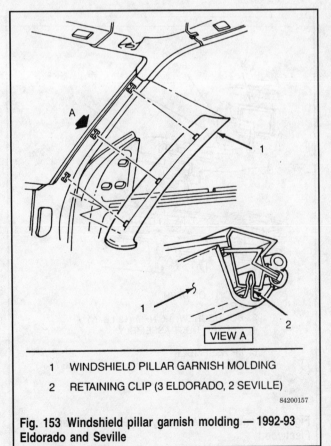

VIEW A

1   WINDSHIELD PILLAR GARNISH MOLDING

2   RETAINING CLIP (3 ELDORADO, 2 SEVILLE)

84200157

Fig. 153 Windshield pillar garnish molding — 1992-93 Eldorado and Seville

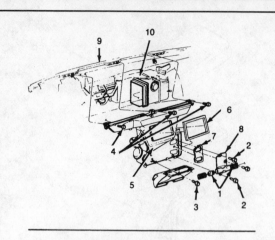

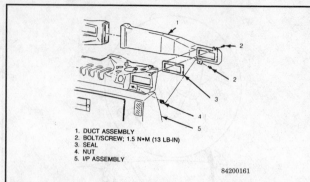

1. DUCT ASSEMBLY
2. BOLT/SCREW; 1.5 N•M (13 LB-IN)
3. SEAL
4. NUT
5. I/P ASSEMBLY

84200161

Fig. 156 Right duct assembly — Deville, Fleetwood and Sixty Special

1   SIDE WINDOW DEFOGGER CONNECTORS

2   SCREW (3 REQ'D)

3   SCREW (2 REQ'D)

4   SCREW (3 REQ'D)

5   DISTRIBUTOR ASSEMBLY

6   SEAL (ADHESIVE BACKED)

7   SEAL

8   SIDE WINDOW DEFOGGER ADAPTER

9   DASH

10 A/C MODULE ASSEMBLY

84200158

Fig. 154 Air distributor — 1990 Deville and Fleetwood

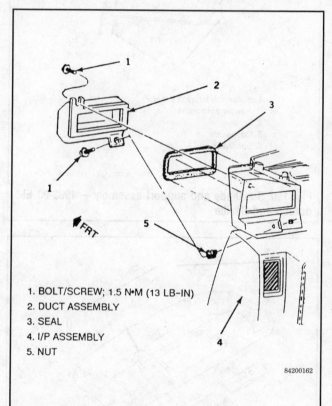

1. BOLT/SCREW; 1.5 N•M (13 LB-IN)
2. DUCT ASSEMBLY
3. SEAL
4. I/P ASSEMBLY
5. NUT

84200162

Fig. 157 Left duct assembly — Deville, Fleetwood and Sixty Special

1990-91 Eldorado and Seville

AIR DISTRIBUTOR

▶ See Figure 163

1. Disconnect the negative battery cable.
2. Remove the console and instrument panel; refer to the procedures in this Section.
3. Remove the center side-glass defroster duct.
4. Remove the floor air duct.
5. Disconnect the wiring harness at the retainers.
6. Label and disconnect the vacuum lines from the actuators.
7. Remove the center instrument panel support bracket.

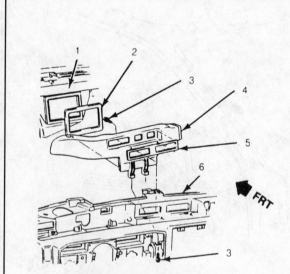

1: FRONT OF DASH
2: SEAL
3: BOLT/SCREW; 1.5 N•M (13 LB-IN)
4: CENTER DUCT ASSEMBLY
5: SEAL
6: I/P ASSEMBLY

84200160

Fig. 155 Center duct assembly — 1990 Deville and Fleetwood

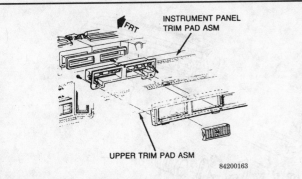

Fig. 158 Center outlet housing — Deville, Fleetwood and Sixty Special

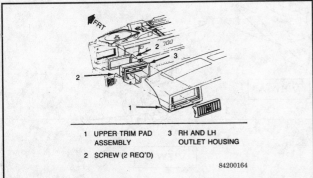

1	UPPER TRIM PAD ASSEMBLY	3 RH AND LH OUTLET HOUSING
2	SCREW (2 REQ'D)	

Fig. 159 Right and left outlet housings — Deville, Fleetwood and Sixty Special

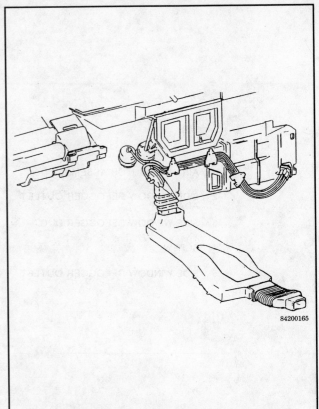

Fig. 160 Air distributor — 1991-93 Deville, Fleetwood and Sixty Special

8. Label and disconnect the 2 vacuum lines from the air distributor. Remove the air distributor retaining screws and remove the air distributor.

9. Installation is the reverse of the removal procedure.

LEFT AND CENTER/RIGHT DUCTS

▶ See Figures 164 and 165

1. Disconnect the negative battery cable.
2. Remove the console and instrument panel; refer to the procedures in this Section.
3. Remove the side window defogger adapter.
4. Remove the center/right duct mounting screws and the duct.
5. Remove the left duct mounting screws and duct.
6. Installation is the reverse of the removal procedure. Tighten the duct mounting screws to 18 inch lbs. (2 Nm).

SIDE WINDOW DEFOGGER DUCT

▶ See Figure 166

1. Disconnect the negative battery cable.
2. Remove the console and instrument panel; refer to the procedures in this Section.
3. Remove the duct connector from the adapter.
4. Remove the adapter retaining screws and the adapter.
5. Remove the duct retaining screw and the side window defogger duct.
6. Installation is the reverse of the removal procedure.

CENTER OUTLET HOUSING

▶ See Figure 167

1. Remove the 2 trim plate screws.
2. Remove the accessory trim plate from the instrument panel.
3. Installation is the reverse of the removal procedure. Tighten the trim plate mounting screws to 18 inch lbs. (2 Nm).

RIGHT OUTLET HOUSING

▶ See Figure 168

1. Rotate the outlet grille completely to one side and pull outward.
2. Remove the outlet housing from the instrument panel upper trim pad.
3. Installation is the reverse of the removal procedure.

LEFT OUTLET HOUSING

▶ See Figure 169

1. Disconnect the negative battery cable.
2. Remove the console and instrument panel; refer to the procedures in this Section.
3. Remove the instrument cluster; refer to Section 6.
4. Remove the dash trim plate screw, air outlet housing screw and the air outlet housing.
5. Installation is the reverse of the removal procedure. Tighten the trim plate and outlet housing retaining screws to 18 inch lbs. (2 Nm).

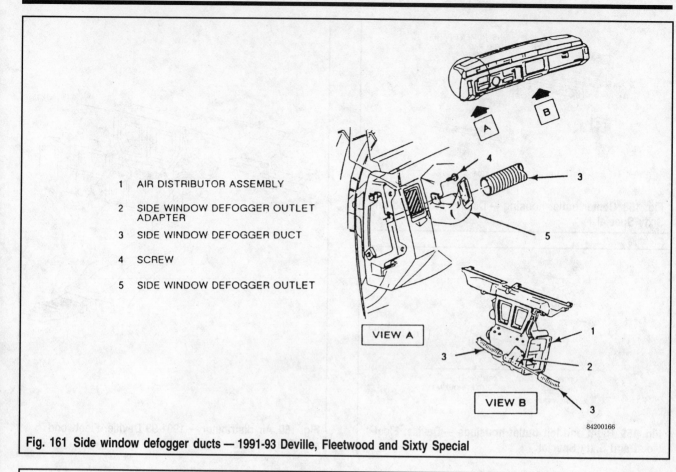

1 AIR DISTRIBUTOR ASSEMBLY

2 SIDE WINDOW DEFOGGER OUTLET
  ADAPTER

3 SIDE WINDOW DEFOGGER DUCT

4 SCREW

5 SIDE WINDOW DEFOGGER OUTLET

VIEW A

VIEW B

84200166

Fig. 161 Side window defogger ducts — 1991-93 Deville, Fleetwood and Sixty Special

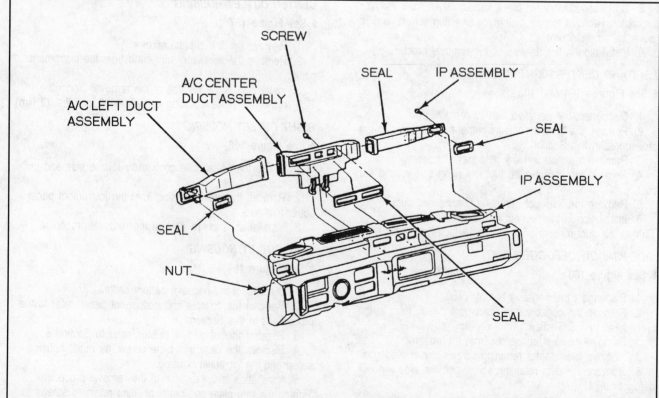

SCREW

A/C CENTER
DUCT ASSEMBLY

SEAL

IP ASSEMBLY

A/C LEFT DUCT
ASSEMBLY

SEAL

IP ASSEMBLY

SEAL

NUT

SEAL

84200167

Fig. 162 Duct assemblies — 1991-93 Deville, Fleetwood and Sixty Special

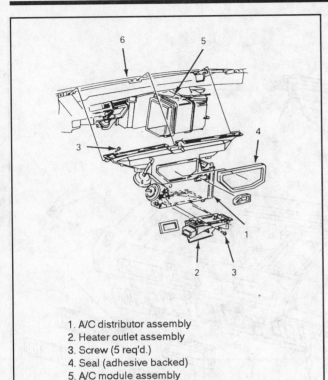

1. A/C distributor assembly
2. Heater outlet assembly
3. Screw (5 req'd.)
4. Seal (adhesive backed)
5. A/C module assembly
6. Dash

84200168

Fig. 163 Air distributor — 1990-91 Eldorado and Seville

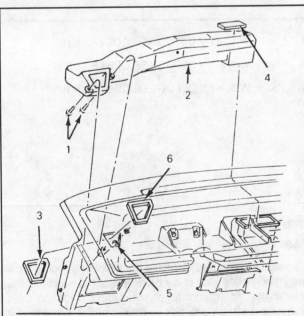

1	SCREW (2 REQ'D)	4	SPACER
2	DUCT ASSEMBLY — L.H.	5	NUT (2 REQ'D)
3	SEAL	6	SEAL

84200169

Fig. 164 Left duct assembly — 1990-91 Eldorado and Seville

1992-93 Eldorado and Seville

AIR DISTRIBUTOR

▶ **See Figure 170**

1. Disconnect the negative battery cable.
2. Remove the console and instrument panel; refer to the procedures in this Section.
3. Remove the emergency brake assembly.
4. Remove the cross car brace.
5. Disconnect the wiring harness at the retainers.
6. Label and disconnect the vacuum lines from the actuators.
7. Label and disconnect the vacuum lines from the air distributor.
8. Remove the air distributor retaining screws and the air distributor.
9. Installation is the reverse of the removal procedure.

DUCTS

▶ **See Figure 171**

1. Disconnect the negative battery cable.
2. Remove the console and instrument panel; refer to the procedures in this Section.
3. Remove the side window defogger adapter.
4. Remove the duct mounting screws and duct.
5. Installation is the reverse of the removal procedure. Tighten the duct mounting screws to 18 inch lbs. (2 Nm).

OUTLETS

▶ **See Figure 172**

Insert a small prybar between the deflector and the duct housing on each side to release the location tabs and slide out.

Door Locks

REMOVAL & INSTALLATION

1990 Deville and Fleetwood

LOCK STRIKER

▶ **See Figures 173 and 174**

1. Mark the position of the striker on the body lock pillar using a pencil.
2. Use tool J-23457, BT 7107 or equivalent, remove the lock striker.

To install:

3. Install the striker to the body using tool J-23457, BT 7107 or equivalent. Align the striker with the pencil marks and tighten the striker bolt to 42 ft. lbs. (55 Nm).
4. If striker adjustment is necessary, proceed as follows:
   a. Make sure the door is properly aligned.
   b. Apply modeling clay or body caulking compound to the lock bolt opening.
   c. Close the door just enough for the striker bolt to form an impression in the clay or caulking compound.

➡**Closing the door completely will make clay removal difficult.**

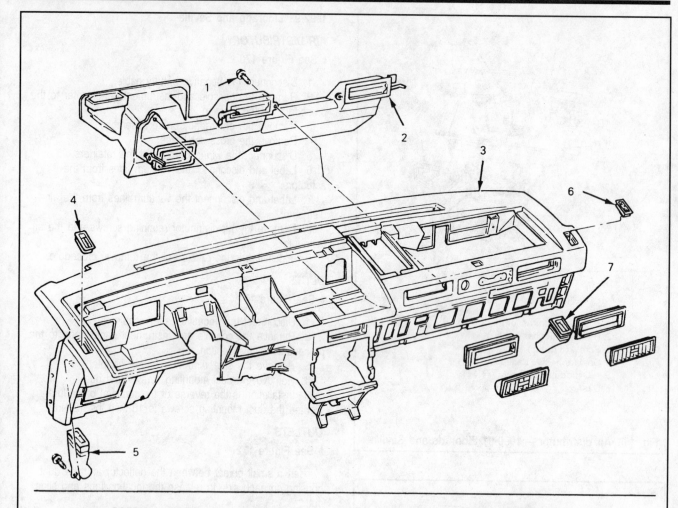

1	SCREW (6 REQ'D)	5	SIDE WINDOW DEFOGGER DUCT — L.H.
2	DUCT ASSEMBLY — AIR DISTRIBUTOR	6	SIDE WINDOW DEFOGGER GRILLE — R.H.
3	INSTRUMENT PANEL	7	SIDE WINDOW DEFOGGER DUCT — R.H.
4	SIDE WINDOW DEFOGGER GRILLE — L.H.		

84200170

Fig. 165 Center/right duct assembly — 1990-91 Eldorado and Seville

d. The striker impression should be centered fore and aft. The minimum allowable measurement for dimension X in Fig. '84200179' is $\frac{3}{32}$ in. (2mm). The maximum allowable measurement for dimension X is $\frac{5}{32}$ in. (4mm). A $\frac{3}{32}$ in. (2mm) spacer, part No. 4469196 or equivalent, can be used for alignment.

e. If adjustment is necessary, insert tool J-23457, BT 7107 or equivalent, into the star-shaped recess in the head of the striker and loosen the striker bolt. Shift the striker as required, then tighten the striker bolt to 42 ft. lbs. (55 Nm).

5. Touch up any exposed unpainted surface on the lock pillar next to the striker, if the striker is outside the pencil marks.

SPRING CLIPS

▶ See Figure 175

Spring clips are used to secure the handle connecting rods and inside locking rods to door lock levers and handle levers. A slot in the clip provides for disengagement of the rod.

1. Use a scratch awl, pick or other thin-bladed tool to slide the clip out of engagement.

2. Remove the rod by pulling it out of the clip.

To install:

3. Press the clip fully on the lever.

4. Press the rod through the hole in the lever until fully engaged by the clip.

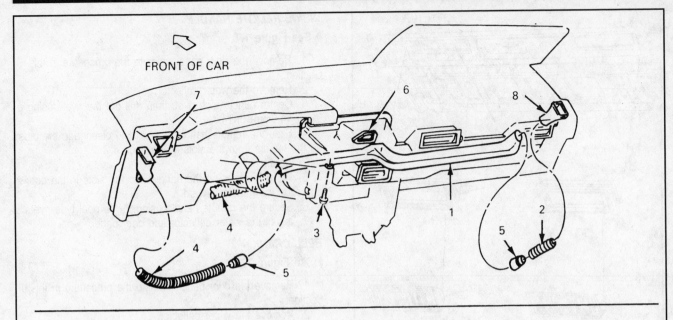

1   ADAPTER   5   CONNECTOR (2 REQ'D)
2   DUCT ASSEMBLY — R.H.   6   SEAL
3   SCREW (2 REQ'D)   7   SIDE WINDOW DEFOGGER DUCT — L.H.
4   DUCT ASSEMBLY — L.H.   8   SIDE WINDOW DEFOGGER DUCT — R.H.

84200171

Fig. 166 Side window defogger duct — 1990-91 Eldorado and Seville

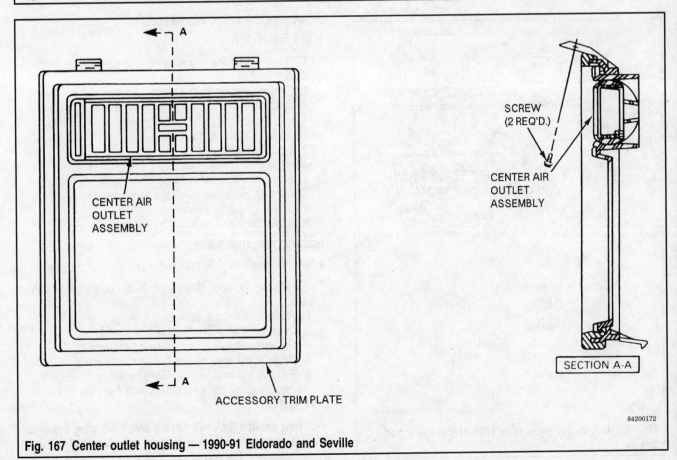

84200172

Fig. 167 Center outlet housing — 1990-91 Eldorado and Seville

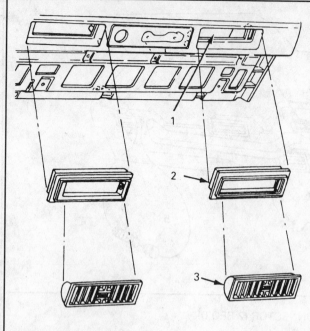

1. Instrument panel
2. Air outlet housing
3. Air outlet assembly

84200173

Fig. 168 Right outlet housing — 1990-91 Eldorado and Seville

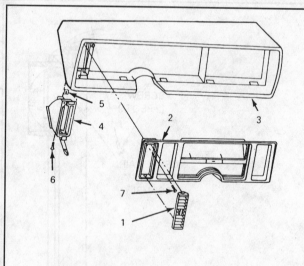

1. Air outlet assembly
2. Dash trim plate
3. Dash pod
4. Air outlet housing
5. Nut
6. Screw
7. Screw

84200174

Fig. 169 Left outlet housing — 1990-91 Eldorado and Seville

INSIDE REMOTE HANDLE

▶ **See Figure 176**

1. Remove the door panel; refer to the procedure in this Section.
2. Remove the water deflector.
3. Center punch each rivet, then drill out the rivets using a ³/₁₆ in. (4.8mm) drill bit.
4. Slide the remote handle rearward to disengage the tabs on the handle from the slots in the door.

To install:

5. Place the tabs on the handle into the slots in the door and slide the handle forward.
6. Secure the remote handle using ³/₁₆ in. peel type rivets.
7. Install the water deflector and door panel.

BELL CRANK

▶ **See Figure 177**

1. Remove the door panel; refer to the procedure in this Section.
2. Remove the water deflector.
3. Disconnect the lock-to-bell crank, actuator and lock switch linkage rods.
4. Use a ³/₁₆ in. (4.8mm) drill bit to drill out the rivet retaining the bell crank to the door.
5. Remove the bell crank.

To install:

6. Attach the bell crank to the door using a ⁵/₁₆ in. rivet.
7. Attach the linkage rods.
8. Install the water deflector and door panel.

POWER DOOR LOCK ACTUATOR

▶ **See Figure 177**

1. Remove the door panel; refer to the procedure in this Section.
2. Remove the water deflector.
3. Disconnect the actuator linkage from the bell crank.
4. Use a ³/₁₆ in. (4.8mm) drill bit to drill out the rivets retaining the actuator to the door.
5. Remove the actuator.

To install:

6. Attach the actuator to the door using ⁵/₁₆ in. rivets.
7. Connect the actuator linkage to the bell crank.
8. Check for proper operation.
9. Install the water deflector and door panel.

DOOR LOCK ASSEMBLY

▶ **See Figures 178, 179 and 180**

1. Remove the door panel; refer to the procedure in this Section.
2. Remove the water deflector.
3. Disconnect all rods attached to the lock.
4. Remove the lock by straightening the tabs.
5. Remove the door ajar switch attaching screw.
6. Remove the door ajar switch by pushing down on the switch to disengage the lip on the switch from the lock.

To install:

➡A new service lock will have a block-out plug installed. Do not operate the lock or remove the plug until the lock is installed and the rod is connected to the lock.

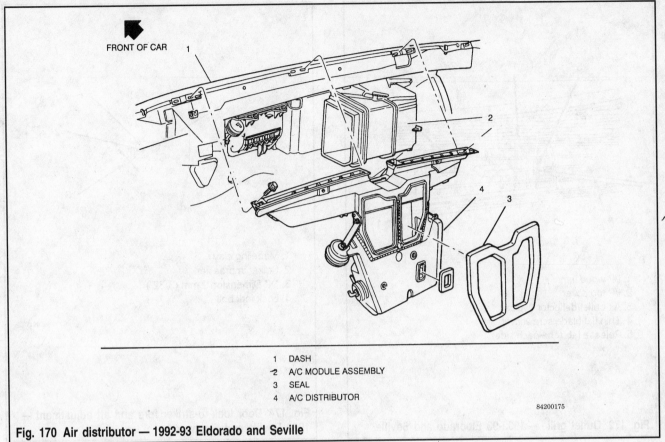

FRONT OF CAR

1 DASH
2 A/C MODULE ASSEMBLY
3 SEAL
4 A/C DISTRIBUTOR

84200175

Fig. 170 Air distributor — 1992-93 Eldorado and Seville

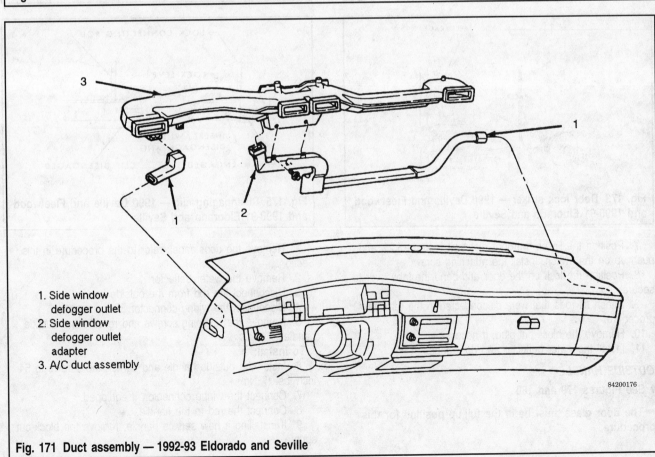

1. Side window defogger outlet
2. Side window defogger outlet adapter
3. A/C duct assembly

84200176

Fig. 171 Duct assembly — 1992-93 Eldorado and Seville

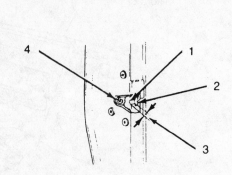

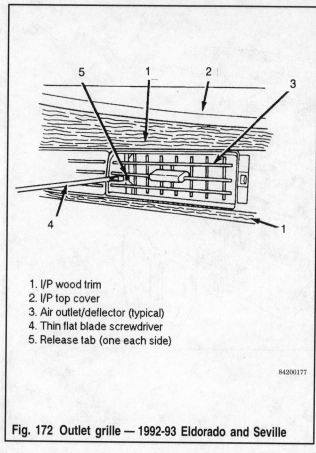

1. I/P wood trim
2. I/P top cover
3. Air outlet/deflector (typical)
4. Thin flat blade screwdriver
5. Release tab (one each side)

84200177

Fig. 172 Outlet grille — 1992-93 Eldorado and Seville

1. Modeling clay
2. Striker impression
3. "X" Dimension 2 mm (3/32")
4. Lock fork bolt

84200179

Fig. 174 Door lock-to-striker fore and aft adjustment — 1990 Deville and Fleetwood

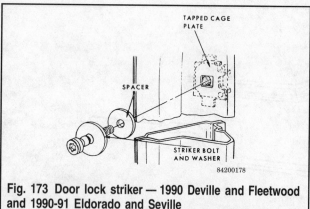

84200178

Fig. 173 Door lock striker — 1990 Deville and Fleetwood and 1990-91 Eldorado and Seville

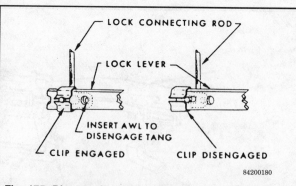

84200180

Fig. 175 Disengaging clip — 1990 Deville and Fleetwood and 1990-91 Eldorado and Seville

7. Position the lip on the door ajar switch to the lock and push up on the switch. Install the attaching screw.

8. Position the lock on the door and bend the tabs over to secure.

9. Attach all rods that were disconnected in the removal procedure.

10. Remove the block-out plug, if necessary.

11. Install the water deflector and door panel.

OUTSIDE HANDLE

▶ See Figures 179 and 180

➡ The door glass must be in the full-up position for this procedure.

1. Remove the door panel; refer to the procedure in this Section.

2. Remove the water deflector.

3. Disconnect the rod from the outside handle.

4. Disconnect the wiring connector, if equipped.

5. Remove the retaining screws and remove the outside handle.

To install:

6. Install the outside handle and tighten the screws to 54 inch lbs. (7 Nm).

7. Connect the wiring connector, if equipped.

8. Connect the rod to the handle.

9. If installing a new service handle, remove the block-out spring.

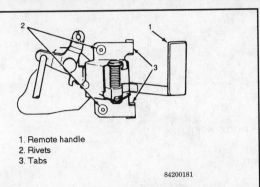

1. Remote handle
2. Rivets
3. Tabs

84200181

Fig. 176 Inside remote handle — Deville, Fleetwood and Sixty Special

10. Check the door lock system for proper operation.
11. Install the water deflector and door panel.

LOCK CYLINDER

▶ See Figure 181

➡ **The door glass must be in the full-up position for this procedure.**

1. Remove the door panel; refer to the procedure in this Section.
2. Remove the water deflector.
3. Disconnect the rod.
4. Disconnect the wiring connector, if equipped.
5. Disconnect or reposition any wiring harnesses that are in the way.

6. Use a flat-bladed tool to remove the lock cylinder retainer and remove the lock cylinder.
To install:
7. Install a gasket over the lock cylinder.
8. Install the lock cylinder, including any wiring harnesses that may be attached.
9. Install the lock cylinder retainer.
10. Connect the wiring connector, if equipped.
11. Connect or reposition any other wiring harnesses, as necessary.
12. Connect the rod.
13. Install the water deflector and door panel.

1991-93 Deville, Fleetwood and Sixty Special

LOCK STRIKER

▶ See Figure 182

1. Mark the position of the striker on the body lock pillar using a pencil.
2. Remove the 2 striker bolts and the lock striker.
To install:
3. Position the lock striker on the lock pillar and install the striker bolts.
4. Align the striker with the pencil marks and tighten the bolts to 18 ft. lbs. (24 Nm).
5. If necessary, align the striker as follows:
   a. Loosen the striker bolts, then snug them so that the striker can still be moved.
   b. Hold the outside handle out and gently push the door against the body to be sure the striker allows a flush fit.

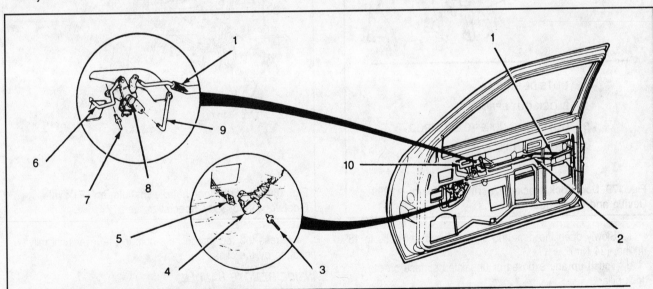

1	BELL CRANK TO LOCK ROD	6	ACTUATOR LINKAGE
2	INSIDE REMOTE TO LOCK ROD	7	BELL CRANK RIVET
3	ACTUATOR RIVET	8	BELL CRANK
4	ACTUATOR	9	LOCK SWITCH LINKAGE
5	CONNECTOR	10	INSIDE REMOTE HANDLE

84200182

Fig. 177 Door lock assembly — 1990 Deville and Fleetwood

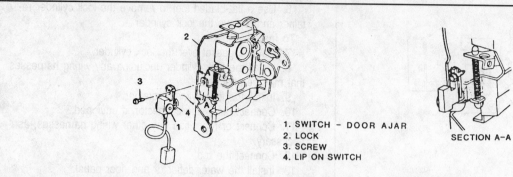

1. SWITCH - DOOR AJAR
2. LOCK
3. SCREW
4. LIP ON SWITCH

SECTION A-A

84200183

Fig. 178 Door lock assembly and door ajar switch — 1990 Deville and Fleetwood and 1990-91 Eldorado and Seville

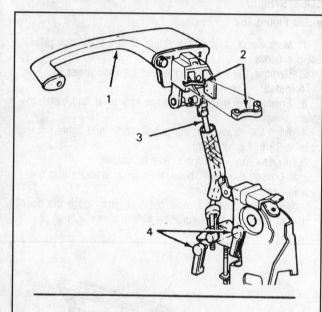

1 . OUTSIDE HANDLE

2 BLOCK-OUT SPRING

3 OUTSIDE HANDLE TO LOCK ROD

4 BLOCK-OUT PLUG

84200184

Fig. 179 Door lock block-out spring and plug — 1990 Deville and Fleetwood

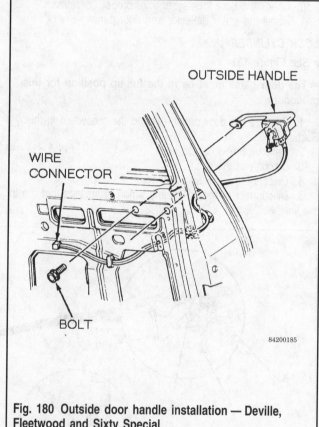

OUTSIDE HANDLE

WIRE CONNECTOR

BOLT

84200185

Fig. 180 Outside door handle installation — Deville, Fleetwood and Sixty Special

c. Slowly open the door and tighten the striker bolts to 18 ft. lbs. (24 Nm).

d. Touch up any exposed or unpainted surface on the lock pillar.

LOCK ROD CLIPS

▶ See Figure 183

1. Remove the clip from the lever by using a scratch awl, pick or other thin-bladed tool and sliding the clip out of engagement.

2. Pull the rod out of the clip.

To install:

3. Press the clip fully on the lever.

4. Press the rod through the hole in the lever until fully engaged by the clip.

INSIDE REMOTE HANDLE

▶ See Figure 176

1. Remove the door panel; refer to the procedure in this Section.

2. Remove the water deflector.

3. Center punch each rivet, then drill out the rivets using a 3/16 in. (4.8mm) drill bit.

4. Slide the remote handle rearward to disengage the tabs on the handle from the slots in the door.

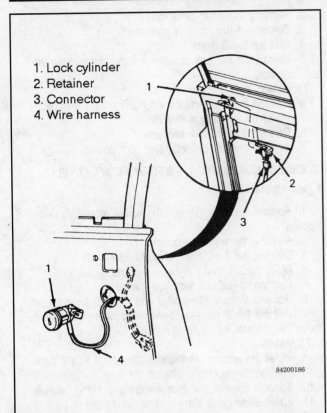

1. Lock cylinder
2. Retainer
3. Connector
4. Wire harness

84200186

Fig. 181 Door lock cylinder installation — Deville, Fleetwood and Sixty Special

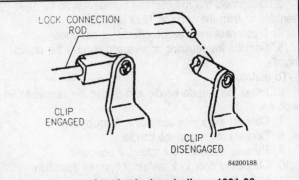

LOCK CONNECTION ROD

CLIP ENGAGED

CLIP DISENGAGED

84200188

Fig. 183 Disengaging the lock rod clip — 1991-93 Deville, Fleetwood and Sixty Special

To install:

5. Place the tabs on the handle into the slots in the door and slide the handle forward.

6. Secure the remote handle using ³⁄₁₆ in. peel type rivets.

7. Install the water deflector and door panel.

OUTSIDE HANDLE

▶ See Figures 180 and 184

➡ **The door glass must be in the full-up position for this procedure.**

1. Remove the door panel; refer to the procedure in this Section.

2. Remove the water deflector.

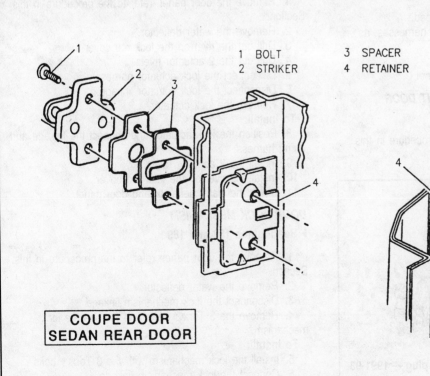

1 BOLT
2 STRIKER

3 SPACER
4 RETAINER

**COUPE DOOR
SEDAN REAR DOOR**

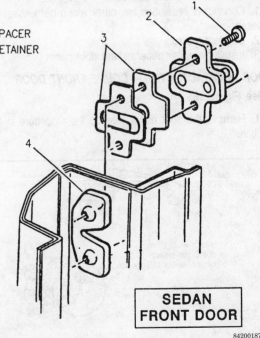

**SEDAN
FRONT DOOR**

84200187

Fig. 182 Door lock striker — 1991-93 Deville, Fleetwood and Sixty Special

3. Disconnect the rod from the outside handle on 1991-92 vehicles or from the latch on 1993 vehicles.

4. Disconnect the wiring connector, if equipped.

5. Remove the retaining screws and remove the outside handle.

To install:

6. Install the outside handle and tighten the screws to 54 inch lbs. (7 Nm).

7. Connect the wiring connector, if equipped.

8. Connect the rod to the handle.

9. Remove the block-out spring, if equipped.

10. Check the door lock system for proper operation.

11. Install the water deflector and door panel.

LOCK CYLINDER

▶ **See Figure 181**

➡ **The door glass must be in the full-up position for this procedure.**

1. Remove the door panel; refer to the procedure in this Section.

2. Remove the water deflector.

3. Disconnect the rod.

4. Disconnect the wiring connector, if equipped.

5. Disconnect or reposition any wiring harnesses that are in the way.

6. Use a flat-bladed tool to remove the lock cylinder retainer and remove the lock cylinder.

To install:

7. Install a gasket over the lock cylinder.

8. Install the lock cylinder, including any wiring harnesses that may be attached.

9. Install the lock cylinder retainer.

10. Connect the wiring connector, if equipped.

11. Connect or reposition any other wiring harnesses, as necessary.

12. Connect the rod.

13. Install the water deflector and door panel.

DOOR LOCK ACTUATOR — COUPE FRONT DOOR

▶ **See Figure 185**

1. Remove the door panel; refer to the procedure in this Section.

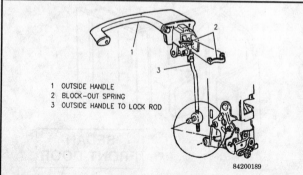

1 OUTSIDE HANDLE
2 BLOCK-OUT SPRING
3 OUTSIDE HANDLE TO LOCK ROD

84200189

Fig. 184 Door lock block-out spring and plug — 1991-93 Deville, Fleetwood and Sixty Special

2. Remove the water deflector.

3. Disconnect the actuator harness.

4. Drill out the 2 rivets.

5. Disconnect the lock actuator linkage and remove the lock actuator.

To install:

6. Position the lock actuator and connect the linkage.

7. Install the actuator with 2 rivets.

8. Connect the actuator harness.

9. Install the water deflector and door panel.

DOOR LOCK ACTUATOR — SEDAN FRONT DOOR

▶ **See Figure 186**

1. Remove the door panel; refer to the procedure in this Section.

2. Remove the water deflector.

3. Drill out the 3 mounting plate-to-door rivets.

4. Disconnect the lock actuator harness.

5. Disconnect the lock actuator linkage.

6. Remove the mounting plate and actuator from the door.

7. Drill out the 2 actuator-to-mounting plate rivets and remove the actuator.

To install:

8. Install the actuator to the mounting plate with 2 rivets.

9. Position the mounting plate in the door.

10. Connect the lock actuator linkage and wiring harness.

11. Install 3 mounting plate-to-door rivets.

12. Install the water deflector and door panel.

DOOR LOCK ACTUATOR — REAR DOOR

▶ **See Figure 187**

1. Remove the door panel; refer to the procedure in this Section.

2. Remove the water deflector.

3. Drill out the rivet on the lock rod cover.

4. Drill out the 2 actuator rivets.

5. Disconnect the lock actuator harness.

6. Disconnect the lock actuator linkage.

7. Remove the lock actuator.

To install:

8. Position the lock actuator and connect the linkage and wiring harness.

9. Install the 2 actuator rivets.

10. Install the rivet on the lock rod cover.

11. Install the water deflector and door panel.

DOOR LOCK MECHANISM

▶ **See Figures 188 and 189**

1. Remove the door panel; refer to the procedure in this Section.

2. Remove the water deflector.

3. Disconnect the lock mechanism linkage.

4. Remove the 3 Torx® bolts and remove the lock mechanism.

To install:

5. Install the lock mechanism with the 3 Torx® bolts.

6. Connect the lock mechanism linkage.

7. Install the water deflector and door panel.

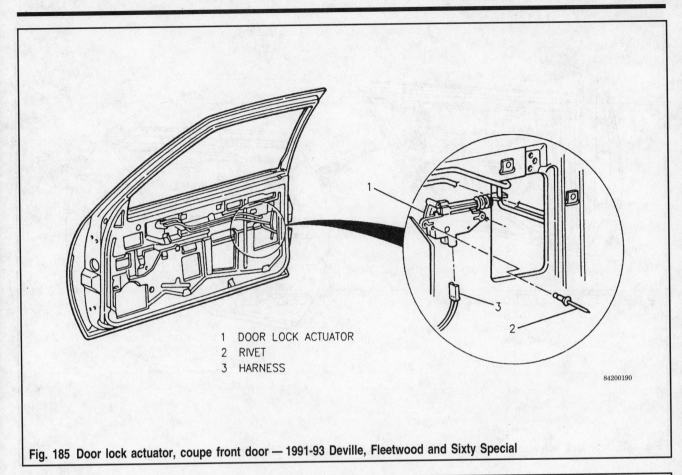

1 DOOR LOCK ACTUATOR
2 RIVET
3 HARNESS

84200190

Fig. 185 Door lock actuator, coupe front door — 1991-93 Deville, Fleetwood and Sixty Special

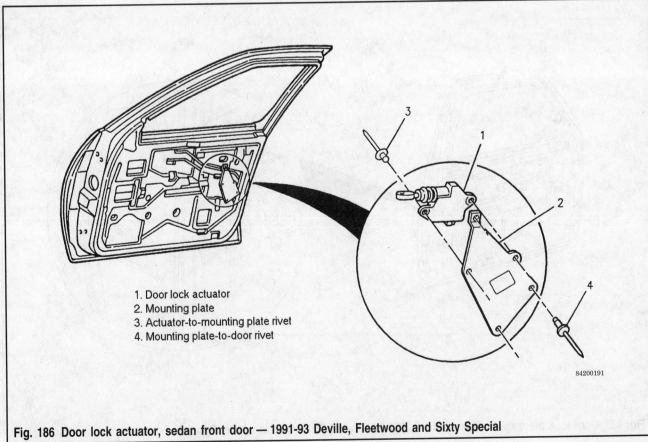

1. Door lock actuator
2. Mounting plate
3. Actuator-to-mounting plate rivet
4. Mounting plate-to-door rivet

84200191

Fig. 186 Door lock actuator, sedan front door — 1991-93 Deville, Fleetwood and Sixty Special

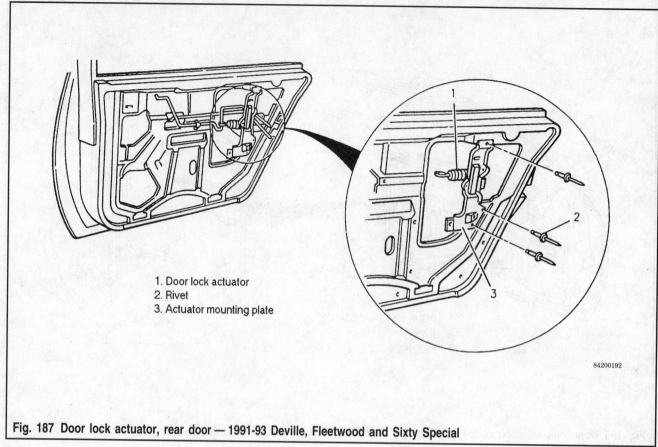

1. Door lock actuator
2. Rivet
3. Actuator mounting plate

84200192

Fig. 187 Door lock actuator, rear door — 1991-93 Deville, Fleetwood and Sixty Special

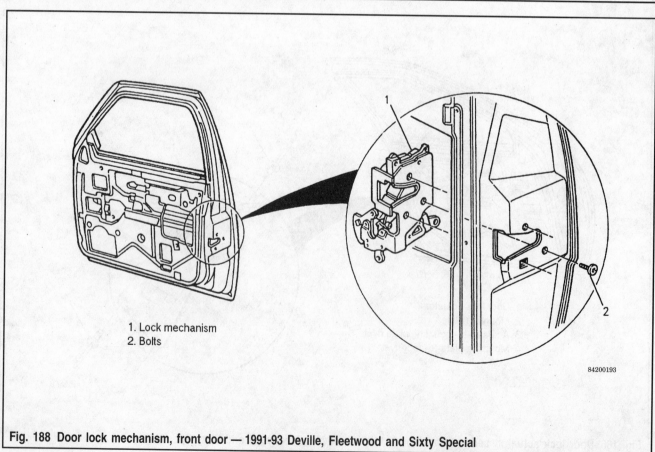

1. Lock mechanism
2. Bolts

84200193

Fig. 188 Door lock mechanism, front door — 1991-93 Deville, Fleetwood and Sixty Special

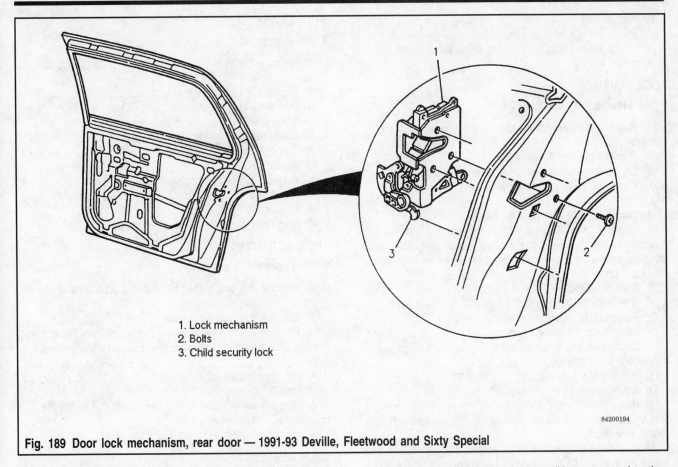

1. Lock mechanism
2. Bolts
3. Child security lock

Fig. 189 Door lock mechanism, rear door — 1991-93 Deville, Fleetwood and Sixty Special

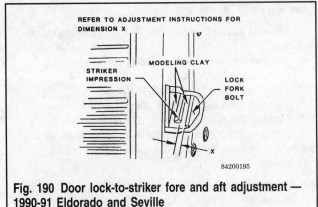

Fig. 190 Door lock-to-striker fore and aft adjustment — 1990-91 Eldorado and Seville

1990-91 Eldorado and Seville

LOCK STRIKER

▶ **See Figures 173 and 190**

1. Mark the position of the striker on the body lock pillar using a pencil.
2. Use tool J-23457, BT 7107 or equivalent, remove the lock striker.

To install:

3. Install the striker to the body using tool J-23457, BT 7107 or equivalent. Align the striker with the pencil marks and tighten the striker bolt to 42 ft. lbs. (55 Nm).
4. If striker adjustment is necessary, proceed as follows:
   a. Make sure the door is properly aligned.

b. Apply modeling clay or body caulking compound to the lock bolt opening.
   c. Close the door just enough for the striker bolt to form an impression in the clay or caulking compound.

➡**Closing the door completely will make clay removal difficult.**

d. The striker impression should be centered fore and aft. The minimum allowable measurement for dimension X in Fig. '84200195' is $3/32$ in. (2mm). The maximum allowable measurement for dimension X is $5/32$ in. (4mm). A $3/32$ in. (2mm) spacer, part No. 4469196 or equivalent, can be used for alignment.
   e. If adjustment is necessary, insert tool J-23457, BT 7107 or equivalent, into the star-shaped recess in the head of the striker and loosen the striker bolt. Shift the striker as required, then tighten the striker bolt to 42 ft. lbs. (55 Nm).
5. Touch up any exposed unpainted surface on the lock pillar next to the striker, if the striker is outside the pencil marks.

SPRING CLIPS

▶ **See Figure 175**

Spring clips are used to secure the handle connecting rods and inside locking rods to door lock levers and handle levers. A slot in the clip provides for disengagement of the rod.

1. Use a scratch awl, pick or other thin-bladed tool to slide the clip out of engagement.
2. Remove the rod by pulling it out of the clip.

To install:

3. Press the clip fully on the lever.

4. Press the rod through the hole in the lever until fully engaged by the clip.

LOCK MODULE

▶ **See Figures 191, 192 and 193**

1. Remove the door panel; refer to the procedure in this Section.

2. Remove the water deflector.

3. On Seville, remove the inner panel cam retaining screws and remove the inner panel cam by sliding off roller of regulator.

4. Disconnect the rod from the handle.

5. Use a ¼ in. (6.3mm) drill bit to drill out the rear run channel retainer rivet. Remove the rear run channel retainer by lifting up on the retainer to disengage the lower retainer from the upper channel.

6. Disconnect the rod from the lock.

7. Use a ³⁄₁₆ in. (4.8mm) drill bit to drill out the 2 rivets.

8. Remove the retaining screws.

9. Disconnect the wiring connector.

10. Disconnect any other electrical connectors present, as necessary (keyless entry, door ajar, etc.).

11. Remove the lock module.

To install:

12. Place the lock module in position through the access hole in the door inner panel, aligning the module to the holes in the door facing.

13. Hold the lock assembly tight against the door facing and install the screws. All screws must be driven at a 90 degree angle to the door facing to prevent cross-threading or stripping of the screws or the door lock attaching holes. Tighten the screws to 48-60 inch lbs. (6.0-7.5 Nm).

14. Install new rivets.

15. Connect the actuator wiring connector.

16. Connect any connectors disconnected in Step 10.

17. Connect the rods to the lock and handle.

18. Engage the tab on the rear run channel retainer with the slot in the upper channel. Secure with a new rivet.

19. On Seville, install the inner panel cam locating over roller of regulator. Install the screws and tighten to 72-96 inch lbs. (9-12 Nm).

20. Install the water deflector and door panel.

INSIDE REMOTE HANDLE

▶ **See Figure 194**

1. Remove the door panel; refer to the procedure in this Section.

2. Remove the water deflector.

3. Center punch each rivet, then drill out the rivets using a ³⁄₁₆ in. (4.8mm) drill bit.

4. Slide the remote handle rearward to disengage the tabs on the handle from the slots in the module assembly.

To install:

5. Place the tabs on the handle into the slots in the module and slide the handle forward.

6. Secure the remote handle using ³⁄₁₆ in. peel type rivets.

7. Install the water deflector and door panel.

BELL CRANK

▶ **See Figure 195**

1. Remove the door panel; refer to the procedure in this Section.

2. Remove the water deflector.

3. Use a ³⁄₁₆ in. (4.8mm) drill bit to drill out the rivet retaining the bell crank to the lock module assembly.

4. Disconnect the inside locking-to-lock rod.

5. Remove the bell crank.

To install:

6. Connect the inside locking-to-lock rod.

7. Attach the bell crank to the lock module assembly using a ⁵⁄₁₆ in. rivet.

8. Install the water deflector and door panel.

LOCK ACTUATOR

▶ **See Figures 191 and 195**

1. Remove the door panel; refer to the procedure in this Section.

2. Remove the water deflector.

3. Remove the screws retaining the actuator to the lock module assembly and disengage the actuator from the bell crank.

4. Remove the actuator.

To install:

5. Connect the actuator to the bell crank and install the actuator retaining screws.

6. Install the water deflector and door panel.

LOCK ASSEMBLY

▶ **See Figures 178, 195 and 196**

1. Remove the door panel; refer to the procedure in this Section.

2. Remove the water deflector.

3. Remove the lock module assembly.

4. Disconnect all rods attached to the lock.

5. Remove the lock by straightening the tabs.

6. Remove the door ajar switch attaching screw.

7. Remove the door ajar switch by pushing down on the switch to disengage the lip on the switch from the lock.

To install:

➡**A new service lock will have a block-out plug installed. Do not operate the lock or remove the plug until the lock is installed and the rod is connected to the lock.**

8. Position the lip on the door ajar switch to the lock and push up on the switch. Install the attaching screw.

9. Position the lock on the lock module and bend the tabs over to secure.

10. Attach all rods that were disconnected in the removal procedure.

11. Install the lock module assembly.

12. The block-out plug is used to adjust the outside handle. With the block-out plug in place, push the outside handle rod up and adjust the barrel nut to fit in the lock lever. Remove the block-out plug.

13. Install the water deflector and door panel.

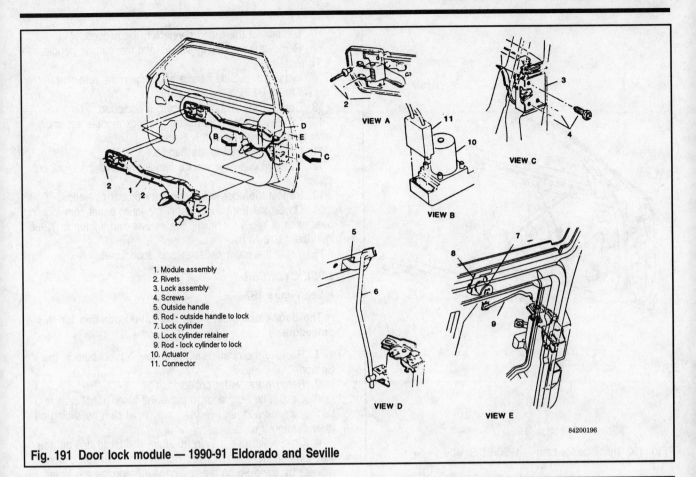

1. Module assembly
2. Rivets
3. Lock assembly
4. Screws
5. Outside handle
6. Rod - outside handle to lock
7. Lock cylinder
8. Lock cylinder retainer
9. Rod - lock cylinder to lock
10. Actuator
11. Connector

84200196

Fig. 191 Door lock module — 1990-91 Eldorado and Seville

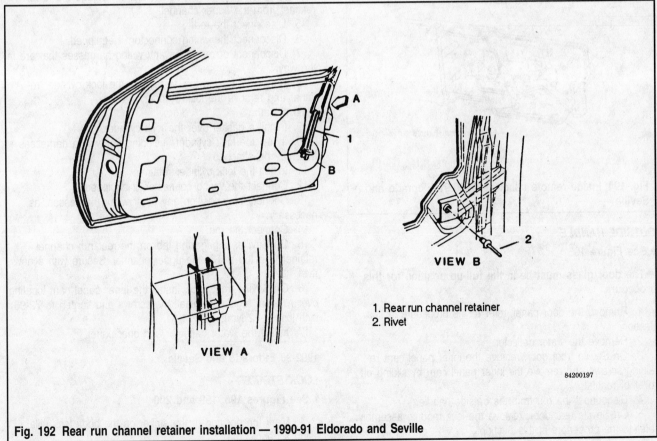

1. Rear run channel retainer
2. Rivet

84200197

Fig. 192 Rear run channel retainer installation — 1990-91 Eldorado and Seville

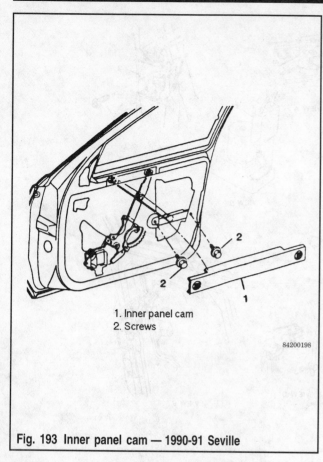

1. Inner panel cam
2. Screws

84200198

Fig. 193 Inner panel cam — 1990-91 Seville

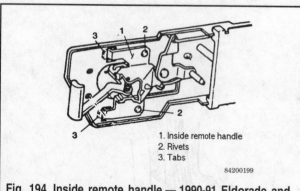

1. Inside remote handle
2. Rivets
3. Tabs

84200199

Fig. 194 Inside remote handle — 1990-91 Eldorado and Seville

OUTSIDE HANDLE

▶ See Figure 196

➥**The door glass must be in the full-up position for this procedure.**

1. Remove the door panel; refer to the procedure in this Section.
2. Remove the water deflector.
3. On Seville front door, remove the inner panel cam retaining screws and remove the inner panel cam by sliding off roller of regulator.
4. Disconnect the rod from the outside handle.
5. On Seville rear door, remove the lock module assembly; refer to the procedure in this Section.

6. Disconnect the wiring connector, if equipped.
7. Remove the retaining screws and the outside handle.

To install:

8. Install the outside handle and tighten the retaining screws to 48-60 inch lbs. (6-8 Nm).
9. Connect the wiring connector, if equipped.
10. On Seville rear door, install the lock module assembly; refer to the procedure in this Section.
11. Connect the rod to the handle.
12. If installing a new service handle, remove the block-out spring.
13. Inspect the door lock system for proper operation.
14. On Seville front door, install the inner panel cam locating over roller of regulator. Install the screws and tighten to 72-96 inch lbs. (9-12 Nm).
15. Install the water deflector and door panel.

LOCK CYLINDER

▶ See Figure 197

➥**The door glass must be in the full-up position for this procedure.**

1. Remove the door panel; refer to the procedure in this Section.
2. Remove the water deflector.
3. On Seville front door, remove the inner panel cam retaining screws and remove the inner panel cam by sliding off roller of regulator.
4. On Seville, use a ¼ in. (6.3mm) drill bit to drill out the rear run channel retainer rivet. Remove the rear run channel retainer by lifting up on the retainer to disengage the lower retainer from the upper channel.
5. Disconnect the rod.
6. Disconnect the wiring connector, if equipped.
7. Disconnect or reposition any wiring harnesses that are in the way.
8. Use a flat-bladed tool to remove the lock cylinder retainer and remove the lock cylinder.

To install:

9. Install a gasket over the lock cylinder.
10. Install the lock cylinder, including any wiring harnesses that may be attached.
11. Install the lock cylinder retainer.
12. Connect the wiring connector, if equipped.
13. Connect or reposition any other wiring harnesses, as necessary.
14. Connect the rod.
15. On Seville, engage the tab on the rear run channel retainer with the slot in the upper channel. Secure with a new rivet.
16. On Seville front door, install the inner panel cam locating over roller of regulator. Install the screws and tighten to 72-96 inch lbs. (9-12 Nm).
17. Install the water deflector and door panel.

1992-93 Eldorado and Seville

LOCK STRIKER

▶ See Figures 198, 199 and 200

1. Mark the position of the striker on the body lock pillar using a pencil.

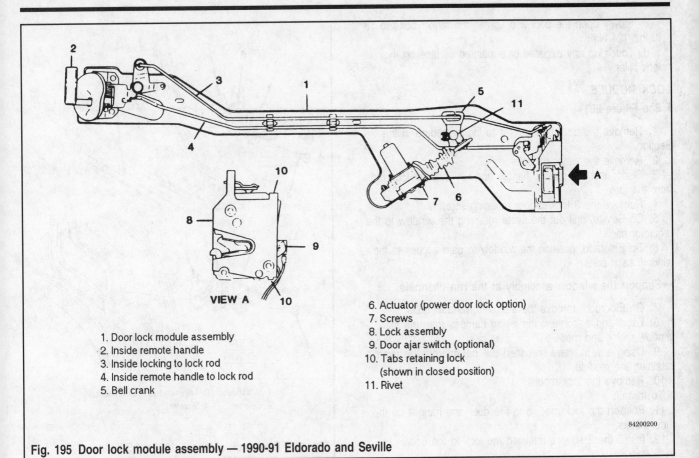

Fig. 195 Door lock module assembly — 1990-91 Eldorado and Seville

1. Door lock module assembly
2. Inside remote handle
3. Inside locking to lock rod
4. Inside remote handle to lock rod
5. Bell crank
6. Actuator (power door lock option)
7. Screws
8. Lock assembly
9. Door ajar switch (optional)
10. Tabs retaining lock
    (shown in closed position)
11. Rivet

84200200

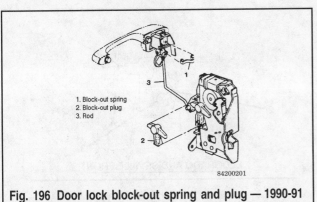

1. Block-out spring
2. Block-out plug
3. Rod

84200201

Fig. 196 Door lock block-out spring and plug — 1990-91 Eldorado and Seville

2. Remove the 2 striker bolts and the lock striker, spacer and washer.

To install:

3. Assemble the washer, spacer and striker.

4. Position the lock striker assembly on the lock pillar and install the striker bolts.

5. Align the striker with the pencil marks and tighten the bolts to 18 ft. lbs. (24 Nm).

6. If necessary, align the striker as follows:

   a. Loosen the striker bolts, then snug them so that the striker can still be moved. Place tool J-39346 or equivalent, over the striker.

   b. Hold the outside handle out and gently push the door flush against the body to locate the striker.

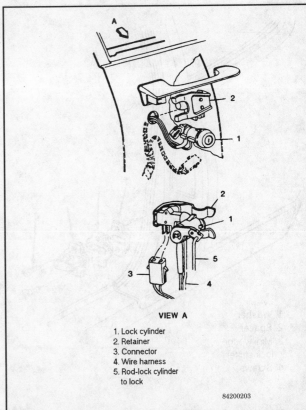

VIEW A

1. Lock cylinder
2. Retainer
3. Connector
4. Wire harness
5. Rod-lock cylinder
   to lock

84200203

Fig. 197 Door lock cylinder installation — 1990-91 Eldorado and Seville

c. Slowly open the door and tighten the striker bolts to 18 ft. lbs. (24 Nm).

d. Touch up any exposed or unpainted surface on the lock pillar.

LOCK MODULE

▶ **See Figure 201**

1. Remove the door panel; refer to the procedure in this Section.

2. Remove the water deflector.

3. Disconnect the outside handle and key cylinder lock rods from the lock.

4. Remove the 3 lock-to-door retaining screws.

5. On Seville, drill out the rivets retaining the window to the regulator sash.

6. On Eldorado, position the window to gain access to the window sash bolts.

➡ **Support the window assembly at the run channels.**

7. On Eldorado, remove the 3 sash-to-window bolts.

8. Label and disconnect the wiring harness from the lock, window motor and module.

9. Using a ¼ in. case hardened drill bit, drill out the rivets retaining the module.

10. Remove the lock module.

To install:

11. Position the lock module to the door and hang it on the inner hooks.

12. Install the 3 screws retaining the lock to the door.

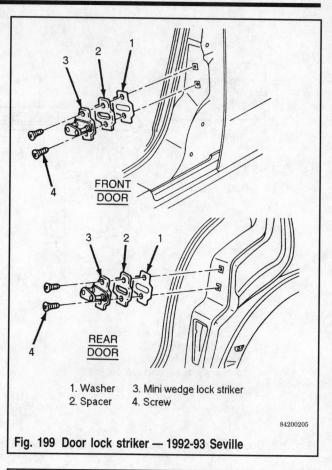

1. Washer   3. Mini wedge lock striker
2. Spacer   4. Screw

Fig. 199 Door lock striker — 1992-93 Seville

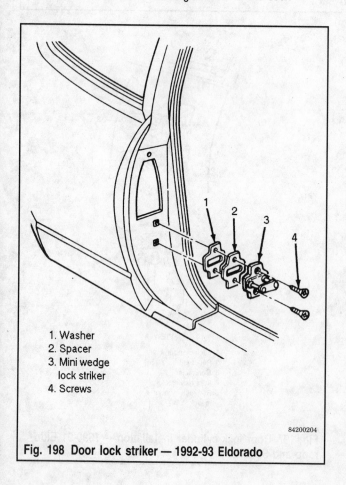

1. Washer
2. Spacer
3. Mini wedge lock striker
4. Screws

84200204

Fig. 198 Door lock striker — 1992-93 Eldorado

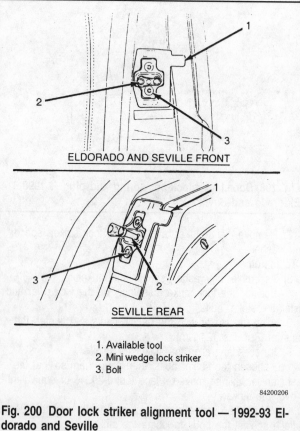

ELDORADO AND SEVILLE FRONT

SEVILLE REAR

1. Available tool
2. Mini wedge lock striker
3. Bolt

84200206

Fig. 200 Door lock striker alignment tool — 1992-93 Eldorado and Seville

13. Install the locating rivets using monobolt type rivets and monobolt rivet head in rivet gun.

➡ **The upper front and upper rear corner rivets are locating rivets. On Eldorado, install the front rivet first, then the rear rivet. On Seville rear door, install the locating rivet first, then working clockwise install the remaining rivets. On Seville front door, install the locating rivet, then the remaining rivets.**

14. Install the remaining rivets.
15. Connect the wiring harness connectors.
16. On Eldorado, install the window sash bolts.
17. On Seville, install the rivets retaining the window to the sash.
18. Connect the outside handle and lock rods to the lock.
19. Install the water deflector and door panel.

INSIDE REMOTE HANDLE

▶ **See Figure 202**

1. Remove the door panel; refer to the procedure in this Section.
2. Remove the water deflector.
3. Center punch each rivet, then drill out the rivets using a ³/₁₆ in. (4.8mm) drill bit.
4. Disengage the tabs on the handle from the slots in the module assembly.
5. Disconnect the lock rods from the handle.
To install:
6. Connect the lock rods to the handle.
7. Place the tabs on the handle into the slots in the module.
8. Secure the remote handle using ³/₁₆ in. peel type rivets.
9. Install the water deflector and door panel.

LOCK RODS

▶ **See Figure 203**

1. Remove the door panel; refer to the procedure in this Section.
2. Remove the water deflector.
3. Remove the lock rod shield, if necessary.
4. Disconnect the rods from the inside remote handle/lock button assembly.
5. Disconnect the rods from the lock assembly and remove the rods.
6. Installation is the reverse of the removal procedure.

LOCK ACTUATOR

▶ **See Figures 204 and 205**

1. Remove the door panel; refer to the procedure in this Section.
2. Remove the water deflector.
3. Remove the lock assembly; refer to the procedure in this Section.
4. Remove the 2 Torx® screws retaining the actuator to the lock assembly and remove the actuator.

To install:

➡ **Before installing the new actuator, the lock assembly must be in the full open position and the teeth on the lock switch (part of the actuator) must be pushed fully toward the actuator arm to prevent damage to the lock switch when the lock assembly is operated.**

5. Release the lock assembly to be sure it is in the full open position. Do this by pushing up on the outside lock rod lever and then pulling on the inside lock handle lever.
6. Before placing the new actuator on the lock assembly, first position the plastic teeth of the lock switch. Push the teeth fully toward the actuator arm so they will mesh correctly with the teeth on the lock assembly when installed. Refer to appropriate illustration.
7. Make sure that the actuating arm rubber bumper is on the actuating arm. Install the actuating arm and bumper into the locking lever, align the lock switch teeth to the gear tooth fork bolt and align the screw holes.
8. Install the Torx® screws and tighten to 6-9 inch lbs. (0.64-1.05 Nm).
9. Manually operate the lock assembly by pushing inward on the fork bolt until it clicks into the fully closed position.

➡ **The lock must operate to the fully closed position without any interference.**

10. Connect the wiring connectors and test operation of the actuator and lock switch. Refer to Fig. '84200212'.
11. Install the lock assembly. Make sure the lock carrier is properly mounted and retained.
12. Install the water deflector and door panel.

LOCK ASSEMBLY

▶ **See Figure 206**

1. Remove the door panel; refer to the procedure in this Section.
2. Remove the water deflector.
3. Remove the lock rod shield from the module.
4. Disconnect the lock rods from the lock.
5. Disconnect the wiring connectors.
6. Remove the 3 retaining screws and the lock assembly.
To install:
7. Install the lock assembly and tighten the screws to 62 inch lbs. (7 Nm).
8. Connect the wiring connectors and the lock rods.
9. Install the lock rod shield.
10. Install the water deflector and door panel.

OUTSIDE HANDLE

▶ **See Figure 207**

➡ **The door glass must be in the full-up position for this procedure.**

1. Remove the door panel; refer to the procedure in this Section.
2. Remove the water deflector.
3. Disconnect the rod from the outside handle.
4. Remove the nut retaining the key cylinder but leave the cylinder in the door.
5. Disconnect the wiring connector.
6. Remove the 2 bolts and the outside handle.

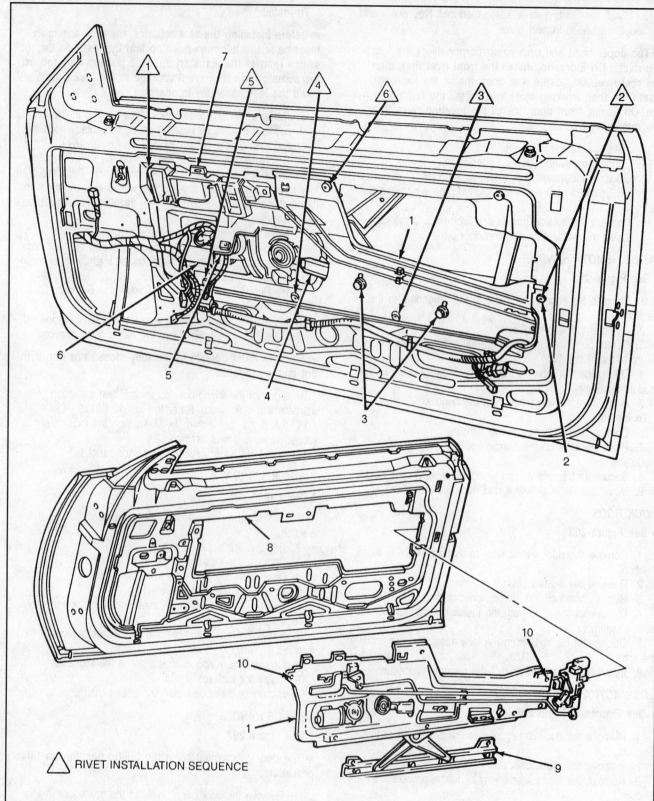

⚠ RIVET INSTALLATION SEQUENCE

1. Door lock module
2. Rivet
3. Inner panel cam retaining bolts
4. Inner panel cam
5. Trim panel retainer
6. Power window motor
7. Inside door handle module
8. Inner door panel
9. Window sash
10. Locating rivet locations

Fig. 201 Door lock module — 1992-93 Eldorado

84200207

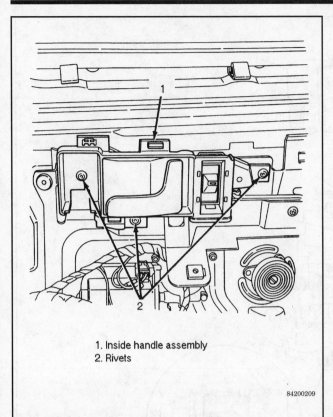

1. Inside handle assembly
2. Rivets

84200209

Fig. 202 Inside remote handle — 1992-93 Eldorado and Seville

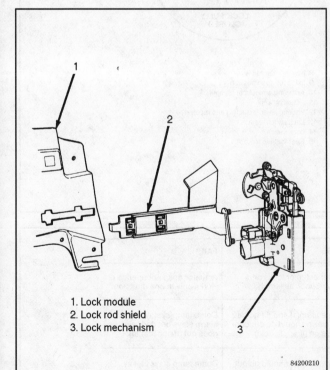

1. Lock module
2. Lock rod shield
3. Lock mechanism

84200210

Fig. 203 Lock rod shield — 1992-93 Eldorado and Seville

To install:

7. Install the outside handle and tighten the bolts to 48-60 inch lbs. (6-8 Nm).

8. Install the nut retaining the key lock cylinder.

9. Connect the wiring connector and connect the rod to the handle.

10. Install the water deflector and door panel.

LOCK CYLINDER

▶ See Figure 208

➡ **The door glass must be in the full-up position for this procedure.**

1. Remove the door panel; refer to the procedure in this Section.

2. Remove the water deflector.

3. Disconnect the lock cylinder-to-lock rod.

4. Disconnect the wiring connector, if equipped.

5. Remove the retaining nut and the lock cylinder.

To install:

6. Install the lock cylinder, including any wiring harnesses that may be attached. Secure with the retaining nut.

7. Connect the wiring connector, if equipped.

8. Connect the lock cylinder-to-lock rod.

9. Install the water deflector and door panel.

Door Glass and Regulator

REMOVAL & INSTALLATION

Deville, Fleetwood and Sixty Special

FRONT DOOR GLASS

▶ See Figure 209

1. Remove the door panel; refer to the procedure in this Section.

2. Remove the water deflector.

3. Remove the door panel upper retainer.

4. Remove the inner belt sealing strip.

5. Remove the front run channel screws.

6. Pull the run channel to the bottom of the door.

7. Pop the guide free from the rear run channel.

8. Remove the glass from the outboard side.

To install:

9. Install the front run channel and screws, finger tight, to the door.

10. Lower the glass into the door from the outboard side of the door frame.

11. Install the guide to the rear run channel.

12. Install the front guide to the front run channel.

13. Adjust the door glass.

14. Install the inner belt sealing strip and retainer.

15. Install the water deflector and door panel.

REAR DOOR GLASS

▶ See Figure 210

1. Remove the door panel; refer to the procedure in this Section.

2. Remove the water deflector.

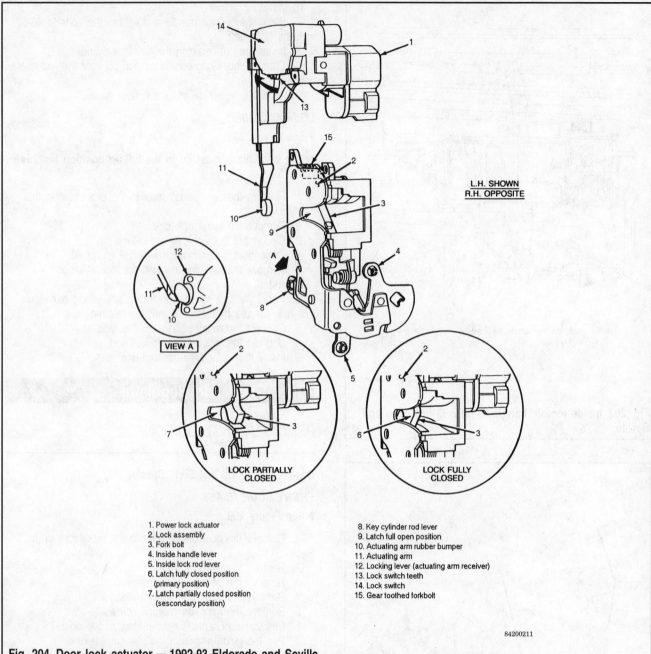

L.H. SHOWN
R.H. OPPOSITE

VIEW A

LOCK PARTIALLY
CLOSED

LOCK FULLY
CLOSED

1. Power lock actuator
2. Lock assembly
3. Fork bolt
4. Inside handle lever
5. Inside lock rod lever
6. Latch fully closed position
   (primary position)
7. Latch partially closed position
   (sescondary position)

8. Key cylinder rod lever
9. Latch full open position
10. Actuating arm rubber bumper
11. Actuating arm
12. Locking lever (actuating arm receiver)
13. Lock switch teeth
14. Lock switch
15. Gear toothed forkbolt

84200211

Fig. 204 Door lock actuator — 1992-93 Eldorado and Seville

OPERATION	ACTION	PASS	FAIL
1.	Operate power door lock switch.	Power actuator locks and unlocks lock assembly.	Actuator does not operate or works only in one direction.
2.	Place latch in partially closed position (secondary position).	Dome lamp(s) should go out; key alarm should go off; door ajar is on (if applicable).	Dome lamp(s) stay lit; key alarm stays on; door ajar goes out (if applicable).
3.	Place latch in fully closed position (primary position).	Dome lamp(s) should go out; key alarm should go off; door ajar is off (if applicable).	Dome lamp stays lit; key alarm stays on; door ajar stays on (if applicable).

84200212

Fig. 205 Door lock actuator operational test — 1992-93 Eldorado and Seville

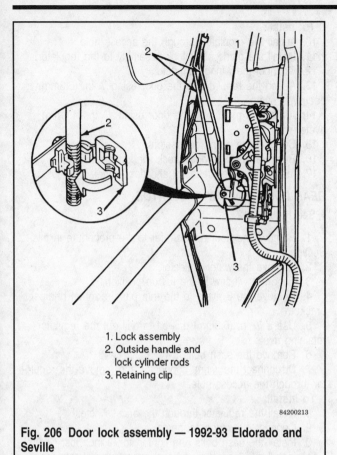

1. Lock assembly
2. Outside handle and
   lock cylinder rods
3. Retaining clip

84200213

Fig. 206 Door lock assembly — 1992-93 Eldorado and Seville

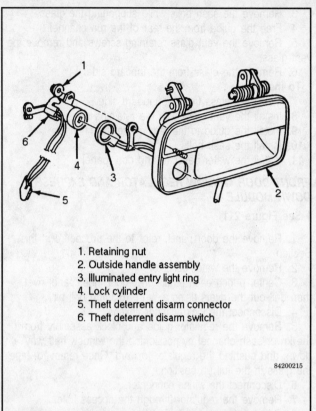

1. Retaining nut
2. Outside handle assembly
3. Illuminated entry light ring
4. Lock cylinder
5. Theft deterrent disarm connector
6. Theft deterrent disarm switch

84200215

Fig. 208 Door lock cylinder — 1992-93 Eldorado and Seville

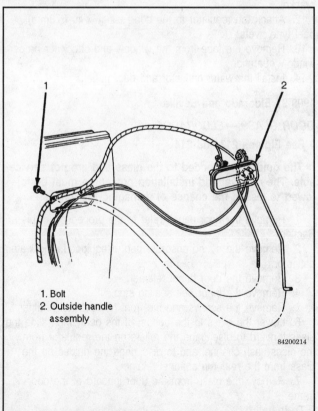

1. Bolt
2. Outside handle
   assembly

84200214

Fig. 207 Outside door handle installation — 1992-93 Eldorado and Seville

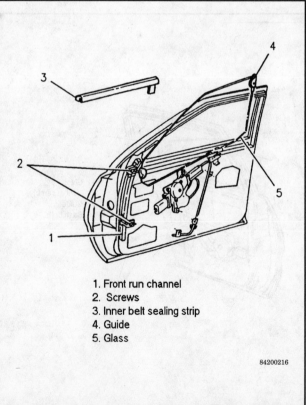

1. Front run channel
2. Screws
3. Inner belt sealing strip
4. Guide
5. Glass

84200216

Fig. 209 Front door glass installation — Deville, Fleetwood and Sixty Special

3. Remove the sash bolts while supporting the glass.
4. Free the guide from the rear of the run channel.
5. Remove the vent glass retaining screws and remove the vent glass.
6. Remove the glass from the inboard side.

To install:

7. Install the glass from the inboard side.
8. Install the vent glass with the retaining screws.
9. Install the guide to the rear of the run channel.
10. Install the sash bolts.
11. Install the water deflector and door panel.

FRONT DOOR WINDOW REGULATOR AND EXPRESS DOWN MODULE

▶ **See Figure 211**

1. Remove the door panel; refer to the procedure in this Section.
2. Remove the water deflector.
3. Center punch each regulator-to-door inner panel rivet, then drill out the rivets using a ¼ in. (6.3mm) drill bit.
4. Disconnect the lock actuator linkage.
5. Remove the regulator guide and block assembly from the lower sash channel by positioning the window half way down, and pushing the regulator forward. Once removed, tape the glass in the full up position.
6. Disconnect the wiring connector.
7. Remove the regulator through the access hole.
8. Drill out the module-to-door inner panel rivets.
9. Disconnect the wiring connector and remove the module.

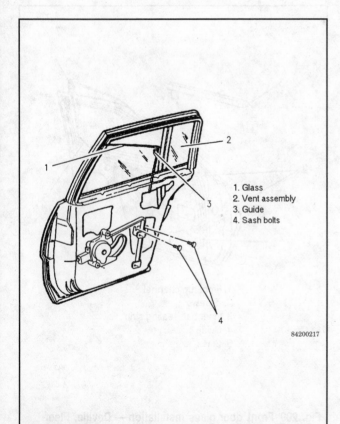

1. Glass
2. Vent assembly
3. Guide
4. Sash bolts

84200217

Fig. 210 Rear door glass installation — Deville, Fleetwood and Sixty Special

To install:

10. Install the regulator through the access hole.
11. Install the guide and block assembly to the regulator.
12. Connect the wiring connector.
13. Attach the regulator to the door using ¼ in. (6.3mm) peel type rivets.
14. Attach the module to the door using ³⁄₁₆ in. (4.8mm) rivets.
15. Connect the wiring connectors.
16. Remove the tape and check window operation.
17. Install the water deflector and door panel.

REAR DOOR WINDOW REGULATOR

▶ **See Figure 212**

1. Remove the door panel; refer to the procedure in this Section.
2. Remove the water deflector.
3. Tape the window in the full up position.
4. Remove the 3 rivets to the trim panel armrest retainer bracket.
5. Use a ¼ in. (6.3mm) drill bit to drill out the regulator retaining rivets.
6. Remove the sash bolts.
7. Disconnect the wiring connector and remove the regulator through the access hole.

To install:

8. Install the regulator through the access hole.
9. Connect the wiring connector.
10. Install the sash bolts and tighten to 79 inch lbs. (9 Nm).
11. Install the 3 rivets to the trim panel armrest retainer bracket.
12. Attach the regulator to the door using ¼ in. (6.3mm) peel type rivets.
13. Remove the tape from the window and check for proper window operation.
14. Install the water deflector and door panel.

1990-91 Eldorado and Seville

DOOR GLASS — ELDORADO

▶ **See Figures 213 and 214**

➡ **The guides are bonded to the glass and are not serviceable. The removal and installation procedure must be followed to lessen the chance of damaging the guides.**

1. Remove the door panel; refer to the procedure in this Section.
2. Remove the sound absorber pad, if equipped, and water deflector.
3. Remove the door panel retainer.
4. Remove the inner belt sealing strip.
5. Remove the screws and the front run channel retainer.
6. Lower the glass to the bottom of the door, then slide the glass forward to disengage the rollers on the regulator from the glass sash channel and to disengage the guides on the glass from the rear run channel retainer.
7. Remove the glass from the door inboard of the door frame.

To install:

8. Install the glass to the door inboard of the door frame.
9. Move the glass to the bottom of the door, engaging the roller on the regulator to the glass sash channel. Slide the

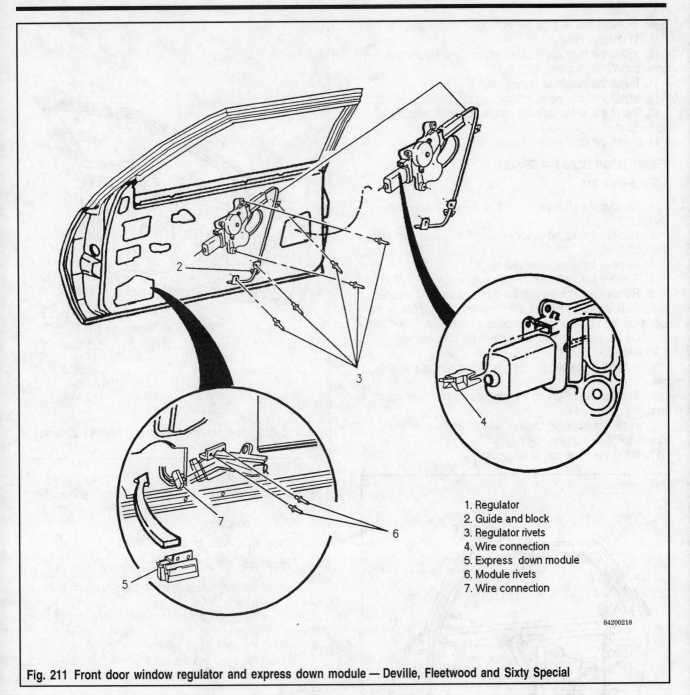

1. Regulator
2. Guide and block
3. Regulator rivets
4. Wire connection
5. Express down module
6. Module rivets
7. Wire connection

84200218

Fig. 211 Front door window regulator and express down module — Deville, Fleetwood and Sixty Special

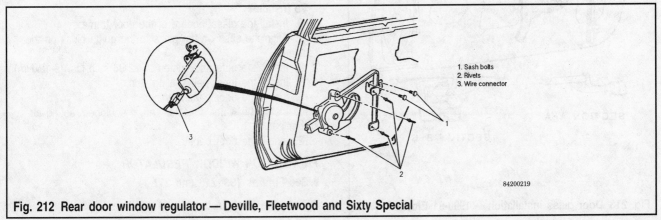

1. Sash bolts
2. Rivets
3. Wire connector

84200219

Fig. 212 Rear door window regulator — Deville, Fleetwood and Sixty Special

glass rearward and engage the rear guide on the glass to the rear run channel retainer.

10. Install the front run channel retainer and tighten the screws to 72-96 inch lbs. (9-12 Nm).

11. Install the inner belt sealing strip.

12. Install the door panel retainer.

13. Install the water deflector and, if equipped, sound absorber pad.

14. Install the door panel.

FRONT DOOR GLASS — SEVILLE

▶ See Figure 214

1. Remove the door panel; refer to the procedure in this Section.

2. Remove the sound absorber pad, if equipped, and water deflector.

3. Remove the door panel retainer.

4. Remove the inner belt sealing strip.

5. Remove the screws and the front run channel retainer.

6. Slide the glass forward, then rearward to disengage the rollers on the regulator from the glass sash channel.

7. Lift the glass up and outboard of the door frame.

To install:

8. Install the glass to the door from outboard of the door frame.

9. Connect the rollers on the regulator to the glass sash channel.

10. Install the front run channel retainer and tighten the screws to 72-96 inch lbs. (9-12 Nm).

11. Install the inner belt sealing strip.

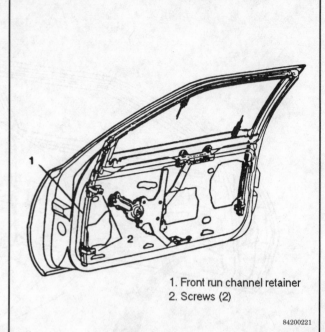

1. Front run channel retainer
2. Screws (2)

84200221

Fig. 214 Front run channel retainer — 1990-91 Eldorado and Seville

12. Install the door panel retainer.

13. Install the water deflector and, if equipped, sound absorber pad.

14. Install the door panel.

REAR DOOR GLASS — SEVILLE

▶ See Figure 215

1. Remove the door panel; refer to the procedure in this Section.

2. Remove the sound absorber pad, if equipped, and water deflector.

3. Remove the door panel retainer.

4. Remove the inner belt sealing strip.

5. Remove the nuts and remove the glass inboard of the door frame.

To install:

6. Install the glass inboard of the door frame.

7. Align the sash on the glass to the guide block on the regulator.

8. Install the nuts and tighten to 72-96 inch lbs. (9-12 Nm).

9. Install the inner belt sealing strip.

10. Install the door panel retainer.

11. Install the water deflector and, if equipped, sound absorber pad.

12. Install the door panel.

FRONT DOOR WINDOW REGULATOR

▶ See Figures 193, 216 and 217

➡ Tape the glass in the full-up position.

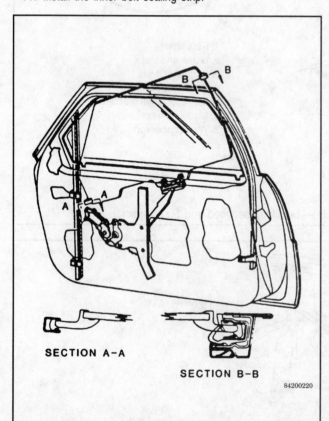

SECTION A-A

SECTION B-B

84200220

Fig. 213 Door glass installation — 1990-91 Eldorado

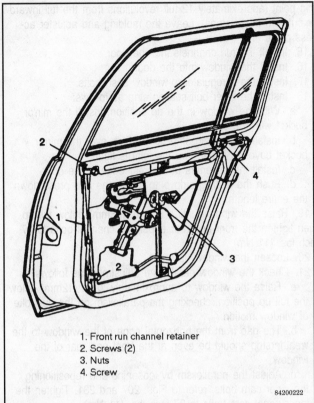

1. Front run channel retainer
2. Screws (2)
3. Nuts
4. Screw

84200222

Fig. 215 Front channel retainer, rear door — 1990-91 Seville

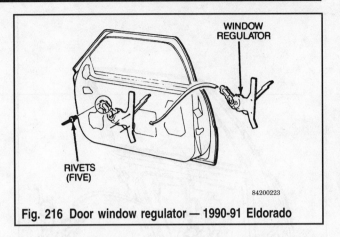

Fig. 216 Door window regulator — 1990-91 Eldorado

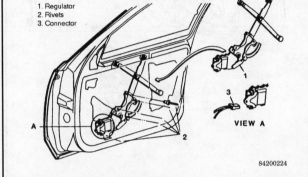

1. Regulator
2. Rivets
3. Connector

84200224

Fig. 217 Front door window regulator — 1990-91 Seville

1. Remove the door panel; refer to the procedure in this Section.
2. Remove the sound absorber pad, if equipped, and water deflector.
3. On Seville, remove the inner panel cam by removing the screws and sliding the inner panel cam off roller of regulator.
4. Drill out the rivets using a ¼ in. (6.3mm) drill bit.
5. Disconnect the wiring connector from the regulator motor and remove the regulator.

✳✳CAUTION

If electric window motor removal from the regulator is required, refer to the procedure in this Section. The regulator lift arm is under tension from the counterbalance spring and can cause personal injury if the sector gear is not locked in position.

To install:
6. Position the regulator to the door panel and connect the wiring connector.
7. Attach the regulator using ¼ x ⅝ peel type rivets.
8. On Seville, position the inner panel cam over roller of regulator. Install the screws and tighten to 72-96 inch lbs. (9-12 Nm).
9. Install the water deflector and, if equipped, sound absorber pad.
10. Install the door panel.

REAR DOOR WINDOW REGULATOR

▶ See Figure 218

➡Tape the glass in the full-up position.

1. Remove the door panel; refer to the procedure in this Section.
2. Remove the sound absorber pad, if equipped, and water deflector.
3. Remove the lock module assembly; refer to the procedure in this Section.
4. Drill out the rivets using a ¼ in. (6.3mm) drill bit.
5. Disconnect the wiring connector from the regulator motor and remove the regulator.
To install:
6. Position the regulator to the door panel and connect the wiring connector.
7. Attach the regulator using ¼ x ⅝ peel type rivets.
8. Install the lock module assembly.
9. Install the water deflector and, if equipped, sound absorber pad.
10. Install the door panel.

1992-93 Eldorado and Seville

DOOR GLASS — ELDORADO

▶ See Figures 201, 219, 220, 221, 222, 223, 224, 225, 226, 227 and 228

1. Remove the door panel; refer to the procedure in this Section.

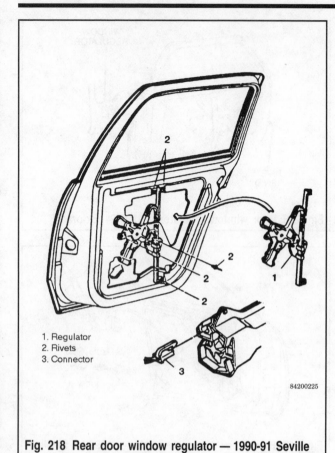

1. Regulator
2. Rivets
3. Connector

84200225

Fig. 218 Rear door window regulator — 1990-91 Seville

2. Remove the water deflector. Note the position of the water deflector prior to removal, as it must be reinstalled in the same position to prevent water leaks.

3. Remove the inner belt sealing strip as follows:

a. Remove the mirror; refer to the procedure in this Section.

b. Remove the screw at mirror bucket end of the sealing strip.

c. Remove the fasteners at the rear edge of the door.

d. Lift upward to remove the sealing strip.

4. Loosen and allow the rear wedge to drop.

5. Remove the window guide blocks.

6. Position the window to gain access to the 3 window sash-to-regulator bolts.

7. Have an assistant hold the window, then remove the 3 window sash-to-regulator bolts.

8. Remove the window from the door.

9. Remove the run channel retaining bolts and lift both run channels up and out of the adjuster.

To install:

10. Place the window and run channels on a bench.

11. Place the guide blocks on the window and loosely secure with the bolts.

12. Place the run channels fully into the guide blocks and adjust the guide block parallelism to run channel. There should be a 1/2 in. (12mm) gap between the edge of the window and the run channel.

13. Set the guide block to the alignment mark on the guide block retainer as illustrated. Tighten the guide blocks.

14. Remove the screw and nut and remove the door lower molding and adjuster access plugs. Set the bevel adjusters to

mid point (approximately 12 full revolutions from the full inward or outward travel stops). Leave the molding and adjuster access plugs off.

15. Install the run channels into the door.

16. Install the window into the door.

17. Install the 3 regulator-to-window sash bolts.

18. Install the inner belt sealing strip as follows:

a. With the window in the up position, install the mirror bucket with the screws.

b. Install the sealing strip hollow bulb over the mirror bucket bayonet. Make sure the joint is tight.

c. Install the fasteners at the rear edge of the door.

d. Push the sealing strip onto the flange and press down the entire length.

19. Raise the window until it is 1 in. (25mm) below full up, then tighten the front and rear upper run channel bolts to 97 inch lbs. (11 Nm).

20. Loosen the window up stops.

21. Check the window parallelism adjustment as follows:

a. Raise the window to approximately 1/2 in. (12mm) below the full up position, checking the parallelism on the upstroke of window motion.

b. The gap from the horizontal edge of the window to the weatherstrip should be even at the front and rear of the window.

c. Adjust the parallelism by loosening and repositioning the inner cam bolts; refer to Figs. 207 and 231. Tighten the inner panel cam bolts to 97 inch lbs. (11 Nm).

22. Loosen the regulator-to-window sash channel bolts and position the window rearward just enough to relieve the pressure of the window to pillar post weatherstrip. Snug the sash channel bolts.

23. Set the rear upstop so the window will pass just under the weatherstrip outer lip and 1mm below the blow out clip as the door is being closed. Set the front upstop to maintain parallelism. Both upstops should contact the guide blocks simultaneously.

24. Check window tip-in as follows:

a. With the door in the open position and the window in the full up position, move the door toward the closed position until the upper rear corner of the window contacts the weatherstrip.

b. The distance from the outer surface of the quarter panel to the door panel outer surface should not exceed 1 1/8 in. (30mm).

c. If necessary, adjust the bevel gear adjusters which are accessed through the bottom of the door. The front and rear adjusters should be turned in equal amounts so that there is sufficient and/or even weatherstrip compression.

d. If the bevel gear adjuster travel is not sufficient to allow the adjustment needed, reposition the front and rear run channel guide blocks inward or outward, as required.

➡**High door closing effort can result if the window tip-in is adjusted too far inward. Door closing effort with the window lowered should increase only slightly with the window fully raised. The window should be cycled and the door closed several times to verify door window performance.**

25. Loosen the regulator-to-window sash channel bolts and position the window forward to achieve water/wind noise seal

at the pillar post weatherstrip. Tighten the regulator-to-sash channel bolts to 97 inch lbs. (11 Nm).

➡️**Moving the window forward too far will increase door closing effort and reduce window clearance to the blow out clip.**

26. With the window in the full up position, check for a smooth transition from bucket at mirror to window. Transition should be checked with slight outward pressure on the window or in the door closed position. Loosen the mirror attachment nuts and bucket attachment screws to reposition the bucket, as needed.

27. With the window still in the full up position, raise the rear wedge until it lightly contacts the rear edge of the window. Tighten the wedge attachment screw to 27 inch lbs. (3 Nm), using a thin flat-bladed tool in the adjustment slot to keep the wedge from rotating when tightened.

28. Install the window adjuster access plugs and the door lower molding.

29. Install the water deflector and door panel.

DOOR WINDOW — SEVILLE

▶ **See Figures 229, 230 and 231**

1. Remove the door panel; refer to the procedure in this Section.

2. Remove the door speaker.

3. Remove the water deflector.

4. Lift upward to remove the inner belt sealing strip.

5. Remove the retaining bolt and the front run channel retainer.

6. Drill out the 2 regulator sash-to-window rivets and remove the window from the door.

To install:

7. Install the window to the door from outboard of the door frame.

8. Install rivets on the regulator-to-window sash channel.

9. Install the front run channel retainer and tighten the bolt to 72-96 inch lbs. (9-12 Nm).

10. Locate the front edge of the inner belt sealing strip over the door flange and press down the entire length of the sealing strip.

11. Install the water deflector.

12. Install the door speaker.

13. Install the door panel.

WINDOW REGULATOR

The window regulator is part of the door lock module; if replacement is necessary, refer to the door lock module removal and installation procedure in this Section.

Electric Window Motor

REMOVAL & INSTALLATION

Deville, Fleetwood and Sixty Special

▶ **See Figure 232**

1. Remove the window regulator; refer to the procedure in this Section.

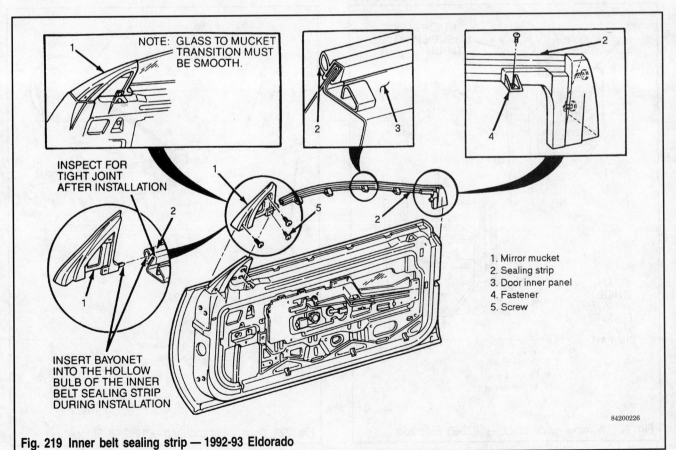

NOTE: GLASS TO MUCKET TRANSITION MUST BE SMOOTH.

INSPECT FOR TIGHT JOINT AFTER INSTALLATION

INSERT BAYONET INTO THE HOLLOW BULB OF THE INNER BELT SEALING STRIP DURING INSTALLATION

1. Mirror mucket
2. Sealing strip
3. Door inner panel
4. Fastener
5. Screw

84200226

Fig. 219 Inner belt sealing strip — 1992-93 Eldorado

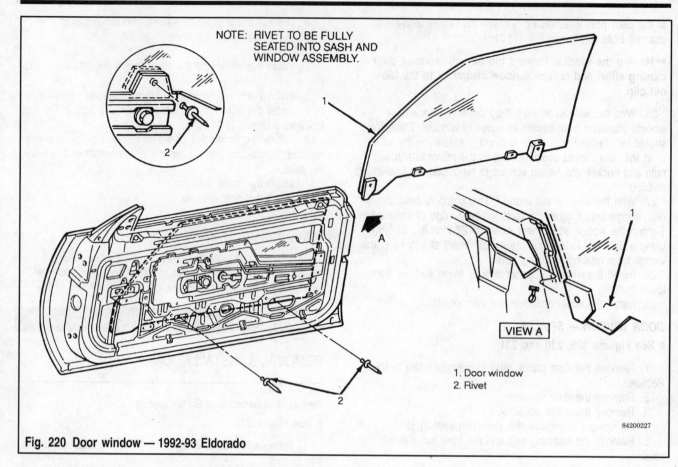

NOTE: RIVET TO BE FULLY SEATED INTO SASH AND WINDOW ASSEMBLY.

VIEW A

1. Door window
2. Rivet

84200227

Fig. 220 Door window — 1992-93 Eldorado

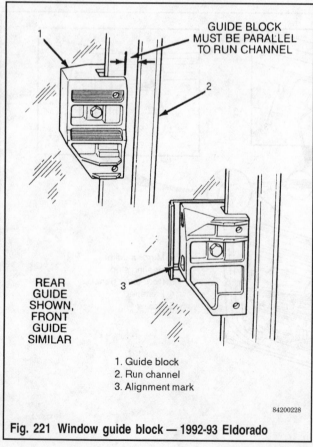

GUIDE BLOCK MUST BE PARALLEL TO RUN CHANNEL

REAR GUIDE SHOWN, FRONT GUIDE SIMILAR

1. Guide block
2. Run channel
3. Alignment mark

84200228

Fig. 221 Window guide block — 1992-93 Eldorado

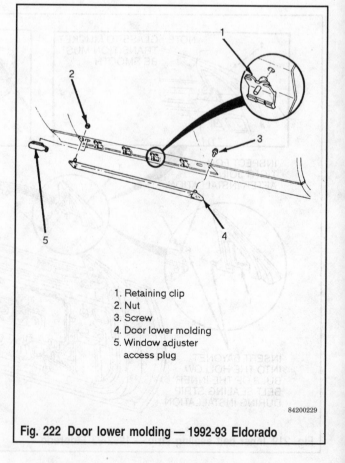

1. Retaining clip
2. Nut
3. Screw
4. Door lower molding
5. Window adjuster access plug

84200229

Fig. 222 Door lower molding — 1992-93 Eldorado

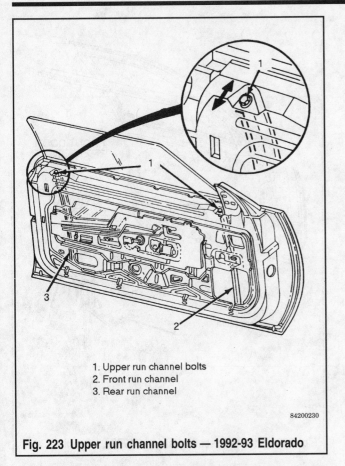

1. Upper run channel bolts
2. Front run channel
3. Rear run channel

84200230

Fig. 223 Upper run channel bolts — 1992-93 Eldorado

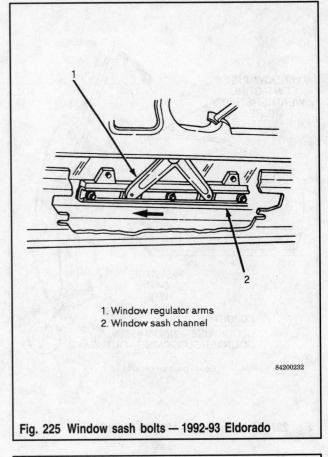

1. Window regulator arms
2. Window sash channel

84200232

Fig. 225 Window sash bolts — 1992-93 Eldorado

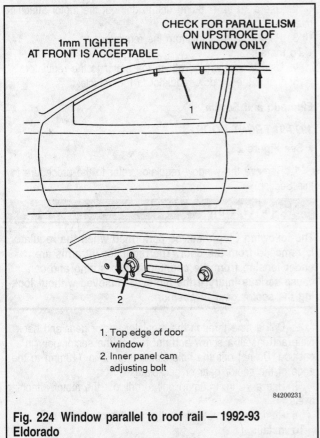

1mm TIGHTER AT FRONT IS ACCEPTABLE

CHECK FOR PARALLELISM ON UPSTROKE OF WINDOW ONLY

1. Top edge of door window
2. Inner panel cam adjusting bolt

84200231

Fig. 224 Window parallel to roof rail — 1992-93 Eldorado

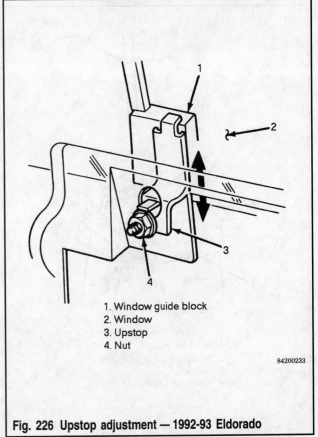

1. Window guide block
2. Window
3. Upstop
4. Nut

84200233

Fig. 226 Upstop adjustment — 1992-93 Eldorado

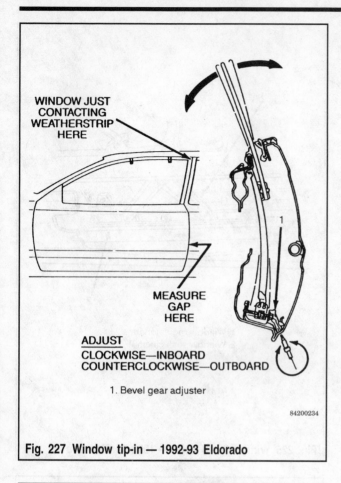

Fig. 227 Window tip-in — 1992-93 Eldorado

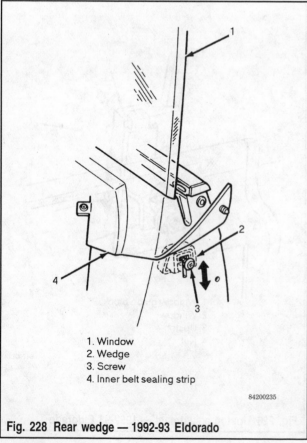

1. Window
2. Wedge
3. Screw
4. Inner belt sealing strip

84200235

Fig. 228 Rear wedge — 1992-93 Eldorado

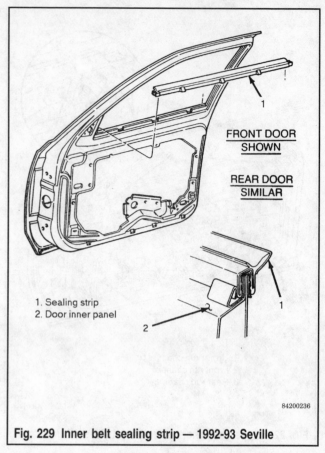

1. Sealing strip
2. Door inner panel

84200236

Fig. 229 Inner belt sealing strip — 1992-93 Seville

2. Use a $^3/_{16}$ in. (4.8mm) drill to drill out the motor attaching rivets.

3. Remove the motor from the regulator.

To install:

4. Use $^3/_{16}$ in. rivets to attach the motor to the regulator.

5. Install the window regulator in the vehicle.

Eldorado and Seville

1990-91 FRONT DOOR

◆ See Figure 233

1. Remove the window regulator; refer to the procedure in this Section.

✲✲CAUTION

The following Step must be performed when the regulator is removed from the door. The regulator lift arms are under tension from the counterbalance spring and can cause serious injury if the motor is removed without locking the sector gear in position.

2. Drill a hole through the regulator sector gear and back plate and install a screw and nut to lock the sector gear in position. Do not drill the hole closer than $^1/_2$ in. (13mm) to the edge of the sector gear or backplate.

3. Use a $^3/_{16}$ in. (4.8mm) drill to drill out the motor attaching rivets.

4. Remove the motor from the regulator.

To install:

5. Use $^3/_{16}$ in. rivets to attach the motor to the regulator.

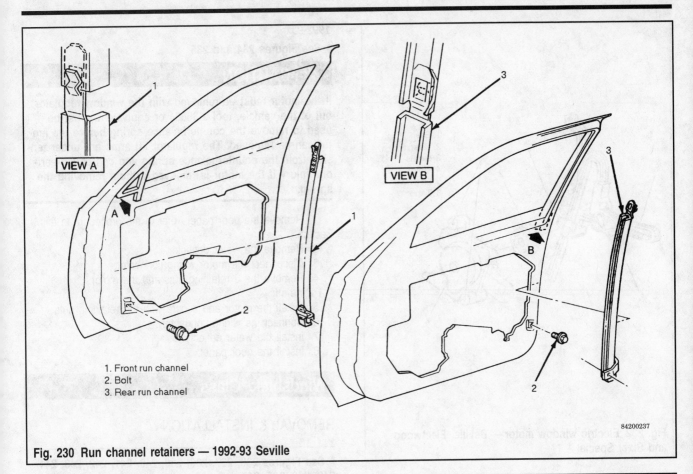

1. Front run channel
2. Bolt
3. Rear run channel

84200237

Fig. 230 Run channel retainers — 1992-93 Seville

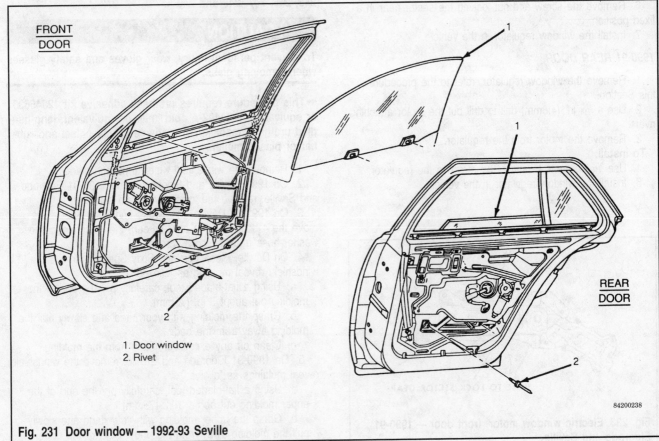

FRONT
DOOR

REAR
DOOR

1. Door window
2. Rivet

84200238

Fig. 231 Door window — 1992-93 Seville

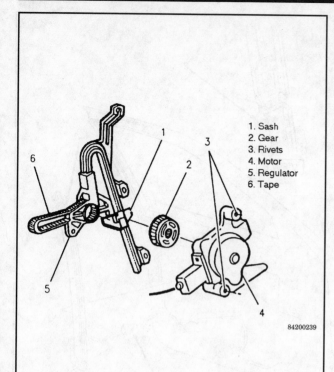

1. Sash
2. Gear
3. Rivets
4. Motor
5. Regulator
6. Tape

Fig. 232 Electric window motor — Deville, Fleetwood and Sixty Special

6. Remove the screw and nut locking the sector gear in a fixed position.

7. Install the window regulator in the vehicle.

1990-91 REAR DOOR

1. Remove the window regulator; refer to the procedure in this Section.

2. Use a ³/₁₆ in. (4.8mm) drill to drill out the motor attaching rivets.

3. Remove the motor from the regulator.

To install:

4. Use ³/₁₆ in. rivets to attach the motor to the regulator.

5. Install the window regulator in the vehicle.

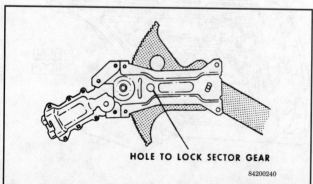

HOLE TO LOCK SECTOR GEAR

Fig. 233 Electric window motor, front door — 1990-91 Eldorado and Seville

1992-93

▶ See Figures 234 and 235

✴✴CAUTION

If the motor must be removed with the window regulator out of the vehicle, tool J-38864 or equivalent, must be used to remove the counterbalance spring before the motor can be removed. The regulator lift arms are under tension from the counterbalance spring and can cause serious injury if the motor is removed without removing the spring.

1. Remove the door panel; refer to the procedure in this Section.

2. Remove the water deflector.

3. Disconnect the motor wiring connector.

4. Remove the 3 retaining nuts and the motor.

To install:

5. Install the motor and secure with the retaining nuts.

6. Connect the wiring connector.

7. Install the water deflector.

8. Install the door panel.

Windshield Glass

REMOVAL & INSTALLATION

▶ See Figures 236, 237, 238, 239, 240, 241, 242, 243, 244, 245, 246, 247, 248 and 249

✴✴CAUTION

To prevent personal injury, wear gloves and safety glasses when removing glass.

➡**This procedure requires urethane adhesive kit 12345633 or equivalent, J-24402-A cold knife or equivalent, long-handled urethane razor knife, urethane corner chisel and rubber or plastic mallet.**

1. Remove the windshield wiper arms and blades.

2. On 1990 Deville and Fleetwood and 1990-91 Eldorado and Seville, remove the lower windshield supports.

3. On 1992-93 Deville, Fleetwood and Sixty Special, remove the 4 bolts and the cowl screen, then disconnect the washer hose from the cowl screen.

4. On Deville, Fleetwood and Sixty Special, remove the windshield reveal molding as follows:

   a. Using a flat-bladed tool, carefully pry the end of the molding out about 3 in. (75mm).

   b. Grasp the molding with your hand and slowly pull the molding away from the body.

   c. Clean off any excess urethane from the molding.

5. On 1990-91 Eldorado and Seville, remove the windshield reveal moldings as follows:

   a. Using a flat-bladed tool, carefully pry the end of the upper molding out about 3 in. (75mm).

   b. Grasp the upper molding with your hand and slowly pull the molding away from the body. Discard the upper molding.

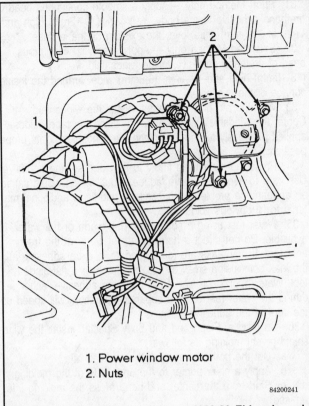

1. Power window motor
2. Nuts

84200241

Fig. 234 Electric window motor — 1992-93 Eldorado and Seville

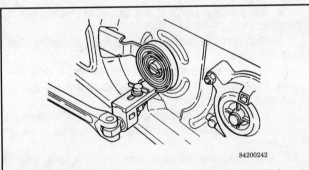

84200242

Fig. 235 Removing the window regulator counterbalance spring (shown with regulator installed in door) — 1992-93 Eldorado and Seville

c. Open the door and remove the door opening drip molding and weatherstrip.

d. Remove the 2 screws and the windshield side molding.

6. On 1992-93 Eldorado, remove the windshield reveal molding and molding retainers as follows:

a. Using a flat-bladed tool, start at the lower corner and pry up on the molding to separate it from the retainer.

b. Continue to slide the tool under the molding, working around the window until it is completely separated.

c. Remove the molding.

d. Slide a plastic scraper or equivalent, between the retainer and window. Push the retainer outward off the window.

e. Pry one end of the retainer out from under the window and grasp the end. Pull away from the window.

7. On 1992-93 Seville, remove the windshield reveal moldings as follows:

a. Pull enough door opening weatherstrip out to gain access to the side reveal molding retaining screws.

b. Remove the 3 screws and the side reveal molding.

c. Using a flat-bladed tool, carefully pry the end of the upper reveal molding away from the windshield. Grasp the end and pull the upper reveal molding from under the windshield.

d. Discard the upper reveal molding.

8. On 1992-93 Deville, Fleetwood and Sixty Special, remove the rearview mirror.

9. If equipped, disconnect the heated windshield wiring harness connector.

10. On 1992-93 Eldorado and Seville, remove the cowl vent panel.

11. Mask off the area around the windshield using 3M protective tape part number 06945 or equivalent, to protect the painted surfaces.

12. Using a razor or utility knife, make a preliminary cut around the entire perimeter of the glass, staying as close to the edge of the glass as possible.

13. Using cold knife J-24402-A or equivalent, carefully cut around the top and sides of the windshield from outside the vehicle, keeping the blade as close to the inside surface of the glass as possible.

14. From inside the vehicle, position the urethane corner chisel into the lower corners of the windshield. Using a mallet, tap the head of the chisel to cut the urethane in the corners.

15. With the aid of an assistant, hold the upper portion of the windshield away from the vehicle, allowing room to cut the urethane between the window frame and the bottom of the windshield with a long-handled urethane razor knife.

16. With the aid of an assistant, remove the windshield from the vehicle.

17. Using a utility knife, trim and level the old urethane on the window frame, leaving approximately $1/8$-$9/16$ in. (3-5mm) of old urethane on the opening. This will serve as a base for the new urethane and during the installation procedure will be referred to as the 'Short Method". Fill the low areas with fresh urethane.

18. Inspect the window frame for any metal damage or irregularity of the metal surface. If these or similar conditions exist, it will be necessary to remove all remaining urethane from the window frame and refinish the frame. During the installation procedure, this will be referred to as the 'Extended Method".

19. If the old windshield is to be reused, trim and level the remaining urethane, leaving a 1-2mm bead of urethane on the glass. If the remaining urethane is loose, damaged, or has voids, remove all urethane from the glass and scrape all traces of black primer from the glass. Apply new primers and urethane as though it were new glass.

To install:

20. Short Method only — Repair any areas on the window frame nicked during windshield removal using the appropriate color touch-up paint. Do not get paint or any other contamination on the remaining urethane base.

21. Clean the inside edges of the windshield with glass cleaner to prevent contamination of the urethane adhesive.

22. Extended Method only — On Eldorado and Seville, cement spacers around the windshield opening as required.

23. On 1992-93 Eldorado, proceed as follows:

a. Snap the reveal molding retainers to the molding.

b. Starting at an upper corner, position the molding to the windshield and retainers.

c. Working down the side of the windshield, press the molding into the retainer until it snaps in firmly.

d. Position the opposite corner and continue snapping the molding into the retainer on the top and remaining sides.

e. Position the lower corners and attach the lower closeouts to the bottom of the windshield. If reusing the molding, apply a small amount of butyl adhesive inside the C channel of the lower closeout prior to assembly.

24. On 1992-93 Seville, install the reveal moldings to the windshield.

➡**On 1992-93 Eldorado and Seville, the reveal moldings must be on the window prior to installation.**

25. On 1990 Deville and Fleetwood and 1990-91 Eldorado and Seville, replace the glass supports.

26. With the aid of an assistant, position the windshield glass in the opening. Apply pieces of masking tape over the edges of the windshield and adjacent body pillar and roof. Slit the tape at the edge of the windshield, then remove the windshield. During installation the tape on the windshield can be aligned with the tape on the body to guide the windshield into the desired position.

27. Extended Method only — Apply urethane bonding body primer to the pinch weld flange.

➡**If performing Short Method, do not apply primer over existing urethane.**

28. Using a clean cloth, apply the clear primer from the urethane adhesive kit to the top and side edges of the windshield and in a band $5/8$ in. (15mm) wide inboard from the edge of the windshield. Apply a $5/8$ in. (15mm) band of primer to the bottom of the windshield below the guide line that is etched into the windshield.

❊❊WARNING

Two glass primers are provided in the urethane adhesive kit, a clear primer and a black primer. The clear primer is always applied to the glass before the black primer. Once the clear primer is applied, wipe off immediately. This primer dries almost instantly and will stain the viewing area of the windshield, so be sure to apply it evenly and keep it away from the viewing area. Do not apply clear primer over black primer.

29. Using a small brush, apply black primer over the same area that the clear primer was applied and allow to dry for 5 minutes.

30. Apply the acoustic strip above the guide line on the windshield.

❊❊WARNING

Failure to install the acoustic strip could cause windshield breakage.

31. Short Method only — Apply a smooth continuous bead of urethane adhesive to the body, $3/8$-$31/64$ in. (10-12mm) high and $1/8$-$9/16$ in. (3-5mm) wide, over the existing urethane base.

32. Extended Method only — Apply a smooth continuous bead of urethane adhesive to the windshield, $1/2$-$9/16$ in. (13-15mm) high and $1/4$-$5/16$ in. (6-8mm) wide, around the inside surface of the windshield.

33. With the aid of an assistant, install the windshield. Center the windshield in the opening, using the tape guides applied previously to carefully place the windshield in its proper position.

34. Press the windshield firmly to flow and set the adhesive. Use care to avoid excessive 'squeeze out'' which would cause an appearance problem. If necessary, paddle in additional material to fill obvious voids in the seal.

35. Water test using a soft spray. Use warm or hot water, if available. Do not direct a hard stream of water at the fresh adhesive. If any leaks are found, paddle in extra adhesive at the leak point using small disposable brush or a flat-bladed tool. Water applied on top of the urethane adhesive, either during the water test or as a separate operation, will speed up the cure of the adhesive.

36. On Deville, Fleetwood and Sixty Special, install the windshield reveal molding as follows:

a. Cut the bottom portion of the molding off.

b. Apply a clear primer to the underside of the molding.

c. Start from the center and hand press the molding into place.

d. Tape the windshield and molding to hold in position.

37. On 1990-91 Eldorado and Seville, install the windshield reveal moldings as follows:

a. Apply a clear primer to the underside of the upper molding.

b. Start from the center and hand press the upper molding into place.

c. Tape the windshield and molding to hold in position.

d. Position the side molding and secure with the 2 screws.

e. Install the door opening drip molding and weatherstrip.

38. Connect the heated windshield wiring harness connector, if equipped.

39. Install the remaining components in the reverse order of removal.

40. The vehicle must remain at normal room temperature for 6 hours to allow the adhesive to cure.

Stationary Glass

REMOVAL & INSTALLATION

❊❊CAUTION

To prevent personal injury, wear gloves and safety glasses when removing glass.

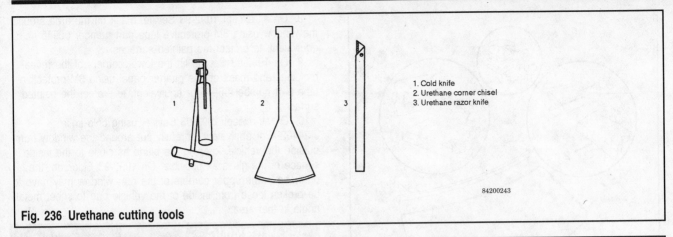

Fig. 236 Urethane cutting tools

1. Cold knife
2. Urethane corner chisel
3. Urethane razor knife

84200243

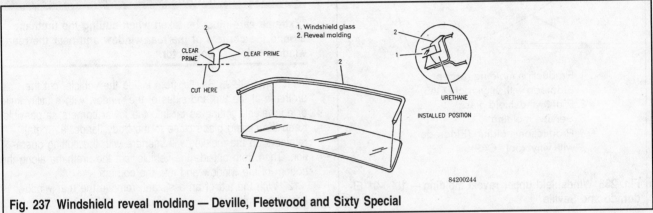

1. Windshield glass
2. Reveal molding

CLEAR PRIME — CLEAR PRIME

CUT HERE

URETHANE

INSTALLED POSITION

84200244

Fig. 237 Windshield reveal molding — Deville, Fleetwood and Sixty Special

Rear Window

EXCEPT DEVILLE, FLEETWOOD AND SIXTY SPECIAL COUPE WITH CB4 OR CF8 ROOF OPTIONAND 1990-91 ELDORADO WITH C10 SPECIAL LANDAU ROOF

▶ **See Figures 236, 243, 248, 250, 251, 252, 253, 254, 255, 256 and 257**

➡**This procedure requires urethane adhesive kit 12345633 or equivalent and J-24402-A cold knife or equivalent.**

1. On 1990 Deville and Fleetwood and 1990-91 Eldorado and Seville, remove the lower glass supports.
2. On Deville, Fleetwood and Sixty Special except hardtop coupe, remove the rear window reveal molding as follows:
    a. Using a flat-bladed tool, carefully pry the end of the molding out about 3 in. (75mm).
    b. Grasp the molding with your hand and slowly pull the molding away from the body.
    c. Clean off any excess urethane from the molding.
3. On Deville, Fleetwood and Sixty Special hardtop coupe, remove the rear window reveal molding as follows:
    a. Remove the rear seat cushion and seat back.
    b. Remove the quarter upper trim panels.
    c. Remove the rear window garnish molding.
    d. Remove the rear shelf with built-in stop lamp assembly.
    e. Remove the reveal molding retaining nuts and the reveal molding.

4. On 1990-91 Eldorado and Seville, remove the rear window reveal moldings as follows:
    a. Using a flat-bladed tool, carefully pry the end of the upper molding out about 3 in. (75mm).
    b. Grasp the upper molding with your hand and slowly pull the molding away from the body. Discard the upper molding.
    c. Open the trunk and pull up on the rubber part of the lower molding.
    d. Remove the retaining clips and screws and remove the lower molding.
5. On 1992-93 Eldorado, remove the rear window reveal molding and molding retainers as follows:
    a. Using a flat-bladed tool, start at the lower corner and pry up on the molding to separate it from the retainer.
    b. Continue to slide the tool under the molding, working around the window until it is completely separated.
    c. Remove the molding.
    d. Slide a plastic scraper or equivalent, between the retainer and window. Push the retainer outward off the window.
    e. Pry one end of the retainer out from under the window and grasp the end. Pull away from the window.
6. On 1992-93 Seville, proceed as follows:
    a. Remove the interior quarter trim panels.
    b. Release the center push-in fastener at the rear of the headliner by carefully pulling downward.
7. Disconnect the rear window defogger harness connector.

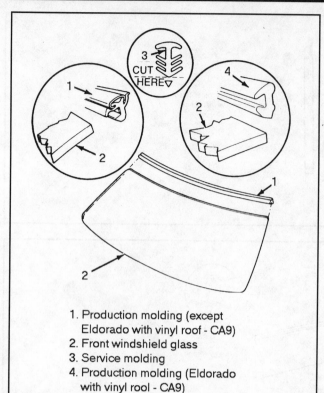

1. Production molding (except Eldorado with vinyl roof - CA9)
2. Front windshield glass
3. Service molding
4. Production molding (Eldorado with vinyl rool - CA9)

84200245

Fig. 238 Windshield upper reveal molding — 1990-91 Eldorado and Seville

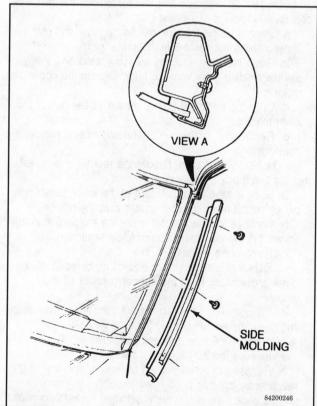

84200246

Fig. 239 Windshield side reveal molding — 1990-91 Eldorado and Seville

8. On all except 1992-93 Seville, mask off the area around the window using 3M protective tape part number 06945 or equivalent, to protect the painted surfaces.

9. On 1992-93 Seville, lift the lower corners of the reveal moldings and mask off the quarter panel using 3M protective tape part number 06945 or equivalent, to protect the painted surfaces.

10. On all except 1992-93 Seville, using cold knife J-24402-A or equivalent, carefully cut around the window from outside the vehicle, keeping the blade as close to the inside surface of the glass as possible. On 1992-93 Eldorado, the urethane in the upper corners of the rear window may have to be broken loose from inside of the vehicle due to sheet metal angle in that area.

✳✳WARNING

Extreme care must be taken when cutting the urethane around the corners of the rear window and near the rear window defogger connector.

11. On 1992-93 Seville, from inside the vehicle, cut the urethane at the top and sides of the window with a utility knife or equivalent, getting as far into the lower corners as possible. Keep the cutting blade close to the body flange, as metal retainers on the molding will interfere with the cutting operation. Then from outside the vehicle, cut the urethane along the bottom of the window and into the corners.

12. With the aid of an assistant, remove the rear window from the vehicle. If the rear window on 1992-93 Seville is to be replaced, remove the reveal moldings.

13. Using a utility knife, trim and level the old urethane on the window frame, leaving approximately $1/8$-$3/16$ in. (3-5mm) of old urethane on the opening. This will serve as a base for the new urethane and during the installation procedure will be referred to as the 'Short Method''. Fill the low areas with fresh urethane.

14. Inspect the window frame for any metal damage or irregularity of the metal surface. If these or similar conditions exist, it will be necessary to remove all remaining urethane from the window frame and refinish the frame. During the installation procedure, this will be referred to as the 'Extended Method''.

15. If the old window is to be reused, trim and level the remaining urethane, leaving 1-2mm of urethane on the glass. If the remaining urethane is loose, damaged, or has voids, remove all urethane from the glass and scrape all traces of black primer from the glass. Apply new primers and urethane as though it were new glass.

To install:

16. Short Method only — Repair any areas on the window frame nicked during window removal using the appropriate color touch-up paint. Do not get paint or any other contamination on the remaining urethane base.

17. Clean the inside edges of the window with glass cleaner to prevent contamination of the urethane adhesive.

18. Extended Method only — cement spacers around the window opening as required.

19. On 1992-93 Eldorado, proceed as follows:

a. Snap the reveal molding retainers to the rear window reveal molding.

b. Starting at an upper corner, position the molding to the window and retainers.

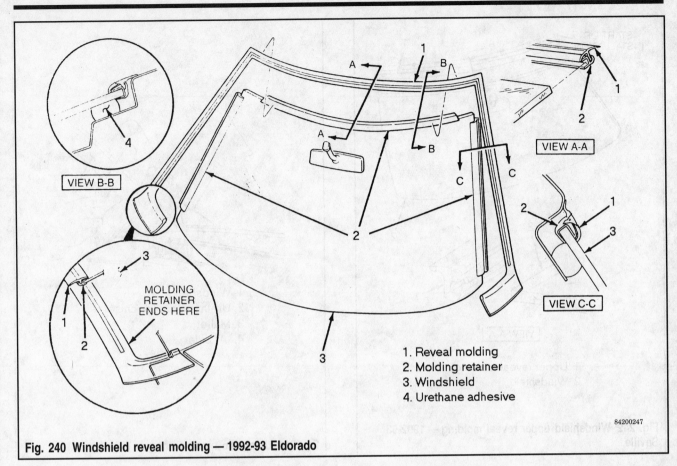

VIEW B-B

MOLDING RETAINER ENDS HERE

VIEW A-A

VIEW C-C

1. Reveal molding
2. Molding retainer
3. Windshield
4. Urethane adhesive

84200247

Fig. 240 Windshield reveal molding — 1992-93 Eldorado

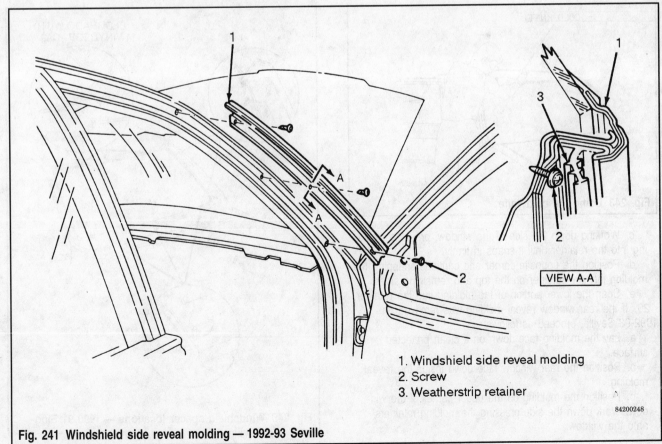

VIEW A-A

1. Windshield side reveal molding
2. Screw
3. Weatherstrip retainer

84200248

Fig. 241 Windshield side reveal molding — 1992-93 Seville

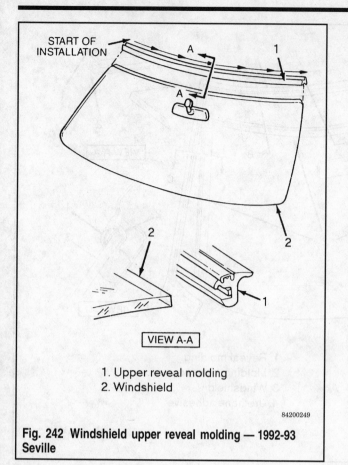

1. Upper reveal molding
2. Windshield

Fig. 242 Windshield upper reveal molding — 1992-93 Seville

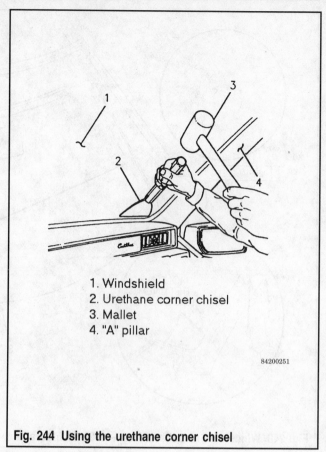

1. Windshield
2. Urethane corner chisel
3. Mallet
4. "A" pillar

Fig. 244 Using the urethane corner chisel

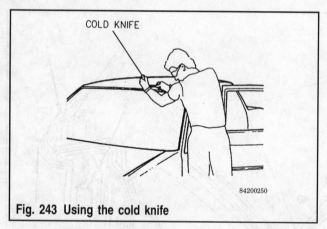

Fig. 243 Using the cold knife

c. Working down the side of the window, press the molding into the retainer until it snaps in firmly.

d. Position the opposite corner and continue snapping the molding into the retainer on the top and remaining sides.

e. Snap the lower portion of the molding into the retainer.

20. If the rear window reveal molding was removed on 1992-93 Seville, proceed as follows:

a. Lay the molding face down on a clean protected surface.

b. Position the rear window face down inside the reveal molding.

c. Position the molding on the upper corner of the window. Work down the side pressing the molding retainers onto the window.

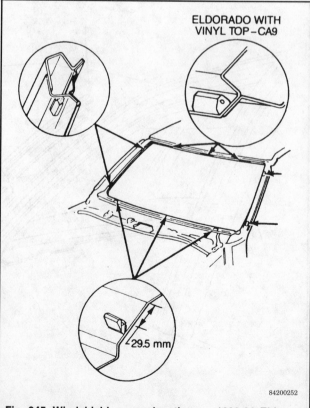

Fig. 245 Windshield spacer locations — 1990-91 Eldorado and Seville

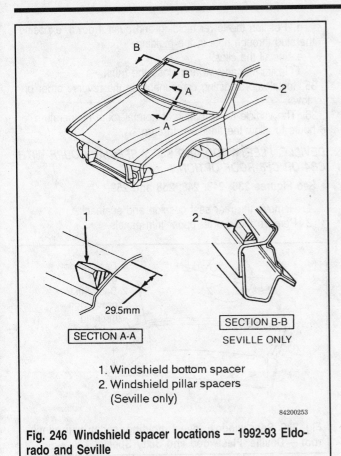

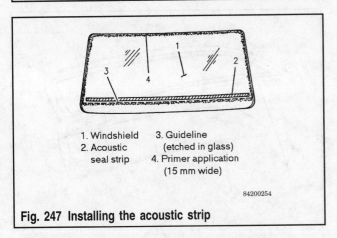

SECTION A-A

29.5mm

SECTION B-B
SEVILLE ONLY

1. Windshield bottom spacer
2. Windshield pillar spacers
   (Seville only)

84200253

Fig. 246 Windshield spacer locations — 1992-93 Eldorado and Seville

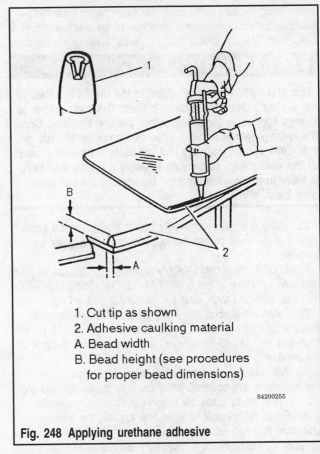

1. Cut tip as shown
2. Adhesive caulking material
A. Bead width
B. Bead height (see procedures
   for proper bead dimensions)

84200255

Fig. 248 Applying urethane adhesive

1. Windshield   3. Guideline
2. Acoustic   (etched in glass)
   seal strip   4. Primer application
                          (15 mm wide)

84200254

Fig. 247 Installing the acoustic strip

84200256

Fig. 249 Installing the windshield

d. Position the lower corner. Continue along the bottom to the opposite lower corner, and install the corner.

e. Pulling slightly so the retainers will clear the window, install the remaining upper corner of the molding to the window. Extreme care must be taken not to break the corner of the molding.

f. Tap the side and top retainers onto the window to secure the molding.

➡**On 1992-93 Eldorado and Seville, the reveal moldings must be on the window prior to installation.**

21. On 1990 Deville and Fleetwood and 1990-91 Eldorado and Seville, replace the glass supports.

22. With the aid of an assistant, position the window glass in the opening. Apply pieces of masking tape over the edges of the window and adjacent body pillar and roof. Slit the tape at the edge of the window, then remove the window. During installation the tape on the window can be aligned with the tape on the body to guide the window into the desired position.

23. Extended Method only — Apply urethane bonding body primer to the pinch weld flange.

➡**If performing Short Method, do not apply primer over existing urethane.**

24. Using a clean cloth, apply the clear primer from the urethane adhesive kit around all edges of the window and in a band ⅝ in. (15mm) wide inboard from the edge of the window.

✳✳WARNING

Two glass primers are provided in the urethane adhesive kit, a clear primer and a black primer. The clear primer is always applied to the glass before the black primer. Once the clear primer is applied, wipe off immediately. This primer dries almost instantly and will stain the viewing area of the windshield, so be sure to apply it evenly and keep it away from the viewing area. Do not apply clear primer over black primer.

25. Using a small brush, apply black primer over the same area that the clear primer was applied and allow to dry for 5 minutes.

26. Short Method only — Apply a smooth continuous bead of urethane adhesive to the body, ⅜³¹/₆₄ in. (10-12mm) high and ⅛-⁹/₁₆ in. (3-5mm) wide, over the existing urethane base.

27. Extended Method only — Apply a smooth continuous bead of urethane adhesive to the window, ½-⁹/₁₆ in. (13-15mm) high and ⁴/₄-⁵/₁₆ in. (6-8mm) wide, around the inside surface of the window.

28. With the aid of an assistant, install the window. Center the window in the opening, using the tape guides applied previously to carefully place the window in its proper position.

29. Press the window firmly to flow and set the adhesive. Use care to avoid excessive 'squeeze out" which would cause an appearance problem. If necessary, paddle in additional material to fill obvious voids in the seal.

30. Water test using a soft spray. Use warm or hot water, if available. Do not direct a hard stream of water at the fresh adhesive. If any leaks are found, paddle in extra adhesive at the leak point using small disposable brush or a flat-bladed tool. Water applied on top of the urethane adhesive, either during the water test or as a separate operation, will speed up the cure of the adhesive.

31. Connect the rear window defogger harness connector.

32. On Deville, Fleetwood and Sixty Special except hardtop coupe, install the rear window reveal molding as follows:

a. Cut the bottom portion of the molding off.

b. Apply a clear primer to the underside of the molding.

c. Start from the center and hand press the molding into place.

d. Tape the windshield and molding to hold in position.

33. On Deville, Fleetwood and Sixty Special hardtop coupe, install the rear window reveal molding as follows:

a. Install the reveal molding with the retaining nuts.

b. Install the rear shelf with built-in stop lamp assembly.

c. Install the rear window garnish molding.

d. Install the quarter upper trim panels.

e. Install the rear seatback and seat cushion.

34. On 1990-91 Eldorado and Seville, install the rear window reveal moldings as follows:

a. Apply a clear primer to the underside of the upper molding.

b. Start from the center and hand press the upper molding into place.

c. Tape the windshield and molding to hold in position.

d. Position the lower molding and push it down, exposing the stud through hole in the molding.

e. Install the clips.

f. Install the screws and close the trunk.

35. Install all remaining components in the reverse order of removal.

36. The vehicle must remain at normal room temperature for 6 hours to allow the adhesive to cure.

DEVILLE, FLEETWOOD AND SIXTY SPECIAL COUPE WITH CB4 OR CF8 ROOF OPTION

▶ See Figures 236, 243, 248, 258 and 259

1. Remove the rear seat cushion and seatback.

2. Remove the quarter upper trim panels.

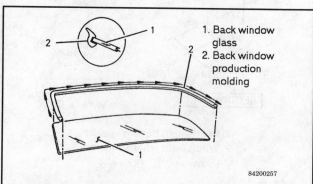

1. Back window glass
2. Back window production molding

Fig. 250 Rear window reveal molding, sedan with vinyl roof — Deville, Fleetwood and Sixty Special

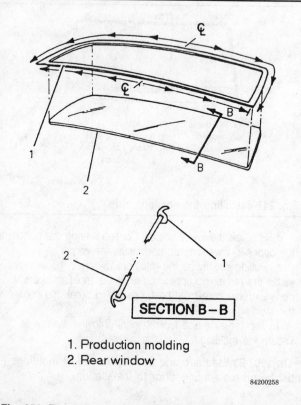

SECTION B–B

1. Production molding
2. Rear window

Fig. 251 Rear window reveal molding, sedan with hardtop — Deville, Fleetwood and Sixty Special

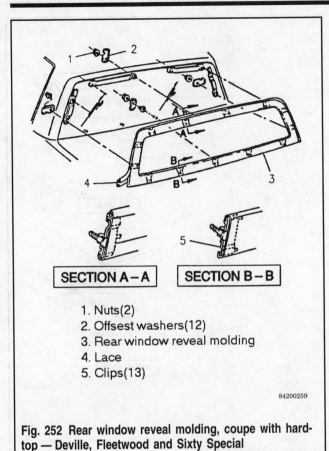

SECTION A–A   SECTION B–B

1. Nuts(2)
2. Offsest washers(12)
3. Rear window reveal molding
4. Lace
5. Clips(13)

84200259

Fig. 252 Rear window reveal molding, coupe with hard-top — Deville, Fleetwood and Sixty Special

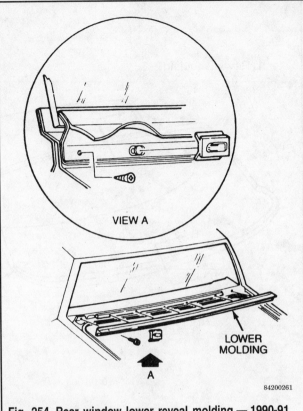

VIEW A

LOWER MOLDING

A

84200261

Fig. 254 Rear window lower reveal molding — 1990-91 Eldorado and Seville

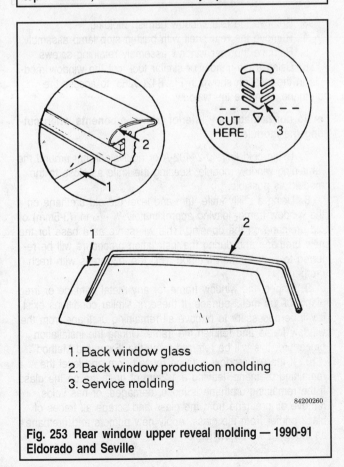

CUT HERE   3

1. Back window glass
2. Back window production molding
3. Service molding

84200260

Fig. 253 Rear window upper reveal molding — 1990-91 Eldorado and Seville

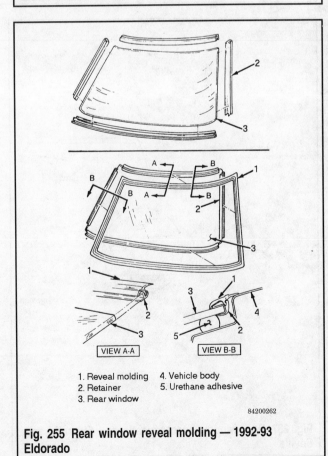

VIEW A-A   VIEW B-B

1. Reveal molding   4. Vehicle body
2. Retainer   5. Urethane adhesive
3. Rear window

84200262

Fig. 255 Rear window reveal molding — 1992-93 Eldorado

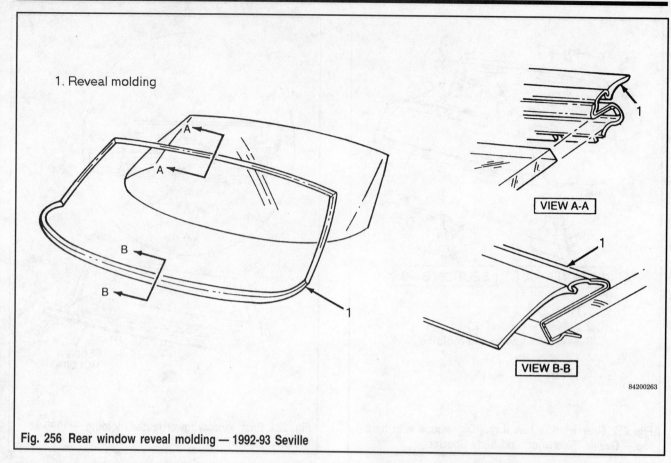

1. Reveal molding

VIEW A-A

VIEW B-B

84200263

Fig. 256 Rear window reveal molding — 1992-93 Seville

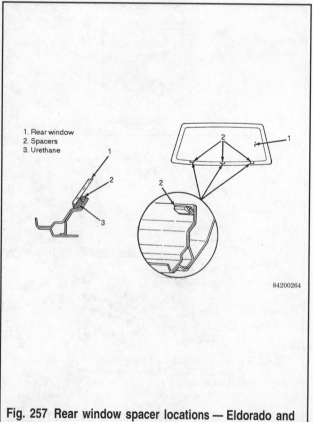

1. Rear window
2. Spacers
3. Urethane

84200264

Fig. 257 Rear window spacer locations — Eldorado and Seville

3. Remove the rear window garnish molding.
4. Remove the rear shelf with built-in stop lamp assembly.
5. Remove the rear window assembly retaining screws.
6. Using a die-grinder or similar tool, cut the window module in the location shown in Fig.'84200265' to access the urethane. Remove the window.

➡**Do not damage any interior trim components when cutting the module.**

7. Using cold knife J-24402-A or equivalent, cut around the remaining window module, keeping the knife as close to the module as possible.
8. Using a utility knife, trim and level the old urethane on the window frame, leaving approximately $\frac{1}{8}$ -$\frac{3}{16}$ in. (3-5mm) of old urethane on the opening. This will serve as a base for the new urethane and during the installation procedure will be referred to as the 'Short Method''. Fill the low areas with fresh urethane.
9. Inspect the window frame for any metal damage or irregularity of the metal surface. If these or similar conditions exist, it will be necessary to remove all remaining urethane from the window frame and refinish the frame. During the installation procedure, this will be referred to as the 'Extended Method''.
10. If the old window is to be reused, trim and level the remaining urethane, leaving a 1-2mm of urethane on the glass. If the remaining urethane is loose, damaged, or has voids, remove all urethane from the glass and scrape all traces of black primer from the glass. Apply new primers and urethane as though it were new glass.

To install:

11. Short Method only — Repair any areas on the window frame nicked during window removal using the appropriate color touch-up paint. Do not get paint or any other contamination on the remaining urethane base.

12. Clean the outside edges of the window module with glass cleaner to prevent contamination of the urethane adhesive.

13. Extended Method only — Apply urethane bonding body primer to the pinch weld flange.

➡️**If performing Short Method, do not apply primer over existing urethane.**

14. Using a clean cloth, apply plastic primer 9985756 or equivalent, around the entire perimeter of the module edge. Once applied, wipe off the excess immediately.

15. Short Method only — Apply a smooth continuous bead of urethane adhesive to the body, $3/8$-$31/64$ in. (10-12mm) high and $1/8$-$3/16$ in. (3-5mm) wide, over the existing urethane base.

16. Extended Method only — Apply a smooth continuous bead of urethane adhesive to the window, $1/2$-$9/16$ in. (13-15mm) high and $1/4$-$5/16$ in. (6-8mm) wide, around the inside surface of the window.

17. With the aid of an assistant, lift the window into the frame using suction cups.

18. Center the window in the opening using the retaining screw holes for alignment.

19. Press the window firmly to flow and set the adhesive. Use care to avoid excessive 'squeeze out" which would cause an appearance problem.

20. Install 3 retaining screws while an assistant holds the window in position. Remove the suction cups and install the remaining screws.

21. Water test using a soft spray. Use warm or hot water, if available. Do not direct a hard stream of water at the fresh adhesive. If any leaks are found, paddle in extra adhesive at the leak point using small disposable brush or a flat-bladed tool. Water applied on top of the urethane adhesive, either during the water test or as a separate operation, will speed up the cure of the adhesive.

22. Install the rear shelf with built-in stop lamp assembly.

23. Install the rear window garnish molding.

24. Install the quarter upper trim panels.

25. Install the rear seatback and seat cushion.

26. The vehicle must remain at normal room temperature for 6 hours to allow the adhesive to cure.

1990-91 ELDORADO WITH C10 SPECIAL LANDAU ROOF

▶ **See Figures 243 and 260**

➡️**The rear window glass extension is secured to the body opening with urethane adhesive. When removal is necessary, damage to the extension may result. A service module (rear window and extension) is available when replacement of the extension is required.**

1. Remove the cap assembly.
2. Remove the rear window garnish molding.
3. Disconnect the rear window defogger wiring connectors.
4. Mask off the area around the rear window extension to protect painted surfaces and to aid in clean-up after installation.

5. Using a utility knife, make a preliminary cut around the entire perimeter of the extension, staying as close to the edge of the extension as possible.

6. Using cold knife J-24402-A or equivalent, cut out the extension, keeping the blade as close to the extension as possible. Remove the rear window extension with the rear window.

7. Clean the glass opening of any loose material. If the extension is to be reinstalled, all urethane must be removed from the extension.

8. Clean the surface of the extension to which adhesive will be applied, by wiping with a clean, alcohol dampened cloth. Allow to air dry.

To install:

9. Prime the rear window glass extension with the black primer from urethane adhesive kit 12345633 or equivalent, and let dry 5 minutes.

10. Apply a smooth continuous bead of adhesive around the edge of the extension where primed.

11. Using suction cups, position the rear window glass extension with the rear window glass in the opening.

12. Press the window firmly to flow and set the adhesive. Use care to avoid excessive 'squeeze out" which would cause an appearance problem. Using a small disposable brush or flat-bladed tool, paddle material around the edge of the extension to ensure a watertight seal. If necessary, paddle in additional material to fill obvious voids in the seal.

13. Water test the rear window at once using a soft spray. Use warm or hot water, if available. Do not direct a hard stream of water at the fresh adhesive. If any leaks are found, paddle in extra adhesive at the leak point using small disposable brush or a flat-bladed tool. Water applied on top of the urethane adhesive, either during the water test or as a separate operation, will speed up the cure of the adhesive.

14. Connect the rear window defogger harness connectors.

15. Install the rear window garnish molding.

16. Install the cap assembly.

17. The vehicle must remain at normal room temperature for 6 hours to allow the adhesive to cure.

Quarter Window

DEVILLE, FLEETWOOD AND SIXTY SPECIAL COUPE EXCEPT ROOF OPTION CB4

▶ **See Figures 248 and 261**

1. Remove the fabric roof cover, if equipped.
2. Mask off the area around the window using 3M protective tape part number 06945 or equivalent, to protect the painted surfaces.
3. Remove the rear seat cushion and seatback.
4. Remove all inside quarter trim.
5. Remove the quarter window retaining nuts.
6. Working inside the vehicle, use cold knife J-24402-A or equivalent, and cut slowly and carefully around the quarter window assembly, keeping the blade as close to the edge of the window as possible.
7. Remove the quarter window.
8. Using a utility knife, trim and level the old urethane on the window frame, leaving approximately $1/8$-$3/16$ in. (3-5mm) of old urethane on the opening. This will serve as a base for the new urethane and during the installation procedure will be re-

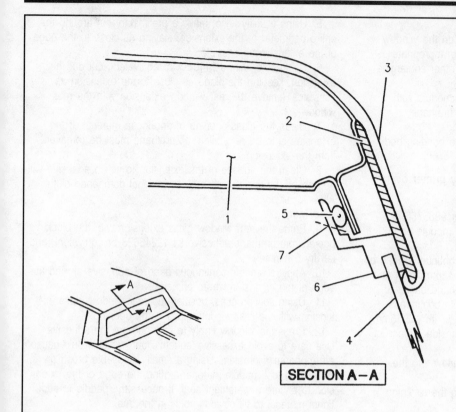

1. Roof of vehicle
2. Fabric roof retainer
3. Fabric roof material
4. Rear window
5. Urethane bead
6. Rear window module
7. Cut module here

SECTION A–A

84200265

Fig. 258 Rear window module removal, coupe with roof options CB4 or CF8 — Deville, Fleetwood and Sixty Special

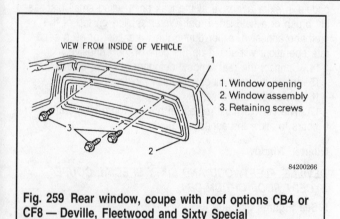

VIEW FROM INSIDE OF VEHICLE

1. Window opening
2. Window assembly
3. Retaining screws

84200266

Fig. 259 Rear window, coupe with roof options CB4 or CF8 — Deville, Fleetwood and Sixty Special

ferred to as the 'Short Method". Fill the low areas with fresh urethane.

9. Inspect the window frame for any metal damage or irregularity of the metal surface. If these or similar conditions exist, it will be necessary to remove all remaining urethane from the window frame and refinish the frame. During the installation procedure, this will be referred to as the 'Extended Method".

To install:

10. Short Method only — Repair any areas on the window frame nicked during window removal using the appropriate color touch-up paint. Do not get paint or any other contamination on the remaining urethane base.

11. Clean the outside edges of the window module with glass cleaner to prevent contamination of the urethane adhesive.

12. Extended Method only — Apply urethane bonding body primer to the pinch weld flange.

➡**If performing Short Method, do not apply primer over existing urethane.**

13. Using a clean cloth, apply plastic primer 9981993 or equivalent, around the entire perimeter of the module edge. Once applied, wipe off the excess immediately.

14. Short Method only — Apply a smooth continuous bead of urethane adhesive around the outside surface of the window frame, $1/4$-$5/16$ in. (6-8mm) high and $1/8$-$3/16$ in. (3-5mm) wide, over the existing urethane base.

15. Extended Method only — Apply a smooth continuous bead of urethane adhesive, $23/64$-$7/16$ in. (9-11mm) high and $3/16$-$9/32$ in. (5-7mm) wide, around the inside surface of the window.

16. Install the quarter window assembly.

17. Press the window firmly to flow and set the adhesive. Use care to avoid excessive 'squeeze out" which would cause an appearance problem.

18. Water test the window using a soft spray. Use warm or hot water, if available. Do not direct a hard stream of water at the fresh adhesive. If any leaks are found, paddle in extra adhesive at the leak point using small disposable brush or a flat-bladed tool. Water applied on top of the urethane adhesive, either during the water test or as a separate operation, will speed up the cure of the adhesive.

19. Install the quarter window retaining nuts.

20. Install the quarter trim.

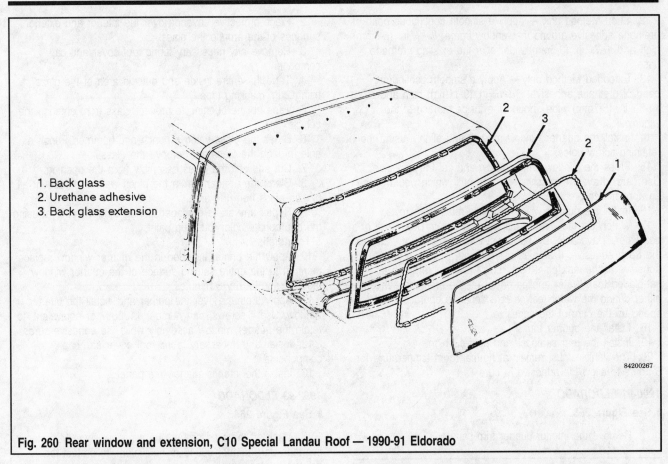

1. Back glass
2. Urethane adhesive
3. Back glass extension

84200267

Fig. 260 Rear window and extension, C10 Special Landau Roof — 1990-91 Eldorado

21. Install the rear seatback and seat cushion.
22. Install the fabric roof cover, if equipped.
23. The vehicle must remain at normal room temperature for 6 hours to allow the adhesive to cure.

DEVILLE, FLEETWOOD AND SIXTY SPECIAL COUPE WITH ROOF OPTION CB4

▶ **See Figures 248 and 262**

1. Remove the rear seat cushion and seatback.
2. Remove all inside quarter trim.
3. Remove the quarter window retaining screws.
4. Using cold knife J-24402-A or equivalent, cut out the quarter window. Stay as close as possible to the pinch weld flange, so as not to damage the module if the module is to be

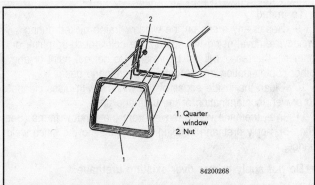

1. Quarter window
2. Nut

84200268

Fig. 261 Quarter window, coupe except roof option CB4 — Deville, Fleetwood and Sixty Special

reused. If the module is damaged, it could cause water leaks and/or wind noise.

5. Remove the quarter window module.
6. Using a utility knife, trim and level the old urethane on the window frame, leaving approximately 1/8-3/16 in. (3-5mm) of old urethane on the opening. This will serve as a base for the new urethane and during the installation procedure will be referred to as the 'Short Method''. Fill the low areas with fresh urethane.
7. Inspect the window frame for any metal damage or irregularity of the metal surface. If these or similar conditions exist, it will be necessary to remove all remaining urethane from the window frame and refinish the frame. During the installation procedure, this will be referred to as the 'Extended Method''.

To install:

8. Short Method only — Repair any areas on the window frame nicked during window removal using the appropriate color touch-up paint. Do not get paint or any other contamination on the remaining urethane base.
9. Clean the outside edges of the window module with glass cleaner to prevent contamination of the urethane adhesive.
10. Extended Method only — Apply urethane bonding body primer to the pinch weld flange.

➡**If performing Short Method, do not apply primer over existing urethane.**

11. Using a clean cloth, apply plastic primer 9985756 or equivalent, around the entire perimeter of the module edge. Once applied, wipe off the excess immediately.

12. Short Method only — Apply a smooth continuous bead of urethane adhesive around the window frame, $1/4$-$5/16$ in. (6-8mm) high and $1/8$-$3/16$ in. (3-5mm) wide, over the existing urethane base.

13. Extended Method only — Apply a smooth continuous bead of urethane adhesive, $23/64$-$7/16$ in. (9-11mm) high and $3/16$-$9/32$ in. (5-7mm) wide, around the inside surface of the window.

14. Install the quarter window module and align it using the retaining screw holes.

15. Press the window firmly to flow and set the adhesive. Use care to avoid excessive 'squeeze out" which would cause an appearance problem.

16. Install the quarter window module retaining screws.

17. Water test the window using a soft spray. Use warm or hot water, if available. Do not direct a hard stream of water at the fresh adhesive. If any leaks are found, paddle in extra adhesive at the leak point using small disposable brush or a flat-bladed tool. Water applied on top of the urethane adhesive, either during the water test or as a separate operation, will speed up the cure of the adhesive.

18. Install the quarter trim.

19. Install the rear seatback and seat cushion.

20. The vehicle must remain at normal room temperature for 6 hours to allow the adhesive to cure.

1990-91 ELDORADO

▶ See Figure 263

1. Remove the interior quarter trim panel.

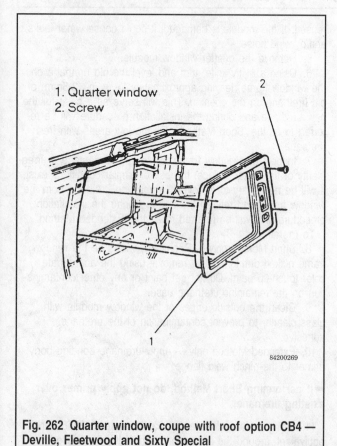

1. Quarter window
2. Screw

84200269

Fig. 262 Quarter window, coupe with roof option CB4 — Deville, Fleetwood and Sixty Special

2. Place protective covering over the interior and exterior surfaces of the around the glass.

3. Remove any necessary fabric roof cover and cap components.

4. Tape the entire inside and outside area of the glass using 2 in. masking tape.

5. Tape up the opening to prevent glass from entering the vehicle.

6. Break the glass using a punch and hammer. Punch a hole through the glass and remove the glass.

7. Cut and pull the glass assembly from the opening.

8. Clean the urethane from the pinch weld and vacuum all broken glass from the area.

9. Repair any areas damaged during window removal using the appropriate color touch-up paint.

To install:

10. Apply the primer included in the quarter window replacement kit to the entire sealing surface of the quarter window module, and let dry 5 minutes.

11. Apply urethane over the primer and install the quarter window. Use 4 screws, part number 1150887 or equivalent, to retain the quarter window assembly while the adhesive cures.

12. Install any necessary fabric roof cover and cap components.

13. Install the interior quarter trim panel.

1992-93 ELDORADO

▶ See Figure 264

1. Mask off the area around the window using 3M protective tape part number 06945 or equivalent, to protect the painted surfaces.

2. Remove the rear seat cushion and seatback.

3. Remove the quarter trim panel.

4. Remove the quarter window retaining screws.

5. Using cold knife J-24402-A or equivalent, from inside the vehicle cut slowly and carefully around the quarter window assembly, keeping the blade as close to the edge of the window assembly as possible.

6. Remove the quarter window.

7. Using a utility knife, trim as much of the old urethane as possible from the window frame, being careful not to nick the paint in or around the bonding surface.

8. Inspect the window frame for any metal damage or irregularity of the metal surface. If these or similar conditions exist, it will be necessary to remove all remaining urethane from the window frame and refinish the frame.

To install:

9. Repair any areas on the window frame nicked during window removal using the appropriate color touch-up paint, or primer if the repair will not be visible. Do not get paint or any other contamination on the remaining urethane base.

10. Clean the inside edges of the window with glass cleaner to prevent contamination of the urethane base.

11. If all urethane was removed from the window frame (See Step 8), apply urethane bonding body primer to the pinch weld flange.

➡**Do not apply primer over existing urethane.**

12. Using a clean cloth, apply plastic primer 9981993 or equivalent, to the rear mounting surface and outboard around

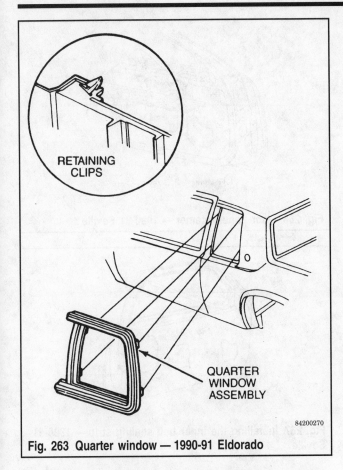

Fig. 263 Quarter window — 1990-91 Eldorado

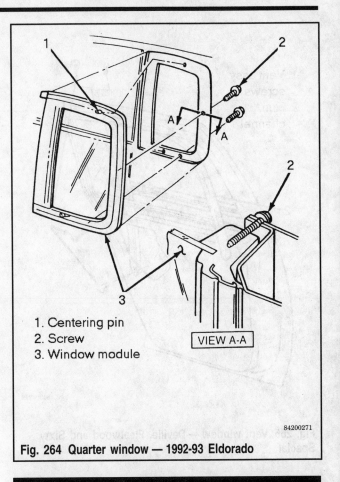

1. Centering pin
2. Screw
3. Window module

VIEW A-A

Fig. 264 Quarter window — 1992-93 Eldorado

the entire perimeter of the module edge. Once applied, wipe off the excess immediately.

13. Apply a smooth continuous bead of urethane adhesive, $^{23}/_{64}$-$^7/_{16}$ in. (9-11mm) high and $^3/_{16}$-$^9/_{32}$ in. (5-7mm) wide, to the mounting surface of the quarter window assembly, where it was primed. Apply add itional urethane on the outboard edge of the module along the rear vertical edge.

14. Install the quarter window assembly, using the centering pins as a guide.

15. Press the window firmly to 'wet out" and set the adhesive. Be sure to seat the lip uniformly and align the module properly to the door belt and window upper reveal moldings. Use care to avoid excessive 'squeeze out" which could cause an appearance problem.

16. Install the 2 window module retaining screws.

17. Water test the window using a soft spray. Use warm or hot water, if available. Do not direct a hard stream of water at the fresh adhesive. If any leaks are found, paddle in extra adhesive at the leak point using a small disposable brush or a flat-bladed tool. Water applied on top of the urethane adhesive, either during the water test or as a separate operation, will speed up the cure of the adhesive.

18. Install the quarter trim.

19. Install the rear seatback and seat cushion.

20. The vehicle must remain at normal room temperature for 6 hours to allow the adhesive to cure.

Vent Windows

REMOVAL & INSTALLATION

Deville, Fleetwood and Sixty Special

▶ See Figure 265

1. Remove the door panel; refer to the procedure in this Section.

2. Remove the water deflector.

3. Remove the sash bolts.

4. Free the guide from the rear run channel allowing the glass to rest as far forward in the door as possible.

5. Remove the vent window retaining screws and the vent window.

To install:

6. Install the vent window with the retaining screws.

7. Attach the guide to the rear run channel.

8. Install the sash bolts.

9. Install the water deflector and the door panel.

Seville

1990-91

▶ See Figures 266, 267, 268 and 269

1. Remove the door panel; refer to the procedure in this Section.

2. Remove the water deflector,

3. Remove the screws and the door panel retainer.

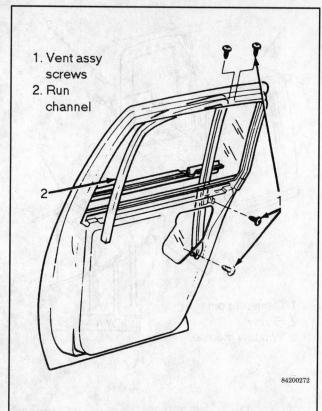

1. Vent assy screws
2. Run channel

Fig. 265 Vent window — Deville, Fleetwood and Sixty Special

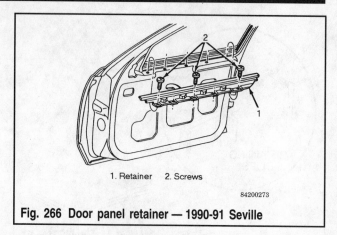

1. Retainer   2. Screws

84200273

Fig. 266 Door panel retainer — 1990-91 Seville

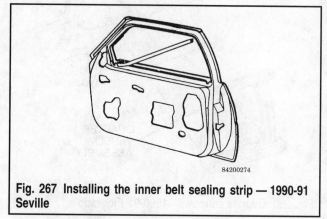

84200274

Fig. 267 Installing the inner belt sealing strip — 1990-91 Seville

4. Remove the inner belt sealing strip by lifting upward.

5. Remove the rear door glass; refer to the procedure in this Section.

6. Use a flat-bladed tool to remove the inner door frame garnish molding.

7. Remove the run channel and vent window retaining screws.

8. Disconnect the run channel, using care and pulling away from the vent window.

9. Remove the vent window.

To install:

10. Attach the vent window to the run channel.

11. Install the vent window and run channel retaining screws.

12. Install the inner door frame garnish molding.

13. Install the rear door glass; refer to the procedure in this Section.

14. Install the front edge of the inner belt sealing strip over the door flange, then press down the entire length of the sealing strip.

15. Install the door panel retainer.

16. Install the water deflector and door panel.

1992-93

▶ **See Figures 229, 270 and 271**

1. Remove the door panel; refer to the procedure in this Section.

2. Remove the water deflector.

3. Remove the inner belt sealing strip by lifting upward.

4. Remove the rear door glass; refer to the procedure in this Section.

5. Use a flat-bladed tool to remove the inner door frame garnish molding.

6. Grasp the front edge of the run channel and pull it loose from the door frame, then remove the remainder of the run channel.

7. Remove the 3 nuts, 5 screws and the vent window.

To install:

8. Install the vent window with the nuts and screws.

9. Apply silicone to the run channel. Install the forward edge of the run channel into position, then install the remainder of the run channel into the door frame using a thin-bladed tool.

10. Install the inner door frame garnish molding.

11. Install the rear door glass; refer to the procedure in this Section.

12. Locate the front edge of the inner belt sealing strip over the door flange, then press down the entire length of the sealing strip.

13. Install the water deflector and door panel.

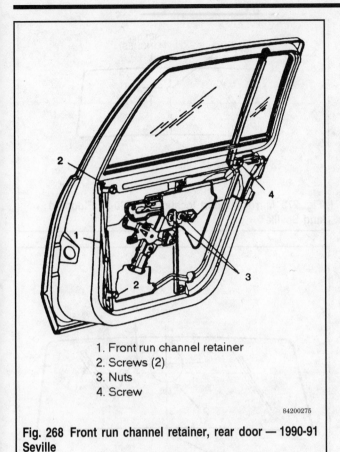

1. Front run channel retainer
2. Screws (2)
3. Nuts
4. Screw

84200275

Fig. 268 Front run channel retainer, rear door — 1990-91 Seville

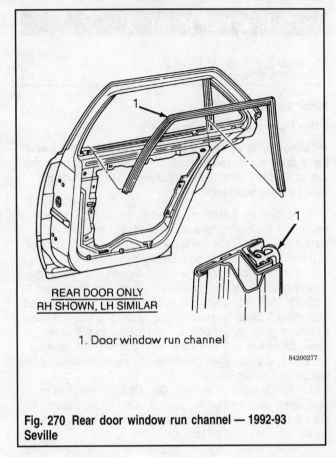

REAR DOOR ONLY
RH SHOWN, LH SIMILAR

1. Door window run channel

84200277

Fig. 270 Rear door window run channel — 1992-93 Seville

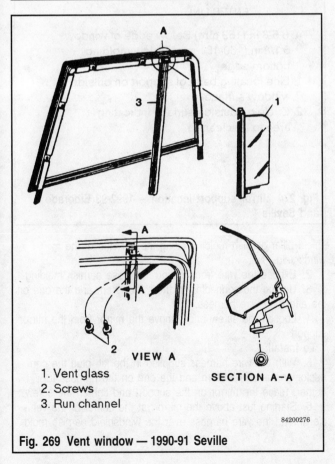

VIEW A

SECTION A-A

1. Vent glass
2. Screws
3. Run channel

84200276

Fig. 269 Vent window — 1990-91 Seville

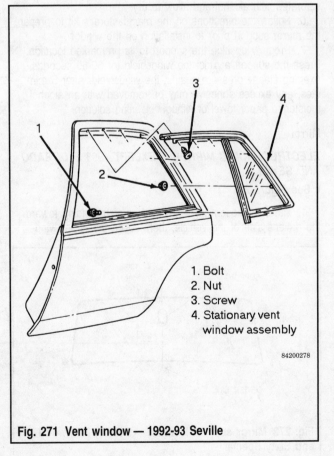

1. Bolt
2. Nut
3. Screw
4. Stationary vent window assembly

84200278

Fig. 271 Vent window — 1992-93 Seville

Inside Rear View Mirror

REMOVAL & INSTALLATION

Mirror Support

▶ See Figures 272, 273, 274 and 275

➡The following procedure provides instructions for installing a detached mirror support. The procedure requires the use of Loctite® Minute-Bond Adhesive 312, two component pack, or equivalent.

1. Refer to the illustrations provided in order to determine the correct position of the mirror support on the windshield. Mark the position of the mirror support on the outside surface of the windshield using a wax marking pencil or crayon.

2. Draw a circle around the mirror support location, on the outside of the windshield, to indicate the area to be cleaned.

3. On the inside windshield surface, clean within the circled area using a paper towel and either scouring cleanser, window cleaner or polishing compound. Rub until the area is completely clean and dry. When dry, clean the area with an alcohol saturated paper towel to remove any traces of scouring powder or cleaning solution.

4. Using a piece of fine grit (320 or 360) emery cloth or sandpaper, sand the bonding surface of the mirror support. If the original support is being reused, all traces of factory installed adhesive must be removed.

5. Wipe the sanded mirror support with a clean paper towel saturated with alcohol and allow to dry.

6. Follow the directions on the manufacturer's kit to prepare the mirror support prior to installation on the window.

7. Properly position the support to its premarked location. Press the support against the windshield for 30-60 seconds, exerting steady pressure against the windshield. After 5 minutes, any excess adhesive may be removed with an alcohol moistened paper towel or window cleaning solution.

Mirror

ELECTROCHROMIC MIRROR — EXCEPT 1993 ELDORADO AND SEVILLE

▶ See Figure 276

1. Carefully loosen the windshield garnish molding toward the driver's side of the vehicle, then loosen the upper wind-

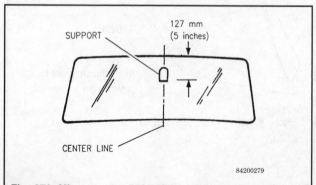

Fig. 272 Mirror support location — Deville, Fleetwood and Sixty Special

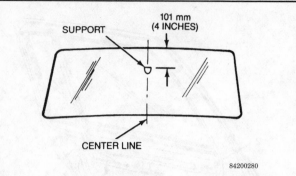

Fig. 273 Mirror support location — 1990-91 Eldorado and Seville

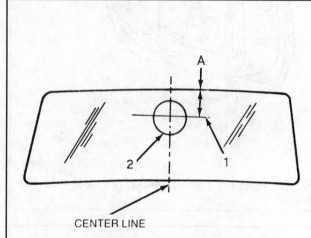

A. 6 5/8 in.(169 mm) Below edge of window.
6 1/8 in.(160-161 mm) Below molding bottom edge
1. Line locating base of support on outside window surface
2. Circle on outside surface indicating area to be cleaned

Fig. 274 Mirror support location — 1992-93 Eldorado and Seville

shield pillar garnish molding along the left side of the windshield.

2. Expose the wire from behind the loose garnish molding.

3. Unplug the connector on the mirror stem and the one on the attaching wire harness.

4. Loosen the screw and remove the mirror from the mirror support.

To install:

5. With the wire harness supplied in the kit, plug the connector on the mirror stem and the one on the harness together. Place the mirror on the support and tighten the screw.

6. Starting just above the mirror, at the center of the vehicle, thread the wire harness over the windshield garnish mold-

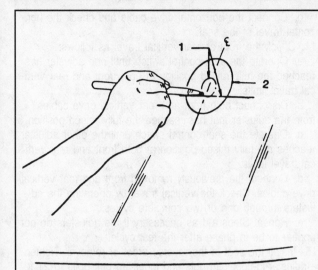

1. Locating circle and base of support line on outside glass surface
2. Circle on outside glass surface indicates area to be cleaned

84200282

Fig. 275 Locating mirror support on windshield — Deville, Fleetwood, Sixty Special and 1990-91 Eldorado and Seville

ing and pull the wire toward you. Be sure enough wire is left going to the connectors and that the wire is not stretched tight.

7. Keeping the wire harness straight, carefully tuck the wire behind the loose garnish moldings.

❊❊WARNING

Be careful not to stretch or pinch the wire. Do not use a sharp tool to force the wire under the molding as this could damage the wire and short the system. Position the protective wire tube under the molding, then carefully tighten the garnish moldings back to their original positions using extreme caution not to pinch or kink the wire harness.

ELECTROCHROMIC MIRROR — 1993 ELDORADO AND SEVILLE

▶ See Figure 277

1. Disconnect the electrical connectors at the rear of the mirror.

2. Twist the mirror to one side and use one hand to support the edge of the mirror against the windshield.

3. Use the other hand to pull the mirror away from the windshield with a quick jerk.

To install:

4. Slide the mirror onto the mirror support. The mirror is fully seated on the support when an audible 'click" is heard.

5. Connect the electrical connectors.

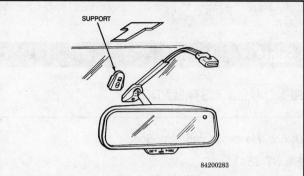

Fig. 276 Electrochromic mirror — except 1993 Eldorado and Seville

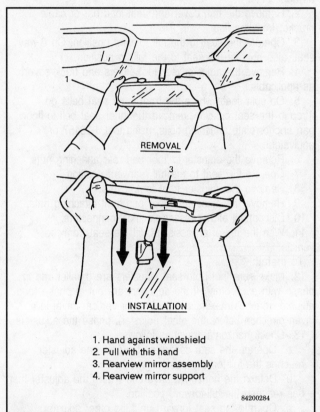

1. Hand against windshield
2. Pull with this hand
3. Rearview mirror assembly
4. Rearview mirror support

84200284

Fig. 277 Electrochromic mirror — 1993 Eldorado and Seville

CONVENTIONAL MIRROR — 1993 ELDORADO AND SEVILLE

▶ See Figure 278

1. Remove the set screw retaining the mirror base to the mirror support.

2. Lift the mirror base from the support.

3. Remove the Torx® screw at the rear of the swivel arm.

To install:

4. Install the lock tooth washer and mirror base to the swivel arm.

5. Install the Torx® screw to the swivel arm and tighten until snug.

6. Install the mirror to the mirror support and install the set screw.

Seats

REMOVAL & INSTALLATION

Deville, Fleetwood and Sixty Special

FRONT SEAT

▶ **See Figures 279, 280, 281 and 282**

1. Disconnect the shoulder belt strap from the guide loop, as applicable.
2. Remove the trim cover and seat load bar or cable bracket from the floor.
3. Operate the seat to the full forward position. On 6-way seat, also operate the seat to the full up position.
4. Remove the adjuster rear foot covers and track covers, as applicable.
5. On split seats where the front inner seat belts go through the seat cushion, remove the inner seat belt-to-floor pan anchor plate attaching bolts, using tool J-23457 or equivalent.
6. Remove the adjuster-to-floor pan rear attaching nuts.
7. Operate the seat to the full rearward position.
8. Remove the adjuster front foot covers.
9. Remove the adjuster-to-floor pan front attaching nuts.
10. Disconnect all necessary electrical connectors.
11. With the aid of an assistant, lift the seat from the vehicle.

To install:

12. Make sure that both seat adjusters are parallel and in phase with each other. If the adjusters are out of phase (one adjuster reaches maximum horizontal or vertical travel in a given direction before the other adjuster), phase the adjusters.
13. Check horizontal travel as follows:
    a. Operate the seat control switch until one adjuster reaches the full-forward position.
    b. Detach the horizontal drive cable from the adjuster that has reached the full-forward position.
    c. Operate the seat forward until the other adjuster reaches the full-forward position.

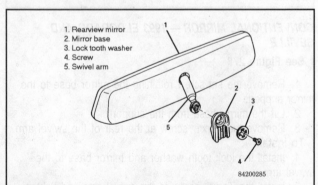

1. Rearview mirror
2. Mirror base
3. Lock tooth washer
4. Screw
5. Swivel arm

84200285

Fig. 278 Conventional mirror — 1993 Eldorado and Seville

    d. Connect the horizontal drive cable and check the horizontal travel of the seat.
14. Check the front or rear vertical travel as follows:
    a. Operate the seat control switch until one adjuster has reached the fully raised position at both front and rear vertical travel limits.
    b. Disconnect both front and rear vertical drive cables from the adjuster that has reached the fully raised position.
    c. Operate the seat control switch until the other adjuster reaches the fully raised position at both front and rear vertical travel limits.
    d. Connect the previously removed front and rear vertical drive cables. Check the vertical travel by operating the adjusters through one or two complete cycles.
    e. Repeat Steps a-d as necessary if the adjusters do not appear to be in phase after the test cycle.
15. Install the seat in the reverse order of removal. Tighten the adjuster-to-floor pan nuts and inner lap belt bolts to 21 ft. lbs. (28 Nm).

✳✳WARNING

When installing the driver seat, be careful not to damage the rear heating and air conditioning floor duct or any electronic module under the carpet.

16. Check operation of the seat for full limits of travel.

REAR SEAT

▶ **See Figure 283**

1. Push the lower forward edge of the seat cushion rearward.
2. Lift upward and pull forward on the seat cushion frame to disengage the cushion frame wires from the retainers on the rear seat pan. Remove the seat cushion.

➡**If it is difficult to disengage the front of the rear seat cushion from the seat pan retainers, grasp the lower edge of the seat cushion at the retainer location on one side of the seat, and exert enough rearward pressure to disengage the seat from the retainers.**

3. At the bottom of the seat back, remove the rear seat lap belts or belt retractor bolts securing the rear seat back.
4. Remove the shoulder belt escutcheons and the 2 bolts retaining the headrest.
5. Remove the seat back.

To install:

6. Position the seat back in the vehicle.
7. Install the 2 headrest retaining bolts and the shoulder belt escutcheons.
8. Install the belt retractor bolts and tighten to 31 ft. lbs. (42 Nm) or the lap belt anchor nuts and tighten to 25 ft. lbs. (35 Nm).
9. Carefully lift the seat cushion into the vehicle, being careful not to damage the adjacent trim. Position the rear edge of the cushion under the seat back while positioning the seat belt straps.
10. Align the frame wire offsets on the front of the seat cushion frame with the retainers on the floor pan. Push the seat cushion rearward until the offsets engage in the retainers;

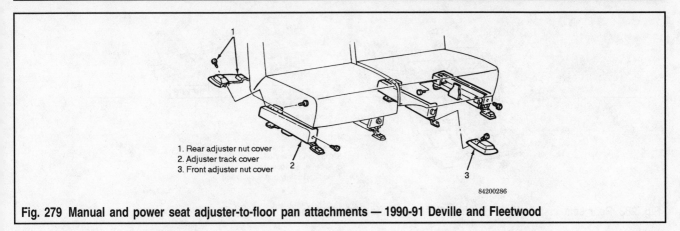

1. Rear adjuster nut cover
2. Adjuster track cover
3. Front adjuster nut cover

84200286

Fig. 279 Manual and power seat adjuster-to-floor pan attachments — 1990-91 Deville and Fleetwood

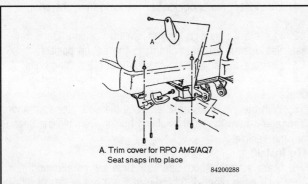

A. Fully driven, seated, and
   not stripped

84200287

Fig. 280 Installing the shoulder belt strap from the guide loop — 1992-93 Deville, Fleetwood and Sixty Special

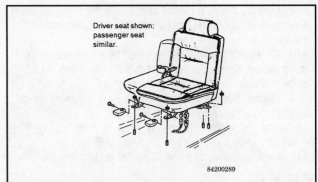

Driver seat shown;
passenger seat
similar.

84200289

Fig. 282 Front seat installation — 1992-93 Deville, Fleetwood and Sixty Special

A. Trim cover for RPO AM5/AQ7
   Seat snaps into place

84200288

Fig. 281 Installing trim covers and load bar bolt — 1992-93 Deville, Fleetwood and Sixty Special

then press down and pull the cushion forward to fully engage the retainers.

➡️**If it is difficult to engage the front of the cushion in the retainers, use the same method described in the removal procedure to engage the cushion in the retainers.**

1990-91 Eldorado and Seville

FRONT SEAT

▶ See Figure 284

1. Disconnect the shoulder belt strap from the seat back.

2. Operate the seat to the full forward position. On 6-way seat, also operate the seat almost to the full up position.
3. Remove the adjuster rear foot covers and track covers.
4. Remove the adjuster-to-floor pan rear attaching nuts.
5. Operate the seat to the full rearward position.
6. Remove the adjuster front foot covers.
7. Remove the adjuster-to-floor pan front attaching nuts.
8. Disconnect all necessary electrical connectors.
9. With the aid of an assistant, lift the seat from the vehicle.

To install:
10. Make sure that both seat adjusters are parallel and in phase with each other. If the adjusters are out of phase (one adjuster reaches maximum horizontal or vertical travel in a given direction before the other adjuster), phase the adjusters.
11. Check horizontal travel as follows:
   a. Operate the seat control switch until one adjuster reaches the full-forward position.
   b. Detach the horizontal drive cable from the adjuster that has reached the full-forward position.
   c. Operate the seat forward until the other adjuster reaches the full-forward position.
   d. Connect the horizontal drive cable and check the horizontal travel of the seat.
12. Check the front or rear vertical travel as follows:
   a. Operate the seat control switch until one adjuster has reached the fully raised position at both front and rear vertical travel limits.
   b. Disconnect both front and rear vertical drive cables from the adjuster that has reached the fully raised position.

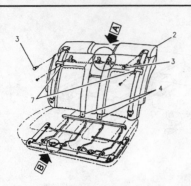

1. Bracket on rear shelf panel
2. Headrest
3. Bolts
4. Rear back retainers
5. Cushion frame wire
6. Retainer on floor pan
7. Bolt and safety belt escutcheon

84200290

Fig. 283 Rear seat installation — Deville, Fleetwood and Sixty Special

c. Operate the seat control switch until the other adjuster reaches the fully raised position at both front and rear vertical travel limits.

d. Connect the previously removed front and rear vertical drive cables. Check the vertical travel by operating the adjusters through one or two complete cycles.

e. Repeat Steps a-d as necessary if the adjusters do not appear to be in phase after the test cycle.

13. Install the seat in the reverse order of removal. Tighten the adjuster-to-floor pan nuts to 21 ft. lbs. (28 Nm).

14. Check operation of the seat for full limits of travel.

REAR SEAT

♦ See Figure 285

1. Remove the rear seat speaker covers, speakers and forward rear compartment trim panel.

2. Remove the nuts securing the seat back studs to the shelf panel supports.

3. Push the lower forward edge of the seat cushion rearward.

4. Lift upward and pull forward on the seat cushion frame to disengage the cushion frame wires from the retainers on the rear seat pan. Remove the seat cushion.

➡ **If it is difficult to disengage the front of the rear seat cushion from the seat pan retainers, grasp the lower edge of the seat cushion at the retainer location on one side of the seat, and exert enough rearward pressure to disengage the seat from the retainers.**

5. Remove the nuts securing the seat back lower loop and center seat belts.

6. Remove the seat back.

To install:

7. Carefully position the seat back in the vehicle.

8. Install the nuts securing the seat back lower loop and center seat belts.

9. Carefully lift the seat cushion into the vehicle, being careful not to damage the adjacent trim. Position the rear edge of the cushion under the seat back.

10. Align the frame wire offsets on the front of the seat cushion frame with the retainers on the floor pan. Push the seat cushion rearward until the offsets engage in the retainers;

then press down and pull the cushion forward to fully engage the retainers.

➡ **If it is difficult to engage the front of the cushion in the retainers, use the same method described in the removal procedure to engage the cushion in the retainers.**

11. Install the nuts securing the seat back studs to the shelf panel support.

12. Install the forward rear compartment trim panel, speakers and speaker covers.

1992-93 Eldorado and Seville

FRONT SEAT

♦ See Figure 286

1. Disconnect the shoulder belt webbing from the seat back.

2. Operate the seat to the full forward position. On 8-way seat, also operate the seat almost to the full up position.

3. Remove the adjuster-to-floor pan rear attaching bolts.

4. Tilt the seat forward and disconnect the electrical connectors.

5. With the aid of an assistant, pull the seat rearward and disengage it from the front retaining hooks. Remove the seat from the vehicle.

To install:

6. Make sure that both seat adjusters are parallel and in phase with each other. If the adjusters are out of phase (one adjuster reaches maximum horizontal or vertical travel in a given direction before the other adjuster), phase the adjusters.

7. Check horizontal travel as follows:

a. Operate the seat control switch until one adjuster reaches the full-forward position.

b. Detach the horizontal drive cable from the adjuster that has reached the full-forward position.

c. Operate the seat forward until the other adjuster reaches the full-forward position.

d. Connect the horizontal drive cable and check the horizontal travel of the seat.

8. Check the front or rear vertical travel as follows:

a. Operate the seat control switch until one adjuster has reached the fully raised position at both front and rear vertical travel limits.

b. Disconnect both front and rear vertical drive cables from the adjuster that has reached the fully raised position.

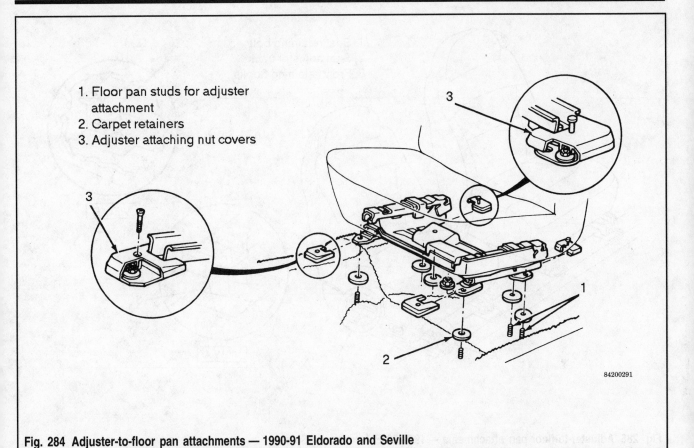

1. Floor pan studs for adjuster attachment
2. Carpet retainers
3. Adjuster attaching nut covers

84200291

Fig. 284 Adjuster-to-floor pan attachments — 1990-91 Eldorado and Seville

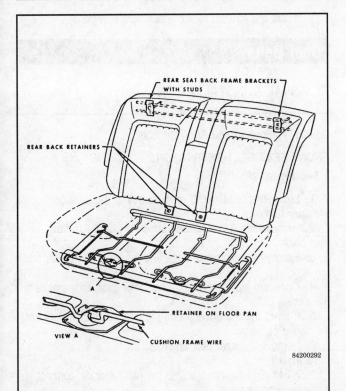

REAR SEAT BACK FRAME BRACKETS WITH STUDS

REAR BACK RETAINERS

RETAINER ON FLOOR PAN

VIEW A

CUSHION FRAME WIRE

84200292

Fig. 285 Rear seat installation — 1990-91 Eldorado and Seville

c. Operate the seat control switch until the other adjuster reaches the fully raised position at both front and rear vertical travel limits.

d. Connect the previously removed front and rear vertical drive cables. Check the vertical travel by operating the adjusters through one or two complete cycles.

e. Repeat Steps a-d as necessary if the adjusters do not appear to be in phase after the test cycle.

9. Position the seat in the vehicle, engaging the front hooks.

10. Tilt the seat forward and connect the electrical connectors.

11. Install the rear attaching bolts and tighten to 21-27 ft. lbs. (28-36 Nm).

12. Connect the shoulder belt webbing to the seat back.

13. Check the seat operation.

REAR SEAT

▶ **See Figure 287**

1. Remove the forward rear compartment trim panel.

2. Remove the nuts securing the seat back studs to the shelf panel support from inside the rear compartment.

3. Push the lower forward edge of the seat cushion rearward.

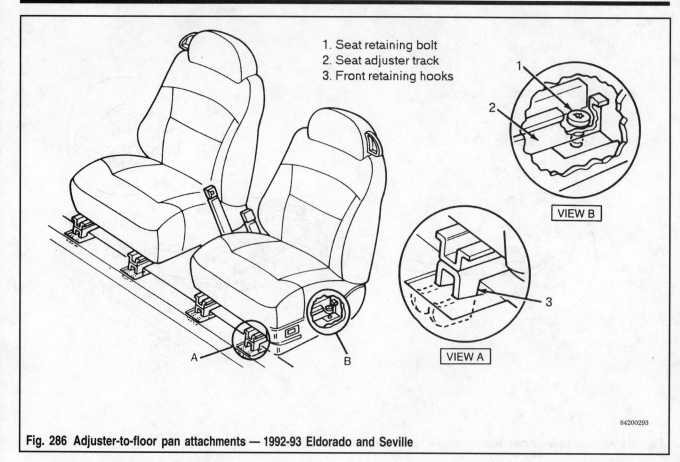

1. Seat retaining bolt
2. Seat adjuster track
3. Front retaining hooks

VIEW B

VIEW A

84200293

Fig. 286 Adjuster-to-floor pan attachments — 1992-93 Eldorado and Seville

4. Lift upward and pull forward on the seat cushion frame to disengage the cushion frame wires from the retainers on the rear seat pan. Remove the seat cushion.

➡**If it is difficult to disengage the front of the rear seat cushion from the seat pan retainers, grasp the lower edge of the seat cushion at the retainer location on one side of the seat, and exert enough rearward pressure to disengage the seat from the retainers.**

5. Remove the nuts securing the seat back lower loop and center seat belts.
6. Remove the seat back.
   To install:
7. Carefully position the seat back in the vehicle.
8. Push the seat back studs into the holes in the shelf panel support, then install the nuts from inside the rear compartment.
9. Install the nuts securing the seat back lower loop and center seat belts.
10. Carefully lift the seat cushion into the vehicle, being careful not to damage the adjacent trim. Position the rear edge of the cushion under the seat back.
11. Align the frame wire offsets on the front of the seat cushion frame with the retainers on the floor pan. Push the seat cushion rearward until the offsets engage in the retainers; then press down and pull the cushion forward to fully engage the retainers.

➡**If it is difficult to engage the front of the cushion in the retainers, use the same method described in the removal procedure to engage the cushion in the retainers.**

12. Install the forward rear compartment trim panel.

Seat Belts

REMOVAL & INSTALLATION

Deville, Fleetwood and Sixty Special

FRONT SEAT BELT RETRACTORS — 2 DOOR

▶ See Figure 288

1. Lower the headliner to gain access to the seat belt shoulder retractor.
2. Remove the 2 screws and shoulder belt guide from the seat back.
3. Remove the 2 anchor bolts and the seat belt shoulder retractor.
4. Open the lap retractor cover access door and remove the anchor bolt.
5. If removing the driver's side lap belt retractor, disconnect the wiring connector.
6. Remove the seat belt lap retractor.
   To install:
7. If installing the driver's side lap belt retractor, connect the wiring connector.
8. Install the seat belt lap retractor and anchor bolt. Tighten the anchor bolt to 31 ft. lbs. (42 Nm).
9. Install the seat belt shoulder retractor with the 2 anchor bolts. Tighten the anchor bolts to 18 ft. lbs. (24 Nm).

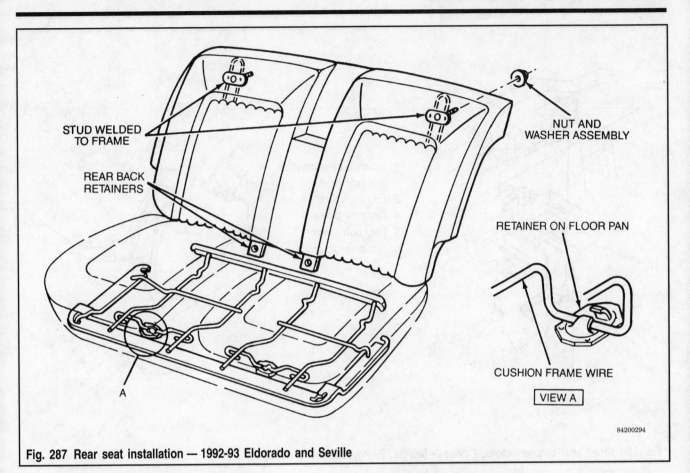

STUD WELDED TO FRAME

NUT AND WASHER ASSEMBLY

REAR BACK RETAINERS

RETAINER ON FLOOR PAN

CUSHION FRAME WIRE

VIEW A

A

84200294

Fig. 287 Rear seat installation — 1992-93 Eldorado and Seville

10. Install the shoulder belt guide and 2 screws.
11. Install the headliner.

FRONT SEAT BELT DUAL RETRACTOR — 4 DOOR

▶ See Figure 289

1. Remove the upper and lower center pillar trim.
2. Remove the anchor bolt and shoulder belt upper guide loop.
3. Remove the screw and shoulder belt lower guide loop.
4. Remove the dual retractor cover screw.
5. Open the retractor cover access door and remove the anchor bolt.
6. If removing the driver's side retractor, disconnect the wiring connector.
7. Remove the seat belt dual retractor.

To install:
8. If installing the driver's side retractor, connect the wiring connector.
9. Align the anti-rotation tab on the back of the retractor with the hole in the rocker panel and position the retractor on the pillar.
10. Install the anchor bolt and tighten to 31 ft. lbs. (42 Nm).
11. Install the dual retractor cover screw.
12. Install the shoulder belt lower guide loop and screw.
13. Install the shoulder belt upper guide loop and anchor bolt. Tighten the bolt to 31 ft. lbs. (42 Nm).
14. Install the upper and lower center pillar trim.

FRONT SEAT CENTER LAP BELT

▶ See Figure 290

1. Remove the screw and anchor bolt cover.
2. Remove the anchor bolt.
3. Separate the belt from the load bar by bending away and discarding the ferrule.
4. Remove the center lap belt.

To install:
5. Route the belt and align the tab on the belt with the slot on the load bar.

✳✳CAUTION

Make sure the anchor bolt is through the load bar and center belt holes. Failure to do so will lead to injury in the event of a collision.

6. Position the belt and load bar over the anchor hole and install the anchor bolt. Tighten the anchor bolt to 31 ft. lbs. (42 Nm).
7. Install the anchor bolt cover and screw.

FRONT SEAT LOAD BAR AND SEAT BELT BUCKLE — FISHER MODEL

▶ See Figure 291

➡The driver and passenger seat belt buckles may be replaced separately if necessary, by removing the nut with the seats still installed.

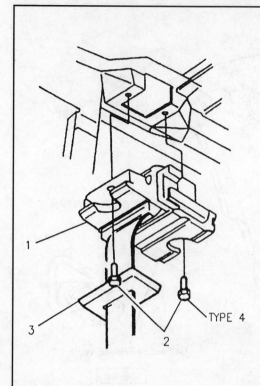

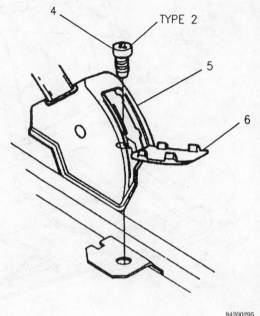

1. Shoulder retractor
2. Anchor bolts
3. Escutcheon
4. Anchor bolts
5. Lap retractor
6. Access door

84200295

Fig. 288 Front seat belt retractors, 2 door — Deville, Fleetwood and Sixty Special

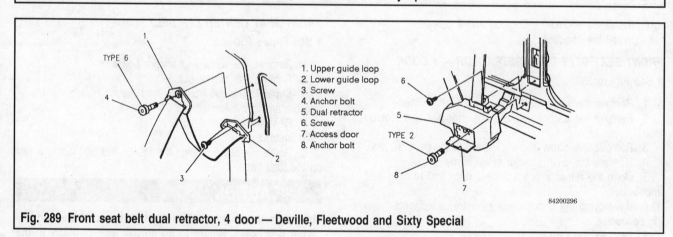

1. Upper guide loop
2. Lower guide loop
3. Screw
4. Anchor bolt
5. Dual retractor
6. Screw
7. Access door
8. Anchor bolt

84200296

Fig. 289 Front seat belt dual retractor, 4 door — Deville, Fleetwood and Sixty Special

1. Remove the front seat; refer to the procedure in this Section.
2. Remove the retaining nut.
3. Drill out the rivet using a 5/16 in. drill bit.
4. Remove the load bar.
5. Remove the nut and the seat belt buckle from the load bar.

To install:

❊❊CAUTION

When reinstalling the load bar, make sure the anchor bolt is through the load bar and center belt holes. The center belt and load bar should be correctly lined up, using the projection on the belt and the notch in the load bar for reference. Failure to do so will lead to injury in the event of a collision.

6.. Attach the load bar to the seat adjuster using a 5/16 in. rivet.
7. Install the nut.
8. Attach the seat belt buckle to the load bar and install the nut. Tighten the nut to 21 ft. lbs. (28 Nm).
9. Install the front seat.

FRONT SEAT LOAD BAR — HANCOCK MODEL

▶ See Figure 291

1. Remove the screws and the cover.

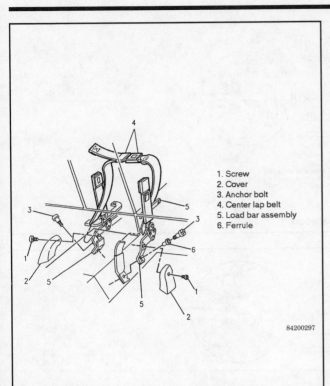

1. Screw
2. Cover
3. Anchor bolt
4. Center lap belt
5. Load bar assembly
6. Ferrule

84200297

Fig. 290 Center lap belt — Deville, Fleetwood and Sixty Special

2. Remove the Torx® bolt.

3. Remove the 2 nuts and the belt load bar assembly.

To install:

4. Position the load bar to the adjuster assembly and install the 2 nuts.

5. Install the Torx® bolt.

6. Install the cover and screw.

FRONT SEAT LOAD CABLE AND SEAT BELT BUCKLE — PNEUMATIC SEAT

▶ **See Figures 292 and 293**

➡The driver and passenger seat belt buckles may be replaced separately if necessary, by removing the nut with the seats still installed.

1. Remove the front seat; refer to the procedure in this Section.

2. Remove the 2 bolts.

3. On 1990-91 vehicles, drill out the rivets using the proper size drill bit.

4. Remove the load cable.

5. Remove the nut and the seat belt buckle from the load cable.

To install:

6. Position the load cable to the seat.

7. On 1990-91 vehicles, install proper size steel rivets. Make sure assembly is secure.

8. Install the 2 bolts.

9. Attach the seat belt buckle to the load cable and install the nut. Tighten to 21 ft. lbs. (28 Nm).

10. Install the front seat.

REAR SEAT RESTRAINT SYSTEM

▶ **See Figure 294**

1. Remove the rear seat cushion; refer to the procedure in this Section.

2. Remove the anchor nuts and lap belts.

3. Remove the shoulder retractor trim cover, if equipped.

4. Remove the rear window trim panel.

5. Remove the anchor bolt and the lap belt retractor.

6. Remove the anchor bolt and the shoulder belt retractor.

To install:

7. Position the tab on the shoulder belt retractor with the hole in the support bracket. Place the shoulder retractor on the support bracket and install the anchor bolt. Tighten the bolt to 31 ft. lbs. (42 Nm).

8. Position the lap retractor on the floor panel so the retractor outboard is against the body metal. Install the anchor bolt and tighten to 31 ft. lbs. (42 Nm).

9. Install the rear window trim panel.

10. Install the retractor trim cover, if equipped.

11. Install the lap belts and anchor nuts. Tighten the nuts to 25 ft. lbs. (35 Nm).

12. Install the rear seat cushion.

Eldorado and Seville

FRONT BELT RETRACTOR ASSEMBLY — ELDORADO

▶ **See Figures 295 and 296**

1. Remove the floor retractor cover on 1990-91 vehicles or carpet retainer on 1992-93 vehicles, then using special tool

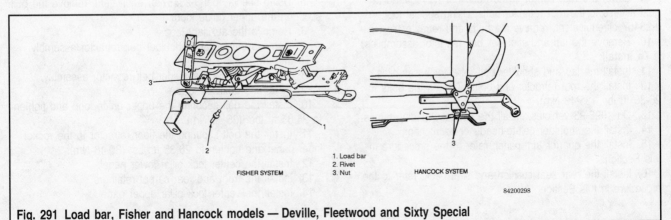

FISHER SYSTEM

HANCOCK SYSTEM

1. Load bar
2. Rivet
3. Nut

84200298

Fig. 291 Load bar, Fisher and Hancock models — Deville, Fleetwood and Sixty Special

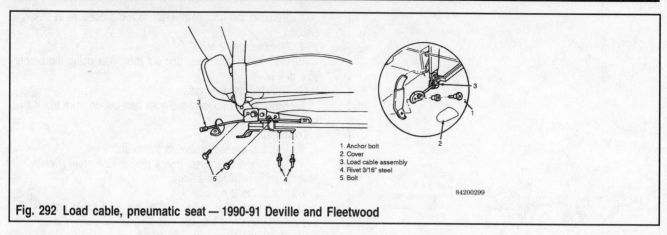

1. Anchor bolt
2. Cover
3. Load cable assembly
4. Rivet 3/16" steel
5. Bolt

84200299

Fig. 292 Load cable, pneumatic seat — 1990-91 Deville and Fleetwood

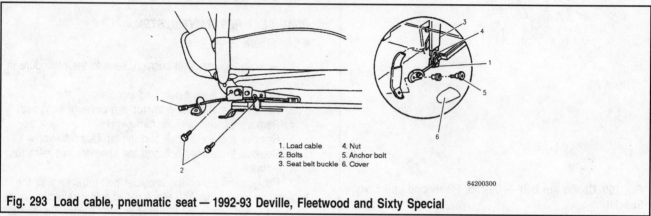

1. Load cable   4. Nut
2. Bolts   5. Anchor bolt
3. Seat belt buckle   6. Cover

84200300

Fig. 293 Load cable, pneumatic seat — 1992-93 Deville, Fleetwood and Sixty Special

J-23457 or equivalent, remove the bolt securing the floor retractor to the inner rocker.

2. Remove the screw from the belt guide on the seat back and slip the belt out of the guide.

3. On 1990-91 vehicles, loosen the windshield pillar and side roof rail garnish molding along the roof rail.

4. On 1992-93 vehicles, remove the windshield pillar garnish molding.

5. Remove the rear seat cushion and seat back; refer to the procedure in this Section.

6. Remove the quarter trim panel; refer to the procedure in this Section.

7. Remove the shoulder belt-to-headliner escutcheon.

8. On 1992-93 vehicles, remove the courtesy/reading lamps.

9. Lower the rear corner of the headliner as required to gain access to the roof retractor bolts. Using special tool J-23457 or equivalent, remove the bolts and retractor.

10. Remove the lap and shoulder belt retractor assemblies.

To install:

11. Install the lap and shoulder belt retractor assemblies.

12. Install the roof retractor and bolts. Tighten the bolts to 26-35 ft. lbs. (35-48 Nm).

13. On 1992-93 vehicles, install the courtesy/reading lamps.

14. Install the shoulder belt-to-headliner escutcheon.

15. Install the quarter trim panel; refer to the procedure in this Section.

16. Install the rear seat cushion and seat back; refer to the procedure in this Section.

17. On 1990-91 vehicles, install the windshield pillar and side roof rail garnish molding. On 1992-93 vehicles, install the windshield pillar garnish molding.

18. Slip the belt into the seat back guide loop and install the bolt securing the guide loop.

19. Install the floor retractor and bolt. Tighten the bolt to 26-36 ft. lbs. (35-48 Nm).

20. Install the floor retractor cover or carpet retainer.

FRONT BELT RETRACTOR ASSEMBLY — 1990-91 SEVILLE

1. Remove the center lock pillar upper panel.

2. Loosen the front and rear carpet retainers.

3. Remove the center lock pillar lower panel.

4. Using special tool J-23457 or equivalent, remove the bolt securing the floor retractor to the rocker inner panel.

5. Using special tool J-23457 or equivalent, remove the bolt securing the upper guide loop.

6. Remove the auxiliary loop.

7. Remove the lap and shoulder belt retractor assembly.

To install:

8. Install the lap and shoulder belt retractor assembly.

9. Install the auxiliary loop.

10. Install the bolt securing the upper guide loop and tighten to 26-35 ft. lbs. (35-48 Nm).

11. Install the bolt securing the floor retractor to the rocker inner panel and tighten to 26-35 ft. lbs. (35-48 Nm).

12. Install the center lock pillar lower panel.

13. Install the front and rear carpet retainers.

14. Install the center lock pillar upper panel.

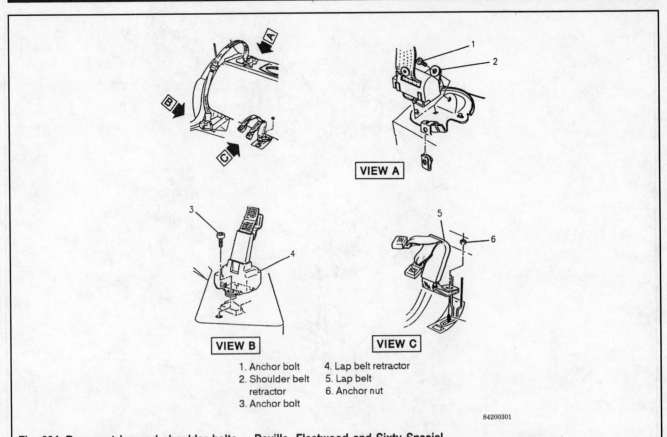

1. Anchor bolt
2. Shoulder belt retractor
3. Anchor bolt
4. Lap belt retractor
5. Lap belt
6. Anchor nut

84200301

Fig. 294 Rear seat lap and shoulder belts — Deville, Fleetwood and Sixty Special

FRONT BELT RETRACTOR ASSEMBLY — 1992-93 SEVILLE

▶ See Figure 297

1. Remove the front and rear primary weatherstrip along the roof.
2. Remove the front courtesy/reading lamp cover.
3. Remove the rear courtesy/reading lamp with the assist handle by removing the 2 screws under the handle.
4. Remove the center lock pillar trim.
5. Remove the carpet retainer.
6. Using special tool J-23457 or equivalent, remove the bolt securing the floor retractor to the rocker inner panel.
7. Remove the height adjuster trim cover by removing the 2 screws under the headliner.
8. Remove the height adjuster guide loop and auxiliary loop bracket.

To install:

9. Install the auxiliary loop bracket and tighten the screws to 44-62 inch lbs. (5-7 Nm).
10. Install the height adjuster guide loop and tighten the bolt to 26-35 ft. lbs. (35-48 Nm).
11. Install the height adjuster trim cover.
12. Install the floor retractor to the inner rocker and tighten the bolt to 26-35 ft. lbs. (35-48 Nm).
13. Install the carpet retainer.
14. Install the center lock pillar trim.
15. Install the rear courtesy/reading lamp and the front courtesy/reading lamp cover.
16. Install the primary weatherstrip.

FRONT SEAT INNER BELTS — 1990-91 ELDORADO AND SEVILLE

Refer to the illustration for front seat inner belt removal and installation. Tighten the bolts to 26-35 ft. lbs. (35-48 Nm).

REAR SEAT LAP AND SHOULDER BELT ASSEMBLY — 1990-91 ELDORADO AND SEVILLE

▶ See Figure 298

1. Remove the rear seat cushion and seat back; refer to the procedure in this Section.
2. On Eldorado, remove the quarter trim panel; refer to the procedure in this Section.
3. On Seville, remove the rear carpet retainer.
4. Remove the anchor bolt and lower retractor.
5. Remove the nut, washer and upper retractor assembly.

To install:

6. Install the upper retractor assembly, washer and nuts. Tighten the nuts to 19-33 ft. lbs. (25-45 Nm).
7. Install the lower retractor and anchor bolt. Tighten the bolt to 26-35 ft. lbs. (35-48 Nm).
8. On Eldorado, install the quarter trim panel; refer to the procedure in this Section.
9. On Seville, install the rear carpet retainer.
10. Install the rear seat cushion and seat back; refer to the procedure in this Section.

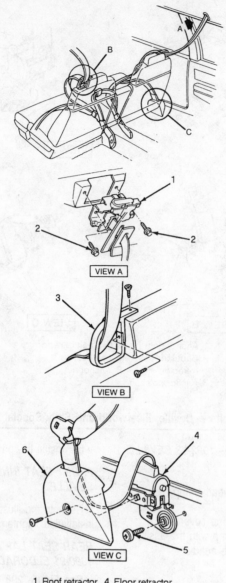

1. Roof retractor   4. Floor retractor
2. Bolt (type 4)   5. Bolt (type 2)
3. Guide   6. Cover

84200302

Fig. 295 Front seat lap and shoulder belts — 1990-91 Eldorado

REAR SEAT LAP AND SHOULDER BELT ASSEMBLY — 1992-93 ELDORADO AND SEVILLE

▶ See Figures 299 and 300

1. Remove the rear seat cushion and seat back; refer to the procedure in this Section.
2. Remove the quarter trim panel; refer to the procedure in this Section.
3. Remove the retractor anchor bolt.
4. Remove the lower anchor bolt.
5. Remove the belt assembly from the vehicle.

To install:

6. Install the belt assembly in the vehicle.
7. Install the lower anchor bolt and tighten to 26-35 ft. lbs. (35-48 Nm).

8. Install the retractor anchor bolt and tighten to 26-35 ft. lbs. (35-48 Nm).
9. Install the quarter trim panel; refer to the procedure in this Section.
10. Install the rear seat cushion and seat back; refer to the procedure in this Section.

REAR SEAT INNER BELTS — 1992-93 ELDORADO AND SEVILLE

1. Remove the rear seat cushion; refer to the procedure in this Section.
2. Remove the rear seat back lower anchor nut(s).
3. Remove the belt(s).

To install:

4. Install the belt(s).

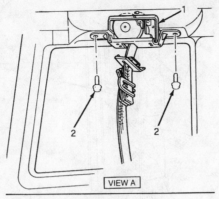

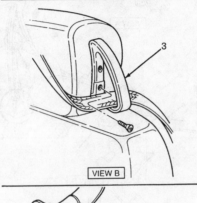

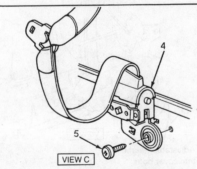

1. Roof retractor
2. Bolt (type 4)
   26-35 ft. lbs.
   (35-48 nm)
3. Guide

4. Floor retractor
5. Bolt (type 2)
   26-35 ft. lbs.
   (35-48 nm)

84200303

Fig. 296 Front seat lap and shoulder belts — 1992-93 Eldorado

5. Install the rear seat back lower anchor nut(s) and tighten to 26-35 ft. lbs. (35-48 Nm).
6. Install the rear seat cushion.

Power Seat Motor

REMOVAL & INSTALLATION

Deville, Fleetwood and Sixty Special
FISHER SYSTEM
▶ See Figure 301

1. Remove the front seat; refer to the procedure in this Section.
2. Place the seat upside down on a clean, protected surface.
3. Disconnect the motor connectors from the motors.

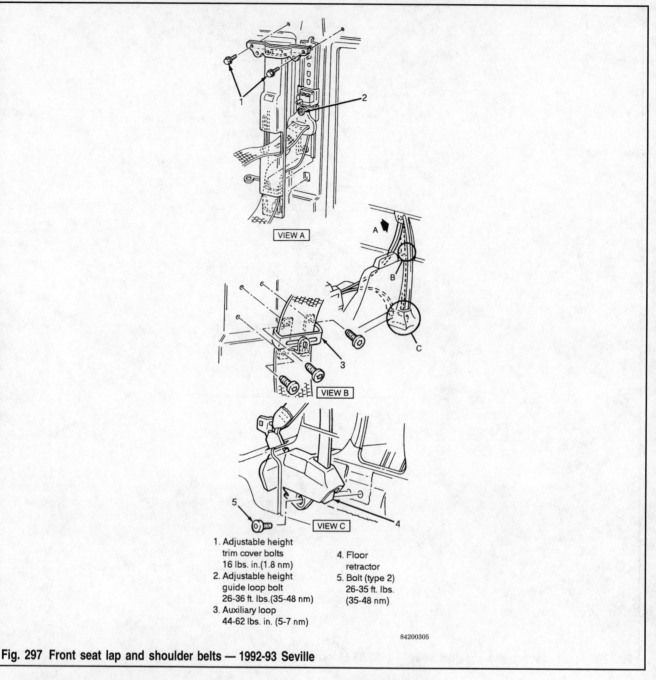

1. Adjustable height
   trim cover bolts
   16 lbs. in.(1.8 nm)
2. Adjustable height
   guide loop bolt
   26-36 ft. lbs.(35-48 nm)
3. Auxiliary loop
   44-62 lbs. in. (5-7 nm)
4. Floor
   retractor
5. Bolt (type 2)
   26-35 ft. lbs.
   (35-48 nm)

84200305

Fig. 297 Front seat lap and shoulder belts — 1992-93 Seville

4. Remove the nut securing the front of the motor support bracket to the inboard adjuster and partially withdraw the assembly from the adjuster and gearnut drives.

5. Remove the drive cables from the motors and complete disassembly of support bracket with motors attached.

6. Grind off peened over end(s) of the grommet assembly securing the motor to the support and separate the motor(s) as required from the support.

7. Installation is the reverse of the removal procedure. Drill out the top end of the grommet assembly using a 5/16 (8mm) drill bit. Attach the grommet assembly to the motor support bracket and secure the motor to the grommet using an 5/16 in. rivet.

HANCOCK SYSTEM

▶ **See Figure 302**

1. Remove the front seat; refer to the procedure in this Section.

2. Place the seat upside down on a clean, protected surface.

3. Remove the adjuster bolts, or clips and pins, as applicable and remove the adjusters as an assembly.

4. Disconnect the electrical connector at the motor.

5. Remove the screw securing the motor assembly support to the motor mounting bracket on the adjuster.

6. Carefully disengage the drive cables from the adjusters, remove the nut from the motor stabilizer rod and the motor assembly from the adjusters. Remove the drive cables from the motor.

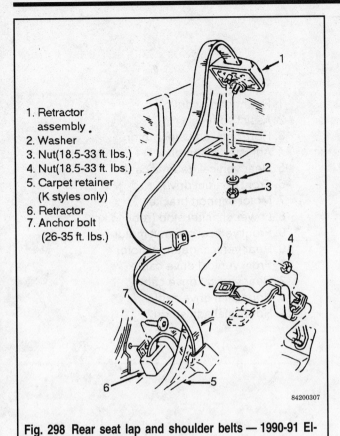

1. Retractor
   assembly.
2. Washer
3. Nut(18.5-33 ft. lbs.)
4. Nut(18.5-33 ft. lbs.)
5. Carpet retainer
   (K styles only)
6. Retractor
7. Anchor bolt
   (26-35 ft. lbs.)

84200307

Fig. 298 Rear seat lap and shoulder belts — Eldorado and Seville

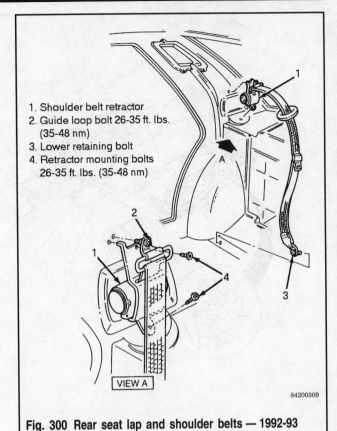

1. Shoulder belt retractor
2. Guide loop bolt 26-35 ft. lbs.
   (35-48 nm)
3. Lower retaining bolt
4. Retractor mounting bolts
   26-35 ft. lbs. (35-48 nm)

VIEW A

84200309

Fig. 300 Rear seat lap and shoulder belts — 1992-93 Seville

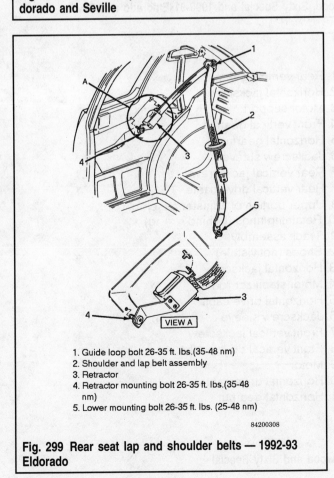

1. Guide loop bolt 26-35 ft. lbs.(35-48 nm)
2. Shoulder and lap belt assembly
3. Retractor
4. Retractor mounting bolt 26-35 ft. lbs.(35-48 nm)
5. Lower mounting bolt 26-35 ft. lbs. (25-48 nm)

VIEW A

84200308

Fig. 299 Rear seat lap and shoulder belts — 1992-93 Eldorado

7. Installation is the reverse of the removal procedure. Prior to installing the motor assembly, make sure the adjusters are in phase (same relative positions) with each other. If necessary, use a suitable tool to remove the appropriate drive cable and adjust the horizontal or vertical gearnuts so that both adjusters are in the same horizontal and vertical positions.

1990-91 Eldorado and Seville

▶ See Figure 301

1. Remove the front seat; refer to the procedure in this Section.

2. Place the seat upside down on a clean, protected surface.

3. Disconnect the motor connectors from the motors.

4. Remove the nut securing the front of the motor support bracket to the inboard adjuster and partially withdraw the assembly from the adjuster and gearnut drives.

5. Remove the drive cables from the motors and complete disassembly of support bracket with motors attached.

6. Grind off peened over end(s) of the grommet assembly securing the motor to the support and separate the motor(s) as required from the support.

7. Installation is the reverse of the removal procedure. Drill out the top end of the grommet assembly using a 5/16 in. (8mm) drill bit. Attach the grommet assembly to the motor support bracket and secure the motor to the grommet using a 5/16 in. rivet.

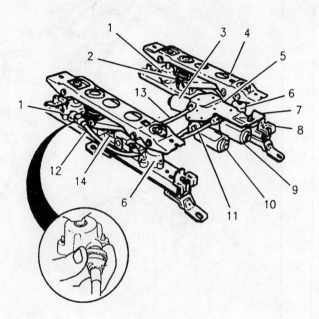

1. Rear gearnut drive
2. Assist springs
3. Horizontal adjuster motor
4. Adjuster assembly
5. Rear vertical gearnut cable
6. Front gearnut drive
7. Motor support bracket
8. Lower channel stop (rebuild kit)
9. Front vertical gearnut motor
10. Rear vertical gearnut motor
11. Front vertical drive cable
12. Rear vertical drive cable
13. Horizontal drive cable
14. Horizontal adjustr drive

84200311

Fig. 301 Power seat adjuster, Fisher system — Deville, Fleetwood, Sixty Special and 1990-91 Eldorado and Seville

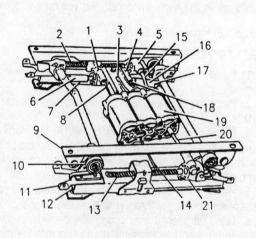

1. Rear vertical gearnut
2. Horizontal jackscrew
3. Motor support
4. Front vertical gearnut
5. Horizontal gearnut
6. Jackscrew sleeve
7. Rear vertical jackscrew
8. Rear vertical drive cable
9. Upper portion of adjuster assembly
10. Retaining rings (behind spring)
11. Track assembly
12. Shoes (not visible)
13. Horizontal jackscrew
14. Motor stabilizer rod
15. Horizontal drive cable
16. Jackscrew sleeve
17. Front vertical jackscrew
18. Front vertical drive cable
19. Motor
20. Horizontal drive cable
21. Horizontal gearnut

84200312

Fig. 302 Power seat adjuster, Hancock system — Deville, Fleetwood and Sixty Special

1992-93 Eldorado and Seville

▶ **See Figure 303**

1. Remove the front seat; refer to the procedure in this Section.

2. Place the seat upside down on a clean, protected surface.

3. Disconnect the motor connectors from the motors.

4. Remove the drive cables from the motors.

5. Remove the nut securing the front of the motor support bracket to the inboard adjuster and partially withdraw the assembly from the adjuster and gearnut drives.

6. Remove the motor.

To install:

7. Install the motor.

8. Install the motor support bracket attaching nut.

9. Install the drive cables.

10. Connect the electrical connector.

11. Install the seat.

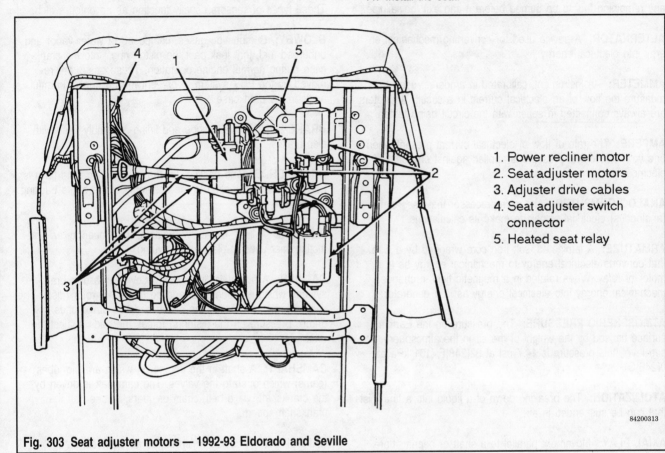

1. Power recliner motor
2. Seat adjuster motors
3. Adjuster drive cables
4. Seat adjuster switch connector
5. Heated seat relay

84200313

Fig. 303 Seat adjuster motors — 1992-93 Eldorado and Seville

GLOSSARY

AIR/FUEL RATIO: The ratio of air to gasoline by weight in the fuel mixture drawn into the engine.

AIR INJECTION: One method of reducing harmful exhaust emissions by injecting air into each of the exhaust ports of an engine. The fresh air entering the hot exhaust manifold causes any remaining fuel to be burned before it can exit the tailpipe.

ALTERNATOR: A device used for converting mechanical energy into electrical energy.

AMMETER: An instrument, calibrated in amperes, used to measure the flow of an electrical current in a circuit. Ammeters are always connected in series with the circuit being tested.

AMPERE: The rate of flow of electrical current present when one volt of electrical pressure is applied against one ohm of electrical resistance.

ANALOG COMPUTER: Any microprocessor that uses similar (analogous) electrical signals to make its calculations.

ARMATURE: A laminated, soft iron core wrapped by a wire that converts electrical energy to mechanical energy as in a motor or relay. When rotated in a magnetic field, it changes mechanical energy into electrical energy as in a generator.

ATMOSPHERIC PRESSURE: The pressure on the Earth's surface caused by the weight of the air in the atmosphere. At sea level, this pressure is 14.7 psi at 32{248}F (101 kPa at 0{248}C).

ATOMIZATION: The breaking down of a liquid into a fine mist that can be suspended in air.

AXIAL PLAY: Movement parallel to a shaft or bearing bore.

BACKFIRE: The sudden combustion of gases in the intake or exhaust system that results in a loud explosion.

BACKLASH: The clearance or play between two parts, such as meshed gears.

BACKPRESSURE: Restrictions in the exhaust system that slow the exit of exhaust gases from the combustion chamber.

BAKELITE: A heat resistant, plastic insulator material commonly used in printed circuit boards and transistorized components.

BALL BEARING: A bearing made up of hardened inner and outer races between which hardened steel balls roll.

BALLAST RESISTOR: A resistor in the primary ignition circuit that lowers voltage after the engine is started to reduce wear on ignition components.

BEARING: A friction reducing, supportive device usually located between a stationary part and a moving part.

BIMETAL TEMPERATURE SENSOR: Any sensor or switch made of two dissimilar types of metal that bend when heated or cooled due to the different expansion rates of the alloys. These types of sensors usually function as an on/off switch.

BLOWBY: Combustion gases, composed of water vapor and unburned fuel, that leak past the piston rings into the crankcase during normal engine operation. These gases are removed by the PCV system to prevent the buildup of harmful acids in the crankcase.

BRAKE PAD: A brake shoe and lining assembly used with disc brakes.

BRAKE SHOE: The backing for the brake lining. The term is, however, usually applied to the assembly of the brake backing and lining.

BUSHING: A liner, usually removable, for a bearing; an anti-friction liner used in place of a bearing.

CALIPER: A hydraulically activated device in a disc brake system, which is mounted straddling the brake rotor (disc). The caliper contains at least one piston and two brake pads. Hydraulic pressure on the piston(s) forces the pads against the rotor.

CAMSHAFT: A shaft in the engine on which are the lobes (cams) which operate the valves. The camshaft is driven by the crankshaft, via a belt, chain or gears, at one half the crankshaft speed.

CAPACITOR: A device which stores an electrical charge.

CARBON MONOXIDE (CO): A colorless, odorless gas given off as a normal byproduct of combustion. It is poisonous and extremely dangerous in confined areas, building up slowly to toxic levels without warning if adequate ventilation is not available.

CARBURETOR: A device, usually mounted on the intake manifold of an engine, which mixes the air and fuel in the proper proportion to allow even combustion.

CATALYTIC CONVERTER: A device installed in the exhaust system, like a muffler, that converts harmful byproducts of combustion into carbon dioxide and water vapor by means of a heat-producing chemical reaction.

CENTRIFUGAL ADVANCE: A mechanical method of advancing the spark timing by using flyweights in the distributor that react to centrifugal force generated by the distributor shaft rotation.

CHECK VALVE: Any one-way valve installed to permit the flow of air, fuel or vacuum in one direction only.

CHOKE: A device, usually a moveable valve, placed in the intake path of a carburetor to restrict the flow of air.

CIRCUIT: Any unbroken path through which an electrical current can flow. Also used to describe fuel flow in some instances.

CIRCUIT BREAKER: A switch which protects an electrical circuit from overload by opening the circuit when the current flow exceeds a predetermined level. Some circuit breakers must be reset manually, while most reset automatically

COIL (IGNITION): A transformer in the ignition circuit which steps up the voltage provided to the spark plugs.

COMBINATION MANIFOLD: An assembly which includes both the intake and exhaust manifolds in one casting.

COMBINATION VALVE: A device used in some fuel systems that routes fuel vapors to a charcoal storage canister instead of venting them into the atmosphere. The valve relieves fuel tank pressure and allows fresh air into the tank as the fuel level drops to prevent a vapor lock situation.

COMPRESSION RATIO: The comparison of the total volume of the cylinder and combustion chamber with the piston at BDC and the piston at TDC.

CONDENSER: 1. An electrical device which acts to store an electrical charge, preventing voltage surges.
2. A radiator-like device in the air conditioning system in which refrigerant gas condenses into a liquid, giving off heat.

CONDUCTOR: Any material through which an electrical current can be transmitted easily.

CONTINUITY: Continuous or complete circuit. Can be checked with an ohmmeter.

COUNTERSHAFT: An intermediate shaft which is rotated by a mainshaft and transmits, in turn, that rotation to a working part.

CRANKCASE: The lower part of an engine in which the crankshaft and related parts operate.

CRANKSHAFT: The main driving shaft of an engine which receives reciprocating motion from the pistons and converts it to rotary motion.

CYLINDER: In an engine, the round hole in the engine block in which the piston(s) ride.

CYLINDER BLOCK: The main structural member of an engine in which is found the cylinders, crankshaft and other principal parts.

CYLINDER HEAD: The detachable portion of the engine, fastened, usually, to the top of the cylinder block, containing all or most of the combustion chambers. On overhead valve engines, it contains the valves and their operating parts. On overhead cam engines, it contains the camshaft as well.

DEAD CENTER: The extreme top or bottom of the piston stroke.

DETONATION: An unwanted explosion of the air/fuel mixture in the combustion chamber caused by excess heat and compression, advanced timing, or an overly lean mixture. Also referred to as "ping".

DIAPHRAGM: A thin, flexible wall separating two cavities, such as in a vacuum advance unit.

DIESELING: A condition in which hot spots in the combustion chamber cause the engine to run on after the key is turned off.

DIFFERENTIAL: A geared assembly which allows the transmission of motion between drive axles, giving one axle the ability to turn faster than the other.

DIODE: An electrical device that will allow current to flow in one direction only.

DISC BRAKE: A hydraulic braking assembly consisting of a brake disc, or rotor, mounted on an axle, and a caliper assembly containing, usually two brake pads which are activated by hydraulic pressure. The pads are forced against the sides of the disc, creating friction which slows the vehicle.

DISTRIBUTOR: A mechanically driven device on an engine which is responsible for electrically firing the spark plug at a predetermined point of the piston stroke.

DOWEL PIN: A pin, inserted in mating holes in two different parts allowing those parts to maintain a fixed relationship.

DRUM BRAKE: A braking system which consists of two brake shoes and one or two wheel cylinders, mounted on a fixed backing plate, and a brake drum, mounted on an axle, which revolves around the assembly.

DWELL: The rate, measured in degrees of shaft rotation, at which an electrical circuit cycles on and off.

ELECTRONIC CONTROL UNIT (ECU): Ignition module, module, amplifier or igniter. See Module for definition.

ELECTRONIC IGNITION: A system in which the timing and firing of the spark plugs is controlled by an electronic control unit, usually called a module. These systems have no points or condenser.

ENDPLAY: The measured amount of axial movement in a shaft.

ENGINE: A device that converts heat into mechanical energy.

EXHAUST MANIFOLD: A set of cast passages or pipes which conduct exhaust gases from the engine.

FEELER GAUGE: A blade, usually metal, of precisely predetermined thickness, used to measure the clearance between two parts.

FIRING ORDER: The order in which combustion occurs in the cylinders of an engine. Also the order in which spark is distributed to the plugs by the distributor.

FLOODING: The presence of too much fuel in the intake manifold and combustion chamber which prevents the air/fuel mixture from firing, thereby causing a no-start situation.

FLYWHEEL: A disc shaped part bolted to the rear end of the crankshaft. Around the outer perimeter is affixed the ring gear. The starter drive engages the ring gear, turning the flywheel, which rotates the crankshaft, imparting the initial starting motion to the engine.

FOOT POUND (ft.lb. or sometimes, ft. lbs.): The amount of energy or work needed to raise an item weighing one pound, a distance of one foot.

FUSE: A protective device in a circuit which prevents circuit overload by breaking the circuit when a specific amperage is present. The device is constructed around a strip or wire of a lower amperage rating than the circuit it is designed to protect. When an amperage higher than that stamped on the fuse is present in the circuit, the strip or wire melts, opening the circuit.

GEAR RATIO: The ratio between the number of teeth on meshing gears.

GENERATOR: A device which converts mechanical energy into electrical energy.

HEAT RANGE: The measure of a spark plug's ability to dissipate heat from its firing end. The higher the heat range, the hotter the plug fires.

HUB: The center part of a wheel or gear.

HYDROCARBON (HC): Any chemical compound made up of hydrogen and carbon. A major pollutant formed by the engine as a byproduct of combustion.

HYDROMETER: An instrument used to measure the specific gravity of a solution.

INCH POUND (in.lb. or sometimes, in. lbs.): One twelfth of a foot pound.

INDUCTION: A means of transferring electrical energy in the form of a magnetic field. Principle used in the ignition coil to increase voltage.

INJECTOR: A device which receives metered fuel under relatively low pressure and is activated to inject the fuel into the engine under relatively high pressure at a predetermined time.

INPUT SHAFT: The shaft to which torque is applied, usually carrying the driving gear or gears.

INTAKE MANIFOLD: A casting of passages or pipes used to conduct air or a fuel/air mixture to the cylinders.

JOURNAL: The bearing surface within which a shaft operates.

KEY: A small block usually fitted in a notch between a shaft and a hub to prevent slippage of the two parts.

MANIFOLD: A casting of passages or set of pipes which connect the cylinders to an inlet or outlet source.

MANIFOLD VACUUM: Low pressure in an engine intake manifold formed just below the throttle plates. Manifold vacuum is highest at idle and drops under acceleration.

MASTER CYLINDER: The primary fluid pressurizing device in a hydraulic system. In automotive use, it is found in brake and hydraulic clutch systems and is pedal activated, either directly or, in a power brake system, through the power booster.

MODULE: Electronic control unit, amplifier or igniter of solid state or integrated design which controls the current flow in the ignition primary circuit based on input from the pick-up coil. When the module opens the primary circuit, the high secondary voltage is induced in the coil.

NEEDLE BEARING: A bearing which consists of a number (usually a large number) of long, thin rollers.

OHM:(Ω) The unit used to measure the resistance of conductor to electrical flow. One ohm is the amount of resistance that limits current flow to one ampere in a circuit with one volt of pressure.

OHMMETER: An instrument used for measuring the resistance, in ohms, in an electrical circuit.

OUTPUT SHAFT: The shaft which transmits torque from a device, such as a transmission.

OVERDRIVE: A gear assembly which produces more shaft revolutions than that transmitted to it.

OVERHEAD CAMSHAFT (OHC): An engine configuration in which the camshaft is mounted on top of the cylinder head and operates the valve either directly or by means of rocker arms.

OVERHEAD VALVE (OHV): An engine configuration in which all of the valves are located in the cylinder head and the camshaft is located in the cylinder block. The camshaft operates the valves via lifters and pushrods.

OXIDES OF NITROGEN (NOx): Chemical compounds of nitrogen produced as a byproduct of combustion. They combine with hydrocarbons to produce smog.

OXYGEN SENSOR: Used with the feedback system to sense the presence of oxygen in the exhaust gas and signal the computer which can reference the voltage signal to an air/fuel ratio.

PINION: The smaller of two meshing gears.

PISTON RING: An open ended ring which fits into a groove on the outer diameter of the piston. Its chief function is to form a seal between the piston and cylinder wall. Most automotive pistons have three rings: two for compression sealing; one for oil sealing.

PRELOAD: A predetermined load placed on a bearing during assembly or by adjustment.

PRIMARY CIRCUIT: Is the low voltage side of the ignition system which consists of the ignition switch, ballast resistor or resistance wire, bypass, coil, electronic control unit and pick-up coil as well as the connecting wires and harnesses.

PRESS FIT: The mating of two parts under pressure, due to the inner diameter of one being smaller than the outer diameter of the other, or vice versa; an interference fit.

RACE: The surface on the inner or outer ring of a bearing on which the balls, needles or rollers move.

REGULATOR: A device which maintains the amperage and/or voltage levels of a circuit at predetermined values.

RELAY: A switch which automatically opens and/or closes a circuit.

RESISTANCE: The opposition to the flow of current through a circuit or electrical device, and is measured in ohms. Resistance is equal to the voltage divided by the amperage.

RESISTOR: A device, usually made of wire, which offers a preset amount of resistance in an electrical circuit.

RING GEAR: The name given to a ring-shaped gear attached to a differential case, or affixed to a flywheel or as part a planetary gear set.

ROLLER BEARING: A bearing made up of hardened inner and outer races between which hardened steel rollers move.

ROTOR: 1. The disc-shaped part of a disc brake assembly, upon which the brake pads bear; also called, brake disc.
2. The device mounted atop the distributor shaft, which passes current to the distributor cap tower contacts.

SECONDARY CIRCUIT: The high voltage side of the ignition system, usually above 20,000 volts. The secondary includes the ignition coil, coil wire, distributor cap and rotor, spark plug wires and spark plugs.

SENDING UNIT: A mechanical, electrical, hydraulic or electromagnetic device which transmits information to a gauge.

SENSOR: Any device designed to measure engine operating conditions or ambient pressures and temperatures. Usually electronic in nature and designed to send a voltage signal to an on-board computer, some sensors may operate as a simple on/off switch or they may provide a variable voltage signal (like a potentiometer) as conditions or measured parameters change.

SHIM: Spacers of precise, predetermined thickness used between parts to establish a proper working relationship.

SLAVE CYLINDER: In automotive use, a device in the hydraulic clutch system which is activated by hydraulic force, disengaging the clutch.

SOLENOID: A coil used to produce a magnetic field, the effect of which is produce work.

SPARK PLUG: A device screwed into the combustion chamber of a spark ignition engine. The basic construction is a conductive core inside of a ceramic insulator, mounted in an outer conductive base. An electrical charge from the spark plug wire travels along the conductive core and jumps a preset air gap to a grounding point or points at the end of the conductive base. The resultant spark ignites the fuel/air mixture in the combustion chamber.

SPLINES: Ridges machined or cast onto the outer diameter of a shaft or inner diameter of a bore to enable parts to mate without rotation.

TACHOMETER: A device used to measure the rotary speed of an engine, shaft, gear, etc., usually in rotations per minute.

THERMOSTAT: A valve, located in the cooling system of an engine, which is closed when cold and opens gradually in response to engine heating, controlling the temperature of the coolant and rate of coolant flow.

TOP DEAD CENTER (TDC): The point at which the piston reaches the top of its travel on the compression stroke.

TORQUE: The twisting force applied to an object.

TORQUE CONVERTER: A turbine used to transmit power from a driving member to a driven member via hydraulic action, providing changes in drive ratio and torque. In automotive use, it links the driveplate at the rear of the engine to the automatic transmission.

TRANSDUCER: A device used to change a force into an electrical signal.

TRANSISTOR: A semi-conductor component which can be actuated by a small voltage to perform an electrical switching function.

TUNE-UP: A regular maintenance function, usually associated with the replacement and adjustment of parts and components in the electrical and fuel systems of a vehicle for the purpose of attaining optimum performance.

TURBOCHARGER: An exhaust driven pump which compresses intake air and forces it into the combustion chambers at higher than atmospheric pressures. The increased air pressure allows more fuel to be burned and results in increased horsepower being produced.

VACUUM ADVANCE: A device which advances the ignition timing in response to increased engine vacuum.

VACUUM GAUGE: An instrument used to measure the presence of vacuum in a chamber.

VALVE: A device which control the pressure, direction of flow or rate of flow of a liquid or gas.

VALVE CLEARANCE: The measured gap between the end of the valve stem and the rocker arm, cam lobe or follower that activates the valve.

VISCOSITY: The rating of a liquid's internal resistance to flow.

VOLTMETER: An instrument used for measuring electrical force in units called volts. Voltmeters are always connected parallel with the circuit being tested.

WHEEL CYLINDER: Found in the automotive drum brake assembly, it is a device, actuated by hydraulic pressure, which, through internal pistons, pushes the brake shoes outward against the drums.

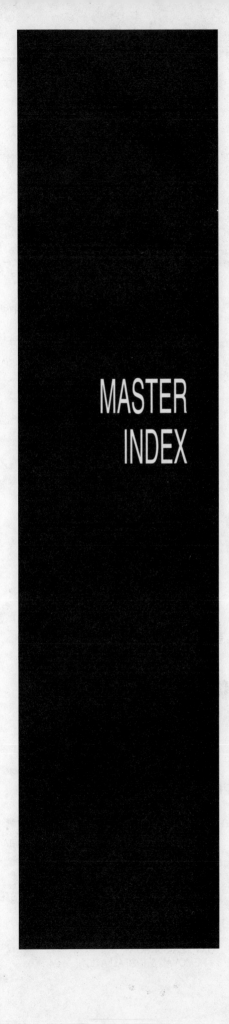

MASTER

INDEX

Total Car Care, continued

Pick-Ups and Montero 1983-95
PART NO. 8666/50500
NISSAN
Datsun 210/1200 1973-81
PART NO. 52300
Datsun 200SX/510/610/710/
810/Maxima 1973-84
PART NO. 52302
Nissan Maxima 1985-92
PART NO. 8261/52450
Maxima 1993-98
PART NO. 52452
Pick-Ups and Pathfinder 1970-88
PART NO. 8585/52500
Pick-Ups and Pathfinder 1989-95
PART NO. 8145/52502
Sentra/Pulsar/NX 1982-96
PART NO. 8263/52700
Stanza/200SX/240SX 1982-92
PART NO. 8262/52750
240SX/Altima 1993-98
PART NO. 52752
Datsun/Nissan Z and ZX 1970-88

PART NO. 8846/52800
RENAULT
Coupes/Sedans/Wagons 1975-85
PART NO. 58300
SATURN
Coupes/Sedans/Wagons 1991-98
PART NO. 8419/62300
SUBARU
Coupes/Sedan/Wagons 1970-84
PART NO. 8790/64300
Coupes/Sedans/Wagons 1985-96
PART NO. 8259/64302
SUZUKI
Samurai/Sidekick/Tracker 1986-98
PART NO. 66500
TOYOTA
Camry 1983-96
PART NO. 8265/68200
Celica/Supra 1971-85
PART NO. 68250
Celica 1986-93
PART NO. 8413/68252

Celica 1994-98
PART NO. 68254
Corolla 1970-87
PART NO. 8586/68300
Corolla 1988-97
PART NO. 8414/68302
Cressida/Corona/Crown/MkII 1970-82
PART NO. 68350
Cressida/Van 1983-90
PART NO. 68352
Pick-ups/Land Cruiser/4Runner 1970-88
PART NO. 8578/68600
Pick-ups/Land Cruiser/4Runner 1989-98
PART NO. 8163/68602
Previa 1991-97
PART NO. 68640
Tercel 1984-94
PART NO. 8595/68700
VOLKSWAGEN
Air-Cooled 1949-69
PART NO. 70200

Air-Cooled 1970-81
PART NO. 70202
Front Wheel Drive 1974-89
PART NO. 8663/70400
Golf/Jetta/Cabriolet 1990-93
PART NO. 8429/70402
VOLVO
Coupes/Sedans/Wagons 1970-89
PART NO. 8786/72300
Coupes/Sedans/Wagons 1990-98
PART NO. 8428/72302

Total Service Series

ATV Handbook
PART NO. 9123
Auto Detailing
PART NO. 8394
Auto Body Repair
PART NO. 7898
Automatic Transmissions/Transaxles
Diagnosis and Repair
PART NO. 8944
Brake System Diagnosis and Repair
PART NO. 8945
Chevrolet Engine Overhaul Manual
PART NO. 8794
Easy Car Care
PART NO. 8042
Engine Code Manual
PART NO. 8851
Ford Engine Overhaul Manual
PART NO. 8793
Fuel Injection Diagnosis and Repair
PART NO. 8946
Motorcycle Handbook
PART NO. 9099
Small Engine Repair
(Up to 20 Hp)
PART NO. 8325
Snowmobile Handbook
PART NO. 9124

Collector's Hard-Cover Manuals

Auto Repair Manual 1993-97
PART NO. 7919
Auto Repair Manual 1988-92
PART NO. 7906
Auto Repair Manual 1980-87
PART NO. 7670
Auto Repair Manual 1972-79
PART NO. 6914
Auto Repair Manual 1964-71
PART NO. 5974
Auto Repair Manual 1954-63
PART NO. 5652

Auto Repair Manual 1940-53
PART NO. 5631
Import Car Repair Manual 1993-97
PART NO. 7920
Import Car Repair Manual 1988-92
PART NO.7907
Import Car Repair Manual 1980-87
PART NO. 7672
Truck and Van Repair Manual 1993-97
PART NO. 7921
Truck and Van Repair Manual 1991-95
PART NO. 7911

Truck and Van Repair Manual 1986-90
PART NO. 7902
Truck and Van Repair Manual 1979-86
PART NO. 7655
Truck and Van Repair Manual 1971-78
PART NO. 7012
Truck Repair Manual 1961-71
PART NO. 6198

System-Specific Manuals

Guide to Air Conditioning Repair and
Service 1982-85
PART NO. 7580
Guide to Automatic Transmission
Repair 1984-89
PART NO. 8054
Guide to Automatic Transmission
Repair 1984-89
Domestic cars and trucks
PART NO. 8053

Guide to Automatic Transmission
Repair 1980-84
Domestic cars and trucks
PART NO. 7891
Guide to Automatic Transmission
Repair 1974-80
Import cars and trucks
PART NO. 7645
Guide to Brakes, Steering, and
Suspension 1980-87
PART NO. 7819

Guide to Fuel Injection and Electronic
Engine Controls 1984-88
Domestic cars and trucks
PART NO.7766
Guide to Electronic Engine Controls
1978-85
PART NO. 7535
Guide to Engine Repair and Rebuilding
PART NO. 7643
Guide to Vacuum Diagrams 1980-86
Domestic cars and trucks
PART NO. 7821

Multi-Vehicle Spanish Repair Manuals

Auto Repair Manual 1992-96
PART NO. 8947
Import Repair Manual 1992-96
PART NO. 8948
Truck and Van Repair Manual
1992-96
PART NO. 8949
Auto Repair Manual 1987-91
PART NO. 8138
Auto Repair Manual
1980-87
PART NO. 7795
Auto Repair Manual
1976-83
PART NO. 7476

2P2VerA